KU-669-337

ELLIOTT AND WOOD'S CASEBOOK ON CRIMINAL LAW

AUSTRALIA
The Law Book Company Ltd.
Sydney : Melbourne : Brisbane

CANADA AND U.S.A.
The Carswell Company Ltd.
Agincourt, Ontario

INDIA
N. M. Tripathi Private Ltd.
Bombay
and
Eastern Law House Private Ltd.
Calcutta and Delhi
M.P.P. House
Bangalore

ISRAEL
Steimatzky's Agency Ltd.
Jerusalem : Tel Aviv : Haifa

MALAYSIA : SINGAPORE : BRUNEI
Malayan Law Journal (Pte.) Ltd.
Singapore

NEW ZEALAND
Sweet and Maxwell (N.Z.) Ltd.
Auckland

PAKISTAN
Pakistan Law House
Karachi

ELLIOTT AND WOOD'S

CASEBOOK ON CRIMINAL LAW

Fourth Edition

by

D. W. ELLIOTT, LL.B.
Solicitor, Professor of Law, University of Newcastle upon Tyne

and

CELIA WELLS, LL.M.
Lecturer in Law at the University of Newcastle upon Tyne

LONDON
SWEET & MAXWELL
1982

First Edition	1963
Second Impression	1967
Second Edition	1969
Second Impression	1971
Third Edition	1974
Fourth Edition	1982

Published by
Sweet & Maxwell Limited of
11 New Fetter Lane, London.
Computerset by MFK Graphic Systems (Typesetting) Limited,
Saffron Walden, Essex.
Printed in Great Britain
by Richard Clay (The Chaucer Press) Limited
Bungay, Suffolk

British Cataloguing in Publication Data
Elliott, D. W.
Elliott and Wood's casebook on criminal law.—
4th ed.
1. Criminal law—England—Cases
I. Title II. Wood, *Sir* John C.
III. Wells, Celia
344.205'0264 KD7868

ISBN 0-421-27740-8
ISBN 0-421-27750-5 Pbk

All rights reserved.
No part of this publication may be reproduced
or transmitted in any form or by any means,
electronic, mechanical, photocopying, recording or
otherwise, or stored in any retrieval system of any nature
without the written permission of the copyright holder
and the publisher, application for which shall be made
to the publisher.

©
Sweet & Maxwell
1982

PREFACE

THE eight years since the third edition have seen much activity in the field of criminal law. The Criminal Law Act 1977, the Theft Act 1978 and the Criminal Attempts Act 1981 are but a few of the more important enactments in that time, each of which bury a large number of formerly important cases. Their places have been taken by new ones, however, for the House of Lords has never been less idle. In a flurry of activity in the mid-70s, the defences of mistake, intoxication and duress received lengthy attention in *Morgan, Majewski, Lynch* and *Abbott*. More recently, the concept of recklessness (one of the basic building bricks of criminal liability) has been extended in *Caldwell*; and the old controversy over the place of foreseen grievous bodily harm in the malice aforethought of murder has been terminated, at least as far as the judges are concerned, by *Cunningham*. Equally productive have been the Law Commission and the Criminal Law Revision Committee; the recommendations of the former as to the mental element in crime, and as to general defences, and of the latter as to offences against the person, including homicide, have involved re-examination of the general principles of liability.

Partly to take account of this re-examination, and partly to give greater emphasis to academic writings, the chapters dealing with general principles have been largely restructured and rewritten. Moreover, statute has required a complete overhaul of the chapter on Inchoate Offences. But no part of the field has remained undisturbed, and virtually every chapter has needed substantial revision, a state of affairs which, although perhaps uncomfortable to anyone trying to master the subject, must be welcomed as demonstrating a continuing vitality in English Criminal Law. It is a matter of regret, however, that the nature of the mental element in crime is still subject to bouts of such severe turbulence as demonstrated in *Caldwell*. It has not been possible to reproduce extracts from some useful comments on that case, in particular Williams, "Recklessness Redefined" [1981] C.L.J. 252. In general we have not included anything published after August 31, 1981, and again we have to thank the various persons and organisations who kindly gave permission for the reproduction of copyright material. We also thank the publishers for providing what we hope will be thought an attractive typographic style.

December, 1981

D. W. ELLIOTT
CELIA WELLS

CONTENTS

	page
Preface	v
Table of Cases	xi
Table of Statutes	xxxiii
Table of Reports and Official Working Papers	xxxix
Abbreviations	xl
Acknowledgments	xli
1. INTRODUCTORY	1
1. The Concept of Crime	1
2. The Form of English Criminal Law	7
2. ACTUS REUS	13
1. Elements of Crime	13
2. Voluntariness	14
3. Omissions	18
4. Causation	24
i. *Sine Qua Non*	26
ii. Imputability	28
5. Coincidence of *Actus Reus* and *Mens Rea*	40
3. MENS REA	43
1. The Requirement of *Mens Rea*	43
2. The Meaning of Terms	46
i. Intention	47
ii. Knowledge	50
iii. Recklessness	50
iv. Negligence	54
v. Law Commission Draft Bill	56
3. Judicial Approaches	62
i. Common Law *Mens Rea*	62
ii. Intention	63
iii. Knowledge	68
iv. Recklessness	71
v. Maliciousness	81
vi. Wilfulness	83
4. Motive	94
5. Mistakes	98
i. Mistake Negating Intent	100
ii. Mistake Affecting Culpability	116
iii. Irrelevant Mistakes	120
6. Strict Liability	128
i. The Evolution of Strict Liability	128
ii. The Present Uncertainty	129
iii. Critique	151
iv. Proposals for Reform	154
4. MENTAL INCAPACITY	157
1. Defences in General	157

2. Insanity 158
i. Unfitness to Plead 159
ii. The Defence of Insanity 162
3. Automatism 167
4. Intoxication 176
5. Proposals for Reform 195

5. DEFENCES 201
1. Duress 201
2. Necessity 227
i. Necessity and Homicide 227
ii. Necessity and Offences other than Homicide 230
iii. Law Commission Recommendations 231
3. Entrapment 233

6. DEGREES OF RESPONSIBILITY 246
1. Accomplices 246
i. Principals and Accessories 246
ii. *Mens Rea* of a Secondary Party 255
iii. Scope of the Common Design 267
iv. Secondary Party Not Convictable as a Principal 274
v. No Principal Offender 278
2. Assisting an Offender and Concealing Information 283
i. Assisting an Offender 283
ii. Concealing Information 288
3. Vicarious Liability 288
4. Corporations 296

7. INCHOATE OFFENCES 303
1. Attempts 303
i. *Actus Reus* 305
ii. Attempting the Impossible 316
iii. Mental Element in Attempt 328
2. Conspiracy 331
i. Conspiracy at Common Law or by Statute 332
ii. Agreement 333
iii. Jurisdiction 336
iv. Parties 339
v. Common Law Conspiracies 343
vi. Statutory Conspiracies 357
viii. Conspiracies to Do the Impossible 359
3. Incitement 360

8. HOMICIDE 366
1. The *Actus Reus* of Homicide 366
2. Murder 368
i. The Penalty for Murder 368
ii. The Mental Element in Murder 368

3. Special Defences 389
i. Provocation 389
ii. Diminished Responsibility 402
4. Self-Defence 411
i. Scope of the Defence 412
ii. Section 3 and the Common Law 418
iii. Reasonable Force 422
iv. Excessive Force 430
5. Involuntary Manslaughter 437
i. Unlawful Act Manslaughter 438
ii. Gross Negligence Manslaughter 449
6. Other Unlawful Homicides 455
i. Infanticide 455
ii. Child Destruction 456
iii. Abortion 456
iv. Suicide 462
7. Reform of the Law of Homicide 463

9. NON-FATAL OFFENCES AGAINST THE PERSON 471
1. Assault and Battery 471
i. *Actus Reus* 471
ii. *Mens Rea* 475
iii. Consent 475
iv. Statutory Assaults 479
2. Malicious Wounding and Wounding with Intent 481
i. Malicious Wounding 481
ii. Wounding with Intent 484
3. Administering Poison 485
4. Sexual Offences 486
i. Rape 486
ii. Other Sexual Offences 491
5. Proposals for Reform 492

10. THEFT AND ROBBERY 494
1. Theft 494
i. Appropriation 495
ii. "Property" 504
iii. "Belonging to Another" 515
iv. "With the Intention of Depriving Permanently" 534
v. Temporary Deprivation 544
vi. "Dishonestly" 555
vii. A New Approach 562
2. Robbery 566

11. FRAUD 571
1. Obtaining Property by Deception 572
i. Obtaining Property Belonging to Another with Intention Permanently to Deprive 573
ii. Deception 573
iii. The Obtaining Must be By the Deception 580
iv. Dishonesty 591

2. Obtaining Pecuniary Advantage by Deception 592
3. Obtaining Services by Deception 593
4. Evasion of Liability by Deception 594
5. Making Off Without Payment 597

12. HANDLING 599
i. Stolen Goods 599
ii. Otherwise than in the Course of Stealing 608
iii. Forms of Handling 611
iv. Knowing or Believing Them to be Stolen Goods 616
v. Dishonestly 620

13. BLACKMAIL 621
i. Demand with Menaces 621
ii. Unwarranted 624

14. BURGLARY AND KINDRED OFFENCES 631
1. Burglary 631
i. Entry 631
ii. As a Trespasser 633
iii. Buildings or Parts of Buildings 640
iv. Intent to Commit an Offence in the Building 641
v. The Ulterior Offence 646
2. Aggravated Burglary 647
3. Going Equipped 649
i. Has with Him 649
ii. When Not in His Place of Abode 650
iii. For Use in the Course of or in Connection with any Burglary, Theft or Cheat 651

15. CRIMINAL DAMAGE
1. Destroying or Damaging Property 653
A. The Simple Offence: Without Danger to Life 654
i. Belonging to Another 654
ii. Without Lawful Excuse 656
iii. Intending to Destroy or Damage any such Property or being Reckless as to Whether any such Property would be Destroyed or Damaged 657
iv. Intending . . . or being Reckless as to Whether any such Property would be Destroyed or Damaged 660
B. The Aggravated Offence: With Danger to Life 660
2. Other Offences 661

Index 663

TABLE OF CASES

[Page references in **bold** indicate the page upon which the section is set out.]

A. (a juvenile) *v.* R. [1978] Crim. L.R. 689 654

Abbott *v.* R. [1977] A.C. 755 .... **217**, 223, 238, 255

Abraham [1973] 1 W.L.R. 1270; 117 S.J. 663; [1973] 3 All E.R. 694; [1974] Crim. L.R. 246; *sub nom.* R. *v.* Abraham (Alan), 57 Cr. App. R. 799, C.A. 412

Advocate (H. M.) *v.* Braithwaite 1945 S.C. (J.) 55 406

—— *v.* Brown 1907 S.C. (J.) 67 161

—— *v.* Ritchie 1926 J.C. 45 173

Ahlers [1915] 1 K.B. 616; 84 L.J.K.B. 901; 112 L.T. 558; 31 T.L.R. 141; 79 J.P. 255; 24 Cox C.C. 623; 11 Cr. App. R. 63 67

Albert *v.* Lavin [1981] 1 All E.R. 628 .... 116, **426**

Allanby and Medford [1974] 1 W.L.R. 1494; 118 S.J. 830; [1974] 3 All E.R. 216; [1975] Crim. L.R. 39; *sub nom.* R. *v.* Allanby (Terence Fitzgerald); R. *v.* Medford (Wayne Elberton Kenmore) 59 Cr. App. R. 189, C.A. 651

Allan [1966] A.C. 1; [1965] 1 Q.B. 130; [1963] 3 W.L.R. 677; 127 J.P. 511; 107 S.J. 596; [1963] 2 All E.R. 897; 47 Cr. App. R. 243, C.C.A. 263, 264

Allen *v.* Whitehead [1930] 1 K.B. 211 .... 293, 295

Allsop (1976) 64 Cr. App. R. 29, C.A. 67, 349

Alphacell *v.* Woodward [1972] A.C. 824; [1972] 2 W.L.R. 1320; [1972] 2 All E.R. 475; 116 S.J. 431; 70 L.G.R. 455; [1972] Crim. L.R. 41, H.L. 146

Ambler [1979] R.T.R. 217, C.A. 553

Ameer and Lucas [1977] Crim. L.R. 104, C.A. 234, 238

Anderson and Morris [1966] 2 Q.B. 110; [1966] 2 W.L.R. 1195; 130 J.P. 318; 110 S.J. 369; [1966] 2 All E.R. 644; 50 Cr. App. R. 216 .... **269**

Anderton *v.* Wish [1980] Crim. L.R. 319, D.C. 499

Andrews *v.* D.P.P. [1937] A.C. 576; 106 L.J.K.B. 370; 53 T.L.R. 663; 101 J.P. 386; 81 S.J. 497; [1937] 2 All E.R. 552; 26 Cr. App. R. 34; 35 L.G.R. 429; *sub nom.* R. *v.* Andrews, 156 L.T. 464; 30 Cox 576 .... 89, 437, **439**, 441, 442, 444, 447, 449, 453, 454

Andrews-Weatherfoil; R. *v.* Sporle; R. *v.* Day [1972] 1 W.L.R. 118; (1971) 115 S.J. 888; 56 Cr. App. R. 31; *sub nom.* R. *v.* Andrews-Weatherfoil [1972] 1 All E.R. 65, C.A. 339

Andrews and Craig [1962] 1 W.L.R. 1474; 127 J.P. 64; 106 S.J. 1013; [1962] 3 All E.R. 961; 47 Cr. App. R. 32 287

Andrews & Hedges [1981] Crim. L.R. 106 597

Anthony [1965] 2 Q.B. 189; [1965] 2 W.L.R. 748; 129 J.P. 168; [1965] 1 All E.R. 440; 49 Cr. App. R. 104 253

Applin *v.* Race Relations Board [1975] A.C. 259; [1974] 2 W.L.R. 541; 118 S.J. 311; [1974] 2 All E.R. 73; 72 L.G.R. 479, H.L.; affirming *sub nom.* Race Relations Board *v.* Applin [1973] 1 Q.B. 815; [1973] 2 W.L.R. 895; 117 S.J. 417; [1973] 2 All E.R. 1190, C.A. 360, 361

Argyll (Duchess) *v.* Argyll (Duke) [1967] Ch. 302; [1965] 2 W.L.R. 790; [1965] 1 All E.R. 611 513

Arrowsmith *v.* Jenkins [1963] 2 Q.B. 561; [1963] 2 W.L.R. 856; [1963] 2 All E.R. 210; 127 J.P. 289; 107 S.J. 215; 61 L.G.R. 312; 79 L.Q.R. 330, D.C. **83**

Ashman (1858) 1 F. & F. 88 .... 372, 375, 387

Aspinall (1876) 2 Q.B.D. 48 337

Assistant Recorder of Kingston-upon-Hull, *ex p.* Morgan [1969] 2 Q.B. 58; [1969] 2 W.L.R. 246; (1968) 133 J.P. 165; 112 S.J. 1005; [1969] 1 All E.R. 416; 53 Cr. App. R. 96, D.C. 360

Aston and Hadley [1970] 1 W.L.R. 1584; [1970] 3 All E.R. 1045; 114 S.J. 906; 55 Cr. App. R. 48, C.A. **580**, 593

Att.-Gen. *v.* Lockwood (1842) 9 M. & W. 378; 6 Jur. 171 .... 131, 138, 141
—— *v.* Whelan [1934] I.R. 518 .... 202, 206, 208, 214, 216
Att.-Gen.'s Reference (No. 1 of 1974) [1974] Q.B. 744; [1974] 2 W.L.R. 891; 118 S.J. 345; [1974] 2 All E.R. 899; 59 Cr. App. R. 203; [1974] Crim. L.R. 165, C.A. ... **599**
—— (No. 1 of 1975) [1975] Q.B. 773; [1975] 3 W.L.R. 11; 119 S.J. 373; [1975] 2 All E.R. 684; 61 Cr. App. R. 118; [1975] R.T.R. 473; [1975] Crim. L.R. 449, C.A. **246**
—— (Nos. 1 and 2 of 1979) [1980] Q.B. 180; [1979] 3 W.L.R. 577; (1979) 123 S.J. 472; [1979] 3 All E.R. 143; (1979) 69 Cr. App. R. 266; [1979] Crim. L.R. 585, C.A. 514, 537, **641**
—— (No. 4 of 1979) (1980) 71 Cr. App. R. 341; [1981] Crim. L.R. 51, C.A. **605**, 616
—— (No. 4 of 1980) [1981] 1 W.L.R. 705; (1981) 125 S.J. 374; [1981] 2 All E.R. 617; (1981) 73 Cr. App. R. 40; [1981] Crim. L.R. 492, C.A. **40**
—— (No. 6 of 1980) [1981] 3 W.L.R. 125; (1981) 125 S.J. 426; [1981] 2 All E.R. 1057; [1981] Crim. L.R. 553; [1981] 1 Q.B. 715; (1981) 73 Cr. App. R. 63, C.A. .. **477**, 491
Att.-Gen. for Northern Ireland's Reference (No. 1 of 1975) [1977] A.C. 105, H.L. (N.I.) **425**
Att.-Gen. for Northern Ireland *v.* Gallagher [1963] A.C. 349; [1961] 3 W.L.R. 619; 105 S.J. 646; [1961] 3 All E.R. 299; 45 Cr. App. R. 316; [77 L.Q.R. 457; 25 M.L.R. 238; 111 L.J. 751; 97 I.L.T. 57], H.L. **192**
Att.-Gen. for South Australia *v.* Brown [1960] A.C. 432; [1960] 2 W.L.R. 588; 104 S.J. 268; [1960] 1 All E.R. 734; 44 Cr. App. R. 100 166,169
Atwal *v.* Massey [1971] 3 All E.R. 881; 56 Cr. App. R. 6, D.C. 617
Austin [1981] 1 All E.R. 374; *sub nom.* R. *v.* Austin, Withers, Fieldsend and Trigwell (1981) 72 Cr. App. R. 104, C.A. **282**, 343
Axtell (1660) Kel. 13; 5 State Tr. 1146; 84 E.R. 1060 222

B. and S. *v.* Leathley [1979] Crim. L.R. 314 640
Bailey (1818) R. & R. 341 632
—— (1977) 66 Cr. App. Rep. 31n. 407, 408
Bainbridge [1960] 1 Q.B. 129; [1959] 3 W.L.R. 656; 123 J.P. 499; [1959] 3 All E.R. 200; 43 Cr. App. R. 194 .... 249, 256, 258
Bank of New South Wales *v.* Piper [1897] A.C. 383; 66 L.J.P.C. 73; 76 L.T. 572; 13 T.L.R. 413; 61 J.P. 660 .... 102, 111, 114, 144, 145
Barnard (1979) 70 Cr. App. R. 28; (1979) 123 S.J. 803; [1980] Crim. L.R. 235, C.A. 336
Barnes *v.* Akroyd (1872) L.R. 7 Q.B. 474; 41 L.J.Q.B. 110; 26 L.T. 692; 20 W.R. 671; 37 J.P. 116 132
Barr [1978] Crim. L.R. 244 .... 546, 553
Barrett [1976] 1 W.L.R. 946; 120 S.J. 402; [1976] 3 All E.R. 895; (1976) 63 Cr. App. R. 174; [1976] Crim. L.R. 576, C.A. 514
Barrow (1868) L.R. 1 C.C.R. 156; 38 L.J.M.C. 20; 19 L.T. 293; 17 W.R. 102; 11 Cox C.C. 191 483
Bastable *v.* Little [1907] 1 K.B. 59 85
Bateman (1925) 94 L.J.K.B. 791; 133 L.T. 730; 41 T.L.R. 557; 89 J.P. 162; 69 S.J. 622; 28 Cox C.C. 33; 19 Cr. App. R. 8 .... 439, 440, 442, **449**, 453
Bayley & Easterbrook [1980] Crim. L.R. 503, C.A. 10
Beard [1977] Crim. L.R. 432, C.A. 181, 182, 184, 185, 193, 914
Beasley (1981) 73 Cr. App. R. 44; [1981] Crim. L.R. 635, C.A. 484
Becerra; R. *v.* Cooper (1975) 62 Cr. App. R. 121; C.A. **270**
Bedder *v.* D.P.P. [1954] 1 W.L.R. 1119; 98 S.J. 556; [1954] 2 All E.R. 801; 38 Cr. App. R. 133 .... 193, 390, 391, 393, 394, 395, 396
Beech (1912) 7 Cr. App. R. 197 484
Belfon (1976) 1 W.L.R. 741, C.A. **65**, 384, 485
Bembridge (1783) 22 State Tr. 1; 3 Doug. K.B. 327; 99 E.R. 679 20
Benge (1865) 4 F. & F. 504 20
Bernhard [1938] 2 K.B. 264; 107 L.J.K.B. 449; 159 L.T. 22; 54 T.L.R. 615; 102 J.P. 282; 82 S.J. 257; [1938] 2 All E.R. 140; 31 Cox C.C. 61; 26 Cr. App. R. 137; 36 L.G.R. 333 626
Betts and Ridley (1930) 144 L.T. 526; 29 Cox C.C. 259; 22 Cr. App. R. 148 ...... **268**, 369
Betts *v.* Stevens [1910] 1 K.B. 1; 79 L.J.K.B. 17; 101 L.T. 564; 73 J.P. 486; 26 T.L.R. 5; 22 Cox C.C. 187; 7 L.G.R. 1052 .... 85, 86
Betty (1964) 48 Cr. App. R. 6, C.C.A. 269, 270

Birtles [1969] 1 W.L.R. 1047; 133 J.P. 573; 113 S.J. 424; [1969] 2 All E.R. 1131n.; *sub nom*. R. *v*. Birtles (Frank Alexander), 53 Cr. App. R. 469, C.A. 238
Bishop (1880) 5 Q.B.D. 259; 49 L.J.M.C. 45; 42 L.T. 240; 28 W.R. 475; 44 J.P. 330; 14 Cox C.C. 404 .... 120, 130, 131
Blaue [1975] 1 W.L.R. 1411; 119 S.J. 589; [1975] 3 All E.R. 466; *sub nom*. R. *v*. Blaue (Robert Konrad) (1975) 61 Cr. App. R. 271; [1975] Crim. L.R. 648, C.A. **31**, 33, 38, 39
Bloxham [1981] 1 W.L.R. 859; [1981] 2 All E.R. 647; (1981) 72 Cr. App. R. 323; [1981] Crim. L.R. 337; [1981] R.T.R. 376, C.A. 615
Board of Trade *v*. Owen [1957] A.C. 602; [1957] 2 W.L.R. 351; 121 J.P. 177; 101 S.J. 186; [1957] 1 All E.R. 411; 41 Cr. App. R. 11; [102 S.J. 189], H.L.; affirming *sub nom*. R. *v*. Owen [1957] 1 Q.B. 174; [1956] 3 W.L.R. 739; 120 J.P. 553; 100 S.J. 769; [1956] 3 All E.R. 432; [1956] C.L.Y. 1764, 1882, 1951, C.C.A.; reversing in part [1956] 3 W.L.R. 252; 100 S.J. 454; 40 Cr. App. R. 103 331
Bogacki [1973] 1 Q.B. 832; [1973] 2 W.L.R. 937; [1973] 2 All E.R. 864; 117 S.J. 355; [1973] R.T.R. 384; [1973] Crim. L.R. 385 548
Boggeln *v*. Williams [1978] 1 W.L.R. 873; (1978) 122 S.J. 94; [1978] 2 All E.R. 1061; (1978) 67 Cr. App. R. 50; [1978] Crim. L.R. 242, D.C. 561
Bolton, H. L. (Engineering) Co. Ltd. *v*. T. J. Graham and Sons Ltd. [1957] 1 Q.B. 159; [1956] 3 W.L.R. 804; 100 S.J. 816; [1956] 3 All E.R. 624; [[1957] J.B.L. 14; 73 L.Q.R. 16; 21 Conv. 77], C.A. 298, 301, 302
Bonner [1970] 1 W.L.R. 838; [1970] 2 All E.R. 97n.; 114 S.J. 188; 54 Cr. App. R. 257, C.A. **520**
Bonollo [1981] V.R. 633 .... 561, 562
Bourne [1939] 1 K.B. 687; 108 L.J.K.B. 471; [1938] 3 All E.R. 615 ...... 456, **457**, 460, 461
—— (1952) 36 Cr. App. R. 125 .... 208, 231, 281
Bow [1977] R.T.R. 6; (1976) 64 Cr. App. R. 54; [1977] Crim. L.R. 176, C.A. **547**, 550
Boyle (1954) 2 Q.B. 292; [1954] 3 W.L.R. 364; 118 J.P. 481; 98 S.J. 559; [1954] 2 All E.R. 721; 38 Cr. App. R. 111 638
Brannan *v*. Peek [1948] 1 K.B. 68; [1948] L.J.R. 405; 63 T.L.R. 592; 112 J.P. 10; 91 S.J. 654; [1947] 2 All 572; 45 L.G.R. 654 235
Bratty *v*. Att.-Gen. for Northern Ireland [1936] A.C. 386; [1961] 3 W.L.R. 965; 105 S.J. 865; [1961] 3 All E.R. 523 .... 16, 163, 167, **168**, 171, 173, 175, 180
Breeze *v*. The State 12 Ohio 146 (1861) 250
Brend *v*. Wood (1946) L.T. 306; 110 J.P. 317; 62 T.L.R. 462 .... 132, 141
Brewster (1979) 69 Cr. App. R. 375; [1979] Crim. L.R. 798, C.A. 531
Brian (1834) 6 C. & P. 349 368
Briggs [1977] 1 W.L.R. 605; [1977] 1 All E.R. 475; (1976) 63 Cr. App. R. 215, C.A. 73, 74, 76, 77
Brindley and Long [1971] 2 Q.B. 300; [1971] 2 W.L.R. 895; 115 S.J. 285; [1971] 2 All E.R. 698; *sub nom*. R. *v*. Brindley (Maureen McKenna); R. *v*. Long (Frank Jones), 55 Cr. App. R. 258, C.A. **286**
Bristol Riots Case (1832) 3 St. Tr. (N.S.) 1 422
Brooks *v*. Mason [1902] 2 K.B. 743 61
Brow [1981] V.R. 783 562
Brown (1899) 63 J.P. 790 .... **363**
—— [1970] 1 Q.B. 105; [1969] 3 W.L.R. 370; [1969] 3 All E.R. 198; 133 J.P. 592; 113 S.J. 639; (1969) 53 Cr. App. R. 527, C.A. 612
Brown and Morley [1968] S.A.S.R. 467 218
Browning *v*. J. W. H. Watson (Rochester) [1953] 1 W.L.R. 1172; 117 J.P. 479; 97 S.J. 591; [1953] 2 All E.R. 775; 51 L.G.R. 597, D.C. 235
Bruce [1975] 1 W.L.R. 1252; 119 S.J. 459; [1975] 3 All E.R. 277; 61 Cr. App. R. 123; [1975] Crim. L.R. 454, C.A. 518
Buck & Buck (1960) 44 Cr. App. R. 213; [1960] Crim. L.R. 730 442
Buckoke *v*. G.L.C. [1971] Ch. 655; [1971] 2 W.L.R. 760; [1971] 2 All E.R. 254; 115 S.J. 174; [1971] R.T.R. 131; 69 L.G.R. 210, C.A. 230
Bull (1839) 9 C. & P. 22; 173 E.R. 723 .... **412**
Bullock [1955] 1 W.L.R. 1; 119 J.P. 65; 99 S.J. 29; [1955] 1 All E.R. 15; 38 Cr. App. R. 151 260
Bundy [1977] 1 W.L.R. 914; (1977) 121 S.J. 252; [1977] 2 All E.R. 382; (1977) 65 Cr. App. R. 239; [1977] R.T.R. 357; [1977] Crim. L.R. 570, C.A. 650

Burles [1947] V.L.R. 392; [1918] A.L.R. 460 113
—— [1970] 2 Q.B. 191; [1970] 2 W.L.R. 597; [1970] 1 All E.R. 642; 114 S.J. 86; 54 Cr. App. R. 196, C.A. 159
Button (1848) 11 Q.B.D. 929; 18 L.J.M.C. 19; 12 L.T.O.S. 309; 13 J.P. 20; 12 Jur. 1017; 3 Cox C.C. 229; 116 E.R. 720 .... 348, 349
—— [1900] 2 Q.B. 597; 69 L.J.Q.B. 901; 83 L.T. 288; 16 T.L.R. 525; 48 W.R. 703; 64 J.P. 600; 44 S.J. 659; 19 Cox C.C. 568 590
Butts *v.* United States (C.C.A. 8th) 18 A.L.R. 143, 273 Fed. 38 240
Byrne *v.* Kinematograph Renters Society [1958] 1 W.L.R. 762; 102 S.J. 509; [1958] 2 All E.R. 579; [102 S.J. 645; 103 S.J. 65, 84; [1959] C.L.J. 30; 21 M.L.R. 661] 638
—— [1960] 2 Q.B. 396; [1960] 3 W.L.R. 440; 104 S.J. 645; [1960] 3 All E.R. 1; 44 Cr. App. R. 246 .... 166, 169, **403**, 407, 408

Caldwell [1981] 1 All E.R. 961, H.L., [1981] Crim. L.R. 393 .... 11, **71**, 77, 79, **190**, 200, 660
Calgarth, the Otarama, the [1927] 638
Cambridgeshire and Isle of Ely County Council *v.* Rust [1972] 2 Q.B. 426; [1972] 3 W.L.R. 226; 116 S.J. 564; [1972] 3 All E.R. 232; 70 L.G.R. 444; [1972] Crim. L.R. 433, D.C. 658
Camplin [1978] A.C. 705; [1978] 2 W.L.R. 679; (1978) 122 S.J. 280; (1978) 67 Cr. App. R. 14; [1978] Crim. L.R. 432; *sub nom.* D.P.P. *v.* Camplin, *The Times*, April 11, 1978; [1978] 2 All E.R. 168, H.L.; affirming [1978] Q.B. 254; [1977] 3 W.L.R. 929; (1977) 121 S.J. 676; [1978] 1 All E.R. 1236; (1977) 66 Cr. App. R. 37; [1977] Crim. L.R. 748, C.A. **389**
—— (1845) 1 C. & K. 746; 1 Den. 89; 5 L.T. (o.s.) 266; 9 J.P. 424; 1 Cox 220 487
Carpenter (1911) 22 Cox 618 592
Carter [1959] V.R. 105 .... 173, 174
Cascoe [1970] 2 All E.R. 833; 54 Cr. App. R. 401, C.A. 389
Case (1850) 1 Den. 580; T. & M. 318; 4 New Sess. Cas. 347; 19 L.J.M.C. 174; 15 L.T. (o.s.) 306; 14 J.P. 339; 14 Jur. 489; 4 Cox C.C. 220 489
Casey *v.* United States 276 U.S. 413; 72 Law Ed. 632 (1928) 240
Cassady *v.* Morris [1975] Crim. L.R. 398 266
Cato; R. *v.* Morris, R. *v.* Dudley [1976] 1 W.L.R. 110; 119 S.J. 775; [1976] 1 All E.R. 260; [1976] Crim. L.R. 59; *sub nom.* R. *v.* Cato (Ronald Philip); R. *v.* Morris (Neil Adrien); R. *v.* Dudley (Melvin) (1975) 62 Cr. App. R. 41, C.A. **26**, 447, **451**, 454, 486
Cattell *v.* Iveson (1858) E.B. & E. 91; 27 L.J.M.C. 167; 4 Jur. (n.s.) 560 2
Chandler [1913] 1 K.B. 125; 82 L.J.K.B. 106; 108 L.T. 352; 29 T.L.R. 83; 77 J.P. 80; 57 S.J. 160; 23 Cox C.C. 330; 8 Cr. App. R. 82 640
—— *v.* D.P.P. [1964] A.C. 763; [1962] 3 W.L.R. 694; 106 S.J. 588; [1962] 3 All E.R. 142; 46 Cr. App. R. 347 .... **94**, 97, 313
Chapman [1974] Crim. L.R. 488, C.A. 518
Charlson [1955] 1 W.L.R. 317; 119 J.P. 283; 99 S.J. 221; [1955] 1 All E.R. 859; 39 Cr. App. R. 37; [73 S.A.L.J. 90] 169, 170
Chisam (1963) 47 Cr. App. R. 130, C.A. 420, 427
Church [1966] 1 Q.B. 59; [1965] 2 W.L.R. 1220; [1965] 2 All E.R. 72; 109 S.J. 371; 129 J.P. 366; 49 Cr. App. R. 206 .... 30, 42, 437, **441**, 443, 444, 445, 446, 447, 449
Churchill *v.* Walton [1967] 2 A.C. 224; [1967] 2 W.L.R. 682; 131 J.P. 277; 111 S.J. 112; [1967] 1 All E.R. 497; 51 Cr. App. R. 212 256
City of Sault Ste Marie (1978) 85 D.L.R. (3d) 161 .... **147**, 151
Clarence (1888) 22 Q.B.D. 23; 58 L.J.M.C. 10; 59 L.T. 780; 5 T.L.R. 61; 37 W.R. 166; 53 J.P. 149; 16 Cox C.C. 511 .... **481**, 489
Clarke [1949] 2 All E.R. 448; 33 Cr. App. R. 216 487
—— [1972] 1 All E.R. 219; 116 S.J. 56; 56 Cr. App. R. 225, D.C. 166
Clarkson [1971] 1 W.L.R. 1402; [1971] 3 All E.R. 344; 115 S.J. 654; 55 Cr. App. R. 445, Cts.-Martial App. Ct. **263**
Clear [1968] 1 Q.B. 670; [1968] 2 W.L.R. 122; [1968] 1 All E.R. 74; 132 J.P. 103; 112 S.J. 67; 52 Cr. App. R. 58, C.A. 622, 623
Clucas [1949] 2 K.B. 226; [1949] L.J.R. 1571; 65 T.L.R. 346; 113 J.P. 355; 93 S.J. 407; [1949] 2 All E.R. 40; 33 Cr. App. R. 136; 47 L.G.R. 563 .... **590**

Cockburn [1968] 1 W.L.R. 281; [1968] 1 All E.R. 466; 132 J.P. 166; 112 S.J. 91; 52 Cr. App. R. 134, C.A. 557, 559, 560, 561
Cocks (1976) 63 Cr. App. R. 79, C.A. 543
Codere (1916) 12 Cr. App. R. 21 .... **164**, 165
Cogan and Leak [1976] 1 Q.B. 217; [1975] 3 W.L.R. 316; 119 S.J. 473; [1975] 2 All E.R. 1059; [1975] Crim. L.R. 584; *sub nom.* R. *v.* Cogan (John Rodney); R. *v.* Leak (Michael Edward) (1975) 61 Cr. App. R. 217, C.A. **279**, 281
Coggins (1873) 29 L.T. 469; 38 J.P. 38; 12 Cox C.C. 517, C.C.R. 609
Cole *v.* Turner (1705) 6 Mod. 149; 87 E.R. 907; Holt K.B. 108 .... **473**
Collins (1864) L. & C. 471; 4 New Rep. 299; 33 L.J.M.C. 177; 10 L.T. 581; 12 W.R. 886; 28 J.P. 436; 10 Jur. (N.S.) 686; 9 Cox C.C. 497 .... 320, 321, 324
—— [1973] 1 Q.B. 100; [1972] 3 W.L.R. 243; [1972] 2 All E.R. 1562; 113 S.J. 897; 54 Cr. App. R. 19, C.A. 632, **633**, 638, 639
Collis-Smith [1971] Crim. L.R. 716, C.A. 582
Collister and Warhurst (1955) Cr. App. R. 100 .... **624**
Comer *v.* Bloomfield [1971] R.T.R. 49; (1970) 55 Cr. App. R. 305, D.C. 307, 310, 311, 315
Commissioner of Police for the Metropolis *v.* Charles [1977] A.C. 177 .... 585, 586, 587
Commonwealth *v.* Cali (1923) 141 N.E. 510 19
—— *v.* Kennedy 170 Mass. 18 (1897) 307
Coney (1882) 8 Q.B.D. 534; 51 L.J.M.C. 66; 46 L.T. 307; 30 W.R. 678; 46 J.P. 404; 15 Cox C.C. 46 .... 262, 263, 478
Cook (1963) 48 Cr. App. R. 98, C.A. 311, 313
Coppen *v.* Moore (No. 2) [1898] 2 Q.B. 306 297
Corcoran *v.* Anderton (1980) 71 Cr. App. R. 104; [1980] Crim. L.R. 385, D.C. **566**
Cotterill *v.* Penn [1936] 1 K.B. 53; 105 L.J.K.B. 1; 153 L.T. 377; 26 T.L.R. 31; 99 J.P. 15; 3 Cr. App. R. 46 101
Cottle [1958] N.Z.L.R. 999 173
Cox (1818) R. & R. 362 372
—— [1968] 1 W.L.R. 308; [1968] 1 All E.R. 386; *sub nom.* R. *v.* Cox (Maurice George) (1967) 111 S.J. 966; 52 Cr. App. R. 130, C.A. 411
Cozens *v.* Brutus [1973] A.C. 854; [1972] 3 W.L.R. 521; [1972] 2 All E.R. 1297; 56 Cr. App. R. 799 .... 558, 613
Cramp (1880) 5 Q.B.D. 307; 49 L.J.M.C. 44; 42 L.T. 442; 28 W.R. 701; 44 J.P. 411; 14 Cox C.C. 401 485
Crane *v.* D.P.P. [1921] 2 A.C. 299; 90 L.J.K.B. 1160; 125 L.T. 642; 85 J.P. 245; 65 S.J. 642; 27 Cox C.C. 43; 15 Cr. App. R. 183; *sub nom.* R. *v.* Crane, 37 T.L.R. 788 160, 161
Croft [1944] 1 K.B. 295; 88 S.J. 152; [1944] 2 All E.R. 483; 113 L.J.K.B. 308; 170 L.T. 312; 60 T.L.R. 226; 29 Cr. App. R. 169, C.C.A. 272
Crofter Hand Woven Harris Tweed Co. Ltd. *v.* Veitch [1942] A.C. 435; 111 L.J.P.C. 117; 166 L.T. 172; 58 T.L.R. 125; [1942] 1 All E.R. 142 376
Crunden (1809) 2 Camp. 89 356
Crutchley (1831) 5 C. & P. 133; 1 Nev. & M.M.C. 282 214
—— (1837) 7 C. & P. 814 .... 214, 368
Cugullere [1961] 1 W.L.R. 858; 125 J.P. 414; 105 S.J. 386; [1961] 2 All E.R. 343; 45 Cr. App. R. 108 647
Cullen (1974), unreported 530
Cullum (1873) L.R. 2 C.C.R. 28; 42 L.J.M.C. 64; 28 L.T. 571; 21 W.R. 687; 37 J.P. 422; 12 Cox C.C. 469 531
Cundy *v.* Le Cocq (1884) 13 Q.B.D. 207; 53 L.J.M.C. 125; 51 L.T. 265; 32 W.R. 769; 48 J.P. 599 .... **130**, 133, 134, 135
Cunliffe *v.* Goodman [1950] 2 K.B. 237; 66 T.L.R. 109; [1950] 1 All E.R. 720; 94 S.J. 179, C.A. 64, 376
Cunningham [1957] 2 Q.B. 396; [1957] 3 W.L.R. 76; 121 J.P. 451; 101 S.J. 503; [1957] 2 All E.R. 412; 41 Cr. App. R. 155 .... 72, 73, 74, 75, 76, 77, **81**, 82, 83
—— [1959] 1 Q.B. 288; [1959] 2 W.L.R. 63; 123 J.P. 134; 103 S.J. 56; [1958] 3 All E.R. 711; 43 Cr. App. R. 79 369
—— [1981] 3 W.L.R. 223; [1981] 2 All E.R. 863; (1981) 125 S.J. 512; [1981] Crim. L.R. 835; (1981) Cr. App. R. 253, H.L. **386**
Curl (1727) 2 Str. 788; 1 Barn. K.B. 29; 17 St. Tr. 153 256

Curley (1909) 2 Cr. App. R. 96, 109 .... **29**
Curr [1968] 2 Q.B. 944; [1967] 2 W.L.R. 595; 131 J.P. 245; 111 S.J. 152; [1967] 1 All E.R. 478; 51 Cr. App. R. 113 .... 360, **361**

Dalloway (1847) 2 Cox 273 .... 18, **28**
Dalton. *See* Percy Dalton Ltd.
Daly [1968] V.R. 257 103
Davey *v.* Lee [1968] 1 Q.B. 366; [1967] 3 W.L.R. 105; 131 J.P. 327; 111 S.J. 212; [1967] 2 All E.R. 423; 51 Cr. App. R. 303 310
Davies *v.* Flackett (1972) 116 S.J. 526; [1973] R.T.R. 8; [1972] Crim. L.R. 708, D.C. **588**
—— *v.* Harvey (1874) L.R. 9 Q.B. 433; 43 L.J.M.C. 121; 30 L.T. 629; 22 W.R. 733; 38 J.P. 661 131
Davis (1881) 14 Cox 563 194
Dawson (1976) 64 Cr. App. R. 170 .... **569**
Dayle [1974] 1 W.L.R. 181; [1973] 3 All E.R. 1151; 117 S.J. 852; [1973] Crim. L.R. 703, C.A. 648
Deakin [1972] 1 W.L.R. 1618; [1972] 3 All E.R. 803; 116 S.J. 944; [1972] Crim. L.R. 781; (1972) 56 Cr. App. R. 841, C.A. **615**
Dee (1884) 14 L.R. Ir. 486; 15 Cox C.C. 579 483
De Freitas *v.* R. (1960) 2 W.I.R. 523 434
Delaval (1763) 3 Burr. 1434; 1 Wm. Bl. 439 356
Denton [1982] 1 All E.R. 65 660
Derbyshire *v.* Howliston [1897] 1 Q.B. 772; 66 L.J.Q.B. 569; 76 L.T. 624; 61 J.P. 374; 45 W.R. 527; 13 T.L.R. 377; 41 S.J. 441; 18 Cox C.C. 609, D.C. 141
Derry *v.* Peek (1889) 14 App. Cas. 337 77
Desmond (1868) *The Times*, April 28 378
Devlin *v.* Armstrong [1971] N.I. 13, C.A. 416, **419**
Dicken (1877) 14 Cox 8 .... 490, 491
Diggin [1980] R.T.R. 83; [1980] Crim. L.R. 656, C.A. 550
D.P.P. *v.* Beard [1920] A.C. 479; 89 L.J.K.B. 437; 122 L.T. 625; 36 T.L.R. 379; 84 J.P. 129; 64 S.J. 340; 26 Cox C.C. 573; 14 Cr. App. R. 159 .... 169, 178, 179, 369
—— *v.* Camplin. *See* Camplin.
—— *v.* Daley [1980] A.C. 237; [1979] 2 W.L.R. 239; [1979] Crim. L.R. 182; *sub nom.* D.P.P. *v.* Daley; D.P.P. *v.* McGhie (1978) 69 Cr. App. R. 39; *sub nom.* D.P.P. *v.* Daley and McGhie (1978) 122 S.J. 861, P.C. 30, 33
—— *v.* Doot [1973] A.C. 807 .... **336**
—— *v.* Majewski [1977] A.C. 443; [[1977] Crim. L.R. 532; 3 Crim. L.J. 13] H.L.; [1976] 2 W.L.R. 623; 120 S.J. 299; [1976] 2 All E.R. 142; (1976) 62 Cr. App. R. 262; [1976] Crim. L.R. 374, H.L. affirming *sub nom.* R. *v.* Majewski [1975] 3 W.L.R. 401; 119 S.J. 560; [1975] 3 All E.R. 296; [1975] Crim. L.R. 570, C.A. .. 175, **176**, 185, 186, 187, 188, 189, 190, 191, 192, 374, 447, 448
—— *v.* Merriman [1973] A.C. 584; [1972] 3 W.L.R. 545; 116 S.J. 745; [1972] 3 All E.R. 42; 56 Cr. App. R. 766; [1972] Crim. L.R. 784, H.L.; reversing *sub nom.* R. *v.* Merriman [1971] 2 Q.B. 310; [1971] 2 W.L.R. 1453; 115 S.J. 466; [1971] 2 All E.R. 424, C.A. 253
—— *v.* Morgan; Same *v.* McDonald; Same *v.* McLarty; Same *v.* Parker [1976] A.C. 182; [1975] 2 W.L.R. 913; 119 S.J. 319; 61 Cr. App. R. 136; *sub nom.* D.P.P. *v.* Morgan [1975] 2 All E.R. 347; [1975] Crim. L.R. 717, H.L.; affirming *sub nom.* R. *v.* Morgan [1975] 1 All E.R. 8, C.A. . 62, **101**, 114, 115, 116, 120, 181, 182, 428, 429, 430, 486
—— *v.* Newbury; D.P.P. *v.* Jones [1977] A.C. 500; [1977] Crim. L.R. 359, H.L. ... 443, **444**
—— *v.* Nock [1978] A.C. 979 ... 10, 319, 320, 321, 322, 323, 324, 331, 359, 365, 644, 645
—— *v.* Ray [1974] A.C. 370; [1973] 3 W.L.R. 359; [1973] 3 All E.R. 131; 117 S.J. 663 **573**, 579, 580
—— *v.* Shannon [1975] A.C. 717; [1974] 3 W.L.R. 155; 118 S.J. 515; 59 Cr. App. R. 250; *sub nom.* R. *v.* Shannon [1974] 2 All E.R. 1009; [1975] Crim. L.R. 703, H.L.; reversing [1974] Crim. L.R. 177, C.A. 339, 340
—— *v.* Smith [1961] A.C. 290; [1960] 3 W.L.R. 546; 124 J.P. 473; 104 S.J. 683; [1960] 3 All E.R. 161; 44 Cr. App. R. 261 ... 10, 180, 369, **371**, 375, 376, 378, 380, 382, 386, 387, 388, 463, 481

D.P.P. *v.* Stonehouse [1978] A.C. 55; [1977] 3 W.L.R. 143; (1977) 121 S.J. 491; [1977] 2 All E.R. 909; (1977) 65 Cr. App. R. 192; [1977] Crim. L.R. 544; H.L. ... 39, 307, 311, 312, 313, 321, 360, 629
—— *v.* Sykes. *See* Sykes *v.* D.P.P.
—— *v.* Turner [1974] A.C. 357; [1973] 3 W.L.R. 352; 57 Cr. App. R. 932, H.L. . 10, 593
—— *v.* Withers [1975] A.C. 849; [1974] 3 W.L.R. 751; 118 S.J. 862; [1974] 3 All E.R. 984; 60 Cr. App. R. 85; [1975] Crim. L.R. 95, H.L.; reversing *sub nom.* R. *v.* Withers [1974] Q.B. 414; [1974] 2 W.L.R. 26; *sub nom.* R. *v.* Withers (Ian Douglas); R. *v.* Withers (Stuart Robert); R. *v.* Gearing (Helen); R. *v.* Withers (Phyllis) (1973) 58 Cr. App. R. 187, C.A. 349, 354
D.P.P. for Northern Ireland *v.* Maxwell (1978) 122 S.J. 758; [1978] 3 All E.R. 1140; [1978] Crim. L.R. 40; *sub nom.* Maxwell *v.* D.P.P. for Northern Ireland (1978) 68 Cr. App. R. 128; *sub nom.* D.P.P. *v.* Maxwell [1978] 1 W.L.R. 1350, H.L.; affirming [1978] Crim. L.R. 422, C.A. (N.I.) 246, **255**
—— *v.* Lynch [1975] A.C. 653; [1975] 2 W.L.R. 641; 119 S.J. 233; 61 Cr. App. R. 6; *sub nom.* Lynch *v.* D.P.P. for Northern Ireland [1975] 1 All E.R. 913; [1975] Crim. L.R. 707, H.L. [1975] N.I. 35 .... 62, 66, 108, **203**, 217, 218, 219, 220, 221, 222, 224, 229
Doherty (1887) 16 Cox C.C. 306 179
Dolan (1855) Dears. 436; 24 L.J.M.C. 59; 1 Jur. (N.S.) 72; 3 W.R. 177; 6 Cox C.C. 449 601, 602
Donnelly *v.* Jackman [1970] 1 W.L.R. 562; (1969) 114 S.J. 130; [1970] 1 All E.R. 987; 54 Cr. App. R. 229; [33 M.L.R. 438; 86 L.Q.R. 298], D.C. 472
Donovan [1934] 2 K.B. 498; 103 L.J.K.B. 683; 152 L.T. 46; 50 T.L.R. 566; 98 J.P. 409; 78 S.J. 601; 30 Cox C.C. 187; 25 Cr. App. R. 1; 55 L.G.R. 439 .... 5, **476**, 478, 491
Doukas [1978] 1 W.L.R. 372; (1978) 122 S.J. 30; [1978] 1 All E.R. 1061; (1977) 66 Cr. App. R. 228; [1978] Crim. L.R. 177, C.A. **582**
Downes (1875) 1 Q.B.D. 25 .... 88, 89
Du Cros *v.* Lambourne [1907] 1 K.B. 40 266
Dudley and Stephens (1884) 14 Q.B.D. 273; 54 L.J.M.C. 32; 52 L.T. 107; 1 T.L.R. 118; 33 W.R. 347; 49 J.P. 69; 15 Cox C.C. 624 .... 208, 210, 214, 216, 229
Duffy [1949] 1 All E.R. 932n. 404
—— [1967] 1 Q.B. 63; [1966] 2 W.L.R. 229; 130 J.P. 137; 110 S.J. 70; [1966] 1 All E.R. 62; 50 Cr. App. R. 68 .... **415**, 420
Duguid (1906) 75 L.J.K.B. 470; 94 L.T. 887; 22 T.L.R. 506; 70 J.P. 294; 50 S.J. 465; 21 Cox C.C. 200 .... 341, **342**, 343
Dunbar [1958] 1 Q.B. 1; [1957] 3 W.L.R. 330; 121 J.P. 506; 101 S.J. 594; [1957] 2 All E.R. 737; 41 Cr. App. R. 182 402
Duncalf and Others [1979] 1 W.L.R. 918; (1979) 123 S.J. 336; [1979] 2 All E.R. 1116; [1979] Crim. L.R. 452; *sub nom.* R. *v.* Duncalf, Carter, Purcell and Waters (1979) 69 Cr. App. R. 206, C.A. 332, **343**
Durham *v.* United States (1954) 214 F. 2d 862 196
Durkin [1973] 1 Q.B. 786; [1973] 2 W.L.R. 741; [1973] 2 All E.R. 872; 117 S.J. 355; [1973] Crim. L.R. 372; 57 Cr. App. R. 637, C.A. 546
Duru and Asghar [1974] 1 W.L.R. 2; (1973) 117 S.J. 7; *sub nom.* R. *v.* Duru [1973] 3 All E.R. 715; (1973) 58 Cr. App. R. 151; *sub nom.* R. *v.* Asghar [1973] Crim. L.R. 701, C.A. 508, 510, 511, **540**, 542
Dyke *v.* Elliot (The Gauntlet) (1872) L.R. 4 P.C. 184; 8 Moo. P.C. (N.S.) 428; 26 L.T. 45; 20 W.R. 497; 17 E.R. 373 141
Dyson [1908] 2 K.B. 454; 77 L.J.K.B. 813; 99 L.T. 201; 24 T.L.R. 653; 72 J.P. 303; 52 S.J. 535; 21 Cox C.C. 669; 1 Cr. App. R. 13 .... **367**
Dytham [1979] Q.B. 722; [1979] 3 W.L.R. 467; (1979) 123 S.J. 621; [1979] 3 All E.R. 641; (1979) 69 Cr. App. R. 387; [1979] Crim. L.R. 666, C.A. **20**

Eagleton (1855) Dears. 376, 515; 24 L.J.M.C. 158; 26 L.T. (O.S.) 7; 4 W.R. 17; 19 J.P. 546; 1 Jur. (N.S.) 940; 6 Cox C.C. 559 .... 305, 306, 307, 310, 311
Easom [1971] 2 Q.B. 315; [1971] 3 W.L.R. 82; [1971] 2 All E.R. 945; 115 S.J. 485; 55 Cr. App. R. 410 .... **535**, 642, 643, 645, 646
Eatch [1980] Crim. L.R. 650 186
Eaton *v.* Cobb [1950] 1 All E.R. 1016; (1950) 114 J.P. 271 84

Eckman *v.* Midland Bank Ltd. [1973] Q.B. 519; [1973] I.C.R. 71; [1973] 3 W.L.R. 284; (1972) 117 S.J. 87; [1973] 1 All E.R. 609; *sub nom.* Goad, *Re v.* Amalgamated Union Engineering Workers (Engineering Section); Eckman *v.* Midland Bank and Hill Samuel & Co. [1973] 1 Lloyd's Rep. 162, N.I.R.C. 507
Eddy *v.* Niman [1981] Crim. L.R. 502 499
Edmeads and Others (1828) 3 C. & P. 390 271
Edwards [1973] 1 All E.R. 152 401
—— *v.* Ddin [1976] 1 W.L.R. 942; 120 S.J. 587; [1976] 3 All E.R. 705; [1976) 63 Cr. App. R. 218; [1976] R.T.R. 508; [1976] Crim. L.R. 580, D.C. 502, **516**, 582
Eggington (1801) 2 Leach C.L. 913; 2 Bos. & P. 508 240
Eldershaw (1828) 3 C. & P. 396 276
Eldredge *v.* U.S. 62 F. 2nd 449 (1932) 273
Ellames [1974] 1 W.L.R. 1391; 118 S.J. 578; [1974] 3 All E.R. 130; [1974] Crim. L.R. 554; *sub nom.* R. *v.* Ellames (Charles John) (1974) 60 Cr. App. R. 7, C.A. **651**
Elliot (1889) 16 Cox 710 20
Ellis *v.* United States 206 U.S. 246; 54 Law Ed. 1047 (1907) 240
Emary *v.* Nolloth [1903] 2 K.B. 264; 72 L.J.K.B. 620; 89 L.T. 100; 67 J.P. 354; 52 W.R. 107; 19 T.L.R. 530; 47 S.J. 567; 20 Cox C.C. 507 291
Evans *v.* Dell (1937) 156 L.T. 240; 53 T.L.R. 310; 101 J.P. 149; 81 S.J. 100; [1937] 1 All E.R. 349; 30 Cox C.C. 558; 35 L.G.R. 105 69
Ewart (1905) 25 N.Z.L.R. 709 149

Fagan *v.* Metropolitan Police Commissioner [1969] 1 Q.B. 439; [1968] 3 W.L.R. 1120; 133 J.P. 16; 112 S.J. 800; [1968] 3 All E.R. 442; 52 Cr. App. R. 700 .... 18, 42, **473**, 478
—— Fagan (1974) unreported 208
Fairclough *v.* Whipp [1951] W.N. 528; [1951] 2 T.L.R. 909; 115 J.P. 612; 95 S.J. 699; [1951] 2 All E.R. 834; 35 Cr. App. R. 138 .... **475**
Farrance [1978] R.T.R. 225; (1977) 67 Cr. App. R. 136; [1978] Crim. L.R. 496, C.A. 319
Farrell (formerly McLaughlin) *v.* Secretary of State for Defence [1980] 1 W.L.R. 172; (1979) 124 S.J. 133; [1980] 1 All E.R. 166; (1979) 70 Cr. App. R. 224, H.L. 418
Faulkner (1877) 13 Cox C.C. 550; I.R. 11 C.L. 8 82
Feely [1973] Q.B. 530; [1973] 2 W.L.R. 201; [1973] 1 All E.R. 341; 117 S.J. 54; [1973] Crim. L.R. 193; 57 Cr. App. R. 312, C.A. **556**, 560, 561, 562, 566, 570, 592, 613, 620, 624
Fennell [1971] 1 Q.B. 428; [1970] 3 W.L.R. 513; [1970] 3 All E.R. 215; 114 S.J. 651; 54 Cr. App. R. 451, C.A. 427
Fenton (1830) 1 Law 179 439
Ferguson *v.* Weaving [1951] 1 K.B. 814; [1951] 1 T.L.R. 465; 115 J.P. 142; 95 S.J. 90; [1951] 1 All E.R. 412; 49 L.G.R. 339 .... 246, 251, **266**, 290
Field [1972] Crim. L.R. 435, C.A. 414
Figures [1976] Crim. L.R. 744 503
Fitzpatrick [1977] N.I. 20, C.C.A. **221**
—— *v.* Kelly (1873) L.R. 8 Q.B. 337; 42 L.J.M.C. 132; 28 L.T. 558; 21 W.R. 681; 38 J.P. 55 131
Flannery and Prendergast [1969] V.R. 31 .... 113, 114
Flattery (1877) 2 Q.B.D. 410; 46 L.J.M.C. 130; 36 L.T. 32; 25 W.R. 398; 13 Cox C.C. 388 .... 483, 489, 490
Fletcher (1859) Bell 63; 28 L.J.M.C. 85; 32 L.T. (O.S.) 388; 7 W.R. 204; 23 J.P. 70; 5 Jur. (N.S.) 179; 8 Cox C.C. 131 .... 116, 240, 243
Forbes and Webb (1865) 10 Cox C.C. 362 .... 101, 480
Ford (1976) unreported 410
Franklin (1883) 15 Cox 163 .... **438**, 442, 444, 447
Fraser *v.* Evans [1969] 1 Q.B. 349; [1968] 3 W.L.R. 1172; 112 S.J. 805; [1969] 1 All E.R. 8, C.A.; reversing *The Times*, September 26, 1968 513
Fretwell (1862) L. & C. 161; 31 L.J.M.C. 145; 6 L.T. 333; 10 W.R. 545; 26 J.P. 499; 8 Jur. (N.S.) 466; 9 Cox C.C. 152 261

Gallagher [1980] Crim. L.R. 723 180
Garlick [1981] Crim. L.R. 178 185

Gaumont British Distributors Ltd. *v.* Henry [1939] 2 K.B. 717 .... **68**, 69
George [1956] Crim. L.R. 52 491
—— (1960) 128 Can. Crim. Cas. 289 182
Ghosh, *The Times*, April 7, 1982 561
Gilks [1972] 1 W.L.R. 1341; [1972] 3 All E.R. 280; 116 S.J. 632; 56 Cr. App. R. 734; [1972] Crim. L.R. 440, C.C.A. 527, 530, **532**, 533
Gill [1963] 1 W.L.R. 841; 127 J.P. 429; 107 S.J. 417; [1963] 2 All E.R. 688; 47 Cr. App. R. 166, C.C.A. 214
Gould [1968] 2 W.L.R. 643; 132 J.P. 209; [1968] 2 Q.B. 65; [1968] 1 All E.R. 849; 52 Cr. App. R. 152 .... 102, 120, 122, 144
Grainge [1974] 1 W.L.R. 619; (1973) 118 S.J. 116; [1974] 1 All E.R. 928; *sub nom.* R. *v.* Grainge (Albert Robert Burns) (1973) 59 Cr. App. R. 3; [1974] Crim. L.R. 180, C.A. 617
Gray *v.* Bar [1971] 2 Q.B. 554; [1971] 2 W.L.R. 1334; [1971] 2 All E.R. 949; 115 S.J. 364; [1971] 2 Lloyd's Rep. 1, C.A. 445, 446, 447
Greenstein; R. *v.* Green [1975] 1 W.L.R. 1353; 119 S.J. 742; [1975] 1 All E.R. 1; *sub nom.* R. *v.* Greenstein (Allan); R. *v.* Green (Monty) (1975) 61 Cr. App. R. 296; [1975] Crim. L.R. 714, C.A. 591
Gregory (1867) L.R. 1 C.C.R. 77; 36 L.J.M.C. 60; 16 L.T. 388; 15 W.R. 774; 31 J.P. 453; 10 Cox C.C. 459 360
Grey (1864) 4 F. & F. 73 350
Griffiths (1974) 60 Cr. App. R. 14, C.A. 70, 617, 619
—— *v.* Studebakers Ltd. [1924] 1 K.B. 102; 93 L.J.K.B. 50; 130 L.T. 215; 40 T.L.R. 26; 87 J.P. 199; 68 S.J. 118; 27 Cox C.C. 565; 21 L.G.R. 796 132
Gugullere [1961] 1 W.L.R. 858 134
Gush [1981] N.Z.L.R. 92 385
Lady Gwendolen, The [1965] P. 294 .... 298, 301

Hadley *v.* Baxendale (1854) 9 Ex. 341 8
Haggard *v.* Mason [1976] 1 W.L.R. 187; (1975) 120 S.J. 7; [1976] 1 All E.R. 337; [1976] Crim. L.R. 51, D.C. 319
Hale (1978) 68 Cr. App. R. 415; [1979] Crim. L.R. 596, C.A. 503, **568**, 611
Hall (1849) 2 C. & K. 947; 1 Den. 381; T. & M. 47; 3 New Sess. Cas. 407; 18 L.J.M.C. 62; 12 L.T. (o.s.) 383; 13 J.P. 55; 13 Jur. 87; 3 Cox C.C. 245 .... **542**
—— (1961) 45 Cr. App. R. 366 442
—— [1973] 1 Q.B. 126; [1972] 3 W.L.R. 381; [1972] 2 All E.R. 1009; 116 S.J. 598; [1972] Crim. L.R. 453; 56 Cr. App. R. 547, C.A. **524**
Halliday (1889) 61 L.T. 701; 6 T.L.R. 109; 38 W.R. 256; 54 J.P. 312 484
Halstead *v.* Patel [1972] 1 W.L.R. 661; [1972] 2 All E.R. 147; 116 S.J. 218; 56 Cr. App. R. 334; [1972] Crim. L.R. 235, D.C. 560
Hamilton (1976) 11 W.I.R. 309 434
Hammett, R. C. Ltd. *v.* London County Council (1933) 97 J.P. 105 .... 298, 300
Hampton *v.* U.S. 425 U.S. 484 (1976) 243
Hands (1887) 16 Cox 188; 56 L.T. 370; 52 J.P. 24; 3 T.L.R. 442, C.C.R. 590
Hardy *v.* Motor Insurers' Bureau [1964] 2 Q.B. 745; [1964] 3 W.L.R. 433; [1964] 2 All E.R. 742; 108 S.J. 422; [1964] 1 Lloyd's Rep. 397 .... 373, 375, 379
Hargreaves *v.* Diddams (1875) L.R. 10 Q.B. 582; 32 L.T. 600; 23 W.R. 828; 40 J.P. 167 132
Harris [1964] Crim. L.R. 54, C.C.A. 266
Harrison *v.* Thornton [1966] Crim. L.R. 388 648
Harry [1972] Crim. L.R. 32 622
Harvey (1980) 72 Cr. App. R. 139 .... **627**, 629
Haughton (1833) 5 C. & P. 559; 1 Nev. & M.M.C. 376 123
—— *v.* Smith (R. D.) [1975] A.C. 476; [1974] 2 W.L.R. 1; [1973] All E.R. 1109; affirming R. *v.* Smith [1973] 2 W.L.R. 942 .... 10, 310, 317, 318, 319, 320, 321, 322, 323, 324, 358, 604, 616, 645
Hayes (1976) 64 Cr. App. R. 82 531
Hayward (1908) 21 Cox 692 .... **29**
Hector (1978) 67 Cr. App. R. 224, C.A. 644
Henshall, John (Quarries) Ltd. *v.* Harvey [1965] 2 Q.B. 233; [1965] 2 W.L.R. 758; 129 J.P. 224; 109 S.J. 152; [1965] 1 All E.R. 725, D.C. 289

Herring *v.* Walround (1681) 2 Chan. Cas. 110 356
Hibbert *v.* McKiernan [1948] 2 K.B. 142; [1948] L.J.R. 1521; 64 T.L.R. 256; 112 J.P. 287; 92 S.J. 259; [1948] 1 All E.R. 860; 46 L.G.R. 238 519
Hickey [1976] 68 D.L.R. (3d) 88 150
Hicklin (1868) L.R. 3 Q.B. 360; 37 L.J.M.C. 89; 18 L.T. 395; 16 W.R. 801; 11 Cox C.C. 19; *sub nom.* Scott *v.* Wolverhampton Justices, 32 J.P. 533 ..... **95**
Higgins (1801) 2 East 5; 102 E.R. 269 ..... 276, 360
Hill *v.* Baxter [1958] 1 Q.B. 277; [1958] 2 W.L.R. 76; 102 S.J. 53; [1958] 1 All E.R. 193 168, 172
Hillen and Pettigrew *v.* I.C.I. (Alkali) Ltd. [1936] A.C. 65 638
Hinchcliffe *v.* Sheldon [1955] 1 W.L.R. 1207; 120 J.P. 13; 99 S.J. 797; [1955] 3 All E.R. 406; [19 M.L.R. 411], D.C. 84
Hircock (1978) 67 Cr. App. R. 278; [1978] Crim. L.R. 184, C.A. 499, 502
Hobbs *v.* L. and S.W. Railway (1875) L.R. 10 Q.B. 111 224
—— *v.* Winchester Corporation [1910] 2 K.B. 471; 79 L.J.K.B. 1123; 102 L.T. 841; 74 J.P. 413; 8 L.G.R. 1072; 26 T.L.R. 557 ..... 135, 136
Hoffman *v.* Thomas [1974] 1 W.L.R. 374; (1973) 118 S.J. 186; [1974] 2 All E.R. 233; [1974] R.T.R. 182; [1974] Crim. L.R. 122, D.C. 231
Holland (1841) 2 Mood. & R. 351 32
Hollis [1971] Crim. L.R. 525 631
Holloway (1849) 2 C. & K. 942; 1 Den. 370; 3 New Sess. Cas. 410; T. & M. 40; 18 L.J.M.C. 60; 12 L.T. (o.s.) 382; 13 J.P. 54; 13 Jur. 86; 3 Cox C.C. 241 ..... **542**, 559
Holmes *v.* D.P.P. [1946] A.C. 588 ..... 390, 391, 394, 395
Holt and Lee [1981] 1 W.L.R. 1000; (1981) S.J. 373; (1981) 2 All E.R. 854; [1981] 73 Cr. App. R. 96; [1981] Crim. L.R. 499, C.A. **595**
Hopper [1915] 2 K.B. 431; 84 L.J.K.B. 1371; 113 L.T. 381; 31 T.L.R. 360; 79 J.P. 335; 59 S.J. 478; 25 Cox C.C. 34; 11 Cr. App. R. 136 400
Horton (1871) 11 Cox C.C. 670 110
Howe (1958) 100 C.L.R. 448; 32 A.L.J.R. 212 ..... 431, 433, 434, 435, 436
Howell and Bentley (1864) 4 F. & F. 160 356
Howells [1977] Q.B. 614; [1977] 2 W.L.R. 716; (1977) 121 S.J. 154; [1977] 3 All E.R. 417; (1977) 65 Cr. App. R. 86; [1977] Crim. L.R. 354, C.A. 121, 147
Howker *v.* Robinson [1973] 1 Q.B. 178; [1972] 3 W.L.R. 234; [1972] 2 All E.R. 786; 116 S.J. 354; [1972] Crim. L.R. 377, D.C. 295
Hudson and Taylor [1971] 2 Q.B. 202; [1971] 2 W.L.R. 1047; [1971] 2 All E.R. 244; 115 S.J. 303; 56 Cr. App. R. 1; 21 New L.J. 845, C.A. **201**, 206, 208, 214
Huggins (1730) 2 Strange 869; 1 Barn. K.B. 358; Fetz-G. 177; 2 Ld. Raym. 1574; 17 State Tr. 309; 94 E.R. 241 288
Hughes (1785) 1 Leach 406 ..... **632**
—— (1857) Dears. & B. 248; 26 L.J.M.C. 202; 29 L.T. (o.s.) 266; 5 W.R. 732; 21 J.P. 438; 3 Jur (N.S.) 696; 7 Cox C.C. 301 20
Hulbert (1979) 69 Cr. App. R. 243, C.A. 616
Humphreys and Turner 130 J.P. 45; [1965] 3 All E.R. 689 ..... 253, 289
Hussey (1924) 41 T.L.R. 205; 89 J.P. 28; 18 Cr. App. R. 160 ..... **416**
Husseyn (1977) 67 Cr. App. R. 131n; *sub nom.* R. *v.* Hussein [1978] Crim. L.R. 219, C.A. 641, 642, 643, 644, 645
Hurley and Murray [1967] V.R. 526 ..... 203, 207, 220
Hyam *v.* D.P.P. [1975] A.C. 55 10, 63, 64, 65, 66, 67, 106, 185, 216, 331, 369, **374**, 384, 385, 386, 387, 388, 485
Hyde and Schneider *v.* U.S. (1911) 255 U.S. 347 307

Indermaur *v.* Dames (1866) L.R. 1 C.P. 274 8
Instan [1893] 1 Q.B. 450; 62 L.J.M.C. 86; 68 L.T. 420; 9 T.L.R. 248; 41 W.R. 368; 57 J.P. 282; 37 S.J. 251; 17 Cox C.C. 602 ..... 20, **21**
Invicta Plastics *v.* Clare [1976] R.T.R. 251 361
Isitt [1978] R.T.R. 211; (1978) 67 Cr. App. R. 44; [1978] Crim. L.R. 159, C.A. 175
Ismail [1977] Crim. L.R. 557, C.A. 618

Jaggard *v.* Dickinson [1981] 2 W.L.R. 118; (1980) 124 S.J. 847; [1980] 3 All E.R. 716; [1980] Crim. L.R. 717, D.C. 116, **187**, 657, 659

James & Son Ltd. *v.* Smee [1955] 1 Q.B. 78; 104 L.J. 730; 218 L.T.J.O. 251; 118 J.P. 536; 98 S.J. 771; [1954] 3 All E.R. 273; 52 L.G.R. 545 .... 136, 289
Jarmain [1946] K.B. 74; 115 L.J. 205; 174 L.T. 85; 62 T.L.R. 33; 89 S.J. 497; [1945] 2 All E.R. 613; 31 Cr. App. R. 39 369
Johnson (1966) 10 W.I.R. 402 432
Johnson and Jones (1841) C. & M. 218 240
Johnson *v.* Phillips [1976] 1 W.L.R. 65; 119 S.J. 645; [1975] 3 All E.R. 682; [1976] R.T.R. 170; [1975] Crim. L.R. 580, D.C. 231
—— *v.* Youden [1950] 1 K.B. 544; [1950] 1 All E.R. 300; 60 T.L.R. (Pt. 1) 395; 114 J.P. 136; 94 S.J. 115; 48 L.G.R. 276 .... 256, 258
Jones [1949] 1 K.B. 194; 64 T.L.R. 616; 113 J.P. 18; 92 S.J. 648; [1948] 2 All E.R. 964; 33 Cr. App. R. 33; 47 L.G.R. 135 287
—— *v.* Brooks [1968] Crim. L.R. 498; 112 S.J. 52 Cr. App. R. 614 310
—— *v.* Secretary of State for Social Services; Hudson *v.* Same [1972] A.C. 944; [1972] 2 W.L.R. 210; (1971) 116 S.J. 57; [1972] 1 All E.R. 145, H.L.; reversing *sub nom.* R. *v.* National Insurance Commissioner, *ex p.* Hudson; R. *v.* National Insurance Commissioner, *ex p.* Jones [1970] 1 Q.B. 477; [1970] 2 W.L.R. 182; 7 K.I.R. 478; *sub nom.* R. *v.* National Insurance Commissioner, *ex p.* Hudson, *ex p.* Lloyd-Jones, 114 S.J. 10; *sub nom.* R. *v.* National Insurance Commissioner, *ex p.* Hudson and Jones [1970] 1 All E.R. 97, C.A.; affirming [1969] 2 W.L.R. 647; 113 S.J. 225; [1969] 2 All E.R. 638n; 6 K.I.R. 123, D.C. 396
Jones and Smith [1976] 1 W.L.R. 672; [1976] 3 All E.R. 54; *sub nom.* R. *v.* Jones (John) and Smith (Christopher), 120 S.J. 299; *sub nom.* R. *v.* Smith (Christopher); R. *v.* Jones (John) (1976) 63 Cr. App. R. 47, C.A. **637**, 639
Jordan (1956) 40 Cr. App. R. 153 .... 32, **34**, 35, 36, 37, 286
Julien (1969) 1 W.L.R. 839; [1969] 2 All E.R. 856; 133 J.P. 489; 113 S.J. 342; 53 Cr. App. R. 407 413

Kaitamaki [1980] N.Z.L.R. 59 486
Kaur *v.* Chief Constable of Hampshire [1981] 1 W.L.R. 578; (1981) 125 S.J. 323; [1981] 2 All E.R. 430; (1981) 72 Cr. App. R. 359; [1981] Crim. L.R. 259, D.C. 499
Kay *v.* Butterworth (1942) 173 L.T. 191; 62 T.L.R. 452; 110 J.P. 75; 89 S.J. 381 172
Kemp [1957] 1 Q.B. 399; [1956] 3 W.L.R. 724; 120 J.P. 457; 100 S.J. 768; [1956] 3 All E.R. 249; 40 Cr. App. R. 121 .... **167**, 169, 172
Kilbride *v.* Lake [1962] N.Z.L.R. 590 17
King [1938] 2 All E.R. 662; (1938) 82 S.J. 569 602
—— [1964] 1 Q.B. 285; [1963] 3 W.L.R. 892; 107 S.J. 832; [1963] 3 All E.R. 561; 48 Cr. App. R. 141 102
Knuller (Publishing, Printing and Promotions) Ltd. *v.* D.P.P. [1973] A.C. 435; [1972] 3 W.L.R. 143; 116 S.J. 545; 56 Cr. App. R. 633, H.L. 212, 345, **350**
Kohn (1979) 69 Cr. App. R. 395; [1979] Crim. L.R. 675, C.A. **506**, 511, 542
Komaroni and Rogerson (1953) 103 L.J. 97; [104 L.J. 211] 307
Kray (Ronald); R. *v.* Kray (Reginald); R. *v.* Kray (Charles); R. *v.* Whitehead; R. *v.* Lambrianou (Christopher); R. *v.* Lambrianou (Anthony); R. *v.* Bender; R. *v.* Foreman; R. *v.* Barrie [1970] 1 Q.B. 125; [1969] 3 W.L.R. 831; 53 Cr. App. R. 569; *sub nom.* R. *v.* Kray, 133 J.P. 719; 113 S.J. 793; [1969] 3 All E.R. 941, C.A. 208, 215, 218
Kromme, De (1892) 17 Cox C.C. 492; 66 L.T. 301 348

La Fontaine *v.* R. (1976) 136 C.L.R. 62 387
Lamb [1967] 2 Q.B. 981; [1967] 3 W.L.R. 888; 131 J.P. 456; 111 S.J. 541; [1967] 2 All E.R. 1282; 51 Cr. App. R. 417 .... 437, **443**, 445, 446, 449
Lambert *v.* California 355 U.S. 225 (1957) 122
Lambie [1981] 2 All E.R. 776; [1981] W.L.R. 78; [1981] 1 All E.R. 332; (1980) 124 S.J. 808; (1980) 71 Cr. App. R. 350; [1980] Crim. L.R. 725, C.A. **584**, 598
Landy; R. *v.* White; R. *v.* Kaye [1981] 1 W.L.R. 355; (1981) S.J. 80; [1981] 1 All E.R. 1172; (1981) 72 Cr. App. R. 237; [1981] Crim. L.R. 326, C.A. 561
Larsonneur (1933) 149 L.T. 542; 97 J.P. 206; 77 S.J. 486; 29 Cox C.C. 673; 24 Cr. App. R. 74; 31 L.G.R. 253 .... **16**, 17
Latimer (1886) 17 Q.B.D. 359; 55 L.J. 135; 54 L.T. 768; 51 J.P. 184; 16 Cox C.C. 70 82, **124**, 126, 268

Launchbury *v.* Morgans. *See* Morgans *v.* Launchbury.
Laverty [1970] 3 All E.R. 432; 54 Cr. App. R. 495, C.A. 581, 588
Lawrence *v.* Metropolitan Commissioner of Police [1972] A.C. 626; [1971] 3 W.L.R. 225; [1971] 2 All E.R. 1253; 115 S.J. 565; 55 Cr. App. R. 471; *sub nom.* Lawrence *v.* Commissioner of Police for the Metropolis [1971] 2 All E.R. 1253; [[1971] C.L.J. 185], H.L.; affirming *sub nom.* R. *v.* Lawrence (Alan) [1971] 1 Q.B. 373; [1970] 3 W.L.R. 1103; *sub nom.* R. *v.* Lawrence, 114 S.J. 864; [1970] 3 All E.R. 933; 55 Cr. App. R. 73, C.A. ... 441, 494, 495, **496**, 498, 499, 500, 502, 516, 534, 572, 616, 647
Lawrence [1981] 2 W.L.R. 524; (1981) 125 S.J. 241; [1981] 1 All E.R. 974; (1981) 73 Cr. App. R. 1; [1981] R.T.R. 217; [1981] Crim. L.R. 409, H.L.; reversing [1980] R.T.R. 443; (1980) 71 Cr. App. R. 291; [145 J.P.N. 228] **78**
Lawrence and Pomroy [1971] Crim. L.R. 645, C.A. **621**, 630
Lederer *v.* Hutchins [1961] W.A.R. 99 75
Lee *v.* Simpson (1847) 3 C.B. 871; 16 L.J.C.P. 105; 11 Jur. 127; 4 Dow. & L. 666 ... 132
Lemon; R. *v.* Gay News [1979] A.C. 617; [1979] 2 W.L.R. 281; (1979) 123 S.J. 163; [1979] 1 All E.R. 898; [1979] Crim. L.R. 311; *sub nom.* Whitehouse *v.* Gay News; Whitehouse *v.* Lemon (1978) 68 Cr. App. R. 381; [143 J.P.N. 300], H.L.; affirming [1979] Q.B. 10; [1978] 3 W.L.R. 404; 62 (1978) 122 S.J. 295; [1978] 3 All E.R. 175; (1978) 67 Cr. App. R. 70, C.A. 62
Lennard's Carrying Co. Ltd. *v.* Asiatie Petroleum Co. Ltd. [1915] A.C. 705; 84 L.J.K.B. 1281; 113 L.T. 195; 31 T.L.R. 294; 59 S.J. 411; 13 Asp. M.L.C. 81; 20 Com. Cas. 283 .... 298, 301
Lesbini [1914] 3 K.B. 1116; 84 L.J.K.B. 1102; 122 L.T. 175; 24 Cox C.C. 516; 11 Cr. App. R. 7 .... 391, 398, 401
Lester and Byast (1955) 39 Cr. App. R. 157 .... **649**
Levett's Case (1638) Cro. Car. 538 118
Lewis *v.* Dickinson [1976] Crim. L.R. 442; [1976] R.T.R. 431, D.C. 86
Lim Chin Aik [1963] A.C. 160; [1963] 1 All E.R. 223 .... 17, 122, **134**, 141, 144
Linnett *v.* Metropolitan Police Commissioner [1946] K.B. 290; 115 L.J.K.B. 513; 174 L.T. 178; 62 T.L.R. 203; 110 J.P. 153; 90 S.J. 211; [1946] 1 All E.R. 380; 44 L.G.R. 95 .... 266, 294
Lipman [1970] 1 Q.B. 152; [1969] 3 W.L.R. 819; [1969] 3 All E.R. 410; 133 J.P. 712; 113 S.J. 670; 53 Cr. App. R. 600, C.A. 174, 447, 448
Lockyer *v.* Gibb [1967] 2 Q.B. 243; [1966] 3 W.L.R. 84; 130 J.P. 306; 110 S.J. 507; [1966] 2 All E.R. 653 .... 152, 520
Lolley's Case (1812) R. & R. 237 131
Lomas (1913) 110 L.T. 239; 30 T.L.R. 125; 78 J.P. 152; 58 S.J. 220; 9 Cr. App. R. 220; 23 Cox C.C. 765 260
London and Globe Finance Corporation Ltd., *Re* [1903] 1 Ch. 728 .. 346, 574, 576, 580
Lord [1905] 69 J.P. 467, C.C.R. 531
Low *v.* Blease (1975) 119 S.J. 695; [1975] Crim. L.R. 513, D.C. 514
Lowe [1973] 1 Q.B. 702; [1973] 2 W.L.R. 481; [1973] 1 All E.R. 805; 117 S.J. 144; [1973] Crim. L.R. 238; 57 Cr. App. R. 365, C.A. ... 90, 91, 92, 441, 447, 453, 455
Lumley (1911) 76 J.P. 208; 22 Cox C.C. 635 378
Lynch *v.* D.P.P. for Northern Ireland. *See* D.P.P. for Northern Ireland *v.* Lynch 255
Lynn (1788) 2 Durn. & E. 733; 2 Term Rep. 73 256

McBride and Turnock [1964] Crim. L.R. 456 101
McCall [1971] Crim. L.R. 237; (1970) 115 S.J. 75; 55 Cr. App. R. 175, C.A. 592
McCarthy [1954] 2 Q.B. 105; [1954] 2 W.L.R. 1044; 98 S.J. 356; [1954] 2 All E.R. 262; 38 Cr. App. R. 74 .... 193, 394
McCormack [1969] 2 Q.B. 442; [1969] 3 W.L.R. 175; 133 J.P. 630; 113 S.J. 507; [1969] 3 All E.R. 371; *sub nom.* R. *v.* McCormack (Patrick Eugene), 53 Cr. App. R. 514, C.A. 491
McCrowther (1746) Fost. 13 202
McCullum (1973) 117 S.J. 525; [1973] Crim. L.R. 582; 57 Cr. App. R. 645, C.A. ... 616
M'Daniel (1755) Fost. C.L. 121 240
McDonough (1962) 106 S.J. 961; 47 Cr. App. R. 37 .... 363, **364**, 365
McEvilly and Lee (1973) 60 Cr. App. R. 150; [1974] Crim. L.R. 239, C.A. 234
McGregor [1962] N.Z.L.R. 1069 .... 396, 397, 398, 399

McHugh [1977] R.T.R. 1; (1976) 64 Cr. App. R. 92; [1977] Crim. L.R. 174, C.A. .. 502, 582
McInnes [1971] 1 W.L.R. 1600; 115 S.J. 655; [1971] 3 All E.R. 295; *sub nom.* R. *v.* McInnes (Walter), 55 Cr. App. R. 55, C.A. 413, 422
McIvor [1972] 1 All E.R. 491 561
McKay [1957] V.R. 560 433
McKnight *v.* Davies (1973) 117 S.J. 940; [1974] R.T.R. 4; [1974] Crim. L.R. 62, D.C. **550**
Macleod *v.* Att.-Gen. for New South Wales [1891] A.C. 455; 60 L.J.P.C. 55; 65 L.T. 321; 7 T.L.R. 703; 17 Cox C.C. 341, P.C. 337
M'Naghten (1843) 10 Cl. & F. 200; 8 E.R. 718; 4 St. Tr. (N.S.) 847; 1 Town St. Tr. 314; 1 C. & K. 130n. 118, 143, **162**, 163, 164, 166, 167, 170, 181, 182
McPherson (1857) Dears. & B. 197; 26 L.J.M.C. 134; 29 L.T. (O.S.) 129; 5 W.R. 525; 21 J.P. 325; 3 Jur. (N.S.) 523; 7 Cox C.C. 281 .... 320, 514, 536
—— (1972) 117 S.J. 13; [1973] Crim. L.R. 191, C.A. 499
McPherson, Farrell and Kajal [1980] Crim. L.R. 654 121
McShane (1977) 66 Cr. App. R. 97; [1977] Crim. L.R. 737; (1977) 121 S.J. 632, C.A. 462
Machent *v.* Quinn [1970] 2 All E.R. 255 514
Mackie (Robert) (1973) 57 Cr. App. R. 453; [1973] Crim. L.R. 438, C.A., affirming [1973] Crim. L.R. 54 .... **29**, 33
Maher *v.* Musson (1934) 52 C.L.R. 100 144
Malcherek & Steel [1981] 1 W.L.R. 690; (1981) 125 S.J. 305; [1981] 2 All E.R. 422; [1981] 73 Cr. App. R. 173; [1981] Crim. L.R. 401 .... **36**, 367
Mancini *v.* D.P.P. [1942] A.C. 1; 111 L.J.K.B. 84; 165 L.T. 353; 58 T.L.R. 25; [1941] 3 All E.R. 272; 28 Cr. App. R. 65 .... 390, 391, 393, 394, **400**, 401
Manley [1933] 1 K.B. 529; 174 L.T.Jo. 491; 49 T.L.R. 130; 24 Cr. App. R. 25; 31 L.G.R. 81 288
Manning (1852) Dears. 21 543
—— (1871) L.R. 1 C.C.R. 338; 41 L.J.M.C. 11; 25 L.T. 573; 36 J.P. 228; 20 W.R. 102; 12 Cox C.C. 106 640
Marcus [1981] 1 W.L.R. 774; (1981) 125 S.J. 396; [1981] 2 All E.R. 833; [1981] Crim. L.R. 490; (1981) 73 Cr. App. R. 49 486
Marsh (1824) 2 B. & C. 717; 4 Dow. & Ry. K.B. 260; 2 Dow. & Ry. M.C. 182 131
Martin (1832) 5 C. & P. 128 .... 31, 82
—— (1881) 8 Q.B.D. 54; 51 L.J.M.C. 36; 45 L.T. 444; 30 W.R. 106; 46 J.P. 288; 14 Cox C.C. 633 .... **124**, 125
Matheson [1958] 1 W.L.R. 474; [1958] 2 All E.R. 87; 42 Cr. App. R. 145 .. 403, 407, 409, 410
Matthews (1950) 66 T.L.R. (Pt. 1) 153; 114 J.P. 73; [1950] 1 All E.R. 137; 34 Cr. App. R. 55; 48 L.G.R. 190 620
Maxwell *v.* D.P.P. for Northern Ireland. *See* D.P.P. for Northern Ireland *v.* Maxwell.
May [1912] 3 K.B. 572; 82 L.J.K.B. 1; 108 L.T. 351; 29 T.L.R. 24; 77 J.P. 31; 23 Cox C.C. 327; 8 Cr. App. R. 63 476
Mayers (1872) 12 Cox 311 487
Mayling [1963] 2 Q.B. 717; [1963] 2 W.L.R. 709; 127 J.P. 269; 107 S.J. 177; [1963] 1 All E.R. 687; 47 Cr. App. R. 102, C.C.A. 356
Mead & Belt (1823) 1 Lewin 184 472
Meade [1909] 1 K.B. 895; 78 L.J.K.B. 476; 25 T.L.R. 359; 73 J.P. 239; 53 S.J. 378; 2 Cr. App. R. 54 .... 184, 193
Mealey and Sheridan (1974) 60 Cr. App. R. 59; [1974] Crim. L.R. 710, C.A. 234
Medland (1851) 5 Cox 292 544
Medley (1834) 6 C. & P. 292 132
Meech; R. *v.* Parslow; R. *v.* Jolliffe [1974] Q.B. 549; [1973] 3 W.L.R. 507; 117 S.J. 713; [1973] Crim. L.R. 771; *sub nom.* R. *v.* Meech [1973] 3 All E.R. 939; *sub nom.* R. *v.* Meech (Arthur James); R. *v.* Parslow (Jonathan Joseph); R. *v.* Jolliffe (Peter William), 58 Cr. App. R. 74, C.A. 499, 502, 503, **526**, 530
Melias Ltd. *v.* Preston [1957] 2 Q.B. 380; [1957] 3 W.L.R. 42; 121 J.P. 444; 101 S.J. 481; [1957] 2 All E.R. 449; 55 L.G.R. 366; [125 J.P.J. 362], D.C. 297
Meredith [1973] Crim. L.R. 253 524
Merriman. *See* D.P.P. *v.* Merriman.
Metharam (1961) 125 J.P. 578; 105 S.J. 632; [1961] 3 All E.R. 200; 45 Cr. App. R. 304 481

Metropolitan Police Commissioner *v.* Streeter (1980) 71 Cr. App. R. 113 604
Middleton (1873) L.R. 2 C.C.R. 38 533
Mieras *v.* Rees [1975] Crim. L.R. 224, D.C. 319
Miller [1954] Q.B. 282; [1954] 2 W.L.R. 138; 118 J.P. 340; 98 S.J. 62; [1954] 2 All E.R. 529; 38 Cr. App. R. 1 .... 480, 487
—— [1975] 1 W.L.R. 1222; 119 S.J. 562; [1975] 2 All E.R. 974; [1975] R.T.R. 479; [1975] Crim. L.R. 723; *sub nom.* R. *v.* Miller (Robert) 61 Cr. App. R. 182, C.A. 121
—— [1976] Crim. L.R. 147, C.A. 550
Mills (1857) 8 Cox 263; D. & B. 205; 26 L.J.M.C. 79; 29 L.T. (O.S.) 114; 21 J.P. 294; 3 Jur. (N.S.) 447; 5 W.R. 528 581
—— [1963] 1 Q.B. 522; [1963] W.L.R. 137; 127 J.P. 176; 107 S.J. 38; [1963] 1 All E.R. 202; 47 Cr. App. R. 49, C.C.A. **333**
Minister of Pensions *v.* Chennell [1947] K.B. 250; [1946] 2 All E.R. 719 35
Mirehouse *v.* Rennell (1833) 1 Cl. & F. 527; 8 Bing. 490; 7 Bli. (N.S.) 241; 1 Moo. & S. 683 356
Mohan [1967] 2 A.C. 187; [1967] 2 W.L.R. 676; 111 S.J. 95; [1967] 2 All E.R. 58 .... 246, **254**
—— [1976] Q.B. 1; [1975] 2 W.L.R. 859; 119 S.J. 219; [1975] 2 All E.R. 193; [1975] R.T.R. 337; [1975] Crim. L.R. 283; *sub nom.* R. *v.* Mohan (John Patrick) 60 Cr. App. R. 272, C.A. 63, 66, 68, 328, 329, 330, 331, 384
Moore (1852) 3 C. & K. 153; 2 Den. 522; 21 L.J.M.C. 199; 16 J.P. 744; 16 Jur. 621; 5 Cox C.C. 555 .... 184, 193
Morden *v.* Porter (1860) 7 C.B. (N.S.) 641; 29 L.J.M.C. 213; 1 L.T. 403; 8 W.R. 262; 25 J.P. 263 132
Morgan [1972] 1 Q.B. 436; [1972] 2 W.L.R. 123; (1971) 116 S.J. 76; [1972] 1 All E.R. 348; *sub nom.* R. *v.* Morgan (Martin Meldrum) (1971) 56 Cr. App. R. 181; [1972] J.C.L. 95, C.A. 178, 186, 187, 188, **284**
—— *v.* Ashcroft [1938] 1 K.B. 49 .... 532, 533
Morgans *v.* Launchbury [1973] A.C. 127 211
Morgentaler *v.* The Queen [1976] 1 S.C.R. 616 231
Morris *v.* Tolman [1923] 1 K.B. 166; 92 L.J.K.B. 215; 128 L.T. 118; 39 T.L.R. 39; 86 J.P. 221; 67 S.J. 169; 27 Cox C.C. 345; 20 L.G.R. 803 278
Most (1881) 7 Q.B.D. 244; 50 L.J.M.C. 113; 44 L.T. 823; 29 W.R. 758; 45 J.P. 696; 14 Cox C.C. 583 360
Mousell Bros. *v.* London and North Western Railway [1917] 2 K.B. 836; 27 L.J.K.B. 82; 118 L.T. 25; 81 J.P. 305; 15 L.G.R. 706 .... 68, 289, 291, 292
Mowatt [1968] 1 Q.B. 421; [1967] 3 W.L.R. 1192; 131 J.P. 463; 111 S.J. 716; [1967] 3 All E.R. 47; 51 Cr. App. R. 402 .... 82, 485
Mowe *v.* Perraton [1952] 1 All E.R. 423; 116 J.P. 139; 96 S.J. 182; 35 Cr. App. R. 194, D.C. 551, 553
Moynes *v.* Coopper [1956] 1 Q.B. 439; [1956] 2 W.L.R. 562; [1956] 1 All E.R. 450; 120 J.P. 147; 100 S.J. 171; 40 Cr. App. R. 20; [1956] Crim. L.R. 516 .... 532, 533
Muir *v.* H.M. Advocate, 1933 S.C. (J.) 46 407
Mulcahy (1868) L.R. 3 H.L. 306 .... 332, 333
Munks [1964] 1 Q.B. 304; [1963] 3 W.L.R. 952; 128 J.P. 77; 107 S.J. 874; [1963] 3 All E.R. 757; 48 Cr. App. R. 56 417
Murphy [1965] N.I. 138 235
—— [1980] 1 Q.B. 434; [1980] 2 W.L.R. 743; (1980) 124 S.J. 189; [1980] 2 All E.R. 325; (1980) 71 Cr. App. R. 33; [1980] R.T.R. 145; [1980] Crim. L.R. 309, C.A. 79, 81
Myers *v.* D.P.P. [1965] A.C. 1001; [1964] 3 W.L.R. 145; 128 J.P. 481; 108 S.J. 519; [1964] 2 All E.R. 881; 48 Cr. App. R. 348; [27 M.L.R. 606; 80 L.Q.R. 457; 81 L.Q.R. 36; 128 J.P.J. 479; 235 L.T. 439; 114 L.J. 768; [1965] C.L.J. 14; 99 I.L.T. 295], H.L.; affirming *sub nom.* R. *v.* Myers, 108 S.J. 221; [1964] 1 All E.R. 877; [128 J.P.J. 377]. C.C.A. 238

National Coal Board *v.* Gamble [1959] 1 Q.B. 11; [1958] 3 W.L.R. 434; 102 S.J. 621; [1958] 3 All E.R. 203 .... **259**, 263, 290
National Insurance Commissioner, *ex p.* Hudson; R. *v.* Industrial Insurance Commissioner, *ex p.* Jones. *See* Jones *v.* Secretary of State for Social Services; Hudson *v.* Same.

Neal *v.* Gribble (1978) 68 Cr. App. R. 9; [1978] R.T.R. 409; [1978] Crim. L.R. 500, D.C. 553
Newell (1980) 71 Cr. App. R. 331; [1980] Crim. L.R. 576, C.A. **397**, 399
Nicholls (1874) 13 Cox 75 .... 20, 23
Nichols *v.* Hall (1873) L.R. 8 C.P. 322; 42 L.J.M.C. 105; 28 L.T. 473; 21 W.R. 579; 37 J.P. 424 .... 131, 134
Nicklin [1977] 1 W.L.R. 403; 121 S.J. 286; [1977] 2 All E.R. 444; (1977) 64 Cr. App. R. 205; [1977] Crim. L.R. 221, C.A. 611

O'Brien (1954) Can. L. Rep. 666 .... 335, 488
—— (1974) 59 Cr. App. R. 222, C.A. 334
O'Connor (1980) 54 A.L.J.R. 349 192
O'Driscoll (1977) 65 Cr. App. R. 50; [1977] Crim. L.R. 560, C.A. 448
Ohlson *v.* Hylton [1975] 1 W.L.R. 724; 119 S.J. 255; [1975] 2 All E.R. 490; [1975] Crim. L.R. 292, D.C. 648
Olugboja [1981] 1 W.L.R. 1382; [1981] 3 All E.R. 443; (1981) 73 Cr. App. R. 344, H.L. 487
Orbell (1703) 6 Mod. Rep. 42; 12 Mod. Rep. 499; 87 E.R. 804 348
Oropesa, The [1943] P. 32; 112 L.J.P. 91; 168 L.T. 364; 59 T.L.R. 103; [1943] 1 All E.R. 211 35
Orpin [1980] 1 W.L.R. 1050; (1980) 124 S.J. 271; [1980] 2 All E.R. 321; (1980) 70 Cr. App. R. 306; [1980] Crim. L.R. 304, C.A.; reversing [1979] Crim. L.R. 722 .... 191, 192
Osborn (1919) 84 J.P. 63 364
O'Shay (1898) 19 Cox 76 .... 489, 490
Ostler *v.* Elliott [1980] Crim. L.R. 585, D.C. 101
Owens *v.* H.M. Advocate 1946 S.C. (J.) 119 .... 420, 427
Oxford *v.* Moss (1978) Cr. App. R. 183; [1979] Crim. L.R. 119, D.C. **512**, 554

Palmer [1971] A.C. 814; [1971] 2 W.L.R. 831; [1971] 1 All E.R. 1077; 115 S.J. 264; 55 Cr. App. R. 223, P.C. 423, 424, **430**, 435, 436
Pappajohn (1980) 111 D.L.R. 1 116
Parker (1910) 74 J.P. 208 625
—— (1963) 111 C.L.R. 610; 37 A.L.J.R. 3 373
—— (Daryl) [1977] 1 W.L.R. 600; (1977) 121 S.J. 353; [1977] 2 All E.R. 37; (1976) 63 Cr. App. R. 211; [1977] Crim. L.R. 102, C.A. 73, 74
Parkes [1973] Crim. L.R. 358 630
Partington *v.* Williams (1975) 120 S.J. 80; (1975) 62 Cr. App. R. 220 .... 319, 645
Payne [1963] 1 W.L.R. 637; 127 J.P. 230; 107 S.J. 97; [1963] 1 All E.R. 848; 47 Cr. App. R. 122; [79 L.Q.R. 476], C.C.A. 234, 239
Pearce unreported, November 21, 1972 527
Pearce [1973] Crim. L.R. 321, C.A. 550
—— *v.* Brooks (1866) L.R. 1 Ex. 213; 4 H. & C. 358; 35 L.J. Ex. 134; 14 L.T. 288; 14 W.R. 614; 30 J.P. 295; 12 Jur. (N.S.) 342 261
Pearks, Gunston & Ward [1902] 2 K.B. 1; 71 L.J.K.B. 656; 87 L.T. 51; 66 J.P. 774; 20 Cox C.C. 279 141
Peart [1970] 2 Q.B. 672; [1970] 3 W.L.R. 63; [1970] 2 All E.R. 823; 114 S.J. 418; 54 Cr. App. R. 374, C.A. **552**, 553
Pembliton (1974) L.R. 2 C.C.R. 119; 43 L.J.M.C. 91; 30 L.T. 405; 22 W.R. 553; 38 J.P. 454; 12 Cox C.C. 607 .... 82, **122**, 124, 125, 126
People *v.* Lewis (1899) 57 Pac. 470 31
Percy Dalton (London) Ltd. [1949] L.J.R. 1626; 65 T.L.R. 326; 93 S.J. 358; [1949] W.N. 198; (1949) 33 Cr. App. R. 102 .... 318, 322, 326, 364, 365
Perkins (1852) 2 Den. 459; 21 L.J.M.C. 152; 16 J.P. 406; 16 Jur. 481; 5 Cox C.C. 554 609
Peter Pan Manufacturing Corp. *v.* Corsets Silhouette [1964] 1 W.L.R. 96; 108 S.J. 97; [1963] 3 All E.R. 402; [1963] R.P.C. 45 513
Phetheon (1840) 9 C. & P. 552 543
Phillips (Glasford) *v.* R. [1969] 2 A.C. 130; [1969] 2 W.L.R. 581; 53 Cr. App. R. 132, P.C. 401
Phipps [1970] R.T.R. 209 .... 551, 552, 553
Pierce Fisheries [1970] 12 D.L.R. (3d) 1591 150

Pierre [1963] Crim. L.R. 513 647
Pinney (1832) 3 B. & Ad. 947; 5 C. & P. 254; 3 State Tr. (N.S.) 11; 1 Nev. & M.M.C. 307; 110 E.R. 349 422
Pitchley (1972) 57 Cr. App. R. 30; [1972] Crim. L.R. 705, C.A. **611**
Pitham & Heyl (1976) 65 Cr. App. R. 45; [1977] Crim. L.R. 285, C.A. 502, 503, **608,** 611
Pittwood (1902) 19 T.L.R. 37 .... **19**
Plummer (1844) 1 C. & K. 600; 8 J.P. 615; 8 Jur. 921 31
Podola [1960] 1 Q.B. 325; [1959] 3 W.L.R. 718; 103 S.J. 856; [1959] 3 All E.R. 418; 43 Cr. App. R. 220 .... **160**, 168
Police *v.* Lavalle [1979] 1 N.Z.L.R. 45 233
Porritt [1961] 1 W.L.R. 1372; 125 J.P. 605; 105 S.J. 991; [1961] 3 All E.R. 463; 45 Cr. App. R. 348; [232 L.T. 119; 78 L.Q.R. 166], C.C.A. 427, 429
Potger (1970) 55 Cr. App. R. 42 .... 592, 593, 647
Poulton [1832] 5 C. & P. 330; 172 E.R. 997 .... **367**
Powell [1963] Crim. L.R. 511 648
—— *v.* MacRae [1977] Crim. L.R. 971, D.C. 531
Prince (1875) L.R. 2 C.C.R. 154; (1875) 13 Cox C.C. 138; 44 L.J.M.C. 122; 32 L.T. 700; 24 W.R. 76; 39 J.P. 676 .... 106, 113, 117, 119, 121, 129, 130, 131
Proprietary Articles Trade Association *v.* Att.-Gen. for Canada [1931] A.C. 324 (P.C.); 100 L.J.P.C. 84; 144 L.T. 577; 47 T.L.R. 250 2
Proudman *v.* Dayman (1941) 67 C.L.R. 536 .... 139, 145, 149
Puffendorf and Plowden 7 Wall. 482 (1869) 486 241
Purdy (1945) 10 J. Cr. L. 182 214

Quick; R. *v.* Paddison [1973] Q.B. 910; [1973] 3 W.L.R. 26; [1973] 3 All E.R. 347; 117 S.J. 371; 57 Cr. App. R. 722; [1973] Crim. L.R. 434, C.A. .. 158, 166, 167, **171**, 175, 279
Quinn (1898) 133 I.L.T. 154, 19 Cox C.C. 78 348
—— *v.* Leathem and Others [1901] A.C. 495; 70 L.J.P.C. 76; 85 L.T. 289; 17 T.L.R. 749; 50 W.R. 139; 65 J.P. 708 333

Rabey (1981) 114 D.L.R. (3d) 193 176
Race Relations Board *v.* Applin. *See* Applin *v.* Race Relations Board.
Radley (Ronald George) R. *v.* Radley (Wilfred George); R. *v.* Radley (Brian) (1973) 58 Cr. App. R. 394; [1974] Crim. L.R. 312, C.A. 348
Ram (1893) 17 Cox C.C. 609 276
Ransford (1874) 31 L.T. 488; 13 Cox C.C. 9 360
Rashid [1977] 1 W.L.R. 298; [1977] 2 All E.R. 237; (1976) 64 Cr. App. R. 201; [1977] Crim. L.R. 237, C.A. 583
Reader (1977) 66 Cr. App. R. 33, C.A. 617
Reeves (1839) 9 C. & P. 25 368
Reynolds *v.* G. H. Austin & Sons Ltd. [1951] 2 K.B. 135; [1951] 1 T.L.R. 614; 115 J.P. 192; 95 S.J. 173; [1951] 1 All E.R. 606; 49 L.G.R. 377 .... **132**, 136
Rice *v.* Connolly [1966] 2 Q.B. 414; [1966] 3 W.L.R. 17; 130 J.P. 322; 110 S.J. 371; [1966] 2 All E.R. 649; [82 L.Q.R. 457; 29 M.L.R. 682], D.C. 84
Richards [1974] Q.B. 776; [1973] 3 W.L.R. 888; 117 S.J. 852; *sub nom.* R. *v.* Richards (Isabelle) [1973] 3 All E.R. 1088; *sub nom.* R. *v.* Richards (Isabelle Christina) (1973) 58 Cr. App. R. 60; [1974] Crim. L.R. 96, C.A. **251**, 283
Ring, Atkins and Jackson (1892) 61 L.J.M.C. 116; 66 L.T. 300; 56 J.P. 552; 8 T.L.R. 326; 17 Cox C.C. 491 .... 318, 320, 321, 536
Roberts (Kenneth) (1971) 115 S.J. 809; [1972] Crim. L.R. 27; (1971) 56 Cr. App. R. 95, C.A. 480
Roberts *v.* Egerton (1874) L.R. 9 Q.B. 494; 43 L.J.M.C. 135; 30 L.T. 633; 22 W.R. 797; 38 J.P. 485 131
Robertson [1977] Crim. L.R. 629 531
—— *v.* Dicicco [1972] R.T.R. 431 579
Robinson [1915] 2 K.B. 342; 84 L.J.K.B. 1149; 113 L.T. 379; 31 T.L.R. 313; 79 J.P. 303; 58 S.J. 366; 24 Cox C.C. 726; 11 Cr. App. R. 124 .... 306, 307, 310, 311, 313, 315
—— [1977] Crim. L.R. 173, C.A. 568
Rolfe (1952) 36 Cr. App. R. 4 471

Roper *v.* Knott [1898] 1 Q.B. 868 654
—— *v.* Taylor's Central Garages [1951] 2 T.L.R. 284 69
Rose (1884) 15 Cox 540 .... **414**, 427
Rothery [1976] Crim. L.R. 691; [1976] R.T.R. 550, C.A. 515
Rouse, William *v.* Bradford Banking Co. Ltd. [1894] A.C. 586 507
Royal College of Nursing of the United Kingdom *v.* D.H.S.S. [1981] 2 W.L.R. 279; (1981) 125 S.J. 149; [1981] 1 All E.R. 545; [1981] Crim. L.R. 322, H.L.; reversing (1980) 124 S.J. 813; [1981] Crim. L.R. 169; (1980) 11 Fam. Law 113, C.A.; reversing (1980) 124 S.J. 615; [1980] Crim. L.R. 714 .... **460**
Russell [1933] V.L.R. 59 266
—— *v.* H.M. Advocate 1946 S.C.(J.) 37 .... 161, 168
Rylands *v.* Fletcher (1868) L.R. 3 H.L. 330 8

S. *v.* Goliath 1972 (3) S.A. 1 216
—— *v.* Nkosiyana (1966) (4) S.A. 655 276
St. George (1840) 9 C. & P. 483; 173 E.R. 921 .... **472**, 474
St. Margaret's Trust Ltd. [1958] 1 W.L.R. 522; 102 S.J. 348; 122 J.P. 312; [1958] 2 All E.R. 289; 42 Cr. App. R. 183 136
Salisbury (1553) 1 Plow. 100; 75 E.R. 159 270
Salvo [1980] V.R. 401 562
Sang [1980] A.C. 402; [1979] 3 W.L.R. 263; (1979) 123 S.J. 552; [1979] 2 All E.R. 1222; (1979) 69 Cr. App. R. 282; [1979] Crim. L.R. 655, H.L.; affirming R. *v.* Sang; R. *v.* Mangan [1979] 2 W.L.R. 439; (1978) 123 S.J. 232; [1979] 2 All E.R. 46; (1978) 68 Cr. App. R. 240; [1979] Crim. L.R. 389, C.A. [[1980] Crim. L.R. 129; 143 J.P.N. 558] **233**, 243, 245
Saunders (1875) 1 Q.B.D. 15; 45 L.J.M.C. 11; 33 L.T. 677; 24 W.R. 348; 13 Cox C.C. 116; *sub nom.* R. *v.* Sargent, 39 J.P.Jo. 760 .... 356, 357
—— (1573) 2 Plowden 473; 75 E.R. 706 .... **267**, 271, 272
Savage 1923 S.C.(J.) 49 406
Sayce *v.* Coupé [1953] 1 Q.B. 1; [1952] W.N. 473; [1952] 2 T.L.R. 664; 116 J.P. 552; 96 S.J. 748; [1952] 2 All E.R. 715 .... **274**, 278
Schmidt (1866) L.R. 1 C.C.R. 15; 55 L.J.M.C. 94; 13 L.T. 679; 30 J.P. 100; 12 Jur. (N.S.) 149; 14 W.R. 286; 10 Cox C.C. 172 .... 601, 602
Scott *v.* Metropolitan Police Commissioner [1975] A.C. 819; [1974] 3 W.L.R. 741; [1974] 3 All E.R. 1032; 60 Cr. App. R. 124; *sub nom.* R. *v.* Scott, 118 S.J. 863; [1975] Crim. L.R. 94, H.L.; affirming *sub nom.* R. *v.* Scott [1974] Q.B. 733; [1974] 2 W.L.R. 379; 118 S.J. 147; [1974] 2 All E.R. 204; [1974] Crim. L.R. 242, C.A. 345, **346**, 514, 554
—— *v.* Shepherd (1773) 2 Wm. Bl. 892; 3 Wils. 403 471
Scully (1824) C. & P. 319; 171 E.R. 1213 .... **413**
Seager *v.* Copydex Ltd. [1967] 1 W.L.R. 923; 111 S.J. 335; [1967] 2 All E.R. 415; 2 K.I.R. 828; [1967] F.S.R. 211; [1967] R.P.C. 349, C.A.; reversing [1967] R.P.C. 349. Petition for leave to appeal to the House of Lords dismissed 513
Senior [1899] 1 Q.B. 283; 68 L.J.Q.B. 175; 79 L.T. 562; 63 J.P. 8; 47 W.R. 367; 15 T.L.R. 102; 43 S.J. 114; 19 Cox C.C. 219 .... 88, 89, 90, 91, 93, 442
Series *v.* Poole [1969] 1 Q.B. 676; [1968] 2 W.L.R. 261; 132 J.P. 82; 111 S.J. 871; [1967] 3 All E.R. 849, D.C. 299, 301
Shannon (1980) 71 Cr. App. R. 192; (1980) 124 S.J. 374; [1980] Crim. L.R. 438, C.A. **422**
Shaw *v.* D.P.P. [1962] A.C. 220; [1961] 2 W.L.R. 897; 125 J.P. 437; 105 S.J. 421; [1961] 2 All E.R. 446; 45 Cr. App. R. 113 .... 4, 345, 350, 351, 352, 353, 354, 355, 356, 357
Sheaf (1927) 134 L.T. 127 526
Shephard [1919] 2 K.B. 125; 88 L.J.K.B. 932; 121 L.T. 393; 35 T.L.R. 366; 83 J.P. 131; 26 Cox C.C. 483; 14 Cr. App. R. 26 .... **362**, 364, 365
Sheppard [1980] 3 W.L.R. 960; (1980) 124 S.J. 864; [1980] 3 All E.R. 899, H.L.; reversing (1980) 70 Cr. App. R. 210, C.A. **86**
Sherras *v.* De Rutzen [1895] 1 Q.B. 918; 64 L.J.M.C. 218; 72 L.T. 839; 11 T.L.R. 369; 43 W.R. 526; 59 J.P. 440; 39 S.J. 451; 18 Cox C.C. 157 .... 68, **130**, 134, 139, 141, 143
Sherriff [1969] Crim. L.R. 260, C.A. 475
Shiartos [1963] 1 W.L.R. 845n. 214

Shippam [1971] Crim. L.R. 434 ... 17
Shoukatallie [1962] A.C. 81; [1961] 3 W.L.R. 1021; 105 S.J. 884; [1961] 3 All E.R. 966 442
Sidley, *sub nom.* Sir Charles Sidley's Case (1663) 1 Sid. 168 ... 356
Simmons *v.* Swift (1826) 5 B. & C. 857; 8 Dow. & Ry. K.B. 693; 5 L.J. (o.s.) K.B. 10 260
Sinclair; R. *v.* Queenswood (Holdings); R. *v.* Smithson (Frederick William) [1968] 1 W.L.R. 1246; *sub nom.* R. *v.* Smithson; R. *v.* Queenswood (Holdings); R. *v.* Sinclair, 112 S.J. 703; *sub nom.* R. *v.* Sinclair, 132 J.P. 527; [1968] 3 All E.R. 241; *sub nom.* R. *v.* Sinclair (William Vernon Squire); R. *v.* Queensway (Holdings); R. *v.* Smithson (Frederick William), 52 Cr. App. R. 618, C.A. Petition for leave to appeal to the House of Lords dismissed ... 348
Skipp [1975] Crim. L.R. 114, C.A. ... 498, 502, 503
Skivington [1968] 1 Q.B. 166; [1967] 2 W.L.R. 665; 111 S.J. 72; 131 J.P. 265; [1967] 1 All E.R. 483 ... 568
Sloggett [1972] 1 Q.B. 430; [1971] 3 W.L.R. 628; [1971] 3 All E.R. 264; 115 S.J. 655; 55 Cr. App. R. 532, C.A. ... **614**
Smart *v.* H.M. Advocate 1975 S.L.T. 65 ... 479
Smith (1914) 11 Cr. App. R. 36 ... 396
—— [1959] 2 Q.B. 35; [1959] 2 W.L.R. 623; 123 J.P. 295; 103 S.J. 353; [1959] 2 All E.R. 193; 43 Cr. App. R. 121 ... 32, **34**, 36, 37
—— (1976) Cr. App. R. 217 ... 619
—— [1979] Crim. L.R. 251 ... 454, 455
—— *Re* (1858) 3 H. & N. 227 ... 246, 251
—— *v.* Hughes, Same *v.* Caiels; Tolan *v.* Hughes, Same *v.* Caiels; Same *v.* Thomas; Same *v.* McKinnon [1960] 1 W.L.R. 830; 104 S.J. 606; 124 J.P. 430; [1960] 2 All E.R. 859; [76 L.Q.R. 487], D.C. ... 357
Smith (Charlotte) (1865) L. & C. 607; 34 L.J.M.C. 153; 12 L.T. 608; 13 W.R. 816; 29 J.P. 532; 11 Jur. (N.S.) 695; 10 Cox C.C. 82 ... 21
Smith (David) [1974] Q.B. 354; [1974] 2 W.L.R. 20; [1974] 1 All E.R. 632, C.A. 100, 107, 111, 112, 122, 188, 189, 429, **657**
Smith (Jesse) (1870) 1 C.C.R. 266 ... 521
Smith (Wesley) [1963] 1 W.L.R. 1200; 128 J.P. 13; 107 S.J. 873; [1963] 3 All E.R. 597, C.C.A. ... 269, 270
Smith (William) (1826) 2 C. & P. 449; 172 E.R. 203 ... **22**, 23
Sneddon *v.* Stevenson [1967] 1 W.L.R. 1051; 131 J.P. 441; 111 S.J. 515; [1967] 2 All E.R. 1277 ... 235
Sockett (1908) 24 T.L.R. 893; 72 J.P. 428; 52 S.J. 729; 1 Cr. App. R. 101 ... 342, 456
Sodeman [1936] 2 All E.R. 1138; [1936] W.N. 190 ... 163, 166
Somerset *v.* Hart (1884) 12 Q.B.D. 360; 53 L.J.M.C. 77; 32 W.R. 594; 48 J.P. 327 .. 294, 295
Sorrells *v.* United States 287 U.S. 435; 77 Law Ed. 413 (1932) ... 233, **239**, 243
Southern Portland Cement Ltd. *v.* Cooper (Rodney John) (an Infant by his next friend Peter Alphonsus Cooper) [1974] A.C. 623; [1974] 2 W.L.R. 152; *sub nom.* Southern Portland Cement *v.* Cooper (1973) 118 S.J. 99; [1974] 1 All E.R. 87, P.C. ... 378
Southport, Mayor of *v.* Morriss [1893] 1 Q.B. 359 ... 224
Sperotto and Salvietti (1970) 71 S.R. (N.S.W.) 334 ... 113
Spriggs [1958] 1 Q.B. 270; [1958] 2 W.L.R. 162; 102 S.J. 89; [1958] 1 All E.R. 309; 42 Cr. App. 69 ... 405
Srinivas Mall Bairoliya *v.* King Emperor (1947) I.L.R. 26 Pat. 460 ... 135
Staines (Linda Irene) (1974) 60 Cr. App. R. 160; [1975] Crim. L.R. 651, C.A. ... 580
State *v.* Hamilton and Laurie 12 Nev. 686 (1878) ... 250
Stark, unreported, October 5, 1967 ... 536, 643
Steane [1947] K.B. 997; 61 L.J.R. 969; 177 L.T. 122; 63 T.L.R. 403; 111 J.P. 337; 91 S.J. 279; [1947] 1 All E.R. 813; 32 Cr. App. R. 61 ... 67, 105, 182, 208, 261
Steele (1977) 65 Cr. App. Rep. 22, C.A. ... **487**
Stephens (1866) L.R. 1 Q.B. 702; 7 B. & S. 710; 35 L.J.Q.B. 251; 14 L.T. 593; 14 W.R. 859; 30 J.P. 822; 12 Jur. (N.S.) 961; 10 Cox C.C. 340 ... 132, 147
Stephenson [1979] Q.B. 695; [1979] 3 W.L.R. 193; (1979) 123 S.J. 403; [1979] 2 All E.R. 1198; (1979) 69 Cr. App. R. 213; [1979] Crim. L.R. 590, C.A. 71, 73, 74, 76, 77, 188, 189
Stevens *v.* Gourlay (1859) 7 C.B. (N.S.) 99 ... 640

Stone [1977] 1 Q.B. 354; [1977] 2 W.L.R. 169; (1976) 121 S.J. 83; [1977] 2 All E.R. 341; (1976) 64 Cr. App. R. 186; *sub nom.* R. *v.* Stone and Dobinson [1977] Crim. L.R. 166, C.A. **22**, 24, **452**, 454, 455
Strasser *v.* Roberge (1980) 103 D.L.R. (3d) 193 151
Stratton (1979) 1 Doug. K.B. 239; 99 E.R. 156, 21 State Tr. 1045 421
Strawbridge [1970] N.Z.L.R. 909 149
Stripp (1979) 69 Cr. App. R. 318, C.A. 175, 176
Subramaniam *v.* Public Prosecutor [1956] 1 W.L.R. 965; 100 S.J. 566, P.C. 202, 214
Sullivan (1945) 30 Cr. App. R. 132 .... 587, 588
—— [1981] Crim. L.R. 46 (C.A.) 82
Surujpaul called Dick *v.* R. [1958] 1 W.L.R. 1050; 102 S.J. 757; [1958] 3 All E.R. 300; 42 Cr. App. R. 266, P.C. 607
Sutcliffe, *The Times*, May 23, 1981 411
Sutton [1977] 1 W.L.R. 1086; (1977) 121 S.J. 676; [1977] 3 All E.R. 476; [1977] Crim. L.R. 569, C.A. 491
Sweet *v.* Parsley [1970] A.C. 132; [1969] 2 W.L.R. 470; 113 S.J. 86; [1969] 1 All E.R. 347 .... 91, 102, 103, 110, 111, 112, 116, 129, **137**, 146, 149
Sykes *v.* D.P.P. [1962] A.C. 528; [1961] 3 W.L.R. 371; 125 J.P. 523; 105 S.J. 566; [1961] 3 All E.R. 33; 45 Cr. App. R. 230, H.L.; [106 S.J. 124; 78 L.Q.R. 40; 25 M.L.R. 301]; affirming *sub nom.* R. *v.* Sykes [1961] 2 Q.B. 9; [1961] 2 W.L.R. 392; 105 S.J. 183; [1961] 1 All E.R. 702, C.C.A. 10, 288
Swietlinski (1981) 117 D.L.R. (3d) 285 448

Tacey (1821) R. & R. 452 654
Tarling *v.* Government of Singapore (1978) 70 Cr. App. R. 77; [1978] Crim. L.R. 490, H.L. [[1979] Crim. L.R. 220]; reversing *The Times*, April 26 & 27, July 30, 1977, D.C. 349
Taylor (1869) L.R. 1 C.C.R. 194 482
—— *v.* Caldwell (1863) 3 B. & S. 826; 2 New Rep. 198; 32 L.J.Q.B. 164; 8 L.T. 356; 27 J.P. 710; 11 W.R. 726; 122 E.R. 309 8
—— *v.* Grainville [1978] Crim. L.R. 482, D.C. 480
Taylor *v.* Mucklow (1973) 117 S.J. 792; [1973] Crim. L.R. 750, D.C. 417
Tesco Supermarkets Ltd. *v.* Nattrass [1972] A.C. 153; [1971] 2 W.L.R. 1166; [1971] 2 All E.R. 127; 115 S.J. 285; 69 L.G.R. 403, H.L. **296**
Thabo Meli *v.* R. [1954] 1 W.L.R. 228; 98 S.J. 77; [1954] 1 All E.R. 373 .... **40**, 443
Thomas *v.* The King (1937) 59 C.L.R. 279 .... 102, 112, 144
Thompson (1869) 21 L.T. 397; 33 J.P. 791; 11 Cox C.C. 362 650
Thomson (1965) 50 Cr. App. R. 1 .... **335**, 336
Thorne *v.* Motor Trade Association [1937] A.C. 797; 106 L.J.K.B. 495; 157 L.T. 399; 53 T.L.R. 810; 81 S.J. 476; [1937] 3 All E.R. 157; 26 Cr. App. R. 51 621
Thornton *v.* Mitchell (1940) 162 L.T. 296; 56 T.L.R. 296; 104 J.P. 108; 84 S.J. 257; [1940] 1 All E.R. 339; 38 L.G.R. 168 .... **278**, 279, 289
Thurborn (1849) 1 Den. 387; 2 C. & K. 311; T. & M. 67; 18 L.J.M.C. 140; 13 J.P. 459; 13 Jur. 499; *sub nom.* R. *v.* Wood, 4 New Mag. Cas. 27; 3 New Sess. Cas. 581; 13 L.T. (o.s.) 548; 3 Cox C.C. 453 556
Tideswell [1905] 2 K.B. 273; 74 L.J.K.B. 725; 93 L.T. 111; 69 J.P. 318; 21 T.L.R. 531; 21 Cox C.C. 10 514
Tolson (1889) 23 Q.B.D. 168; 58 L.J.M.C. 97; 60 L.T. 899; 5 T.L.R. 465; 37 W.R. 716; 54 J.P. 4, 20; 16 Cox C.C. 530 .... 103, 106, 107, 111, 112, 113, **116**, 129, 139, 143, 144, 145, 178, 181
Tomlin [1954] 2 Q.B. 274; [1954] 2 W.L.R. 1140; 118 J.P. 354; 98 S.J. 374; [1954] 2 All E.R. 272; 38 Cr. App. R. 82, C.C.A. 514
Traill *v.* Baring (1864) 4 De G.J. & Sm. 318; [1936] Ch. 575 578
Treacy *v.* D.P.P. [1971] A.C. 537; [1971] 2 W.L.R. 112; 115 S.J. 12; [1971] 1 All E.R. 110; 55 Cr. App. R. 113, H.L. **623**, 624, 632
Tuberville *v.* Savage (1669) 1 Mod. Rep. 3; 86 E.R. 684; 2 Keb. 345 .... **471**
Twose (1879) 14 Cox C.C. 327 659
Turner (No. 2) [1971] 1 W.L.R. 901; [1971] 2 All E.R. 441; [1971] R.T.R. 396 ... **522**, 524
Tyler [1891] 2 Q.B. 588 289
Tyler and Price (1838) 8 C. & P. 616 .... 208, 213, 220, 279

Tyrrell [1894] 1 Q.B. 710; 63 L.J.M.C. 58; 70 L.T. 41; 10 T.L.R. 167; 42 W.R. 255; 38 S.J. 130; 17 Cox C.C. 716 .... **274**, 277, 278

United States *v.* Healey (D.C.) 202 Fed. 349 (1913) 240
—— *v.* Holmes 26 Fed. Cas. 360 (1842) 229
—— *v.* Kirby 7 Wall. 482 (1869) 241
—— *v.* Russell 93 S. Ct. 1637 (1973) 243

Vane *v.* Yiannopoulos [1965] A.C. 486; [1964] 3 W.L.R. 1218; 129 J.P. 50; 108 S.J. 937; [1964] 3 All E.R. 82; 63 L.G.R. 91 .... 289, **290**, 296
Venna [1976] Q.B. 421; [1975] 3 W.L.R. 737; 119 S.J. 679; [1975] 3 All E.R. 788; [1975] Crim. L.R. 701; *sub nom.* R. *v.* Venna (Henson George) (1975) 61 Cr. App. R. 310, C.A. 62, 180, 475
Vickers [1957] 2 Q.B. 664; [1957] 3 W.L.R. 326; 121 J.P. 510; 101 S.J. 593; [1957] 2 All E.R. 741; 41 Cr. App. R. 189 .... **370**, 372, 373, 380, 382, 383, 386, 388
Villensky [1892] 2 Q.B. 597; 61 L.J.M.C. 218; 8 T.L.R. 780; 41 W.R. 160; 56 J.P. 824; 36 S.J. 745 601
Vinagre (1979) 69 Cr. App. R. 104, C.A. 403, **409**, 411

Walker [1962] Crim. L.R. 458 334
Walkington (1979) 1 W.L.R. 1169; (1979) 123 S.J. 704; [1979] 2 All E.R. 716; (1979) 68 Cr. App. R. 427; [1979] Crim. L.R. 526, C.A. 640, 644, 646
Wallett [1968] 2 Q.B. 367; [1968] 2 W.L.R. 1199; 132 J.P. 318; 112 S.J. 232; [1968] 2 All E.R. 296; 52 Cr. App. R. 271 .... 374, 375
Walters and Others [1979] R.T.R. 220; (1979) 69 Cr. App. R. 115, C.A. 344, 345
Walters *v.* Lunt [1951] W.N. 472; 115 J.P. 512; 95 S.J. 625; [1951] 2 All E.R. 645; 35 Cr. App. R. 94; 49 L.G.R. 809 .... 280, 364
Walton *v.* The Queen [1977] 3 W.L.R. 902; (1977) 121 S.J. 728; [1978] 1 All E.R. 542; [1978] A.C. 788; (1978) 66 Cr. App. R. 25; [1977] Crim. L.R. 747, P.C. 403, **407**
Ward (1836) 4 A. & E. 384; 1 Har. & W. 703; 6 Nev. & M. 38; 5 L.J.K.B. 221 2
—— (1872) L.R. 1 C.C.R. 356; 41 L.J.M.C. 69; 26 L.T. 43; 20 W.R. 392; 36 J.P. 453; 12 Cox C.C. 123 .... 123, 125
Warner *v.* Metropolitan Police Commissioner [1969] 2 A.C. 256; [1968] 2 W.L.R. 1303; 132 J.P. 378; 112 S.J. 378; [1968] 2 All E.R. 356; 52 Cr. App. R. 373 .. 102, 112, 114, 138, 141, 143, 647, 661
—— (1970) 55 Cr. App. R. 93, C.A. **538**, 540, 543
Watmore *v.* Jenkins [1962] 2 Q.B. 572; [1962] 3 W.L.R. 463; 126 J.P. 432; 106 S.J. 492; [1962] 2 All E.R. 868; 60 L.G.R. 325, D.C. 173
Webb [1969] 2 Q.B. 278; [1969] 2 W.L.R. 1088; 133 J.P. 437; 113 S.J. 304; [1969] 2 All E.R. 626; 53 Cr. App. R. 360, C.A. 159
Welsh (1869) 11 Cox C.C. 336 391
—— [1974] R.T.R. 478, C.A. 515
West (1848) 2 Car. & Kir. 784; 11 L.T. (o.s.) 49; 2 Cox C.C. 500 368
Weston (1879) 14 Cox C.C. 346 427
Wheat and Stocks [1921] 2 K.B. 119; 90 L.J.K.B. 583; 124 L.T. 830; 37 T.L.R. 417; 85 J.P. 203; 65 S.J. 554; 26 Cox C.C. 717; 15 Cr. App. R. 134 145
Wheeler [1967] W.L.R. 1531; 132 J.P. 41; 111 S.J. 850; [1967] 3 All E.R. 829; 52 Cr. App. R. 28 412
Whitchurch and Others (1890) 24 Q.B.D. 420; 59 L.J.M.C. 77; 62 L.T. 124; 6 T.L.R. 177; 54 J.P. 472; 16 Cox C.C. 743 .... 274, **341**, 342, 456
White (1859) 1 F. & F. 665 .... 70, 616, 618
—— [1910] 2 K.B. 124; 79 L.J.K.B. 854; 102 L.T. 784; 26 T.L.R. 466; 74 J.P. 318; 54 S.J. 523; 22 Cox C.C. 325; 4 Cr. App. R. 257 318
Whitehouse (alias Savage) (1941) 1 W.W.R. 112 271
Whitehouse [1977] Q.B. 868; [1977] 2 W.L.R. 925; 121 S.J. 171; [1977] 3 All E.R. 737; (1977) 65 Cr. App. R. 33; [1977] Crim. L.R. 689, C.A. **275**, 362
Wibberley [1966] 2 Q.B. 214; [1966] 2 W.L.R. 1; 130 J.P. 58; 109 S.J. 877; [1965] 3 All E.R. 718; 50 Cr. App. R. 51, C.C.A. 551, 552
Williams (1836) 7 C. & P. 354 592
—— [1923] 1 K.B. 340; 92 L.J.K.B. 230; 128 L.T. 128; 39 T.L.R. 131; 87 J.P. 67; 67 S.J. 263; 27 Cox C.C. 350; 17 Cr. App. R. 56 .... **489**

Williams [1953] 1 Q.B. 660; [1953] 2 W.L.R. 937; 117 J.P. 251; 97 S.J. 318; [1953] 1 All E.R. 1068; 37 Cr. App. R. 71, C.C.A. 557, 558, 559, 560, 561
Willmott *v.* Atack [1977] 1 Q.B. 498; [[1977] Crim. L.R. 187] **84**, 86
Willis [1972] 1 W.L.R. 1605; 116 S.J. 944; [1972] 3 All E.R. 797, C.A. 611
Wilson [1955] 1 W.L.R. 493; 119 J.P. 216; 99 S.J. 321; [1955] 1 All E.R. 744; 39 Cr. App. R. 12 472
—— *v.* Inyang [1951] 2 K.B. 799; [1951] 2 T.L.R. 553; 115 J.P. 411; 95 S.J. 562; [1951] 2 All E.R. 237; 49 L.G.R. 654 .... 101, 107, 262
Windle [1952] 2 Q.B. 826; [1952] 1 T.L.R. 1344; 116 J.P. 365; 96 S.J. 379; [1952] 2 All E.R. 1; 36 Cr. App. R. 85 .... **165**
Winson [1969] 1 Q.B. 371; [1968] 2 W.L.R. 113; (1968) 112 S.J. 71; [1968] 1 All E.R. 197, C.A. 293
With *v.* O'Flanagan [1936] Ch. 575; 105 L.J.Ch. 247; 154 L.T. 634; 80 S.J. 285; [1936] 1 All E.R. 727, C.A. 578
Woodman [1974] Q.B. 758; [1974] 2 W.L.R. 821; 118 S.J. 346; [1974] 2 All E.R. 955; [1974] Crim. L.R. 441; *sub nom.* R. *v.* Woodman (George Eli) (1974) 59 Cr. App. R. 200, C.A. **518**, 520
Woodrow (1846) 15 M. & W. 404; 2 New Mag. Cas. 1; 2 New Sess. Cas. 346; 16 L.J.M.C. 122; 10 J.P. 791 .... 131, 147
Woodward *v.* Koessler [1958] 1 W.L.R. 1255; 123 J.P. 14; 102 S.J. 879; [1958] 3 All E.R. 557 648
Woolmington *v.* D.P.P. [1935] A.C. 462; 104 L.J.K.B. 433; 153 L.T. 232; 51 T.L.R. 446; 79 S.J. 401; 25 Cr. App. R. 72 .... 139, 145, 149, 150, 168
Woolcock [1977] Crim. L.R. 104, 161, C.A. 654
Wyat (1705); Fortes Rep. 127; 2 Ld. Raym. 1189; 11 Mod. Rep. 53; 88 E.R. 880 20

Yates (1853) 6 Cox C.C. 441 348
Yeandel *v.* Fisher [1966] 1 Q.B. 440; [1965] 3 W.L.R. 1002; 129 J.P. 546; 109 S.J. 593; [1965] 3 All E.R. 158 138
Young (1878) 14 Cox 114 487
Yule [1964] 1 Q.B. 5; [1963] 3 W.L.R. 285; 127 J.P. 469; 107 S.J. 497; [1963] 2 All E.R. 780; 47 Cr. App. R. 229, C.C.A. 525

TABLE OF STATUTES

[Page references in **bold** indicate the page upon which the section is set out.]

1532 Killing & Thief Act (24 Hen. 8, c. 5) 414
1800 Criminal Lunatics Act (39 & 40 Geo. 3, c. 94) 161
s. 2 160
1803 Lord Ellenborough's Act (43 Geo. 3, c. 58) 381, 382, 383, 387, 458
1824 Vagrancy Act (5 Geo. 4, c. 83)—
s. 4 .... 309, 310, 316
1832 Anatomy Act (2 & 3 Will. 4, c. 75)—
s. 10 515
1839 Metropolitan Police Act (2 & 3 Vict., c. 47)—
s. 44 .... 293, 294
1845 Lunatics Act (8 & 9 Vict., c. 100)—
s. 44 120
1851 Prevention of Offences Act (14 & 15 Vict., c. 19)—
s. 4 482
1857 Lunacy (Scotland) Act (20 & 21 Vict., c. 71)—
s. 87 161
1861 Accessories and Abettors Act (24 & 25 Vict., c. 94)—
s. 8 ...... 246, 247, 248, 249, 250, 280
Larceny Act (24 & 25 Vict., c. 96) 505, 521
s. 3 347
s. 82 347
s. 83 347
s. 84 347
s. 97 599
Malicious Damage Act (24 & 25 Vict., c. 97) ... 72, 73, 74, 75, 653
s. 13
s. 18 .... 66, 68
s. 20 66
s. 51 123
Forgery Act (24 & 25 Vict., c. 98)—
s. 3 571
Offences against Person Act (24 & 25 Vict., c. 100) 479
s. 4 .... 360, 362

1861 Offences against Person Act —*cont.*
s. 18 .... 18, 52, 182, 220, 252, 484, 492
s. 20 ...... 82, 125, 181, 252, **481**, 492
s. 23 .... 81, 82, 83, 448, **485**, 493
s. 24 .... 485, 493
s. 31 417
s. 35 330
s. 36 492
ss. 36–40 492
s. 37 492
s. 38 .... **479**
s. 39 492
s. 40 492
ss. 42–47 492
s. 47 ...... 52, 181, 471, **480**, 481, 492
s. 49 119
s. 55 .... 113, 119, 121
s. 56 ...... 119, 282, 283, 342, 343
s. 57 .... 113, 117, 118, 144
s. 58 ...... 341, **456**, 458, 460, 461
s. 59 .... **457**, 460, 461
1868 Larceny and Embezzlement Act (31 & 32 Vict., c. 116) 521
Poor Law Amendment Act (31 & 32 Vict., c. 122)—
s. 32 88
1869 Debtors Act (32 & 33 Vict., c. 82)—
s. 13 571
1872 Licensing Act (35 & 36 Vict., c. 94)—
s. 13 130
s. 14 130
s. 16 130
(1) 131
(2) 130, 131, 132
1874 False Personation Act (37 & 38 Vict., c. 36)—
s. 1 571
1875 Falsification of Accounts Act (38 & 39 Vict., c. 24) 347
1885 Criminal Law Amendment Act (48 & 49 Vict., c. 69) 119, 274, 275, 483
s. 3 (2) 489, 490

1885 Criminal Law Amendment Act—*cont.*
s. 4 .... 119, 275
s. 5 .... 119, 274, 275
(1) 491
s. 6 119
s. 7 119
s. 16 490
1887 Merchandise Marks Act (50 & 51 Vict., c. 28)—
s. 2 297
1889 Prevention of Cruelty to, and Protection of, Children Act (52 & 53 Vict., c. 44) 88
1893 Sale of Goods Act (56 & 57 Vict., c. 71) 516
s. 18 517
s. 18 r. 5 260
s. 19 517
1906 Prevention of Corruption Act (6 Edw. 7, c. 34)—
s. 1 514
1907 Criminal Appeal Act (7 Edw. 7, c. 23) 9, 161
s. 19 (*a*) 160
1908 Children Act (8 Edw. 7, c. 67) 88, 92
1911 Official Secrets Act (1 & 2 Geo. 5, c. 28)—
s. 1 94
1913 Forgery Act (3 & 4 Geo. 5, c. 27) 309
1915 Indictment Act (5 & 6 Geo. 5, c. 90)—
s. 5 536
1916 Larceny Act (6 & 7 Geo. 5, c. 50) 494, 522, 567, 570
s. 1 .... 494, 534
(1) ... 496, 556, 557, 558, 559
(2) (*a*) 556
(i) 533
s. 2 (1) (*c*) 556
s. 3 (1) 556
s. 20 (1) (iv) 525, 526
s. 25 631
s. 26 631
s. 27 631
s. 28 650
s. 29 (1) 621
(i) 625
s. 30 .... 624, 625
s. 32 571
(1) 571, 590, 591
s. 33 .... 70, 599
(1) 280
s. 40 (4) 521
1920 Dangerous Drugs Act (10 & 11 Geo. 5, c. 46) 140
1921 Licensing Act (11 & 12 Geo. 5, c. 74)—
s. 4 266
1925 Dramatic and Musical Performers' Protection Act (15 & 16 Geo. 5, c. 46)—
s. 1 (*a*) 68
Criminal Justice Act (15 & 16 Geo. 5, c. 86)—
s. 47 210
1926 Sale of Food (Weights and Measures) Act (16 & 17 Geo. 5, c. 63)—
s. 5 (2) 300
s. 12 (5) 300
1929 Infant Life (Preservation) Act (19 & 20 Geo. 5, c. 34)—
s. 1 .... **456**
(1) 456, 458
1930 Road Traffic Act (20 & 21 Geo. 5, c. 43) 551
s. 11 440
s. 12 .... 440, 441
s. 28 551
s. 72 132
1933 Children and Young Persons Act (23 Geo. 5, c. 12) ... 19, 86
s. 1 .... 86, 87, 91, 92, 93
(1) .. 86, 88, 89, 90, 91, 93, 94, 441, 453
(2) (*a*) 88, 89, 92, 93
1934 Road Traffic Act (24 & 25 Geo. 5, c. 50)—
s. 25 (1) (*b*) 132
s. 34 440
1936 Public Order Act (1 Edw. 8 & 1 Geo. 6, c. 6)—
s. 5 558
1938 Infanticide Act (1 & 2 Geo. 6, c. 36)—
s. 1 .... **455**
1942 Tobacco Act (5 & 6 Vict., c. 93)—
s. 13 274
1945 Family Allowances Act (8 & 9 Geo. 6, c. 41)—
s. 9 .... 361, 362
s. 9 (*b*) 361
1948 Companies Act (11 & 12 Geo. 6, c. 58) 301
1951 Rivers (Prevention of Pollution) Act (14 & 15 Geo. 6, c. 66)—
s. 2 (1) (*a*) 146
1952 Magistrates' Court Act (15 & 16 Geo. 6 & 1 Eliz. 2, c. 55)—
s. 35 250
s. 81 61
Sched. I, para. 20 361

1953 Prevention of Crime Act (1 & 2 Eliz. 2, c. 14)—
s. 1 .... 134, 648
(1) 309
Licensing Act (1 & 2 Eliz. 2, c. 46) 292
Post Office and Telegraph (Money) Act (2 & 3 Eliz. 2, c. 4)—
s. 53 553
1954 Protection of Birds Act (2 & 3 Eliz. 2, c. 30) 505
1956 Sexual Offences Act (4 & 5 Eliz. 2, c. 69) 103, 277
s. 1 .... 103, 486
(1) 102
(2) **489**
s. 3 (1) 489
s. 5 .... **491**
s. 6 (1) 491
(3) 491
s. 10 .... 276, 277
s. 11 .... 276, 277
(1) 275
s. 14 491
s. 15 491
s. 37 486
s. 44 486
Sched. 2 486
1957 Homicide Act (5 & 6 Eliz. 2, c. 11) ... 158, 185, 368, 380, 381, 383, 386, 387, 388, 390, 391, 392, 393, 404, 410
s. 1 .... 91, **369**, 380
(1) 370, 371, 373, 387
s. 2 ...... 195, **402**, **403**, 404, 406, 407, 437, 465
(1) 402, 404, 405
s. 3 ...... 193, **389**, 390, 392, 394, 395, 396, 401
s. 4 .... **462**, 463, 468
(1) 462
(3) 462
s. 5 388
(2) 373
1958 Prevention of Fraud (Investments) Act (6 & 7 Eliz. 2, c. 45) 77
1959 Highways Act (7 & 8 Eliz. 2, c. 25)—
s. 121 (1) 83, 84, 86
s. 127 658
Obscene Publications Act (7 & 8 Eliz. 2, c. 66)—
s. 2 (3) 355
(4) 356
s. 4 353
Mental Health Act (7 & 8 Eliz. 2, c. 72)—
s. 60 (2) 197
1960 Administration of Justice Act (8 & 9 Eliz. 2, c. 65)—
s. 1 (2) 497
Indecency with Children Act (8 & 9 Eliz. 2, c. 33) 476
Road Traffic Act (8 & 9 Eliz. 2, c. 16)—
s. 186 299
s. 217 .... 547, 548
1961 Suicide Act (9 & 10 Eliz. 2, 60) **462**
s. 1 462
s. 2 463
(1) 266, 462, 463
(2) 462
(4) 463
Licensing Act (9 & 10 Eliz. 2, c. 61) 292
s. 21 293
s. 22 293
(1) 290, 292, 293
(*a*) 290, 292, 293
1962 Road Traffic Act (10 & 11 Eliz. 2, c. 59)—
s. 20 299
1963 Deer Act (c. 33) 505
1964 Licensing Act (c. 26)—
s. 169 (1) 296
Police Act (c. 48) 85
s. 51 .... 85, 427, **480**
(1) 85, 101
(3) 84, 101
Obscene Publications Act (c. 74) 354
Criminal Procedure (Insanity) Act (c. 84) **159**
s. 1 159
s. 4 159
s. 5 (1) 159
s. 6 .... **402**
1965 Dangerous Drugs Act (c. 15)—
s. 3 (2) 338
s. 5 .... 140, 145
(*b*) 137
s. 6 (2) 136
(3) 136, 137
s. 8 140
(*d*) 140
Law Commissions Act (c. 22)—
s. 3 11
Murder (Abolition of Death Penalty) Act (c. 71) ... 368, 384
s. 1 (2) 368, 466
1967 Road Traffic Regulation Act (c. 21)—
s. 79 231
Criminal Law Act (c. 58) 182, 235, 237, 303, 418
s. 1 .... 247, 280

1967 Criminal Law Act—*cont.*
s. 2 .... 479, 547
s. 3 .... **418**, 419, 421, 469
(1) 422
s. 4 .... **283**, 284, 652
(1) ... 284, 285, 286, 287, 325
(3) 285
s. 5 .... **288**
(1) 288, 325
(2) 288, 307, 345
s. 6 536
(3) 285, 484
s. 8 329
Sched. 3 .... **484**
Criminal Law (Northern Ireland) Act (c. 58)—
s. 3 .... 418, 419, 421
(1) 418
Sexual Offences Act (c. 60) 350, 351, 353, 354
s. 1 (1) 350
Criminal Justice Act (c. 80) 382, 447
s. 3 412
s. 8 ...... 61, 62, 76, 91, 110, 112, 178, 180, 183, 185, 186, 190, 373, 374, 375, 386, 429, 447, 648
Vessels Protection Act (c. 85) 547
Abortion Act (c. 87) .. 457, 460, 461
s. 1 461
(1) 457, 461
(3) 461
s. 4 (1) 461
s. 5 (2) 461
s. 6 .... 460, 466
1968 Criminal Appeal Act (c. 19)—
s. 2 (1) 114, 581, 629
(3) 279
s. 3 581
s. 12 159
s. 33 (2) 497
Criminal Appeal (Northern Ireland) Act (c. 21)—
s. 13 209
s. 14 209
s. 38 209
Firearms Act (c. 27)—
s. 1 121
s. 58 (2) 121
Trade Descriptions Act (c. 29) 296
s. 11 (2) 296, 297, 300, 302
s. 20 .... 298, 300, 302
(1) 297, 302
s. 23 .... 297, 298, 302
s. 24 .... 298, 300, 302
(1) 296, 297, 299
(*a*) 298
(*b*) 298
(2) (*b*) 302
1968 Theatres Act (c. 54) 353
s. 3 353
Theft Act (c. 60) ... 11, 309, 355, 496, 508, 513, 514, 519, 521, 522, 524, 534, 539, 555, 559, 562, 569, 605, 609, 614, 623, 624, 637, 638, 645
s. 1 ...... **495**, 509, 516, 517, 521, 534, 538, 539, 557
(1) 347, 496, 497, 498, 501, 513, 519, 521, 530, 532, 538, 555, 557, 558, 564, 572, 609, 642, 645
s. 2 .... **555**, 556, 566, 591
(1) 497, 523, 532, 555, 556, 591
(*a*) 555
(*b*) 526, 555
(*c*) 555
(2) 555, 556
s. 3 .... **495**, 521, 568
(1) 495, 497, 502, 503, 532, 555, 567
(2)–(4) 573
s. 4 .... 495, **504**, 654
(1) 505, 513, 541, 573
s. 5 .... 495, 497, **515**, 517, 521
(1) 515, 517, 519, 522, 523, 530
(2) 515, 517
(3) 502, 515, 517, 524, 525, 526, 527, 528, 529, 530, 531, 532
(4) 501, 515, 529, 530, 532, 533, 534, 556
(5) 515
s. 6 . **537**, 538, 539, 540, 542, 543
s. 6 (1) 496, 508, 512, 513, 535, 537, 539, 542, 543
(2) 537, 543, 544
s. 8 .... 503, 566, 568, 611
(1) 566, 570
(2) 566, 570
s. 9 .... **631**, 634, 636, 641, 644
(1) 631, 644
(*a*) 641, 642, 644, 645, 646, 649
(*b*) 637, 638, 642, 646, 649
(2) 642
s. 10 .... **647**, 648
(1) 649
s. 11 .... **545**, 553
(1) 545
(2) 545, 546
(3) 545, 546
(4) 546
s. 12 ..... 545, **547**, 548, 549, 550, 551, 552, 553
(1) 316, 547, 549, 552, 649

1968 Theft Act—*cont.*
s. 12—*cont.*
(2) 547
(3) 547
(4) 547
(5) 547
(6) 547
(7) 547, 553
(*a*) 547
(*b*) 547
s. 13 514
s. 15 ...... 77, 311, 508, **572**, 580, 582, 593, 647, 649, 655
(1) 497, 498, 555, 572, 591, 604
(3) 542
(4) 331, 573
s. 16 .... 574, 589, 591, **592**
(1) 584
(*a*) 593
(2) (*a*) 573, 580, 581
(*c*) 581
(3) 573
s. 17 .... 347, 655
s. 20 655
s. 21 .... 353, **621**
(1) 630
(*a*) 626, 627
(*b*) 622
s. 22 ..... 503, **599**, 606, 610, 611, 619
(1) 70, 71, 604, 609, 611, 614, 615, 616
s. 24 .... 317, 606
(1)–(3) 604
(2) **604**, 606, 608, 613
(*a*) 606, 607
(3) 600, 603
(4) **604**
s. 25 .... 582, **649**, 650, 651
(1) 650, 651, 652
(3) 651
s. 34 .... **630**
(1) 572, 573
(2) **604**, 606, 613
(*a*) 630
(i) 630
(*b*) 606
Sched. 1 505
Race Relations Act (c. 71) 360
1971 Misuse of Drugs Act (c. 38) 146, 319
Criminal Damage Act (c. 48) 11, 71, 72, 74, 75, 76, 80, 107, 189, 309, 429, 653, 658, 659
s. 1 .... 72, 75, 79, 80, **653**
(1) 71, 72, 73, 75, 79, 100, 111, 187, 188, 189, 191, 192, 657, 658, 659, 660

1971 Criminal Damage Act—*cont.*
s. 1—*cont.*
(2) 71, 75, 76, 190, 191, 661
(*a*) 72, 75
(*b*) ... 71, 72, 75, 190, 192
(3) 192
s. 2 .... 656, **661**
(1) 76
s. 3 .... 656, **661**
s. 4 .... **653**
s. 5 .. 188, 189, 429, **656**, 657, 658
(2) 187, 188, 189, 190, 657, 658, 660
(*a*) 658, 660
(3) 112, 187, 188, 189, 657, 658
(5) 657, 658
s. 10 .... **654**
(1) 505
1972 Road Traffic Act (c. 20) 249, 279, 330
s. 1 .... 78, 79, 80, 441
s. 2 .... 79, 80, 441
s. 3 .... 79, 80, 441
s. 6 17
(1) 247, 319
s. 99 121
(6) 121
s. 190 (1) 316
Criminal Justice Act (c. 71)—
s. 36 .... 10, 246, 477, 599, 600
(1) 606
1973 Northern Ireland (Emergency Provisions) Act (c. 53) 259
1974 Trade Union and Labour Relations Act (c. 52) 332
1975 Conservation of Wild Creatures and Wild Plants Act (c. 48) 508
Salmon and Freshwater Fisheries Act (c. 51) 505
1976 Sexual Offences (Amendment) Act (c. 82) 114
s. 1 .... 62, 281
(1) **486**
(2) 61
1977 Torts (Interference with Goods) Act (c. 32)—
s. 3 (6) 309
s. 6 (2) 309
s. 7 (4) 309
Protection from Eviction Act (c. 43)—
s. 1 417
Criminal Law Act (c. 45) **332**, 340, 341, 342, 343, 344
s. 1 ...... 303, 325, 332, 343, 344, 359

1977 Criminal Law Act—*cont.*
s. 1—*cont.*
(1) 344, 345, 357, 359
(2) 344, 358, 359
s. 2 (1) 341
(2) 343
s. 5 .... 332, 345
(1) 345
(3) 345
(7) 360
(8) 340
s. 6 417
s. 8 309
s. 28 598
s. 50 .... 78, 441
s. 54 277
Part I 303
1978 Theft Act (c. 31) 514, 593, 621
s. 1 .... 555, **593**, 594, 598
s. 2 .... **594**, 595, 598
(1) 595, 596
(*a*) 594, 596, 597
(*b*) 594, 595, 597
(*c*) 594, 595, 596
(2) 594
(3) 594, 597
(4) 594

1978 Theft Act—*cont.*
s. 3 .... **597**, 595, 598
s. 4 .... 593, **598**
(1) 606
s. 5 573
(1) 573
(5) 573, 593
Protection of Children Act (c. 37) 492
1980 Magistrates' Courts Act (c. 43)—
s. 44 246
1981 Criminal Attempts Act (c. 47) **303**, 359
s. 1 326
(1) 315
(4) 331, 360
s. 3 (4) 331
(5) 331
s. 4 (3) 315
s. 5 359
(1) 332
s. 6 (1) 304
s. 8 316
s. 9 .... **316**
s. 10 333

REPORTS AND OFFICIAL WORKING PAPERS

Law Commission

Reports No. 10: Imputed Criminal Intent, 373
29: Criminal Damage, 655
83: Defences of General Application, 225–226, 231–232, 244
89: Mental Element in Crime, 50, 54, 56–62, 70, 154
102: Attempts, etc., 304, 305–314, 317–325, 328–331

Working Papers No. 43: Parties, Complicity and Liability for the Acts of Another, 278, 281
50: Inchoate Offences, 304, 306

Criminal Law Revision Committee

Reports 8th: Theft and Related Offences, 544, 545, 556, 571, 591, 599, 608, 610, 616, 624–626
14th: Offences against the Person, 63, 198–200, 466–469, 492–493

Working Paper (1980): Sexual Offences, 489

American Law Institute: Model Penal Code (1962)

s. 1.04 (Classification of offences), 155
2.03 (Causation), 28
2.05 (Strict liability), 156
2.08 (Recklessness/intoxication), 180
2.13 (Entrapment), 243
3.04 (Self-defence), 414

ABBREVIATIONS

Archbold	Archbold's *Criminal Pleading, Evidence and Practice* (40th ed., by Mitchell, 1979).
Blackstone	*Commentaries on the Laws of England*, by Sir William Blackstone (1765) (Chitty's ed., 1826).
Butler Committee	Report of The Committee on Mentally Abnormal Offenders, Cmnd. 6244, 1975.
C.L.J.	*Cambridge Law Journal*.
Col. L.R.	*Columbia Law Review*.
Crim. L.Q.	*Criminal Law Quarterly*.
Crim. L.R.	*Criminal Law Review*.
Edwards	*Mens Rea in Statutory Offences*, by J. L. L. J. Edwards (1955).
Fletcher	*Rethinking Criminal Law*, by George P. Fletcher (1978).
Glazebrook	*Reshaping the Criminal Law*, P. Glazebrook (ed.) (1978).
Gross	*A Theory of Criminal Justice*, by Hyman Gross (1978).
Hale	*Pleas of the Crown*, by Sir Matthew Hale (1682).
Hall	*General Principles of Criminal Law*, by Jerome Hall (2nd ed., 1960).
Harv. L.R.	*Harvard Law Review*.
Kenny	Kenny's *Outlines of Criminal Law* (19th ed., by J. W. C. Turner, 1966).
L.Q.R.	*Law Quarterly Review*.
M.L.R.	*Modern Law Review*.
Model Penal Code	American Law Institute, *Model Penal Code*, Proposed Official Draft, 1962.
Perkins	*Criminal Law*, by Rollo M. Perkins (1957).
Russell	*Russell on Crime* (12th ed., by J. W. C. Turner, 1964).
Smith and Hogan	*Criminal Law*, by J. C. Smith and Brian Hogan (4th ed., 1978).
Stephen, H.L.C.	*A History of the Common Law of England*, by Sir James Fitzjames Stephen (1883).
U.T.L.J.	*University of Toronto Law Journal*.
Williams, C.L.G.P.	*Criminal Law, The General Part*, by Glanville Williams (2nd ed., 1961).
Williams, Proof of Guilt	*The Proof of Guilt, A study of the English Criminal Trial*, by Glanville Williams (3rd ed., 1963).
Williams, T.C.L.	*Textbook of Criminal Law*, by Glanville Williams (1978).

ACKNOWLEDGMENTS

Grateful acknowledgment is made to the following authors and publishers for permission to quote from their works:

ASHWORTH, A. J.: "Self-defence and the Right to Life" [1975] C.L.J. 282, 284, 302.

BRETT AND WALLER: *Criminal Law Text and Cases* (4th ed., Butterworths), p. 145.

BUXTON, R.: "The New Murder" [1980] Crim. L.R. 521, 524.

COHEN, M.: "Questions of Impossibility" [1980] Crim. L.R. 773.

CROSS, PROF. SIR RUPERT: "Centenary Reflections on Prince's Case" (1975) 91 L.Q.R. 540; "Murder under Duress" (1978) 28 U.T.L.J. 369.

DENNIS, I.: "Manslaughter by Omission" (1980) *Current Legal Problems* 255, 264; "The Elements of Attempt" [1980] Crim. L.R. 758–768.

DUFF, R. A.: "Recklessness" [1980] Crim. L.R. 282; "Implied and Constructive Malice in Murder" (1979) 95 L.Q.R. 418.

FINGARETTE, H.: "Diminished Mental Capacity as a Criminal Law Defence" (1974) 37 M.L.R. 264.

FLETCHER, G. P.: *Rethinking Criminal Law* (1978, Little, Brown & Co., Boston).

GALLIGAN, D. J.: "The Return to Retribution in Penal Theory—Crime, Proof and Punishment," *Essays in Memory of Sir Rupert Cross* (1981, Butterworths), pp. 144, 146.

GLAZEBROOK, P. R.: "Criminal Omissions: The Duty Requirement in Offences against the Person" (1960) 76 L.Q.R. 386, 387.

GLAZEBROOK P. R. (ed.): *Reshaping the Criminal Law* (Essays in honour of Glanville Williams) (1978, Stevens & Sons):
Ashworth, A. J.: "Transferred Malice in Unforeseen Circumstances"
Cross, Prof. Sir Rupert: "The Reports of the Criminal Law Commissioners (1833–1849) and the Abortive Bills of 1853"
Griew, E. J.: "Consistency, Communication and Codification: Reflections on Two *Mens Rea* Words"
Smith, A. T. H.: "On *Actus Reus* and *Mens Rea*"
Smith, J.C.: "Aid, Abet, Counsel or Procure"
Thomas, D. A.: "Form and Function in Criminal Law."

GRIEWE, E.: *The Theft Acts 1968 and 1978* (3rd ed., Sweet & Maxwell).

HART, H. L. A.: *Punishment and Responsibility* (© Oxford University Press, 1968), p. 90, by permission of Oxford University Press.

HUTCHINSON A. C.: "Note on Sault Ste. Marie" (1979) *Osgoode Hall Law Journal* 415, 429, footnote 78.

JUSTICE: "Breaking the Rules" (1980), § 4.12.

KENNY: *Freewill and Responsibility* (R.K.P., 1978, Routledge and Kegan Paul Ltd.).

LLOYD, D.: *Introduction to Jurisprudence* (4th ed., Stevens & Sons).

MACKENNA, SIR BERNARD: "Blackmail: A Criticism" [1966] Crim. L.R. 467.

MODERN PENAL CODE: Proposed Official Draft (1962, The American Law Institute, Philadelphia).

PAULUS, I.: "Strict Liability: Its Place in Public Welfare Offences" (1978) 20 Crim. L.Q. 445.

SAYRE, F. B.: "Public Welfare Offences" (1933) *Columbia Law Review* 55.

SMITH, PROF. J. C.: "Criminal Damage" [1981] Crim. L.R. 393; "Intent: A Reply" [1978] Crim. L.R. 14; *The Law of Theft* (4th ed., Butterworths).

SMITH AND HOGAN: *Criminal Law* (4th ed., Butterworths).

SPENCER, J. R.: "The Theft Act 1978" [1979] Crim. L.R. 24; "The Metamorphosis of section 6 of the Theft Act" [1977] Crim. L.R. 653.

WALKER, N.: *Crime and Punishment in Britain* (1965, Edinburgh University Press).

WASIK, M.: "Duress and Criminal Responsibility" [1977] Crim. L.R. 453; "*Mens Rea*, Motive and the Problem of 'Dishonesty' in the Law of Theft" [1979] Crim. L.R. 543.

WILLIAMS, PROF. GLANVILLE: *Textbook of Criminal Law* (1978, Stevens & Sons); *Criminal Law: The General Part* (2nd ed., Stevens & Sons); "The Definition of Crime" (1955) *Current Legal Problems* 107; "Appropriation: A Single or Continuous Act?" [1978] Crim. L.R. 69; "Temporary Appropriation should be Theft" [1981] Crim. L.R. 129; "Theft, Consent and Illegality" [1977] Crim. L.R. 127; "The Government's Proposals on Criminal Attempts" (1981) N.L.J. 80 (Butterworths).

CHAPTER 1

INTRODUCTORY

	PAGE		PAGE
1. The Concept of Crime	1	2. The Form of English Criminal Law	7

THIS chapter is concerned briefly to sketch some of the assumptions underlying criminal law, and then to look, equally briefly, at the present form of English criminal law. As will be seen, in form it is a mixture of common law and statutory rules, with some progress discernible in the direction of complete codification.

1. THE CONCEPT OF CRIME

Williams, "The Definition of Crime" (1955) Current Legal Problems 107

"Is the effort [to define crime] worth making? The answer is that lawyers must try to clarify the notion of 'crime,' because it suffuses a large part of the law. For example: there is generally no time limit for criminal proceedings, whereas civil proceedings become statute-barred after a certain time. Criminal and civil proceedings are commenced differently, and often in different courts. A criminal prosecutor generally need not be the victim of the wrong, and a private criminal prosecutor is for many purposes not regarded as a party to the proceedings; he is certainly not 'master' of the proceedings in the sense that he can drop them at will; these rules are different in civil cases. The law of procedure may generally be waived in civil but not in criminal cases. There are many differences in the law of evidence, and several in respect of appeal....

... The common-sense approach is to consider whether there are any intrinsic differences between the acts constituting crimes and civil wrongs respectively. It is perhaps natural to suppose that since 'a crime' differs from 'a civil wrong,' there must be something *in* a crime to make it different from a civil wrong.

As everybody knows, there is one serious hindrance to a solution of this kind. This is the overlap between crime and tort. Since the same act can be both a crime and a tort, as in murder and assault, it is impossible to divide the two branches of the law by reference to the type of act. So also it is impossible to divide them by reference to the physical consequences of the act, for if the act is the same the physical consequences must be the same.

It has occurred to some that there is a possible escape from this difficulty. Although the act, and its consequences, are the same, the act and consequences have a number of different characteristics or aspects; and it may be possible to identify some of these characteristics as criminal and some as civil. Pursuing this line of thought, two separate aspects have been seized upon as identifying crime: the aspect of moral wrong and the aspect of damage to the public....

The proposition that crime is a moral wrong may have this measure of truth: that the average crime is more shocking, and has graver social consequences, than the average tort. Yet crimes of strict responsibility can be committed without moral wrong, while torts and breaches of trust may be, and often are, gross moral wrongs.

Even where a forbidden act is committed intentionally, a court deciding that it is a crime is not committed to the proposition that it is a moral wrong. Thus in holding that a summary proceeding for an offence under the Game Act was criminal in character, Lord Campbell C.J. said: 'It is our business, not to estimate the degree of moral guilt in the act of the appellant, but to see how such act is treated by the legislature. . . . I cannot be bound by any opinion I may form of the morality of that act: but I must see what it is that the legislature has chosen to punish': *Cattell* v. *Ireson* (1858) E.B. & E. at pp. 97–98. There are crimes of great gravity in the legal calendar, such as mercy-killing and eugenic abortion, which are disputably moral wrongs, though they are indisputably crimes. The same is true of numerous summary offences. Lord Atkin put the situation pungently. 'The criminal quality of an act cannot be discerned by intuition; nor can it be discovered by reference to any standard but one: is the act prohibited with penal consequences? Morality and criminality are far from coextensive; nor is the sphere of criminality necessarily part of a more extensive field covered by morality—unless the moral code necessarily disapproves of all acts prohibited by the state, in which case the argument moves in a circle': *Proprietary Articles Trade Association* v. *Att.-Gen. for Canada* [1931] A.C. 324 (P.C.).

The second intrinsic difference between crimes and civil wrongs found by some writers is in respect of the damage done. In tort there is almost invariably actual damage to some person, whereas in crime such damage is not essential, the threat being to the community as a whole. . . . Again there are formidable objections. Some torts do not require damage (such as trespass and libel), while many crimes do involve private damage. Some crimes are punished as an affront to the moral feelings of the community although they cause no damage to the community as a whole. This is true of the group of crimes having in differing degrees a religious aspect: blasphemy, attempted suicide, abortion, bigamy. It is also largely true of obscenity and adult homosexuality. Even murder need not cause public damage: for example, when a mother kills her infant child. This creates no general sense of insecurity; the only material loss to society is the loss of the child, and whether that is economically a real loss or a gain depends on whether the country is under- or over-populated at the time. Evidently, the social condemnation of infant-killing rests on non-utilitarian ethics. Some forms of public nuisance, too, are crimes although they positively benefit the community: *Ward* (1836) 4 Ad. & El. 384.

Even where an act injures the community, it need not be exclusively a crime. Thus some crimes, as has already been pointed out, may be made the occasion either of a criminal prosecution or of a civil action (generally a relator action) for an injunction by the Attorney-General; in the latter event the crime is treated not as a crime but as a civil wrong to the public. There are civil public wrongs that are not crimes, for which there is no remedy but a relator action, as where statutory powers are being exceeded. Indeed, an ordinary tort to property may be committed against public property and so become a public wrong.

We have rejected all definitions purporting to distinguish between crimes and other wrongs by reference to the sort of thing that is done or the sort of physical, economic or social consequences that follow from it. Only one possibility now remains. A crime must be defined by reference to the *legal* consequences of the act. We must distinguish, primarily, not between crimes and civil wrongs but between criminal and civil proceedings. A crime then becomes an act that is capable of being followed by criminal proceedings, having one of the types of outcome (punishment, etc.) known to follow these proceedings. . . .

As stated at the outset, there are many differences of procedure between crimes and civil wrongs. Often these differences are of no help in distinguishing between the two, because they are consequential differences—it is only when you know that the act is a crime or a civil wrong respectively that you know which procedure to select. However, some elements in procedure do assist in making the classification. When Parliament passes a statute forbidding certain conduct, it may refer in terms to certain procedural matters—such as trial on indictment, or summary conviction—which indicate that the act is to be a crime. Again, when it is disputed whether a given proceeding, such as a proceeding for a penalty, is criminal or civil, a point can be scored by showing that this proceeding has been held in the past to be governed by some procedural rule which is regarded as indicative of a criminal or civil proceeding, as the case may be. For example, the fact that a precedent decides that a new trial may be granted in a particular proceeding indicates that the proceeding is civil, since new trials are not granted in criminal cases. On the other hand a precedent deciding that evidence of character is admissible in a certain proceeding indicates that it is criminal, since evidence of character is not admissible in civil cases, apart from certain quite definite exceptions.

Since the courts thus make use of the whole law of procedure in aid of their task of classification, an attempt to define crime in terms of one item of procedure only is mistaken. This remark applies to the test of crime adopted by Kenny, following Austin and Clark, which links crime with the ability of the Crown to remit the sanction. This test tells you whether an act is a crime only if you already know whether the sanction is remissible by the Crown. Almost always, however, the latter has to be deduced from the former, instead of vice versa. Thus Kenny defines *ignotum per ignotius*. This objection would not be open if Kenny's chosen procedural test were made available *along with all the others*. The procedural test does not give full assistance unless one is allowed to use the whole law of procedure.

. . . In short, a crime is an act capable of being followed by criminal proceedings having a criminal outcome, and a proceeding or its outcome is criminal if it has certain characteristics which mark it as criminal. In a marginal case the court may have to balance one feature, which may suggest that the proceeding is criminal, against another feature, which may suggest the contrary."

P. J. Fitzgerald, "A Concept of Crime" [1960] Crim. L.R. 257, 259

"In the question what is a crime there seems to be entangled three different though related questions.

1. The question may be simply the request of the non-lawyer as to how he is to tell whether an act is a crime or not. Here we may give an imperative definition by saying that a crime is a breach of the criminal law. Though dismissed by Glanville Williams as circular, such a definition is useful firstly in emphasising that a crime is not necessarily a moral wrong and vice versa. Secondly, its value is that it directs attention away from abstract speculation on the nature of the act and focuses it on the need to study the provisions of the criminal law itself. . . .

2. The request for a definition of crime may be the request of the non-lawyer to be told what it means for the law to lay down that certain conduct shall be criminal. In other words he may want to know the effect of the law providing that an act is a crime. Here lies the usefulness of the definition proposed by Glanville Williams which distinguishes criminal wrongs from other legal wrongs. . . .

3. The quest for a definition of crime may be a more sophisticated question, of a lawyer reflecting on the criminal law, namely, what have all crimes in common other than the fact that they are breaches of the criminal law? In so far as the motive behind such a question is the desire for a simple test to decide whether conduct is criminal or not without reference to the provisions of the law, Glanville Williams' discussion is helpful and illuminating in demonstrating that this is a search for the unattainable. But what may lie behind the question 'What is a crime?' may be the idea that Parliament and still more the courts have not created

crimes arbitrarily or irrationally. Given that the aim of the criminal law is to announce that certain acts are not to be done, and to bring about that fewer of these acts are done, what is the principle or principles that have led the criminal law to prohibit the acts it has prohibited? . . ."

Lloyd, Introduction to Jurisprudence (4th ed.), pp. 54–59

"A good deal of controversy has arisen in recent years as to whether the fact that conduct is, by common standards, regarded as immoral, in itself justifies making that conduct punishable by law. This controversy was set off by the opinion expressed in the Wolfenden Committee Report on Prostitution and Homosexuality (Cmnd. 247, 1957), which in effect re-asserted the answer given by John Stuart Mill, that legal coercion can only be justified for the purpose of preventing harm to others. Accordingly, on this view, there is a moral or ethical limit beyond the appropriate reach of the law. Mill's thesis had been attacked by the great Victorian judge, Stephen, in his *Liberty, Equality and Fraternity*, and the issue was now rekindled by Lord Devlin's critique of *Wolfenden* in a lecture called 'The Enforcement of Morals' delivered in 1959. Lord Devlin has subsequently returned to this theme a number of times [see Devlin, *The Enforcement of Morals*, O.U.P., 1965]. He has argued that there is a public morality which provides the cement of any human society, and that the law, especially the criminal law, must regard it as its primary function to maintain this public morality. Whether in fact in any particular case the law should be brought into play by specific criminal sanctions must depend upon the state of public feeling. Conduct which arouses a widespread feeling of reprobation, a mixture of 'intolerance, indignation and disgust', deserves to be suppressed by legal coercion in the interests of the integrity of society. For this purpose, Lord Devlin has recourse to the common law jury idea, the notion that the 'man in the jury-box' supplies an adequate standard of current morality for the purpose of assessing the limits of legal intervention. The juryman after all does not give a snap judgment; his verdict is the outcome of argument and deliberation after, perhaps, listening to expert evidence and receiving guidance from an experienced judge. And as for reliance upon feeling, this was the ordinary man's best guide where a choice had to be made between a number of reasonable conclusions. He therefore stigmatises as an 'error of jurisprudence' the view in the Wolfenden Report that there is some single principle explaining the division between crime and sin, such as that based upon Mill's notion of what may lead to harmful consequences to third persons.

Devlin concluded that if vice were not suppressed society would crumble: 'The suppression of vice is as much the law's business as the suppression of subversive activities.'

Such a thesis appears to have received some support from the remarkable decision of the House of Lords in the so-called *Ladies' Directory Case*, (*Shaw* v. *D.P.P.* [1962] A.C. 220), but has been strenuously opposed by Professor Hart (H. L. A. Hart, *Law, Liberty and Morality*, O.U.P., 1963). Hart has outlined (35 Univ. of Chicago Law Review 1, 11–13), in the first place, 'the types of evidence that might conceivably be relevant to the issue.' One could examine 'crude historical evidence', look at disintegrated societies and enquire whether disintegration was preceded by a malignant change in their common morality, considering further any 'causal connection'. Such a survey would have formidable difficulties for, even supposing, which is most unlikely, that moral decadence was responsible for the decline of Rome, would such evidence be persuasive in considering modern technological societies? Hart puts his faith rather in the evidence of social psychology. Depending on one's ideology, the way of viewing the alternatives to the maintenance of a common morality, this could take one of two forms. One view would be *permissiveness*: one would show how this led to a weakening of individual capacity for self-control and contributed to an increase in violence and dishonesty. But the other side of the coin is *moral pluralism*. Would this lead to antagonism, to a society in the state of nature depicted by Hobbes [see *Leviathan*, Pt. 1, Chap. 13 ('. . . the life of man, solitary, poor, nasty, brutish, and short').] or rather to mutual tolerance, to co-existence of divergent moralities? What evidence there is comes down firmly in favour of co-existence. Having removed the foundations of Devlin's thesis, Hart then sets about to demolish the structure erected upon them. He dismisses as fantastic the notion that all morality forms 'a single seamless web' so that deviation from any one part will almost inevitably produce destruction of the whole. The mere fact that conventional morality may change in a permissive direction does not mean that society is going to be destroyed or subverted. Again, Lord Devlin assumes a degree of moral solidarity in society, which may have existed in mid-Victorian England, but is hardly discernible at the present time. Hart goes on to point out that the real solvent to social morality is not the failure of the law to endorse its restrictions, but rather the operation of free critical discussion, and he goes on to point out the dangers to democracy which might flow from the notion that free discussion should be prohibited on account of its impact on the prevalent social morality. That the moral notions of the majority are matters to which the legislature must pay close account seems beyond question, but what Mill had in mind was that at all costs the idea that the majority had a moral right to dictate how everyone else should live, was something which needed to be resisted. It is essential, therefore, from a libertarian point of view, that public indignation, while given due weight, should be subject to the overriding tests of rational and critical appraisal.

Nevertheless, Hart accepts the need for the law to enforce some morality and the real area of dispute is where the line should be drawn. Mill drew it at harm to others. Hart extends the role of the law by his acceptance of 'paternalism', in addition to Mill's reliance on harmful consequences to others (*Law, Liberty and Morality*, pp. 30–34). So, where Devlin justified *R.* v. *Donovan* [1934] 2 K.B. 498, *post*, p. 476) as enforcement of morality, Hart sees the decision as a concession to paternalism. Hart never defines paternalism and Devlin has been critical of its vagueness. 'What, also, I did not foresee was that some of the crew who sail under Mill's flag of liberty would mutiny and run paternalism up the mast.' (*The Enforcement of Morals*, p. 132.) Although Devlin is unable to distinguish paternalism and the enforcement of morals, there is a distinction which centres on the decision-making process of those who are subject to the law. Paternalism thus may intervene to stop self-inflicted harm such as the results of drug-taking or cigarette smoking or of the refusal to use crash helmets or seat belts, not because of a wish to enforce conventional morality, but because of doubts as to the capacity of the 'victim' to make a rational decision, especially where he is mentally disturbed (according to conventional morality) or physically ill.

But Hart goes further than this. He admits, with Devlin, that some shared morality is essential to society, what he calls 'universal values' (*Law, Liberty, and Morality*, p. 71). If *any* society is to survive, if any legal system is to function, then there must be rules prohibiting, for example, murder. But is abortion or euthanasia murder? The standard case remains uncontroversial, the marginal situation is no nearer solution. Hart further argues, in a later formulation (35 Univ. of Chicago Law Review, p. 10), that rules essential for a *particular* society (monogamy might be an example) might also be enforced. 'For any society there is to be found . . . a central core of rules or principles which constitutes its pervasive and distinctive style of life.' And he continues: 'it then becomes an open and empirical question whether any particular moral rule is so organically connected with the central core that its preservation is required as a vital bastion.' At this stage a point has been reached where there is not much to choose between the two main contestants. (For further viewpoints in this controversy see E.

Rostow [1960] C.L.J. 174, reprinted in *The Sovereign Prerogative* (1962); Hughes, 71 Yale L.J. 662, reprinted in Summers, *Essays in Legal Philosophy* (1968), p. 183; Summers (1963) 38 N.Y.U.L. Rev. 1201; Henkin (1963) 63 Col. L. Rev. 393; Samek, 49 Can. Bar Rev. 188.)"

Note

Quite apart from this quarrel about what the criminal law should prohibit, there is another controversy about what should be done with individuals who defy such prohibitions as the criminal law has.

Galligan, "The Return to Retribution in Criminal Theory," in "Crime Proof and Punishment"; Essays in Memory of Sir Rupert Cross (1981), pp. 144, 146 et seq.

"If one were to attempt to explain the principal functions of that complex amalgam of institutions, persons, rules, and practices which we loosely refer to as the system of criminal justice, then two particular things would seem to call out for special attention. First, criminal justice is concerned centrally with trying, convicting and punishing those who are guilty of breaking the criminal law. Secondly, such systems are concerned to punish those who are convicted with a view to upholding the authority and effectiveness of the criminal law by sanctions that seek to deter, to prevent, to reform, or to incapacitate. These two tasks will often, but not necessarily, be compatible with each other. One view of criminal justice is to emphasise the forward-looking or utilitarian functions while another view sees the backward-looking or retributive aspect as primary. How one perceives the system will largely determine how one explains it and the kind of justifications that one finds acceptable . . . .

Utilitarian accounts usually begin with the assumption that the central purpose of criminal justice is to reduce crime. This purpose is achieved by taking coercive action against selected individuals, usually those who have broken the law and who can be held personally responsible for so doing. There is an increasing body of offences which do not require responsibility in the usual legal sense, but nevertheless, with respect to the main corpus of criminal laws there is still a meticulous concern to be sure that before a person is punished he is guilty in the sense that he is responsible. But why should this be so? It is an important aspect of forward-looking explanations of criminal justice that the punishment of wrongdoers is not itself part of the general aim or purpose. Rather, confinement of impositions to the guilty law-breaker is a costly constraint on pursuit of the general reductivist aim. One approach faces this problem by suggesting that these constraints are misguided, in that inquiries into matters of personal responsibility are inevitably very crude, and unfairly selective in that there are large areas where action is taken without the requirement of responsibility. According to this view criminal justice should not be thought of as significantly different from other methods of social protection, such as confining dangerous mental defectives. Society has an interest in protecting itself from the person who has or is likely to commit serious crime and may legitimately take whatever preventive action is necessary. Although such an understanding of criminal justice has been anathema to most, a few modifications show it in a much better light. A modified approach might see considerable advantages such as economy, humanitarianism and the reduction of suffering in retaining the basic constraints on the aim of reducing crime, but since these would be conditional they could be departed from if to do so would provide better service to the general aim. It is worth noting that much of the practice of criminal justice is indeed compatible with this position for while coercion is normally based on responsibility, it is also often departed from if we bear in mind the preventive powers of the police and courts, the areas of strict and vicarious liability and the means available for confining mental defectives.

Views of this kind, however, have never dominated explanations of criminal justice. Most forward-looking accounts of criminal justice, no matter how different in other respects, seek to show that while the general purpose of criminal justice is forward looking, the responsibility constraints on that purpose are explicable, justifiable and necessary. Since Bentham's famous but flawed defence of punishing only those responsible for their actions, a range of increasingly subtle and sophisticated explanations have been advanced. There is, for example, the pragmatist argument that as a matter of practicalities it would be virtually impossible to design an efficacious system of criminal justice that did not limit the distribution of sanctions to the responsible offender. Alternatively there is the suggestion that the purpose of criminal justice is not only reduction-through-deterrence, but also reduction-through-respect for the law. Unless the administration of criminal justice is in accordance with values esteemed in the community then respect for law is hardly to be earned and naturally most people think that a man should only be punished if he is guilty. There is much to be said for this view; notice however that it puts forward the responsibility constraint not as an independent value in itself, but of value because it maximises the efficacy of law. . . .

Finally, it is a frequently heard criticism of utilitarian accounts that since the aim is crime control, there are difficulties in finding principles that limit the amount of punishment that may be inflicted on any offender. To the practical reformer this is the central issue, for recent penal history has shown the difficulty of controlling punishment distributed according to forward-looking goals. Retributive accounts, with their emphasis on punishment according to deserts, is naturally an attractive alternative to the unruly policies of rehabilitation and deterrence. . . .

Retributive explanations emphasise the concern of the criminal justice system to punish those who break the law. The core of the idea of retribution is the moral notion that the wrongdoer ought to be punished. Thus a system that is centrally concerned with punishing offenders is retributive. In explaining the practice of criminal justice in this way, the retributive approach avoids the difficulties in explanation that beset forward-looking accounts. There is no need to distinguish between aim and distribution since the aim provides the criterion of distribution. The person who has not broken the law, or who could not help breaking it, or who can offer some other acceptable excuse is not a wrongdoer and is not liable for punishment. In other words within the context of criminal justice as we know it, punishment means inflicting sanctions on wrongdoers. This does not imply that coercion is never used against people in other ways; all it claims is that the reasons for coercing wrongdoers are different from the reasons that would explain other areas of coercion.

Put in this bald way, retribution includes both a description of criminal justice and a justification. Just as the Utilitarian sees criminal justice as primarily concerned with reducing crime, so the retributivist sees the punishment of offenders as the dominant purpose. The logic of punishment consists in singling out an offender, condemning him for his offence and imposing punitive treatment upon him. The retributivist sees these three elements as part of one unified and justifiable social process: the offender has done wrong which, by punishment, is somehow righted. In short, the distinctive feature of retribution as a justifying principle, is that it provides a basis not just for singling out and condemning the offender, but also for inflicting punitive treatment. . . ."

2. THE FORM OF ENGLISH CRIMINAL LAW

In some Commonwealth jurisdictions, *e.g.* Queensland, the criminal law is in the form of a code. In England and Wales, despite an attempt in that direction in the nineteenth century, no general criminal code has appeared. Although the great bulk of the law relating to particular offences is embodied in Acts of Parliament, some of them so elaborate and comprehensive as to be describable as partial codifications, it remains true that the general part of the law, *i.e.* that dealing with principles common to all crimes, was not enacted on some particular occasion by the legislature, but was developed over the centuries by the judges.

The history of judicial law-making in English criminal law is one of stunted development. This is not to say that it rested on no rational principles, but that the principles did not enjoy the prolonged period of active development and refinement in the nineteenth century such as occurred in, *e.g.* contract law. It is true that, unlike the criminal law, much of the civil law was at first cribbed and confined by the rigidities of the formulary system and the artificialities of pleading, but that system seems to have involved its practitioners in habits of ratiocination without atrophying their creative powers. At all events when the old restraints were loosened and then cast aside, the subsequent development of the law, helped as it was by constant pressure from mercantile interests, was ordered, continuous and comparatively rapid.

By contrast, criminal law at the close of the eighteenth century was "principled," perhaps over-principled, in that the authoritative works of such as Hale, Hawkins and Foster had appeared and had been accorded authority by the courts. These works were written by practitioners, usually working judges with extensive experience, and they extracted principles out of that experience and the experience of earlier working judges such as Kelyng. The criminal law thus underwent a crystallisation, which was not undone by any reform of the ground rules such as occurred on the civil side. The civil law's period of development and refinement was not matched by anything similar in criminal law. During the nineteenth century, such appeal to principle as occurred in reported judgments consisted in the parrotting of the institutional writers, who enjoyed (and still do enjoy) an influence denied to other legal text books. Few, if any, thorough reviews and rationalisations and syntheses of earlier decisions, like those in *Taylor* v. *Caldwell* or *Hadley* v. *Baxendale* in contract, or *Rylands* v. *Fletcher* or *Indermaur* v. *Dames* in tort, occurred in criminal law. Such movement as there was in the field was due to the frequent, but unthought-out, contributions of Parliament, which body was indeed coming to be thought of as the only proper innovator when the life or liberty of the subject was concerned. In the result, the middle of the twentieth century found many of the central concepts of criminal law, such as complicity, still unarticulated.

A further, apparent, reason for this stunted growth was the absence of appeal decisions and reports of appeal decisions. There was no appeal as of right by the accused and no appeal at all by the Crown from the result of a trial on indictment. Such reviews as took place of first instance decisions were the deliberations of the Court for Crown Cases Reserved, which were dominated by the daily triers of crime, the puisne judges. This is not to deny the appearance of an occasional judge of stature and influence, such as Stephen; but to make the contrast with the position in civil law at any rate since 1875. The facilities for appeal were improved by the setting up of the Court of Criminal Appeal in 1907. But any hopes that the new arrangements would provide coherent, modern, principles were frustrated, because those who held these hopes failed to take account of the attitude of the judges themselves, particularly the puisnes, and of the fact that the operation of the new system was left almost entirely in the hands of those puisne judges.

To take the latter point first, the Court of Criminal Appeal consisted in the Lord Chief Justice and a fluctuating selection of judges of the Queen's Bench Division. Apart from the Lord Chief Justice, there were no senior judges, removed from the daily handling of trials, to keep an oversight of the way in which the criminal law developed. Nor was this want of oversight supplied by the House of Lords. Although theoretically that court of last resort was available in criminal matters, its influence was minimal. The *fiat* of the Attorney-General was needed, certifying that the decision appealed against involved a point of law of *exceptional* public importance; which meant that between 1907 and 1960 appeals to the House of Lords in criminal matters were few and far between, there being only 21 reported in those 53 years. Not until 1966 was the position at the first level of appeal remedied, when the Court of Criminal Appeal was abolished and replaced by the Court of Appeal (Criminal Division). This usually sits in two courts, the first with the Lord Chief Justice, a Lord Justice of Appeal and a puisne judge, the second with one Lord Justice of Appeal and two puisnes. Appeal to the House of Lords was put on its present footing in 1960. The necessity for the Attorney-General's *fiat* was abolished, and appeal now lies from the Court of Appeal (Criminal Division) if (i) the Court of Appeal certifies a point of law of *general* public importance, and (ii) either that Court or the House of Lords gives leave to appeal on the ground that the point is one which ought to be considered by the House of Lords. Appeals to the House of Lords have become very common, and the influence of that tribunal on the criminal law has been pronounced, if controversial. The same puisne judges who had the handling of appeals from convictions on indictment also heard appeals from petty sessions, which were and are by way of case stated to the Queen's Bench Divisional Court, consisting in at least two Queen's Bench judges sitting together. There was no further appeal until 1960, when appeals to the House of Lords were allowed subject to exactly the same conditions as those governing appeals from the Court of Appeal (Criminal Division).

As to the attitude of the judges, they preferred the old system. In *The Judge* (O.U.P., 1979), Lord Devlin notes the dislike with which many judges greeted the Criminal Appeal Act 1907: "They felt that the verdict of a jury properly directed in law—they would always of course correct the law—should be unassailable and that to allow an appeal from it cast an unnecessary doubt on its reliability. This feeling, coupled with the normal judicial distrust of innovation resulted in a very narrow exercise of the new powers" (p. 112). And later he writes of their reluctance to make case law. "[It] goes back a long way. At the root of it there is, I think, the idea that criminal justice ought to be made to measure.... Doubtless it is the judicial unwillingness to make any case law at all which accounts for the sloppiness with which it is made, when it is.... Discussion of general principle is not encouraged. Cases relating to *mens rea* as an element of crime live in a shambles from which academic writers try to rescue them." (pp. 185–186).

The attitude of the judges to academic prompting and criticism was for a long time one of lordly indifference. Indeed there was a period when this attitude was inevitable because no respectable academic opinion confronted them. It was not until 1902, when C. S. Kenny produced his *Outlines of Criminal Law*, that a text appeared which was more than a mere chap-book or practitioner's *aide-mémoire*; and not until 1953, when Glanville Williams' *The Criminal Law: the General Part* appeared, that any textbook got below the surface of English criminal law. The latter work stimulated academic interest in a subject which was formerly much neglected by English academic lawyers, and at length the judges began to notice what was written in books other than the practitioner's Bible, *Archbold's Criminal Pleading*. It is now common to find judicial citations of, *e.g.* Smith and Hogan's *Criminal Law*, Glanville Williams' *Textbook*, and the writings of Smith, and Griew, on Theft. Usually the references are complimentary or at least respectful, but occasionally irritation at what are felt as academic pin-pricks is revealed: see Commentary on *R.* v. *Bayley & Easterbrook* [1980] Crim. L.R. 503.

Two further points can be made on the subject of the judges' role in law-making in the area of criminal law. One is that there was until 1972 no provision for any appeal from a jury's acquittal. This had the drawback that if a doubtful point of law constantly manifested itself in instructions to acquit by trial judges, there was no way in which the point could be considered by appellate courts. This drawback was removed by the Criminal Justice Act 1972, s. 36, which provides that where a person tried on indictment has been acquitted, and the Attorney-General desires an opinion of the Court of Appeal on a point of law which has arisen in the case, he may refer the point to the Court and they shall give an opinion on it. The opinion does not in any way affect the acquittal, but the section does allow the new, improved, court of first appeal to pass on a wider range of points than formerly.

The second point concerns the court of final appeal, the House of Lords. This has been much more active since 1960 than it was before, but its contribution has not pleased everyone. Professor J. C. Smith ([1981] Crim. L.R. 393) describes its record in criminal cases as dismal. He notes that all too often their Lordships' decisions have had to be reversed by legislation, citing *D.P.P.* v. *Smith* [1961] A.C. 290; *D.P.P.* v. *Sykes* [1962] A.C. 528; *D.P.P.* v. *Turner* [1974] A.C. 357; *Haughton* v. *Smith* [1975] A.C. 476, and *D.P.P.* v. *Nock* [1978] A.C. 979. Glanville Williams ([1981] Crim. L.R. 582), after giving credit for some beneficial decisions, considers it a nice question whether, on balance, the appellate jurisdiction of the House of Lords in criminal cases is worth the expense to the community. He identifies part of the trouble as the extreme width of the jurisdiction. "Few lawyers, even the most competent, would care to be asked for opinions of momentous consequence on an absolutely unlimited range of problems. It is particularly inapt that a Chancery judge should have the casting vote in the House of Lords in a criminal case, as Lord Cross did in *Hyam* v. *D.P.P.* [1975] A.C. 55." He suggests that the Court of Appeal, augmented on occasions by the attendance of Law Lords, ought to be the final appellate Court. "All judges fall into error from time to time, but, whatever the theory of precedent may say, the Court of Appeal is slightly better at correcting its mistakes than the House of Lords, about whose pronouncements there is an awful finality."

Professor Smith (*op. cit.*) prophesies that *R.* v. *Caldwell* [1981] 1 All E.R. 961 might well join the ranks of decisions which have to be reversed by statute, "for it plainly defeats the intention of the Law Commission which was responsible for drafting the [Criminal Damage Act 1971] . . . and it conflicts with the proposals of the Criminal Law Revision Committee in their report on the law of offences against the person." Even a short description of the present state of English criminal law would not be adequate without mention of these two bodies, the activities of which have gone some way towards making that law more rational and ordered.

In English law, criminal law is peculiar in having two standing bodies actively devoted to its reform. The Criminal Law Revision Committee was set up in 1959 by the Home Secretary as a standing committee to examine such aspects of the criminal law as he might refer to it and to make recommendations for revision if thought necessary. This committee of part-time lawyer members has made no pretensions, nor indeed has it had the power, to examine the criminal law as a whole. However it has produced a number of reports on particular areas, usually resulting in legislation, *e.g.* the Theft Act 1968. In 1965 the Law Commissions Act established a permanent body of salaried Commissioners to keep the whole of the law, civil and criminal, under review "with a view to its systematic development and reform, including in particular the codification of such law, the elimination of anomalies, the repeal of obsolete and unnecessary enactments, the reduction of the number of separate enactments and generally the simplification and modernisation of the law" (s. 3). In pursuance of this remit, the Law Commission announced an ambitious programme for the codification of criminal law, but in the event soon found itself examining and reporting on particular areas of the law, which reports have sometimes resulted in legislation, *e.g.* the Criminal Damage Act 1971. Commonly the Law Commission sets up a Working Party to make a preliminary examination of a topic and produce a Working Paper. The Law Commission's Report usually endorses the conclusions in the Working Paper, but not always, *e.g.* Law Com. No. 102 on attempts.

Since after 1965 in practice both bodies were considering and making proposals about particular areas of the law, it might have been decided that the Criminal Law Review Committee was redundant. However the Home Secretary has continued to refer matters to it. Both bodies continue to produce reports on particular areas, not always entirely in step with each other. The criminal law is the better for their efforts, and would be further improved if Parliamentary time were found to embody all their reports in legislation. However, codification still seems a long way away. It can be argued that reforming particular parts of the law before producing a code covering the general principles of liability is putting the cart before the horse. This way of proceeding has, however, proved unavoidable. The fact of the matter is that the Law Commission has not been able to find the great amount of time needed to think about general principles, as it recognised in 1981 by setting up a small team of senior academics to undertake the preliminary work for the codification of the general parts of the criminal law.

CHAPTER 2

ACTUS REUS

	PAGE		PAGE
1. Elements of Crime	13	4. Causation	24
2. Voluntariness	14	5. Coincidence of *Actus Reus* and *Mens Rea*	40
3. Omissions	18		

1. ELEMENTS OF CRIME

THE terms *actus reus* and *mens rea* when used to describe the elements of a criminal offence are deceptively simple. Not only is there a host of conceptual pitfalls concealed within each, but there is also no agreement amongst lawyers as to the precise divide between them.

A. T. H. Smith, "On Actus Reus and Mens Rea" in Reshaping the Criminal Law (ed. Glazebrook), pp. 95–107

"As the elliptic statements of the basic ingredients of criminal liability that they are frequently taken to be, both expressions [*actus reus* and *mens rea*] are incomplete and misleading. While the term *mens rea* is used in at least three distinct senses, so that failure to distinguish clearly between them leads inevitably to confusion, the terminology of *actus reus* tends to conceal the important principles that are at stake when the courts are deciding what sorts of conduct deserve condemnation as criminal. I do not mean to suggest that the traditional terminology should be abandoned; rather I would argue that a sharper awareness of its limitations might help us to see more clearly what the preconditions to criminal liability really are, and how far they really reflect the principles they are commonly supposed to encapsulate. . . .

This division of crime into its constituent parts is an exercise of analytical convenience: the concepts of *actus reus* and *mens rea* are simply tools, useful in the exposition of the criminal law. Great care should, therefore, be taken to avoid determining questions of policy by reference to definition and terminology. Such observations as that the maxim *actus non facit reum nisi mens sit rea* serves the 'important purpose of stressing two basic requirements of criminal liability', make *actus reus* and *mens rea* seem rather more than analytical tools. They have been converted from the descriptive to the normative: to propositions that criminal liability *should* be based on harmful conduct, and *should* require a mental element. . . .

The raw material of any crime is the particular social mischief that the legislator is seeking to suppress. But for ascertaining the *actus reus* of any given offence, the starting point for the courts is the statute, or, as it may still be, the common law definition. Questions of statutory interpretation must be solved before the exact scope of the proscribed activity can be known. Where the defendant's conduct can fairly be described as coming within the terms of the proscribed activity, an offence has, prima facie, been committed: liability will ensue unless he advances some explanation of his conduct which shows that it was justified, in which case there is no *actus reus*. As one writer puts it, 'the *actus reus* is a defeasible concept.' But some lawyers are content to say that the requirements of *actus reus* are satisfied whenever the terms of the definition are fulfilled. The danger of taking such a very limited view of what is entailed in the *actus reus*, is that it may too readily be concluded that the harm that the law seeks to prevent has occurred. Much depends on the view taken of the role of defences....

Glanville Williams [C.L.G.P., p. 20] inclines to the view that all the elements of a crime are divisible into either *actus reus* or *mens rea* and holds that the *actus reus* includes absence of defence. By implication, therefore, all defences are a denial that the prosecution has proved a requisite part of its case. Although they nowhere clearly articulate the point, Professors Smith and Hogan seem to prefer the view that the constituent ingredients of crime are threefold, and include defences which are themselves composites of physical (or external) and mental elements. This mode of analysis is becoming increasingly widespread amongst academic writers, and has been carried furthest by Professor Lanham [[1976] Crim. L.R. 276]. He says that:

> as a matter of analysis we can think of a crime as being made up of three ingredients, *actus reus*, *mens rea* and (a negative element) absence of a valid defence. Some defences (*e.g.* alibi) negative the *actus reus*. Some defences (*e.g.* I did not mean to do it) negative the *mens rea*. A third group of defences (*e.g.* self-defence) operate without negativing either positive element, in effect as a confession and avoidance. But there is a fourth kind of defence (*sic*) which is perfectly capable of standing as a confession and avoidance but which normally will negative one or other (or both) of the *actus reus* and *mens rea*.

According to this view, then *actus reus* and *mens rea* do not encapsulate all the ingredients of a crime."

Most writers seem agreed that the "act" implied in the phrase "*actus reus*" does not stop at bodily movements or overt acts. "Some acts can only be engaged in, some can only be performed, some only are done, and there are even some that can only take place; and this suggests the richness and variety of those bits of the world that we may choose to regard as acts." (Gross, p. 133). Williams takes the view that "the proposition that an offence requires an act requires to be so qualified by exceptions that its utility comes to seem doubtful.... It is therefore less misleading to say that a crime requires some *external state of affairs* that can be categorised as criminal." (T.C.L., p. 31).

2. VOLUNTARINESS

H. L. A. Hart, "Act of Will and Responsibility" in Punishment and Responsibility (1968), p. 90

"*The General Doctrine*

In this lecture I propose to air some doubts which I have long felt about a doctrine, concerning criminal responsibility, which has descended from the philosophy of conduct of the eighteenth century, through Austin, to modern English writers on the criminal law. This is the doctrine that, besides the elements of knowledge of circumstances and foresight of consequences, in terms of which many writers define *mens rea*, there is another 'mental' or at least psychological element which is required for responsibility: the accused's 'conduct' (including his omissions where these are criminally punishable) must, so it is said, be voluntary and not involuntary. This element in responsibility is more fundamental than *mens rea* in the sense of knowledge of circumstances or foresight of consequences; for even where *mens rea* in that sense is not required, and responsibility is 'strict' or 'absolute'..., this element, according to some modern writers, is still required....

In many textbooks there are general assertions that for *all* criminal responsibility conduct must be 'voluntary', 'conduct [must be] the result of the exercise of his will' there must be an 'act with its element of will,' 'an act due to the deliberate exercise of the will.' Yet, surely, even if there is any such general doctrine, these phrases are very dark. What does doctrine mean? What after all is the will?...

We know now what the general doctrine means: it defines an act in terms of the simplest thing we can do: this is the minimum feat of contracting our muscles. Conduct is 'voluntary' or 'the expression of an act of will' if the muscular contraction which, on the physical side, is the initiating element in what are loosely thought of as simple actions, is caused by a desire for the same contractions. This is all the mysterious element of the 'will' amounts to: it is this which is the minimum indispensable link between mind and body required for responsibility even where responsibility is strict....

... The ... theory that has got into our law books through Austin is first, nonsensical when applied to omissions, and secondly cannot characterise what is amiss even in involuntary interventions; for the desire to move our muscles, which it says is missing there, is not present in normal voluntary action either."

Consider Hart's alternative definition under which he seeks to classify those acts generally regarded as not voluntary:

"... We could characterise involuntary movements such as those made in epilepsy, or in a stroke, or mere reflex actions to blows or stings, as movements of the body which occurred although they were not appropriate, *i.e.*, required for any action (in the ordinary sense of action) which the agent believed himself to be doing."

Williams, Textbook of Criminal Law, p. 33

"Lawyers sometimes speak of a voluntary act meaning only that it was willed. Since every act is by definition willed, there is no need to call it voluntary.

The element of volition in an act has greatly exercised the philosophers. I can look at my hand, say to myself "Hand, move to the left," and then cause it to move to the left. But that is not the way in which I usually live and move: I do not consciously direct orders to my muscles. Two philosophers, Ryle and Melden, have attempted to argue away the notion of will. They build their case upon the difficulty of identifying conscious volitions accompanying bodily movement. Certainly it would be false to assume that every act is the result of deliberation: I may scratch my nose while thinking, without knowing I am doing it or recollecting I have done it. Even when the act is conscious, introspection does not show a conscious exercise of will preceding conduct. When I move my arms, say in writing a letter, I do not consciously decide to move them before moving them. It is true that electrical impulses run from the motor nerve cells in the spinal cord through the nerve fibres to the muscles; and these muscles are under the control of my brain. But the mental functioning that controls movement is not conscious determination, and it takes place at practically the same time as the movement. Will is the mental activity accompanying the type of bodily movement that we call an act. It is, of course, possible to will the absence of an act, as when we sit still.

A bodily movement is said to be willed, generally speaking, when the person in question could have refrained from it if he had so willed, that is, he could have kept still. Movements that are the result of epilepsy, for example, are involuntary or unwilled because the person concerned cannot by any mental effort avoid them. Whatever the difficulties in explaining what we mean by volition, everyone realises the important difference between doing something and having something happen to one; and this distinction is a basic postulate of a moral view of human behaviour."

Note

Voluntariness and Consciousness

It is not *necessary* for a person to be unconscious before his or her acts are said to be involuntary. A person suffering from St. Vitus Dance, or having a muscle spasm, is acting involuntarily under either the Hart "inappropriateness" formula, or the Williams' "inability to refrain" test. Nor is unconsciousness in itself *sufficient* to avoid liability. As Lord Denning said in *Bratty* v. *A.-G. for Northern Ireland* [1963] A.C. 386, 410: "It is not every involuntary act which leads to a complete acquittal." This dictum applies in particular where the defendant is responsible for his or her own incapacity. A separate defence of automatism has thus developed with its own limitations. There is also a connection between some instances of automatism and insanity. For these two reasons automatism is dealt with below in Chapter 4. But what happens when the defendant is conscious but still claims he or she acted involuntarily? Does the concept of voluntariness cover more than muscle twitches? The following case has often been criticised for ignoring the requirement of a voluntary act.

R. v. Larsonneur
(1933) 97 J.P. 206
Court of Criminal Appeal

The defendant, a French subject, landed in the United Kingdom with a French passport. This was indorsed with conditions prohibiting her employment here. On March 22 these conditions were varied by a condition requiring her to leave the United Kingdom that day. This she did, going to the Irish Free State. The Irish authorities ordered her deportation and she was brought to Holyhead in the custody of the Irish police and she was there handed over to the English police. She was charged that "she being an alien to whom leave to land in the United Kingdom contrary to Articles 1(3) (*g*) and 18 (1) (*b*) of the Aliens Order, 1920, as amended by S.R. & O. No. 326 of 1923 and 715 of 1931." She was convicted at London Sessions and appealed.

Lord Hewart C.J.: The fact is, as the evidence shows, that the appellant is an alien. She has a French passport, which bears this statement under the date March 14, 1933. "Leave to land granted at Folkestone this day on condition that the holder does not enter any employment, paid or unpaid, whilst in the United Kingdom," but on March 22 that condition was varied and one finds these words: "The condition attached to the grant of leave to land is hereby varied so as to require departure from the United Kingdom not later than March 22, 1933." Then follows the signature of an Under-Secretary of State. In fact, the appellant went to the Irish Free State and afterwards, in circumstances which are perfectly immaterial, so far as this appeal is concerned, came back to England. She was at Holyhead on April 21, 1933, practically a month after the day limited by the condition of her passport. . . .

Appeal dismissed

Note

Part of the problem with this case is that the prohibition related to a state of affairs rather than a physical act. One way of solving the apparent injustice is by the implication of *mens rea* into the offence: as in *Lim Chin Aik* v. *R.*, *post*, p. 134. But it may still be possible to reconcile the case with the doctrine of a voluntary act. Lanham defends the decision, though not the reasoning, in "Larsonneur Revisited" [1976] Crim. L.R. 276. He suggests that Miss Larsonneur was herself responsible for her seemingly unfortunate fate, and no more deserved acquittal than a person who becomes an automaton through drink or drugs. It appears from a confession which she made to the police that Miss Larsonneur had gone to Ireland to arrange a marriage between herself and an Englishman, and had been told by the Irish police to leave by April 17: "Miss Larsonneur's story . . . reveals that the defendant brought upon herself the act of compulsion which led to her being charged. . . . No-one could claim that *Larsonneur* stood as a shining example of jurisprudence. But it can hardly be regarded as the last word in judicial depravity. If Miss Larsonneur had been dragged kicking and screaming from France into the United Kingdom by kidnappers and the same judgment had been given by the Court of Criminal Appeal, the defence of unforeseeable compulsion would truly have been excluded and the case would be the worst blot on the pages of the modern criminal law. But she wasn't and it wasn't and it isn't."

Even if Miss Larsonneur's conviction was not in accordance with the doctrine of voluntary conduct, it may be questioned whether the doctrine is the appropriate instrument with which to apportion criminal responsibility. A driver whose drinks have, unbeknown to him or her, been "laced," resulting in an excessive blood-alcohol concentration will not avoid conviction under the Road Traffic Act 1972, s. 6: *R.* v. *Shippam* [1971] Crim. L.R. 434. The rationale here does not seem to be that the drinking was self-induced (*cf.* "involuntary" intoxication as a defence to non-alcohol-related crimes, *post*, p. 176) but that the "driving" was voluntary. This suggests that the doctrine is still a little unpolished.

Compare *Kilbride* v. *Lake* [1962] N.Z.L.R. 590. Kilbride's conviction for failing to display a current warrant of fitness was quashed by the New Zealand Court of Criminal Appeal on the ground that the omission was not within his conduct, knowledge or control, since the warrant was there when he parked his car and inexplicably not there when he returned.

The critics of Larsonneur might be expected to welcome this display of antipodean juristic maturity but an argument is put forward by Budd and Lynch, in "Voluntariness, Causation and Strict Liability" [1978] Crim. L.R. 74 that "it is a form of involuntariness quite unlike those forms usually referred to in the law. . . . If one believes that strict liability, although entailing the conviction of the morally blameless, is nevertheless beneficial to society, then there is no purpose in excluding from its ambit those who can demonstrate that some unforeseeable intervening event produced the result, or those who can show that they lacked the physical 'opportunity to act otherwise,' whether on the extended *Kilbride* v. *Lake* definition or in the more limited sense of their being in a state of automatism."

It seems that "voluntariness" is a slippery concept which raises, but does not answer, all sorts of questions about culpability.

For further exploration of the utility of strict liability, see Chapter 3, p. 151.

3. OMISSIONS

P. R. Glazebrook, "Criminal Omissions: The Duty Requirement in Offences Against the Person" (1960) 76 L.Q.R. 386 at 387

"Although a failure to act may have as serious consequences as an act, and although any difference between acts and omissions is often denied, the distinction is deeply embedded in the law. This fact is no less inescapable because there is no precise test for distinguishing an act from an omission. Human conduct may often be described in either positive or negative terms, though usually one way rather than the other will appear more natural. . . . But difficult cases there will be, and their very existence leads to the imposition of liability for omissions. A man is in his spring cart; the reins are not in his hands, but lying on the horse's back. While the horse trots down a hill a young child runs across the road in front of the cart, is knocked down and killed. Had the man held the reins he could have pulled the horse up. Did he kill the child by driving the cart recklessly, or by recklessly failing to drive the cart?"

The facts of the case cited in the last sentence are those of *R.* v. *Dalloway* (*post*, p. 28).

One distinction which is important is that between offences whose essence is an omission and those which, though usually committed by a postive act, can also be committed by omission.

Fletcher, Rethinking Criminal Law (1978), p. 421

"Both 'acts' and 'omissions' can be brought under the general rubric of 'conduct'. . . . If there is a special problem in punishing omissions, we can learn what it is only by examining the contexts in which lawyers conventionally talk about 'omissions' or 'failing to act'. In fact, there is a radical cleavage between two forms of liability for 'omissions'. According to one type, the focus of liability is a breach of statutory obligation to act [appropriate English examples would be failure to display a vehicle tax disc, failure to report an accident]. . . . We shall call this the field of liability for 'breach of duty to act'. The contrasting field is the imposition of liability for failing to intervene, when necessary, to prevent the occurrence of a serious harm such as death or the destruction of property . . . we shall refer to this second type of liability as 'commission by omission'. The substantive difference [between the two] is that liability for breach of a statutory duty does not presuppose the occurrence of harm. . . . In contrast, the death of the victim is essential for committing homicide by omission. . . . The gravamen of liability for 'breach of duty' is the breach itself; for commission by omission, the occurrence of a particular result."

The discussion here is concerned with the second type of liability identified by Fletcher. Not all offences are susceptible of commission by omission. Most of the cases concern murder or manslaughter although liability could arise in a similar way for causing grievous bodily harm under section 20 of the Offences Against the Person Act 1861. It was thought that assault required a positive act but this is now in doubt: see *Fagan* v. *Metropolitan Police Commissioner* [1969] 1 Q.B. 439, *post*, p. 473.

The American case of *Commonwealth* v. *Cali* (1923) 141 N.E. 510 took a similar approach to the defendant's failure to put out a fire, which had started accidentally.

Not all omissions give rise to liability: *Williams*, T. C. L., p. 34: "At first sight it may seem strange to say that an offence can be committed by an omission. If there is an act, someone acts; but if there is an omission, everyone (in a sense) omits. We all omit to do everything in the world that is not done.

In common speech, whether a not-doing is described as an omission depends upon whether a person would in those circumstances ordinarily be expected to have acted. And where the expectation is recognised and sanctioned by the law, we say that there is a legal duty to act."

Liability for failing to intervene

It is generally recognised that the attitude adopted by the common law is well summarised in the passage below.

Lord Macaulay's Works (ed. Lady Trevelyan), Vol. VII, p. 497

"It is, indeed, most highly desirable that men should not merely abstain from doing harm to their neighbours, but should render active services to their neighbours. In general, however, the penal law must content itself with keeping men from doing positive harm, and must leave to public opinion, and to the teachers of morality and religion, the offence of furnishing men with motives for doing positive good. It is evident that to attempt to punish men by law for not rendering to others all the service which it is their duty to render to others would be preposterous. We must grant impunity to the vast majority of those omissions which a benevolent morality would pronounce reprehensible, and must content ourselves with punishing such omissions only when they are distinguished from the rest by some circumstance which marks them out as peculiarly fit objects of penal legislation."

It is possible to recognise three strands: duties arising out of contract, duties of parents to children (under common law and under the Children and Young Persons Act 1933), and duties arising from the assumption of care for the helpless and infirm. For a case on wilful neglect under the 1933 Act see *Sheppard*, *post*, p. 86.

R. v. Pittwood
(1902) 19 T.L.R. 37
Taunton Assizes

The defendant was a gatekeeper on the Somerset and Dorset Railway. He had to keep the gate shut whenever a train was passing during the period 7 a.m. to 7 p.m. One afternoon the gate was open and a hay cart which was crossing the line was hit by a train. One man was killed and another was seriously injured. Witnesses testified that the road was an accommodation road and not a public road. The accused was charged with manslaughter.

Wright J., without calling upon the prosecution, gave judgment. He said he was clearly of opinion that in this case there was gross and criminal negligence, as the man was paid to keep the gate shut and protect the public. In his opinion there were three grounds on which the verdict could be supported: (1) There might be cases of misfeasance and cases of mere non-feasance. Here it was quite clear there was evidence of misfeasance as the prisoner directly contributed to the accident. (2) A man might incur criminal liability from a duty arising out of contract. The learned judge quoted in support of this *R.* v. *Nicholls* (1875) 13 Cox 75; *R.* v. *Elliott* (1889) 16 Cox 710; *R.* v. *Benge* (1865) 4 F. & F. 594; *R.* v. *Hughes* (1857) Dears. & B. 248. The strongest case of all was, perhaps, *R.* v. *Instan*, [*post*, p. 21] and that case clearly governed the present charge. (3) With regard to the point that this was only an occupation road, he clearly held that it was not, as the company had assumed the liability of protecting the public whenever they crossed the road. . . .

Verdict: Guilty

R. v. Dytham

[1979] 3 All E.R. 641
Court of Appeal

The defendant, a police constable, was on duty in uniform near a club when a man was ejected from the club and kicked to death by a "bouncer." D. took no steps to intervene and drove off. He appealed against conviction for misconduct whilst acting as an officer of justice.

LORD WIDGERY C.J.: . . . [T]he argument . . . ran deep into constitutional and jurisprudential history. The effect of it was that not every failure to discharge a duty which devolved on a person as the holder of a public office gave rise to the common law offence of misconduct in that office. As counsel for the appellant put it, non-feasance was not enough. There must be a malfeasance or at least a misfeasance involving an element of corruption. In support of this contention a number of cases were cited from 18th and 19th century reports. It is the fact that in nearly all of them the misconduct asserted involved some corrupt taint; but this appears to have been an accident of circumstances and not a necessary incident of the offence. Misconduct in a public office is more vividly exhibited where dishonesty is revealed as part of the dereliction of duty. Indeed in some cases the conduct impugned cannot be shown to have been misconduct unless it was done with a corrupt or oblique motive. . . .

[I]n Stephen's Digest of the Criminal Law are to be found these words:

> "Every public officer commits a misdemeanour who wilfully neglects to perform any duty which he is bound either by common law or by statute to perform provided that the discharge of such duty is not attended with greater danger than a man of ordinary firmness and activity may be expected to encounter."

In support of this proposition *R.* v. *Wyat* (1705) 1 Salk. 380 is cited as well as *R.* v. *Bembridge* (1783) 3 Doug. K.B. 327, a judgment of Lord Mansfield. The neglect must be wilful and not merely inadvertent; and it must be culpable in the sense that it is without reasonable excuse or jusitification.

In the present case it was not suggested that the appellant could not have summoned or sought assistance to help the victim or to arrest his assailants. The charge as framed left this answer open to him. Not surprisingly he did not seek to avail himself of it, for the facts spoke strongly against any such answer. The allegation made was not of mere non-feasance but of deliberate failure and wilful neglect. This involves an element of culpability which is not restricted to corruption or dishonesty but which must be of such a degree that the misconduct impugned is calculated to injure the public interest so as to call for condemnation and punishment. Whether such a situation is revealed by the evidence is a matter that a jury has to decide.

Appeal dismissed

R. v. Instan
[1893] 1 Q.B. 450
Court for Crown Cases Reserved

> The defendant lived with her aunt who was 73 years old. The aunt was healthy until shortly before her death. During the last 12 days of her life she had gangrene in her leg and could not fend for herself, move about nor summon help. Only the defendant knew of this condition. She appeared not to have given her aunt any food nor did she seek medical or nursing aid. She was charged with manslaughter and convicted.

LORD COLERIDGE C.J.: We are all of opinion that this conviction must be affirmed. It would not be correct to say that every moral obligation involves a legal duty; but every legal duty is founded on a moral obligation. A legal common law duty is nothing else than the enforcing by law of that which is a moral obligation without legal enforcement. There can be no question in this case that it was the clear duty of the prisoner to impart to the deceased so much as was necessary to sustain life of the food which she from time to time took in, and which was paid for by the deceased's own money for the purpose of the maintenance of herself and the prisoner; it was only through the instrumentality of the prisoner that the deceased could get the food. There was, therefore, a common law duty imposed upon the prisoner which she did not discharge.

Nor can there be any question that the failure of the prisoner to discharge her legal duty at least accelerated the death of the deceased, if it did not actually cause it. There is no case directly in point; but it would be a slur upon and a discredit to the administration of justice in this country if there were any doubt as to the legal principle, or as to the present case being within it. The prisoner was under a moral obligation to the deceased from which arose a legal duty towards her; that legal duty the prisoner has wilfully and deliberately left unperformed, with the consequence that there has been an acceleration of the death of the deceased owing to the non-performance of that legal duty. It is unnecessary to say more than that upon the evidence this conviction was most properly arrived at.

Conviction affirmed

Note

Consider the two following cases in the light of the following extract from the judgment of Erle C.J., in *R.* v. *Charlotte Smith* (1865) 10 Cox 82, where a master was charged with the homicide of his servant by, amongst other things, neglecting to give her sufficient food or wholesome lodgings. "The law is undisputed that, if a person having the care or custody of another who is helpless, neglects to supply him with the necessaries of life and thereby causes or accelerates his death, it is a criminal offence. But the law is clear, that if a person having the exercise of free will, chooses to stay in a service where bad food and lodging is provided, and death is thereby caused, the master is not criminally liable."

R. v. William Smith

(1826) 2 C. & P. 449; 172 E.R. 203
Gloucester Assizes

The defendants were two brothers and a sister. They had lived with their mother and with a helpless idiot brother. The mother died and it was alleged that the idiot brother was neglected and suffered in health. The defendants were charged with assault and false imprisonment.

BURROUGH J.: I am clearly of opinion that on the facts proved there is no assault and no imprisonment in the eye of the law, and all the rest of the charge is non-feasance. In the case of *Squires* and his wife for starving the apprentice, the husband was convicted, because it was his duty to maintain the apprentice, and the wife was acquitted, because there was no such obligation on her. I expected to have found in the will of the father that the defendants were bound, if they took the father's property, to maintain his brother; but, under the will, they are only bound to pay him £50 a year, and not bound to maintain him. William Smith appears to have been the owner of the house, and Thomas and Sarah were mere inmates of it, as their idiot brother might be: as to these latter, there could clearly be no legal obligation on them: and how can I tell the jury that either of the defendants had such a care of this unfortunate man as to make them criminally liable for omitting to attend to him. There is strong proof that there was some negligence; but my point is, that omission, without a duty, will not create an indictable offence. There is a deficiency of proof of the allegation of care, custody and control, which must be taken to be legal care, custody and control. Whether an indictment might be so framed, as to suit this case, I do not know; but on this indictment I am clearly of opinion that the defendants must be acquitted.

Verdict: Not guilty

R. v. Stone and Dobinson

[1977] 1 Q.B. 354
Court of Appeal

S., who was 67, partially deaf, nearly blind and of low intelligence, cohabited with D., aged 43, who was described as ineffectual and inadequate. Also living with them was S.'s mentally subnormal son. S.'s younger sister, E., came to live there in 1972, suffering from anorexia nervosa. She stayed in her room most of the time though she was known to creep down and cook herself something to eat when S. and D. went to the pub.

S. and D. attempted to find her doctor in Spring 1975 though she refused to tell them his name. In July, D. and a neighbour washed F. who, by this time, was confined to bed and lying amidst her own excrement. The defendants were unable to use the telephone and a neighbour was unsuccessful in getting a local doctor to visit F. No-one was informed of F.'s condition, even though a social worker came to the house from time to time to visit S.'s son. F. died in August. The pathologist's report suggested that she had been in need of urgent medical attention for days, if not weeks. S. and D. appealed against their convictions for manslaughter.

GEOFFREY LANE L.J.: There is no dispute, broadly speaking, as to the matters on which the jury must be satisfied before they can convict of manslaughter in circumstances such as the present. They are (1) that the defendant undertook the care of a person who by reason of age or infirmity was unable to care for himself;

(2) that the defendant was grossly negligent in regard to his duty of care; (3) that by reason of such negligence the person died....

[Counsel for the appellants] submitted that the evidence which the judge had suggested to the jury might support the assumption of a duty by the appellants does not, when examined, succeed in doing so. He suggests that the situation here is unlike any reported case. Fanny came to this house as a lodger. Largely, if not entirely due to her own eccentricity and failure to look after herself or feed herself properly, she became increasingly infirm and immobile and eventually unable to look after herself. Is it to be said, asks Mr. Coles rhetorically, that by the mere fact of becoming infirm and helpless in these circumstances she casts a duty on her brother and the appellant Dobinson....? The suggestion is that, heartless though it may seem, this is one of those situations where the appellants were entitled to do nothing; where no duty was cast upon them to help, any more than it is cast upon a man to rescue a stranger from drowning, however easy such a rescue might be.

... Whether Fanny was a lodger or not she was a blood relation of the appellant Stone; she was occupying a room in his house; the appellant Dobinson had undertaken the duty of trying to wash her, of taking such food to her as she required. There was ample evidence that each appellant was aware of the poor condition she was in by mid-July. It was not disputed that no effort was made to summon an ambulance or the social services or the police....

This was not a situation analogous to the drowning stranger. They did make efforts to care. They tried to get a doctor; they tried to discover the previous doctor. The appellant Dobinson helped with the washing and the provision of food. All these matters were put before the jury in terms which we find it impossible to fault. The jury were entitled to find that the duty had been assumed. They were entitled to conclude that once Fanny became helplessly infirm, as she had by July 19, the appellants were, in the circumstances, obliged either to summon help or else to care for Fanny themselves....

Appeal dismissed

Questions

1. Can this case be distinguished from *R.* v. *William Smith, ante*, p. 22? Does the following statement of principle by Brett J. in *R.* v. *Nicholls* (1875) 13 Cox 75 help?

> "If a grown up person chooses to undertake the charge of a human creature helpless either from infancy, simplicity, lunacy or other infirmity, he is bound to execute that charge without (at all events) *wicked* negligence."

2. Would Stone and Dobinson have been liable if F. was Stone's sister-in-law (*i.e.* his brother's wife)?

3. Would they have been liable if they had made no efforts to help at all?

4. Did Stone and Dobinson *cause* F.'s death? Farrier's Note at (1978) 41 M.L.R. 211, n. 6 raises the question whether the restrictive policy adopted in *Blaue, post*, p. 31, should apply where the causal conduct consists of an omission.

Note

These cases raise the question whether the duties on which liability for omissions is founded should not be more clearly specified. The New

Zealand Crimes Act of 1961, for example, contains an exhaustive list of "duties tending to the preservation of life" (ss. 151–154). In its Report on Offences Against the Person (1980, Cmnd. 7844) the Criminal Law Revision Committee suggests seven categories of common law duties to act. *Stone and Dobinson* belongs to the category: "members of a household in which a person becomes infirm and helpless may be held to have assumed a duty to that person."

A further possible category is "where the defendant has himself put another in danger by a wrongful act, he is probably under a duty not to leave that person in danger." This vagueness is, however, perceived a virtue, § 255:

"Most of us are of opinion that the extent of the duty to act should be left undefined so that the courts can apply the common law to omissions. The main reason for this view is that the boundaries of the common law are not clearly marked and there would be difficulty in setting them out in statutory form. The flexibility of the present law is a definite advantage and we consider it important that the Offences Against the Person Bill should preserve a simplicity of form. The American Model Penal Code, in section 2.01(3), contains a provision of the type which would be required in an Offences Against the Person Bill if our proposal to leave the duties to act to the common law is accepted. Section 2.01(3) provides as follows:

> 'Liability for the commission of an offence may not be based on an omission unaccompanied by action unless:
>
> (a) the omission is expressly made sufficient by the law defining the offence; or
>
> (b) a duty to perform the omitted act is otherwise imposed by law.'

Professor Williams dissents from this recommendation. The law relating to omissions is obscure in many ways, and he holds it to be wrong that the courts should be able to decide retrospectively that a person was under a particular duty, and to punish him for not performing it. Moreover, he thinks that it should be for Parliament, not the judges, to decide the occasions when people are legally required to bestir themselves on behalf of others. Important questions of morality and social policy are involved. For example, there have recently been three prosecutions for manslaughter of a person who failed to provide medical help for a sick relative, even though the relative was clearly resisting offers of medical help. Such prosecutions, in Professor Williams' opinion, overlook the right of self-determination: there can be no duty to force attention on a patient when the patient has the right to reject it. This is only one of the points on which the law needs clarification."

4. CAUSATION

Brett and Waller, Criminal Law Text and Cases (4th ed., 1978), p. 145

"Many philosophers have devoted great effort to elucidating the notion of causation. In particular, Hume and Mill have made great contributions in this field of enquiry, and from time to time one finds echoes of or borrowings from their work in judgments and legal writings. It is fair to say, however, that their views (and those of other philosophers also) are concerned with causal statements of general application, such as scientific laws. They are thus of comparatively slight value to lawyers, who are concerned with isolated events in the past which cannot be reproduced in the present or future. . . .

For our purposes it is enough to say that when the law treats a particular act or omission as the cause of an event it makes a choice. It does so for the purpose of attributing the responsibility for that event to a particular person, or of denying that he is responsible for it.

This, however, leaves unanswered the question: how is the choice made? The currently fashionable answer (in many other legal contexts as well as in this) is that the judges resort to considerations of 'policy'. But that tells us very little, and it may indeed be positively misleading. For it conjures up a picture of the judge consciously considering various possible choices and selecting what he thinks to be the 'best' one ('best' here having some rather vague reference to notions of supposed social utility). And it is reasonably clear that this is not what the judge does, either consciously or (as some would argue) unconsciously.

We think that a more accurate way of answering the question is to say that the judges make use of the common sense notions of the ordinary man (Hart and Honoré, in their *Causation in the Law* (1959), adopt broadly the same view). Nor, indeed, is there any good reason why they should not do so. The ordinary common sense notions of causation and responsibility can be shown to have, in most respects, a sound moral basis. . . .

The cases and books make use of a number of phrases in the attempt to clarify these common sense notions. Many of these, however, do little more than state a conclusion which has been reached rather than the reasons for reaching it—as when it is said that the law looks to 'proximate' causes as opposed to 'remote' causes, the notions of proximity and remoteness being taken as self-explanatory, likewise it is sometimes said that the law seeks for the 'primary' cause, or even the 'legal' cause, or that it seeks for the *causa causans* (causing, or operative cause)."

Williams (T.C.L., pp. 326–328) elucidates the meaning of some of these phrases:

"A convenient English equivalent of the term causation *sine qua non* is but-for causation (properly speaking, but-for . . . not causation). For a factor to be a but-for cause, one must be able to say that *but for* the occurrence of the antecedent factor the event would *not* have happened. . . .

When causation is in issue, the defendant's act (or omission) must be shown to be not only a but-for cause but also an imputable or legal cause of the consequence. Imputable causes are *some* of the but-for causes. In other words, the defendant's act, being a but-for cause, must be sufficiently closely connected with the consequence to involve him in responsibility. The lawyer is interested in the causal parentage of events, not in their causal ancestry. . . .

Several attempts have been made to find a suitable name for this second notion of cause. To call it the 'direct' or 'proximate' cause (as is often done) is misleading, because several stages may intervene between the so-called direct cause and the effect. D may send poisoned chocolates to V, who lives at the other side of the world; if V eats the chocolates and dies, the law will certainly regard D as responsible for the death, though his act was far removed in space and considerably removed in time from its effect. To call D's act the 'effective' cause is unhelpful because every cause must by definition be effective—if an act is not effective to produce a given result, it is not a cause of it. 'Substantial' is a less misleading adjective, but it is not illuminating.

Sometimes (looking at the situation backwards instead of forwards) imputable causation is stated in terms of 'remoteness of consequence'. To say that a particular consequence is 'too remote' is only another way of saying that the defendant's act (or omission) is not an imputable cause.

. . . When one has settled the question of but-for causation, the further test to be applied to the but-for cause in order to qualify it for legal recognition is not a test of causation but a moral reaction. The question is whether the result can fairly be said to be imputable to the defendant. If the term 'cause' must be used, it can best be distinguished as the 'imputable' or 'responsible' or 'blamable' cause, to indicate the value-judgment involved. The word 'imputable' is here chosen as best representing the idea. Whereas the but-for cause can generally be demonstrated scientifically, no experiment can be devised to show that one of a number of concurring but-for causes is more substantial or important than another, or that one person who is involved in the causal chain is more blameworthy than another."

The remainder of the discussion of causation is divided as follows:

i. *Sine qua non*
ii. Imputability
  (a) Fright and flight
  (b) Weak or intractable victims
  (c) Intervening causes
iii. An alternative approach

i. Sine qua non

R. v. Cato
[1976] 1 W.L.R. 110
Court of Appeal

> C. and his victim F., were friends. F. invited C. to have a "fix" of his heroin. Each filled his own syringe and then asked the other to inject it into him. This procedure was repeated several times during one night. F. died the next morning. One of the grounds on which C. appealed against his conviction for manslaughter concerned causation.

LORD WIDGERY C.J.: . . . At the trial there was quite a volume of expert evidence. First, there was a pathologist who conducted the . . . preliminary examination of the body and discovered there was insufficient evidence of natural disease to account for death and that an autopsy would be necessary. Then there was other further and detailed investigation of specimens of various parts of the body which showed . . . a quantity of morphine in the body consistent with the injections of heroin which had been taken, according to their confessions, through the night. But it was noteworthy, so the expert said, that there was no morphine in the blood—a pointer, as we understand it, to a longer interval between the injection and the death than would have appeared to have occurred having regard to the recital of the facts that I have given. Furthermore, Dr. Robinson, who was called on behalf of the defence, strongly made the point that there was not enough morphine visibly present in the samples to account for death because it was not a fatal dose. She had not seen the samples or worked on them herself because she had come into the case later than that, but she clearly took the view that although there was morphine in the body, and although the morphine may have contributed to the death, it was not exclusively responsible for it because there was, as she had said, a missing factor; and she concluded that there was a missing factor because in her view the size of the dose received by the deceased Farmer was insufficient to cause death. . . .

It seems to us that the first and most important single factor to which counsel for the appellant directed our attention was concerned with causation, that is to say with the link alleged to exist between the injection of heroin and the death of Farmer. . . .

He pointed out that the medical evidence did not at any point say "This morphine killed Farmer"; the actual link of that kind was not present. The witnesses were hesitant to express such a view and often recoiled from it, saying it was not for them to state the cause of death. It is perfectly true . . . that the expert evidence did not in positive terms provide a link, but it was never intended to. The expert witnesses here spoke to factual situations, and the conclusions and deductions therefrom were for the jury. The first question was: was there sufficient evidence upon which the jury could conclude, as they must have concluded, that adequate causation was present?

When one looks at the evidence it is important to realise that no other cause of Farmer's death was supplied. Dr. Robinson thought that there might have been another drug, and she said at one stage it might have been cocaine, but there was never any cocaine found in the body. The only cause of death actually supplied by the evidence was morphine. No natural disease was present and no other drug was identified. Furthermore, the symptoms and the external appearance of the body, and the nature of the final terminal cause, was consistent with poison by the administration of heroin in the way which was described. . . .

Of course behind this whole question of the sufficiency of evidence of causation is the fact that it was not necessary for the prosecution to prove that the heroin was the only cause. As a matter of law, it was sufficient if the prosecution could establish that it was *a* cause, provided it was a cause outside the de minimis range, and effectively bearing upon the acceleration of the moment of the victim's death. When one has that in mind it is, we think, really possible to say that if the jury had been directed to look for heroin as a cause, not de minimis but a cause of substance, and they came back with a verdict of not guilty, the verdict could really be described as a perverse one. The whole background of the evidence was the other way and there certainly was ample evidence, given a proper direction, upon which a charge of manslaughter could be supported.

But what about the proper direction? [the jury had been asked: "Did [the] injection of heroin by [the appellant] cause, contribute to or accelerate the death of Farmer?"] It will be noted that in none of the versions which I have quoted of the judge's direction on this point, nor in any of those which I have not quoted which appear in the summing up, is there any reference to it being necessary for the cause to be a substantial one. It is said in clear terms . . . that the jury can consider whether the administration of the heroin was a cause or contributed to or accelerated the death, and in precise terms the word "contributed" is not qualified to show that a substantial contribution is required. . . .

Before pursuing that, it is worth reminding oneself that some of the more recent dicta in the textbooks about this point do not support as strongly as was once the case the theory that the contribution must be substantial. In Smith and Hogan, *Criminal Law*, 3rd ed. (1973), p. 217 there is this rather interesting extract:

> "It is commonly said by judges and writers that, while the accused's act need not be the sole cause of the death, it must be a substantial cause. This appears to mean only that a minute contribution to the cause of death will not entail responsibility. It may therefore be misleading to direct a jury that D is not liable unless his conduct was a 'substantial' cause. Killing is merely an acceleration of death and factors which produce a very trivial acceleration will be ignored."

Whether that be so or not, and we do not propose to give that passage the court's blessing today at all events, if one looks at the circumstances of the present case with any real sense of reality, we think there can be no doubt that when the judge was talking about contribution the jury knew perfectly well that he was talking about something more than the mere de minimis contribution. We have given this point particular care in our consideration of the case because it worried us to some extent originally, but we do feel in the end, having looked at all the circumstances, that there could not have been any question in this case of the jury making the mistake of thinking that the contribution would suffice if it were de minimis. . . .

Appeal dismissed

Model Penal Code

"S.2.03 (1) Conduct is the cause of a result when:

(a) it is an antecedent but for which the result in question would not have occurred; and
(b) the relationship between the conduct and result satisfies any additional causal requirements imposed by the Code or by the law defining the offence."

ii. Imputability

The *Model Penal Code* continues:

"S.2.03 (2) When purposely or knowingly causing a particular result is an element of an offense, the element is not established if the actual result is not within the purpose or the contemplation of the actor unless: . . .

(b) the actual result involves the same kind of injury or harm as that designed or contemplated and is not too remote or accidental in its occurrence to have a just bearing on the actor's liability or on the gravity of his offense."

S.2.03 (3) contains a similar provision 'when recklessly or negligently causing a particular result is an element of an offense.'

R. v. Dalloway
(1847) 2 Cox 273
Stafford Assizes

A child ran in front of the defendant's cart and was killed. The reins were not in the defendant's hands but loose on the horse's back.

ERLE J., in summing up to the jury, directed them that a party neglecting an ordinary caution, and, by reason of that neglect, causing the death of another, is guilty of manslaughter; that if the prisoner had reins, and by using the reins could have saved the child, he was guilty of manslaughter; but that if they thought he could not have saved the child by pulling the reins, or otherwise by their assistance, they must acquit him.

Not guilty

Note

This case could also be seen as illustrating the but-for principle. The difficulty here is that the presence of the cart *was* a *sine qua non* of the child's death but D's negligent driving was not.

Problems can also arise where D's act was not the direct cause of death (where, for example, fright exacerbates a medical condition or V dies escaping from D), or where D's act does not cause instantaneous death and a complex chain of causation develops (through, for example, negligent medical care).

(a) *Fright and flight*

R. v. Hayward
(1908) 21 Cox 692
Maidstone Assizes

The defendant returned home in a state of violent excitement. He was heard to express the intention of "giving his wife something" when she came in. When she did arrive there were sounds of an altercation and shortly afterwards the woman ran from the house into the road, closely followed by the defendant. She fell into the roadway and the accused kicked her on the left arm. She died and a medical examination showed that the bruise on her arm, caused by the kick, was not the cause of death. The deceased woman was in good health apart from a persistent thyrus gland. Medical evidence was given that a person subject to this condition might die from a combination of fright or strong emotion and physical exertion. The defendant was charged with manslaughter.

RIDLEY J.: . . . directed the jury that if they believed the witnesses there was a sufficient chain of evidence to support a conviction of manslaughter. He pointed out that no proof of actual physical violence was necessary, but that death from fright alone, caused by an illegal act, such as threats of violence, would be sufficient. The abnormal state of the deceased's health did not affect the question whether the prisoner knew or did not know of it if it were proved to the satisfaction of the jury that the death was accelerated by the prisoner's illegal act.

Verdict: Guilty

R. v. Curley
(1909) 2 Cr. App. R. 109
Court of Criminal Appeal

The appellant had been indicted for murder and convicted of manslaughter. He was heard to be quarrelling with the woman with whom he lived. She was heard to cry from her bedroom "Let me out," "murder" and "police." The appellant was heard to go into the room, the window was thrown up. It appeared that the woman jumped from the window.

JELF J: Appellant told the officer, "I ran at her to hit her. I didn't quite touch her. Out she jumped." On that statement a verdict of murder might well have been returned, but it was mercifully reduced to one of manslaughter. The jumping out of the window was contributed to by the appellant's unlawful act. . . .

Appeal dismissed

R. v. Mackie
(1973) 57 Cr. App. R. 453
Court of Appeal

M was convicted of the manslaughter of a boy aged three whom he was looking after. It was alleged that the boy fell downstairs while running away in fear of being ill-treated.

STEPHENSON L.J. read the judgment of the Court:
Where the injuries are not fatal, the attempt to escape must be the natural

consequence of the assault charged, not something which could not be expected, but something which any reasonable and responsible man in the assailant's shoes would have foreseen. Where the injuries are fatal, the attempt must be the natural consequence of an unlawful act and that unlawful act "must be such as all sober and reasonable people would inevitably recognise must subject the other person to, at least, the risk of some harm resulting therefrom, albeit not serious harm": *Church* (1965) 49 Cr. App. R. 206 at p. 213;...

In this case there were two complications: (1) the victim was a child of three and regard must be had to his age in considering whether his reaction was well-founded or well-grounded on an apprehension of immediate violence (in the language of the old cases appropriate to adults) and therefore reasonably to be expected. (2) This defendant was in the position of a parent, which may have entitled him to "assault" the child by smacking or threatening him without breaking the law, and it was not every act which might be expected to cause slight harm to the boy that would be unlawful for a man in his parental position; he might have to do some act in the interests of the boy's own safety, for instance, to keep him away from the upstairs window. The purpose of correcting the child—and perhaps the sole justification for correcting a young child—is to deter; how else can the kind parent of a nervous child save it from danger than by in some degree hurting or frightening it? How far was it reasonable, and therefore lawful, for the appellant to go in punishing this child was one of the questions the jury had to decide. Whether the boy "over-reacted" (as Mr. Back put it) in a way which the appellant could not reasonably be expected to have foreseen was another.

... At the end of the summing-up the judge came back to these questions in suggesting what the vital points might be: "First, was the boy in fear of Mackie? Secondly, did that cause him to try to escape? Thirdly, if he was in fear, was that fear well-founded? If it was well-founded, was it caused by the unlawful conduct of the accused, that is, by conduct for which there was no lawful excuse even on the part of a man in the position of a father, ...

We think that the judge directed the jury clearly and correctly as to the law laid down in the cases....

Appeal dismissed

Note

This approach to "manslaughter by 'flight'" was confirmed by the Privy Council in *D.P.P.* v. *Daley* [1979] 2 W.L.R. 239. Lord Keith of Kinkel summarised it thus:

"[T]he essential ingredients of the prosecution's proof of a charge of manslaughter, laid upon the basis that a person has sustained fatal injuries while trying to escape from assault ... are: (1) that the victim immediately before he sustained the injuries was in fear of being hurt physically; (2) that this fear was such that it caused him to try to escape; (3) that whilst he was trying to escape, and because he was trying to escape he met his death; (4) that his fear of being hurt there and then was reasonable and was caused by the conduct of the defendant; (5) that the defendant's conduct which caused the fear was unlawful; and (6) that his conduct was such as any sober and reasonable person would recognise as likely to subject the victim to at least the risk of some harm resulting from it, albeit not a serious harm. Their Lordships have to observe that it is unnecessary to prove the defendant's knowledge that his conduct was unlawful."

Why should the deceased's fear have to be reasonable? A more extreme example of V "escaping" to his own death occurred in the Californian case of *People* v. *Lewis* (1899) 57 Pac. 470. A few minutes after he received a gun shot wound in the abdomen from which he would inevitably have died the deceased cut his own throat. The prosecution conceded (although the Court itself doubted this) that the gun shot wound was not, at the time he died, directly contributing to the death. Temple J. said this:

"But, if the deceased did die from the effect of the knife wound alone, no doubt the defendant would be responsible, if it was made to appear, and the jury could have found from the evidence, that the knife wound was caused by the wound inflicted by the defendant, in the natural course of events. If the relation was causal, and the wounded condition of the deceased was not merely the occasion upon which another cause intervened, not produced by the first wound, or related to it in other than in a causal way, then defendant is guilty of a homicide. But, if the wounded condition only afforded an opportunity for another unconnected person to kill, the defendant would not be guilty of a homicide, even though he had inflicted a mortal wound. In such case, I think, it would be true that the defendant was thus prevented from killing. . . ."

(b) *Weak or intractable victims*

It is a general rule of criminal liability that defendants take their victims as they find them. Thus in *R.* v. *Plummer* (1844) 1 C. & K. 600, where a husband had denied shelter to his wife who died soon afterwards, Gurney B. said, "It does not appear in evidence what her disease was, or that she was afflicted with that mortal illness under which she laboured, or that she was suffering from diarrhoea which caused her death; but he was, nevertheless, informed that she was very ill, and had not shelter. If you should be of opinion that her death was caused or accelerated by his conduct you will say that he is guilty (of manslaughter)." And in *R.* v. *Martin* (1832) 5 C. & P. 128 Parke J. said, "It is said, that the deceased was in a bad state of health; but that is perfectly immaterial, as, if the prisoner was so unfortunate as to accelerate her death, he must answer for it." This principle applies where, for religious or other reasons, the victim refuses medical help.

R. v. Blaue
[1975] 1 W.L.R. 1411
Court of Appeal

The appellant stabbed a woman; the wound penetrated her lung. At the hospital she was told that a blood transfusion and surgery were necessary to save her life. She refused to have a transfusion as it was contrary to her beliefs as a Jehovah's Witness. She died the next day. Medical evidence indicated that she would not have died had she accepted the medical treatment.

LAWTON L.J.: . . . Towards the end of the trial and before the summing up started counsel on both sides made submissions as to how the case should be put to the jury. Counsel then appearing for the defendant invited the judge to direct the jury to acquit the defendant generally on the count of murder. His argument was that her refusal to have a blood transfusion had broken the chain of causation between the stabbing and her death. As an alternative he submitted that the jury should be left to decide whether the chain of causation had been broken. Mr. Herrod submitted that the judge should direct the jury to convict, because no facts were in issue and when the law was applied to the facts there was only one possible verdict, namely, manslaughter by reason of diminished responsibility.

When the judge came to direct the jury on this issue he did so by telling them that they should apply their common sense. He then went on to tell them they would get some help from the cases to which counsel had referred in their speeches. He reminded them of what Lord Parker C.J. had said in *R.* v. *Smith* [1959] 2 Q.B. 35, 42 and what Maule J. had said 133 years before in *R.* v. *Holland* (1841) 2 Mood. & R. 351, 352. He placed particular reliance on what Maule J. had said. The jury, he said, might find it "most material and most helpful." He continued:

> "This is one of those relatively rare cases, you may think, with very little option open to you but to reach the conclusion that was reached by your predecessors as members of the jury in *R.* v. *Holland*, namely, 'yes' to the question of causation that the stab was still, at the time of the girl's death, the operative cause of death—or a substantial cause of death. However, that is a matter for you to determine after you have withdrawn to consider your verdict."

Mr. Comyn has criticised that direction on three grounds: first, because *R.* v. *Holland* should no longer be considered good law; secondly, because *R.* v. *Smith*, when rightly understood, does envisage the possibility of unreasonable conduct on the part of the victim breaking the chain of causation; and thirdly, because the judge in reality directed the jury to find causation proved although he used words which seemed to leave the issue open for them to decide.

In *R.* v. *Holland*, 2 Mood. & R. 351, the defendant in the course of a violent assault, had injured one of his victim's fingers. A surgeon had advised amputation because of the danger to life through complications developing. The advice was rejected. A fortnight later the victim died of lockjaw. Maule J. said, at p. 352: "the real question is, whether in the end the wound inflicted by the prisoner was the cause of death." That distinguished judge left the jury to decide that question as did the judge in this case. They had to decide it as juries always do, by pooling their experience of life and using their common sense. They would not have been handicapped by a lack of training in dialectic or moral theology.

Maule J's direction to the jury reflected the common law's answer to the problem. He who inflicted an injury which resulted in death could not excuse himself by pleading that his victim could have avoided death by taking greater care of himself: see *Hale's Pleas of the Crown* (1800 ed.), pp. 427–428. The common law in Sir Matthew Hale's time probably was in line with contemporary concepts of ethics. A man who did a wrongful act was deemed *morally* responsible for the natural and probable consequence of that act. Mr. Comyn asked us to remember that since Sir Matthew Hale's day the rigour of the law relating to homicide has been eased in favour of the accused. It has been—but this has come about through the development of the concepts of intent, not by reason of a different view of causation. Well known practitioner's textbooks, such as *Halsbury's Laws of England*, 3rd ed., vol. 10 (1955), p. 706 and *Russell on Crime*, 12th ed. (1964), vol. 1, p. 30 continue to reflect the common law approach. Textbooks intended for students or as studies in jurisprudence have queried the common law rule; see Hart and Honoré, *Causation in Law* (1959), pp. 320–321 and Smith and Hogan, *Criminal Law*, 3rd ed. (1973), p. 214.

There have been two cases in recent years which have some bearing upon this topic: *R.* v. *Jordan* (1956), [below] and *R.* v. *Smith*, [below]. The physical cause of death in this case was the bleeding into the pleural cavity arising from the penetration of the lung. This had not been brought about by any decision made by the deceased but by the stab wound.

Mr. Comyn tried to overcome this line of reasoning by submitting that the jury should have been directed that if they thought the deceased's decision not to have a blood transfusion was an unreasonable one, then the chain of causation would have been broken. At once the question arises—reasonable by whose standards? Those of Jehovah's Witnesses? Humanists? Roman Catholics? Protestants of Anglo-Saxon descent? The man on the Clapham omnibus? But he might well be an admirer of Eleazar who suffered death rather than eat the flesh of swine (2 Maccabees, ch.6, vv.18–31) or of Sir Thomas More who, unlike nearly all his contemporaries was unwilling to accept Henry VIII as Head of the Church of England. Those brought up in the Hebraic and Christian traditions would probably be reluctant to accept that these martyrs caused their own deaths.

As was pointed out to Mr. Comyn in the course of argument, two cases, each raising the same issue of reasonableness because of religious beliefs, could produce different verdicts depending on where the cases were tried. A jury drawn from Preston, sometimes said to be the most Catholic town in England, might have different views about martyrdom to one drawn from the inner suburbs of London. Mr. Comyn accepted that this might be so: it was, he said, inherent in trial by jury. It is not inherent in the common law as expounded by Sir Matthew Hale and Maule J. It has long been the policy of the law that those who use violence on other people must take their victims as they find them. This in our judgment means the whole man, not just the physical man. It does not lie in the mouth of the assailant to say that the victim's religious beliefs which inhibited him from accepting certain kinds of treatment were unreasonable. The question for decision is what caused her death. The answer is the stab wound. The fact that the victim refused to stop this end coming about did not break the causal connection between the act and death. . . .

Appeal dismissed

Williams, Note (1976) C.L.J. 15

"Although the case follows the precedents, . . . it fails to notice that all of them dated from a time when medical science was in its infancy, and when operations performed without hygiene carried great danger to life. It was therefore open to the court for the benefit of the defendant to consider the question afresh, and there were several reasons for doing so.

It had been held in the law of tort that the test of reasonable foresight applies to facts like those in *Blaue*, but the court refused to bring the criminal law into line. The criminal law should avoid the appearance of harshness, and to make it more stringent than the civil law in the matter of causation is surprising. Lawton L.J., speaking for the court, explained the difference between crime and tort by saying that 'the criminal law is concerned with the maintenance of law and order and the protection of the public generally.' This overlooks that Blaue was in any event punishable severely for wounding with intent. What social purpose is served by giving an attacker *extra* punishment because the person attacked unreasonably refused treatment?"

The Court of Appeal's objection to a test of reasonable refusal was countered by K. J. M. Smith, Note (1976) 92 L.Q.R. 30 at 31: ". . . [It] might be contended that this problem arises when an objective test is applied in the criminal law, yet it does not prevent the courts arriving at an appropriate standard. . . ." The same writer also suggests that the Court of Appeal is inconsistent in allowing an unreasonable "flight" to break the chain of causation (see *Mackie* and *Daley*, *ante*, p. 30) and asks "Is there some essential distinction to be drawn between passive and active behaviour by a victim?"

(c) *Intervening causes*

R. v. Jordan
(1956) 40 Cr. App. R. 153
Court of Criminal Appeal

The appellant stabbed the deceased in the abdomen. The deceased was taken promptly to hospital and the wound was stitched. A few days later he died. Jordan was convicted of murder at Leeds Assizes and on appeal sought to adduce further medical evidence. This evidence disclosed that the wound, which had penetrated the intestine in two places, was mainly healed at the time of death. At the hospital terramycin was administered to prevent infection. The deceased was found to be intolerant to this antibiotic. A doctor who was unaware of this ordered its continuance. Two fresh witnesses also testified that abnormal quantities of liquid had been given intravenously. This caused the lungs to become waterlogged and pulmonary oedema was discovered.

HALLETT J.: . . . We are disposed to accept it as the law that death resulting from any normal treatment employed to deal with a felonious injury may be regarded as caused by the felonious injury, but we do not think it necessary to examine the cases in details or to formulate for the assistance of those who have to deal with such matters in the future the correct test which ought to be laid down with regard to what is necessary to be proved in order to establish causal connection between the death and the felonious injury. Not only one feature, but two separate and independent features, of treatment were, in the opinion of the doctors, palpably wrong and these produced the symptoms discovered at the post-mortem examination which were the direct and immediate cause of death, namely, the pneumonia resulting from the condition of oedema which was found.

Conviction quashed

R. v. Smith
[1959] 2 Q.B. 35
Courts-Martial Appeal Court

The appellant, a soldier, was charged with, and convicted of, the murder of a fellow soldier during the course of a fight between the men of two regiments who shared the same barrack room. The deceased received two bayonet wounds, one in the arm and one in the back which pierced the lung and caused haemorrhage. Another soldier tried to carry the wounded man to the medical reception station. He twice dropped him on the ground. At the station the medical officer and his orderly were extremely busy. There were two other stabbed men to deal with as well as others with minor injuries. The medical staff did not know of the haemorrhage nor was the serious nature of the injury realised. A transfusion of saline solution was tried but failed and when breathing seemed impaired, oxygen and artificial respiration were given. This treatment was "thoroughly bad" and might well have affected his chance of recovery. There was medical evidence at the trial that haemorrhage of this type tends to stop. Had there been a blood transfusion available chances of recovery were assessed as high as 75 per cent. by a medical witness for the defence.

Lord Parker C.J.: In these circumstances Mr. Bowen urged that not only was a careful summing-up required, but that a correct direction to the court would have been that they must be satisfied that the death of Private Creed was a natural consequence and the sole consequence of the wound sustained by him and flowed directly from it. If there was, says Mr. Bowen, any other cause, whether resulting from negligence or not, if, as he contends here, something happened which impeded the chance of the deceased recovering, then the death did not result from the wound. The court is quite unable to accept that contention. It seems to the court that if at the time of death the original wound is still an operating cause and a substantial cause, then the death can properly be said to be the result of the wound, albeit that some other cause of death is also operating. Only if it can be said that the original wounding is merely the setting in which another cause operates can it be said that the death did not result from the wound. Putting it another way, only if the second cause is so overwhelming as to make the original wound merely part of the history can it be said that the death does not flow from the wound.

There are a number of cases in the law of contract and tort on these matters of causation, and it is always difficult to find a form of words when directing a jury or, as here, a court which will convey in simple language the principle of causation. It seems to the court enough for this purpose to refer to one passage in the judgment of Lord Wright in *The Oropesa* [1943] P. 32, 39, where he said: "To break the chain of causation it must be shown that there is something which I will call ultroneous, something unwarrantable, a new cause which disturbs the sequence of events, something which can be described as either unreasonable or extraneous or extrinsic." To much the same effect was a judgment on the question of causation given by Denning L.J. in *Minister of Pensions* v. *Chennell* [1947] K.B. 250.

Mr. Bowen placed great reliance on a case decided in the Court of Criminal Appeal, *R.* v. *Jordan* [*ante*, p. 34] and in particular on a passage in the headnote which says, ". . . that death resulting from any normal treatment employed to deal with a felonious injury may be regarded as caused by the felonious injury, but that the same principle does not apply where the treatment is abnormal." Reading those words into the present case, Mr. Bowen says that the treatment that this unfortunate man received from the moment that he was struck to the time of his death was abnormal. The court is satisfied that *Jordan's* case was a very particular case depending upon its exact facts. It incidentally arose on the grant of an application to call further evidence, and leave having been obtained, two well-known medical experts gave evidence that in their opinion death had not been caused by the stabbing but by the introduction of terramycin after the deceased had shown that he was intolerant to it, and by the intravenous introduction of abnormal quantities of liquid. It also appears that at the time when that was done the stab wound which had penetrated the intestine in two places had mainly healed. In those circumstances the court felt bound to quash the conviction because they could not say that a reasonable jury, properly directed, would not have been able on that to say that there had been a break in the chain of causation; the court could only uphold the conviction in that case if they were satisfied that no reasonable jury could have come to that conclusion.

In the present case it is true that the judge-advocate did not in his summing-up go into the refinements of causation. Indeed, in the opinion of this court he was probably wise to refrain from doing so. He did leave the broad question to the court whether they were satisfied that the wound had caused the death in the sense that the death flowed from the wound, albeit that the treatment he received was in the light of after-knowledge a bad thing. In the opinion of this court that was on the facts of the case a perfectly adequate summing-up on causation; I say "on the facts of the case" because, in the opinion of the court, they can only lead to one conclusion: a man is stabbed in the back, his lung is pierced and haemorrhage results; two hours later he dies of haemorrhage from that wound; in the interval there is no time for a careful examination, and the treatment given turns out in the light of subsequent knowledge to have been inappropriate and, indeed, harmful. In those circumstances no reasonable jury or court could, properly directed, in our view possibly come to any other conclusion than that the death resulted from the original wound. Accordingly the court dismisses this appeal.

Appeal dismissed

Note

One ground upon which these two cases on improper medical treatment can be reconciled is that the accused must take as normal medical treatment given in an emergency when the medical staff is under pressure even though later it appears that this treatment was quite wrong. A test on these lines might be—did the medical treatment reach a reasonable standard in the particular conditions? Many difficulties still arise. If the attack was outside a doctor's surgery in a busy street but the wound proved fatal for want of elementary but immediate attention because (a) the doctor was out, or (b) he refused to leave his patients, is the chain of causation still intact? If, as has been suggested, the description of *Jordan's* case as "a particular case depending upon its exact facts" is to be read as disapproval of the principle in *Jordan's* case, then does *Smith's* case go so far as to insist that only where, say, the wound is nearly healed will the chain be broken? If the ground for distinguishing cases is that in one the wound is still capable of causing death, whilst in the other it is not, does this not put the decision upon the question of the time when the erroneous treatment was given?

Question

If A, who is seriously injured in an attack, is given, in error, a fatal injection immediately he or she is admitted to hospital, whereas B, who has been similarly injured is given the wrong injection two weeks later, it may follow that the first death is a homicide by the assailant and the second is not. A's assailant is denied the chance to show that the wound, although of a mortal type, would not have killed A.

The Court of Appeal in *R.* v. *Malcherek*, below, further endorsed *Smith*, rather than *Jordan*.

R. v. Malcherek
R. v. Steel
[1981] 2 All E.R. 422
Court of Appeal

These two cases raised the same question. M. stabbed his wife with a kitchen knife causing a deep abdominal wound. S. was accused of attacking a girl causing grave head injuries. Both victims were put on life support machines during normal courses of treatment. In each case the machines were switched off after a number of tests indicated that brain death had occurred. Both M. and S. were convicted at their trials for murder. The ground of M.'s appeal and S.'s application for leave to appeal was that the judge should not have withdrawn the question of causation from the jury. S. also sought leave to adduce further medical evidence that the doctors in each case had not complied with all the royal medical colleges' suggested criteria for establishing brain death.

LORD LANE C.J.: [After stating the facts] . . . This is not the occasion for any decision as to what constitutes death. Modern techniques have undoubtedly resulted in the blurring of many of the conventional and traditional concepts of death. A person's heart can now be removed altogether without death supervening; machines can keep the blood circulating through the vessels of the body until a new heart can be implanted in the patient, and even though a person is no longer able to breathe spontaneously a ventilating machine can, so to speak, do his breathing for him, as is demonstrated in the two cases before us. There is, it seems, a body of opinion in the medical profession that there is only one true test of death and that is the irreversible death of the brain stem, which controls the basic functions of the body such as breathing. When that occurs it is said the body has died, even though by mechanical means the lungs are being caused to operate and some circulation of blood is taking place.

We have had placed before us, and have been asked to admit, evidence that in each of these two cases the medical men concerned did not comply with all the suggested criteria for establishing such brain death. Indeed, further evidence has been suggested and placed before us that those criteria or tests are not in themselves stringent enough. However, in each of these two cases there is no doubt that whatever test is applied the victim died; that is to say, applying the traditional test, all body functions, breathing and heartbeat and brain function came to an end, at the latest, soon after the ventilator was disconnected.

The question posed for answer to this court is simply whether the judge in each case was right in withdrawing from the jury the question of causation. Was he right to rule that there was no evidence on which the jury could come to the conclusion that the assailant did not cause the death of the victim?

The way in which the submissions are put by counsel for Malcherek on the one hand and by counsel for Steel on the other is as follows: the doctors, by switching off the ventilator and the life support machine, were the cause of death or, to put it more accurately, there was evidence which the jury should have been allowed to consider that the doctors, and not the assailant, in each case may have been the cause of death.

In each case it is clear that the initial assault was the cause of the grave head injuries in the one case and of the massive abdominal haemorrhage in the other. In each case the initial assault was the reason for the medical treatment being necessary. In each case the medical treatment given was normal and conventional. At some stage the doctors must decide if and when treatment has become otiose. This decision was reached, in each of the two cases here, in circumstances which have already been set out in some detail. It is no part of the task of this court to inquire whether the criteria, the Royal Medical College confirmatory tests, are a satisfactory code of practice. It is no part of the task of this court to decide whether the doctors were, in either of these two cases, justified in omitting one or more of the so called "confirmatory tests". The doctors are not on trial: Steel and Malcherek respectively were.

There are two comparatively recent cases which are relevant to the consideration of this problem. [His Lordship then considered *R.* v. *Smith, ante,* p. 34, and *R.* v. *Jordan, ante,* p. 34].

In the view of this court, if a choice has to be made between the decision in *R.* v. *Jordan* and that in *R.* v. *Smith,* which we do not believe it does (*R.* v. *Jordan* being a very exceptional case), then the decision in *R.* v. *Smith* is to be preferred.

The only other case to which reference has been made, it having been drawn to our attention by counsel for Steel, is *R.* v. *Blaue,* [*ante,* p. 31] . . .

The passage . . . is the last paragraph of the judgment of Lawton L.J. [1975] 1 W.L.R. 1411 at 1416:

> "The issue of the cause of death in a trial for either murder or manslaughter is one of fact for the jury to decide. But if, as in this case, there is no conflict of evidence and all the jury has to do is apply the law to the admitted facts, the judge is entitled to tell the jury what the result of that application will be. In this case the judge would have been entitled to have told the jury that the appellant's stab wound was an operative cause of death. The appeals fails."

There is no evidence in the present case here that at the time of conventional death, after the life support machinery was disconnected, the original wound or injury was other than a continuing, operating and indeed substantial cause of the death of the victim, although it need hardly be added that it need not be substantial to render the assailant guilty. There may be occasions, although they will be rare, when the original injury has ceased to operate as a cause at all, but in the ordinary case if treatment is given bona fide by competent and careful medical practitioners, then evidence will not be admissible to show that the treatment would not have been administered in the same way by other medical practitioners. In other words, the fact that the victim has died, despite or because of medical treatment for the initial injury given by careful and skilled medical practitioners, will not exonerate the original assailant from responsibility for the death. It follows that so far as the ground of appeal in each of these cases relates to the direction given on causation, that ground fails. It also follows that the evidence which it is sought to adduce now, although we are prepared to assume that it is both credible and was not available properly at the trial (and a reasonable explanation for not calling it at the trial has been given), if received could, under no circumstances, afford any ground for allowing the appeal.

The reason is this. Nothing which any of the two or three medical men whose statements are before us could say would alter the fact that in each case the assailant's actions continued to be an operating cause of the death. Nothing the doctors could say would provide any ground for a jury coming to the conclusion that the assailant in either case might not have caused the death. The furthest to which their proposed evidence goes, as already stated, is to suggest, first, that the criteria or the confirmatory tests are not sufficiently stringent and, second, that in the present case they were in certain respects inadequately fulfilled or carried out. It is no part of this court's function in the present circumstances to pronounce on this matter, nor was it a function of either of the juries at these trials. Where a medical practitioner adopting methods which are generally accepted comes bona fide and conscientiously to the conclusion that the patient is for practical purposes dead, and that such vital functions as exist (for example, circulation) are being maintained solely by mechanical means, and therefore discontinues treatment, that does not prevent the person who inflicted the initial injury from being responsible for the victim's death. Putting it in another way, the discontinuance of treatment in those circumstances does not break the chain of causation between the initial injury and the death.

Although it is unnecessary to go further than that for the purpose of deciding the present point, we wish to add this thought. Whatever the strict logic of the matter may be, it is perhaps somewhat bizarre to suggest, as counsel have impliedly done, that where a doctor tries his conscientious best to save the life of a patient brought to hospital in extremis, skilfully using sophisticated methods, drugs and machinery to do so, but fails in his attempt and therefore discontinues treatment, he can be said to have caused the death of the patient. . . .

Appeal and applications dismissed

Smith, Note (1981) Crim. L.R. 401, 403

"The judge acted in accordance with the opinion of the court in *Blaue* in withdrawing the question of causation from the jury; but *Blaue* was decided before *Stonehouse* [1977] 2 All E.R. 909 where the House of Lords, by a majority of three to two, held that a question of fact must be left to the jury even where the evidence admits of only one reasonable answer, which is that the fact has been established by the prosecution. The direction given by the trial judge in that case as to whether there was an attempt seems to have been very similar to that given in the present case as whether there was causation. If that is so, the direction was wrong in law; but the practical effect is nil, because the conviction would be upheld under the proviso since, *ex hypothesi*, no reasonable jury could have arrived at any other conclusion."

For the special year and a day rule in homicide, see *post*, p. 367.

iii. An alternative approach

Fletcher, Rethinking Criminal Law, pp. 362, 368

"It would be plausible to define a law protecting life in terms that made the occurrence of death irrelevant. The critical issue would be an act endangering life. An attempt to kill, particularly if manifested unequivocally in the actor's behaviour, would be treated the same as an actual killing. Conduct highly dangerous to human life would be treated as equivalent to reckless homicide. The rationale for eliminating the issues of causation and death would be that the purpose of the law should be to punish and to deter blameworthy assaults on the interest in life. The actual occurrence of death and its causal attribution are irrelevant to the sets of acts that should be deterred, and it is also irrelevant to the criteria rendering the accused blameworthy for his conduct. The man who shoots at an apparently alive but dead patient, is arguably no less blameworthy than the assassin who has the bad luck to shoot and kill a living patient. . . .

There is no easy solution to the problem of causation. The metaphysics of proximate cause, degrees of contribution and intervening causes will continue to affect even the most rational penal system. The reasons are several. First, the inquiry into causation is categorical. A death is attributable to someone or it is not. There is no room for a compromise verdict as there is in the assessment of culpability for criminal homicide. Secondly, the issue of causation, along with the elements of acting and the occurrence of death, goes to the foundation of liability. . . .

A third significant factor is that the courts are bound to render these appellate decisions in an all-or-nothing fashion without having a general theory to guide their assessment whether in close cases they should find for the defendant or the prosecution. . . .

Rooted in the practice of tainting, the causal inquiry bears neither on the definition of conduct that should be deterred nor on the criteria for justly blaming someone who endangers human life."

Question

Consider whether any of the above cases would have been decided differently had the question not been one of causation but of an act endangering life, as suggested by Fletcher.

5. COINCIDENCE OF ACTUS REUS AND MENS REA

Thabo Meli v. The Queen
[1954] 1 W.L.R. 228
Privy Council

The deceased was taken to a hut by the appellants where he was struck over the head with intent to kill him. His unconscious body was then rolled over a small cliff to make the death appear to be an accident. Medical evidence indicated that the appellants had not succeeded in killing the deceased in the hut but that he had died from exposure.

LORD REID: The point of law which was raised in this case can be simply stated. It is said that two acts were necessary and were separable: first, the attack in the hut; and, secondly, the placing of the body outside afterwards. It is said that, while the first act was accompanied by *mens rea*, it was not the cause of death; but that the second act, while it was the cause of death, was not accompanied by *mens rea*; and on that ground it is said that the accused are not guilty of any crime, except perhaps culpable homicide.

It appears to their Lordships impossible to divide up what was really one transaction in this way. There is no doubt that the accused set out to do all these acts in order to achieve their plan and as parts of their plan; and it is too refined a ground of judgment to say that, because they were under a misapprehension at one stage and thought that their guilty purpose had been achieved before in fact it was achieved, therefore they are to escape the penalties of the law....

Appeal dismissed

Attorney General's Reference (No. 4 of 1980)
[1981] 2 All E.R. 617
Court of Appeal

The Attorney General sought the court's opinion on the following point of law: whether a person who has committed a series of acts against another culminating in the death of that person, each act in the series being either unlawful and dangerous or an act of gross criminal negligence, is entitled to be acquitted of manslaughter on the ground that it cannot be shown which of such acts caused the death of the deceased.

ACKNER L.J. for the court:

[This reference] raises yet again the problem of the supposed corpse, and the facts, which I take from the terms of the reference itself, are inevitably macabre.

The deceased was the fiancée of the accused and for some months before her death they had lived together in a maisonette consisting of two floors of a house connected by two short flights of carpeted wooden stairs. The deceased was employed locally and was last seen at work on 17th January 1979 at about 5 pm. Thereafter no one, other than the accused, ever saw her alive again.

The deceased met her death on 18th January 1979, although this fact was not known until over three weeks later when the defendant so informed a friend. His account, the first of a number, was that in the course of an argument on the evening of 17th January he had slapped her on the face causing her to fall downstairs and bang her head. He said that he had then put her to bed but discovered next morning that she was dead. He then took her body to his home town and buried her.

On the following day . . . he gave his second account, telling the same friend that after the deceased had 'fallen downstairs' he had dragged her upstairs by a piece of rope tied round her neck. He subsequently cut up her body with a saw before burying it. The next day, on the advice of his friend, the accused went to see a superior and gave an account similar to the one he had given his friend.

We now come to the statements which he made to the police. On 27th February, having consulted solicitors, the accused was interviewed by the police at his solicitors' office. He began by giving the police substantially the same account that he had given to his friend and his superior but added that instead of burying the deceased he had 'dumped' the various parts of her body on a tip. At the police station later that day he amplified this statement by saying that the incident when the deceased 'fell downstairs' occurred at about 7 pm on 17th January and that it was the following day, when he found her motionless, that he pulled her upstairs by a rope around her neck and then cut up her body in the bathroom. On the following day after much questioning by the police he changed his account stating that everything had happened on Thursday, 18th January at about 7 am. This is what he then said happened. (i) He and the deceased had an argument on the landing in the course of which each slapped the other; he seized the deceased and shook her hard; she dug her nails into him and he pushed her away instinctively, causing her to fall backwards over the handrail, down the stairs head first onto the floor. (ii) He went downstairs immediately to find her motionless and on a very cursory examination discovered no pulse, and no sign of breath but frothy blood coming from her mouth. (iii) Almost immediately thereafter he dragged her upstairs by a rope tied around her neck, placed her in the bath and cut her neck with a penknife to let out her blood, having already decided to cut up her body and dispose of the pieces.

He agreed that his previous account was untrue and he made a detailed voluntary statement along the lines set out in (i), (ii) and (iii) above describing how subsequently he had cut up and disposed of her body.

. . .

Subsequently the police discovered evidence which corroborated the accused's account of how, where and when he had cut up the body. They also found the saw he had used and the shopkeeper who sold it to him. However, the body of the deceased was never found, only some minute fragments of bone, which were discovered in the maisonette. There was thus no expert evidence as to the cause of death. The deceased died either as a result of being pushed and thus caused to fall backwards over the handrail and backwards down the stairs head first onto the floor, or by being strangled with the rope, or having her throat cut. The Crown conceded that it was not possible for them to prove whether the deceased died as the result of the 'fall' downstairs or from what the accused did to the deceased thereafter.

At the close of the Crown's case counsel for the accused stated that he proposed to submit that on the facts proved there was no case of manslaughter capable of going to the jury. It is not easy to follow from the transcript the exact basis of his submissions, but what he appears to have been contending was that (a) it was not possible for the jury to be sure what caused the deceased's death and (b) whether the death was caused as a result of her 'fall' down the stairs or from what the accused subsequently did, believing her to be dead, in neither event was there a *prima facie* case of manslaughter.

The judge, although expressing his reluctance to accept that the accused could be in a better position as a result of his dismembering the body of the deceased, appeared to have been very concerned at what he described as 'an insuperable problem of sentencing', were the accused to be convicted of manslaughter. He expressed the view that the real criminality of the accused's behaviour was in disposing of the body, a view which this court is unable to accept. These views appear to have influenced his decision, which was to withdraw the case from the jury and to direct an acquittal on the ground that the Crown had failed to prove the cause of the death of the deceased.

On the above facts this reference raises a single and simple question, viz, if an accused kills another by one or other of two or more different acts each of which, if it caused the death, is a sufficient act to establish manslaughter, is it necessary in order to found a conviction to prove which act caused the death? The answer to the question is No, it is not necessary to found a conviction to prove which act caused the death. No authority is required to justify this answer, which is clear beyond argument, as was indeed immediately conceded by counsel on behalf of the accused.

What went wrong in this case was that counsel made jury points to the judge and not submissions of law. He was in effect contending that the jury should not convict of manslaughter if the death had resulted from the 'fall', because the push which had projected the deceased over the handrail was a reflex and not a voluntary action, as a result of her digging her nails into him. If, however, the deceased was still alive when he cut her throat, since he then genuinely believed her to be dead, having discovered neither pulse nor sign of breath, but frothy blood coming from her mouth, he could not be guilty of manslaughter because he had not behaved with gross criminal negligence. What counsel and the judge unfortunately overlooked was that there was material available to the jury which would have entitled them to have convicted the accused of manslaughter, whichever of the two sets of acts caused her death. It being common ground that the deceased was killed by an act done to her by the accused and it being conceded that the jury could not be satisfied which was the act which caused the death, they should have been directed in due course in the summing up, to ask themselves the following questions: (i) 'Are we satisfied beyond reasonable doubt that the deceased's "fall" downstairs was the result of an intentional act by the accused which was unlawful and dangerous?' If the answer was No, then they would acquit. If the answer was Yes, then they would need to ask themselves a second question, namely: (ii) 'Are we satisfied beyond reasonable doubt that the act of cutting the girl's throat was an act of gross criminal negligence?' If the answer to that question was No, then they would acquit, but if the answer was Yes, then the verdict would be guilty of manslaughter. The jury would thus have been satisfied that, whichever act had killed the deceased, each was a sufficient act to establish the offence of manslaughter.

The facts of this case did not call for 'a series of acts direction' following the principle in *Thabo Meli* v. *R* [above]. We have accordingly been deprived of the stimulating questions whether the decision in *R* v. *Church* [*post*, p. 441] correctly extended that principle to manslaughter, in particular to 'constructive manslaughter' and if so whether that view was part of the ratio decidendi.

Determination accordingly

Note

For other examples of the problem of separate acts or a series, see *R.* v. *Church*, *post*, p. 441 and *Fagan* v. *Metropolitan Police Commissioner*, *post*, p. 473, and Marston, "Contemporaneity of Act and Intention in Crimes" (1970) 86 L.Q.R. 208.

Chapter 3

MENS REA

	PAGE		PAGE
1. The Requirement of *Mens Rea*	43	3. Judicial Approaches (*contd.*)	
2. The Meaning of Terms	46	iv. Recklessness	71
i. Intention	47	v. Maliciousness	81
ii. Knowledge	50	vi. Wilfulness	83
iii. Recklessness	50	4. Motive	94
iv. Negligence	54	5. Mistakes	98
v. Law Commission Draft Criminal Liability (Mental Element) Bill	56	i. Mistake negating intent	100
		ii. Mistake affecting culpability	116
		iii. Irrelevant mistakes	120
3. Judicial Approaches	62	6. Strict Liability	128
i. Common Law *Mens Rea*	62	i. The Evolution of Strict Liability	128
ii. Intention	63	ii. The Present Uncertainty	129
iii. Knowledge	68	iii. Critique	151
		iv. Proposals for Reform	154

1. THE REQUIREMENT OF MENS REA

Williams, Criminal Law: The General Part, p. 30

"*Nature of the requirement of mens rea*

There is no need here to go into the remote history of *mens rea;* suffice it to say that the requirement of a guilty state of mind (at least for the more serious crimes) had been developed by the time of Coke, which is as far back as the modern lawyer needs to go. 'If one shoot at any wild fowl upon a tree, and the arrow killeth any reasonable creature afar off, without any evil intent in him, this is *per infortunium.*'

It may be said that any theory of criminal punishment leads to a requirement of some kind of *mens rea*. The deterrent theory is workable only if the culprit has knowledge of the legal sanction; and if a man does not foresee the consequence of his act he cannot appreciate that punishment lies in store for him if he does it. The retributive theory presupposes moral guilt; incapacitation supposes social danger; and the reformative aim is out of place if the offender's sense of values is not warped.

However, the requirement as we have it in the law does not harmonise perfectly with any of these theories. It does not quite fit the deterrent theory, because a man may have *mens rea* although he is ignorant of the law. On the deterrent theory, ignorance of the law should be a defence; yet it is not. Again, the requirement does not quite conform to the retributive theory, because the *mens rea* of English law does not necessarily connote an intention to engage in moral wrongdoing. A crime may be committed from the best of motives and yet remain a crime. (In this respect the phrase *mens rea* is somewhat misleading). There are similar difficulties with incapacitation and reform.

What, then, does legal *mens rea* mean? It refers to the mental element necessary for the particular crime, and this mental element may be either *intention* to do the immediate act or bring about the consequence or (in some crimes) *recklessness* as to such act or consequence. In different and more precise language, *mens rea* means intention or recklessness as to the elements constituting the *actus reus*. These two concepts, intention and recklessness, hold the key to the understanding of a large part of criminal law. Some crimes require intention and nothing else will do, but most can be committed either intentionally or recklessly. Some crimes require particular kinds of intention or knowledge.

Outside the class of crimes requiring *mens rea* there are some that do not require any particular state of mind but do require negligence. Negligence in law is not necessarily a state of mind; and thus these crimes are best regarded as not requiring *mens rea*. However, negligence is a kind of legal fault, and in that respect they are akin to crimes requiring *mens rea*.

Yet other crimes do not even require negligence. They are crimes of strict or vicarious responsibility, and, like crimes of negligence, they constitute exceptions to the adage *Actus non facit reum nisi mens sit rea*."

Recently, writers have drawn attention to some of the dangers of assuming that "*mens rea*" is a merely descriptive term.

A. T. H. Smith "On Actus Reus and Mens Rea" in Reshaping the Criminal Law (ed. Glazebrook), p. 103

"The idea that *mens rea* is in some sense a basic or indispensable ingredient of criminal liability is deeply rooted. For example, Stroud stated that:

> the guilt of an act charged against a prisoner must always depend upon two conditions . . . [which] . . . may be called the condition of illegality (*actus reus*) and the condition of culpable intentionality (*mens rea*). (*Mens Rea* (London, 1914), p. 7.)

Kenny's view was that:

> no external conduct, however serious or even fatal its consequences may have been, is ever punished unless it is produced by some form of *mens rea*. (*Outlines of Criminal Law* (2nd ed.) (Cambridge, 1904), p. 39).

These writers explicitly discount the phenomenon of strict liability, and they should not be taken to task for failing to elucidate matters with which they were not concerned. Nevertheless, by insisting that *mens rea is* a necessary constituent of crime, they distort the function that that concept really performs. A fully descriptive account of criminal responsibility would be forced to acknowledge that there are many instances where liability is imposed without proof of *mens rea* as to at least some elements in the *actus reus*.

It may be helpful to identify three of the purposes for which the expression *mens rea* is used. It is, first, an expositional tool, when used in sentences such as "the *mens rea* of X offence is Y", where Y might be (depending on the offence in question) intention, recklessness, malice, dishonesty, an intent to defraud or deceive. We could substitute the expression "mental element" without any change of meaning. This is the use to which Stephen referred when he said that

> the maxim about "*mens rea*" means no more than that the definition of all or nearly all crimes contains not only an outward and visible element, but a mental element, varying according to the different nature of different crimes. (*A History of the Criminal Law of England* (London, 1883), vol. ii, p. 95).

In addition the term is used, as has already been seen, to denote traditional *mens rea*, a catalogue of more or less blameworthy mental states of intention, recklessness and negligence from which the legislator, in defining crime, is free to pick and choose to suit his requirements.

The expression *mens rea* performs, however, another function by acting as an ideal towards which the legal system should evolve. A balance of modern opinion favours imposing liability on the basis of fault, subjectively assessed, and a considerable body of literature criticises such strict liability and constructive liability for deviating from this ideal. Such criticisms are premised on a view of criminal responsibility which has fault as its basis. But when traditional *mens rea* is referred to as the "fault" element, this fault principle and a purely technical usage are conflated. The two by no means necessarily coincide, since traditional *mens rea* refers only to awareness of circumstances and to the contemplation of particular results. It does not follow that, because a person foresees or intends he is necessarily at fault: the intention may have been formed in a variety of exculpating circumstances such as under provocation, duress or necessity. As the expression of a fault principle, then, traditional *mens rea* is no more than a rule of thumb. Even as a description of the present law, it is necessary to look for a more embracing fault principle within which the existing excuses can be subsumed. This more fundamental principle has been formulated by Professor Hart in these terms:

> unless a man has the capacity and a fair opportunity or chance to adjust his behaviour to the law its penalties ought not to be applied to him. (*Punishment and Responsibility* (Oxford, 1968), p. 181).

This, he argues, is not only a rationale for most of the excuses which the law already admits; it might also act as a critical principle to ask of the law more than it already concedes.

An account of criminal liability that treats traditional *mens rea* as a necessary fault requirement is thus deficient in two respects. It overlooks the phenomenon of strict liability, and it takes no account of a number of efficacious excuses which do not negative the element of awareness or cognition."

Fletcher, Rethinking Criminal Law, pp. 396–397

"*Descriptive and Normative Uses of the Same Terms*

One of the persistent tensions in legal terminology runs between the descriptive and normative uses of the same terms. Witness the struggle over the concept of malice. The term has a high moral content, and when it came into the law as the benchmark of murder, it was presumably used normatively and judgmentally. Yet Fitzjames Stephen and succeeding generations of English jurists have sought to reduce the concepts of malice to the specific mental states of intending and knowing. California judges, in contrast, have stressed the normative content of malice in a highly judgmental definition, employing terms like 'base, anti-social purpose' and 'wanton disregard for human life.' For the English, malice is a question of fact: did the actor have a particular state of consciousness (intention or knowledge)? In California, malice is a value judgment about the actor's motives, attitudes and personal capacity.

If the English have tried to reduce the normative concept of malice to a state of fact, other commentators and courts seek to invest nominally descriptive terms with moral force. Though the terms 'intent', 'state of mind', and 'mental state' appear to be descriptive, legislators and courts use these terms to refer to issues that require normative judgment....

The confusion between normative and descriptive language is so pervasive in Anglo-American criminal law that it affects the entire language of discourse. There appear to be very few terms that are exempt from the ambiguity. The term 'intent' may refer either to a state of intending (regardless of blame) or it may refer to an intent to act under circumstances (such as failing to inquire about the age of a sexual partner) that render an act properly subject to blame. The term 'criminal intent' does not resolve the ambiguity, for a criminal intent may simply be the intent to do the act, which, according to the statutory definition, renders the act 'criminal', i.e., punishable under the law. There may be nothing morally blameworthy in keeping a pair of brass knuckles as a conversation piece, yet that intent renders the act punishable and, in this sense, is a criminal intent.

It is obvious that the very word 'criminal' is affected by the same tension between descriptive and normative illocutionary force. When used normatively, 'criminal' refers to the type of person who by virtue of his deeds deserves to be branded and punished as a criminal. When used descriptively, as in the phrase 'criminal act' it may refer simply to any act that the legislature has declared to be 'criminal'. Thus the term 'criminal intent' may mean the intent to act under circumstances that make it just to treat the actor as a criminal in the pejorative sense. . . . But it is equally plausible to use the term 'criminal intent' to refer to the intent or knowledge sufficient to commit a crime as defined by the legislature. The adjective 'criminal' in this context simply means that the intent is sufficient to render the act punishable under the statute. . . .

There is no term fraught with greater ambiguity than that venerable Latin phrase that haunts Anglo-American criminal law: *mens rea*. Glanville Williams defines *mens rea* to mean 'the mental element necessary for the particular crime.' Of course, the term 'mental element' may be employed either descriptively or normatively, yet in this context it seems clear that Williams means to refer to a factual state of affairs. Intent, used descriptively, is an example of a required 'mental element.' In another passage, Williams argues that the issue of duress should not be seen as negating either intention or *mens rea*. Thus he would conclude, . . . that someone who was acquitted on grounds of duress nonetheless acted with *mens rea*. However prestigious this line of analysis might be, the courts fortunately remain unimpressed. Engaged as they are in the processes of judgment and condemnation, the courts repeatedly stress the normative content of *mens rea*, ...

This tension between descriptive and normative usage carries significance for the structuring of issues in the criminal law. Descriptive theorists, like Stephen, Turner, Williams and others in the English tradition, are apt to see problems of insanity, duress and mistake as extrinsic to the analysis of *mens rea* and criminal intent. Normative theorists, in contrast, are able to integrate these 'defensive' issues into their formulation of the minimum conditions for liability. If *mens rea* raises a normative issue of just and appropriate blame, then there is no *mens rea* or 'criminal intent' when the intentional commission of the offence is excused by reason of duress, insanity, or reasonable mistake about an attendant circumstance (e.g., the age of the girl in statutory rape)."

2. THE MEANING OF TERMS

Both common law and statute employ a bewildering array of words and phrases with which to indicate the mental element required. Amongst those used are: "intentionally," "with intent to," "purposely," "knowingly," "recklessly," "wilfully" and "maliciously." To this lack of agreed terminology in the actual definition of offences is added the further confusion that the terms themselves have been subjected to a variety of interpretations. The next section, *post*, p. 62, looks at the judicial approach to some of these phrases currently used by the law.

The concepts involved can be broadly reduced to the following mental elements: intention, knowledge, recklessness and negligence. This section of the chapter is concerned with an explanation of these.

(References are made below to the Law Commission Draft Criminal Liability (Mental Element) Bill which was appended to the Report on the Mental Element in Crime (Law Com. No. 89, HMSO 1978). The Bill is reproduced in full, *post*, p. 56.)

i. Intention

Clause 2, Draft Bill, *post*, p. 57.

Fletcher, Rethinking Criminal Law, pp. 442–448

"The basic cleavage in the states of mind used in criminal legislation is between those that focus on the actor's goal (wilfulness, intention, purposefulness) and those that focus on the risk that the actor creates in acting (recklessness and negligence). The difficult problem confronted in all legal systems is working out the precise boundary between these two clusters of mental states—or, more precisely, between these two ways of committing offences. . . .

The problem of distinguishing 'intention' and 'recklessness' arises because in both cases the actor is aware that his conduct might generate a specific result. . . .

[T]here would be little dispute about distinguishing 'intention' from 'recklessness' if the former were not a term of art, encompassing many situations that we would not call 'intentional' in ordinary language. . . .

If a prisoner in an effort to escape blows up the prison wall with knowledge that guards are present and one of the latter dies in the explosion, we would not say that the prisoner intentionally killed the guard. Yet in legal systems across the Western world, the concept of 'intention' is interpreted broadly to include these probable side-effects of intentional conduct. This willingness to sweep in probable side-effects is what generates the problem of demarcation relative to recklessness. If the side-effects are not very probable—say, there are no guards visible at the time of the explosion—the killing might well be considered reckless rather than intentional. . . .

[W]hen is there a problem of distinguishing 'intention' from 'recklessness'? The problematic cases arise in the pattern of harmful consequences. In the case of these offences, a specific palpable result is a condition of the offence, and the question is whether if the actor takes a very high risk of bringing about that result, he can be held accountable as though he intended the result. If the statute proscribes only intentional commission of the offence, or if the intentional commission is punished more severely, this is a matter of practical importance.

There are two distinct foci in efforts to distinguish between bringing about a result intentionally and bringing it about recklessly. One approach is to stress the relative degree of risk that the result will occur; the other, to stress the actor's attitude toward the risk. Let us attempt to apply these diverse perspectives in two hypothetical situations:

A. The prison-break hypothetical: the prisoner blows up a wall in order to escape. A guard is either killed or injured. Is the prisoner liable for intentional homicide or battery?

B. The stewardess on a hijacked airplane, renders a parachute defective in the expectation that the hijacker, a known and feared terrorist, might use the chute. He does and is either killed or injured.

To assess whether the injury or death in these cases is to be regarded as intended, we can proceed simply by assessing the relative probability that the explosion would hit the guard or that the hijacker would use the chute. Most legal systems would treat the side-effect of an explosion, if sufficiently probable, as a case of directly 'intending the result'. The parachute case is more subtle, as is the case of a prison break where the risk of injuring a guard is low.

To analyse these cases comparatively, we have to bring into the open an important doctrinal difference between German and Soviet law, on the one hand, and Anglo-American (and possibly French) law on the other. The former systems draw the distinction between intentional and negligent conduct by including *dolus eventualis* within the contours of intending a particular result. *Dolus eventualis* is defined as a particular subjective posture toward the result. The tests for this subjective posture vary; the possibilities include everything from being 'indifferent' to the result, to 'being reconciled' with the result as a possible cost of attaining one's goal. The implication is that recklessness (or 'conscious negligence' as it is called in German and Soviet law) requires an affirmative aversion to the harmful side-effect.

If we apply the definitions of the Model Penal Code to the case of the defective parachute, the issue of killing 'purposely' would turn on whether the stewardess' 'conscious object' was to cause the death of the hijacker; killing 'knowingly' would depend on whether she was 'practically certain' he would use the chute and fall to his death. Given the appropriate interpretations of 'conscious object' and 'causing death' we might be able to find a purposeful or knowing killing under these definitions. The standard of *dolus eventualis* would point more clearly to liability for intentional killing. Why does the stewardess render the parachute defective if she does not want the hijacker to use it? Thus her subjective emotional posture toward the killing would be controlling.

The difference between the standard of the Model Penal Code and *dolus eventualis* would emerge in a variation of the prison break case in which the killing of the guard was unlikely. If it is not the actor's conscious object to kill and if he is not 'practically certain' that death will result, then the Code would not permit a finding of killing 'purposely' or 'knowingly'. But the actor's subjective posture might be just as incriminating. He might be indifferent or 'reconciled' to harming people in the blast, and thus even if the thought that the likelihood of personal injury was very low, he would act with *dolus eventualis*.

The doctrine of *dolus eventualis* has vast repercussions in German and Soviet theory. If a rapist puts his hand over his victim's mouth with indifference to her fate and she dies, the killing is intentional. This broad conception of 'intentional' killing explains why these systems can dispense with a doctrine of felony-murder. As to the intent required for attempted offences, German law treats *dolus eventualis* as sufficient for liability. This means that if a man shoots into a room full of people without the intent to injure anyone but indifferent to whether he does, he is guilty of at least attempted murder.

So far as the Anglo-American conception of intention is concerned, there is no doctrine with the sweep of *dolus eventualis*. It is very unlikely that in a case of low probability of harm, an English or American court would find an intentional killing, arson or battery. The orientation of the system is toward actual risk and knowledge of risk, not the inner posture of the actor. . . .

The comparative analysis of *dolus eventualis* is extremely subtle. That the concept is missing in the Anglo-American literature prompts us to look for surrogates, such as the felony-murder rule. We should also recall that in the common law, intentional killing is not the only basis for establishing the most egregious form of criminal homicide. A review of the Anglo-American law of murder reveals criteria of risk-taking, sufficient for murder, that closely resembles the criteria for *dolus eventualis*. For example, the Model Penal Code treats reckless killing, 'manifesting extreme indifference to the value of human life', as equivalent to purposeful and knowing killing. Thus the factor of 'indifference to life' need not bear on the definition of 'intention' if the functional outcome for the law of murder is the same.

The basic question is whether the actor's attitude alone can warrant classification at a higher level of culpability than would be supported by the risk he creates. Can the lust for death compensate for a low risk of harm? It is important that the Model Penal Code inserts the issue of 'indifference' only to qualify the standard of recklessness. Yet the German literature, in contrast, suggests that if the actor regards death 'as possible' and he acts with *dolus eventualis*, the killing would be intentional even if the risk of death is not as great as that required for negligent homicide. Thus if the risk were low in the parachute case, the stewardess might be prima facie accountable either for intentional homicide, or for no crime at all, but not negligent homicide. That negligent homicide is not 'included' in intentional killing points to a structural difference between the two systems; but it is one that should be checked against a rigorous examination of all the German cases."

Rupert Cross, "Reports of the Criminal Law Commissioners (1833–49) and the Abortive Bills of 1853" in Reshaping the Criminal Law (ed. Glazebrook), p. 5

". . . The lesson to be learnt from the treatment of the mental element is that the all important question of the moral basis of proposals for the reform of significant parts of the substantive criminal law requires careful consideration and on no occasion since the publication of the Commissioners' reports has it been given such consideration at an official level in this country. R. S. Wright's memorandum accompanying his code, the report of the Royal Commission on the draft code of 1878 and, to-date, the Law Commission's working papers, as well as the reports of the Criminal Law Revision Committee, are deficient in moral discourse. As the commissioners said:

> Penal laws cannot be made commensurate with the moral law, but they are designed to promote the same objects, so far as they extend; they are derived from the same great origins, and without the aid of morals they are but vain and unprofitable.

It is not suggested that the proposals of the modern law reformers lack a moral basis as sound as, if not sounder than, the suggestions of the commissioners, but the case needs to be put rather than taken for granted. . . .

Without wishing to detract in any way from the value of the semantic arguments presented in such modern documents as the Law Commission's Working Paper No. 31 concerning the legal definitions of intention and recklessness, and the extent to which it is desirable, for legal purposes, to go beyond the ordinary meaning of intention, one may perhaps be permitted to stress the fact that, even for a lawyer, morals are more important than semantics. Of course it is possible to make out a case for distinguishing between the man who directly intends a forbidden result and the man who consciously takes an unjustified risk of its occurrence, but arguments of the kind mentioned by the commissioners of 1833 and 1845 must be met. To revert to the pistol case, [the author had earlier cited the example of one 'who selects a pistol from a number of which, to his knowledge, only one is loaded, points it at the head of another, draws the trigger and kills him'] let us suppose that the criminal, despairing of any other means of disposing of his enemy, had selected his weapon hoping against hope that it was the one which was loaded. If his hopes were fulfilled, he would have directly intended his enemy's death and it is difficult to believe that anyone would wish to deny that he was guilty of murder. Is there any moral difference, and should there be any legal difference, if he had selected the pistol and pointed it at his victim in order to frighten him, to experience the thrill of finding out whether he had chosen the one which was loaded, or in the hope of winning a bet?

According to [the Law Commission] . . . the ordinary meaning of intention should be extended to cover the case of the man who has no substantial doubt that his act will produce a particular result, although it ought not to extend to the man who believes that the result is probable. If these bodies have their way, the upshot will be that someone who sets fire to a house knowing that its sole occupant is a helpless baby will be guilty of murder if the baby is burnt to death and the jury finds that he had no substantial doubt that this would happen, although his only concern was with the insurance money, while he will only be guilty of manslaughter if the jury thinks that he may have been telling the truth when he said 'I believed that the baby would probably be burnt, but I thought there was just a chance that he would be saved, although I didn't really care because I was hell bent on getting the money.' Do we have to put up with this kind of distinction? The commissioners of 1833 and 1845 would have said 'No.' If the answer is 'Yes', it is up to those who give that answer to justify it."

[The proposals of the Law Commission in its final Report (No. 89) did not substantively differ from those in the Working Paper].

More extensive criticisms of the Law Commission's proposals are contained in two articles by R. A. Duff [1980] Crim. L.R. 147 and 404.

ii. Knowledge

Clause 3, Draft Bill, *post*, p. 57.

The Law Commission, Report on the Mental Element in Crime, Law Com. 89 (1978)

"§ 47. On the whole, we have come to the conclusion that knowledge should be treated in a similar way to intention and for substantially similar reasons. With regard to the position of the person who is shown deliberately to have shut his eyes to the existence of the relevant circumstances of an offence, and claims that he did not actually *know* of their existence, we consider that a jury or court would generally infer, and so find as a fact, that he *had no substantial doubt* that those circumstances existed."

Note

The recommended definition of intention applies only to results. The equivalent mental state in relation to circumstances is covered by the word knowledge. Some "result-crimes" also contain relevant circumstances and the failure to extend the definition of intention to such legally relevant circumstances is criticised by Williams ([1978] Crim. L.R. 589–590). Clause 3 (2) (*c*) does not help where there is no clear implication that knowledge is required for liability. Recklessness, however, is used in relation to both results and circumstances.

iii. Recklessness

Clause 4, Draft Bill, *post*, p. 58.

Law Com. 89

"§ 57. A few simple examples may serve to illustrate the practical result of the test of recklessness which we are recommending—

(*a*) A man is kicking a football along a pavement. To avoid some children and without thinking of any risk involved, he kicks the ball to one side. The ball breaks a window. He is not guilty of recklessly damaging property (although of course he could be civilly liable for negligence).

(*b*) An amateur handyman has built a high fence in his garden. He admits that when he built it he foresaw the fence might conceivably blow down and cut his neighbour. In fact, owing to his lack of technical expertise in the construction of high fences, the fence is blown down by the wind and injures his neighbour, cutting him on the face. If it would not be unreasonable for a person, with the defendant's appreciation of the degree of the risk involved, to take that risk, the defendant would not be liable for causing injury recklessly.

(*c*) A professional variety artist, with many years of accident-free experience of juggling, is performing before an audience with a dozen Indian clubs. He admits that he foresaw that in such a performance he might misjudge a throw and wound a spectator but, in view of his long experience and skill, he thought there was no more than a very remote risk of a spectator being so injured. He in fact misjudges a throw, as a result of which a spectator is wounded. He is only reckless for the purposes of criminal liability if it is unreasonable for such a performer, who estimates the risk of injury as very slight, to take it.

(*d*) The case is as in (*b*) above, except that the builder is a professional craftsman, who has built a number of high fences of similar technical construction several of which he has had to repair after they have been blown down by the wind and one of which caused personal injury by its fall. If (as seems on the facts an inevitable inference) he foresaw when building the fence in question that there was a risk it would blow down and cause injury and (as further seems likely) it is found to be unreasonable for him to have taken that risk, he has been reckless for the purposes of criminal liability."

R. A. Duff, "Recklessness" [1980] Crim. L.R. 282

"A widely held view about the meaning and significance of 'recklessness' in criminal law can be expressed in these five propositions.

(1) 'Recklessness' differs from 'intention' and 'negligence' in involving *conscious risk-taking*. One who is 'reckless' as to the existence of some fact need neither intend nor be certain of the existence of that fact; but he must at least realise that it *might* exist.

(2) A 'reckless' agent consciously takes a risk which is *unreasonable* or *unjustified*. The standard of reasonableness is 'objective' (the agent need not himself think the risk unreasonable): but it must be applied to the risk which he actually realised. We must show not just that it was unreasonable to take the risk which he in fact took, or which he could and should have realised he was taking, but that it was unreasonable to take the kind of degree of risk which he realised he was taking.

(3) It is neither necessary nor sufficient that he realise that it is 'probable' that the relevant fact exists: if the harm he risks is sufficiently serious, and his action sufficiently worthless, he may be 'reckless' even though he knows the harm to be unlikely; if his action is sufficiently valuable he may be justified, and thus not 'reckless', in acting in the knowledge that the relevant harm will 'probably' ensue. The 'reckless' agent must realise that there is *a* risk—that it is at least *possible* that the relevant fact exists: but whether he is 'reckless' depends not just on how likely it is, to his knowledge, that the fact exists, but on whether it is reasonable to take that risk in the course of the activity in which he is engaged.

(4) He need not be 'indifferent' to the existence of the fact as to which he is 'reckless'. He may hope that it does not exist, take *some* precautions against it, and act only in the belief that it probably does not exist: but he is still 'reckless', despite his beliefs and precautions, if the risk he knows he is taking is unreasonable.

(5) 'Recklessness' is usually a necessary and sufficient condition of criminal liability. While we may sometimes base liability on negligence, or even make it to some degree 'strict', a guilty agent must usually be at least 'reckless' as to every element of the *actus reus*; and while we may sometimes require that a guilty agent act with 'intention' or 'knowledge' as to some element, we will usually, and rightly, hold an agent as guilty if he is 'reckless' as to any relevant fact as if he acts with 'intention' or 'knowledge'.

These propositions are reflected in the Law Commission's proposals for a statutory definition of 'recklessness'....

....

I will argue that 'recklessness' as a generally necessary and sufficient condition of criminal liability, cannot be defined as the Commission define it: that their definition is too wide, in counting *every* conscious and unreasonable risk-taker as 'reckless'; and too narrow, in counting an agent 'reckless' only if he *realises* the risk he is taking. An adequate discussion of the sense in which, and the extent to which, 'recklessness' should be a necessary or sufficient condition of criminal liability would require an examination of a whole range of offences, which is impossible here. I will talk mainly about offences of violence against the person: not because these are necessarily typical, but because to show that the Commission's definition is inadequate for this kind of offence is enough to show that it should not be accepted as a *general* definition of 'recklessness'.

The Commission's category of 'recklessness' is extraordinarily wide. The builder who knowingly and unreasonably takes the risk that the fence he erects *might* blow down and cause injury has the same *mens rea* as an agent who does what he knows will very probably, but not certainly, cause injury. Of course, the less likely it is that injury will actually ensue, the less likely it is that he will find himself guilty of an offence: but if injury does ensue, he must be guilty of the same offence (*e.g.* of assault occasioning actual bodily harm). His sentence may reflect the lesser seriousness of the risk he takes: but 'this will not fully remove the stigma of being convicted of that offence.' I suggest that this makes the category of 'recklessness', as a basis of criminal liability, too wide.

Imagine three authors, each of whom, frustrated in his work, flings his typewriter out of his study window. *Alan* knows quite well that his neighbour is sunbathing outside the window, and 'has no substantial doubt' that the typewriter will hit and injure him; he does not *aim* to hit him, but is not moved by the thought that he will injure him. *Andrew* knows that it is quite probable that his neighbour is there and thus quite probable that he will injure him: he hopes he is not there, but acts in the expectation that he will probably injure him. *Arnold* knows there is a chance that his neighbour is there, and thus that he might injure him: but he knows he is probably indoors, and hopes and expects that he will probably not hit him. Assume that in each case it is unreasonable for the author to take the risk he takes, and that in each case the neighbour *is* outside the window, and is injured by the typewriter.

If we interpret the Offences Against the Person Act 1861 in line with the Commission's definitions, then depending on the nature and seriousness of the anticipated and the actual injury all three would be guilty of assault under section 47, and perhaps of wounding or inflicting grievous bodily harm under section 20, while Alan alone might be guilty of wounding with intent to cause grievous bodily harm under section 18.... But the difference between Alan and Andrew is surely less significant, and that between Andrew and Arnold more significant, than this classification suggests....

Now neither Alan nor Andrew 'actually intend' to cause injury: both may regret, welcome, or be indifferent to the injury they cause....

We could say that, while Andrew's action can properly be described simply as 'injuring his neighbour', Arnold's is more properly described as one of 'risk-taking' or 'endangering his neighbour': for these descriptions specify the results which each expects to bring about. . . .

I suggest that Andrew should, but Arnold should not, be guilty of assault or of 'causing injury recklessly.' If we wish to distinguish an agent who 'has no substantial doubt' that he will cause injury from one who realises that he will probably but not certainly do so (though this difference between Alan and Andrew is hardly significant), we may say that Alan causes injury 'intentionally' while Andrew causes it 'recklessly'. But we should then find another category for Arnold, such as 'conscious negligence': which is not to say he is guilty of no offence, but rather that it should at worst be a lesser offence than Andrew's, more akin to an offence of negligence. For while Andrew is not far removed from that paradigm of malicious (oblique) 'intent' which Alan instantiates, Arnold is a long way from that paradigm: his action does not manifest a sufficiently serious disregard for his neighbour's safety.

But this is not to say that 'recklessness', as a basis of liability for this kind of offence, must *always* involve the realisation that the relevant fact *probably* exists: for there are other ways in which an agent can manifest a sufficiently serious disregard for another's safety. In my examples so far, the agent was 'reckless' as to a *contingent* circumstance (his neighbour's presence) or consequence (the injury to his neighbour) of his intended action: there is no *essential* connection between the defenestration of a typewriter and the presence of someone who might be injured by it. But in other cases there is a closer connection between the agent's intended action and the fact as to which he may be held reckless: and he may then be held reckless, and thus criminally liable, even if he rightly believes that it is unlikely, though possible, that that fact exists.

Suppose that Arnold throws out his typewriter not (just) to vent his frustration, but to frighten his neighbour out of his habit of sunbathing outside the window. It is not part of Arnold's intention, nor crucial to his enterprise, that the neighbour actually be there and be injured: indeed, he acts in the belief that he is probably *not* there. But it is part of his intention, and crucial to his enterprise, that the neighbour *might* be there and *might* be injured (and that the neighbour realise this): for only thus could his action have its intended effect. He now *intends*, as he did not before, to endanger his neighbour: the possibility (though not the actuality) of injury is now *part* of his intended action, not merely a contingent circumstance of it. He now manifests a more serious, 'reckless', disregard for his neighbour's safety, and can properly be held guilty of assault if he causes injury: for by intending to create a risk of injury he relates himself more closely as an agent to, and makes himself fully responsible for, the injury which in fact ensues.

But I suggest that 'recklessness' as a generally sufficient basis of criminal liability, should not be defined so widely that it includes *every* conscious and unreasonable risk-taker. We should require, at least in the kinds of case discussed here, either that he realise that it is *probable*, not just possible, that the relevant fact exists; or that that fact is so essentially and significantly connected to his intended action that we can properly count him 'reckless' as to it even when he realises only that it is possible. If neither of these conditions obtain, he is too remote from the paradigms of 'malicious intent': he is 'consciously negligent' rather than 'reckless'.

The Commission also require that a reckless agent *realise* the risk he takes, and that judgments of his recklessness be based on the risk he realises. Thus a fourth frustrated author, Arthur, who does not (though he should) even realise that his neighbour might be outside, is 'negligent' not 'reckless'. They think it important to retain this 'real mental element' in 'recklessness', and must thus suppose that the presence or absence of this 'mental element' makes an important difference to the nature and degree of the agent's guilt. . . .

The problem here is generated by the belief that, if 'recklessness' is to have a suitably 'subjective' rather than a reprehensibly 'objective' meaning, it must involve a realisation of the relevant risk. But that belief is wrong. Some failures of attention or realisation may manifest, not mere stupidity or 'thoughtlessness', but the same indifference or disregard which characterises the conscious risk-taker as reckless. . . .

In general, the extent to which I notice or realise the various aspects of my action, its context, and its results, is a function as much of my attitudes and values as of my powers of observation and attention: to say that I forgot or did not realise something may be to admit that I thought it unimportant, and thus to convict myself of a serious lack of concern for it. . . . A man may be reckless even though, and even partly *because,* he does not realise the risk which is in fact an essential and significant aspect of this action.

This is not to say that we should adopt an 'objective' rather than a 'subjective' definition of 'recklessness', if this means that we should ignore the agent's own attitudes, intentions, and beliefs: but rather that the kind of practical attitude which is central to the notion of recklessness may be revealed in his failure to realise a risk as much as in his conscious risk-taking. The task of course remains of distinguishing such reckless failures of attention from those which should be classed rather as negligent or stupid: but I hope I have said enough to show that the Commission's definition of 'recklessness' attaches a significance to the agent's actual realisation of the risk he takes which is not always appropriate."

Questions

1. In the above extract, is Duff arguing that English law should adopt the notion of "*dolus eventualis*" which Fletcher describes (*ante*, p. 48)?

2. If the Law Commission had wanted to include the kind of "attitude" described by Duff in its definition of recklessness, would the following provision in the Model Penal Code have been appropriate?:

> s. 210.2 (1) ". . . Criminal homicide constitutes murder when: . . . (*b*) it is committed recklessly under circumstances manifesting extreme indifference to the value of human life."

iv. Negligence

Law Com. 89

"§ 67. In Working Paper No. 31 not only were intention, knowledge and recklessness provided with definitions which it was proposed should apply to existing and future offences, but also 'negligence'. The definition of 'negligence' was as follows—

> 'A person is negligent if he fails to exercise such care, skill or foresight as a reasonable man in his situation would exercise.'

§ 68. Whereas, however, there is a considerable measure of uncertainty as to the meaning in law of intention, knowledge, and recklessness both as to results and, more particularly, as to circumstances, there has not been any comparable uncertainty as to the legal meaning of negligence. We therefore make no recommendation for any general statutory definition of negligence. We are not of course here referring to the very different question, as to which there has been uncertainty, whether in respect of any particular requirement of an offence it is sufficient to establish liability for that offence that the defendant has been negligent, whether some higher degree of 'fault' is necessary or whether in respect of that requirement the offence is one of strict liability. We mention this latter question in later paragraphs of this report."

Negligence and mens rea

The Law Commission recommended that, where a statute indicates no particular required mental state, intention or recklessness should be presumed as the minimum basis of liability (s. 5, Draft Bill, *post*, p. 59).

Williams, Criminal Law: the General Part, pp. 102–103

"Although negligence has occasionally been treated as a form of *mens rea*, there seems to be every argument against this view. (1) Negligence is not by definition a state of mind, except in the negative feature of absence of intention, ... It would be linguistically objectionable to describe something that is not a mental state as *mens*. (2) *Mens rea* is a general requirement for crime at common law; but negligence is not usually sufficient. In other words, negligence is not the kind of *mens rea* that characterises the ordinary run of crimes. This is because the justification for punishing thoughtlessness is not so strong as the justification for punishing foresight. (3) If negligence were admitted as a form of *mens rea*, the consequence might be that judges would come to extend the number of crimes that can be committed in this way. This would be a most undesirable result of the 'jurisprudence of conceptions', since crimes of negligence should not be created except after full consideration of the issues of policy and justice that are involved."

Fletcher, Rethinking Criminal Law, pp. 504 et seq.

"[N]o set of terms enjoys as much confusion as the notions of objectivity and subjectivity in the theory of liability. The question is repeatedly put, whether a standard, say of negligence or provocation, is objective or subjective. The question is perfectly appropriate, yet what is surprising is the way it is so readily answered. Leading writers, such as Glanville Williams, Herbert Packer and Jerome Hall, are quick to reply that negligent homicide is punished on the basis of an objective or external standard. The implication is that this feature renders negligence a suspect basis of liability; unlike cases of 'subjective fault' negligence is akin to strict liability. In other contexts 'objective' and 'subjective' are cast about as though they were dice with only one face of meaning. In fact they have several faces, and any discussion that fails to acknowledge this diversity of meaning proves to be loaded in favour of unarticulated and undefended theories of liability. . . .

Any time a standard, say of negligence, is identified as 'objective' the implication is that the standard could not serve as a proper ground for blaming the particular individual to whom the standard is applied. Objective standards are identified as 'social' rather than individual standards. If fault is found according to an objective standard, the implication is that the fault is 'social' rather than individual. It follows that some injustice to the individual is inherent in the criminal law, for, as Holmes argued, the law 'undoubtedly treat[s] the individual as the means to an end, and use[s] him as a tool to increase the general welfare at his own expense.' (The Common Law 1881, 46–7). Thus if the criminal law must be justified on this ground, there is nothing particularly disturbing about standards of strict liability, the felony-murder rule, and other devices that might be insensitive to the actual desert of the offender. All of these devices are like objective standards of liability, for they 'sacrifice the individual to the general good.' It follows from this account of the criminal law that the only sound rationale for punishment is social protection, not the distribution of punishment according to individual culpability. . . .

The thesis that knowing and intentional acts are authentic instances of culpable conduct, but negligence is anomalous as an external standard, conceals a confusion between 'being culpable' and 'feeling culpable'. That one act with a sense of guilt—with knowledge that one is doing wrong—is neither necessary nor sufficient for culpability. The state of the actor's mind or conscience is a factual claim. Guilt, fault and culpability are normative judgments, based on an evaluation of the actor's conduct and state of mind. To reason from premise about the actor's intent to a conclusion about his fault, culpability or blameworthiness, we need this additional premise:

> If someone is acting wrongfully and he believes that he is doing wrong, then he is culpable for what he is doing.

Though this proposition is generally true, it is defeased by the full range of excusing conditions, including duress, necessity and insanity. What the actor thinks or believes hardly entails culpability in violating the law. If the act is beyond her control—if her 'will is overborne'—subjective awareness of wrongdoing is hardly sufficient for fairly blaming the actor. . . .

Once the normative dimension of culpability comes into focus, the difference between intentional and negligent wrongdoing no longer appears critical. Judging both forms of acting as culpable requires normative assessment in the light of possible excusing conditions. There may be some clear cases of intentional killing, where the normative question is easily resolved. But, there are also cases of negligent risk-taking where it is equally clear that the actor should have been more attentive to the risk. There might be more controversy about inadvertent risk-creation than there is about most cases of intentional wrongdoing, but this difference of degree should not obscure the commonality of normative judgment as the foundation for judgments of personal accountability."

v. Law Commission Draft Bill

Law Com. No. 89

"*Criminal Liability (Mental Element) Bill*

Draft of a Bill to establish, in relation to offences created by or by virtue of Acts of Parliament passed after 1980, rules as to the effect of certain words used to define states of mind and as to the states of mind or standards of conduct required for liability where those words are not used; to provide that a person charged with such an offence is in certain cases not to be guilty of it if he believed in the existence of circumstances whose existence would have meant that he was not guilty; and to make further provision with respect to the proof of intention, knowledge, recklessness and foresight for the purpose of criminal liability.

Be it enacted by the Queen's most Excellent Majesty, by and with the advice and consent of the Lords Spiritual and Temporal, and Commons, in this respect Parliament assembled, and by the authority of the same, as follows:—

1. Standard tests for questions of criminal liability

(1) A court or jury determining whether a person has committed an offence created by a provision—

(*a*) which is contained in or made by virtue of an Act of Parliament passed after 31st December, 1980, and

(*b*) which employs one of the key words specified in this Act.

shall use the standard test under this Act for which that key word is appropriate when answering any question relating to him specified in subsection (2) below, unless the provision creating the offence declares that the test is not to be used.

(2) The questions mentioned in subsection (1) above are—

(*a*) the question of intention;

(*b*) the question of knowledge;

(*c*) the question of recklessness as to result; and

(*d*) the question of recklessness as to circumstances.

(3) In this Act, in relation to any person—
'the question of intention' means the question whether he intended a particular result of his conduct;
'the question of knowledge' means the question whether he knew of any relevant circumstances;
'the question of recklessness as to result' means the question whether he was reckless as to whether his conduct would have any particular result; and
'the question of recklessness as to circumstances' means the question whether he was reckless as to whether any relevant circumstances existed.

(4) The standard tests for the questions specified in subsection (3) above are respectively specified in sections 2, 3, 4 (1) and 4 (2) below.

Notes

Clause 1

1. Clause 1 provides for the use of standard tests (specified in Clauses 2, 3, 4 (1) and 4 (2)) in determining, in relation to liability for criminal offences created in the future, whether a person—
(*a*) intended a result of his conduct;
(*b*) knew of a circumstance;
(*c*) was reckless as to a result of his conduct; or
(*d*) was reckless as to whether a circumstance existed;
where the offence-creating provision uses one of the key words indicating intention, knowledge or recklessness (subsection (1)).

2. The standard tests apply (unless specifically excluded) where the key words are used in offences created by Acts passed after a specified date, or by instruments made under such Acts. The date will, in fact, be fixed so as to allow time for the legislation to be studied fully by those drafting offences, and the date in subsection (1) is simply by way of illustration.

3. The standard tests will also apply where any question of intention, knowledge or recklessness arises by reason of Clause 5.

2. Intention

(1) The standard test of intention is—
Did the person whose conduct is in issue either intend to produce the result or have no substantial doubt that his conduct would produce it?

(2) The appropriate key words are—
(*a*) the verb 'to intend' in any of its forms; and
(*b*) 'intent', 'intention', 'intentional' and 'intentionally'.

Notes

Clause 2

1. Subsection (1) provides the standard test of intention.
2. Subsection (2) specifies the key words which import the above test.

3. Knowledge

(1) The standard test of knowledge is—
Did the person whose conduct is in issue either know of the relevant circumstances or have no substantial doubt of their existence?

(2) The appropriate key words are—
(*a*) the verb 'to know' in any of its forms;
(*b*) 'knowledge' and 'knowingly'; and
(*c*) any of the words mentioned in section 2 (2) above, if used so as to imply that the person whose conduct is in issue cannot intend to produce a particular result unless he knows some particular fact or facts.

Notes

Clause 3

1. Subsection (1) provides the standard test of knowledge.
2. Subsection (2) specifies the key words which import the above test.
3. The standard test of knowledge applies not only when any of the 'knowledge' words specified in paragraphs (*a*) and (*b*) of subsection (2) is used, but also by virtue of paragraph (*c*) when any of the 'intention' words specified in clause 2 (2) is used so as to imply that knowledge of circumstances is required for liability. For example, where it is an offence for a person *intentionally* to administer a harmful substance to another, and the word 'intentionally' is construed as requiring that the person administering the substance must know that it is harmful, the test of knowledge is that in subsection (1).

4. Recklessness

(1) The standard test of recklessness as to result is—

Did the person whose conduct is in issue foresee that his conduct might produce the result and, if so, was it unreasonable for him to take the risk of producing it?

(2) The standard test of recklessness as to circumstances is—

Did the person whose conduct is in issue realise that the circumstances might exist and, if so, was it unreasonable for him to take the risk of their existence?

(3) The appropriate key words for both tests are 'reckless', 'recklessness' and 'recklessly'.

(4) The question whether it was unreasonable for the person to take the risk is to be answered by an objective assessment of his conduct in the light of all relevant factors, but on the assumption that any judgment he may have formed of the degree of risk was correct.

Notes

Clause 4

1. Subsection (1) provides the standard test of recklessness as to result. This involves asking two questions.
   (*a*) The first question—Did the person concerned foresee that his conduct might produce the result?—relates to the state of mind of that person and is to be decided on a subjective basis. If it is answered in the negative the second question will not arise.
   (*b*) The second question—Was it unreasonable for the person to take the risk of his conduct producing that result?—is to be answered objectively, considering whether the risk ought to have been taken (see also subsection (4)).
2. Subsection (2) provides the standard test of recklessness as to circumstances. This also involves asking two questions.
   (*a*) The first question—Did the person concerned realise that the circumstances might exist?—is to be decided on a subjective basis, and, again, if it is answered in the negative the second question will not arise.
   (*b*) The second question—Was it unreasonable to take the risk of the circumstances existing?—is to be answered objectively, considering whether the risk ought to have been taken (see also subsection (4)).
3. Subsection (3) specifies the key words which import the above tests.
4. Subsection (4), apart from providing that the question of whether it was unreasonable to take the risk is to be answered by an objective assessment of the conduct of the person in question, requires the assessment to be made on the assumption that any judgment the person may have formed of the degree of risk

was correct. Thus if it is found that a person thought that it was very probable his conduct would cause a particular prohibited result there may be little difficulty in holding that it was unreasonable for him to take the risk of causing that result. Yet where it is found that a person thought there was only the very slightest risk of his conduct causing that result it may be held, in the same circumstances, that it was not unreasonable for him to take the risk of causing that result. If it is found that the person formed no judgment of the degree of the risk, the question of whether it was unreasonable to take the risk will be decided by objective criteria.

5. Cases where the standard tests apply without the use of key words

(1) This section has effect where an offence is created by a provision contained in or made by virtue of an Act of Parliament passed after 31st December 1980 unless the provision creating the offence declares that it is not to have effect.

(2) Subject to subsection (4) below, a person is not guilty of an offence in relation to which this section has effect unless the prosecution establish that, using the standard test, an affirmative answer is to be given in respect of all relevant circumstances—

(*a*) to the question of knowledge, or
(*b*) to the question of recklessness as to circumstances.

(3) Subject to subsection (4) below, where a person can only be guilty of an offence in relation to which this section has effect if his conduct produces a particular result, he is not guilty of it unless the prosecution establish that, using the standard test, an affirmative answer is to be given in respect of that result—

(*a*) to the question of intention, or
(*b*) to the question of recklessness as to result.

(4) Where a provision creating an offence contains words indicating in respect of a particular circumstance or result—

(*a*) that a person can only commit the offence if he has a particular state of mind or if he does not comply with an objective standard of conduct, or
(*b*) that a person can commit it whatever the state of his mind or the standard of his conduct, or
(*c*) that there is an exemption from liability if a person does not have a particular state of mind or complies with an objective standard of conduct,

subsection (2) or (3) above shall be disregarded in relation to that circumstance or result.

Notes

Clause 5

1. This clause gives effect to the recommendation in paragraph 89 of the report that in any future offence, where there is no provision for fault or for strict liability in relation to a requirement of the offence, there should, in relation to that requirement, be a presumption that liability depends upon intention or recklessness as to any result of conduct, and upon knowledge of, or recklessness as to, any circumstance.

2. The presumptions apply, unless specifically excluded, to offences created by or under Acts passed after the date specified in clause 1 (1) (*subsection* (1)).

3. Where the presumptions apply they are that—

(*a*) in relation to all relevant circumstances the prosecution must establish either knowledge or recklessness on the part of the defendant (subsection (2)), and (*b*) in relation to the result of the defendant's conduct the prosecution must establish that he intended the result or was reckless as to it (subsection (3)),

and in each case the standard tests in clauses 2, 3, 4 (1) and 4 (2) are to be applied in determining whether there was intention, knowledge or recklessness.

4. The presumptions do not, however, apply if in relation to any circumstance or result—

(*a*) it is provided that a particular state of mind, or failure to observe an objective standard of conduct, is a requirement of the offence—*e.g.*, if it were made an offence (as by s. 19 of the Allotments Act 1922) by negligence to cause damage to an allotment garden (subsection (4) (*a*));

(*b*) it is provided that the offence can be committed regardless of the defendant's state of mind, or his observance of an objective standard of conduct—*e.g.*, if it were made an offence to be in possession of an explosive, whether or not the defendant knew that what he had in his possession was an explosive (subsection (4) (*b*)); or

(*c*) there is provided an exemption from liability if the defendant does not have a particular state of mind or if he complies with an objective standard of conduct—*e.g.*, if it were made an offence to pollute a river, subject to a defence that the defendant had taken all reasonable precautions against doing so (subsection (4) (*c*)).

In these cases there is no place for a presumption to operate.

6. Defence of belief in exempting circumstances

(1) This section has effect where an offence is created by a provision contained in or made by virtue of an Act of Parliament passed after 31st December 1980 unless the provision creating the offence declares that it is not to have effect.

(2) Subject to subsection (3) below, if the provision creating such an offence specifies exempting circumstances, a person charged with the offence is not guilty of it if at the time of the conduct alleged to constitute the offence he believed that exempting circumstances existed.

(3) Subsection (2) above does not apply where the provision contains words indicating that a person charged with the offence is not guilty of it if, in relation to any exempting circumstances, he had a particular state of mind or complied with an objective standard of conduct.

(4) For the purposes of this section a provision specifies exempting circumstances if it specifies, by way of defence, exception, proviso, excuse or qualification, circumstances the establishment of which has the effect that a person charged with the offence cannot be guilty of it.

(5) Any requirement as to proof of the existence of exempting circumstances shall apply also as to proof of belief in their existence.

Notes

Clause 6

1. This clause gives effect to the recommendation in paragraph 91 of the report that in any future offence, where liability is subject to a defence or exemption, the defendant should not be liable if he believed that any circumstance existed which, had it in fact existed, would have provided him with that defence or exemption.

2. The clause has effect where an offence-creating provision provides a defence, exception, proviso, excuse or qualification if a prescribed factual circumstance exists—*e.g.*, if it were made an offence knowingly to supply liquor to children, but subject to a defence that the liquor was in a properly corked and sealed vessel.

3. In such a case subsection (2) provides, in effect, for a defence—additional to that specifically provided by the offence-creating provision—that the defendant

believed that the liquor was in a properly corked and sealed vessel; *cf.*, *Brooks* v. *Mason* [1902] 2 K.B. 743.

4. Subsection (2) does not, however, apply where the exempting provision itself indicates that a person is not liable if he had a particular state of mind or complied with an objective standard of conduct in relation to an exempting circumstance—*e.g.*, if in the above case the defence provided was that the liquor was in a properly corked and sealed vessel or the defendant believed *on reasonable grounds* that it was in a properly corked and sealed vessel (subsection (3)).

5. By subsection (5) the burden of proving the defendant's belief that the exempting circumstance existed is the same as the burden of proving that the circumstance itself existed. Thus, where there is a persuasive burden on the defendant in relation to an exemption (as there is, for example, by virtue of section 81 of the Magistrates' Courts Act 1952), a defendant wishing to rely upon his belief in facts that would have brought him within the exemption has a similar burden in relation to his belief.

7. Proof of intention, knowledge, recklessness and foresight

(1) A court or jury determining whether a person has committed an offence—

(*a*) shall not be bound in law to infer that any question specified in the first column of the Table below is to be answered in the affirmative by reason only of the existence of the factor specified in the second column as appropriate to that question, but

(*b*) shall treat that factor as relevant to that question, and decide the question by reference to all the evidence, drawing such inferences from the evidence as appear proper in the circumstances.

TABLE

Questions	*Appropriate factors*
1. Whether the person charged with the offence— (*a*) intended to produce a particular result by his conduct; (*b*) was reckless as to whether his conduct would produce a particular result; (*c*) foresaw that his conduct might produce a particular result.	1. The fact that the result was a natural and probable result of such conduct.
2. Whether he knew a particular fact.	2. The presence of circumstances leading to the inference that a reasonable man in his situation would have known the fact.
3. Whether he was reckless as to whether particular circumstances existed.	3. The presence of circumstances leading to the inference that a reasonable man in his situation would have realised that the circumstances might exist.

(2) Section 8 of the Criminal Justice Act 1967 and section 1 (2) of the Sexual Offences (Amendment) Act 1976 (which are superseded by this section) are hereby repealed.

(3) This section shall come into force at the expiration of a period of 2 months beginning with the date on which this Act is passed.

Notes

Clause 7

1. This clause widens and generalises section 8 of the Criminal Justice Act 1967. That section provides for a subjective, as against an objective, test in determining whether a defendant intended or foresaw the result of his actions. This clause applies the same test also to knowledge of facts or circumstances, and to recklessness as to results or as to facts or circumstances, thus giving effect to paragraph 98 of the report. The operation of this clause is not restricted to instruments made after the passing of the Bill.

2. *Subsection* (1) (*a*) provides that a court, considering in relation to a defendant any of the questions listed in column 1 of the Table in the subsection, shall not be bound in law to treat as conclusive of that question the factor listed in column 2 as appropriate to that question. The subsection goes on in paragraph (*b*), however, to make clear that in relation to each of those questions the appropriate factor is relevant and is to be taken into account with all the evidence.

3. The repeal by *subsection* (2) of the legislation mentioned there does not change the law, which is comprehensively covered by the new clause.

4. This clause comes into force 2 months after the Bill is passed (*subsection* (3))."

3. JUDICIAL APPROACHES

Lord Simon of Glaisdale in *D.P.P. for Northern Ireland* v. *Lynch* [1975] A.C. 653, 688, speaking in a wider context than the issue of duress, with which that case was primarily concerned, said—

"A principal difficulty in this branch of the law is the chaotic terminology, whether in judgments, academic writings or statutes. Will, volition, motive, purpose, object, view, intention, intent, specific intent or intention, wish, desire; necessity, coercion, compulsion, duress—such terms which do indeed overlap in certain contexts, seem frequently to be used interchangeably, without definition, and regardless that in some cases the legal usage is a term of art differing from the popular usage. As if this were not enough, Latin expressions which are themselves ambiguous, and often overlap more than one of the English terms, have been freely used—especially animus and (most question-begging of all) mens rea."

i. Common law mens rea

Usually, proof of either intention or recklessness will suffice for common law crimes. This has been held to be so for assault: "We see no reason in logic or law why a person who recklessly applies physical force to the person of another should be outside the criminal law of assault. In many cases the dividing line is barely distinguishable." (James L.J. in *R.* v. *Venna* [1975] 3 All E.R. 788, 794). The House of Lords in *D.P.P.* v. *Morgan*, *post*, p. 101 came to the same conclusion as regards rape. (This has since been put on a statutory footing by the Sexual Offences (Amendment) Act 1976, s. 1.)

Confusion has arisen where common law *mens rea* has been described as "intention." It is not always clear whether the word is used loosely, and therefore misleadingly, as a synonym for *mens rea*, or in a technical sense distinguishing it from recklessness. So, for example, in *R.* v. *Lemon* [1979] A.C. 617, 638 Lord Diplock, although dissenting on the question whether blasphemous libel required a mental element beyond the intention to publish said this:

"The fear that, by retaining as a necessary element of the mens rea of the offence the intention of the publisher to shock and arouse resentment among believing Christians, those who are morally blameworthy will be unjustly acquitted appears to me to manifest a judicial distrust of the jury's capability of appreciating the meaning which in English criminal law is ascribed to the expression 'intention' of the accused. When Stephen was writing in 1883, he did not then regard it as settled law that, where intention to produce a particular result was a necessary element of an offence, no distinction is to be drawn in law between the state of mind of one who does an act because he desires it to produce that particular result and the state of mind of one who, when he does the act, is aware that it is likely to produce that result but is prepared to take the risk that it may do so, in order to achieve some other purpose which provided his motive for doing what he did. It is by now well-settled law that both states of mind constitute 'intention' in the sense in which that expression is used in the definition of a crime whether at common law or in a statute. Any doubts on this matter were finally laid to rest by the decision of this House in *R.* v. *Hyam* [1975] A.C. 55."

Fuller extracts from *Hyam* are set out *post*, p. 374. For present purposes, two observations are appropriate. First, it is not so easy as Lord Diplock suggests to state quite what *Hyam* did decide as to the meaning of intention. The Criminal Law Revision Committee in its Report on Offences Against the Person had some difficulty in summarising the effect of the case:

"The effect of that decision is that it is murder if a person kills by doing an act—

(i) intending to kill; or
(ii) intending to cause serious bodily harm; or
(iii) knowing that death is a [highly] probable result of the act; or
(iv) knowing that serious bodily harm is a [highly] probable result of the act [provided that the act is 'aimed at' someone]

....

the word 'highly' is added in square brackets because that was how the judge directed the jury in *Hyam*, and the House of Lords' decision was that his direction was correct; but Lord Cross thought that the use of the word 'highly' was too favourable to the defendant, and Lords Diplock and Kilbrandon also thought that knowledge or ordinary probability or likelihood was enough. Secondly, these two Law Lords dissented, holding that it was necessary for the prosecution to prove that the defendant knew that the injury he foresaw was one likely to cause death." (§§ 17, 18, 14th Report, Cmnd. 7844 (1980).

The second observation is that, as the cases below illustrate, *Hyam* was concerned with the *mens rea* of murder, and not necessarily with the meaning of intention in other crimes.

ii. Intention

There are some crimes where recklessness is not enough and intention is required. In *R.* v. *Mohan* [1976] Q.B. 1, a case on attempt, the Court of Appeal was faced with the argument that in *Hyam*, above and *post*, p. 374, a case on murder, the House of Lords had given intention a meaning which was to be generally applicable in the criminal law. The court disposed of this argument, as follows:

"James L.J.: The first question we have to answer is: what is the meaning of 'intention' when that word is used to describe the mens rea in attempt? ...

In *R.* v. *Hyam* [1975] A.C. 55 [*post*, p. 374] Lord Hailsham of St. Marylebone

L.C., at p. 74, cited with approval the judicial interpretation of 'intention' or 'intent' applied by Asquith J., in *Cunliffe* v. *Goodman* [1950] 2 K.B. 237, p. 253: 'An "intention" to my mind connotes a state of affairs which the party intending; I will call him X—does more than merely contemplate: it connotes a state of affairs which, on the contrary, he decides so far as in him lies to bring about and which, in point of possibility, he has a reasonable prospect of being able to bring about by his own act of volition.'

If that interpretation of 'intent' is adopted as the meaning of *mens rea* in the offence of attempt, it is not wide enough to justify the direction in the present case. The direction, taken as a whole, can be supported as accurate only if the necessary *mens rea* includes not only specific intent, but also the state of mind of one who realises that, if his conduct continues, the likely consequence is the commission of the complete offence and who continues his conduct in that realisation, or the state of mind of one who, knowing that continuation of his conduct is likely to result in the commission of the complete offence, is reckless as to whether or not that is the result.

In *R.* v. *Hyam* (*supra*), . . . it was suggested in argument that the fact that a state of affairs is correctly foreseen as a highly probable consequence of what is done is the same thing as the fact that the state of affairs is intended. Lord Hailsham rejected that argument.

Viscount Dilhorne (at p. 82) said: 'While I do not think it necessary in this case to decide whether such knowledge establishes the necessary intent, for if [the trial judge] was wrong about that it is not such a misdirection as would warrant the quashing of the conviction as, even if it did not establish intent, it was correct in that such knowledge amounted to malice aforethought. I am inclined to the view that [the judge] was correct. A man may act with a number of intentions. If he does it deliberately and intentionally, knowing that when he does it it is highly probable that grievous bodily harm will result, I think most people would say, and be justified in saying, that whatever other intention he may have had as well he at least intended grievous bodily harm.'

Lord Diplock (at p. 86) said: 'This appeal raises two questions. The first is common to all crimes of this class. It is: what is the attitude of mind of the accused towards the particular evil consequence of his physical act that must be proved in order to constitute the offence.' By 'crimes of this class' his Lordship was referring to the class of crime 'in which the mental element or *mens rea* necessary to constitute the offence in English law includes the attitude of mind of the accused, not only towards his physical act itself which is the *actus reus* of the offence—as is the case with manslaughter—but also towards a particular evil consequence of that act.'

As to the first, and for present purposes the only relevant, question his Lordship said: 'I do not desire to say any more than that I agree with those of your Lordships who take the uncomplicated view that in crimes of this class no distinction is to be drawn in English law between the state of mind of one who does an act because he desires it to produce a particular evil consequence and the state of mind of one who does the act knowing full well that it is likely to produce that consequence, although it may not be the object he was seeking to achieve by doing the act. What is common to both these states of mind is a willingness to produce the particular evil consequence: and this in my view is the *mens rea* needed to satisfy a requirement whether imposed by statute or existing at common law, that in order to constitute the offence with which the accused is charged he must have acted with the intent to produce a particular evil consequence or, in the ancient phrase which still survives in crimes of homicide, with malice aforethought.'

The speech of Lord Cross of Chelsea (at p. 95) is, as we read it, confined to the consideration of the state of mind, malice aforethought, relevant to the charge of murder and the reasoning is not applied to any wider class of crime. His Lordship, for the purposes of the case, accepted as an accurate statement of the law of malice aforethought Article 223 of Stephen's *Digest of the Criminal Law* (original edition 1877) which includes both (a) intention to kill or to cause grievous bodily harm and (b) knowledge that the act which causes death will probably cause death or grievous bodily harm. The only criticism he thought could be directed at the summing-up was that by inserting 'highly' before 'probable' it was unduly favourable to the accused. There is no passage relevant for present purposes in the speech of Lord Kilbrandon whose conclusions were the same as those of Lord Diplock.

We do not find in the speeches of their lordships in the case of *R.* v. *Hyam* (*supra*) anything which binds us to hold that *mens rea* in the offence of attempt is proved by establishing beyond reasonable doubt that the accused knew or correctly foresaw that the consequences of his act unless interrupted would 'as a high degree of probability', or would be 'likely' to, be the commission of the complete offence. Nor do we find authority in that case for the proposition that a reckless state of mind is sufficient to constitute the *mens rea* in the offence of attempt. . . ."

See also the following case on wounding with intent to cause grievous bodily harm.

R. v. Belfon
(1976) 1 W.L.R. 741
Court of Appeal

> The appellant had pushed a girl to the ground. A group of people who came to her aid were set upon by the appellant and another man. The appellant slashed one of the group with an open razor causing severe injuries to his forehead and wounds to his chin and chest. He was convicted, *inter alia*, of wounding with intent to cause grievous bodily harm.

WIEN J. read the judgment of the court:

For over a century judges have almost daily directed juries as to the essential elements required to constitute the offence of wounding with intent to do grievous bodily harm contrary to section 18 of the Offences Against the Person Act 1861. There has never been any need to explain what "intent" means since the specific intent is defined in the section. Juries do not seem to have experienced any difficulty in understanding the word "intent" without further explanation and convictions under this section are frequent.

In the instant case the judge directed the jury in the following terms: "The law about intent is this . . . A person intends the consequences of his voluntary act in each of two quite separate cases; first when he desires those consequences and secondly when he foresees that they are likely to follow from his act but he commits the act recklessly irrespective of appreciating that those results will follow."

This appeal raises the question whether that direction with yet a further elaboration was correct. The elaboration was as follows: "Let us apply that particular general principle in the case of wounding. A man who in fact wounds another man is guilty of doing so with intent to cause him serious injury if either he wishes to cause him serious injury and that is therefore why he does what he does, or alternatively he foresees that serious injury is likely to result from his using whatever implement he does use in the way that he does and he nevertheless does that injury recklessly, notwithstanding his foresight that serious injury is likely to result. So what you have to ask yourselves when you have to decide what a defendant did in a particular case is this. Did he do it either intending in the sense of wishing that serious injuries should result or even if not that, did he at the time as a matter of fact foresee that serious injury was probably going to result and yet went on and did the act recklessly, ignoring his foresight that really serious injury was a likely consequence of what he was doing? If either of those matters be the case then he is guilty of the necessary intent but unless it is proved that one or other of those matters is true of the case then the necessary intent is lacking." ....

Prior to the case of *R.* v. *Hyam* [*post*, p. 374] one ventures to think that it would never have occurred to a judge to explain what "intent" meant when directing a jury in a case of wounding with intent. He would have told the jury that what has to be proved is (1) a wounding of a person concerned, (2) that the wounding was deliberate and without justification, that is that it was not by way of accident or self-defence, (3) that the wounding was committed with intent to do really serious bodily harm and (4) that the necessary intent must have been in the mind of the accused, that is the intent of a reasonable or sensible man is irrelevant, for the test is a subjective one, and not objective. Nothing more than this was ever called for except in certain cases where an explanation of "wounding" was desirable.

Why then did this learned judge depart from the usual practice? The Court can only assume that he has been influenced by certain opinions expressed by their Lordships in *Hyam* (*supra*). ... it must be emphasised that *Hyam's* case was concerned with the *mens rea* necessary to establish murder....

In cases of wounding with intent it has never been considered that recklessness was to be equated with the particular kind of harm that is intended in order to constitute an offence described in section 18 of the Act of 1861....

[His Lordship then discussed the meaning of 'maliciously' in section 18.]

One may now turn to the question of foreseeability—not in relation to section 20 of the Act of 1861 where, because no specific intent is required, the word "maliciously" of itself imports an awareness or the foreseeability that some minor harm might result, but in relation to section 18. Some comments by their Lordships in *Hyam's* case (*supra*) might give credence to the view that foreseeability of the risk of serious injury can indeed be equated with an intention to cause grievous bodily harm....

It may be anomalous that to establish the crime of murder it need be necessary only to show that the accused foresaw that his deliberate acts were likely to expose his victim to the risk of grievous bodily harm whereas to establish an offence under section 18 of the Act of 1861 it must be proved that there was an intent to cause grievous bodily harm. It is not the first time that this Court has been faced with an anomalous situation. Such a situation can arise where the offence charged is an attempt to commit a crime. To prove attempted murder nothing less than an intent to kill will do. To prove an attempt to commit any crime the prosecution has to prove a specific intent. It is not sufficient to establish that the accused knew or foresaw that the consequences of his act would be likely to result in the commission of the complete offence....

[His Lordship cited *Mohan* (*ante*, p. 63)].

Counsel for the Crown, in the instant case, derives support for his contention (though he does not seek it) from what was said by Lord Simon of Glaisdale in *Director of Public Prosecutions for Northern Ireland* v. *Lynch* [1975] A.C. 653, which concerned a defence of duress on a charge of murder by a person accused as a principal in the second degree. At p. 698 he said in reference to the second certified question, which in part dealt with willingness to participate in the crime of murder, "An example is wounding with intent to do grievous bodily harm. The *actus reus* is the wounding: and the prosecution must start by proving a corresponding *mens rea*—namely, that the accused foresaw the wounding as a likely consequence of his act. But this crime is defined in such a way that its *mens rea* goes beyond foresight of the *actus reus;* so that the prosecution must in addition prove that the accused foresaw that the victim would, as a result of the act, probably be wounded in such a way as to result in serious physical injury to him."

This Court attaches considerable weight to the opinion of Lord Simon. Nevertheless his remarks were *obiter*. They were expressed in a dissenting speech and so far as one can tell no argument was addressed to him, for it was not necessary to do so, as to whether one was entitled to enlarge on the intent necessary in the offence of wounding with intent to do grievous bodily harm. At any rate we do not find in that speech or in any of the speeches of their Lordships in *Hyam's* case (*supra*) anything which obliges us to hold that the "intent" in wounding with intent is proved by foresight that serious injury is likely to result from a deliberate act. There is certainly no authority that recklessness can constitute an intent to do grievous bodily harm. Adding the concept of recklessness to foresight not only does not assist but will inevitably confuse a jury. Foresight and recklessness are evidence from which intent may be inferred but they cannot be equated either separately or in conjunction with intent to do grievous bodily harm.

We consider that the directions given by the judge in this case were wrong in law. Had he refrained from elaborating on the meaning of intent he would have given a quite adequate direction. It is unnecessary in such a case as this to do anything different from what has been done for many years.

Appeal allowed

Note

The decision in *Allsop* (1976) 64 Cr. App. R. 29 suggests that the Court of Appeal has not been altogether consistent in rejecting the notion of constructive intent which the House of Lords adopted in *Hyam*. In construing the phrase "with intent to defraud" on a charge of conspiracy to defraud, the court approved the view of Lord Diplock in *Hyam* that no distinction is to be drawn between a person who desires to produce a particular consequence and one who knows his or her act was likely to produce that consequence ([1976] A.C. 55, 86). However, J.C. Smith in a comment in [1976] Crim. L.R. 738 wrote: "It is respectfully submitted that conspiracy requires an intent to defraud and the proposition of Lord Diplock in *Hyam* is too wide to be regarded as a satisfactory definition of intent. . . . It does not follow that if the above criticisms are right, the actual decision in the present case is wrong." The defendant would have been guilty without resort to the notion of constructive intent. What, then, is the meaning of "real" intent?

J. C. Smith, "Intent: A Reply" [1978] Crim. L.R. 14, at p. 21

"Most of the authorities in favour of real intention suggest that only desired consequences are intended. There is, however, an ambiguity about 'desired'. A man may desire result (a) and not desire result (b). If he knows he can only cause (a) by causing (b) as well and decides that he will cause (a), is (b) a desired consequence? Opinions might differ. It is thought that, whether or not (b) was desired, it ought to be regarded as intended; and this is the point of extending the definition of intention to consequences which are foreseen as certain. By this test, of course, *Ahlers* [1915] 1 K.B. 616 and *Steane* [1947] K.B. 997 did intend to assist the enemy. Sending the Germans home and reading the script *were* acts of assistance to the enemy; and the accused intended to do those acts. In this sort of case, the result is absolutely certain; if (a) happens, (b) happens as well. Similarly where the accused, having no desire to break a window, throws a stone at P whom he knows to be standing behind a window. In these cases there is no reason to qualify in any way the requirement of certainty; but there are other cases where it is theoretically possible for (a) to occur and (b) not to occur. This is the bomb-in-the-aircraft case. Only a miracle can save the crew, but miraculous escapes do occasionally occur. Yet death is not merely probable but 'a moral certainty.' The accused is not merely taking a risk of killing, even a serious risk; he is killing as surely as if he was shooting his victim through the head. Hence the introduction of the 'no substantial doubt' test.

The Law Commission . . . view is thus to some extent a compromise. . . . This is the position adopted in *Mohan*: the result need not be desired. On its face it might be thought that there is some degree of contradiction in the proposition of the court: how can one use all one's power to bring something about without desiring it? I have the best of reasons for believing that what the court had in mind is this: D has no desire to harm the policeman, P, in any way. He only wishes to escape his questions. He drives his car at him hoping he will get out of the way, which he does. But if, not having any desire to harm P but only to escape, he recognises that to harm him is the only way of escape and he drives at him intending to run him down, that is an attempt to harm him without the desire to do so.

This being so for attempts, it must also be so for statutory requirements of ulterior intent, such as that in section 18 since it would be unreasonable to suppose that the statutory requirement of intent is more rigorous than that in attempts.

It is submitted that this represents what the law is and what the law ought to be."

See *post*, p. 537 for a discussion of "conditional" intent.

iii. Knowledge

Gaumont British Distributors Ltd. v. Henry
[1939] 2 K.B. 717
King's Bench Division

G.B. was charged under section 1 (*a*) of the Dramatic and Musical Performers' Protection Act 1925, with knowingly making a record of a musical work without the consent in writing of the peformers. No relevant consent had been given, but G.B. had never thought about the question of consent. G.B. was convicted and appealed by way of case stated.

LORD HEWART C.J.: I am not suggesting for a moment that in a case like this the difficult topic of *mens rea* comes in. There is a mass of well known cases on the topic of *mens rea*. It is usual in such cases to refer in particular to *Sherras* v. *De Rutzen* [*post*, p. 130], and to *Mousell Brothers Ltd.* v. *London & North Western Ry.* [1917] 2 K.B. 836. But when one finds put up as a danger signal or a signpost at the very forefront of the first section of this statute the words "If any person knowingly" does certain things, it seems to me that discussions about *mens rea* are of something less than academic interest. The knowledge on the part of the alleged offender is described prominently as an essential ingredient of the offence. The other essential ingredient is that that which he does must be knowingly done without the consent in writing of the performers. The knowledge, which is part of the essence of the offence, extends to knowledge of the absence of consent on the part of the performers.

Taking that view of the true meaning of this section, we thought it right after the hearing on the former occasion to request the learned magistrate to communicate to us the answer to the plain question which was then submitted to him in writing. That question was: "Whether the appellants knew at the time of the making of the record that the consent in writing of the performers had not been obtained." The answer, which was given in writing and is now before me, was in these words: "The defendants never applied their minds to the question whether the consent in writing of the performers had or had not been given, because the responsible manager, Mr. Bromige, was ignorant of the requirements of the Act." ... In my opinion, the answer which the learned magistrate has written out shows that it would not be correct to say in this case that the appellants knowingly made a record without the consent in writing of the performers. The answer seems to be that they did not know that there was absence of consent; they did not apply their minds to the question whether it had or had not been given. It seems to be of the nature of an affirmative finding that there was an absence of consent. At any rate the learned magistrate manifestly refrains from finding that the appellants did know at the time of the making of the record that the consent in writing had not been obtained. On that question and that answer ... I think that the proper conclusion is that the finding is in favour of the appellants.

I desire to add emphatically that no colour can be obtained from this case, or from the argument, or from any opinion which is present to my mind, that the wholesome and fundamental principle *ignorantia juris neminem excusat* is in any degree or in any sense to be modified or departed from. ... I should be very sorry, directly or indirectly, even to appear to add any colour to the suggestion, if it were made—as I do not think it is—that in circumstances of this kind ignorance of the law might excuse. The way in which the topic of the appellants' knowledge came in was solely with reference to the words "knowingly makes any record without the consent in writing of the performers," and the contention was a contention of fact. According to a true view of the evidence of fact in this case it was incorrect to say that the appellants did knowingly without the consent in writing of the performers that which was done.

Appeal allowed

Question and Note

In *Gaumont British Distributors* v. *Henry*, what does Lord Hewart mean when he says "I am not suggesting for a moment that in a case like this the difficult topic of *mens rea* comes in?"

Degrees of Knowledge

In *Roper* v. *Taylor's Central Garages* [1951] 2 T.L.R. 284, Devlin J.: "There are, I think, three degrees of knowledge which it may be relevant to consider in cases of this kind. The first is actual knowledge, which the justices may find because they infer it from the nature of the act done, for no man can prove the state of another man's mind; and they may find it even if the defendant gives evidence to the contrary. They may say, 'We do not believe him; we think that this was his state of mind.' They may feel that the evidence falls short of that, if they do they have then to consider what might be described as knowledge of the second degree; whether the defendant was, as it has been called, shutting his eyes to an obvious means of knowledge. Various expressions have been used to describe that state of mind. I do not think it necessary to look further, certainly not in cases of this type, than the phrase which Lord Hewart C.J. used in a case under this section, *Evans* v. *Dell* (1937) 53 T.L.R. 310, where he said (at p. 313): '... the respondent deliberately refrained from making inquiries, the results of which he might not care to have.'

The third kind of knowledge is what is generally known in law as constructive knowledge: it is what is encompassed by the words 'ought to have known' in the phrase 'knew or ought to have known.' It does not mean actual knowledge at all; it means that the defendant had in effect the means of knowledge. When, therefore, the case of the prosecution is that the defendant failed to make what they think were reasonable inquiries it is, I think, incumbent on them to make it plain which of the two things they are saying. There is a vast distinction between a state of mind which consists of deliberately refraining from making inquiries the result of which the person does not care to have, and a state of mind which is merely neglecting to make such inquiries as a reasonable and prudent person would make. If that distinction is kept well in mind I think that justices will have less difficulty than this case appears to show they have had in determining what is the true position. The case of shutting the eyes is actual knowledge in the eyes of the law: the case of merely neglecting to make inquiries is not knowledge at all—it comes within the legal conception of constructive knowledge, a conception which, generally speaking, has no place in the criminal law."

However, something strange has happened to the meaning of "knowing or believing" goods to be stolen in the offence of handling stolen goods in section 22 (1) of the Theft Act 1968. James L.J. in *Griffiths* [1974] 60 Cr. App. Rep. 14, at p. 18:

"To direct the jury that the offence is committed if the defendant, suspecting that the goods were stolen, deliberately shut his eyes to the circumstances as an alternative to knowing or believing the goods were stolen is a misdirection. To direct the jury that, in common sense and in law, they may find that the defendant knew or believed the goods to be stolen because he deliberately closed his eyes to the circumstances is a perfectly proper direction."

See *post*, Chapter 12, for more extensive discussion of this offence, but note the confusion as to the effect of the handling cases on the word "knowingly" in other offences.

Law Com. No. 89

"§ 19: The concept of 'intention' which we have discussed in the preceding paragraphs is normally used in the context of the criminal law in respect of certain results. Some offences, however, involve no results, although all offences prescribe certain circumstances to be present before criminal liability can be established. The question which then arises is what mental state, if any, is required of the accused in relation to those circumstances, and further (which is the question particularly relevant to this report) how is such a mental state to be indicated. It would probably be generally agreed that the highest (in the sense of the most demanding) mental requirement in respect of circumstances is that the person concerned should 'know' or 'have knowledge of' those circumstances. But the meaning of 'knowledge' in relation to the prescribed circumstances of an offence has in law given rise to uncertainty, which has encouraged glosses on the meaning of 'knowledge' and sometimes the provision of alternatives to the requirement of knowledge involving some lesser degree of cognition. Thus, at common law and under section 33 of the Larceny Act 1916, it was an essential ingredient of the offence of receiving stolen goods that the accused received the goods 'knowing' them to have been stolen. In *R.* v. *White* (1859) 1 F. & F. 665 Bramwell B. told the jury that 'the knowledge . . . need not be such knowledge as would be acquired if the prisoner had actually seen the lead stolen; it is sufficient if you think the circumstances were such, accompanying the transaction, as to make the prisoner believe that it had been stolen.' The comparable 'handling' offence created by section 22 (1) of the Theft Act 1968 substituted 'knowing or believing' for 'knowing.' Cases under the 1968 Act have made it clear that 'knowing or believing' in effect means actually knowing or being convinced in one's mind that the property has been stolen. But, even if the mental state in respect of section 22 (1) of the Theft Act is now relatively clear, the question arises whether other offences, where the requirement is simply one of 'knowing' impose a stricter requirement than is demanded in an offence which is framed in terms of 'knowing *or believing*.'"

iv. Recklessness

Before *Caldwell*, below, there was a brief period of calm when the Court of Appeal endorsed the Law Commission's approach to recklessness: *R.* v. *Stephenson* [1979] Q.B. 695. Both cases concern criminal damage.

R. v. Caldwell
[1981] 1 All E.R. 961
House of Lords

In pursuit of a grievance which he thought he had against the proprietor of a hotel, the respondent set fire to the hotel. There were 10 guests living there at the time. The fire was discovered before any serious damage occurred. The appeal was mainly concerned with his defence of intoxication, as to which see *post*, p. 190, but the House took the opportunity to consider the meaning of recklessness in the Criminal Damage Act 1971.

LORD DIPLOCK: ... [The respondent] was indicted at the Central Criminal Court on two counts of arson under section 1 (1) and (2) respectively, of the Criminal Damage Act 1971. That section reads as follows:

"1.—(1) A person who without lawful excuse destroys or damages any property belonging to another intending to destroy or damage any such property or being reckless as to whether any such property would be destroyed or damaged shall be guilty of an offence.

(2) A person who without lawful excuse destroys or damages any property, whether belonging to himself or another....

(*a*) intending to destroy or damage any property or being reckless as to whether any property would be destroyed or damaged; and

(*b*) intending by the destruction or damage to endanger the life of another or being reckless as to whether the life of another would be thereby endangered;

shall be guilty of an offence.

(3) An offence committed under this section by destroying or damaging property by fire shall be charged as arson."

Count 1 contained the charge of the more serious offence under section 1 (2) which requires intent to endanger the life of another or recklessness as to whether the life of another would be endangered. To this count the respondent pleaded not guilty....

Count 2 contained the lesser offence under section 1 (1) to which the respondent pleaded guilty.

The recorder directed the jury that self-induced drunkenness was not a defence to count 1, and the jury convicted him on this count. ... [u]nder section 1 (2) (*b*) there are two alternative states of mind as respects endangering the life of another.... One is intention that a particular thing should happen in consequence of the *actus reus*, viz., that the life of another person should be endangered, (this was not relied on by the Crown in the instant case). The other is recklessness as to whether that particular thing should happen or not. The same dichotomy of *mentes reae*, intention and recklessness, is to be found throughout the section; in subsection (1) and paragraph (*a*) of subsection (2) as well as in paragraph (*b*); and "reckless" as descriptive of a state of mind must be given the same meaning in each of them.

My Lords, the Criminal Damage Act 1971 replaced almost in their entirety the many and detailed provisions of the Malicious Damage Act 1861. Its purpose, as stated in its long title was to *revise* the law of England and Wales as to offences of damage to property. As the brevity of the Act suggests, it must have been hoped that it would also simplify the law.

In the Act of 1861, the word consistently used to describe the *mens rea* that was a necessary element in the multifarious offences that the Act created was "maliciously"—a technical expression, not readily intelligible to juries, which became the subject of considerable judicial exegesis. This culminated in a judgment of the Court of Criminal Appeal in *R.* v. *Cunningham*, (*post*, p. 81) which approved, as an accurate statement of the law, what had been said by Professor Kenny in his *Outlines of Criminal Law* (1st Edn., 1902):

> "In any statutory definition of a crime, 'malice' must be taken . . . as requiring either (1) an actual intention to do the particular *kind* of harm that in fact was done; or (2) recklessness as to whether such harm should occur or not (*i.e.* the accused has foreseen that the particular kind of harm might be done and yet has gone on to take the risk of it)."

My Lords, in this passage Professor Kenny was engaged in defining for the benefit of students the meaning of "malice" as a term of art in criminal law. To do so he used ordinary English words in their popular meaning. Among the words he used was "recklessness", the noun derived from the adjective "reckless", of which the popular or dictionary meaning is: careless, regardless, or heedless, of the possible harmful consequences of one's acts. It presupposes that if thought were given to the matter by the doer before the act was done, it would have been apparent to him that there was a real risk of its having the relevant harmful consequences; but, granted this, recklessness covers a whole range of states of mind from failing to give any thought at all to whether or not there is any risk of those harmful consequences, to recognising the existence of the risk and nevertheless deciding to ignore it. Conscious of this imprecision in the popular meaning of recklessness as descriptive of a state of mind, Professor Kenny, in the passage quoted, was, as it seems to me, at pains to indicate by the words in brackets the particular species within the genus reckless states of mind, that constituted "malice" in criminal law. This parenthetical restriction on the natural meaning of recklessness was necessary to an explanation of the meaning of the adverb "maliciously" when used as a term of art in the description of an offence under the Malicious Damage Act 1861 (which was the matter in point in *R.* v. *Cunningham*); but it was not directed to and consequently has no bearing on the meaning of the adjective "reckless" in section 1 of the Criminal Damage Act 1971. To use it for that purpose can, in my view, only be misleading.

My Lords, the restricted meaning that the Court of Appeal in *R.* v. *Cunningham* had placed on the adverb "maliciously" in the Malicious Damage Act 1861 in cases where the prosecution did not rely upon an actual intention of the accused to cause the damage that was in fact done called for a meticulous analysis by the jury of the thoughts that passed through the mind of the accused at or before the time he did the act that caused the damage, in order to see on which side of a narrow dividing line they fell. If it had crossed his mind that there was a risk that someone's property might be damaged but, because his mind was affected by rage or excitement or confused by drink, he did not appreciate the seriousness of the risk or trusted that good luck would prevent its happening, this state of mind would amount to malice in the restricted meaning placed upon that term by the Court of Appeal; whereas if, for any of these reasons, he did not even trouble to give his mind to the question whether there was any risk of damaging the property, this state of mind would not suffice to make him guilty of an offence under the Malicious Damage Act 1861.

Neither state of mind seems to me to be less blameworthy than the other; but if the difference between the two constituted the distinction between what does and what does not in legal theory amount to a guilty state of mind for the purposes of a statutory offence of damage to property, it would not be a practicable distinction for use in a trial by jury. The only person who knows what the accused's mental processes were is the accused himself—and probably not even he can recall them accurately when the rage or excitement under which he acted has passed, or he has sobered up if he were under the influence of drink at the relevant time. If the accused gives evidence that because of his rage, excitement or drunkenness the risk of particular harmful consequences of his acts simply did not occur to him, a jury would find it hard to be satisfied beyond reasonable doubt that his true mental process was not that, but was the slightly different mental process required if one applies the restricted meaning of "being reckless as to whether" something would happen, adopted by the Court of Appeal in *R.* v. *Cunningham*.

My Lords, I can see no reason why Parliament when it decided to revise the law as to offences of damage to property should go out of its way to perpetuate fine and impracticable distinctions such as these, between one mental state and another. One would think that the sooner they were got rid of, the better.

When cases under section 1 (1) of the new Act, in which the prosecution's case was based upon the accused having been "reckless as to whether . . . property would be destroyed or damaged", first came before the Court of Appeal, the question as to the meaning of the expression "reckless" in the context of that subsection appears to have been treated as soluble simply by posing and answering what had by then, unfortunately, become an obsessive question among English lawyers. Is the test of recklessness "subjective" or "objective"? The first two reported cases, in both of which judgments were given off the cuff, are first *R.* v. *Briggs* [1977] 1 W.L.R. 605, *R.* v. *Parker (Daryl)* [1977] 1 W.L.R. 600. Both classified the test of recklessness as "subjective". This led the court in *Briggs* to say: "A man is reckless in the sense required when he carries out a deliberate act knowing that there is some risk of damage resulting from that act but nevertheless continues in the performance of that act." This leaves over the question whether the risk of damage may not be so slight that even the most prudent of men would feel justified in taking it, but it excludes that kind of recklessness that consists of acting without giving any thought at all to whether or not there is any risk of harmful consequences of one's act; even though the risk is great and would be obvious if any thought were given to the matter by the doer of the act. *Parker*, however, opened the door a chink by adding as an alternative to the actual knowledge of the accused that there is some risk of damage resulting from his act and his going on to take it, a mental state described as "closing his mind to the obvious fact" that there is such a risk.

R. v. *Stephenson* [1979] 1 Q.B. 695, the first case in which there was full argument, though only on one side, and a reserved judgment, slammed the door again upon any less restricted interpretation of "reckless" as to whether particular consequences will occur than that originally approved in *Briggs*. The appellant, a tramp, intending to pass the night in a hollow in the side of a haystack, had lit a fire to keep himself warm; as a result of this the stack itself caught fire. At his trial, he was not himself called as a witness but a psychiatrist gave evidence on his behalf that he was schizophrenic and might not have had the same ability to foresee or appreciate risk as a mentally normal person. The judge had given to the jury the direction on the meaning of reckless that had been approved in *Parker*. The argument for the appellant on the appeal was that this let in an objective test whereas the test should be entirely subjective. It was buttressed by copious citation from previous judgments in civil and criminal cases where the expression "reckless" or "recklessness" had been used by judges in various contexts. Counsel for the Crown expressed his agreement with the submissions for the appellant. The judgment of the court contains an analysis of a number of the cited cases, mainly in the field of civil law. These cases do not disclose a uniform judicial use of the terms; and as respects judicial statements made before the current vogue for classifying all tests of legal liability as either objective or subjective they are not easily assignable to one of those categories rather than the other. The court, however, reached its final conclusion by a different route. It made the assumption that although Parliament in replacing the Act of 1861 by the Act of 1971 had discarded the word "maliciously" as descriptive of the *mens rea* of the offences of which the *actus reus* is damaging property, in favour of the more explicit phrase "intending to destroy or damage any such property or being reckless as to whether any such property would be destroyed", it nevertheless intended the words to be interpreted in precisely the same sense as that in which the single adverb "maliciously" had been construed by Professor Kenny in the passage that received the subsequent approval of the Court of Appeal in *R.* v. *Cunningham*.

My Lords, I see no warrant for making any such assumption in an Act whose declared purpose is to revise the then existing law as to offences of damage to property, not to perpetuate it. "Reckless" as used in the new statutory definition of the *mens rea* of these offences is an ordinary English word. It had not by 1971 become a term of legal art with some more limited esoteric meaning than that which it bore in ordinary speech—a meaning which surely includes not only deciding to ignore a risk of harmful consequences resulting from one's acts that one has recognised as existing, but also failing to give any thought to whether or not there is any such risk in circumstances where, if any thought were given to the matter, it would be obvious that there was.

If one is attaching labels, the latter state of mind is neither more nor less "subjective" than the first. But the label solves nothing. It is a statement of the obvious; *mens rea* is, by definition, a state of mind of the accused himself at the time he did the physical act that constitutes the *actus reus* of the offence; it cannot be the mental state of some non-existent, hypothetical person.

Nevertheless, to decide whether someone has been "reckless" whether harmful consequences of a particular kind will result from his act, as distinguished from his actually intending such harmful consequences to follow, does call for some consideration of how the mind of the ordinary prudent individual would have reacted to a similar situation. If there were nothing in the circumstances that ought to have drawn the attention of an ordinary prudent individual to the possibility of that kind of harmful consequence, the accused would not be described as "reckless" in the natural meaning of that word for failing to address his mind to the possibility; nor, if the risk of the harmful consequences was so slight that the ordinary prudent individual upon due consideration of the risk would not be deterred from treating it as negligible, could the accused be described as "reckless" in its ordinary sense if, having considered the risk, he decided to ignore it. (In this connection the gravity of the possible harmful consequences would be an important factor. To endanger life must be one of the most grave). So to this extent, even if one ascribes to "reckless" only the restricted meaning, adopted by the Court of Appeal in *Stephenson* and *Briggs*, of foreseeing that a particular kind of harm might happen and yet going on to take the risk of it, it involves a test that would be described in part as "objective" in current legal jargon. Questions of criminal liability are seldom solved by simply asking whether the test is subjective or objective.

In my opinion, a person charged with an offence under section 1 (1) of the Criminal Damage Act 1971 is "reckless as to whether or not any property would be destroyed or damaged" if (1) he does an act which in fact creates an obvious risk that property will be destroyed or damaged and (2) when he does the act he either has not given any thought to the possibility of there being any such risk or has recognised that there was some risk involved and has nonetheless gone on to do it. That would be a proper direction to the jury; cases in the Court of Appeal which held otherwise should be regarded as overruled.

Where the charge is under section 1 (2) the question of the state of mind of the accused must be approached in stages, corresponding to paragraphs (*a*) and (*b*). The jury must be satisfied that what the accused did amounted to an offence under section 1 (1), either because he actually intended to destroy or damage the property or because he was reckless (in the sense that I have described) as to whether it might be destroyed or damaged. Only if they are so satisfied must the jury go on to consider whether the accused also either actually intended that the destruction or damage of the property should endanger someone's life or was reckless (in a similar sense) as to whether a human life might be endangered. . . .

[LORDS KEITH OF KINKEL and ROSKILL agreed with LORD DIPLOCK].

LORD EDMUND-DAVIES, (with whom LORD WILBERFORCE agreed): . . . The words "intention" and "recklessness" have increasingly displaced in statutory crimes the word "maliciously", which has frequently given rise to difficulty in interpretation. [His Lordship then cited the passage from *Cunningham*, quoted by Lord Diplock, *supra*].

My Lords, my noble and learned friend, Lord Diplock, somewhat dismissively describes Professor Kenny as having been "engaged in defining for the benefit of students the meaning of 'malice' as a term of art in criminal law", adding:

"To do so he used ordinary English words in their *popular* meaning. Among the words he used was 'recklessness', the noun derived from the adjective 'reckless', of which the popular or dictionary meaning is "careless, regardless, or heedless, of the possible harmful consequences of one's acts." It presupposes that *if* thought were given to the matter by the doer before the act was done, *it would have been apparent to him* that there was a real risk of its having the relevant harmful consequences. . . . This parenthetical restriction on the natural meaning of recklessness was necessary to an explanation of the adverb 'maliciously' when used as a term of art in the description of an offence under the Malicious Damage Act 1861 (which was the matter in point in *R.* v. *Cunningham*); but it was not directed to and consequently has no bearing on the meaning of the adjective 'reckless' in section 1 of the Criminal Damage Act 1971." (Emphasis added).

I have to say that I am in respectful, but profound, disagreement. The law in action compiles its own dictionary. In time, what was originally the common coinage of speech acquires a different value in the pocket of the lawyer than when in the layman's purse. Professor Kenny used lawyers' words in a lawyers' sense to express his distillation of an important part of the established law relating to *mens rea*, and he did so in a manner accurate not only in respect of the law as it stood in 1902 but also as it has been applied in countless cases ever since, both in the United Kingdom and in other countries where the common law prevails; see, for example in Western Australia, *Lederer* v. *Hutchins* [1961] W.A.R. 99, and, in the United States of America, Jethro Brown's "General Principles of Criminal Law", 2nd Edition, 1960, 115. And it is well known that the Criminal Damage Act 1971 was in the main the work of the Law Commission, who, in their Working Paper No. 31 (1970) defined recklessness by saying:

"A person is reckless if, (a) knowing that there is a risk that an event may result from his conduct or that a circumstance may exist, he takes that risk, and (b) it is unreasonable for him to take it, having regard to the degree and nature of the risk which he knows to be present."

It was surely with this contemporaneous definition and the much respected decision of *Cunningham* in mind that the draftsman proceeded to his task of drafting the Criminal Damage Act 1971.

It has therefore to be said that, unlike negligence, which has to be judged objectively, recklessness involves foresight of consequences, combined with an objective judgment of the reasonableness of the risk taken. And recklessness *in vacuo* is an incomprehensible notion. It *must* relate to foresight of risk of the particular kind relevant to the charge preferred, which, for the purpose of section 1 (2), is the risk of endangering life and nothing other than that.

So if a defendant says of a particular risk, "It never crossed my mind", a jury could not on those words alone properly convict him of recklessness simply because they considered that the risk *ought* to have crossed his mind, though his words might well lead to a finding of negligence. But a defendant's admission that he "closed his mind" to a particular risk could prove fatal, for "A person cannot, in any intelligible meaning of the words, "close his mind to a risk" unless he first realises that there is a risk; and if he realises that there is a risk, that is the end of the matter." (Glanville Williams, Textbook of Criminal Law, p. 79).

In the absence of exculpatory factors, the defendant's state of mind is therefore all-important where recklessness is an element in the offence charged, and section 8 of the Criminal Justice Act 1967 has laid down that:

> "A court or jury, in determining whether a person has committed an offence,—
> (*a*) shall not be bound in law to infer that he intended *or foresaw* a result of his actions by reason only of its being a natural and probable consequence of those actions; but
> (*b*) shall decide whether he did intend *or foresee* that result by reference to all the evidence, drawing such inferences from the evidence as appear proper in the circumstances."

My Lords, it is unnecessary to examine at length the proposition that ascertainment of the state of mind known as "recklessness" is a *subjective* exercise, for the task was expansively performed by Geoffrey Lane L.J. (as he then was) in *Stephenson* [1979] 1 Q.B. 695. And, indeed, that was the view expressed by the learned recorder herself in the instant case when, citing *Briggs* [1977] 1 All E.R. 475, at 477, she directed the jury at one stage in these terms:

> ". . . It may be the most useful function that I can perform if I read to you the most recent (I hope) definition of 'recklessness' . . . by a superior court . . .
> A man is reckless . . . when he carries out a deliberate act, knowing that there is some risk of damage resulting from that act, but "nevertheless continues in the performance of that act" . . . That came, in fact, in a case of straight arson and damage to property, but in this case you would probably feel that you had to add after the words to fit this section of the Act, "some risk of damage to life", . . . because that is what we are concerned with. I see both counsel nod assent to that. So, we can stay on common ground. . . ."

[The House dismissed the appeal on the grounds that self-induced intoxication was not a defence to section 2 (1) where the charge was based on recklessness, see *post*, p. 190.]

Appeal dismissed

Questions

1. Do you agree with Lord Diplock that to ask a jury to distinguish between a defendant who foresaw a risk and one who ought to have foreseen a risk calls for "meticulous analysis"?

2. Is the distinction referred to in question 1 above any more demanding than that required in order to determine whether a person formed the *mens rea* of murder?

3. Is Lord Diplock's attitude to subjective and objective liability similar to that of Fletcher, *ante*, p. 55?

4. If "reckless" is an "ordinary English word" (Lord Diplock) is it not strange that the majority in *Caldwell* "prevails not only over the weighty dissent of Lords Wilberforce and Edmund-Davies but also over the substantial body of judicial opinion in the cases of *Briggs, Stephenson* and other cases in the Court of Appeal and the Divisional Court." (Smith [1981] Crim. L.R. 393)? One possible answer to this question would be that "even 'ordinary' words (and especially abstract words) are variously understood—everyone may 'know what they mean' but, without knowing it, use them with different meanings." (Griew, "Consistency, Communication and Codification: Reflections on Two Mens Rea Words" in Glazebrook, pp. 57, 58.)

Note

J. C. Smith in his commentary on *Caldwell*, [1981] Crim. L.R. 393–394: "Parliament has had ample notice of, and has clearly approved of, or at least acquiesced in, the meaning attributed by law reform bodies to recklessness. The Eighth Report of the Criminal Law Revision Committee presented to Parliament in 1966 discussed it in connection with reckless deception. The Committee expressly rejected the objective (*pace* Lord Diplock) meaning attributed to the word under the Prevention of Fraud (Investments) Act 1958 and said 'In our opinion it is right that deception for the purpose of the offences under clause 12 [now s. 15 of the Theft Act 1968] should cover recklessness in the sense of not caring whether the statement is true or false (the kind of recklessness which counts for deception for the purposes of the civil law, as in *Derry* v. *Peek* (1889) 14 App. Cas. 337), but not mere carelessness.' The Law Commission Working Paper No. 23 of 1969 on Malicious Damage made the provisional proposals of the Law Commission crystal clear. Having reviewed the law as stated in *Cunningham*, ('recklessness in relation to [the act's] *foreseen* consequences') they said 'Our provisional proposals . . . are designed to adhere to this pattern.' The final report of the Law Commission on Criminal Damage, (Law Com. No. 29) expressly stated that they proposed to adopt *Cunningham*: 'We consider . . . that the same elements as are required at present should be retained, but that they should be expressed with greater simplicity and clarity:' (para. 44)—a passage at which the Law Commissioners must now be looking ruefully for it appears that they would have attained their object by sticking to the archaic 'maliciously.'

As Lord Edmund-Davies pointed out, the Law Commission Working Paper no. 31 on the Mental Element in Crime spelt out the meaning which their Working Party attributed to recklessness in the clearest possible terms in June 1970, before Parliament considered the Criminal Damage Bill. That has been confirmed by the Commission's final report on the Mental Element in Crime (Law Com. No. 89). The Criminal Law Revision Committee have expressly adopted the same meaning of recklessness in their Report on Offences against the Person (Cmnd. 7844, para. 11), presented to Parliament in 1980.

What has the majority to offer against this overwhelming evidence as to Parliament's actual intentions? Lord Diplock points out that the purpose of the Criminal Damage Act, as stated in its long title, was 'to *revise* the law' (his Lordship's italics) and he could 'see no reason why Parliament when it decided to revise the law . . . should go out of its way to perpetuate fine and impracticable distinctions. . . .' With all possible respect, this is a pathetically inadequate reason for ignoring the readily available evidence. The Criminal Damage Act made a massive revision of the law, apart from the mental element; almost the only aspect of the law it found to be satisfactory in substance though not in form. The Courts do not look at the Parliamentary debates (in theory, at least) and had they done so in the present case, they would have found no support for the majority opinion. Some doubts were expressed in the House of Commons about the meaning of recklessness and Mr. Mark Carlisle (H.C.Deb. Vol. 817, col. 1461) answered these by saying that, as he understood it, the word covered the offender who 'did not necessarily intend to cause the damage but could not care less whether he caused it or not'—a state of mind which certainly seems to require knowledge of the risk. In general, however, Parliament seems to have been content to accept the Report and the Bill drafted by the Law Commission (to which numerous flattering references were made). Beyond any doubt, the intention of the framers was correctly interpreted by *Briggs, Stephenson* and Lords Wilberforce and Edmund-Davies and is defeated by the decision of the majority.

. . . .

Lord Diplock describes these terms ['objective' and 'subjective'] as 'jargon' and both he and Lord Hailsham in *Lawrence* are critical of their use. The unnecessary use of jargon is certainly to be deplored and such a charge, coming from Lord Diplock, who has admitted to a reputation for 'gratuitous philological exhibitionism' [1968] 1 All E.R. at 108 and has coined such terms as 'synallagmatic contracts' and 'anticipatory secondary obligations' must be taken seriously. 'Objective' and 'subjective' by comparison are relatively simple, well-understood terms which are conveniently used to distinguish between conclusive presumptions as to a mental state and an actual mental state, and between standards of conduct and states of mind. Such distinctions have constantly to be made in expounding the criminal law and the present case does nothing to lessen their significance. It is feared that their continued use is something their Lordships will have to put up with. Indeed, after expressing his distaste, Lord Hailsham went on almost immediately to speak of 'objectively blameworthy' conduct."

An area which gives rise to problems is "reckless" driving in section 1 of the Road Traffic Act 1972 (as substituted by section 50 of the Criminal Law Act 1977). Here the "recklessness" is not related to consequences or circumstances but to conduct, and thus raises the question: "reckless" as to what?

R. v. Lawrence

[1981] 1 All E.R. 974

House of Lords

The facts appear in the speech of Lord Diplock.

LORD HAILSHAM delivered a speech in which he expressed agreement with Lord Diplock.

LORD DIPLOCK: On Good Friday, 13th April 1979, after night had fallen, the respondent ("the driver") was riding his motor cycle along an urban street in Lowestoft. The street was subject to a 30 m.p.h. speed limit and there was a good deal of other traffic using it at the time. The driver ran into and killed a pedestrian who was crossing the road to return from an off-licence shop to her car which was parked on the opposite side of the street. The driver was in due course tried upon indictment for the offence of causing her death by driving a motor vehicle on a road recklessly, contrary to section 1 of the Road Traffic Act 1972.

Apart from the very tragic consequences of this accident the case that the jury had to try was about as simple and straightforward as any case can be in which the charge is one of driving recklessly. The only question of fact that was in issue was the speed at which the driver was travelling immediately before the impact. The prosecution's case was that the motor cycle was being driven at between 60 and 80 m.p.h. and probably much nearer to the latter. The case for the defence was that the speed of the motor cycle was no more than 30 or, at most, 40 m.p.h. and probably nearer to the former.

All that the jury had to do was to make up their minds whether, upon that evidence, they were satisfied beyond reasonable doubt that the driver was in fact driving along this urban street, on which it was not disputed there was a good deal of other traffic, at a speed somewhere between 60 and 80 m.p.h. If they were so satisfied, even the defence did not suggest that any sensible jury could come to any other conclusion than that he was driving recklessly; whereas, if they thought that his own estimate of his speed at 30 to 40 m.p.h. might be right, they ought to have found him not guilty, for the prosecution had not relied upon any other aspect of his driving as constituting recklessness, apart from excessive speed. . . .

In the course of his summing-up the deputy circuit judge gave to the jury a direction as to what amounted in law to "driving recklessly". This direction the Court of Appeal described with justification, but also with the utmost sympathy, as confused. And so it was, because it sought to combine the very recent definition of "driving recklessly" in section 2 of the Road Traffic Act 1972 that had been given by Eveleigh L.J. in *R.* v. *Murphy* [1980] 1 Q.B. 434 ("the *Murphy* definition") with the definition of "reckless" in section 1 (1) of the Criminal Damage Act 1971 that had been given by Geoffrey Lane L.J. in *R.* v. *Stephenson* [1979] 1 Q.B. 695. This latter definition has been the subject of disapproval by this House in the immediately preceding appeal, *R.* v. *Caldwell* [*ante*, p. 71].

The jury too must have found the direction confusing for, after three and a half hours' retirement, they sought further elucidation from the judge. In substance he repeated to them the *Murphy* direction and, after a further short retirement, the jury, by a majority of eleven to one, brought in a verdict of guilty.

The *Murphy* direction is in the following terms:

> "A driver is guilty of driving recklessly if he deliberately disregards the obligation to drive with due care and attention or is indifferent as to whether or not he does so and thereby creates a risk of an accident which a driver driving with due care and attention would not create."

Whether the *Murphy* direction is correct or not is the subject of the third question of law involved in the instant case that the Court of Appeal, in giving leave to appeal, have certified as being of general public importance. The other two are

> "1. Is *mens rea* involved in the offence of driving recklessly? and
> 2. If yes, what is the mental element required?"

[His Lordship then explained the legislative history of sections 1, 2 and 3 of the Road Traffic Act 1972. Section 2 covers reckless driving and section 3 driving without due care and attention].

The context in which the word "reckless" appears in section 1 of the Criminal Damage Act 1971 differs in two respects from the context in which the word "recklessly" appears in sections 1 and 2 of the Road Traffic Act 1972, as now amended. In the Criminal Damage Act 1971 the *actus reus*, the physical act of destroying or damaging property belonging to another, is in itself a tort. It is not something that one does regularly as part of the ordinary routine of daily life, such as driving a car or a motor cycle. So there is something out of the ordinary to call the doer's attention to what he is doing and its possible consequences, which is absent in road traffic offences. The other difference in context is that in section 1 of the Criminal Damage Act 1971 the *mens rea* of the offences is defined as being reckless as to whether particular harmful consequences would occur, whereas in sections 1 and 2 of the Road Traffic Act 1972, as now amended, the possible harmful consequences of which the driver must be shown to have been heedless are left to be implied from the use of the word "recklessly" itself. In ordinary usage "recklessly" as descriptive of a physical act such as driving a motor vehicle which can be performed in a variety of different ways, some of them entailing danger and some of them not, refers not only to the state of mind of the doer of the act when he decides to do it but also qualifies the manner in which the act itself is performed. One does not speak of a person acting "recklessly", even though he has given no thought at all to the consequences of his act, unless the act is one that presents a real risk of harmful consequences which anyone acting with reasonable prudence would recognise and give heed to. So the *actus reus* of the offence under sections 1 and 2 is not simply driving a motor vehicle on a road, but driving it in a manner which in fact creates a real risk of harmful consequences resulting from it. Since driving in such a manner as to do no worse than create a risk of causing inconvenience or annoyance to other road users constitutes the lesser offence under section 3, the manner of driving that constitutes the *actus reus* of an offence under sections 1 and 2 must be worse than that; it must be such as to create a real risk of causing physical injury to someone else who happens to be using the road or damage to property more substantial than the kind of minor damage that may be caused by an error of judgment in the course of parking one's car.

The *Murphy* direction, as it seems to me, is defective in this respect before one comes to any question of *mens rea*. By referring to the duty to drive with "due care and attention" which is a direct quotation from section 3, it makes the standard of driving that must be maintained, in order to avoid the more serious offence of driving recklessly, the same as in the less serious offence under section 3 and thus perpetuates the very mischief which the 1977 amendments were intended to remedy. . . .

I turn now to the *mens rea*. My task is greatly simplified by what has already been said about the concept of recklessness in criminal law in *R.* v. *Caldwell*. Warning was there given against adopting the simplistic approach of treating all problems of criminal liability as soluble by classifying the test of liability as being either "subjective" or "objective". Recklessness on the part of the doer of an act does presuppose that there is something in the circumstances that would have drawn the attention of an ordinary prudent individual to the possibility that his act was capable of causing the kind of serious harmful consequences that the section which creates the offence was intended to prevent, and that the risk of those harmful consequences occurring was not so slight that an ordinary prudent individual would feel justified in treating them as negligible. It is only when this is so that the doer of the act is acting "recklessly" if before doing the act, he either fails to give any thought to the possibility of there being any such risk or, having recognised that there was such risk, he nevertheless goes on to do it.

In my view, an appropriate instruction to the jury on what is meant by driving recklessly would be that they must be satisfied of two things:

First, that the defendant was in fact driving the vehicle in such a manner as to create an obvious and serious risk of causing physical injury to some other person who might happen to be using the road or of doing substantial damage to property; and

Second, that in driving in that manner the defendant did so without having given any thought to the possibility of there being any such risk or, having recognised that there was some risk involved had nonetheless gone on to take it.

It is for the jury to decide whether the risk created by the manner in which the vehicle was being driven was both obvious and serious and, in deciding this, they may apply the standard of the ordinary prudent motorist as represented by themselves.

If satisfied that an obvious and serious risk was created by the manner of the defendant's driving, the jury are entitled to infer that he was in one or other of the states of mind required to constitute the offence and will probably do so; but regard must be given to any explanation he gives as to his state of mind which may displace the inference. . . .

Since the deputy circuit judge gave to the jury what was substantially the *Murphy* direction itself and also a somewhat confused version of it and both of these stated the law too unfavourably to the driver, this appeal must in my view be dismissed.

Appeal dismissed

LORD FRASER OF TULLYBELTON, LORD ROSKILL and LORD BRIDGE OF HAWICK all agreed with the speeches of LORD HAILSHAM and LORD DIPLOCK.

v. Maliciousness

R. v. Cunningham
[1957] 2 Q.B. 396
Court of Criminal Appeal

> C. stole a gas meter from the cellar of a house and in doing so fractured a gas pipe. Gas escaped, percolated through the cellar wall to the adjoining house, and entered a bedroom with the result that W., when she was asleep, inhaled a considerable quantity of the gas. C. was convicted of unlawfully and maliciously causing W. to take a noxious thing, so as thereby to endanger her life contrary to section 23 of the Offences Against the Person Act 1861. The judge directed the jury that "maliciously" meant "wickedly"—doing "something which he has no business to do and perfectly well knows it."

BYRNE J. read the judgment of the court:

The act of the appellant was clearly unlawful and therefore the real question for the jury was whether it was also malicious within the meaning of section 23 of the Offences Against the Person Act 1861.

Before this court Mr. Brodie has taken three points, all dependent upon the construction of that section. Section 23 provides: "Whosoever shall unlawfully and maliciously administer to or cause to be administered to or taken by any other person any poison or other destructive or noxious thing, so as thereby to endanger the life of such person, or so as thereby to inflict upon such person any grievous bodily harm, shall be guilty of felony. . . ."

Mr. Brodie argued, first, that mens rea of some kind is necessary. Secondly, that the nature of the mens rea required is that the appellant must intend to do the particular kind of harm that was done, or, alternatively, that he must foresee that that harm may occur yet nevertheless continue recklessly to do the act. Thirdly, that the judge misdirected the jury as to the meaning of the word "maliciously".

He cited the following cases: *R.* v. *Pembliton* [*post*, p. 122] *R.* v. *Latimer* [*post*, p. 124] and *R.* v. *Faulkner* (1877) 13 Cox C.C. 550. In reply, Mr. Snowden, on behalf of the Crown, cited *R.* v. *Martin* [*post*, p. 124].

We have considered those cases, and we have also considered, in the light of those cases, the following principle which was propounded by the late Professor C. S. Kenny in the first edition of his Outlines of Criminal Law published in 1902 and repeated in 1952: "In any statutory definition of a crime, malice must be taken not in the old vague sense of wickedness in general but as requiring either (1) An actual intention to do the particular kind of harm that in fact was done; or (2) recklessness as to whether such harm should occur or not (i.e., the accused has foreseen that the particular kind of harm might be done and yet has gone on to take the risk of it). It is neither limited to nor does it indeed require any ill will towards the person injured". The same principle is repeated by Mr. Turner in his 10th edition of Russell on Crime at p. 1592.

We think that this is an accurate statement of the law. It derives some support from the judgments of Lord Coleridge C.J. and Blackburn J. in *Pembliton's* case (1874) L.R. 2 C.C.R. 119. In our opinion the word "maliciously" in a statutory crime postulates foresight of consequence. . . .

With the utmost respect to the learned judge, we think it is incorrect to say that the word "malicious" in a statutory offence merely means wicked. We think the judge was, in effect, telling the jury that if they were satisfied that the appellant had acted wickedly—and he had clearly acted wickedly in stealing the gas meter and its contents—they ought to find that he had acted maliciously in causing the gas to be taken by Mrs. Wade so as thereby to endanger her life.

In our view it should have been left to the jury to decide whether, even if the appellant did not intend the injury to Mrs. Wade, he foresaw that the removal of the gas meter might cause injury to someone but nevertheless removed it. We are unable to say that a reasonable jury, properly directed as to the meaning of the word "maliciously" in the context of section 23, would without doubt have convicted.

In these circumstances this court has no alternative but to allow the appeal and quash the conviction.

Appeal allowed

Note

The meaning of "maliciously" was further explored in *R.* v. *Mowatt* [1968] 1 Q.B. 421; a case on section 20 of the Offences Against the Person Act (unlawfully and maliciously wounding or inflicting grievous bodily harm).

Diplock L.J., p. 426: "In the offence under section 20, . . . the word 'maliciously' does import upon the part of the person who unlawfully inflicts the wound or other grievous bodily harm an awareness that his act may have the consequence of causing some physical harm to some other person. That is what is meant by "the particular kind of harm" [in the quotation from Kenny in *Cunningham*, above]. It is quite unnecessary that the accused should have foreseen that his unlawful act might cause physical harm of the gravity described in the section, i.e., a wound or serious physical injury. It is enough that he should have foreseen that some physical harm to some person, albeit of a minor character, might result."

An intention to cause fear is not foresight of the same "kind of harm" and therefore not "malicious": *R.* v. *Sullivan* [1981] Crim. L.R. 46 (C.A.).

An important limitation was placed on the meaning of "maliciously" by the Court of Appeal in *Cato* (*ante*, p. 26). In considering whether *Cato* "maliciously" administered a noxious thing (*i.e.* the heroin) contrary to section 23 of the 1861 Act, Lord Widgery C.J. said [1976] 1 W.L.R. 110, at p. 120:

"No doubt the requirement of foresight is correct in the *Cunningham* type of case where the injury to the victim was done indirectly: done, as it was in that case, by the escape of gas making itself felt in a wholly different part of the house. No doubt if the injury to the victim is indirect, then the element of foresight arises and the element of foresight will be taken from the words of Byrne J. in the *Cunningham* case. But these problems do not arise when the act complained of is done directly to the person of the victim, as it was in this case. We think in this case where the act was entirely a direct one that the requirement of malice is satisfied if the syringe was deliberately inserted into the body of Farmer, as it undoubtedly was, and if the appellant at a time when he so inserted the syringe knew that the syringe contained a noxious substance. That is enough, we think, in this type of direct injury case to satisfy the requirement of maliciousness."

It can be argued that section 23 itself covers "direct" and "indirect" methods in using the words "whosoever shall unlawfully and maliciously *administer to* or *cause to be administered to* . . ." and that if "maliciously" qualifies the second phrase (indirect) it must also qualify the first (direct) (emphasis added).

Williams, T.C.L., p. 175: "*Cunningham* is well on the way to becoming so 'distinguished' that it never applies."

vi. Wilfulness

Arrowsmith v. Jenkins
[1963] 2 Q.B. 561
Divisional Court

The defendant addressed a public meeting on the highway and was convicted on an information alleging wilful obstruction of the highway, by standing on it and causing others to congregate.

LORD PARKER C.J.: The sole question here is whether the defendant has contravened section 121 (1) of the Highways Act of 1959. That section provides: "If a person, without lawful authority or excuse, in any way wilfully obstructs the free passage along a highway he shall be guilty of an offence and shall be liable in respect thereof to a fine not exceeding forty shillings."

I am quite satisfied that section 121 (1) of the Act of 1959, on its true construction, is providing that if a person, without lawful authority or excuse, intentionally as opposed to accidentally, that is, by an exercise of his or her free will, does something or omits to do something which will cause an obstruction or the continuance of an obstruction, he or she is guilty of an offence. Mr. Wigoder, for the defendant, has sought to argue that if a person—and I think that this is how he puts it—acts in the genuine belief that he or she has lawful authority to do what he or she is doing then, if an obstruction results, he or she cannot be said to have wilfully obstructed the free passage along a highway.

Quite frankly, I do not fully understand that submission. It is difficult, certainly, to apply in the present case. I imagine that it can be put in this way: that there must be some mens rea in the sense that a person will only be guilty if he knowingly does a wrongful act. I am quite satisfied that that consideration cannot possibly be imported into the words "wilfully obstructs" in section 121 (1) of the Act of 1959. If anybody, by an exercise of free will, does something which causes an obstruction, then an offence is committed. There is no doubt that the defendant did that in the present case.

Appeal dismissed

Cf. Eaton v. *Cobb* [1950] 1 All E.R. 1016.

Willmott v. Atack
[1977] 1 Q.B. 498
Divisional Court

P.C. Atack was trying to arrest a reluctant suspect. W., a friend of the suspect, twice intervened in order to persuade his friend to "go quietly." W. was convicted of wilfully obstructing a constable under section 51 (3) of the Police Act 1964.

Croom-Johnson J.: The actual wording of section 51 (3) might perhaps be read at this point:

> "Any person who resists or wilfully obstructs a constable in the execution of his duty, or a person assisting a constable in the execution of his duty, shall be guilty of an offence . . ."

That is so far as is material. The point which is taken is that the phrase "wilfully obstructs" means that it is not enough that there should be an intention merely to do something which happens to result in there being an obstruction, but that it is also necessary that it should import some form of hostility towards the police.

Obstruction has been considered in a great many cases and one has to approach it so far as its definition is concerned in what is now regarded and has been adopted in this court as the correct test, which was laid down by Lord Goddard C.J. in *Hinchliffe* v. *Sheldon* [1955] 1 W.L.R. 1207, where he said, at p. 1210:

> "Obstructing, for the present purpose, means making it more difficult for the police to carry out their duties. It is obvious that the defendant here was detaining the police by giving a warning; he was making it more difficult for the police to get entry into the premises, and the justices were entitled to find as they did, and therefore the appeal is dismissed."

That phrase, of making it more difficult for the police to discharge their duties, was adopted in this court in *Rice* v. *Connolly* [1966] 2 Q.B. 414, where Lord Parker C.J. said, at p. 419:

> "To carry the matter a little further, it is in my view clear that 'obstruct' under section 51 (3) of the Police Act 1964 is the doing of any act which makes it more difficult for the police to carry out their duty. That description of obstructing I take from *Hinchliffe* v. *Sheldon*."

I would adopt it in the present case.

The question is then: is it necessary for there to have been an intention for the acts of the appellant to have been to make it more difficult for the police to carry out their duties rather than, as appears to have been found by the Crown Court here, an intention on his part to make it more easy for the police to carry out their duties? If there was no hostility so far the intervention by the appellant was concerned, and indeed there appears to be a clear finding of fact as to what the intention of the appellant was on each of the occasions when he did interfere, what is the answer to the question. "Should there be an intention not merely to do the act but also that the act should be one of hindering the police rather than helping them?" One turns at this point to *Betts* v. *Stevens* [1910] 1 K.B. 1, which was a case arising out of the warnings given once upon a time by AA patrolmen to those who were exceeding the speed limit of the existence of a nearby police trap. Darling J., dealing with the question of intention, said at p. 8:

> "The gist of the offence to my mind lies in the intention with which the thing is done. In my judgment in *Bastable* v. *Little* [1907] 1 K.B. 59, I used these words: 'In my opinion it is quite easy to distinguish the cases where a warning is given with the object of preventing the commission of a crime from the cases in which the crime is being committed and the warning given in order that the commission of the crime may be suspended while there is danger of detection.' I desire to repeat those words. Here I think it is perfectly plain upon the facts found by the magistrates in this case that the object of Betts' intervention was that the offence which was being committed should be suspended or desisted from merely whilst there was danger of the police detecting it and taking evidence of it, and that therefore he was obstructing the police in their duty to collect evidence of an offence which had been committed and was being permitted. [Then comes an important passage:] He did that wilfully in order to obstruct them in their duty, and not in order to assist them in the performance of their duty nor in order to prevent a motorist upon the road from committing an offence."

The point is clearly taken by Darling J. in that case.

It is suggested that if any other construction than the one which the appellant is urging were placed on the words 'wilfully obstructs' in the subsection, the result would be that any well-meaning bystander who saw the police, for example, having difficulty making an arrest and went to try and help them, would find, if he should unfortunately be the unwitting cause of the criminal escaping through his intervention, that he had himself committed a criminal offence. When one looks at the whole context of s. 51, dealing as it does with assaults on constables in sub-s. (1) and concluding in sub-s. (3) with resistance and wilful obstruction in the execution of the duty, I am of the view that the interpretation of this subsection for which the appellant contends is the right one. It fits the words 'wilfully obstructs' in the context of the subsection, and in my view there must be something in the nature of a criminal intent of the kind which means that it is done with the idea of some form of hostility to the police with the intention of seeing that what is done is to obstruct, and that it is not enough merely to show that he intended to do what he did and that it did, in fact, have the result of the police being obstructed.

That is my view on the question of law which has been left for the court to consider. What is now to happen to this appeal? The court at Croydon in respect of both of these charges applied a view of the law which, in my view, is the wrong one. Whereas I would say that it is not fatal to a conviction for wilful obstruction in respect of the first interference that there should have been an acquittal for assault on the same occasion, yet having regard to the finding of the facts as to the appellant's intentions which have been made in para. 10 of the case, the Crown Court applied the wrong test on the charge of obstruction and accordingly I would be in favour of quashing this conviction.

MAY J.: I agree. The word 'wilfully' has been inconsistently interpreted in various Acts which define criminal offences. In some cases it has been held to import a requirement of mens rea. In other Acts it has not. The question in the present case is whether in the relevant section of the Police Act 1964 mens rea is imported by the use of the term 'wilfully' or not.

I agree with Croom-Johnson J. that when one looks at the judgment of Darling J. in the earlier case of *Betts* v. *Stevens* [1910] 1 K.B. 1, where he said: "The gist of the offence to my mind lies in the intention with which the thing is done", it is clear that 'wilfully' in this particular Act does import a requirement of mens rea. Taking that view of the proper construction of the Act, and for the reasons on the facts given by Croom-Johnson J. in his judgment, I agree that this appeal should be allowed.

[Lord Widgery C.J. concurred].

Conviction quashed

For discussion of the word "wilfully" in relation to mistake, see *post*, p. 101.

Questions

1. Is the word "wilfully" in section 121 (1) of the Highways Act 1959 redundant? *cf. Lewis* v. *Dickinson* [1976] Crim. L.R. 442.

2. Was the issue for the court in *Wilmott* v. *Atack* simply, as May J. implies, a choice between either importing *mens rea* into the offence or not at all? For further discussion, see Ross "Two Cases on Obstructing a Constable" [1977] Crim. L.R. 187. For the relevance of knowing whether the person is a police officer, see *post*, p. 101. As the case of *Sheppard*, below, illustrates, the courts have also struggled in their search for an appropriate interpretation of "wilful" in the context of "wilful neglect" under the Children and Young Persons Act 1933.

R. v. Sheppard
[1980] 3 All E.R. 899
House of Lords

The youngest child of Mr. and Mrs. S. died at the age of 16 months from malnutrition and hypothermia. Three appointments to see a paediatrician had been made by the Health Visitor but the appellants had failed to attend. They were convicted of causing cruelty by wilful neglect under section 1 of the Children and Young Persons Act 1933. The Court of Appeal felt bound by authority to uphold the direction of the trial judge that no element of foresight of harm was necessary for the offence, but granted leave to appeal to the House of Lords.

Lord Diplock: My Lords, the appellants ('the parents') were convicted in the Crown Court at Northampton of an offence under s. 1 (1) of the Children and Young Persons Act 1933 of wilfully neglecting their infant child, Martin, between 1st July 1978 and 29th January 1979 in a manner likely to cause him unnecessary suffering or injury to health.

The child, who had been a slow developer, died, at the age of 16 months, on 28th January 1979 of hypothermia associated with malnutrition, a condition which increased the susceptibility of infants to hypothermia. If Martin had received timely medical attention his life might well have been saved. For five days or more before his death he had probably suffered from gastroenteritis which had caused him to vomit up and so fail to ingest the food that had been offered to him; but the details of such symptoms of serious illness as were apparent during the period before his death do not affect the question which falls to be decided by your Lordships in this appeal and is a question of law alone.

The gravamen of the charge against the parents was that they had failed to provide Martin with adequate medical aid on several occasions during the seven months to which the charge related and, in particular, during the week immediately preceding his death. In the light of the trial judge's instructions given to the jury as to the law applicable to the offence charged, it can safely be inferred from the verdicts of guilty that the jury found (1) that injury to Martin's health had in fact been caused by the failure by each of the parents to have him examined by a doctor in the period prior to his death and (2) that any reasonable parents i.e. parents endowed with ordinary intelligence and not indifferent to the welfare of their child, would have recognised from the manifest symptoms of serious illness in Martin during that period that a failure to have him examined by a doctor might well result in unnecessary suffering or injury to his health.

The parents, a young couple aged 20 and 22 respectively, occupied poor accommodation, particularly as respects heating, where the family, which included another (older) child, subsisted on a meagre income. They would appear, on the evidence, to have been of low intelligence. Their real defence, if it were capable of amounting to a defence in law, was that they did not realise that the child was ill enough to need a doctor; they had observed his loss of appetite and failure to keep down his food, but had genuinely thought that this was due to some passing minor upset to which babies are prone, from which they recover naturally without medical aid and which medical treatment can do nothing to alleviate or to hasten recovery.

We do not know whether the jury would have thought that this explanation of the parents' failure to have Martin examined by a doctor might be true. In his instructions the judge had told the jury that to constitute the statutory offence with which the parents were charged it was unnecessary for the Crown to prove that at the time when it was alleged the parents should have had the child seen by a doctor either they in fact knew that their failure to do so involved a risk of causing him unnecessary suffering or injury to health or they did not care whether this was so or not. . . .

The Court of Appeal, regarding themselves as bound by the same line of authority, felt compelled to dismiss the parents' appeal. . . . . . but certified as the point of law of general public importance involved in their decision to dismiss the appeal:

> "What is the proper direction to be given to a jury on a charge of wilful neglect of a child under s. 1 of the Children and Young Persons Act 1933 as to what constitutes the necessary mens rea of the offence?"

The relevant provisions of s. 1 are in the following terms:

'(1) If any person who has attained the age of sixteen years and has the custody, charge, or care of any child or young person under that age, wilfully assaults, ill-treats, neglects, abandons, or exposes him, or causes or procures him to be assaulted, ill-treated, neglected, abandoned, or exposed, in a manner likely to cause him unnecessary suffering or injury to health (including injury to or loss of sight, or hearing, or limb, or organ of the body, and any mental derangement), that person shall be guilty of a misdemeanour, and shall be liable—(a) on conviction on indictment, to a fine, or alternatively, or in addition thereto, to imprisonment for any term not exceeding two years. . . .

(2) For the purposes of this section—(a) a parent or other person legally liable to maintain a child or young person shall be deemed to have neglected him in a manner likely to cause injury to his health if he has failed to provide adequate food, clothing, medical aid or lodging for him, or if, having been unable otherwise to provide such food, clothing, medical aid or lodging, he has failed to take steps to procure it to be provided under enactments applicable in that behalf. . . .'

A provision in the same terms as s. 1 (1) has been on the statute book since the Prevention of Cruelty to, and Protection of, Children Act 1889.

Section 1 (2) (a) on the other hand has its legislative origin in s. 32 of the Poor Law Amendment Act 1868. This made it a summary offence for a parent to 'wilfully neglect to provide adequate Food, Clothing, Medical Aid or Lodging for his Child . . . whereby the Health of such Child shall have been or shall be likely to be seriously injured.' It was the only relevant provision that was in force when *R.* v. *Downes* (1875) 1 Q.B.D. 25 was decided. It was repealed by the Prevention of Cruelty to, and Protection of, Children Act 1889 and for nineteen years, which covered the date when *R.* v. *Senior* [1899] 1 Q.B. 283 was decided, there was no corresponding provision on the statute book until its reappearance in its present form but without the adverb 'seriously' as a 'deeming' provision in the Children Act 1908.

My Lords, the language in which the relevant provisions of the 1933 Act are drafted consists of ordinary words in common use in the English language. If I were to approach the question of their construction untrammelled (as the House is) by authority I should have little hesitation in saying that where the charge is one of wilfully neglecting to provide a child with adequate medical aid, which in appropriate cases will include precautionary medical examination, the prosecution must prove (1) that the child did in fact need medical aid at the time at which the parent is charged with having failed to provide it and (2) either that the parent was aware at that time that the child's health might be at risk if it were not provided with medical aid or that the parent's unawareness of this fact was due to his not caring whether the child's health were at risk or not.

In view of the previous authorities, however, which reach a different conclusion, it becomes necessary to analyse more closely the wording and structure of s. 1 (1) and (2) (a). . . .

The presence of the adverb 'wilfully' qualifying all five verbs, 'assaults, ill-treats, neglects, abandons, or exposes', makes it clear that any offence under s. 1 requires *mens rea*, a state of mind on the part of the offender directed to the particular act or failure to act that constitutes the *actus reus* and warrants the description 'wilful'. The other four verbs refer to positive acts, 'neglect' refers to failure to act, and the judicial explanation of the state of mind denoted by the statutory expression 'wilfully' in relation to the doing of a positive act is not necessarily wholly apt in relation to a failure to act at all. The instant case is in the latter category, so I will confine myself to considering what is meant by wilfully neglecting a child in a manner likely to cause him unnecessary suffering or injury to health. . . .

The *actus reus* of the offence with which the accused were charged in the instant case does not involve construing the verb 'neglect' for the offence fell within the deeming provision; and the only question as respects the *actus reus* was: did the parents fail to provide for Martin in the period before his death medical aid that was in fact adequate in view of his actual state of health at the relevant time? This, as it seems to me, is a pure question of objective fact to be determined in the light of what has become known *by the date of the trial* to have been the child's actual state of health at the relevant time. It does not depend on whether a reasonably careful parent, with knowledge of those facts only which such a parent might reasonably be expected to observe for himself, would have thought it prudent to have recourse to medical aid. . . . If failure to use the hypothetical powers of observation, ratiocination and foresight of consequences [of the reasonable man] is to constitute an ingredient of a criminal offence it must surely form part not of the *actus reus* but of the *mens rea*.

It does not, however, seem to me that the concept of the reasonable parent . . . has any part to play in the *mens rea* of an offence in which the description of the *mens rea* is contained in the single adverb 'wilfully'. In the context of doing a child a positive act (assault, ill-treat, abandon or expose) that is likely to have specified consequences (to cause him unnecessary suffering or injury to health), 'wilfully', which must describe the state of mind of the actual doer of the act, may be capable of bearing the narrow meaning that the wilfulness required extends only to the doing of the physical act itself which in fact results in the consequences described, even though the doer thought that it would not and would not have acted as he did had he foreseen a risk that those consequences might follow. Although this is a possible meaning of 'wilfully', it is not the natural meaning even in relation to positive acts defined by reference to the consequences to which they are likely to give rise; and, in the context of the section, if this is all the adverb 'wilfully' meant it would be otiose. Section 1 (1) would have the same effect if it were omitted; for even in absolute offences (unless vicarious liability is involved) the physical act relied on as constituting the offence must be wilful in the limited sense, for which the synonym in the field of criminal liability that has now become the common term of legal art is 'voluntary'.

So much for 'wilfully' in the context of a positive act. To 'neglect' a child is to omit to act, to fail to provide adequately for . . . its physical needs. . . . For reasons already given the use of the verb 'neglect' cannot, in my view, of itself import into the criminal law the civil law concept of negligence. The *actus reus* in a case of wilful neglect is simply a failure, for whatever reason, to provide the child whenever it in fact needs medical aid with the medical aid it needs. Such a failure as it seems to me could not be properly described as 'wilful' unless the parent *either* (1) had directed his mind to the question whether there was some risk (though it might fall far short of a probability) that the child's health might suffer unless he were examined by a doctor and provided with such curative treatment as the examination might reveal as necessary, and had made a conscious decision, for whatever reason, to refrain from arranging for such medical examination, *or* (2) had so refrained because he did not care whether the child might be in need of medical treatment or not.

As regards the second state of mind, this imports the concept of recklessness which is a common concept in *mens rea* in criminal law. It is not to be confused with negligence in the civil law of tort (see *Andrews* v. *Director of Public Prosecutions* [1937] A.C. 576 at 582–583). In speaking of the first state of mind I have referred to the parent's knowledge of the existence of some risk of injury to health rather than of probability. The section speaks of an act or omission that is 'likely' to cause unnecessary suffering or injury to health. This word is imprecise. It is capable of covering a whole range of possibilities from 'it's on the cards' to 'it's more probable than not'; but, having regard to the ordinary parent's lack of skill in diagnosis and to the very serious consequences which may result from failure to provide a child with timely medical attention, it should in my view be understood as excluding only what would fairly be described as highly unlikely.

I turn now to the authorities. [His Lordship referred to *R.* v. *Downes* (1875) 1 Q.B.D. 25].

To the judgment of Lord Russell C.J. in *R.* v. *Senior* [1899] 1 Q.B. 283, may be ascribed the origin of the construction of s. 1 (1) of the Children and Young Persons Act 1933 that has since been followed. This case also was one of failure by a member of the sect of Peculiar People to provide medical attention for his infant child. In considering this judgment it is important to remember (1) that the section of the 1894 Act that Lord Russell C.J. was construing did not contain the deeming provisions that are to be found in s. 1 (2) (a) of the 1933 Act and (2) that the parent knew that the child's physical suffering might be alleviated by medical treatment but had deliberately refrained from having recourse to it because he thought to do so would be sinful as showing unwillingness to accept God's will in relation to the child.

So here there was not any question of the accused parent being unaware that risk to the child's health might be involved in his failure to provide it with medical aid. He deliberately refrained from having recourse to medical aid with his eyes open to the possible consequences to the child's physical health. He broke the law because he sincerely believed that to comply with its command would be sinful and would be against the interests of the child's spiritual welfare. In an extempore judgment directed only to a deliberate breach of the law on conscientious grounds, it is not surprising that Lord Russell C.J. felt able to deal with the construction of the statute shortly. He said ([1899] 1 Q.B. 283 at 290–291):

> "'Wilfully' means that the act is done deliberately and intentionally, not by accident or inadvertence, but so that the mind of the person who does the act goes with it. Neglect is the want of reasonable care—that is, the omission of such steps as a reasonable parent would take, such as are usually taken in the ordinary experience of mankind. . . ."

My Lords, there was at that time no specific reference in the statute to the provisions of adequate food, clothing, medical aid or lodging. The word 'neglects' was quite general, qualified only by the requirement that it must be in such a manner as to be likely to cause the child unnecessary suffering or injury to health. One cannot quarrel with Lord Russell C.J.'s statement that 'neglect is want of reasonable care' if all that that means is that a reasonable parent who was mindful of the physical welfare of his child and *possessed of knowledge of all the relevant facts* would have taken steps that the accused omitted to take to avoid the risk of unnecessary suffering by the child or injury to his health. The danger of the statement is that it invites confusion between, on the one hand, neglect and, on the other hand, negligence, which calls for consideration not of what steps should have been taken for that purpose in the light of the facts as they actually were but of what steps would have been appropriate in the light of those facts only which the accused parent either knew at the time of his omission to take them or would have ascertained if he had been as mindful of the welfare of his child as a reasonable parent would have been.

Lord Russell C.J.'s brief explanation of the meaning of 'wilfully' is confined to positive physical acts. In relation to these he equiparates wilful acts with acts that would now be described as 'voluntary'. I do not myself think that this was right even in relation to positive physical acts of which the statutory definition included the characteristic that they were likely to have certain consequences; but its meaning in relation to positive acts is clear. I find its meaning obscure, however, in relation to a failure to do a physical act where the failure is not deliberate or intentional in the sense that consideration had been given whether or not to do it and a conscious choice made not to do it. To speak of the mind going with the act is inappropriate to omissions, but the contrast drawn between 'deliberately and intentionally' and 'by inadvertence' is at least susceptible of the meaning that if the accused has not addressed his mind to the question whether or not to do the physical act he is accused of omitting to do his failure to do the act is not to be treated as 'wilful'.

R. v. *Senior*, however, appears to have been treated as having decided that if the child did in fact need medical treatment it did not matter whether the accused parent actually knew or ought to have known that medical treatment was needed; he was nonetheless guilty of the offence of wilfully neglecting the child if all that he knew was that the child had not been seen by a doctor. This appears from the judgment of the Court of Appeal in *R.* v. *Lowe* [1973] Q.B. 702 at 707. So *R.* v. *Senior* has been regarded as deciding that the offence under s. 1 (1) of the 1933 Act is an absolute offence.

My Lords, I have already said why I do not think that *R.* v. *Senior* did so decide, ...

[W]hat your Lordships are faced with is a consistent practice of the courts, extending over many years without any reported exceptions, of treating *R.* v. *Senior* as if it were a binding authority for the proposition that the statutory offence of wilfully neglecting a child by failing to provide him with adequate medical aid is an absolute offence.

In many fields of law I should hesitate long before recommending this House to overturn a long-standing judicial acceptance of a particular meaning for a statutory provision. *Communis error facit lex* is often a good maxim in promoting legal certainty in matters in which people arrange their affairs in reliance on the accepted meaning of a law. But three reasons persuade me not to apply the maxim in the instant case. The climate of both parliamentary and judicial opinion has been growing less favourable to the recognition of absolute offences over the last few decades, a trend to which s. 1 of the Homicide Act 1957 and s. 8 of the Criminal Justice Act 1967 bear witness in the case of Parliament, and in the case of the judiciary is illustrated by the speeches in this House in *Sweet* v. *Parsley* [*post,* p. 137]. Secondly, the Court of Appeal in the instant case has expressed its own feeling of unease about the present state of the authorities by which it regards itself as bound and has granted leave to appeal in order that those authorities may be reviewed by your Lordship's House. Thirdly, and most importantly, the common error, as I believe it to have been, has operated to the disadvantage of the accused and to correct it will spare from criminal conviction those only who are free from any moral guilt.

To give to s. 1 (1) of the 1933 Act the meaning which I suggest it bears would not encourage parents to neglect their children nor would it reduce the deterrent to child neglect provided by the section. It would afford no defence to parents who do not bother to observe their children's health or, having done so, do not care whether their children are receiving the medical examination and treatment that they need or not; it would involve the acquittal of those parents only who through ignorance or lack of intelligence are genuinely unaware that their child's health may be at risk if it is not examined by a doctor to see if it needs medical treatment. And, in view of the abhorrence which magistrates and juries feel for cruelty to helpless children, I have every confidence that they would not readily be hoodwinked by false claims by parents that it did not occur to them that an evidently sick child might need medical care.

In the instant case it seems likely that on the evidence of the jury, if given the direction which I have suggested as correct, would have convicted one or both of the accused; but I do not think it possible to say with certainty that they would. It follows that in my opinion these appeals must be allowed and that the certified question should be answered: "The proper direction to be given to a jury on a charge of wilful neglect of a child under s. 1 of the Children and Young Persons Act 1933 by failing to provide adequate medical aid is that the jury must be satisfied (1) that the child did in fact need medical aid at the time at which the parent is charged with failing to provide it (the *actus reus*) and (2) either that the parent was aware at that time that the child's health might be at risk if it was not provided with medical aid or that the parent's unawareness of this fact was due to his not caring whether his child's health was at risk or not (the *mens rea*).

LORD EDMUND-DAVIES: . . . .

R. v. *Senior* [1899] 1 Q.B. 283 was the starting point of a long series of cases culminating in the Court of Appeal judgment in *R.* v. *Lowe* [1973] Q.B. 702 that, in the words of Phillimore L.J.:

> "It did not matter what [the father of the deceased child] ought to have realised as the possible consequences of his failure to call a doctor—the sole question was whether his failure to do so was deliberate and thereby occasioned the results referred to in [s. 1 of the 1933 Act]."

By attaching no importance to the mental ingredient of wilfulness, *R.* v. *Lowe* and all similar decisions must, in my respectful judgment, be regarded as wrongly decided....

The justice (and, with respect, the common sense) of the matter is surely that, as Professor Glanville Williams has put it in his Textbook of Criminal Law (1978, p. 88):

> "We do not run to a doctor whenever a child is a little unwell. We invoke medical aid only when we think that a doctor is reasonably necessary and may do some good. The requirement of wilfulness means, or should mean, that a parent who omits to call in the doctor to his child is not guilty of the offence if he does not know that the child needs this assistance."

But to that must be added that a parent reckless about the state of his child's health, not caring whether or not he is at risk, cannot be heard to say that he never gave the matter a thought and was therefore not wilful in not calling in a doctor. In such circumstances recklessness constitutes mens rea no less than positive awareness of the risk involved in failure to act.

My Lords, the supremacy of this House in its unprecedented task of interpreting s. 1 of the 1933 Act should not be regarded as fettered by its legislative ancestry or its judicial history in subordinate courts, as to which the Court of Appeal, Criminal Division, in the present case obviously felt some disquiet. That is understandable, for the extensive interpretation hitherto accepted involves rejection of the presumption in favour of a strict construction of criminal statutes which grew up in the eighteenth century and has persisted to this day. That interpretation has again found favour, this time with some of your Lordships, but I respectfully find it unacceptable. And, notwithstanding its conformity to that given in countless cases over the last eighty years, the direction to the jury in the present case cannot in my judgment be upheld.

Nor do I consider that to depart from it would lessen the law's protection of the welfare of children. For my part, I have confidence in the vigilance and ability of magistrates and juries to detect cases of wilful neglect. The stronger the objective indications of neglect, the more difficult for defendants to repel the conclusion that they *must* have known of the plight of the children in their charge, or, at least, that they had been recklessly regardless of their welfare. And, as my noble and learned friend Lord Keith, has said, feckless parents who fall into neither of those categories are not (and, in the nature of things, cannot be) deterred by the law as hitherto understood from neglecting their children. To perpetuate the prevailing approach cannot therefore be said to be either in the children's interest or in accordance with justice to those having children in their charge.

What verdicts the jury would have returned had they been directed substantially in the terms indicated in the speech of my noble and learned friend Lord Diplock (which I respectfully adopt) must remain a matter of conjecture. In sentencing the accused the trial judge said that it was 'a bad case of child neglect'. But he added that the evidence did not show that the parents had been persistently and deliberately cruel, that neither of them had foreseen the child's death, and that 'you simply failed during the last month to obtain the necessary and available medical assistance.'

In my judgment, the possibility that a miscarriage of justice has occurred cannot be eliminated, and I would therefore allow this consolidated appeal.

Lord Fraser: [After a review of the legislative and judicial history of the offence his Lordship continued]: The next significant stage in the history comes with the Children Act 1908 which repealed earlier legislation and re-enacted the provision against neglecting a child in a manner likely to cause unnecessary suffering or injury to health etc. and added a deeming proviso in terms substantially identical with those of s. 1 (2) (a) of the 1933 Act. Since 1908 there has been no change in the legislation which is relevant for present purposes. The effect of the deeming proviso introduced in 1908 is in my opinion merely to provide that failure to provide adequate food, medical aid etc. shall constitute neglect contrary to the Act, and to leave the meaning of the word 'wilfully' unaffected. As to what is meant by 'adequate' medical aid in sub-s. (2) (a), one asks: 'adequate for what?' It cannot mean adequate to prevent the likelihood of injury to the child's health, or adequate in the light of what is known at the date of the trial to have prevented injury to health, because in some cases no amount of medical aid would prevent injury to health, which is defined in sub-s. (1) as 'including injury to or loss of sight, or hearing, or limb, or organ of the body, and any mental derangement'. To read 'adequate' in such an absolute sense would mean that every parent whose child died would be guilty of neglect, though not necessarily of wilful neglect. That cannot be right. Neglect must convey some implication of omission to perform a duty. In a case where in spite of the best medical aid the child suffered injury to health, or death, it would surely be an abuse of language to say that the parent had behaved with (non-wilful) neglect. Moreover, it would throw an unduly heavy burden on the word 'wilfully' in the context. In my opinion 'adequate' medical aid (or food, clothing or lodging) means such as ordinary reasonable careful parents would have provided in the circumstances as known to the accused. That agrees with the explanation of the word in the 1894 Act given by Lord Russell C.J. in *R.* v. *Senior* and I see nothing in subsequent legislation to change the meaning of 'wilfully' or 'neglect' there explained. Quite the contrary. If Parliament had wished to alter or correct those meanings, that could easily have been done in the 1933 Act, but it was not. . . .

My Lords, in view of the long period for which the explanation in *R.* v. *Senior* has been accepted and the large number of cases in which it has been applied, apparently with approval, by many learned judges, I would be very hesitant about overruling it now even if I thought it wrong. But I do not. The provisions of what is now s. 1 of the 1933 Act are intended by Parliament for the protection of children who are unable to look after themselves and are in the care of older people. There is nothing unreasonable in their being stringent and objective. If the offence required proof that the particular parents were aware of the probable consequences of neglect, then the difficulty of proof against stupid or feckless parents would certainly be increased and so I fear might the danger to their children. Such parents would not necessarily be unaffected by the existence of an absolute offence; they might not be able to appreciate when their child needed medical care whenever the child showed any signs of ill-health, even though the signs might seem to them to be trivial. I recognise that the climate of opinion has recently become less favourable than it once was to the recognition of absolute offences, but I do not think that such change of climate as has taken place justifies us in departing from a construction of this provision which has been consistently followed by the courts since 1899, and which is, at the very least, not manifestly wrong. Especially in these times when parental responsibility for children tends to be taken all too lightly, such a sharp change towards relaxation of the law on the subject seems to me appropriate only for the legislature and not for the courts.

In these circumstances I regret that I am unable to agree with the direction which has commended itself to the majority of my noble and learned friends as being appropriate for this type of case. I would dismiss the appeal.

[LORD KEITH delivered an opinion in which he agreed with LORD DIPLOCK; LORD SCARMAN gave a dissenting opinion agreeing with LORD FRASER].

Appeal allowed

Questions

1. Do you agree with Lord Diplock that, if the word "wilfully" were given a narrow meaning extending only to the doing of the positive act,

and not its consequences,it would be otiose in section 1 (1)? Is a parent who admonishes a child with a slap committing a voluntary act? Is it therefore a "wilful" assault? Or is it not an assault at all because it is "lawful"?

2. If the parent in question 1 is not committing an assault because parents are allowed to use reasonable disciplinary measures, is Lord Diplock right to assert it is only in the "*mens rea*" of an offence that the reasonable man concept will be found?

3. Both Lord Fraser and Lord Scarman believed that the deterrent effect of the offence would be reduced if the prosecution had to prove foresight of the consequences of neglect. Can this hypothesis be tested?

4. MOTIVE

Chandler v. Director of Public Prosecutions
[1964] A.C. 763
House of Lords

> C. and other appellants were members of a group seeking to further the aims of the Campaign for Nuclear Disarmament. They planned to sit on Wethersfield airfield and so prevent aircraft from taking off. They made their intentions clear but they were prevented from entering the airfield. They were charged and convicted of an offence under section 1 of the Official Secrets Act 1911, which makes it a felony "If any person for any purpose prejudicial to the safety or interests of the state—(*a*) approaches ... any prohibited place...." Wethersfield airfield was a prohibited place. The appellants claimed that their campaign was in the interests of the state and that they had no guilty intent. The Court of Criminal Appeal rejected the appeal.

LORD RADCLIFFE: ... All controversies about motives or intentions or purposes are apt to become involved through confusion of the meaning of the different terms and it is perhaps not difficult to show by analysis that the ideas conveyed by these respective words merge into each other without a clear line of differentiation. Nevertheless, a distinction between motive and purpose, for instance, is familiar enough in ordinary discussion and there are branches of law in which the drawing of such a distinction is unavoidable. The Act of Parliament in this case has introduced the idea of a purpose as a determining element in the identification of the offence charged and lawyers, therefore, whose function it is to attribute meanings to words and to observe relevant distinctions between different words, cannot escape from this duty merely by saying that "purpose" is a word which has no sharply defined content. They must do the best they can to find what its content is in the context of this Act.

For my part I cannot say that I see any very great difficulty in doing so here. I do not think that the ultimate aims of the appellants in bringing about this demonstration of obstruction constituted a purpose at all within the meaning of the Act. I think that those aims constituted their motive, the reason why they wanted the demonstration, but they did not qualify the purpose for which they approached or sought to enter the airfield. Taking this view, I do not think that the distinction between immediate purposes and long-term purposes is the most satisfactory one that can be made. If the word "purpose" is retained at all to describe both object and motive, I think that direct and indirect purposes best describe the distinction which should be placed before a jury, since those adjectives are less likely to confuse the issue. In the result, I am of opinion that if a person's direct purpose in approaching or entering is to cause obstruction or interference, and such obstruction or interference is found to be of prejudice to the defence dispositions of the state, an offence is thereby committed, and his indirect purposes or his motives in bringing about the obstruction or interference do not alter the nature or content of his offence.

It is important to note that the case we are dealing with is one in which the appellants intended to bring about obstruction of the airfield for the sake of having an obstruction. Nothing short of an obstruction would have suited their purpose. That was the kind of demonstration that they desired and it was their intention to use the obstruction as an instrument for furthering their general campaign in favour of nuclear disarmament. I do not regard such a case, in which obstruction is directly intended, as comparable with hypothetical cases put to us in argument in which obstruction, though intended, is only an indirect purpose of entry upon a prohibited place. Is a man guilty of an offence, it was asked, if he rushes onto an airfield intending to stop an airplane taking off because he knows that a time-bomb has been concealed on board? I should say that he is not, and for the reason that his direct purpose is not to bring about an obstruction but to prevent a disaster, the obstruction that he causes being merely a means of securing that end.

The other question involved in this appeal is as to the evidence admitted or rejected by the trial judge. . . . The question seems to me to come down to this: When a man has avowed that his purpose in approaching an airfield forming part of the country's defence system was to obstruct its operational activity, what, if any, evidence is admissible on the issue as to the prejudicial nature of his purpose? In my opinion the correct answer is, virtually none. This answer is not surprising if certain considerations that lie behind the protection of official secrets are borne in mind. The defence of the state from external enemies is a matter of real concern, in time of peace as in days of war. The disposition, armament and direction of the defence forces of the state are matters decided upon by the Crown and are within its jurisdiction as the executive power of the state. So are treaties and alliances with other states for mutual defence. An airfield maintained for the service of the Royal Air Force or of the air force of one of Her Majesty's allies is an instrument of defence, as are the airplanes operating from the airfield and their armament.

It follows, I think, that if a man is shown to the satisfaction of the jury to have approached an airfield with the direct purpose of obstructing its operational use, a verdict of guilty must result, provided that they are also satisfied that the airfield belongs to Her Majesty and was at the relevant date part of the defence system maintained by the Crown for the protection of the realm.

Appeal dismissed

R. v. Hicklin

(1868) 11 Cox 19

Court of Queen's Bench

The defendant was charged with having in his possession a number of copies of an obscene book. The magistrates found this proved and ordered their destruction. On appeal to the Recorder the order was quashed on the ground that the books were not kept by the defendant for gain nor to prejudice good morals but to expose the errors of the Church of Rome. The prosecutor appealed.

COCKBURN C.J.: It seems to me, the effect of this work is mischievous, and against the law; and is not to be justified because the immediate object of the party is not to deprave the public mind, but it may be to destroy and extirpate Roman Catholicism. I think the old, sound and honest maxim that "you shall not do evil that good may come," is applicable in law as well as in morals; and here we have a certain and positive evil produced for the purpose of effecting an uncertain, remote and very doubtful good. I think, therefore, the case for the order is made out, and although I quite concur in thinking that the motive of the parties who published this work, however mistaken, was an honest one, yet I cannot suppose but what they had that intention which constitutes the criminality of the act—at any rate that they knew perfectly well that this work must have the tendency which in point of law makes it an obscene publication, namely, the tendency to corrupt the minds and morals of those into whose hands it might come. The mischief of it, I think, cannot be exaggerated, but it is not upon that I take my stand in the judgment I pronounce. I am of opinion, as the learned Recorder has found, that this is an obscene publication; I take it where a man published a work manifestly obscene, he must be taken to have had the intention which is implied from that act, and that as soon as you have an illegal act thus established, *quoad* the intention, and *quoad* the act itself, it does not lie in the mouth of the man who does it to say, "Well, I was breaking the law, but I was breaking it for some wholesome and salutary purpose." The law does not allow that. You must abide by the law, and if you accomplish your object, you must do it in a legal manner, or let it alone. You must not do it in a manner which is illegal. I think, therefore, that the Recorder's judgment must be reversed, and the conviction must be allowed to stand.

Judgment accordingly

cf. R. v. *Bourne* (*post*, p. 457).

Wasik, "Mens Rea, Motive, and the Problem of 'Dishonesty' in the Law of Theft" [1979] Crim. L.R. 543

". . . Austin described motive as the 'spring of action.' (Lectures on Jurisprudence (4th edn. 1879) at p. 165). He then proceeded to distinguish motive from intention, the central requirement of *mens rea*, by declaring simply: 'The intention is the aim of the act, of which the motive is the spring.' This analysis has been accepted into the criminal law. So, where X steals Y's property, X's intention is said to be to take that property unlawfully, and his motive might be, for example, greed. Motive is thus used to mean an emotion prompting an act. When used in this sense, motive must always precede intention in time. As Kenny has remarked: 'One cannot have an intention for a motive, but one can have a motive for an intention.' (Action, Emotion and Will (1963) at p. 87). Kenny then goes on to suggest that motive can thus be regarded as 'backward-looking' and intention as 'forward-looking'. It has proved necessary, however, to designate this kind of motive as 'motive *in esse*' or 'motive proper', as the law has recognised the existence of a second function of motive in human conduct. Salmond was one of the first to point out this second meaning, where motive means 'a part of intention: Intentions are divisible into immediate intentions and ulterior intentions. The former relate to the unlawful act itself, the latter to the object for the sake of which the act is done.' So, where X, motivated by greed, steals Y's property, his reasons for perpetrating the theft have also been referred to as motive. The 'motive in prospect' is, however, 'forward-looking' rather than 'backward-looking.'

. . . [L]awyers have largely ignored the additional complexities of motive. Motive is declared emphatically, and almost *de rigueur*, to be irrelevant to criminal responsibility though it is conceded that it may be crucial in determining a man's sentence. It is true that some writers have ventured to suggest that motive is really a part of intention, or a species of intent, but many others have been anxious to refute such suggestions. A more common modern approach is to argue that if 'motive' were always confined to its first meaning of 'motive *in esse*', and 'motive in prospect' were invariably known as 'ulterior intent', then motive and intention would, by definition be mutually exclusive. On one level this is an attractive proposal, because it seems to reinforce the distinction between the concepts of *mens rea* and motive. Making such a distinction certainly tends towards jurisprudential tidiness, but it cannot conceal the impression that the division may sometimes be an unrealistic one. This modern 'semantic' approach brings with it the concession that in some cases 'motive in prospect' *is* relevant to criminal responsibility. Thus, in the case of burglary, for example, an intentional entry is required, together with an 'ulterior intent' of committing a certain kind of crime within the premises. Yet once it is conceded that 'motive in prospect' can in some cases be relevant to responsibility, it is arguable that 'motive *in esse*' must also become relevant, since the two varieties of motive are undoubtedly closely linked. Indeed, Bentham argued that there was *always* such a link:

> 'Motive refers necessarily to action. It is a pleasure, pain, or other event that prompts an action. Motive, then, in one sense of the word, must be previous to such event. But for a man to be governed by a motive, he must in every case look beyond that event which is called his action; he must look to the consequences of it: and it is only in this way that the idea of pleasure, of pain, or of any other event, can give birth to it.'

Making verbal distinctions between the two varieties of motive, or between motive and intention, though useful for analysis in many cases, should not be allowed to conceal the links which exist between them. A philosopher who has subjected the terms to protracted analysis has reached this conclusion, (Kenny, *op. cit.*, pp. 86–93):

> 'Motives and intentions are clearly connected, and it is not easy to make any sharp distinction between them . . . a report of an intention fills in in detail part of a pattern which a report of motive sketches out in general.'

In the vast majority of cases where the defence has raised the issue of the accused's motive as being relevant to his responsibility, the judiciary have re-emphasised the traditional irrelevance of motive; but in some more recent cases the judges, in seeking to implement an increasingly subjectively—orientated criminal law, have found such distinctions more difficult to make, [The author referred to *Chandler* v. *D.P.P.* (*ante*)]. . . .

Even if the importance of retaining independent standards in the law is agreed upon, the argument that all matters of motive should thereby be excluded in the determination of criminal responsibility overstates the size of the potential problem. It is part of my contention that in a significant number of cases motive is already taken into account, and that in such cases the motives do not threaten to undermine the law. Perhaps it is inevitable that a system of criminal law which embodies independent standards whilst also seeking to base liability upon subjective fault akin to moral responsibility, will tend to take a rather inconsistent line on the relevance of the accused's motive for committing the criminal act. It is suggested here that this inconsistency is illustrated in English law by the repeated articulation of the general exclusionary rule, while at the same time motive really *is* admitted as relevant to responsibility in a significant, and increasing, number of cases.

Where, for example, an excuse in law does not operate by negativing a positive element in an offence, *mens rea* or *actus reus*, the efficacy of the excuse often turns upon something which appears to be part of the accused's motive for committing the criminal offence. Motives of fear and self-preservation are surely of fundamental importance in the cases of duress and self-defence, and those of anger and fear are crucial in the case of provocation. 'Good motive' is taken into account in homicide by way of partial excuse under the diminished responsibility rules. . . . [O]ne of the most significant examples [is] the issue of dishonesty in theft and related offences.

Liability for theft requires that the prosecution prove beyond reasonable doubt that the accused acted dishonestly when he appropriated property belonging to another with the intention of permanently depriving the other party of the property. It seems indisputable that 'dishonesty' (or 'honesty') is a very different kind of concept than, say, intention. While intention can meaningfully be described as a 'mental element', 'honesty' rather reflects a code of social conduct which is ethically based, the main tenets of which are claimed to be widely shared in a civilised society.

. . . The element of dishonesty provides the accused with an opportunity to account for his conduct in a fuller and more meaningful way than if the offence was phrased purely in terms of *mens rea*. 'Dishonesty' thus gives the accused a chance to explain 'why' the alleged offence occurred instead of just 'how' it occurred (*i.e.* for certain reasons rather than intentionally or recklessly), and this appears to admit explanations involving the accused's motive for committing the act charged."

5. MISTAKES

Fletcher, Rethinking Criminal Law, pp. 683–691

"The most difficult problems in criminal theory are generated by dissonance between reality and belief, between the objective facts and the actor's subjective impression of the facts. . . . [W]e turn to the vast set of problems connected with the facts being incriminating, but the actor's beliefs, innocent. This is the general problem of mistake and ignorance about conduct that nominally violates a legal prohibition. If the actor knows of the circumstances in these cases, he surely would be liable for his conduct; but if he does not know, we confront the general theoretical question about the extent to which his ignorance provides an excuse for his legal violation. . . .

The literature of the common law, along with that of other legal systems, has long tended to divide mistakes into two categories: mistakes of fact and mistakes of law. Our hope will be to show that this form of classification is insensitive to the wide variety of mistakes that can arise in criminal cases. As we shall see in the following schema of mistakes, questions of fact and law arise, recede and interweave at every turn. The structural position of the mistake proves to be as significant as whether the mistake is one of law or fact. Here, then, is a sampling of mistakes, organized according to structural categories of liability:

A. *Mistakes about elements of the definition*

This category encompasses a wide variety of mistakes. Let us assume for the time being that the objective elements, about which the actor is mistaken, adhere to the definition of the offense rather than to claims of justification and excuse.

1. A mistaken belief that what one is shooting at is a bear when in fact it is a fellow hunter.
2. A mistaken belief that one's sexual partner is over age when in fact she is not.
3. A mistaken judgment about whether particular conduct falls within a known offense.
4. A mistaken belief that conduct of a particular type—say, private homosexual conduct between consenting adults—has been legalized in the particular jurisdiction.

B. *Mistakes related to justificatory claims*

5. A mistaken belief that one is being attacked by an aggressor. One responds in putative self-defense.
6. A mistaken belief that deadly force is permissible, if necessary, to apprehend a petty thief.
7. A mistaken belief that, as a teacher, one has the right to use corporal punishment as a disciplinary measure.

C. *Mistakes about excusing conditions*

8. A mistaken belief that unless one commits perjury, one will be killed by the defendant under prosecution.
9. A mistaken belief that the excuse of duress encompasses homicide as well as lesser offences.
10. A mistaken belief that the jurisdiction recognizes the excuse of necessity as well as duress. The actor relies on this belief in escaping from prison in order to avoid a homosexual rape.

D. *Mistakes in cases of negligent risk-taking*

11. A mistaken belief that conduct will decrease rather than increase the risks, say, of a railroad collision. Having misread the timetable, a switchman switches the track so as to put the trains on a collision course.
12. A mistaken belief about the relative costs and benefits of a particular course of conduct. A nightclub owner mistakenly concludes that the safety benefits of additional fire escapes are more than offset by the financial cost and their aesthetic disadvantages.
13. A mistaken belief that only risks to persons, and not to property, constitute punishable negligence.

Twelve of these categories derive from applying a refined version of the distinction between fact and law in each of these structural categories. The refinement recognizes that some mistakes are based on misperceptions of the world (cases 1, 5, 8, and 11); and others on a false belief about the enactment or abolition of a legal norm (cases 4, 7, 10, and 13). The middle category raises questions both of fact and of law: the mistake goes to the application of an existing legal norm to a particular set of facts (cases 3, 6, 9, and 12). So far as one works with merely two categories—fact and law—this middle range of cases is forced into one inapt category or the other.

More important even than this refinement of mistakes of fact and law into three categories instead of two is the recognition that the object of the mistake might influence the analysis of liability. The claim is that it should matter whether the mistake is about an element of the definition, a claim of justification, a claim of excuse or the creation of risk. These four categories intersect with the three types of mistakes and generate twelve of the problematic cases. The point of this chapter is to show that each of these categories raises special problems of analysis. . . .

Outcomes in the Analysis of Mistakes. The problematic cases have to be mapped onto three possible legal outcomes. If the mistake is made in good faith, then: (1) the mistake might bar liability altogether; (2) the mistake might bar liability only if the making of the mistake (or the inadvertence) is itself free from culpability; or (3) the mistake might have no effect at all on the outcome of the case.

A. Mistakes Negating Intent. The first outcome derives from an analysis of the intent required for liability. If the intent required for homicide is the intent to kill a human being, then a mistake as to whether one is shooting at a human being precludes a finding of intentional homicide. If the intent required for larceny is the intent to deprive the owner of his property, then the belief that one is taking one's own book or umbrella precludes an intent to deprive the owner (for the taker thinks he is the owner). The logic of this argument is simple. The required intent is 'the intent to do A'; if the actor believes that not A is the case, then he cannot have the 'intent to do A.'

It follows from the logic of this argument that any mistake—reasonable or unreasonable—precludes a finding of the required intent. The use of this strategy presupposes, of course, a determination of the intent required for the offense.

It is important to note that the impact of a successful use of this strategy depends on whether the offense is subject to prosecution on the basis of negligence. . . .

B. Mistakes Negating Culpability. The second outcome—that the actor benefits only from faultless or reasonable mistakes—might surface in one of three doctrinal forms. First, if the prosecution is for an offense that can be committed negligently, then the mistake is of no avail if it is negligently made. . . .

Alternatively, the mistake might have to meet the criteria of reasonableness in any case in which it pertains to an element extrinsic to the required intent. In our hypothetical case 2, for example, a court might plausibly require that for the accused statutory rapist to be acquitted, his mistake about the age of the girl must be reasonable. The argument for this outcome is that the mistake is an excuse negating the actor's culpability rather than a mental element of the definition. The definition is satisfied and the act is wrongful, but the mistake negates the actor's accountability for the wrongful act. . . .

. . . . The effect in these cases is to treat an unreasonable mistake as though it were equivalent to knowledge of that element of the offense. It is obvious that someone who makes a good-faith, but unreasonable mistake about the age of a sexual partner is not as culpable as someone who means to seduce a young girl, and yet the law lumps the two together. . . .

The third context in which the requirement of reasonableness asserts itself is in mistaken claims of justificatory facts, particularly the mistaken claim that defensive force is necessary to avert an apparently aggressive attack . . . [see *post*, Chap. 8].

The first two strategies for recognizing mistakes are readily summed up as alternative forms of logical negation. If the mistake negates the required intent, then any good-faith mistake will suffice; if it merely negates the actor's culpability, then the mistake must be reasonable—that is, the making of the mistake must be free from culpability. . . .

C. Irrelevant Mistakes. The third possible outcome is that the mistake, even if reasonable, should have no exculpatory effect at all. This outcome is most readily defended where the mistake does not bear on the actor's culpability. . . .

The maxim that mistakes of law do not excuse specifies a category of irrelevant mistakes even though a mistake about the legality of one's conduct bears on whether one can be fairly blamed for violating the law.

Mistakes are sometimes genuinely irrelevant to a just determination of liability and sometimes, as in many cases of mistake of law, they are deemed irrelevant for practical or utilitarian reasons."

Fletcher's classification provides a useful framework for the English cases on mistake.

i. Mistake Negating Intent

James L.J. in *R.* v. *Smith (David)* [1974] Q.B. 354 said of section 1 (1) of the Criminal Damage Act 1971:

"Construing the language of [the] section we have no doubt that the *actus reus* is 'destroying or damaging any property belonging to another'. It is not possible to exclude the words 'belonging to another' which describe the 'property'. Applying the ordinary principles of *mens rea*, the intention and recklessness and the absence of lawful excuse required to constitute the offence have reference to property belonging to another. It follows that, in our judgment, no offence is committed under this section if a person destroys or causes damage to property belonging to another if he does so in the honest though mistaken belief that the property is his own, and provided that the belief is honestly held it is irrelevant to consider whether or not it is a justifiable belief."

A mistaken belief that the person obstructed is not a police constable affords a defence to section 51 (3) of the Police Act 1964 (wilful obstruction of a police constable in the execution of his duty): *Ostler* v. *Elliott* [1980] Crim. L.R. 585. But the same mistaken belief will be of no avail under section 51 (1) of that Act (assaulting a police constable in the execution of his duty): *Forbes* (1865) 10 Cox C.C. 362; *McBride and Turnock* [1964] Crim. L.R. 456. In *Ostler* v. *Elliott* (*supra*) and also in *Wilson* v. *Inyang* [1951] 2 K.B. 799 the courts appeared to lay special emphasis on the word "wilfully" in the decision to allow mistake to negate *mens rea*. But consistency is lacking even where the word "wilfully" is used. See, for example, *Cotterill* v. *Penn* [1936] 1 K.B. 53: "unlawfully and wilfully killing a house pigeon." D thought the bird he shot at was a wood pigeon. Lord Hewart C.J.: "Although the statute says 'unlawfully and wilfully', it does not require the element of *mens rea* beyond the point that the facts must show an intention on the part of the person accused to do the act forbidden, which was here that of shooting. It seems to me to be immaterial that the bird which the respondent shot was of a different kind from that which he thought he was shooting. If the section had used the word 'maliciously' the state of mind of the person charged would have been relevant. But using the terms 'unlawfully and wilfully' the section seems to me only to mean that the person accused intended to shoot and that the shooting was without lawful excuse." Even if the courts were consistent about the meaning of "wilfully", this approach tends to divert attention from the question: which parts of the definition of an offence (all, some, none?) are qualified by the requirement of a mental element? It was this question which was faced in the case below.

D.P.P. v. Morgan
[1976] A.C. 182
House of Lords

The appellant invited three friends to have intercourse with his wife telling them that her signs of resistance were not to be interpreted as lack of consent: she enjoyed it better that way. The friends were charged with rape, the appellant with aiding and abetting. They appealed against the direction of the trial judge that their belief in her consent must be reasonable.

LORD CROSS OF CHELSEA: . . . The question of law which is raised by the appeal is whether the judge was right in telling the jury that, if they came to the conclusion that Mrs. Morgan had not consented to the intercourse in question but that the defendants believed or may have believed that she was consenting to it, they must nevertheless find the defendants guilty of rape if they were satisfied that they had no reasonable grounds for so believing. . . .

The Sexual Offences Act 1956 which provides by section 1 (1) that it is an offence "for a man to rape a woman" contains no definition of the word "rape". No one suggests that rape is an "absolute" offence to the commission of which the state of mind of the defendant with regard to the woman's consent is wholly irrelevant. The point in dispute is as to the quality of belief which entitles the defendant to be acquitted and as to the "evidential" burden of proof with regard to it. . . .

Finally, I must refer to an alternative submission, made by counsel for the appellant—namely, that in *R.* v. *Tolson, post*, p. 116, the court was wrong in saying that to afford a defence to a charge of bigamy the mistaken belief of the defendant had to be based on reasonable grounds. It is, of course true that the question whether a mistaken belief honestly held but based on no reasonable grounds would have afforded a defence was not argued in that case. There had been several conflicting decisions by judges on assize—one saying that an honest belief would be a defence, others that a belief on reasonable grounds would be a defence, and yet others that not even a belief on reasonable grounds would be a defence. In *R.* v. *Tolson*, Stephen J. asked the jury whether they thought that the defendant in good faith and on reasonable grounds believed her husband to be dead at the date of her second marriage. Having obtained an affirmative answer he then, in order to get the point settled by the Court of Crown Cases Reserved, directed the jury—contrary to his own opinion—that such a belief would not be a defence and, after they had duly convicted Mrs. Tolson, sentenced her to one day's imprisonment. On her appeal against her conviction, her counsel was not, of course, concerned to dispute the view that a mistaken belief had to be based on reasonable grounds, since the jury had held that his client had had reasonable grounds for her belief, and the question whether an honest belief would have been enough was never argued. If it had been argued, it is possible that some of the judges who were in the majority—though having regard to the way in which he framed his question, I do not think that Stephen J. would have been one of them—might have held that a mistaken belief honestly but unreasonably held was enough. But *R.* v. *Tolson* was decided over 80 years ago. It is accepted as a leading authority in the law of bigamy not only in this country (see *R.* v. *King* [1964] 1 Q.B. 285 and *R.* v. *Gould* [1968] 2 Q.B. 65) but also in Australia (see *Thomas* v. *The King* (1937) 59 C.L.R. 279). Moreover, the phrase "an honest and reasonable belief entertained by the accused of the existence of facts, which, if true, would make the act charged against him innocent" (23 Q.B.D. 168, 181) has been adopted on several occasions as a definition of *mens rea* generally applicable to cases where the offence is not an absolute one but the words defining it do not expressly or impliedly indicate that some particular *mens rea* is required to establish it: see *Bank of New South Wales* v. *Piper* [1897] A.C. 383; by Lord Reid in *R.* v. *Warner* [1969] 2 A.C. 256, 268 and by Lord Diplock in *Sweet* v. *Parsley* [1970] A.C. 132, 164, 165. Counsel did not refer us to any case in which the propriety of the inclusion of the element of "reasonableness" has been doubted; and its inclusion was, in fact, approved in *R.* v. *King* [1964] 1 Q.B. 285 and by Lord Diplock in *Sweet* v. *Parsley*. So, even if I had been myself inclined to think that the inclusion of the element of reasonableness was wrong, I would not have thought it right for us to call it in question in this case. In fact, however, I can see no objection to the inclusion of the element of reasonableness in what I may call a "*Tolson*" case. If the words defining an offence provide either expressly or impliedly that a man is not to be guilty of it if he believes something to be true, then he cannot be found guilty if the jury think that he may have believed it to be true, however inadequate were his reasons for doing so. But, if the definition of the offence is on the face of it "absolute" and the defendant is seeking to escape his prima facie liability by defence of mistaken belief, I can see no hardship to him in requiring the mistake—if it is to afford him a defence—to be based on reasonable grounds. As Lord Diplock said in *Sweet* v. *Parsley* [1970] A.C. 132 [*post*, p. 137] there is nothing unreasonable in the law requiring a citizen to take reasonable care to ascertain the facts relevant to his avoiding doing a prohibited act. To have intercourse with a woman who is not your wife is, even today, not generally considered to be a course of conduct which the law ought positively to encourage and it can be argued with force that it is only fair to the woman and not in the least unfair to the man that he should be under a duty to take reasonable care to ascertain that she is consenting to the intercourse and be at the risk of a prosecution if he fails to take such care. So if the Sexual Offences Act 1956 had made it an offence to have intercourse with a woman who was not consenting to it, so that the defendant could only escape liability by the application of the "*Tolson*" principle, I would not have thought the law unjust.

But, as I have said, section 1 of the Act of 1956 does not say that a man who has sexual intercourse with a woman who does not consent to it commits an offence; it says that a man who rapes a woman commits an offence. Rape is not a word in the use of which lawyers have a monopoly and the first question to be answered in this case, as I see it, is whether according to the ordinary use of the English language a man can be said to have committed rape if he believed that the woman was consenting to the intercourse and would not have attempted to have it but for this belief, whatever his grounds for so believing. I do not think that he can. Rape, to my mind, imports at least indifference as to the woman's consent. I think, moreover, that in this connection the ordinary man would distinguish between rape and bigamy. To the question whether a man who goes through a ceremony of marriage with a woman believing his wife to be dead, though she is not, commits bigamy, I think that he would reply "Yes,—but I suppose that the law contains an escape clause for bigamists who are not really to blame." On the other hand, to the question whether a man, who has intercourse with a woman believing that she is consenting to it, though she is not, commits rape, I think that he would reply "No. If he was grossly careless then he may deserve to be punished but not for rape." That being my view as to the meaning of the word "rape" in ordinary parlance, I next ask myself whether the law gives it a different meaning. There is very little English authority on the point but what there is—namely, the reported directions of several common law judges in the early and middle years of the last century—accords with what I take to be the ordinary meaning of the word. The question has been canvassed in a number of recent cases in New South Wales and Victoria but there is only one of them—*R.* v. *Daly* [1968] V.R. 257—that I find of much assistance. In none of the others do the judges advert to the fact that to include an intention to have intercourse whether or not the woman consents in the definition of rape and to say that a reasonable mistake with regard to consent is an available defence to a charge of rape are two incompatible alternatives which cannot be combined in a single direction to a jury—as, incidentally, the judge combined them in one passage in his summing up in this case. In *R.* v. *Daly* the court, as well as drawing that distinction which I regard as fundamental, indicated pretty clearly that it thought—as I do—that the former approach to the problem was the right one. For these reasons, I think that the summing up contained a misdirection. . . .

LORD HAILSHAM OF ST. MARYLEBONE: . . . [In summing up,] the learned Judge said:

> "First of all, let me deal with the crime of rape. What are its ingredients? What have the prosecution to prove to your satisfaction before you can find a defendant guilty of rape? The crime of rape consists in having unlawful sexual intercourse with a woman without her consent and by force. By force.

Those words mean exactly what they say. It does not mean there has to be a fight or blows have to be inflicted. It means that there has to be some violence used against the woman to overbear her will or that there has to be a threat of violence as a result of which her will is overborne. You will bear in mind that force or the threat of force carries greater weight when there are four men involved than where there is one man involved. In other words, measure the force in deciding whether force is used. One of the elements to which you will have regard is the number of men involved in the incident.

Further, the prosecution have to prove that each defendant intended to have sexual intercourse with this woman without her consent, not merely that he intended to have intercourse with her but that he intended to have intercourse without her consent. Therefore if the defendant believed or may have believed that Mrs. Morgan consented to him having sexual intercourse with her, then there would be no such intent in his mind and he would not be guilty of the offence of rape, but such a belief must be honestly held by the defendant in the first place. He must really believe that. And, secondly, his belief must be a reasonable belief; such a belief as a reasonable man would entertain if he applied his mind and thought about the matter. It is not enough for a defendant to rely upon a belief, even though he honestly held it, if it was completely fanciful; contrary to every indication which could be given which would carry some weight with a reasonable man. And, of course, the belief must be not a belief that the woman would consent at some time in the future, but a belief that at the time when intercourse was taking place or when it began that she was then consenting to it."

No complaint was made of the first paragraph where the learned judge is describing what, to use the common and convenient solecism, is meant by the actus reus in rape. Nor is there any complaint by the appellants of the judge's first proposition describing the mental element.

It is upon the second proposition about the mental element that the appellants concentrate their criticism. An honest belief in consent, they contend, is enough. It matters not whether it be also reasonable. No doubt a defendant will wish to raise argument or lead evidence to show that his belief was reasonable, since this will support its honesty. No doubt the prosecution will seek to cross examine or raise arguments or adduce evidence to undermine the contention that the belief is reasonable, because, in the nature of the case, the fact that a belief cannot reasonably be held is a strong ground for saying that it was not in fact held honestly at all. Nonetheless, the appellants contend, the crux of the matter, the factum probandum, or rather the fact to be refuted by the prosecution, is honesty and not honesty plus reasonableness. In making reasonableness as well as honesty an ingredient in this "defence" the judge, say the appellants, was guilty of a misdirection.

My first comment upon this direction is that the propositions described "in the first place" and "secondly" in the above direction as to the mental ingredient in rape are wholly irreconcileable. In practice this was accepted by both counsel for the appellants and for the respondent, counsel for the appellants embracing that described as "in the first place" and counsel for the respondent embracing the "secondly", and each rejecting the other as not being a correct statement of the law. In this, in my view, they had no alternative.

If it be true, as the learned judge says "in the first place," that the prosecution have to prove that

"each defendant intended to have sexual intercourse without her consent, not merely that he intended to have intercourse with her but that he intended to have intercourse without her consent," the defendant must be entitled to an acquittal if the prosecution fail to prove just that. The necessary mental ingredient will be lacking and the only possible verdict is "not guilty." If, on the other hand, as is asserted in the passage beginning "secondly," it is necessary for any belief in the woman's consent to be "a reasonable belief" before the defendant is entitled to an acquittal, it must either be because the mental ingredient in rape is not "to have intercourse and to have it without her consent" but simply "to have intercourse" subject to a special defence of "honest and reasonable belief," or alternatively to have intercourse without a reasonable belief in her consent. Counsel for the Crown argued for each of these alternatives, but in my view each is open to insuperable objections of principle. No doubt it would be possible, by statute, to devise a law by which intercourse, voluntarily entered into, was an absolute offence, subject to a "defence" or belief whether honest or honest and reasonable, of which the "evidential" burden is primarily on the defence and the "probative" burden on the prosecution. But in my opinion such is not the crime of rape as it has hitherto been understood. The prohibited act in rape is to have intercourse without the victim's consent. The minimum mens rea or guilty mind in most common law offences, including rape, is the intention to do the prohibited act, and that is correctly stated in the proposition stated "in the first place" of the judge's direction. In murder the situation is different, because the murder is only complete when the victim dies, and an intention to do really serious bodily harm has been held to be enough if such be the case.

The only qualification I would make to the direction of the learned judge's "in the first place" is the refinement for which, as I shall show, there is both Australian and English authority, that if the intention of the accused is to have intercourse nolens volens, that is recklessly and not caring whether the victim be a consenting party or not, that is equivalent on ordinary principles to an intent to do the prohibited act without the consent of the victim.

The alternative version of the learned judge's direction would read that the accused must do the prohibited act with the intention of doing it without an honest and reasonable belief in the victim's consent. This in effect is the version which took up most of the time in argument, and although I find the Court of Appeal's judgment difficult to understand, I think it the version which ultimately commended itself to that court. At all events I think it the more plausible way in which to state the learned judge's "secondly." In principle, however, I find in unacceptable. I believe that "mens rea" means "guilty or criminal mind", and if it be the case, as seems to be accepted here, that mental element in rape is not knowledge but intent, to insist that a belief must be reasonable to excuse is to insist that either the accused is to be found guilty of intending to do that which in truth he did not intend to do, or that his state of mind, though innocent of evil intent, can convict him if it be honest but not rational. . . .

I believe the law on this point to have been correctly stated by Lord Goddard C.J. in *R.* v. *Steane* [1947] K.B. 997, 1004, when he said:

> ". . . if on the totality of the evidence there is room for more than one view as to the intent of the prisoner, the jury should be directed that it is for the prosecution to prove the intent to the jury's satisfaction, and if, on a review of the whole evidence, they either think that the intent did not exist or they are left in doubt as to the intent, the prisoner is entitled to be acquitted."

That was indeed, a case which involved a count where a specific, or, as Professor Smith has called it, an ulterior, intent was, and was required to be, charged in the indictment. But, once it be accepted that an intent of whatever description is an ingredient essential to the guilt of the accused I cannot myself see that any other direction can be logically acceptable. Otherwise a jury would in effect be told to find an intent where none existed or where none was proved to have existed. I cannot myself reconcile it with my conscience to sanction as part of the English law what I regard as logical impossibility, and, if there were any authority which, if accepted would compel me to do so, I would feel constrained to declare that it was not to be followed. However for reasons which I will give, I do not see any need in the instant case for such desperate remedies.

The beginning of wisdom in all the "mens rea" cases to which our attention was called is, as was pointed out by Stephen J. in *R.* v. *Tolson*, 23 Q.B.D. 168, 185, that "mens rea" means a number of quite different things in relation to different crimes. Sometimes it means an intention, e.g., in murder, "to kill or to inflict really serious injury." Sometimes it means a state of mind or knowledge, e.g., in receiving or handling goods "knowing them to be stolen." Sometimes it means both an intention and a state of mind, e.g. "dishonestly and without a claim of right made in good faith with intent permanently to deprive the owner thereof." Sometimes it forms part of the essential ingredients of the crime without proof of which the prosecution, as it were, withers on the bough. Sometimes it is a matter, of which, though the "probative" burden may be on the Crown, normally the "evidential" burden may usually (though not always) rest on the defence, e.g., "self-defence" and "provocation" in murder, though it must be noted that if there is material making the issue a live one, the matter must be left to the jury even if the defence do not raise it. Moreover, of course, a statute can, and often does, create an absolute offence without any degree of mens rea at all. It follows from this, surely, that it is logically impermissible, as the Crown sought to do in this case, to draw a necessary inference from decisions in relation to offences where mens rea means one thing, and cases where it means another, and in particular from decisions on the construction of statutes, whether these be related to bigamy, abduction or the possession of drugs, and decisions in relation to common law offences. It is equally impermissible to draw direct or necessary inferences from decisions where the mens rea is, or includes, a state of opinion, and cases where it is limited to intention (a distinction I referred to in *R.* v. *Hyam* [*post*, p. 374] or between cases where there is a special "defence", like self-defence or provocation and cases where the issue relates to the primary intention which the prosecution has to prove.

Once one has accepted, what seems to be abundantly clear, that the prohibited act in rape is non-consensual sexual intercourse, and that the guilty state of mind is an intention to commit it, it seems to me to follow as a matter of inexorable logic that there is no room either for a "defence" of honest belief or mistake, or of a defence of honest and reasonable belief or mistake. Either the prosecution proves that the accused had the requisite intent, or it does not. In the former case it succeeds, and in the latter it fails. Since honest belief clearly negatives intent, the reasonableness or otherwise of that belief can only be evidence for or against the view that the belief and therefore the intent was actually held, and it matters not whether, to quote Bridge J. in the passage cited above, "the definition of a crime includes no specific element beyond the prohibited act." If the mental element be primarily an intention and not a state of belief it comes within his second proposition and not his third. Any other view, as for insertion of the word "reasonable" can only have the effect of saying that a man intends something which he does not.

By contrast, the appellants invited us to overrule the bigamy cases from *R.* v. *Tolson* [*post*, p. 116], onwards and perhaps also *R.* v. *Prince*, L.R. 2 C.C.R. 154 (the abduction case) as wrongly decided at least in so far as they purport to insist that a mistaken belief must be reasonable. The arguments for this view are assembled, and enthusiastically argued, by Professor Glanville Williams in his treatise on *Criminal Law*, 2nd ed. (1961), between pages 176 and 205, and by Smith and Hogan (see *Smith and Hogan* at pp. 148, 149 of their textbook).

Although it is undoubtedly open to this House to reconsider *R.* v. *Tolson* and the bigamy cases, and perhaps *R.* v. *Prince* which may stand or fall with them, I must respectfully decline to do so in the present case. Nor is it necessary that I should. I am not prepared to assume that the statutory offences of bigamy or abduction are necessarily on all fours with rape, and before I was prepared to undermine a whole line of cases which have been accepted as law for so long, I would need argument in the context of a case expressly relating to the relevant offences. I am content to rest my view of the instant case on the crime of rape by saying that it is my opinion that the prohibited act is and always has been intercourse without consent of the victim and the mental element is and always has been the intention to commit that act, or the equivalent intention of having intercourse willy-nilly not caring whether the victim consents or no. A failure to prove this involves an acquittal because the intent, an essential ingredient, is lacking. It matters not why it is lacking if only it is not there, and in particular it matters not that the intention is lacking only because of a belief not based on reasonable grounds. I should add that I myself am inclined to view *R.* v. *Tolson* as a narrow decision based on the construction of a statute, which prima facie seemed to make an absolute statutory offence, with a proviso, related to the seven year period of absence, which created a statutory defence. The judges in *R.* v. *Tolson* decided that this was not reasonable, and, on general jurisprudential principles, imported into the statutory offence words which created a special "defence" of honest and reasonable belief of which the "evidential" but not the probative burden lay on the defence. I do not think it is necessary to decide this conclusively in the present case. But if this is the true view there is a complete distinction between *Tolson* and the other cases based in statute and the present.

I may also add that I am not impressed with the analogy based on the decision in *Wilson* v. *Inyang* [1951] 2 K.B. 799, 803 which has attracted the attention of some academic authors. That clearly depends on the construction of the words "wilfully and falsely" where they are used in the relevant statute. Also, though I get some support from what I have been saying from the reasoning of the decision in *R.* v. *Smith (David)* [1974] Q.B. 354, I nevertheless regard that case as a decision on the Criminal Damage Act 1971, rather than a decision covering the whole law of criminal liability.

For the above reasons I would answer the question certified in the negative, but would apply the proviso to the Criminal Appeal Act on the ground that no miscarriage of justice has or conceivably could have occurred.

LORD SIMON OF GLAISDALE: The problem which faces your Lordships arises when the accused raises a case fit for the jury's consideration that he believed that the woman was consenting to sexual intercourse, though in fact she was not doing so. Does an honest *but unreasonable* belief that the woman is consenting to sexual intercourse suffice to negative the charge of rape?

The answer to this question depends, in my view, on the following matters: first, a distinction between crimes of basic and of ulterior intent; secondly, a distinction between probative and evidential burdens of proof; thirdly, the inter-relationship of these two distinctions; fourthly, ascertainment whether rape is a crime of basic or ulterior intent; and, fifthly, the general policy of the criminal law when the prosecution has provisionally discharged the burden of proving actus reus and mens rea, and the accused then alleges a belief, albeit erroneous, in a state of facts which would, if true, negative the actus reus and the mens rea provisionally proved by the prosecution. After examining these five matters I shall endeavour to determine the reasons for what I believe to be the general policy of the criminal law in such circumstances.

I turn to examine, first, the distinction between crimes of basic and of ulterior intent, having taken the latter expression from *Smith and Hogan*. I leave aside, as irrelevant, crimes of absolute liability; and I propose to use the terms actus reus and mens rea in the senses which I indicated in *D.P.P. for Northern Ireland* v. *Lynch* [1975] A.C. 653. By "crimes of basic intent" I mean those crimes whose definition expresses (or, more often, implies) a mens rea which does not go beyond the actus reus. The actus reus generally consists of an act and some consequence. The consequence may be very closely connected with the act or more remotely connected with it: but with a crime of basic intent the mens rea does not extend beyond the act and its consequence, however remote, as defined in the actus reus. I take assault as an example of a crime of basic intent where the consequence is very closely connected with the act. The actus reus of assault is an act which causes another person to apprehend immediate and unlawful violence. The mens rea corresponds exactly. The prosecution must prove that the accused foresaw that his act would probably cause another person to have apprehension of immediate and unlawful violence, or would possibly have that consequence, such being the purpose of the act, or that he was reckless as to whether or not his act caused such apprehension. This foresight (the term of art is "intention") or recklessness is the mens rea in assault. For an example of a crime of basic intent where the consequence of the act involved in the actus reus as defined in the crime is less immediate, I take the crime of unlawful wounding. The act is, the squeezing of a trigger. A number of consequences (mechanical, chemical, ballistic and physiological) intervene before the final consequence involved in the defined actus reus—namely, the wounding of another person in circumstances unjustified by law. But again here the mens rea corresponds closely to the actus reus. The prosecution must prove that the accused foresaw that some physical harm would ensue to another person in circumstances unjustified by the law as a probable (or possible and desired) consequence of his act, or that he was reckless as to whether or not such consequence ensued.

On the other hand there are crimes of ulterior intent—"ulterior" because the mens rea goes beyond contemplation of the actus reus. For example, in the crime of wounding with intent to cause grievous bodily harm, the actus reus is the wounding. The prosecution must prove a corresponding mens rea (as with unlawful wounding), but the prosecution must go further: it must show that he foresaw that serious physical injury would probably be a consequence of his act, or would possibly be so, that being a purpose of his act. The crime of wounding with intent to cause grievous bodily harm could be committed without any serious physical injury being caused to the victim. This is because there is no actus reus corresponding to the ulterior intent. One of the questions which has to be answered in this appeal is whether rape is a crime of basic or ulterior intent.

A second relevant distinction known to the modern law is that between probative and evidential burdens of proof. Though the terminology has changed, this distinction goes back to a seminal article by Denning J. in (1945) 41 L.Q.R. 379, entitled "Presumptions and Burdens". In the criminal law the probative burden of every issue lies on the prosecution (except for the single common law exception of insanity and some statutory exceptions). But the prosecution may adduce evidence sufficient, at a certain stage in the trial, to discharge provisionally the probative burden and thus call for some explanation on behalf of the accused (generally by evidence; though forensic analysis discounting the prosecution's case sometimes suffices): the evidential burden has shifted, though the probative burden remains on the prosecution. Again, the accused may raise a case fit for the consideration of the jury on a fresh issue. For example, although the prosecution may have provisionally discharged the onus of proving an assault, the accused may raise an issue of self-defence in a form fit for the consideration of the jury: if so, the evidential burden of disproving it will shift to the prosecution, which has, of course, also (once the defence is raised in a form fit for the consideration of the jury) the probative burden of disproving it. In this way the evidential burden of proof will often shift backwards and forwards during a trial, the probative burden remaining throughout upon the prosecution.

The third matter for consideration is the interaction between these two distinctions—between crimes of basic and ulterior intent, on the one hand, and between probative and evidential burdens of proof on the other. Such interaction occurs because proof of the actus reus generally raises a presumption of a corresponding mens rea, an act being usually performed with foresight of its probable consequences. I emphasise the words "generally" and "usually"; because the inference may not be a natural one in some circumstances. For example, a different inference as to intention may be drawn from proof that the accused drove his elbow hard into the stomach of a stranger in a crowded train from where it is proved that he did the same act when alone with the stranger in the course of an angry argument. If the crime is one of basic intent, so that the mens rea does not extend beyond the actus reus, proof of the actus reus is therefore, generally, sufficient prima facie proof of the mens rea to shift the evidential burden of proof. Thus, if the prosecution proves that the accused squeezed the trigger of a firearm and thereby wounded a victim, this will often be sufficient proof not only of the actus reus of unlawful wounding but also of the necessary mens rea—i.e., that the accused foresaw the wounding as a likely consequence of his act or was reckless as to whether it ensued—so as to cause the evidential burden to shift and thus to call for some explanation on behalf of the accused. But if the crime is one of ulterior intent, proof of the actus reus tells little about the mens rea in so far as it extends beyond the actus reus; so that the evidential burden does not necessarily shift on proof of the actus reus. To prove that A wounded B, even intentionally, does not of itself raise a presumption that A thereby intended to cause serious physical injury to B.

This brings me to the fourth question—namely, whether rape is a crime of basic or ulterior intent. Does it involve an intent going beyond the actus reus? *Smith and Hogan*, 3rd ed. (1973), p. 47, says No. I respectfully agree. The actus reus is sexual intercourse with a woman who is not in fact consenting to such intercourse. The mens rea is knowledge that the woman is not consenting or recklessness as to whether she is consenting or not. That it is nothing more can be seen by postulating an offence of rape with an ulterior intent. The offence with which the 4th Earl of Bothwell was popularly charged by his contemporaries was rape with intent to procure marriage. If this were a crime—and several 18th century crimes of abduction are near analogues—the crime would be one of ulterior intent. But comparison with such a postulated crime shows that rape itself involves no mens rea going beyond the actus reus.

If this is right, proof of the actus reus in rape—that is, proof of sexual intercourse with a woman who did not consent to it—will generally be sufficient prima facie proof to shift the evidential burden. If the evidential burden shifts in this way, the accused must either prove that his conduct was involuntary (which is irrelevant in the crime of rape) or he must negative the inference as to mens rea which might be drawn from the actus reus. Assuming that the prosecution has proved sexual intercourse with a woman who did not in fact consent to it, in general the only way in which the accused can shift back the evidential burden is by showing a belief in a state of affairs whereby the actus would not be reus. In the context of rape, the accused in such circumstances must, in other words, show that he believed that the woman was consenting. To say that he must show that he believed it "honestly" is tautologous but useful as emphasising a distinction. The question is whether he must show that he believed it reasonably, and if so, why. . . .

It remains to consider why the law requires, in such circumstances, that the belief in a state of affairs whereby the actus would not be reus must be held on reasonable grounds. One reason was given by Bridge J. in the Court of Appeal:

> "The rationale of requiring reasonable grounds for the mistaken belief must lie in the law's consideration that a bald assertion of belief for which the accused can indicate no reasonable ground is evidence of insufficient substance to raise any issue requiring the jury's consideration."

I agree; but I think there is also another reason. The policy of the law in this regard could well derive from its concern to hold a fair balance between victim and accused. It would hardly seem just to fob off a victim of a savage assault with such comfort as he could derive from knowing that his injury was caused by a belief, however absurd, that he was about to attack the accused. A respectable woman who has been ravished would hardly feel that she was vindicated by being told that her assailant must go unpunished because he believed, quite unreasonably, that she was consenting to sexual intercourse with him. The policy behind section 6 of the Sexual Offences Act is presumably that Parliament considered that a girl under 16 is generally unlikely to be sufficiently mature to realise the full implications of sexual intercourse; so that her protection demands that a belief by a man under the age of 24 that she herself was over the age of 16 should not be only an honest but also a reasonable belief.

All the foregoing accords, I trust and believe, with the passage in the speech of my noble and learned friend, Lord Diplock, in *Sweet* v. *Parsley* [1970] A.C. 132, 164E-G which was cited by Bridge J.

I would therefore answer the question certified for your Lordships' consideration, Yes. But even did I consider that it should be answered No, I would, for the reasons given by my noble and learned friends, think this a suitable case to apply the proviso.

I would therefore dismiss the appeal.

Lord Edmund-Davies: . . . In the absence of contrary evidence, the accused may be presumed to have appreciated the significance of circumstances which must have come to his notice. But it does not follow inexorably that he in fact did so, and *R.* v. *Horton* (1871) 11 Cox C.C. 670, a bigamy case, is but one example of failure in this respect. The presumption is not conclusive and, unless it emerges that there is a weight of authority compelling a different conclusion, I should have considered that the honest belief of an accused charged with rape that the woman was willing, being wholly inconsistent with the criminal intention necessary to constitute the crime, would call for his acquittal. The more unreasonable such a belief in the proved circumstances of the case, the slimmer the chances of the jury's thinking that it was ever entertained. Nevertheless, if, after hearing all the evidence (and, in most cases, particularly that of the accused himself), they did not reject out of hand the plea of honest belief, even though they were alive to its unreasonableness, I should have thought that they were duty bound to acquit. Honest belief, however foolishly formed, that the woman was willing seems to me incompatible with an intention to rape her. Here, as in any other crime where knowledge is an essential ingredient, this should connote actual knowledge and not merely what the accused ought to have known. As Smith and Hogan, *Criminal Law* put it, 3rd ed., p. 150:

> ". . . it is now established by section 8 of the Criminal Justice Act 1967 that a failure to foresee the material results of one's conduct is a defence whether reasonable or not. It is odd that a different rule should prevail with respect to circumstances, the more particularly since foresight of results frequently depends on knowledge of circumstances. . . . Such a distinction seems unjustifiable. Its existence points in favour of a rule allowing as a defence any honest mistake which negatives mens rea, whether reasonable or not."

Does the law, then, compel one to say that a man should be convicted as a rapist though the jury remain unconvinced that rape was in his mind? . . .

Finally, in relation to the critical comments of Professor Glanville Williams that crimes requiring mens rea ought not to be capable of being committed by inattention, it is important to recall that in *Sweet* v. *Parsley* [1970] A.C. 132, Lord Diplock said in this House, at p. 163:

> "... the importance of the actual decision of the nine judges who constituted the majority in *R.* v. *Tolson*, ... was that it laid down as a general principle of construction of any enactment, which creates a criminal offence, that, even where the words used to describe the prohibited conduct would not in any other context connote the necessity for any particular mental element, they are nevertheless to be read as subject to the implication that a necessary element in the offence is the absence of a belief, held honestly and upon reasonable grounds, in the existence of facts which, if true, would make the act innocent. As was said by the Privy Council in *Bank of New South Wales* v. *Piper* [1897] A.C. 383, 389, 390, the absence of mens rea really consists in such a belief by the accused."

At pp. 164–165:

> "It has been objected that the requirement laid down in *R.* v. *Tolson*, 23 Q.B.D. 168 and the *Bank of New South Wales* v. *Piper* [1897] A.C. 383 that the mistaken belief should be based on reasonable grounds introduces an objective mental element into mens rea. This may be so, but there is nothing novel in this. The test of the mental element of provocation which distinguishes manslaughter from murder has always been at common law and now is by statute the objective one of the way in which a reasonable man would react to provocation. There is nothing unreasonable in requiring a citizen to take reasonable care to ascertain the facts relevant to his avoiding doing a prohibited act."

These words express the general approach of the criminal law adopted over a wide spectrum, by courts applying the common law both here and overseas, approved to the extent already indicated by this House and by courts of inferior jurisdiction, and in respect of a variety of offences. What Professor Glanville Williams has described as "the hoary error that a mistake to afford a defence to a criminal charge must be reasonable" ((1951) 14 M.L.R. 485) is not only old but widely accepted. I indicated at an early stage the approach which I should have been inclined to adopt in relation to the direction on mens rea given in the present case had I felt free to do so. It is, of course, true to say that there is no direct decision of this House which compels my Lords now to uphold that direction, which has been so vigorously attacked by appellants' counsel. That being so, Professor J. C. Smith has invited us ([1975] Crim. L.R. 42) to hold that it was a clear misdirection. In support, he cited the recent Court of Appeal decision in *R.* v. *Smith (David)* [1974] Q.B. 354, where a man charged under section 1 (1) of the Criminal Damage Act 1971, with damaging another's property without lawful excuse pleaded that he thought it was his own. The Crown urged that, in order to establish "lawful excuse" as a defence, it must be shown that the defendant honestly but mistakenly believed *on reasonable grounds* that the facts were such that, had they existed, his conduct would have been lawful. But, in giving the judgment of the court allowing the appeal, James L.J. stressed that the statutory offence under section 1 relates to "A person who without lawful excuse destroys or damages any property belonging to another", and added at p. 360:

> "Applying the ordinary principles of mens rea, the intention and recklessness and the absence of lawful excuse required to constitute the offence have reference to property belonging to another. It follows that in our judgment no offence is committed under this section if a person destroys or causes

> damage to property belonging to another if he does so in the honest though mistaken belief that the property is his own, and provided that the belief is honestly held it is irrelevant to consider whether or not it is a justifiable belief."

It is, however, not without significance that, in relation to another section of the Act (section 5 (3)), which afforded a defence if at the material time the accused believed that the person entitled to consent to the destruction or damage of the property in question had consented, it was expressly provided that: "For the purposes of this section it is immaterial whether a belief is justified or not if it is honestly held." That exculpatory provision had *no* application to the defence relied upon in the case, namely, that the accused believed that the property he had damaged was his own, a defence which therefore had to be judged in accordance with general principles. As to these, Professor Smith commented that [1975] Crim. L.R. 42, 43:

> "The ordinary principles of mens rea should certainly be no less applicable to the common law offence of rape than to the statutory offences of criminal damage."

R. v. *Smith (David)* was a special case and at some future date the question involved in it may have to be reconsidered. Be that as it may, had I felt free to do so I would have acceded to the invitation extended by Professor Smith to this House [1975] Crim. L.R. 42 that we "should decide that a mistake of a relevant fact is a defence if the mistake was honest and genuine, even if it was also unreasonable." But regard must be had to the uniformity of approach over a wide area and for a long time—*R.* v. *Tolson*, *post*, p. 116, it should be remembered, was decided nearly 90 years ago. Paying such regard, the conclusion I have come to is that the necessary course is to uphold, as being in accordance with established law, the direction given in this case by the learned trial judge as to the necessity for the mistake of fact urged to be based on reasonable grounds. The approach which I should have preferred must, I think, wait until the legislature reforms this part of the law, just as it did in relation to the former presumption of intending the reasonable consequence of one's actions by section 8 of the Criminal Justice Act 1967. The proponents of such reform will doubtless have regard to the observations of Lord Reid in *Sweet* v. *Parsley* [1970] A.C. 132 at p. 150. On the other hand, those who oppose the notion that honest belief should per se suffice, on the ground that it facilitates the raising of bogus defences, should bear in mind the observations of Dixon J. in *Thomas* v. *The King*, 59 C.L.R. 279, 309 cited with approval by Lord Reid in *R.* v. *Warner* [1969] 2 A.C. 256, 274. But, the law being as it now is and for a long time has been, I find myself obliged to say that the certified point of law should be answered in the affirmative. . . .

In my judgment, in the light of all the evidence in this extraordinary case, no reasonable jury could have failed to convict all four accused even had they been directed as counsel for the appellants urges they should. Accordingly, even had I acceded to the submission that there was a misdirection, I should have held that no miscarriage of justice resulted in respect of any of the accused. I would therefore still have said, as I now do, that the appeals of all four should be dismissed.

Lord Fraser of Tullybelton: . . . Most offences, whether at common law or under statute, include some mental element, but the description of the offence normally refers only to the prohibited act, leaving the mental element to be implied. . . .

All the definitions of rape quoted to us which made any reference to the state of mind required of the rapist included a statement to the effect that: "one of the elements of the crime of rape is an intention on the part of an accused person to have intercourse without consent." I take that quotation from *R.* v. *Flannery and Prendergast* [1969] V.R. 31, 32, decided by the full Court in Victoria.

The argument for the Crown in support of an affirmative answer to the question in this case was not supported by any English decision on rape. It was supported by reference to English decisions in relation to other offences which are more or less analogous to rape, and to Australian decisions on rape, some of which I have already referred to. The English case upon which most reliance was placed was *R.* v. *Tolson* [*post,* p. 116], which was concerned with bigamy, and which decided that a bona fide belief *on reasonable grounds* in the death of the husband at the time of the second marriage afforded a good defence to the indictment of bigamy. The main argument in the case was concerned with the question whether a mistaken belief could be a defence to a charge of bigamy at all, and comparatively little attention was given to the subsidiary point of whether the belief had to be based upon reasonable grounds. The case seems to me therefore of only limited assistance for the present purpose. We were invited to overrule *Tolson* but, as it has stood for over 80 years, and has been followed in many later cases, I would not favour that course. But in my opinion the case is distinguishable from the present. Bigamy was a statutory offence under the Offences Against the Person Act 1861, section 57. So far as appears from the words of the section, bigamy was an absolute offence, except for one defence set out in a proviso, and it is clear that the mental element in bigamy is quite different from that in rape. In particular, bigamy does not involve any intention except that intention to go through a marriage ceremony, unlike rape in which I have already considered the mental element. So, if a defendant charged with bigamy believes that his spouse is dead, his belief does not involve the absence of any intent which forms an essential ingredient in the offence, and it is thus not comparable to the belief of a defendant charged with rape that the woman consents. The difficulty of arguing by analogy from one offence to another is strikingly illustrated by reference to the case of *R.* v. *Prince* (1875) 13 Cox C.C. 138. That case dealt with abduction of a girl under the age of 16, an offence created by section 55 of the Act of 1861. Bramwell B., with whom five other judges concurred, held that a mistaken and reasonable belief by the defendant that the abducted girl was aged 16 or more was no excuse, because abduction of a young girl was immoral as well as illegal, although a mistaken and reasonable belief by the defendant that he had the consent of the girl's father would have been an excuse. If such differences can exist about mistaken beliefs of different facts in one offence, it is surely dangerous to argue from one offence to another. No doubt a rapist, who mistakenly believes that the woman is consenting to intercourse, must be behaving immorally, by committing fornication or adultery. But those forms of immoral conduct are not intended to be struck at by the law against rape; indeed, they are not now considered appropriate to be visited with penalties of the criminal law at all. There seems to be no reason why they should affect the consequences of the mistaken belief.

I feel more difficulty about the Australian, and especially the Victorian, rape cases. I have already referred to their definition of the crime of rape as including an intention to have intercourse against the consent of the woman. Notwithstanding that, certain of them contain judicial dicta that a mistaken belief by the accused that the woman was consenting was no defence unless based upon reasonable grounds (see *R.* v. *Burles* [1947] V.L.R. 392, 402), but in none of these cases did the precise point with which we are now concerned arise for decision. In some of them the court accepted that mens rea would be excluded by the mistaken belief only if it was based on reasonable grounds. But they did so either because authorities which they considered binding on them "constrained" them to do so (*R.* v. *Sperotto and Salvietti* (1970) 71 S.R. (N.S.W.) 334, 339), or by reference to particular authorities without separate consideration of the point (*R.*

v. *Flannery and Prendergast* [1969] V.R. 31, 34). Accordingly, those cases do not contribute any additional argument tending to resolve the logical difficulty to which I have referred in considering the learned judge's direction in this case, and which seems to me insuperable. The authority referred to in *Flannery* was *R.* v. *Warner* [1969] 2 A.C. 256 where Lord Reid at p. 276C quoted with approval the following words from *Bank of New South Wales* v. *Piper* [1897] A.C. 383:

> "the absence of mens rea really consists of an *honest and reasonable* belief entertained by the accused of the existence of facts which if true, would make the act charged against him innocent." (My italics).

Later in his speech Lord Reid said, at p. 280C:

> "Mens rea or its absence is a subjective test, and any attempt to substitute an objective test for serious crime has been successfully resisted."

With the greatest respect I cannot see how it could be a subjective test, if the absence of mens rea includes the essentially objective element of being reasonable.

For these reasons, I am of the opinion that there is no authority which compels me to answer the question in this case in what I would regard as an illogical way. I would therefore answer the question in the negative—that is in favour of the accused. But, for the reasons stated by my noble and learned friends, Lord Hailsham of St. Marylebone and Lord Edmund-Davies, I would apply the proviso to the Criminal Appeal Act 1968, section 2 (1), and I would refuse the appeal.

Appeals dismissed

Note

Although the decision in *D.P.P.* v. *Morgan* was on the whole welcomed by legal academics it was widely denounced in the Press. As a result a Committee, chaired by Heilbron J., was set up to consider the implications of the case. The Committee's Report (Cmnd. 6352 (1976)) accepted the decision as consistent with the subjective approach to the mental element in crime, but recommended that the offence of rape be statutorily defined. This was implemented in the Sexual Offences (Amendment) Act 1976.

Three different academic reactions are discernible. There are those who welcomed the decision but wished it had gone further; those who felt it achieved the right balance and those who remained unconvinced that it was right to exclude reasonableness. The extracts below illustrate each of these points of view.

Smith and Hogan, Criminal Law (4th ed.), p. 183

"One unfortunate aspect of the discussion of the bigamy cases in *Morgan* is that it suggests a very strict approach to the problem of the implication of *mens rea* into statutory offences. . . . These *dicta* . . . suggest that, where a statute uses no words expressly importing *mens rea,* the mental element which the court will require the prosecution to prove will be minimal—to go through a ceremony of marriage, to have sexual intercourse etc., and that it will then be for the accused to introduce evidence sufficient to raise a doubt whether he did not, on reasonable grounds, have a belief inconsistent with some material element in the *actus reus.*"

Rupert Cross, "Centenary Reflections on Prince's Case" (1975) 91 L.Q.R. 540 at 551

"I have made suggestions which may, I fear, antagonise, for opposite reasons, two bodies of opinion to which I am accustomed to pay respect. The first is the opinion of a number of academic lawyers who are, if the expression can be permitted, 'in total bondage to the subjectivist bug'; the second is the opinion of that section of the press which, if the expression can be permitted, is 'dedicated to the vindication of outrages.'

There are academics who think that mistake of fact should always be a defence however unreasonable it may be; but, to say the least, I have toyed with the view that there are situations in which the law may properly require that the mistake should be a reasonable one. One such situation is that in which the mistake is pleaded as a total excuse for a deliberate resort to violence. Surely it is arguable that gross failure to exercise a reasonable judgment in these circumstances should be punished, so long as it is never forgotten that 'detached reflection cannot be demanded in the presence of an uplifted knife.' Another situation in which the law may properly require that a mistake of fact should be reasonable is perhaps that of intercourse with girls beneath the age of 16. The object of the legislation on this subject is to protect young girls against themselves. If their consent to the intercourse is immaterial, why should their statements with regard to their age provide an over-credulous accused with a defence. The requirement of reasonableness may at least do a little to insure that men do not jump to conclusions they desire to reach.

I can understand why the decision in *Morgan* came as a shock to those who rightly consider it to be one of the functions of the criminal law to vindicate the outrage of rape, although it is probably true to say that the case is exceptional. The number of situations in which a jury could entertain no reasonable doubt concerning the prosecutrix's evidence of protest and resistance and, at the same time, give any credence to the accused's assertion that he nonetheless believed her to be consenting to intercourse must be small. . . . [O]ne reason why the maximum punishment for rape is life imprisonment is that the common man considers rapists to be very wicked people. Someone who believes, albeit without reasonable cause, that the woman is consenting may well be stupid and insensitive, but he is not wicked in the sense in which the rapist is wicked."

Fletcher, Rethinking Criminal Law, p. 703

"There are some cases in which any mistake is sufficient to preclude liability, others in which the mistake prevails only if free from fault. An adequate method would help us classify cases into these two groups. Yet [in *D.P.P.* v. *Morgan*] both Lord Cross' reliance on ordinary language and Lord Hailsham's reliance on textbook definitions prove to be little more than tools for rationalizing the result in this case, and it is not even clear that the rationalization favors the right result. . . .

If we can determine the elements of the definition, then the claim is that the required intent encompasses these and only these elements. But how do we determine whether non-consent is part of the definition of rape? The definition, it will be recalled, is the minimal set of elements necessary to incriminate the actor. Consider the following scale of elements arranged in order of ascending incrimination:

1. touching
2. sexual contact
3. forcible sexual contact
4. non-consensual, forcible sexual contact

It is difficult to argue that touching per se is incriminating. . . . Sexual contact is obviously different. Intimate touching of the genitals is hardly routine; the touching requires a good reason. The reason, or the justification, might be the consent of the person touched or it might be the necessity of performing an operation in an emergency situation. This seems to me to be sufficient to regard the definition of rape as sexual penetration, with consent functioning as a ground for regarding the sexual act as a shared expression of love rather than as an invasion of bodily integrity.

The case in *Morgan* is even clearer, for the penetration was forcible. It is conceivable that a woman would enjoy being taken by force and that her consent would justify the forcible penetration. But it would be implausible to treat non-consent as well as force as necessary conditions for rendering the sexual act suspect. There seems to be little doubt that under the circumstances of *Morgan*, the consent of the woman should have functioned as a justification. And if that is the case, it is wrong to regard the intent required for rape as encompassing a belief in non-consent. If the perpetrators were mistaken about the supposed justification for forcible intercourse, their wrongful act might well be excused. But if the focus is on excusing their conduct, it is appropriate to require—in this case as in *Tolson* and *Sweet*—that their mistake be free from fault. If they were personally culpable in believing Morgan's lies about his wife, they could hardly claim their acts were blameless and therefore properly excused.

One might be tempted to think that the actual decision in *Morgan*, holding that any mistake about consent bars liability, expresses the mores of the new sexual morality. The stigma of fornication has softened; therefore one should have to show more in order to make out a case that sexual acts are socially unacceptable. It seems to follow that what makes rape wrong is non-consent, and therefore non-consent should be included in the definition of the defense. This argument is seductive, but . . . changing attitudes toward chastity hardly diminish the evil of rape. Indeed one can well argue the opposite view.

The more seriously one takes the sexual autonomy of adult men and women, the more incriminating an act of forcible intercourse of the type prosecuted in *Morgan*. Further, if consensual sexual acts are socially acceptable, it does not follow that non-consent is a necessary component of the definition and therefore encompassed in the required intent."

See also Sellers, "Mens Rea and the Judicial Approach to Bad Excuses" (1978) 41 M.L.R. 245, and Richard S. Tur (1981) 1 Ox. J. Leg. Stud. 432 where he discusses a decision of the Canadian Supreme Court, *R.* v. *Pappajohn* (1980) 111 D.L.R. 1 that the jury need not be directed on honest mistake unless there is some external evidence (such as Morgan's advice to his friends about his wife's "simulated resistance") to support it.

For further evidence of the "definitional approach" (*Fletcher, above*) see *Jaggard* v. *Dickinson, post*, p. 187, and *Albert* v. *Lavin, post*, p. 426.

Question

Rupert Cross is prepared to countenance a requirement of reasonableness where "mistake is pleaded as a total excuse for a deliberate resort to violence." Would this not include rape?

ii. Mistake Affecting Culpability

R. v. Tolson
(1889) 23 Q.B.D. 168
Court for Crown Cases Reserved

The defendant was deserted by her husband, and afterwards heard that he had been lost at sea. Five years after last seeing her husband, the defendant went through a ceremony of marriage with another man.

Her husband was still alive. She was convicted of bigamy, a felony under section 57, Offences Against the Person Act 1861, which is set out in the judgment of Cave J. below. Her conviction was quashed by a majority of nine judges to five.

CAVE J.: . . . At common law an honest and reasonable belief in the existence of circumstances, which, if true, would make the act for which a prisoner is indicted an innocent act has always been held to be a good defence. This doctrine is embodied in the somewhat uncouth maxim "*Actus non facit reum, nisi mens sit rea.*" Honest and reasonable mistake stands in fact on the same footing as absence of the reasoning faculty, as in infancy, or perversion of that faculty, as in lunacy. Instances of the existence of this common law doctrine will readily occur to the mind. So far as I am aware it has never been suggested that these exceptions do not equally apply in the case of statutory offences unless they are excluded expressly or by necessary implication. In *R.* v. *Prince* (1875) L.R. 2 C.C.R. 154, in which the principle of mistake underwent much discussion, it was not suggested by any of the judges that the exception of honest and reasonable mistake was not applicable to all offences, whether existing at common law or created by statute. As I understand the judgments in that case the difference of opinion was as to the exact extent of the exception. . . .

It is argued, however, that, assuming the general exception to be as stated, yet the language of the Act (24 & 25 Vict. c. 100, s. 57), is such that that exception is necessarily excluded in this case. Now, it is undoubtedly within the competence of the legislature to enact that a man shall be branded as a felon and punished for doing an act which he honestly and reasonably believes to be lawful and right; just as the legislature may enact that a child or a lunatic shall be punished criminally for an act which he has been led to commit by the immaturity or perversion of his reasoning faculty. But such a result seems so revolting to the moral sense that we ought to require the clearest and most indisputable evidence that such is the meaning of the Act. It is said that this inference necessarily arises from the language of the section in question, and particularly of the proviso. The section (omitting immaterial parts) is in these words: "Whosoever, being married, shall marry any other person during the life of the former husband or wife, . . . shall be guilty of felony . . . : provided that nothing in this section contained shall extend . . . to any person marrying a second time whose husband or wife shall have been continually absent from such person for the space of seven years then last past, and shall not have been known by such person to be living within that time. . . ." It is argued that the first part is expressed absolutely; but, surely, it is not contended that the language admits of no exception, and therefore that a lunatic who, under the influence of a delusion, marries again, must be convicted; and, if an exception is to be admitted where the reasoning faculty is perverted by disease, why is not an exception equally to be admitted where the reasoning faculty, although honestly and reasonably exercised, is deceived? But it is said that the proviso is inconsistent with the exception contended for; and, undoubtedly, if the proviso covers less ground or only the same ground as the exception, it follows that the legislature has expressed an intention that the exception shall not operate until after seven years from the disappearance of the first husband. But if, on the other hand, the proviso covers more ground than the general exception, surely it is no argument to say that the legislature must have intended that the more limited defence shall not operate within the seven years because it has provided that a less limited defence shall only come into operation at the expiration of those years.

What must the accused prove to bring herself within the general exception? She must prove facts from which the jury may reasonably infer that she honestly and on reasonable grounds believed her first husband to be dead before she married again. What must she prove to bring herself within the proviso? Simply that her husband has been continually absent for seven years; and, if she can do that, it will be no answer to prove that she had no reasonable grounds for believing him to be dead or that she did not honestly believe it. Unless the prosecution can prove that she knew her husband to be living within the seven years she must be acquitted. The honesty and reasonableness of her belief is no longer in issue. Even if it could be proved that she believed him to be alive all the time, as distinct from knowing him to be so, the prosecution must fail. The proviso, therefore, is far wider than the general exception; and the intention of the legislature, that a wider and more easily established defence should be open after seven years from the disappearance of the husband, is not necessarily inconsistent with the intention that a different defence, less extensive and more difficult of proof, should be open within the seven years.

STEPHEN J.: My view of the subject is based upon a particular application of the doctrine usually, though I think not happily, described by the phrase "*non est reus, nisi mens sit rea.*" . . . The principle involved appears to me, when fully considered, to amount to no more than this. The full definition of every crime contains expressly or by implication a proposition as to a state of mind. Therefore, if the mental element of any conduct alleged to be a crime is proved to have been absent in any given case, the crime so defined is not committed; or, again, if a crime is fully defined, nothing amounts to that crime which does not satisfy that definition. Crimes are in the present day much more accurately defined by statute or otherwise than they formerly were. The mental element of most crimes is marked by one of the words "maliciously," "fraudulently," "negligently," or "knowingly," but it is the general—I might, I think, say, the invariable—practice of the legislature to leave unexpressed some of the mental elements of crime. In all cases whatever, competent age, sanity and some degree of freedom from some kinds of coercion are assumed to be essential to criminality, but I do not believe they are ever introduced into any statute by which any particular crime is defined.

The meaning of the words "malice," "negligence" and "fraud" in relation to particular crimes has been ascertained by numerous cases. Malice means one thing in relation to murder, another in relation to the Malicious Mischief Act, and a third in relation to libel, and so of fraud and negligence.

With regard to knowledge of fact, the law, perhaps, is not quite so clear, but it may, I think, be maintained that in every case knowledge of fact is to some extent an element of criminality as much as competent age and sanity. To take an extreme illustration, can anyone doubt that a man who, though he might be perfectly sane, committed what would otherwise be a crime in a state of somnambulism, would be entitled to be acquitted? And why is this? Simply because he would not know what he was doing. A multitude of illustrations of the same sort might be given. I will mention one or two glaring ones. *Levett's Case*, (1638) Cro. Car. 538, decides that a man who, making a thrust with a sword at a place where, upon reasonable grounds, he supposed a burglar to be, killed a person who was not a burglar, was held not to be a felon, though he might be (it was not decided that he was) guilty of killing *per infortuniam*, or possibly, *se defendendo*, which then involved certain forfeitures. In other words, he was in the same situation as far as regarded the homicide as if he had killed a burglar. In the decision of the judges in *M'Naghten's Case* [*post*, p. 162], it is stated that if under an insane delusion one man killed another, and if the delusion was such that it would, if true, justify or excuse the killing, the homicide would be justified or excused. This could hardly be if the same were not law as to a sane mistake. . . .

It is said, first, that the words of 24 & 25 Vict. c. 100, s. 57, are absolute, and that the exceptions which that section contains are the only ones which are intended to be admitted, and this it is said is confirmed by the express proviso in the section—an indication which is thought to negative any tacit exception. It is also supposed that the case of *R.* v. *Prince* (1875) L.R. 2 C.C.R. 154, decided on section 55, confirms this view. I will begin by saying how far I agree with these views. First, I agree that the case turns exclusively upon the construction of section 57 of 24 & 25 Vict. c. 100. Much was said to us in argument on the old statute, 1 Jac. 1, c. 11. I cannot see what this has to do with the matter. Of course, it would be competent to the legislature to define a crime in such a way as to make the existence of any state of mind immaterial. The question is solely whether it has actually done so in this case.

In the first place I will observe upon the absolute character of the section. It appears to me to resemble most of the enactments contained in the Consolidation Acts of 1861, in passing over the general mental elements of crime which are presupposed in every case. Age, sanity and more or less freedom from compulsion, are always presumed, and I think it would be impossible to quote any statute which in any case specifies these elements of criminality in the definition of any crime. It will be found that either by using the words wilfully and maliciously, or by specifying some special intent as an element of particular crimes, knowledge of fact is implicitly made part of the statutory definition of most modern definitions of crime, but there are some cases in which this cannot be said. Such are section 55, on which *R.* v. *Prince* was decided, section 56, which punishes the stealing of "any child under the age of fourteen years," section 49, as to procuring the defilement of any "woman or girl under the age of twenty-one," in each of which the same question might arise as in *R.* v. *Prince*; to these I may add some of the provisions of the Criminal Law Amendment Act of 1885. Reasonable belief that a girl is sixteen or upwards is a defence to the charge of an offence under sections 5, 6 and 7, but this is not provided for as to an offence against section 4, which is meant to protect girls under thirteen.

It seems to me that as to the construction of all these sections the case of *R.* v. *Prince* is a direct authority. It was the case of a man who abducted a girl under sixteen, believing, on good grounds, that she was above that age. Lord Esher, then Brett J., was against the conviction. His judgment establishes at much length, and, as it appears to me, unanswerably, the principle above explained, which he states as follows: "That a mistake of facts on reasonable grounds, to the extent that, if the facts were as believed, the acts of the prisoner would make him guilty of no offence at all, is an excuse, and that such an excuse is implied in every criminal charge and every criminal enactment in England."

Lord Blackburn, with whom nine other judges agreed, and Lord Bramwell, with whom seven others agreed, do not appear to me to have dissented from this principle, speaking generally; but they held that it did not apply fully to each part of every section to which I have referred. Some of the prohibited acts they thought the legislature intended to be done at the peril of the person who did them, but not all.

The judgment delivered by Lord Blackburn proceeds upon the principle that the intention of the legislature in section 55 was "to punish the abduction unless the girl was of such an age as to make her consent an excuse."

Lord Bramwell's judgment proceeds upon this principle: "The legislature has enacted that if anyone does this wrong act he does it at the risk of her turning out to be under sixteen. This opinion gives full scope to the doctrine of the *mens rea*. If the taker believed he had her father's consent, though wrongly, he would have no *mens rea*; so if he did not know she was in anyone's possession nor in the care or charge of anyone. In those cases he would not know he was doing the act forbidden by statute."

All the judges, therefore, in *R.* v. *Prince* agreed on the general principle, though they all, except Lord Esher, considered that, the object of the legislature being to prevent a scandalous and wicked invasion of parental rights (whether it was to be regarded as illegal apart from the statute or not), it was to be supposed that they intended that the wrongdoer should act at his peril.

As another illustration of the same principle, I may refer to *R.* v. *Bishop* (1880) 5 Q.B.D. 259. The defendant in that case was tried before me for receiving more than two lunatics into a house not duly licensed, upon an indictment on 8 & 9 Vict. c. 100, s. 44. It was proved that the defendant did receive more than two persons, whom the jury found to be lunatics, into her house, believing honestly, and on reasonable grounds, that they were not lunatics. I held that this was immaterial, having regard to the scope of the Act, and the object for which it was apparently passed, and this court upheld that ruling.

The application of this to the present case appears to me to be as follows. The general principle is clearly in favour of the prisoner, but how does the intention of the legislature appear to have been against them? It could not be the object of Parliament to treat the marriage of widows as an act to be if possible prevented as presumably immoral. The conduct of the [woman] convicted was not in the smallest degree immoral, it was perfectly natural and legitimate. Assuming the facts to be as [she] supposed, the infliction of more than a nominal punishment on [her] would have been a scandal. Why, then, should the legislature be held to have wished to subject [her] to punishment at all. . . .?

It is argued that the proviso that a remarriage after seven years' separation shall not be punishable, operates as a tacit exclusion of all other exceptions to the penal part of the section. It appears to me that it only supplies a rule of evidence which is useful in many cases, in the absence of explicit proof of death. But it seems to me to show not that belief in the death of one married person excuses the marriage of the other only after seven years' separation, but that mere separation for that period had the effect which reasonable belief of death caused by other evidence would have at any time. It would to my mind be monstrous to say that seven years' separation should have a greater effect in excusing a bigamous marriage than positive evidence of death, sufficient for the purpose of recovering a policy of assurance or obtaining probate of a will, would have. . . .

Conviction quashed

[A reasonable belief that the first marriage has been dissolved has also been held to be a defence to bigamy: *R.* v. *Gould* [1968] 1 All E.R. 849.]

Note

Until the decision in *D.P.P.* v. *Morgan* no-one could be sure whether what was in issue in the bigamy cases was the reasonableness of the mistake, or the relevance of a mistake which happened to be reasonable (as are most credible mistakes). In either case it would have been open to the House of Lords to bring bigamy within the *ratio* of *Morgan*. What justifications are there for convicting for bigamy a person who mistakenly believes he or she is free to marry?

See *post*, p. 425 for a discussion of reasonable mistakes in self-defence.

iii. Irrelevant Mistakes

(a) Mistake and Strict Liability
(b) Ignorance of the Law
(c) Transferred Malice

Mistakes can only be relevant in crimes which require proof of some mental element. As the preceding sections indicate, the courts, in allocating mistake to one category or another, are making decisions as to what that mental element is and to what parts of the *actus reus* it is to apply. The rules deduced from the cases can be stated without reference to mistake as such. Thus of bigamy it can be said that proof of intention is necessary for the act of getting married while as to the circumstances of being married only negligence is needed. Where an offence is interpreted as not even requiring negligence as to an element of the *actus reus* it is said to be an offence of strict liability. *Prince*, below, illustrates how the creation of such an offence renders the mistake of no legal consequence.

The converse of the opening statement of the above paragraph is not true: mistakes are sometimes irrelevant in *mens rea* crimes. Ignorance of the law is often no defence. In these cases, as in *Prince*, the mistake is *rendered* irrelevant by the law even though, had things been as the defendant supposed, there would have been no offence. However, in cases of transferred malice, the mistake is legally irrelevant because it is immaterial to D's culpability whether the victim is the intended one or someone else.

(a) *Mistake and strict liability*

R. v. Prince (1875) L.R. 2 C.C.R. 154: Section 55 of the Offences Against the Person Act 1861 provides that it is an offence "unlawfully [to] take . . . any unmarried girl, being under the age of 16 years, out of the possession and against the will of her father. . . ." Prince was convicted under this section despite having reasonable grounds to believe the girl concerned was over 16. The following passage is from the judgment of Blackburn J. in which 9 other judges concurred (at L.R. 2 C.C.R. 154, 170): "The question . . . is reduced to this, whether the words in s. 55 [*supra*], are to be read as if they were 'being under the age of sixteen, and he knowing she was under that age.' No such words are contained in the statute, nor is there the word 'maliciously', 'knowingly', or any other word used that can be said to involve a similar meaning." See also *R.* v. *McPherson* [1980] Crim. L.R. 654.

R. v. Miller [1975] *1 W.L.R. 1222:* The offence of driving a motor vehicle on a road while disqualified under section 99 (6) of the Road Traffic Act 1972 was held to have been committed despite the defendant's belief that he was driving on a private road. James L.J., p. 1226: "[W]e have reached the clear conclusion that section 99 . . . provides an offence which is proved once the prosecution establish the facts which were not disputed in the present case, namely, that there was driving by a person who was at that time disqualified . . . and that it is not relevant for a defendant to raise the question of his state of mind in order to show . . . a mistaken belief as to the nature of the place where the driving was taking place."

R. v. Howells [*1977*] *2 W.L.R. 716:* It is an offence under section 1 of the Firearms Act 1968 to possess a revolver without a firearm certificate. Under section 58 (2) this does not apply to antique firearms, "purchased . . . or possessed as a curiosity or ornament." D thought he possessed an antique; in fact it was a modern reproduction. His appeal against conviction was dismissed by the Court of Appeal, Brown L.J., p. 725: "This court has reached the decision that s. 1 should be construed strictly . . . to allow a defence of honest and reasonable belief that the firearm was an antique and therefore excluded would be likely to defeat the clear intention of the Act."

Question

If the draft Criminal Liability (Mental Element) Bill, *ante*, p. 56, were in force, would clause 6 have helped the defendant in *Howells*, above?

(b) *Ignorance of the law*

R. v. *Smith, ante,* p. 100 and *R.* v. *Gould, ante,* p. 120 indicate that mistake of civil law can preclude a person from having the requisite mental element for a particular offence. Ignorance of the law in the sense of not realising that a particular act is prohibited is rarely a defence. People are presumed to know the law. Two justifications have been advanced for this constructive knowledge:

Oliver Wendell Holmes, The Common Law (1881), p. 48:
"[T]o admit the excuse at all would be to encourage ignorance . . . and justice to the individual is rightly outweighed by the larger interests on the other side of the scales."

Hall, p. 382:
"If that plea [mistake of law] were valid, the consequence would be: wherever a defendant in a criminal case thought the law was thus and so, he is to be treated as though the law were thus and so, i.e. *the law actually is thus and so.* But such a doctrine would contradict the essential requisites of a legal system. . . ." (italics in original).

Hall's view seems logically attractive but does any defence of mistake, whether of fact or law, alter either factual reality or the law itself? In any case, this view fails to recognise that ignorance of the law does sometimes affect culpability. When an offence is confined to a particular class of prohibited persons and the means of discovering who is in that class are obscure, ignorance may be excused: Lord Evershed in *Lim Chin Aik* v. *The Queen, post,* p. 134, [1963] A.C. 160, 171: "[T]he maxim [ignorance of the law is no excuse] cannot apply to such a case as the present where it appears that there is . . . no provision . . . for the publication in any form of an order of the kind made in the present case or any other provision designed to enable a man by appropriate inquiry to find out what 'the law' is." The United States' Supreme Court has allowed a defence of ignorance to an offence of "failing to register as a convicted person": *Lambert* v. *California* 355 U.S. 225 (1957). The Court drew a distinction between crimes of commission, where ignorance could never be a defence, and crimes of omission, where it may be, unless the failure to act is under circumstances which should alert the doer to the consequences of such failure. Mr. Justice Douglas said, at p. 232: "Were it otherwise, the evil would be as great as it is when the law is written in print too fine to read, or in language foreign to the community." Can this be reconciled with Holmes's statement above? See, generally, A. J. Ashworth, "Excusable Mistake of Law" [1974] Crim. L.R. 652.

(c) *Transferred malice*

R. v. Pembliton
(1874) L.R. 2 C.C.R. 119
Court for Crown Cases Reserved

The defendant was a member of a group who were fighting outside the public-house called The Grand Turk. He picked up a large stone and threw it at those with whom he had been fighting. The stone passed over their heads and broke a window of the public-house. The defendant was indicted for "unlawfully and maliciously" committing damage under the Malicious Damage Act 1861, s. 51. The jury found that he had intended to strike the persons at whom he aimed the stone and that he did not intend to break the window.

Underhill, for the prosecution. The finding of the jury as to the intent is surplusage; directly it is proved that he threw the stone which caused the damage without just cause, the offence is established.

[Lush L.J.: That omits the word "maliciously".]

In this Act there are a number of sections in which intent is a necessary ingredient to the offence, and in all of them this is expressed. Thus a distinction is drawn by the legislature, and if intent had been necessary here it would have been inserted. The common law rule as to malice is applicable here, and the consideration arises whether "the fact has been attended with such circumstances as are the ordinary symptoms of a wicked, depraved, malignant spirit": Foster's *Crown Cases*, p. 256; *Russell on Crime*, 4th edn., Vol. I, 667. Then here the jury have found that the prisoner was actuated by malice.

[Blackburn J.: But only of a particular kind, and not against the person injured.]

In *R.* v. *Ward* (1872) L.R. 1 C.C.R. 356 the prisoner was charged with wounding with intent, and convicted of malicious wounding, though his intention was to frighten, not to shoot the prosecutor.

[Blackburn J.: There was evidence of malice in that case and so the conviction was upheld, but here the express finding of the jury negatives malice.]

In *R.* v. *Haughton* (1833) 5 C. & P. 559 the prisoner set fire to a cowhouse not knowing a cow was in it, and was convicted of maliciously burning the cow. So in Hale's *Pleas of the Crown*, p. 474, throwing a stone over a wall with intent to do hurt to people passing and killing one of them is treated as murder.

[Blackburn J.: Lord Coke, 3 Inst., p. 56, puts the case of a man stealing a deer in a park, shooting at the deer, and by the glance of the arrow killing a boy that is hidden in a bush, and calls this murder; but can one say that ruling would be adopted now?]

The test is whether the act is malicious in itself as in the case of a person wilfully riding an unruly horse into a crowd: East, *Pleas of the Crown*, p. 231.

[Blackburn J.: I should have told the jury that if the prisoner knew there were windows behind, and that the probable consequence of his act would be to break one of them, that would be evidence for them of malice. The jury might perhaps have convicted on such a charge, but we have to consider their actual findings.]

The fifty-eighth section, which renders it immaterial that there should be malice against the owner of the property or otherwise, applies.

[Lord Coleridge C.J.: No, that means against the owner, or someone not the owner.]

Lord Coleridge C.J.: I am of the opinion that the evidence does not support the conviction. The indictment is under [section 51, Malicious Damage Act 1861] which deals with malicious injuries to property, and the section expressly says that the act is to be unlawful and malicious. There is also the fifty-eighth section, which makes it immaterial whether the offence has been committed from malice against the owner of the property or otherwise, that is, from malice against someone not the owner of the property. In both these sections it seems to me that what is intended by the statute is a wilful doing of an intentional act. Without saying that if the case had been left to them in a different way the conviction could not have been supported, if, on these facts, the jury had come to a conclusion that the prisoner was reckless of the consequence of his act, and might reasonably have expected that it would result in breaking the window, it is sufficient to say that the jury have expressly found the contrary. . . .

BLACKBURN J.: We have not now to consider what would be malice aforethought to bring a given case within the common law definition of murder; here the statute says that the act must be unlawful and malicious, and malice may be defined to be "where any person wilfully does an act injurious to another without lawful excuse." Can this man be considered, on the case submitted to us, as having wilfully broken a pane of glass? The jury might perhaps have found on this evidence that the act was malicious, because they might have found that the prisoner knew that the natural consequence of his act would be to break the glass, and although that was not his wish, yet that he was reckless whether he did it or not; but the jury have not so found, and I think it is impossible to say in this case that the prisoner has maliciously done an act which he did not intend to do.

Conviction quashed

R. v. Latimer
(1886) 17 Q.B.D. 359
Court for Crown Cases Reserved

L., who was quarrelling with C. in a public-house aimed a blow at C. with his belt. The belt glanced off C. and severely injured R. In answer to questions by the recorder the jury found that the striking of R. was purely accidental and not such a consequence of the blow as the prisoner ought to have expected to follow. They also found that the blow was unlawful and malicious. L. was found guilty of unlawful and malicious wounding.

LORD COLERIDGE C.J.: We are of opinion that this conviction must be sustained. It is common knowledge that a man who has an unlawful and malicious intent against another, and, in attempting to carry it out, injures a third person, is guilty of what the law deems malice against the person injured, because the offender is doing an unlawful act, and has that which the judges call general malice, and that is enough.... So, but for *R.* v. *Pembliton* (above), there would not have been the slightest difficulty. Does that case make any difference? I think not, and, on consideration, that it was quite rightly decided. But it is clearly distinguishable, because the indictment in *R.* v. *Pembliton* was on the Act making unlawful and malicious injury to property a statutory offence punishable in a certain way, and the jury expressly negatived, the facts expressly negatived, any intention to do injury to property, and the court held that under the Act making it an offence to injure any property there must be an intent to injure property. *R.* v. *Pembliton*, therefore, does not govern the present case, and on no other ground is there anything to be said for the prisoner.

Conviction affirmed

R. v. Martin
(1881) 8 Q.B.D. 54
Court for Crown Cases Reserved

Shortly before the end of a theatrical performance the defendant, with the intention of causing terror in the minds of persons leaving the theatre, put out the lights on a staircase which a large number would descend. He also put an iron bar across a doorway with the intention of obstructing the exit. As a result several persons were injured. He was charged with unlawfully and maliciously inflicting grievous bodily harm and was convicted. The jury found these intentions in reply to questions put to them.

LORD COLERIDGE C.J.: I am unable to entertain any doubt as to the propriety of this conviction. The prisoner was indicted under [section 20 of the Offences Against the Person Act 1861], which enacts that "whosoever shall unlawfully and maliciously wound, or inflict any grievous bodily harm upon any other person, either with or without any weapon or instrument, shall be guilty of misdemeanour, etc." [He then stated the facts.]

Upon these facts the prisoner was convicted, and the jury found all that was necessary to sustain the conviction. The prisoner must be taken to have intended the natural consequences of that which he did. He acted "unlawfully and maliciously," not that he had any personal malice against the particular individuals injured, but in the sense of doing an unlawful act calculated to injure, and by which others were in fact injured. Just as in the case of a man who unlawfully fires a gun among a crowd, it is murder if one of the crowd is thereby killed. The prisoner was most properly convicted.

STEPHEN J.: I am entirely of the same opinion, but I wish to add that the recorder seems to have put the case too favourably for the prisoner, for he put it to the jury to consider whether the prisoner did the act "as a mere piece of foolish mischief." Now, it seems to me, that if the prisoner did that which he did as a piece of foolish mischief unlawfully and without excuse, he did it "wilfully," that is "maliciously," within the meaning of the statute. I think it important to notice this as the word "malicious" is capable of being misunderstood. Lord Blackburn (then Mr. Justice Blackburn) in the cases of *R.* v. *Ward* (1872) L.R. 1 C.C.R. 356 at p. 360 and *R.* v. *Pembliton,* above, lays it down that a man acts "maliciously" when he wilfully and without lawful excuse does that which he knows will injure another.

Conviction affirmed

Question

The defendant in *Martin,* above, had no mental element in relation to any particular person. Was the decision in *Latimer, supra,* decided in a similar vein?

A. J. Ashworth, "Transferred Malice and Punishment for Unforeseen Consequences" in Reshaping the Criminal Law (ed. Glazebrook), pp. 77–94

"The central case for application of transferred malice is where D does an act which is intended to injure O but which accidentally injures P. But how much further does the doctrine go, and what are its outer limits? On principle it seems clear that, just as the doctrine transfers D's intention from O to P, so it should equally operate to transfer recklessness from O to P. If D does an act which he realises might injure O (whose presence he either foresees as probable or knows as certain), and D's act results in injury to P (whose presence he did not foresee), a consistent application of the doctrine would render D liable for the injury to P.

Before discussing whether the doctrine of transferred malice is consistent with general principles of criminal liability, it is appropriate to consider whether the doctrine is really necessary. The laws of South Africa and of some Australian states do without transferred malice. What, if anything, would be lost if the doctrine were abolished here? Does our criminal law offer any acceptable alternative methods of dealing with these cases? There are two obvious possibilities—liability for the crime attempted (thus ignoring the accidental result), and liability for the actual result based on recklessness— and these will be examined in turn. If it be assumed for present purposes that sentences for attempts are not materially lower than sentences for completed crimes, and that the sentences for two offences which form part of the same transaction should be concurrent, the practical importance of the discussion is clear.

A conviction for attempt is possible in virtually all cases which fall within the doctrine of transferred liability. D will invariably have taken sufficient steps towards committing the offence against his intended victim for there to be the *actus reus* of an attempt, and *mens rea* will be undisputed. In *Latimer*, for example, D could quite simply have been convicted of the attempted unlawful wounding of O; and likewise in *Pembliton* there were strong grounds for convicting D of attempted unlawful wounding of persons in the crowd. A feature of the cases on transferred malice is the frequency with which D, in expressing his regret about injuring P, admits that he intended to harm O. In such circumstances a charge of attempt in relation to O would seem so straightforward that it is hard to understand why transferred malice is so frequently invoked. An underdeveloped law of attempts and restrictive rules of procedure may have justified the doctrine as an expedient in earlier centuries, but neither reason has applied for 100 years now....

In many of the cases to which transferred malice applies, the harm to P was quite unforeseen. But in some of them, D could be held liable for the harm to P without invoking transferred malice—on the basis that, in attempting to harm O, he was reckless as to harming P....

It is often said that in *Pembliton* the jury should have found D reckless as to damaging the window, and that this would have spared counsel and the courts much fruitless argument. But the real fault surely lay with the prosecutor: D intended and attempted to injure persons with a stone, he should properly be charged, convicted and sentenced for an offence against the person, not as a property offender. The damage to the window is an irrelevance; and a conviction for malicious damage would have been an inadequate characterisation of his criminality....

The doctrine could, then, be abolished without material loss to criminal justice; and it is desirable that it should be. For, quite apart from any problems over the consistency of the doctrine with general principles of criminal liability, it attributes significance to matters of chance and results in a mischaracterisation of D's criminality which could simply and effectively be avoided by charging an attempt. What, then, are the objections to using the law of attempts?

The first is that it would be wrong for a person who intended to cause harm of a certain kind and did cause such harm to escape with a lighter sentence merely because he was charged with an attempt. This objection assumes that the sentence for an attempt will be lighter than for the completed crime, and it appears that the assumption is well-founded. What little judicial authority exists on the question of sentencing for attempted crime suggests that English courts pay less regard to the intended than to the actual consequences of D's actions. This tendency is also apparent in decisions on the relevance of unforeseen consequences to sentencing....

The first objection to using the law of attempts is therefore well-founded in fact, but it is nevertheless submitted that it should not succeed. Rather, the sentencing policy of the courts is wrong and should be changed. Some of the arguments advanced in favour of lower sentences for attempted than for completed crimes apply only where D has not done all the acts he intended to do—such as the argument that the lower sentence supplies D with an incentive not to take the final steps to consummate the crime—and not to cases where D has done all the acts he intended to do but has failed to produce the desired result. A more general argument which does apply to the "transferred malice" situation is that since those who attempt crimes expect to be successful, the deterrent efficacy of the law is not greatly weakened by imposing lighter sentences for attempts; but that would be to regard general prevention as more important than individual prevention, an order of priority which many (including the present writer) would oppose. Perhaps the most popular reason for punishing completed crimes more severely than attempts, shared (as we have seen) by some judges, is that it is important to take account of the harm actually caused by the offence. Exactly why the harm actually caused should be important to sentence when it was *unforeseen* is not, however, clear. . . .

A second objection, in a similar vein and with similar weaknesses, is that even if the punishment were the same, it is more appropriate to convict of the completed crime in the "transferred malice" situation. Where D set out to cause harm of a certain kind and did cause harm of that kind, it seems empty and insufficient to convict him of a mere attempt. He has actually caused a loss to the community of the kind he intended to cause, and that fact should be recorded. Once again, however, this reasoning leans too heavily on results which may be entirely a matter of chance. In a system based on subjective liability, the legal label attached to D's offence should generally reflect his intentional act and not the chance result.

The argument here is, therefore, that it is more appropriate to charge an attempt than to pursue a conviction for the completed offence by means of transferred malice. In terms of social defence through criminal punishment nothing should be lost, because the sentence for the attempt should be the same as for the completed crime. Both on a retributive theory and on a theory of individual deterrence, the sentence should be governed by the result D intended to produce and not by the seriousness of that which eventuated. Moreover, to allow an unintended result to influence the classification of D's offence is to move closer to constructive liability than subjective liability.

There remains the question whether it is fair to describe the result in a 'transferred malice' situation as unintended. Is the doctrine really 'an arbitrary exception to normal principles?' [Williams, C.L.G.P., p. 134]. Can it be impugned on grounds of logic, as well as on the ground of appropriateness?

The simplest argument which is used to bring transferred malice within normal principles of *mens rea* is that D intended to cause the *actus reus* of a crime and did cause the *actus reus* of that crime. If D intended to kill and did kill, it cannot be correct to describe the killing as unintended merely because the victim was P instead of O. This argument, as Glanville Williams observes,

> sounds plausible only because part of the real intention is omitted. Although the result in the sense of a killing was intended, the result in the sense of a killing of P was not intended. After all, the accused is not indicted for killing in the abstract; he is indicted for killing P; and it should therefore, on a strict view, be necessary to establish *mens rea* in relation to the killing of P.

That view, which gives pride of place to the form of indictment and to ordinary language, has been challenged by Smith and Hogan:

> The answer to this, it is submitted, is that D's act is unintentional only in a respect which is immaterial. The test of materiality in a difference of result is whether it affects the existence of the *actus reus* which D intended. . . . The *actus reus* of murder is the killing of a human being—*any* human being—under the Queen's Peace, and his identity is irrelevant.

The difference between the two positions is clear. Glanville Williams points out that D is charged with murdering P or with unlawfully wounding P, and that it would be logical to require *mens rea* in relation to that specified result. The commonsense attraction of this view is demonstrated by the fact that in ordinary language we would never say that 'D intentionally killed P' if we knew that D was aiming at O, and by the specific findings of juries in the decided cases. Smith and Hogan, on the other hand, point out that many offences are so defined as to proscribe the causing of the *actus reus* to 'any person,' and that there are already two clear exceptions to any supposed requirement of full *mens rea* in relation to the actual result caused—if D causes the *actus reus* by a different mode than he intended he is nonetheless liable, and if D is mistaken as to the identity of his victim he is held liable on the basis that he intended to cause the *actus reus* to the person he aimed at. But the mere fact that there are already two respects in which full *mens rea* as to the actual result is not required cannot of itself lend support to a third exception: some would dispute the wisdom of the rule that causing the intended *actus reus* by an unintended mode does not affect D's liability, and the rule that a mistake in the identity of the victim is immaterial because D certainly intended to kill the man at whom he shot can be justified on the purely practical ground that there might otherwise be no offence of which D could be convicted. This leaves only the question whether the logic of a subjective principle of *mens rea* is satisfied by an intention to cause the *actus reus* of the offence to some person, or whether that logic requires an intention to cause the *actus reus* to the person actually harmed. The answer is that neither proposition is deducible from the general principles of *mens rea*: it depends upon how one chooses to define those principles, and that choice will be influenced by one's view about the solution of the particular problem presented by the transferred malice situation.

Greater attention among prosecutors to intended harm rather than accidental results would achieve considerable improvement, especially in those cases in which the courts will otherwise apply the doctrine of transferred malice. But, a wider problem arises under the broad codified offences such as criminal damage. Here principles of sentencing become especially important. The proper effect on sentence of an unsuccessful intention and an unintended result must be settled, and, in particular, the grip of the notion that sentences are rightly proportioned to the actual consequences of D's actions must be loosened. Both in general, and in cases which now fall within the doctrine of transferred malice, the touchstone of sentencing should be the intended and not the actual result."

6. STRICT LIABILITY

i. The Evolution of Strict Liability

"Justice," the British Section of the International Commission of Jurists, has estimated that, of the 7,200 separate offences listed in Stone's Justices' Manual for 1975, over half did not require proof of a mental element. (Justice, *Breaking the Rules* (1980)).

Sayre, "Public Welfare Offences" (1933) 33 Col. L.R. 55

"The growth of a distinct group of offences punishable without regard to any mental element dates from about the middle of the nineteenth century. Before this, convictions for crime without proof of a *mens rea* are to be found only occasionally, chiefly among the nuisance cases. In the early days newspaper proprietors might also be punished . . . for libel without proof of *mens rea*, for in libel prosecutions actual criminal knowledge on the part of the owners or publishers of newspapers would often be a matter so difficult to ascertain as to make proof well-nigh impossible. Yet to treat as criminal newspaper owners who were altogether innocent of any criminal intent seemed so harsh and unjust a doctrine and so out of accord with established legal principles that in 1836 an act of

Parliament was passed to make this no longer possible [Lord Campbell's Act: s. 7 allowed a newspaper proprietor to escape liability by proving that the publication was made "without his authority, consent or knowledge."] But apart from exceptional isolated cases criminal liability depended upon proof of a criminal intent. . . .

The decisions permitting convictions of light police offences without proof of a guilty mind came just at the time when the demands of an increasingly complex social order required additional regulation of an administrative character unrelated to questions of personal guilt; the movement also synchronised with the trend of the day away from nineteenth century individualism toward a new sense of the importance of collective interests. The result was almost inevitable. The doctrine first evolved in the adulterated food and liquor cases came to be recognised as a special class of offence for which no *mens rea* was required. . . . The interesting fact that the same development took place in both England and the United States at about the same time strongly indicates that the movement has been not merely an historical accident but the result of the changing social conditions and beliefs of the day. . . .

The problem is how to draw the line between those offences which do and those which do not require *mens rea*. Clearly, it will not depend on whether the crime happens to be a common law or statutory offence. . . . Some courts have suggested that the line depends upon the distinction between *mala in se* and *mala prohibita*; and this seems to depend essentially upon whether or not the offence is inherently immoral. But this also is . . . unsound. . . . Many offences which are held not to require proof of *mens rea* are highly immoral; and many requiring it are not inherently immoral at all. . . .

Neither can the dividing line be drawn according to the gravity or the lightness of the offence. Petty larceny is a much lighter and less dangerous offence than selling narcotics or poisoned food, yet the former requires *mens rea* and the latter not. . . .

How then can one determine practically which offences do and which do not require *mens rea*, when the statute creating the offence is . . . silent? . . . . [T]wo cardinal principles stand out upon which the determination must turn.

The first relates to the character of the offence. All criminal enactments in a sense serve the double purpose of singling out wrongdoers for the purpose of punishment or correction and of regulating the social order. But often the importance of the one far outweighs the other. . . .

The second criterion depends upon the possible penalty. If this be serious . . . the individual interest of the defendant weighs too heavily to allow conviction without proof of a guilty mind. . . . Crimes punishable with prison sentences, therefore, ordinarily require proof of a guilty intent."

ii. The Present Uncertainty

Williams, T.C.L., p. 910:

"In general, the authorities on strict liability are so conflicting that it is impossible to abstract any coherent principle on when this form of liability arises and when it does not."

However, it is possible to detect trends. It can be said that up to 1969 and the case of *Sweet* v. *Parsley* (*post*, p. 137), the stricter approach exemplified in *Prince* (*ante*, p. 121), requiring close attention to the actual statutory words, generally prevailed over the more liberal attitude implicit in *Tolson* (*ante*, p. 116). But consistency was, and still is, lacking.

Cundy v. Le Cocq

(1884) 13 Q.B.D. 207
Queen's Bench Division

C., a licensed victualler, sold liquor to a person who was drunk. C. was unaware of the drunkenness, but he was nevertheless convicted of unlawfully selling liquor to a drunken person, contrary to section 13 of the Licensing Act 1872. C. appealed to the Divisional Court.

STEPHEN J.: I am of opinion that this conviction should be affirmed. Our answer to the question put to us turns upon this, whether the words of the section under which this conviction took place, taken in connection with the general scheme of the Act, should be read as constituting an offence only where the licensed person knows or has means of knowing that the person served with intoxicating liquor is drunk, or whether the offence is complete where no such knowledge is shown. I am of opinion that the words of the section amount to an absolute prohibition of the sale of liquor to a drunken person, and that the existence of a bona fide mistake as to the condition of the person served is not an answer to the charge, but is a matter only for mitigation of the penalties that may be imposed. I am led to that conclusion both by the general scope of the Act, which is for the repression of drunkenness, and from a comparison of the various sections under the head "offences against public order." Some of these contain the word "knowingly", as for instance section 14, which deals with keeping a disorderly house, and section 16, which deals with the penalty for harbouring a constable. Knowledge in these and other cases is an element in the offence; but the clause we are considering says nothing about the knowledge of the state of the person served. I believe the reason for making this prohibition absolute was that there must be a great temptation to a publican to sell liquor without regard to the sobriety of the customer, and it was thought right to put upon the publican the responsibility of determining whether his customer is sober. Against this view we have had quoted the maxim that in every criminal offence there must be a guilty mind; but I do not think that maxim has so wide an application as it is sometimes considered to have. In old time, and as applicable to the common law or to earlier statutes, the maxim may have been of general application; but a difference has arisen owing to the greater precision of modern statutes. It is impossible now, as illustrated by the cases of *R.* v. *Prince* [*ante*, p. 121] 154, and *R.* v. *Bishop* (1880) 5 Q.B.D. 259, to apply the maxim generally to all statutes, and the substance of all the reported cases is that it is necessary to look at the object of each Act that is under consideration to see whether and how far knowledge is of the essence of the offence created. Here, as I have already pointed out, the object of this part of the Act is to prevent the sale of intoxicating liquor to drunken persons, and it is perfectly natural to carry that out by throwing on the publican the responsibility of determining whether the person supplied comes within that category.

I think, therefore, the conviction was right and must be affirmed.

Conviction affirmed

Sherras v. De Rutzen

[1895] 1 Q.B. 918
Queen's Bench Division

S., a licensed victualler, was convicted under section 16 (2) of the Licensing Act 1872, for having unlawfully supplied liquor to a police constable on duty without having the authority of a superior officer of such constable for so doing. S. reasonably believed that the constable was off duty. He appealed to quarter sessions and thence to the Divisional Court.

DAY J.: I am clearly of opinion that this conviction ought to be quashed. This police constable comes into the appellant's house without his armlet, and with every appearance of being off duty. The house was in the immediate neighbourhood of the police-station, and the appellant believed, and he had very natural grounds for believing, that the constable was off duty. In that belief he accordingly served him with liquor. As a matter of fact, the constable was on duty—but does that fact make the innocent act of the appellant an offence? I do not think it does. He had no intention to do a wrongful act; he acted in the bona fide belief that the constable was off duty. It seems to me that the contention that he committed an offence is utterly erroneous. An argument has been based on the appearance of the word "knowingly" in subsection (1) of section 16, and its omission in subsection (2). In my opinion the only effect of this is to shift the burden of proof. In cases under subsection (1) it is for the prosecution to prove the knowledge, while in cases under subsection (:2) the defendant has to prove that he did not know. That is the only inference I draw from the insertion of the word "knowingly" in the one subsection and its omission in the other.

It appears to me that it would be straining the law to say that this publican, acting as he did in the bona fide belief that the constable was off duty, and having reasonable grounds for that belief, was nevertheless guilty of an offence against the section for which he was liable both to a penalty and to have his licence indorsed.

WRIGHT J.: I am of the same opinion. There are many cases on the subject, and it is not very easy to reconcile them. There is a presumption that *mens rea*, an evil intention, or a knowledge of the wrongfulness of the act, is an essential ingredient in every offence; but that presumption is liable to be displaced either by the words of the statute creating the offence or by the subject-matter with which it deals, and both must be considered: *Nichols* v. *Hall* (1873) L.R. 8 C.P. 322. One of the most remarkable exceptions was in the case of bigamy. It was held by all the judges, on the statute 1 Jac. 1, c. 11, that a man was rightly convicted of bigamy who had married after an invalid Scotch divorce, which had been obtained in good faith, and the validity of which he had no reason to doubt: *Lolly's Case* (1812) R. & R. 237. Another exception, apparently grounded on the language of a statute, is *Prince's Case* (1875) L.R. 2 C.C.R. 154, where it was held by fifteen judges against one that a man was guilty of abduction of a girl under sixteen, although he believed, in good faith and on reasonable grounds, that she was over that age. Apart from isolated and extreme cases of this kind, the principal classes of exceptions may perhaps be reduced to three. One is a class of acts which, in the language of Lush J. in *Davies* v. *Harvey* (1874) L.R. 9 Q.B. 433, are not criminal in any real sense, but are acts which in the public interest are prohibited under a penalty. Several such instances are to be found in the decision on the Revenue Statutes, e.g., *Att.-Gen.* v. *Lockwood* (1842) 9 M. & W. 378, where the innocent possession of liquorice by a beer retailer was held to be an offence. So under the Adulteration Acts, *R.* v. *Woodrow* (1846) 15 M. & W. 404 as to innocent possession of adulterated tobacco; *Fitzpatrick* v. *Kelly* (1873) L.R. 8 Q.B. 337, and *Roberts* v. *Egerton* (1874) L.R. 9 Q.B. 494, as to the sale of adulterated food. So under the Game Acts, as to the innocent possession of game by a carrier: *R.* v. *Marsh* (1824) 2 B. & C. 717. So as to the liability of a guardian of the poor, whose partner, unknown to him, supplied goods for the poor: *Davies* v. *Harvey* (1874) L.R. 9 Q.B. 433. To the same head may be referred *R.* v. *Bishop* (1880) 5 Q.B.D. 259, where a person was held rightly convicted of receiving lunatics in an unlicensed house, although the jury found that he honestly and on reasonable grounds believed that they were not lunatics. Another class comprehends some, and perhaps all, public nuisances: *R.* v. *Stephens* (1866) L.R. 1 Q.B. 702, where the employer was held liable on indictment for a nuisance caused by workmen without his knowledge and contrary to his orders; and so in *R.* v. *Medley* (1834) 6 C. & P. 292, and *Barnes* v. *Akroyd* (1872) L.R. 7 Q.B. 474. Lastly, there may be cases in which, although the proceeding is criminal in form, it is really only a summary mode of enforcing a civil right: see *per* Williams and Willes JJ. in *Morden* v. *Porter* (1860) 7 C.B. (N.S.) 641, as to unintentional trespass in pursuit of game; *Lee* v. *Simpson* (1847) 3 C.B. 871, as to unconscious dramatic piracy; and *Hargreaves* v. *Diddams* (1875) 10 Q.B. 582, as to a bona fide belief in a legally impossible right to fish. But, except in such cases as these, there must in general be guilty knowledge on the part of the defendant, or of someone whom he has put in his place to act for him, generally, or in the particular matter, in order to constitute an offence. It is plain that if guilty knowledge is not necessary, no care on the part of the publican could save him from a conviction under section 16, subsection (2), since it would be as easy for the constable to deny that he was on duty when asked, or to produce a forged permission from his superior officer, as to remove his armlet before entering the public-house. I am, therefore, of opinion that this conviction ought to be quashed.

Conviction quashed

Question

Do the two cases above represent a conflict of authority, as Glanville Williams suggests (C.L.G.P., p. 223)? Or can a rationale be found in the distinction between the risk of serving a drunk, and that of serving a constable on duty? See the case below.

Reynolds v. G. H. Austin & Sons Ltd.
[1951] 2 K.B. 135
King's Bench Division

A women's guild organised an outing and arranged with a company, who carried on the business of operating motor-coaches, to convey in a motor-coach a party at a fixed price per person. The organiser of the outing caused to be exhibited in a shop an advertisement giving particulars of the trip which stated "Few tickets left. Apply within." The company had no knowledge and no reasonable means of discovering that any such advertisement had been made. The outing took place and the company, who held no road service licence covering the journey in question, were charged with having used the motor-coach in contravention of section 72 of the Act of 1930 on the ground that by the condition of section 25, subsection (1) (*b*), of the Act of 1934, such journey "must be made without previous advertisement to the public of the arrangements therefor." The information was dismissed and the prosecutor appealed.

DEVLIN J.: ... The main weight of the case for the prosecutor rests on the contention that this statute belongs to a class in which *mens rea* should be dispensed with. There is no doubt that some of the provisions of the Road Traffic Acts do fall within that class: see, for example, *Griffiths* v. *Studebakers Ltd.* [1924] 1 K.B. 102. It may seem, on the face of it, hard that a man should be fined, and, indeed, made subject to imprisonment, for an offence which he did not know that he was committing. But there is no doubt that the legislature has for certain purposes found that hard measure to be necessary in the public interest. The moral justification behind such laws is admirably expressed in a sentence by Dean Roscoe Pound in his book *The Spirit of the Common Law,* at p. 52: see *The Law Quarterly Review,* Vol. 64, p. 176. "Such statutes," he says, "are not meant to punish the vicious will but to put pressure upon the thoughtless and inefficient to do their whole duty in the interest of public health or safety or morals." Thus a man may be made responsible for the acts of his servants, or even for defects in his business arrangements, because it can fairly be said that by such sanctions citizens are induced to keep themselves and their organisations up to the mark. Although, in one sense, the citizen is being punished for the sins of others, it can be said that, if he had been more alert to see that the law was observed, the sin might not have been committed. But if a man is punished because of an act done by another, whom he cannot reasonably be expected to influence or control, the law is engaged, not in punishing thoughtlessness or inefficiency, and thereby promoting the welfare of the community, but in pouncing on the most convenient victim. Without the authority of express words, I am not willing to conclude that Parliament can intend what would seem to the ordinary man (as plainly it seemed to the justices in this case) to be the useless and unjust infliction of a penalty. . . .

I think it a safe general principle to follow (I state it negatively, since that is sufficient for the purposes of this case), that where the punishment of an individual will not promote the observance of the law either by that individual or by others whose conduct he may reasonably be expected to influence then, in the absence of clear and express words, such punishment is not intended.

There is another way in which the matter may be tested. In the case of statutes which apparently dispense with *mens rea,* it is sometimes said that it is the doing of an act which is absolutely prohibited that itself supplies the *mens rea.* In many such cases it is impossible to do the prohibited act without being conscious of it; and though in such cases there may be no moral guilt if the accused does not know that he was doing wrong, this is an excuse which the law cannot permit. In other cases it is possible, by taking heed, to avoid the doing of the prohibited act. In *Cundy* v. *Le Cocq,* [*ante,* p. 130] in which the decision turned partly on the wording of the Act, it was also said that the object of the Act was to put upon the publican the responsibility of determining for himself whether a person supplied with drink was sober or not, and so conceivably to punish him for an error of judgment. But in the present case, as I have pointed out, not only are there no means of knowledge open to the accused but there are no data available to him on which he could arrive at any determination whether the law was likely to be broken or not. Even after the event it would need a judicial inquiry, covering the past activities of the organiser and each of the passengers, before it could be determined whether it had been broken. An express carriage is not a type of vehicle which can be identified by observation. No driver on one of these expeditions could answer the question whether or not he was driving an express carriage. In truth, an express carriage is an abstract conception. A vehicle may begin as an ordinary vehicle and become an express carriage in the course of its journey if a passenger insists on dismounting. It is a creature of statute; and a creature which, in its habits of appearing and disappearing (and, I suspect, of leaving a grin behind it at the legal complications which its behaviour may cause), has many of the attributes of the Cheshire cat. In these circumstances, it would be going further than any decided case has yet gone, and further than I am willing to go without the clearest authority, to construe the statute as imposing an absolute prohibition.

Appeal dismissed

Lim Chin Aik v. The Queen
[1963] A.C. 160
Privy Council

By section 6 of the Immigration Ordinance 1952 of the State of Singapore: "(2) It shall not be lawful for any person other than a citizen of Singapore to enter the colony from the Federation or having entered the colony from the Federation to remain in the colony if— . . . (*b*) such person has been prohibited by order made under section 9 of this Ordinance from entering the colony; . . .

"(3) Any person who contravenes the provisions of subsection (2) of this section shall be guilty of an offence against this Ordinance."

Section 9, in the case of an order directed to a single individual, contained no provision for publishing the order or for otherwise bringing it to the attention of the person named.

The appellant was charged with and convicted of contravening section 6 (2) of the Immigration Ordinance by remaining in Singapore (after having entered) when he had been prohibited from entering by an order made by the Minister under section 9. At the trial there was no evidence from which it could properly be inferred that the order had in fact come to the notice or attention of the appellant. He appealed, ultimately to the Privy Council.

Lord Evershed: That proof of the existence of a guilty intent is an essential ingredient of a crime at common law is not at all in doubt. The problem is of the extent to which the same rule is applicable in the case of offences created and defined by statute or statutory instrument. Their Lordships were very properly referred to a number of cases, including the often-cited *Nichols* v. *Hall* (1873) L.R. 8 C.P. 322 and *Cundy* v. *Le Cocq* [*ante,* p. 130], and covering a considerable period ending with the decision last year of the Court of Criminal Appeal in *R.* v. *Cugullere* [1961] 1 W.L.R. 858. As was observed by Wright J. at the beginning of his judgment in the case of *Sherras* v. *De Rutzen* [*ante,* p. 130] to which their Lordships will presently make further reference, the difficulty of the problem is enhanced by the fact that many of the cases are not easy to reconcile. Thus it has been held that a licensee of a public-house commits an offence under the licensing legislation of serving alcoholic liquor to a drunken man even though he was unaware of the customer's condition (*Cundy* v. *Le Cocq*): but that a licensee does not commit the offence under the same legislation of serving drinks to a police constable on duty if he reasonably supposed that the constable was in fact off duty (see *Sherras's case* above mentioned): and in the latest case above cited the Court of Criminal Appeal held that the terms of section 1 of the Prevention of Crime Act 1953, "Any person who without lawful authority or reasonable excuse, the proof whereof shall lie on him, has with him in any public place any offensive weapon shall be guilty of an offence" must be read as if the word "knowingly" were written before the word "has".

Mr. Gratiaen founded his argument upon the formulation of the problem contained in the judgment of Wright J. in *Sherras's* case. The language of that learned and experienced judge was as follows: "There is a presumption that *mens rea,* or evil intention or knowledge of the wrongfulness of the act, is an essential ingredient in every offence, but that presumption is liable to be displaced either by the words of the statute creating the offence or by the subject-matter with which it deals, and both must be considered."

It is to be observed that in that case the court held the presumption not to be displaced even though the word "knowingly" which was not found in the subsection involved in the case did appear in another subsection of the same section. Their Lordships add that the circumstance last mentioned was regarded by Day J. in his judgment in the same case as shifting the onus of proof to the defendant (which onus the learned judge held to have been discharged). The question of onus does not, as already stated, arise in the present case. Their Lordships think it right, however, to say that they should not be thought to assent to Day J.'s proposition. . . .

Their Lordships accept as correct the formulation cited from the judgment of Wright J. They are fortified in that view by the fact that such formulation was expressly accepted by Lord du Parcq in delivering the judgment of the Board in the case in 1947 of *Srinivas Mall Bairoliya* v. *King-Emperor* (1947) I.L.R. 26 Pat. 460, a case which unfortunately has not found its way into the Law Reports. That was a case in which one of the appellants had been charged with an offence under the rules made by virtue of the Defence of India Act, 1939, consisting of the sale of salt at prices exceeding those prescribed under the rules, the sales having in fact been made without that appellant's knowledge by one of his servants. The Indian High Court had held the appellant to be nonetheless liable upon the terms of the rules; but the Board rejected the view of the High Court. Lord de Parcq, after citing with approval the judgment already quoted of Lord Wright J., also adopted the language of Lord Goddard C.J. in the case of *Brend* v. *Wood* (1946) 62 T.L.R. 462, D.C.: "It is in my opinion of the utmost importance for the protection of the liberty of the subject that a court should always bear in mind that unless a statute either clearly or by necessary implication rules out *mens rea* as a constituent part of a crime a defendant should not be found guilty of an offence against the criminal law unless he has got a guilty mind."

The adoption of these formulations of principle does not, however, dispose of the matter. . . . The difficulty remains of their application. What should be the proper inferences to be drawn from the language of the statute or statutory instrument under review—in this case of sections 6 and 9 of the Immigration Ordinance? More difficult, perhaps, still what are the inferences to be drawn in a given case from the "subject-matter with which [the statute or statutory instrument] deals"?

Where the subject-matter of the statute is the regulation for the public welfare of a particular activity—statutes regulating the sale of food and drink are to be found among the earliest examples—it can be and frequently has been inferred that the legislature intended that such activities should be carried out under conditions of strict liability. The presumption is that the statute or statutory instrument can be effectively enforced only if those in charge of the relevant activities are made responsible for seeing that they are complied with. When such a presumption is to be inferred, it displaces the ordinary presumptions of *mens rea*. Thus sellers of meat may be made responsible for seeing that the meat is fit for human consumption and it is no answer for them to say that they were not aware that it was polluted. If that were a satisfactory answer, then as Kennedy L.J. pointed out in *Hobbs* v. *Winchester Corporation* [1910] 2 K.B. 471, the distribution of bad meat (and its far-reaching consequences) would not be effectively prevented. So a publican may be made responsible for observing the condition of his customers, *Cundy* v. *Le Cocq* [*ante*, p. 130].

But it is not enough in their Lordships' opinion merely to label the statute as one dealing with a grave social evil and from that to infer that strict liability was intended. It is pertinent also to inquire whether putting the defendant under strict liability will assist in the enforcement of the regulations. That means that there must be something he can do, directly or indirectly, by supervision or inspection, by improvement of his business methods or by exhorting those whom he may be expected to influence or control, which will promote the observance of the regulations. Unless this is so, there is no reason in penalising him, and it cannot be inferred that the legislature imposed strict liability merely in order to find a luckless victim. This principle has been expressed and applied in *Reynolds* v. *G. H. Austin & Sons Ltd.* [*ante*, p. 132] and *James & Son Ltd.* v. *Smee* [1955] 1 Q.B. 78. Their Lordships prefer it to the alternative view that strict liability follows simply from the nature of the subject-matter and that persons whose conduct is beyond any sort of criticism can be dealt with by the imposition of a nominal penalty. This latter view can perhaps be supported to some extent by the dicta of Kennedy L.J. in *Hobbs* v. *Winchester Corporation*, and of Donovan J. in *R.* v. *St. Margaret's Trust Ltd.* [1958] 1 W.L.R. 522. But though a nominal penalty may be appropriate in an individual case where exceptional lenience is called for, their Lordships cannot, with respect, suppose that it is envisaged by the legislature as a way of dealing with offenders generally. Where it can be shown that the imposition of strict liability would result in the prosecution and conviction of a class of persons whose conduct could not in any way affect the observance of the law, their Lordships consider that, even where the statute is dealing with a grave social evil, strict liability is not likely to be intended.

Their Lordships apply these general observations to the Ordinance in the present case. The subject-matter, the control of immigration, is not one in which the presumption of strict liability has generally been made. Nevertheless, if the courts of Singapore were of the view that unrestricted immigration is a social evil which it is the object of the Ordinance to control most rigorously, their Lordships would hesitate to disagree. That is a matter peculiarly within the cognisance of the local courts. But Mr. Le Quesne was unable to point to anything that the appellant could possibly have done so as to ensure that he complied with the regulations. It was not, for example, suggested that it would be practicable for him to make continuous inquiry to see whether an order had been made against him. Clearly one of the objects of the Ordinance is the expulsion of prohibited persons from Singapore, but there is nothing that a man can do about it if, before the commission of the offence, there is no practical or sensible way in which he can ascertain whether he is a prohibited person or not.

Mr. Le Quesne, therefore, relied chiefly on the text of the Ordinance and their Lordships return, accordingly, to the language of the two material sections. It is to be observed that the Board is here concerned with one who is said (within the terms of section 6 (3) to have "contravened" the subsection by "remaining" in Singapore (after having entered) when he had been "prohibited" from entering by an "order" made by the Minister containing such prohibition. It seems to their Lordships that, where a man is said to have contravened an order or an order of prohibition, the common sense of the language presumes that he was aware of the order before he can be said to have contravened it. Their Lordships realise that this statement is something of an over-simplification when applied to the present case; for the "contravention" alleged is of the unlawful act, prescribed by subsection (2) of the section, of remaining in Singapore after the date of the order of prohibition. Nonetheless it is their Lordships' view that, applying the test of ordinary sense to the language used, the notion of contravention here alleged is more consistent with the assumption that the person charged had knowledge of the order than the converse. But such a conclusion is in their Lordships' view much reinforced by the use of the word "remains" in its context. It is to be observed that if the respondent is right a man could lawfully enter Singapore and could thereafter lawfully remain in Singapore until the moment when an order of prohibition against his entering was made; that then, instanter, his purely passive conduct in remaining—that is, the mere continuance, quite unchanged, of his previous behaviour, hitherto perfectly lawful—would become criminal. These considerations bring their Lordships clearly to the conclusion that the sense of the language here in question requires for the commission of a crime thereunder *mens rea* as a constituent of such crime; or at least that there is nothing in the language used which suffices to exclude the ordinary presumption. Their

Lordships do not forget the emphasis placed by Mr. Le Quesne on the fact that the word "knowingly" or the phrases "without reasonable cause" or "without reasonable excuse" are found in various sections of the Ordinance (as amended) but find no place in the section now under consideration—see, for example, sections 16 (4), 18 (4), 19 (2), 29, 31 (2) and 56 (*d*) and (*e*) of the Ordinance. In their Lordships' view the absence of such a word or phrase in the relevant section is not sufficient in the present case to prevail against the conclusion which the language as a whole suggests. In the first place, it is to be noted that to have inserted such words as "knowingly" or "without lawful excuse" in the relevant part of section 6 (3) of the Act would in any case not have been sensible. Further, in all the various instances where the word or phrase is used in the other sections of the Ordinance before-mentioned the use is with reference to the doing of some specific act or the failure to do some specific act as distinct from the mere passive continuance of behaviour theretofore perfectly lawful. Finally, their Lordships are mindful that in the *Sherras* case itself the fact that the word "knowingly" was not found in the subsection under consideration by the court but was found in another subsection of the same section was not there regarded as sufficient to displace the ordinary rule.

Appeal allowed

Sweet v. Parsley
[1970] A.C. 133
House of Lords

S. was convicted by magistrates of being concerned in the management of certain premises which were used for the purpose of smoking cannabis or cannabis resin, contrary to section 5 (*b*) of the Dangerous Drugs Act 1965. She appealed, ultimately, to the House of Lords. The facts appear from the judgment of Lord Reid.

LORD REID: My Lords, the appellant was convicted at Woodstock Petty Sessions on September 14, 1967, on a charge that on June 16, 1967, she was concerned in the management of certain premises at Fries Farm, Oxfordshire, which were used for the purpose of smoking cannabis contrary to section 5 (*b*) of the Dangerous Drugs Act 1965. She was fined £25 and ordered to pay £12 18s 0d costs. It appears from the case stated by the justices that the tenant of this farm had sublet the farmhouse to her at a rent of £28 per four weeks. She was a teacher at a school in Oxford and she had intended to reside in this house and travel daily by car to Oxford. This proved to be impracticable so she resided in Oxford and let rooms in the house at low rents to tenants allowing them the common use of the kitchen. She retained one room for her own use and visited the farm occasionally to collect her letters, to collect rent from her tenants and generally to see that all was well. Sometimes she stayed overnight but generally she did not.

On June 16, while she was in Oxford, the police went to the premises with a search warrant. They found receptacles hidden in the garden which contained cannabis resin and L.S.D. They also found in the kitchen, cigarette ends containing cannabis, and an ornamental hookah pipe which belonged to the appellant and which had, admittedly without her knowledge, been used for smoking this substance.

The justices found that "she did not enter the rooms of tenants except by invitation and she had no reason to go into their rooms. Her own room was occasionally used in her absence by other persons who lived in the house. She had no knowledge whatever that the house was being used for the purpose of smoking cannabis or cannabis resin. Once or twice when staying overnight at the farmhouse the appellant shouted if there was excessive noise late at night but otherwise she did not exercise any control over the tenants except that she collected rent from them."*

A Divisional Court dismissed her appeal, holding that she had been concerned in the management of those premises. The reasons given for holding that she was managing the property were that she was in a position to choose her tenants: that she could put them under as long or as short a tenancy as she desired and that she could make it a term of any letting that smoking of cannabis was not to take place. All these reasons would apply to every occupier who lets out parts of his house or takes in lodgers or paying guests. But this was held to be an absolute offence following the earlier decision in *Yeandel* v. *Fisher* [1966] 1 Q.B. 440.

How has it come about that the Divisional Court has felt bound to reach such an obviously unjust result? It has in effect held that it was carrying out the will of Parliament because Parliament has chosen to make this an absolute offence. And, of course, if Parliament has so chosen the courts must carry out its will, and they cannot be blamed for any unjust consequences. But has Parliament so chosen?

I dealt with this matter at some length in *Warner* v. *Metropolitan Police Commissioner* [1969] 2 A.C. 256. On reconsideration I see no reason to alter anything which I there said. But I think that some amplification is necessary. Our first duty is to consider the words of the Act: if they show a clear intention to create an absolute offence that is an end of the matter. But such cases are very rare. Sometimes the words of the section which creates a particular offence make it clear that *mens rea* is required in one form or another. Such cases are quite frequent. But in a very large number of cases there is no clear indication either way. In such cases there has for centuries been a presumption that Parliament did not intend to make criminals of persons who were in no way blameworthy in what they did. That means that whenever a section is silent as to *mens rea* there is a presumption that, in order to give effect to the will of Parliament, we must read in words appropriate to require *mens rea*.

Where it is contended that an absolute offence has been created, the words of Alderson B. in *Attorney-General* v. *Lockwood* (1842) 9 M. & W. 378, 398, have often been quoted: "The rule of law, I take it, upon the construction of all statutes, and therefore applicable to the construction of this, is, whether they be penal or remedial, to construe them according to the plain, literal, and grammatical meaning of the words in which they are expressed, unless that construction leads to a plain and clear contradiction of the apparent purpose of the Act, or to some palpable and evident absurdity."

That is perfectly right as a general rule and where there is no legal presumption. But what about the multitude of criminal enactments where the words of the Act simply make it an offence to do certain things but where everyone agrees that there cannot be a conviction without proof of *mens rea* in some form? This passage, if applied to the present problem, would mean that there is no need to prove *mens rea* unless it would be "a plain and clear contradiction of the apparent purpose of the Act" to convict without proof of *mens rea*. But that would be putting the presumption the wrong way round: for it is firmly established by a host of authorities that *mens rea* is an essential ingredient of every offence unless some reason can be found for holding that that is not necessary.

It is also firmly established that the fact that other sections of the Act expressly require *mens rea*, for example because they contain the word "knowingly", is not in itself sufficient to justify a decision that a section which is silent as to *mens rea* creates an absolute offence. In the absence of a clear indication in the Act that an offence is intended to be an absolute offence, it is necessary to go outside the Act

* Lord Reid's statement of the facts does not appear in [1970] A.C., but see [1969] 2 W.L.R. 472.

and examine all relevant circumstances in order to establish that this must have been the intention of Parliament. I say "must have been" because it is a universal principle that if a penal provision is reasonably capable of two interpretations, that interpretation which is most favourable to the accused must be adopted.

What, then, are the circumstances which it is proper to take into account? In the well-known case of *Sherras* v. *De Rutzen* [*ante*, p. 130], Wright J. only mentioned the subject-matter with which the Act deals. But he was there dealing with something which was one of a class of acts which "are not criminal in any real sense, but are acts which in the public interest are prohibited under a penalty". It does not in the least follow that when one is dealing with a truly criminal act it is sufficient merely to have regard to the subject-matter of the enactment. One must put oneself in the position of a legislator. It has long been the practice to recognise absolute offences in this class of quasi-criminal acts, and one can safely assume that, when Parliament is passing new legislation dealing with this class of offences, its silence as to *mens rea* means that the old practice is to apply. But when one comes to acts of a truly criminal character, it appears to me that there are at least two other factors which any reasonable legislator would have in mind. In the first place a stigma still attaches to any person convicted of a truly criminal offence, and the more serious or more disgraceful the offence the greater the stigma. So he would have to consider whether, in a case of this gravity, the public interest really requires that an innocent person should be prevented from providing his innocence in order that fewer guilty men may escape. And equally important is the fact that fortunately the Press in this country are vigilant to expose injustice and every manifestly unjust conviction made known to the public tends to injure the body politic by undermining public confidence in the justice of the law and of its administration. But I regret to observe that, in some recent cases where serious offences have been held to be absolute offences, the court has taken into account no more than the wording of the Act and the character and seriousness of the mischief which constitutes the offence.

The choice would be much more difficult if there were no other way open than either *mens rea* in the full sense or an absolute offence; for there are many kinds of case where putting on the prosecutor the full burden of proving *mens rea* creates great difficulties and may lead to many unjust acquittals. But there are at least two other possibilities. Parliament has not infrequently transferred the onus as regards *mens rea* to the accused, so that, once the necessary facts are proved, he must convince the jury that on balance of probabilities he is innocent of any criminal intention. I find it a little surprising that more use has not been made of this method: but one of the bad effects of the decision of this House in *Woolmington* v. *Director of Public Prosecutions* [1935] A.C. 462, may have been to discourage its use. The other method would be in effect to substitute in appropriate classes of cases gross negligence for *mens rea* in the full sense as the mental element necessary to constitute the crime. It would often be much easier to infer that Parliament must have meant that gross negligence should be the necessary mental element than to infer that Parliament intended to create an absolute offence. A variant of this would be to accept the view of Cave J. in *R.* v. *Tolson* [*ante*, p. 116]. This appears to have been done in Australia where authority appears to support what Dixon J. said in *Proudman* v. *Dayman* (1941) 67 C.L.R. 536, 540: "As a general rule an honest and reasonable belief in a state of facts which, if they existed, would make the defendant's act innocent affords an excuse for doing what would otherwise be an offence." It may be that none of these methods is wholly satisfactory but at least the public scandal of convicting on a serious charge persons who are in no way blameworthy would be avoided.

If this section means what the Divisional Court have held that it means, then hundreds of thousands of people who sublet part of the premises or take in lodgers or are concerned in the management of residential premises or institutions are daily incurring a risk of being convicted of a serious offence in circumstances where they are in no way to blame. For the greatest vigilance cannot prevent tenants, lodgers or inmates or guests whom they bring in from smoking cannabis cigarettes in their own rooms. It was suggested in argument that this appellant brought this conviction on herself because it is found as a fact that when the police searched the premises there were people there of the "beatnik fraternity." But surely it would be going a very long way to say that persons managing premises of any kind ought to safeguard themselves by refusing accommodation to all who are of slovenly or exotic appearance, or who bring in guests of that kind. And unfortunately drug taking is by no means confined to those of unusual appearance.

Speaking from a rather long experience of membership of both Houses, I assert with confidence that no Parliament within my recollection would have agreed to make an offence of this kind an absolute offence if the matter had been fully explained to it. So, if the court ought only to hold an offence to be an absolute offence where it appears that that must have been the intention of Parliament, offences of this kind are very far removed from those which it is proper to hold to be absolute offences.

I must now turn to the question what is the true meaning of section 5 of the 1965 Act. It provides: "If a person (*a*) being the occupier of any premises, permits those premises to be used for the purpose of smoking cannabis or cannabis resin or of dealing in cannabis or cannabis resin (whether by sale or otherwise); (*b*) is concerned in the management of any premises used for any such purpose as aforesaid; he shall be guilty of an offence against this Act." We are particularly concerned with paragraph (*b*), and the first question is what is meant by "used for any such purpose". Is the "purpose" the purpose of the smoker or the purpose of the management? When in *Warner's* case, I dealt briefly with *Yeandel's* case, I thought it was the purpose of the smoker, but fuller argument in this present case brought out that an identical provision occurs in section 8 (*d*) which deals with opium. This latter provision has been carried on from the Dangerous Drugs Act 1920, and has obviously been copied into the later legislation relating to cannabis. It would require strong reasons—and there are none—to justify giving this provision a new meaning in section 5 different from that which it had in the 1920 Act and now has in section 8 of the 1965 Act. I think that in section 8 it is clear that the purpose is the purpose of the management. The first purpose mentioned is the purpose of the preparation of opium for smoking which can only be a purpose of the management. I believe that opium cannot be smoked casually anywhere at any time as can a cannabis cigarette. The section is dealing with "opium dens" and the like when the use of opium is the main purpose for which the premises are used. But it is a somewhat strained use of language to say that an ordinary room in a house is "used for the purpose" of smoking cannabis when all that happens is that some visitor lights a cannabis cigarette there. Looking to the origin and context of this provision, I have come to the conclusion that it cannot be given this wide meaning. No doubt this greatly reduces the scope of this provision when applied to the use of cannabis. But that is apt to happen when a draftsman simply copies an existing provision without regard to the different circumstances in which it is to operate. So, if the purpose is the purpose of the management, the question whether the offence with regard to opium in 1920, and now with regard to cannabis, is absolute can hardly arise. It could only arise if, although the manager not only knew about cannabis smoking and conducted the premises for that purpose, some person concerned in the management had no knowledge of that. One would first have to decide whether a person who is not actually assisting in the management can be regarded as being "concerned in the management," although ignorant of the purpose for which the manager was using the premises. Even if such a person could be regarded as "concerned in the management," I am of opinion that, for the reasons which I have given, he could not be convicted without proof of *mens rea.*

I would allow the appeal and quash the appellant's conviction.

LORD MORRIS OF BORTH-Y-GEST: My Lords, it has frequently been affirmed and should unhesitatingly be recognised that it is a cardinal principle of our law that *mens rea,* an evil intention or a knowledge of the wrongfulness of the act, is in all ordinary cases an essential ingredient of guilt of a criminal offence. It follows from this that there will not be guilt of an offence created by statute unless there is *mens rea* or unless Parliament has by the statute enacted that guilt may be established in cases where there is no *mens rea.*

To this effect were the words of Wright J. in *Sherras* v. *De Rutzen,* [*ante,* p. 130] and in *Derbyshire* v. *Houliston* in [1897] 1 Q.B. 772. In the judgment of the Privy Council in *Lim Chin Aik* v. *The Queen* [*ante,* p. 134] the principle was amply expressed. It was said (*ante,* p. 134): "That proof of the existence of a guilty intent is an essential ingredient of a crime at common law is not at all in doubt."

But as Parliament is supreme it is open to Parliament to legislate in such a way that an offence may be created of which someone may be found guilty though *mens rea* is lacking. There may be cases in which, as Channell J. said in *Pearks, Gunston & Tee Ltd.* v. *Ward* [1902] 2 K.B. 1, 11: ". . . the Legislature has thought it so important to prevent the particular act from being committed that it absolutely forbids it to be done; and if it is done the offender is liable to a penalty whether he had any *mens rea* or not, and whether or not he intended to commit a breach of the law."

Thus in diverse situations and circumstances and for any one of a variety of reasons Parliament may see fit to create offences and make people responsible before criminal courts although there is an absence of *mens rea.* But I would again quote with appreciation (as I did in *Warner's* case [1969] 2 A.C. 256) the words of Lord Goddard C.J., in *Brend* v. *Wood* (1946) L.T. 306, 307, when he said: "It is of the utmost importance for the protection of the liberty of the subject that a court should always bear in mind that, unless a statute, either clearly or by necessary implication, rules out *mens rea* as a constituent part of a crime, the court should not find a man guilty of an offence against the criminal law unless he has a guilty mind."

The intention of Parliament is expressed in the words of an enactment. The words must be looked at in order to see whether either expressly or by necessary implication they displace the general rule or presumption that *mens rea* is a necessary prerequisite before guilt of an offence can be found. Particular words in a statute must be considered in their setting in the statute and having regard to all the provisions of the statute and to its declared or obvious purpose. In 1842 in *Att.-Gen.* v. *Lockwood* (1842) 9 M. & W. 378, 398 Alderson B. said: "The rule of law, I take it, upon the construction of all statutes . . . is, whether they be penal or remedial, to construe them according to the plain, literal, and grammatical meaning of the words in which they are expressed, unless that construction leads to a plain and clear contradiction of the apparent purpose of the Act, or to some palpable and evident absurdity."

It must be considered, therefore, whether by the words of a penal statute it is either express or implied that there may be a conviction without *mens rea* or, in other words, whether what is called an absolute offence is created.

In *Dyke* v. *Elliott. The "Gauntlet"* (1872) L.R. 4 P.C. 184, 191 it was said: "No doubt all penal statutes are to be construed strictly, that is to say, the court must see that the thing charged as an offence is within the plain meaning of the words used, and must not strain the words on any notion that there has been a slip, that there has been a casus omissus, that the thing is so clearly within the mischief that it must have been intended to be included and would have been included if thought of. On the other hand, the person charged has a right to say that the thing charged, although within the words, is not within the spirit of the enactment. But where the thing is brought within the words and within the spirit, there a penal enactment is to be construed, like any other instrument, according to the fair common-sense meaning of the language used, and the court is not to find or make any doubt of ambiguity in the language of a penal statute, where such doubt or ambiguity would clearly not be found or made in the same language in any other instrument."

The inquiry must be made, therefore, whether Parliament has used words which expressly enact or impliedly involve that an absolute offence is created. Though sometimes help in construction is derived from noting the presence or the absence of the word "knowingly," no conclusive test can be laid down as a guide in finding the fair, reasonable and commonsense meaning of language. But in considering whether Parliament has decided to displace what is a general and somewhat fundamental rule it would not be reasonable lightly to impute to Parliament an intention to create an offence in such a way that someone could be convicted of it who by all reasonable and sensible standards is without fault. . . .

LORD PEARCE: My Lords, the prosecution contend that any person who is concerned in the management of premises where cannabis is in fact smoked even once, is liable, though he had no knowledge and no guilty mind. This is, they argue, a practical act intended to prevent a practical evil. Only by convicting some innocents along with the guilty can sufficient pressure be put upon those who make their living by being concerned in the management of premises. Only thus can they be made alert to prevent cannabis being smoked there. And if the prosecution have to prove knowledge or *mens rea*, many prosecutions will fail and many of the guilty will escape. I find that argument wholly unacceptable.

The notion that some guilty mind is a constituent part of crime and punishment goes back far beyond our common law. And at common law *mens rea* is a necessary element in a crime. Since the Industrial Revolution the increasing complexity of life called into being new duties and crimes which took no account of intent. Those who undertake various industrial and other activities, especially where these affect the life and health of the citizen, may find themselves liable to statutory punishment regardless of knowledge or intent, both in respect of their own acts or neglect and those of their servants. But one must remember that normally *mens rea* is still an ingredient of any offence. Before the court will dispense with the necessity for *mens rea* it has to be satisfied that Parliament so intended. The mere absence of the word "knowingly" is not enough. But the nature of the crime, the punishment, the absence of social obloquy, the particular mischief and the field of activity in which it occurs, and the wording of the particular section and its context, may show that Parliament intended that the act should be prevented by punishment regardless of intent or knowledge.

Viewing the matter on these principles, it is not possible to accept the prosecution's contention. Even granted that this were in the public health class of case, such as, for instance, are offences created to ensure that food shall be clean, it would be quite unreasonable. It is one thing to make a man absolutely responsible for all his own acts and even vicariously liable for his servants if he engaged in a certain type of activity. But it is quite another matter to make him liable for persons over whom he has no control. The innocent hotel-keeper, the lady who keeps lodgings or takes paying guests, the manager of a cinema, the warden of a hostel, the matron of a hospital, the house-master and matron of a boarding school, all these, it is conceded, are, on the prosecution's argument, liable to conviction the moment that irresponsible occupants smoke cannabis cigarettes. And for what purpose is this harsh imposition laid on their backs? No vigilance by night or day can make them safe. The most that vigilance can attain is advance knowledge of their own guilt. If a smell of cannabis comes from a sitting-room, they know that they have committed the offence. Should they then go at once to the police and confess their guilt in the hope that they will not be prosecuted? They may think it easier to conceal the matter in the hope that it may never be found out. For if, though morally innocent, they *are* prosecuted they may lose their livelihood, since thereafter, even though not punished, they are objects of suspicion. I see no real, useful object achieved by such hardship to the innocent. And so wide a possibility of injustice to the innocent could not be justified by any benefit achieved in the determent and punishment of the guilty. If, therefore, the words creating the offence are as wide in their application as the prosecution contend, Parliament cannot have intended an offence to which absence of knowledge or *mens rea* is no defence. . . .

LORD DIPLOCK: The expression "absolute offence" . . . is an imprecise phrase currently used to describe an act for which the doer is subject to criminal sanctions even though when he did it he had no *mens rea*, but *mens rea* itself also lacks precision and calls for closer analysis than is involved in its mere translation into English by Wright J. in *Sherras* v. *de Rutzen* [*ante*, p. 130] as "evil intention or a knowledge of the wrongfulness of the act"—a definition which suggests a single mental element common to all criminal offences and appears to omit thoughtlessness which, at any rate if it amounted to a reckless disregard of the nature or consequences of an act, was a sufficient mental element in some offences at common law.

A more helpful exposition of the nature of *mens rea* in both common law and statutory offences is to be found in the judgment of Stephen J. in *R.* v. *Tolson* [*ante*, p. 116]. He said: "The full definition of every crime contains expressly or by implication a proposition as to a state of mind. Therefore, if the mental element of any conduct alleged to be a crime is proved to have been absent in any given case, the crime so defined is not committed; or, again, if a crime is fully defined, nothing amounts to that crime which does not satisfy that definition."

Where the crime consists of doing an act which is prohibited by statute the proposition as to the state of mind of the doer which is contained in the full definition of the crime must be ascertained from the words and subject-matter of the statute. The proposition, as Stephen J. pointed out, may be stated explicitly by the use of such qualifying adverbs as "maliciously", "fraudulently", "negligently" or "knowingly"—expressions which in relation to different kinds of conduct may call for judicial exegesis. And even without such adverbs the words descriptive of the prohibited act may themselves connote the presence of a particular mental element. Thus, where the prohibited conduct consists in permitting a particular thing to be done the word "permit" connotes at least knowledge or reasonable grounds for suspicion on the part of the permittor that the thing will be done and an unwillingness to use means available to him to prevent it and, to take a recent example, to have in one's "possession" a prohibited substance connotes some degree of awareness of that which was within the possessor's physical control: *Warner* v. *Commissioner of Police* [1969] 2 A.C. 256.

But only too frequently the actual words used by Parliament to define the prohibited conduct are in themselves descriptive only of a physical act and bear no connotation as to any particular state of mind on the part of the person who does the act. Nevertheless, the mere fact that Parliament has made the conduct a criminal offence gives rise to *some* implication about the mental element of the conduct proscribed. It has, for instance, never been doubted since *M'Naghten's Case* [*post*, p. 162] that one implication as to the mental element in any statutory offence is that the doer of the prohibited act should be sane within the M'Naghten rules; yet this part of the full definition of the offence is invariably left unexpressed by Parliament. Stephen J. in *R.* v. *Tolson*, [*ante*, p. 116] suggested other circumstances never expressly dealt with in the statute where a mental element to be implied from the mere fact that the doing of an act was made a criminal offence would be absent, such as where it was done in a state of somnambulism or under duress, to which one might add inevitable accident. But the importance of the actual decision of the nine judges who constituted the majority in *R.* v. *Tolson*, [*ante*, p. 116] which concerned a charge of bigamy under section 57 of the Offences Against the Person Act 1861, was that it laid down as a general principle of construction of any enactment, which creates a criminal offence, that, even where the words used to describe the prohibited conduct would not in any other context connote the necessity for any particular mental element, they are nevertheless to be read as subject to the implication that a necessary element in the offence is the absence of a belief, held honestly and upon reasonable grounds, in the existence of facts which, if true, would make the act innocent. As was said by the Privy Council in *Bank of New South Wales* v. *Piper* [1897] A.C. 383, 389, 390, the absence of *mens rea* really consists in such a belief by the accused.

This implication stems from the principle that it is contrary to a rational and civilised criminal code, such as Parliament must be presumed to have intended, to penalise one who has performed his duty as a citizen to ascertain what acts are prohibited by law (*ignorantia juris non excusat*) and has taken all proper care to inform himself of any facts which would make his conduct lawful.

Where penal provisions are of general application to the conduct of ordinary citizens in the course of their everyday life the presumption is that the standard of care required of them in informing themselves of facts which would make their conduct unlawful, is that of the familiar common law duty of care. But where the subject-matter of a statute is the regulation of a particular activity involving potential danger to public health, safety or morals in which citizens have a choice as to whether they participate or not, the court may feel driven to infer an intention of Parliament to impose by penal sanctions a higher duty of care on those who choose to participate and to place upon them an obligation to take whatever measures may be necessary to prevent the prohibited act, without regard to those considerations of cost or business practicability which play a part in the determination of what would be required of them in order to fulfil the ordinary common law duty of care. But such an inference is not lightly to be drawn, nor is there any room for it unless there is something that the person on whom the obligation is imposed can do directly or indirectly, by supervision or inspection, by improvement of his business methods or by exhorting those whom he may be expected to influence or control, which will promote the observance of the obligation [see *Lim Chin Aik* v. *R.*, *ante*, p. 134].

The numerous decisions in the English courts since *R.* v. *Tolson* in which this later inference has been drawn rightly or, as I think, often wrongly, are not easy to reconcile with others where the court has failed to draw the inference, nor are they always limited to penal provisions designed to regulate the conduct of persons who choose to participate in a particular activity as distinct from those of general application to the conduct of ordinary citizens in the course of their everyday life. It may well be that had the significance of *R.* v. *Tolson* been appreciated here, as it was in the High Court of Australia, our courts, too, would have been less ready to infer an intention of Parliament to create offences for which honest and reasonable mistake was no excuse.

Its importance as a guide to the construction of penal provisions in statutes of general application was recognised by Dixon J. in *Maher* v. *Musson* (1934) 52 C.L.R. 100, 104, and by the majority of the High Court of Australia in *Thomas* v. *The King* (1937) 59 C.L.R. 279. It is now regularly adopted in Australia as a general principle of construction of statutory provisions of this kind.

By contrast, in England the principle laid down in *R.* v. *Tolson* has been overlooked until recently (see *R.* v. *Gould* [1968] 2 Q.B. 65) partly because the *ratio decidendi* was misunderstood by the Court of Criminal Appeal in *R.* v. *Wheat and Stocks* [1921] 2 K.B. 119 and partly, I suspect, because the reference in *R.* v. *Tolson* to the mistaken belief as being a "defence" to the charge of bigamy was thought to run counter to the decision of your Lordships' House in *Woolmington* v. *D.P.P.* [1935] A.C. 462. That expression might have to be expanded in the light of what was said in *Woolmington's* case, though I doubt whether a jury would find the expansion much more informative than describing the existence of the mistaken belief as a defence to which they should give effect unless they felt sure either that the accused did not honestly hold it or, if he did, that he had no reasonable grounds for doing so.

Woolmington's case affirmed the principle that the onus lies upon the prosecution in a criminal trial to prove all the elements of the offence with which the accused is charged. It does not purport to lay down how that onus can be discharged as respects any particular elements of the offence. This, under our system of criminal procedure, is left to the common sense of the jury. *Woolmington's* case did not decide anything so irrational as that the prosecution must call evidence to prove the absence of any mistaken belief by the accused in the existence of facts which, if true, would make the act innocent, any more than it decided that the prosecution must call evidence to prove the absence of any claim of right in a charge of larceny. The jury is entitled to presume that the accused acted with knowledge of the facts, unless there is some evidence to the contrary originating from the accused who alone can know on what belief he acted and on what ground the belief, if mistaken, was held. What *Woolmington's* case did decide is that where there is any such evidence the jury after considering it and also any relevant evidence called by the prosecution on the issue of the existence of the alleged mistaken belief should acquit the accused unless they feel sure that he did not hold the belief or that there were no reasonable grounds upon which he could have done so.

This, as I understand it, is the approach of Dixon J. to the onus of proof of honest and reasonable mistaken belief as he expressed it in *Proudman* v. *Dayman* (1941) 67 C.L.R. 536, 541. Unlike the position where a statute expressly places the onus of proving lack of guilty knowledge on the accused, the accused does not have to prove the existence of mistaken belief on the balance of probabilities; he has to raise a reasonable doubt as to its non-existence.

It has been objected that the requirement laid down in *R.* v. *Tolson* [*ante,* p. 116] and the *Bank of New South Wales* v. *Piper* [1897] A.C. 383 that the mistaken belief should be based on reasonable grounds introduces an objective mental element into *mens rea.* This may be so, but there is nothing novel in this. The test of the mental element of provocation which distinguishes manslaughter from murder has always been at common law and now is by statute the objective one of the way in which a reasonable man would react to provocation. There is nothing unreasonable in requiring a citizen to take reasonable care to ascertain the facts relevant to his avoiding doing a prohibited act.

It is, then, with these principles in mind that I approach the construction of section 5 of the Dangerous Drugs Act 1965, under which Miss Sweet was charged. It contains separate prohibitions in paragraphs (*a*) and (*b*) respectively. The offence under (*a*), with which Miss Sweet was not charged, can only be committed by the occupier of premises. The act of the occupier which is prohibited is to "permit" those premises to be used for the purpose of smoking cannabis or cannabis resin or of dealing in cannabis or cannabis resin. Here the word "permits", used to define the prohibited act, in itself connotes as a mental element of the prohibited conduct knowledge or grounds for reasonable suspicion on the part of the occupier that the premises will be used by someone for that purpose and an unwillingness on his part to take means available to him to prevent it. As regards this offence there is no need to have recourse to the more general implication as to the need for *mens rea* where the words are in themselves descriptive only of a physical act.

In paragraph (*b*) the phrase "concerned with the management of any premises", unlike the phrase "being the occupier of any premises" in paragraph (*a*), is not descriptive of a class of person to whom a particular kind of conduct subsequently defined is prohibited. It is part of the definition of the offence itself. The conduct prohibited is to be "concerned in the management of premises used for the purpose of smoking cannabis", etc. What, if any, mental element does this compound phrase connote? The premises of which it is an offence to be concerned in the management are defined not by reference merely to what happens on them (*e.g.*, "Premises on which cannabis is smoked") but by the purpose for which they are used. "Purpose" connotes an intention by some person to achieve a result desired by him. Whose purpose must it be that the premises should be used for smoking cannabis? The answer is, in my opinion, to be found in the words "is concerned in the management." To manage or to be concerned in the management itself connotes control or direction of an activity to achieve a result desired by those who control or direct the activity. In my opinion, in the compound phrase "is concerned in the management of premises used for the purpose of smoking cannabis", etc., the purpose described must be the purpose of the person concerned in the management of the premises.

But at its highest against Miss Sweet the words of the paragraph are ambiguous as to whose is the relevant purpose. That ambiguity in a penal statute which, on the alternative construction that it would be sufficient if the purpose to use the premises for smoking cannabis were that of anyone who in fact smoked cannabis, would render her liable, despite lack of any knowledge or acquiescence on her part, should be unhesitatingly resolved in her favour.

Appeal allowed

[The Misuse of Drugs Act 1971 incorporated "knowingly" in this offence.]

Note

Although *Sweet* v. *Parsley* represented a distinct change in judicial attitude, it is difficult to assess its effect. What is involved in the field of so-called "regulatory offences" is a vast number of diverse statutory provisions which are not easily accommodated under the umbrella of general principle. How, in any case, is the distinction to be drawn between the "quasi" and the "truly" criminal act? In *Alphacell* v. *Woodward* [1972] A.C. 824, the House of Lords upheld a conviction under section 2 (1) (*a*) of the Rivers (Prevention of Pollution) Act 1951 ("causing" polluted matter to enter a river) although there was proof neither of knowledge nor negligence. A second or subsequent conviction under this section carries with it the possibility of a sentence of imprisonment. The case illustrates the tension between the principle of confining criminal liability to "quasi" criminal offences and the principle of protecting the public from potentially dangerous activities. Lord Salmon, at p. 848: "Section 2 (1) (*a*) . . . is undoubtedly a penal section. [The appellants contend] that it follows that if it is capable of two or more meanings then the meaning most favourable to the subject should be adopted. . . . I do not agree. It is of the utmost public importance that our rivers should not be polluted. The risk of pollution, particularly from the vast and increasing number of riparian industries is very great." Individuals who engage in potentially dangerous pastimes, such as the possession of firearms, may also find themselves subject to the rigours of strict liability: *R.* v. *Howells* [1977] 2 W.L.R. 716 [*ante,* p. 121]. The Canadian Supreme Court has recently produced a three-fold classification of crimes: see the case below.

R. v. City of Sault Ste Marie

(1978) 85 D.L.R. (3d) 161
Supreme Court of Canada

The City of Sault Ste Marie entered into an agreement with C. Co. Ltd. to dispose of all the city's refuse. As a direct result of the methods of disposal used by the company, the Root River and Cannon Creek became polluted. The company was convicted under section 32 (1) of the Ontario Water Resources Act. The question arose whether the City should also be convicted under section 32 (1) which provided: "[E]very municipality or person that discharges or deposits, or causes or permits the discharge . . . of any material . . . into any water . . . that may impair the quality of water, is guilty of an offence."

DICKSON J. FOR THE COURT: In the present appeal the Court is concerned with offences variously referred to as "statutory", "public welfare", "regulatory", "absolute liability", or "strict responsibility", which are not criminal in any real sense, but are prohibited in the public interest. Although enforced as penal laws through the utilization of the machinery of the criminal law, the offences are in substance of a civil nature and might well be regarded as a branch of administrative law to which traditional principles of criminal law have but limited application. They relate to such everyday matters as traffic infractions, sales of impure food, violations of liquor laws, and the like. In this appeal we are concerned with pollution.

The mens rea point

The distinction between the true criminal offence and the public welfare offence is one of prime importance. Where the offence is criminal, the Crown must establish a mental element, namely that the accused who committed the prohibited act did so intentionally or recklessly, with knowledge of the facts constituting the offence, or with wilful blindness toward them. Mere negligence is excluded from the concept of the mental element required for conviction. Within the context of a criminal prosecution a person who fails to make such inquiries as a reasonable and prudent person would make, or who fails to know facts he should have known, is innocent in the eyes of the law.

In sharp contrast, "absolute liability" entails conviction on proof merely that the defendant committed the prohibited act constituting the *actus reus* of the offence. There is no relevant mental element. It is no defence that the accused was entirely without fault. He may be morally innocent in every sense, yet be branded as a malefactor and punished as such.

Public welfare offences obviously lie in a field of conflicting values. It is essential for society to maintain, through effective enforcement, high standards of public health and safety. Potential victims of those who carry on latently pernicious activities have a strong claim to consideration. On the other hand, there is a generally held revulsion against punishment of the morally innocent.

Public welfare offences evolved in mid-19th century Britain (*R.* v. *Woodrow* (1846) 15 M. & W. 404, and *R.* v. *Stephens* (1866) L.R. 1 Q.B. 702) as a means of doing away with the requirement of *mens rea* for petty police offences. The concept was a judicial creation, founded on expediency. That concept is now firmly embedded in the concrete of Anglo-American and Canadian jurisprudence, its importance heightened by the ever-increasing complexities of modern society.

Various arguments are advanced in justification of absolute liability in public welfare offences. Two predominate. Firstly, it is argued that the protection of social interests requires a high standard of care and attention on the part of those who follow certain pursuits and such persons are more likely to be stimulated to maintain those standards if they know that ignorance or mistake will not excuse them. The removal of any possible loophole acts, it is said, as an incentive to take precautionary measures beyond what would otherwise be taken, in order that mistakes and mishaps be avoided. The second main argument is one based on administrative efficiency. Having regard to both the difficulty of proving mental culpability and the number of petty cases which daily come before the Courts, proof of fault is just too great a burden in time and money to place upon the prosecution. To require proof of each person's individual intent would allow almost every violator to escape. This, together with the glut of work entailed in proving *mens rea* in every case would clutter the docket and impede adequate enforcement as virtually to nullify the regulatory statutes. In short, absolute liability, it is contended, is the most efficient and effective way of ensuring compliance with minor regulatory legislation and the social ends to be achieved are of such importance as to override the unfortunate by-product of punishing those who may be free of moral turpitude. In further justification, it is urged that slight penalties are usually imposed and that conviction for breach of a public welfare offence does not carry the stigma associated with conviction for a criminal offence.

Arguments of greater force are advanced against absolute liability. The most telling is that it violates fundamental principles of penal liability. It also rests upon assumptions which have not been, and cannot be, empirically established. There is no evidence that a higher standard of care results from absolute liability. If a person is already taking every reasonable precautionary measure, is he likely to take additional measures, knowing that however much care he takes, it will not serve as a defence in the event of breach? If he has exercised care and skill, will conviction have a deterrent effect upon him or others? Will the injustice of conviction lead to cynicism and disrespect for the law, on his part and on the part of others? These are among the questions asked. The argument that no stigma attaches does not withstand analysis, for the accused will have suffered loss of time, legal costs, exposure to the processes of the criminal law at trial and, however one may downplay it, the opprobrium of conviction. It is not sufficient to say that the public interest is engaged and, therefore, liability may be imposed without fault. In serious crimes, the public interest is involved and *mens rea* must be proven. The administrative argument has little force. In sentencing, evidence of due diligence is admissible and therefore the evidence might just as well be heard when considering guilt. . . .

Public welfare offences involve a shift of emphasis from the protection of individual interests to the protection of public and social interests. The unfortunate tendency in many past cases has been to see the choice as between two stark alternatives: (i) full *mens rea*; or (ii) absolute liability. In respect of public welfare offences (within which category pollution offences fall) where full *mens rea* is not required, absolute liability has often been imposed. English jurisprudence has consistently maintained this dichotomy: see "Criminal Law, Evidence and Procedure", 11 Hals., 4th ed., pp. 20–2, para. 18. There has, however, been an attempt in Australia, in many Canadian Courts, and indeed in England, to seek a middle position, fulfilling the goals of public welfare offences while still not punishing the entirely blameless. There is an increasing and impressive stream of authority which holds that where an offence does not require full *mens rea*, it is nevertheless a good defence for the defendant to prove that he was not negligent. . . .

The case which gave the lead in this branch of the law is the Australian case of *Proudman* v. *Dayman* (1941) 67 C.L.R. 536, where Dixon J., said, at p. 540:

> It is one thing to deny that a necessary ingredient of the offence is positive knowledge of the fact that the driver holds no subsisting licence. It is another to say that an honest belief founded on reasonable grounds that he is licensed cannot exculpate a person who permits him to drive. As a general rule an honest and reasonable belief in a state of facts which, if they existed, would make the defendant's act innocent affords an excuse for doing what would otherwise be an offence.

This case, and several others like it, speak of the defence as being that of reasonable mistake of fact. The reason is that the offences in question have generally turned on the possession by a person or place of an unlawful status, and the accused's defence was that he reasonably did not know of this status: *e.g.* permitting an unlicensed person to drive, or lacking a valid licence oneself, or being the owner of property in a dangerous condition. In such cases, negligence consists of an unreasonable failure to know the facts which constitute the offence. It is clear, however, that in principle the defence is that all reasonable care was taken. In other circumstances, the issue will be whether the accused's behaviour was negligent in bringing about the forbidden event when he knew the relevant facts. Once the defence of reasonable mistake of fact is accepted, there is no barrier to acceptance of the other constituent of a defence of due diligence.

The principle which has found acceptance in Australia since *Proudman* v. *Dayman, supra,* has a place also in the jurisprudence of New Zealand: see *The Queen* v. *Strawbridge* [1970] N.Z.L.R. 909; *The King* v. *Ewart* (1905) 25 N.Z.L.R. 709.

In the House of Lords case of *Sweet* v. *Parsley* (*ante,* p. 137), Lord Reid noted the difficulty presented by the simplistic choice between *mens rea* in the full sense and an absolute offence. He looked approvingly at attempts to find a middle ground. Lord Pearce, in the same case, referred to the "sensible half-way house" which he thought the Courts should take in some so-called absolute offences. The difficulty, as Lord Pearce saw it, lay in the opinion of Viscount Sankey, L.C. in *Woolmington* v. *Director of Public Prosecutions* [1935] A.C. 462, if the full width of that opinion were maintained. Lord Diplock, however, took a different and, in my opinion, a preferable view, [1970] A.C. 132 at p. 164:

> *Woolmington's* case did not decide anything so irrational as that the prosecution must call evidence to prove the absence of any mistaken belief by the accused in the existence of facts which, if true, would make the act innocent, any more than it decided that the prosecution must call evidence to prove the absence of any claim of right in a charge of larceny. The jury is entitled to presume that the accused acted with knowledge of the facts, unless there is some evidence to the contrary originating from the accused who alone can know on what belief he acted and on what ground the belief, if mistaken, was held.

In *Woolmington's* case the question was whether the trial judge was correct in directing the jury that the accused was required to prove his innocence. Viscount Sankey L.C., referred to the strength of the presumption of innocence in a criminal case and then made the statement, universally accepted in this country, that there is no burden on the prisoner to prove his innocence; it is sufficient for him to raise a doubt as to his guilt. I do not understand the case as standing for anything more than that. It is to be noted that the case is concerned with criminal offences in the true sense; it is not concerned with public welfare offences. It is somewhat ironic that *Woolmington's* case, which embodies a principle for the benefit of the accused, should be used to justify the rejection of a defence of reasonable care for public welfare offences and the retention of absolute liability, which affords the accused no defence at all. There is nothing in *Woolmington's* case, as I comprehend it, which stands in the way of adoption, in respect of regulatory offences, of a defence of due care, with burden of proof resting on the accused to establish the defence on the balance of probabilities. . . .

It may be suggested that the introduction of a defence based on due diligence and the shifting of the burden of proof might be better implemented by legislative act. In answer, it should be recalled that the concept of absolute liability and the creation of a jural category of public welfare offences are both the product of the judiciary and not of the Legislature. The development to date of this defence, in the numerous decisions I have referred to, of Courts in this country as well as in Australia and New Zealand, has also been the work of Judges. The present case offers the opportunity of consolidating and clarifying the doctrine.

The correct approach, in my opinion, is to relieve the Crown of the burden of proving *mens rea,* having regard to *Pierce Fisheries* [1970] 12 D.L.R. (3d) 1591, and to the virtual impossibility in most regulatory cases of proving wrongful intention. In a normal case, the accused alone will have knowledge of what he has done to avoid the breach and it is not improper to expect him to come forward with the evidence of due diligence. This is particularly so when it is alleged, for example, that pollution was caused by the activities of a large and complex corporation. Equally, there is nothing wrong with rejecting absolute liability and admitting the defence of reasonable care.

In this doctrine it is not up to the prosecution to prove negligence. Instead, it is open to the defendant to prove that all due care has been taken. This burden falls upon the defendant as he is the only one who will generally have the means of proof. This would not seem unfair as the alternative is absolute liability which denies an accused any defence whatsoever. While the prosecution must prove beyond a reasonable doubt that the defendant committed the prohibited act, the defendant must only establish on the balance of probabilities that he has a defence of reasonable care.

I conclude, for the reasons which I have sought to express, that there are compelling grounds for the recognition of three categories of offences rather than the traditional two:

1. Offences in which *mens rea,* consisting of some positive state of mind such as intent, knowledge, or recklessness, must be proved by the prosecution either as an inference from the nature of the act committed, or by additional evidence.
2. Offences in which there is no necessity for the prosecution to prove the existence of *mens rea*; the doing of the prohibited act *prima facie* imports the offence, leaving it open to the accused to avoid liability by proving that he took all reasonable care. This involves consideration of what a reasonable man would have done in the circumstances. The defence will be available if the accused reasonably believed in a mistaken set of facts which, if true, would render the act or omission innocent, or if he took all reasonable steps to avoid the particular event. These offences may properly be called offences of strict liability. Mr. Justice Estey so referred to them in *Hickey* [1976] 68 D.L.R. (3d) 88.
3. Offences of absolute liability where it is not open to the accused to exculpate himself by showing that he was free of fault.

Offences which are criminal in the true sense fall in the first category. Public welfare offences would, *prima facie,* be in the second category. They are not subject to the presumption of full *mens rea.* An offence of this type would fall in the first category only if such words as "wilfully", "with intent", "knowingly", or "intentionally" are contained in the statutory provision creating the offence. On the other hand, the principle that punishment should in general not be inflicted on those without fault applies. Offences of absolute liability would be those in respect of which the Legislature had made it clear that guilt would follow proof merely of the proscribed act. The over-all regulatory pattern adopted by the Legislature, the subject-matter of the legislation, the importance of the penalty, and the precision of the language used will be primary considerations in determining whether the offence falls into the third category.

The Divisional Court of Ontario concluded that s. 32 (1) created a *mens rea* offence.

The words "cause" and "permit" fit much better into an offence of strict liability than either full *mens rea* or absolute liability. Since s. 32 (1) creates a public welfare offence, without a clear indication that liability is absolute, and without any words such as "knowingly" or "wilfully" expressly to import *mens rea*, application of the criteria which I have outlined above undoubtedly places the offence in the category of strict liability.

Appeals dismissed and a new trial ordered

[This classification has not proved to be free of difficulty. See *Strasser* v. *Roberge* (1980) 103 D.L.R. (3d) 193.]

iii. Critique

It is evident from the cases in the preceding section that a number of justifications are advanced for the imposition of strict liability. In *Sault Ste Marie* (above) the two predominant arguments were seen as improved standards of prevention (*i.e.* the public will be better protected from the inherent risks in certain activities), and greater administrative efficiency (*i.e.* that efficacious enforcement is only possible where there is no burden on the prosecution to prove a mental element). On their own both these arguments could be used to favour the abolition of *mens rea* in all crimes. (See Barbara Wootton, *Crime and the Criminal Law* (Stevens, 2nd ed., 1981), chap. 2.)

Two further glosses are thus added. On the one hand it is suggested that strict liability does not eliminate fault as a basis of liability but that the fault element is determined at an earlier stage of the criminal process. Such an argument can lead to different conclusions. (See Paulus, Thomas and Smith, below.) On the other hand, it is said that, since these offences are not "true" crimes, the concept of *mens rea* is not required to prevent the injustice of punishing the "morally" innocent. This approach leads to difficulties in deciding whether it is the nature of the prohibited activity or the fact that no mental element is required which renders these "quasi" crimes. A vicious circle may arise in which strict liability is imposed to protect the public from the risks inherent in certain activities, while that protection is undermined by sentencing lightly defendants who, by virtue of the use of discretionary enforcement policies, have at the very least been negligent. (See Walker, below.) At a different level of analysis, it can be questioned whether either strict liability or negligence acts as an incentive to greater safety precautions (Hutchinson, below).

Ingeborg Paulus, "Strict Liability: Its Place in Public Welfare Offences" (1978) 20 Crim. L.Q. 445:

"*Theoretical* legal reasoning repeatedly stresses that strict liability . . . is unjust and holds persons liable for offences for which they are morally blameless. Yet empirical researchers assessing the law in action are not alarmed about strict liability offences and their enforcement.... [W]henever studies have been made investigating the workings of strict liability, the persons involved in the administration of public welfare offences, especially those concerning food and drug laws, have stressed that strict liability generally does not penalize offenders who are not also clearly guilty.... [T]he personnel in charge of enforcement rarely prosecute unless they find an element of fault or *mens rea* present in the offence. But the *availability* of strict liability prosecutions greatly facilitates their work."

[The studies referred to are: Smith and Pearson, "The Value of Strict Liability" [1969] Crim. L.R. 5; W. G. Carson, "Some Sociological Aspects of Strict Liability and the Enforcement of Factory Legislation" (1970) 33 M.L.R. 396; F. J. Remington, *et al.*, "Liability Without Fault Criminal Statutes" [1965] Wis. L.R. 625. To these can be added: Law Commission, Pub. Working Paper No. 30, Strict Liability and the Enforcement of the Factories Act 1961 (1970) and Law Reform Commission of Canada, "Studies in Strict Liability" (Ottowa, 1974)].

D. A. Thomas, "Form and Function in Criminal Law" in Glazebrook, p. 30:

"The effect of imposing strict liability is not necessarily to eliminate fault as a requirement of liability, but to delegate to the enforcer both the responsibility of deciding what kind of fault will in general justify a prosecution (with the certainty of conviction) and the right to determine whether in the circumstances of the particular case that degree of fault is present. The main objections to the concept of strict liability are thus procedural rather than substantive, and the questions to be addressed to the proponent of a statute creating an offence of strict liability are: 'Why is it not possible to incorporate into the definition of the offence the nature of the fault which is likely in practice to be required as a condition precedent to prosecution, and why is it not possible for the existence of this fault to be determined in accordance with the normal processes of the law?' At the very least, there can be no justification for enacting an offence of strict liability which is not balanced by a provision allowing the question whether fault existed or not to be raised in the trial as an affirmative defence, and any offence of strict liability where the gravity of the offence would be enhanced by the offender's knowledge of the relevant circumstances should be the lowest step in a hierarchy of offences including similar offences requiring proof of knowledge or intent."

J. C. Smith [1966] Crim. L.R. 505, commenting on *Lockyer* v. *Gibb* [1967] 2 Q.B. 243, a case on possession of drugs where the defendant did not know that what she possessed *was* a drug:

"The interpretation of statutes so as to create offences of strict liability in fact creates difficulties of sentencing which have not been faced up to by the courts. Take a case in which the accused is tried on indictment. The judge tells the jury to convict if they are satisfied that (i) D knew he was in possession of the thing, and (ii) the thing is a dangerous drug. They convict. If these are the only facts proved against D it would be quite scandalous to do other than give him an absolute discharge. If D ought to have known the thing was a drug, then he is in some degree blameworthy; if he in fact knew it was a drug, he is more blameworthy. But the jury need not consider these questions. How does the judge know on what basis he should sentence? He is discouraged from asking the jury the question at all. The judge presumably makes up his own mind. His view of the facts may differ completely from that of the jury—if they have a view. Thus what is really the fundamental issue of fact in the case is withdrawn from the jury and decided by the judge alone. The position in the case of a magistrates' court is a little easier because the magistrates at least know on what facts the conviction is based; but it is unsatisfactory that they may come to the sentencing stage without having considered whether the accused bears any moral responsibility whatever for the 'offence' which has been committed. This question must be considered before a sentence can be imposed. Presumably it is dealt with in the informal way in which other findings of fact relating only to sentence are handled. But this is hardly satisfactory, when it is really the most fundamental issue of fact in the case which is being considered. On what basis was the fine of £10 in the present case imposed? The magistrate must have thought that the defendant was in some degree blameworthy or he would presumably have granted an absolute discharge. Yet he was evidently not satisfied beyond reasonable doubt that the defendant knew that the substance was a dangerous drug. Did he then fine her because she ought to have known? Or was he satisfied with a lower degree of proof (she probably knew)?"

Nigel Walker, Crime and Punishment in Britain (1965), p. 33:

"The number of people killed or injured in road accidents each year is more than ten times the numbers involved in all the forms of assault recorded in the Criminal Statistics. Many of these casualties were due to the victim's own negligence or disobedience of rules; but even if we allow for this by halving the figures, it is clear that anti-social use of vehicles is a much more important source of death, bereavement, physical suffering and disablement than any intentional forms of violence. Yet the penal system treats motoring offences far less seriously than crimes of violence or even of dishonesty. Inadvertence is the excuse offered by most people accused of illegal parking, speeding or disobeying traffic signals, and that partly because this defence is so hard to disprove, partly in the hope of making the negligent driver less negligent, the law has been drafted so that even negligent transgressions are offences. This encourages the impression that *most* such transgressions are merely negligent, although it is very doubtful whether this is so."

Allan C. Hutchinson, Note on Sault Ste Marie (1979), 17 Osgoode Hall Law Journal 415, 429 (fn. 78):

"An application of the presently favoured 'economic perspective', as represented by Richard A. Posner and other members of the so-called Chicago School, to the problem offers some interesting insights into the relative efficiency of strict liability and negligence as methods of combating the type of harm and safeguarding the interests that public welfare offences are intended to protect. According to such an analysis, where the primary object of an offence is accident prevention, as is the case with public welfare offences, there is little to choose between strict liability and negligence. Whichever basis of liability is employed, the standard of care taken by the potential injurer is likely to be influenced almost exclusively by the result of balancing the cost of precautions against the predicted cost of the penalty. If the preventive costs are lower, then precautions will be taken whether the offence is one of negligence or strict liability. But if the penalty is lower, then neither negligence nor strict liability is likely to encourage the taking of precautions. Therefore, the choice of liability standards has no effect on the level of safety achieved. Moreover, it is possible, yet surprising to many, that, if either basis of liability is to bring about some long term effect, the imposition of strict liability is more likely than negligence to result in an improvement in accident prevention. As regards negligence, liability is usually determined on the existing state of sophistication of the technology of accident prevention and, as such, presents little or no incentive to advance such knowledge by investing in its research and development. On the other hand, strict liability may engender greater safety, as there is more of an incentive to encourage and engage in the research into and the development of precautionary measures:

> If [for example, a railroad company] were liable for all accidents . . . , it would compare the liability that it could not avoid by means of existing safety precautions with the feasibility of developing new precautions that would reduce that liability. If safety research and development seemed likely to reduce accident costs by more than the cost of research and development, the [company] would undertake it. . . . (Posner, *The Economic Analysis of Law* (2d ed. Boston: Little, Brown, 1977) at 138).

Such an approach is overly simplistic. The validity of the argument is contingent on two dubious assumptions: that penalties will remain minimal and unrealistic, and that the intangible costs (i.e., loss of reputation in the community, political embarrassment, unsettling of shareholders) will be negligible. Moreover, it fails to take into account the possible and positive gains that are available if the polluter shows himself to be a morally and socially responsible member of the community. There is much more to law and life than the cold and relentless logic of economic reasoning."

iv. Proposals for Reform

Clause 5, Law Commission Draft Bill (*ante*, p. 59).

Law Com. No. 89

"§ 73. Earlier in this report we have referred to the uncertainty which can arise in the construction of a statutory offence. This uncertainty arises when it is not indicated what mental state (if any) is needed of a defendant in respect of one or more of the requirements of the offence before he can be guilty of that offence. And we have pointed out that it is an undue simplification of the problem in such a case to regard the choice before the courts as one between on the one hand reading into the offence a requirement of some form of mental element and on the other treating the offence as one imposing strict liability. It may well be that on a proper construction, where all the requirements of the offence (other than the requirement of "fault") are satisfied, it can only be committed by a defendant who has failed to conform to an objective standard of reasonable behaviour; in other words the offence involves something akin to negligence. We have also pointed out that, whatever requirement as to a mental element or as to negligence a court reads into an offence, there is the further question as to what should be the burden of proof in respect of that requirement.

§ 74. It is unnecessary to consider the ways that can be devised to resolve the uncertainty which may arise in the circumstances discussed in the last paragraph. But first we emphasise that that uncertainty only arises where it is not clear from the language used to formulate an offence whether in respect of any matters relevant to the commission of that offence a particular mental state, some objective standard of conduct or strict liability is involved.

§ 75. *We therefore recommend* that, in respect of an offence which is created by a provision in or under a statute passed on or after the appointed day, it should be expressly stated to what extent liability depends on intention, knowledge or recklessness (which we hope, as stated in paragraph 72 (*b*) above, will be the terms used, wherever possible, to indicate any mental state required), depends on an objective standard of conduct (whether expressed as liability for negligence or in some other way) or is intended to be strict.

§ 76. With regard to existing offences, Proposition 6 in Working Paper No. 31 was in the following terms—

> "Subject to any specific exceptions, where the existing law does not require a particular degree of fault in respect of an element of the offence, that offence nevertheless requires negligence in the defendant as to that element. In such cases, unless otherwise expressly provided, negligence may be treated as established in the absence of any evidence to the contrary. Where the fault proved by the evidence is of a higher degree than negligence, negligence shall be taken as established."

§ 77. In paragraph 70 above we have explained why we have been unable to accept the proposal that the recommended definitions of intention, knowledge and recklessness should apply to existing offences. We also cannot recommend the adoption of Proposition 6. It is true that the proposition is 'subject to any specific exceptions', but the determination of those exceptions over the whole field of the criminal law would involve a similar enquiry to that which, with its attendant difficulties and disadvantages, would be necessary if our recommendations regarding intention, knowledge and recklessness were to be applied to existing offences. With regard to Proposition 6 we are strengthened in our conclusion by the consideration that many of the offences which raise difficulty as to whether they ought as a matter of policy to involve a mental element, negligence or strict liability are found in legislation of a 'regulatory' kind, which requires fairly frequent reconsideration and reformulation by Parliament. When such reformulation takes place in future, if the recommendations so far made in this report are accepted, we think the legislator will be assisted in knowing what would be the effect of referring in a future offence to intention, knowledge or recklessness."

See Hogan [1978] Crim. L.R. 593 for some rigorous criticism of the Law Commission's proposals.

The Model Penal Code

"s. 1.04 (1) An offense defined by this Code or by any other statute of this State, for which a sentence of [death or of] imprisonment is authorized, constitutes a crime. Crimes are classified as felonies, misdemeanours or petty misdemeanours.

. . . .

(5) An offense defined by this Code or by any other statute of this State constitutes a violation if it is so designated in this Code or in the law defining the offense or if no other sentence than a fine, or fine and forfeiture or other civil penalty is authorized upon conviction or if it is defined by a statute other than this Code which now provides that the offense shall not constitute a crime. A violation does not constitute a crime and conviction of a violation shall not give rise to any disability or legal disadvantage based on conviction of a criminal offense.

s. 2.05 (1) The requirements of culpability prescribed by Sections 2.01 and 2.02 [of which the minimum is negligence] do not apply to:

(a) offenses which constitute violations, unless the requirement involved is included in the definition of the offense or the Court determines that its application is consistent with effective enforcement of the law defining the offense; or
(b) offenses defined by statutes other than the Code, insofar as a legislative purpose to impose absolute liability for such offenses or with respect to any material element thereof plainly appears.

Justice, Breaking the Rules, 1980

[In recommending a similar division between "crimes" and "contraventions" in this country, *Justice* envisages the following:]

"§ 4.12 In practice, the sort of procedure we have in mind would work something like this:—

(a) whenever the public authority charged with responsibility for the relevant sector of public conduct obtained evidence amounting to a *prima facie* case of a contravention, it would notify the alleged contravenor by letter and invite his explanation;
(b) failing a satisfactory explanation within a fixed time, the authority would impose a prescribed penalty, and notify the contravenor what his options are;
(c) those options would be either to comply with the penalty imposed (e.g. to pay a fine) or, if he challenged the imposition of the penalty, to give notice of his objection (on a form supplied to him) to his local Magistrates' Court;
(d) if such a notice is given, the burden would be on the authority to satisfy the Magistrates' Court, by sworn evidence and beyond reasonable doubt, that the alleged contravenor had committed the contravention complained of."

Question

The Law Commission proposal would create a presumption in favour of *mens rea* which Parliament could expressly rebut. The M.P.C. and "Justice" propose that "offences" of strict liability should be separately classified. Would either of these proposals tend to increase the incidence of strict liability? Is either approach preferable?

Chapter 4

MENTAL INCAPACITY

	PAGE		PAGE
1. Defences in General	157	3. Automatism	167
2. Insanity	158	4. Intoxication	176
i. Unfitness to Plead	159	5. Proposals for Reform	195
ii. The Defence of Insanity	162		

1. DEFENCES IN GENERAL

A. T. H. Smith, "On Actus Reus and Mens Rea" in Reshaping the Criminal Law (ed. Glazebrook), p. 97

"When speaking colloquially lawyers are inclined to call any reason advanced by a defendant in support of an acquittal a 'defence.' These include such explanations as alibi, infancy, mistake, accident, and insanity. When they use the term more precisely, they point out that automatism—for example—is not really a defence at all, but a denial that the prosecution has proved part of its case: the prosecution has failed to show that the defendant acted with *mens rea*. It has now been accepted by no less a body than the House of Lords that, where the definition of any particular crime includes intention or recklessness, any mistake that has the effect of preventing the formation of these states of mind must exculpate, whether it be a reasonable mistake or not. This is so because mistake prevents the formation of the particular *mens rea* which must be established as part of the prosecution case. Duress, necessity, self-defence, and infancy, on the other hand, are said to be properly described as 'defences', because they do not negative either traditional *mens rea* or *actus reus*, but operate in some way independently. . . .

It is possible to make a distinction between defences which are justificatory in character, and those which are excuses. It has not found much favour in Anglo-American jurisprudence, partly no doubt because of Stephen's emphatic assertion that it 'involves no legal consequences,' a reproach guaranteed to deprive it of any significance it might otherwise have enjoyed. Briefly stated, the distinction is that we excuse the actor because he is not sufficiently culpable or at fault, whereas we justify an act because we regard it as the most appropriate course of action in the circumstances, even though it may result in harm that would, in the absence of the justification, amount to a crime. It does not follow that, because the distinction between the two is not formally taken in our law that it is altogether without significance, particularly when the law is in a state of flux. The reasons why, and the circumstances in which, we are prepared to excuse may be altogether different from the corresponding reasons for justification. We admit excuses as 'an expression of compassion for one of our kind caught in a maelstrom of circumstances.' A plea of justification, by contrast, is founded upon the law's preference, in social and policy terms, for one course of action rather than another.

Where a defendant successfully pleads a defence such as prevention of crime or self-defence, he argues that what he did was not unlawful, and he is able to point to a specific rule—in the one case of statutory origin, and in the other, in common law—to substantiate his plea. It may be, however, that a plea of justification has not crystallised into one of these specific defences, but is of a more nebulous sort.

For example, although it appears that there is no general defence of necessity in that there is no rule to which a defendant can appeal to justify his having chosen to bring about a proscribed harm, there is nevertheless a principle infiltrating the legal system, given efficacy through a variety of legal inlets, that where a person is placed by force of circumstance in the position of having to choose between two evils, his act is justified if he chooses the lesser one. In that somewhat fitful sense, necessity operates as a 'defence.' Some would say that a person who commits a *prima facie* unlawful act as a result of necessity is not blameworthy or at fault and hence lacks *mens rea*. But it does not necessarily follow that we exculpate him for that reason. An alternative explanation is that where the act done is the lesser of two evils, it is justified or lawful—that there was no *actus reus* notwithstanding that the conduct falls literally within the terms of the definition of the offence.

Analysis of crime in terms of *actus reus* and *mens rea*, and the mechanical application of statutes, tend to obscure the principles of harm and illegality on which criminal liability is based. Unless these principles find expression either in the definition of the crime itself (*e.g.* by the inclusion of 'unlawfully') or in some express exculpatory rule, it seems that our legal system is incapable of giving effect to them. Whereas the judges are adept at interpreting legislation in such a way as to introduce traditional *mens rea*, if necessary by reading words into the statutes, they will only infrequently allow considerations of principle to override the plain words of a statute. Only by providing in a code for a defence of necessity, therefore, is it possible to ensure that this principle is preserved in a form in which it will invariably prevail."

Note

The scheme adopted in this book attempts to reflect the distinction between excuse and justification although some defences do not necessarily fit neatly into such a classification: see duress (*post*, p. 201). Thus, insanity, automatism and intoxication are considered in this chapter, duress and necessity in the next. Provocation and diminished responsibility, because they are only available in murder, and self-defence, because it mostly arises in murder, are dealt with in Chapter 8.

2. INSANITY

The law relating to mental abnormality and its effect upon criminal liability has developed in three branches of the criminal law. It is to be found in the consideration of individual responsibility for acts where the problem of automatic states of mind has led to a body of case law that is discussed *post*, p. 167; statute, Homicide Act 1957, has provided for the defence of diminished responsibility which applies only to the crime of murder and is discussed *post*, p. 402.

This section is concerned with the law's treatment of insanity itself which is, theoretically at least, a complete defence to liability. In practice, because of the consequence of a finding of insanity, it is a defence which is rarely raised. In 1978, for example, two people were found insane, although a further 12 were found to be unfit to plead: people "would rather be thought bad than mad." (Williams, T. C. L., p. 595). In seeking a legal definition of insanity the courts are often, if only implicitly, attempting to protect the public from the danger presented by some forms of mental abnormality. The dual purposes of individual excuse and social protection have sometimes led the courts into difficulties: see *R.* v. *Quick* (*post*, p. 171). The double edged quality of the defence is also reflected in the statutory provisions in relation to verdict, appeal and disposal. A special verdict of "not guilty by reason of insanity" is given (Criminal Procedure (Insanity) Act 1964, s. 1), but an appeal is possible (Criminal Appeal Act 1968, s. 12). A finding of insanity or of unfitness to plead results in the defendant's compulsory admission to a hospital specified by the Home Secretary (Criminal Procedure (Insanity) Act 1964, s. 5 (1)).

i. Unfitness to Plead

Criminal Procedure (Insanity) Act 1964

Section 4: "(1) Where on the trial of a person the question arises (at the instance of the defence or otherwise) whether the accused is under disability, that is to say under any disability such that apart from this Act it would constitute a bar to his being tried, the following provisions shall have effect.

(2) The court, if having regard to the nature of the supposed disability the court are of opinion that it is expedient so to do and in the interests of the accused, may postpone consideration of the said question (hereinafter referred to as 'the question of fitness to be tried') until any time up to the opening of the case for the defence, and if before the question of fitness to be tried falls to be determined the jury return a verdict of acquittal on the count or each of the counts on which the accused is being tried that question shall not be determined.

(3) Subject to the foregoing subsection, the question of fitness to be tried shall be determined as soon as it arises.

(4) The question of fitness to be tried shall be determined by the jury; and—

(a) where it falls to be determined on the arraignment of the accused, then if the trial proceeds the accused shall be tried by a jury other than that which determined the question;

(b) where it falls to be determined at any later time it shall be determined by a separate jury or by the jury by whom the accused is being tried, as the court may direct.

(5) Where in accordance with subsection (2) or (3) of this section it is determined that the accused is under disability, the trial shall not proceed or further proceed."

Section 5: "(1) Where— . . . (*c*) a finding is recorded that the accused is under disability the court shall make an order that the accused be admitted to such hospital as may be specified by the Secretary of State."

Note

These rules are not without difficulty. Their purpose was put succinctly in *R.* v. *Webb* [1969] 2 Q.B. 278 by Sachs L.J.:

"Before the passing of the 1964 Act, the issue of fitness to plead had of necessity to be disposed of before arraignment. If the jury found unfitness to plead, then the order of the court was in all cases that the defendant be detained at Her Majesty's pleasure. One of the main objects of the Act was, of course, to enable the accused to avoid this much dreaded order in cases where the defence was in a position to demolish the prosecution case by cross-examination or upon some point of law before the time came for the defence to be opened."

It appears that a trial judge has to balance the disability of the accused by the apparent strength of the prosecution case—a far from easy task, see *R.* v. *Burles* [1970] 2 Q.B. 191.

R. v. Podola
[1960] 1 Q.B. 325
Court of Criminal Appeal

The appellant was charged with killing Detective P., being a police officer acting in the execution of his duty. Before he was arraigned, the appellant's counsel raised the preliminary issue of the accused's fitness to plead. Edmund-Davies J. ruled upon this preliminary issue that it was for the defence to establish that the accused was so insane as to be unfit to stand his trial, and upon the defence being unable to do so, the trial proceeded and the appellant was convicted of capital murder. He did not appeal, but the Home Secretary, being of the opinion that a question of law was raised by the case, namely the onus of proof on the issue of fitness to plead, referred the whole case to the Court of Criminal Appeal for determination under section 19(a) of the Criminal Appeal Act 1907.

Lord Parker C.J.: If a convicted person appeals against his conviction on the ground that the hearing of the preliminary issue was open to objection for error in law, so that he should never have been tried on the substantive charge at all, we are of opinion that this court has jurisdiction to entertain the appeal. In such a case it seems to us that the principles laid down in *Crane* v. *D.P.P.* [1921] 2 A.C. 299; 15 Cr. App. R. 183 are applicable.

In our judgment, the appellant in the present case could have appealed against his conviction upon the ground that in the hearing of the preliminary issue the judge misdirected the jury, and therefore that he should never have been tried upon the main charge at all. It follows that this court has jurisdiction to hear and determine the case referred.

[With regard to the onus of proof] the principles may be stated as follows:

1. In all cases in which a preliminary issue as to the accused person's sanity is raised, whether that issue is contested or not, the jury should be directed to consider the whole of the evidence and to answer the question "Are you satisfied upon that evidence that the accused person is insane so that he cannot be tried upon the indictment?" If authority were needed for the principle, it is to be found in the very words of the section itself.

2. If the contention that the accused is insane is put forward by the defence and contested by the prosecution, there is, in our judgment, a burden upon the defence of satisfying the jury of the accused's insanity. In such a case, as in other criminal cases in which the onus of proof rests upon the defence, the onus is discharged if the jury are satisfied on the balance of probabilities that the accused's insanity has been made out.

3. Conversely, if the prosecution alleges and the defence disputes insanity, there is a burden upon the prosecution of establishing it.

In our judgment, therefore, the direction of Edmund-Davies J. in the present case on the subject of onus of proof was right.

We have, however, thought it necessary, in the circumstances of the case, to consider whether the alleged state of mind of the appellant would have brought him within the provisions of section 2 of the Criminal Lunatics Act 1800, had the jury found that the state of mind was a genuine one.

In considering this problem it is important to stress that the appellant, in the proceedings at the Central Criminal Court, relied solely on an hysterical amnesia preventing him from remembering events during the whole of the period material to the question whether he committed the crime alleged. There was no suggestion that his mind in other respects was not a completely normal mind. His case on this point was that this defect of memory rendered him unable properly to instruct his advisers, with the consequence that he could not make "a proper defence."

This defect, it was argued, rendered the applicant insane within the meaning of the Act of 1800.

This case is the first attempt in England to assert that hysterical amnesia covering the period of the events which are the subject of the indictment renders a man insane so that he cannot be tried. The matter has, however, come before the courts in Scotland. In 1907 there was the case of *H.M. Advocate* v. *Brown* in the High Court of Justiciary: 1907 S.C. (J.) 67 [and] in 1946 the case of *Russell* v. *H.M. Advocate* in the High Court of Justiciary: 1946 S.C. (J.) 37.

[In that case] the Lord Justice-Clerk in the course of his judgment said at p. 46: "The only grounds associated with the abnormal personal condition of the accused which our law and practice have ever recognised as the basis of a plea in bar are (a) insanity (either in the ordinary sense or in the special sense of the Lunacy (Scotland) Act 1857, s. 87)" where the words are similar to the words of the Act of 1800 "and (b) the condition of a deaf mute. There is no trace in either Scotland or England of a plea in bar founded on the loss of memory by a sane and otherwise normal accused person."

Later he said, at p. 48: "The conclusions which I feel bound to draw are that loss of memory may be an important element in leading to the conclusion that an accused person is insane.... But, if it falls short of that, loss of memory in a person otherwise normal and sane plays its full part if it is sufficiently proved in increasing the onus on the Crown and in raising doubts to which it may be the duty of the jury to give effect in a verdict of acquittal after investigation of the whole case. But as our law stands it can have no further or other effect."

We agree with the opinions stated and the conclusions arrived at in the case of *Russell* v. *H.M. Advocate, supra*. The word used in the Act of 1800 is the word "insane." It is true that in the case of a deaf mute the word "insane" does not strictly apply, but we cannot see that it is in accordance either with reason or common sense to extend the meaning of the word to include persons who are mentally normal at the time of the hearing of the proceedings against them, and are perfectly capable of instructing their solicitors as to what submission their counsel is to put forward with regard to the commission of the crime.

Accordingly, this appeal is dismissed.

Appeal dismissed

Note

In *Crane* v. *D.P.P., supra*, C. was indicted for receiving stolen goods and M. was indicted separately for stealing and for receiving them. Both prisoners were improperly tried together and convicted. C. appealed on the ground of misdirection and misreception of evidence and the Court of Criminal Appeal ordered a new trial to be held. On a further appeal the House of Lords held that the proceedings at the trial were a nullity but that C. had so far been convicted as to be able to appeal. It was also held that the Court of Criminal Appeal had jurisdiction under the Criminal Appeal Act 1907, to hear such appeal and to make any order to enable justice to be done. Their lordships dismissed the appeal and affirmed the order of the Court of Criminal Appeal.

ii. The defence of insanity

M'Naghten's Case
(1843) 10 Cl. & F. 200; 8 E.R. 718

M'Naghten was indicted for murder and acquitted on the ground of insanity. In consequence debates took place in the House of Lords, and it was decided to take the opinion of the judges as to the nature and extent of the unsoundness of mind which would excuse the commission of a felony of this sort. Five questions were put to the judges in the terms set out in the following extract from their opinions.

TINDAL C.J. (Delivering the opinion of all the judges except Maule J.): The first question proposed by your Lordships is this: "What is the law respecting alleged crimes committed by persons afflicted with insane delusion in respect of one or more particular subjects or persons: as, for instance, where at the time of the commission of the alleged crime the accused knew he was acting contrary to law, but did the act complained of with a view, under the influence of insane delusion, of redressing or revenging some supposed grievance or injury, or of producing some supposed public benefit?"

In answer to which question, assuming that your Lordships' inquiries are confined to those persons who labour under such partial delusions only, and are not in other respects insane, we are of opinion that, notwithstanding the party accused did the act complained of with a view, under the influence of insane delusion, of redressing or revenging some supposed grievance or injury, or of producing some public benefit, he is nevertheless punishable according to the nature of the crime committed, if he knew at the time of committing such crime that he was acting contrary to law; by which expression we understand your Lordships to mean the law of the land.

Your Lordships are pleased to inquire of us, secondly, "What are the proper questions to be submitted to the jury, where a person alleged to be afflicted with insane delusion respecting one or more particular subjects or persons, is charged with the commission of a crime (murder, for example), and insanity is set up as a defence?" And, thirdly, "In what terms ought the question to be left to the jury as to the prisoner's state of mind at the time when the act was committed?" And as these two questions appear to us to be more conveniently answered together, we have to submit our opinion to be, that the jurors ought to be told in all cases that every man is to be presumed to be sane, and to possess a sufficient degree of reason to be responsible for his crimes, until the contrary be proved to their satisfaction; and that to establish a defence on the ground of insanity, it must be clearly proved that, at the time of the committing of the act, the party accused was labouring under such a defect of reason, from disease of the mind, as not to know the nature and quality of the act he was doing; or, if he did know it, that he did not know he was doing what was wrong. The mode of putting the latter part of the question to the jury on these occasions has generally been, whether the accused at the time of doing the act knew the difference between right and wrong: which mode, though rarely, if ever, leading to any mistake with the jury, is not, as we conceive, so accurate when put generally and in the abstract, as when put with reference to the party's knowledge of right and wrong in respect to the very act with which he is charged. If the question were to be put as to the knowledge of the accused solely and exclusively with reference to the law of the land, it might tend to confound the jury, by inducing them to believe that an actual knowledge of the law of the land was essential in order to lead to a conviction: whereas the law is administered upon the principle that everyone must be taken conclusively to know it, without proof that he does know it. If the accused was conscious that the act was one which he ought not to do, and if that act was at the same time contrary to the law of the land, he is punishable: and the usual course therefore has been to leave the question to the jury, whether the party accused had a sufficient degree of reason to know that he was doing an act that was wrong: and this course we think is correct, accompanied with such observations and explanations as the circumstances of each particular case may require.

The fourth question which your Lordships have proposed to us is this: "If a person under an insane delusion as to existing facts, commits an offence in consequence thereof, is he thereby excused?" To which question the answer must, of course, depend on the nature of the delusion: but, making the same assumption as we did before, namely, that he labours under such partial delusion only, and is not in other respects insane, we think he must be considered in the same situation as to responsibility as if the facts with respect to which the delusion exists were real. For example, if under the influence of his delusion he supposes another man to be in the act of attempting to take away his life, and he kills that man, as he supposes, in self-defence, he would be exempt from punishment. If this delusion was that the deceased had inflicted a serious injury to his character and fortune, and he killed him in revenge for such supposed injury, he would be liable to punishment.

The question lastly proposed by your Lordships is: "Can a medical man conversant with the disease of insanity, who never saw the prisoner previously to the trial, but who was present during the whole trial and the examination of all the witnesses, be asked his opinion as to the state of the prisoner's mind at the time of the commission of the alleged crime, or his opinion whether the prisoner was conscious at the time of doing the act that he was acting contrary to law, or whether he was labouring under any and what delusion at the time?" In answer thereto, we state to your Lordships, that we think the medical man, under the circumstances supposed, cannot in strictness be asked his opinion in the terms above stated, because each of those questions involves the determination of the truth of the facts deposed to, which it is for the jury to decide, and the questions are not mere questions upon a matter of science, in which such evidence is admissible. But where facts are admitted or not disputed, and the question becomes substantially one of science only, it may be convenient to allow the question to be put in that general form, though the same cannot be insisted on as a matter of right.

Question and Note

Do you agree with Glanville Williams that "the three M'Naghten questions are principally concerned with *mens rea*" (T.C.L., p. 593)?

M'Naghten places the burden of proof on the defendant. It was held in *R.* v. *Sodeman* [1936] 2 All E.R. 1138 that this requires proof on a balance of probability. Both the Criminal Law Revision Committee (11th Report, Cmnd. 4991 (1972), § 1.40) and the Butler Committee on Mentally Abnormal Offenders (Cmnd. 6244 (1975), § 18.39) recommended that this burden should be on the prosecution. See *Bratty, post,* p. 168, for an explanation of the working of the burden of proof where insanity is run with other defences.

R. v. Codere
(1916) 12 Cr. App. R. 21
Court of Criminal Appeal

The appellant had been convicted of murder. Insanity was the only defence raised at the trial. Under section 5(4) of the Criminal Appeal Act 1907, the Court of Criminal Appeal have power to quash the sentence and order the appellant to be detained as insane.

LORD READING C.J.: . . . Mr. Foote (on behalf of Codere) has addressed an argument to us based on *M'Naghten's Case*, which is the classic authority on the subject, which in substance resolved itself into this, that we must assume that when the law says that the question is whether the accused was labouring under such a defect of reason, from disease of the mind, as not to know the nature and quality of the act he was doing, we must read "nature" to have reference to the physical act, and "quality" to refer to the morality of the act, and that therefore the jury should be asked if he knew he was doing wrong. The argument advanced is that the judge ought to tell the jury that "quality" means, "Did the accused person know that the act was immoral?" and when one stops and asks the meaning of "immoral" we get to the first of the difficulties which faced Mr. Foote.

It is said that "quality" is to be regarded as characterising the moral, as contrasted with the physical, aspect of the deed. The court cannot agree with that view of the meaning of the words "nature and quality." The court is of opinion that in using the language "nature and quality" the judges were only dealing with the physical and moral aspects of the act. That is the law as it has been laid down by judges in many directions to juries, and as the court understands it to be at the present time.

We then come to the second branch of the test, namely, if he knew the physical nature of the act did he know that he was doing wrong? Mr. Foote has argued that it is not enough that he knew the act was contrary to law and punishable by law, and that, even if he did know that . . . yet the jury ought to have been told that they must find a special verdict (of guilty but insane) . . . unless they came to the conclusion that he knew that the act was morally wrong. The question of the distinction between morally and legally wrong opens wide doors. In a case of this kind, namely, killing, it does not seem debatable that the appellant could have thought that the act was not morally wrong, judged by the ordinary standards, when the act is punishable by law, and is known by him to be punishable by law. It was suggested at one time in the course of argument that the question should be judged by the standard of the accused, but it is obvious that this proposition is wholly untenable, and would tend to excuse crimes without number, and to weaken the law to an alarming degree. It is conceded now that the standard to be applied is whether according to the ordinary standard adopted by reasonable men the act was right or wrong. . . . Once it is clear that the appellant knew that the act was wrong in law, then he was doing an act which he was conscious he ought not to do, and as it was against the law, it was punishable by law; assuming, therefore, that he knew the nature and quality of the act, he was guilty of murder, and was properly convicted.

The difficulty no doubt arises over the words "conscious that the act was one which he ought not to do," but, looking at all the answers in *M'Naghten's Case*, it seems that if it is punishable by law it is an act which he ought not to do, and that is the meaning in which the phrase is used in that case. There may be minor cases before a court of summary jurisdiction where that view may be open to doubt, but in cases such as these the true view is what we have just said.

Application dismissed

R. v. Windle
[1952] 2 Q.B. 826
Court of Criminal Appeal

The appellant gave his wife a fatal dose of aspirin. He admitted that he had done so, and said he supposed he would hang for it. The appellant's only defence was that of insanity. At the trial, Devlin J. ruled that there was no evidence to go to the jury on the defence of insanity.

LORD GODDARD C.J.: The point we have to decide in this case can be put into a very small compass. We are asked to review what are generally known as the M'Naghten Rules, and possibly to make new law. . . . The argument before us has really been on what is the meaning of the word "wrong". . . . Mr. Shawcross (for Windle) . . . suggested that the word "wrong" as it was used in the M'Naghten Rules, did not mean contrary to law but has some kind of qualified meaning, such as morally wrong, and that if a person was in such a state of mind through a defect of reason that, although he knew that what he was doing was wrong in law, he thought that it was beneficial or kind or praiseworthy, that would excuse him.

Courts of law can only distinguish between that which is in accordance with law and that which is contrary to law. There are many acts which, to use an expression which is to be found in some of the old cases, are contrary to the law of God and man. For instance, in the Decalogue will be found the laws "Thou shalt not kill" and "Thou shalt not steal". Those acts are contrary to the law of man and also to the law of God. If the seventh commandment is taken, "Thou shalt not commit adultery", although that is contrary to the law of God, so far as the criminal law is concerned it is not contrary to the law of man. That does not mean that the law encourages adultery; I only say that it is not a criminal offence. The law cannot embark on the question, and it would be an unfortunate thing if it were left to juries to consider whether some particular act was morally right or wrong. The test must be whether it is contrary to law. . . .

In the opinion of the court there is no doubt that in the M'Naghten Rules "wrong" means contrary to law and not "wrong" according to the opinion of one man or of a number of people on the question of whether a particular act might or might not be justified. In the present case, it could not be challenged that the appellant knew that what he was doing was contrary to law, and that he realised what punishment the law provided for murder.

Appeal dismissed

Questions

1. Consider the questions raised by these last two cases. Is what is legally wrong always morally wrong? In *Codere* the judge was prepared to conceive of a negative answer only in minor crimes dealt with by courts of summary jurisdiction.

2. Must the defence establish that the accused did not know the act was legally wrong, or morally wrong, or both?

3. *Codere* approves the test "the ordinary standard adopted by reasonable men," *Windle* indicates that the test is "whether it is contrary to law." Does this alter the law? Was the creation of a new test essential for the decision in *Windle*?

4. If the test is one of insanity is an objective test of any sort appropriate? Consider the passage in *Codere* which indicates that a subjective standard would "weaken the law to an alarming degree."

Note

The basis of the rules is "defect of reason." This might be thought to be the result of the state of medical knowledge at the time of their formulation. "[T]he M'Naghten test . . . was based on the now obsolete belief in the pre-eminent role of reason in controlling social behaviour. It therefore requires evidence of the cognitive capacity. . . . Contemporary psychiatry and psychology emphasise that man's social behaviour is determined more by how he has learned to behave than by what he knows or understands. (Butler Committee, § 18.6).

There is, however, no sign of a judicial inclination to modify this part of the rules in the light of modern understanding. Thus in *R.* v. *Clarke* [1972] 1 All E.R. 219, a rare shoplifting case in which the defence of insanity was raised, Ackner J. said: "It may be that on the evidence of this case . . . the appellant suffered from a disease of the mind. . . . However . . . the evidence fell very far short either of showing that she suffered from a defect of reason or the consequences of that defect in reason, if any, were that she was unable to know the nature and quality of the act she was doing. The M'Naghten Rules . . . do not apply . . . to those who retain the power of reasoning but who in moments of confusion of absent-mindedness fail to use their powers to the full." (But see *Quick, post*, p. 171, for a more modern approach to "disease of the mind.")

And when the defence of uncontrollable impulse was raised in *Sodeman* v. *R.* [1936] 2 All E.R. 1138, the Privy Council (at p. 1140), rejected the proposition "that the rules in *M'Naghten's Case* are no longer to be treated as an exhaustive statement of the law with regard to insanity, and that there is to be engrafted upon those rules another rule that where a man knows that he is doing what is wrong, nonetheless he may be held to be insane if he is caused to do the act by an irresistible impulse produced by disease."

This was further explained in *Attorney-General for South Australia* v. *Brown* [1960] A.C. 432 where, in an appeal to the Privy Council, Lord Tucker said (at p. 449) "At various times in the past attempts have been made to temper the supposed harshness or unscientific nature of the M'Naghten Rules. These attempts were supported by the high authority of Sir James Fitz-James Stephen, but in the end the Rules remain in full force and their harshness has in this country been to some extent alleviated by the recent legislative enactment affording the defence of diminished responsibility. . . .

"Their Lordships must not, of course, be understood to suggest that in a case where evidence has been given (and it is difficult to imagine a case where such evidence would be other than medical evidence) that irresistible impulse is a symptom of the particular disease of the mind from which a prisoner is said to be suffering and as to its effect on his ability to know the nature and quality of his act or that his act is wrong it would not be the duty of the judge to deal with the matter in the same way as any other relevant evidence given at the trial."

For the way in which "irresistible impulse" has been treated in the defence of diminished responsibility, see *R.* v. *Byrne, post*, p. 403.

The "defect of reason" must arise "from a disease of the mind." The question may arise whether a person's state of automatism (where clearly reason is not only defective but completely absent) arises from a disease of the mind. These cases are dealt with in the next section. A similar problem can be seen in the section on intoxication, *post*, p. 192. On the connection between these three defences see *Fingarette*, *post*, p. 195.

3. AUTOMATISM

The defence of automatism arises initially as one form of denial that the prosecution has proved that the *actus reus* was voluntary (see *ante*, p. 16). But acquittal will not necessarily follow. If the origin of the automatic state is a disease of the mind, a finding of insanity will result. *Kemp*, *Bratty* and *Quick* below illustrate the problems facing the courts in this borderland between the two defences. Where the origin is self-induced intoxication, the defendant is subject to the limitations of that defence: see *Majewski*, *post*, p. 176. Even where the defendant's state is attributable to neither of those factors a person who is at fault in losing the capacity for voluntary control of his or her actions cannot rely on this defence: *Quick*, below. This imports a similar notion to that which qualifies intoxication as a denial of *mens rea*: self-induced incapacity may be culpable.

Thus it is only in extremely confined circumstances that the defence can be successfully raised. See Williams, T.C.L., 609–613 for a description of the common causes of automatism.

R. v. Kemp
[1957] 1 Q.B. 399
Bristol Assizes

> The defendant was charged with causing grievous bodily harm to his wife. He suffered from arteriosclerosis which had not given rise to general mental trouble but caused temporary loss of consciousness during which state the attack was made. He did not plead insanity.

DEVLIN J.: In this case it is conceded that everything [in the third and fourth answers in *M'Naghten's Case*] applies here, except for "disease of the mind." . . . The law is not concerned with the brain but with the mind, in the sense that "mind" is ordinarily used, the mental faculties of reason, memory and understanding. If one read for "disease of the mind" "disease of the brain", it would follow that in many cases pleas of insanity would not be established because it could not be proved that the brain had been affected in any way, either by degeneration of the cells or in any other way. In my judgment the condition of the brain is irrelevant and so is the question of whether the condition of the mind is curable or incurable, transitory or permanent. There is no warranty for introducing those considerations into the definition in the M'Naghten Rules. Temporary insanity is sufficient to satisfy them. It does not matter whether it is incurable and permanent or not.

I think that the approach of Mr. Lee (for the Crown) to the definition in the Rules is the right one. He points out the order of the words "a defect of reason, from disease of the mind." The primary thing that has to be looked for is the defect of reason. "Disease of the mind" is there for some purpose, obviously, but the prime thing is to determine what is admitted here, namely, whether or not there is a defect of reason. In my judgment, the words "from disease of the mind" are not to be construed as if they were put in for the purpose of distinguishing between diseases which have a mental origin and diseases which have a physical origin, a distinction which in 1843 was probably little considered. They were put in for the purpose of limiting the effect of the words "defect of reason." A defect of reason is by itself enough to make the act irrational and therefore normally to exclude responsibility in law. But the Rule was not intended to apply to defects of reason caused simply by brutish stupidity without rational power. It was not intended that the defence should plead "although with a healthy mind he nevertheless had been brought up in such a way that he had never learned to exercise his reason, and therefore he is suffering from a defect of reason." The words ensure that unless the defect is due to a diseased mind and not simply to an untrained one there is insanity within the meaning of the Rule.

Hardening of the arteries is a disease which is shown on the evidence to be capable of affecting the mind in such a way as to cause a defect, temporarily or permanently, of its reasoning, understanding and so on, and so is in my judgment a disease of the mind which comes within the meaning of the Rules.

Verdict: Guilty but insane

Bratty v. A.-G. for Northern Ireland

[1963] A.C. 386
House of Lords

> The appellant strangled a girl. He said in a statement to the police that when he was with her he had "a terrible feeling" and "a sort of blackness" came over him. At the trial there was medical evidence that he might have been suffering from psychomotor epilepsy. To a charge of murder he raised three defences: automatism, lack of intent for murder, and insanity. The judge refused to leave the first two to the jury, and they rejected the plea of insanity. This was affirmed by the Court of Criminal Appeal in Northern Ireland. He appealed to the House of Lords.

VISCOUNT KILMUIR and LORD MORRIS OF BORTH-Y-GEST delivered speeches dismissing the appeal with which LORDS TUCKER and HODSON agreed.

LORD DENNING: My Lords, in the case of *Woolmington* v. *Director of Public Prosecutions* [1935] A.C. 462, 482, Viscount Sankey L.C. said that "when dealing with a murder case the Crown must prove (a) death "as a result of a voluntary act of the accused", and (b) malice of "the accused." The requirement that it should be a voluntary act is essential, not only in a murder case, but also in every criminal case. No act is punishable if it is done involuntarily: and an involuntary act in this context—some people nowadays prefer to speak of it as "automatism"—means an act which is done by the muscles without any control by the mind, such as a spasm, a reflex action or a convulsion; or an act done by a person who is not conscious of what he is doing, such as an act done whilst suffering from concussion or whilst sleep-walking. . . .

The term "involuntary act" is, however, capable of wider connotations: and to prevent confusion it is to be observed that in the criminal law an act is not to be regarded as an involuntary act simply because the doer does not remember it. When a man is charged with dangerous driving, it is no defence to him to say "I don't know what happened. I cannot remember a 'thing'", see *Hill* v. *Baxter* [1958] 1 Q.B. 277. Loss of memory afterwards is never a defence in itself, so long as he was conscious at the time . . . . see *Russell* v. *H.M. Advocate* 1946 S.C. (J.) 37; *Reg.* v. *Podola* [*ante*, p. 160]. Nor is an act to be regarded as an involuntary act simply because the doer could not control his impulse to do it. When a man is charged with murder, and it appears that he knew what he was doing, but he could not resist it, then his assertion " I couldn't help myself" is no defence in itself, see *Attorney-General for South Australia* v. *Brown* (1960) A.C. 432: though it may go towards a defence of diminished responsibility, in places where that defence is available, see *R.* v. *Byrne* [*post*, p. 403]: but it does not render his act involuntary so as to entitle him to an unqualified acquittal. Nor is an act to be regarded as an involuntary act simply because it is unintentional or its consequences are unforeseen. When a man is charged with dangerous driving, it is no defence for him to say, however truly, "I did not mean to drive dangerously".... But even though it is absolutely prohibited, nevertheless he has a defence if he can show that it was an involuntary act in the sense that he was unconscious at the time and did not know what he was doing....

Another thing to be observed is that it is not every involuntary act which leads to a complete acquittal. Take first an involuntary act which proceeds from a state of drunkenness. If the drunken man is so drunk that he does not know what he is doing, he has a defence to any charge, such as murder or wounding with intent, in which a specific intent is essential, but he is still liable to be convicted of manslaughter or unlawful wounding for which no specific intent is necessary, see *Beard* [1920] A.C. 479.

Again, if the involuntary act proceeds from a disease of the mind, it gives rise to a defence of insanity, but not to a defence of automatism. Suppose a crime is committed by a man in a state of automatism or clouded consciousness due to a recurrent disease of the mind. Such an act is no doubt involuntary, but it does not give rise to an unqualified acquittal, for that would mean that he would be let at large to do it again. The only proper verdict is one which ensures that the person who suffers from the disease is kept secure in a hospital so as not to be a danger to himself or others. That is a verdict of guilty but insane.

Once you exclude all the cases I have mentioned, it is apparent that the category of involuntary acts is very limited.

[There] is the singular case of *R.* v. *Charlson* [1955] 1 W.L.R. 317. Stanley Charlson, a devoted husband and father, hit his ten-year-old son on the head with a hammer and threw him into the river and so injured him. There was not the slightest cause for the attack. He was charged with causing grievous bodily harm with intent, and with unlawful wounding. The evidence pointed to the possibility that Charlson was suffering from a cerebral tumour in which case he would be liable to a motiveless outburst of impulsive violence over which he would have no control at all. Now comes the important point—no plea of insanity was raised, but only the defence of automatism. Barry J. directed the jury in these words: "If he did not know 'what he was doing, if his actions were purely automatic and his mind had no control over the movement of his limbs, if he was in the same position as a person in an epileptic fit then no responsibility rests upon him at all, and the proper verdict is 'Not Guilty'". On that direction the jury found him not guilty. In striking contrast to *Charlson's* case is *R.* v. *Kemp* [*ante*, p. 167]....

My Lords, I think that Devlin J. was quite right in *Kemp's* case in putting the question of insanity to the jury, even though it had not been raised by the defence. When it is asserted that the accused did an involuntary act in a state of automatism, the defence necessarily puts in issue the state of mind of the accused man: and thereupon it is open to the prosecution to show what his true state of mind was. The old notion that only the defence can raise a defence of insanity is now gone. The prosecution are entitled to raise it and it is their duty to do so rather than allow a dangerous person to be at large....

Upon the other point discussed by Devlin J., namely, what is a "disease of the mind" within the M'Naghten Rules, I would agree with him that this is a question for the judge. The major mental diseases, which the doctors call psychoses, such as schizophrenia, are clearly diseases of the mind. But in *Charlson's* case, Barry J. seems to have assumed that other diseases such as epilepsy or cerebral tumour are not diseases of the mind, even when they are such as to manifest themselves in violence. I do not agree with this. It seems to me that any mental disorder which has manifested itself in violence and is prone to recur is a disease of the mind. At any rate it is the sort of disease for which a person should be detained in hospital rather than be given an unqualified acquittal. . . .

In the present case the defence raised both automatism and insanity. And herein lies the difficulty because of the burden of proof. If the accused says he did not know what he was doing, then, so far as the defence of automatism is concerned, the Crown must prove that the act was a voluntary act, see *Woolmington's* case. But so far as the defence of insanity is concerned, the defence must prove that the act was an involuntary act due to disease of the mind, see *M'Naghten's* case [ante, p. 162].

. . . I think that the difficulty is to be resolved by remembering that, whilst the *ultimate* burden rests on the Crown of proving every element essential in the crime, nevertheless in order to prove that the act was a voluntary act, the Crown is entitled to rely on the *presumption* that every man has sufficient mental capacity to be responsible for his crimes: and that if the defence wish to displace that presumption they must give some evidence from which the contrary may reasonably be inferred. Thus a drunken man is presumed to have the capacity to form the specific intent necessary to constitute the crime, unless evidence is given from which it can reasonably be inferred that he was incapable of forming it. . . .

The presumption of mental capacity of which I have spoken is a provisional presumption only. It does not put the legal burden on the defence in the same way as the presumption of sanity does. It leaves the legal burden on the prosecution, but nevertheless, until it is displaced, it enables the prosecution to discharge the ultimate burden of proving that the act was voluntary. Not because the presumption is evidence itself, but because it takes the place of evidence. In order to displace the presumption of mental capacity, the defence must give sufficient evidence from which it may reasonably be inferred that the act was involuntary. The evidence of the man himself will rarely be sufficient unless it is supported by medical evidence which points to the cause of the mental incapacity. . . .

When the only cause that is assigned for an involuntary act is drunkenness, then it is only necessary to leave drunkenness to the jury, with the consequential directions, and not to leave automatism at all. When the only cause that is assigned for it is a disease of the mind, then it is only necessary to leave insanity to the jury, and not automatism. When the cause assigned is concussion or sleep-walking, there should be some evidence from which it can reasonably be inferred before it should be left to the jury. . . .

Once a proper foundation is thus laid for automatism, the matter becomes at large and must be left to the jury. As the case proceeds, the evidence may weigh first to one side and then to the other: and so the burden may appear to shift to and fro. But at the end of the day the legal burden comes into play and requires that the jury should be satisfied beyond reasonable doubt that the act was a voluntary act.

I am clearly of opinion that, if the act of George Bratty was an involuntary act, as the defence suggested, the evidence attributed it solely to a disease of the mind and the only defence open was the defence of insanity. There was no evidence of automatism apart from insanity. There was, therefore, no need for the judge to put it to the jury. And when the jury rejected the defence of insanity, they rejected the only defence disclosed by the evidence. . . .

I would, therefore, dismiss the appeal.

Appeal dismissed

R. v. Quick and Paddison
[1973] Q.B. 910
Court of Appeal

The appellant, who was a diabetic, was a psychiatric nurse. He was charged with assaulting a patient at the hospital where he worked. He said he could not remember the incident but that on the day it occurred he had taken his prescribed insulin, a small breakfast, some whisky, a quarter of a bottle of rum, and had no lunch. Medical evidence showed he was suffering at the time from hypoglycaemia, a deficiency of blood sugar after an injection of insulin. The appellant changed his plea to guilty after the judge rejected his defence of automatism on the grounds that the only defence open to him was insanity.

LAWTON L.J., for the court: In its broadest aspects these appeals raise the question what is meant by the phrase 'a defect of reason from disease of the mind' within the meaning of the M'Naghten Rules. More particularly the question is whether a person who commits a criminal act whilst under the effects of hypoglycaemia can raise a defence of automatism, as the appellants submitted was possible, or whether such a person must rely on a defence of insanity if he wishes to relieve himself of responsibility for his acts, as Bridge J. ruled. . . .

The evidence on which the judge ruled came partly from witnesses for the prosecution and partly from Quick's own evidence and that of a consultant physician, Dr. Cates, who was called on his behalf.

The following answer by Dr. Cates sums up his evidence about hypoglycaemia and his opinion whether Quick could have been doing what he was proved to have been doing in the course of a suggested hypoglycaemic reaction:

> "If a patient is going unconscious with a falling blood sugar, for a while he will be aggressive, for a while he will be more aggressive, for a while he may start being physically violent and then he will be in a semi-conscious state when he could be . . . struggling and resisting people's efforts to give him sugar. Then he may have a fit, then he may stay deeply unconscious for quite a while. It would sound from the evidence . . . that this man developed an increasing effect of a falling blood sugar from some time in the afternoon till when he collapsed after the episode of attack. At least the events fit with that."

Dr. Cates said that there were a number of causes for this. The doctor may have prescribed too much insulin; the patient may have eaten too little or have been over active. He accepted that on the occasion when Green was attacked, Quick's own conduct that day may well have caused a severe fall in blood sugar.

The question which the judge's ruling [that insanity was the only plea open] raises is one on which it seems that there is no direct English or Commonwealth authority and only a few which bear indirectly on it. We are grateful to counsel for the depth of their researches.

Our examination of such authorities as there are must start with *Bratty* v. *Attorney-General for Northern Ireland*, *supra*, because the judge ruled as he did in reliance on that case. The House of Lords . . . accepted that automatism as distinct from insanity could be a defence if there was a proper foundation in the evidence for it. In this case, if Quick's alleged condition could have been caused by hypoglycaemia Bridge J's ruling was right. The question remains, however, whether a mental condition arising from hypoglycaemia does amount to a disease of the mind. All their Lordships based their speeches on the basis that such medical evidence as there was pointed to Bratty suffering from a 'defect of reason from disease of the mind' and nothing else. Lord Denning discussed in general terms what constitutes a disease of the mind [His Lordship then quoted the passage on 'disease of the mind', *supra*].

If this opinion is right and there are no restricting qualifications which ought to be applied to it, Quick was setting up a defence of insanity. He may have been at the material time in a condition of mental disorder manifesting itself in violence. Such manifestations had occurred before and might recur. The difficulty arises as soon as the question is asked whether he should be detained in a mental hospital? No mental hospital would admit a diabetic merely because he had a low blood sugar reaction; and common sense is affronted by the prospect of a diabetic being sent to such a hospital when in most cases the disordered mental condition can be rectified quickly by pushing a lump of sugar or a teaspoonful of glucose into the patient's mouth.

The 'affront to common sense' argument, however, has its own inherent weakness, as counsel for the Crown pointed out. If an accused is shown to have done a criminal act whilst suffering from a 'defect of reason from disease of the mind', it matters not 'whether the disease is curable or incurable . . . temporary or permanent' (see *R.* v. *Kemp* [*ante*, p. 167], *per* Devlin J.). If the condition is temporary, the Secretary of State may have a difficult problem of disposal; but what happens to those found not guilty by reason of insanity is not a matter for the courts.

In *R.* v. *Kemp*, where the violent act was alleged to have been done during a period of unconsciousness arising from arteriosclerosis, counsel for the accused submitted that his client had done what he had during a period of mental confusion arising from a physical, not a mental disease. Devlin J. rejected this argument saying:

> "It does not matter, for the purposes of the law, whether the defect of reasoning is due to a degeneration of the brain or to some other form of mental derangement. That may be a matter of importance medically, but it is of no importance to the law, which merely has to consider the state of mind in which the accused is, not how he got there."

Applied without qualification of any kind, Devlin J's statement of the law would have some surprising consequences. Take the not uncommon case of the rugby player who gets a kick on the head early in the game and plays on to the end in a state of automatism. If, whilst he was in that state, he assaulted the referee it is difficult to envisage any court adjudging that he was not guilty by reason of insanity. Another type of case which could occur is that of the dental patient who kicks out whilst coming round from an anaesthetic. The law would be in a defective state if a patient accused of assaulting a dental nurse by kicking her whilst regaining consciousness could only excuse himself by raising the defence of insanity.

In *Hill* v. *Baxter* [1958] 1 Q.B. 277, the problem before the Divisional Court was whether the accused had put forward sufficient evidence on a charge of dangerous driving to justify the justices adjudging that he should be acquitted, there having been no dispute that at the time when his car collided with another one he was at the driving wheel. At the trial the accused had contended that he became unconscious as a result of being overcome by an unidentified illness. The court (Lord Goddard C.J., Devlin and Pearson JJ.) allowed an appeal by the prosecution against the verdict of acquittal. In the course of examining the evidence which had been put forward by the accused the judges made some comments of a general nature. Lord Goddard C.J. referred to some observations of Humphreys J. in *Kay* v. *Butterworth* (1945) 173 L.T. 191 which seemed to indicate that a man who became unconscious whilst driving due to the onset of a sudden illness should not be made liable at criminal law and went on as follows, at 282,

> "I agree that there may be cases when the circumstances are such that the accused could not really be said to be driving at all. Suppose he had a stroke or an epileptic fit, both instances of what may properly be called Acts of God; he might well be in the driver's seat even with his hands on the wheel but in such a state of unconsciousness that he could not be said to be driving. . . . In this case, however, I am content to say that the evidence falls far short of what would justify a court holding that this man was in some automatous state."

Lord Goddard C.J. did not equate unconsciousness due to a sudden illness, which must entail the malfunctioning of the mental process of the sufferer, with disease of the mind, and in our judgment no one outside the court of law would. Devlin J. in his judgment at 285 accepted that some temporary loss of consciousness arising *accidentally* (the italics are ours) did not call for a verdict based on insanity. It is not clear what he meant by 'accidentally'. The context suggests that he may have meant 'unexpectedly' as can happen with some kind of virus infections. He went on as follows:

> "If, however, disease is present the same thing may happen again and therefore since 1800 the law has provided that persons acquitted on this ground should be subject to restraint."

If this be right anyone suffering from a tooth abscess who knows from past experience that he reacts violently to anaesthetics because of some constitutional bodily disorder which can be attributed to disease might have to go on suffering or take the risk of being found insane unless he could find a dentist who would be prepared to take the risk of being kicked by a recovering patient. It seems to us that the law should not give the words 'defect of reason from disease of the mind' a meaning which would be regarded with incredulity outside the court.

The last of the English authorities is *Watmore* v. *Jenkins* [1962] 2 Q.B. 572. . . . In the course of the argument in that case counsel for the accused is reported as having submitted, on the basis of how Lord Murray had directed the jury in *H.M. Advocate* v. *Ritchie* 1926 J.C. 45:

> "Automatism is a defence to a charge of dangerous driving provided that a person takes reasonable steps to prevent himself from acting involuntarily in a manner dangerous to the public. It must be caused by some factor which he could not reasonably foresee and not by a self-induced incapacity. . . ."

Subject to the problem of whether the conduct said to have been done in a state of automatism was caused by a disease of the mind, we agree with this submission. In this case, had the jury been left to decide whether the appellant Quick at the material time was insane, or in a state of automatism or just drunk, they probably would not have had any difficulty in making up their minds.

[His Lordship then referred to some Commonwealth cases].

. . . .

In this quagmire of law seldom entered nowadays save by those in desperate need of some kind of defence, *Bratty* v. *Attorney-General for Northern Ireland, supra*, provides the only firm ground. Is there any discernible path? We think there is—judges should follow in a common sense way their sense of fairness. This seems to have been the approach of the New Zealand Court of Appeal in *R.* v. *Cottle* [1958] N.Z.L.R. 999, and of Sholl J. in *R.* v. *Carter* [1959] V.R. 105. In our judgment no help can be obtained by speculating (because that is what we would have to do) as to what the judges who answered the House of Lords' questions in 1843 meant by disease of the mind, still less what Sir Matthew Hale meant in the second half of the 17th century [(1682) Vol. J, Ch. IV.] A quick backward look at the state of medicine in 1843 will suffice to show how unreal it would be to apply the concepts of that age to the present time. Dr. Simpson had not yet started his experiments with chloroform, the future Lord Lister was only 16 and laudanum was used and prescribed like aspirins are today. Our task has been to decide what the law means now by the words 'disease of the mind'. In our judgment the fundamental concept is of a malfunctioning of the mind caused by disease. A malfunctioning of the mind of transitory effect caused by the application to the body of some external factor such as violence, drugs, including anaesthetics, alcohol and hypnotic influences cannot fairly be said to be due to disease. Such malfunctioning, unlike that caused by a defect of reason from disease of the mind, will not always relieve an accused from criminal responsibility. A self-induced incapacity will not excuse [see *R.* v. *Lipman*, [1970] 1 Q.B. 152 nor will one which could have been reasonably foreseen as a result of either doing, or omitting to do something, as, for example, taking alcohol against medical advice after using certain prescribed drugs, or failing to have regular meals whilst taking insulin. From time to time difficult borderline cases are likely to arise. When they do, the test suggested by the New Zealand Court of Appeal in *R.* v. *Cottle* [1958] N.Z.L.R. 999 is likely to give the correct result, viz. can this mental condition be fairly regarded as amounting to or producing a defect of reason from disease of the mind?

In this case Quick's alleged mental condition, if it ever existed, was not caused by his diabetes but by his use of the insulin prescribed by his doctor. Such malfunctioning of the mind as there was, was caused by an external factor and not by a bodily disorder in the nature of a disease which disturbed the working of his mind. It follows in our judgment that Quick was entitled to have his defence of automatism left to the jury and that Bridge J's ruling as to the effect of the medical evidence called by him was wrong. Had the defence of automatism been left to the jury, a number of questions of fact would have had to be answered. If he was in a confused mental condition, was it due to a hypoglycaemic episode or to too much alcohol? If the former, to what extent had he brought about his condition by not following his doctor's instructions about taking regular meals? Did he know that he was getting into a hypoglycaemic episode? If Yes, why did he not use the antidote of eating a lump of sugar as he had been advised to do? On the evidence which was before the jury Quick might have had difficulty in answering these questions in a manner which would have relieved him of responsibility for his acts. We cannot say, however, with the requisite degree of confidence, that the jury would have convicted him. It follows that this conviction must be quashed on the ground that the verdict was unsatisfactory.

Appeal allowed

Questions

1. Do you agree that Quick's hypoglycaemic state was not "caused by his diabetes"? How would the "external cause" approach cope with a defendant who has an illness which can be perfectly controlled by prescribed drugs but which, without them, would render him or her susceptible to states of automatism? See Butler Committee, pp. 224–225.

2. Lawton L.J. said that the court's task was to decide "what the law means now by the words 'disease of the mind'." Should "defect of reason" be approached in the same way?

3. Is it correct to say that self-induced incapacity through drink or drugs will not excuse? Should such incapacity not excuse crimes of specific intent? See *post*, p. 186.

Note

In *R.* v. *Isitt* (1978) 67 Cr. App. R. 44, a dangerous driving case, the Court of Appeal held that the trial judge was correct to rule that evidence that the appellant was suffering from 'hysterical fugue' which made him unaware of legal restrictions or matters of moral concern provided no defence. Although the appellant had little merit in his case since he had clearly been drinking, some of the remarks made by Lawton L.J. about automatism are of interest, at p. 49:

"There are people ... whose minds go with the acts which they are doing, but whose minds do not function properly.... If the malfunctioning of the mind produces the consequences set out in ... M'Naghten's case then the accused has the defence of insanity. At the other end of the mental spectrum, in cases in which the accused acts during an epileptic attack, the mind does not function at all. What the accused does in those circumstances is involuntary. Acts performed involuntarily have come to be known as automatism ... on the psychiatrist's evidence, it is clear that he was accepting that the appellant's mind was working to some extent. In the course of argument it was suggested from the bench that perhaps in law there is a grey area between insanity and automatism, and if there is such a grey area—and we think there is—this case would undoubtedly ... come within it. Such value, if any, as [the] psychiatric evidence had would have been in mitigation of penalty and not by way of a defence in law."

Quick was not referred to in the above case, nor in *R.* v. *Stripp* (1979) 69 Cr. App. R. 318 which gave rise to some perplexing *obiter dicta* from the Court of Appeal. The appellant was convicted of a number of driving offences, including drunken driving. He had arrived at Walworth bus station as a passenger. He left at the wheel of a 'bus although he had never driven anything but a scooter before. His defence was that he had been concussed when the first 'bus swerved and caused him to hit his head. The Court of Appeal held that the trial judge was wrong both to allow the defence of automatism to be put to the jury as no 'proper foundation' had been laid for it (see *Bratty, ante,* p. 168) and to direct the jury that the defence of automatism was not available where the concussion was caused solely or substantially by the appellant being intoxicated. On this latter point, Ormrod L.J., for the court said, at p. 323:

"[I]t is clear, on the authorities, that once a proper foundation for a defence [of automatism] has been laid, the burden, which is always on the prosecution, to prove that the acts were voluntary, becomes an active burden.... If it was a question of two causes operating, we venture to think that the prosecution would not be able to discharge the burden of proof."

Does this ignore *Quick, supra,* and *D.P.P.* v. *Majewski, post,* p. 176?

In *Stripp* and *Isitt* the Court of Appeal seems to be failing to separate two questions: what in physical terms can amount to non-insane automatism, and what factors should affect culpability. As to the first question there seems to be a danger in positing, as Lawton L.J. does in *Isitt*, an epileptic fit as the paradigm example of automatism. *Quick,* for example, had not lost complete control of his movements: was his mind "working to some extent"? It might be helpful to include under automatism both states of unconsciousness and some states of clouded consciousness. It may then have been right on the facts of *Isitt* to hold that his behaviour did not come within either. But it cannot be enough to say that it fell outside the band of recognised automatic behaviour merely because it was *more* conscious than that of a person in an epileptic fit. The Canadian courts have been more open to arguments that disturbances of consciousness from non-organic causes should be recognised as automatism. See R. D. Mackay, "Non-Organic Automatism—Some Recent Developments" [1980] Crim. L.R. 350. The Canadian Supreme Court recently held that "dissociated" behaviour resulting from a "psychological blow" (in this case discovering that a much-admired member of the opposite sex thought the appellant a "nothing") could amount to automatism. But if, as in this case, the defendant's reaction was abnormal and had had "its source primarily in [his] psychological and emotional make-up" it would come within the category of "disease of the mind" even though the medical evidence suggested that the defendant was not dangerous and required no further treatment: *Rabey* v. *R.* (1981) 114 D.L.R. (3d) 193.

Once the question of which dissociated states are legally recognised as giving rise to the possibility of a defence of automatism, the second question could then come into play: should the defendant nevertheless be held responsible for his or her involuntariness? Reference could appropriately be made here to the extract from A. T. H. Smith, *ante*, (p. 13), in which he makes a plea for a question of *actus reus* and *mens rea* not to be seen as the sole determinants of culpability. This plea appears to be all the more necessary in the light of the reasoning given in *Stripp*.

4. INTOXICATION

D.P.P. v. Majewski
[1976] 2 W.L.R. 623
House of Lords

M. appealed against convictions of assault occasioning actual bodily harm and assault of a police constable in the execution of his duty on the ground that he was too intoxicated, through a combination of drugs and alcohol, to form the appropriate *mens rea*.

LORD ELWYN-JONES L.C.: ... The appellant gave evidence and said that on a Saturday, 17th February 1973, he bought, not on prescription, about 440 Dexadrine tablets ('speeds') and early on Sunday morning consumed about half of them. That gave him plenty of energy until he 'started coming down'. He did not sleep throughout Sunday. On Monday evening at about 6.00 p.m. he acquired a bottle full of sodium nembutal tablets which he said were tranquillisers—'downers', 'barbs' —and took about eight of them at about 6.30 p.m. He and his friends then went to the Bull. He said he could remember nothing of what took place there save for a flash of recollection of [one of his friends] kicking a window. All he recollected of the police cell was asking the police to remove his handcuffs and then being injected.

In cross-examination he admitted he had been taking amphetamines and barbiturates, not on prescription, for two years, in large quantities. On occasions he drank barley wine or Scotch. He had sometimes 'gone paranoid'. This was the first time he had 'completely blacked out.'

Dr. Bird, called for the defence, said that the appellant had been treated for drug addiction since November 1971. There was no history in his case of psychiatric disorder or diagnosable mental illness, but the appellant had a personality disorder. Dr. Bird said that barbiturates and alcohol are known to potentiate each other and to produce rapid intoxication and affect a person's awareness of what was going on. In the last analysis one could be rendered unconscious and a condition known as pathological intoxication can occur, but it is uncommon and there are usually well-marked episodes. It would be possible, but unlikely, to achieve a state of automatism as a result of intoxication with barbiturates and alcohol or amphetamines and alcohol. Aggressive behaviour is greater. After a concentration of alcohol and barbiturates it was not uncommon for 'an amnesic patch' to ensue.

In cross-examination, Dr. Bird said he had never in practice come across a case of 'pathological intoxication' and it is an unusual condition. It is quite possible that a person under the influence of barbiturates, amphetamines or alcohol or all three in combination may be able to form certain intentions and execute them, punching and kicking people, and yet afterwards be unable to remember anything about it. During such 'disinhibited behaviour' he may do things which he would not do if he was not under the influence of the various sorts of drink and drugs about which evidence has been given.

The Court of Appeal dismissed the appeal against conviction but granted leave to appeal to your Lordships' House certifying that the following point of law of general public importance was involved:

> "Whether a defendant may properly be convicted of assault not withstanding that, by reason of his self-induced intoxication, he did not intend to do the act alleged to constitute the assault.'

Self-induced alcoholic intoxication has been a factor in crimes of violence, like assault, throughout the history of crime in this country. But voluntary drug taking with the potential and actual dangers to others it may cause has added a new dimension to the old problem with which the courts have had to deal in their endeavour to maintain order and to keep public and private violence under control. To achieve this is the prime purpose of the criminal law. I have said 'the courts', for most of the relevant law has been made by the judges. A good deal of the argument in the hearing of this appeal turned on that judicial history, for the crux of the case for the Crown was that, illogical as the outcome may be said to be, the judges have evolved for the purpose of protecting the community a substantive rule of law that, in crimes of basic intent as distinct from crimes of specific intent, self-induced intoxication provides no defence and is irrelevant to offences of basic intent, such as assault.

The case of counsel for the appellant was that there was no such substantive rule of law and that if there was, it did violence to logic and ethics and to fundamental principles of the criminal law which had been evolved to determine when and where criminal responsibility should arise. His main propositions were as follows: (i) No man is guilty of a crime (save in relation to offences of strict liability) unless he has a guilty mind. (ii) A man who, though not insane, commits what would in ordinary circumstances be a crime when he is in such a mental state (whether it is called 'automatism' or 'pathological intoxication' or anything else) that he does not know what he is doing, lacks a guilty mind and is not criminally culpable for his actions. (iii) This is so whether the charge involves a specific (or 'ulterior') intent or one involving only a general (or 'basic') intent. (iv) The same principle applies whether the automatism was the result of causes beyond the control of the accused or was self-induced by the voluntary taking of drugs or drink. (v) Assaults being crimes involving a guilty mind, a man who in a state of automatism unlawfully assaults another must be regarded as free from blame and be entitled to acquittal. (vi) It is logically and ethically indefensible to convict such a man of assault; it also contravenes s. 8 of the Criminal Justice Act 1967. (vii) There was accordingly a fatal misdirection.

A great deal of the argument in the hearing of the appeal turned on the application to the established facts of what Cave J. in *R.* v. *Tolson* [*ante*, p. 116] called 'the somewhat uncouth maxim "actus non facit reum, nisi mens sit rea"'....

[His Lordship quoted from Stephen J's judgment in *Tolson, ante,* p. 116, and from Lord Simon's speech in *Morgan, ante,* p. 101, on the meaning of "basic intent"].

If a man consciously and deliberately takes alcohol and drugs not on medical prescription, but in order to escape from reality, to go 'on a trip', to become hallucinated, whatever the description may be, and thereby disables himself from taking the care he might otherwise take and as a result by his subsequent actions causes injury to another—does our criminal law enable him to say that because he did not know what he was doing he lacked both intention and recklessness and accordingly is entitled to an acquittal?

Originally the common law would not and did not recognise self-induced intoxication as an excuse. Lawton L.J. spoke of the 'merciful relaxation' to that rule which was introduced by the judges during the 19th century, and he added:

> "Although there was much reforming zeal and activity in the 19th century Parliament never once considered whether self-induced intoxication should be a defence generally to a criminal charge. It would have been a strange result if the merciful relaxation of a strict rule of law had ended, without any Parliamentary intervention, by whittling it away to such an extent that the more drunk a man became, provided he stopped short of making himself insane, the better chance he had of acquittal.... The common law rule still applied but there were exceptions to it which Lord Birkenhead L.C., *D.P.P.* v. *Beard* [1920] A.C. 479, tried to define by reference to specific intent."

There are, however, decisions of eminent judges in a number of Commonwealth cases in Australia and New Zealand (but generally not in Canada nor in the United States), as well as impressive academic comment in this country, to which we have been referred supporting the view that it is illogical and inconsistent with legal principle to treat a person who of his own choice and volition has taken drugs and drink, even though he thereby creates a state in which he is not conscious of what he is doing, any differently from a person suffering from the various medical conditions like epilepsy or diabetic coma and who is regarded by the law as free from fault. However, our courts have for a very long time regarded in quite another light the state of self-induced intoxication. The authority which for the last half century has been relied on in this context has been the speech of Lord Birkenhead L.C. in *Director of Public Prosecutions* v. *Beard*, at 494:

> "Under the law of England as it prevailed until early in the nineteenth century voluntary drunkenness was never an excuse for criminal misconduct; and indeed the classic authorities broadly assert that voluntary drunkenness must be considered rather an aggravation than a defence. This view was in terms based upon the principle that a man who by his own voluntary act debauches and destroys his will power, shall be no better situated in regard to criminal acts than a sober man."

Lord Birkenhead L.C. made an historical survey of the way the common law from the 16th century on dealt with the effect of self-induced intoxication on criminal responsibility. This indicates how, from 1819 on, the judges began to mitigate the severity of the attitude of the common law in such cases as murder and serious violent crime when the penalties of death or transportation applied or where there was likely to be sympathy for the accused, as in attempted suicide.

Lord Birkenhead L.C., at 499, concluded that (except in cases where insanity was pleaded) the decisions he cited—

> "establish that where a specific intent is an essential element in the offence, evidence of a state of drunkennes rendering the accused incapable of forming such an intent should be taken into consideration in order to determine whether he had in fact formed the intent necessary to constitute the particular crime. If he was so drunk that he was incapable of forming the intent required he could not be convicted of a crime which was committed only if the intent was proved. . . . In a charge of murder based upon intention to kill or to do grievous bodily harm, if the jury are satisfied that the accused was, by reason of his drunken condition, incapable of forming the intent to kill or to do grievous bodily harm . . . he cannot be convicted of murder. But nevertheless unlawful homicide has been committed by the accused, and consequently he is guilty of unlawful homicide without malice aforethought, and that is manslaughter: *per* Stephen J. in *Doherty's Case* (1887) 16 Cox C.C. 306, 307. [He concluded the passage:] the law is plain beyond all question that in cases falling short of insanity a condition of drunkenness at the time of committing an offence causing death can only, when it is available at all, have the effect of reducing the crime from murder to manslaughter."

From this it seemed clear—and this is the interpretation which the judges have placed on the decision during the ensuing half-century—that it is only in the limited class of cases requiring proof of specific intent that drunkenness can exculpate. Otherwise in no case can it exempt completely from criminal liability.

Unhappily what Lord Birkenhead L.C. described as 'plain beyond question' becomes less plain in the later passage in his speech at 504, on which counsel for the appellant not unnaturally placed great emphasis. It reads:

> "I do not think that the proposition of law deduced from these earlier cases is an exceptional rule applicable only to cases in which it is necessary to prove a specific intent in order to constitute the graver crime—e.g., wounding with intent to do grievous bodily harm or with intent to kill. It is true that in such cases the specific intent must be proved to constitute the particular crime, but this is, on ultimate analysis, only in accordance with the ordinary law applicable to crime, for, speaking generally (and apart from certain special offences), a person cannot be convicted of a crime unless the mens was rea. Drunkenness, rendering a person incapable of the intent, would be an answer, as it is for example in a charge of attempted suicide."

Why then would it not be an answer in a charge of manslaughter, contrary to the earlier pronouncement? In my view these passages are not easy to reconcile, but I do not dissent from the reconciliation suggested by my noble and learned friend Lord Russell of Killowen. Commenting on the passage in 1920 shortly after it was delivered, however, Stroud wrote, (1920) 36 L.Q.R. at 270:

> "The whole of these observations . . . suggest an extension of the defence of drunkenness far beyond the limits which have hitherto been assigned to it. The suggestion, put shortly, is that drunkenness may be available as a defence, upon any criminal charge, whenever it can be shown to have affected *mens rea*. Not only is there no authority for the suggestion; there is abundant authority, both ancient and modern, to the contrary."

It has to be said that it is on the latter footing that the judges have applied the law before and since *Beard's* case and have taken the view that self-induced intoxication, however gross and even if it has produced a condition akin to automatism, cannot excuse crimes of basic intent such as the charges of assault which have given rise to the present appeal.

[His Lordship quoted Lord Denning in *Gallagher, post*, p. 192, and in *Bratty, ante*, p. 168].

In no case has the general principle of English law as described by Lord Denning in *Gallagher's* case and exposed again in *Bratty's* case been overruled in this House and the question now to be determined is whether it should be.

I do not for my part regard that general principle as either unethical or contrary to the principles of natural justice. If a man of his own volition takes a substance which causes him to cast off the restraints of reason and conscience, no wrong is done to him by holding him answerable criminally for any injury he may do while in that condition. His course of conduct in reducing himself by drugs and drink to that condition in my view supplies the evidence of mens rea, of guilty mind certainly sufficient for crimes of basic intent. It is a reckless course of conduct and recklessness is enough to constitute the necessary mens rea in assault cases: see *R.* v. *Venna* [*post*, p. 475], *per* James L.J. The drunkenness is itself an intrinsic, an integral part of the crime, the other part being the evidence of the unlawful use of force against the victim. Together they add up to criminal recklessness. On this I adopt the conclusion of Stroud that:

> "It would be contrary to all principle and authority to suppose that drunkenness [and what is true of drunkenness is equally true of intoxication by drugs] can be a defence for crime in general on the ground that 'a person cannot be convicted of a crime unless the *mens* was *rea*.' By allowing himself to get drunk and thereby putting himself in such a condition as to be no longer amenable to the law's commands, a man shows such regardlessness as amounts to *mens rea* for the purpose of all ordinary crimes."

This approach is in line with the American Model Code, s.2.08 (2),

> "When recklessness establishes an element of the offence, if the actor, due to self-induced intoxication, is unaware of a risk of which he would have been aware had he been sober, such unawareness is immaterial."

Acceptance generally of intoxication as a defence (as distinct from the exceptional cases where some additional mental element above that of ordinary mens rea has to be proved) would in my view undermine the criminal law and I do not think that it is enough to say, as did counsel for the appellant, that we can rely on the good sense of the jury or of magistrates to ensure that the guilty are convicted. It may well be that Parliament will at some future time consider, as I think it should, the recommendation in the Butler Committee Report on Mentally Abnormal Offenders that a new offence of 'dangerous intoxication' should be created [*post*, p. 198]. But in the meantime it would be irresponsible to abandon the common law rule, as 'mercifully relaxed', which the courts have followed for a century and a half. . . .

The final question that arises is whether s. 8 of the Criminal Justice Act 1967 has had the result of abrogating or qualifying the common law rule. That section emanated from the consideration the Law Commission gave to the decision of the House in *D.P.P.* v. *Smith* [1961] A.C. 290. Its purpose and effect was to alter the law of evidence about the presumption of intention to produce the reasonable and probable consequences of one's acts. It was not intended to change the common law rule. In referring to 'all the evidence' it meant all the *relevant* evidence. But if there is a substantive rule of law that in crimes of basic intent, the factor of intoxication is irrelevant (and such I hold to be the substantive law), evidence with regard to it is quite irrelevant. Section 8 does not abrogate the substantive rule and it cannot properly be said that the continued application of that rule contravenes the section. For these reasons, my conclusion is that the certified question should be answered Yes, that there was no misdirection in this case and that the appeal should be dismissed.

My noble and learned friends and I think it may be helpful if we give the following indication of the general lines on which in our view the jury should be directed as to the effect on the criminal responsibility of the accused of drink or drugs or both, whenever death or physical injury to another person results from something done by the accused for which there is no legal justification and the offence with which the accused is charged is manslaughter or assault at common law or the statutory offence of unlawful wounding under s. 20, or of assault occasioning actual bodily harm under s. 47 of the Offences Against the Person Act 1861.

In the case of these offences it is no excuse in law that, because of drink or drugs which the accused himself had taken knowingly and willingly, he had deprived himself of the ability to exercise self-control, to realise the possible consequences of what he was doing or even to be conscious that he was doing it. As in the instant case, the jury may be properly instructed that they 'can ignore the subject of drink or drugs as being in any way a defence to' charges of this character.

[LORD DIPLOCK agreed with the speech of Lord Elwyn-Jones and with Lord Russell's explanation of *Beard*.]

LORD SIMON also agreed but added 'by way of marginal comment': . . . a considerable difficulty in this branch of the law arises from the terminology which has been used. I do not suggest that the criminal law should be founded on Byzantine linguistic refinements. The primary test for its efficacy is that it should be found by experience to extend, on the one hand, an effective protection to the public and, on the other, justice to the accused. Nevertheless, it is desirable that it should, in addition, if possible, be so framed as to be comprehensible by statements of coherent and cohesive general rules. For this, and for juristic analysis generally, it is desirable that the terms used should be defined, unambiguous and used consistently.

There is an immediate difficulty. Fundamental to the criminal law is the concept of mens rea. But, first, this phrase is taken from a legal maxim phrased in highly elliptical Latin. Secondly, apart from the quite exceptional case of one type of treason, there is no such thing as a 'guilty mind'. The criminal law prohibits certain defined conduct (actus reus). But it goes on to say that a person who perpetrates such conduct is not criminally responsible, in general, unless such conduct is accompanied by a wrongful state of mind which is expressed or implied in the definition of the offence (mens rea). This wrongful state of mind can vary greatly with the various offences contained in the criminal code, as is shown by the quotations by my noble and learned friend, Lord Elwyn-Jones L.C., from the judgment of Stephen J. in *R.* v. *Tolson*. Mens rea is therefore on ultimate analysis the state of mind stigmatised as wrongful by the criminal law which, when compounded with the relevant prohibited conduct, constitutes a particular offence. There is no juristic reason why mental incapacity (short of *M'Naghten* insanity) brought about by self-induced intoxication, to realise what one is doing or its probable consequences should not be such a state of mind stigmatised as wrongful by the criminal law; and there is every practical reason why it should be.

But, in order to understand this branch of the law in general and *D.P.P.* v. *Beard* in particular, it is desirable to have further tools of analysis. A term that appears frequently in discussion of this aspect of the law and crucially in *Beard* is 'specific intent'. Smith and Hogan, Criminal Law, 3rd edn., 1973, 47 justly criticise this term as potentially ambiguous, since it has been used in three different senses. The first sense is that particular state of mind which, when compounded with prohibited conduct, constitutes a particular offence. This is an unnecessary and misleading usage; and, since 'specific intent' has been frequently and usefully employed in other senses, should merely be abandoned. A second sense in which 'specific intent' has been used is what in *D.P.P.* v. *Morgan* [*ante*, p. 101] I called 'ulterior intent', having taken the term from Smith and Hogan. I needed that particular concept for the analysis on which I ventured in *D.P.P.* v. *Morgan;* unfortunately, my argument failed to command the assent of the majority of the appellate committee, or, on further appeal, some academic commentators and the Advisory Group on the Law of Rape (1975) Cmnd. 6352. But I would not wish it to be thought that I consider 'ulterior intent' as I defined it in *Morgan* as interchangeable with 'specific intent' as that term was used by Stephen, for example, in his Digest, by Lord Birkenhead L.C. in *Beard* or by Lord Denning and others in commenting on *Beard*. 'Ulterior intent', which I can here summarily describe as a state of mind contemplating consequences beyond those defined in the actus reus, is merely one type of 'specific intent' as that term was used by Lord Birkenhead L.C. etc. 'Ulterior intent' does not accurately describe the state of mind in the crime of doing an act likely to assist the enemy (*R.* v. *Steane* [1947] K.B. 997) or causing grievous bodily harm with intent to do some grievous bodily harm (Offences Against the Person Act 1861, s. 18, as amended by the Criminal Law Act 1967) or even murder. None of these requires by its definition contemplation of consequences extending beyond the actus reus.

I still have the temerity to think that the concept of 'crime of basic intent' is a useful tool of analysis; and I explained what I meant by it in the passage in *Morgan* generously cited by my noble and learned friend, Lord Elwyn-Jones L.C. It stands significantly in contrast with 'crime of specific intent' as that term was used by Stephen's Digest and by Lord Birkenhead L.C. in *Beard*. The best description of 'specific intent' in this sense that I know is contained in the judgment of Fauteux J. in *R.* v. *George* (1960) 128 Can. Crim. Cas. 289, 301:

> "In considering the question of *mens rea*, a distinction is to be made between (i) intention as applied to acts considered in relation to their purposes and (ii) intention as applied to acts apart from their purposes. A general intent attending the commission of an act is, in some cases, the only intent required to constitute the crime while, in others, there must be, in addition to that general intent, a specific intent attending the purpose for the commission of the act."

In short, where the crime is one of 'specific intent' the prosecution must in general prove that the purpose for the commission of the act extends to the intent expressed or implied in the definition of the crime. . . .

As I have ventured to suggest, there is nothing unreasonable or illogical in the law holding that a mind rendered self-inducedly insensible (short of *M'Naghten* insanity), through drink or drugs, to the nature of a prohibited act or to its probable consequences is as wrongful a mind as one which consciously contemplates the prohibited act and foresees its probable consequences (or is reckless whether they ensue). The latter is all that is required by way of mens rea in a crime of basic intent. But a crime of specific intent requires something more than contemplation of the prohibited act and foresight of its probable consequences. The mens rea in a crime of specific intent requires proof of a purposive element. This purposive element either exists or not; it cannot be supplied by saying that the impairment of mental powers by self-induced intoxication is its equivalent, for it is not. So that the 19th century development of the law as to the effect of self-induced intoxication on criminal responsibility is juristically entirely acceptable; and it need be a matter of no surprise that Stephen stated it without demur or question.

Lord Salmon: . . . [A]n assault committed accidentally is not a criminal offence. A man may, e.g., thoughtlessly throw out his hand to stop a taxi, or open the door of his car and accidentally hit a passer-by and perhaps unhappily cause him quite serious bodily harm. In such circumstances, the man who caused the injury would be liable civilly for damages but clearly he would have committed no crime.

There are many cases in which injuries are caused by pure accident. I have already given examples of such cases: to these could be added injuries inflicted during an epileptic fit, or whilst sleep-walking, and in many other ways. No one, I think, would suggest that any such case could give rise to criminal liability.

It is argued on behalf of the appellant that a man who makes a vicious assault may at the material time have been so intoxicated by drink or drugs that he no more knew what he was doing than did any of the persons in the examples I have given and that therefore he too cannot be found guilty of a criminal offence.

To my mind there is a very real distinction between such a case and the examples I have given. A man who by voluntarily taking drink and drugs gets himself into an aggressive state in which he does not know what he is doing and then makes a vicious assault can hardly say with any plausibility that what he did was a pure accident which should render him immune from any criminal liability. Yet this in effect is precisely what counsel for the appellant contends that the learned judge should have told the jury.

A number of distinguished academic writers support this contention on the ground of logic. As I understand it, the argument runs like this. Intention, whether special or basic (or whatever fancy name you choose to give it), is still intention. If voluntary intoxication by drink or drugs can, as it admittedly can, negative the special or specific intention necessary for the commission of crimes such as murder and theft, how can you justify in strict logic the view that it cannot negative a basic intention, e.g. the intention to commit offences such as assault and unlawful wounding? The answer is that in strict logic this view cannot be justified. But this is the view that has been adopted by the common law of England, which is founded on common sense and experience rather than strict logic. There is no case in the 19th century when the courts were relaxing the harshness of the law in relation to the effect of drunkenness on criminal liability in which the courts ever want so far as to suggest that drunkenness, short of drunkenness producing insanity, could ever exculpate a man from any offence other than one which required some special or specific intent to be proved.

[His Lordship then discussed *Beard*.]

As I have already indicated, I accept that there is a degree of illogicality in the rule that intoxication may excuse or expunge one type of intention and not another. This illogically is, however, acceptable to me because the benovelent part of the rule removes undue harshness without imperilling safety and the stricter part of the rule works without imperilling justice. It would be just as ridiculous to remove the benevolent part of the rule (which no one suggests) as it would be to adopt the alternative of removing the stricter part of the rule for the sake of preserving absolute logic. Absolute logic in human affairs is an uncertain guide and a very dangerous master. The law is primarily concerned with human affairs. I believe that the main object of our legal system is to preserve individual liberty. One important aspect of individual liberty is protection against physical violence. . . .

If, as I think, this long-standing rule was salutary years ago when it related almost exclusively to drunkenness, and hallucinatory drugs were comparatively unknown, how much more salutary is it today when such drugs are increasingly becoming a public menace? My Lords, I am satisfied that this rule accords with justice, ethics, and common sense. . . . I agree with my noble and learned friend, Lord Elwyn-Jones L.C., that, for the reasons he gives, s. 8 of the Criminal Justice Act 1967 does not touch the point raised in this appeal, and I also agree that direction along the lines laid down by my noble and learned friend Lord Elwyn-Jones L.C., should be given by trial judges to juries in the kind of cases to which my noble and learned friend refers.

My Lords, for these reasons, I would dismiss the appeal.

[LORD EDMUND-DAVIES delivered a speech in favour of dismissing the appeal].

LORD RUSSELL OF KILLOWEN: . . . There are two aspects of *Beard's* case [1920] A.C. 479, which have given rise to misunderstanding as to what was there said. One misunderstanding is that a passage in the speech of Lord Birkenhead L.C. is inconsistent with and indeed contradictory of the main tenor thereof. The other is that it lays down or assumes that rape is a crime of specific intent.

The first aspect to which I have referred is related to the following passage of the report:

> "I do not think that the proposition of law deduced from these earlier cases is an exceptional rule applicable only to cases in which it is necessary to prove a specific intent in order to constitute the graver crime—e.g., wounding with intent to do grevious bodily harm or with intent to kill. It is true that in such cases the specific intent must be proved to constitute the particular crime, but this is, on ultimate analysis, only in accordance with the ordinary law applicable to crime, for, speaking generally (and apart from certain special offences), a person cannot be convicted of a crime unless the mens was rea. Drunkenness, rendering a person incapable of the intent, would be an answer, as it is for example in a charge of attempted suicide. In *R.* v. *Moore* (1852) 3 Car & Kir 319, drunkenness was held to negative the intent in such a case, and Jervis C.J. said: 'If the prisoner was so drunk as not to know what she was about, how can you say that she intended to destroy herself?' "

In my opinion this passage is not to be taken as stating in effect the opposite of the whole previous tenor of the speech in the course of denying the applicability of the statement in *R.* v. *Meade* [1909] 1 K.B. 895. The clue to the cited passage appears to me to be in the words 'in order to constitute the graver crime'. In my opinion the passage cited does no more than to say that special intent cases are not restricted to those crimes in which the absence of a special intent leaves available a lesser crime embodying no special intent, but embrace all cases of special intent even though no alternative lesser criminal charge is available. And the example given of attempted suicide is just such a case.

The second aspect of *Beard* to which I have referred relates to two passages. The first is:

> "My Lords, drunkenness in this case could be no defence unless it could be established that Beard at the time of committing the rape was so drunk that he was incapable of forming the intent to commit it, which was not in fact, and manifestly, having regard to the evidence, could not be contended. For in the present case the death resulted from two acts or from a succession of acts, the rape and the act of violence causing suffocation. These acts cannot be regarded separately and independently of each other. The capacity of the mind of the prisoner to form the felonious intent which murder involves is in other words to be explored in relation to the ravishmnent; and not in relation merely to the violent act which gave effect to the ravishment."

The second is: "There was certainly no evidence that he was too drunk to form the intent of committing rape."

In my opinion these passages do not indicate an opinion that rape is a crime of special intent. All that is meant is that conscious rape is required to supply "the felonious intent which murder involves." For the crime of murder special or particular intent is always required for the necessary malice aforethought. This may be intent to kill or intent to cause grievous bodily harm: or in a case such as *Beard* of constructive malice, this required the special intent *consciously to commit* the violent felony of rape in the course and furtherance of which the act of violence causing death took place. *Beard* therefore, in my opinion does not suggest that rape is a crime of special or particular intent.

I too would dismiss this appeal.

Appeal dismissed

[It should be pointed out that felony—murder, with which Beard was concerned, was abolished by the Homicide Act 1956].

Questions

1. Lord Elwyn-Jones states that self-induced intoxication is "a reckless course of conduct" and that "recklesness is enough to constitute the necessary *mens rea* in assault cases." In what sense(s) is the word "reckless" being used in these two statements?
2. Although Lord Simon agreed with Lord Elwyn-Jones he also said "*Mens rea* is . . . the state of mind stigmatised as wrongful by the criminal law. . . . There is no juristic reason why mental incapacity . . . brought about by self-induced intoxication, to realise what one is doing . . . should not be such a state of mind stigmatised as wrongful." Is this compatible with describing such intoxication as "reckless"?
3. If the only purpose of section 8 of the Criminal Justice Act 1967 was to "alter the law of evidence," how could it be said to have affected the substantive law in relation to the *mens rea* of murder in *R.* v. *Hyam, post*, p. 374? See Lynn, (1978) 29 N.I.L.Q. 133.
4. Lord Salmon and Lord Edmund-Davies admitted that the decision was illogical. Do you agree? See Dashwood: "Logic and the Lords in Majewski" [1977] Crim. L.R. 532 and 591, and Sellers: "*Mens Rea* and the Judicial Approach to Bad Excuses" (1978) 41 M.L.R. 245.

Note

It is clear from *Garlick* [1981] Crim. L.R. 178 that when intoxication is raised as a defence to a crime of specific intent the question in issue is not whether the defendant was incapable of forming the intent but whether, even if still capable, he or she did form that intent.

But it is not entirely clear from *Majewski* what status, if any, evidence of intoxication has in defence to a charge of a basic intent offence.

Williams, Textbook of Criminal Law, pp. 426, 428

"There are three possible opinions as to the law since *Majewski*.

1. On a charge of assault, evidence of intoxication is inadmissible, being irrelevant. On this view the jury will not hear or know of the evidence, even though it is logically relevant to the question they have to decide: whether the defendant had the requisite mental element. But it is not the usual practice to exclude evidence relevant to culpability and sentence, even though it is irrelevant to guilt. Nothing in *Majewski* suggests that the law of evidence is affected; so we may assume that it is not.
2. The jury hear the evidence of intoxication, but the judge directs them that they must decide whether the act was intentional or reckless without paying

regard to the evidence that the defendant was tipsy at the time. This would be asking the jury to decide an entirely artificial issue.

3. The jury hear the evidence as in (2), but the judge directs them that since the defendant has given evidence of intoxication in order to support a defence of lack of *mens rea*, the question of *mens rea* is now excluded, and liability is strict. This would be a workable rule (though how it can be reconciled with section 8 of the Act of 1967 remains mysterious).

Legal difficulties aside, the third rule is best. It must be confined to cases where the evidence of intoxication is adduced by the defence. It cannot apply where the evidence is adduced by the prosecution, who cannot be allowed to exclude the issue of *mens rea* by such an expedient. But in all probability the second theory represents the law."

But see *R.* v. *Eatch* [1980] Crim. L.R. 650 which reports a judge at Nottingham Crown Court adopting approach number (3) above.

What are crimes of specific intent?

Williams, Textbook of Criminal Law, pp. 428 et seq.

"In allocating crimes to one category or the other, the courts adopt a Humpty Dumpty attitude. . . . The House of Lords [in *Majewski*] did not collectively commit itself to a solution of the problem. The Lord Chancellor cited with approval a passage from the speech of Lord Simon in *Morgan*, declaring that "crimes of basic intent" are those "whose definition expresses (or more often, implies) a *mens rea* which does not go beyond the *actus reus*"; but he failed to note that Lord Simon's view was rejected by a majority of the House in *Morgan*, and he did not go into the difficulty caused by that view. Lord Simon said that an *actus reus* for his purposes included a "consequence, however remote, as defined in the *actus reus*". The definition is easy to misunderstand, because it is against common sense. It is presumably meant to exclude the type of crime where the law requires a certain consequence to be intended or foreseen *without requiring that the consequence should actually occur* (attempt, theft [in that the owner need not in fact be permanently deprived], burglary in one of its forms, forgery). These last are crimes of specific intent. In contrast, crimes of basic intent are those where no consequence is referred to, or, if one is referred to, it must occur before the crime is regarded as committed (murder, wounding with intent). In the latter, the consequence is part of the required *actus reus* (taking that expression in a broad sense), while in the former it pertains only to the *mens rea*. But, if this is the distinction, it not only attaches a very peculiar meaning to "specific intent" but fails to explain the law. Everyone agrees that murder and wounding with intent are crimes of specific intent, not basic intent, for the purpose of the intoxication rule. Lord Simon's test would make them crimes of basic intent.

Since Lord Simon's definition patently does not work, there must arise a temptation to amend it in the hope of making it work. In a subsequent case, Lord Salmon, speaking for the whole Appellate Committee, altered Lord Simon's definition of crimes of basic intent by amputating the reference to the consequence. He said that "what is called a basic intention . . . is an intention to do the acts which constitute the crime". (*Newbury* [1977] A.C. at 509). This omits any reference to consequences. (Whether the noble lord's omission was intentional it is impossible to say, owing to the general slackness of thought in this area; but let us take the statement at its face value, as lawyers deserve to have their statements taken). Crimes of basic intent now mean those in which the *mens rea* relates only to the bodily movement and its circumstances. *Per contra*, a crime of specific intent is one in which the *mens rea* relates also to specified consequences. This may look a more hopeful line. It restores what at first sight appears to be a sensible meaning to the phrase "crimes of specific intent". Murder and wounding with intent are now crimes of specific intent within the definition, because they both require *mens rea* as to a consequence, whereas the crime of knowingly possessing explosives is a crime of basic intent, since no consequence need be intended or foreseen. Fully acceptable; but it again fails to explain the intoxication rule. The definition would make handling stolen goods a crime of basic intent, whereas this is held to be a crime of specific intent. Conversely with assault. The grand object of the judges is somehow to get assault into the category of crimes of basic intent. But, on Lord Salmon's definition, an assault causing the apprehension of harm (psychic assault) would be a crime of specific intent. Such an assault is not committed unless the victim is actually caused to feel apprehension. If he is unaware of what is going on there is no assault. Additionally, the defendant must intend (or at least be reckless as to) the apprehension. So if a crime of basic intent means a crime in which the required *mens rea* relates only to the defendant's movement, a psychic assault is not a crime of basic intent but a crime of specific intent.

In *Majewski*, all of their lordships held that assault is invariably a crime of basic intent; they did not distinguish between different manifestations of assault. Lord Simon, in the passage in *Morgan* quoted with approval both by the Lord Chancellor and by Lord Edmund-Davies, specifically held that an assault causing apprehension (a psychic assault) is a crime of basic intent.

But the difficulty goes beyond psychic assaults, because many physical assaults would not be crimes of basic intent. Suppose that A throws a stone at B, or fires a shot at him, hitting him. On the same definition of a crime of basic intent, this would be a crime of specific intent. A is not guilty of physical assault unless he intended or was reckless as to the consequence of hitting B.

In short, the doctrine of "basic intent" plays tricks with words. "Basic intent" is a meaningless expression which the courts use when they wish to impose a restriction on the *mens rea* doctrine. They distinguish between offences on grounds of policy, while pretending to derive the distinction from definitions. The policy is to admit the relevance of intoxication to charges of murder and of wounding with intent, while denying its relevance to the fallback charges of manslaughter and assault (with its compounds)."

The two cases extracted below indicate the difficulties faced in determining which offences (or, as it now seems, parts of offences) allow a defence of intoxication.

Jaggard v. Dickinson
[1980] 3 All E.R. 716
Queen's Bench Division

The appellant went to a house late one night. She was drunk. She thought it was a house belonging to a friend. She believed, correctly, that her friend would not object to her breaking in. It was the wrong house. She appealed against a conviction under section 1 (1) of the Criminal Damage Act 1971, on the ground that, despite her intoxication, she was entitled to rely on the defence of lawful excuse under s. 5 (2) and (3) of the Act.

Mustill J.: S. 1 (1) of the 1971 Act. . . reads as follows:

"A person who without lawful excuse destroys or damages any property belonging to another intending to destroy or damage any such property or being reckless as to whether any such property would be destroyed or damaged shall be guilty of an offence."

At the hearing before the magistrates the appellants relied on the following provisions of s. 5 of the 1971 Act:

> "(2) A person charged with an offence to which this section applies shall, whether or not he would be treated for the purposes of this Act as having a lawful excuse apart from this subsection, be treated for those purposes as having a lawful excuse—(*a*) if at the time of the act or acts alleged to constitute the offence he believed that the person or persons whom he believed to be entitled to consent to the destruction of or damage to the property in question had so consented, or would have so consented to it if he or they had known of the destruction or damage and its circumstances ... (3) For the purposes of this section it is immaterial whether a belief is justified or not if it is honestly held. . . ."

It is convenient to refer to the exculpatory provisions of s. 5 (2) as if they created a defence while recognising that the burden of disproving the facts referred to by the subsection remains on the prosecution. The magistrates held that the appellant was not entitled to rely on s. 5 (2) since the belief relied on was brought about by a state of self-induced intoxication.

In support of the conviction counsel for the respondent advanced an argument which may be summarised as follows (i) Where an offence is one of "basic intent", in contrast to one of "specific intent", the fact that the accused was in a state of self-induced intoxication at the time when he did the acts constituting the actus reus does not prevent him from possessing the mens rea necessary to constitute the offence: see *D.P.P. v. Morgan* [*ante*, p. 101] *D.P.P.* v. *Majewski* [*ante*, p. 176]. (ii) Section 1 (1) of the 1971 Act creates an offence of basic intent: see *R.* v. *Stephenson* [1979] Q.B. 695. (iii) Section 5 (3) has no bearing on the present issue. It does not create a separate defence, but is no more than a partial definition of the expression "without lawful excuse" in s. 1 (1). The absence of lawful excuse forms an element in the mens rea: see *R.* v. *Smith* [1974] Q.B. 354 at 360. Accordingly, since drunkenness does not negative mens rea in crimes of basic intent, it cannot be relied on as part of a defence based on s. 5 (2).

Whilst this is an attractive submission, we consider it to be unsound, for the following reasons. In the first place, the argument transfers the distinction between offences of specific and of basic intent to a context in which it has no place. The distinction is material where the defendant relies on his own drunkenness as a ground for denying that he had the degree of intention or recklessness required in order to constitute the offence. Here, by contrast, the appellant does not rely on her drunkenness to displace an inference of intent or recklessness; indeed she does not rely on it at all. Her defence is founded on the state of belief called for by s. 5 (2). True, the fact of the appellant's intoxication was relevant to the defence under s. 5 (2) for it helped to explain what would otherwise have been inexplicable, and hence lent colour to her evidence about the state of her belief. This is not the same as using drunkenness to rebut an inference of intention or recklessness. Belief, like intention or recklessness, is a state of mind; but they are not the same states of mind.

Can it nevertheless be said that, even if the context is different, the principles established by *Majewski* ought to be applied to this new situation? If the basis of the decision in *Majewski* had been that drunkenness does not prevent a person from having an intent or being reckless, then there would be grounds for saying that it should equally be left out of account when deciding on his state of belief. But this is not in our view what *Majewski* decided. The House of Lords did not conclude that intoxication was irrelevant to the fact of the defendant's state of mind, but rather that, whatever might have been his actual state of mind, he should for reasons of policy be precluded from relying on any alteration in that state brought about by self-induced intoxication. The same considerations of policy apply to the intent or recklessness which is the mens rea of the offence created by s. 1 (1) and that offence is accordingly regarded as one of basic intent (see *R.* v. *Stephenson*). It is indeed essential that this should be so, for drink so often plays a part in offences of criminal damage, and to admit drunkenness as a potential means of escaping liability would provide much too ready a means of avoiding conviction. But these considerations do not apply to a case where Parliament has specifically required the court to consider the defendant's actual state of belief, not the state of belief which ought to have existed. This seems to us to show that the court is required by s. 5 (3) to focus on the existence of the belief, not its intellectual soundness; and a belief can be just as much honestly held if it is induced by intoxication as if it stems from stupidity, forgetfulness or inattention.

It was, however, urged that we could not properly read s. 5 (2) in isolation from s. 1 (1), which forms the context of the words"without lawful excuse" partially defined by s. 5 (2). Once the words are put in context, so it is maintained, it can be seen that the law must treat drunkenness in the same way in relation to lawful excuse (and hence belief) as it does to intention and recklessness, for they are all part of the mens rea of the offence. To fragment the mens rea, so as to treat one part of it as affected by drunkenness in one way and the remainder as affected in a different way, would make the law impossibly complicated to enforce.

If it had been necessary to decide whether, for all purposes, the mens rea of an offence under s. 1 (1) extends as far as an intent (or recklessness) as to the existence of a lawful excuse, I should have wished to consider the observations of James L.J., delivering the judgment of the Court of Appeal in *R.* v. *Smith* [1974] Q.B. 354 at 360. I do not however find it necessary to reach a conclusion on this matter and will only say that I am not at present convinced that, when these observations are read in the context of the judgment as a whole, they have the meaning which the respondent has sought to put on them. In my view, however, the answer to the argument lies in the fact that any distinctions which have to be drawn as to the relevance of drunkenness to the two subsections arises from the scheme of the 1971 Act itself. No doubt the mens rea is in general indivisible, with no distinction being possible as regards the effect of drunkenness. But Parliament has specifically isolated one subjective element, in the shape of honest belief, and has given it separate treatment and its own special gloss in s. 5 (3). This being so, there is nothing objectionable in giving it special treatment as regards drunkenness, in accordance with the matural meaning of its words.

In these circumstances, I would hold that the magistrates were in error when they decided that the defence furnished to the appellant by s. 5 (2) was lost because she was drunk at the time. I would therefore allow the appeal.

DONALDSON J.: I agree . . . The law in relation to self-induced intoxication and crimes of basic intent is without doubt an exception to the general rule that the prosecution must prove the actual existence of the relevant intent, be it basic or specific (see *R.* v. *Stephenson* [1979] Q.B. 695 at 704 *per* Geoffrey Lane L.J.). And in s. 5 Parliament has very specifically extended what would otherwise be regarded as "lawful excuse" by providing that it is immaterial whether the relevant belief is justified or not provided that it is honestly held. The justification for what I may call the *Majewski* exception, although it is much older than that decision, is said to be that the course of conduct inducing the intoxication supplies the evidence of mens rea (see [1977] A.C. 443 at 474–475) *per* Lord Elwyn-Jones L.C. It seems to me that to hold that this substituted mens rea overrides so specific a statutory provision involves reading s. 5 (2) as if it provided that "for the purpose of this section it is immaterial whether a belief is justified or not if it is honestly held provided that the honesty of the belief is not attributable only to self-induced intoxication." I cannot so construe the section and I too would therefore allow the appeal.

Appeal allowed,
Conviction quashed

Questions

1. Mustill J. suggests that *Majewski* decided that, although drunkenness can prevent a person forming the requisite intention or recklessness for a crime of basic intent, as a matter of policy the defendant cannot rely on such lack of *mens rea*. Does this accord with the opinion of Lord Elwyn-Jones in *Majewski*, in which Lords Diplock, Simon and Kilbrandon concurred?

2. Is section 5 (2) of the 1971 Act the equivalent, in relation to circumstances, of section 8 of the Criminal Justice Act 1967, in relation to consequences?

Note

Section 1 (2) of the Criminal Damage Act 1971 provides:

> "A person who without lawful excuse destroys or damages any property, whether belonging to himself or another. . . .
> (*a*) intending to destroy or damage any property or being reckless as to whether any property would be destroyed or damaged; and
> (*b*) intending by the destruction or damage to endanger the life of another or being reckless as to whether the life of another would be thereby endangered;
> shall be guilty of an offence."

In *R.* v. *Caldwell* (below), the House of Lords held that whether this is a crime of specific or basic intent depends on the basis of the charge.

R. v. Caldwell
[1981] 1 All E.R. 961
House of Lords

The facts appear *ante*, p. 71.

The certified question was as follows: "Whether evidence of self-induced intoxication can be relevant to the following questions—(a) Whether the defendant intended to endanger the life of another; and (b) Whether the defendant was reckless as to whether the life of another would be endangered, within the meaning of 'section 1 (2) (b) of the Criminal Damage Act 1971."

LORD DIPLOCK: As respects the charge under section 1 (2) the prosecution did not rely upon an actual intent of the respondent to endanger the lives of the residents but relied upon his having been reckless whether the lives of any of them would be endangered. His act of setting fire to it was one which the jury were entitled to think created an obvious risk that the lives of the residents would be endangered; and the only defence with which your Lordships are concerned is that the respondent had made himself so drunk as to render him oblivious of that risk.

If the only mental state capable of constituting the necessary *mens rea* for an offence under section 1 (2) were that expressed in the words "intending by the destruction or damage to endanger the life of another," it would have been necessary to consider whether the offence was to be classified as one of "specific" intent for the purposes of the rule of law which this House affirmed and applied in *R.* v. *Majewski*, and this it plainly is. But this is not, in my view, a relevant inquiry where "being reckless as to whether the life of another would be thereby endangered" is an alternative mental state that is capable of constituting the necessary *mens rea* of the offence with which he is charged.

The speech of the Lord Chancellor in *Majewski* with which Lord Simon of Glaisdale, Lord Kilbrandon and I agreed, is authority that self-induced intoxication is no defence to a crime in which recklessness is enough to constitute the necessary *mens rea*. . . .

Reducing oneself by drink or drugs to a condition in which the restraints of reason and conscience are cast off was held to be a reckless course of conduct and an integral part of the crime. The Lord Chancellor accepted as correctly stating English law the provision in section 208 of the American Model Penal Code:

> "When recklessness establishes an element of the offence, if the actor, due to self-induced intoxication, is unaware of a risk of which he would have been aware had he been sober, such unawareness is immaterial."

So, in the instant case, the fact that the respondent was unaware of the risk of endangering the lives of residents in the hotel owing to his self-induced intoxication, would be no defence if that risk would have been obvious to him had be been sober.

. . . [T]he Court of Appeal in the instant case regarded the case as turning upon whether the offence under section 1 (2) was one of "specific" intent or "basic" intent. Following a recent decision of the Court of Appeal by which they were bound, *R.* v. *Orpin* (1980) 70 Cr. App. R. 306, they held that the offence under section 1 (2) was one of "specific" intent in contrast to the offence under section 1 (1) which was of basic intent. This would be right if the only *mens rea* capable of constituting the offence were an actual intention to endanger the life of another. For the reasons I have given, however, classification into offences of "specific" and "basic" intent is irrelevant where being reckless as to whether a particular harmful consequence will result from one's act is a sufficient alternative *mens rea*. I would give the following answers to the certified questions:

(*a*) If the charge of an offence under section 1 (2) of the Criminal Damage Act 1971 is framed so as to charge the defendant only with "*intending* by the destruction or damage" [of the property] "to endanger the life of another", evidence of self-induced intoxication can be relevant to his defence.

(*b*) If the charge is, or includes, a reference to his "being reckless as to whether the life of another would thereby be endangered," evidence of self-induced intoxication is not relevant.

LORDS KEITH of KINKEL and ROSKILL agreed with this statement of the law. LORD WILBERFORCE agreed with LORD EDMUND-DAVIES.

LORD EDMUND-DAVIES: [T]he view expressed by my noble and learned friend Lord Diplock "that the speech of the Lord Chancellor in *Majewski* is authority that self-induced intoxication is no defence to a crime in which recklessness is enough to constitute the necessary *mens rea*" . . . is a view which, with respect, I do not share. In common with all noble and learned Lords hearing that appeal, Lord Elwyn-Jones L.C. adopted the well-established (though not universally favoured) distinction between basic and specific intents. *Majewski* related solely to charges of assault, undoubtedly an offence of basic intent, and the Lord Chancellor made it clear that his observations were confined to offences of that nature. . . . My respectful view is that *Majewski* accordingly supplies no support for the proposition that, in relation to crimes of specific intent (such as section 1 (2) (*b*) of the 1971 Act) incapacity to appreciate the degree and nature of the risk created by his action which is attributable to the defendant's self-intoxication is an irrelevance. The Lord Chancellor was dealing simply with crimes of basic intent, and in my judgment it was strictly within that framework that he adopted the view expressed in the American Penal Code [s. 2.08] and recklessness as an element in crimes of specific intent was, I am convinced, never within his contemplation.

For the foregoing reasons, the Court of Appeal were in my judgment right in quashing the conviction under section 1 (2) (*b*) and substituting a finding of guilty of arson contrary to section 1 (1) and (3) of the 1971 Act.

. . . [I]t was recently predicted that, "There can hardly be any doubt that *all* crimes of recklessness except murder will now be held to be crimes of basic intent within *Majewski*." (Glanville Williams, "Textbook of Criminal Law", 1978, p. 431). That prophecy has been promptly fulfilled by the majority of your Lordships, for, with the progressive displacement of "maliciously" by "intentionally or recklessly" in statutory crimes, that will surely be the effect of the majority decision in this appeal. That I regret, for the consequence is that, however grave the crime charged, if recklessness can constitute its *mens rea* the fact that it was committed in drink can afford no defence. It is a very long time since we had so harsh a law in this country. Having revealed in *Majewski* (p. 495B–497C) my personal conviction that, on grounds of public policy, a plea of drunkenness cannot exculpate crimes of basic intent and so exercise unlimited sway in the criminal law, I am nevertheless unable to concur that your Lordships' decision should now become the law of the land. For, as Eveleigh L.J. said in *Orpin (supra,* at p. 312):

> ". . . there is nothing inconsistent in treating intoxication as irrelevant when considering the liability of a person who has willed himself to do that which the law forbids (for example, to do something which wounds another), and yet to make it relevant when a further mental state is postulated as an aggravating circumstance making the offence even more serious."

By way of postscript I would add that the majority view demonstrates yet again the folly of totally ignoring the recommendations of the Butler Committee (Report on Mentally Abnormal Offenders. Cmnd. 6244, 1975, paras. 18, 53–58).

Appeal dismissed

Note

See *post*, p. 198 for the Butler Committee recommendations.

The High Court of Australia is the only court of final appeal in the common law world to have departed from *Majewski*. In *R.* v. *O'Connor* (1980) 54 A.L.J.R. 349 a four-to-three majority held that self-induced intoxication could be a defence to any crime.

The case below illustrates that, even in crimes of specific intent, intoxication may not avail as a defence.

Attorney-General for Northern Ireland v. Gallagher
[1963] A.C. 349
House of Lords

The respondent was convicted of the murder of his wife. The defence was that of insanity under the M'Naghten Rules or, in the alternative, that at the time of the commission of the crime the respondent was by reason of drink incapable of forming the intent required in murder and was therefore guilty only of manslaughter. The respondent had indicated an intention to kill his wife before taking the alcohol. The Court of Criminal Appeal in Northern Ireland allowed an appeal on the ground that the judge in his summing-up directed the jury to apply the tests laid down in the M'Naghten Rules to the time when alcohol was taken and not to the time when the actual murder was committed.

LORD DENNING: My Lords, this case differs from all others in the books in that the accused man, whilst sane and sober, before he took to the drink, had already made up his mind to kill his wife. This seems to me to be far worse—and far more deserving of condemnation—than the case of a man who, before getting drunk, kills another by an act which he would not dream of doing when sober. Yet by the law of England in this latter case his drunkenness is no defence even though it has distorted his reason and his will-poower. So why should it be a defence in the present case? And is it made any better by saying that the man is a psychopath?

The answer to the question is, I think, that the case falls to be decided by the general principle of English law that, subject to very limited exceptions, drunkenness is no defence to a criminal charge, nor is a defect of reason produced by drunkenness. This principle was stated by Sir Matthew Hale in his *Pleas of the Crown* , I, p. 32, in words which I would repeat here: "This vice" (drunkenness) "doth deprive men of the use of reason, and puts many men into a perfect, but temporary, phrenzy.... By the laws of England such a person shall have no privilege by this voluntary contracted madness, but shall have the same judgment as if he were in his right senses."

The general principle can be illustrated by looking at the various ways in which drunkenness may produce a defect of reason:

(a) It may impair a man's powers of perception so that he may not be able to foresee or measure the consequences of his actions as he would if he were sober. Nevertheless he is not allowed to set up his self-induced want of perception as a defence. Even if he did not himself appreciate that what he was doing was dangerous, nevertheless, if a reasonable man in his place, who was not befuddled with drink, would have appreciated it, he is guilty: see *R.* v. *Meade* [1909] 1 K.B. 895, as explained in *D.P.P.* v. *Beard* [1920] A.C. 479.

(b) It may impair a man's power to judge between right or wrong, so that he may do a thing when drunk which he would not dream of doing while sober. He does not realise he is doing wrong. Nevertheless he is not allowed to set up his self-induced want of moral sense as a defence. In *Beard's* case Lord Birkenhead L.C. distinctly ruled that it was not a defence for a drunken man to say he did not know he was doing wrong.

(c) It may impair a man's power of self-control so that he may more readily give way to provocation than if he were sober. Nevertheless he is not allowed to set up his self-induced want of control as a defence. The acts of provocation are to be assessed, not according to their effect on him personally, but according to the effect they would have on a reasonable man in his place. The law on this point was previously in doubt (see the cases considered in *Beard's* case), but it has since been resolved by *R.* v. *McCarthy* [1954] 2 Q.B. 105, *Bedder* v. *D.P.P.* [1954] 1 W.L.R. 1119 and section 3 of the Homicide Act 1957.

The general principle which I have enunciated is subject to two exceptions:

1. If a man is charged with an offence in which a specific intention is essential (as in murder, though not in manslaughter), then evidence of drunkenness, which renders him incapable of forming that intention, is an answer: see *Beard's* case. This degree of drunkenness is reached when the man is rendered so stupid by drink that he does not know what he is doing (see *R.* v. *Moore* (1852) 3 C. & K. 153), as where, at a christening, a drunken nurse put the baby behind a large fire,

taking it for a log of wood (*Gentleman's Magazine,* 1748, p. 570); and where a drunken man thought his friend (lying in his bed) was a theatrical dummy placed there and stabbed him to death (*The Times,* January 13, 1951). In each of those cases it would not be murder. But it would be manslaughter.

2. If a man by drinking brings on a distinct disease of the mind such as delirium tremens, so that he is temporarily insane within the M'Naghten Rules, that is to say, he does not at the time know what he is doing or that it is wrong, then he has a defence on the ground of insanity: see *R.* v. *Davis* (1881) 14 Cox 563 and *Beard's* case.

Does the present case come within the general principle or the exceptions to it? It certainly does not come within the first exception. This man was not incapable of forming an intent to kill. Quite the contrary. He knew full well what he was doing. He formed an intent to kill, he carried out his intention and he remembered afterwards what he had done. And the jury, properly directed on the point, have found as much, for they found him guilty of murder. Then does the case come within the second exception? It does not, to my mind, for the simple reason that he was not suffering from a disease of the mind brought on by drink. He was suffering from a different disease altogether. As the Lord Chief Justice observed in his summing-up: "If this man was suffering from a disease of the mind, it wasn't of a kind that is produced by drink."

So we have here a case of the first impression. The man is a psychopath. That is, he has a disease of the mind which is not produced by drink. But it is quiescent. And whilst it is quiescent he forms an intention to kill his wife. He knows it is wrong but still he means to kill her. Then he gets himself so drunk that he has an explosive outburst and kills his wife. At that moment he knows what he is doing but he does not know it is wrong. So in that respect—in not knowing it is wrong—he has a defect of reason at the moment of killing. If that defect of reason is due to the drink, it is no defence in law. But if it is due to the disease of the mind, it gives rise to a defence of insanity. No one can say, however, whether it is due to the drink or to the disease. It may well be due to both in combination. What guidance does the law give in this difficulty? That is, as I see it, the question of general public importance which is involved in this case.

My Lords, I think the law on this point should take a clear stand. If a man, whilst sane and sober, forms an intention to kill and makes preparation for it, knowing it is a wrong thing to do, and then gets himself drunk so as to give himself Dutch courage to do the killing, and whilst drunk carries out his intention, he cannot rely on this self-induced drunkenness as a defence to a charge of murder, nor even as reducing it to manslaughter. He cannot say that he got himself into such a stupid state that he was incapable of an intent to kill. So also when he is a psychopath, he cannot by drinking rely on his self-induced defect of reason as a defence of insanity. The wickedness of his mind before he got drunk is enough to condemn him, coupled with the act which he intended to do and did do. A psychopath who goes out intending to kill knowing it is wrong, and does kill, cannot escape the consequences by making himself drunk before doing it. That is, I believe, the direction which the Lord Chief Justice gave to the jury and which the Court of Criminal Appeal found to be wrong. I think it was right and for this reason I would allow the appeal.

I would agree, of course, that if before the killing he had discarded his intention to kill or reversed it—and then got drunk—it would be a different matter. But when he forms the intention to kill and without interruption proceeds to get drunk and carry out his intention, then his drunkenness is no defence and nonetheless so because it is dressed up as a defence of insanity. There was no evidence in this case of any interruption and there was no need for the Lord Chief Justice to mention it to the jury.

I need hardly say, of course, that I have here only considered the law of Northern Ireland. In England a psychopath such as this man might now be in a position to raise a defence of diminished responsibility under section 2 of the Homicide Act 1957. . . .

Appeal allowed

Question

What has Lord Denning in mind when he speaks of the interruption of intent to kill? If there is a previous, clearly expressed, seriously intended intent to kill, what interruption will suffice to establish that this has been discarded? Even if a discarding can be successfully shown, will not the earlier intention serve to rebut the presumption raised by the drunkenness that the man was incapable of forming the specific intent required?

5. PROPOSALS FOR REFORM

Although there may be nothing in common between the insane defendant, the automaton or the drunkard, they often present common problems to the courts. In terms of traditional principles of criminal liability the mental disabilities of each mean that either the actus reus or the mens rea cannot be fully proved (or sometimes both). Yet the courts have to balance the demands of individual justice against those of social protection.

Fingarette, "Diminished Mental Capacity as a Criminal Law Defence" (1974) 37 M.L.R. 264

"The concept which I propose as central, as generic to the entire domain of the relevant law, indeed as defining that domain, is *'diminished mental capacity'*. A second, related concept, also basic to the analysis, is that of the *'context of origin'* of the diminished mental capacity. Both these concepts take their sense, as will be seen, in a legal context, the context of assessing criminal responsibility. They are not medical concepts, though medical evidence may be relevant.

The entire legal doctrine based on these concepts is, I believe, an elaboration of deeply rooted and entirely reasonable common sense intuitions. These might be rendered explicitly, though somewhat formally, as follows. A person's mind may be deranged in ways that make him unable to conduct himself rationally with respect to some standard. If so, he is not responsible in his conduct with respect to that standard. If, when we look to the context in which this irrationality had its origin, we find that he became irrational in this way through no fault of his own, he should not be held responsible at all for the conduct in respect of that standard. Therefore he cannot be in that respect culpable. However, if he was culpable with respect to the origin of this condition of diminished mental capacity, then he cannot totally escape responsibility and culpability for his offending conduct. In the latter case, the specific kind and degree of ultimate culpability will depend, systematically, on the way in which his originating culpability is related to the impaired state of mind, to the resulting offending act, and to the relevant standards. Finally, whether the verdict is that the diminished mental capacity originated through the accused's own fault or not, this prior irrationality with respect to a criminal law standard warrants appropriate court imposed restraints and medical regimen unless and until the likelihood of any further such diminished mental capacity is past. [In *Mental Disabilities and Criminal Responsibilities*, California, 1979, Fingarette replaced this term with 'disabilities of mind']."

Report of the Committee on Mentally Abnormal Offenders (the Butler Committee) 1975, Cmnd. 6244

"*A Revised Special Verdict*

1. *Experience of Revised Formulations in America*

18.14. In considering what recommendations we should make, we have found our point of departure in the remark of the Royal Commission on Capital Punishment (Cmnd. 8932, § 291), that many offenders who know what they are doing and that it is wrong and therefore are not within the scope of the M'Naghten Rules are nevertheless undoubtedly so severely disordered that they ought not to be held responsible for their actions. The problem we have to deal with is to devise a formula to provide for them. In other common-law countries efforts have been made to extend the "insanity" defence by interpretation or statutory additions or restatement. For example, the knowledge of wrong test has been widened by asking whether the defendant was so mentally disordered that he was unable to appreciate the reasons why his act was regarded as wrong, or that he was unable to feel that it was wrong. Among other formulations we have considered have been the "Durham" formula, (propounded in *Durham* v. *United States* (1954) 214 F. 2d 862), under which "the accused is not criminally responsible if his unlawful act was the product of mental disease or mental defect", and the proposal in the American Law Institute's Model Penal Code (1959) that the question be whether the defendant, as a result of mental disease or defect, lacked substantial capacity either to appreciate the criminality of his conduct or to conform his conduct to the requirements of law.

18.15. The "Durham" formula has created difficulties of interpretation in its application to the unlawful act as the "product" of the mental condition, and in relation to psychopaths whom psychiatrists could testify to be suffering from mental disease or defect. The expression "mental disease" itself has gone out of general use in this country, and in any case it does not help to distinguish between minor and major disorders. The author of the "Durham" formula, Judge Bazelon, has described his own reasons for favouring its abandonment in the following terms:

> "In the end, after 18 years, I favored the abandonment of the Durham rule because in practice it had failed to take the issue of criminal responsibility away from the experts. Psychiatrists continued to testify to the naked conclusion instead of providing information about the accused so that the jury could render the ultimate moral judgment about blameworthiness. Durham had secured little improvement over M'Naghten."

A drawback of the Durham formula is that it encouraged psychiatrists to draw inferences which are not for doctors to draw. This was a problem which we had to overcome in devising a new defence.

18.16. The Model Penal Code proposal is open to the same objection as Durham in its reference to "mental disease or defect", but its second limb raises other problems. In particular the test of capacity to conform has to face a well-known philosophical criticism. How can one tell the difference between an impulse which is irresistible and one which is merely not resisted? . . .

Summary of Conclusions

. . . .

4. We propose a new formulation of the special verdict, namely "not guilty on evidence of mental disorder", the grounds for which should comprise two elements: (*a*) a *mens rea* element approximating to the first limb of the M'Naghten Rules ("Did he know what he was doing?"); (*b*) specific exemption from convic-

tion for defendants suffering, at the time of the act or omission charged, from severe mental illness or severe subnormality. (§§ 18.17–18.18.)

5. Magistrates' courts should be allowed to return the special verdict. It will not be necessary to retain section 60 (2) of the Mental Health Act. (§ 18.19.)

The first element

6. The jury (or magistrates) should return a verdict of "not guilty on evidence of mental disorder" if they find that the defendant did the act or made the omission charged but (by reason of the evidence of mental disorder) they do not find that the state of mind required for the offence has been proved and they further find that on the balance of probability the defendant was mentally disordered at the time. (§ 18.20.)

7. The first element would apply to any mental disorder but should exclude transient states not related to other forms of mental disorder and arising solely as a consequence of the administration, mal-administration or non-administration of alcohol, drugs or other substances, or from physical injury. All other cases now regarded as non-insane automatism would be within the special verdict. Thus the distinction between conditions which are now legally regarded as "insanity" and those dealt with as "non-insane automatism" would be clearly drawn. (§§ 18.22–23.)

8. The M'Naghten "knowledge of wrong" test should not be included in terms in the new special verdict, but it will be covered in substance in the second element. (§ 18.24.)

9. The new formulation of the first element may have the effect of widening the scope of the special verdict to cover certain categories of mentally disordered persons (including the subnormal) who would now obtain a complete acquittal; but under our recommendations the court's discretionary powers of disposal will enable account to be taken of the individual circumstances of each case. (§ 18.25.)

The second element

10. We recommend that statutory exemption from punishment should be provided for defendants who, although they were suffering from severe mental disorder at the time of the act or omission charged, do not come within the compass of the first element because they were able to form intentions and carry them out. We propose that the special verdict in the terms set out in Conclusion 6 above should be returned if at the time of the act or omission charged the offender was suffering from severe mental illness or severe abnormality. We suggest a definition of severe mental illness, which we propose should be incorporated in the statute, subject to the possibility of revision by statutory instrument. (§§ 18.26–18.36.)

[18.35. We propose the following definition:

"A mental illness is severe when it has one or more of the following characteristics:—

(*a*) Lasting impairment of intellectual functions shown by failure of memory, orientation, comprehension and learning capacity.

(*b*) Lasting alteration of mood of such degree as to give rise to delusional appraisal of the patient's situation, his past or his future, or that of others, or to lack of any appraisal.

(*c*) Delusional beliefs, persecutory, jealous or gradiose.

(*d*) Abnormal perceptions associated with delusional misinterpretation of events.

(*e*) Thinking so disordered as to prevent reasonable appraisal of the patient's situation or reasonable communication with others."]

Offences committed while intoxicated

19. We suggest measures to deal with people who become violent when voluntarily intoxicated. We propose that it should be an offence for a person while voluntarily intoxicated to do an act (or make an omission) that would amount to a dangerous offence if it were done or made with the requisite state of mind for such offence. The offence would not be charged in the first instance but the jury would be directed to find on this offence in the event of intoxication being successfully raised as a defence to the offence originally charged. We define "dangerous" and "voluntary intoxication" for this purpose. We suggest penalties for the new offence. (§§ 18.51–18.59).

[18.55. A dangerous offence for this purpose should be defined as one involving injury to the person (actual bodily harm) or death or consisting of a sexual attack on another, or involving the destruction of or causing damage to property so as to endanger life. A dangerous offence is to be regarded as charged if the jury can convict of it under the indictment.

18.56. "Voluntary intoxication" would be defined to mean intoxication resulting from the intentional taking of drink or a drug knowing that it is capable in sufficient quantity of having an intoxicating effect; provided that intoxication is not voluntary if it results in part from a fact unknown to the defendant that increases his sensitivity to the drink or drug. The concluding words would provide a defence to a person who suffers from hypoglycaemia, for example, who does not know that in that condition the ingestion of a small amount of alcohol can produce a state of altered consciousness, as well as to a person who has been prescribed a drug on medical grounds without warning of the effect it may produce. We do not think it necessary to define intoxication, drink or drug, because this offence would be a fall-back offence, relevant only when the defendant has been acquitted on another charge by reason of evidence of intoxication.

18.57. These provisions would mean that the offence would be one of strict liability (not requiring proof of a mental element or other fault) in respect of the objectionable behaviour, but would require the fault element of becoming voluntarily intoxicated. A mistaken belief in a circumstance of excuse (such as that the victim was about to attack so that the force was necessary by way of defence, or that the victim consented) would not be a defence unless a sober person might have made the same mistake."]

The Criminal Law Revision Committee, 14th Report

"261. One of the defects in the Butler Committee proposal is, in our opinion, the problem of the nomenclature of the offence. A conviction of the Butler Committee offence would merely record a conviction of an offence of committing a dangerous act while intoxicated. This is insufficient. The record must indicate the nature of the act committed, for example whether it was an assault or a killing. It would be unfair for a defendant who has committed a relatively minor offence while voluntarily intoxicated to be labelled as having committed the same offence as a defendant who has killed. The penalty suggested is also in our opinion insufficient to deal with serious offences such as killings or rapes while voluntarily intoxicated by drink or drugs.

262. Professors Smith and Glanville Williams support the proposal of a separate offence because in the first place they consider it to be a fundamental principle that a person should not be convicted of an offence requiring recklessness when he was not in fact reckless. In such a case the verdict of the jury and the record of the court do not represent the truth. Secondly, they think it important that the verdict of the jury should distinguish between an offender who was reckless and one who was not because that is relevant to the question of sentence. In their opinion there is a great difference between, for example, a man who knew that there was a grave risk of causing death and one who was unaware that there

was any risk of any injury whatever to the person but was intoxicated. The fault of the former was in recklessly doing the act which caused injury to the person: the fault of the latter was in becoming intoxicated. They agree that the same maximum penalty should be available to the judge in these two cases, because, exceptionally, an intoxicated offender may be such a public danger as to require the imposition of the maximum, but think that often the two cases ought to be dealt with differently.

263. For these reasons Professors Smith and Glanville Williams provided an improved version of the Butler Committee proposal for the consideration of the Committee. In the interests of conciseness and clarity their proposal is set out in the following propositions: it is not intended to be a final legislative draft.

(1) Intoxication shall be taken into account for the purpose of determining whether the person charged had formed an intention, specific or otherwise, in the absence of which he would not be guilty of the offence.

(2) Where a person is charged with an offence and he relies on evidence of voluntary intoxication, whether introduced by himself or by any other party to the case, for the purpose of showing that he was not aware of a risk where awareness of that risk is, or is part of, the mental element required for conviction of the offence, then, if:

(a) the jury are not satisfied that he was aware of the risk, but

(b) the jury are satisfied

(i) that all the elements of the offence other than any mental element have been proved, and

(ii) that the defendant would, in all the circumstances of the case, have been aware of the risk if he had not been voluntarily intoxicated,

the jury shall find him not guilty of the offence charged but guilty of doing the act while in a state of voluntary intoxication.

(3) Where a person charged with an offence relies on evidence of voluntary intoxication, whether introduced by himself or by any other party to the case, for the purpose of showing that he held a belief which, in the case of a sober person, would be a defence to the offence charged, then, if:

(a) the jury are of opinion that he held that belief or may have held it, and

(b) are satisfied that the belief was mistaken and that the defendant would not have made the mistake had he been sober, the jury shall find him not guilty of the offence charged but guilty of doing the act while in a state of voluntary intoxication.

(4) Where the offence charged consists of an omission, the verdict under (2) and (3) above shall be of making the omission while intoxicated.

(5) A person convicted under (2) or (3) above shall, where the charge was of murder, be liable to the same punishment as for manslaughter; and in any other case shall be liable to the same punishment as that provided by the law for the offence charged.

264. If there is to be a separate offence of doing the *actus reus* of an offence while voluntarily intoxicated we are all agreed that the proposal set out above is to be preferred to that of the Butler Committee. The majority of us feel, however, that that proposal would also create problems. The separate offence would add to the already considerable number of matters which a jury often has to consider when deciding whether the offences charged have been proved, and some of us feel that the separate offence would make the jury's task even more difficult than it is at present in some cases, particularly where the charge is murder. . . .

266. We all agree that the present law is right in requiring that the defendant should be acquitted of intentionally causing the *actus reus* if, on account of voluntary intoxication, a requisite "specific intent" cannot be established. Furthermore, we consider that the present law needs amendment in so far as it relates to so called offences of "basic" intent. The majority of us therefore went on

to consider whether we could improve upon the common law principle and avoid the problems of "specific" and "basic" intent. We found the germ of our eventual proposal in the American Model Penal Code, Article 2, section 2.08 (2) of which provides:

> "When recklessness establishes an element of the offence, if the actor, due to self-induced intoxication, is unaware of a risk of which he would have been aware had he been sober, such unawareness is immaterial."

267. Our recommendation is that the common law rules being rules of general application should be replaced by a statutory provision on the following lines:

(1) that evidence of voluntary intoxication should be capable of negativing the mental element in murder and the intention required for the commission of any other offence; and
(2) in offences in which recklessness constitutes an element of the offence, if the defendant owing to voluntary intoxication had no appreciation of a risk which he would have appreciated had he been sober, such lack of appreciation is immaterial.

Questions

1. Has the House of Lords in *Caldwell*, *ante*, p. 190 effectively adopted the proposal of the Criminal Law Revision Committee, *supra*, § 267?
2. Which of the solutions do you prefer?
3. Fletcher, p. 514, writes of "the vices for which we are held accountable . . . as contrasted with the impediments that mitigate and excuse our wrongdoing." Is this a helpful notion with which to approach the problems raised in this chapter?

For the wider context of this problem see David Farrier, *Drugs and Intoxication* (Sweet and Maxwell, 1980).

CHAPTER 5

DEFENCES

	PAGE		PAGE
1. Duress	201	(iii) Law Commission Recommendations	231
2. Necessity	227	3. Entrapment	233
(i) Necessity and Homicide	227		
(ii) Necessity and Offences Other Than Homicide	230		

1. DURESS

Wasik, "Duress and Criminal Responsibility" [1977] Crim. L.R. 453

"There seems to be general agreement among lawyers that criminal responsibility should follow when an individual chooses to perform an act proscribed by the criminal law, when he has both the capacity and a fair opportunity or chance to adjust his behaviour to conform with the law. It follows that no individual should be held responsible if he had no opportunity to choose an alternative to breaking the law. As the philosophers put it: there should be no ascription of responsibility to the accused unless "he could have acted otherwise." Much attention has been paid to this requirement by philosophers but lawyers, by contrast, have not shown a great deal of interest. Perhaps the main reason for this is the practical rarity of such problems. It is much more common for an accused to plead mistake or lack of intention as an excuse than to plead that he had no choice but to act as he did. Cases in which the defence of duress is raised are probably the most frequent of this small group. . . .

A comparison has sometimes been made between the defence of duress and that of automatism. The suggestion is that in duress, the accused claims that there was no act by *him;* in automatism the accused claims that there was no *act* by him. Both defences are then seen as containing what may in loose terminology be called "an involuntary act" on the part of the accused. But this is misleading, as the element of voluntariness is quite different in the two excuses. Where the defence of automatism succeeds, the accused has had no opportunity at all to exercise choice with regard to the performing of the act, and thus he cannot be held responsible for it. . . . By contrast, in duress, there is an issue of choice. If a man is threatened with physical injury unless he assists in a criminal enterprise, he has the choice (albeit a difficult one) of assisting in the crime or facing the consequences. The question here is whether the accused had a fair opportunity to make the choice."

R. v. Hudson and Taylor
[1971] 2 Q.B. 202
Court of Appeal

H. and T. who were aged 17 and 19 respectively, were charged with perjury in a case in which they were witnesses to an unlawful wounding incident. They admitted that they had given false evidence but raised the defence of duress. This took the form of threats before the trial that unless they did so they would be "cut up." The recorder directed the jury that the defence was not available since the threat was not immediate. On appeal the Crown contended that the plea should have failed on the additional ground that they should have sought police protection before the trial.

Lord Widgery C.J.: . . . it is clearly established that duress provides a defence in all offences including perjury (except possibly treason or murder as a principal) if the will of the accused has been overborne by threats of death or serious personal injury so that the commission of the alleged offence was no longer the voluntary act of the accused. This appeal raises two main questions: first, as to the nature of the necessary threat and, in particular, whether it must be "present and immediate"; secondly, as to the extent to which a right to plead duress may be lost if the accused has failed to take steps to remove the threat as, for example, by seeking police protection.

It is essential to the defence of duress that the threat shall be effective at the moment when the crime is committed. The threat must be a "present" threat in the sense that it is effective to neutralise the will of the accused at that time. Hence an accused who joins a rebellion under the compulsion of threats cannot plead duress if he remains with the rebels after the threats have lost their effect and his own will has had a chance to re-assert itself (*McCrowther's Case* (1746) Fost. 13; and *A.-G.* v. *Whelan* [1934] I.R. 518). Similarly a threat of future violence may be so remote as to be insufficient to overpower the will at the moment when the offence was committed, or the accused may have elected to commit the offence in order to rid himself of a threat hanging over him and not because he was driven to act by immediate and unavoidable pressure. In none of these cases is the defence of duress available because a person cannot justify the commission of a crime merely to secure his own peace of mind.

When, however, there is no opportunity for delaying tactics, and the person threatened must make up his mind whether he is to commit the criminal act or not, the existence at that moment of threats sufficient to destroy his will ought to provide him with a defence even though the threatened injury may not follow instantly, but after an interval. This principle is illustrated by *Subramaniam* v. *Public Prosecutor* [1956] 1 W.L.R. 965, when the appellant was charged in Malaya with unlawful possession of ammunition and was held by the Privy Council to have a defence of duress, fit to go to the jury, on his plea that he had been compelled by terrorists to accept the ammunition and feared for his safety if the terrorists returned.

In the present case the threats of Farrell were likely to be no less compelling, because their execution could not be effected in the court room, if they could be carried out in the streets of Salford the same night. Insofar, therefore, as the recorder ruled as a matter of law that the threats were not sufficiently present and immediate to support the defence of duress we think that he was in error. He should have left the jury to decide whether the threats had overborne the will of the appellants at the time when they gave the false evidence.

Counsel for the Crown, however, contends that the recorder's ruling can be supported on another ground, namely, that the appellants should have taken steps to neutralise the threats by seeking police protection either when they came to court to give evidence, or beforehand. He submits on grounds of public policy that an accused should not be able to plead duress if he had the opportunity to ask for protection from the police before committing the offence and failed to do so. The argument does not distinguish cases in which the police would be able to provide effective protection, from those when they would not, and it would, in effect, restrict the defence of duress to cases where the person threatened had been kept in custody by the maker of the threats, or where the time interval between the making of the threats and the commission of the offence had made recourse to the police impossible. We recognise the need to keep the defence of duress within reasonable bounds but cannot accept so severe a restriction on it. The duty, of the person threatened, to take steps to remove the threat does not seem to have arisen in an English case but in a full review of the defence of duress in the Supreme Court of Victoria (*R.* v. *Hurley, R.* v. *Murray* [1967] V.R. 526), a condition of raising the defence was said to be that the accused "had no means, with safety to himself, of preventing the execution of the threat."

In the opinion of this court it is always open to the Crown to prove that the accused failed to avail himself of some opportunity which was reasonably open to him to render the threat ineffective, and that on this being established the threat in question can no longer be relied on by the defence. In deciding whether such an opportunity was reasonably open to the accused the jury should have regard to his age and circumstances, and to any risks to him which may be involved in the course of action relied on.

In our judgment the defence of duress should have been left to the jury in the present case, as should any issue raised by the Crown and arising out of the appellants' failure to seek police protection. The appeals will, therefore, be allowed and the convictions quashed.

Appeals allowed

The two cases below concern the availability of the defence of duress on a charge of murder.

D.P.P. v. Lynch
[1975] A.C. 653
House of Lords

The appellant was the driver of a car which contained members of the IRA in Northern Ireland on an expedition in which they shot and killed a police officer. He said that he was not a member of the IRA and was convinced that he would be shot if he did not obey the leader of the group. The trial judge held that the defence of duress was not available to an aider and abettor of murder. The Court of Criminal Appeal in Northern Ireland dismissed his appeal.

LORD MORRIS OF BORTH-Y-GEST: . . . The case against the appellant was that he was a principal in the second degree. He had not done any of the actual shooting which killed the police constable. The case against him was that he had aided and abetted the killing. . . . The main contention of the appellant and one of the main lines of his defence at the trial was that all that he had done had been done under duress and that he was entitled to be acquitted. . . .

So the question presents itself whether the issue of duress should have been left to the jury. If on the facts the conclusion could be that the appellant only participated to the extent that he did because he was forced to participate should he be held guilty? There are two aspects of the question, viz., (a) whether there was evidence upon which it would be open to a jury to say that there was duress and (b) if there was, and if a jury considered that there had been duress, whether duress can avail as a defence to a charge which is presented as a charge of murder.

It is important to remember that in this case we are concerned with an alleged principal in the second degree, and that the particular points of law which are raised are framed in reference to an aider and abettor. We are concerned with duress in the form of threats (either expressly made or by conduct indicated) to kill the person threatened or to cause serious personal physical injury to him. I limit my decision to the facts of the present case. . . .

In a series of decisions and over a period of time courts have recognised that there can be circumstances in which duress is a defence. In examining them and more particularly in approaching the issue raised in this appeal the question naturally presents itself—why and on what basis can duress be raised? If someone acts under duress—does he intend what he does? Does he lack what in our criminal law is called mens rea? If what he does amounts to a criminal offence ought he to be convicted but be allowed in mercy and in mitigation to be absolved or relieved from some or all of the possible consequences?

The answer that I would give to these questions is that it is proper that any rational system of law should take fully into account the standards of honest and reasonable men. By those standards it is fair that actions and reactions may be tested. If then someone is really threatened with death or serious injury unless he does what he is told to do is the law to pay no heed to the miserable, agonising plight of such a person? For the law to understand not only how the timid but also the stalwart may in a moment of crisis behave is not to make the law weak but to make it just. In the calm of the court-room measures of fortitude or of heroic behaviour are surely not to be demanded when they could not in moments for decision reasonably have been expected even of the resolute and the well disposed.

In posing the case where someone is "really" threatened I use the word "really" in order to emphasise that duress must never be allowed to be the easy answer of those who can devise no other explanation of their conduct nor of those who readily could have avoided the dominance of threats nor of those who allow themselves to be at the disposal and under the sway of some gangster-tyrant. Where duress becomes an issue courts and juries will surely consider the facts with care and discernment.

In my view the law has recognised that there can be situations in which duress can be put forward as a defence. Someone who acts under duress may have a moment of time, even one of the utmost brevity, within which he decides whether he will or will not submit to a threat. There may consciously or subconsciously be a hurried process of balancing the consequences of disobedience against the gravity or the wickedness of the action that is required. The result will be that what is done will be done most unwillingly but yet intentionally. Terminology may not, however, much matter. The authorities show that in some circumstances duress may excuse and may therefore be set up as a special defence.

A tenable view might be that duress should never be regarded as furnishing an excuse from guilt but only where established as providing reasons why after conviction a court could mitigate its consequences or absolve from punishment. Some writers including Stephen (see *History of the Criminal Law in England* (1883), vol. 2, pp. 107–108) have so thought. It is, however, much too late in the day, having regard to the lines of authority, to adopt any such view. But apart from this—would such an approach be just? I think not. It is said that if duress could not be set up as a defence there would be difficulties in the way of bringing evidence of the relevant facts and circumstances before the court. I am not greatly impressed by this. A judge could ensure that after a conviction full opportunity would be given to adduce all material evidence. If, however, what a person has done was only done because he acted under the compulsion of a threat of death or of serious bodily injury it would not in my view be just that the stigma of a conviction should be cast on him. As Blackstone put it (*Commentaries on the Laws of England* (1862), vol. 4, p. 23):

> ". . . it is highly just and equitable that a man should be excused for those acts which are done through unavoidable force and compulsion."

The law must, I think, take a common sense view. If someone is forced at gunpoint either to be inactive or to do something positive—must the law not remember that the instinct and perhaps the duty of self-preservation is powerful and natural? I think it must. A man who is attacked is allowed within reason to take necessary steps to defend himself. The law would be censorious and inhumane which did not recognise the appalling plight of a person who perhaps suddenly finds his life in jeopardy unless he submits and obeys.

The issue in the present case is therefore whether there is any reason why the defence of duress, which in respect of a variety of offences has been recognised as a possible defence, may not also be a possible defence on a charge of being a principal in the second degree to murder. I would confine my decision to that issue. It may be that the law must deny such a defence to an actual killer, and that the law will not be irrational if it does so.

Though it is not possible for the law always to be worked out on coldly logical lines there may be manifest factual differences and contrasts between the situation of an aider and abettor to a killing and that of the actual killer. Let two situations be supposed. In each let it be supposed that there is a real and effective threat of death. In one a person is required under such duress to drive a car to a place or to carry a gun to a place with knowledge that at such place it is planned that X is to be killed by those who are imposing their will. In the other situation let it be supposed that a person under such duress is told that he himself must there and then kill X. In either situation there is a terrible agonising choice of evils. In the former to save his life the person drives the car or carries the gun. He may cling to the hope that perhaps X will not be found at the place or that there will be a change of intention before the purpose is carried out or that in some unforeseen way the dire event of a killing will be averted. The final and fatal moment of decision has not arrived. He saves his own life at a time when the loss of another life is not a certainty. In the second (if indeed it is a situation likely to arise) the person is told that to save his life he himself must personally there and then take an innocent life. It is for him to pull the trigger or otherwise personally to do the act of killing. There, I think, before allowing duress as a defence it may be that the law will have to call a halt. May there still be force in what long ago was said by Hale?

> "Again, if a man be desperately assaulted, and in peril of death, and cannot otherwise escape, unless to satisfy his assailant's fury he will kill an innocent person then present, the fear and actual force will not acquit him of the crime and punishment of murder, if he commit the fact; for he ought rather to die himself, than kill an innocent."

(see *Hale's Pleas of the Crown*, vol. 1, p. 51). Those words have over long periods of time influenced both thought and writing but I think that their application may have been unduly extended when it is assumed that they were intended to cover all cases of accessories and aiders and abettors.

Writers on criminal law have generally recorded that whatever may be the extent to which the law has recognised duress as a defence it has not been recognised as a defence to a charge of murder (see *Russell on Crime*, 12th ed. (1964), p. 90; *Kenny's Outlines of Criminal Law*, 19th ed. (1966), p. 70; *Glanville Williams, Criminal Law*, 2nd ed. (1961), p. 759, and *Smith and Hogan, Criminal Law*, 3rd ed. (1973), pp. 164–168).

It may be a matter for consideration whether the offences of being accessory before the fact to murder and of aiding and abetting murder might not be constituted as separate offences involving a liability to the imposition of life imprisonment but not as a mandatory sentence.

I fully appreciate that, particularly at the present time, situations may arise where the facts will be much less direct and straightforward than those which, as examples, I have described. I see no advantage in giving illustrations of them. They will be situations presenting greater difficulties of fact than those presented in the present case. But where there have been threats of the nature that really have compelled a person to act in a particular way and he has only acted because of them I think that the approach of the law should be to recognise that the person may be excused in the cases that I have supposed.

It is most undesirable that, in the administration of our criminal law, cases should arise in which, if there is a prosecution leading to a conviction, a just conclusion will only be attained by an exercise thereafter of the prerogative of granting a pardon. I would regret it, therefore, if upon an application of legal principles such cases could arise. Such principles and such approach as will prevent them from arising would seem to me to be more soundly based. . . .

[His Lordship then cited many English and Commonwealth authorities on the defence of duress.]

Having regard to the authorities to which I have referred it seems to me to have been firmly held by our courts in this country that duress can afford a defence in criminal cases. A recent pronouncement was that in the Court of Appeal in 1971 in the case above referred to (*R.* v. *Hudson* [1971] 2 Q.B. 202) [see above]. The court stated that they had been referred to a large number of authorities and to the views of writers of textbooks. In the judgment of the court delivered by Lord Parker C.J. and prepared by Widgery L.J. the conclusion was expressed, at p. 206, that

> ". . . it is clearly established that duress provides a defence in all offences including perjury (except possibly treason or murder as a principal)."

We are only concerned in this case to say whether duress could be a possible defence open to Lynch who was charged with being an aider and abettor. Relying on the help given in the authorities we must decide this as a matter of principle. I consider that duress in such a case can be open as a possible defence. Both general reasoning and the requirements of justice lead me to this conclusion. . . .

The question arises as to what is the proper course to follow. The appellant did not have the opportunity of having his defence of duress considered. I think that he should have it. His conviction should be quashed but having regard to all the circumstances I consider that the interests of justice require that there should be a re-trial. I would remit the case to the Court of Criminal Appeal to make the appropriate order.

I would allow the appeal accordingly.

Lord Wilberforce: It is clear that a possible case of duress, on the facts, could have been made. I say "a possible case" because there were a number of matters which the jury would have had to consider if this defence had been left to them. Among these would have been whether Meehan, though uttering no express threats of death or serious injury, impliedly did so in such a way as to put the appellant in fear of death or serious injury; whether, if so, the threats continued to operate throughout the enterprise; whether the appellant had voluntarily exposed himself to a situation in which threats might be used against him if he did not participate in a criminal enterprise (the appellant denied that he had done so); whether the appellant had taken every opportunity open to him to escape from the situation of duress.

In order to test the validity of the judge's decision to exclude this defence, we must assume on this appeal that these matters would have been decided in favour of the appellant.

What, then, does exclusion of the defence involve? It means that a person, assumedly not himself a member of a terrorist group, summoned from his home, with explicit or implied threats of death or serious injury at gunpoint, to drive armed men on what he finds to be a criminal enterprise, having no opportunity to escape, but with the certainty of being shot if he resists or tries to get away, is liable to be convicted of murder. The same would be true of a bystander in a street, or an owner of a car, similarly conscripted, once it is shown that he, or she, knew the nature of the enterprise. One may multiply examples of the possible involvement of persons, whom the normal man would regard as without guilt, under threats of death or violence, in violent enterprises—examples unfortunately far from fanciful at this time. Does the law require all these to be charged with murder and call for their conviction? It would be our duty to accept such a law if it existed, but we are also entitled to see if it does.

Does then the law forbid admission of a defence of duress on a charge of murder whether as a principal in the first degree or as a principal in the second degree or as an accessory? Consistently with the method normal in the development of the common law, an answer to this question must be sought in authority, and in the principles upon which established authority is based. I look first at the principle. The principle upon which duress is admitted as a defence is not easy to state. Professor Glanville Williams indeed doubts whether duress fits in to any accepted theory: it may, in his view, stand by itself altogether outside the definition of will and act. The reason for this is historical. Duress emerged very early in our law as a fact of which account has to be taken, particularly in times of civil strife where charges of treason were the normal consequence of defeat, long before the criminal law had worked out a consistent or any theory of "mens rea" or intention. At the present time, whatever the ultimate analysis in jurisprudence may be, the best opinion, as reflected in decisions of judges and in writers, seems to be that duress per minas is something which is superimposed upon the other ingredients which by themselves would make up an offence, i.e. upon act and intention.

"Coactus volui" sums up the combination: the victim completes the act and knows that he is doing so; but the addition of the element of duress prevents the law from treating what he has done as a crime. . . .

[The appellant] may have had the necessary intention to involve him as an aider and abettor but his intention may have been produced by threats which he could not resist.

I referred above to judicial decisions: it is certainly the case that, in recent years, and subsequently to *Stephen, History of the Criminal Law in England* (1883) (and in spite of that eminent author's views) the defence of duress has been judicially admitted in relation to a variety of crimes: inter alia, treason, receiving, stealing, malicious damage, arson, perjury. In all of these crimes there would have to be proved, in addition to an actus reus, an element of intention. Yet this defence has been admitted. This makes it clear beyond doubt, to my mind, that if the defence is to be denied in relation to murder, that cannot be because the crime of murder—as distinct from other crimes—involves the presence of intention: it must be so for some other reason. If the proposition is correct at all that duress prevents what would otherwise constitute a crime from attracting criminal responsibility, then that should be correct whatever the crime.

What reason then can there be for excepting murder? One may say—as some authorities do (*cf. A.-G.* v. *Whelan* [1934] I.R. 518, 526 *per* Murnaghan J., *R.* v. *Hurley and Murray* [1967] V.R. 526, 543 *per* Smith J.) that murder is the most heinous of crimes: so it may be, and in some circumstances, a defence of duress in relation to it should be correspondingly hard to establish. Indeed, to justify the deliberate killing by one's own hand of another human being may be something that no pressure or threat even to one's own life which can be imagined can justify—no such case ever seems to have reached the courts. But if one accepts the test of heinousness, this does not, in my opinion, involve that all cases of what is murder in law must be treated in the same way. Heinousness is a word of degree, and that there are lesser degrees of heinousness, even of involvement in homicide, seems beyond doubt. An accessory before the fact, or an aider or abettor, may (not necessarily must) bear a less degree of guilt than the actual killer: and even if the rule of exclusion is absolute, or nearly so in relation to the latter, it need not be so in lesser cases. Nobody would dispute that the greater the degree of heinousness of the crime, the greater and less resistible must be the degree of pressure, if pressure is to excuse. Questions of this kind where it is necessary to weigh the pressures acting upon a man against the gravity of the act he commits are common enough in the criminal law, for example with regard to provocation and self-defence: their difficulty is not a reason for a total rejection of the defence. To say that the defence may be admitted in relation to some degrees of murder, but that its admission in cases of direct killing by a first degree principal is likely to be attended by such great difficulty as almost to justify a ruling that the defence is not available, is not illogical. It simply involves the recognition that by sufficiently adding to the degrees, one may approach an absolute position.

So I find no convincing reason, on principle, why, if a defence of duress in the criminal law exists at all, it should be absolutely excluded in murder charges whatever the nature of the charge; hard to establish, yes, in case of direct killing so hard that perhaps it will never be proved: but in other cases to be judged, strictly indeed, on the totality of facts. Exclusion, if not arbitrary, must be based either on authority or policy. I shall deal with each.

As to authority, this has been fully examined by others of your Lordships and I shall not duplicate the process. The stream is reasonably clear if not deep. I do not think it open to controversy (i) that a defence of duress is known to English law and has been so known since the 14th century. (In one form or another it seems to be admitted in all common law and civil law jurisdictions): (ii) that the defence is admitted in English law as absolving from guilt, not as diminishing responsibility or as merely mitigating the punishment. Some authors do indeed suggest the latter, at least in relation to homicide (*cf. East's Pleas of the Crown* (1803), p. 225) and there may be a case (not an unanswerable case) for saying, generally, that this ought to be the law. It clearly, however, is not the law and, particularly where sentence is mandatory, whether of death or life imprisonment, Parliamentary action would be necessary if proof of duress were to operate upon the sentence. It would also be necessary if duress were to be admitted as diminishing responsibility: (iii) that there is no direct English judicial authority against its application to charges of murder. There is the judgment of Lord Coleridge C.J. in the "necessity" case of *R.* v. *Dudley and Stephens,* 14 Q.B.D. 273 [*post*, p. 227]: there are obiter dicta (*A.-G.* v. *Whelan* [1934] I.R. 518, 526; *R.* v. *Steane* [1947] K.B. 997, 1005; *R.* v. *Bourne* (1952) 36 Cr. App. R. 125, 128), some of eminent judges, in favour of exclusion, but these follow the writers, who in turn follow Hale. That great writer—and the same is true of Stephen—would recognise that legal thought and practice has moved far since his time. . . .

That the defence may be admissible in cases of murder other than as a principal was indicated by the Court of Appeal presided over by Lord Parker C.J. in a judgment prepared by Widgery L.J. in *R.* v. *Hudson* [1971] 2 Q.B. 202, 206 [above]. That judgment was a considered judgment after relevant authorities had been fully cited: (iv) that there are two cases in which the defence of duress had arisen in relation to charges of murder not being murder by a principal of the first degree. The first is *R.* v. *Kray (Ronald),* 53 Cr. App. R. 569. . . . The other was an unreported case recently tried (by judge alone) in Northern Ireland (*R.* v. *Fagan* (1974) MacDermott J.)—also involving an involuntary car driver. The charge seems to have been one of aiding and abetting an attempted murder or possibly of attempted murder, which would make it a stronger case, and the defence was admitted. On the other side is *R.* v. *Tyler,* 8 C. & P. 616 in which Lord Denman C.J. is reported to have charged the jury in terms more widely expressed than was necessary and in which the facts could not, properly regarded, be considered as amounting to duress. . . .

[His Lordship then cited some Commonwealth authorities.]

The conclusion which I deduce is that although, in a case of actual killing by a first degree principal the balance of judicial authority at the present time is against the admission of the defence of duress, in the case of lesser degrees of participation, the balance is, if anything, the other way. At the very least, to admit the defence in such cases involves no departure from established decisions. . . .

The broad question remains how this House, clearly not bound by any precedent, should now state the law with regard to this defence in relation to the facts of the present case. I have no doubt that it is open to us, on normal judicial principles, to hold the defence admissible. We are here in the domain of the common law: our task is to fit what we can see as principle and authority to the facts before us, and it is no obstacle that these facts are new. The judges have always assumed responsibility for deciding questions of principle relating to criminal liability and guilt, and particularly for setting the standards by which the law expects normal men to act. In all such matters as capacity, sanity, drunkenness, coercion, necessity, provocation, self-defence, the common law, through the judges, accepts and sets the standards of right-thinking men of normal firmness and humanity at a level which people can accept and respect. The House is not inventing a new defence: on the contrary, it would not discharge its judicial duty if it failed to define the law's attitude to this particular defence in particular circumstances. I would decide that the defence is in law admissible in a case of aiding and abetting murder, and so in the present case. I would leave cases of direct killing by a principal in the first degree to be dealt with as they arise.

It is said that such persons as the appellant can always be safeguarded by action of the executive which can order an imprisoned person to be released. I firmly reject any such argument. A law, which requires innocent victims of terrorist threats to be tried for murder and convicted as murderers, is an unjust law even if the executive, resisting political pressures, may decide, after it all, and within the permissible limits of the prerogative to release them. Moreover, if the defence is excluded in law, much of the evidence which would prove the duress would be inadmissible at the trial, not brought out in court, and not tested by cross-examination. The validity of the defence is far better judged by a jury, after proper direction and a fair trial, than by executive officials; and if it is said that to allow the defence will be to encourage fictitious claims of pressure I have enough confidence in our legal system to believe that the process of law is a better safeguard against this than inquiry by a government department.

I would allow the appeal and answer the first certified question in the affirmative. This involves no more than saying that a defence of duress was admissible in law. Since, as I have explained, that defence has yet to be made good in fact, and since a number of elements have to be proved to a jury's satisfaction, I would, under sections 13 and 38 of the Criminal Appeal (Northern Ireland) Act 1968 order a new trial and remit the case to the Court of Criminal Appeal for directions to be given under section 14 of the Act.

LORD SIMON OF GLAISDALE: . . . In my opinion no distinction can be based on the degree of participation. I have already rehearsed the arguments in support of the concept of duress as a defence (the absence of moral blameworthiness and the inappropriateness of punishment in such circumstances); there are no different arguments relating to "necessity" as a defence: and none affords any ground for distinguishing between principals in the first or second degrees respectively. It is, with all respect, irrational to say, "The man who actually pulls the trigger is in a class by himself: he is outside the pale of any such defence as I am prepared to countenance." He cannot on any sensible ground be put in a class by himself: the man who pulls the trigger because his child will be killed otherwise is deserving of exactly the same consideration as the man who merely carries the gun because he is frightened. Moreover, in general, as *Smith and Hogan, Criminal Law*, 3rd ed. (1973), p. 166, states in this very connection:

> "The difficulty about adopting a distinction between the principal and secondary parties as a rule of law is that the contribution of the secondary party to the death may be no less significant than that of the principal."

So the question must be faced whether there is a sustainable distinction in principle between "necessity" and duress as defences to a charge of murder as a principal. In the circumstances where either "necessity" or duress is relevant, there are both actus reus and mens rea. In both sets of circumstances there is power of choice between two alternatives; but one of those alternatives is so disagreeable that even serious infraction of the criminal law seems preferable. In both the consequence of the act is intended, within any permissible definition of intention. The only difference is that in duress the force constraining the choice is a human threat, whereas in "necessity" it can be any circumstance constituting a threat to life (or, perhaps, limb). Duress is, thus considered, merely a particular application of the doctrine of "necessity": see *Glanville Williams on Criminal Law*, 2nd ed. (1961), p. 760. In my view, therefore, if your Lordships were to allow the instant appeal, it would be necessary to hold that *R.* v. *Dudley and Stephens* [*post*, p. 227] either was wrongly decided or was not a decision negativing "necessity" as a defence to murder; and, if the latter, it would be further incumbent, I think, to define "necessity" as a criminal defence, and lay down whether it is a defence to all crimes, and if not why not. It would, in particular, be necessary to consider Hale's dissent from Bacon as to the starving man stealing a loaf of bread. It would be a travesty of justice and an invitation to anarchy to declare that an innocent life may be taken with impunity if the threat to one's own life is from a terrorist but not when from a natural disaster like ship- or plane-wreck.

In my respectful submission such questions—why, if duress is available as a defence to a principal in the second degree, it should not also be available to a principal in the first degree; and what is the difference in principle between "necessity" and duress that should make the latter but not the former a defence to murder—cannot simply be shrugged off by an assertion that one's judgment goes no further than the facts instantly under consideration. One of the tests of the validity of a legal rule is to see whether its implications stand up to examination. A refusal to submit a rule to such an examination can only be justified if anomaly is considered as a positive virtue in the law.

But the law for a long time recognised . . . a defence by a wife, in relation to certain crimes committed in her husband's presence, that she acted in obedience of his orders. The fiction of the law, raising a strong presumption, was that she thereby acted under his coercion. . . .

"Coercion" in its popular sense denotes an external force which cannot be resisted and which impels its subject to act otherwise than he would wish. . . . It was this state of mind which was presumed by the law to be that of a wife performing certain acts prohibited by law in the presence of her husband; and the law held her to be thereby excused.

Both the doctrine itself and its limitations are of crucial significance in relation to duress. As early as Bracton's *De Legibus* (f.151b) the doctrine was held not to apply to "heinous deeds" (*atrocioribus*): see Professor Thorne's edition for the Selden Society, vol. II, p. 428. Hale (*Pleas of the Crown*, vol. 1, p. 45) stated specifically that it did not apply to murder or treason, citing *The Earl and Countess of Somerset's* cases (1616) 2 St. Tr. 951, 966 in respect of murder—the Countess being an accessory. The report of the Committee on the Responsibility of the Wife for Crimes committed under the coercion of husband (Cmd. 1677 of 1922) stated that the presumption applied to all felonies except murder (p. 3). The exceptions of treason and murder were given specific statutory endorsement when the *presumption* of coercion was abolished by section 47 of the Criminal Justice Act 1925, the *doctrine* being otherwise affirmed:

> "Any presumption of law that an offence committed by a wife in the presence of her husband is committed under the coercion of the husband is hereby abolished, but on a charge against a wife for any offence other than treason or murder it shall be a good defence to prove that the offence was committed in the presence of, and under the coercion of, the husband."

(The Criminal Justice Act (Northern Ireland) 1945 is in similar terms). The exact scope and effect of this provision, and its interrelationship with the doctrine of duress, are obscure in the extreme; and different interpretations have been proffered, without any consensus emerging. But two things at least are clear: first, Parliament recognised "coercion" as a subsisting defence in law; and, secondly, Parliament refused to recognise it as a defence to charges of treason or murder, without differentiating between degrees of participation. Since "coercion" was defined neither by the antecedent law nor by the statute, I take it that it is used in its ordinary sense, as it is in the law of probate, and which I have just discussed. The state of mind produced, and which excuses from liability, is thus the same for both "coercion" and duress—namely, "This is not my wish, but I must do it"—and in both the constraint is due to external human pressure. The difference lies, first, in the method of pressure (for duress it is limited to threats, whereas for "coercion" it extends to any force overbearing the wish); and, secondly, that there is authority to the effect that duress is a defence to certain types of treason, whereas "coercion" is not. But neither of these differences justifies any differentiation between "coercion" and duress as a defence to murder: and the two concepts (duress and "coercion") are, indeed, habitually treated by jurists as cognate. If, therefore, "coercion" constitutes no defence to a charge of murder, it would be anomalous were duress to do so. . . .

. . . But, of course, no discussion can have any claim to adequacy which does not extend to the authorities. Fortunately, I am absolved from reviewing them in detail, since that has been done by my noble and learned friends. My only misgiving is that such an impressive muster should be sent packing so ignominiously. Poor Hale, poor Blackstone; wretched Russell and Kenny; poor, poor Lord Denman. But at least they are in good company. There are all those famous jurists, headed by Stephen, who drew up the draft code of 1879 under the fond belief that they were codifying the common law. And all those framers of the Commonwealth codes, and the commentators on them, under the same illusion. And Americans too. They are like the denizens of the first circle of Hell, who, for all their wisdom and virtue, lived in such benighted times as to have forfeited salvation. So, too, these great lawyers are too eminent to go altogether unacknowledged: they are recognised with a courtly bow, but their words are lost in the gale of juristic change. For, in truth, their voices were unanimous that duress is no defence to murder. What is to be set against them? A dissenting judgment of Bray C.J., which boggles at murder as a principal in the first degree and adds (almost alone) attempted murder to the exception. A case of accessory before the fact where the issue was virtually uncontested. A passing reference in a Privy Council case where the point did not fall for decision. One unreported trial in England and another in Northern Ireland. A judgment in Roman-Dutch law. If the first question for your Lordships' consideration is to be answered Yes, it is overturning the consensus of centuries. I am all for recognising frankly that judges do make law. And I am all for judges exercising this responsibility boldly at the proper time and place—that is, where they can feel confident of having in mind, and correctly weighed, all the implications of their decision, and where matters of social policy are not involved which the collective wisdom of Parliament is better suited to resolve (see *Launchbury* v. *Morgans* [1973] A.C. 127, 136F–137A, 137G). I can hardly conceive of circumstances less suitable than the instant for five members of an appellate committee of your Lordships' House to arrogate to ourselves so momentous a law-making initiative.

LORD KILBRANDON: . . . It is my misfortune that while I agree with those of your Lordships who consider that the law is in a very unsatisfactory state, and is in urgent need of restatement, I remain convinced that the grounds on which the majority propose that the conviction of the appellant be set aside involve changes in the law which are outside the proper functions of your Lordships in your judicial capacity. If duress per minas has never been admitted as a defence to a charge of murder, and if the proposal that it should now be so admitted be approved, it seems to me that your Lordships, in countenancing a defence for many years authoritatively (though not in your Lordship's House) denied, would be doing what, in the converse, was firmly and properly disapproved in *R.* v. *Knuller, (Publishing, Printing and Promotions) Ltd.* [1973] A.C. 435. Instead of, for reasons of public policy, declaring criminal for the first time conduct until then not so described, your Lordships would be for the first time declaring the existence of a defence to a criminal charge which had up to now by judges, text writers, and law teachers throughout the common law world, been emphatically repudiated.

I am putting the matter in this way, because I want to emphasise in the comparatively brief observations I have to make that since, first, in my opinion, the learned judge's charge was right, and secondly that the substance of the law which he laid down is hard to defend, we are therefore in the realm of law reform; in my judgment it is an impermissible, or at least an undesirable, mode of law reform to use the occasion of an appeal in a decided case for the purpose of declaring that changing conditions and enlarging opinions have rendered the ratio decidendi of the lower court obsolete and therefore suceptible of being set aside. This is perhaps a technical way of looking at the matter. But there is a much wider aspect. It seems to me to be clear that the effect of the opinions of the majority of your Lordships would be to change what has during many generations of judges, teachers, practitioners and students been regarded as the common law. If they were all wrong, I can imagine no more plausible justification for that rather dubious brocard communis error facit ius. It would in my opinion be a necessary preliminary to the reform of that generally accepted version of the common law that consultations, on a far wider basis than discussions among lawyers, including the arguments of counsel before the highest tribunal, should have taken place and been seriously considered. If there is one lesson which has been learned since the setting up of the Law Commissions it is this, that law reform by lawyers for lawyers (unless in exceptionally technical matters) is not socially acceptable. An alteration in a fundamental doctrine of law, such as this appeal proposes, could not properly be given effect to save after the widest reference to interests, both social and intellectual, far transcending those available in the judicial committee of your Lordship's House. Indeed general public opinion is deeply and properly concerned. It will not do to claim that judges have the duty—call it the privilege—of seeing to it that the common law expands and contracts to meet what the judges conceive to be the requirements of modern society. Modern society rightly prefers to exercise that function for itself, and this it conveniently does through those who represent it in Parliament. And its representatives nowadays demand, or should demand, that they be briefed by all those who can qualify an interest to advise them. The fascinating discussions of policy which adorn the speeches of your Lordships—and to which I intend to make a short and undistinguished addition—are themselves highly illustrative of what I mean. They may perhaps be taken as the ultimate in the distillation of legal policy-opinion, but that is not enough. I will not take time to enumerate the various other disciplines and interests whose views are of equal value in deciding what policy should inform the legislation, necessary if reform of the law is really called for, giving effect to the defence of duress per minas in all crimes including murder. In the absence of such consultations I do not think it would be right to decide an appeal in such a way as to set aside the common understanding of the law. . . .

I would . . . refuse this appeal.

LORD EDMUND-DAVIES: . . . .

I. SHOULD DURESS BE A DEFENCE TO ANY CRIME?

In *R.* v. *Tyler*, 8 C. & P. 616, 620–621, Lord Denman C.J., said:

> ". . . the law is, that no man, from a fear of consequnces to himself, has a right to make himself a party to committing mischief on mankind. . . . It cannot be too often repeated, that the apprehension of personal danger does not furnish any excuse for assisting in doing any act which is illegal."

It has been said that, despite the unqualified nature of these observations, they must be read as applying only to the murder charge then being tried. But, over forty years later, Stephen wrote in *History of the Criminal Law in England*, vol. 2, pp. 107–108:

> "Criminal law is itself a system of compulsion on the widest scale. It is a collection of threats of injury to life, liberty and property if people do commit crimes. Are such threats to be withdrawn as soon as they are encountered by opposing threats? The law says to a man intending to commit murder, If you do it I will hang you. Is the law to withdraw its threat if someone else says, If you do not do it I will shoot you? Surely it is at the moment when temptation to crime is strongest that the law should speak most clearly and emphatically to the contrary. It is, of course, a misfortune for a man that he should be placed between two fires, but it would be a much greater misfortune for society at large if criminals could confer impunity upon their agents by threatening them with death or violence if they refused to execute their commands. If impunity could be so secured a wide door would be opened to collusion, and encouragement would be given to associations of malefactors, secret or otherwise. No doubt the moral guilt of a person who commits a crime under compulsion is less than that of a person who commits it freely, but any effect which is thought proper may be given to this circumstance by a proportional mitigation of the offender's punishment. These reasons lead me to think that compulsion by threats ought in no case whatever to be admitted as an excuse for crime, though it may and ought to operate in mitigation of punishment in most though not in all cases."

Well, such an approach at least makes for neatness. No matter how terrifying the circumstances which have impelled a man (and which, indeed, might well have impelled *most* men) to transgress the criminal law, he must be convicted. Crutchley (5 C. & P. 133) should therefore have been convicted of malicious damage during the threshing machine riots, even though he had been compelled by a mob to strike a blow at the machines. Instead, his defence of duress was upheld. The trouble about such neatness is that it may work intolerable injustice in individual cases, for, as Professor Glanville Williams has observed (*Criminal Law*, p. 755, para. 245):

> "*Crutchley* was a case where justice demanded not merely a mitigation of punishment, but no punishment at all; nor would there have been any sound reason for registering even a technical conviction."

Apart from the obloquy involved in the mere fact of conviction, in the nature of things there can be no assurance that even a completely convincing plea of duress will lead to an absolute discharge. And even the exercise of the royal prerogative involves the notion that there must have been a degree of wrong-doing, for were it otherwise no "pardon" would be called for. Furthermore, as the appellant's counsel cogently submitted, if duress is excluded at the trial, it may well be that (unlike in the present case) no evidence on the point will be given, and there would accordingly be no satisfactory means of deciding whether the plea had any substance. In such circumstances, a decision by the Home Secretary adverse to the accused might understandably be regarded as unsatisfactory, for he might well have concluded that duress had not been made out rather than that the prosecution had established its unacceptability, which is indisputably the correct approach.

Stephen himself cannot be acquitted of contributing to the lack of neatness and consistency in this branch of the law. He was a member of the Royal Commission whose draft criminal code of 1879—that is, four years before his *History* appeared—purported to express "what we think is the existing law, and what at all events we suggest ought to be the law." Section 23 provided that:

> "Compulsion by threats of immediate death or grievous bodily harm ... shall be an excuse for the commission of any offence other than high treason ..., murder, piracy, offences deemed to be piracy, attempting to murder, assisting in rape, forcible abduction, robbery, causing grievous bodily harm and arson. . . ."

These exceptions are substantially greater than those of *Hale's Pleas of the Crown*, vol. 1, p. 50, who excepted only treason, murder and robbery. Of the several writers quoted to us, none (save Stephen) goes so far as to assert that duress neither affords nor should afford a defence to *any* criminal charge. Similarly, each of the many codes cited follows the pattern of providing that duress is a defence to all crimes save a specified few, while section 2.09 of the American Law Institute's Model Penal Code excludes the plea of duress from *no* criminal charge and in this respect resembles section 40 of the German Draft Penal Code of 1961.

II. When is the Plea of Duress Available?

Despite the views of old (and not so old) writers, there has been for some years an unquestionable tendency towards progressive latitude in relation to the plea of duress. Thus, it may be invoked in some types of treason (*R.* v. *Purdy* (1945) 10 J. Cr. L. 182), in receiving (*A.-G.* v. *Whelan* [1934] I.R. 518), in stealing (*R.* v. *Gill* [1963] 1 W.L.R. 841), in malicious damage (*R.* v. *Crutchley*, 5 C. & P. 133), in arson (*R.* v. *Shiartos*, noted in *R.* v. *Gill* [1963] 1 W.L.R. 841), in unlawful possession of ammunition (*Subramaniam* v. *Public Prosecutor* [1956] 1 W.L.R. 965), and in perjury (*R.* v. *Hudson* [1971] 2 Q.B. 202 [above]). Indeed, in the last-mentioned case, Lord Parker C.J. said, at p. 206, that

> "... it is clearly established that duress provides a defence in all offences including perjury (except possibly treason or murder as a principal) if the will of the accused has been overborne by threats of death or serious personal injury so that the commission of the alleged offence was no longer the voluntary act of the accused."

But, as in some types of treason, complicity in murder has, at least until recent times, been put into a category of its own. . . . And in this context, one should not overlook the eloquent observations of Lord Coleridge C.J., in *R.* v. *Dudley and Stephens* 14 Q.B.D. 273, 288 [*post*, p. 227] in relation to the defence of necessity:

> "It must not be supposed that in refusing to admit temptation to be an excuse for crime it is forgotten how terrible the temptation was; how awful the suffering; how hard in such trials to keep the judgment straight and the conduct pure. We are often compelled to set up standards we cannot reach ourselves, and to lay down rules which we could not ourselves satisfy. But a man has no right to declare temptation to be an excuse, though he might himself have yielded to it, nor allow compassion for the criminal to change or weaken in any manner the legal definition of the crime."

But even this seemingly clear stream has been made opaque by the decision in *R.* v. *Kray (Ronald)*, 53 Cr. App. R. 569, where Barry, one of the accused, was charged with being an accessory before the fact to the murder of one McVitie. The Crown's case was that Barry had carried to a certain destination a gun which he well knew Reginald Kray intended to use to murder McVitie. Barry admitted these allegations, but pleaded that he had so acted on the order of the Krays, because he feared for the safety of himself and his family if he disobeyed them. Objections were raised to the admissibility of certain parts of Barry's evidence, but counsel both for the Krays and for the Crown conceded that duress was available to a person charged (as Barry was) with being an accessory before the fact to murder, though not to a person charged as a principal. In dismissing the Krays' appeal against conviction for murder, Widgery L.J., as he then was, said, at p. 578:

> "We are . . . satisfied that Barry had a viable defence . . . that by reason of threats he was so terrified that he ceased to be an independent actor, and that the evidence of violent conduct by the Krays which Barry put before the court was accordingly relevant and admissible."

The question that immediately arises is: Can a distinction properly be made between the action of Barry in carrying the murder weapon to the scene of the crime and the action of Lynch in driving Meehan and his criminal colleagues to and from the scene of the shooting and waiting around the corner while the murdering was being committed? Can the styling of the one "accessory before the fact" and the other "principal in the second degree" of itself make any difference to their criminality? If both acted in terror of imminent death or grave injury, should the one go scot free and the other be convicted of murder and receive the mandatory sentence of life imprisonment? Professor J. C. Smith ("A Note on Duress" [1974] Crim. L.R. 349, 351) has little doubt how these questions should be answered:

> "A party who is absent may in fact have played a more significant role in the killing than one who is present and, if both were acting under duress, it would be wrong that the former should be able to rely on that defence and the latter not. . . . If duress is once admitted as a possible defence to an accessory, then it is difficult to find a logical limit to the availability of the defence."

III. What is the Basis of the Plea of Duress?

Of the two theories regarding the nature of the plea of duress canvassed below and before this House, I prefer the view of Professor Glanville Williams (*Criminal Law*, p. 751, para. 242) that:

> "True duress is not inconsistent with act and will as a matter of legal definition, the maxim being coactus volui. Fear of violence does not differ in kind from fear of economic ills, fear of displeasing others, or any other determinant of choice, it would be inconvenient to regard a particular type of motive as negativing will."

At the end of the day, the defence of duress is probably best evaluated without reference to its supposed relation to either actus reus or mens rea, for, in the words of Professor Turpin [1972] C.L.J. 205, "not every morally exculpatory circumstance has a necessary bearing on these legal ingredients of crime."

IV. WHY SHOULD DURESS NOT BE AVAILABLE IN MURDER?

If the circumstances are such that "the ordinary power of human resistance" is overborne, why should they not render excusable even the unlawful killing of an innocent person? Several reasons have been advanced for asserting that no duress, however terrible, can save such a participator in unlawful killing as the appellant from being convicted of murder. One of these has already been referred to and is epitomised by the observation of Lord Coleridge C.J., in *R.* v. *Dudley and Stephens*, 14 Q.B.D. 273, 287 that: "To preserve one's life is generally speaking a duty, but it may be the plainest and the highest duty to sacrifice it." Such an approach was elaborately dealt with in *S.* v. *Goliath*, 1972 (3) S.A. 1 where the Appellate Division held that on a charge of murder compulsion can be a complete defence. In giving the majority judgment, Rumpff J. developed the submission of defence counsel, at p. 6 that, "the criminal law, should not be applied as if it were a blueprint for saintliness but rather in a manner in which it can be obeyed by the reasonable man," by saying:

> "It is generally accepted . . . that for the ordinary person in general his life is more valuable than that of another. Only those who possess the quality of heroism will intentionally offer their lives for another. Should the criminal law then state that compulsion could never be a defence to a charge of murder, it would demand that a person who killed another under duress, whatever the circumstances, would have to comply with a higher standard than that demanded of the average person. I do not think that such an exception to the general rule which applies in criminal law is justified." (S.A.L.R. (1973) (3) 465, 480.)

It has also to be remembered that lack of "heroism" may not necessarily be selfishly self-directed, for the duress exerted may well extend to and threaten the lives and safety of others. . . .

V. CONCLUSION

Having considered the available material to the best of my ability, I find myself unable to accept that any ground in law, logic, morals or public policy has been established to justify withholding the plea of duress in the present case. To say, as Murnaghan J. did in *A.-G.* v. *Whelan* [1934] I.R. 518, 526, that ". . . murder is a crime so heinous that . . . in such a case the strongest duress would not be any justification" is, with respect, to beg the whole question. That murder has a unique gravity most would regard as not open to doubt, but the degree of legal criminality or blameworthiness involved in participation therein depends upon all the circumstances of the particular case, just as it does whenever the actus reus and the mens rea necessary to constitute any other offence are established. In homicide, the law already recognises degrees of criminality, notwithstanding that unlawful killing with malice aforethought has unquestionably taken place. In non-homicidal cases, the degree of criminality or blameworthiness can and should be reflected in the punishment meted out, a course which the mandatory life sentence for murder prohibits. . . . For the reasons I have sought to advance, I can find no valid ground for preventing the appellant Lynch from presenting the plea of duress, and I would therefore be for allowing his appeal. By doing so, I consider that this House would be paying due regard to those "contemporary views of what is just, what is moral, what is humane" which my noble and learned friend, Lord Diplock, described in *R.* v. *Hyam* [1975] A.C. 55, 89 [*post*, p. 374] as constituting "the underlying principle which is the justification for retaining the common law as a living source of rules binding upon all members of contemporary society in England."

Appeal allowed
Retrial ordered

[At Lynch's retrial his defence of duress was rejected by the jury and he was again convicted.]

Questions

1. Do you agree with Lord Simon that duress is a type of necessity? What arguments can be used to distinguish the two claims? See *post*, p. 229.
2. Should judicial extension of a defence be viewed in the same light as judicial extension of an offence? Lord Kilbrandon's view can be contrasted with that of Williams, *post*, p. 232.
3. On what basis can a distinction be drawn between principals in the first and second degrees? See the case below.

Abbott v. The Queen
[1977] A.C. 755
Privy Council

> The appellant claimed the defence of duress on a charge of murder as a principal in the first degree. There was evidence that he was afraid that if he did not carry out the orders of one Malik to kill the girl, Gale Benson, either he or his mother would have been killed. He had dug a hole for the body, held the girl while she was stabbed by others, and, with others, had filled in the hole while she was dying, but still alive.
> Both the trial judge and the Court of Appeal of Trinidad and Tobago held that duress was not available.

LORD SALMON delivered the majority judgment of their Lordships:
Whilst their Lordships feel bound to accept the decision of the House of Lords in *Lynch's* case they find themselves constrained to say that had they considered (which they do not) that that decision is an authority which requires the extension of the doctrine to cover cases like the present they would not have accepted it.
. . . .
The majority of the noble and learned Lords who decided *Lynch's* case certainly said nothing to support the contention now being made on behalf of the appellant. At best, from the appellant's point of view, they left the point open. Indeed there are passages in some of their speeches which suggest that duress can be of no avail to a charge of murder as principal in the first degree.
[His Lordship quoted from the speeches of Lords Morris of Borth-y-Gest and Wilberforce.]
It seems to their Lordships that if one adds these passages . . . to those of the two noble and learned Lords who dissented in *Director of Public Prosecutions for Northern Ireland* v. *Lynch* [above] the majority of the House was of the opinion that duress is not a defence to a charge of murder against anyone proved to have done the actual killing. However this may be, their Lordships are clearly of the opinion that in such a case, duress, as the law now stands, affords no defence. For reasons which will presently be explained, their Lordships whilst loyally accepting the decision in *Lynch's* case, are certainly not prepared to extend it.
When the noble and learned Lords Simon Glaisdale and Kilbrandon stated in

their dissenting speeches in *Lynch's* case that the drawing of an arbitrary line between murder as a principal in the first degree and murder as a principal in the second degree cannot be justified either morally or juridically, they clearly meant that since, rightly, it had always been accepted that duress was not a defence to a charge of murder as a principal in the first degree, the cases and dicta (e.g. Bray C.J. in *R.* v. *Brown and Morley* [1968] S.A.S.R. 467 and *R.* v. *Kray (Ronald)* 53 Cr. App. R. 569) which suggested that duress could amount to a defence to a charge of murder in the second degree should not be followed. The noble and learned Lords were clearly not conceding that if, contrary to their view, duress was capable of being a defence to a charge of murder as a principal in the second degree it should therefore be capable of being a defence to a charge of murder as a principal in the first degree.

. . . *Lynch's* case made duress available as a complete defence to anyone charged with murder as a principal in the second degree, but left untouched what for hundreds of years has never been doubted, namely that on a charge of murder, duress is of no avail to a man who does the actual killing.

Counsel for the appellant has argued that the law now presupposes a degree of heroism of which the ordinary man is incapable and which therefore should not be expected of him and that modern conditions and concepts of humanity have rendered obsolete the rule that the actual killer cannot rely on duress as a defence. Their Lordships do not agree. In the trials of those responsible for wartime atrocities such as mass killings of men, women or children, inhuman experiments on human beings, often resulting in death, and like crimes, it was invariably argued for the defence that these atrocities should be excused on the ground that they resulted from superior orders and duress: if the accused had refused to do these dreadful things, they would have been shot and therefore they should be acquitted and allowed to go free. This argument has always been universally rejected. Their Lordships would be sorry indeed to see it accepted by the common law of England.

It seems incredible to their Lordships that in any civilised society acts such as the appellant's, whatever threats may have been made to him, could be regarded as excusable or within the law. We are not living in a dream world in which the mounting wave of violence and terrorism can be contained by strict logic and intellectual niceties alone. Common sense surely reveals the added dangers to which in this modern world the public would be exposed, if the change in the law proposed on behalf of the appellant were affected. It might well, as the noble and learned Lord Simon of Glaisdale said in *Lynch's* case, prove to be a charter for terrorists, gang leaders and kidnappers. . . .

We have been reminded that it is an important part of the judge's role to adapt and develop the principles of the common law to meet the changing needs of time. We have been invited to exercise this role by changing the law so that on a charge of murder in the first degree, duress shall entitle the killer to be acquitted and go scot-free. Their Lordships certainly are very conscious that the principles of the common law must not be allowed to become sterile. The common law, as has often been said, is a living organism. . . . Their Lordships however are firmly of the opinion that the invitation extended to them on behalf of the appellant goes far beyond adapting and developing the principles of the common law. What has been suggested is the destruction of a fundamental doctrine of our law which might well have far-reaching and disastrous consequences for public safety to say nothing of its important social, ethical and maybe political implications. Such a decision would be far beyond their Lordships' powers even if they approved—as they certainly do not—of this revolutionary change in the law proposed on behalf of the appellant. Judges have no power to create new criminal offences; nor in their Lordships' opinion, for the reasons already stated, have they the power to invent a new defence to murder which is entirely contrary to fundamental legal doctrine accepted for hundreds of years without question. If a policy change of such a fundamental nature were to be made it could, in their Lordships' view, be made only by Parliament. Whilst their Lordships strongly uphold the right and indeed the duty of the judges to adapt and develop the principles of the common law in an orderly fashion they are equally opposed to any usurpation by the courts of the functions of Parliament....

LORD WILBERFORCE and LORD EDMUND-DAVIES dissenting:

The starting point in this appeal must be the decision of the House of Lords in *D.P.P. for Northern Ireland* v. *Lynch* [above] which decision was not available to the trial judge in this case or to the Court of Appeal. This established that on a murder charge the defence of duress is open to a person accused as a principal in the second degree. Not only has the actual decision in *Lynch* to be respected but also its implications, for it was based upon a consideration in some depth of topics scarcely adverted to by their Lordships in the present appeal. The question that immediately arises is whether any acceptable distinction can invariably be drawn between a principal in the first degree to murder and one in the second degree, with the result that the latter may in certain circumstances be absolved by his plea of duress, while the former may never even advance such a plea.

The simple fact is that *no* acceptable basis of distinction has even now been advanced. In *Lynch* Lord Simon of Glaisdale and Lord Kilbrandon who dissented, adverted to the absence of any valid distinction as a ground for holding that duress should be available to *neither*....

Great stress has been laid by the majority of their Lordships upon the apparent unanimity with which great writers of the past have rejected duress as a defence. But, on any view, they have to be read with circumspection in these days, for the criminal courts have long accepted duress as an available defence to a large number of crimes from which those same writers withheld it. This, again, is a topic extensively canvassed in *D.P.P. for Northern Ireland* v. *Lynch* and, while no purpose would be served by traversing it again, the point is one to be borne in mind in assessing the present day authority of writers of earlier centuries and of Stephen in the last century. Their work needs to be looked at with a fresh eye and with a readiness to regard it as at least conceivable that what Hale and others propounded as the law in their days does not necessarily hold good today. This is in fact what the courts, in the cases cited in *Lynch*, have been doing continuously over the last century. In the result, it is inaccurate to treat *Lynch* as having invented an entirely new defence contrary to fundamental legal doctrine. As Lord Wilberforce said, at p. 685:

> "The House is not inventing a new defence; on the contrary, it would not discharge its judicial duty if it failed to define the law's attitude to this particular defence in particular circumstances."

And, *Lynch* having been decided as it was, it is still less permissible to claim that acceptance of this appellant's submissions threatens, in their Lordships' words, "the destruction of a fundamental doctrine of our law."

Something must be said about the significance attached by the majority of their Lordships to the absence of any direct decision that it is open to principals in the first degree to murder to advance a plea of duress. As to this, two observations need to be made: (i) There is little use in looking back earlier than 1898, for until then an accused could not give evidence on his own behalf; and to advance such a plea without any opportunity of explaining to the jury why he acted as he did would be to attempt something foredoomed to failure. It is significant, too, that the increasingly humane attitude of the courts in relation to duress has developed since the gag on accused persons was removed. (ii) As was pointed out in *Lynch*, the balance of such judicial authority as exists was against the admission of the defence of duress in cases of first degree murder. But this balance was a weak one and one which both of us thought might have to yield in an actual case. While there are in the law reports a number of obiter dicta (that is, in cases where murder was not charged) to the effect that duress is not available in murder, apparently in only one case has it been directly so held. The one exception is nearly 140 years old—*R.* v. *Tyler* (1838) 8 C. & P. 616 where Lord Denman C.J., using unqualified terms which certainly cannot be regarded as accurately stating the law of today, said, at p. 620:

> "It cannot be too often repeated, that the apprehension of personal danger does not furnish any excuse for assisting in doing any act which is illegal."

Apart from the unqualified and therefore unacceptable generality of those words, the decision is for additional reasons an unsatisfactory guide to the proper outcome of the present appeal: see *D.P.P. for Northern Ireland* v. *Lynch*. It has further to be borne in mind that the present case involves a feature (viz. threats of death to an innocent third person) which has not been considered in the United Kingdom, or so far as we are aware, elsewhere in the Commonwealth except in the Victoria case of *R.* v. *Hurley and Murray* [1967] V.R. 526.

Lynch having been decided as it was, the most striking feature of the present appeal is the lack of any indication, in the judgment of the majority *why* a flat declaration that in no circumstances whatsoever may the actual killer be absolved by a plea of duress makes for sounder law and better ethics. In truth, the contrary is the case. For example D attempts to kill P but, though injuring him, fails. When charged with attempted murder he may plead duress (*R.* v. *Fagan* (unreported), September 20 1974, and several times referred to in *Lynch*). Later P dies and D is charged with his murder; if the majority of their Lordships are right, he now has no such plea available. Again, no one can doubt that our law would today allow duress to be pleaded in answer to a charge, under section 18 of the Offences Against the Person Act 1861, of wounding with intent. Yet, here again, should the victim die after the conclusion of the first trial, the accused when faced with a murder charge would be bereft of any such defence. It is not the mere lack of logic that troubles one. It is when one stops to consider why duress is *ever* permitted as a defence even to charges of great gravity that the lack of any moral reason justifying its *automatic* exclusion in such cases as the present becomes so baffling and so important.

The majority have deemed it right to resurrect in the present appeal objections to the admissibility of a plea of duress which, if accepted, would leave *Lynch* with only vestigial authority, even though the decisions resulted from their demolition. One example of this is the alleged ease with which bogus pleas of duress can be advanced, and the so-called "charter for terrorists, gang leaders and kidnappers" originally raised by Lord Simon of Glaisdale in *D.P.P. for Northern Ireland* v. *Lynch* just as though the plea of duress had merely to be raised for an acquittal automatically to follow. But the realistic view is that, the more dreadful the circumstances of the killing, the heavier the evidential burden of an accused advancing such a plea, and the stronger and more irresistible the duress needed before it could be regarded as affording any defence. . . .

To hold that a principal in the first degree in murder is never in any circumstances to be entitled to plead duress, whereas a principal in the second degree may, is to import the possibility of grave injustice into the common law. Such a conclusion should not be arrived at unless supported by compelling authority or by the demands of public policy shown to operate differently in the two cases. There are no authorities compelling this Board so to hold, nor are there reasons of public policy present in this case which are lacking in the case of principals in the second degree.

It has to be said with all respect that the majority opinion of their Lordships amounts, in effect, to side-stepping the decision in *Lynch* and even were that constitutionally appropriate, to do it without advancing cogent grounds.

Appeal dismissed

Note

Dennis, "Duress, Murder and Criminal Responsibility" (1980) 96 L.Q.R. 208, 237: "The decision in *Lynch* should logically have been extended to give a defence of duress to a person charged with murder as a principal in the first degree, and there were no convincing reasons of morality, principle or policy why it should not have been." But Wasik, in "Duress and Criminal Responsibility" [1977] Crim. L.R. 453, 462, concludes that "It seems more coherent, on balance, that duress should be an issue relevant to mitigation only. . . . The artificial distinction concerning murder . . . should be removed. This would necessitate the abolition of the mandatory penalty for murder . . . [on which] change is not likely to come soon. It is submitted that a good alternative would be to allow duress to operate to reduce murder to manslaughter."

R. v. Fitzpatrick

[1977] N.I. 20

Court of Criminal Appeal in Northern Ireland

The appellant shot and killed a man during an armed robbery. He and his accomplice were members of the IRA. He was charged with murder, robbery and membership of a proscribed organisation. He pleaded duress. He was induced to join the IRA when he was 19 in the belief that civil war was imminent. He said he knew that the IRA was an illegal organisation and that he might be required to take part in serious crimes. When he tried to leave the IRA after nine months he was put against a wall, kicked, and told to take part in a robbery. When he said he would leave the country he was told his parents would be shot.

LOWRY L.C.J.: The first ground of appeal in this court was:

"1. The learned trial judge erred in law and misdirected himself on the question of the availability of the defence of duress.

(a) The learned trial judge was wrong in directing himself that such defence was not available to an accused person who had voluntarily joined a terrorist organisation which engaged in violence.

(b) If the dicta in *R.* v. *Lynch* and the other authorities are open to the interpretation put upon them by the trial judge, the learned trial judge misdirected himself by concluding that subsequent attempts by the accused to dissociate himself from such organisation were of no avail in laying a basis for restoring the defence of duress in this case. The evidence as to how the accused joined the Irish Republican Army and his effort to leave were not seriously contested."

As to ground 1 (a), we consider that the learned trial judge properly directed himself and that he correctly applied the legal principles to the facts.

Counsel on both sides have informed us that the point is devoid of judicial authority and we have not found anything to suggest the contrary. Therefore we have to decide, in the absence of judicial decisions, what is the common law. Assistance may be sought from the opinions of text-writers, judicial dicta and the reports of Commissions and legal committees, and from analogies with legal systems which share our common law heritage, with a view to considering matters of general principle and arriving at the answer.

[His Lordship then referred to the Canadian Criminal Code, s. 17, the New Zealand Crimes Act 1961, s. 24, the Queensland Criminal Code (1899), s. 31 (4), the Tasmanian Criminal Code, s. 20, the New York Penal Code (1967), s. 35, the Royal Commission Draft Code (1879), s. 23 and *Perkins on Criminal Law* (1957), s. 35.]

We consider that the widespread adoption of such limiting provisions with regard to duress shows that the framers of the codes and drafts which we have mentioned considered that this exclusory doctrine was already part of the common law and the Law Commission's recommendation [Working Paper No. 55, § 26] indicates the view of a distinguished body of jurists (whose recommendations are in general favourable to duress as a defence), that participation in unlawful associations or conspiracies should disqualify the accused from relying on it. . . .

We turn now to *R.* v. *Lynch* [*ante,* p. 203] for such indications as may be deduced from the opinions delivered in the House of Lords.

[His Lordship quoted from the speeches in that case.]

We recognise that the issue which we have to decide was not before the House in *R.* v. *Lynch* and that we cannot seek to extract a binding rule from the passages we have cited, but we believe that their lordships' observations collectively tend towards a rejection of the present appellant's argument.

Lord Edmund-Davies' reference to Lord Diplock's observations in *Hyam's* case helpfully reminds us of the common law approach to a problem when, as here, there is a lack of judicial authority. We are not here dealing with the doctrine of precedent or custom, for none has been established, but with the use of analogy and the observance of what Sir Frederick Pollock in his essay on Judicial Caution and Valour called "the duty of the Court to keep the rules of law in harmony with the enlightened common sense of the nation." This is not a subject which is governed by any doctrines that can be recognised as "rules of the common law," and therefore we must resort to what we believe, within a framework of fairness and justice to the individual, to represent expediency, reasonableness and widely accepted notions of morality. The codes and draft codes to which we have referred and the signs of what is accepted as the common law in the United States furnish, in our opinion, strong indications of the answer to which these criteria should lead us in relation to the questions we have to decide. As Cardozo J. pointed out when considering The Nature of the Judicial Process, "The final cause of law is the welfare of society." So far as we may derive assistance from analogy, we have been referred to the law on voluntary drunkenness as affecting criminal responsibility and to the ineffectiveness of pleading the orders of a superior when answering to a criminal charge: *R.* v. *Axtell* (1660) Kel. 13, where this plea was, not surprisingly, of little avail to one of the regicides. One might also perhaps have regard to the *volenti* principle in relation to tortious liability.

In the Law Commission's Working Paper No. 55 it is stated (correctly, as we respectfully consider) that the defence of duress may be regarded as a concession to human infirmity in the face of an overwhelming evil threatened by another (para. 3). In this respect it differs from the doctrine of duress in contract, where the principle is to restore the innocent victim of duress to his rightful position vis-a-vis the other party to the contract who has coerced him into an unfair bargain. Again, returning to the criminal sphere, the defence of duress differs from those of self-defence and provocation, since self-defence exculpates the perpetrator who defends himself against a wrongful attacker and the defence of provocation, which is also concerned with the wrongful behaviour of the victim towards the perpetrator, may mitigate the punishment and can reduce murder to manslaughter. In criminal law, therefore, the defence of duress does not derive from the wrongful conduct of the other party to a contract or of a victim who has himself provoked the criminal act of the accused, but enures for the benefit of a person who has been compelled by the coercion of a third party to commit a crime against society and against an *innocent* victim. Accordingly, it is reasonable to expect that the accused, if he is to benefit from this defence, should himself be morally innocent.

The defence of duress is based on a balance of moral factors. It abandons what may be called the higher morality which adopts the view that death is preferable to dishonour and that man has a paramount duty, at whatever cost to himself, not to inflict unjustified harm on his fellow man. In relation to first degree murder at least, an analogous principle apparently still holds (*R.* v. *Abbott* [above]) but it is applied more pragmatically than ethically, since a first degree murderer whose only intention was to inflict serious personal injury is morally less culpable than an accomplice in a planned murder, or indeed than a person who attempts to murder. Generally speaking, however, the defence of duress looks to a practical morality. Crime deliberately committed is excusable if the coercive threat to the perpetrator is more than he can be expected to resist. Thus moral excusability erases the criminality of the guilty act and the guilty mind, because the crime was committed, and the conscious intention to commit it was formed, under a compulsion so strong that it is said that the perpetrator ought not to be expected to resist it. Putting the matter thus one can appreciate an argument for saying that duress if proved should merely be reflected in the severity of the punishment and not in exculpation of the crime, but it is now too late to pretend that this approach would reflect the common law. And yet the authorities show that the availability of duress as a defence is quite strictly, and in a sense arbitrarily, limited by reference to the nature of the threats which may be relied on by the accused as constituting duress, even though other kinds of threats might be still more oppressive and effective. This limitation is, incidentally, maintained in the codes and draft codes to which we have referred.

If a person behaves immorally by, for example, committing himself to an unlawful conspiracy, he ought not to be able to take advantage of the pressure exercised on him by his fellow criminals in order to put on when it suits him the breastplate of righteousness. An even more rigorous view which, as we have seen, prevails in the United States, but does not arise for consideration in this case, is that, if a person is culpably negligent or reckless in exposing himself to the risk of being subjected to coercive pressure, he too loses the right to call himself innocent by reason of his succumbing to that pressure.

A practical consideration is that, if some such limit on the defendant's duress does not exist, it would be only too easy for every member of an unlawful conspiracy and for every member of a gang except the leader to obtain an immunity denied to ordinary citizens. Indeed, the better organised the conspiracy and the more brutal its internal discipline, the surer would be the defence of duress for its members. It can hardly be supposed that the common law tolerates such an absurdity.

In making this last observation we are not saying that the ease with which a defence can be put up is a reason for not allowing that defence and impartially considering it when made. Still less do we subscribe to any doctrine that, when society is threatened, the ordinary protection of the common law can, except by statute, be withheld even from those who are alleged to have conspired against it: "Amid the clash of arms the laws are not silent." On the other hand what we are contemplating here is the possibility that any band of criminals could so organise their affairs in advance as to confer mutual immunity in respect of any crime to which duress provides a defence. . . .

We are continually reminded that the method of the common law is not to draw lines or to attempt exhaustive definitions. It is often enough to say that one knows on which side of the line a case falls without drawing the line itself: *Hobbs* v. *L. & S.W. Rly.* (1875) L.R. 10 Q.B. 111, 121, *per* Blackburn J., *Mayor of Southport* v. *Morriss* [1893] 1 Q.B. 359, 361, *per* Lord Coleridge C.J. It may be tempting to go further and try to draw up a system, but it is not always wise. This court is satisfied that there are circumstances in which persons who associate with violent criminals and voluntarily expose themselves to the risk of compulsion to commit criminal acts cannot according to the common law avail themselves of the defence of duress. We are further satisfied that, wherever the line should be drawn, this appellant falls on the side of it where that defence is not available to him.

. . . [W]e guard ourselves against the use of any expression which might tend to confine the application of that principle to illegal, in the narrow sense of proscribed, organisations. A person may become associated with a sinister group of men with criminal objectives and coercive methods of ensuring that their lawless enterprises are carried out and thereby voluntarily expose himself to illegal compulsion, whether or not the group is or becomes a proscribed organisation.

Nor indeed, so far as the facts are concerned, do we consider that the evidence of the nature and activities of the relevant organisations has necessarily to be the same formal and precise character as it apparently was in this case.

As to ground 1 (b), which we have set out above but which did not seem to be pressed in this court, here again we agree with the trial judge. To say that the appellant could revive for his own benefit the defence of duress by trying to leave the organisation is no more cogent an argument than saying that he tried unavailingly to resist the order to carry out a robbery. In each case the answer is the same: if a person voluntarily exposes and submits himself, as the appellant did, to illegal compulsion, he cannot rely on the duress to which he has voluntarily exposed himself as an excuse either in respect of the crimes he commits against his will or in respect of his continued but unwilling association with those capable of exercising upon him the duress which he calls in aid.

The second ground of appeal claiming that the appellant ought to have been acquitted because the Crown failed to discharge the onus of proof in relation to the defence of duress need not be considered, because it is framed simply as a consequence of the hoped-for success of ground 1.

The third ground of appeal was:

> "3. By reason of the foregoing matters the learned trial judge precluded himself from dealing with the charge of murder on the basis that the reason for the accused being in the premises taking part in an armed robbery was because of duress and while the duress itself did not extend to forcing the accused to commit a killing none the less it was a relevant factor on the issue as to whether the killing could have amounted to an unlawful homicide not murder that the accused was forced to take part in an armed robbery with a loaded weapon whereby through the accused's fear at the scene or by mischance a person might be shot."

This ground is based on the fallacy of confusing the unwillingness of the accused to commit a robbery with his alleged lack of intent to commit a crime which (having regard to its fatal consequences) amounted to murder. The distinction between the unwillingness to commit a crime and the absence of criminal intent has been exhaustively analysed in the judgment of the majority in this court in *R.* v. *Lynch* [1975] N.I. 35 which on this point was unanimously accepted by the House of Lords. In this case, not only was the accused not subjected to duress to commit murder or to inflict serious personal injury on the deceased, but, even if he had been subjected to such duress, he would still have committed the guilty act with a guilty mind. . . .

Appeal dismissed

Law Commission Report on Defences of General Application, No. 83, 1977

"*The arguments against a defence of duress*

§ 2.14. Those who favour the conclusion that duress should not afford a defence which absolves from criminal liability contend that it can never be justifiable for a person to do wrong, in particular to do serious harm to another, merely to avoid some harm to himself; that it is not for the individual to balance the doing of wrong against the avoidance of harm to himself. They argue that duress does not destroy the will or negative intention in the legal sense, but that it merely deflects the will so that intention conflicts with the wish; in short that it provides a motive for the wrongful act and that motive is, on general principle, irrelevant to whether a crime has been committed. On the more practical aspect it is said that the criminal law is itself a system of threats of pains and penalties, which would be undermined if some countervailing system of threats were allowed to override it, and that to allow this to happen would be to provide a charter for terrorists, gang leaders and kidnappers, allowing criminals of notorious violence to confer on others by terrorism immunity from the criminal law. . . .

The arguments for a defence of duress

§ 2.16 The main opposing argument is that the law should not insist upon condemning a person who acts under compulsion which he is unable to resist; that in doing so it would be making excessive demands on human nature and imposing penalties in circumstances where they are unjustified as retribution and irrelevant as a deterrent. The law must recognise that the instinct and perhaps the duty of self-preservation is powerful and natural, and that it would be "censorious and inhumane [if it] did not recognise the appalling plight of a person who perhaps suddenly finds his life in jeopardy unless he submits and obeys." This argument is most cogently advanced by the majority in Lynch's case and convinces us that it would be quite unjust that a person who has committed an offence only because of threats which he could not withstand (subject to qualifications as to the nature of the threats) should face trial and conviction with the obloquy inherent therein.

§ 2.17 We do not think that it is sufficient in the true case of duress for account to be taken of the duress by the exercise of some discretionary power, whether in regard to the bringing of proceedings, by mitigation of punishment, by the use of the power of the Parole Board or by the exercise of the royal prerogative of pardon. From its very nature duress is a question appropriate for determination by a jury after consideration of all the circumstances including the nature of the offence and the characteristics of the defendant as shown in the evidence and his appearance before them. While these features are, of course, before the trial judge, they may not necessarily be available in the same detail to the prosecutor, the Parole Board or those advising the Sovereign. Further, as Lord Edmund-Davies points out [in *Lynch*], in the nature of things there can be no assurance that even a completely convincing plea of duress will lead to an absolute discharge, and, of course, such a course would not be possible where the sentence is a mandatory one. . . .

§ 2.19 On the more practical point that the defence of duress offers a charter to thugs and terrorists by exonerating those whom they may intimidate from the crimes they may be forced to commit, we would point out that, over the many years that duress has been accepted as a defence, the few reported cases in which it has arisen for consideration, and the even fewer occasions when it has apparently been successfully relied upon, seem to indicate that the fears are without serious foundation. It is after all a defence of last resort, which entails acceptance of participation in the offence, and a degree of courage is required to advance the defence if the threats are really serious and convincing because of the possibility of reprisals against the defendant or those close to him. Finally, protection against the likelihood of the defence succeeding where it should not lies in the safeguard of the decision of a properly instructed jury. It is, perhaps, significant that Lynch was convicted when he was retried for aiding and abetting the murder of a policeman by driving the murderer to and from the scene. . . .

Conclusion as to duress as a defence

§ 2.21 In our view it would not be right now for the criminal law to insist that in no circumstances should duress ever be a defence to criminal liability. . . .

To what offences should duress apply?

. . . .

§ 2.43 It has been suggested that there is much to be said for the view that on a charge of murder duress, like provocation, should not entitle the accused to a complete acquittal but should reduce murder to manslaughter and thus give the court power to pass whatever sentence might be appropriate. It is our view, however, that where the requirements of the defence as we have defined it are present there is no justification for any finding of guilt against a defendant, any more than there is in the case where self-defence has been established. The nature of the duress which will exonerate will, on our recommendations, vary with the nature of the offence, and where the duress is so compelling that the defendant could not reasonably have been expected to resist it, perhaps being a threat not to the defendant himself but to an innocent hostage dear to him, it would in our view be unjust that the defendant should suffer the stigma of a conviction even for manslaughter. We do not think that any social purpose is served by requiring the law to prescribe such standards of determination and heroism.

§ 2.44 We recommend that duress should be available as a defence to a defendant charged with murder as an actual perpetrator. This makes it unnecessary to consider whether any convincing distinction can be drawn between that case and the case of a defendant charged with murder as an aider and abettor.

Summary of recommendations

§ 2.46

(1) . . . .

(2) . . . .

(3) . . . .

(4) The defendant must believe that—

(*a*) the harm threatened is death or serious personal injury, whether physical or mental (paragraphs 2.25 and 2.27);

(*b*) the threat will be carried out immediately, or, if not immediately, before he can have any real opportunity of seeking official protection (paragraph 2.31); and

(*c*) there is no other way of avoiding or preventing the harm threatened (paragraph 2.27).

(5) The threat must be such that the defendant could not reasonably be expected to resist it in all the circumstances of the case, including the nature of the offence, the defendant's belief as to the three matters in subparagraph (4) above, and any other relevant circumstances personal to him (paragraph 2.28).

(6) . . . .

(7) . . . .

(8) The defence should be excluded where the defendant is voluntarily and without reasonable cause in a situation in which he knows he will or may be subjected to duress to induce him to commit such an offence as that with which he is charged (paragraph 2.38)."

Note

In "Murder under Duress," (1978) 28 U.T.L.J. 369, Sir Rupert Cross considered the Law Commission's proposals "to be better than the provisions of any code of which I am aware" but expressed doubts about the proviso that the threat must be such that the defendant could not reasonably be expected to resist, p. 379:

> "If the Law Commission's proposals are adopted, the jurors will not only have to perform considerable feats of empathy; they will also be confronted with serious problems when deciding whether the defendant could reasonably have been expected to resist the threats. What are to be counted among his relevant 'personal circumstances'? Are the facts that he is old, undistinguished, and unimportant, as contrasted with the youth, distinction, and importance of the person he is ordered to kill, to be taken into consideration? What if a police officer entrusted with the task of guarding a house occupied by A assists someone who threatens him with serious personal injury or death to enter the house in the certain knowledge that A will be killed by that person? It is arguable that the defence of duress should never be available in such circumstances.
>
> In spite of these queries and many others that could be raised, there is perhaps no better way of deciding the issue whether the defendant's freedom of choice was grossly impaired by duress than by asking the jury whether, in all the circumstances of the case, he could reasonably have been expected to resist the threats. But this assumes that the criminal law with regard to excuses should be fully codified. Is there not something to be said for a clause containing a declaration that duress shall be a defence to all charges, together perhaps with a definition of the term, leaving the judges to fill in details concerning the applicability of the defence? The days of the judicial creation of offences are fortunately over, but, in situations in which the common law is undeveloped, why curtail the existing powers of the judiciary?"

See also the comment by A. T. H. Smith, [1978] Crim. L.R. 122. It is interesting to compare the Law Commission's proposals on duress with its stance on necessity, see *post*, p. 231.

2. NECESSITY

(i) Necessity and Homicide

R. v. Dudley and Stephens
(1884) 14 Q.B.D. 273
Queen's Bench Division

> D and S and a boy were cast away from a ship on the high seas and drifted for twenty days in an open boat. They had hardly any food or water during that time, and fearing they would all die soon unless they obtained some sustenance D and S killed the boy, who was likely to die first anyway, and ate his flesh. Four days later they were rescued, and were subsequently indicted for the boy's murder. The jury found the facts of the case in a special verdict and the case was adjourned for argument before five judges.

LORD COLERIDGE C.J.: ... Now it is admitted that the deliberate killing of this unoffending and unresisting boy was clearly murder, unless the killing can be justified by some well-recognised excuse admitted by the law. It is further admitted that there was in this case no such excuse, unless the killing was justified by what has been called "necessity." But the temptation to the act which existed here was not what the law has ever called necessity. Nor is this to be regretted. Though law and morality are not the same, and many things may be immoral which are not necessarily illegal, yet the absolute divorce of law from morality would be of fatal consequence; and such divorce would follow if the temptation to murder in this case were to be held by law an absolute defence of it. It is not so. To preserve one's life is generally speaking a duty, but it may be the plainest and the highest duty to sacrifice it. War is full of instances in which it is a man's duty not to live, but to die. The duty, in case of shipwreck, of a captain to his crew, of the crew to the passengers, of soldiers to women and children, as in the noble case of the *Birkenhead*; these duties impose on man the moral necessity, not of the preservation, but of the sacrifice of their lives for others, from which in no country, least of all, it is to be hoped, in England, will men shrink, as indeed, they have not shrunk. It is not correct, therefore, to say that there is any absolute or unqualified necessity to preserve one's life. "*Necesse est ut eam, non ut vivam,*" is a saying of a Roman officer quoted by Lord Bacon himself with high eulogy in the very chapter on necessity to which so much reference has been made. It would be a very easy and cheap display of common-place learning to quote from Greek and Latin authors, from Horace, from Juvenal, from Cicero, from Euripides, passage after passage, in which the duty of dying for others has been laid down in glowing and emphatic language as resulting from the principles of heathen ethics; it is enough in a Christian country to remind ourselves of the Great Example whom we profess to follow. It is not needful to point out the awful danger of admitting the principle which has been contended for. Who is to be the judge of this sort of necessity? By what measure is the comparative value of lives to be measured? Is it to be strength, or intellect, or what? It is plain that the principle leaves to him who is to profit by it to determine the necessity which will justify him in deliberately taking another's life to save his own. In this case the weakest, the youngest, the most unresisting, was chosen. Was it more necessary to kill him than one of the grown men? The answer must be "No." . . .

It must not be supposed that in refusing to admit temptation to be an excuse for crime it is forgotten how terrible the temptation was; how awful the suffering; how hard in such trials to keep the judgment straight and the conduct pure. We are often compelled to set up standards we cannot reach ourselves, and to lay down rules which we could not ourselves satisfy. But a man has no right to declare temptation to be an excuse, though he might himself have yielded to it, nor allow compassion for the criminal to change or weaken in any manner the legal definition of the crime. It is therefore our duty to declare that the prisoners' act in this case was wilful murder, that the facts as stated in the verdict are no legal justification of the homicide; and to say that in our unanimous opinion the prisoners are upon this special verdict guilty of murder.

Sentence of death
Commuted later to six months' imprisonment

Question

Consider and compare the following examples often found in text-books:

A shipwrecked sailor, clinging to a plank which will only support the weight of one man, prevents another from grasping the plank, so that that other dies by drowning.

The man on the plank is pushed off by the swimmer, who takes his place, leaving him to drown.

The lower of two roped rock-climbers slips and falls. The upper is not strong enough to hold him, and to save himself from a certain fall, cuts the lower man free, so that he falls to his death.

Note

In *U.S.* v. *Holmes* (1842) 26 Fed. Cas. 360, the accused was convicted of the manslaughter of 16 passengers whom he had thrown out of an overcrowded lifeboat. The judge would it seems have allowed a defence of necessity if the choice had been made by the drawing of lots.

The extracts below illustrate the moral and philosophical challenge which necessity as a defence to homicide presents.

Cross "Murder under Duress" (1978) 28 U.T.L.J. 369, at 377

"Speaking of the hypothetical case of the two shipwrecked mariners struggling for a plank only large enough for one, [Kant] said: 'A penal law applying to such a situation could never have the effect intended, for the threat of an evil that is still uncertain (being condemned to death by a judge) cannot outweigh the fear of an evil that is certain (being drowned). Hence we must judge that, although an act of self-preservation through violence is not inculpable, it is still unpunishable.' . . .

[I]n the context, I find myself wholly unable to distinguish this defence from that of duress, and I feel bound to say that the English Law Commission has achieved the apotheosis of absurdity by recommending that our proposed criminal code should provide for a defence of duress while excluding any general defence of necessity. Surely Lord Simon of Glaisdale was speaking in unanswerable terms when he said in the course of his dissenting speech in *Lynch* [*ante*, p. 203] 'It would be a travesty of justice and an invitation to anarchy to declare that an innocent life may be taken with impunity if the threat to one's own life is from a terrorist but not when from a natural disaster like ship- or plane-wreck.'"

Kenny, Freewill and Responsibility (1978, Routledge & Kegan Paul), pp. 36–38

"In everyday language people are often said to be compelled to do things when no actual force is used but the actions are performed to avert the threat of violent action or imminent disaster. These are cases where it will be natural for the agent to say that he 'had no choice' . . . but in fact the action is a voluntary one, arising out of a choice between evils. When the choice . . . is posed as a result of the wrongful threats of another, lawyers speak of 'duress'; when it arises through the operation of natural causes, they prefer to speak of 'necessity.' . . . To me the decision [in *Dudley & Stephens]* seems ethically sound. . . . The principle that one should never intentionally take innocent life would be contested by supporters of euthanasia. . . . The decision in *Dudley and Stephens* can be justified by the narrower principle that one should not take innocent life in order to save one's own life. This principle seems to me, as it did to Lord Coleridge in 1884, to be correct: it seems likely to reduce the overall number of innocent deaths. Certainly I would rather be in an open boat with companions who accepted the principle than in company with lawyers who accepted necessity as a defence to murder.

The moral objection to necessity as a defence applies equally to duress. *Dudley and Stephens*, it seems, is still authoritative in law. There seems something paradoxical in a state of law which refused necessity as a defence to murder, but which allows duress even though all the objections to allowing necessity apply equally to allowing duress, while the allowance of duress is open to the further objection that it puts a premium on murderous threats."

Williams, C.L.G.P., § 237

". . . . Where it is merely a case of life for life, the doctrine of necessity must generally be silent, because the two lives must be accounted equal in the eye of the law and there is nothing to choose between them. Necessity cannot justify in such circumstances; but they may go so strongly in alleviation that the accused is discharged without punishment (where this is possible) or pardoned. The technical conviction merely records that in the eye of the law the act was wrongful. The necessary and reasonable consequence of this view is that resistance to the act on the part of the victim is lawful.

It seems that the position is different where the killing results in a net saving of life. Here it seems that the killing should be regarded as not merely excusing from punishment but as legally justifying. We need a general rule, and one allowing necessity as a defence to homicide where the minority are killed to preserve the majority is on the whole more satisfactory than the opposite.

A strong instance of this kind of justification is the action of a ship's captain in a wreck. He can determine who are to enter the first lifeboat; he can forbid overcrowding; and it makes no difference that the passengers who are not allowed to enter the lifeboat will inevitably perish with the ship. The captain, in choosing who are to live, is not guilty of killing those who remain. He would not be so guilty even though he kept some of the passengers back from the boat at revolver-point. . . ."

A.L.I., Model Penal Code, s. 3.02

Conduct which the actor believes necessary to avoid a harm or evil to himself is justifiable provided that (1) the harm or evil sought to be avoided by such conduct is greater than that sought to be prevented by the law defining the offence charged. . . .

See also Gross, *A Theory of Criminal Justice* (Oxford, 1979), pp. 26, 27.

(ii) Necessity and offences other than homicide

The evils between which the choice is being made do not of course have to involve loss of life. In two cases the question has arisen, collaterally, whether necessity of lessening the risk to life can be argued as a defence to a minor traffic infraction. In *Buckoke* v. *G.L.C.* [1971] Ch. 655 the Court of Appeal had to consider the lawfulness of London Fire Brigade Order No. 144/8 which stated that drivers of fire engines were under an obligation to obey traffic light signals but went on to give advice as to the precautions to observe if a driver 'decides to proceed against the red light.' Lord Denning at pp. 668, 669:

"During the argument I raised the question: Might not the driver of a fire engine be able to raise the defence of necessity? I put this illustration: A driver of a fire escape with ladders approaches the traffic lights. He sees 200 yards down the road a blazing house with a man at an upstairs window in extreme peril. The road is clear in all directions. At that moment the lights turn red. Is the driver to wait for 60 seconds, or more, for the lights to turn green? If the driver waits for that time, the man's life will be lost. I suggested to both counsel that the driver might be excused in crossing the lights to save the man. He might have the defence of necessity. Both counsel denied it. They would not allow him any defence in law. The circumstances went to mitigation, they said, and did not take away his guilt. If counsel are correct—and I accept that they are—nevertheless such a man should not be prosecuted. He should be congratulated. . . .

I take it, therefore, that the commissioner of police can give a policy direction to his men saying they need not prosecute a fireman for crossing the lights at red when there is no danger. If the commissioner of police can do this, I see no reason why the chief officer of the fire brigade should not do likewise. He can say to his men: "So long as you stop and see that all is clear before crossing the lights, no disciplinary action will be taken against you." That is a justifiable administrative step taken by him in the public interest."

[The particular question in this case is of academic interest only since drivers of fire engines, police cars and ambulances are now allowed in emergencies to regard red traffic lights as warnings to give way (Traffic Signs Regulations and General Directions, S.I. 1975 No. 1536 reg. 34 (1) (b)). They are also permitted to exceed speed limits (Road Traffic Regulation Act 1967, s. 79).]

However, the aversion of the common law to a necessity principle is not complete. In *Johnson* v. *Phillips* [1976] 1 W.L.R. 65, a motorist was instructed by a police officer to reverse the wrong way down a narrow one-way street in order to allow ambulances access to injured persons further up the street. On his refusal he was charged with wilful obstruction of a constable in the execution of his duty. Wien J., p. 69:

"The precise question that has to be answered in the instant case may be put thus: has a constable in purported exercise of his power to control traffic on a public road the right under common law to disobey a traffic regulation such as going the wrong way along a one-way street? If he himself has that right then it follows that he can oblige others to comply with his instructions to disobey such a regulation. If, for example, a bomb had been planted in The Windsor public house and the exit from Cannon Street had in some way been blocked, could he lawfully reverse a police vehicle and oblige any other motorist then present in the road to reverse his own vehicle? The answer is yes, provided that in the execution of his duty he was acting to protect life or property: see *Hoffman* v. *Thomas* [1974] 1 W.L.R. 374, 379. . . . In the judgment of this court a constable would be entitled, and indeed under a duty, to give such instruction if it were reasonably necessary for the protection of life or property."

Williams (Commenting on Law Commission Report No. 83 [post] [1978] Crim. L.R. 128 at 131)

"It perhaps says something about the attitude of the bench to legal defences that this solitary decision represents an acceptance of necessity as a reason not for acquitting but for convicting. . . . On a narrow interpretation the decision justifies the driver in reversing in such circumstances only when required to do so by the police. But is it seriously suggested that a driver would be guilty of an offence if he reversed on his own initiative to allow the passage of ambulances? And what defence could he possibly have under the present law except that of necessity?"

The Supreme Court of Canada has recognised a common law defence of necessity: *Morgentaler* v. *The Queen* [1976] 1 S.C.R. 616. See Leigh, "Necessity and the Case of Dr. Morgentaler" [1978] Crim. L.R. 151. See also *Bourne, post,* p. 457.

(iii) Law Commission Recommendations

Law Com. No. 83

"§ 4.28 The principal difference between duress and necessity, as we have noted, lies in the source of the threatened harm: in the case of the former it always proceeds from another's wrongdoing. This difference was noted by the [Working

Paper, No. 55], which also pointed out that necessity, in contrast to duress is most frequently discussed in the case of minor offences. Neither difference, it suggested 'can be regarded as an adequate juristic basis for permitting one defence to be raised but denying the other' (para. 29). So far as the second difference is concerned, we have come to the conclusion that the difficulties attaching to a general defence extending to minor offences would outweigh its advantages, and that it is preferable for awkward situations which involve technical breaches of such offences to be dealt with by other means. The other difference requires a further brief comment at this stage.

§ 4.29 Any general defence ought, we think, to be capable of dealing with the exceptional and difficult case, and to apply to all offences save any to which, on rational and defensible grounds, an exception is thought to be desirable. In the case of duress, the form of defence we are recommending does, we believe, cope with the exceptional and difficult cases which may arise out of the various forms of illegal threats made by one person against another, and it is limited in such a way that we consider it requires no exceptions to be made as regards the offences in respect of which the defence may be raised.

§ 4.30 . . . It is probable that situations where necessity may be in issue are so diverse as not to be readily classifiable; and in this respect the difference between, on the one hand, necessity and, on the other, duress and other defences applicable in more narrowly defined circumstances, such as self-defence, is perhaps more fundamental than the Working Party appreciated. . . .

§ 4.31 Furthermore, even if a general defence were thought feasible there are a number of offences, among them the most serious of all, in relation to which, as we have seen, the operation of the defence would have to be excluded. Those exceptions, in particular those relating to murder and some serious offences against the person, would be necessary because of the unexplored implications the defence would have for sensitive questions of ethics and social responsibility, or because of the unacceptable results which might ensue from the application of the defence in special cases. Such exceptions, made necessary by expediency rather than principle, weigh further against the view that a general defence is desirable.

. . . .

§ 4.33 We have indicated that any general defence might sometimes be uncertain in operation; that various qualifications would be needed to the generality of its operation; that, in respect of some important offences, such as murder, exceptions to its application would be required, while in respect of minor offences, it would be preferable for no defence to be available; and, finally, that in respect of yet other offences, there is probably little need for any defence. These considerations lead us to recommend that there should be no general defence of necessity in the Code. We indicated at the outset that it is very improbable that any such defence exists at common law. For the avoidance of doubt, we recommend that, if any such defence does exist, it should be abolished."

[*cf.* the Model Penal Code, *ante*, p. 230 and Cross, *ante*, p. 229.]

Williams [1978] Crim. L.R. 128: commenting on the Law Commission's proposal that any defence of necessity which may exist should be abolished:

"The . . . proposal seems to exhibit a misunderstanding of the rationale of codification. This is to enable the citizen to know (at least if he takes legal advice) what conduct is penalised, so that he may not have to guess whether what he does is punishable. There will always be a degree of uncertainty in the application of the law, but the object is to take from the courts their powers of extending the area of legal prohibition except to the extent that these powers are inherent in the judicial process. Of late years the courts have themselves surrendered their power to add to offences under the head of public mischief, but they retain the power of extensive interpretation of common law crimes of vague ambit, like public mischief and the corruption of public morals. Reducing these offences to statutory form will clarify them one way or the other.

It by no means follows that it should be any part of the purpose of a code to get rid of open-ended defences, or to fetter the power of the courts to create new defences in the name of the common law. That the courts have power to enlarge defences is sometimes denied by the judges, just as they deny in terms their power to enlarge offences; but history records some examples of the former activity as well as innumerable examples of the latter."

3. ENTRAPMENT

The police, or other agents of law enforcement, may face difficulties in securing evidence of the commission of offences, particularly those which are "victim-less" or "consensual" such as soliciting or drug trafficking. Paradoxically, in pursuance of their legitimate function of preventing crime, such officers of the state may become involved in the actual commission of an offence. The Law Commission's Report on Defences of General Application, (No. 83, 1978) recognised that "in many situations such involvement is perfectly legitimate ... [for example] in offences concerned with the sale of liquor, the readiness of the holder of a licence to sell otherwise than in accordance with its terms may be properly tested by purchases made by ... the police." (§ 5.1). The paradox arises where that readiness is not present and, as a result of police enticement, a person is persuaded to commit an offence which would not otherwise have been committed. "The problem becomes acute where the participant is an informer, knowledgeable in the workings of the underworld (hence able to provide opportunities for entrapment) and anxious to give 'bodies' to the police in exchange for concessions in the criminal process." (Oscapella, "A Study of Informers in England" [1980] Crim. L.R. 136.) In the United States a defence of entrapment has been developed by the Supreme Court in cases where police involvement has crossed the line dividing detection and instigation: *Sorrells* v. *U.S.* (*post*, p. 239). No common law jurisdiction has followed this lead although the New Zealand Court of Appeal has held that where this line is crossed the evidence should be inadmissible: *Police* v. *Lavalle* [1979] 1 N.Z.L.R. 45. The House of Lords has, however, recently confirmed, see the case below, that English law neither recognises a defence of entrapment nor a discretion to exclude evidence so obtained as a result of entrapment.

R. v. Sang
[1979] 3 W.L.R. 263
House of Lords

The appellant was charged with conspiracy to utter counterfeit United States banknotes, and of unlawful possession of such forged banknotes. He alleged that he was approached while in prison by a police informer who acted in concert with a police officer in inducing him to commit a crime which he would not otherwise have committed. Before the prosecution opened its case, the defence asked the trial judge to consider, on a *voir dire*, whether the accused's involvement in the alleged offences

> arose out of the activities of an agent provocateur. The judge refused to hold a *voir dire* on the grounds that, even if these allegations were proved, he had no discretion to exclude the evidence. The appellant pleaded guilty and his appeal against the judge's ruling was dismissed both by the Court of Appeal and the House of Lords.

LORD DIPLOCK: ... Faced, as he was, by recent decisions of the Criminal Division of the Court of Appeal that "entrapment" is no defence in English law (*R.* v. *McEvilly, R.* v. *Lee* (1973) 60 Cr. App. R. 150; *R.* v. *Mealey, R.* v. *Sheridan* (1974) 60 Cr. App. R. 59), counsel for the appellant sought to achieve by a different means the same effect as if it were. He submitted that if the judge were satisfied at a "trial within a trial" that the offence was instigated by an agent provocateur acting on the instructions of the police and, but for this, would not have been committed by the accused, the judge had a discretion to refuse to allow the prosecution to prove its case by evidence.

In support of this submission counsel was able to cite a number of dicta from impressive sources which, on the face of them, suggest that judges have a very wide discretion in criminal cases to exclude evidence tendered by the prosecution on the ground that it has been unfairly obtained. In addition there is one actual decision of the Court of Criminal Appeal in *R.* v. *Payne* [1963] 1 W.L.R. 637, where a conviction was quashed on the ground that the judge ought to have exercised his discretion to exclude admissible evidence on that ground, though this was not a case of entrapment. Moreover there had also been a recent decision at the Central Criminal Court (*R.* v. *Ameer, R.* v. *Lucas* [1977] Crim. L.R. 104) in a case which did involve an agent provocateur where Judge Gillis, after a lengthy trial within a trial, had exercised his discretion by refusing to allow the prosecution to call any evidence to prove the commission of the offence by the accused.

In order to avoid what promised to be a lengthy trial within a trial, which would be fruitless if Judge Buzzard were to rule as a matter of law that he had no discretion to exclude relevant evidence tendered by the prosecution to prove the commission of the offence, even though it had been instigated by an agent provocateur and was one which the accused would never have committed but for such inducement, the judge first heard legal submissions on this question. He ruled that even on that assumption he had no discretion to exclude the prosecution's evidence. In consequence of this ruling the appellant withdrew his plea of not guilty and pleaded guilty.

It is only fair to the police to point out that there never was a trial within a trial. The judge's ruling made it unnecessary to go into the facts relating to the appellant's claim that he was induced by a police informer to commit a crime of a kind which but for such persuasion he would never have committed; so no evidence was ever called to prove that there had been any improper conduct on the part of the police or of the prosecution.

The appeal to the Court of Appeal . . . was dismissed. . . . [T]hey certified as the point of law of general importance involved in their decision a much wider question than is involved in the use of agents provocateurs. It is:

> "Does a trial judge have a discretion to refuse to allow evidence, being evidence other than evidence of admission, to be given in any circumstances in which such evidence is relevant and of more than minimal probative value?"

I understand this question as enquiring what are the circumstances, if there be any, in which such a discretion arises; and as not being confined to trials by jury. . . . The decisions in *R.* v. *McEvilly, R.* v. *Lee* and *R.* v. *Mealy, R.* v. *Sheridan* that there is no defence of "entrapment" known to English law are clearly right. Many crimes are committed by one person at the instigation of others. From earliest times at common law those who counsel and procure the commission of the offence by the person by whom the actus reus itself is done have been guilty themselves of an offence, and since the abolition by the Criminal Law Act 1967 of the distinction between felonies and misdemeanours can be tried, indicted and punished as principal offenders. The fact that the counsellor and procurer is a policeman or a police informer, cannot affect the guilt of the principal offender; both the physical element (actus reus) and the mental element (mens rea) of the offence with which he is charged are present in his case.

My Lords, this being the substantive law on the matter, the suggestion that it can be evaded by the procedural device of preventing the prosecution from adducing evidence of the commission of the offence, does not bear examination. Let me take first the summary offence prosecuted before magistrates where there is no practical distinction between a trial within a trial. There are three examples of these in the books, *Brannan* v. *Peek* [1948] 1 K.B. 68; *Browning* v. *J. W. H. Watson (Rochester)* [1953] 1 W.L.R. 1172; *Sneddon* v. *Stevenson* [1967] 1 W.L.R. 1051. Here the magistrates in order to decide whether the crime had in fact been instigated by an agent provocateur acting on police instructions would first have to hear evidence which ex hypothesi would involve proving that the crime had been committed by the accused. If they decided that it had been so instigated, then, despite the fact that they had already heard evidence which satisfied them that it had been committed, they would have a discretion to prevent the prosecution from relying on that evidence as proof of its commission. How does this differ from recognising entrapment as a defence, but a defence available only at the discretion of the magistrates?

Where the accused is charged on indictment and there is a practical distinction between the trial and a trial within a trial, the position, as it seems to me, would be even more anomalous if the judge were to have a discretion to prevent the prosecution from adducing evidence before the jury to prove the commission of the offence by the accused. If he exercised the discretion in favour of the accused he would then have to direct the jury to acquit. How does this differ from recognising entrapment as a defence, but a defence for which the necessary factual foundation is to be found not by the jury but by the judge and even where the factual foundation is so found the defence is available only at the judge's discretion.

My Lords, this submission goes far beyond a claim to a judicial discretion to exclude evidence that has been obtained unfairly or by trickery; nor in any of the English cases on agents provocateurs that have come before appellate courts has it been suggested that it exists. What it really involves is a claim to a judicial discretion to acquit an accused of any offences in connection with which the conduct of the police incurs the disapproval of the judge. The conduct of the police where it has involved the use of an agent provocateur may well be a matter to be taken into consideration in mitigation of sentence; but under the English system of criminal justice it does not give rise to any discretion on the part of the judge himself to acquit the accused or to direct the jury to do so, notwithstanding that he is guilty of the offence. Nevertheless the existence of such a discretion to exclude the evidence of an agent provocateur does appear to have been acknowledged by the Courts-Martial Appeal Court of Northern Ireland in *R.* v. *Murphy* [1965] N.I. 138. That was before the rejection of "entrapment" as a defence by the Court of Appeal in England; and Lord McDermott C.J. in delivering the judgment of the court relied on the dicta as to the existence of a wide discretion which appeared in cases that did not involve an agent provocateur. In the result he held that the court-martial had been right in exercising its discretion in such a way as to admit the evidence.

I understand your Lordships to be agreed that whatever be the ambit of the judicial discretion to exclude admissible evidence it does not extend to excluding evidence of a crime because the crime was instigated by an agent provocateur. In so far as *R.* v. *Murphy* suggests the contrary it should no longer be regarded as good law.

I turn now to the wider question that has been certified. It does not purport to be concerned with self-incriminatory admissions made by the accused himself after commission of the crime, though in dealing with the question I will find it necessary to say something about these. What the question is concerned with is the discretion of the trial judge to exclude all other kinds of evidence that are of more than minimal probative value. . . .

[His Lordship considered the authorities including the following statement of Lord Goddard C.J. in *Kuruma Son of Kaniu* v. *R.* [1955] A.C. 197 at 204: "No doubt in a criminal case the judge always has a discretion to disallow evidence if the strict rules of admissibility would operate unfairly against the accused. . . . If, for instance, some admission of some piece of evidence, e.g. a document, had been obtained from a defendant by a trick, no doubt the judge might properly rule it out."]

[I]t has to be recognised that there is an unbroken series of dicta in judgments of appellate courts to the effect that there is a judicial discretion to exclude admissible evidence which has been "obtained" unfairly or by trickery or oppressively, although except in *R.* v. *Payne* [1963] 1 W.L.R. 637 there never has been a case in which those courts have come across conduct so unfair, so tricky or so oppressive as to justify them in holding that the discretion ought to have been exercised in favour of exclusion. In every one of the cases to which your Lordships have been referred where such dicta appear, the source from which the evidence sought to be excluded had been obtained has been the defendant himself or (in some of the search cases) premises occupied by him; and the dicta can be traced to a common ancestor in Lord Goddard C.J.'s statement in *Kuruma Son of Kaniu* v. *R.* which I have already cited. That statement was not, in my view, ever intended to acknowledge the existence of any wider discretion than to exclude (1) admissible evidence which would probably have a prejudicial influence on the minds of the jury that would be out of proportion to its true evidential value and (2) evidence tantamount to a self-incriminatory admission which was obtained from the defendant, after the offence had been committed, by means which would justify a judge in excluding an actual confession which had the like self-incriminating effect. As a matter of language, although not as a matter of application, the subsequent dicta go much further than this; but in so far as they do so they have never yet been considered by this House.

My Lords, I propose to exclude, as the certified question does, detailed consideration of the role of the trial judge in relation to confessions and evidence obtained from the defendant after commission of the offence that is tantamount to a confession. It has a long history dating back to the days before the existence of a disciplined police force, when a prisoner on a charge of felony could not be represented by counsel and was not entitled to give evidence in his own defence either to deny that he had made the confession, which was generally oral, or to deny that its contents were true. The underlying rationale of this branch of the criminal law, though it may originally have been based on ensuring the reliability of confessions is, in my view, now to be found in the maxim, nemo debet prodere se ipsum, no one can be required to be his own betrayer, or in its popular English mistranslation "the right to silence." That is why there is no discretion to exclude evidence which the accused has been induced to produce voluntarily if the method of inducement was unfair.

Outside this limited field in which for historical reasons the function of the trial judge extended to imposing sanctions for improper conduct on the part of the prosecution before the commencement of the proceedings in inducing the accused by threats, favour of trickery to provide evidence against himself your

Lordships should, I think, make it clear that the function of the judge at a criminal trial as respects the admission of evidence is to ensure that the accused has a fair trial according to law. It is no part of a judge's function to exercise disciplinary powers over the police or prosecution as respects the way in which evidence to be used at the trial is obtained by them. If it was obtained illegally there will be a remedy in civil law; if it was obtained legally but in breach of the rules of conduct for the police, this is a matter for the appropriate disciplinary authority to deal with. What the judge at the trial is concerned with is not how the evidence sought to be adduced by the prosecution has been obtained but with how it is used by the prosecution at the trial. . . .

I would accordingly answer the question certified in terms which have been suggested by my noble and learned friend, Viscount Dilhorne, in the course of our deliberations on this case. (1) A trial judge in a criminal trial has always a discretion to refuse to admit evidence if in his opinion its prejudicial effect outweighs its probative value. (2) Save with regard to admissions and confessions and generally with regard to evidence obtained from the accused after commission of the offence, he has no discretion to refuse to admit relevant admissible evidence on the ground that it was obtained by improper or unfair means. The court is not concerned with how it was obtained. It is no ground for the exercise of discretion to exclude that the evidence was obtained as the result of the activities of an agent provocateur.

I would dismiss this appeal.

[VISCOUNT DILHORNE delivered a speech in favour of dismissing the appeal.]

LORD SALMON: [His Lordship stated that English law recognises no defence of entrapment, and continued:] It is only fair to observe that in the present case there was not a shred of evidence that the police sergeant was an agent provocateur. Even if he had been told by an informer that the accused was a hardened dealer in forged bank notes, it would, I think, have been his duty to carry out a test to discover whether this information was correct, which events show that it obviously was. No doubt, the accused would not have committed the crime of trying to sell forged bank notes to the police had he known it was the police. There can, however, be little doubt that he would have tried to sell the forged notes to anyone else whom he "considered safe."

I would now refer to what is, I believe, and hope, the unusual case in which a dishonest policeman, anxious to improve his detection record, tries very hard with the help of an agent provocateur to induce a young man with no criminal tendencies to commit a serious crime, and ultimately the young man reluctantly succumbs to the inducement. In such a case, the judge has no discretion to exclude the evidence which proves that the young man has committed the offence. He may, however, according to the circumstances of the case, impose a mild punishment on him or even give him an absolute or conditional discharge and refuse to make any order for costs against him. The policeman and the informer who had acted together in inciting him to commit the crime should however both be prosecuted and suitably punished. This would be a far safer and more effective way of preventing such inducements to commit crimes from being made, than a rule that no evidence should be allowed to prove that the crime in fact had been committed.

At common law the person who successfully persuades or induces ("counsels or procures") another to commit an offence has always himself been guilty of a criminal offence and, since the Criminal Law Act 1967, he can be indicted and punished as a principal offender. He is regarded as being as guilty as the man he has incited to commit the crime, and often far more culpable.

It is perhaps worth observing that the law relating to crimes caused by duress is quite different from the law relating to crimes caused by incitement. As the law now stands, a man who commits any offence under duress except murder in the first degree is entitled to a clear acquittal. I think that serious consideration should be given to reforming this branch of the law particularly in view of the mounting wave of terrorism; but this could only be done by statute. I respectfully agree with that great criminal lawyer Sir James Fitzjames Stephen when he wrote, History of the Criminal Law of England (1883), vol. 2, p. 108: "... compulsion by threats ought in no case whatever to be admitted as an excuse for crime, though it may and ought to operate in mitigation of punishment in most though not in all cases." The punishment would certainly vary according to the circumstances of the case; sometimes it might be minimal: see the majority judgment in *Abbott* v. *The Queen* [1977] A.C. 755 [*ante*, p. 217].

It follows that *R.* v. *Ameer, R.* v. *Lucas* [1977] Crim. L.R. 104 which laid down that a trial judge has a discretion to exclude evidence of the accused's guilt called by the Crown because it had been improperly obtained by the activities of an agent provocateur was wrongly decided and should be overruled.

... [S]o far as this appeal is concerned, the answer to [the certified] question can only be obiter.... I consider that it is a clear principle of the law that a trial judge has the power and the duty to ensure that the accused has a fair trial. Accordingly, amongst other things, he has a discretion to exclude legally admissible evidence if justice so requires: see Lord Reid's speech in *Myers* v. *D.P.P.* [1965] A.C. 1001 at 1024. [His Lordship then gave examples relating to confessions and other evidence obtained from the accused after the commission of the offence.] ...

I recognise that there may have been no categories of cases, other than those to which I have referred, in which technically admissible evidence proffered by the Crown has been rejected by the court on the ground that it would make the trial unfair. I cannot, however, accept that a judge's undoubted duty to ensure that the accused has a fair trial is confined to such cases. In my opinion the category of such cases is not and never can be closed except by statute. I understand that the answer given by my noble and learned friend, Lord Diplock, to the certified question accepts the proposition which I have just stated. On that basis, I respectfully agree with that answer.

My Lords, I would dismiss the appeal.

[Lord Fraser of Tullybelton delivered a speech in which he favoured dismissing the appeal and answering the question in the way proposed by Lord Diplock.]

Lord Scarman: ... It would be wrong in principle to import into our law a defence of entrapment. Incitement is no defence in law for the person incited to crime, even though the inciter is himself guilty of crime and may be far the more culpable. It would confuse the law and create unjust distinctions if incitement by a policeman or an official exculpated him whom they incited to crime whereas incitement by others, perhaps exercising much greater influence, did not. There are other more direct, less anomalous, ways of controlling police and official activity than by introducing so dubious a defence into the law. The true relevance of official entrapment into the commission of crime is on the question of sentence when its mitigating value may be high: see *R.* v. *Birtles* [1969] 1 W.L.R. 1047....

The role of the judge is confined to the forensic process. He controls neither the police nor the prosecuting authority. He neither initiates nor stifles a prosecution. Save in the very rare situation, which is not this case, of an abuse of the process of the court (against which every court is in duty bound to protect itself), the judge is concerned only with the conduct of the trial. The Judges' Rules, for example, are not a judicial control of police interrogation, but notice that, if certain steps are not taken, certain evidence, otherwise admissible, may be excluded at the trial. The judge's control of the criminal process begins and ends with trial, though his influence may extend beyond its beginning and conclusion. It follows that the prosecution has rights, which the judge may not override. The right to prosecute and the right to lead admissible evidence in support of its case are not subject to judicial control. Of course when the prosecutor reaches court he becomes subject to the directions as to the conduct of the trial by the judge, whose duty it then is to see that the accused has a fair trial according to law.

What does "fair" mean in this context? It relates to the process of trial. No man is to be compelled to incriminate himself: nemo tenetur se ipsum prodere. No man is to be convicted save on the probative effect of legally admissible evidence. No admission or confession is to be received in evidence unless voluntary. If legally admissible evidence be tendered which endangers these principles (as, for example, in *R.* v. *Payne*), the judge may exercise his discretion to exclude it, thus ensuring that the accused has the benefit of principles which exist in the law to secure him a fair trial; but he has no power to exclude admissible evidence of the commission of a crime, unless in his judgment these principles are endangered.

In the light of these principles this appeal presents no difficulty. . . . I agree with the answer to the certified question in the terms proposed by my noble and learned friends, Lord Diplock and Viscount Dilhorne. . . .

Appeal dismissed

Sorrells v. United States
287 U.S. 435 (1932)
Supreme Court of the United States

> S. was convicted of possessing and selling intoxicating liquor in violation of the National Prohibition Act. His defence that he was instigated to commit the offence by a government agent was not left to the jury, the court ruling as a matter of law that there was no entrapment. The Circuit Court of Appeals affirmed the judgment but the Supreme Court granted a certiorari limited to the question whether the evidence was sufficient to go to the jury upon the issue of entrapment.

HUGHES C.J.: It is clear that the evidence was sufficient to warrant a finding that the act for which defendant was prosecuted was instigated by the prohibition agent, that it was the creature of his purpose, that defendant had no previous disposition to commit it but was an industrious, law-abiding citizen, and that the agent lured defendant, otherwise innocent, to its commission by repeated and persistent solicitation in which he succeeded by taking advantage of the sentiment aroused by reminiscences of their experiences as companions in arms in the World War. Such a gross abuse of authority given for the purpose of detecting and punishing crime, and not for the making of criminals, deserves the severest condemnation, but the question whether it precludes prosecution or affords a ground of defence, and, if so upon what theory, has given rise to conflicting opinions.

It is well settled that the fact that officers or employees of the Government merely afford opportunities or facilities for the commission of the offense does not defeat the prosecution. Artifice and stratagem may be employed to catch those engaged in criminal enterprises. . . . The appropriate object of this permitted activity, frequently essential to the enforcement of the law, is to reveal the criminal design; to expose the illicit traffic, the prohibited publication, the fraudulent use of the mails, the illegal conspiracy, or other offenses, and thus to disclose the would-be violators of the law. A different question is presented when the criminal design originates with the officials of the Government, and they implant in the mind of an innocent person the disposition to commit the alleged offense and induce its commission in order that they may prosecute.

The Circuit Court of Appeals reached the conclusion that the defense of entrapment can be maintained only where, as a result of inducement, the accused is placed in the attitude of having committed a crime which he did not intend to commit, or where, by reason of the consent implied in the inducement, no crime has in fact been committed: 57 F. (2d) p. 974. As illustrating the first class, reference is made to the case of a sale of liquor to an Indian who was disguised so as to mislead the accused as to his identity: *United States* v. *Healy* (D.C.) 202 Fed. 349. In the second class are found cases such as those of larceny or rape where want of consent is an element of the crime: *R.* v. *Fletcher* (1859) 8 Cox 131; *R.* v. *M'Daniel* (1755) Fost. C.L. 121, 127, 128. There may also be physical conditions which are essential to the offense and which do not exist in the case of a trap, as, for example, in the case of a prosecution for burglary where it appears that by reason of the trap there is no breaking: *R.* v. *Eggington* (1801) 2 Leach C.L. 913; *R.* v. *Johnson* (1841) C. & M. 218. But these decisions applying accepted principles to particular offenses do not reach, much less determine, the present question. Neither in reasoning nor in effect do they prescribe limits for the doctrine of entrapment.

While this court has not spoken on the precise question, the weight of authority in the lower federal courts is decidedly in favour of the view that in such a case as the one before us the defense of entrapment is available. . . .

. . . The Federal courts have generally approved the statement of Circuit Judge Sanborn in the leading case of *Butts* v. *United States* (C.C.A. 8th) 18 A.L.R. 143, 273 Fed. 38, as follows: "The first duties of the officers of the law are to prevent not to punish crime. It is not their duty to incite to and create crime for the sole purpose of prosecuting and punishing it. Here the evidence strongly tends to prove, if it does not conclusively do so, that their first and chief endeavour was to cause, to create, crime in order to punish it, and it is unconscionable, contrary to public policy, and to the established law of the land to punish a man for the commission of an offence of the like of which he had never been guilty, either in thought or in deed, and evidently never would have been guilty of if the officers of the law had not inspired, incited, persuaded and lured him to attempt to commit it." . . .

The validity of the principle as thus stated and applied is challenged both upon theoretical and practical grounds. The argument, from the standpoint of principle, is that the court is called upon to try the accused for a particular offense which is defined by statute and that, if the evidence shows that this offense has knowingly been committed, it matters not that its commission was induced by officers of the Government in the manner and circumstances assumed. It is said that where one intentionally does an act in circumstances known to him, and the particular conduct is forbidden by the law in those circumstances, he intentionally breaks the law in the only sense in which the law considers intent. *Ellis* v. *United States*, 206 U.S. 246, 257. Moreover, that as the statute is designed to redress a public wrong, and not a private injury, there is no ground for holding the Government estopped by the conduct of its officers from prosecuting the offender. To the suggestion of public policy the objectors answer that the legislature, acting within its constitutional authority, is the arbiter of public policy and that, where conduct is expressly forbidden and penalized by a valid statute, the courts are not at liberty to disregard the law and to bar a prosecution for its violation because they are of the opinion that the crime has been instigated by government officials.

It is manifest that these arguments rest entirely upon the letter of the statute. They take no account of the fact that its application in the circumstances under consideration is foreign to its purpose; that such an application is so shocking to the sense of justice that it has been urged to stop the prosecution in the interest of the Government itself, to protect it from the illegal conduct of its officers and to preserve the purity of its courts. *Casey* v. *United States*, 276 U.S. 413. But can an application of the statute having such an effect—creating a situation so contrary to the purpose of the law and so inconsistent with its proper enforcement as to invoke such a challenge—fairly be deemed to be within its intendment?

Literal interpretation of statutes at the expense of the reason of the law and producing absurd consequences or flagrant injustice has frequently been condemned. . . . The court (in *U.S.* v. *Kirby*, 7 Wall. 482 (1869)), said: "All laws should receive a sensible construction. General terms should be so limited in their application as not to lead to injustice, oppression, or an absurd consequence. It will always, therefore, be presumed that the legislature intended exceptions to its language which would avoid results of this character. The reason of the law in such cases should prevail over its letter." And the court supported this conclusion by reference to the classical illustrations found in *Puffendorf and Plowden, ibid.*, pp. 486, 487. . . .

We think that this established principle of construction is applicable here. We are unable to conclude that it was the intention of the Congress in enacting this statute that its processes of detection and enforcement should be abused by the instigation by government officials of an act on the part of persons otherwise innocent in order to lure them to its commission and to punish them. We are not forced by the letter to do violence to the spirit and purpose of the statute. This, we think, has been the underlying and controlling thought in the suggestions in judicial opinions that the Government in such a case is estopped to prosecute or that the courts should bar the prosecution. If the requirements of the highest public policy in the maintenance of the integrity of administration would preclude the enforcement of the statute in such circumstances as are present here, the same considerations justify the conclusion that the case lies outside the purview of the Act and that its general words should not be construed to demand a proceeding at once inconsistent with that policy and abhorrent to the sense of justice. This view does not derogate from the authority of the court to deal appropriately with abuses of its process and it obviates the objection to the exercise by the court of a dispensing power in forbidding the prosecution of one who is charged with conduct assumed to fall within the statute. . . .

Objections to the defense of entrapment are also urged upon practical grounds. But considerations of mere convenience must yield to the essential demands of justice. The argument is pressed that if the defense is available it will lead to the introduction of issues of collateral character relating to the activities of the officials of the Government and to the conduct and purpose of the defendant previous to the alleged offense. . . . The predisposition and criminal design of the defendant are relevant. But the issues raised and the evidence adduced must be pertinent to the controlling question whether the defendant is a person otherwise innocent whom the Government is seeking to punish for an alleged offense which is the product of the creative activity of its own officials. If that is the fact, common justice requires that the accused be permitted to prove it. The Government in such a case is in no position to object to evidence of the activities of its representatives in relation to the accused, and if the defendant seeks acquittal by reason of entrapment he cannot complain of an appropriate and searching inquiry into his own conduct and predisposition as bearing upon that issue. . . .

We are of the opinion that upon the evidence produced in the instant case the defense of entrapment was available and that the trial court was in error in holding that as a matter of law there was no entrapment and in refusing to submit the issue to the jury.

Roberts J.: Society is at war with the criminal classes, and courts have uniformly held that in waging this warfare the forces of prevention and detection may use traps, decoys, and deception to obtain evidence of the commission of crime. Resort to such means does not render an indictment thereafter found a nullity nor call for the exclusion of evidence so procured. . . . But the defense here asserted involves more than obtaining evidence by artifice or deception. Entrapment is the conception and planning of an offense by an officer, and his procurement of its commission by one who would not have perpetrated it except for the trickery, persuasion, or fraud of the officer. Federal and state courts have held that substantial proof of entrapment as thus defined calls for the submission of the issue to the jury and warrants an acquittal. The reasons assigned in support of this procedure have not been uniform. Thus it has been held that the acts of its officers estop the Government to prove the offense. The result has also been justified by the mere statement of the rule that where entrapment is proved the defendant is not guilty of the crime charged. Often the defense has been permitted upon grounds of public policy, which the courts formulate by saying they will not permit their process to be used in aid of a scheme for the actual creation of a crime by those whose duty is to deter its commission.

This court has adverted to the doctrine, but has not heretofore had occasion to determine its validity, the basis on which it should rest, or the procedure to be followed when it is involved. The present case affords the opportunity to settle these matters as respects the administration of the federal criminal law.

There is common agreement that where a law officer envisages a crime, plans it, and activates its commission by one not theretofore intending its perpetration, for the sole purpose of obtaining a victim through indictment, conviction and sentence, the consummation of so revolting a plan ought not to be permitted by any self-respecting tribunal. Equally true is this whether the offense is one at common law or merely a creature of statute. Public policy forbids such sacrifice of decency. The enforcement of this policy calls upon the court, in every instance where alleged entrapment of a defendant is brought to its notice, to ascertain the facts, to appraise their effect upon the administration of justice, and to make such order with respect to the further prosecution of the cause as the circumstances require.

This view calls for no distinction between crimes *mala in se* and statutory offenses of lesser gravity; requires no statutory construction, and attributes no merit to a guilty defendant; but frankly recognises the true foundation of the doctrine in the public policy which protects the purity of government and its processes. . . .

A new method of rationalising the defense is now asserted. This is to construe the Act creating the offense by reading in a condition or proviso that if the offender shall have been entrapped into crime the law shall not apply to him. So, it is said, the true intent of the legislature will be effectuated. This seems a strained and unwarranted construction of the statute; and amounts, in fact, to judicial amendment. It is not merely broad construction, but addition of an element not contained in the legislation. . . . This amounts to saying that one who with full intent commits the act defined by law as an offense is nevertheless by virtue of the unspoken and implied mandate of the statute to be adjudged not guilty by reason of someone else's improper conduct. It is merely to adopt a form of words to justify action which ought to be based on the inherent right of the court not to be made the instrument of wrong.

It is said that this case warrants such a construction of the applicable Act, but that the question whether a similar construction will be required in the case of other more serious crimes is not before the court. Thus no guide or rule is announced as to when a statute shall be read as excluding a case of entrapment; and no principle of statutory construction is suggested which would enable us to say that it is excluded by some statutes and not by others. . . .

Recognition of the defense of entrapment as belonging to the defendant and as raising an issue for decision by the jury called to try him upon plea of the general issue, results in the trial of a false issue wholly outside the true rule which should be applied by the courts. It has been generally held, where the defendant has proved an entrapment, it is permissible for the Government to show in rebuttal that the officer guilty of incitement of the crime had reasonable cause to believe the defendant was a person disposed to commit the offense. This procedure is approved by the opinion of the court. The proof received in rebuttal usually amounts to no more than that the defendant had a bad reputation, or that he had been previously convicted. . . .

The recognised procedure, in effect, pivots conviction in such cases, not on the commission of the crime charged, but on the prior reputation or some former act or acts of the defendant not mentioned in the indictment.

The applicable principle is that courts must be closed to the trial of a crime instigated by the Government's own agents. No other issue, no comparison of equities as between the guilty official and the guilty defendant, has any place in the enforcement of this overruling principle of public policy.

Judgment reversed

Notes

The United States view on entrapment is by no means accepted uncritically. The view taken in *Sorrell's* case is the subject of strong dissent of a substantial minority in *U.S.* v. *Russell*, 93 S.Ct. 1637 (1973) and the Supreme Court recently affirmed that the defence does not apply when there is a predisposition to commit the crime, *Hampton* v. *U.S.* 425 U.S. 484 (1976).

One view of the defence as developed in the United States is that it is "torn by conflicting interpretations, one of which relates the issue to culpability and another, which denies the relationship" (*Fletcher*, p. 543). He continues, "There is no single theory of the defense that can explain both (1) the exclusion of entrapment by private parties and (2) the limitation to suspects not 'predisposed' to commit the offense." In the commentary to the Model Penal Code's draft of the defence it is described as "a complaint by the accused against the State for employing a certain kind of unsavoury enforcement" (Tentative Draft No. 9, p. 14). The Code provides, s. 2.13:

"(1) A public law enforcement official or a person acting in cooperation with such an official perpetrates an entrapment if for the purpose of obtaining evidence of the commission of an offense, he induces or encourages another person to engage in conduct constituting such offense by either:

(a) making knowingly false representations designed to induce the belief that such conduct is not prohibited; or
(b) employing methods of persuasion or inducement which create a substantial risk that such an offense will be committed by persons other than those who are ready to commit it.

(2) Except as provided in Subsection (3) of this Section, a person prosecuted for an offense shall be acquitted if he proves by a preponderance of evidence that his conduct occurred in response to an entrapment. The issue of entrapment shall be tried by the Court in the absence of the jury.

(3) The defense afforded by this Section is unavailable when causing or threatening bodily injury is an element of the offense charged and the prosecution is based on conduct causing or threatening such injury to a person other than the person perpetrating the entrapment."

It is clear, after the decision in *R.* v. *Sang* (*ante*, p. 233) that any recognition of entrapment as a defence in this country would have to be the result of legislative initiative. The Law Commission, however, in its Report on Defences of General Application, rejected such a proposal on the following grounds:

"§ 5.37 A defendant who would not have committed an offence but for inducement by others to do so is, in respect of the actus reus and any necessary mens rea, in no different position from any other criminal: he has committed the offence. Whether the inducement comes from fellow-criminals or from any other source can from the point of view of his guilt make no difference, except, perhaps, in the hypothetical case of a police officer inciting, openly in his capacity as a police officer, the commission of an offence. It is true that, when committing an offence under duress, the defendant is also usually regarded as possessing the necessary mens rea, but in such a case he is absolved from liability because of the overwhelming pressure directed against him. Normally, no such pressure is involved in cases of entrapment. From his viewpoint, then, a defence of entrapment where the inducement is alleged is solely that of the police or informers corresponds with no moral distinction in his behaviour. It appears to us that the proponents of the defence of entrapment seek to control admittedly unacceptable conduct on the part of the State's law-enforcement agencies, not by penalising them or otherwise preventing the repetition of such conduct, but by absolving the defendant. This is in our view illogical. A proper reflection of the defendant's guilt in any case of entrapment, whether or not officially inspired, can be effected by the practice of mitigating the penalty; and if the entrapment is clearly the result of conduct by the police or informers, that mitigation may in an appropriate case extend so far as an unconditional discharge."

Controlling entrapment through a discretionary exclusionary rule of evidence was also rejected by the Law Commission, § 5.29:

"... The defendant's allegation is, not that the evidence has been unfairly obtained, but that a conviction for the offence itself is "unfair," in that it would not have occurred but for the pressure or persuasion of the State's own law enforcement officers or their agents. In our view, the extension of a discretionary power relating to admission of evidence to the case where what is really in issue is whether it is "fair" that the proceedings should have been instituted at all is wholly illogical, and, indeed, raises issues going far beyond the merely evidential."

However, the Law Commission did suggest that "further consideration be given to the creation of a new offence of entrapment, which would penalise anyone who takes the initiative in instigating or persuading another person to commit an offence." (§ 5.54).

The exclusionary rule is favoured by the Australian Law Reform Commission: Report No. 2: *Criminal Investigation* (1975), § 229. Somewhat surprisingly, the Report of the Royal Commission on Criminal Procedure, Cmnd. 8092 (1981) does not advert to this aspect of police activity at all.

On entrapment generally, see Heydon, "The Problems of Entrapment" [1973] C.L.J. 268, and Barlow, "Entrapment and the Common Law: Is there a Place for the American Doctrine of Entrapment?" (1978) 41 M.L.R. 266.

Questions

1. If, as the Law Commission suggests, there is no moral distinction

between the behaviour of one entrapped by the police and one induced by another criminal, what is the basis on which the entrapped defendant's guilt is to be mitigated at the sentencing stage? See Ashworth's comment at [1978] Crim. L.R. 137.

2. It was suggested in *Sang* that an exclusionary rule in relation to evidence obtained by entrapment would amount to an admission of a defence of entrapment by the back-door. Compare this view with the following: "Those who advocate the discretion to exclude evidence obtained by entrapment do not advocate that if entrapment exists, the court should have a discretion to exclude *all* otherwise admissible evidence. The discretion advocated is simply to exclude evidence which proceeds from the entrapment. If D commits a crime (e.g. selling heroin) at E's instigation, the discretion would be to exclude E's evidence but not that of O, an observer who witnessed sales. . . ." (Heydon, "Unfairly Obtained Evidence in the House of Lords" [1980] Crim. L.R. 129.)

Chapter 6

DEGREES OF RESPONSIBILITY

	PAGE		PAGE
1. Accomplices	246	2. Assisting an Offender and Concealing Information	283
i. Principals and Accessories	246	i. Assisting an Offender	283
ii. *Mens Rea* of a Secondary Party	255	ii. Concealing Information	288
iii. Scope of the Common Design	267	3. Vicarious Liability	288
iv. Secondary Party Not Convictable as a Principal	274	4. Corporations	296
v. No Principal Offender	278		

1. ACCOMPLICES

i. Principles and Accessories

Note

One who participates in a crime, which he does not actually commit either personally or through the medium of an innocent agent, is nevertheless punishable if he aids, abets, counsels and procures the principal offender to commit the crime. See Accessories and Abettors Act 1861, s. 8, in the judgment of Lord Widgery C.J. below, and as to summary offences, Magistrates' Courts Act 1980, s. 44.

The words "aid and abet, counsel and procure" may all be used together to charge a person who is alleged to have participated in an offence otherwise than as the principal in the first degree or as an accessory after the fact: *Re Smith* (1858) 3 H. & N. 227; *Ferguson* v. *Weaving*, *post*, p. 266. Such a person may also be charged as a principal: see *Maxwell* v. *D.P.P. for Northern Ireland*, *post*, p. 255. Indeed, if two persons are present at the commission of a crime, and it is not clear which committed the crime and which did no more than help, it is not normally necessary to show which was the actual perpetrator in order to convict them both: see *Mohan* v. *R.*, *post*, p. 254.

Attorney-General's Reference (No. 1 of 1975)

[1975] Q.B. 773
Court of Appeal

The facts appear in the judgment.

LORD WIDGERY C.J.: This case comes before the court on a reference from the Attorney-General, under section 36 of the Criminal Justice Act 1972, and by his reference he asks the following question:

> "Whether an accused, who surreptitiously laced a friend's drinks with double measures of spirits when he knew that his friend would shortly be driving his car home, and in consequence his friend drove with an excessive

> quantity of alcohol in his body and was convicted of the offence under section 6 (1) of the Road Traffic Act 1972, is entitled to a ruling of no case to answer on being later charged as an aider and abettor, counsellor and procurer, on the ground that there was no shared intention between the two, that the accused did not by accompanying him or otherwise positively encourage the friend to drive, or on any other ground"

. . . The present question has no doubt arisen because in recent years there have been a number of instances where men charged with driving their motor cars with an excess quantity of alcohol in the blood have sought to excuse their conduct by saying that their drinks were "laced", as the jargon has it; that is to say, some strong spirit was put into an otherwise innocuous drink and as a result the driver consumed more alcohol than he had either intended to consume or had the desire to consume. The relevance of all that is not that it entitles the driver to an acquittal because such driving is an absolute offence, but that it can be relied on as a special reason for not disqualifying the driver from driving. Hence no doubt the importance which has been attached in recent months to the possibility of this argument being raised in a normal charge of driving with excess alcohol.

The question requires us to say whether on the facts posed there is a case to answer and, needless to say, in the trial from which this reference is derived the judge was of the opinion that there was no case to answer and so ruled. We have to say in effect whether he is right.

The language in the section which determines whether a "secondary party", as he is sometimes called, is guilty of a criminal offence committed by another embraces the four words "aid, abet, counsel or procure". The origin of those words is to be found in section 8 of the Accessories and Abettors Act 1861, which provides:

> "Whosoever shall aid, abet, counsel or procure the commission of any misdemeanor, whether the same be a misdemeanor at common law or by virtue of any Act passed or to be passed, shall be liable to be tried, indicted and punished as a principal offender."

Thus, in the past, when the distinction was still drawn between felony and misdemeanor, it was sufficient to make a person guilty of a misdemeanor if he aided, abetted, counselled or procured the offence of another. When the difference between felonies and misdemeanors was abolished in 1967, section 1 of the Criminal Law Act 1967 in effect provided that the same test should apply to make a secondary party guilty either of treason or felony.

Of course it is the fact that in the great majority of instances where a secondary party is sought to be convicted of an offence there has been a contact between the principal offender and the secondary party. Aiding and abetting almost inevitably involves a situation in which the secondary party and the main offender are together at some stage discussing the plans which they may be making in respect of the alleged offence, and are in contact so that each knows what is passing through the mind of the other.

In the same way it seems to us that a person, who counsels the commission of a crime by another, almost inevitably comes to a moment when he is in contact with that other, when he is discussing the offence with that other and when, to use the words of the statute, he counsels the other to commit the offence.

The fact that so often the relationship between the secondary party and the principal will be such that there is a meeting of minds between them caused the trial judge in the case from which this reference is derived to think that this was really an essential feature of proving or establishing the guilt of the secondary party and, as we understand his judgment, he took the view that in the absence of some sort of meeting of minds, some sort of mental link between the secondary party and the principal, there could be no aiding, abetting or counselling of the offence within the meaning of the section.

So far as aiding, abetting and counselling is concerned we would go a long way with that conclusion. It may very well be, as I said a moment ago, difficult to think of a case of aiding, abetting or counselling when the parties have not met and have not discussed in some respects the terms of the offence which they have in mind. But we do not see why a similar principle should apply to procuring. We approach section 8 of the Act of 1861 on the basis that the words should be given their ordinary meaning, if possible. We approach the section on the basis also that if four words are employed here, "aid, abet, counsel or procure", the probability is that there is a difference between each of those four words and the other three, because, if there were no such difference, then Parliament would be wasting time in using four words where two or three would do. Thus, in deciding whether that which is assumed to be done under our reference was a criminal offence we approach the section on the footing that each word must be given its ordinary meaning.

To procure means to produce by endeavour. You procure a thing by setting out to see that it happens and taking the appropriate steps to produce that happening. We think that there are plenty of instances in which a person may be said to procure the commission of a crime by another even though there is no sort of conspiracy between the two, even though there is no attempt at agreement or discussion as to the form which the offence should take. In our judgment the offence described in this reference is such a case.

If one looks back at the facts of the reference: the accused surreptitiously laced his friend's drink. This is an important element and, although we are not going to decide today anything other than the problem posed to us, it may well be that, in similar cases where the lacing of the drink or the introduction of the extra alcohol is known to the driver quite different considerations may apply. We say that because, where the driver has no knowledge of what is happening, in most instances he would have no means of preventing the offence from being committed. If the driver is unaware of what has happened, he will not be taking precautions. He will get into his car seat, switch on the ignition and drive home, and, consequently, the conception of another procuring the commission of the offence by the driver is very much stronger where the driver is innocent of all knowledge of what is happening, as in the present case where the lacing of the drink was surreptitious.

The second thing which is important in the facts set out in our reference is that, following and in consequence of the introduction of the extra alcohol, the friend drove with an excess quantity of alcohol in his blood. Causation here is important. You cannot procure an offence unless there is a causal link between what you do and the commission of the offence, and here we are told that in consequence of the addition of this alcohol the driver, when he drove home, drove with an excess quantity of alcohol in his body.

Giving the words their ordinary meaning in English, and asking oneself whether in those circumstances the offence has been procured, we are in no doubt that the answer is that it has. It has been procured because, unknown to the driver and without his collaboration, he has been put in a position in which in fact he has committed an offence which he never would have committed otherwise. We think that there was a case to answer and that the trial judge should have directed the jury that an offence is committed if it is shown beyond reasonable doubt that the defendant knew that his friend was going to drive, and also knew that the ordinary and natural result of the additional alcohol added to the friend's drink would be to bring him above the recognised limit of 80 milligrammes per 100 millilitres of blood.

It was suggested to us that, if we held that there may be a procuring on the facts of the present case, it would be but a short step to a similar finding for the generous host, with somewhat bibulous friends, when at the end of the day his friends leave him to go to their own homes in circumstances in which they are not fit to drive and in circumstances in which an offence under the Road Traffic Act 1972 is committed. The suggestion has been made that the host may in those circumstances be guilty with his guests on the basis that he has either aided, abetted, counselled or procured the offence.

The first point to notice in regard to the generous host is that that is not a case in which the alcohol is being put surreptitiously into the glass of the driver. That is a case in which the driver knows perfectly well how much he has to drink and where to a large extent it is perfectly right and proper to leave him to make his own decision.

Furthermore, we would say that, if such a case arises, the basis on which the case will be put against the host is, we think, bound to be on the footing that he has supplied the tool with which the offence is committed. This, of course, is a reference back to such cases as those where oxy-acetylene equipment was bought by a man knowing it was to be used by another for a criminal offence: see *R.* v. *Bainbridge* [1960] 1 Q.B. 129. There is ample and clear authority as to the extent to which supplying the tools for the commission of an offence may amount to aiding and abetting for present purposes.

Accordingly, so far as the generous host type of case is concerned we are not concerned at the possibility that difficulties will be created, as long as it is borne in mind that in those circumstances the matter must be approached in accordance with well known authority governing the provision of the tools for the commission of an offence, and never forgetting that the introduction of the alcohol is not there surreptitious, and that consequently the case for saying that the offence was procured by the supplier of the alcohol is very much more difficult.

Our decision on the reference is that the question posed by the Attorney-General should be answered in the negative.

Opinion accordingly

Question

What bearing does the opinion of the Court have on the "my drink was laced" plea mentioned by Lord Widgery as the reason why the referred question had arisen?

J. C. Smith, "Aid, Abet, Counsel or Procure" in Reshaping the Criminal Law, ed. Glazebrook, 1978, pp. 122–125

"The formula adopted in section 8 of the Accessories and Abettors Act 1861 and other nineteenth and twentieth century statutes is the most modern in a long line from very early times. . . .

Other earlier and later statutes, however, use different formulae in which the words, 'helping', 'maintaining', 'commanding', 'contriving', 'assisting', 'directing' and 'hiring' and others recur. . . .

Foster (Crown Law, p. 121) agreed that it is true that penal statutes must be strictly construed but said that 'it is equally true that we are not to be governed by the sound, but by the well-known, true, legal import of the words'. He reviewed the large variety of words used in various statutes to describe the activity of accessories and concluded that such words are technical expressions to be given their legal meaning.

> From these different modes of expression, all plainly descriptive of the same offence, I think one may safely conclude, that in the construction of statutes which oust clergy in the case of *Participes Criminis*, we are not to be governed

> by the bare sound, but by the true legal import of the words. And also, that every person who cometh within the description of these statutes, various as they are in point of expression, is in the judgment of the legislature an accessory before the fact; unless he is present at the fact, and in that case he is undoubtedly a principal.

According to this highly authoritative view, the actual words used are of no significance once it is clear that they were intended to incorporate the common law concepts of secondary participation. That these are concepts of the common law is clear. It was recognised by Coke, Hale and the subsequent writers of authority that it was not necessary for a statute to provide for the liability of secondary parties. It was sufficient for Parliament to prescribe the offence and liability for secondary participation followed by implication. Yet, for some reason, Parliament sometimes made express provision and sometimes did not. When express provision was made, there was no consistency in the terminology used: but whatever the words, the same concept of the common law applied.

What then of the words used in section 8 of the Accessories and Abettors Act 1861, and section 35 of the Magistrates' Court Act 1952? According to C. S. Greaves, the editor of the third and fourth editions of *Russell on Crime*, and the draftsman of the 1861 legislation, section 8 'is really only a declaration of the common law on the subject.' This opinion has been followed by the courts on several occasions. It is submitted that this is the right view and that as Sir Francis Adams puts it: 'Nothing is to be gained by attempting to distinguish between the meaning of different words used in this connection.'"

Notes

1. The person who commits the crime, either personally or through an innocent agent, is called the principal or the first principal, or (the old expression which is still occasionally used), the principal in the first degree. At common law secondary parties in felonies were called principals in the second degree and accessories before the fact. These terms are now obsolete, a fact which must be borne in mind reading cases decided before 1967, but the difference between the two kinds of secondary parties to all offences is probably still precisely as it was in the case of felonies. The difference depended entirely on whether the secondary party was present during the commission of the crime.

2. *Blackstone*, Book IV, p. 33: "A principal . . . in the second degree, he is who is present, aiding and abetting the fact to be done. Which presence need not always be an actual immediate standing by, within sight and hearing of the fact; but there may also be a constructive presence as where one commits a robbery or murder, and another keeps watch or guard at some convenient distance."

3. If A and B agree to pilfer from a shop, and A goes round the corner to a call box and telephones the shopkeeper thus causing the latter to go into the rear room so that the shop is left unattended while B steals some object, A renders assistance so as to be a principal in the second degree. Does it make any difference that A makes the call from the other end of the country? In *Breeze* v. *The State*, 12 Ohio 146 (1861), A entertained a shopkeeper at a convivial gathering, while his confederates B and C broke into the shop. And in *State* v. *Hamilton and Laurie*, 12 Nev. 686 (1878), A was stationed on a mountain top 30 or 40 miles from an intended ambush of a stage coach. By means of a controlled fire, he signalled the approach

of the stage coach to his confederates, who were enabled to ambush it. In both cases A was held guilty as a principal in the second degree.

4. In *Ferguson* v. *Weaving* (for facts, see *post*, p. 266), the defendant, although "absent," was charged with aiding, abetting, counselling and procuring. Lord Goddard C.J.:

"At the hearing an application was made to amend the information against the respondent by the deletion of the words 'aid and abet', so that the information charged her only with counselling and procuring the commission of the offences. Before us it was contended on her behalf that, even if the facts on which the prosecution relied were accepted, they could only establish a case of aiding and abetting, and that there was no evidence that the respondent in any way counselled or procured the commission of the said offences. It is well known that the words 'aid and abet' are apt to describe the action of a person who is present at the time of the commission of an offence and takes some part therein. He is then described as an aider and abettor, whereas the words 'counsel and procure' are appropriate to a person who, though not present at the commission of the offence, is an accessory before the fact. That all these words may be used together to charge a person who is alleged to have participated in an offence otherwise than as a principal in the first degree was established by *Re Smith* (1858) 3 H. & N. 227. Whether, where the words 'counsel and procure' alone are used, there must be a proof of something more than would establish a case of being an accessory before the fact is not one which we feel necessary to decide in this case. . . . As we are satisfied that the respondent cannot be convicted as a participant, to use a compendious expression, in the offences charged against the persons who consumed the intoxicating liquor, we give no decision on it."

5. *Smith, "Aid, Abet, Counsel or Procure," supra, p. 127*: It is submitted that the true position is as follows. The distinction between "aiding and abetting" and "counselling and procuring", like that between principal and accessory, depends on one consideration only, namely whether the defendant was present (again in the large sense in which the common law understood that term) or absent. Notwithstanding the ordinary meaning of the words, the distinction does not turn in any way on the nature of the acts done by the defendant. Any act which would amount to "aiding and abetting" if done while present at the crime would amount to "counselling and procuring" if done while absent. Any act which would amount to "counselling and procuring" when done in the absence of the principal would amount to "aiding and abetting" if done while present at the crime. . . . If it is right to regard the words "aid and abet" as indicative of the liability of a person present and the words "counsel and procure" as indicative of the liability of a person absent, it is obvious that these are highly technical terms. It is inconsistent so to treat the words in one context and yet to regard them as words of ordinary meaning in another.

6. For a case where the extent of a party's liability apparently depended on whether she was present or absent, see below.

R. v. Richards
[1974] Q.B. 776
Court of Appeal

Mrs. R. told B. and S. that she would give them £5 if they would beat up her husband so that he would be in a hospital for a month. They planned the attack together, but, in Mrs. R.'s absence, B. and S. carried out the assault, in which they did not seriously injure the husband. They were all three charged with wounding the husband with intent to cause him grievous bodily harm, contrary to section 18 of the Offences against the Person Act 1861, and alternatively with unlawful wounding, contrary to section 20 of the same Act. B. and S. were found guilty of unlawful wounding, but Mrs. R. was convicted of wounding with intent to cause grievous bodily harm. She appealed.

James L.J.: . . . On the evening of February 25, 1973, the defendant's husband, Mr. Richards, left his home in Weymouth in order to go to work. Shortly afterwards in a lane not far away he was attacked by two men, who were wearing black balaclavas over their heads. He was struck on the back of his head. He tried to escape but was grabbed by the coat sleeves. Eventually he struggled free from his assailants. The medical evidence was that he sustained a laceration on the top of his scalp which required two stitches. There was no need for him to be detained in hospital; it was not a serious injury in fact.

On February 26 the defendant was arrested and at the police station she explained that, according to her, her marriage had been deteriorating, she had become very depressed and started drinking. She was asked if it was at her suggestion that her co-accused Bryant (known as Alan) and Squires (known as Paul) attacked her husband, and to that she replied that she had made the suggestion but in fact she did not want them to hurt him. She said: "All I wanted was for us to get together again. I thought if he was hurt, he would turn to me for affection." But in her statement she admitted in these words: "I told them that I wanted them to beat him up bad enough to put him in hospital for a month." She agreed that she had told them that she would give them £5 if they would beat up her husband. She also admitted that she had suggested the appropriate time that her husband might be attacked, namely, when he went out to work and that she would give a signal by putting on the kitchen light in the house where they lived so that those lying in wait would know when he was setting off for work. As it turned out, there was a power cut at the time so she could not put the light on; she had to hold a candle up to the window, but she played her part as she had promised.

None of the accused gave evidence at the trial and they were content to rest upon the basis that the jury might find them guilty of the second less serious offence. Thus in the upshot the two persons who committed the acts which were the foundation of the offence alleged in count 2 were guilty of an offence under section 20; the defendant, who committed no physical act upon the victim herself at all, was convicted of the more serious offence.

Mr. Aplin's submissions are brief. He says that looking at the facts of this case the defendant is in the position of one who aided and abetted, or counselled and procured, to use the old language, the other two to commit the offence, and that she cannot be guilty of a graver crime than the crime of which the two co-accused were guilty. There was only one offence that was committed, committed by the co-accused, an offence under section 20, and therefore there is no offence under section 18 of the Act of which his client can properly be found guilty on the facts of this case.

Mr. Purvis has referred us to a number of authorities in support of his submissions and argument that it is possible, and it should be on the facts of this case, that a person who did no physical act herself by way of assault should nevertheless be guilty of the graver crime of wounding with intent if it is established that she had that specific intent, although persons who were acting at her counselling and command did not have the specific intent that she had and therefore are not themselves guilty of the graver offence.

In support of this argument Mr. Purvis invites our attention first to *R.* v. *Merriman* [1973] A.C. 584 and in particular to a passage in the speech of Lord Diplock. After Lord Diplock had referred to the authorities of *Hale, Pleas of the Crown* (1778), vol. 2, p. 173 and *Hawkins' Pleas of the Crown*, 8th ed. (1824), vol. 2, p. 331, he said, at p. 607:

> "I conclude, therefore, that whenever two or more defendants are charged in the same count of an indictment with any offence which men can help one another to commit it is sufficient to support a conviction against any and each of them to prove *either* that he himself did a physical act which is an essential ingredient of the offence charged" (and I interrupt to stress those words "of the offence charged") "*or* that he helped another defendant to do such an act, *and*, that in doing the act or in helping the other defendant to do it, he himself had the necessary criminal intent."

Mr. Purvis says the words "had the necessary criminal intent" in that passage can be applied to the position of the defendant, she being one who intended the other to do something to her husband that would amount to an injury sufficient to put him in hospital for a month.

Then (without attempting to cite in any detail all the authorities to which we have been referred, for it is not necessary to do so in the light of the view we have formed as to the facts of this particular case), Mr. Purvis invites our attention to *Smith and Hogan, Criminal Law*, 2nd ed. (1969), in particular at p. 90, para. 5. Paragraph 6 is a section which deals with accomplices, and in particular on p. 92, after reference to *Russell on Crime*, 12th ed. (1964), and again citing from *Hawkins*, p. 439, one finds:

> ". . . if there were malice in the abettor, and none in the person who struck the party, it will be murder as to the abettor, and manslaughter only as to the other."

There the person who is an abettor, using the old word again, not actually doing the physical act himself, is said to be guilty possibly of the more serious crime than the crime of which the person acting is guilty. But it is right to observe that *Hawkins*, the authority for that proposition there cited, confines that to a case in which the person who is said to be capable of being guilty of the more serious offence is an abettor, a different situation from one who is in the position of an accessory, though as to accessories on the same page [*Smith and Hogan, Criminal Law*, p. 92] *Hawkins* thought, it is said:

> ". . . that the abettor might be guilty of a greater crime than the principal in the first degree, he was emphatic that the rule was otherwise with respect to accessories before the fact": then quoting *Hawkins*, at p. 442, it continues: "'I take it to be an uncontroverted rule (that the offence of the accessory can never rise higher than that of principal); it seeming incongruous and absurd that he who is punished only as a partaker of the guilt of another, should be adjudged guilty of a higher crime than the other.'"

It is convenient to cite again from p. 93 of *Smith and Hogan, Criminal Law* because this puts in a very short compass an essential part of Mr. Purvis's argument:

> "The true principle, it is suggested,"—Mr. Purvis says this is right—"is that where the principal has caused an *actus reus*, the liability of each of the secondary parties should be assessed according to his own *mens rea*. If there is no *actus reus*, then certainly no one can be convicted."

We have been helpfully invited again to look at *R.* v. *Anthony* [1965] 2 Q.B. 189; *R.* v. *Humphreys and Turner* [1965] 3 All E.R. 689, and the passage in *Archbold Criminal Pleading Evidence & Practice*, 38th ed. (1973), para. 4136, p. 1562 is drawn to our attention where it is said, citing as authority for the proposition *R.* v. *Burton* (1875) 13 Cox C.C. 71:

> "If an aider and abettor and a principal in an offence are indicted together as principals, the aider and abettor may be convicted, although the principal is acquitted: . . .".

Mr. Purvis says that here one can properly look at the *actus reus*, that is the physical blows struck upon Mr. Richards, and separately the intention with which the blows were struck. The defendant, he says, is responsible for the blows being struck, the *actus reus*, because they were struck at her request by the co-accused. If, as Mr. Purvis says is the case, the specific intention of the defendant was different from the specific intention if any proved to be entertained on the part of the co-accused, then it is proper that the defendant should be convicted of the section 18 offence if that specific intention goes so far as to amount to intent to cause grievous bodily harm, although that intention was never in the minds of the persons who committed the acts at her request.

We do not take that view. Looking at the facts of this case the acts were perpetrated at some distance from where the defendant was. She was not truly in a position which would earlier have been described as an abettor of those who did the acts. There is proved on the evidence in this case one offence and one offence only, namely, the offence of unlawful wounding without the element of specific intent. We do not think it right that one could say that that which was done can be said to be done with the intention of the defendant who was not present at the time and whose intention did not go to the offence which was in fact committed. That is the short point in the case as we see it. If there is only one offence committed, and that is the offence of unlawful wounding, then the person who has requested that offence to be committed, or advised that that offence be committed, cannot be guilty of a graver offence than that in fact which was committed.

For those reasons we think that this conviction cannot stand. On the other hand it is quite clear that the defendant was guilty of the offence which was in fact committed, namely, an offence of unlawful wounding, and Mr. Aplin does not seek to suggest otherwise. In fact the defendant acknowledged it by her attempted plea at the trial, so what this court will do is to quash the conviction that was sustained and substitute a conviction for unlawful wounding.

Appeal allowed

Questions

1. What do you think the Court's attitude would have been if Mrs. Richards had been held to be "present"?
2. Was the Court justified in treating her as "absent"?
3. *Ought* the liability of a person in her position to turn upon presence or absence?

Mohan v. R.
[1967] 2 A.C. 187
Privy Council

> D. was quarrelling with M., when R., who was D.'s father, ran out of his house and attacked M. with a cutlass. While R. was chasing M., D. went off and returned with another cutlass. Both struck many blows at M., who collapsed and later died. He was found to be wounded in the back and in the leg. It appeared that death was caused only by the leg wound.

D. and R. were convicted of murder, and appealed on the ground that, as there was no evidence of a pre-arranged plan to attack M., the Crown must show which of them struck the fatal blow.

LORD PEARSON: [The appellants' argument] will be considered on the hypothesis that the death may have been caused solely by the leg wound. The question then arises whether each of the appellants can be held responsible for the leg wound, when it may have been inflicted by the other of them. There is conflicting evidence as to which of them struck the blow on M.'s leg, the evidence for the prosecution tending to show that the appellant D. struck it and the evidence for the defence tending to show that the appellant R. struck it. There is uncertainty on that point.

Also it cannot be inferred with any certainty from the evidence that the appellants had a pre-arranged plan for their attack on M.

It is, however, clear from the evidence for the defence as well as from the evidence for the prosecution, that at the material time both the appellants were armed with cutlasses, both were attacking M., and both struck him. It is impossible on the facts of this case to contend that the fatal blow was outside the scope of the common intention. The two appellants were attacking the same man at the same time with similar weapons and with the common intention that he should suffer grievous bodily harm. Each of the appellants was present, and aiding and abetting the other of them in the wounding of M.

That is the feature which distinguishes this case from cases in which one of the accused was not present or not participating in the attack or not using any dangerous weapon, but may be held liable as a conspirator or an accessory before the fact or by virtue of a common design if it can be shown that he was party to a pre-arranged plan in pursuance of which the fatal blow was struck. In this case one of the appellants struck the fatal blow, and the other of them was present aiding and abetting him. In such cases the prosecution do not have to prove that the accused were acting in pursuance of a pre-arranged plan.

Appeals dismissed

Question

A and B were involved in the death of C, one holding him while the other stabbed him. Jointly charged with murder, they both give evidence of duress. It cannot be shown who was the stabber. What is the position? See *Lynch* v. *D.P.P. for Northern Ireland*, and *Abbott* v. *R.*, *ante*, pp. 203, 221.

ii. Mens Rea of a Secondary Party

Maxwell v. Director of Public Prosecutions for Northern Ireland
(1978) 68 Cr. App. R. 128
House of Lords

The facts are set out in the speech of Lord Hailsham

LORD HAILSHAM OF ST. MARYLEBONE: My Lords, in my opinion this appeal should be dismissed. The appellant was the owner and driver of the guide car in what subsequently turned out to be a terrorist attack by members of the criminal and illegal organisation known as the Ulster Volunteer Force (UVF) on a public house owned by a Roman Catholic licensee at 40, Grange Road, Toomebridge and known as the Crosskeys Inn. The attack was carried out on the night of January 3, 1976 by the occupants of a Cortina car and took the form of throwing a pipe bomb containing about five pounds of explosive into the hallway of the public house. The attack failed because the son of the proprietor had the presence of mind to pull out the burning fuse and detonator and throw it outside the premises where the detonator exploded either because the fuse had reached the detonator or on contact with the ground.

The appellant was tried on October 13, 1976, on an indictment containing four counts to two of which he pleaded guilty. This appeal is concerned with the remaining two counts (numbered 1 and 2) on which he was convicted at the Belfast City Commission by MacDermott J. sitting without a jury.

The two counts are as follows:

First Count

Statement of Offence

Doing an act with intent, contrary to section 3 (a) of the Explosive Substances Act 1883.

Particulars of Offence

"James Charles Maxwell, on January 3, 1976, in the county of Antrim, unlawfully and maliciously did an act with intent to cause by explosive substances, namely a pipe bomb, an explosion in the United Kingdom of a nature likely to endanger life or cause serious injury to property, in that he placed the said pipe bomb with fuse lit inside the premises known as the Crosskeys Inn, at Toomebridge, in the said county."

Second Count

Statement of Offence

Possession of explosive substance with intent, contrary to section 3 (b) of the Explosive Substances Act 1883.

Particulars of Offence

"James Charles Maxwell, on January 3, 1976, in the county of Antrim, unlawfully and maliciously had in his possession or under his control a pipe bomb with intent by means thereof to endanger life or cause serious injury to property in the United Kingdom or to enable any other person by means thereof to endanger life or cause serious injury to property in the United Kingdom."

It will be seen that, in the above counts, the accused was charged, as the general law permits, as a principal, but the real case against him was that, as the driver of the guide car, he was what used to be known as an accessory before the fact. Although no complaint is made about the form of the counts I agree with the view expressed by my noble and learned friend Viscount Dilhorne of the desirability in these cases of aiding, abetting, counselling or procuring, of drawing the particulars of offence in such a way as to disclose with greater clarity the real nature of the case that the accused has to answer.

The only substantial matter to be discussed in the appeal is the degree of knowledge required before an accused can be found guilty of aiding, abetting, counselling, or procuring. To what extent must the accused be proved to have particular knowledge of the crime in contemplation at the time of his participation and which was ultimately committed by its principal perpetrators? For myself I am content for this purpose to adopt the words of Lord Parker C.J. in *R.* v. *Bainbridge* [1960] 1 Q.B. 129 when, after saying that it is not easy to lay down a precise form of words which will cover every case, he observed at p. 134 "... there must not be merely suspicion but knowledge that a crime of the type in question was intended ..." and the words of Lord Goddard C.J. in *Johnson* v. *Youden* [1950] 1 K.B. 544, 546, endorsed by this House in *Churchill* v. *Walton* [1967] 2 A.C. 224, 236 that "Before a person can be convicted of aiding and abetting the commission of an offence he must at least know the essential matters which constitute that offence." The only question in debate in the present appeal is whether the degree of knowledge possessed by the appellant was of the "essential matters constituting" the offence in fact committed, or, to put what in the context of the instant case is exactly the same question in another form, whether the appellant knew that the offence in which he participated was "a crime of the type" described in the charge.

For that purpose I turn to two passages in the findings of fact of the learned judge. The first is as follows: "In my judgment, the facts of this case make it clear to me that the accused knew the men in the Cortina car were going to attack the Inn and had the means of attacking the Inn with them in their car. The accused may not, as he says, have known what form the attack was going to take, but in my judgment he knew the means of the attack, be they bomb, bullet or incendiary device, were present in that car."

In the second passage MacDermott J. said: "In my judgment, the accused knew that he was participating in an attack on the Inn. He performed an important role in the execution of that attack. He knew that the attack was one which would involve the use of means which would result in danger to life or damage to property. In such circumstances, where an admitted terrorist participates actively in a terrorist attack, having knowledge of the type of attack intended, if not of the weapon chosen by his colleagues, he can in my view be properly charged with possession of the weapon with which it is intended that life should be endangered or premises seriously damaged."

The learned judge also found *inter alia* that the word "job" (as used in the appellant's statements) is "synonymous with military action which raises, having regard to the proven activities of the UVF, the irresistible inference [that] the attack would be one of violence in which people would be endangered or premises seriously damaged."

There was no dispute that there was ample evidence to support all these findings and it follows that the only question is whether the passages contain some self-misdirection in point of law. As to this I agree with the opinion of Sir Robert Lowry C.J. (in the Court of Criminal Appeal for Northern Ireland) when he said [1978] 1 W.L.R. 1363, 1375: "The facts found here show that the appellant, as a member of an organisation which habitually perpetrates sectarian acts of violence with firearms and explosives, must, as soon as he was briefed for his role, have contemplated the bombing of the Crosskeys Inn as not the only possibility but one of the most obvious possibilities among the jobs which the principals were likely to be undertaking and in the commission of which he was intentionally assisting. He was therefore in just the same situation, so far as guilty knowledge is concerned, as a man who had been given a list of jobs and told that one of them would be carried out."

The only argument attacking this passage of any substance directed to your Lordships on the part of the appellant was to the effect that since at the time of the commission of the offence there was no generalised offence of terrorism as such the state of ignorance which must be assumed in favour of the accused as to the precise weapon (*e.g.* bomb, bullets, or incendiary device) or type of violence to be employed in the concerted "job" contemplated was such as to make him ignorant of some or all of the "essential ingredients" of the two offences charged in the particulars of offence in which a "pipe bomb" is specified, and one at least of which, had it been committed, would or at least might have been laid under a separate penal provision.

I regard this point as frankly unarguable. I would consider that bullet, bomb, or incendiary device, indeed most if not all types of terrorist violence, would all constitute offences of the same "type" within the meaning of *R.* v. *Bainbridge* and that so far as *mens rea* is concerned "the essential ingredients" of all and each of the offences within the other authorities I have cited were each and all contained within the guilty knowledge of the appellant at the time of his participation. The fact that, in the event, the offence committed by the principals crystallised into one rather than the other of the possible alternatives within his contemplation only means that in the event he was accessory to that specific offence rather than one of the others which in the event was not the offence committed. Obviously there must be limits to the meaning of the expression "type of offence" and a minimum significance attached to the expression "essential ingredients" in this type of doctrine, but it is clear that if an alleged accessory is perfectly well aware that he is participating in one of a limited number of serious crimes and one of these is in fact committed he is liable under the general law at least as one who aids, abets, counsels or procures that crime even if he is not actually a principal. Otherwise I can see no end to the number of unmeritorious arguments which the ingenuity of defendants could adduce. This disposes of the present appeal, which seems to me to be as lacking in serious plausibility as it is wholly devoid of substantial merits. I should perhaps add that I was at one time doubtful whether some distinction could be drawn between counts 1 and 2. But counsel for the appellant did not attempt to draw such a distinction, and, for the reasons given by my noble and learned friend Lord Scarman, I am of the opinion that in this case omission was the better part of valour.

LORD SCARMAN: My Lords, I also would dismiss this appeal. The question it raises is as to the degree of knowledge required by law for the attachment of criminal responsibility to one who assists another (or others) to commit or attempt crime.

In *Johnson* v. *Youden* [1950] 1 K.B. 544 the Divisional Court held that before a person can be convicted of aiding and abetting the commission of an offence he must at least know the essential matters which constitute the offence. He does not have to know that the facts constitute an offence: for ignorance of the law is no defence. In *R.* v. *Bainbridge* the Court of Criminal Appeal (for England and Wales) held that it was not necessary that the accused should know the particular crime intended or committed by those whom he assisted, and upheld a direction in which the judge had made it clear that it was enough if the accused knew the type of crime intended.

Counsel for the appellant submits that, if *R.* v. *Bainbridge* is to be followed, there is no evidence in the present case that the appellant knew the particular type of crime intended, *i.e.* doing an act with intent to cause an explosion of the nature likely to endanger life or cause serious injury to property. Counsel is really submitting that, if his client's conviction be upheld on either of the two counts with which his appeal is concerned (count 1, doing an act with intent to cause an explosion, and count 2, possession of an explosive substance with intent), your Lordships will be extending the law beyond the decision in *R.* v. *Bainbridge* and that, even if that decision be good law, such extension is unjustifiable.

I think *R.* v. *Bainbridge* was correctly decided. But I agree with counsel for the appellant that in the instant case the Court of Criminal Appeal in Northern Ireland has gone further than the Court of Criminal Appeal for England and Wales found it necessary to go in *R.* v. *Bainbridge*. It is not possible in the present case to declare that it is proved, beyond reasonable doubt, that the appellant knew a bomb attack upon the Inn was intended by those whom he was assisting. It is not established, therefore, that he knew the particular type of crime intended. The Court, however, refused to limit criminal responsibility by reference to knowledge by the accused of the type or class of crime intended by those whom he assisted. Instead, the Court has formulated a principle which avoids the uncertainties and ambiguities of classification. The guilt of an accessory springs, according to the Court's formulation, "from the fact that he contemplates the commission of one (or more) of a number of crimes by the principal and he intentionally lends his assistance in order that such a crime will be committed": *per* Sir Robert Lowry C.J. "The relevant crime," the Lord Chief Justice continues, "must be within the contemplation of the accomplice, and only exceptionally would evidence be found to support the allegation that the accomplice had given the principal a completely blank cheque."

The principle thus formulated has great merit. It directs attention to the state of mind of the accused—not what he ought to have in contemplation, but what he did have: it avoids definition and classification while ensuring that a man will not be convicted of aiding and abetting any offence his principal may commit, but only one which is within his contemplation. He may have in contemplation only one offence, or several: and the several which he contemplates he may see as alternatives. An accessory who leaves it to his principal to choose is liable, provided always the choice is made from the range of offences from which the accessory contemplates the choice will be made. Although the court's formulation of the principle goes further than the earlier cases, it is a sound development of the law and in no way inconsistent with them. I accept it as good judge-made law in a field where there is no statute to offer guidance.

Upon the facts as found by the trial judge (there was no jury because of the Northern Ireland (Emergency Provisions) Act 1973), the appellant knew he was guiding a party of men to the Crosskeys Inn on a UVF military-style "job", *i.e.* an attack by bomb, incendiary or bullet on persons or property. He did not know the particular type of offence intended, but he must have appreciated that it was very likely that those whom he was assisting intended a bomb attack on the Inn.

If the appellant contemplated, as he clearly did, a bomb attack as likely, he must also have contemplated the possibility that the men in the car, which he was leading to the Inn, had an explosive substance with them. Though he did not know whether they had it with them or not, he must have believed it very likely that they did. In the particular circumstances of this case, the inference that the two offences of possessing the explosive and using it with intent to cause injury or damage were within the appellant's contemplation is fully justified upon the evidence. The appellant was rightly convicted, and I would dismiss his appeal.

Appeal dismissed

National Coal Board v. Gamble
[1959] 1 Q.B. 11
Queen's Bench Division

The National Coal Board had an instalment contract with the Central Electricity Authority for a supply of coal to be delivered at a colliery into lorries sent by a carrier on behalf of the authority. In pursuance of this contract W. Ltd., a carrier, sent a lorry in the charge of its servant M. into the colliery. The method of loading was for a lorry-driver to place his lorry under the Board's hopper and tell the hopper operator to stop when the driver thought he had enough coal on his lorry. The lorry was then driven to the colliery weighbridge which was in the charge of H., a servant of the Board. H., after weighing the lorry and its load, would give the driver a ticket showing the weight of coal loaded, which ticket operated as a delivery note, so that the sale of the load of coal was then complete and the property in the coal passed from the Board to the purchaser.

M. went through this procedure, but when H. weighed his lorry and load he discovered that they together exceeded the maximum permitted weight for a vehicle being driven on a road. H. drew M.'s attention to

> this fact, and there was also a large notice at the door of the weighbridge office warning drivers that the Board was not responsible for the use of any vehicle on a road which was loaded beyond its authorised capacity. On being asked by H. if he intended to take this load (which he could easily have offloaded) M. said that he would risk it. H. then handed M. the weighbridge ticket and M. drove the overloaded lorry out of the colliery onto a road, thereby committing an offence against the Motor Vehicles (Construction and Use) Regulations 1955.
>
> The Board were charged with and convicted of aiding, abetting, counselling and procuring the carrier W. Ltd. to commit the offence under the Regulations. The board appealed.

DEVLIN J.: A person who supplies the instrument for a crime or anything essential to its commission aids in the commission of it; and if he does so knowingly and with intent to aid, he abets it as well and is therefore guilty of aiding and abetting. I use the word "supplies" to comprehend giving, lending, selling or any other transfer of the right of property. In a sense a man who gives up to a criminal a weapon which the latter has a right to demand from him aids in the commission of the crime as much as if he sold or lent the article. But this has never been held to be aiding in law: see *R.* v. *Lomas* (1913) 110 L.T. 239; and *R.* v. *Bullock* [1955] 1 W.L.R. 1. The reason, I think, is that in the former case there is in law a positive act and in the latter only a negative one. In the transfer of property there must be either a physical delivery or a positive act of assent to a taking. But a man who hands over to another his own property on demand, although he may physically be performing a positive act, in law is only refraining from detinue. Thus in law the former act is one of assistance voluntarily given and the latter is only a failure to prevent the commission of the crime by means of forcible detention, which would not even be justified except in the case of felony. Another way of putting the point is to say that aiding and abetting is a crime that requires proof of *mens rea*, that is to say, of intention to aid as well as of knowledge of the circumstances, and proof of the intent involves proof of a positive act of assistance voluntarily done.

These considerations make it necessary to determine at what point the property in the coal passed from the Board and what the Board's state of knowledge was at that time. If the property had passed before the Board knew of the proposed crime, there was nothing they could legally do to prevent the driver of the lorry from taking the overloaded lorry out onto the road. If it had not, then they sold the coal with knowledge that an offence was going to be committed. (His lordship repeated the facts as found in the case.)

In these circumstances, the property in the coal passed on delivery to the carrier in accordance with Rule 5 of section 18 of the Sale of Goods Act, 1893. If the delivery was complete after loading and before weighing, the Board has not until after delivery any knowledge that an offence had been committed. But where weighing is necessary for the purpose of the contract, as, for example, in order to ascertain the price of an instalment, the property does not pass until the weight has been agreed. In *Simmons* v. *Swift* (1826) 5 B. & C. 857, the parties agreed to buy and sell "the bark stacked at Redbrook at £9. 5s. per ton." It was held that the property did not pass until the bark had been weighed and the price ascertained. Bayley J. said that the concurrence of the seller was necessary and he might insist on keeping possession until the bark had been weighed.

It was contended on behalf of the Board that H had no option after weighing but to issue a ticket for the amount then in the lorry. I think this contention is unsound. In the circumstances of this case the loading must be taken as subject to adjustment; otherwise, if the contract were for a limited amount, the seller might make an over-delivery or an under-delivery which could not thereafter be rectified and the carrier might be contractually compelled to carry away a load in excess of that legally permitted. I think that delivery of the coal was not completed until after the ascertained weight had been assented to and some act was done signifying assent and passing the property. The property passed when H asked M whether he intended to take the load and M said he would risk it and when mutual assent was, as it were, sealed by the delivery and acceptance of the weighbridge ticket. He could, therefore, after he knew of the overload, have refused to transfer the property in the coals.

This is the conclusion to which the justices came. Mr. Thompson submits on behalf of the Board that it does not justify a verdict of guilty of aiding and abetting. He submits, first, that even if knowledge of the illegal purpose had been acquired before delivery began, it would not be sufficient for the verdict; and secondly, that if he is wrong about that, the knowledge was acquired too late and the Board was not guilty of aiding and abetting simply because H failed to stop the process of delivery after it had been initiated.

On his first point Mr. Thompson submits that the furnishing of an article essential to the crime with knowledge of the use to which it is to be put does not of itself constitute aiding and abetting; there must be proved in addition a purpose or motive of the defendant to further the crime or encourage the criminal. Otherwise, he submits, there is no *mens rea*.

I have already said that in my judgment there must be proof of an intent to aid. I would agree that proof that the article was knowingly supplied is not conclusive evidence of intent to aid. *R.* v. *Fretwell* (1862) L. & C. 161, is authority for that. *R.* v. *Steane* [1947] K.B. 997, in which the defendant was charged with having acted during the war with intent to assist the enemy contrary to the Defence Regulations then in force, makes the same point. But *prima facie*—*R.* v. *Steane* makes this clear also—a man is presumed to intend the natural and probable consequences of his acts, and the consequence of supplying essential material is that assistance is given to the criminal. It is always open to the defendant, as in *R.* v. *Steane*, to give evidence of his real intention. But in this case the defence called no evidence. The *prima facie* presumption is therefore enough to justify the verdict, unless it is the law that some other mental element besides intent is necessary to the offence.

This is what Mr. Thompson argues, and he describes the additional element as the purpose or motive of encouraging the crime. No doubt evidence of an interest in the crime or of an express purpose to assist it will greatly strengthen the case of the prosecution. But an indifference to the result of the crime does not of itself negative abetting. If one man deliberately sells to another a gun to be used for murdering a third, he may be indifferent about whether the third man lives or dies and interested only in the cash profit to be made out of the sale, but he can still be an aider and abettor. To hold otherwise would be to negative the rule that *mens rea* is a matter of intent only and does not depend on desire or motive.

The authorities, I think, support this conclusion, though none has been cited to us in which the point has been specifically argued and decided....

The same principle has been applied in civil cases where the seller has sued upon a contract for the supply of goods which he knew were to be used for an illegal purpose. In some of the authorities there is a suggestion that he could recover on the contract unless it appeared that in addition to knowledge of the purpose he had an interest in the venture and looked for payment to the proceeds of the crime. But in *Pearce* v. *Brooks* (1866) L.R. 1 Ex. 213, Pollock C.B. stated the law as follows:

> "I have always considered it as settled law that any person who contributes to the performance of an illegal act by supplying a thing with the knowledge that it is going to be used for that purpose, cannot recover the price of the thing so supplied. If, to create that incapacity, it was ever considered neces-

> sary that the price should be bargained or expected to be paid out of the fruits of the illegal act (which I do not stop to examine), that proposition has been overruled by the cases I have referred to, and has now ceased to be law."

The case chiefly relied on by Mr. Thompson was *R.* v. *Coney* (1882) 8 Q.B.D. 534. In that case the defendants were charged with aiding and abetting an illegal prize fight at which they had been present. The judgments all refer to "encouragement", but it would be wrong to conclude from that that proof of encouragement is necessary to every form of aiding and abetting. Presence on the scene of the crime without encouragement or assistance is no aid to the criminal; the supply of essential material is. Moreover, the decision makes it clear that encouragement can be inferred from mere presence. Cave J., who gave the leading judgment, said of the summing-up: "It may mean either that mere presence unexplained is evidence of encouragement, and so of guilt, or that mere presence unexplained is conclusive proof of encouragement, and so of guilt. If the former is the correct meaning I concur in the law so laid down; if the latter, I am unable to do so." This dictum seems to me to support the view I have expressed. If voluntary presence is *prima facie* evidence of encouragement and therefore of aiding and abetting, it appears to me to be *a fortiori* that the intentional supply of an essential article must be *prima facie* evidence of aiding and abetting.

As to Mr. Thompson's alternative point, I have already expressed the view that the facts show an act of assent made by H after knowledge of the proposed illegality and without which the property would not have passed. If some positive act to complete delivery is committed after knowledge of the illegality, the position in law must, I think, be just the same as if the knowledge had been obtained before the delivery had been begun. Of course, it is quite likely that H was confused about the legal position and thought that he was not entitled to withhold the weighbridge ticket. There is no *mens rea* if the defendant is shown to have a genuine belief in the existence of circumstances which, if true, would negative an intention to aid; see *Wilson* v. *Inyang* [1951] 2 K.B. 799; but this argument, which might have been the most cogent available to the defence, cannot now be relied upon, because H was not called to give evidence about what he thought or believed.

Appeal dismissed

Notes

1. Lord Goddard C.J. delivered a concurring judgment. Slade J. dissented on the ground that the alleged aider must have assisted or encouraged the principal offender. "It is not sufficient that the alleged abettor should be proved to have done some act, or to have made some omission, without which the principal offender could not have committed the offence; nor is it sufficient that such act or omission had the effect of facilitating the commission of the offence or that it in fact operated on the mind of the principal offender so as to decide him to commit it. The prosecution must prove that the act or omission upon which they rely as constituting the alleged aiding and abetting was done or made with a view to assisting or encouraging the principal offender to commit the offence or, in other words, with the motive of endorsing the commission of the offence." His Lordship considered that the facts found by the magistrates did not support the inference that H. meant to encourage M. in any way.

2. Devlin J.'s discussion becomes heavily involved with the civil law of sale, the passing of property, and the ability of a seller to sue on a contract

tainted by illegality. It seems inappropriate for the criminal law to be entangled with the civil law this way. No doubt Slade J.'s solution, requiring a positive motive of endorsing the commission of the offence, is too lax, at any rate where a serious crime is substantially facilitated by the sale. But could not the law take some account of the triviality of the offence aided and/or of the aid supplied? A gunsmith selling a gun to a man he knows is about to commit an armed robbery is one thing, but a garage attendant selling a gallon of petrol to a motorist whose road fund licence has expired seems quite another.

3. On the necessity for "encouragement," denied by Devlin J., see *R.* v. *Allan* [1965] 1 Q.B. 130, 138:

"Indeed, in our judgment, encouragement in one form or another is a minimal requirement before an accused person may properly be regarded as a principal in the second degree to any crime. It is true that, in *National Coal Board* v. *Gamble* Devlin J. referring to *Coney* said:

> '. . . it would be wrong to conclude . . . that proof of encouragement is necessary to every form of aiding and abetting.'

But when the facts of that case are examined, it does not, in our judgment, affect the validity of the proposition which we have stated, for there the accused had intentionally supplied an article essential to the perpetration of the crime charged, and this Devlin J. described as an *a fortiori* case to that of voluntary presence. In that case, there was what was judicially described as 'proof of intent to aid', which may properly be regarded as but one of the numerous possible manifestations of encouragement."

R. v. Clarkson

[1971] 1 W.L.R. 1402
Court-Martial Appeal Court

> The accused were charged with aiding and abetting three offences of rape. The evidence was that the accused, who had been drinking heavily, heard a disturbance in a room. They went in and stood watching whilst a woman was raped. They gave neither physical assistance nor verbal encouragement. They were convicted and appealed.

MEGAW L.J.: ". . . Let it be accepted, and there was evidence to justify this assumption, that the presence of those two defendants in the room where the offence was taking place was not accidental in any sense and that it was not by chance, unconnected with the crime, that they were there. Let it be accepted that they entered the room when the crime was committed because of what they had heard, which indicated that a woman was being raped, and they remained there.

R. v. *Coney* (1882) 8 Q.B.D. 534, decided that non-accidental presence at the scene of the crime is not conclusive of aiding and abetting. The jury has to be told by the judge, or in this case the court-martial has to be told by the judge advocate, in clear terms what it is that has to be proved before they can convict of aiding and abetting; what it is of which the jury or the court-martial, as the case may be, must be sure as matters of inference before they can convict of aiding and abetting in such a case where the evidence adduced by the prosecution is limited to non-accidental presence.

What has to be proved is stated in *R.* v. *Coney* by Hawkins J. in a well-known passage in his judgment, at p. 557:

> "In my opinion, to constitute an aider and abettor some active steps must be taken by word, or action, with the intent to instigate the principal, or principals. Encouragement does not of necessity amount to aiding and abetting, it may be intentional or unintentional, a man may unwittingly encourage another in fact by his presence, by misinterpreted words, or gestures, or by his silence, or non-interference or he may encourage intentionally by expressions, or gestures, or actions intended to signify approval. In the latter case he aids and abets, in the former he does not. It is no criminal offence to stand by, a mere passive spectator of a crime, even of a murder. Non-interference to prevent a crime is not itself a crime. But the fact that a person was voluntarily and purposely present witnessing the commission of a crime, and offered no opposition to it, though he might reasonably be expected to prevent and had the power so to do, or at least to express his dissent, might under some circumstances, afford cogent evidence upon which a jury would be justified in finding that he wilfully encouraged and so aided and abetted. But it would be purely a question for the jury whether he did so or not."

It is not enough, then, that the presence of the accused has, in fact, given encouragement. It must be proved that the accused intended to give encouragement; that he *wilfully* encouraged. In a case such as the present, more than in many other cases where aiding and abetting is alleged, it was essential that that element should be stressed; for there was here at least the possibility that a drunken man with his self-discipline loosened by drink, being aware that a woman was being raped, might be attracted to the scene and might stay on the scene in the capacity of what is known as a voyeur; and, while his presence and the presence of others might in fact encourage the rapers or discourage the victim, he, himself, enjoying the scene or at least standing by assenting, might not intend that his presence should offer encouragement to rapers and would-be rapers or discouragement to the victim; he might not realise that he was giving encouragement; so that, while encouragement there might be, it would not be a case in which, to use the words of Hawkins J., the accused person "wilfully encouraged".

A further point is emphasized in passages in the judgment of the Court of Criminal Appeal in *R.* v. *Allan* [1965] 1 Q.B. 130, 135, 138. That was a case concerned with participation in an affray. The court said, at p. 135:

> "in effect, it amounts to this: that the judge thereby directed the jury that they were duty bound to convict an accused who was proved to have been present and witnessing an affray if it was also proved that he nursed an intention to join in if help was needed by the side he favoured and this notwithstanding that he did nothing by words or deeds to evince his intention and outwardly played the role of a purely passive spectator. It was said that, if that direction is right, where A and B behave themselves to all outward appearances in an exactly similar manner, but it be proved that A had the intention to participate if needs be, whereas B had no such intention, then A must be convicted of being a principal in the second degree to the affray, whereas B should be acquitted. To do that, it is objected, would be to convict A on his thoughts, even though they found no reflection in his actions."

The other passage in the judgment is at p. 138:

> "In our judgment, before a jury can properly convict an accused person of being a principal in the second degree to an affray, they must be convinced

> by the evidence that, at the very least, he by some means or other encouraged the participants. To hold otherwise would be, in effect, as the appellants' counsel rightly expressed it, to convict a man on his thoughts, unaccompanied by any physical act other than the fact of his mere presence."

From that it follows that mere intention is not in itself enough. There must be an intention to encourage; and there must also be encouragement in fact, in cases such as the present case.

So we come to what was said by the judge advocate. First there was the guidance which he gave to the court after the submissions had been made at the close of the prosecution's case. The relevance of that to the matters which the court now has to decide has already been mentioned. There is a passage in that guidance in which the judge advocate said:

> "You have been told correctly the position as regards an aider and abettor, and that is all that the accused is charged with in these three charges. To be an aider and abettor, a person need not take any active steps in the commission of a crime, but he must be in a position to render assistance or encouragement by actual or constructive presence, and he must share a common intention with them that the crime should be committed. An illustration is that of a jeweller's shop. One man will throw a brick through the window and somebody else will snatch the valuables inside. It might be said that they were the people who actually committed the offence itself, but on such an occasion there will be somebody standing by with a motor car to enable the others to make their getaway. Probably someone is on the corner to make sure there is no policeman about to arrive on the scene. One or two others may be present to thrust out a leg and trip up anybody who may interfere or get in the way, if necessary, of those who will go in pursuit. They are sharing a common intention that the offence should be committed and they are aiders and abettors. Other people may be standing by, but the mere fact that a person watches and just stands by without sharing the common purpose of the others, is not guilty of aiding and abetting."

The judge advocate draws the analogy which is commonly drawn where direction is given of two persons jointly indicted, for example, of committing burglary. One actually enters the house and the other stands outside to keep watch. That analogy, in the view of this court, is misleading in relation to what was involved in the present case. For it presupposes a prior meeting of minds between the persons concerned as to the crime to be committed. The man who stands outside and does not go in is guilty of burglary; but it cannot in such a case properly be said that he has taken no active step in the commission of the offence. He has gone to the place where he is, and he has conducted himself as he does, as a part of the joint plan which, in its totality, is intended to procure commission of the crime.

In the view of this court the echo of that false analogy unfortunately continued throughout when the judge advocate came to sum up the matter to the court-martial. . . . This court has come to the conclusion that the court might have misunderstood the relevant principles that ought to be applied. It might have been left under the impression that it could find these two defendants guilty on the basis of their continuing, non-accidental presence, even though it was not sure that the necessary inferences to be drawn from the evidence included (i) an intention to encourage and (ii) actual encouragement. While we have no doubt that those inferences could properly have been drawn in respect of each defendant on each count, so that verdicts of guilty could properly have been returned, we cannot say that the court-martial, properly directed, would necessarily have drawn those inferences. Accordingly the convictions of the defendants Clarkson and Carroll must be quashed.

Appeals allowed

Questions

1. Is the knowing supply of the means of committing a crime *evidence* of encouragement, or the *equivalent* of encouragement?
2. What difference might it make which it is?
3. If A is able to control B's behaviour, and does not do so, with the result, expected by A, that B commits a crime, what is the significance, on a charge of aiding, abetting, counselling or procuring B's crime, of A's failure?
4. Ought it to make any difference whether A's power to control B is a legal one or merely a physical or psychological one? See *Cassady* v. *Morris* [1975] Crim. L.R. 398: *Du Cros* v. *Lambourne* [1907] 1 K.B. 40; *R.* v. *Harris* [1964] Crim. L.R. 54.
5. A's wife B tells him that she is going to kill herself and their infant children. A protests but does nothing to stop B, who throws her children into a river and jumps in herself, so that they are all drowned. Has A aided, abetted, counselled or procured (i) the murder of the children, (ii) the suicide of B? See Suicide Act 1961, s. 2 (1), *post*, p. 462 (*cf. R.* v. *Russell* [1933] V.L.R. 59).

Ferguson v. Weaving

[1951] 1 K.B. 814

King's Bench Division

> Section 4 of the Licensing Act, 1921, makes it an offence for any person, except during the permitted hours, to consume on licensed premises any intoxicating liquor. In a large public-house managed by W, customers were found consuming liquor outside permitted hours and were convicted of an offence under the section. There was no evidence that W knew that the liquor was being consumed, which had been supplied by waiters employed by her who had neglected to collect the glasses in time. A charge against W of counselling and procuring the customers' offence was dismissed and the prosecutor appealed.

LORD GODDARD C.J.: There can be no doubt that this court has more than once laid it down in clear terms that before a person can be convicted of aiding and abetting the commission of an offence, he must at least know the essential matters which constitute the offence. . . . The magistrate in this case has acquitted the licensee of any knowledge of the matters which constituted the principal offence, but it is said that the cases established that the knowledge of her servants must be imputed to her. . . . We now turn to (these) cases. . . . It is unnecessary to go through them all because the principle which applies was laid down, not for the first time, in *Linnett* v. *Metropolitan Police Commissioner* [1946] K.B. 290. All the cases on the subject were quoted, and, in giving judgment, I said: "The principle underlying these decisions does not depend upon the legal relationship existing between master and servant or between principal and agent; it depends on the fact that the person who is responsible in law, as, for example, a licensee under the licensing Acts, has chosen to delegate his duties, powers and authority to another."

We will assume for the purpose of this case that the licensee had delegated to the waiters the conduct and management of the concert room, and if the Act had made it an offence for a licensee knowingly to permit liquor to be consumed after hours, then the fact that she had delegated management and control of the concert room to the waiters would have made their knowledge her knowledge. In this case there is no substantive offence in the licensee at all. The substantive offence is committed only by the customers. She can aid and abet the customers if she knows that the customers are committing the offence, but we are not prepared to hold that knowledge can be imputed to her so as to make her not a principal offender, but an aider and abettor. So to hold would be to establish a new principle in criminal law and one for which there is no authority. If Parliament had desired to make a licensee guilty of an offence by allowing persons to consume liquor after hours it would have been perfectly easy so to provide in the section. But a doctrine of criminal law that a licensee who has knowledge of the facts is liable as a principal in the second degree is no reason for holding that if she herself has no knowledge of the facts but that someone in her employ and to whom she may have entrusted the management of the room did know them, this makes her an aider and abettor. As no duty is imposed on her by the section to prevent the consumption of liquor after hours there was no duty in this respect that she could delegate to her employees. While it may be that the waiters could have been prosecuted for aiding and abetting the consumers, as to which we need express no opinion, we are clearly of opinion that the licensee could not be. To hold to the contrary would, in our opinion, be an unwarranted extension of the doctrine of vicarious responsibility in criminal law."

Appeal dismissed

Note

For vicarious liability, see *post*, p. 288.

iii. Scope of the Common Design

R. v. Saunders and Archer

(1573) 2 Plowden 473; 75 E.R. 706
Warwick Assizes

John Saunders had a wife whom he intended to kill, in order that he might marry another woman with whom he was in love, and he opened his design to . . . Alexander Archer, and desired his assistance and advice in the execution of it, who advised him to put an end to her life by poison. With this intent the said Archer bought the poison, *viz.*, arsenick and roseacre, and delivered it to the said John Saunders to give to his wife, who accordingly gave it to her, being sick, in a roasted apple, and she eat a small part of it, and gave the rest to . . . Eleanor Saunders, an infant, about three years of age, who was the daughter of her and the said John Saunders her husband. And the said John Saunders seeing it, blamed his wife for it, and said that apples were not good for such infants; to which his wife replied that they were better for such infants than for herself: and the daughter eat the poisoned apple, and the said John Saunders, her father, saw her eat it, and did not offer to take it from her lest he should be suspected, and afterwards the wife recovered, and the daughter died of the said poison.

Whether or no this was murder in John Saunders, the father, was somewhat doubted, for he had no intent to poison his daughter, nor had he any malice against her, but on the contrary he had a great affection for her, and he did not give her the poison, but his wife ignorantly gave it her, and although he might have taken it from the daughter, and so have preserved her life, yet the not taking it from her did not make it a felony, for it was all one whether he had been present or absent, as to this point, inasmuch as he had no malice against the daughter, nor any inclination to do her any harm. But at last the said justices, upon consideration of the matter, and with the assent of Saunders, Chief Baron, who had the examination of the said John Saunders before, and who had signified his opinion to the said justices . . . were of opinion that the said offence was murder in the said John Saunders. And the reason thereof . . . was because the said John Saunders gave the poison with an intent to kill a person, and in the giving of it he intended that death should follow. And when death followed from his act, although it happened in another person than her whose death he directly meditated, yet it shall be murder in him, for he was the original cause of the death.

But the most difficult point in this case, and upon which the justices conceived greater doubt than upon the offence of the principal, was, whether or no Archer should be adjuged accessory to the murder. For the offence which Archer committed was the aid and advice which he gave to Saunders, and that was only to kill his wife, and no other, for there was no parol communication between them concerning the daughter, and although by the consequences which followed from the giving of the poison by Saunders the principal, it so happened that the daughter was killed, yet Archer did not precisely procure her death, nor advise him to kill her, and therefore whether or no he should be accessory to this murder which happened by a thing consequential to the first act, seemed to them to be doubtful. . . . Upon conference before had with the justices of both Benches, they were agreed that they ought not to give judgment against the said Alexander Archer, because they took the law to be that he could not be adjudged accessory to the said offence of murder, for that he did not assent that the daughter should be poisoned, but only that the wife should be poisoned, which assent cannot be drawn further than he gave it, for the poisoning of the daughter is a distinct thing from that to which he was privy, and therefore he shall not be adjudged accessory to it. . . .

Question

If Saunders had been absent when his wife gave the poisoned apple to their daughter, he would still have been guilty, as the cases on transferred malice show, in particular, *R.* v. *Latimer, ante,* p. 124. Moreover, Archer would now become liable as a party to the murder, as the next case shows. Why does the law treat Archer differently depending upon whether Saunders, who is guilty in any event, knew or did not know of the giving of the apple to his child?

R. v. Betts and Ridley
(1930) 22 Cr. App. R. 148
Court of Criminal Appeal

B. and R. agreed that B. should rob A. by pushing him down and seizing the bag he was carrying, while R. would wait round the corner in a car wherein B. could make his escape. B. struck A. with such force that he died. Both were convicted of murder and appealed.

AVORY J.: It is clear law that it is not necessary that the party, to constitute him a principal in the second degree, should be actually present, an eyewitness or ear-witness of the transaction. He is, in construction of law, present aiding and abetting if, with the intention of giving assistance, he is near enough to afford it, should the occasion arise. . . . [Being a principal in the second degree] he is at least as responsible as . . . an accessory before the fact, and in *Foster's Crown Cases*, at p. 369, dealing with an accessory before the fact, it is said: "Much has been said by writers who have gone before me, upon cases where a person supposed to commit a felony at the instigation of another hath gone beyond the terms of such instigation, or hath, in the execution varied from them. If the principal totally and substantially varieth, if being solicited to commit a felony of one kind he wilfully and knowingly committeth a felony of another, he will stand single in that offence, and the person soliciting shall not be involved in his guilt . . . but if the principal in substance complieth with the temptation, varying only in circumstances of time or place, or in the manner of execution, in these cases the person soliciting to the offence will, if absent, be an accessory before the fact, if present a principal." It appears to the court in this that the case of R. comes precisely within this description.

Appeals dismissed

R. v. Anderson and Morris
[1966] 2 Q.B. 110
Court of Criminal Appeal

The accused were convicted of the murder of one Welch, in circumstances which appear in the summing-up cited below. Morris appealed.

LORD PARKER C.J.: What is complained of is a passage in the summing-up. . . . The material direction is: "If you think there was a common design to attack Welch but it is not proved, in the case of Morris, that he had any intention to kill or cause grievous bodily harm, but that Anderson, without the knowledge of Morris, had a knife, took it from the flat and at some time formed the intention to kill or cause grievous bodily harm to Welch and did kill him—an act outside the common design to which Morris is proved to have been a party—then you would or could on the evidence find it proved that Anderson committed murder and Morris would be liable to be convicted of manslaughter provided you are satisfied that he took part in the attack or fight with Welch. . . ."

[Counsel for the Appellant] submits that that was a clear misdirection. He would put the principle of law to be invoked in this form: that where two persons embark on a joint enterprise, each is liable for the acts done in pursuance of that joint enterprise, that that includes liability for unusual consequences if they arise from the execution of the agreed joint enterprise but (and this is the crux of the matter) that, if one of the adventurers goes beyond what has been tacitly agreed as part of the common enterprise, his co-adventurer is not liable for the consequences of that unauthorised act. Finally, he says it is for the jury in every case to decide whether what was done was part of the joint enterprise, or went beyond it and was in fact an act unauthorised by that joint enterprise.

In support of that, he refers to a number of authorities to which the court finds it unnecessary to refer in detail, which in the opinion of this court show that at any rate for the last 130 or 140 years that has been the true position. This matter was in fact considered in some detail in *R.* v. *Smith (Wesley)* [1963] 1 W.L.R. 1200, heard by a court of five judges presided over by Hilbery J., in which Slade J. gave the judgment of the court. *R.* v. *Smith (Wesley)* was referred to at some length in the later decision in this court in *R.* v. *Betty* (1964) 48 Cr. App. R. 6, it is unnecessary to go into that case in any detail. It followed the judgment of Slade J. in *R.* v. *Smith (Wesley)*, and it did show the limits of the general principle which Mr. Lane invokes in the present case. In *R.* v. *Smith (Wesley)* the co-adventurer who in fact killed was known by the defendant to have a knife, and it was clear on the facts of that case that the common design involved an attack on a man, in that case a barman, in which the use of a knife would not be outside the scope of the concerted action. Reference was there made to the fact that the case might have been different if in fact the man using the knife had used a revolver, a weapon which he had, unknown to Smith.

The court in *R.* v. *Betty* approved entirely of what had been said in *R.* v. *Smith (Wesley)*, and in fact added to it. In passing, it is to be observed that, as Mr. Lane has pointed out, the headnote to *R.* v. *Betty* may go somewhat further and may have led the judge in the present case to think that there were no such limits to the principle.

[Counsel for the Crown], on the other hand, while recognising that he cannot go beyond this long string of decided cases, has said really that they are all part and parcel of a much wider principle which he put in this form, that if two or more persons engaged in an unlawful act and one suddenly develops an intention to kill whereby death results, not only is he guilty of murder, but all those who have engaged in the unlawful act are guilty of manslaughter. He recognises that the present trend of authority is against that proposition, but he goes back to *Salisbury's* case (1553) 1 Plow. 100. In that case a master had lain in wait to attack a man, and his servants, who had no idea of what his, the master's, idea was, joined in the attack, whereby the man was killed. It was held there that those servants were themselves guilty of manslaughter.

The court is by no means clear on the facts as reported that Salisbury's case is really on all fours, but it is in the opinion of the court quite clear that the principle is wholly out of touch with the position today. It seems to this court that to say that adventurers are guilty of manslaughter when one of them has departed completely from the concerted action of the common design and has suddenly formed an intent to kill and has used a weapon and acted in a way which no party to that common design could suspect is something which would revolt the conscience of people today.

[Counsel for the Crown], in his attractive argument, points to the fact that it would seem to be illogical that, if two people had formed a common design to do an unlawful act and death resulted by an unforeseen consequence, they should be held, as they would undoubtedly be held, guilty of manslaughter; whereas if one of them in those circumstances had in a moment of passion decided to kill, the other would be acquitted altogether. The law, of course, is not completely logical, but there is nothing really illogical in such a result, in that it could well be said as a matter of common sense that in the latter circumstances the death resulted or was caused by the sudden action of the adventurer who decided to kill and killed. Considered as a matter of causation, there may well be an overwhelming supervening event which is of such a character that it will relegate into history matters which would otherwise be looked upon as causative factors. Looked at in that way, there is really nothing illogical in the result to which [counsel for the Crown] points.

Conviction quashed

R. v. Becerra

(1975) 62 Cr. App. R. 212
Court of Appeal

B. broke into a house with C. and G., intending to steal. B. gave a knife to C. to use if necessary on anyone interrupting them. The tenant of the upstairs flat L. came down to investigate the noise. B. said, "There's a bloke coming. Let's go," jumped out of the window and ran away. C. stabbed L. with the knife, killing him. At his trial for murder, B. contended that he had withdrawn from the joint adventure before the attack on L. The jury were directed that his words and departure through the window were insufficient to constitute a withdrawal. B. was convicted, and sought leave to appeal.

Roskill L.J.: Mr. Owen [for the appellant] says that in that passage which I have just read, the learned judge in effect, though perhaps not in so many words, withdrew the defence of "withdrawal" from the jury, because the learned judge was saying to the jury that the only evidence of Becerra's suggested "withdrawal" was the remark, if it were made, "Come on let's go," coupled with the fact of course that Becerra then went out through the window and ran away and that that could not in those circumstances amount to "withdrawal" and therefore was not available as a defence, even if they decided the issue of common design against Becerra. It is upon that passage in the summing-up that Mr. Owen has principally focused his criticism.

It is necessary, before dealing with that argument in more detail, to say a word or two about the relevant law. It is a curious fact, considering the number of times in which this point arises where two or more people are charged with criminal offences, particularly murder or manslaughter, how relatively little authority there is in this country upon the point. But the principle is undoubtedly of long standing.

Perhaps it is best first stated in *R.* v. *Saunders and Archer* (*ante*, p. 267), in a note by *Plowden*, p. 476, thus: "... for if I command one to kill J.S. and before the Fact done I go to him and tell him that I have repented, and expressly charge him not to kill J.S. and he afterwards kills him, there I shall not be Accessory to this Murder, because I have countermanded my first Command, which in all Reason shall discharge me, for the malicious Mind of the Accessory ought to continue to do ill until the Time of the Act done, or else he shall not be charged; but if he had killed J.S. before the Time of my Discharge or Countermand given, I should have been Accessory to the Death, notwithstanding my private Repentance."

The next case to which I may usefully refer is some 250 years later, but over 150 years ago: *R.* v. *Edmeads and Others* (1828) 3 C. & P. 390, where there is a ruling of Vaughan B. at a trial at Berkshire Assizes, upon an indictment charging Edmeads and others with unlawfully shooting at game keepers. At the end of his ruling the learned Baron said on the question of common intent, at p. 392, "that is rather a question for the jury; but still, on this evidence, it is quite clear what the common purpose was. They all draw up in lines, and point their guns at the game-keepers, and they are all giving their countenance and assistance to the one of them who actually fires the gun. If it could be shewn that either of them separated himself from the rest, and showed distinctly that he would have no hand in what they were doing, the objection would have much weight in it."

I can go forward over 100 years. Mr. Owen (to whose juniors we are indebted for their research into the relevant Canadian and United States cases) referred us to several Canadian cases, to only one of which is it necessary to refer in detail, a decision of the Court of Appeal of British Columbia in *R.* v. *Whitehouse* (alias *Savage*) (1941) 1 W.W.R. 112. I need not read the headnote. The Court of Appeal held that the trial judge concerned in that case, which was one of murder, had been guilty of misdirection in his direction to the jury on this question of "withdrawal". The matter is, if I may most respectfully say so, so well put in the leading judgment of Sloan J.A., that I read the whole of the passage at pp. 115 and 116: "Can it be said on the facts of this case that a mere change of mental intention and a quitting of the scene of the crime just immediately prior to the striking of the fatal blow will absolve those who participate in the commission of the crime by overt acts up to that moment from all the consequences of its accomplishment by the one who strikes in ignorance of his companions' change of heart? I think not. After a crime has been committed and before a prior abandonment of the common enterprise may be found by a jury there must be, in my view, in the absence of exceptional circumstances, something more than a mere mental change of intention and physical change of place by those associates who wish to dissociate themselves from the consequences attendant upon their willing assistance up to the moment of the actual commission of that crime. I would not attempt to define too closely what must be done in criminal matters involving participation in a common unlawful purpose to break the chain of causation and responsibility. That must depend upon the circumstances of each case but it seems to me that one essential element ought to be established in a case of this kind: Where practicable and reasonable there must be timely communication of the intention to abandon the common purpose from those who wish to dissociate themselves from the contemplated crime to those who desire to continue in it. What is 'timely communication' must be determined by the facts of each case but where practicable and reasonable it ought to be such communication, verbal or otherwise, that will serve unequivocal notice upon the other party to the common unlawful cause that if he proceeds upon it he does so without the further aid and assistance of those who withdraw. The unlawful purpose of him who continues alone is then his own and not one in common with those who are no longer parties to it nor liable to its full and final consequences." The learned judge then went on to cite a passage from 1 Hale's *Pleas of the Crown* 618 and the passage from *R.* v. *Saunders and Archer* to which I have already referred.

In the view of each member of this Court, that passage, if we may respectfully say so, could not be improved upon and we venture to adopt it in its entirety as a correct statement of the law which is to be applied in this case.

The last case, an English one, is *R.* v. *Croft* [1944] 1 K.B. 295, a well-known case of a suicide pact where, under the old law, the survivor of a suicide pact was charged with and convicted of murder. It was sought to argue that he had withdrawn from the pact in time to avoid liability (as the law then was) for conviction for murder.

The Court of Criminal Appeal, comprising Lawrence J. (as he then was), Lewis and Wrottesley JJ. dismissed the appeal and upheld the direction given by Humphreys J. to the jury at the trial. Towards the end of the judgment Lawrence J. said (pp. 297 and 298): ". . . counsel for the appellant complains—although I do not understand that the point had ever been taken in the court below—that the summing-up does not contain any reference to the possibility of the agreement to commit suicide having been determined or countermanded. It is true that the learned judge does not deal expressly with that matter except in a passage where he says: 'Even if you accept his statement in the witness-box that the vital and second shot was fired when he had gone through that window, he would still be guilty of murder if she was then committing suicide as the result of an agreement which they had mutually arrived at that that should be the fate of both of them, and it is no answer for him that he altered his mind after she was dead and did not commit suicide himself.' . . . the authorities, such as they are, show in our opinion, that where a person has acted as an accessory before the fact, he must give express and actual countermand or revocation of the advising, counselling, procuring, or abetting which he had given before."

It seems to us that those authorities make plain what the law is which has to be applied in the present case.

We therefore turn back to consider the direction which the learned judge gave in the present case to the jury and what was the suggested evidence that Becerra had withdrawn from the common agreement. The suggested evidence is the use by Becerra of the words "Come on let's go," coupled, as I said a few moments ago, with his act in going out through the window. The evidence, as the judge pointed out, was that Cooper never heard that nor did the third man. But let it be supposed that that was said and the jury took the view that it was said.

On the facts of this case, in the circumstances then prevailing, the knife having already been used and being contemplated for further use when it was handed over by Becerra to Cooper for the purpose of avoiding (if necessary) by violent means the hazards of identification, if Becerra wanted to withdraw at that stage, he would have to "countermand", to use the word that is used in some of the cases or "repent" to use another word so used, in some manner vastly different and vastly more effective than merely to say "Come on, let's go" and go out through the window.

It is not necessary, on this application, to decide whether the point of time had arrived at which the only way in which he could effectively withdraw, so as to free himself from joint responsibility for any act Cooper thereafter did in furtherance of the common design, would be physically to intervene so as to stop Cooper attacking Lewis, as the judge suggested, by interposing his own body between them or somehow getting in between them or whether some other action might suffice. That does not arise for decision here. Nor is it necessary to decide whether or not the learned judge was right or wrong, on the facts of this case, in that passage which appears at the bottom of p. 206, which Mr. Owen criticised: "and at least take all reasonable steps to prevent the commission of the crime which he had agreed the others should commit." It is enough for the purposes of deciding this application to say that under the law of this country as it stands, and on the facts (taking them at their highest in favour of Becerra), that which was urged as amounting to withdrawal from the common design was not capable of amounting to such withdrawal. Accordingly Becerra remains responsible, in the eyes of the law, for everything that Cooper did and continued to do after Becerra's disappearance through the window as much as if he had done them himself.

Application refused

Note

"A declared intent to withdraw from a conspiracy to dynamite a building is not enough, if the fuse has been set; he must step on the fuse," *per* McDermott J. in *Eldredge* v. *U.S.*, 62 F. 2nd 449 (1932). But at an earlier stage, indicating dissent ought to be enough; indeed it can be argued that mere withdrawal (known to the others) without dissent, ought to be enough. It must be remembered that the withdrawing person remains guilty of conspiracy and, in appropriate cases, incitement and attempt.

Questions

(1) If help or encouragement in preparing or committing the crime is what the law seeks to punish, how ought the law to deal with A in the following cases?

(i) A, a fortnight before the planned crime is to take place, tells B and C that he will be unable to be present, but he wishes them well.

(ii) B and C wait for A at the beginning of the expedition, but in the end get tired of waiting and go off and commit the crime without him.

2. In (ii) above ought it to make any difference whether the reason why A has not turned up as agreed is that he has (a) repented, or (b) become afraid that their plan is known to the police, or (c) been arrested by the police?

3. It is difficult, in the case of some forms of participation, to imagine how there can be a withdrawal. A lends safe-cutting gear to B and C,

whom he knows are going to use the gear in safe-breaking. A repents and tells the police; but he has lost touch with B and C, and no-one is able to stop them committing 50 safe-breaks all over the country. Is A implicated in all 50 crimes?

4. Would it make any difference in (3) if A could prove that B and C promised him that they would use the gear for safe-breaking once and once only? (see Glanville Williams: *Criminal Law: The General Part*, §§ 127, 134).

iv. Secondary Party Not Convictable as a Principal

Sayce v. Coupe
[1953] 1 Q.B. 1
Queen's Bench Division

C. was charged with aiding, abetting, counselling and procuring a person unknown to sell tobacco otherwise than as a licensed retailer of tobacco contrary to section 13 of the Tobacco Act 1842 as amended. It appeared that C. had purchased the tobacco from a person who was not a licensed retailer. The magistrates dismissed the charge, and the prosecutor appealed.

Lord Goddard C.J.: [Counsel for the accused] has argued that because the statute does not make it an offence to buy, but only makes it an offence to sell, we ought to hold that the offence of aiding and abetting the sale ought not to be preferred or could not be preferred. It is obvious that it can be preferred. The statute does not make it an offence to buy, but obviously, on ordinary general principles of criminal law, if in such case a person knows the circumstances and knows, therefore, that an offence is being committed and takes part in, or facilitates the commission of the offence, he is guilty as a principal in the second degree, for it is impossible to say that a person who buys does not aid and abet the sale.

Appeal allowed

R. v. Tyrrell
[1894] 1 Q.B. 710
Court for Crown Cases Reserved

Tyrrell, a girl aged between 13 and 16, was convicted of aiding and abetting one Ford to commit the misdemeanour of having unlawful carnal knowledge of her, which was an offence under Criminal Law Amendment Act 1885, s. 5. (See now, Sexual Offences Act 1956, s. 6.)

Counsel for the accused: Under [the Offences against the Person Act 1861], section 58 [*post*, p. 341], a woman is not indictable for administering poison or other noxious thing to herself with intent to procure abortion, unless she is with child when she does so; but she is liable to conviction and punishment if, with the same intent, she administers poison, etc. to another woman, though the other be not with child. . . . *R.* v. *Whitchurch* [*post*, p. 341] . . . therefore has no application here. It is impossible that the legislature, in passing the Criminal Law Amendment Act, 1885, can have intended that the women and girls for whose protection it was passed should be liable to prosecution and punishment under it. Part I, in which section 5 comes, is headed "Protection of Women and Girls."

A girl under 16 is treated as of so immature a mind as not to be capable of consenting. The Act assumes that she has no *mens rea*, and she cannot, therefore, be treated as capable of aiding and abetting. If a girl is liable to be convicted of aiding and abetting an offence under section 5 she is also liable to conviction for aiding and abetting the felony made punishable by section 4, and she would then be liable to be sentenced to penal servitude for life, because an accessory before the fact to a felony may be punished as a principal. The result would be to render the Act inoperative, because girls would not come forward to give evidence. The Criminal Law Amendment Act, 1885, s. 5, created no new offence, and for 600 years it has never been suggested that such an offence as that charged against the defendant could be committed at common law.

LORD COLERIDGE C.J.: The Criminal Law Amendment Act, 1885, was passed for the purpose of protecting women and girls against themselves. At the time it was passed there was a discussion as to what point should be fixed as the age of consent. That discussion ended in a compromise, and the age of consent was fixed at 16. With the object of protecting women and girls against themselves the Act of Parliament has made illicit connection with a girl under that age unlawful; if a man wishes to have such illicit connection he must wait until the girl is 16, otherwise he breaks the law; but it is impossible to say that the Act, which is absolutely silent about aiding and abetting or soliciting or inciting, can have intended that the girls for whose protection it was passed should be punishable under it for the offences committed upon themselves. I am of opinion that this conviction ought to be quashed.

MATHEW J.: I am of the same opinion. I do not see how it would be possible to obtain convictions under the statute if the contention for the Crown were adopted, because nearly every section which deals with offences in respect of women and girls would create an offence in the woman or girl. Such a result cannot have been intended by the legislature. There is no trace in the statute of any intention to treat the woman or girl as criminal.

Conviction quashed

R. v. Whitehouse
[1977] Q.B. 868
Court of Appeal

W. pleaded guilty to a charge of inciting his 15-year-old daughter to commit incest with him. On appeal against sentence, the Court of Appeal gave him leave to appeal against conviction on the view that he may have pleaded guilty to an offence which was unknown to the law.

SCARMAN L.J.: ... We can turn now to consider whether the indictment disclosed an offence known to the law. The count standing by itself does disclose such an offence because the count merely alleges incitement to commit incest. But when one goes on to the particulars one sees that the defendant is charged with inciting his daughter, a girl aged 15, to commit incest with him. The Crown recognises that there are difficulties in the drafting of the indictment. The Crown recognises that under section 11 of the Sexual Offences Act 1956 a girl aged 15 cannot commit incest. The relevant subsection is (1) and I read it:

> "It is an offence for a woman of the age of 16 or over to permit a man whom she knows to be her ... father ... to have sexual intercourse with her by her consent."

It is of course accepted by the Crown that at common law the crime of incitement consists of inciting another person to commit a crime. When one looks at this indictment in the light of the particulars of the offence pleaded, one sees that it is charging the defendant with inciting a girl to commit a crime which in fact by statute she is incapable of committing. If therefore the girl was incapable of committing the crime alleged, how can the defendant be guilty of the common law crime of incitement? The Crown accepts the logic of that position and does not seek in this court to rely on section 11 of the Act of 1956 or to suggest that this man could be guilty of inciting his daughter to commit incest, to use the old phrase, as a principal in the first degree. But the Crown says that it is open to them upon this indictment to submit that it covers the offence of inciting the girl to aid and abet the man to commit the crime of incest upon her. Section 10 of the Act of 1956 makes it an offence for a man to have sexual intercourse with a woman whom he knows to be his daughter, and the Crown says that upon this indictment it is possible to say that the defendant has committed an offence known to the law the offence being that of inciting his daughter under the age of 16 to aid and abet him to have sexual intercourse with her.

. . . We are prepared to assume, for the purposes of this appeal, that the indictment can be cured, and accordingly we now read the indictment as an indictment charging this man with the offence of inciting a girl of 15 to aid and abet him to commit incest with her.

Is there such an offence known to the law? The difficulty arises from two features of the law to which I have already referred. First, at common law the crime of incitement consists of inciting another person to commit a crime. This was laid down in *R.* v. *Higgins* (1801) 2 East 5 many years ago and is well described in the very beginning of chapter 10 of *Smith and Hogan, Criminal Law*, 3rd ed. (1973), p. 172. The authors cite a passage from *S.* v. *Nkosiyana* 1966 (4) S.A. 655, 658, which includes this sentence: "An inciter is one who reaches and seeks to influence the mind of another to the commission of a crime." The second difficult feature of the law is section 11 of the Act of 1956 to which I have already referred. A woman under the age of 16 cannot commit the crime of incest. But, says the Crown, a man can commit incest, and so they go on to make their submission that a girl of 15 can aid and abet him to do so.

There is no doubt of the general principle, namely, that a person, provided always he or she is of the age of criminal responsibility, can be guilty of aiding or abetting a crime even though it be a crime which he or she cannot commit as a principal in the first degree. There are two famous illustrations in the books of this principle. A woman can aid and abet a rape so as herself to be guilty of rape, and a boy at an age where he is presumed impotent can nevertheless aid and abet a rape. The cases, which are very well known, are first in time *R.* v. *Eldershaw* (1828) 3 C. & P. 396. In that case Vaughan B., in the course of a six line judgment, the brevity of which I wish I could emulate, says "This boy being under 14, he cannot, by law, be found guilty of a rape, except as a principal in the second degree." So much for the boy.

The position in regard to a woman is stated by Bowen L.J. in one line and a half in *R.* v. *Ram* (1893) 17 Cox C.C. 609, where two prisoners, a Mr. and Mrs. Ram, were indicted jointly for rape upon Annie Edkins of the age of 13. It was submitted that the woman could not be indicted for rape. Bowen L.J. declined to quash the indictment for rape as against the female prisoner.

Those cases clearly establish, and have been regarded for a very long time as establishing, the general principle to which I have referred.

But what if the person alleged to be aiding and abetting the crime is herself the victim of the crime? This poses the short question with which this appeal is concerned. Before we consider it we would comment that, if indeed it be the law that this girl aged 15 can be guilty of incest as the aider and abettor of a man who is seeking to have intercourse with her, then one has the strange situation that, although she cannot be guilty of the crime of incest under the section which formulates the conditions under which a woman may be found guilty of that crime, yet through this doctrine of aiding and abetting she can be guilty of the offence when it is committed by a man. That is an odd conclusion, but not necessarily to be rejected because of its oddity.

The important matters in our judgment are these. First this girl, aged 15, belongs to a class which is protected, but not punished, by sections 10 and 11 of the Sexual Offences Act 1956, and secondly the girl is alleged to be the victim of this notional crime. The whole question has an air of artificiality because nobody is suggesting either that the father has committed incest with her or that she has aided and abetted him to commit incest upon her. What is suggested is that the father has committed the crime of incitement because by his words and conduct he has incited her to do that which, of course, she never has done.

The question in our judgment is determined by authority. It is, strictly speaking, persuasive authority only because it deals with a different Act of Parliament, but it is a decision by a strong court which has declared a principle which is as applicable to the statutory provision with which we are concerned as to that with which that case was concerned. The case is *R.* v. *Tyrrell,* [*ante,* p. 274]. [After reciting the facts and quoting the judgment of Coleridge J.C.J.]. In our judgment it is impossible, as a matter of principle, to distinguish *R.* v. *Tyrrell* from the present case. Clearly the relevant provisions of the Sexual Offences Act 1956 are intended to protect women and girls. Most certainly, section 11 is intended to protect girls under the age of 16 from criminal liability, and the Act as a whole exists, in so far as it deals with women and girls exposed to sexual threat, to protect them. The very fact that girls under the age of 16 are protected from criminal liability for what would otherwise be incest demonstrates that this girl who is said to have been the subject of incitement was being incited to do something which, if she did it, could not be a crime by her.

One can only avoid that conclusion if one can pray in aid the doctrine of aiding and abetting and apply it to the crime committed by a man under section 10. But *R.* v. *Tyrrell* makes it clear that to do that would be to impose criminal liability upon persons whom Parliament has intended should be protected, not punished.

We have therefore come to the conclusion, with regret, that the indictment does not disclose an offence known to the law because it cannot be a crime on the part of this girl aged 15 to have sexual intercourse with her father, though it is of course a crime, and a very serious crime, on the part of the father. There is here incitement to a course of conduct, but that course of conduct cannot be treated as a crime by the girl. Plainly a gap or lacuna in the protection of girls under the age of 16 is exposed by this decision. It is regrettable indeed that a man who importunes his daughter under the age of 16 to have sexual intercourse with him but does not go beyond incitement cannot be found guilty of a crime. . . . It may be that the legislature will consider it desirable to stop that gap. But in our judgment, applying the principles of the common law relating to the crime of incitement, and taking note of the decision of *R.* v. *Tyrrell* in relation to legislation similar to the Sexual Offences Act 1956, we have to declare the existence of the lacuna to which I have referred. There was incitement; but it was not incitement to crime. The girl's notional crime—because she never did commit it—is unknown to the law and therefore there can be no offence by him, the inciter. . . .

Appeal against conviction allowed

Notes

1. Section 54 of the Criminal Law Act 1977 now makes it an offence for a man or boy to incite to have sexual intercourse with him a girl under the

age of 16 whom he knows to be his grand-daughter, daughter, sister or half-sister.

2. The rationale of *Tyrrell* and *Whitehouse* appears to be that the statute never meant to include under-age girls, because it was passed for their protection (although it may be doubted if that was the reason for section 10 of the Sexual Offences Act 1956). Other reasons could in appropriate cases be advanced for concluding that a statute was not intended to cover particular classes of people; but English law appears to take no account of them: see *Sayce* v. *Coupe, ante*. Law Com. W.P. 43 proposes that "a person does not become an accessory to an offence if the offence is so defined that his conduct in it is inevitably incidental to its commission and such conduct is not expressly penalized" (Proposition 8). This would cover such cases as *Sayce* v. *Coupe*, and form a better reason for excluding young girls in sexual cases. See, generally, Hogan, *"Victims as Parties to Crime"* [1962] Crim. L.R. 683.

Questions

1. "Most certainly, section 11 is intended to protect girls under the age of 16 from criminal liability"; *per* Scarman L.J. *ante*, p. 277. Is that the same 'kind' of protection as formed the basis of Coleridge L.C.J.'s judgment in *R.* v. *Tyrrell*?

2. If a brother persuades his sister, aged 15, to offer to have sexual intercourse with their father, may he be convicted of (a) inciting incest?; (b) attempted incest?—see *post*, p. 303; (c) conspiring to commit incest?—see *post*, p. 343.

v. No Principal Offender

Thornton v. Mitchell
[1940] 1 All E.R. 339
King's Bench Division

> A bus driver reversed his bus according to the signals of his conductor, who failed to notice some persons standing behind the bus. The driver could not possibly see behind the bus and had to rely on the signals of the conductor. The persons standing behind the bus were injured. The driver was charged with careless driving, and the conductor with aiding and abetting, counselling and procuring the commission of that offence. The charge against the driver was dismissed, but the conductor was convicted. He appealed.

Lord Hewart C.J.: [The justices] say in para. 8: "We being of opinion that the conductor [had been very negligent] held that he was guilty of aiding, abetting, counselling and procuring the said Hollindrake to drive without due care and attention, and accordingly we inflicted a fine." In my opinion, this case is *a fortiori* on *Morris* v. *Tolman* [1923] 1 K.B. 166, to which our attention has been directed. I will read one sentence from the judgment of Avory J. at p. 171: ". . . in order to convict, it would be necessary to show that the respondent was aiding and abetting the principal, but a person cannot aid another in doing something which that other has not done."

That I think is the very thing which these justices have decided that the bus conductor did. In one breath they say that the principal did nothing which he should not have done and in the next breath they hold that the bus conductor aided and abetted the driver in doing something which had not been done or in not doing something which he ought to have done. I really think that, with all respect to the ingenuity of counsel for the respondent, the case is too plain for argument.

Appeal allowed

Notes

1. In many comparable situations the person charged with aiding and abetting will not escape merely because the "principal" has a good defence, *e.g.* absence of *mens rea*; because the innocence of the "principal" will mean that the other party himself was the perpetrator of the crime through the medium of an innocent agent. Suppose A tells B to take C's chattel, saying that C has sold it to him (A), which is not the case. If A is charged with aiding and abetting B in the commission of theft, B's innocence will mean that A stole the chattel, using B as an innocent agent; and A may be convicted as principal. And where A, who was sane, aided B, who was insane, to murder a police constable, it was held that although A could not be guilty of aiding and abetting B, he could be convicted as a principal in the first degree: *R.* v. *Tyler and Price* (1838) 8 C. & P. 616.

2. The reason why the bus conductor in *Thornton* v. *Mitchell* could not be convicted of careless driving as principal was because it was impossible to construe the word "drive" in the relevant section of the Road Traffic Act as referring to the conduct of anyone other than the immediate driver. See, Williams, *Textbook*, p. 318. There would seem to be limits beyond which the concept of agency will not stretch. However, see next case.

R. v. Cogan and Leak

[1976] 1 Q.B. 217
Court of Appeal

> L. forced his wife to have sexual intercourse with C. C. was charged with rape and L. was charged with aiding, abetting, counselling and procuring C. to commit rape. C. was acquitted of rape on it appearing that he did not know that L.'s wife was not consenting to the intercourse. L. was convicted and appealed.

LAWTON L.J.: . . . Leak's appeal against conviction was based on the proposition that he could not be found guilty of aiding and abetting Cogan to rape his wife if Cogan was acquitted of that offence as he was deemed in law to have been when his conviction was quashed: see section 2 (3) of the Criminal Appeal Act 1968. Leak's counsel, Mr. Herrod, conceded however, that his proposition had some limitations. The law on this topic lacks clarity as a perusal of some of the textbooks shows: see *Smith and Hogan, Criminal Law,* 3rd ed. (1973), pp. 106–109; *Glanville Williams, Criminal Law,* 2nd ed. (1961), pp. 386–390, 406–408; *Russell on Crime,* 12th ed. (1964), vol. 1, p. 128. We do not consider it appropriate to review the law generally because, as was said by this court in *R.* v. *Quick* [1973] Q.B. 910, 923, when considering this kind of problem:

> "The facts of each case . . . have to be considered and in particular what is alleged to have been done by way of aiding and abetting."

The only case which Mr. Herrod submitted had a direct bearing upon the problem of Leak's guilt was *Walters* v. *Lunt* [1951] 2 All E.R. 645. In that case the respondents had been charged, under section 33 (1) of the Larceny Act 1916, with receiving from a child aged seven years, certain articles knowing them to have been stolen. In 1951, a child under eight years was deemed in law to be incapable of committing a crime: it followed that at the time the charge had not been proved. That case is very different from this because here one fact is clear—the wife had been raped. Cogan had had sexual intercourse with her without her consent. The fact that Cogan was innocent of rape because he believed that she was consenting does not affect the position that she was raped.

Her ravishment had come about because Leak had wanted it to happen and had taken action to see that it did by persuading Cogan to use his body as the instrument for the necessary physical act. In the language of the law the act of sexual intercourse without the wife's consent was the *actus reus*: it had been procured by Leak who had the appropriate *mens rea*, namely, his intention that Cogan should have sexual intercourse with her without her consent. In our judgment it is irrelevant that the man whom Leak had procured to do the physical act himself did not intend to have sexual intercourse with the wife without her consent. Leak was using him as a means to procure a criminal purpose.

Before 1861 a case such as this, pleaded as it was in the indictment, might have presented a court with problems arising from the old distinctions between principals and accessories in felony. Most of the old law was swept away by section 8 of the Accessories and Abettors Act 1861 and what remained by section 1 of the Criminal Law Act 1967. The modern law allowed Leak to be tried and punished as a principal offender. In our judgment he could have been indicted as a principal offender. It would have been no defence for him to submit that if Cogan was an "innocent" agent, he was necessarily in the old terminology of the law a principal in the first degree, which was a legal impossibility as a man cannot rape his own wife during cohabitation. The law no longer concerns itself with niceties of degrees in participation in crime; but even if it did Leak would still be guilty. The reason a man cannot by his own physical act rape his wife during cohabitation is because the law presumes consent from the marriage ceremony: see *Hale, Pleas of the Crown* (1778), vol. 1, p. 629. There is no such presumption when a man procures a drunken friend to do the physical act for him. Hale C.J. put this case in one sentence, at p. 629:

> "... tho in marriage she hath given up her body to her husband, she is not to be by him prostituted to another": see *loc. cit.*

Had Leak been indicted as a principal offender, the case against him would have been clear beyond argument. Should he be allowed to go free because he was charged with "being aider and abettor to the same offence"? If we are right in our opinion that the wife had been raped (and no one outside a court of law would say that she had not been), then the particulars of offence accurately stated what Leak had done, namely, he had procured Cogan to commit the offence. This would suffice to uphold the conviction. We would prefer, however, to uphold it on a wider basis. In our judgment convictions should not be upset because of mere technicalities of pleading in an indictment. Leak knew what the case against him was and the facts in support of that case were proved. But for the fact that the jury thought that Cogan in his intoxicated condition might have mistaken the wife's sobs and distress for expressions of her consent, no question of any kind would have arisen about the form of pleading. By his written statement Leak virtually admitted what he had done. As Judge Chapman said in *R.* v. *Humphreys* [1965] 3 All E.R. 689, 692:

> "It would be anomalous if a person who admitted to a substantial part in the perpetration of a misdemeanour as aider and abettor could not be convicted on his own admission merely because the person alleged to have been aided and abetted was not or could not be convicted."

In the circumstances of this case it would be more than anomalous: it would be an affront to justice and to the common sense of ordinary folk. It was for these reasons that we dismissed the appeal against conviction. . . .

Appeal against conviction dismissed

Questions

1. If the person who had forced Mrs. Leak to submit to intercourse with Cogan had been her *sister*, rather than her husband, would the result have been the same? See section 1 of the Sexual Offences (Amendment) Act 1976, *post*, p. 486.
2. In *R.* v. *Bourne* (1952) 36 Cr. App. R. 125, the C.C.A. upheld a conviction of a husband for aiding and abetting his wife to commit buggery with a dog, although the facts showed that the wife, who was the only possible first principal, would have been able to raise the defence of duress had she been charged with committing buggery with the dog. The reason given was that a plea of duress admits the crime but prays to be excused punishment on the grounds of duress. Is the stated reason an acceptable one? See *ante*, p. 203.
3. Would the doctrine of agency have offered a better solution to the problems posed in *R.* v. *Bourne*?
4. Does the decision in *R.* v. *Cogan & Leak* coincide with or go further than the position advocated below?

Law Com. W.P. 43: Parties, Complicity and Liability for the Acts of Another

"*Proposition 2*: (1) A principal in an offence is one who, with any necessary fault element, does the acts constituting the external elements of the offence.

2. A person does such an act not only when he does it himself but also when he (a) acts through an innocent agent . . .

Proposition 3: (1) A person acts through an innocent agent when he intentionally causes the external elements of the offence to be committed by (or partly by) a person who is himself innocent of the offence charged by reason of lack of a required fault element, or lack of capacity.

(2) A person is not guilty of committing an offence through an innocent agent when (a) the law provides or implies that the offence can be committed only by one who complies with a particular description which does not apply to that person, or specifies the offence in terms implying personal conduct on the part of the offender. . . ."

Note

The doctrine employed in *R.* v. *Bourne*, above, that although the principal actor may have a complete defence, there is nonetheless a crime, to which secondary participants can be parties, is sometimes less artificial than it was in that case. See next case.

R. v. Austin

[1981] 1 All E.R. 374
Court of Appeal

A child of three years was in the lawful custody of her mother J.K. R.K., the father, got an order from a Maryland Court awarding control of the child to him, which order was not enforceable in England. R.K. employed A and others to help him take the child by force. R.K. snatched the child from J.K. in a street in Winchester, and while A and others confused the pursuit, reached Heathrow and was able to leave the country with the child. A and others were convicted of child stealing and appealed.

WATKINS L.J.: At the close of the case for the Crown in the Crown Court at Winchester counsel for the appellants . . . made a number of concessions on behalf of the appellants. He has repeated them to this court. They are: (1) that each of these appellants aided and abetted King in taking Lara away from the possession of her mother; (2) that the child was taken by King by the use of force on the mother and on the child. It was also conceded that they all knew the child was in the lawful possession of the mother, since there was no order in this country which affected her right to that at the material time and the order of the American court could not affect it in any practical way. It was also admitted that they had the intention to deprive the mother of possession of the child.

Having regard to those admissions and the background of this affair, one looks at s. 56 of the 1861 [Offences Against the Person] Act which provides:

"Whosoever shall unlawfully . . . by force . . . take away . . . any child under the age of fourteen years, with intent to deprive any parent . . . of the possession of such child . . . shall be liable, at the discretion of the court . . . to be imprisoned: Provided, that no person who shall have claimed any right to the possession of such child, or shall be the mother or shall have claimed to be the father of an illegitimate child, shall be liable to be prosecuted by virtue hereof on account of the getting possession of such child . . ."

. . . A parent who seeks, especially when there is no order of a court in existence affecting the ordinary common law right of possession of parents to a child, to take away that child from the other parent by force will inevitably commit the offence of child stealing under s. 56, unless it be shown that at the time there was lawful excuse for the use of the force as a means of taking the child away. Accordingly, apart from the proviso, King on the known facts could have had no defence if charged with this offence.

Undoubtedly King could properly have claimed a right of possession to the child and so have gained the protection of the proviso. What would have been the effect of that? The effect would have been that, although he had committed the offence of child stealing, because he was the child's father and could claim a right to possession of the child, he would not have been prosecuted. It is submitted on the appellant's behalf that the proviso also protects a class of persons wide enough to include those who aid a person such as the father of the child in gaining possession of his child by force. They become his agents for the purpose. Many persons have from time to time the temporary possession of a child as agents of parents. Why are they not protected to the same extent as parents when regaining possession as agents of parents?

In our view the only sensible construction of the proviso allows of its protection being granted to a small class of persons only, which includes the father and the mother of the child, whether the child be legitimate or illegitimate or a guardian appointed by a testamentary document, or by an order conferring the status of guardianship, or a person to whom is granted an order conferring some form of care, control, custody or access. We can think of no other who could claim exemption from prosecution by reason of the proviso.

What of these appellants? They had no good reason for doing what they did. They had no right to assert, and no interest in, the possession of the child. They were the paid hirelings of King to aid him in the commission of a criminal offence, namely stealing a child, and with him they committed it as aiders and abettors. While King may shelter behind the proviso, there is no room there for them. Parliament in its wisdom undoubtedly decided that the mischiefs of matrimonial discord which are unhappily so widespread should not give rise to wholesale criminal prosecutions arising out of disputes about children, about who should have possession and control of them. That and that alone is the reason for the existence of the proviso to s. 56. Thus, as we have said, its application is confined to the select class of persons we have endeavoured to define. . . .

Appeals dismissed

Note

For the position where the principal offender is not guiltless, but less guilty than the secondary party, see *R.* v. *Richards*, *ante*, p. 251.

2. ASSISTING AN OFFENDER AND CONCEALING INFORMATION

i. Assisting an Offender

Criminal Law Act 1967, section 4

"(1) Where a person has committed an arrestable offence, any other person who, knowing or believing him to be guilty of the offence or of some other arrestable offence, does without lawful authority or reasonable excuse any act with intent to impede his apprehension or prosecution shall be guilty of an offence.

(2) If on the trial of an indictment for an arrestable offence the jury are satisfied that the offence charged (or some other offence of which the accused might on that charge be found guilty) was committed, but find the accused not guilty of it, they may find him guilty of any offence under subsection (1) above of which they are satisfied that he is guilty in relation to the offence charged (or that other offence).

(3) A person committing an offence under subsection (1) above with intent to impede another person's apprehension or prosecution shall on conviction on indictment be liable to imprisonment according to the gravity of the other person's offence, as follows:

(*a*) if that offence is one for which the sentence is fixed by law, he shall be liable to imprisonment for not more than ten years;

(*b*) if it is one for which a person (not previously convicted) may be sentenced to imprisonment for a term of fourteen years, he shall be liable to imprisonment for not more than seven years;

(*c*) if it is not one included above but is one for which a person (not previously convicted) may be sentenced to imprisonment for a term of ten years, he shall be liable to imprisonment for not more than five years;

(*d*) in any other case, he shall be liable to imprisonment for not more than three years."

Note

At common law, one who, after a felony had been committed, helped the felon to evade justice was termed an accessory after the fact. It was no specific offence to aid one who had committed a misdemeanour or summary offence. The offence in section 4 applies only in the case of arrestable offences, which by section 2 of the same Act means offences for which the sentence is fixed by law or for which a first offender may be sentenced to five years' imprisonment or attempts to commit such offences. It is still no specific offence to assist one who has committed a non-arrestable offence.

R. v. Morgan
[1972] 1 Q.B. 436
Court of Appeal

The defendant, knowing that P. had killed a man, arranged a hide-out for him. Subsequently P. was charged with murder and in count 2 of the same indictment the defendant was charged under section 4 (1) of the Criminal Law Act 1967 that he had arranged for P. to stay in a flat intending to impede his arrest, knowing or believing P. to be guilty of murder. At the trial P.'s defence was that he had been provoked by his victim and the jury were invited on his behalf to return a verdict of manslaughter. The prosecutor obtained leave to amend count 2 by substituting "unlawful killing" for "murder." P. was convicted of murder and the defendant was convicted of impeding P.'s apprehension.

On appeal, the defendant contended that count 2 as amended was defective in that there was no arrestable offence of "unlawful killing", and that a count charging an offence under section 4 (1) of the Act of 1967 should specify the arrestable offence committed by the person assisted by the defendant.

BRIDGE J.: The submission made on behalf of the defendant is that it is essential when charging an offence under section 4 (1) of the Act of 1967, to specify correctly the particular offence actually committed by the person whom the accused has assisted. It is common ground that under the old law when charging an accessory after the fact to felony it was necessary to specify both the particular felony which had been committed and that this was known to the accessory. The statute clearly changes the law in the latter respect. Under section 4 (1) it matters not that the assistant does not know the nature of the other person's offence. But we see nothing in the language of the subsection to suggest an intention to change the law so that it should no longer be necessary to specify the particular offence committed. In any event, the later provisions of section 4, in our judgment, really put the matter beyond doubt. Under subsection (3) a scale of maximum penalties is laid down for offences under subsection (1), which varies "according to the gravity of the other person's offence". Thus, for example, to assist a murderer carries a maximum of 10 years' imprisonment; to assist a manslaughterer a maximum of only seven years'. Again, by subsection (5) it is the character of the offence committed by the person who receives assistance which determines whether or not the assistant may be tried summarily. It must follow that the actual offence needs to be specified in the charge so that the court's jurisdiction to entertain it and the maximum punishment to which the accused will be liable on conviction may be known at the outset. Accordingly, counsel for the defendant makes good his complaint that count 2 as amended was defective.

The next question is whether this irregularity led to any miscarriage of justice. We have heard argument as to what steps in relation to the defendant ought to have been taken to cover the contingency that Phillips might be convicted of either murder or manslaughter. Counsel for the defendant at one stage submitted that the contingency could only be met by alternative counts. He said that at the stage of this trial when the question arose, it was too late to amend the indictment to introduce a new count against the defendant. In the end, however, counsel on both sides before us have accepted that in truth no amendment was necessary, because the situation was covered by section 6 (3) of the Criminal Law Act 1967, which provides, so far as material:

> "Where, on a person's trial on indictment for any offence except treason or murder, the jury find him not guilty of the offence specifically charged in the indictment, but the allegations in the indictment amount to or include (expressly or by implication) an allegation of another offence falling within the jurisdiction of the court of trial, the jury may find him guilty of that other offence. . . ."

This language is applicable to the situation envisaged because the allegation "A having killed B with intent (murder) you, X, assisted A" obviously includes the allegation "A having killed B without intent (manslaughter) you X, assisted A."

Accordingly, if the court had been referred to section 6 (3) instead of being asked to allow the offending amendment, the jury could have been properly directed to convict the defendant, if satisfied (1) that Phillips was guilty of murder or manslaughter; (2) that the defendant knew or believed that Phillips was guilty of one or other of those offences or of any other arrestable offence and (3) that the defendant assisted Phillips with intent to impede his apprehension.

In fact, the directions given by the judge to the jury in relation to count 2 as amended, were in substance either to that effect or (in so far as they differed) to an effect more favourable to the accused. The vice of uncertainty or ambiguity in the amended count was of no practical consequence, because the jury's verdict that Phillips was guilty of murder on the first count made clear for the purposes of section 4 (3) the scale of gravity of the defendant's offence of assisting him. The defendant was in no way prejudiced by the circumstance that the route to his conviction was technically a deviation. The correct route, had it been followed, would inevitably have led to the same result. In our judgment there was no miscarriage of justice. We uphold the conviction.

We wish to refer to a further submission made by Mr. Salts, on behalf of the defendant. He says that in any case under section 4 (1) the court must know before passing sentence not only what offence was committed by the person assisted, but also what the assistant knew or believed it to be; and to this end, he submits, the jury must be asked for a special verdict. We cannot accept this. It appears to us that the deliberate policy of the legislature embodied in section 4 is that those who assist fugitives from justice act at their peril. The graver the fugitive's offence the heavier is the punishment to which the assistant renders himself liable irrespective of his state of knowledge. We do not, of course, mean to imply that the state of mind of the accused may not be a material factor in mitigation or that the court might not in an exceptional case think it useful to invite the jury to return a special verdict on the point. But this cannot be the norm and it was wholly unnecessary in the present case.

It is fair to add, however, that Mr. Salts' submission on this point derives some support from the actual form of the indictment, which, by alleging that the defendant acted with intent to impede Phillips' apprehension "for the arrestable offence of murder", appeared to make the defendant's knowledge of the nature of the offence material. This allegation went beyond what was necessary to prove an offence under the subsection. A count in an indictment particularising an offence under section 4 (1) will be sufficient if it states that the other person has committed a specified arrestable offence and that the accused, knowing or believing him to be guilty of that or some other arrestable offence, has without lawful authority or reasonable excuse done the act particularised with intent to impede the other person's apprehension or prosecution.

For the reasons stated earlier in this judgment, the appeal against conviction is dismissed.

Appeal dismissed

Question

A stabbed P who was removed unconscious to hospital, where he later died. A was hidden by B, to whom he confessed what he had done. A was charged with murder and B with doing acts likely to impede A's arrest, knowing or believing A to be guilty of murder. At the trial, evidence was given that P died, not of the stab wound which was beginning to heal, but of grossly negligent medical treatment (see *R.* v. *Jordan, ante*, p. 34). What verdicts may be returned against A and against B?

R. v. Brindley and Long

[1971] 2 Q.B. 300

Court of Appeal

B. and L. were convicted of doing an act contrary to section 4 (1) of the Criminal Law Act 1967 in the circumstances outlined in the judgment. They applied for leave to appeal.

LYELL J.: . . . The facts were that on the night of November 21, 1969, two lorries containing loads of brass ingots and spirits were stolen from a yard behind the Silverline Garage, the forecourt of which abutted on the A.13 road. In the forecourt were petrol pumps and a kiosk for the attendant to shelter in when not serving petrol. The evidence showed that the lorries must have been taken from the yard shortly before 10 p.m. that night and that they must have been driven away across the forecourt of the garage. It was not in dispute that the defendant Brindley was on duty until 10.30 p.m. as the petrol pump attendant, and that the occupier of the premises next door to the garage had come and told her that strangers had got into his garden and escaped over the wall towards the yard. He offered to investigate the yard to see that everything was all right. She said that she would go, and came back and reported that nothing was amiss.

Two days after the theft she was interviewed by the police and stated that no lorries had left the yard at the material time. She repeated that in evidence but admitted that, if two lorries had crossed the forecourt, she must have seen them. The prosecution's case was that the statement was untrue, that she saw the lorries, knew they were stolen, and made the statement untruthfully without lawful authority or reasonable excuse, with intent to impede the apprehension or prosecution of the thief or thieves. She admitted that she knew one Morphew who was jointly charged with her with the theft of the lorries. She was, however, acquitted of the charge of theft.

The defendant Long was also interviewed by the police and made two statements. In the first he said that, while he was at the garage with the defendant Brindley, he had seen no lorries cross the forecourt. Later he made a further statement in which he admitted that he had in fact seen two lorries driven from the yard across the forecourt of the garage at the material time.

Both now apply for leave to appeal against their convictions.

The defendant Long puts forward two grounds. [His Lordship considered a ground of application not material to this report, and continued:] The defendant

Long's second ground of appeal, and the only ground put forward on behalf of Brindley, was that the judge misdirected the jury as to what was required to be proved under section 4 (1) of the Criminal Law Act 1967. First it was argued that the prosecution had to prove that the accused knew who had committed the principal offence and that he did an act relating to that person.

In view of the court there is no foundation for that contention. What has to be proved is as follows: first, that a person has committed an arrestable offence; second, that another person knew or believed that the first person had committed it; third, that the second person did an act with intent to impede the apprehension or prosecution of the first person; fourth, that the act was done without lawful authority or reasonable excuse.

The unsoundness of the defendants' contention is perhaps best demonstrated by a simple example. A smash-and-grab raid is carried out in a quiet street and the person or persons committing it run off. Another person sees it. A police car comes by shortly after, the driver sees the broken window, asks the man who has seen the offence committed which way the offenders went and he replies that they went up the street when in fact they went down. That evidence is clearly enough for a jury to convict the bystander of an offence under the section. Anyone who sees a smash-and-grab raid being committed must know that a theft has been committed, and he has seen the person or persons who did it. He sends the police in the wrong direction, so giving the offenders more time to escape. It would then be for the jury to consider whether they are sure he sent the police the wrong way to make it more difficult to catch the thieves and whether there could be any lawful authority or reasonable excuse for his act. It is frivolous to suggest that in such circumstances the bystander needed to know the identity of the thieves before he could be convicted.

Finally it is said that the judge should have directed the jury to consider whether the accused may have had some other intent than that of impeding arrest or prosecution. In the judgment of this court there was no duty to do so. His only duty was to direct the jury as to the intent which had to be proved, and direct them that they had to be sure it had been proved, unless some other intent was suggested by the defendant. None was suggested here and there was a proper direction as to what the prosecution had to do.

For these reasons the applications are refused.

Applications refused

Note

No other "intent" was suggested by Brindley or Long. Suppose they had given evidence that the reason why they had lied was that they had been promised £1,000 each by the thieves if they lied. In cases on accessories before the fact (*R.* v. *Jones* [1949] 1 K.B. 194; *R.* v. *Andrews & Craig* [1962] 1 W.L.R. 1474), it was held that the accused's overriding purpose had to be to assist the felon, not, *e.g.* to make money for himself.

Question

A asked B, an old friend, to help him lie low because the police were looking for him. B agreed and hid A. A did not tell B why he was lying low, but B assumed that A, who was a life-long forger, had been forging again. What is B's liability if: (i) A had been forging?; (ii) A had wounded a man in a pub brawl?

ii. Concealing Information

Criminal Law Act 1967, section 5

(1) Where a person has committed an arrestable offence, any other person who, knowing or believing that the offence or some other arrestable offence has been committed, and that he has information which might be of material assistance in securing the prosecution or conviction of an offender for it, accepts or agrees to accept for not disclosing that information any consideration other than the making good of loss or injury caused by the offence, or the making of reasonable compensation for that loss or injury, shall be liable on conviction on indictment to imprisonment for not more than two years.

(2) Where a person causes any wasteful employment of the police by knowingly making to any person a false report tending to show that an offence has been committed, or to give rise to apprehension for the safety of any persons or property, or tending to show that he has information material to any police inquiry, he shall be liable on summary conviction to imprisonment for not more than six months or to a fine of not more than two hundred pounds or to both.

(3) No proceedings shall be instituted for an offence under this section except by or with the consent of the Director of Public Prosecutions.

(4). . . . .

(5) The compounding of an offence other than treason shall not be an offence otherwise than under this section.

Notes

1. The offence in section 5 (1) corresponds to the common law misdemeanour of compounding a felony, that is, agreeing for a consideration not to prosecute a felon or to impede his prosecution. As with the common law misdemeanour, the statutory offence is not limited to bargains with the criminal, but covers bargains with third parties, *e.g.* a bargain with the criminal's father that the criminal will not be prosecuted. The common law covered all such bargains, if they related to felonies, but section 5 (1), which relates to arrestable offences, allows certain bargains as lawful.

2. A mere failure to disclose an offence of which one knows is now no offence; until the abolition of the distinction between felonies and misdemeanours, it was, if the non-disclosed offence was a felony, the misdemeanour of misprision of felony: see *Sykes* v. *D.P.P.* [1962] A.C. 528.

3. The offence in section 5 (2) was a common law misdemeanour: see *R.* v. *Manley* [1933] 1 K.B. 529.

3. VICARIOUS LIABILITY

R. v. Huggins (1730) 2 Strange 869: H, the Warden of the Fleet prison was charged with aiding and abetting B, a turnkey, in the murder of A, a prisoner who was so neglected by B that he died. The jury found a special verdict and the case was argued before all the judges. "It is a point not to be disputed but that in criminal cases the principal is not answerable for the act of the deputy, as he is in civil cases; they must each answer for their own acts and stand or fall by their own behaviour. All the authors that treat of criminal proceedings, proceed on the foundation of this distinction; that to affect the superior by the act of the deputy, there must be the command of the deputy, which is not found in this case. The duress in this case consisted in the first taking him against his consent, and putting him in that room, and the keeping him there so long without necessaries, which was the occasion of his death. Now none of these circumstances are found as against the prisoner. The jury does not say he directed his being put into the room; that he knew how long he had been there, that he was without the necessaries in the indictment, or was ever kept there after the time the prisoner saw him, which was fifteen days before his death. . . ." Judgment: Not Guilty.

Mousell Bros. v. London and North Western Ry. [1917] 2 K.B. 836, 845 (C.A.):

ATKIN J.: "I think that the authorities cited . . . make it plain that while *prima facie* a principal is not to be made criminally responsible for the acts of his servants, yet the legislature may prohibit an act or enforce a duty in such words as to make the prohibition or the duty absolute; in which case the principal is liable if the act is in fact done by his servants. To ascertain whether a particular Act of Parliament has that effect or not regard must be had to the object of the statute, the words used, the nature of the duty laid down, the person upon whom it is imposed, the person by whom it would in ordinary circumstances be performed, and the person upon whom the penalty is imposed. If authority for this is necessary it will be found in the judgment of Bowen L.J. in *R.* v. *Tyler* [1891] 2 Q.B. 588, 592."

Notes

1. Discovering the Parliamentary intention involves first asking whether strict liability was intended (on this, see *ante,* p. 128) because on the whole if *mens rea* is required for a conviction, a guiltless master cannot be convicted (although *Mousell's* case is itself an exception, the offence being "giving a false account with intent to avoid toils," which was held to import vicarious liability). If the statute contains such words as "knowingly," "maliciously," "fraudulently," the master is not usually fixed with the knowledge or malice or fraud of his servant. And if the offence consists of "permitting," "suffering" or "allowing" something to happen, a master does not do so merely because his servant permits, suffers or allows: see *James & Son* v. *Smee* [1955] 1 Q.B. 78. All this is however, subject to the doctrine of delegation, as to which see *Vane* v. *Yiannopoulos,* below.

2. Even if the offence is one of strict liability, much depends on the key verb used in the statute to describe the conduct prohibited: some activities by a servant can be attributed to the master with more plausibility than others. "Using" is apt for vicarious liability, so if a servant uses a vehicle on his master's business, the master will often be held to be using it: see *James & Son* v. *Smee: John Henshall (Quarries) Ltd.* v. *Harvey* [1965] 2 Q.B. 233. Compare "driving"—only the actual driver can be said to be doing this: *cf. Thornton* v. *Mitchell, ante,* p. 278.

Williams, Criminal Law: The General Part, § 96, p. 281 (citations omitted)

". . . It seems we are now to witness the compiling of a new 'judicial dictionary' which will distinguish between those verbs in respect of which the servant's conduct can be regarded as the master's, and those in which it cannot. We must take it as settled by authority that a sale or use or (perhaps) presentation of a play by a servant, if within the general scope of his authority (though forbidden in the precise circumstances), is a sale or use or presentation by the master. On the other hand, it has been held that a representation made by the servant in the course of selling is not a representation by the master. A servant's 'ill-treating' of an animal cannot be attributed to his master. A receiving by a servant does not make his master guilty of 'receiving' stolen goods. So also a giving of credit by a servant is not a giving of credit by the master, and a demand for an illegal premium by a servant is not a demand by the master. Although the point has not been expressly decided, it seems that a master could not be convicted of an offence of 'driving' a vehicle through his servant, for in law it is only the actual driver who drives. Yet it has been held that a bus company 'carries' its passenger and is apparently responsible for an offence in relation to carriage committed by the conductor. . . .

To make the law more difficult still, the same verb may possibly be construed to create vicarious responsibility in a 'public welfare offence' but not in one of the traditional crimes. Thus when a servant is in *de facto* possession of a thing on behalf of his master, the possession may be attributed to the master for the purpose of a public welfare offence, and yet not attributed to him for the purpose of the crime of receiving stolen goods. This way of reconciling the authorities may lead to the somewhat surprising conclusion that the presentation of an unlicensed stage play is a 'public welfare offence'. Again, the context of the verb may modify its meaning: for example, the word 'use' may be restricted by the purport of the section to persons of a particular class.

Note

Except when the master is a company and the servant is a director (as to which see *post*, p. 296), whether or not the offence is one where vicarious liability is held to be intended, it seems that in no case, not even a case of delegated management, will a master be primarily or vicariously liable for *aiding and abetting* an offence, without personal knowledge of the essential matters constituting the offence. On such a charge, the acts and knowledge of the servant are not imputed to the master (see *Ferguson* v. *Weaving, ante,* p. 266) *N.C.B.* v. *Gamble, ante,* p. 259, is not an authority to the contrary, because there the master invited the court to identify him with the servant whose acts and knowledge constituted the aiding and abetting (see [1959] 1 Q.B. 26).

Vane v. Yiannopoullos
[1965] A.C. 486
House of Lords

By section 22 (1) of the Licensing Act 1961: "If—(a) the holder of a justices' on-licence knowingly sells or supplies intoxicating liquor to persons to whom he is not permitted by the conditions of the licence to sell or supply it . . . he shall be guilty of an offence."

The licensee of a restaurant had been granted a justices' on-licence subject to the condition that intoxicating liquor was to be sold only to persons ordering meals. He employed a waitress, whom he had instructed to serve drinks only to customers ordering meals, but on one occasion, whilst he was on another floor of the restaurant, the waitress served drinks to two youths who did not order a meal. The licensee did not know of that sale. He was charged with knowingly selling intoxicating liquor on the premises to persons to whom he was not permitted to sell, contrary to section 22 (1) (*a*) of the Act. The magistrate dismissed the information and the prosecutor appealed, ultimately to the House of Lords.

LORD EVERSHED (after reviewing many cases cited by the appellant): But the effect of these numerous cases appears to my mind to be that (subject to the exception which follows) where the scope and purpose of the relevant Act is the maintenance of proper and accepted standards of public order in licensed premises or other comparable establishments, there arises under the legislation what Channell J. [in *Emary* v. *Nolloth* [1903] 2 K.B. 264] called a "quasi-criminal offence" which renders the licensee or proprietor criminally liable for the acts of his servants, though there may be no *mens rea* on his part. On the other hand, where the relevant regulation imports the word "knowingly" as a condition of liability on the part of the licensee or proprietor the result will be different. "Knowledge", that is *mens rea* in a real sense, on the part of the licensee or proprietor should normally be established as a fact if he is to be held liable under the statute. To this second proposition it appears, however, that, for better or worse, it should now be accepted that something further may be added—namely, that in the absence of proof of actual knowledge, nevertheless the licensee or proprietor may be held liable if he be shown, in the language of the judgments to which I have referred, in a real sense, effectively to have "delegated" his proprietary or managerial functions. If it be asked what is meant by delegation, it may be said . . . that the expression will cover cases where the licensee or proprietor has handed over all the effective management of his premises, where he in truth connives at or wilfully closes his eyes to what in fact is being done. But I prefer to attempt nothing further in the way of definition applicable to any of the classes of case which have arisen; for I venture, for my part, to think that in the light of the numerous authorities the answer to any given case will generally depend upon the common sense of the jury or magistrate concerned, in light of what I believe can now be fairly and sensibly derived from the effect of the numerous cases referred to in the argument, to some of which I have alluded. On the one hand, where there is absent from the statutory prohibition the word "knowingly" applied to the licensee, I think that it should now be accepted that he may yet be held, and properly held, liable for breaches of the conditions of the licence committed by his servants in conscious disregard of those conditions, in spite of his own innocence, where a contrary view would, in the language of Viscount Reading C.J. [in *Mousell Brothers, Ltd.* v. *London and North Western Railway Co.* [1917] 2 K.B. 836], be regarded as fairly likely to stultify what, upon its fair construction, was the purpose of the legislation. On the other hand, where statutory liability on the licensee's part is qualified by the word "knowingly" (or some similarly clear term) then actual knowledge—that is, *mens rea*—is *prima facie* required. But I also think, in light of the cases which have come before the Divisional Court during the present century, that it is right and sensible to hold that, even in the absence of that knowledge on the licensee's part, he may yet fairly and sensibly be held liable where he has in truth and reality "delegated" his powers, functions and responsibilities in the sense indicated in the examples which I have cited from the authorities. I do not attempt any further definition. As I have said, I think the result in any given case will depend upon the common sense of the jury or magistrate in light of what I think to be the effect of the numerous decisions.

So far, however, as the present case is concerned, I feel no doubt that the decision of the Divisional Court was right. There was clearly no "knowledge" in the strict sense proved against the licensee: I agree also with the Lord Chief Justice that there was no sufficient evidence of such "delegation" on his part of his powers, duties and responsibilities to render him liable on that ground. I would therefore without hesitation dismiss the appeal.

Lord Morris of Borth-y-Gest: My Lords, the principle "respondeat superior" finds no place in our criminal law. If a master tells or authorises his servant to do some particular act any criminal liability in the master that might result, either as a principal or as an accessory, springs from the authorisation and not simply from the relationship of master and servant. Parliament may, however, in an infinite variety of ways provide that there is to be criminal liability in one who has personally no *mens rea* or in one who personally has not committed an *actus reus*. The question is whether Parliament has done this in section 22 (1) (a).

It is open to Parliament to provide that a particular act is wrongful and that a person who does the act is guilty of an offence. In general our criminal law requires that there should be *mens rea* in order to establish guilt. Parliament may, however, enact that *mens rea* is not necessary. There may be strict liability. So also it might be enacted that a person is guilty of an offence if his servant or agent does some act and does it with *mens rea*. It might be enacted that a person is guilty of an offence if some other person not his servant or agent does some act and does it with *mens rea*. It might be enacted that a person is guilty of an offence if there is *mens rea* either in him or in the person doing the act. It might be enacted that a person is guilty of an offence if an act is done by some other person even though there is no *mens rea* in anyone. My Lords, the cases cited by Mr. Buzzard in his careful argument provide illustrations of the ways in which courts have interpreted particular sections of particular Acts. I do not propose to refer to them in detail. I do not feel that they ought to determine the construction of the section of the Act of 1961 now being considered. The decisions may seem to be divergent. There is, however, no present need to express a preference for some of them rather than for others. The section of the Act of 1961 now under consideration had no ancestry in earlier Licensing Acts. Even if it had, I am not prepared to accept that there are any canons of construction which are specially applicable to legislation dealing with licensing, or that in such legislation the principle "*respondeat superior*" commands some exceptional yet general acceptance. If in some of the decided cases there are words suggesting that evil consequences would flow if conclusions were reached different from those pronounced, such words must be read (for otherwise they could hardly be justified) as denoting that in the process of construing the words used by Parliament in particular contexts the purpose that was in the mind of Parliament was not to be forgotten. In *Mousell Brothers, Ltd.* v. *London & North Western Railway Co.* [1917] 2 K.B. 836, 845, Atkin J. (as he then was) said: "I think that the authorities cited . . . make it plain that while *prima facie* a principal is not to be made criminally responsible for the acts of his servants, yet the legislature may prohibit an act or enforce a duty in such words as to make the prohibition or the duty absolute; in which case the principal is liable if the act is in fact done by his servants. To ascertain whether a particular Act of Parliament has that effect or not regard must be had to the object of the Statute, the words used, the nature of the duty laid down, the person upon whom it is imposed, the person by whom it would in ordinary circumstances be performed, and the person upon whom the penalty is imposed."

I do not find it necessary to express any opinion in regard to the cases which distinguish between what has been called total and partial delegation. I know of no statutory wording which while pointing to "delegation" distinguishes between servants and agents with major responsibility and those with lesser responsibility. The holder of a licence, it is said, may be criminally liable in some circumstances for the acts of a manager of licensed premises (who may or may not be his own servant) if the manager is in control but will not be liable for what is done by a servant who is not in control. I think that further consideration of these matters need not now arise. While finding myself in agreement with the conclusion of the learned magistrate I base my agreement merely upon an interpretation of the wording of section 22 (1) (a) of the Act of 1961. That Act contained new provisions as to licences for restaurants and guest houses and it amended the Licensing Act of 1953. The Act of 1953, which was an Act that consolidated a number of licensing enactments, contained many variations of wording.

. . . In section 21 (of the 1961 Act) it is provided that "the holder of the licence or his servant shall not knowingly sell" to a person under 18. The section now to be interpreted is the section which follows. The words of section 22 (1) (a) include the word "knowingly". There is no express mention of any servant or agent of the holder of the licence. As a matter of construction it seems to me that in the context of section 22 (1) the presence of the word "knowingly" requires knowledge in the holder of the licence: it requires that he should know that there is a sale to someone to whom (as he knows) he is not permitted to sell. The contention of the appellant is that an offence is committed by the holder of the licence if there is a sale either personally by him or by someone acting on his behalf, provided that either he or such other person knows that the sale is to someone to whom he is not permitted to sell. Having regard to the wording of other sections, I consider that different and much clearer wording was needed in section 22 (1) to convey the meaning contended for by the appellant. In a penal section there should be certainty. The interpretation urged by the appellant involves reading words into the subsection which are not there. I would dismiss the appeal.

Appeal dismissed

Notes

1. Although the decision to dismiss the prosecutor's appeal was unanimous, their Lordships differed in their reasons. Lords Reid and Hodson agreed with Lord Evershed that a partial delegation, unlike a complete delegation, is not enough to make a master liable in the absence of knowledge of his delegate's acts; but Lord Donovan agreed with Lord Morris in doubting whether the law does make a distinction between the two kinds of delegation and in resting his decision on the precise wording of section 22, especially as contrasted with the different wording of the immediately preceding section 21.

2. In view of this hesitation in the House of Lords, in *R.* v. *Winson*, Lord Parker C.J. took the opportunity to reiterate that the law does make such a distinction, and went into its nature and history.

R. v. Winson [1969] *1 Q.B. 371, 382 (C.A.)*: Lord Parker C.J.:—"It is therefore necessary to look a little further back into the inception of this doctrine. It is to be observed in the first instance that this doctrine is something quite independent of the principles which come into play when Parliament has created an absolute offence; when an absolute offence has been created by Parliament, then the person on whom a duty is thrown is responsible, whether he has delegated or whether he has acted through a servant; he is absolutely liable regardless of any intent or knowledge or *mens rea*. The principle of delegation comes into play, and only comes into play, in cases where, although the statute uses words which import knowledge or intent such as in this case 'knowingly' or in some other cases 'permitting' or 'suffering' and the like, cases to which knowledge is inherent, nevertheless it has been held that a man cannot get out of his responsibilities which have been put upon him by delegating those responsibilities to another.

Though not the first case by any means on the subject, the first case to which attention is drawn is that of *Allen* v. *Whitehead* [1930] 1 K.B. 211, D.C. The offence in question there was knowingly permitting or suffering prostitutes to meet together on premises contrary to section 44 of the Metropolitan Police Act, 1839. In that case the occupier and licensee of a refreshment house did not manage the refreshment house himself but employed a manager for that purpose. A number of women known to the manager to be prostitutes resorted to the refreshment house. In that case, as here, the occupier and licensee said, 'It was not knowingly on my part. I was not there, I had appointed a manager'. Lord Hewart C.J. said (at p. 220):

> 'I think that this provision in this statute would be rendered nugatory if the contention raised on behalf of this respondent were held to prevail. That contention was this, that as the respondent did not himself manage the refreshment house and had no personal knowledge that prostitutes met together and remained therein, and had not been negligent in failing to notice these facts, and had not wilfully closed his eyes to them, he could not in law be held responsible.'

He went on to say (at p. 221)

> 'He had transferred to the manager the exercise of discretion in the conduct of the business, and it seems to me that the only reasonable conclusion is, regard being had to the purposes of this Act, that the knowledge of the manager was the knowledge of the keeper of the house.'

Branson J. put the matter very succinctly. He said (at p. 221)

> 'I agree. The essence of the respondent's case was that he had no personal knowledge of the fact that prostitutes were meeting and remaining upon these premises. It is found that his manager knew, and Lord Coleridge C.J. said in *Somerset* v. *Hart* (1884) 12 Q.B.D. 360, D.C. "that a man may put another in his position so as to represent him for the purpose of knowledge." I think that is what the respondent has done here and that, consequently, the contention set up by the respondent fails.'

It is just worth referring to *Somerset* v. *Hart* itself, if only because that was decided on the basis that there had been no valid delegation. The offence there concerned gaming, that the licensee of premises had suffered gaming to take place on the premises. In fact he had not delegated the management to anybody else, but a servant of his employed on the premises, without any connivance or wilful blindness on the part of the licensee, had suffered gaming to take place. In the course of the argument Lord Coleridge said (at p. 362)

> 'How can a man suffer a thing done when he does not know of it? It is true that a man may put another in his position so as to represent him for the purpose of knowledge, but there is no evidence of such delegation here.'

In his judgment Lord Coleridge said (at p. 364)

> 'I quite agree that the provisions of an Act which is passed in the interests of public morality and order should receive a reasonably liberal construction. I do not say that proof of actual knowledge on the part of the landlord is necessary. Slight evidence might be sufficient to satisfy the magistrates that the landlord might have known what was taking place if he had pleased, but where no actual knowledge is shown there must, as it seems to me, be something to show either that the gaming took place with the knowledge of some person clothed with the landlord's authority, or that there was something like connivance on his part, that he might have known but purposely abstained from knowing.'

Finally, of the more important authorities on this point there is the case of *Linnett* v. *Metropolitan Police Commissioner*, [1946] K.B. 290, D.C. The offence there was 'knowingly permitting disorderly conduct contrary to section 44 of the Metropolitan Police Act'. In fact the licensee of the premises had absented himself from the premises and left the control to another man. It was held that although he, the licensee, had no knowledge, the man he had appointed manager or controller did have knowledge and on the principle of delegation he, the licensee, was liable. Lord Goddard C.J. said (at p. 294)

'The principle underlying these decisions does not depend upon the legal relationship existing between master and servant or between principal and agent; it depends on the fact that the person who is responsible in law, as for example, a licensee under the Licensing Acts, has chosen to delegate his duties, powers and authority to another.'

He goes on to refer to *Somerset* v. *Hart* and points out that in that case there had been no delegation of control, but that it was merely a case, as indeed was *Vane* v. *Yiannopoullos* of a servant acting behind the back of the licensee. He ends up by saying (at p. 295)

'Where there is such delegation, [that is, true delegation] then the knowledge of the servant or agent becomes that of the master or principal.

In this case there was no relationship of master and servant between the appellant and Baker. They were joint licensees. If one licensee chooses to say to his co-licensee, although not his servant: "We are both licensees and both keepers of this house, but I am not going to take any part in the management of this house, I leave the management to you", he is putting his co-licensee into his own place to exercise his own powers and duties and he must, therefore, accept responsibility for what is done or known by his co-licensee in that exercise. That is the principle which underlies all the cases to which I have referred. I am far from saying, and I do not wish it to be thought that I am saying, that where a statute provides that in any business a certain act permitted by the manager shall be an offence on the part of the manager if it is done with his knowledge, that if that act takes place whilst the manager himself is carrying on that business and is in charge of that business but without his knowledge, so that he was powerless to prevent it, that person necessarily commits the offence. But if the manager chooses to delegate the carrying on of the business to another, whether or not that other is his servant, then what that other does or what he knows must be imputed to the person who put the other into that position.'

That is the doctrine of delegation which does form part of our law and no one in the House of Lords has said that it does not."

Note

The justification for the doctrine (mentioned by Lord Hewart L.C.J. in *Allen* v. *Whitehead*) is that otherwise the statute would be rendered nugatory. The argument is that, since the statute covers only the licensee and not the servant or delegate, if the licensee could plead ignorance and escape on that ground, the law would have no one to shoot at. The servant could not be guilty—not under the statute, because it does not apply to him, nor as an aider and abettor since there is no principal (see *ante*, p. 278). One would think that if the statute expressly covers "the licensee or his servant" the delegation principle would not be invoked, since its justification is absent. But it is held otherwise. In *Howker* v. *Robinson* [1973] 1 Q.B. 178, 184, Bristow J. said: "The effect of the addition of the words 'or his servant' ... is simply to add the servant as an additional target for prosecution. Once a principle of law or canon of construction has been established and has become part of the law, it has to be applied even if the circumstances which appear to have led to its adoption do not exist in the particular case in which its application is in question."

In *Howker* v. *Robinson*, the licensee was in the next room when his servant sold liquor to a boy aged 14. Section 169 (1) Licensing Act 1964 forbade this by "the holder of the licence or his servant." The licensee's conviction was upheld, the Division Court holding itself bound by the magistrates' finding of fact that the responsibility for ensuring the law was complied with had been delegated to the barman by the licensee. Since the licensee was nearer to his servant than the licensee in *Vane* v. *Yiannopoullos*, it can be argued that the magistrates were not entitled to make that "finding of fact."

4. CORPORATIONS

Tesco Supermarkets Ltd. v. Nattrass
[1972] A.C. 153
House of Lords

> T.S. Ltd. was charged with an offence under the Trade Descriptions Act 1968. It sought to raise a defence under section 24 (1) on the grounds that the commission of the offence was due to the act or default of another person, namely the manager of the store at which it was committed, and it exercised all due diligence to avoid the commission of the offence. The magistrates found that the company had set up a proper system, so it had exercised all due diligence; but the manager, who had failed to carry out his part under the system, was not "another person." The company, on conviction, appealed to the Divisional Court which held that the manager was "another person" but the company had not exercised all due diligence. The company appealed to the House of Lords.

Lord Pearson: My Lords, in September 1969, the company (Tesco Supermarkets Ltd.) was selling Giant Size packets of Radiant washing powder at a price of 2s 11d., being a reduced price 1s. below the price of 3s. 11d. which was the ordinary price normally recommended by the manufacturers. Affixed to the window of the company's shop at Northwich in Cheshire was a large poster, of which the upper part bore the legent "Radiant 1s. off Giant Size 2s. 11d." Advertisements to the same effect had been inserted in local and national newspapers. Initially there was at the shop a stock of "flash packs," that is to say, Giant Size packets of the washing powder bearing the legend "1s. off recommended price."

Things went wrong on September 25 and 26, 1969. The stock of such "flash packs" was exhausted. On the evening of September 25 Miss Rogers, an assistant at the shop, discovered that no such "flash packs" remained on display, and she filled up the "fixture" with ordinary packets of the washing powder marked with the ordinary price of 3s. 11d. and she failed to inform the shop manager, Mr. Clement, of the dearth of "flash packs" or the action which she had taken. Mr. Clement failed to check the washing powder "fixture" on September 26, notwithstanding his entry in his weights and measures book for that morning "All special offers O.K." On the morning of September 26, a customer entered the shop expecting to find a "flash pack" at 2s. 11d. but was able to find only a packet offered at the ordinary price of 3s. 11d. and he had to buy it at that price.

The relevant provisions of the Trade Descriptions Act 1968 are as follows:

Section 11 (2):

> "If any person offering to supply any goods gives, by whatever means, any indication likely to be taken as an indication that the goods are being offered

> at a price less than that at which they are in fact being offered he shall, subject to the provisions of this Act, be guilty of an offence."

Section 20 (1):

> "Where an offence under this Act which has been committed by a body corporate is proved to have been committed with the consent and connivance of, or to be attributable to any neglect on the part of, any director, manager, secretary or other similar officer of the body corporate, or any person who was purporting to act in any such capacity, he as well as the body corporate shall be guilty of that offence and shall be liable to be proceeded against and punished accordingly."

Section 23:

> "Where the commission by any person of an offence under this Act is due to the act or default of some other person that other person shall be guilty of the offence, and a person may be charged with and convicted of the offence by virtue of this section whether or not proceedings are taken against the first mentioned person."

Section 24 (1):

> "In any proceedings for an offence under this Act it shall, subject to subsection (2) of this section, be a defence for the person charged to prove—(a) that the commission of the offence was due to a mistake or to reliance on information supplied to him or to the act or default of another person, an accident or some other cause beyond his control; and (b) that he took all reasonable precautions and exercised all due diligence to avoid the commission of such an offence by himself or any person under his control."

In my opinion, the first conclusions to be drawn from the application of these provisions to the facts of the present case are as follows:

(1) An offence was committed under section 11 (2).

(2) *Prima facie* the company has committed and is liable for the offence, because the company through its servants offered to supply the goods and gave the indication of the reduced price. The case is similar to *Coppen* v. *Moore* (No. 2) [1898] 2 Q.B. 306, decided under the Merchandise Marks Act 1887, s. 2, where Lord Russell C.J. said, at pp. 312–313:

> "The question, then, in this case, comes to be narrowed to the simple point, whether upon the true construction of the statute here in question the master was intended to be made criminally responsible for acts done by his servants in contravention of the Act, where such acts were done, as in this case, within the scope or in the course of their employment. In our judgment it was clearly the intention of the legislature to make the master criminally liable for such acts, unless he was able to rebut the *prima facie* presumption of guilt by one or other of the methods pointed out in the Act."

Also relevant is the judgment of Lord Goddard C.J. in *Melias Ltd.* v. *Preston* [1957] 2 Q.B. 380.

(3) In the present case the company was the master of the persons who committed the acts or defaults whereby the offence was committed, and as in *Coppen* v. *Moore* (No. 2) [1898] 2 Q.B. 306 the company may rebut the presumption of guilt in one or other of the methods pointed out by the Act. Section 11 (2) is expressly made "subject to the provisions of this Act" and therefore is subject to section 24 (1). The company has sought to prove under section 24 (1) (a) that

"the commission of the offence was due . . . to the act or default of another person," naming Mr. Clement as the other person. In order to complete its defence the company must also prove that the company took all reasonable precautions and exercised all due diligence to avoid the commission of such an offence by itself or any person under its control. The question in this appeal is whether the company has proved those two points.

Your Lordships are not concerned in this appeal with the questions whether Miss Rogers and Mr. Clement or either of them could be held liable under section 23 for the commission of the offence, and whether they or either of them would have a defence under section 24. I express no opinion on those questions.

The magistrates have said in paragraph 7 of the case stated that they were of opinion that

> "(ii) the commission of the offence was due to the act or default of the said Clement by his failure to see that the appellants' policy was correctly carried out and/or to correct the errors of the staff under him; (iii) the appellants had exercised all due diligence in devising a proper system for the operation of the said store and by securing so far as was reasonably practicable that it was fully implemented and thus had fulfilled the requirements of section 24 (1) (b); (iv) the appellants could not rely upon the act or default of the said Clement as he was not 'another person' within the meaning of section 24 (1) (a); . . ."

In giving their reasons for the opinion in (iv) they said that they reached the conclusion that the original act or default was that of Miss Rogers and the act or default of Mr. Clement was in his failure to instruct or supervise her; Mr. Clement represented the company in his supervisory capacity and for his lack of due diligence the company was responsible on the principle laid down in *R. C. Hammett Ltd.* v. *London County Council* (1933) 97 J.P. 105; accordingly, Mr. Clement was not "another person" for the purposes of section 24 (1) (a) of the Act.

The magistrates' opinion that Mr. Clement was not "another person"—a person other than the company—seems to me to be clearly unsustainable. It would be immediately obvious in the case of an individual proprietor of a business and the manager of one of his shops. It is less obvious in the case of a company which can only act through servants or agents and has generally in the law of tort and sometimes in criminal law vicarious responsibility for what they do on its behalf. But vicarious responsibility is very different from identification. There are some officers of a company who may for some purposes be identified with it, as being or having its directing mind and will, its centre and ego, and its brains. *Lennard's Carrying Co. Ltd.* v. *Asiatic Petroleum Co. Ltd.* [1915] A.C. 705, 713; *H. L. Bolton (Engineering) Co. Ltd.* v. *T. J. Graham & Sons Ltd.* [1957] 1 Q.B. 159, 171–173; *The Lady Gwendolen* [1965] P. 294, 343. The reference in section 20 of the Trade Descriptions Act 1968 to "any director, manager, secretary or other similar officer of the body corporate" affords a useful indication of the grades of officers who may for some purposes be indentifiable with the company, although in any particular case the constitution of the company concerned should be taken into account. With regard to the word "manager" I agree with Fisher J. [1971] 1 Q.B. 133 who said, in his judgment in the present case, at p. 142, that the word refers to someone in the position of managing the affairs of the company, and would not extend to include a person in the position of Mr. Clement. In the present case the company has some hundreds of retail shops, and it would be far from reasonable to say that every one of its shop managers is the same person as the company.

The Divisional Court, although they affirmed the conviction and dismissed the company's appeal, took a view that was different from that of the magistrates.

They held that Mr. Clement was "another person" distinct from the company, so that the company proved its point under paragraph (a) of section 24 (1). But they held that the company failed under paragraph (b). Their reasoning was that, although the company had devised a proper system for taking precautions and exercising due diligence to avoid the commission of an offence, the company had delegated the function of operating the system to employees, of whom Mr. Clement was one; that Mr. Clement had operated the system negligently; the company was responsible for the negligent operation of the system by one of its delegates; and so the company failed to prove that it had taken all reasonable precautions and exercised all due diligence to prevent the commission of the offence. Some extracts from the judgment of Fisher J. [1971] 1 Q.B. 133 will show clearly how the Divisional Court reached their conclusion. He said, at p. 143:

> "The taking of such precautions and the exercise of such diligence involves, or may involve, two things. First the setting up of an efficient system for the avoidance of offences under the Act. Secondly the proper operation of that system. Inevitably the second part, the operation of the system, will in most cases have to be delegated by the company to employees falling outside those mentioned in section 20. The question which this court has to consider is whether a company can be said to have satisfied the requirements of paragraph (b) if it satisfies the justices that it has set up an efficient system, or a system which cannot be criticised, or whether it is deprived of the defence under that section if it is shown that there has been a failure by someone to whom the duty of carrying out the system was delegated properly to carry out that function."

Later he said, at p. 145:

> "if it be the case that the manager was a person to whom [the appellants] had delegated in respect of that particular shop their duty to take all reasonable precautions and exercise all due diligence to avoid the commission of such an offence, and if the manager had failed properly to carry out that duty, then [the appellants] are unable to show that they have satisfied paragraph (b) of section 24 (1)."

The conclusion was, at p. 146:

> "It seems clear to me that a person in the position of the manager of a shop, a supermarket, is properly to be considered as being a person to whom [the appellants] had, so far as concerned that shop, delegated their duty of taking all reasonable precautions and exercising all due diligence to avoid the commission of an offence; and it seems to me that in the light of the findings which I have just read, it was impossible for the justices to find that [the appellants] had satisfied the requirements of section 24 (1) (b)."

Fisher J. also cited the case of *Series* v. *Poole* [1969] 1 Q.B. 676, in which it was held that the defendant was liable under section 186 of the Road Traffic Act 1960, and had failed to prove a defence under section 20 of the Road Traffic Act 1962, when he had "delegated" the checking of certain records to a lady secretary and she had been negligent in the performance of that task. In his judgment in that case Lord Parker C.J. had said at pp. 683–684:

> "If I can go by stages, the absolute obligation under section 186 of the Act of 1960 is a personal obligation, personal in this sense, that if an employer, acting perfectly reasonably, puts some competent person in charge to perform his, the employer's duty, the employer remains liable if the servant fails

> in his duty. . . . He may, as I have said, acting perfectly reasonably appoint somebody else to perform his duty, his alter ego, and in that case, as it seems to me, if the alter ego fails in his duty the employer is liable. Equally, if the employer seeks to rely on the defence under section 20, he must show that the alter ego has observed due diligence."

Clearly the Divisional Court's decision was based on the theory of "delegation". One has to examine the meaning of the word "delegation" in relation to the facts of this case and the provisions of the Trade Descriptions Act 1968, ss. 11 (2) and 24. In one sense the meaning is as wide as the principle of the master's vicarious liability for the acts and omissions of his servants acting within the scope of their employment. In this sense the master can be said to "delegate" to every servant acting on his behalf all the duties which the servant has to perform. But that cannot be the proper meaning here. If the company "delegated" to Miss Rogers the duty of filling the fixture with appropriate packets of washing powder, and "delegated" to Mr. Clement the duty of supervising the proper filling of fixtures and the proper exhibition or withdrawal of posters proclaiming reduced prices, then any master, whether a company or an individual, must be vicariously liable for all the acts and omissions of all its or his servants acting on its or his behalf. That conclusion would defeat the manifest object of section 24 which is to enable defendants to avoid vicarious liability where they were not personally at fault.

Section 24 requires a dividing line to be drawn between the master and any other person. The defendant cannot disclaim liability for an act or omission of his ego or his alter ego. In the case of an individual defendant, his ego is simply himself, but he may have an alter ego. For instance, if he has only one shop and he appoints a manager of that shop with full discretion to manage it as he thinks fit, the manager is doing what the employer would normally do and may be held to be the employer's alter ego. But if the defendant has hundreds of shops, he could not be expected personally to manage each one of them and the manager of one of his shops cannot in the absence of exceptional circumstances be considered his alter ego. In the case of a company, the ego is located in several persons, for example, those mentioned in section 20 of the Act or other persons in a similar position of direction or general management. A company may have an alter ego, if those persons who are or have its ego delegate to some other person the control and management, with full discretionary powers, of some section of the company's business. In the case of a company, it may be difficult, and in most cases for practical purposes unnecessary, to draw the distinction between its ego and its alter ego, but theoretically there is that distinction.

Mr. Clement, being the manager of one of the company's several hundreds of shops, could not be identified with the company's ego nor was he an alter ego of the company. He was an employee in a relatively subordinate post. In the company's hierarchy there were a branch inspector and an area controller and a regional director interposed between him and the board of directors.

It was suggested in the argument of this appeal that in exercising supervision over the operations in the shop Mr. Clement was performing functions of management and acting as a delegate and alter ego of the company. But supervision of the details of operations is not normally a function of higher management: it is normally carried out by employees at the level of foremen, chargehands, overlookers, floor managers and "shop" managers (in the factory sense of "shop"). Also reference was made to the case of *R. C. Hammett Ltd.* v. *London County Council* (1933) 97 J.P. 105, in which, when the reported arguments are taken into account the ground of decision appears to have been that, for the purposes of the Sale of Food (Weights and Measures) Act 1926, ss. 5 (2) and 12 (5), the employer had to show due diligence on behalf of all the employees concerned except the actual offender. In my opinion, there was no justification for drawing the line of division between the company and its employees at that point, and the case was wrongly decided. As to the case of *Series* v. *Poole* [1969] 1 Q.B. 676, the decision of the Divisional Court seems to have been in accordance with the general merits of the case, but the treatment of the secretary as an alter ego of the employer is difficult to uphold, when she had merely been instructed by him to check the records and had failed to do so diligently.

I would allow the appeal.

LORD DIPLOCK: . . . My Lords, a corporation incorporated under the Companies Act 1948 owes its corporate personality and its powers to its constitution, the memorandum and articles of association. The obvious and the only place to look to discover by what natural persons its powers are exercisable, is in its constitution. The articles of association, if they follow Table A, provide that the business of the company shall be managed by the directors and that they may "exercise all such powers of the company" as are not required by the Act to be exercised in general meeting. Table A also vests in the directors the right to entrust and confer upon a managing director any of the powers of the company which are exercisable by them. So it may also be necessary to ascertain whether the directors have taken any action under this provision or any other similar provision providing for the co-ordinate exercise of the powers of the company by executive directors or by committees of directors and other persons, such as are frequently included in the articles of association of companies in which the regulations contained in Table A are modified or excluded in whole or in part.

In my view, therefore, the question: what natural persons are to be treated in law as being the company for the purpose of acts done in the course of its business, including the taking of precautions and the exercise of due diligence to avoid the commission of a criminal offence, is to be found by identifying those natural persons who by the memorandum and articles of association or as a result of action taken by the directors, or by the company in general meeting pursuant to the articles, are entrusted with the exercise of the powers of the company.

This test is in conformity with the classic statement of Viscount Haldane L.C. in *Lennard's Carrying Co. Ltd.* v. *Asiatic Petroleum Co. Ltd.* [1915] A.C. 705. The relevant statute in that case, although not a criminal statute, was in *pari materia,* for it provided for a defence to a civil liability which excluded the concept of vicarious liability of a principal for the physical acts and state of mind of his agent.

There has been in recent years a tendency to extract from Denning L.J.'s judgment in *H.L. Bolton (Engineering) Co. Ltd.* v. *T. J. Graham & Sons Ltd.* [1957] 1 Q.B. 159, 172, 173 his vivid metaphor about the "brains and nerve centre" of a company as contrasted with its hands, and to treat this dichotomy, and not the articles of association, as laying down the test of whether or not a particular person is to be regarded in law as being the company itself when performing duties which a statute imposes on the company.

In the case in which this metaphor was first used Denning L.J. was dealing with acts and intentions of directors of the company in whom the powers of the company were vested under its articles of association. The decision in that case is not authority for extending the class of persons whose acts are to be regarded in law as the personal acts of the company itself, beyond those who by, or by action taken under, its articles of association are entitled to exercise the powers of the company. In so far as there are dicta to the contrary in *The Lady Gwendolen* [1965] P. 294, they were not necessary to the decision and, in my view, they were wrong. . . .

Appeal allowed

Lennard's Carrying Co. Ltd. v. *Asiatic Petroleum Co. Ltd.* [1915] A.C. 705, *per* Viscount Haldane L.C. at p. 713: "Did what happened take place without the actual fault or privity of the owners of the ship who were the appellants? My Lords, a corporation is an abstraction. It has no mind of its own any more than it has a body of its own; its active and directing will must consequently be sought in the person of somebody who for some purposes may be called an agent, but who is really the directing mind and will of the corporation, the very ego and centre of the personality of the corporation. That person may be under the direction of the shareholders in general meeting; that person may be the board of directors itself, or it may be, and in some companies it is so, that that person has an authority co-ordinate with the board of directors given to him under the articles of association, and is appointed by the general meeting of the company, and can only be removed by the general meeting of the company. . . . The fault or privity is the fault or privity of somebody who is not merely a servant or agent for whom the company is liable upon the footing *respondeat superior*, but somebody for whom the company is liable because his action is the very action of the company itself."

H.L. Bolton (Engineering) Co. Ltd. v. *T. J. Graham & Sons Ltd.* [1957] 1 Q.B. 159, *per* Denning L.J. at p. 172: "A company may in many ways be likened to a human body. It has a brain and nerve centre which controls what it does. It also has hands which hold the tools and act in accordance with directions from the centre. Some of the people in the company are mere servants and agents who are nothing more than hands to do the work and cannot be said to represent the mind or will. Others are directors and managers who represent the directing mind and will of the company, and control what it does. The state of mind of these managers is the state of mind of the company and is treated by the law as such."

Note

On vicarious liability, see, *ante*, p. 288.

Questions

1. Section 11 (2) of the Trade Descriptions Act 1968, defining the offence, is held to intend vicarious liability, while section 24 (2) (*b*), defining the defence, is held not to do so. How would you summarise the legislative policy requiring this result? Is it an intelligible policy in an area where the subjects and objects of the law are large national corporations and individual shoppers respectively?

2. If the lack of due diligence in the Tesco case could as a matter of fact be traced up to a member of the main board of directors, what would be the position of that director? What would be his position in the absence of section 20 (1)?

3. Statute makes it an offence for a manufacturer of widgets to sell any widgets in the making of which blotto has been used. The statute contains no provisions corresponding to sections 20, 23, 24 of the Trade Descriptions Act. Widgets Ltd., is a manufacturer of widgets. Alan is a managing and sales director of Widgets Ltd., Bob is the director in charge of production and Con is a salesman employed by the company. A consignment of widgets was sold to one of the company's customers. The sale was arranged by Con who, unlike Alan, knew that Bob had used blotto in their manufacture. Consider the criminal liability of all concerned.

CHAPTER 7

INCHOATE OFFENCES

	PAGE
1. Attempts	303
i. *Actus Reus*	305
ii. Attempting the Impossible	316
iii. Mental Element in Attempt	328
2. Conspiracy	331
i. Conspiracy at Common Law or by Statute	332
ii. Agreement	333
2. Conspiracy (*cont.*)	
iii. Jurisdiction	336
iv. Parties	339
v. Common Law Conspiracies	343
vi. Statutory Conspiracies	357
vii. Conspiracies to do the Impossible	359
3. Incitement	360

Note

Intending to commit an offence is not itself an offence, but one who sets out to commit an offence may commit one of the inchoate crimes of attempt, conspiracy or incitement. They were common law crimes and incitement still is, but attempt is now defined and punished in the Criminal Attempts Act 1981, and conspiracy in Part I of the Criminal Law Act 1977, as amended by the Criminal Attempts Act 1981

1. ATTEMPTS

Criminal Attempts Act 1981

"Section 1: (1) If, with intent to commit an offence to which this section applies, a person does an act which is more than merely preparatory to the commission of the offence, he is guilty of attempting to commit the offence.

(2) A person may be guilty of attempting to commit an offence to which this section applies even though the facts are such that the commission of the offence is impossible.

(3) In any case where—

(a) apart from this subsection a person's intention would not be regarded as having amounted to an intent to commit an offence; but

(*b*) if the facts of the case had been as he believed them to be, his intention would be so regarded,

then, for the purposes of subsection (1) above, he shall be regarded as having had an intent to commit that offence.

(4) This section applies to any offence which, if it were completed, would be triable in England and Wales as an indictable offence, other than—

(a) conspiracy (at common law or under section 1 of the Criminal Law Act 1977 or any other enactment);

(*b*) aiding, abetting, counselling, procuring or suborning the commission of an offence;

(c) offences under section 4 (1) (assisting offenders) or 5 (1) (accepting or agreeing to accept consideration for not disclosing information about an arrestable offence) of the Criminal Law Act 1967.

Section 4: (3) Where, in proceedings against a person for an offence under section 1 above, there is evidence sufficient in law to support a finding that he did an act falling within subsection (1) of that section, the question whether or not his act fell within that subsection is a question of fact."

Notes

1. In the common law of attempt, there was much uncertainty surrounding the definition of the *actus reus*, especially in cases where the crime attempted was, for one reason or another, impossible to commit. To a much lesser degree, some uncertainty was also attached to the *mens rea*. The difficulties are outlined in Law. Com. No. 102, below. The Act reproduces, but not exactly, the Law Commission's proposals to deal with those difficulties. The common law of attempt is abolished: Section 6 (1), Criminal Attempts Act 1981.

2. The Law Commission, after deciding that the three separate inchoate offences should be retained, and that a general law of attempt (rather than the redefinition of every offence to make it wide enough to catch preparatory as well as completed conduct) was still needed (§§ 2.4–2.6), considered whether the concept of *attempt* should be retained.

Law Com. No. 102

"§ 2.7 The final preliminary question is, assuming that an inchoate offence is needed in the field presently covered by the law of attempt, whether that concept should be retained or whether some other concept should be substituted for it. We have already pointed out that the main justification for the retention of inchoate offences is the need to permit the law to impose criminal sanctions in certain cases where a crime has been contemplated but not in fact committed. It is, however, a fundamental principle of our law that it should not seek to penalise the mere intention to commit a crime. As the Working Party said (1973) W.P. 50, § 65—

> 'The mere intention in a serious case constitutes a social danger, but provided that it remains no more than intention, no intervention is justifiable. It is only when some act is done which sufficiently manifests the existence of the social danger present in the intent that authority should intervene. It is necessary to strike a balance in this context between individual freedom and the countervailing interest of the community.'

In some cases, as the Working Party pointed out, the problem of balancing social and individual interests—

> 'has been met by the adoption of a technique other than the law of attempt, for example, by the creation of offences of procurement, possession, threats and going equipped. Provisions of this kind, however, relate only to specific crimes and particular types of attempt in relation to these crimes. They do not purport to offer more than a partial remedy. There are in a few instances specific attempts in statutes creating the substantive offence, relating for the most part to sexual offences, but this is not the practice in more recent codifying Acts. Within a limited sphere (for example, official secrets) another solution has been found by going back a stage further than the earliest stage at which the present law of attempt seeks to operate and providing that acts 'preparatory to' the commission of substantive offences shall in themselves constitute offences. Generally, however, English law has hitherto not travelled back this far in the chain of causation unless the preparatory act itself constitutes a substantive offence, as where forgery is committed as a preliminary step in an ultimate intended offence of deception.'

§ 2.8 Another relevant consideration is that, if it is accepted that some kind of inchoate offence is needed to penalise conduct at present dealt with by the law of attempt, it is worth retaining that name for the offence. Not only is the word 'attempt' one which is in everyday use, but it may cogently be argued that the conduct which the law should aim to penalise is, broadly speaking, that which the layman would regard as 'attempting' to commit an offence. This desirable coincidence of social policy and ordinary language could not survive a drastic expansion of the meaning of 'attempt' to encompass all preparatory acts.

§ 2.9 . . . We therefore conclude that the Working Party were correct in their view that the concept of attempt should be retained in preference to any possible alternative."

i. Actus Reus

Note

The problem of defining a criminal attempt at common law continuously troubled judges and writers. The Law Commission regarded it as important to get as precise a definition as possible, so as to avoid penalising conduct so distant from the ultimate objective that the balance of the needs of society and the individual would be upset. For that reason, it rejected the suggestion that *any* act intended by the accused to further his intent to commit a crime should be punishable. In formulating its own criterion of criminality, it reviewed various theories of attempt.

Law Com. No. 102

[*Footnotes to this extract are numbered as in original document.*]

1. The attempt theories

(a) *The "first stage" theory*

§ 2.22 The "first stage" test in its pure form seizes on the first overt act done towards the commission of the offence as the criterion. It appears to be adopted by some Continental Codes, which refer to "acts exhibiting the commencement of the execution" of crimes, although this form of words might be regarded as equally consistent with an "unequivocality" test. It also met with a measure of approval in the English draft code of 1879, Stephen's *Digest of the Criminal Law* Article 29, and the Indian Penal Code. In these latter cases, however, it seems to have been qualified by the additional test of proximity. In its pure form the "first stage" test appears to lay undue stress upon the intention of the defendant in that, given proof of intention to commit an offence, many quite innocent acts can be regarded as overt acts done towards the commission of the offence. For example the buying of a particular nib or pen with which to forge a signature may be an overt act towards committing the forgery, if the intention to forge is established. It was for this reason that the Working Party considered that this test would not be acceptable. We have seen that generally English law rejects a test which is based on an act of mere preparation (§ 2.7 above) and that, save in isolated examples, this line of development has not been followed. A concept of attempt based on the "first stage" theory would appear to follow that line too closely, and we agree with the Working Party's rejection of it.

(b) *The "final stage" theory*

§ 2.24 The "final stage" theory admits of no attempt unless and until the intending offender had done all that is necessary for him to do in order to bring his crime to completion. At one time it met with approval in English law and was certainly adopted by Parke B. as decisive in *R.* v. *Eagleton* where he stated (1855) 6 Cox C.C. 559, 571, that—

"The mere intention to commit a misdemeanour is not criminal. Some act is required and we do not think all acts towards committing a misdemeanour are indictable. Acts remotely leading towards the commission of the offence are not to be considered as attempts to commit it, but acts immediately connected with it are; *and if, in this case . . . any further step on the part of the defendant had been necessary to obtain payment. . . . we should have thought that the obtaining credit . . . would not have been sufficiently proximate to the obtaining of the money. But, on the statement of this case, no other act on the part of the defendant would have been required. It was the last act, depending on himself, towards the payment of money, and therefore, it ought to be considered as an attempt."*

This passage, in whole or in part, has been much quoted. In the present context, it is the part which we have italicised that is material. This part was apparently crucial to the decision of the Court of Criminal Appeal in *R.* v. *Robinson*, although the court did not in fact cite it in its judgment.[60] . . .

§ 2.25 The Working Party summarised objections to basing the law of attempt on this approach in the following terms (§ 71)—

"In the first place, it is difficult, from a practical point of view, to see how it could be applied to certain serious crimes. On a strict application of the test, attempted rape, for example, would not be possible and it is this approach which may well have been responsible for the conclusion that there could not be a verdict of attempting to demand money with menaces because 'either there is a demand or there is not'. More importantly, however, it seems to us that the theory allows too many persons who might be thought deserving of punishment (as in *Robinson's* case) to escape it; and, furthermore, allows intending offenders to advance far in their conduct before effective intervention can take place."

The approach has been criticised elsewhere and we think the Working Party rightly rejected it.

(c) *The "unequivocal act" theory*

§ 2.26 This theory in its pure form requires that the act itself, without regard to any statement of intention, either contemporaneous or subsequent, must unequivocally demonstrate the intention to commit the relevant offence. It was propounded by Salmond and was enacted in the New Zealand Crimes Act 1908, but was found not to work satisfactorily in practice. In some instances, the act demonstrated unequivocally the intent to commit an offence, but was so distant from the execution of it that on a common-sense view it was impossible to regard it as an attempt. In others, the conduct was clearly carried out in execution of the offence but could not be regarded as unequivocally pointing to the intention. The test was therefore discarded by the New Zealand Crimes Act 1961, s. 72 (3), and we do not ourselves favour it. Nevertheless, elements of the test have found their way into English cases, to which we refer again below.

(d) *The "proximity" test*

§ 2.27 In so far as English law subscribes to any one theory or approach (a matter which we examine further below), that of "proximity" may be regarded as dominant, although the case law discloses elements of all the approaches so far considered. But the requirement of the proximity of the conduct to the completed offence, and the distinction between this and acts of preparation, is a common

[60] [1915] 2 K.B. 342. The facts of this much-criticised case are given in § 2.29, n. 72, below. The whole of the quoted passage from *R.* v. *Eagleton* was cited in the argument for the appellant, but the court cited in its judgment only the unitalicised part: *ibid.*, p. 348.

thread throughout most reported cases, whether or not in conjunction with other requirements. This is often expressed by reference to the decision of Parke B. in *R.* v. *Eagleton*. Frequently the citation is limited to the statement that "acts remotely leading towards the commission of the offence are not to be considered as attempts to commit it, but acts immediately connected with it are." On this basis the courts have sometimes held that, as the defendant had done all that it was necessary for him to have done, his act was sufficiently proximate to the offence attempted; in others, the courts have concluded that, since there was still an opportunity for the defendant to change his mind, the stage of mere preparation had not been passed.

§ 2.28 Variants on the proximity test have been advanced in certain other common law jurisdictions. In the United States, for example, Holmes J. enunciated in *Commonwealth* v. *Kennedy* the well-known test. "As the aim of the law is not to punish sins but is to prevent certain external results, the act done must come pretty near to accomplishing that result before the law will notice it" 48 N.E. 770 (Mass. 1897). Elsewhere (*Hyde* v. *U.S.* 225 U.S. 347, 388 (1911)) he suggested that his notion of "dangerous proximity to success" required consideration in each case of public policy, for example "the nearness of the danger, the greatness of the harm, and the degree of apprehension felt." In so far as this embodies the idea that the defendant must have done nearly everything that he could towards his aim, it differs little from the proximity test as it is presently understood; but the objective elements in the test, relating to surrounding circumstances rather than the defendant's own acts, are in our view not helpful in defining the critical stage of his conduct.

§ 2.29 It is true to say, as our Working Party did, § 73, that no precise test has been evolved for determining whether an act is sufficiently proximate to the offence to constitute the actus reus of an attempt. Because of the imprecision of these words and because their application in practice resulted in the conduct in such cases as *R.* v. *Robinson*,[72] *R.* v. *Komaroni*[73] and *Comer* v. *Bloomfield*[74] being held not to constitute an attempt, the majority of the Working Party felt that a new formulation of the actus reus was required. The Working Paper therefore provisionally proposed as a solution the "substantial step" approach, which we now consider in detail.

(e) *The "substantial step" test*

§ 2.30 The Working Party's proposal (§§ 74 *et seq.*) was that the actus reus of an attempt should be defined as conduct which is a substantial step towards the commission of the ultimate offence. It should be for the judge to direct the jury as

[72] [1915] 2 K.B. 342: here a jeweller insured his stock for £1,200 against theft, concealed stock on the premises, tied himself up with string and called for help. He told police who broke in that he had been knocked down and his safe robbed. He confessed when the property was found later, but his conviction for attempting to obtain money by false pretences was quashed. Had he prepared a claim form or communicated the facts on which a claim was to be based to the insurance company it seems clear that he would have been convicted; *ibid.* at p. 348. Proceedings on similar facts could today be brought under the Criminal Law Act 1967, s. 5 (2) (false reports wasteful of police employment). The case is criticised by Lord Edmund-Davies in *D.P.P.* v. *Stonehouse* [1978] A.C. 55, 85: see para. 2.41, below.

[73] (1953) Law Journal, vol. 103, p. 97: the defendants trailed a lorry for some 130 miles even giving assistance to it when it broke down, waiting for a chance to steal it and its load: held no attempt, only a continuous act of preparation.

[74] (1970) 55 Cr. App. R. 305: the defendant drove his vehicle into a wood to hide it and enquired of the insurers whether a claim would lie for its loss: held, no attempt to obtain money by deception. See further, as to this and the preceding cases, para. 2.39, below.

a question of law as to whether particular conduct did or did not constitute a substantial step. Conduct constituting preparation for the commission of an offence might, according to circumstances, amount to a substantial step on these proposals. Recognising the degree of imprecision that this working might import, and also being aware that it might be regarded as penalising conduct too far removed from the contemplated offence, the Working Party proposed that legislation should include a list of illustrations which, while not exhaustive, would in law constitute substantial steps.[76] On the other hand they would not give any indication of what was too remote from the offence attempted to be regarded as a substantial step.

§ 2.31 Although there is little authority in English law for the approach favoured by the Working Party, there are several codes which use the concept of the substantial step. Thus the Draft Code for the Australian Territories provides as the sole test of attempt "conduct which is or which [the defendant] believes to be a substantial step towards the commission of the offence." A number of examples similar to but not identical with those proposed by the Working Party are set out as indicating, without being exhaustive, circumstances which are in law sufficient to constitute a substantial step. A somewhat similar formulation is found in the New York Revised Penal Law, Article 110, namely "with intent to commit a crime, [engaging] in conduct which tends to effect the commission of a crime."

§ 2.33 It seems to us that the introduction of the concept of a "substantial step" together with illustrative examples in new legislation could only be justified if there were fundamental defects in the existing law, or if it could be demonstrated that the courts had in a substantial number of cases reached decisions at variance with the social purposes of the law of attempt outlined at the beginning of this section of the Report. At the time when the Working Party was considering the law of attempt, the unsatisfactory way in which the test of proximity appeared to be working accounted for the desire of the Working Party to introduce a fresh concept, but as we indicate below the position has changed to some extent in the intervening period. Considered on its own merits, it seems to us that the definition of what constitutes a "substantial step" is incapable of further description or elucidation. The Working Party tried to surmount this difficulty in two ways. In the first place, it suggested that it should be for the judge to direct the jury as a matter of law whether the particular conduct did or did not constitute a substantial step. We deal in more detail below with the functions of the judge and jury in the law of attempt. It suffices to state here that in our view the question whether the defendant's conduct amounts to an attempt is a question of fact which should be for the jury to decide. Secondly, the Working Party suggested the provision of examples which would be illustrative, but not exhaustive of what constitutes a substantial step. If, as we believe, provision of such examples is necessary because it is inherently impossible to define further what is meant by a "substan-

[76] The illustrations were as follows: (a) committing an assault for the purpose of the intended offence: (b) lying in wait for, searching out or following the contemplated victim or object of the intended offence: (c) enticing or seeking to entice the contemplated victim of the intended offence to go to the place contemplated for its commission: (d) reconnoitring the place contemplated for the commission of the intended offence: (e) unlawful entry upon a structure vehicle or enclosure, or remaining thereon unlawfully for the purpose of committing or preparing to commit the intended offence: (f) acquiring, preparing or equipping oneself with materials to be employed in the commission of the offence, which are specially designed for such unlawful use or which serve no lawful purpose in the circumstances: (g) preparing or acting a falsehood for the purpose of an offence of fraud or deception: (h) soliciting any person, whether innocent or not, to engage in conduct constituting an external element of the offence.

tial step," the test in our view stands self-condemned: either the examples are superfluous because they fall within the natural meaning of "substantial," or they amount to a highly artificial concept of what is "substantial" because the conduct which they illustrate would not ordinarily be regarded as a substantial step towards the commission of an offence. Furthermore, even if the examples were allowed to remain as part of the test, some of those proposed by the Working Party are probably unsatisfactory as they stand and in our view would inevitably be subject to interpretation and accretion through reported cases. At the same time, examples (d) reconnoitring, and (f) acquiring and preparing materials for use in committing an offence, lie far outside the law of attempt as at present understood, and amount only to preparation. The courts have little or no experience of the use of legislative illustrations in the criminal law and it seems to us that there would be a considerable degree of uncertainty as to how they could be used in practice.[86] For example, in situations which both fell outside the presently accepted bounds of attempt and were not analogous to the illustrations, could the judge in his direction nonetheless quote any of them he chose as an aid to the jury? The test provides no clue to the answer. This uncertainty, together with the drawbacks of the examples which we have mentioned, suggests that there would be serious dangers of the development of a body of case-law widening the ambit of the law of attempt to an unacceptable extent. Irrespective of this possibility, we regard the provision of a vague test together with illustrations as an unsatisfactory way of reforming the law.

§ 2.35 In considering examples of the substantial step which would at present be regarded only as preparatory acts, it is also necessary to bear in mind the existing law, particularly in relation to possession offences. There are provisions penalising the possession of an offensive weapon in a public place which have recently been extended to possession of a weapon of offence while trespassing on private property.[88] The Forgery Act 1913, the Theft Act 1968 and the Criminal Damage Act 1971 also contain possession offences. In these areas, at any rate, the law penalises by means of specific offences some of the conduct with which it would otherwise be possible to deal, under the substantial step test, by means of specific examples stretching the meaning of attempt far beyond its accepted usage. Provision of such specific offences seems to us to be the preferable approach; and provision of a general offence based on the "substantial step" concept would entail an unnecessary overlap with those offences.

§ 2.36 The proposition that some of the examples of a substantial step supported by the Working Party extend far beyond the law of attempt as at present understood and amount only to preparation is particularly true of example (d), "reconnoitring the place contemplated for the commission of the intended offence." There is an added danger in adopting an example such as this that the law of attempt would be capable of being used in situations which, if they should be penalised at all, should be the subject of a specific offence. For example, some of the ground covered by (d) is dealt with at present by that part of section 4 of the

[86] Where illustrations are used in legislation upon civil law matters (*e.g.* in the Torts (Interference with Goods) Act 1977, ss. 3 (6), 6 (2) and 7 (4)) their purpose is usually to clarify and exemplify provisions which might otherwise be difficult to understand. This contrasts with the illustrations of what constitutes a substantial step which, as we have noted, seem to be designed to provide substance to an inherently vague concept which cannot be elucidated by other means.

[88] The Prevention of Crime Act 1953, s. 1 (1) penalises anyone who without lawful authority or excuse "has with him in any public place any offensive weapon." The Criminal Law Act 1977, s. 8 based on clause 9 of the draft Bill annexed to (1976) Law Com. No. 76 *Report on Conspiracy and Criminal Law Reform,* penalises anyone on any premises as a trespass, after having entered as such, if, without lawful authority or reasonable excuse, he "has with him on the premises any weapon of offence."

Vagrancy Act 1824 which penalises "every suspected person or reputed thief, frequenting any street or any highway or any place adjacent to a street or highway with intent to commit an arrestable offence." Whatever the criticisms which may be made of the "suspected person" offence, we do not think that it would be legitimate simply to replace it by an artificial extension of the law of attempt. Cosmetic changes of this sort conceal rather than clarify the true state of the law. If there is a need for the law to be extended beyond the accepted bounds of the law of attempt, in our view this is a matter which requires separate consideration in relation to the specific types of conduct which it is sought to penalise. As we have noted this is the approach which has already been adopted in several instances.

§ 2.37 The substantial step approach was put forward because of the advantage it would have in penalising certain conduct held in the past not to amount to an attempt. As we have noted, this would be achieved by very substantially widening the present law and by materially altering the functions of the judge and jury in the law of attempt in a way which we consider unacceptable. Without this alteration we believe the concept would render the law more uncertain than it is at present. With it, it would confine questions of fact and degree in particular cases in the straitjacket of precedent. In our view the disadvantages of the approach discussed in the preceding paragraphs greatly outweigh any advantage to be gained from it, and we do not recommend its adoption.

2. The present law reconsidered

§ 2.38 The cases mentioned in our preceding survey have all been cited as decisions on the issue of the actus reus in the English law of attempt and, as we have seen, they draw upon more than one of the theories referred to above. We think it necessary to examine recent decisions with a view to determining the currently accepted view of the issue. As will be seen this has undergone some change.

§ 2.39 In 1973, when Working Paper No. 50 was published, the law was taken to be settled by a trio of Divisional Court cases [The Law Commission considered *Davey* v. *Lee* [1968] 1 Q.B. 366; *Jones* v. *Brooks* (1968) 52 Cr. App. R. 614; and *Comer* v. *Bloomfield* (1970) 55 Cr. App. R. 305]. It is evident from this outline of the cases that the proximity test was not working well. Its application was confused by the introduction of elements of other incompatible approaches and by the lack of any agreed principle upon which to decide what was sufficiently proximate. This in turn resulted in a random appeal to authorities, including such unsatisfactory cases as *R.* v. *Robinson* where the result reached would, to the man in the street, appear to be contrary to common sense.

§ 2.40 Since 1973 the law has been considered in two cases in the House of Lords, in both of which reference was made to the issue of the actus reus in attempt. In *Haughton* v. *Smith* [1975] A.C. 476 Lord Hailsham, after quoting in full from *R.* v. *Eagleton* and also the various tests set out in *Davey* v. *Lee* said (at p. 492)—

> "The act relied on as constituting the attempt must not be an act merely preparatory to commit the completed offence, but must bear a relationship to the completion of the offence referred to in *R.* v. *Eagleton* . . . as being 'proximate' to the completion of the offence and in *Davey* v. *Lee* . . . as being 'immediately and not merely remotely connected' with the completed offence."

Lord Reid said (at p. 499)—

> "It is well settled that mere preparation is not criminal. . . . It can be said that the accused must have begun to perpetrate the crime. But no words, unless

> so general as to be virtually useless, can be devised which will fit the immense variety of possible cases. Any attempted definition would, I am sure, do more harm than good. It must be left to common sense to determine in each case whether the accused has gone beyond mere preparation."

§ 2.41 In *D.P.P.* v. *Stonehouse* [1978] A.C. 55, one of the questions at issue was whether the defendant's conduct was such as could constitute an attempt. In that case the defendant, having insured his life in England for the benefit of his wife, faked his death and disappeared. If he had not been discovered before his wife was paid by the insurers, "the full offence would have been that he dishonestly and by deception enabled his wife to obtain insurance money by the false pretence that he had drowned," (at p. 87 *per* Lord Edmund-Davies) contrary to section 15 of the Theft Act 1968. In holding that the defendant's acts did suffice for an attempt, four of the speeches referred to the first and the most quoted part of Parke B's dictum in *R.* v. *Eagleton*, three of them with a measure of approval, Lord Diplock adding that "the offender must have crossed the Rubicon and burnt his boats," and Lord Salmon defining an attempt also on the lines of Article 29 of Stephen's Digest. Lord Edmund-Davies, however, criticised both the *Eagleton* dictum and the *Digest* formulation, doubting whether the former had been properly applied in *R.* v. *Robinson*. He thought that the court had been wrong in that case to treat all the preceding acts of the defendant as mere preparation, and that the ruling that there could be no conviction for an attempt to obtain by deception unless the deception had come to the knowledge of the intended victim should not be followed. He also disapproved of the view that a defendant must necessarily be guilty of an attempt if he has done the last act which he expects to do and which it is necessary for him to do to achieve the consequence aimed at, since he may nonetheless have engaged only in preparation. Lord Edmund-Davies considered that Stonehouse's conduct was sufficiently proximate to constitute the attempt because the faking of his death, in relation to the offence charged was intended to produce the result, was the final act which he could perform and went a substantial distance towards the attainment of his goal.

§ 2.42 We draw three conclusions from this brief review of recent cases. In the first place, the "unequivocal act" approach is no longer to be applied even though it only recently made an appearance as an element of the test of what constitutes the actus reus; secondly, the correct test is that of proximity although there is no agreement on how this should be formulated; and thirdly, there must now be some doubt as to whether *R.* v. *Robinson*, and *a fortiori Comer* v. *Bloomfield*, were correctly decided.

§ 2.43 *Stonehouse* does clarify certain other matters which, although not bearing on the immediate issue, have the effect of further developing the law of attempt. In the first place, it seems clear on the facts of the case that an act may be proximate enough to render the person doing it liable for an attempt even if there is a further act to be done to effect the crime, which is to be done by an innocent agent. Secondly, the facts of the case lend support to the view that, provided the defendant acts as principal, the last act which it is in his power to do towards the commission of an offence will always be sufficiently proximate to it to constitute an attempt.

§ 2.44 Finally, the House of Lords also settled the respective roles of judge and jury in trials for attempts. In *R.* v. *Cook* Lord Parker C.J. stated (1963) 48 Cr. App. R. 98, 102, that "while in every case it is for the judge to rule whether there is any evidence capable of constituting an attempt, it is always for the jury to say whether they accept it as amounting to an attempt." This approach was endorsed by a majority of the House of Lords in *D.P.P.* v. *Stonehouse*: "in every case where a jury may be entitled to convict, the application of the law to the facts is a matter for the jury and not for the judge" [1978] A.C. 55, 94, *per* Lord Keith of Kinkel.

3. Recommendations as to the actus reus

§ 2.45 In the light of the case law, the opinions of writers and the various approaches to the actus reus already described, we must make it clear that in our view there is no magic formula which can now be produced to define precisely what constitutes an attempt. . . . Of the various approaches, only the "proximity" test has produced results which may be thought broadly acceptable. Its disadvantages are that hitherto it has not worked well in some cases, and that it is imprecise. It shares the latter disadvantage with all other approaches but its flexibility does enable difficult cases to be reconsidered and their authority questioned. Further, where cases are so dependent on what are sometimes fine differences of degree, we think it is eminently appropriate for the question whether the conduct in a particular case amounts to an attempt to be left to the jury. This suggests that a relatively simple definition based on the "proximity" approach is the best which can be hoped for.

(a) *Content of the actus reus*

§ 2.46 The first element in a statutory test of proximity should be the drawing of the distinction between acts of preparation and acts which are sufficiently proximate to the offence. This is a truism repeated in many cases including the most recent. It is nonetheless useful because it recognises that certain forms of conduct, in almost all circumstances which can be envisaged, do not amount to an attempt. Possession of implements for the purpose of committing an offence is an obvious example which, as we have noted, is at present dealt with by other means. Reconnoitring the place contemplated for the commission of the intended offence is another example of conduct which it is difficult to regard as more than an act of preparation: it would not ordinarily be called an attempt.

§ 2.47 The definition of sufficient proximity must be wide enough to cover two varieties of cases; first, those in which a person has taken all the steps towards the commission of a crime which he believes to be necessary as far as he is concerned for that crime to result,[127] such as firing a gun at another and missing. Normally such cases cause no difficulty. Secondly, however, the definition must cover those instances where a person has to take some further step to complete the crime, assuming that there is evidence of the necessary mental element on his part to commit it; for example, when the defendant has raised the gun to take aim at another but has not yet squeezed the trigger. We have reached the conclusion that, in regard to these cases, it is undesirable to recommend anything more complex than a rationalisation of the present law.

§ 2.48 In choosing the words to be used to describe this rationalisation of the present law, we have had to bear in mind that they will be the subject of consideration and interpretation by the courts. For this reason we have rejected a number of terms which have already been used with some frequency in reported cases, such as acts which are "proximate to," or "closely connected" or "immediately connected" with the offence attempted. The literal meaning of "proximate" is "nearest, next before or after (in place, order, time, connection of thought, causation, etc.)." Thus, were this term part of a statutory description of the *actus reus* of attempt, it would clearly be capable of being interpreted to exclude all but the "final act"; this would not be in accordance with the policy outlined above. The term "immediately connected" is in our view inappropriate for the same reason. And acts which may be "closely connected" in the sense that they have advanced a considerable way towards the completed offence may

[127] This is on the assumption that he is the actual perpetrator; if his part in the commission is a minor one, none of his acts may get beyond the stage of preparation: see *D.P.P.* v. *Stonehouse* [1978] A.C. 55, 86, *per* Lord Edmund-Davies, and § 2.41, above.

nonetheless bear no qualitative resemblance to the acts required for completion. For example, it is arguable that what the appellant in *R.* v. *Robinson* had done had no close qualitative connection with what remained to be done—making a claim on the insurance company—even though in terms of quantity his conduct as a whole had advanced far towards his objective. This potential ambiguity therefore precludes use of that term.

§ 2.49 The foregoing considerations lead us to *recommend* as the most appropriate form of words to define the *actus reus* of attempt *any act which goes so far towards the commission of the offence attempted as to be more than an act of mere preparation.*

(b) *Issues of law and fact*

§ 2.50 The final element of the offence of attempt which requires consideration in the present context is the respective functions of the judge and jury. We have noted that the "substantial step" approach would require the judge to direct the jury as a matter of law as to whether particular conduct, if proved, constitutes a substantial step. (§ 2.30) . . . Since then, the majority in *D.P.P.* v. *Stonehouse* has, as we have noted, approved the decision in *R.* v. *Cook* in which Lord Parker C.J. stated that, "while in every case it is for the judge to rule whether there is any evidence capable of constituting an attempt, it is always for the jury to say whether they accept it as amounting to an attempt. That involves . . . a careful direction in every case on the general principle with regard to what acts constitute attempts": (1963) 48 Cr. App. R. 98, 102. We agree with this view: as factual situations may be infinitely varied and the issue of whether an accused's conduct has passed beyond mere preparation to commit an offence may depend upon all the surrounding circumstances, it is appropriate to leave the final issue to be decided as a question of fact, although "the judge may sum up in such a way as to make it plain that he considers that the accused is guilty and should be convicted." *D.P.P.* v. *Stonehouse* [1978] A.C. 55, 80, *per* Lord Salmon. Furthermore, this division of function between judge and jury is in accord with the principle that it is for the judge to tell the jury what the law is, but for the jury to say whether on the facts the accused has been brought within the provisions of the offence with which he has been charged. If the conduct is such that in law it cannot constitute more than an act of preparation the judge must direct the jury to acquit. . . .

§ 2.51 There has been criticism of the present tendency to leave the application of words in statutes to the jury as a question of fact, on the ground that this opens the way to perverse verdicts of acquittal. We think that this argument ignores the accepted function of the jury when the question is whether the accused's conduct falls within non-technical words used to characterise the elements of an offence. The criticism would have more substance if it could be said that the facts of one case were in all respects identical to another, but "a lawyer may think that the result of applying the law correctly to a certain factual situation is perfectly clear, but nevertheless the evidence may give rise to nuances which he has not observed, but which are apparent to the collective mind of a lay jury."; *ibid* at p. 94, *per* Lord Keith of Kinkel. Although the risk of perverse verdicts cannot altogether be eliminated, "the risk that directions to convict may lead to quashings can be obviated by clarity in identifying the contested issue, by commenting on the evidence (maybe even in strong terms, provided that they fall short of a direction, as Lord Devlin stressed in *Chandler* v. *Director of Public Prosecutions* [1964] A.C. 763, 806) and by then trusting the jury to play their constitutional part in the criminal process"; [1978] A.C. 55, 88, *per* Lord Edmund-Davies. Thus the risk is one which is more apparent than real.

§ 2.52 The difficulties which have occurred in the past in defining the respective functions of judge and jury in relation to the *actus reus* of attempt lead us to the view that, although the issue may be regarded as settled at common law by a majority decision of the House of Lords, legislation which creates a new statutory offence of attempt ought to deal with it in specific terms. Accordingly *we recommend* a provision to the effect that the question whether an act done by the defendant is capable of being an attempt should be a question of law; the question whether that act (accompanied by the required mental element) amounts in all the circumstances to an attempt should be a question of fact.

Glanville Williams, "The Government's Proposals on Criminal Attempts" (1981) 131 New L.J. 70

"The Bill, following the Law Commission, proposes to abandon talk of the proximity of attempts. In future we are to speak only of acts that are merely preparatory and those that are attempts. It is inconvenient to be deprived in this way of a single adjective to describe the quality of an act that makes it an attempt because it is more than merely preparatory, and no one knows whether censoring out the language of proximity is going to make any practical difference. In the eyes of the common law any act going beyond mere preparation is a proximate act of attempt, just as a proximate act of attempt is an act going beyond mere preparation; but the language of proximity is now to be taboo. The idea apparently is that by refraining from talk of proximity you will increase the number of acts that are regarded as attempts and decrease the number that are regarded as mere preparation, even though there is to be no legislation to say this."

Dennis, "The Elements of Attempt" [1980] Crim. L.R. 758, 768

"These proposals give rise to a number of misgivings.

1. *Imprecision*. Even given the premise that precise definition is impossible, the Law Commission's test is more open-textured than any of the common law tests which it replaces. The form of words chosen does very little more than indicate that some acts do constitute attempts ('more than preparatory') and some acts do not ('preparatory'). The descriptive words '[an act] which goes so far towards the commission of the offence' do not constitute a qualitative distinction between these two categories: they merely indicate that a scale of conduct is in contemplation, and that at some point along it a line is drawn to fix the threshold of liability.

What the Law Commission have done then is to take a principle—that in order to preserve a balance between the interests of the individual and those of society not all acts towards the commission of an offence should be punishable—and erect it into a rule to be applied by the tribunal to resolve individual cases, but without giving it any further content. How is this principle/rule to be applied?

One radical answer would have been to take the current fashion to extremes, and to turn the whole issue over to the jury, asking them to construe the word 'preparatory' as an ordinary word of the English language. All they would then need to do would be to decide whether the defendant's acts went beyond their understanding of that term. It appears, however, that the Law Commission do not wish to go as far as this. The judge is to retain control in the first instance of the limits of preparation. 'If the conduct is such that *in law it cannot constitute more than an act of preparation* the judge must direct the jury to acquit.' (Emphasis supplied). To this extent then the application of the test is a matter of law, but no guidance is given in the draft Bill on how this question of law should be determined. We may assume that a judge will decide, for example, that evidence of 'reconnoitring the place intended for the commission of the offence' is evidence of an act of preparation only, but on what basis is he to reach this conclusion? Certainly he will be in some difficulty if he turns to the pre-existing common law because the

Law Commission have cogently criticised all the common law theories and endeavoured to replace them with the codified offence.

2. *Role of the Jury*. Pursuing this theme, how are the jury to apply the test if the evidence passes the judge? (We may assume that [section 4 (3)] does have the effect of requiring the issue of whether D's conduct fell within [section 1 (1)] to be left to the jury, although it does not actually say so). They are still being given a very large issue to decide, and it is submitted that the 'question of fact' represents a considerable extension of that term. It normally refers to the finding of primary facts (did D practise a deception?), evaluation of primary facts against a fixed standard (was the force used by D reasonable?), and, more controversially, the determination of statutory words where they are used as ordinary words of the English language (was D dishonest?). In this case the jury are *not* being asked to decide the meaning of the word attempt, or any other word, as a matter of ordinary language. Rather they are being asked expressly to determine whether D's act fell within a subsection of a criminal statute. Putting the matter in these terms connotes a question of interpretation and classification, and it is submitted that it is simply leaving too much to the jury to ask them to perform the task with such an imprecise criterion.

The practical risks involved are those of perverse verdicts and inconsistent verdicts. Perverse verdicts of acquittal may occur where the law is, or should be, clear that a sufficient act of attempt has taken place, as where D has committed the last act he intended to commit. The Law Commission anticipate this objection and argue that the risk can be obviated by clarity in identifying the contested issue and by commenting on the evidence, if necessary in strong terms. Fair enough, but there is still no guidance on how the contested issue could be clarified in a direction, and what benefit is gained by leaving the question open if the answer is clear?

Inconsistent verdicts are a much more serious danger. The Law Commission commented at the beginning of this section of the Report that 'in the absence of any definition of the conduct required for an attempt, there would be little assistance which a judge could give in directing the jury, and this could lead to unacceptable discrepancies and very marked inconsistencies in jury verdicts in similar cases.' (§ 2.19) It has been argued that the test in [section] 1 (1) does not take the definition of attempt very much further. In the absence of any statutory guidance on how the test is to be interpreted, there is a real risk that different juries may adopt different criteria to deal with essentially similar material facts. Suppose that the facts of *Robinson* and of *Comer* v. *Bloomfield* recur. The judge leaves the issue to the jury in both cases, realising that the Law Commission wished the boundaries of "preparation" to be altered so that the conduct in these cases was at least capable of amounting to an attempt. Jury A convict on the facts of *Robinson*, arguing that this was an elaborate deception showing firmness of purpose, and that it was not necessary that the deception should have come to the notice of the intended victim of the fraud. Jury B acquit on the facts of *Comer* v. *Bloomfield* arguing that the accused had not actually made a claim for the loss of his vehicle and that his enquiry about it was not an act showing clear unlawful purpose. If this example is not far fetched, the result brings the law into disrepute, since the accused in case B had clearly gone further than the accused in case A."

Questions

1. It is permissible to cite to a jury decisions by earlier juries in other cases with facts similar to those in the instant case?

2. Two separate cases of alleged attempts came before the Bogtown Magistrates. In A's case, the magistrates dismissed the charge because in

their view the act disclosed by the evidence could not in law constitute more than an act of preparation. In B's case, the magistrates dismissed the charge because in their view, although the act disclosed by the evidence *could* amount to more than an act of preparation, in fact it did not do so. From the point of view of the prosecutors, who wish to appeal, what is the difference between these two cases?

3. C was charged with attempted theft. The evidence disclosed that C reconnoitred a place where valuable goods were with the intention of coming back later when the goods were unguarded and stealing them. The judge left the question of whether C's acts were more than merely preparatory to the jury, and they convicted. On appeal against conviction, what authorities or arguments can C use to persuade the Court of Appeal that the conviction was wrong?

Note

Section 4 of the Vagrancy Act 1824, referred to in § 2.26 above, is now repealed in so far as it relates to suspected persons or reputed thieves loitering with intent to commit an arrestable offence: section 8. In its place, section 9 enacts a more narrowly drawn preparatory offence.

Criminal Attempts Act 1981, section 9

(1) A person is guilty of the offence of vehicle interference if he interferes with a motor vehicle or trailer or with anything carried in or on a motor vehicle or trailer with the intention that an offence specified in subsection (2) below shall be committed by himself or some other person.

2. The offences mentioned in subsection (1) above are—

(a) theft of the motor vehicle or trailer or part of it;

(b) theft of anything carried in or on the motor vehicle or trailer; and

(c) an offence under section 12 (1) of the Theft Act 1968 (taking and driving away without consent);

and, if it is shown that a person accused of an offence under this section intended that one of those offences should be committed, it is immaterial that it cannot be shown which it was.

(3) A person guilty of an offence under this section shall be liable on summary conviction to imprisonment for a term not exceeding three months or to a fine not exceeding £500 or to both.

(4) A constable may arrest without warrant anyone who is or whom he with reasonable cause suspects to be guilty of an offence under this section.

(5) In this section "motor vehicle" and "trailer" have the meanings assigned to them by section 190 (1) of the Road Traffic Act 1972.

ii. Attempting the Impossible

Note

The common law gave extremely confused and contradictory answers to the question of whether a person can be convicted of attempt where he intends to commit an offence known to the law believing that circumstances are such that the offence will be committed but where, unknown to him, they are in fact such that the means adopted or proposed are inadequate or the object is unattainable. Examples are, where A, intending to handle stolen goods, handles goods which in fact are not stolen; where B, intending to steal an umbrella, takes an umbrella which in fact belongs to himself; or where C, intending to steal the contents of a pocket, puts his hand into the pocket which turns out to be empty. Much of the confusion and uncertainty was due to the House of Lords decision in *Haughton* v. *Smith* [1975] A.C. 476; and the Law Commission recognised that any attempt to unravel the tangle into which the law had got itself must start with a discussion of that decision.

Law Com. No. 102

[Footnotes to this extract are numbered as in original document.]

1. The present law

(a) *Haughton* v. *Smith*

§ 2.54 In *Haughton* v. *Smith* police officers stopped an overloaded van and, finding that it contained stolen goods, took the driver to the police station. The taking of the goods into police possession meant that they reverted to lawful custody and so ceased to be stolen goods, but the police officers decided to permit the van and goods to continue to a service area on a motorway, accompanied and followed by police officers. There the defendant took a leading part in arranging for future disposal of the goods. He was convicted of attempting to handle stolen goods. . . . For the reasons given in § 2.55, below, the Court of Appeal quashed the defendant's conviction but certified as a point of law for decision by the House of Lords the following: "If stolen goods are returned to lawful custody and thus cease to be stolen by virtue of section 24 of the Theft Act 1968, can a person who subsequently dishonestly handles goods believing them to be stolen be guilty of the offence of attempting to handle stolen goods?" The Crown's appeal to the House of Lords was unanimously dismissed for the reasons discussed in §§ 2.56–2.61, below.

§ 2.55 The Court of Appeal had distinguished between two categories of cases—

> "The first class is the type of case where the accused has embarked on a course of conduct which, if completed, will result in an offence but for some reason breaks off that course of conduct and never completes the action required to amount to the offence. . . . The second class . . . is where the accused has meticulously and in detail followed every step of his intended course believing throughout that he was committing a criminal offence and when in the end it is found that he has not committed a criminal offence because in law that which he planned and carried out does not amount to a criminal offence at all." [1975] A.C. 476, 481, *per* Lord Widgery C.J. (C.A.).

In the first class, where the accused's conduct if completed would have amounted to a crime, the Court of Appeal placed by way of example the picking of an empty pocket; the efforts of a would-be burglar, disturbed by the police, who has been trying to break open a window; and those of a would-be safebreaker who finds the safe too difficult to open. In such cases the court considered that a charge of attempt could properly be laid. But in the second class, where the accused's intended course of conduct was completed and did not amount to a substantive crime, it considered that no charge of attempt would lie. The court took the view that the case before them belonged to the second class. In reaching this conclusion the court found of a particular value a dictum of Birkett J. giving the judgment of the Court of Criminal Appeal in *R.* v. *Percy Dalton (London) Ltd.*[153]:

> "Steps on the way to the commission of what would be a crime, if the acts were completed, may amount to attempts to commit that crime, to which, unless interrupted, they would have led; but steps on the way to the doing of something, which is thereafter done and which is no crime, cannot be regarded as attempts to commit a crime."

§ 2.56 The House of Lords, while reaching the same conclusion on the facts of the case as the Court of Appeal, enunciated principles governing the question of impossibility in attempts which have wider implications. . . .

§ 2.58 Before the decision of the House of Lords in *Haughton* v. *Smith* it was widely thought that if a person has as his objective the commission of a crime which in the circumstances is physically incapable of being committed, he may nevertheless be liable for an attempt to commit that crime. Thus in *R.* v. *Ring, Atkins and Jackson* (1892) 61 L.J.M.C. 116, it had been held, contrary to earlier decisions, that a man could be guilty of an attempt to steal from a pocket which was in fact empty. Lord Hailsham, however, with whose speech Lords Morris and Salmon were in agreement, while saying that he was expressing "no concluded opinion," regarded the reasoning in the decisions before *Ring* as sound, which led him to the conclusion, referred to above, that "in general" there could be no attempt to do what in fact was impossible of achievement. He went on to discuss whether a charge of attempted murder would lie where a man stabs a corpse or a bolster in a bed, believing it is occupied by his living enemy, or if a man fires into an empty room thinking his intended victim is present in it. He concluded, again with the qualification "in general" that no charge of attempt would lie in such cases. He accepted that where a man used inadequate means to achieve his objective he would be guilty of an attempt and appears to have left open the question where inadequacy of means (to use his example, a non-fatal dose of cyanide)[164] becomes impossibility of achieving an objective (as when water is administered in mistake for cyanide).

§ 2.59 Lord Reid in *Haughton* v. *Smith* was more emphatic than Lord Hailsham in rejecting the possibility of bringing a charge of attempt where the crime attempted could not be committed. If a crime is impossible in the circumstances, then in his view no acts could be proximate to it and hence there would be no attempt. To hold otherwise would be to punish people for their guilty intentions. Discussing one of the hypothetical cases raised by Lord Hailsham he went so far as to say that the law "cannot be so asinine" as to make a man liable for attempted murder if he stabs a corpse thinking it is a living person. Nevertheless Lord Reid conceded that there will be "borderline cases" where inadequate means to achieve an objective are used or where a person shoots at a place recently occupied by his intended victim.

§ 2.60 Viscount Dilhorne also gave a very wide scope to impossibility in ruling out a charge of attempt. There could be no charge of attempt if the crime could not be committed either as a result of physical impossibility or by reason of legal impossibility. In either case the defendant would not be convicted of an attempt

[153] (1949) 33 Cr. App. R. 102, 110. The facts of the case were that the defendants sold a certain weight of pears at a price below the permitted maximum. But they thought the weight was less than it in fact was and that they were selling at a price above that maximum. The court held that in these circumstances it was not possible to charge the defendants with attempting to sell at a price in excess of the permitted maximum.

[164] In *R.* v. *White* [1910] 2 K.B. 124, a man who administered such a dose was held guilty of attempted murder.

if, had he succeeded in doing all that he attempted to do, he would not have been liable for the full offence. "Conduct which is not criminal is not converted into criminal conduct by the accused believing that a state of affairs exists which does not exist." Applying these principles, Viscount Dilhorne took the view that a person could not be liable for attempting to handle stolen goods which were not in fact stolen (the issue in the instant case), for attempting to steal when taking his own umbrella thinking it belongs to someone else, or (in so far as he declined to treat *R.* v. *Ring* as authoritative) for attempting to steal from a pocket which was in fact empty.

(b) *Subsequent cases*

§ 2.61 The law regarding impossibility in attempts appeared therefore to be left by the decision in *Haughton* v. *Smith* as follows: (1) no charge of attempt to handle stolen goods will lie where the goods in question are not in fact stolen; (2) subject to some possible qualifications of indefinite extent, no charge of attempt will lie where what is attempted is in fact impossible of achievement. Subsequent cases at first tended to emphasise the wide impact of *Haughton* v. *Smith* rather than to limit its significance. In *Partington* v. *Williams* (1975) 62 Cr. App. R. 220, the defendant took a wallet from a drawer in the office of her employers and looked in it with the intention of stealing any money it might contain. In fact it contained none. She was convicted of attempting to steal, but the conviction was quashed on appeal. The commission of the substantive offence was in the circumstances impossible. The Divisional Court considered that the wide principles enunciated by the House of Lords in *Haughton* v. *Smith* were not *obiter,* and in particular that the earlier cases on all fours with the instant case were to be regarded as overruled. In this respect, however, the House of Lords in *D.P.P.* v. *Nock* [1978] A.C. 979, took the view that, for reasons which we set out below, the Divisional Court had misinterpreted *Haughton* v. *Smith.*

§ 2.64 Another consequence of *Haughton* v. *Smith* is the very fine distinctions which the courts now have to draw, sometimes in relation to matters of fact and sometimes in relation to the offences charged. In *R.* v. *Farrance* (1977) 67 Cr. App. R. 136, the defendant had been convicted of attempting to drive when he had a blood alcohol concentration above the prescribed limit contrary to section 6 (1) of the Road Traffic Act 1972. The facts were that the clutch of his car had burnt out, so that although the defendant could operate the engine he could not drive the car. The Court of Appeal upheld the conviction on the grounds that a burnt out clutch was only an impediment to the commission of a crime, similar to the inadequate burglar's tool or the would-be poisoner's insufficient dose. It is not clear what the court's answer would have been if the car had had no petrol or if its transmission had completely seized up. The second category is illustrated by the contrast between *Mieras* v. *Rees* [1975] Crim. L.R. 224, and *Haggard* v. *Mason* [1976] 1 W.L.R. 187. In the first of these cases, the defendant was held on appeal to the Divisional Court not guilty of *attempting to supply* a certain controlled drug contrary to the Misuse of Drugs Act 1971 when he had supplied a different substance in the belief that it was that controlled drug. In the second case, the Divisional Court held that the defendant was rightly convicted of *offering to supply* a certain controlled drug, when he had offered to supply a different substance in the belief that it was that controlled drug. The facts of the two cases are indistinguishable: in both cases the defendant sold a substance which both he and his purchaser believed to be a particular controlled drug and in neither case was the drug either that particular drug or any controlled drug. The distinction therefore lay solely in the different nature of the offences charged. . . .

§ 2.65 In *D.P.P.* v. *Nock* the House of Lords held, . . . that the principles underlying *Haughton* v. *Smith* were as applicable to the inchoate crime of conspiracy as they were to the inchoate crime of attempt. However the House of

Lords in *D.P.P.* v. *Nock* (where the appellants agreed to obtain cocaine, a controlled drug the production of which was an offence by separating it out from a powder which in fact contained no cocaine) explained the principles underlying *Haughton* v. *Smith* in a more restrictive way than had hitherto generally been thought possible. The appellants were held not guilty of conspiracy only because the agreement was to pursue a *specific course of conduct* which when carried out could not produce cocaine and so could not constitute a crime; they would have been guilty if they had simply agreed to go into business as cocaine producers even if in pursuance of that agreement they attempted to produce cocaine from a substance which could not yield it. This reasoning was also applicable to attempts. According to Lord Scarman in *Nock*, the House of Lords did not commit themselves in *Haughton* v. *Smith* to the "sweeping ... proposition ... that he who, with intent to steal, picks a pocket but finds nothing to steal, must be acquitted of attempted theft." The true position, according to Lord Diplock, was that in that case they did not say that the actual decision in *R.* v. *Ring* was wrong, only that Lord Coleridge C.J. was in error in repudiating the authority of *R.* v. *McPherson* (1857) Dears. & B. 197 and *R.* v. *Collins* (1864) 9 Cox C.C. 497. The first of these two cases was concerned with an attempt to steal goods specified in the indictment which had in fact been removed before the defendant broke into the house. In the second, "the offence charged was restricted to an attempt to steal from the person of a woman unknown property located in the very pocket in which one of the accused had put his hand," when there was no affirmative proof that there was anything in the pocket. On the other hand in *R.* v. *Ring* the charge was of attempting to steal from the person of a person unknown, which was "an attempt to steal from the person generally.' Lord Diplock concluded that "under an indictment drafted in suitably broad terms I see no reason why even the solitary pickpocket should not be convicted of attempted theft without the prosecution needing to prove that the particular pockets or handbags in which he was seen to put his hand in fact contained something which he would have stolen if he could."

Impossibility in other systems of law

[After considering the state of the law in various other systems] § 2.84 It is evident from this survey of the ways in which attempting the impossible is treated in foreign systems of law that the vast majority differ from the approach now adopted in England and Wales following the decision in *Haughton* v. *Smith*. Of those which we have examined, only New Zealand and, with apparent reluctance, South Australia clearly limit the situations in which it is an offence to attempt to commit a crime which in the circumstances it is impossible to commit. In all other instances, both in common law and civil law systems, factual impossibility is apparently no bar to a charge of attempt. Against this background, we now examine the policy and practical implications of the law of England and Wales.

3. Consideration of the present law

§ 2.85 In paragraphs 2.61–2.64 we referred to the fine distinctions and practical difficulties which have arisen following the decision of the House of Lords in *Haughton* v. *Smith*. In *D.P.P.* v. *Nock*, however, the House of Lords suggested, as summarised in § 2.65, that the effect of the earlier decision was less wide than had generally been thought. The suggestion was that if an attempt to commit a crime were charged in "sufficiently broad terms" the actual impossibility of completing the crime aimed at in the particular manner adopted would not preclude a conviction for an attempt to commit that crime. As Lord Diplock said [1978] A.C. 979, 993:

"The crime which the pickpocket sets out to commit is not confined to stealing from a particular person or *a fortiori* from a particular pocket in a particular person's clothes or from a particular article carried by a particular person. When he converts intention into attempt by the proximate act of extending his hand to a particular pocket or article, failure at this point to effect his intention of stealing, because where he first puts his hand there is nothing to steal, does not mean that the course of conduct that he intended to pursue would have ended with this initial failure and would not have continued until he had found something to steal in some similar place and stolen it."

The underlying policy consideration would appear to be that person who has a general intent to commit a crime is a social danger and should be liable for attempt to commit it even if the particular attempt in the course of which he has been caught was in fact impossible, whereas there is not social danger in a man setting out to commit only one crime in a particular context if the commission of the crime in that context is in fact impossible. . . .

§ 2.86 We have pointed out that in *Nock* the House of Lords supported the early decisions in *R.* v. *Ring* and *R.* v. *Collins,* in the sense that it considered that both could be regarded as rightly decided on the form of the indictments in those cases. But the rationale for the case of *Ring* suggested by the House of Lords does entail the substitution of a general intention to commit crimes of a particular class for a specific intention to commit one crime in particular circumstances. This surely undermines the doctrine that proximate acts are a necessary element in liability for attempt; for clearly the basis of the law of attempt is not mere guilty intention but guilty intention together with proximate acts, and the substitution of a general intention to commit crimes inevitably links the appropriate *mens rea* less directly to the acts relied on as the *actus reus* of the attempt. The extracts which we have quoted above from Lord Diplock's speech seem to suggest that the act of putting the hand into a particular person's empty pocket is evidence of the "proximity" of that act, not to the attempt to steal from that person, but to the stealing thereafter from the pocket of some other person in which the intending thief might actually succeed in finding money or something worth stealing. This explanation is in our view difficult to reconcile with the concept of proximity as explained by the House of Lords in other recent cases [*Haughton* v. *Smith,* and *D.P.P.* v. *Stonehouse, supra,* §§ 2.54, 2.41]

§ 2.87 . . . We conclude that if there is any basis for the criticisms made of the decision of the House of Lords in *Haughton* v. *Smith,* they do not appear to be satisfactorily met by the explanation of that decision later made by the House of Lords in *D.P.P.* v. *Nock.* The basic question we have to consider is therefore whether the law as laid down in *Haughton* v. *Smith* is satisfactory.

§ 2.88 We think it would have been helpful if in *Haughton* v. *Smith* a clearer distinction had been made between a case in which factual impossibility as a defence to a charge of attempt is in issue and a case where as an inevitable logical deduction from "the principle of legality"[1] no question of a criminal attempt can arise. The latter type of case arises where a person solely by reason of an error as to the general criminal law believes that certain conduct constitutes a criminal offence. For example, the defendant is under the mistaken impression that it is a criminal offence to have sexual intercourse with a girl over 16 but under 18; neither such intercourse nor *a fortiori* attempting it is a criminal attempt. There has been general agreement among commentators on Working Paper No. 50 as well

[1] See Jerome Hall, *General Principles of Criminal Liability,* 1960, p. 586: "unless the intended end is a legally proscribed harm, causing it is not criminal, hence any conduct falling short of that is not a criminal attempt."

as by courts and legal writers in this country and overseas that any charge of criminal attempt is inappropriate in such a case.

§ 2.89 Some courts have however stated the "principle of legality" mentioned in the preceding paragraph in language which, although capable of covering that principle and for that reason attracting ready agreement, is in fact used for a somewhat different purpose. A much cited dictum in this connection is that of Birkett J. in *R.* v. *Percy Dalton*. . . . "Steps on the way to the doing of something, which is thereafter done, and which is no crime, cannot be regarded as attempts to commit a crime" clearly disposes of any charge of attempt in respect of a man who has sexual intercourse with a girl of 16 believing that it is an offence to have intercourse with a girl of that age. But if the "doing of something" refers solely to the physical action of the accused and does not include the results at which that action is aimed, then there will be a very much wider range of cases where no charge of attempt will be possible. Thus in *Haughton* v. *Smith* the intention to handle *stolen* property was disregarded; what was taken as excluding a charge of attempt was that the intended physical acts of the defendant in relation to the property did not amount to a criminal offence, not because he was mistaken as to the law about handling stolen property but because he had been ignorant of the history of the goods in question. Similarly, in *D.P.P.* v. *Nock* where the issue related to conspiracy rather than attempt, the emphasis was put, not on the ultimate object which was to make cocaine (clearly an illegal act), but on the specifically limited agreement to work on a particular substance (which since it contained no cocaine was not illegal) even though the intended but actually unattainable objective was to obtain cocaine.

§ 2.90 It seems that the interpretation put by the House of Lords on Birkett J.'s dictum in *R.* v. *Percy Dalton*, which greatly narrows the field in which a charge of attempt may be brought, was ultimately influenced by a consideration of policy which is emphatically stated by Lord Reid in *Haughton* v. *Smith*:

> "The theory is really an attempt to punish people for their guilty intentions. The man who stabs the corpse may be as deserving of punishment as a man who attempts to murder a living person. The accused in the present case may be as deserving of punishment as he would have been if the goods had still been stolen goods. But such a radical change in the principles of our law should not be introduced in this way even if it were desirable."

We do not however think that to disregard impossibility in relation to attempts would necessarily be so revolutionary a departure from the basic principles of English law as Lord Reid suggested. It would not mean that a man would be liable for an attempt by reason of his intent alone. An attempt would still require a proximate act as well as an intent although the proximity of the act would have to be judged in the light of the facts as the defendant believed them to be. Thus suppose A intends to kill B by means of what he believes to be a bottle of poison. In any possible charge of attempted murder A's guilty intention would certainly loom large but it would by no means be the only ingredient. There would also have to be evidence of an *actus reus* sufficient to amount to an attempt, of which an extreme example would be his act of administering the contents of the bottle; that act would be judged in the light of what he believe it to contain.

§ 2.91 It is true that the decision of principle of the House of Lords in *Haughton* v. *Smith* was subject to the important qualification that an attempt which fails by reason of the insufficiency of the means adopted may be criminal; but it seems to us that the qualification is not only of indeterminate extent but also difficult to rationalise from the point of view of policy. A number of examples may be given which indicate its drawbacks. Lord Hailsham of St. Marylebone L.C. himself recognised that it may be difficult to distinguish between impossibility of means and impossibility of the objective sought, giving as one example a case where from one point of view it might be said that only the means were insufficient, because a gun has too short a range to reach the intended victim, or from another point of view that the objective could not be achieved because the victim was too far off. Lord Hailsham was confident that in this particular case an attempt would clearly be criminal, but Lord Reid seemed to think that the effect of impossibility on a charge of attempt, as far as the position of the intended victim was concerned, would be a matter of degree; on that basis it would follow that one could not attempt to kill another who was a mile off with a revolver, however much one intended the crime and however complete one's belief in the range of one's weapon. Again, Lord Hailsham gave Turner J.'s example of a man "who walks into a room intending to steal, say a specific diamond ring, and finds the ring is no longer there but has been removed by the owner to the bank." He was of the opinion that in such a case no charge of attempted theft would lie. Yet it is only necessary slightly to elaborate the facts to see what arbitrary lines of policy are thus determined. If the owner of the ring, suspecting an attempt to steal it, changes the lock on the door, the would-be thief who tries out his now useless key on the lock has only used inadequate means and can be guilty of an attempt to steal; but if the owner has removed the ring to the bank the would-be thief is not guilty. The facts of *D.P.P.* v. *Nock* suggest similar inconsistencies: it is clear that the defendants were not convicted of attempting to produce cocaine because the powder they were attempting to separate contained no cocaine. Yet if the powder had in fact partly consisted of cocaine and their failure was due to an optimistic use of an inadequate and inappropriate reagent, it seems that they would have been guilty of an attempt. Finally, one may contrast the case of the intending murderer who doses his victim with too weak a solution of poison with that of another who administers an entirely innocent liquid. Both believe that what they are giving is lethal. The only possible explanation which can be given for holding the former guilty of attempted murder and the latter not guilty is that the actions of the former were in some sense more dangerous than those of the latter. The explanation itself poses the question of how weak the mixture has to be before it becomes innocent.

§ 2.92 Results as capricious as these do not seem acceptable in the criminal law, yet it is common ground among the proponents of the principle in *Haughton* v. *Smith* that it is subject to the qualification that liability for attempt should attach where the only reason for failure to commit the full crime is the adequacy of the means employed. This qualification seems to us so uncertain in its application as to throw doubt on the principle itself. . . .

§ 2.95 The problem we are considering is not easy of solution, not least because both the proponents and opponents of the principle in *Haughton* v. *Smith* regard commonsense as their ally. There are borderline cases whichever approach is adopted. Lord Reid regarded the answers to the questions he posed in *Haughton* v. *Smith* in relation to the man who stabbed a corpse and the man who married a women whose husband he believed to be alive as too clear for argument. We respectfully disagree. We agree with Lord Reid that the man who picks an empty pocket cannot be convicted of theft. We further agree that "the ordinary man would say without stopping to think—of course he was attempting to steal"; but, in so far as Lord Reid implied that after stopping to think the ordinary man would reach a different conclusion, we again respectfully disagree. We think that he would still take the view that this was attempted theft and we consider that the law should reflect this belief.

§ 2.96 We think it would be generally accepted that if a man possesses the appropriate mens rea and commits acts which are sufficiently proximate to the actus reus of a criminal offence, he is guilty of attempting to commit that offence. Where, with that intention, he commits acts which, if the facts were as he believed them to be, would have amounted to the actus reus of the full crime or would have been sufficiently proximate to amount to an attempt, we cannot see why this failure to appreciate the true facts should, in principle relieve him of liability for the attempt. We stress that this solution to the problem does not punish people simply for their intentions. The necessity for proof of proximate acts remains. The fact that the impossibility of committing the full crime reduces the social danger is adequately reflected in the generally milder penalty which an attempt attracts instead of that for the full offence. And even if it is conceded that there may be some reduction in the social danger in cases of impossibility, it has to be borne in mind that a certain social danger undoubtedly remains. Defendants in cases such as *Haughton* v. *Smith* and *Nock* are prepared to do all they can to break the criminal law even though in the circumstances their attempts are doomed to failure; and if they go unpunished, they may be encouraged to do better at the next opportunity. Finally, if the solution under consideration is accepted, it makes it possible to dispense with the doctrine of "inadequate means" and with strained efforts to catch those who might otherwise escape by resort to broadly drawn indictments and an "inferred general intention."

§ 2.97 If it is right in principle that an attempt should be chargeable even though the crime which it is sought to commit could not possibly be committed, we do not think that we should be deterred by the consideration that such a change in our law would also cover some extreme and exceptional cases in which a prosecution would be theoretically possible. An example would be where a person is offered goods at such a low price that he believes that they are stolen, when in fact they are not; if he actually purchases them, upon the principles which we have discussed he would be liable for an attempt to handle stolen goods. Another case which has been much debated is that raised in argument by Bramwell B. in *R.* v. *Collins*. If A takes his own umbrella, mistaking it for one belonging to B and intending to steal B's umbrella, is he guilty of attempted theft? Again, on the principles which we have discussed he would in theory be guilty, but in neither case would it be realistic to suppose that a complaint would be made or that a prosecution would ensue. On the other hand, if our recommendations were formulated so as to exclude such cases, then it might well be impossible to obtain convictions in cases such as *Haughton* v. *Smith*, where a defendant handles goods which were originally stolen, intending to handle stolen goods, but where, unknown to him, the goods had meanwhile been restored to lawful custody. . . .

§ 2.98 A possible difficulty of another kind which we have considered is the distinction which it will be necessary to draw between impossibility arising from misapprehension as to the facts and impossibility arising from a misapprehension of the law in situations which at first sight appear to be similar. As we have seen, if the defendant believes, because of a mistake of law, that certain conduct constitutes an offence when it is not, he should not be liable for attempt if he acts in accordance with his intent. For example, the defendant intends to smuggle certain goods through the customs in the belief that they are dutiable; under the relevant law those goods are in fact not dutiable. He has made no mistake as to the nature of the goods: his error is solely one of law, and if he imports them he should not be liable for an attempt improperly to import goods without paying duty, since he had no intent to commit an offence known to the law. The position is different if the defendant is asked while abroad to smuggle into the country goods which he is assured by the person making the request are goods which are actually dutiable, but which are not in fact dutiable because they are not what he believes them to be. Here the defendant's error arises solely from his misapprehension as to the nature of the goods; it is a pure error of fact. He has every intention of committing an offence on the facts as he believes them to be, and if he succeeds in importing the goods or in getting sufficiently close to his objective, he must be liable for attempt upon the principles which we have been considering.

Fine as the distinction appears to be in these cases, it is one which is in our view vital to make. Provided that any legislation giving effect to the principle of factual impossibility makes the distinction sufficiently clear, we think that careful consideration of the facts of each case will eliminate potential difficulties.

4. Conclusions and recommendations

§ 2.99 Our conclusion is that the fact that it is impossible to commit the crime aimed at should not preclude a conviction for attempt. The experience of other countries and consideration of the conditions in this country do not suggest to us that such a principle will cause serious difficulty, whereas we are strongly of the view that a contrary principle, with its necessarily somewhat indeterminate exceptions and limitations, can and does cause difficulty, uncertainty and anomalies in the administration of the criminal law. Furthermore, we believe the law as it stands at present is out of line with what the majority of people would, if questioned, understand the law to be.

§ 2.100 The policy which we *recommend* may be summed up as follows—

(1) the fact that an offence which is intended cannot in fact be committed should not preclude a conviction for attempt to commit that offence if the defendant

(a) intends to commit the offence; and

(b) takes action which, but for the existence of facts or circumstances making commission of the offence impossible, would either constitute the intended offence or an attempt to commit it;

but (2) pursuing a course of action which does not constitute an offence should not become an attempt to commit an offence because, by reason only of an error as the general law, the defendant believes that that course of action does constitute an offence; and action which falls short of that full course of action should not constitute an attempt to commit an offence because, by reason only of an error as to the general law, the defendant believes that the course of conduct if completed would constitute an offence.

Appendix A: Draft Criminal Attempts Bill, Clause 1

(1) If, with intent to commit a relevant offence, a person does an act—

(a) which goes so far towards the commission of that offence as to be more than a merely preparatory act, or

(b) which would fall within paragraph (a) above but for the existence of any facts or circumstances which render the commission of that offence impossible.

he is guilty of attempting to commit that offence.

(2) For the purpose of subsection (1) above, an intent to commit a relevant offence includes an intention to do something which, if the facts or circumstances of the particular case were as the accused believes them to be, would amount to an intent to commit a relevant offence.

(3) In subsection (1) above, "relevant offence" means an offence (including a summary offence) which, if it were completed, would be triable in England and Wales other than—

(a) conspiracy (whether it is an offence at common law, or under section 1 of the Criminal Law Act 1977 or any other enactment);

(b) aiding, abetting, counselling, procuring or suborning the commission of an offence;

(c) offences under section 4 (1) (assisting offenders) or section 5 (1) (concealing arrestable offences) of the Criminal Law Act 1967.

Note

Section 1 of Criminal Attempts Act 1981 (see, ante, p. 303) enacts the provision of this Clause in a somewhat different form.

Questions

1. Statute makes it an offence for a male aged 14 years or over to have sexual intercourse with a girl under the age of 16 years. Which of the following cases can amount to criminal attempts?
   (a) A, aged 21, believing B to be 15, has sexual intercourse with her. In fact, B is 16.
   (b) A, believing *he* is 16, has intercourse with B whom he knows is 15. In fact A is 13.
   (c) A, aged 21, tries to have intercourse with B, whom he knows is 15. A does not know that the law forbids the intercourse he is attempting.

2. Statute makes it an offence to sell certain goods at above a certain price per lb.
   (a) A tried to sell goods to B at a price which A knew to be unlawful if they weighed 46 lbs. as A thought they did. (Compare *R.* v. *Percy Dalton* § 2.55, above). In fact the goods weighed 48 lbs. so that the price proposed would not have been unlawful if the sale had been completed. Has A committed a criminal attempt?
   (b) Would it make any difference if A did not know that the price he proposed to charge for what he thought was 50 lbs. was unlawful.
   (c) Does the answer to (b) depend upon whether the offence is one of strict liability so far as the price is concerned?

3. After distinguishing two cases of intention to smuggle goods which are not dutiable, the Law Commission says, "Fine as the distinction appears to be in these cases, it is one which is in our view vital to make." (§ 2.98 above). *Why* is it vital to make this distinction?

4. Pursuant to the distinction it draws between two kinds of would-be smuggler, the Law Commission declares its policy not to convict the one who makes only a mistake of law (§ 2.100 (2)). How has that policy been effectuated in the draft Bill and the Criminal Attempts Act? (*Ante*, p. 303.)

5. On its general approach to the problem of impossible attempts, the Law Commission says: "We stress that this solution to the problem does not punish people simply for their intentions." (§ 2.96). Do you agree? See below.

Cohen, "Questions of Impossibility" [1980] Crim. L.R. 773

"The Law Commission accept that the criminal law should retain a general law of attempt (§§ 2.6–2.9). The choice then becomes whether to adopt a 'subjectivist' or an 'objectivist' approach in the area of impossibility. As Williams has said, 'The ambit that is given to the law of attempt depends very much upon the view taken of the social policy of the matter. . . .' Put rather crudely, the 'objectivists' would punish only dangerous *acts*, while the 'subjectivists' would punish dangerous *actors*. There is, among the writers, a good deal of support for both views in either a pure or modified form. The Law Commission, in going for the 'subjectivist' approach, have, it is submitted, made the right choice.

Consider the 'objectivists' objections to the 'subjectivist' approach. First it is said that D should not be convicted for he has done no harm. But as Buxton has pointed out, [1973] Crim. L.R. 656, 669, this argument proves too much, for according to it there should logically be no conviction whenever D is unsuccessful in carrying out his intention, whether because he is arrested before committing the full offence, or withdraws, or fails through the use of inadequate means.

Secondly, it is said that the 'subjectivist' would punish mere intention. Hughes has said (1967) N.Y.U.L. Rev. 1005, 1024:

> '... To say that attempted murder can be *doing anything* while thinking (mistakenly) that you are going to cause X ... provides no criteria whatsoever for characterising an act as an attempt other than the mistaken view under which it is being done, and is thus ... tantamount to punishment for intention alone....'

But Williams, it is submitted, convincingly refutes this view, when he says, 'there is more than intention: there is conduct that carries very far the endeavour to carry out the intention, on the facts as the defendant believed them to be ...,' (Textbook of Criminal Law, 399) and thus 'If there is a *mens rea*, it is capable of establishing as an *actus reus* an act that would otherwise be not only legally but morally and socially innocent. Consequently, it is false to say that, because an act is "objectively" innocent it cannot be a criminal attempt' (Criminal Law: The General Part, 643).

Thirdly it is said that to convict of attempt in cases of impossibility is to use the criminal law as a means of preventive detention. Yet some of the 'objectivists' are prepared for the law to be used in this way in some cases—for example, Professor Smith would punish the inadequate means cases, and Temkin would punish all attempts to kill and to cause grievous bodily harm.

The weakness of the 'objectivist' position is that it would fail to punish some defendants who have manifested their social dangerousness. Much of the 'objectivists' antipathy to the 'subjectivist' view is caused by the fact that in extreme cases the 'subjectivist' view will lead to unfair results. Both the Working Party and the Law Commission recognise this, as indeed do the 'subjectivist' writers. But extreme cases are, by their nature, rare, and it may be a mistake to base a general approach on them.

Let us consider some of the extreme cases. Take first the case of Lady Eldon, who believes she is smuggling French lace. Assume it is an offence to import French lace without paying the duty. Unknown to her, what she has is English lace, which is not dutiable. The 'subjectivists' would convict her of attempting to avoid the payment of duty on French lace; the 'objectivists' would say that this was unjustifiable. But let us alter the facts. What if Lady Eldon thought she was importing heroin but, unknown to her, it was talcum powder? This may make the 'objectivists' pause for thought. Suppose then that the authorities have been watching Lady Eldon's trips abroad for some time, strongly suspecting, and rightly, that she is a courier for heroin but has, so far, been clever enough to avoid apprehension. Is this revamped Lady Eldon not now socially dangerous? ...

What is being submitted is that the 'objectivists' are being seduced by the relative harmlessness of the extreme examples. They would throw away a device that would enable conviction in those analytically indistinguishable cases where, on any view, D is a social danger. The price for not convicting the relatively harmless would be that the criminal law would be impotent to deal with the wicked and the dangerous."

iii. Mental element in attempt

Law Com. No. 102

[Footnotes to this extract are numbered as in original document.]

1. The Working Party's formulation and the present law

§ 2.11 As a matter of analysis the Working Party thought it useful to consider separately the defendant's mental state as to the *consequences* of his acts and, where circumstances are elements of an offence, as to the *circumstances* in which he carried them out. The Working Party's discussion carried through this distinction into the formulation of the mental element.[21] Thus, to take some simple examples, attempted murder would, on the Working Party's test, require the intention to bring about the consequences specified by the offence of murder, that is, the death of another; an intent to cause grievous bodily harm would not be enough on this test, even though the offence of murder is committed if the defendant kills another with intent only to cause grievous bodily harm. On the other hand attempted theft would not necessarily require knowledge that the property which the defendant intended to appropriate belonged to another; mere recklessness would be enough, since recklessness as to this element of the offence is sufficient for theft.

§ 2.12 The Working Party's formulation of the mental element for attempt was criticised as being unduly complex. We agree with this criticism. The separation of elements of an offence into circumstances and consequences may in some instances be a useful means of analysing them. But to ask in the case of every offence what is a circumstance and what is a consequence is in our view a difficult and artificial process which may sometimes lead to confusion. Since a new statutory offence of attempt in place of the common law will (subject to express exceptions) apply to all existing offences, it seems to us that the terminology of "circumstances" and "consequences" will not be appropriate. Save as an aid to analysis, we therefore do not use this terminology in our discussion of the mental element.

§§ 2.13 Since the issue of the Working Paper, the mental element in attempt has been considered by the Court of Appeal in *R.* v. *Mohan* [1976] Q.B. 1. The defendant was alleged to have driven a car at a policeman intending to injure him. He was charged with attempting to cause grievous bodily harm with intent and upon that charge he was acquitted. He was also charged with attempting by wanton driving to cause bodily harm to the policeman. The jury was directed that it was sufficient for the prosecution to prove that the defendant was reckless as to whether bodily harm would be caused by wanton driving, and found him guilty. The conviction was quashed by the Court of Appeal (Criminal Division). The Court in its judgment stated that—

> "The attraction of this [approach] is that it presents a situation in relation to attempts to commit a crime which is simple and logical, for it requires in proof of the attempt no greater burden in respect of *mens rea* than is required in proof of the completed offence. The argument in its extreme form is that an attempt to commit a crime of strict liability is in itself a strict liability

[21] (1973) Working Paper No. 50, § 89, where the mental element for attempt was formulated as follows: "(a) *As to consequences*. Where a particular consequence must be brought about before the offence in question is committed, an attempt to commit that offence is committed only when the actor intends that consequence. (b) *As to circumstances*. Where what a person attempts to do will not be criminal unless a certain circumstance exists, he is guilty of an attempt to commit that offence only when he has knowledge of or (where recklessness is all that the substantive offence requires) is reckless as to the existence of that circumstance."

offence. It is argued that the contrary view involves the proposition that the offence of attempt includes *mens rea* when the offence which is attempted does not and in that respect the attempt takes on a graver aspect than, and requires an additional burden of proof beyond that which relates to, the complete offence." (at p. 6).

The Court's answer to this argument is contained in the following passage—

"An attempt to commit a crime is itself an offence. Often it is a grave offence. Often it is as morally culpable as the completed offence which is attempted but not in fact committed. Nevertheless it falls within the class of conduct which is preparatory to the commission of a crime and is one step removed from the offence which is attempted. The court must not strain to bring within the offence of attempt conduct which does not fall within the well established bounds of the offence. On the contrary, the court must safeguard against extension of those bounds save by the authority of Parliament. The bounds are presently set by requiring proof of specific intent, a decision to bring about, in so far as it lies within the accused's power, the commission of the offence which it is alleged the accused attempted to commit, no matter whether the accused desired that consequence of his act or not." (at p. 11).

In establishing whether in any particular case such intent is present, the Court pointed to the requirements of section 8 of the Criminal Law Act 1967, and commented—

"upon the question whether or not the accused had the necessary intent in relation to a charge of attempt, evidence tending to establish directly, or by inference, that the accused knew or foresaw that the likely consequence, and, even more so, the highly probable consequence, of his act—unless interrupted—would be the commission of the completed offence, is relevant material for the consideration of the jury. In our judgment, evidence of knowledge of likely consequences, or from which knowledge of likely consequence can be inferred, is evidence by which intent may be established but it is not, in relation to the offence of attempt, to be equated with intent. If the jury find such knowledge established they may and, using common sense, they probably will find intent proved, but it is not the case that they must do so."

This case appears to us to have removed some of the difficulties raised by earlier cases, and the extracts from the Court's judgment quoted above have been of value in our consideration of how to formulate the law for the future.

2. Conclusions and recommendations

§ 2.14 In our view, an indication of the most appropriate way in which to express for the future the mental element of a new statutory offence of attempt is to be found in the Court of Appeal's dictum in *R.* v. *Mohan* that the bounds of the mental element require "proof of specific intent, a decision to bring about, in so far as it lies within the accused's power, the commission of the offence which it is alleged the accused attempted to commit." At the time of the attempt, the completed offence has of course not yet taken place: it is a future occurrence, even though in some instances the temporal difference may be small. It therefore seems to us that it is not only in accord with the decision in *R.* v. *Mohan* but right in principle that the concept of the mental element in attempt should be expressed as an intent to bring about each of the constituent elements of the offence attempted. Put more simply, this may be stated as an intent to commit the offence attempted.

§ 2.15 Some illustrations may indicate how this concept might be expected to work in practice. If a defendant who is interrupted while forcing the window of a house is accused of attempted burglary, it will be necessary to show that at the time of the attempted entry he intended to enter a building as a trespasser with the further intent required by the offence of theft of appropriating property of another. If a defendant is accused of an attempt to commit the offence under section 35 of the Offences against the Person Act 1861 of causing bodily harm by wanton driving in charge of a vehicle, it will be necessary to establish that he intended by that means to cause such harm. And to take an instance where the completed offence is one of strict liability, where a defendant is charged with an attempt to have intercourse with a girl under the age of thirteen, it will be necessary to show that he intended to have intercourse with a girl under that age. The mental elements for the completed offences in these examples require varying degrees of knowledge of circumstances and intent to do the proscribed acts, stretching from strict liability to full knowledge and intent; but the mental element for the attempt to commit them may in each case be described as an intent that the offence shall be brought about. This intention will in practice be established by proof of the defendant's intention to bring about the consequences, and of his knowledge of the factual circumstances, expressly or implicitly required by the definition of the substantive offence.

§ 2.16 It should be noted that a requirement of proof of intent to commit the offence attempted is in no way intended to derogate from the general principle that ignorance of the law is no defence to a charge of an attempted (or indeed any) crime. In the example cited above, it does not follow from the requirement that there should be an intent to have intercourse with a girl under thirteen that the defendant must also be aware that such conduct is an offence. This distinction between the intention to do something which, if done, is an offence and the knowledge that, if done, an offence is committed is of particular importance in the sphere of "regulatory" legislation, where the offences are frequently of strict liability and triable only summarily. On any charge of attempt to commit such offences it will be necessary to prove that the defendant intended to carry out the forbidden act, whether or not he knew that the act would amount to an offence. In some common offences, such as certain of the offences under the Road Traffic Act 1972, this might well restrict the occasions upon which it would be possible to charge an attempt. For example, if the defendant was stopped when on the point of driving off in his motor car which had defective brakes, he could not be convicted of attempting to use a car which "does not comply with regulations" unless there was proof of his intention to drive with defective brakes, although the completed offence does not require knowledge that the brakes are defective. In our view this is the right result: while there are many instances in which legislation has imposed strict liability where the proscribed conduct is completed, there is less justification for imposing such liability if the defendant neither intended to do nor succeeded in completing the forbidden act. As the Court of Appeal pointed out in *R.* v. *Mohan*, an attempt "is one step removed from the offence which is attempted," and care has therefore to be taken to avoid bringing "within the offence of attempt conduct which does not fall within the well-established bounds of the offence."

§ 2.17 In our *Report on the Mental Element in Crime* (Law Com. No. 89, *ante*, p. 57) we recommend that whenever a person's conduct was in issue, the test of whether he "intended" a result of his conduct should be whether he *intended* to produce the result or *whether he had no substantial doubt* that his conduct would produce it (*ibid*, § 44). But we pointed out in that Report that our recommendations would not preclude the use in future legislation of the term intention in a different sense. There are in our view two reasons for departing from that test in the context of attempt. In the case of attempt, what is intended is not a "result" of "conduct" but commission of the complete offence. The formulation used in our *Report on the Mental Element* is therefore not appropriate to the mental element which we propose for attempt and cannot easily be adapted to it in legislative terms. More fundamentally, implicit in attempt is the "decision to bring about, in so far as it lies within the accused's power, the commission of the offence." (*R.* v. *Mohan*, above.) This confirms that what is required is an actual intent to commit the offence attempted. There is no room for the broader concept of intent which in our *Report on the Mental Element in Crime* we describe as having no substantial doubt as to the results of conduct. We therefore do not recommend adoption of the terminology used in that Report, and see no need for any special definition of intent in the present context.

§ 2.18 For the reasons given in the foregoing paragraphs, we *recommend* that the mental element for the offence of attempt should be defined as an intent to commit the offence attempted.

Note

In § 2.16 above, the Law Commission discusses attempted offences of strict liability, including these triable only summarily. Later in the Report, the Commission recommends that it should be an offence to attempt a summary offence, thereby extending the common law (§ 2.105, and see Draft Clause 1, *ante,* p. 325). However, the Criminal Attempts Act 1981 covers attempts at indictable offences only (s. 1 (4)). This means that it is only an offence to attempt a summary offence if the statute creating the offence specifically makes it so. In deciding whether such an attempt has been committed, a court will work to the same definition as for an attempt to commit an indictable offence: see s. 3 (4) (5).

Questions

1. A places a bomb on an aircraft in order to collect on the insurance policy. He foresees the deaths of the passengers and crew as certain if the bomb explodes, but he does not actively wish for their deaths. The bomb fails to explode. Is A guilty of attempted murder? See *Hyam* v. *D.P.P. post,* p. 374.
2. B asks for money from C, making a representation which B is aware may well be false, although he does not know that it is false. (See Theft Act 1968, s. 15 (4), *post,* p. 572). In fact the representation is false, but C does not believe B and does not give him money. Is B guilty of attempting to obtain money by deception?
3. D, who had been given a commission by a dealer to locate and steal a certain Old Master painting, was discovered trying to break into Barchester Towers. D confessed that he hoped the painting was there, although he did not know that it was; his object in locating it was to steal it. In fact the painting was in Barchester Towers. Is D guilty of attempting burglary with intent to steal? (See *post,* p. 641, on conditional intention.)
4. In (3), would it make any difference if the painting were not in Barchester Towers?

2. CONSPIRACY

D.P.P. v. Nock [1978] A.C. 979, 997: "Lord Tucker [in *B.O.T.* v. *Owen* [1957] A.C. 602], by stressing the 'auxiliary' nature of the crime of conspiracy, and by explaining its justification as being to prevent the commission of substantive offence, has placed the crime firmly in the same class and category as attempts to commit a crime. Both are criminal because they are steps towards the commission of a substantive offence. The distinction between the two is that whereas a 'proximate' act is that which constitutes the crime of attempt, agreement is the necessary ingredient in conspiracy. The importance of the distinction is that agreement may, and usually will, occur well before the first step which can be said to be an attempt. The law of conspiracy thus makes possible an earlier intervention by the law to prevent the commission of the substantive offence.": *per* Lord Scarman.

Note

Conspiracy was a common law offence, consisting of "the agreement of two or more to do an unlawful act, or to do a lawful act by unlawful means": *per* Willes J. in *Mulcahy* v. *R.* (1868) L.R. 3 H.L. 306. "Unlawful" in this context covered all crimes, even summary offences, some torts, fraud, the corruption of public morals and the outraging of public decency. The aim of the Law Commission (Law Com. No. 76, § 1.113) is to confine conspiracy to agreements to commit crimes. This aim is partially achieved by sections 1 and 5 of the Criminal Law Act 1977 (see below). However, pending a comprehensive review of offences of fraud and of the law relating to obscenity and indecency, conspiracies to defraud, and to corrupt public morals or outrage public decency, are preserved. See *R.* v. *Duncalf*, below.

i. Conspiracy at Common Law or by Statute

Criminal Law Act 1977

Section 1: *The offence of conspiracy* (1) Subject to the following provisions of this Part of this Act, if a person agrees with any other person or persons that a course of conduct shall be pursued which, if the agreement is carried out in accordance with their intentions, either—

(a) will necessarily amount to or involve the commission of any offence or offences by one or more of the parties to the agreement, or
(b) would do so but for the existence of facts which render the commission or the offence or any of the offences impossible,

he is guilty of conspiracy to commit the offence or offences in question. [Substituted, as to conspiracies entered into or continuing to exist after 31st August, 1981, by Section 5 (1) Criminal Attempts Act 1981].

(2) Where liability for any offence may be incurred without knowledge on the party of the person committing it of any particular fact or circumstance necessary for the commission of the offence, a person shall nevertheless not be guilty of conspiracy to commit that offence by virtue of subsection (1) above unless he and at least one other party to the agreement intend or know that that fact or circumstance shall or will exist at the time when the conduct constituting the offence is to take place.

(3) Where in pursuance of any agreement the acts in question in relation to any offence are to be done in contemplation or furtherance of a trade dispute (within the meaning of the Trade Union and Labour Relations Act 1974) that offence shall be disregarded for the purposes of subsection (1) above provided that it is a summary offence which is not punishable with imprisonment.

(4) In this Part of this Act "offence" means an offence triable in England and Wales, except that it includes murder notwithstanding that the murder in ques-

tion would not be so triable if committed in accordance with the intentions of the parties to the agreement.

Section 5: *Abolitions, savings, transitional provisions, consequential amendments and repeals.* (1) Subject to the following provisions of this section, the offence of conspiracy at common law is hereby abolished.

(2) Subsection (1) above shall not affect the offence of conspiracy at common law so far as relates to conspiracy to defraud, and section 1 above shall not apply in any case where the agreement in question amounts to a conspiracy to defraud at common law.

(3) Subsection (1) above shall not affect the offence of conspiracy at common law if and in so far as it may be committed by entering into an agreement to engage in conduct which—

(a) tends to corrupt public morals or outrages public decency; but
(b) would not amount to or involve the commission of an offence if carried out by a single person otherwise than in pursuance of an agreement.

(7) Incitement to commit the offence of conspiracy (whether the conspiracy incited would be an offence at common law or under section 1 above or any other enactment) shall cease to be offences. [As amended by Criminal Attempts Act 1981, Section 10.]

ii. Agreement

R. v. Mills
(1962) 47 Cr. App. R. 49
Court of Criminal Appeal

D asked M to abort her, they agreed a price, and she went to visit him with the money. They were in conversation, with D still undecided whether to go on, when the police entered M's flat. M was convicted of conspiracy to procure a miscarriage and appealed.

Lord Parker C.J.: At the end of the case for the prosecution Mr. Clarke submitted to the learned judge that there was no evidence on the count of conspiracy to leave to the jury. His case, quite shortly, before the learned judge was that the stage had not been reached when intention had developed into agreement. The well-known cases of *Mulcahy* (1868) L.R. 3 H.L. 306 and *Quinn* v. *Leathem and Others* [1901] A.C. 495 were referred to. In the end, the learned judge overruled the submission, and thereupon the appellant elected to give his evidence.

. . . This court is quite clearly of opinion that there was ample evidence to support the verdict and that the verdict cannot be said to be unreasonable. In particular, it was open to the jury to find, as no doubt they did, that at the very early stage on the telephone there was an agreement in the sense that what both parties intended became an agreement with a common design. There was the fact that he knew she wanted an abortion, that the price was arranged and that no visit was to take place until she had the £25, the fact that he said that when she had got it he would take her, and finally the instruments found boiling in the kettle when the police came into the room. Mr. Clarke, by way of an alternative, has advanced this proposition, as I understand it, that, whenever an arrangement which otherwise would amount to an agreement has in it some form of reservation, it cannot amount to an agreement so as to found the crime of conspiracy. He would go so far as to say that if the arrangement was of a specific nature—let us say to break into a particular house on a particular day at a particular time by a particular means—yet if either expressly or impliedly there was a reservation that that would not be attempted if a policeman was outside the door, even so there was no agreement on which to found a conspiracy to housebreak. This court is quite clearly of the opinion that that is wrong. If that were so, no doubt nobody could ever be convicted of conspiracy at all. He suggests that that follows from the fact that an agreement for the purposes of conspiracy is of the same nature as an agreement in civil proceedings but, as it seems to this court, an agreement in civil proceedings is quite clearly no less an agreement because the parties have introduced reservations and exceptions either express or implied. No doubt in many cases it may be a very fine line whether the parties at the particular moment under consideration are merely negotiating or whether they have reached an agreement to do something if it is possible or propitious to do it, and it may be that those cases will be decided largely on the form of the reservation. If the reservation is no more than if a policeman is not there, it would be impossible to say that there had not been an agreement. On the other hand, if the matters left outstanding and reserved are of a sufficiently substantial nature, it may well be that the case will fall on the other side of the fence, and it will be said that the matter is merely a matter of negotiation.

A somewhat similar case came before this court in the case of *Walker* [1962] Crim. L.R. 458. There, on the evidence of one of the prisoners, he had dropped out of the project, if I may use a neutral term, before it had been put into effect, the project being to steal the wages of a particular firm. The question was whether at the time when he had dropped out of the project an agreement had been arrived at so as to form a conspiracy or whether the matter was still in a state of negotiation. Much reliance has been placed upon that case, in which this court said: "The court has come to the conclusion in this case that, while it is perhaps impossible to say that there was no evidence from which an agreement could be inferred, what is contained in the statement is at least just as consistent with the matter having consisted purely of negotiation." That was the view of the court on the facts of that case, and on the facts of the present case the court is satisfied that there was ample evidence upon which the jury on this summing-up could hold that an agreement had been arrived at. So far as the first count is concerned, therefore, this court sees no reason to interfere.

(The appeal was allowed on another count)

R. v. O'Brien (1974) 59 Cr. App. R. 222: A was found photographing the outside of a prison. At his house were discovered documents and plans which suggested an intention to assist in an escape of S, who was held in the prison. On appeal, it was held that there was no sufficient evidence of any conspiracy: "The essence of a conspiracy is an agreement, and persons do not commit a criminal offence merely by talking about the possibility of committing some wrongful or unlawful act unless they reach the stage when they have agreed to commit that act if it lies in their power. If the jury considered the background of this case and the inferences to be drawn, they could quite properly, and no doubt would, have drawn the inference that O'Brien had told them a pack of lies and that he had gone to Winson Green in order to take a photograph of the wall for such value as that photograph might be in an escape. They might very well have drawn the inference that it was most unlikely that O'Brien would have done all this entirely by himself without consulting his friends in Luton because he was clearly well known in the Irish nationalist circles in that town. But the point about which the jury must have been in considerable difficulty, had the matter been explained to them, was in saying that the only possible inference to be drawn here was not merely that O'Brien had discussed a prison break with his friends, but that O'Brien had agreed to undertake a prison break with his friends."

R. v. Thomson
(1965) 50 Cr. App. R. 1
Nottinghamshire Assizes

T. was being tried for conspiracy, and sought a ruling that a secret intention on his part not to co-operate with his alleged co-conspirators would constitute a defence.

LAWTON J.: In this case, in which the defendant is charged with conspiracy to defraud it has become necessary for me to rule whether it is a defence for the defendant to say, as the jury might infer he had said in two statements made by him in July 1963, that he had led his alleged co-conspirators to believe that he was agreeing with them to carry out an unlawful purpose when in fact he had no intention of doing anything of the kind.

The problem perhaps can be put in general terms, *viz.*, on a charge of conspiracy, must the prosecution prove not only an agreement between the alleged conspirators to carry out an unlawful purpose, as signified by words or other means of communication between them, but also that they had an intention to carry out the unlawful purpose?

The researches of counsel seem to show that this problem has never been resolved by any English court, but it has been before the Supreme Court of Canada in *O'Brien* (1954) Can. L. Rep. 666 and before courts in Texas and Tennessee. The Canadian Supreme Court decided, by a majority of three to two, that the prosecution had to prove in each of the alleged conspirators an intention at the time when the agreement was made to carry out the unlawful purpose. This decision was reached after the court had considered the common law of conspiracy. The Texas and Tennessee courts seem to have reached the same conclusion as the Supreme Court of Canada, but I have no first-hand knowledge of their decisions. I agree with the view of the majority of the Supreme Court of Canada. . . .

When a man makes an agreement, he assents with his mind to the offer of the other party and communicates his assent to the other party by words or conduct. For the purposes of the law of contract, the words or conduct by which a man manifests his assent are binding on him and the law does not allow him to say that his mind did not go with his conduct. The criminal law, however, is concerned with punishing wrongdoing; the essential element in any crime, other than in the limited class of absolute offences, is a guilty mind. Evidence that the accused person acted and spoke as if he was making and had made an agreement may provide cogent evidence of a guilty mind; but it is only evidence and can be rebutted by other evidence.

It follows, in my judgment that in the crime of conspiracy there must be the element of a guilty mind. . . .

If the facts show, as the jury might on the evidence in this case infer that they do, that the defendant manifested his assent to a criminal enterprise, but that his mind did not go with his assent, then it seems to me that the element of the guilty mind is missing and, accordingly, on those facts he would be entitled to be acquitted, and I propose to direct the jury accordingly.

Ruling accordingly

In *R.* v. *O'Brien* (*ante*, p. 334) the Court of Appeal was dealing, *obiter*, with the argument that, O. being charged with conspiring with L. and others, the fact that L. was a police informer who had no intention of going through with the agreement ought to provide O. with a defence. Widgery L.C.J.: "We do not accept the submission that the fact that one party to an apparent agreement has no intention of playing his part in itself prevents the other guilty-minded conspirators from being guilty of the offence charged against them."

Question

Is this dictum inconsistent with the ruling in *R.* v. *Thomson*?

R. v. Barnard (1979) 70 Cr. App. R. 28. A reconnoitred a jeweller's shop and discussed stealing from it with B & C. Later A discovered that his usual *modus operandi* was impossible, so he withdrew, but passed on his observations to B and C so that they could do the job their way, which involved attacking the shop-keeper with an iron bar. In holding that there was no sufficient evidence to convict A of conspiracy to steal, the Court of Appeal added (p. 34): "If the indictment had been drawn in a different way and had he been charged with robbery, it may be ... that there was sufficient evidence to bring him before the jury on the ground that he incited the robbers to do what they did. What there was no sufficient evidence of was that he had formed a conspiracy to rob."

iii. Jurisdiction

D.P.P. v. Doot
[1973] A.C. 807
House of Lords

> Six American citizens, in Europe, planned to import cannabis into the United States by way of England. One of the vans containing the drug was found at Southampton, another at Liverpool. They were all convicted of importing prohibited drugs and did not appeal on this. They were also charged with conspiring to import dangerous drugs. The defence to that charge was that the conspiracy had been entered into abroad. The trial judge overruled the submission, but the Court of Appeal took a different view and quashed the conviction. The Crown appealed further.

Lord Wilberforce: ... Often in conspiracy cases the implementing action is itself the only evidence of the conspiracy—this is the doctrine of overt acts. Could it be said, with any plausibility, that if the conclusion or a possible conclusion to be drawn from overt acts in England was that there was a conspiracy, entered into abroad, a charge of conspiracy would not lie? Surely not: yet, if it could, what difference should it make if the conspiracy is directly proved or is admitted to have been made abroad? The truth is that, in the normal case of a conspiracy carried out, in this country, the location of the formation of the agreement is irrelevant: the attack upon the laws of this country is identical wherever the conspirators happened to meet; the "conspiracy" is a complex, formed indeed, but not separably completed, at the first meeting of the plotters.

A legal principle which would enable concerting law breakers to escape a conspiracy charge by crossing the Channel before making their agreement or to bring forward arguments, which we know can be subtle enough, as to the location of agreements, or, conversely, which would encourage the prosecution into allegation or fiction of a renewed agreement in this country, all this with no compensating merit, is not one which I could endorse....

Lord Pearson: A conspiracy involves an agreement expressed or implied. A conspiratorial agreement is not a contract, not legally binding, because it is unlawful. But as an agreement it has its three stages, namely (1) making or formation (2) performance or implementation (3) discharge or termination. When the conspiratorial agreement has been made, the offence of conspiracy is complete, it has been committed, and the conspirators can be prosecuted even though no performance has taken place: *R.* v. *Aspinall*, 2 Q.B.D. 48, *per* Brett J.A., at pp. 58–59. But the fact that the offence of conspiracy is complete at that stage does not mean that the conspiratorial agreement is finished with. It is not dead. If it is being performed, it is very much alive. So long as the performance continues, it is operating, is being carried out by the conspirators, and it is governing or at any rate influencing their conduct. The conspiratorial agreement continues in operation and therefore in existence until it is discharged (terminated) by completion of its performance or by abandonment or frustration or however it may be.

On principle, apart from authority, I think (and it would seem the Court of Appeal also thought) that a conspiracy to commit in England an offence against English law ought to be triable in England if it has been wholly or partly performed in England. In such a case the conspiracy has been carried on in England with the consent and authority of all the conspirators. It is not necessary that they should all be present in England. One of them, acting on his own behalf and as agent for the others, has been performing their agreement, with their consent and authority, in England. In such a case the conspiracy has been committed by all of them in England. Be it granted that "All crime is local" and "The jurisdiction over the crime belongs to the country where the crime is committed . . .": *per* Lord Halsbury L.C. in *Macleod* v. *A.G. for New South Wales* [1891] A.C. 455, 458. The crime of conspiracy in the present case was committed in England, personally or through an agent or agents, by all the conspirators.

The balance of authority is in favour of the view that the English courts have jurisdiction in a case such as this . . .

LORD SALMON: . . . If a conspiracy is entered into abroad to commit a crime in England, exactly the same public mischief is produced by it as if it had been entered into here. It is unnecessary for me to consider what the position might be if the conspirators came to England for an entirely innocent purpose unconnected with the conspiracy. If, however, the conspirators come here and do acts in furtherance of the conspiracy, for example, by preparing to commit the planned crime, it cannot, in my view, be considered contrary to the rules of international comity for the forces of law and order in England to protect the Queen's peace by arresting them and putting them on trial for conspiracy whether they are British subjects or foreigners and whether or not conspiracy is a crime under the law of the country in which the conspiracy was born. It was unusual until recently to have any direct evidence of conspiracy. Conspiracy was usually proved by what are called overt acts, being acts from which an antecedent conspiracy is to be inferred. Where and when the conspiracy occurs is often unknown and seldom relevant. Today, however, it is possible to have direct evidence such as tape recordings or oral agreements. Suppose a case in which evidence existed of a conspiracy hatched abroad by bank robbers to raid a bank in London, or by terrorists to carry out some violent crime at an English airport, or by drug pedlars to smuggle large quantities of dangerous drugs on some stretch of the English coast. Suppose the conspirators came to England for the purpose of carrying out the crime and were detected by the police reconnoitring the place where they proposed to commit it, but doing nothing which by itself would be illegal, it would surely be absurd if the police could not arrest them then and there but had to take the risk of waiting and hoping to be able to catch them as they were actually committing or attempting to commit the crime. Yet that is precisely what the police would have to do if a conspiracy entered into abroad to commit a crime here were not in the circumstances postulated recognised by our law as a criminal offence which our courts had any jurisdiction to try.

I do not believe that any civilised country, even assuming that its own laws do not recognise conspiracy as a criminal offence, could today have any reasonable objection to its nationals being arrested, tried and convicted by English courts in the circumstances to which I have referred. Today, crime is an international problem—perhaps not least crimes connected with the illicit drug traffic—and there is a great deal of cooperation between the nations to bring criminals to justice. Great care also is taken by most countries to do nothing which might help their own nationals to commit what would be crimes in other countries: see, for example, section 3 (2) of the Dangerous Drugs Act 1965. . . .

There can be no doubt but that the respondents' conduct in conspiring in Belgium or Morocco to commit crimes in England caused harm in this country because the respondents carried out those very crimes in furtherance of that conspiracy. No one suggests that to charge the respondents with those crimes in our courts could violate the rules of international comity; nor do I think that anyone could suppose that the inclusion of a charge in respect of the conspiracy could offend those rules whatever other criticisms might be made of it.

It is, unfortunately, by no means unlikely that cases may arise in the future in which there will be conclusive evidence of persons having conspired abroad to commit serious crimes in England and then having done acts here in furtherance of the conspiracy and in preparation for the commission of those crimes yet none of these acts will in itself be unlawful. Although such a case would be very different from the present, if the reasoning upon which I have based this opinion is sound it follows that such persons could properly be arrested and tried for conspiracy in our courts.

My Lords, even if I am wrong in thinking that a conspiracy hatched abroad to commit a crime in this country may be a common law offence because it endangers the Queen's peace, I agree that the convictions for conspiracy against these respondents can be supported on another ground, namely, that they conspired together in this country notwithstanding the fact that they were abroad when they entered into the agreement which was the essence of the conspiracy. That agreement was and remained a continuing agreement and they continued to conspire until the offence they were conspiring to commit was in fact committed. Accordingly, when Watts, Loving and Fay sailed into English territorial waters they were still agreeing and conspiring to import into this country the dangerous drugs which a little later they smuggled ashore. Moreover, they were agreeing, not only on their own behalf but also on behalf and with the authority of Doot and Shannahan. Therefore, they were, all five of them, guilty of conspiring in England. It is irrelevant for this purpose that they had originally entered into the conspiracy abroad and that an offence of conspiracy is committed at the moment when the agreement to commit a crime is first made.

If, however, a conspiracy is entered into abroad by a number of conspirators to commit a series of crimes in England and only one conspirator comes to this country and commits one of the planned crimes, it would, I think, be unrealistic to regard him as agreeing with himself, whilst here, on behalf of each of the other conspirators. It is true that he would be committing an act in furtherance of the conspiracy, indeed, one of the very crimes which, whilst abroad, all the conspirators had conspired to commit. The act, however, would not be an ingredient of the crime of conspiracy, but only evidence of the existence of the conspiracy entered into abroad. If another of the conspirators who had perhaps masterminded the whole conspiracy later came here to obtain information useful to enable the other planned crimes to be committed, he would be immune from a charge of conspiracy however overwhelming the evidence of conspiracy might be if conspiracy abroad to commit a crime in England cannot be a common law offence: neither he nor anyone on his behalf would have conspired in England. This is why I have taken up time in explaining why, on principle, conspiracy abroad to commit a crime in England may, in my view, be a common law offence certainly when acts in furtherance of it are committed in this country.

My Lords, for the reasons I have indicated, I would allow the appeal.

Appeal allowed

Questions

1. A and B in France agree to steal a picture from the National Gallery, the theft to be committed on an agreed date.

(a) Six months before the agreed date, A comes to England to reconnoitre the position of the picture. Can A be convicted of conspiracy?
(b) After A had reconnoitred the picture's position, B comes to England for a wholly innocent purpose. Can B be convicted of conspiracy?
(c) B comes to England for an innocent purpose before A has started to reconnoitre. Can B be convicted of conspiracy?
(d) B comes to England for an innocent purpose, before A has started to reconnoitre, but after the picture has been accidentally destroyed. Can B be convicted of conspiracy?

2. A in England telephoned B in France and they agreed that he would steal a picture in the National Gallery. Would there a be a conspiracy, and if so, where would it be made, and does it matter anyway?

3. A and B in England agree to steal a picture from the Louvre. Can they be convicted of conspiracy in England? (See C.L.A. 1977, s. 1 (4), *ante*, p. 332).

iv. Parties

1. *At least two conspirators*

Notes

It takes two to agree, so if A is adjudged not to have agreed with B, it would appear to follow that B has not agreed with A. From this it was thought to be a rule that if A were acquitted of conspiracy with B, a conviction of B for conspiracy with A (if there were no other conspirators involved) could not possibly stand. This alleged rule was abolished by the House of Lords in *D.P.P.* v. *Shannon* [1975] A.C. 717, where the following passage from *R.* v. *Andrews-Weatherfoil Ltd.* [1972] 1 W.L.R. 118, 125 was approved.

"As long as it is possible for persons concerned in a single offence to be tried separately, it is inevitable that the verdicts returned by the two juries will on occasion appear to be inconsistent with one another. Such a result may be due to differences in the evidence presented at the two trials or simply to the different views which the juries separately take of the witnesses. . . . When inconsistent verdicts are returned by the same jury, the position is usually more simple. If the inconsistency shows that the single jury was confused, or self contradictory, its conclusions are unsatisfactory or unsafe and neither verdict is reliable. Very often, however, an apparent inconsistency reflects no more than the jury's strict adherence to the judge's direction that they must consider each case separately and that evidence against one may not be admissible against the other: for example, where there is a signed confession. So too, where the verdicts are returned by different juries the inconsistency does not, of itself, indicate that the jury which returned the verdict was confused or misled or reached an incorrect conclusion on the evidence before it. The verdict 'not guilty' includes 'not proven.'"

The decision in *D.P.P.* v. *Shannon* was confirmed by Criminal Law Act 1977:

"Section 5: (8) The fact that the person or persons who, so far as appears from the indictment on which any person has been convicted of conspiracy, were the only other parties to the agreement on which his conviction was based have been acquitted of conspiracy by reference to that agreement (whether after being tried with the person convicted or separately) shall not be a ground for quashing his conviction unless under all the circumstances of the case his conviction is inconsistent with the acquittal of the other person or persons in question.

(9) Any rule of law or practice inconsistent with the provisions of subsection (8) above is hereby abolished."

2. *Effect of exempt parties*

Notes

If A is charged with conspiring with B to commit a crime, and it appears that B would incur no liability for the crime if it were consummated, two questions arise.

The first question is, does B's exemption in respect of the contemplated crime mean that he cannot be convicted of *conspiring* to commit the crime?

If his "exemption" is because he did not know the crime was to be committed, then he cannot be guilty of conspiracy in that his agreement did not extend to the commission of the crime. Section 1 (2) of the Criminal Law Act 1977 makes express provision for this if the offence is one of strict liability.

If B has some personal exemption which prevents him (whatever his state of mind) from being convicted as first principal of the contemplated crime, then, as seen (*ante*, p. 274) this does not always prevent him from being convicted as a secondary party to that crime. There is no reason why he should not be guilty of conspiracy to commit a crime to which he could be a secondary party. But if B could not be guilty either as a principal or as a secondary party, he ought not to be convicted of conspiring to commit the crime. The policy of the law which excluded B from liability as a party to the crime ought, to be consistent, to exclude him from liability for conspiracy to commit the crime. The Law Commission, agreeing with its Working Party, so recommended (see Law Com. No. 76, § 1.56). Clause 2 of their Draft Bill reads:

"2 (1) A person shall not by virtue of section 1 above be guilty of conspiracy in relation to any particular offence if he is a person who, by virtue of—

(a) any limitation on the description of persons who are capable, in law, of committing that offence; or
(b) any exemption from prosecution provided in relation to that offence;

would not be guilty of an offence or (as the case may be) liable to be prosecuted if he were to do the acts in question under the agreement in relation to that offence himself."

However in the Criminal Law Act 1977, this was replaced by the following:

"s. 2 (1) A person shall not by virtue of section 1 above be guilty of conspiracy to commit any offence if he is an intended victim of that offence."

Questions

1. If the facts of *R.* v. *Whitchurch* (below) occurred again today, ought the decision to be the same as in that case?

2. What, today, ought to be the answer to the question Lord Alverstone C.J. leaves open in *R.* v. *Duguid* (*post*, p. 342)?

R. v. Whitchurch and Others

(1890) 24 Q.B.D. 420
Court for Crown Cases Reserved

A, B and Elizabeth Cross were convicted of conspiring to procure the miscarriage of Cross by unlawfully using instruments on her. The defendants all thought that Cross was pregnant but in fact she was not. The question was reserved as to whether the conviction of Cross was right, in view of the fact that it would not be an offence under section 58 of the Offences against the Person Act, 1861, for a woman who was not pregnant to use such instruments on herself with intent to procure a miscarriage.

LORD COLERIDGE, C.J.: I am of opinion that the conviction ought to be affirmed. The question arises on an indictment charging a woman, who, we must take it, was not in fact with child, with conspiring with others to procure abortion on herself. There might have been something to be said if the indictment had been for an attempt to procure abortion, for in that case the words of the section would not apply. This, however, is an entirely different case. The prisoner is charged with the offence of conspiracy—that is, a combination to commit a felony—and I cannot entertain the slightest doubt that if three persons combine to commit a felony they are all guilty of conspiracy, although the person on whom the offence was intended to be committed could not, if she stood alone, be guilty of the intended offence.

HAWKINS J.: I am of the same opinion.

The prisoner is not charged with using instruments, or administering drugs to herself, for the purpose of procuring abortion, but with conspiring with others to procure abortion. It is clear that she could not lawfully call in other persons to do that which when done by them is a crime punishable with penal servitude. What she did was a conspiracy to commit a criminal act.

Conviction affirmed

Offences against the Person Act, 1861, s. 58: "Every woman being with child, who, with intent to procure her own miscarriage, shall unlawfully administer to herself any poison or other noxious thing, or shall unlawfully use any instrument or other means whatsoever with the like intent, and whosoever, with intent to procure the miscarriage of any woman, whether she be or be not with child, shall unlawfully administer to her or cause to be taken by her any poison or other noxious thing, or shall unlawfully use any instrument or other means whatsoever with the like intent, shall be guilty of felony."

Note also *R.* v. *Sockett* (1908) 24 T.L.R. 893, where the court held that in circumstances similar to those in *Whitchurch*, the woman could be convicted of aiding and abetting the other defendants.

Note

The second question is, does B's exemption from liability for the crime contemplated, mean that A is not guilty of conspiracy with him? If B's "exemption" is because he did not know the crime was to be committed, then, as seen (*ante*) the whole agreement between A and B did not involve the commission of the crime and it must follow that A has not agreed in the terms required by section 1. As to other exemptions, authority is sparse, but see below.

R. v. Duguid
(1906) 75 L.J.K.B. 470
Court of Crown Cases Reserved

> Duguid and X were charged with conspiring with Mrs. Chetwynd, the mother of a child, to remove the child from the custody of the father, who was the lawful guardian. Such removal would be an offence under the Offences against the Person Act 1861, s. 56 (see below). X was acquitted, but D was convicted, and objected on the ground that as the only other conspirator was the mother, who had an immunity from prosecution for the offence which the conspiracy contemplated, he could not be guilty of conspiracy.

LORD ALVERSTONE C.J.: I express no opinion as to the effect of the proviso in the section upon a person in the position of Mrs. Chetwynd either as bearing upon an offence under the section or on a conspiracy to carry it into effect. That would depend very largely on the way in which the indictment was framed and on the evidence given in support of it. But no immunity of one of the persons which would prevent her from being proceeded against in respect of acts done by herself has any bearing on the question whether a conspiracy between her and another person to do an unlawful act is an offence against the criminal law.

Conviction affirmed

Offences against the Person Act 1861, s. 56: "Whosoever shall unlawfully, either by force or fraud, lead or take away . . . any child under the age of fourteen years, with intent to deprive any parent, guardian, or other person having the lawful care or charge of such child or the possession of such child . . . shall be guilty of felony . . . provided that no person who shall have claimed any right to the possession of such child, or shall be the mother or shall have claimed to be the father of an illegitimate child, shall be liable to be prosecuted by virtue hereof on account of the getting possession of such child, or taking such child out of the possession of any person having the lawful charge thereof."

Law Com. No. 76

1.57 . . . It might appear at first sight that there is no reason why [the non-exempt party] should not be prosecuted for conspiracy. Where one person is by statute expressly exempted from liability for his or her activity, for example, the exception in section 56 of the Offences against the Person Act 1861, it may nevertheless be thought desirable that the non-exempt party in a conspiracy to do the prohibited act should be penalised for agreeing to do what would be an offence on his part. On balance, however, we have come to the conclusion that the non-exempt party should in none of the cases under discussion be liable for conspiracy. This will eliminate the theoretical problems which attend the alternative solution, such as whether all the necessary elements of conspiracy can be held to exist where one party to the alleged agreement is, by reason of mental disorder, incapable of forming the necessary intent.

Draft Bill, Clause 2 (2)

A person shall not by virtue of section 1 above be guilty of conspiracy in relation to any offence or offences if the only other person or persons with whom he agrees are persons of any one or more of the following descriptions, that is to say—

(a) his spouse;
(b) a person under the age of criminal responsibility;
(c) a person exempt under subsection (1) above [*see ante*, p. 340] from liability for conspiracy in relation to that offence or each of those offences; and
(d) an intended victim of that offence or of each of those offences.

However in the Criminal Law Act 1977, this was replaced by the following:

"Section 2: (2) A person shall not by virtue of section 1 above be guilty of conspiracy to commit any offence or offences if the only other person or persons with whom he agrees are (both initially and at all times during the currency of the agreement) persons of any one or more of the following descriptions, that is to say—

(a) his spouse;
(b) a person under the age of criminal responsibility; and
(c) an intended victim of that offence or of each of those offences."

Questions

1. Would the decision in *R.* v. *Duguid* be the same today?
2. What should be the position if A is charged with conspiring with B who, by reason of mental disorder, is incapable of forming the necessary intent?

Note

See *R.* v. *Austin, ante,* p. 282 where it was held that non-exempt parties were guilty of *aiding and abetting* an offence under section 56, O.A.P.A.

v. Common Law Conspiracies

R. v. Duncalf and Others
(1979) 69 Cr. App. R. 206
Court of Appeal

The appellants were charged with conspiracy to steal contrary to section 1 Criminal Law Act 1977. The prosecution case was that they were seen to enter some 11 shops within a period of 45 minutes, their object being to see what they could steal from the shops in question. They were convicted and appealed.

ROSKILL L.J.: The main ground of appeal was that these five appellants had been charged with and convicted of an offence which did not exist. It was argued that because their intention was dishonest and they had as their objective the ultimate defrauding of the shopkeepers concerned, they should have been charged, not with conspiracy to steal contrary to section 1 of the 1977 Act, but with conspiracy to defraud contrary to the common law, an offence expressly preserved by section 5 (2) of that Act. In short, therefore, it was said that whenever the conspiracy charged contains an element of dishonesty and thus of intent to defraud, the conspiracy must be charged as a conspiracy to defraud contrary to the common law or possibly as a conspiracy to steal contrary to the common law, and not as a conspiracy to commit one or more of the specific offences in fact agreed upon such as theft or robbery or forgery or obtaining property by deception, as the case might be, envisaged by section 1 (1) of the 1977 Act.

This is not the first occasion upon which this submission has been advanced. It was seemingly first advanced at Nottingham Crown Court in *Quinn's* case [1978] Crim. L.R. 750 before Drake J. on October 24, 1978—curiously enough the day after the conviction of these appellants. There the indictment contained two counts, the first of conspiracy to steal at common law. The learned judge was invited to rule which of the two counts should be proceeded with. The learned judge, a note of whose ruling appears in [1978] Crim. L.R. 750, ruled that the correct count upon which to proceed was the second and that inasmuch as conspiracy to defraud included conspiracy to steal, while the offence could have been charged as conspiracy to defraud by conspiring to steal, it was nevertheless correct to charge the offence as conspiracy to steal at common law....

Subsequently in *Walters and Others* [1979] R.T.R. 220 a similar point came before this Court. The offence in question was there charged as conspiracy to defraud contrary to common law. It was argued that the conspiracy should have been charged under section 1 of the 1977 Act and not as conspiracy at common law by virtue of section 5 (2) of that Act. This Court rejected that argument. The learned Lord Chief Justice, after setting out the relevant sections of the 1977 Act, said at p. 223: "We are not going to lay down any final conclusions about this case. When a new point of this kind has to be developed, it is better if it is developed slowly. We shall look at the circumstances of this case and see how the statutory provisions work out in relation to it." This the Court proceeded to do and then the Lord Chief Justice added: "One can note as an interested spectator in passing that Drake J. had similar matters to decide sitting as a judge at first instance in October last, in *Quinn*. I do not intend to read the whole of what was said by Drake J., but, faced with this prospect, he took the firm view, which personally I support as at present advised, that it is perfectly proper to regard a conspiracy to steal as something within a conspiracy to defraud, and accordingly, therefore, if truly the offence is conspiracy to steal, the indictment is not rendered invalid merely because it charges a conspiracy to defraud. In many ways it must be preferable that the conspiracy to defraud should be regarded as the greater container, as it were, and able to mop up conspiracy to steal if and when that is convenient having regard to the nature of the case."

We think it is clear that this Court on that occasion was not giving any decision upon the matter which we now have to decide, even though it indicated tentative approval of the view taken by Drake J. . . .

The [long] title of the Criminal Law Act 1977 states as the first purpose of the Act that it is "An Act to amend the law of England and Wales with respect to criminal conspiracy; to make new provision in that law in place of the provisions of the common law . . ." Pausing there one moment, if the effect of section 5 (2) is to require all offences of conspiracy to steal, to rob, to forge or to obtain property by deception to continue to be charged as offences at common law because of the saving of the common law offence of conspiracy to defraud, the statute plainly has achieved little of its avowed objective.

It seems to us that the structure of this part of the 1977 Act is a little curious. One might have expected section 5 (1) to appear as section 1 (1), the common law offence of conspiracy being abolished (subject, of course, to the provisions of s. 5 (2) and 5 (3)) before the new statutory offence was created by section 1 (1). But the draftsman has in his wisdom decided otherwise. The Act starts in section 1 (1) by defining the new offence of conspiracy, the definition being stated to be subject to the following provisions of this part of the Act. Though the side-note to section 1 (1) is of course no part of the statute, it seems to us plain that the very language of this subsection coupled with the provisions of section 5 (1) abolishing the common law offence of conspiracy (subject of course to ss. 5 (2) and 5 (3) and to the remaining subsections of s. 5) shows that the definition in section 1 (1) is and was intended to be an exhaustive definition.

If this approach be right, then the presence of section 5 (2) and for that matter of section 5 (3) must, we think, be regarded as a limited qualification upon that abolition and upon the creation of that new statutory offence. But with profound respect to those who have taken a different view, it seems to us wrong to allow that qualification to prevail so as largely to emasculate the two main enacting provisions. The qualification should surely be read as preserving only that which requires to be preserved in order that a lacuna should not be left in the law. If section 1 (1) and section 5 (1) had been left standing without the savings in section 5 (2) there would have been a lacuna, because a conspiracy to defraud *simpliciter* could not fall within section 1 (1): see *Scott* v. *Metropolitan Police Commissioner* [*post*, p. 346] and if those two subsections had been left without the parallel saving in section 5 (3), the decision in *Shaw* v. *D.P.P.* [1962] A.C. 220, later confirmed in *Knuller (Publishing, Printing and Promotions) Ltd* [*post*, p. 350], might have been seemingly reversed in a statute which, though reforming the law of criminal conspiracy, was not concerned with the law relating to obscene publications.

Much reliance was placed in argument before us upon the penultimate paragraph of the speech of Viscount Dilhorne in *Scott's* case [*post*, p. 346]: "... in my opinion it is clearly the law that an agreement by two or more by dishonesty to deprive a person of something which is his or to which he is or would be or might be entitled and an agreement by two or more by dishonesty to injure some proprietary right of his, suffices to constitute the offence of conspiracy to defraud." It was said that Parliament must have intended to use the phrase "conspiracy to defraud" in section 5 (2) in the sense in which Viscount Dilhorne had there defined it, and therefore section 5 (2) must be given a meaning wide enough to embrace every conspiracy the objective of which was dishonestly to injure some proprietary or other right of the victim.

If section 5 (2) is to be literally construed, this argument has obvious force. But we do not think it right to give so strict or literal a construction to the subsection when the effect of so doing would be so largely to destroy the obvious purpose of this Act, and a sensible construction can, as we think, be given to both section 5 (2) and section 5 (3) as preserving the old law to, but only to, such extent as is necessary to ensure that a lacuna was not left in the law by section 1 (1). There may well be cases where it is still proper to charge a conspiracy to defraud at common law, as was done in *Walters and Others* (*supra*) rather than a conspiracy to commit one or more specific offences contrary to section 1 of the 1977 Act. But where, as in the instant case, the obvious purpose of the conspiracy was to steal, we think that the Act requires such a conspiracy to be charged as such contrary to section 1. Similarly where the purpose of the conspiracy was to rob or to forge or to obtain property by deception, we think the conspiracy should be charged as a conspiracy contrary to section 1. Mr. Harrison for the appellants frankly accepted that this argument involved that section 1 could only operate where the conspiracy in question was to commit some act of violence unaccompanied by any intention to deprive the victim of that violence of his property. In short, his argument involved a differentiation between a conspiracy to rob or to commit aggravated burglary on the one hand, and a conspiracy to commit murder or grievous bodily harm on the other. We do not think that the language of this statute requires so artificial a distinction. In the result we think that the instant offence was properly charged as one of conspiracy to steal contrary to section 1 of the 1977 Act and we do not find it necessary to consider what the position would have been as regards the nullity argument had our decision been otherwise. It follows that, with great respect, we find ourselves unable to agree with Drake J.'s ruling in *Quinn* or with the dictum tentatively approving that ruling in *Walters and Others*.

Appeals dismissed

Scott v. Metropolitan Police Commissioner
[1975] A.C. 819
House of Lords

S. agreed with employees of cinema owners temporarily to abstract, without permission of the owners, films, without the knowledge or consent of the copyright owners, for the purpose of making infringing copies and distributing them on a commercial basis. He was convicted of conspiracy to defraud the copyright owners, and appealed.

VISCOUNT DILHORNE: The Court of Appeal certified that a point of law of general public importance was involved in the decision to dismiss the appeal against conviction on count one, namely,

> "Whether on a charge of conspiracy to defraud, the Crown must establish an agreement to deprive the owners of their property by deception; or whether it is sufficient to prove an agreement to prejudice the rights of another or others without lawful justification and in circumstances of dishonesty."

Before the House Mr. Blom-Cooper put forward three contentions, his main one being that which he had advanced unsuccessfully before the Court of Appeal and Judge Hines that there could not be a conspiracy to defraud without deceit. . . .

Mr. Blom-Cooper's main submission was based on the well known dicta of Buckley J. in *In re London and Globe Finance Corporation Ltd.* [1903] 1 Ch. 728, 732:

> "To deceive is, I apprehend, to induce a man to believe that a thing is true which is false, and which the person practising the deceit knows or believes to be false. To defraud is to deprive by deceit: it is by deceit to induce a man to act to his injury. More tersely it may be put, that to deceive is by falsehood to induce a state of mind; to defraud is by deceit to induce a course of action."

Mr. Blom-Cooper, while not submitting that an intent to defraud necessarily includes an intent to deceive, nevertheless submitted that a man could not be defrauded unless he was deceived. Buckley J.'s definition was, he said, exhaustive and as the conspiracy charged in count one did not involve any deceit of the companies and persons who owned the copyright and the distribution rights of the films which had been copied, the conviction on that count could not, he submitted, stand.

In a great many and it may be the vast majority of fraud cases the fraud has been perpetrated by deceit and in many cases Buckley J.'s dicta have been quoted in charges to juries. It does not, however, follow that it is an exhaustive definition of what is meant by "defraud." Buckley J. had to decide when a prima facie case had been shown "of doing some or one of the acts" mentioned in sections 83 and 84 of the Larceny Act 1861 "with intent to deceive or defraud." He did not have to make or to have to attempt to make an exhaustive definition of what was meant by "defraud."

Stephen, History of the Criminal Law of England (1883), vol. 2, contains the following passage, at p. 121:

> "Fraud—There has always been a great reluctance amongst lawyers to attempt to define fraud, and this is not unnatural when we consider the number of different kinds of conduct to which the word is applied in connection with different branches of it. I shall not attempt to construct a definition which will meet every case which might be suggested, but there is little danger in saying that whenever the words 'fraud' or 'intent to defraud' or 'fraudulently' occur in the definition of a crime two elements at least are essential to the commission of the crime: namely, first, deceit or an intention to deceive or in some cases mere secrecy; and, secondly, either actual injury or possible injury or an intent to expose some person either to actual injury or to a risk of possible injury by means of that deceit or secrecy."

Stephen thus recognises that a fraud may be perpetrated without deceit by secrecy and that an intent to defraud need not necessarily involve an intent to deceive. In vol. 3 of his *History* at p. 121 he says that:

> "Offences relating to property fall into two principal classes, namely, fraudulent offences which consist in its misappropriation, and mischievous offences which consist in its destruction or injury. Theft is the typical fraudulent offence, . . ."

The definition of the common law offence of simple larceny had as one of its elements the fraudulent taking and carrying away (see *Hawkins' Pleas of the Crown*, 6th ed. (1777), Book I, p. 134; *East's Pleas of the Crown*, vol. II (1803), p. 553). "Fraudulently" is used in the definition of larceny by a bailee in section 3 of the Larceny Act 1861 (24 & 25 Vict. c. 96) and in the definition of larceny in section 1 of the Larceny Act 1916. Theft always involves dishonesty. Deceit is not an ingredient of theft. These citations suffice to show that conduct to be fraudulent need not be deceitful.

The Criminal Law Revision Committee in their Eighth Report on "Theft and Related Offences" (1966) (Cmnd. 2977) in paragraph 33 expressed the view that the important element of larceny, embezzlement and fraudulent conversion was "undoubtedly the dishonest appropriation of another person's property"; in paragraph 35 that the words "dishonestly appropriates" meant the same as "fraudulently converts to his own use or benefit, or the use or benefit of any other person," and in paragraph 39 that "dishonestly" seemed to them a better word than "fraudulently."

Parliament endorsed these views in the Theft Act 1968, which by section 1 (1) defined theft as the dishonest appropriation of property belonging to another with the intention of permanently depriving the other of it. Section 17 of that Act replaces section 82 and 83 of the Larceny Act 1861 and the Falsification of Accounts Act 1875. The offences created by those sections and by that Act made it necessary to prove that there had been an "intent to defraud." Section 17 of the Theft Act 1968 substitutes the words "dishonestly with a view to gain for himself or another or with intent to cause loss to another" for the words "intent to defraud."

If "fraudulently" in relation to larceny meant "dishonestly" and "intent to defraud" in relation to falsification of accounts is equivalent to the words now contained in section 17 of the Theft Act 1968 which I have quoted, it would indeed be odd if "defraud" in the phrase "conspiracy to defraud" has a different meaning and means only a conspiracy which is to be carried out by deceit.

In the course of the argument many cases were cited. It is not necessary to refer to all of them. Many were cases in which the conspiracy alleged was to defraud by deceit. Those cases do not establish that there can only be a conspiracy to defraud if deceit is involved and there are a number of cases where that was not the case.

In *R.* v. *Orbell* (1703) 6 Mod. Rep. 42 the indictment stated that the defendants had fraudulently and per conspirationem, to cheat J.S. of his money, got him to lay a certain sum of money upon a foot race and prevailed with the party to run "booty." No false representation was made to J.S. and he was not led to believe something to be true which was in fact false.

In *R.* v. *Button* (1848) 3 Cox C.C. 229 the defendants were charged with conspiracy to use their employers' vats and dyes to dye articles which they were not entitled to dye, to secure profits for themselves and so to defraud their employer of profit. There was no false pretence and no deceit of their employer by inducing him to believe something to be true which was false.

In *R.* v. *Yates* (1853) 6 Cox C.C. 441 the defendant was charged with conspiracy by false pretences and subtle means and devices to extort from T.E. a sovereign and to cheat and defraud him thereof. There was no evidence of any false pretence but Crompton J. held that the words "false pretences" might be rejected as surplusage and held that the defendant might be convicted of conspiracy to extort and defraud. Again, in this case, there was no deceit of T.E. inducing him to believe something to be true which was false.

In *R.* v. *De Kromme* (1892) 17 Cox C.C. 492 the defendant was indicted for soliciting a servant to conspire to cheat and defraud his master by selling his master's goods at less than their proper price. Lord Coleridge C.J. said that if the servant had sold the goods at less than their proper price, his employer would have been defrauded. The conviction was upheld. The conspiracy which the defendant was charged with inciting did not involve any deceit of the employer.

In *R.* v. *Quinn* (1898) 19 Cox C.C. 78 the defendants were convicted of conspiring to cheat and defraud the Great Northern Railway of Ireland of fares by abstracting return half tickets and selling them to members of the public. Again, there was no deceit of their employers.

In *R.* v. *Radley* (1973) 58 Cr. App. R. 394 the defendants were convicted of conspiring to defraud a company *inter alia* by stealing the property of that company. The Court of Appeal upheld their conviction and it was never suggested that the conviction was bad on the ground that no deceit of the company was involved.

Indeed, in none of these cases was it suggested that the conviction was bad on the ground that the conspiracy to defraud did not involve deceit of the person intended to be defrauded. If that had been a valid ground for quashing the conviction it is, I think, inconceivable that the point would not have been taken, if not by counsel, by the court....

In the course of delivering the judgment of the Court of Appeal in *R.* v. *Sinclair* [1968] 1 W.L.R. 1246, where the defendants had been convicted of conspiracy to cheat and defraud a company, its shareholders and creditors by fraudulently using its assets for purposes other than those of the company and by fraudulently concealing such use, James J. said at p. 1250:

> "To cheat and defraud is to act with deliberate dishonesty to the prejudice of another person's proprietary right."

Again, one finds in this case no support for the view that in order to defraud a person that person must be deceived.

One must not confuse the object of a conspiracy with the means by which it is intended to be carried out. In the light of the cases to which I have referred, I have come to the conclusion that Mr. Blom-Cooper's main contention must be rejected. I have not the temerity to attempt an exhaustive definition of the meaning of "defraud." As I have said, words take colour from the context in which they are used, but the words "fraudulently" and "defraud" must ordinarily have a very similar meaning. If as I think, and as the Criminal Law Revision Committee appears to have thought, "fraudulently" means "dishonestly," then "to defraud" ordinarily means, in my opinion, to deprive a person dishonestly of something which is his or of something to which he is or would or might but for the perpetration of the fraud be entitled. . . .

In this case the accused bribed servants of the cinema owners to secure possession of films in order to copy them and in order to enable them to let the copies out on hire. By so doing Mr. Blom-Cooper conceded they inflicted more than nominal damage to the goodwill of the owners of the copyright and distribution rights of the films. By so doing they secured for themselves profits which but for their actions might have been secured by those owners just as in *R.* v. *Button* the defendants obtained profits which might have been secured by their employer. In the circumstances it is, I think, clear that they inflicted pecuniary loss on those owners.

Appeal dismissed

R. v. Allsop (1977) 64 Cr. App. R. 29 (a conspiracy case): *per* Shaw L.J. at pp. 31, 32: "Generally the primary objective of fraudsmen is to advantage themselves. The detriment which results to their victims is secondary to that purpose and is incidental. It is 'intended' only in the sense that it is a contemplated outcome of the fraud that is perpetrated. If the deceit which is employed imperils the economic interest of the person deceived, this is sufficient to constitute fraud even though in the event no actual loss is suffered and notwithstanding that the deceiver did not desire to bring about actual loss. . . . Interests which are imperilled are less valuable in terms of money than those same interests when they are secure and protected. Where a person intends by deceit to induce a course of conduct in another which puts that other's economic interests in jeopardy, he is guilty of fraud even though he does not intend or desire that actual loss should ultimately be suffered by that other in this context."

Questions

1. A, employed on commission by B, agreed with others to lie to B to induce B to take on greater business, with greater profits to B and thus greater commission to A. Is he guilty of conspiracy to defraud?

2. A and B, company directors, agree not to tell the shareholders of a dealing which brings profits to A and B, and which the shareholders have a right to be told of, so that they can claim the profits from A and B. A and B (rightly) believe that no shareholder will object to being kept in the dark or will wish to claim the profits. Are they guilty of conspiracy to defraud? (See *Tarling* v. *Government of Singapore* (1978) 70 Cr. App. R. 77, *per* Lord Salmon, at p. 132).

Note

An agreement to deceive a public official to breach his duty is a conspiracy to defraud: *D.P.P.* v. *Withers* [1975] A.C. 842.

Knuller v. D.P.P.
[1973] A.C. 435
House of Lords

The accused were directors of a company which published an "underground" magazine called *IT*. It contained advertisements by homosexuals inviting others to meet them for the purpose of homosexual practices. The charge consisted of two counts: (i) conspiracy to corrupt public morals and (ii) conspiracy to outrage public decency. The accused having been convicted on both counts, they appealed, ultimately to the House of Lords.

Lord Simon of Glaisdale: My Lords, Count 1: *Conspiracy to Corrupt Public Morals* ... In *Shaw* v. *D.P.P.* [1962] A.C. 220 your Lordships' House, dismissing an appeal from the Court of Criminal Appeal, upheld a conviction on a count of conspiracy to corrupt public morals; and in so doing established as a matter of law "that such an offence is known to the common law" (Viscount Simonds at p. 266). In that case the conspiracy consisted of an agreement to publish a pamphlet (entitled "The Ladies' Directory") in which female prostitutes advertised their various sexual services. In the course of the speeches in that case Viscount Simonds said, at p. 268:

> "Let it be supposed that at some future, perhaps, early, date homosexual practices between adult consenting males are no longer a crime. Would it not be an offence if, even without obscenity, such practices were publicly advocated and encouraged by pamphlet and advertisement? Or must we wait until Parliament finds time to deal with such conduct? I say, my Lords, that if the common law is powerless in such event, then we should no longer do her reverence."

and Lord Tucker said, at p. 285:

> "Suppose Parliament tomorrow enacts that homosexual practices between adult consenting males is no longer to be criminal, is it to be said that a conspiracy to further and encourage such practices amongst adult males should not be the subject of a criminal charge fit to be left to a jury?"

Lord Morris of Borth-y-Gest (p. 291) and Lord Hodson (p. 292) expressly agreed with the speeches of Viscount Simonds and Lord Tucker. But the passages I have just cited were obiter. Obiter dicta are a source of law, though not a compelling source in the way that the ratio decidendi of a case is within the doctrine of precedent; and the Court of Appeal in the instant case naturally attached importance to the dicta I have cited coming from the sources they did and concurred in as they were. However, the trial judge in the instant case did not direct the jury with reference to these passages; but left it at large to the jury to determine on the evidence whether a conspiracy to corrupt public morals had been proved. One of the advertisements ran: "Young gay [i.e., homosexual] male desperately needs to earn £40 as soon as possible. Will do anything legal. Genuine replies only please." In its context this could hardly be read as other than an offer of sexual prostitution; it differs from the advertisements in "The Ladies' Directory" only in that it was apparently made by a male rather than a female. Another of the advertisements in the instant case ran: "Young dolly boy seeks sugar daddy. Photo appreciated."

It was at one stage argued before your Lordships on behalf of the appellants that the Sexual Offences Act 1967 had as regards the instant case abrogated the decision in *Shaw* v. *D.P.P.* or had made the instant case distinguishable from it. Section 1 (1) of the Sexual Offences Act 1967 reads:

> "Notwithstanding any statutory or common law provision, but subject to the provisions of the next following section, a homosexual act in private shall not be an offence provided that the parties consent thereto and have attained the age of 21 years."

("The next following section" provided that homosexual acts between members of the crews of United Kingdom merchant ships should continue to be offences.) The argument for the appellants based on the Sexual Offences Act 1967, was twofold: first, that the words "Notwithstanding any . . . common law provision," were inserted in order to refer to the common law offence of conspiracy to corrupt public morals by an agreement to encourage or facilitate private homosexual acts between male persons over 21—i.e., in order to overrule the decision in *Shaw* v. *D.P.P.* pro tanto; secondly, and alternatively, that, Parliament having sanctioned such conduct, it could not be a conspiracy to corrupt public morals to agree to encourage or facilitate it.

[After rejecting the first argument.] As for the second argument . . . although Parliament decided that homosexual acts in private between persons over the age of 21 should no longer be offences either at common law or by statute, it does not appear that Parliament was even neutral in its attitude towards such conduct. In the first place, there is the exception of homosexual acts in merchant ships to which I have already referred. In the second place, notwithstanding the recommendation of the Wolfenden Committee on which the statute was founded (Cmnd. No. 247 of 1957), the Act did not extend to Scotland. In the third place, by section 4 it continues to be an offence for A to procure a male B to commit buggery or an act of gross indecency with a male C, notwithstanding that both B and C are consenting adults over 21 years of age and that the act is in private . . . It is, in my view, impossible to spell out of the Sexual Offences Act 1967 any indication that Parliament regarded the sort of conduct which was the subject-matter of the indictment in the instant case as no longer susceptible of corruption of public morals.

In the end counsel for the appellants abandoned any argument that the instant case was distinguishable from *Shaw* v. *D.P.P.* either by reason of the Sexual Offences Act 1967, or otherwise; and rested his case on the contention that your Lordships should decline to follow *Shaw* v. *D.P.P.* He did not traverse the field of the case law which was closely covered in the speeches in *Shaw* v. *D.P.P.* but rather argued that it was objectionable that our law should recognise any such offence as conspiracy to corrupt public morals. I do not myself find it necessary for judgment in this appeal to express any opinion whether the decision in *Shaw* v. *D.P.P.* was (in an abstract juridical sense) "correct in law" or as to its desirability. In my view, the appeal turns on how far your Lordships are justified in altering the law as previously established.

The sanction for your Lordships' departure from a rule of law laid down by a previous decision of your Lordships' House rests on an announcement made on July 26, 1966, by Lord Gardiner L.C. with the approval of all the Lords of Appeal in Ordinary at that time [*Practice Statement (Judicial Precedent)* [1966] 1 W.L.R. 1234] . . .

[The] terms were as follows:

> "Their Lordships regard the use of precedent as an indispensable foundation upon which to decide what is the law and its application to individual cases. It provides at least some degree of certainty upon which individuals can rely in the conduct of their affairs, as well as a basis for orderly development of legal rules.
>
> "Their Lordships nevertheless recognise that too rigid adherence to precedent may lead to injustice in a particular case and also unduly restrict the proper development of the law. They propose, therefore, to modify their

> present practice and, while treating former decisions of this House as normally binding, to depart from a previous decision when it appears right to do so.
>
> "In this connection they will bear in mind the danger of disturbing retrospectively the basis on which contracts, settlements of property and fiscal arrangements have been entered into and also the especial need for certainty as to the criminal law.
>
> "This announcement is not intended to affect the use of precedent elsewhere than in this House."

I draw particular attention to the words "the especial need for certainty as to the criminal law."...

But it was argued for the appellants that *Shaw* v. *D.P.P.* itself introduced uncertainty into the law; that overruling it would introduce a greater certainty; so that your Lordships would not be thereby offending against the limitations of the declaration of July 26, 1966. It was urged, in particular, that leaving it at large to the jury to say whether the conduct alleged is corrupting of public morals involves that no one can know until a particular jury returns its verdict whether or not an offence has been committed; whereas certainty in law demands that any citizen should know in advance whether a contemplated course of conduct offends against the law. To this argument there are, I think, two answers. First, this sort of certainty cannot be vouchsafed by a system of law such as ours which depends in so many of its rules on the finding by a tribunal of fact whether the conduct in question viewed as a whole has reached a certain standard or degree —frequently the standard of the reasonable man. Secondly, the type of certainty alleged to be wanting as a result of the decision in *Shaw* v. *D.P.P.* was not the type of certainty referred to in the declaration of July 26, 1966.

Certainty is a desirable feature of any system of law. But there are some types of conduct desirably the subject-matter of legal rule which cannot be satisfactorily regulated by specific statutory enactment, but are better left to the practice of juries and other tribunals of fact. They depend finally for their juridical classification not upon proof of the existence of some particular fact, but upon proof of the attainment of some degree. The law cannot always say that if fact X and fact Y are proved (both of which will generally be known not only to the tribunal of adjudication, but also, in advance, to the persons involved) legal result Z will ensue. Often the law can only say that if conduct of a stipulated standard is attained (or, more often, is not attained) legal result Z will ensue; and whether that standard has been attained cannot be with certainty known in advance by the persons involved, but has to await the evaluation of the tribunal of fact. This is, indeed, so characteristic a feature of English law that examples, even though drawn from many different spheres of jurisprudence, give an inadequate impression of how pervasive it is. Has an act been done, or a contract performed, or a duty discharged, within a reasonable time? Are goods reasonably fit for a particular purpose?... Has the defendant so conducted himself that a reasonable person would assume that he was making a representation of fact meant to be acted on?... Has A exercised proper care for the safety of those to whom the law says he owes a duty of care (the standard varying according to the legal relationship of the persons in question)? Had B reasonable and probable cause for arresting C, or preferring a prosecution against him? What sum is required to compensate D for the injuries he has suffered? Has reasonable notice to quit been given? Has consent to assignment been unreasonably withheld? Is the proposed assignee a proper and responsible person?... Has a testator made reasonable provision for a dependant; and, if not, what would be reasonable provision?... Has one spouse behaved in such a way that the other cannot reasonably be expected to continue in cohabitation? For the purpose of a charge to tax in respect of shortfall in distribution by a close company, how much was necessary or advisable for the maintenance and development of the business? . . . Has an employer complied with the manifold requirements of the Factories Acts so far as is reasonably practicable? What is reasonable overtime in industrial law? For the purpose of the Regulations for Preventing Collisions at Sea, was there in general due regard to the observance of good seamanship? Was the vessel proceeding at a moderate speed? Was a proper look-out being maintained? Is it just and equitable that a company should be wound up or a partnership dissolved? Is a trade mark likely to cause confusion? . . .

The law does not return an answer in advance to any of these questions, which arise both at common law and under statute: all must await the answer of the tribunal. They could be almost indefinitely multiplied.

Nor are such situations limited to civil law. . . . Whether conduct causing death falls so far short of a proper duty of care as to amount to manslaughter cannot be known until the jury returns its verdict. . . . The driver of a motor vehicle may be accompanied by leading and junior counsel and by his solicitor as well; but he will still not know whether or not he has committed the offence of driving in a manner dangerous to the public or without due care and attention or without reasonable consideration for others or at an excessive speed until jury or justices so find. . . . Similarly with those many offences which depend on whether admitted conduct was perpetrated dishonestly. Again, did the accused convene an assembly in such a manner as to cause reasonable people to fear a breach of the peace? Did the alleged blackmailer have reasonable grounds for making the demand and was the use of menaces a proper means of reinforcing it? (Theft Act 1968, section 21.) Was it a public mischief that the accused conspired to effect? Did the accused publish an article or perform a theatrical play which had a tendency to deprave or corrupt? If so, was its publication or performance nevertheless on balance for the public good by reason of any of the matters set out in section 4 of the Obscene Publications Act 1959 or section 3 of the Theatres Act 1968? In none of these cases, which again could be greatly multiplied, can it in advance be said with certainty whether an offence has been committed: and those who choose, in such situations, to sail as close as possible to the wind inevitably run some risk.

But, in any case, the type of "uncertainty" invoked by the appellants is not that with which the declaration of July 26, 1966 was concerned. The context was the doctrine of precedent. The declaration was, in other words, concerned with that certainty which comes from following rules of law already judicially determined, not with any such certainty as many come from the abrogation of those judicially determined rules of law which involve issues of fact and degree. *Shaw* v. *D.P.P.* laid down with certainty that the offence of conspiracy to corrupt public morals was part of our criminal law. Parliament, in the Theatres Act 1968, recognised that this had been so established. A number of persons have been prosecuted and convicted on this basis. It was not contended that the rule had led to any injustice.

But over and above the limitations constitutionally imposed by the terms and context of the declaration of July 26, 1966, there are three additional features in the instant case which render it particularly undesirable, in my respectful submission, for your Lordships to depart from the decision in *Shaw* v. *D.P.P.* In the first place, your Lordships are concerned with highly controversial issues, on which there is every sign that neither public nor parliamentary opinion is settled. It is a matter of high debate how far the law should concern itself at all with "morality." The ambivalence in society's attitude towards homosexualism is sufficiently indicated by the provisions of the Sexual Offences Act 1967 to which I have already drawn attention. Nor has the decision itself in *Shaw* v. *D.P.P.* lacked critics and champions. Of course, courts of law do not shrink from decisions which are liable to be controversial when judicial duty demands such decisions. But your Lordships are here in a field where the decisions—at any rate, policy decisions—are better left to Parliament, if such is possible. Certainly, it is the sort of matter in which it is most undesirable that there should be, in effect, an appeal from one Appellate Committee of your Lordships' House to another. In default of any decision by Parliament to reverse the judgment in *Shaw* v. *D.P.P.* the determination in particular cases is in the hands of that microcosm of democratic society, the jury.

A second particular reason why this is, over and above constitutional convention, in my view an unsuitable issue for the exercise of your Lordships' law-making powers is that there have been several occasions when Parliament itself had the opportunity, had it wished to avail itself of it, to abrogate the decision in *Shaw* v. *D.P.P.*; the Obscene Publications Act 1964 . . . the Sexual Offences Act 1967, and the Criminal Law Act 1968. As my noble and learned friend, Lord Reid, said in *Shaw* v. *D.P.P.* [1962] A.C. 22), 275: "Where Parliament fears to tread it is not for the courts to rush in."

Thirdly, virtually all the objections which have been advanced against the offence of conspiracy to corrupt public morals are equally applicable to the offence of conspiracy to effect a public mischief. . . . It would hardly be possible to reconsider *Shaw* v. *D.P.P.* without also reconsidering the offence of conspiracy to effect a public mischief.[1] . . .

It follows, in my view, that your Lordships should follow *Shaw* v. *D.P.P.* on the matter as to which it constituted a direct authority—namely, that the offence of conspiracy to corrupt public morals is part of the criminal law of England. But there are certain other matters which either appear in that case as obiter dicta or which have been ascribed to the decision (in my view, unnecessarily and wrongly) to which I would wish to refer. First, there are some expressions in the majority speeches which indicate that not only was the offence of conspiracy to corrupt public morals established as a matter of continuous legal history in English law, but also that it was desirable that this should be so. I do not think that those expressions of view were necessary for the decision. Although courts of law are sometimes faced with making policy decisions (in the sense that there is sometimes a choice to be made between two tenable views of the law), I have already indicated that I think that in the instant field they should if possible be avoided and rather left to Parliament. Secondly, there are some suggestions in the speeches in *Shaw* v. *D.P.P.* that the courts have still some role to play in the way of general superintendence of morals. This was a phrase used in various 18th- and 19th-century cases, "superintendence of" meaning "jurisdiction over." Whatever may have been the position in the 18th century—and there is more than one clear indication that the courts of common law then assumed that they were fitted for and bound to exercise such a role—I do not myself believe that such is any part of their present function. As will appear, I do not think that "conspiracy to corrupt public morals" invites a general tangling with codes of morality. Thirdly, in this connection, it has been suggested that the speeches in *Shaw* v. *D.P.P.* indicated that the courts retain a residual power to create new offences. I do not think they did so. Certainly, it is my view that the courts have no more power to create new offences than they have to abolish those already established in the law; both tasks are for Parliament. What the courts can and should do (as was truly laid down in *Shaw* v. *D.P.P.*) is to recognise the applicability of established offences to new circumstances to which they are relevant. Fourthly, I have already indicated my view that *Shaw* v. *D.P.P.* is not authority for the proposition that male homosexualism, or even its facilitation or encouragement, are themselves as a matter of law corrupting of public morals. It is for the jury to decide as a

[1] Nevertheless the matter was reconsidered in *D.P.P.* v. *Withers* [1975] A.C. 842, when it was held that a conspiracy to effect a public mischief was an offence unknown to the law.

matter of fact whether the conduct alleged to be the subject-matter of the conspiracy charged is in any particular case corrupting of public morals. Lastly, it was suggested in argument before your Lordships that, if *Shaw* v. *D.P.P.* were not overruled, it would be open to juries to convict if they thought that the conduct in question was liable to "lead morally astray." But all that was decided in *Shaw* v. *D.P.P.* was that, in the general context of the whole of the summing up in that case, the use of the phrase "lead morally astray" was not a misdirection. *Shaw* v. *D.P.P.* must not be taken as an authority that "corrupt public morals" and "lead morally astray" are interchangeable expressions. On the contrary, "corrupt" is a strong word. The Book of Common Prayer, following the Gospel, has "... where rust and moth doth corrupt." The words "corrupt public morals" suggest conduct which a jury might find to be destructive of the very fabric of society.

Having scrutinised the summing up in the instant case in the light of the foregoing reservations, in my view there was no misdirection; the conviction on count 1 must be upheld; and the appeal on this part of the case dismissed.

Count 2: Conspiracy to Outrage Public Decency

... At a late stage in his reply counsel [for the appellants] accepted the suggestion that there was no such offence known to the common law; there were merely certain specific offences violating public decency which were not applications of any more general class—namely, keeping a disorderly house, mounting an indecent exhibition and indecent exposure. Apart from his arguments on law, counsel argued that the jury was insufficiently directed as to the necessary element of publicity, and that the Court of Appeal was wrong in holding that the facts proved established sufficient publicity to constitute the offence.

The following questions, therefore, arise on this part of the case: (1) is there a general common law offence of outraging public decency, or only the particular offences which the cases establish? (2) Is there a common law offence of conspiring to outrage public decency? (3) If (1) or (2) are answered in the affirmative, are they inapplicable to newspapers or books either (a) because they have never been so applied, or (b) because of section 2 (3) of the Obscene Publications Act 1959? (4) If (1) or (2) are answered in the affirmative, what are the requirements of the law as to publicity in order for the offence(s) to be established? In particular, is there sufficient publicity if either (a) the object in question is not seen simultaneously by more than one person, but only by one at a time, or (b) it is on the inside of a newspaper or book? (5) Do any other ingredients of the offence(s) (if they exist) need emphasis? (6) Was the direction to the jury on this part of the case misleading or inadequate?

(1) It is, in general, the difference between mature and rudimentary legal systems that the latter deal specifically with a number of particular and unrelated instances, whereas the former embody the law in comprehensive, cohesive and rational general rules. The law is then easier to understand and commands a greater respect. Fragmentation, on the other hand, leads to anomalous (and therefore inequitable) distinctions and to hedging legal rules round with technicalities that are only within the understanding of an esoteric class. The general development of English law (like that of other mature systems) has been towards the co-ordination of particular instances into comprehensive and comprehensible general rules. The evolution of the compendious tort of negligence from a number of disparate forms of action is a well-known example from the common law: the Theft Act 1968 may be regarded as a statutory counterpart. (I must, however, add the rider that English law has never felt bound to carry every rule to its logical conclusion in the face of convenience.) But the common law proceeds generally by distilling from a particular case the legal principle on which it is decided, and that legal principle is then generally applied to the circumstances of other cases to which the principle is relevant as they arise before the courts. As

Parke B, said, giving the advice of the judges to your Lordships' House on *Mirehouse* v. *Rennell* (1833) 1 Cl. & F. 527, 546 . . .:

> "Our common law system consists in the applying to new combinations of circumstances those rules of law which we derive from legal principles and judicial precedents; and for the sake of attaining uniformity, consistency and certainty, we must apply those rules, where they are not plainly unreasonable or inconvenient, to all cases which arise; and we are not at liberty to reject them, and to abandon all analogy to them, in those to which they have not yet been judicially applied, because we think that the rules are not as convenient and reasonable as we ourselves could have devised."

Secondly, the decided cases look odd standing on their own. Indecent exposure (*R.* v. *Crunden* (1809) 2 Camp. 89), acts of sexual indecency in public (*R.* v. *Mayling* [1963] 2 Q.B. 717), indecent words (*R.* v. *Saunders* (1875) 1 Q.B.D. 15), disinterring a corpse (*R.* v. *Lynn* (1788) 2 Durn. & E. 733), selling a wife (cited in *R.* v. *Delaval* (1763) 3 Burr. 1434, 1438), exhibiting deformed children (*Herring* v. *Walround* (1681) 2 Chan. Cas. 110), exhibiting a picture of sores (*R.* v. *Grey* (1864) 4 F. & F. 73), procuring a girl apprentice to be taken out of the custody of her master for the purpose of prostitution (*R.* v. *Delaval*: see also count 4 in *R.* v. *Howell and Bentley* (1864) 4 F. & F. 160, 161, conspiracy to procure a girl of 17 to become a common prostitute)—all these have been held to be offences. They have a common element in that, in each, offence against public decency was alleged to be an ingredient of the crime (except *Grey*, where it was said to be "disgusting and offensive," "so disgusting that it is calculated to turn the stomach"); but otherwise they are widely disparate; this suggests that they are particular applications of a general rule whereby conduct which outrages public decency is a common law offence. Even keeping a disorderly house can be considered a manifestation of conduct which outrages public decency. (The alternative is to regard all as manifestations of public nuisance.)

Thirdly, in *R.* v. *Delaval*, (the case of the female apprentice) the court proceeded on the basis that *R.* v. *Sidley* (1663) *sub nom. Sir Charles Sidley's Case*, 1 Sid 168 (where the accused stood naked on a balcony and urinated on the crowd below) and *R.* v. *Curl* (1727) 2 Str. 788 (obscene and indecent libel) were precedents (they had both "been guilty of offences against good manners" (3 Burr. 1434, 1439)): this strongly suggests a general class embracing all three decisions, rather than a number of isolated instances . . .

I would add, lastly, that, subject to the riders to which I refer later, it does not seem to me to be exorbitant to demand of the law that reasonable people should be able to venture into public without their sense of decency being outraged.

I think that the authorities establish a common law offence of conduct which outrages public decency.

(2) If there is a common law offence of conduct which outrages public decency, a conspiracy to outrage public decency is also a common law offence, as an agreement to do an illegal act. In *Shaw* v. *D.P.P.* . . . Viscount Simonds seems to have considered that the conduct there in question was indictable also as a conspiracy "to affront public decency." . . .

(3) As for whether such an offence is applicable to books and newspapers, the argument based on section 2 (4) of the Obscene Publications Act 1959 is concluded against the appellants by the construction put upon that subsection in *Shaw* v. *D.P.P.* . . .

(4) I turn, then, to the requirement of publicity. *R.* v. *Mayling* shows that the substantive offence (and therefore the conduct the subject of the conspiracy) must be committed in public, in the sense that the circumstances must be such that the alleged outrageously indecent matter could have been seen by more than

one person, even though in fact no more than one did see it. If it is capable of being seen by one person only, no offence is committed.

It was at one time argued for the appellants that the matter must have been visible to two or more people simultaneously; and that an article in a newspaper did not fulfil this requirement. But this point was rightly abandoned, and I need not examine it further.

It was argued for the Crown that it was immaterial whether or not the alleged outrage to decency took place in public, provided that the sense of decency of the public or a substantial section of the public was outraged. But this seems to me to be contrary to many of the authorities which the Crown itself relied on to establish the generic offence. The authorities establish that the word "public" has a different connotation in the respective offences of conspiracy to corrupt public morals and conduct calculated to, or conspiracy to, outrage public decency. In the first it refers to certain fundamental rules regarded as essential social control which yet lack the force of law: when applicable to individuals, in other words, "public" refers to persons in society. In the latter offences, however, "public" refers to the place in which the offence is committed. This is borne out by the way the rule was framed by my noble and learned friend, Lord Reid, in *Shaw* v. *D.P.P.* It is also borne out by what is presumably the purpose of the legal rule—namely, that reasonable people may venture out in public without the risk of outrage to certain minimum accepted standards of decency.

On the other hand, I do not think that it would necessarily negative the offence that the act or exhibit is superficially hid from view, if the public is expressly or impliedly invited to penetrate the cover. Thus, the public touting for an outrageously indecent exhibition in private would not escape: see *R.* v. *Saunders.* Another obvious example is an outrageously indecent exhibit with a cover entitled "Lift in order to see . . ." This sort of instance could be applied to a book or newspaper; and I think that a jury should be invited to consider the matter in this way. The conduct must at least in some way be so projected as to have an impact in public: *cf. Smith* v. *Hughes* [1960] 1 W.L.R. 830.

(5) There are other features of the offence which should, in my view, be brought to the notice of the jury. It should be emphasised that "outrage," like "corrupt," is a very strong word. "Outraging public decency" goes considerably beyond offending the susceptibilities of, or even shocking, reasonable people. Moreover the offence is, in my view, concerned with recognised minimum standards of decency, which are likely to vary from time to time. Finally, notwithstanding that "public" in the offence is used in a locative sense, public decency must be viewed as a whole; and I think the jury should be invited, where appropriate, to remember that they live in a plural society, with a tradition of tolerance towards minorities, and that this atmosphere of toleration is itself part of public decency.

(6) The Court of Appeal said of the direction on count 2 that it might be that it was not wholly satisfactory. I would myself go further. I regard it as essential that the jury should be carefully directed, on the lines that I have ventured to suggest, on the proper approach to the meaning of "decency" and "outrage" and the element of publicity required to constitute the offence. The summing up was generally a careful and fair one, but I think it was defective in these regards; and I therefore do not think it would be safe to allow the conviction on count 2 to stand.

[Lord Diplock dissented on count 1, Lord Morris on count 2. Lords Reid and Diplock thought that conspiracy to outrage public decency was not an offence known to the law.]

Appeal Dismissed on Count 1. Allowed on Count 2

vi. Statutory Conspiracies

See section 1 (1) of the Criminal Law Act 1977 (*ante*, p. 332).

Notes

1. The object of the subsection plainly is to see to it that (apart from conspiracies to defraud or to corrupt public morals or outrage public decency) nothing is a conspiracy unless the parties agreed to commit a crime. The subsection, which has not yet been judicially passed on, is not well drafted and appears to need very liberal interpretation if it is to confine conspiracy to what was intended by the Law Commission (Law Com. No. 76, § 1.113).

2. *"If a person agrees with any other person that a course of conduct shall be pursued which will necessarily amount to the commission of any offence."* It seems that "course of conduct" must be construed to mean not only the *acts* contemplated by the parties but also the results looked for by them and the circumstances known or believed in or hoped for by them. This is because, on the statutory wording, what is agreed must *necessarily* result in a crime. Since in life few things are inevitable, the contemplated crime might not be produced by the agreed-on acts. *E.g.* A and B agree to shoot at C, hoping to kill him. If "course of conduct" means firing guns towards C, A and B could object that pursuing this course of conduct will not necessarily result in murder, because they might miss C or only wound him. Yet they must surely be guilty of conspiracy to murder. If the whole agreement was carried out in accordance with their intentions, C would be killed and it would be murder. The same would appear to be true of circumstances. If A and B agree to handle goods which they know to be stolen, it may be that by the time they handle them, the goods will have ceased to be stolen goods. They cannot be allowed to object that they did not conspire to handle merely because it is possible that the circumstances may change.[1]

3. *"If the agreement is carried out in accordance with their intentions."* This must mean in accordance with their *joint* intention, otherwise an innocent party would be guilty merely because the other party intends a crime. *E.g.* A asks B to set fire to some bracken in which A knows that C is lying hidden. B, not knowing of the presence of C, agrees. If B does what he has agreed to do, and C is killed, A will be guilty of homicide (although B will not). On a strict reading of the subsection, by agreeing to do what will be a crime by A, B is guilty of conspiracy to murder or to unlawfully kill C. But it cannot be said it was part of *B*'s intention that C should be killed: and it is inconceivable that B could be guilty of conspiracy to commit murder. (It would follow that A would not be guilty of conspiracy to murder either; but he would be guilty of attempt, through an innocent agent.)

4. If one party does not know of a circumstance which makes the contemplated result a crime, he cannot be guilty of conspiring to commit that crime. Section 1 (2) declares this, if the *crime* is one which can be committed without knowledge of the circumstances (*i.e.* a crime of strict liability as to that circumstance). Nothing is said about agreements to commit crimes of full *mens rea*, so that it may be argued that with these crimes, ignorance of a circumstance making the agreed-on result criminal

[1] Even if circumstances *did* change in fact and it became impossible to handle stolen goods, that would not, at common law, prevent a conviction of conspiracy to handle stolen goods: see *Haughton* v. *Smith* [1975] A.C. 476, *per* Lord Hailsham, at p. 489.

is no excuse, if the other party knew and would therefore commit the crime if he carried out the agreement. But it is thought that this paradox cannot have been intended, and that section 1 (2) is merely put in to remove all doubt, to emphasize that even with a crime of strict liability, an unknowing party is not a conspirator. *A fortiori* with a *mens rea* crime.

(See Smith and Hogan, pp. 219 *et seq.*: Williams, *Textbook*, Chap. 15, §§ 7, 8).

5. The enactment of the Criminal Attempts Act 1981 afforded an opportunity to clear up these obscurities in section 1 (1) of the Criminal Law Act 1977. The Law Commission used the opportunity to propose amendments on conspiracies to do the impossible, as to which see below, but made no other proposals to amend section 1 (1). See Glanville Williams' draft section below.

vii. Conspiracies to do the Impossible

1. On the position at common law, see *D.P.P.* v. *Nock* [1978] A.C. 979 (Law Com. No. 102, § 2.65, *ante*, p. 319). The Law Commission decided that problems of impossibility in conspiracy were so similar to those in attempts that proposals for conspiracy should be parallel to those made for attempts: Law Com. No. 102, § 3.8 (see § 2.100, *ante*, p. 325, for their policy on impossible attempts). Their amendments to section 1 of the Criminal Law Act (effected by section 5 of the Criminal Attempts Act) consist in effect in the addition of subsection 1 (*b*) (*ante*, p. 332) and are much shorter than either what was proposed or what was enacted for impossible attempts. (See Draft Bill, Clause 1, *ante*, p. 325, and section 1 of the Criminal Attempts Act, *ante*, p. 303).

2. A comprehensive recasting of section 1 of the Criminal Law Act, taking account of both the impossibility difficulties and the relevant problems in that section as originally drafted (see Notes 2–4, *ante*, p. 358) was proposed by Glanville Williams *(1981) N.L.J. 80, 130*:

"(1) Subject to the following provisions of this Part of this Act, if a person agrees with any other person or persons that an offence or offences shall be committed by one or more of the parties to the agreement, he is guilty of conspiracy to commit the offence or offences in question.

(2) A person shall be guilty of a conspiracy to commit an offence by virtue of subsection (1) above if and only if he and at least one other party to the agreement intends, knows, believes, hopes or has no substantial doubt that—

(a) (where a result is specified in the offence) the result will occur, and
(b) (where a fact is specified in the offence as being present or absent) the fact is or will be present or absent as the case may be. 'Specified in the offence' means specified in the definition of the offence or in any defence allowed by law.

(2A) Subsection (2) above applies whether or not an offence which is the object of the conspiracy requires proof of knowledge of a fact or of the non-existence of a fact.

(2B) It is immaterial to a charge of conspiracy under subsection (1) above that the existence or non-existence of any facts renders the commission of the offence impossible.

(2C) A person cannot be convicted of conspiring to commit an offence if, owing to his mistake of law, he wrongly believes that what he is conspiring to do will, when he succeeds, amount to that offence."

3. INCITEMENT

Notes

1. Counselling a crime which is not committed does not make the counsellor an aider and abettor in the counselled crime: *R.* v. *Gregory* (1867) L.R. 1 C.C.R. 77; but the counsellor is guilty of the offence of incitement. "But it is argued, that a mere intent to commit evil is not indictable, without an act done; but is there not an act done, when it is charged that the defendant solicited another to commit a felony? The solicitation is an act": *per* Lord Kenyon C.J. in *R.* v. *Higgins* (1801) 2 East 5.

2. The solicitation is an act by the incitor: but no act at all is required from the incitee. "It matters not that no steps have been taken towards the commission of the attempt or of the substantive offence. It matters not, in other words, whether the incitement had any effect at all. It is merely the incitement or the attempting to incite which constitutes the offence": *per* Lord Widgery C.J. in *R.* v. *Assistant Recorder of Kingston-upon-Hull* [1969] 2 Q.B. 58.

3. Attempting to incite occurs when the solicitation (*e.g.* in a letter) does not reach the mind of the incitee: see *R.* v. *Ransford* (1874) 13 Cox 9. An incitement made by A to B to commit a crime necessarily involved inciting B to conspire with A, an attempt by A to conspire with B, and an attempt by A to counsel or procure an offence by B. These three offences, being redundant, have been abolished: see section 5 (7) of the Criminal Law Act 1977; section 1 (4) of the Criminal Attempts Act 1981, *ante*, p. 303). A's incitement cannot ordinarily involve an attempt by him to commit the substantive crime. Incitement requires that B, the incitee, must know he is being asked to commit a crime (see *R.* v. *Curr* below). If B knows, it follows that the actual attempt at the crime is to be done by him and A's urging is not more than merely preparatory. A's urging may well be more than merely preparatory if B is innocent (see *D.P.P.* v. *Stonehouse*, Law Com. No. 102, § 243, *ante*, p. 311), but B's innocence means that there is no incitement by A.

R. v. Most (1881) 7 Q.B.D. 244 (C.C.C.R.): M. published in London an article in a newspaper urging readers in foreign countries to assassinate their Heads of State. *Held*, incitement to murder under section 4 of the Offences Against the Person Act 1861.

Race Relations Board v. Applin [1973] Q.B. 815, 825 (C.A.): A. sent a circular to W.'s neighbours, complaining about W.'s taking coloured foster children. His object was to get W. to take white foster children only. The question was whether this was an incitement of W. to do an unlawful act under the Race Relations Act 1968. Lord Denning M.R.: "[It was suggested] that to 'incite' means to urge or spur on by advice, encouragement or persuasion, and not otherwise. I do not think the word is so limited, at any rate in the present context. A person may 'incite' another to do an act by threatening or by pressure, as well as by persuasion." A. had therefore incited W.

Invicta Plastics v. Clare [1976] R.T.R. 251 (Div. Ct.): I.P. advertised for sale a device which was not illegal to own, but was illegal to operate without a licence, which was unlikely to be given. The device, when operated by a car driver, gave him warning when a police radar trap was set. *Held*, approving Lord Denning's remarks in *Applin's* case (above), I.P. incited readers of the advertisement to commit an offence under the Wireless Telegraphy Act 1949.

R. v. Curr
[1968] 2 Q.B. 944
Court of Appeal

> Curr lent money and in return took as security family allowance vouchers which the borrower signed for him. He got another woman to cash these vouchers for him at a Post Office. He was charged with (*inter alia*) soliciting this woman to commit a summary offence under section 9 (*b*) of the Family Allowances Act 1945 (see below). Curr appealed against his conviction at quarter sessions.

FENTON ATKINSON J.: The facts shortly were these, that he was in fact a trafficker in family allowance books. His method was to approach some married woman who had a large family of children and lend her money on the security of her family allowance book. A woman would borrow from him, let us say, £6, and would sign three of the vouchers in her family allowance book to the value of, let us say £9, and hand over the book to him as security. He then had a team of women agents whom he sent out to cash the vouchers, and he would pocket the proceeds in repayment of the loans and thereafter return the books.... He agreed quite frankly that he knew he was not legally entitled to receive these payments, and that it could be risky....

Count 3 was of soliciting the commission of a summary offence contrary to section 9 (b) of the Act of 1945.... Mr. Kershaw (for Curr) took a preliminary point on that count that incitement to commit a summary offence is not in fact an indictable offence, and he referred to some old authorities which might lend some countenance to that view. But it appears to this court that Parliament in the Magistrates' Courts Act, 1952, in paragraph 20 of Schedule I, has in fact recognised incitement of this kind as an indictable offence, and it is not necessary, therefore, to go further into that matter, all the more because Mr. Kershaw's main point is this, that the offence the commission of which the defendant is said to have solicited is not an absolute statutory offence, but it is one requiring knowledge on the part of the female agent that she is doing something unlawful in receiving the allowance.

Section 9 is headed "Penalty for obtaining or receiving payment wrongfully," and provides:

> "If any person—... (b) obtains or receives any such sum as on account of an allowance, either as in that person's own right or as on behalf of another, knowing that it was not properly payable, or not properly receivable by him or her; that person shall be liable on summary conviction to imprisonment for a term not exceeding three months or to a fine not exceeding fifty pounds ..."

Mr. Kershaw's argument was that if the woman agent in fact has no guilty knowledge, knowing perhaps nothing of the assignment, or supposing that the defendant was merely collecting for the use and benefit of the woman concerned, then she would be an innocent agent, and by using her services in that way the defendant would be committing the summary offence himself, but would not be inciting her to receive money knowing that it was not receivable by her. He contends that it was essential to prove, to support this charge, that the woman agent in question . . . knew that the allowances were not properly receivable by her. [Counsel for the Crown's] answer to that submission was that the woman agent must be presumed to know the law, and if she knew the law, she must have known, he contends, that the allowance was not receivable by her. . . .

The argument is that in no other circumstances [than those set out in the book, *e.g.* during illness] may an agent lawfully collect for the use and benefit of the book holder. . . .

In our view the prosecution argument here gives no effect to the word "knowing" in section 9 (b), and in our view the defendant could only be guilty on count 3 if the woman solicited, that is, the woman agent sent to collect the allowance, knew that the action she was asked to carry out amounted to an offence. . . . But the assistant recorder never [dealt] with the question of the knowledge of the woman agents, and in the whole of the summing-up dealing with this matter he proceeded on the assumption that either guilty knowledge in the woman agent was irrelevant, or, alternatively, that any woman agent must be taken to have known that she was committing an offence under section 9 (b).

Appeal allowed

Note

In *R.* v. *Whitehouse* [1977] Q.B. 868 (see *ante*, p. 275), A urged B to commit incest, which B was not legally able to commit as either a principal or a secondary party. It was held that A was not guilty of incitement.

Question

As a general rule, is it incitement to urge someone to be a secondary party to a crime?

R. v. Shephard
[1919] 2 K.B. 125
Court of Criminal Appeal

> S. wrote a letter to a woman, who was six weeks gone with child, in which he said: "When the kiddie is born, you must lie on it in the night. Do not let it live." The child was in due course born alive. Later S. was convicted of incitement to murder under section 4 of the Offences against the Person Act 1861.

BRAY J.: In this case the appellant was convicted on a count framed under section 4 of the Offences against the Person Act, 1861, which makes it an offence to solicit any person to murder "any other person." The appellant undoubtedly did solicit the woman Shephard to murder her child if and when it should be born, and the question is whether the case falls within the section having regard to the fact that at the date when the letter containing the solicitation was written the child was unborn and therefore could not be the subject of murder. We must look at the matter from a common sense point of view, and, so looking at it, we cannot entertain a doubt that it does. All that is essential to bring a case within the section is that there should be a person capable of being murdered at the time when the act of murder is to be committed. If there is such a person then in existence it is quite immaterial that the person was not in existence at the date of the incitement. Here the child was in fact born alive, so that the event happened upon which the act was to be done. That is enough to satisfy the section. We do not decide whether the appellant could have been convicted if the child had not been born alive. It is not necessary to decide that. In the event which has happened the appellant was properly convicted and the appeal must be dismissed.

Appeal dismissed

Questions

1. If the child had been born dead, could S. have been convicted?
2. If S. had been tried before the child was born, could he have been convicted?
3. If, unknown to S., the foetus was dead when he wrote the letter, could he have been convicted? See *R.* v. *McDonough* (1962) 47 Cr. App. R. 37, *post*, p. 364.

R. v. Brown
(1899) 63 J.P. 790
Central Criminal Court

> B. was charged with inciting, counselling, procuring and aiding one Harriet Smith, being a woman with child, to commit a certain misdemeanour to wit unlawfully to attempt to administer to herself certain noxious things capable of procuring an abortion. In the course of the trial, the point was taken that if the accused knew the substance in question was harmless, there was no offence by him.

DARLING J.: After Mr. Gill and Lord Coleridge had submitted that there was no evidence to go to the jury and had raised the point as to what constitutes a criminal attempt, the Attorney-General submitted that the rule should be that it was immaterial whether the thing supplied and taken by the women would effect abortion or not, and further that the inciting to commit a felony would be complete, whatever the state of mind might be of the person inciting as to the drug the women were incited to take. This case raises the question what is and what is not a criminal attempt to do a thing and how far the person inciting is criminally responsible. I do not intend to define what is a criminal attempt or what is inciting to commit a crime. Dealing with this particular case only, if the woman believing she is taking a noxious thing within the statute, does, with intent to procure abortion, take a thing that is in fact harmless she is guilty of an attempt to procure an abortion within the statute. Further, I come to the conclusion, though I do not think it is necessary to this case, that if a person, himself believing the thing to be a noxious drug, incites a woman to take it, he is guilty, although the commission of the crime in the manner proposed is impossible. But if the thing supplied is to his knowledge not capable of procuring abortion, such person in not guilty of inciting her to commit an offence under the statute although he knows that she will take it in the belief that it is a noxious thing in order to procure abortion. (He went on to hold that there was evidence that the thing was noxious and that B knew it was noxious and left the question to the jury.)

Verdict: Guilty

Questions

If Darling J. is right when he says that, if a woman believing she is taking a noxious thing within the statute, does, with intent to procure abortion, take a thing that is in fact harmless she is guilty of an attempt to procure abortion (as to which, see *ante*, p. 303), why is it no crime to incite her to do this? Does the case decide that it is no offence to incite a crime which one intends to frustrate? What crime, exactly, was it which Brown intended to frustrate? (See section 58 of the Offences against the Person Act 1861, *ante*, p. 341.)

R. v. McDonough
(1962) 47 Cr. App. R. 37
Court of Appeal

McD. was convicted of soliciting R. to receive four lamb carcasses, knowing the same to have been stolen. There was no evidence that at the material date there were any such carcasses to receive. (According to [1963] Crim. L.R. 203, McD. admitted that he sold a cold-store ticket to R, to enable him to get certain stolen carcasses from the cold store: but no such carcasses were in the store). McD. appealed.

ASHWORTH J.: In substance, what is argued for the appellant is this, that in this case of a charge of soliciting or inciting to receive stolen goods, guilt cannot be established unless it is shown affirmatively that at the time of the solicitation there were stolen goods of the type mentioned. In other words, what is contended is that if A says to B: "I am going to steal goods tomorrow, and they will be in such-and-such a place; will you receive them?", and B says: "Yes," that is no offence by A of soliciting to receive because at the time of the solicitation the goods had not been stolen.

[After considering *Walters* v. *Lunt* (1951) 35 Cr. App. R. 94, and *R.* v. *Osborn* (1919) 84 J.P. 63.] The third case, which was near the problem involved in the present appeal, was *R.* v. *Shephard* [*ante*, p. 362]. In that case a man was charged on September 2; "with having solicited and endeavoured to persuade Cicely Maria Shephard thereafter to murder a newly born child lately before then born of her body." What is important is that this court was quite certainly of opinion that the offence alleged could be established notwithstanding the fact that the child to be murdered by the woman had not then been born. In other words, incitement of a prospective mother to murder her child when born is an offence within the statute. By parity of reasoning, one would suppose that a solicitation to receive stolen goods is likewise an offence notwithstanding that the goods themselves have not been stolen at the date of the incitement.

The last case to which, in order to do justice to Mr. Kaye's careful argument, reference should be made also in this court, *R.* v. *Percy Dalton (London), Ltd.*, (1949) 33 Cr. App. R. 102 [*ante*, p. 318] and, the sentence on which Mr. Kaye relied appears at p. 110: "Steps on the way to the commission of what would be a crime, if the acts were completed, may amount to attempts to commit that crime, to which, unless interrupted, they would have led; but steps on the way to the doing of something, which is thereafter done, and which is no crime, cannot be regarded as attempts to commit a crime."

As it seems to this court, the principle there stated is one which, if I may humbly say so, is obviously right, but is very far removed from the problem involved in the present case.

Returning now to what is in fact the problem here: could the appellant in the present case properly be charged with inciting to receive notwithstanding that at the date of his solicitation there were no stolen carcasses? In the view of this court the answer is plainly yes, and the learned Recorder was right. It may be that this particular point has not previously been the subject-matter of a reported decision, but in the view of this court there is only one logical answer to the question when it is analysed, and that is the answer which I have just given. Accordingly, this appeal is dismissed.

Appeal dismissed

Questions

1. Is the principle stated in *R.* v. *Percy Dalton Ltd.* still right?
2. If McD. thought that the lamb carcasses were already in the cold store, is the case on all fours with *R.* v. *Shephard*?
3. Could R. be convicted of (a) attempting and (b) conspiracy to handle stolen goods?

Note

It was thought by some that *R.* v. *McDonough*, on inciting the impossible, could not stand with the House of Lords decision in *Haughton* v. *Smith*, on attempting the impossible. However, in *D.P.P.* v. *Nock*, it was distinguished from *Houghton* v. *Smith*; and on that ground and because the law laid down in *R.* v. *McDonough* accorded, in the Law Commission's view, with what the law on impossible attempts and conspiracies ought to be, the Commission made no proposals at all on inciting the impossible (Law Com. No. 102, § 4.2).

Chapter 8

HOMICIDE

	PAGE		PAGE
1. Actus Reus of Homicide	366	5. Involuntary Manslaughter	437
2. Murder	368	i. Unlawful Act Manslaughter	438
i. The Penalty for Murder	368	ii. Gross Negligence Manslaughter	449
ii. The Mental Element in Murder	368	6. Other Unlawful Homicides	455
3. Special Defences	389	i. Infanticide	455
i. Provocation	389	ii. Child Destruction	456
ii. Diminished Responsibility	402	iii. Abortion	456
4. Self-Defence	411	iv. Suicide	462
		7. Reform of the Law of Homicide	463

The true homicides are murder, manslaughter, infanticide, and causing death by reckless driving (as to the latter, see *ante*, p. 78). Suicide was an offence until the Suicide Act 1961; some aspects of the crime still remain. Child destruction is a near-homicide which is always dealt with as a homicide. Abortion, similarly, approximates to homicide and is best dealt with in this section.

1. The Actus Reus of Homicide

The common element in homicides is the *actus reus*.

"Unlawfully killing a reasonable person who is in being and under the King's Peace, the death following within a year and a day": Coke, 3 Inst. 47.

Discussing homicide at the time of Bracton (c. 1256) Pollock and Maitland, *History of English Law*, Vol. II, p. 476, says: "Homicide is the crime of which there is most to be said, but the practicable English law that lies beneath the borrowed Italian trappings is rough and simple. In a few cases homicide is absolutely justifiable and he who commits it will suffer no ill. One such case is the execution of a lawful sentence of death. . . . The man who commits homicide by misadventure or in self-defence deserves but needs a pardon. Bracton cannot conceal this from us and it is plain from multitudinous records of Henry III's reign. If the justices have before them a man who, as a verdict declares, has done a deed of this kind, they do not acquit him, nor can they pardon him, they bid him hope for the king's mercy. . . . On the patent rolls of Henry III pardons for those who have committed homicide by misadventure, in self-defence, or while of unsound mind are common."

Accidental death and death by misadventure involve a coroner's inquest but no criminal charge. Self-defence is a defence to a charge of homicide which will be discussed below (see p. 411) and assault (see p. 479). The principal problem in determining the *actus reus* in homicide is that of causation. This is a general problem, basic to criminal liability, although the majority of cases concern homicide. These have been discussed above (see p. 24). Peculiar to the homicide, however, is the year and a day rule (see the case below). There is also the question of what is a life "in being."

R. v. Dyson
[1908] 2 K.B. 454
Court of Criminal Appeal

The appellant was indicted for the manslaughter of his child. The evidence was that in November 1906 he beat the child into unconsciousness and its skull was fractured. For this offence he received a sentence of four months' imprisonment in the magistrates' court. In December 1907 the appellant again beat the child and severely bruised its face and head. In February 1908 the child developed traumatic meningitis and died in March 1908. By this time the marks of the injuries inflicted in December 1907 had disappeared. The medical evidence was that the fractured skull was the main cause of death but that the later acts of violence would accelerate the death. The defence contended that the fracture was the sole cause of death. The appellant was found guilty and appealed against conviction.

Lord Alverstone C.J.: The jury convicted the prisoner, who appeals against that conviction upon the ground that the judge misdirected the jury in that he left it to them to find the prisoner guilty if they considered the death to have been caused by the injuries inflicted in 1906.

That was clearly not a proper direction, for, whatever one may think of the merits of such a rule of law, it is still undoubtedly the law of the land that no person can be convicted of manslaughter where the death does not occur within a year and a day after the injury was inflicted, for in that event it must be attributed to some other cause. . . . The proper question to have been submitted to the jury was whether the prisoner accelerated the child's death by the injuries which he inflicted in December 1907.

Conviction quashed

Questions

1. Is this rule of remoteness necessary? The Criminal Law Revision Committee's 14th Report on Offences Against the Person (Cmnd. 7844, 1980) suggested that "it would be wrong for a person to remain almost indefinitely at risk for prosecution for murder. A line has to be drawn somewhere and in our opinion the present law operates satisfactorily" (§ 39).

2. Should there be a definition of death? See R. v. *Malcherek*, *ante*, p. 36, Williams, T.C.L., pp. 233–237, and CLRC, 14th Report, § 37.

R. v. Poulton
(1832) 5 C. & P. 330; 172 E.R. 997
Central Criminal Court

The defendant had given birth to a child. Its body was found with a ligature round its neck. Three medical witnesses called for the prosecution all said that although the child had breathed they could not tell whether the child had been completely born, as breathing can take place during birth. The defendant was charged with murder.

LITTLEDALE J.: With respect to birth the being born must mean that the whole body is brought into the world: and it is not sufficient that the child respires in the progress of the birth. Whether the child was born alive depends mainly upon the evidence of the medical man. None of them say that the child was born alive; they only say that it had breathed....

Not guilty of murder

Note

The period 1830–1840 saw many cases on this point reported by Carrington and Payne, *e.g. R.* v. *Brain* (1834) 6 C. & P. 349, *R.* v. *Crutchley* (1837) 7 C. & P. 814 and *R.* v. *Reeves* (1839) 9 C. & P. 25, which last case added the point that the umbilical cord need not be severed for there to be a life in being. This legal test is not apparently in accord with medical opinion where the emphasis is on breathing; see Stanley B. Atkinson, "Life, Birth and Live Birth" (1904) 20 L.Q.R. 134, 141 *et seq*. As long as the child has "lived" it does not matter that the injuries causing its death occurred while it was still in the womb: *R.* v. *West* (1848) 2 Car. & Kir. 784. See also child destruction and abortion, *post*, p. 456.

2. MURDER

i. The Penalty for Murder

"The punishment for murder in the old days was a mandatory death sentence; now, by a quirk of language, it was to be a mandatory life sentence" (Williams, T.C.L., p. 206). Capital punishment for murder was abolished by the Murder (Abolition of the Death Penalty) Act 1965 which replaced the unhappy compromise of partial abolition established by the Homicide Act 1957.

The unusual feature of the penalty for murder is that it is mandatory. The judge has no discretion other than to recommend that the convicted person be detained in prison for a specified minimum term of years (1965 Act, s. 1 (2)). The mandatory sentence, whether death or life, has been a crucial factor in the shaping of the law of homicide, insanity and diminished responsibility. Any discussion of reform of the law of homicide is forced to take account of this. See *post*, p. 463.

ii. The Mental Element in Murder

R. A. Duff, "Implied and Constructive Malice in Murder" (1979) 95 L.Q.R. 418

"Murder, in English law, is 'unlawful killing with malice aforethought.' But if we ask what 'malice aforethought' either does or should amount to, we find complete agreement only on two propositions: that 'malice aforethought' is a term of art, in which neither word carries its ordinary meaning; for murder need involve neither malice, as normally (extra-legally) understood, nor premeditation: and that a man acts with malice aforethought if he aims to cause death or knows that his action will certainly cause death. Beyond that, nothing is certain. Twenty-five years ago one could give a more confident account of how the law actually stood. Malice aforethought could be *expressed* in the intention to kill or the knowledge that his action would probably cause death; it could be *implied* by the intention to cause grievous bodily harm or the knowledge that his action would probably cause such harm; or it could be *constructed* from his wilful engagement in any felony involving the use or threat of violence against the person. The doctrine of constructive malice had historically been rather wider than this, counting as murder any killing which was caused in the course of a felony: but the courts had come to limit its application to cases in which the felony involved the use or threat of violence against the person, and perhaps even to cases in which the violence used or threatened was such that some serious bodily harm was in fact likely to ensue.

But events since then, culminating in *Hyam's case* [*post*, p. 374] in 1974, have rendered the law of murder far less clear."

Note

That the *mens rea* of murder has caused the House of Lords much difficulty in the last 20 years is perhaps not surprising for two reasons. Apart from treason, murder is considered the most heinous of all criminal offences yet "many ... factors affect the gravity of the offence. The defendant's motive may be of the greatest significance. An intentional killing done out of compassion may be much less reprehensible than a merely reckless killing committed in the course of a robbery" (CLRC, 14th Report, § 19). An additional factor is that drawing the line for murder directly affects that for manslaughter but the issue is rarely seen in these terms. The failure to do so was particularly noticeable in *R.* v. *Hyam, post*, p. 374:

[T]he members of the House of Lords at no point examine the functions of drawing a formal legal distinction between different offences aimed at penalising the same broad category of social harm." (M. D. Farrier, "The Distinction Between Murder and Manslaughter in its Procedural Context" (1976) 41 M.L.R. 414, 415).

The rules as to *mens rea* are subject to the Homicide Act 1957, which abolished the two heads of constructive malice and so overruled formerly important decisions such as *D.P.P.* v. *Beard* [1920] A.C. 479, *R.* v. *Betts & Ridley* (1930) 22 Cr. App. R. 148 and *R.* v. *Jarmain* (1945) 31 Cr. App. R. 39, so far as they dealt with constructive malice. Implied malice (intention or foresight of *grievous bodily harm*) still exists, although there is some judicial opinion against it, see *Hyam* and *Cunningham, post*, pp. 374 and 386.

An early preoccupation was whether the *mens rea* of murder should be a matter of subjective or objective proof: see the note following *D.P.P.* v. *Smith, post*, p. 373. This case, although now discredited on this point, is also useful for its discussion of the meaning of grievous bodily harm. *R.* v. *Hyam*, below, illustrates the problems of defining the border between murder and manslaughter. It raises both the question whether some form of recklessness is enough for murder and whether it is sufficient for that state of mind (intention/recklessness) to be in relation to grievous bodily harm, without any contemplation of death. See Chapter 3, *ante*, p. 62, for a discussion of intention and recklessness.

Homicide Act 1957, section 1

"(1) Where a person kills another in the course or furtherance of some other offence, the killing shall not amount to murder unless done with the same malice aforethought (express or implied) as is required for a killing to amount to murder when not done in the course or furtherance of another offence.

(2) For the purposes of the foregoing subsection, a killing done in the course or for the purpose of resisting an officer of justice or of resisting or avoiding or preventing a lawful arrest, or of affecting or assisting an escape or rescue from legal custody, shall be treated as a killing in the course or furtherance of an offence."

R. v. Vickers
[1957[2 Q.B. 664
Court of Criminal Appeal

The appellant broke into a shop intending to steal. He was seen by the occupant of the living quarters above, an elderly woman of 72. He struck her many blows and kicked her in the face. She died as a result. The appellant was convicted of capital murder.

Lord Goddard C.J.: . . . The point that has been raised on the appellant's behalf turns entirely on section 1 (1) of the Homicide Act, 1957, which came into force this year. As there was not complete unanimity among the members of the court at the first hearing of the case, I assembled a full court of five members and the judgment I am about to deliver is the judgment of the court. The court has been much indebted to Mr. Brabin for the learned and careful argument which he has put forward on behalf of the appellant, and the matter has now been thoroughly explored, and the court is now able to give this decision which will be a guidance to courts in the future. I should also like to say that in the opinion of the court the summing-up of Hinchcliffe J. was quite impeccable.

The marginal note to that section (s. 1 (1)), which, of course, is not part of the section but may be looked at as some indication of its purpose, is: "Abolition of 'constructive malice'".

"Constructive malice" is an expression which I do not think will be found in any particular decision, but it is to be found in the textbooks, and is something different from implied malice. The expression "constructive malice" is generally used where a person causes death during the course of carrying out a felony which involves violence—that always amounted to murder. There may be many cases in which a man is not intending to cause death, as, for instance, where he gives a mere push and a person falls and strikes his head or falls down the stairs and breaks his neck, and although the push would never have been considered in the ordinary way as an act which would be likely to cause death, yet if it was done in the course of carrying out a felony it would amount to murder. Another illustration of "constructive malice" would be if a man raped a woman, and she died in the course of the struggle. The fact that he may only have used a moderate or even small degree of violence in the struggle would have been no defence to a charge of murder, because if he caused death, he did so during the commission of the felony of rape. Another instance of constructive malice which was always held sufficient to amount to murder was if a police officer was killed in the execution of his duty. If a person was resisting arrest before the Act of 1957 and caused the death of a police officer, although he might only have used a little violence on the officer he was guilty of murder. Murder is, of course, killing with malice aforethought, but "malice aforethought" is a term of art. It has always been defined in English law as, either an express intention to kill, as could be inferred when a person, having uttered threats against another, produced a lethal weapon and used it on a victim, or implied, where, by a voluntary act, the accused intended to cause grievous bodily harm to the victim and the victim died as the result. If a person does an act which amounts to the infliction of grievous bodily harm he cannot say that he only intended to cause a certain degree of harm. It is called *malum in se* in the old cases and he must take the consequences. If he intends to inflict grievous bodily harm and that person dies, that has always been held in English law, and was at the time this Act was passed, sufficient to imply the malice aforethought which is a necessary constituent of murder.

It will be observed that the section preserves implied malice as well as express malice, and the words "Where a person kills another in the course or furtherance of some other offence" cannot, in our opinion, be referred to the infliction of the grievous bodily harm if the case which is made against the accused is that he killed a person by having assaulted the person with intent to do grievous bodily harm, and from the bodily harm he inflicted that person dies. The "furtherance of some other offence" must refer to the offence he was committing or endeavouring to commit other than the killing, otherwise there would be no sense in it. It was always the English law, as I have said, that if death was caused by a person in the course of committing a felony involving violence that was murder. Therefore, in the present case it is perfectly clear that the words "Where a person kills another in the course or furtherance of some other offence" must be attributed to the burglary he was committing. The killing was in the course or furtherance of that burglary. He killed that person in the course of the burglary because he realised that the victim recognised him and he therefore inflicted grievous bodily harm on her, perhaps only intending to render her unconscious, but he did intend to inflict grievous bodily harm by the blows he inflicted upon her and by kicking her in the face, of which there was evidence. The section goes on: "the killing shall not amount to murder unless done with the same malice aforethought (express or implied) as is required for a killing to amount to murder when not done in the course or furtherance of another offence." It would seem clear, therefore, that the legislature is providing that where one has a killing committed in the course or furtherance of another offence, that other offence must be ignored. What have to be considered are the circumstances of the killing, and if the killing would amount to murder by reason of the express or implied malice, then that person is guilty of capital murder. It is not enough to say he killed in the course of the felony unless the killing is done in a manner which would amount to murder ignoring the commission of felony. It seems to the court, therefore, that in the present case, a burglar attacked a householder to prevent recognition. The householder died as the result of blows inflicted upon her—blows or kicks or both—and if this section had not been passed there could be no doubt that the appellant would have been guilty of murder. He is guilty of murder because he has killed a person with the necessary malice aforethought being implied from the fact that he intended to do grievous bodily harm. . . .

The court desires to say quite firmly that in considering the construction of section 1 (1) it is impossible to say that the doing of grievous bodily harm is the other offence which is referred to in the first line and a half of the section. One has to show, independently of the fact that the accused is committing another offence, that the act which caused the death was done with malice aforethought as implied by law. The existence of express or implied malice is expressly preserved by the Act and, in our opinion, a perfectly proper direction was given by Hinchcliffe J. to the jury, and accordingly this appeal fails and is dismissed.

Appeal dismissed

Director of Public Prosecutions v. Smith
[1961] A.C. 290
House of Lords

The appellant was driving a car containing some stolen property when a policeman told him to draw into the kerb. Instead he accelerated and the constable clung on to the side of the car. The car followed an erratic course and the policeman fell off in front of another car and was killed. The appellant drove on for 200 yards, dumped the stolen property, and then returned. He was charged with capital murder. He was convicted but the Court of Criminal Appeal quashed the conviction for capital murder and substituted one for manslaughter. The Crown appealed to the House of Lords, which restored the conviction for capital murder.

Viscount Kilmuir L.C.: . . . In his final direction to the jury the trial judge, Donovan J., said: "If you are satisfied that . . . he must as a reasonable man have contemplated that grievous bodily harm was likely to result to that officer . . . and that such harm did happen and the officer died in consequence, then the accused is guilty of capital murder. . . . On the other hand, if you are not satisfied that he intended to inflict grievous bodily harm upon the officer—in other words, if you think he could not as a reasonable man have contemplated that grievous bodily harm would result to the officer in consequence of his actions—well, then, the verdict would be guilty of manslaughter."

The last criticism of the summing-up which was raised before your Lordships was in regard to the meaning which the learned judge directed the jury was to be given to the words "grievous bodily harm." The passages of which complaint is made are the following: "When one speaks of an intent to inflict grievous bodily harm upon a person, the expression grievous bodily harm does not mean for that purpose some harm which is permanent or even dangerous. It simply means some harm which is sufficient seriously to interfere with the victim's health or comfort."

"In murder the killer intends to kill, or to inflict some harm which will seriously interfere for a time with health or comfort."

"If the accused intended to do the officer some harm which would seriously interfere at least for a time with his health and comfort, and thus perhaps enable the accused to make good his escape for the time being at least that would be murder too."

The direction in these passages was clearly based on the well-known direction of Willes J. in *R.* v. *Ashman* (1858) 1 F. & F. 88 and on the words used by Graham B. in *R.* v. *Cox* (1818) R. & R. 362 (C.C.R.). Indeed, this is a direction which is commonly given by judges in trials for the statutory offence under section 18 of the Offences Against the Person Act 1861, and has on occasions been given in murder trials: *cf. R.* v. *Vickers* [1957] 2 Q.B. 664.

My Lords, I confess that whether one is considering the crime of murder or the statutory offence, I can find no warrant for giving the words "grievous bodily harm" a meaning other than that which the words convey in their ordinary and natural meaning. "Bodily harm" needs no explanation, and "grievous" means no more and no less than "really serious". . . .

It was, however, contended before your lordships on behalf of the respondent, that the words ought to be given a more restricted meaning in considering the intent necessary to establish malice in a murder case. It was said that the intent must be to do an act "obviously dangerous to life" or "likely to kill." It is true that in many of the cases the likelihood of death resulting has been incorporated into the definition of grievous bodily harm, but this was done, no doubt, merely to emphasise that the bodily harm must be really serious, and it is unnecessary, and I would add inadvisable, to add anything to the expression "grievous bodily harm" in its ordinary and natural meaning.

To return to the summing-up in the present case, it is true that in the two passages cited the learned judge referred to "grievous bodily harm" in the terms used by Willes J. in *R.* v. *Ashman*, but in no less than four further passages, and in particular in the vital direction given just before the jury retired he referred to "serious hurt" or "serious harm." Read as a whole, it is, I think, clear that there was no misdirection. Further, on the facts of this case it is quite impossible to say that the harm which the respondent must be taken to have contemplated could be anything but of a very serious nature coming well within the term "grievous bodily harm."

Before leaving this appeal I should refer to a further contention which was but faintly adumbrated, namely, that section 1 (1) of the Homicide Act 1957, had abolished malice constituted by a proved intention to do grievous bodily harm, and that, accordingly, *R.* v. *Vickers*, [*ante*, p. 370], which held the contrary, was wrongly decided. As to this it is sufficient to say that in my opinion the Act does not in any way abolish such malice. The words in parenthesis in section 1 (1) of the Act and a reference to section 5 (2) make this clear beyond doubt.

Appeal allowed

Note

The body of Viscount Kilmuir's speech (not quoted here) laid down the much more controversial rule that the intent to cause death or grievous bodily harm was purely objective, *i.e.* it was sufficient if a reasonable man would foresee it, even if the accused did not foresee or intend it. There was a brief period of intense judicial and academic activity—see especially Glanville Williams, "Constructive Malice Revived" (1960) 23 M.L.R. 605; R. J. Buxton, "The Retreat from Smith" [1966] Crim. L.R. 195; *Hardy* v. *Motor Insurers' Bureau* [1964] 2 Q.B. 745 and in the Australian High Court, *Parker* v. *The Queen* (1963) 111 C.L.R. 610.

The matter was referred to the Law Commission which produced a Report "Imputed Criminal Intent (*Director of Public Prosecutions* v. *Smith*)" in 1967:

"E. Summary of Proposals

22(*a*) A 'subjective' and not an 'objective' test should be applied in ascertaining the intent required in murder. A jury should be free to infer such an intent from the fact that death or grievous bodily harm (if the intent to inflict grievous bodily harm be retained in murder) was the natural probable consequence of the accused's actions, and often the case for such an inference will as a matter of common sense and experience be very strong; but the jury should not be bound to draw such an inference.

(*b*) The same 'subjective' test should be applied in regard to all other offences where it is necessary to ascertain the existence of intent or foresight.

(*c*) An intent to inflict grievous bodily harm should no longer be retained as an alternative to an intent to kill in the crime of murder. A killing should not amount to murder unless there is an intent to kill. But it should be made clear that, where a man does not have the purpose to kill in any event, he may nevertheless have the intent to kill, if, at the time when he takes the action in fact resulting in death, he is willing by that action to kill in accomplishing some purpose other than killing."

The first two proposals have been dealt with as suggested by the Law Commission in the Criminal Justice Act 1967, s. 8:

"A court or jury, in determining whether a person has committed an offence,—

(*a*) shall not be bound in law to infer that he intended or foresaw a result of his actions by reason only of its being a natural and probable consequence of those actions; but

(*b*) shall decide whether he did intend or foresee that result by reference to all the evidence, drawing such inferences from the evidence as appear proper in the circumstances."

The third proposal is further discussed, *post*, p. 385. But its omission means that section 8 does not refer to murder. The section has been interpreted as abolishing that part of *D.P.P.* v. *Smith* which suggested that the *mens rea* of murder could be satisfied by an objective test: *R.* v. *Wallett* [1968] 2 Q.B. 367 and *R.* v. *Hyam*, below. There are difficulties in so holding especially in the light of the view taken in *D.P.P.* v. *Majewski*, *ante*, p. 176, that section 8 concerns only rules of evidence, and not the substantive law.

Smith and Hogan, Criminal Law (4th ed.), p. 290

"*Smith* laid down a rule of the substantive law of murder and not a rule of evidence. This is clear from subsequent decisions which confined the case to the law of murder. If it had laid down a principle of proof, then it might have been expected to apply on charges of attempted murder, malicious wounding and other offences; but the courts held that this was not so. According to ordinary principles of interpretation, then, it would appear that s. 8 did no more than affirm that the 'intention to do something unlawful to someone' must be subjectively proved—a matter which was never in doubt, anyway. It is clear, however, that *Smith* was disliked by the judges and was being largely ignored even before the Criminal Justice Act. It is hardly surprising, therefore, to find that the courts gave the section the effect which it was undoubtedly intended to have, even though, on a proper construction, it is difficult to see how it can bear that meaning."

R. v. Hyam

[1975] A.C. 55

House of Lords

> The appellant was the lover of Jones. She became suspicious of his relationship with another woman. When she heard that he was intending to go on holiday with the woman the appellant went to her house. She poured petrol through the letter box and then pushed newspaper in. She lit the paper and caused a fierce fire. She left without raising the alarm. Two girls who were in the house with their mother were killed. The appellant said that she merely intended to frighten the woman. There was evidence that before setting the fire she had checked that Jones was at his own home so that he did not come to any harm. She was convicted of murder and appealed, basing her appeal largely upon the direction of the trial judge on the necessary intent in murder.

LORD HAILSHAM OF ST. MARYLEBONE: ... In my view the one point in this case is the intention which it is necessary to impute to an accused person in order to find him guilty of the crime of murder. Is it simply the intention to kill or cause grievous bodily harm (in the sense of really serious injury) as is commonly assumed, or is it enough that he intends wilfully to expose another to the risk of death or grievous bodily harm in the sense of really serious injury? I do not believe that knowledge or any degree of foresight is enough. Knowledge or foresight is at the best material which entitles or compels a jury to draw the necessary inference as to intention. But what is that intention? It is acknowledged that intention to achieve the result of death or grievous bodily harm in the sense of really serious injury is enough to convict. But may the intention wilfully to expose a victim to the serious risk of death or really serious injury also be enough?

The Court of Appeal . . . certified . . . the following point of law of general public importance, namely, the question:

> "Is malice aforethought in the crime of murder established by proof beyond reasonable doubt that when doing the act which led to the death of another the accused knew that it was highly probable that that act would result in death or serious bodily harm?"

. . . It is beyond question that the actual decision in *Smith* [[1961] A.C. 290, [*ante*, p. 371]] has given rise to a series of wholly irreconcilable interpretations. There have been maximalising interpretations, notably from its critics, and minimalising interpretations, usually from its defenders. . . .

I am not going to endeavour to decide between these rival and wholly irreconcilable interpretations for the very good reason that I believe that each can be justified by particular phrases to be found in the report. What is beyond question is that an attempt to revive the decision in toto without interpreting it de novo would be to introduce confusion and not lucidity into the law. Far better to recognise that Parliament in 1967, after considering a report by the Law Commission, decided that it was better to turn its back on what was rightly or wrongly taken as the main argumentation of *Smith*, and to impose the rule of a subjective test both as to foresight of the consequences and as to intention, as section 8 of the Criminal Justice Act 1967 appears to do, while yet retaining the intention to cause grievous bodily harm (in the sense explained) as a possible alternative to intent to kill as the essential mental element in the crime of murder. Such at least is the proper inference to be drawn from the decision of Parliament to enact the first and the failure of Parliament to enact the second of the two draft clauses in the Law Commission's recommendations [*ante*, p. 373], and such at least appears to have been the view of the Court of Appeal in *R.* v. *Wallett* [1968] 2 Q.B. 367. . . .

. . . At the end of the day there are, I think, two reasons against formally overruling *Smith* [*ante*, p. 371] in virtue of our practice direction as suggested by the authors of Smith and Hogan [*Criminal Law*, 3rd ed.]. The first is that in view of the diversity of interpretation it is difficult to know exactly what one is overruling. Indeed, if the extreme minimalising interpretations be adopted, there is little or nothing to overrule, or indeed little enough to require the intervention of Parliament in 1967. The second is that there are at least two passages in *Smith* of permanent value which on any view ought not to be overruled. The first is the passage at the end of Lord Kilmuir's opinion (at p. 372) which disposes at least in this context of the doctrine of *Ashman*, 1 F. & F. 88, regarding the nature of grievous bodily harm, and thus excludes the possibility of "murder by pinprick". The second is the earlier passage where Lord Kilmuir says, at p. 327: "The unlawful and voluntary act must clearly be aimed at someone in order to eliminate cases of negligence or of careless or dangerous driving." There is also a more important third element latent in the decision to which I will return later, and which seems to justify the result, if not all the reasoning.

The view taken above of *Smith* and of the Act of 1967 is not enough to dispose of the present appeal. For, whatever may be said by way of criticism of the crucial passage in the judge's direction, it was impeccable at least in this, that it applied the jury's mind to a subjective test of what was the state of mind of the accused. The question raised by Ackner J.'s charge to the jury is not whether he revived the passages in *Smith* which seem to suggest an objective test, but (i) whether, on the assumption that the test is subjective, foresight of the probable consequences is an alternative species of malice aforethought to intention, or, as Pearson L.J. clearly suggests in *Hardy* v. *Motor Insurers' Bureau* [1964] 2 Q.B. 745, 764, whether foresight of the probable consequences is only another way of describing intention and (ii) on the assumption that foresight can be used as an alternative to or equivalent of intention whether a high degree of probability in that which is foreseen is enough. This seems to me the point in this case, and I do not find it altogether easy to decide. In order to equip myself to do so, I must embark on a brief inquiry into the meaning of some ordinary words. It has been pointed out more than once that "motive" has two distinct but related meanings. I do not claim to say which sense is correct. Both are used, but it is important to realise that they are not the same. In the first sense "motive" means an emotion prompting an act. This is the sense in which I used the term when I said that the admitted motive of the appellant was jealousy of Mrs. Booth. The motive for murder in this sense may be jealousy, fear, hatred, desire for money, perverted lust, or even, as in so-called "mercy killings," compassion or love. In this sense motive is entirely distinct from intention or purpose. It is the emotion which gives rise to the intention and it is the latter and not the former which converts an *actus reus* into a criminal act. Thus as Smith and Hogan point out (*Criminal Law*, 3rd ed., p. 53): "The mother who kills her imbecile and suffering child out of motives of compassion is just as guilty of murder as is the man who kills for gain." [See also the discussion on this used by Viscount Maugham in *Crofter Hand Woven Harris Tweed Co. Ltd.* v. *Veitch* [1942] A.C. 435, 452.] On the other hand, "motive" can mean a "kind of intention" [see Glanville Williams, *Criminal Law* (*The General Part*), 2nd ed., p. 48]. In this sense, in his direction to the jury, the judge (quoted above, and in the judgment of the Court of Appeal) has said: "It matters not if her motive was to frighten Mrs. Booth." See also the discussion of this sense by Lord Wright in *Crofter Hand Woven Harris Tweed Co. Ltd.* v. *Veitch*, at p. 469. I agree with the Court of Appeal that it is desirable, to avoid confusion, to use the word "motive" in this context always in the first sense, and I have attempted to do so.

It is, however, important to realise that in the second sense too motive, which in that sense is to be equated with the ultimate "end" of a course of action, often described as its "purpose" or "object", although "a kind of intention," is not co-extensive with intention, which embraces, in addition to the end, all the necessary consequences of an action including the means to the end and any consequences intended along with the end. In the present case the appellant's "motive"—in the second sense—may have been to frighten Mrs. Booth. This does not exclude, and the jury must have affirmed, the intention to expose the sleepers in the house to the high probability of grievous bodily harm and in many cases it may involve an actual intention to kill or cause grievous bodily harm. Thus, also, in a Victorian melodrama the villain's motive—in the second sense—or his "end," his "purpose", "object" or "intention" may have been to acquire an inheritance. But this does not exclude, and may involve, the intention to slay the rightful heir, or abduct his sister. Or again, in the Law Commission's report [No. 10 (1967)] on *Smith* the example is given where the end is to be paid insurance moneys, the means is to blow up an aircraft in flight, and the inseparable consequence is the death of passengers and crew.

I know of no better judicial interpretation of "intention" or "intent" than that given in a civil case by Asquith L.J. (*Cunliffe* v. *Goodman* [1950] 2 K.B. 237) when he said, at p. 253: "An 'intention' to my mind connotes a state of affairs which the party 'intending'—I will call him X—does more than merely contemplate: it connotes a state of affairs which, on the contrary, he decides, so far as in him lies, to bring about, and which, in point of possibility, he has a reasonable prospect of being able to bring about, by his own act of volition." If this be a good definition of "intention" for the purposes of the criminal law of murder, and so long as it is held to include the means as well as the end and the inseparable consequences of the end as well as the means, I think it is clear that "intention" is clearly to be distinguished alike from "desire" and from foresight of the probable consequences. As the Law Commission pointed out in their disquisition on *Smith* [Law Commission Report No. 10], a man may desire to blow up an aircraft in flight in order to obtain insurance moneys. But if any passengers are killed he is guilty of murder, as their death will be a moral certainty if he carries out his intention. There is no difference between blowing up the aircraft and intending the death of some or all of the passengers. On the other hand, the surgeon in a heart transplant operation may intend to save his patient's life, but he foresees a high degree of probability that he will cause his death, which he neither intends nor desires, since he regards the operation not as a means of killing his patient, but as the best, and possibly the only, means of ensuring his survival.

If this be the right view of the meaning of words, the question certified in this case must, strictly speaking, be answered in the negative.

. . . But this, again, does not dispose of the matter. Another way of putting the case for the Crown was that, even if it be conceded that foresight of the probable consequences is not the same thing as intention, it can, nevertheless, be an alternative type of malice aforethought, equally effective as intention to convert an unlawful killing into murder. This view, which is inconsistent with the view that foresight of a high degree of probability is only another way of describing intention, derives some support from the way in which the proposition is put in *Stephen's Digest of Criminal Law*, art. 223, where it is said that malice aforethought for the purpose of the law of murder includes a state of mind in which there is "knowledge that the act which causes death will probably cause the death of, or grievous bodily harm to, some person, whether such person is the person actually killed or not, although such knowledge is accompanied by indifference whether death or grievous bodily harm is caused or not, or by a wish that it may not be caused; . . . ." If this be right, Ackner J.'s direction can be justified on the grounds that such knowledge is itself a separate species of malice aforethought, and not simply another way of describing intention. I must, however, qualify the negative answer I have proposed to the question certified as of general public importance. For the reasons I have given, I do not think that foresight as such of a high degree of probability is at all the same thing as intention, and, in my view, it is not foresight but intention which constitutes the mental element in murder. It is the absence of intention to kill or cause grievous bodily harm which absolves the heart surgeon in the case of the transplant, notwithstanding that he foresees as a matter of high probability that his action will probably actually kill the patient. It is the presence of an actual intention to kill or cause grievous bodily harm which convicts the murderer who takes a very long shot at his victim and kills him notwithstanding that he thinks correctly as he takes his aim that the odds are very much against his hitting him at all.

But what are we to say of the state of mind of a defendant who knows that a proposed course of conduct exposes a third party to a serious risk of death or grievous bodily harm, without actually intending those consequences, but nevertheless and without lawful excuse deliberately pursues that course of conduct regardless whether the consequences to his potential victim take place or not? In that case, if my analysis be correct, there is not merely actual foresight of the probable consequences, but actual intention to expose his victim to the risk of those consequences whether they in fact occur or not. Is that intention sufficient to reduce the crime to manslaughter notwithstanding a jury's finding that they are sure that it was the intention with which the act was done? In my opinion, it is not and in this my opinion corresponds with the opinion of the Commissioners on the Criminal Law, Fourth Report (1839), when they said:

> "Again it appears to us that it ought to make no difference in point of legal distinction whether death results from a direct intention to kill or from wilfully doing an act of which death is the probable consequence."

And again in a later passage: "It is the wilful exposure of life to peril that constitutes the crime." The heart surgeon exposes his patient to the risk, but does everything he can to save his life, regarding his actions as the best or only means of securing the patient's survival. He is, therefore, not exposing his patient to the risk without lawful excuse or regardless of the consequences. The reckless motorist who is guilty of manslaughter but not murder, is not at least ordinarily aiming his actions at anyone in the sense explained in Smith [1961] A.C. 290, 327. If he were, it is quite possible that, as in Smith, he might be convicted of murder. In the field of guilty knowledge it has long been accepted both for the purposes of criminal and civil law that ". . . a man who deliberately shuts his eyes to the truth will not be heard to say that he did not know it." (See per Lord Reid in *Southern Portland Cement Ltd*. v. *Cooper* [1974] A.C. 623, 638.) Cannot the same be said of the state of intention of a man who, with actual appreciation of the risks and without lawful excuse, wilfully decides to expose potential victims to the risk of death or really serious injury regardless of whether the consequences take place or not? This seems to me to be the truth underlying the statement of the law in Stephen's Digest, the summing up of Cockburn C.J. in *R*. v. *Desmond*, The Times, April 28, 1868, and of Avory J. in *R*. v. *Lumley*, 22 Cox C.C. 635 and of those phrases in Smith [1961] A.C. 290 in which it seems to be said that a rational man must be taken to intend the consequences of his acts. It is not a revival of the doctrine of constructive malice or the substitution of an objective for a subjective test of knowledge or intention. It is the man's actual state of knowledge and intent which, as in all other cases, determines his criminal responsibility. Nor, for the like reason, does this set up an irrebuttable presumption. It simply proclaims the moral truth that if a man, in full knowledge of the danger involved, and without lawful excuse, deliberately does that which exposes a victim to the risk of the probable grievous bodily harm (in the sense explained) or death, and the victim dies, the perpetrator of the crime is guilty of murder and not manslaughter to the same extent as if he had actually intended the consequence to follow, and irrespective of whether he wishes it. This is because the two types of intention are morally indistinguishable, although factually and logically distinct, and because it is therefore just that they should bear the same consequences to the perpetrator as they have the same consequences for the victim if death ensues." . . . I, therefore, propose the following propositions in answer to the question of general public importance.

(1) Before an act can be murder it must be "aimed at someone" as explained in *D.P.P*. v. *Smith*, and must in addition be an act committed with one of the following intentions, the test of which is always subjective to the actual defendant: (i) The intention to cause death; (ii) The intention to cause grievous bodily harm in the sense of that term explained in *Smith* [*ante*, p. 371] *i.e.* really serious injury; (iii) Where the defendant knows that there is a serious risk that death or grievous bodily harm will ensue from his acts, and commits those acts deliberately and without lawful excuse, the intention to expose a potential victim to that risk as the result of those acts. It does not matter in such circumstances whether the defendant desires those consequences to ensue or not, and in none of these cases does it matter that the act and the intention were aimed at a potential victim other than the one who succumbed. (2) Without an intention of one of these three types the mere fact that the defendant's conduct is done in the knowledge that grievous bodily harm is likely, or highly likely to ensue from his conduct is not by itself enough to convert a homicide into the crime of murder. Nevertheless, for the reasons I have given in my opinion the appeal fails and should be dismissed.

Viscount Dilhorne: . . . In his *Digest of the Criminal Law*, published in 1877, in art. 223, Sir James Stephen defined "malice aforethought" as involving the following states of mind:

> "(*a*) An intention to cause the death of, or grievous bodily harm to, any person, whether such person is the person actually killed or not; (*b*) Know-

ledge that the act which causes death will probably cause the death of, or grievous bodily harm to, some person, whether such person is the person actually killed or not, although such knowledge is accompanied by indifference whether death or grievous bodily harm is caused or not, or by a wish that it may not be; [(*c*) and (*d*) dealt with constructive malice].

The Royal Commission on Capital Punishment (1949–1953) in their report (Cmd. 8932) said, at p. 27, that this was the statement of the modern law most commonly cited as authoritative. The Royal Commission did not dissent from but endorsed Stephen's statement that such knowledge amounted to malice aforethought. In paragraph 76 (p. 28) five propositions were stated which, the report said, were commonly accepted. The fifth proposition was:

"(*v*) It is murder if one person kills another by an intentional act which he knows to be likely to kill or to cause grievous bodily harm, . . . and may either be recklessly indifferent as to the results of his act or may even desire that no harm should be caused by it."

The propositions, the report said, fell within paragraphs (*a*) and (*b*) of article 223 of *Stephen's Digest* and "... it has been generally agreed that they are properly included in the category of murder" (paragraph 77 (p. 29)) and in paragraph 473 (p. 163) it is stated:

"Under the existing law as stated by Stephen, the question the jury have to consider in such a case is whether the accused knew or was aware of the likely consequences of his act; and we think that the law is sound. . . ."

Stephen in his *Digest* treated such knowledge as a separate head of malice aforethought and distinct from those in which intent is necessary. The Royal Commission treated it as justifying a conviction of murder even if the accused did not intend to kill or to do grievous bodily harm. If this view is right, then Ackner J. was wrong in telling the jury that proof of such knowledge established the necessary intent.

On the other hand, Lord Devlin in a lecture he gave in 1954 (reported at [1954] Crim. L.R. 661) said, at pp. 666–667, that where a man has decided that certain consequences would probably happen, then

"for the purposes of the law he intended them to happen, and it does not matter whether he wanted them to happen or not . . . it is criminal intent in the strict sense."

Pearson L.J. appears to have been of the same opinion for in *Hardy* v. *Motor Insurers' Bureau* [1964] 2 Q.B. 745 he said, at pp. 763–764:

"Then this is the syllogism. No reasonable man doing such an act could fail to foresee that it would in all probability injure the other person. The accused is a reasonable man. Therefore he must have foreseen, when he did the act, that it would in all probability injure the other person. Therefore he had the intent to injure the other person."

Whether or not it be that the doing of the act with the knowledge that certain consequences are highly probable is to be treated as establishing the intent to bring about those consequences, I think it is clear that for at least 100 years such knowledge has been recognised as amounting to malice aforethought. . . .

While I do not think that it is strictly necessary in this case to decide whether such knowledge establishes the necessary intent, for, if Ackner J. was wrong about that, it is not such a misdirection as would warrant the quashing of the conviction as, even if it did not establish intent, it was correct in that such knowledge amounted to malice aforethought, I am inclined to the view that Ackner J. was correct. A man may do an act with a number of intentions. If he does it deliberately and intentionally, knowing when he does it that it is highly probable that grievous bodily harm will result, I think most people would say and be justified in saying that whatever other intentions he may have had as well, he at least intended grievous bodily harm.

I now turn to the second contention advanced on behalf of the appellant. This has two facets: first, that the reference to the intent to cause grievous bodily harm has been based on the law that killing in the course or furtherance of a felony is murder, and that when the Homicide Act 1957 was enacted abolishing constructive malice it meant that it no longer sufficed to establish intent to do grievous bodily harm; and, secondly, that, if intent to do grievous bodily harm still made a killing murder, it must be intent to do grievous bodily harm of such a character that life was likely to be endangered.

Committing grievous bodily harm was for many, many years, and until all felonies were abolished, a felony. Consequently so long as the doctrine of constructive malice was part of the law of England, to secure a conviction for murder it was only necessary to prove that the death resulted from an act committed in the course of or in furtherance of the commission of grievous bodily harm. But when one looks at the cases and the old textbooks, one does not find any indication that proof of intent to do grievous bodily harm was an ingredient of murder only on account of the doctrine of constructive malice. Indeed, one finds the contrary. . . .

This was recognised in the report of the Royal Commission on Capital Punishment (1953) (Cmd. 8932). Their five propositions stated in paragraph 76 which were, so the report said, generally accepted to be properly included in the category of murder, were

> ". . . all cases where the accused either *intended* to cause death or grievous bodily harm or *knew* that his act was likely to cause death or grievous bodily harm."

The Royal Commission went on to recommend the abolition of constructive malice, and in paragraph 123 suggested a clause for inclusion in a Bill to bring that about.

Section 1 of the Homicide Act 1957 is in all material respects similar to the clause proposed. It would, indeed, be odd if the Royal Commission by recommending the abolition of constructive malice had in fact proposed the abolition of intent to do grievous bodily harm as an ingredient of murder when the commission had not intended and did not recommend that. Parliament may, of course, do more by an Act than it intends but if, as in my opinion was the case, intent to do grievous bodily harm was entirely distinct from constructive malice, then the conclusion that Parliament did so by the Homicide Act 1957 must be rejected. In my opinion *R.* v. *Vickers* [*ante*, p. 370] was rightly decided and this House was right in saying that that was so in *D.P.P.* v. *Smith* [*ante*, p. 371].

I now turn to the second facet of the appellant's contention, namely, that the words "grievous bodily harm" are to be interpreted as meaning harm of such a character as is likely to endanger life. . . .

Our task is to say what, in our opinion, the law is, not what it should be. In the light of what I have said, in my opinion, the words "grievous bodily harm" must, as Viscount Kilmuir said [in *D.P.P.* v. *Smith*, *ante*, p. 371] be given their ordinary and natural meaning and not have the gloss put on them for which the appellant contends. . . .

To change the law to substitute "bodily injury known to the offender to be likely to cause death" for "grievous bodily harm" is a task that should . . . be left to Parliament if it thinks such a change expedient. . . . I share the view of the majority of the Royal Commission that such a change would not lead to any great difference in the day-to-day administration of the law.

For these reasons in my opinion this appeal should be dismissed.

Lord Diplock: . . . This appeal raises two separate questions. The first is common to all crimes of this class. It is: what is the attitude of mind of the accused towards the particular evil consequence of his physical act that must be proved in order to constitute the offence? The second is special to the crime of murder. It is: what is the relevant evil consequence of his physical act which causes death, towards which the attitude of mind of the accused must be determined on a charge of murder?

Upon the first question I do not desire to say more than that I agree with those of your Lordships who take the uncomplicated view that in crimes of this class no distinction is to be drawn in English law between the state of mind of one who does an act because he desires it to produce a particular evil consequence, and the state of mind of one who does the act knowing full well that it is likely to produce that consequence although it may not be the object he was seeking to achieve by doing the act.

. . . I turn then to the second question. I believe that all your Lordships are agreed that if the English law of homicide were based on concepts that are satisfactory, both intellectually and morally, the crime of murder ought to be distinguished from less heinous forms of homicide by restricting it to cases where the consequence of the act, which the accused desired or foresaw as likely, was the death of a human being. Where we differ is as to whether it is still open to this House to declare in its judicial capacity that this is now the law of England, or whether to define the law of murder thus would involve so basic a change in the existing law that it could only properly be made by Act of Parliament. For my part I think that Parliament itself has, by the Homicide Act 1957, made it constitutionally permissible for this House so to declare, and I believe that this House ought to do so . . .

[T]he now familiar expression "grievous bodily harm" appears to owe its place in the development of the English law of homicide to its use in 1803 in Lord Ellenborough's Act (43 Geo. 3, c. 58), which made it a felony to shoot at, stab or cut any other person "with intent . . . to murder, . . . maim, disfigure, or disable, . . . or . . . do some other grievous bodily harm . . ." [section 1]. . . .

If what was written before the 19th century about the degree of violence that must have been intended by the accused in order to support a charge of murder is to be properly understood, there are several matters to be borne in mind.

(1) It must be remembered that, judged by present day standards, we are dealing with a violent age. Men were used to carrying deadly weapons and not slow to resort to them. So, at the beginning of the period Coke did not classify as murder a killing on "a sudden falling out." Later when this defence became merged in the general doctrine of provocation most of the cases with which the writers were preoccupied involved the use of deadly weapons and it is not without significance that Lord Ellenborough's Act itself was concerned only with shooting, stabbing and cutting.

(2) Medical and surgical science were in a very primitive state. Any bodily injury, particularly if it involved risk of sepsis through an open wound, might well prove mortal although today the likelihood of its resulting in death would be insignificant. It was not until the last quarter of the 19th century that antiseptics came into general use.

(3) Until the 19th century the common law did not recognise unconsummated attempts to commit a crime as being criminal offences in themselves. So in relation to the crime of murder judges were dealing with bodily injuries which had in fact been fatal, and so demonstrated to have been of a kind which could endanger life.

(4) As stated by Foster J. it was accepted law in the 18th century that once the fact of killing was proved the onus lay upon the prisoner to prove facts negativing

malice aforethought unless such facts arose out of the evidence produced against him.

(5) Until as late as 1898 persons accused of murder were incompetent to give evidence in their own defence. So the actual intent with which they had done the act which had in fact caused death could only be a matter of inference from the evidence of other witnesses as to what the accused had done or said. In drawing this inference from what he had done it was necessary to assume that the accused was gifted with the foresight and reasoning capacity of a "reasonable man" and, as such, must have foreseen as a possible consequence of his act, and thus within his intention, anything which, in the ordinary course of events, might result from it.

Bearing these considerations in mind, I for my part find it impossible to say with confidence whether or not by the close of this period judges, when in connection with malice aforethought they used various expressions connoting physical injuries, did so with the unexpressed major premise in mind: "All physical injuries, at any rate if they are serious, are likely to endanger life" and so equated intent to cause serious physical injuries with intent to endanger life. Probably they did not at the beginning of the period. . . . For my part, I am satisfied that the decision of this House in *D.P.P.* v. *Smith* was wrong in so far as it rejected the submission that in order to amount to the crime of murder the offender, if he did not intend to kill, must have intended or foreseen as a likely consequence of his act that human life would be endangered. . . . I think the reason why this House fell into error was because it failed to appreciate that the concept of "intention to do grievous bodily harm" only became relevant to the common law crime of murder as a result of the passing of Lord Ellenborough's Act in 1803 and the application to the new felony thereby created of the then current common law doctrine of constructive malice. This led this House to approach the problem as one of the proper construction of the words "grievous bodily harm" which because, though *only* because, of the doctrine of constructive malice had over the past 100 years become part of the standard definition of *mens rea* in murder, as well as part of the statutory definition of *mens rea* in the statutory felony of causing grievous bodily harm with intent to cause grievous bodily harm. I do not question that in the statutory offence "grievous bodily harm" bears the meaning ascribed to it by this House in *D.P.P.* v. *Smith* but the actual problem which confronted this House in *D.P.P.* v. *Smith* and the Court of Criminal Appeal in *R.* v. *Vickers* [*ante*, p. 370] was a much more complex one. . . .

It was, I venture to think, a comparable failure to appreciate the significance of the accidents of history in the development of English criminal law that led this House in the same case to adopt the objective test of intention as to the consequences of a voluntary act, *i.e.* that part of the decision that is now overruled by the Criminal Justice Act 1967. Intention can only be subjective. It was the actual intention of the offender himself that the objective test was designed to ascertain. So long as the offender was not permitted to give evidence of what his actual intention was, the objective test provided the only way, imperfect though it might be, of ascertaining this.

Lord Cross of Chelsea: . . . I agree with my noble and learned friend, Lord Kilbrandon, that now that murder no longer attracts the death penalty it would be logical to replace the two crimes of murder and manslaughter by a single offence of unlawful homicide; but there are considerations, in which logic plays little part, which tell against the making of such a change—and as long as one has the two separate crimes one has to decide on which side of the line any given state of mind falls. . . . The first question to be answered is whether if an intention to kill—using intention in the strict sense of the word—is murder—as it plainly is—doing an unlawful act with knowledge that it may well cause death ought also to be murder. I have no doubt whatever that it ought to be . . . [I]f it is the law that an intention to cause grievous bodily harm—using intention in the strict sense of the word—is "malice aforethought", whether or not one realises that one's act may endanger life, then I think that it is right that the doing of an act which one realises may well cause grievous bodily harm should also constitute malice aforethought whether or not one realises that one's act may endanger life. . . . In the result, therefore, I think that the only criticism which can be directed against Ackner J.'s summing up is that by the insertion of the word "highly" before "probable" it was unduly favourable to Mrs. Hyam.

It was not until counsel for the appellant was in the middle of his reply that I appreciated that he was contending as an alternative to his main argument that *R.* v. *Vickers* [*ante*, p. 370] had been wrongly decided. My failure to appreciate this may well have been partly due to the fact that I have never before had to grapple with this obscure and highly technical branch of the law, but the fact that the Solicitor-General did not deal with this point at all in his argument is some indication that counsel, if he was intending to make it in his opening, did not lay much stress on it at that stage. Moreover, although by the close of the argument I could see that it was a serious point, it was only when I read the speech of my noble and learned friend, Lord Diplock, that I fully appreciated the historical and logical basis for it. Briefly the argument, as I understand it, runs as follows—that the Court of Criminal Appeal was wrong when it said in *R.* v. *Vickers* that an intention to inflict grievous bodily harm had itself "*always*" supplied the necessary "malice" to support a conviction for murder whether or not the accused realised that what he was doing was likely to endanger life; that such an intention only came to supply the necessary malice after the intentional infliction of grievous bodily harm had been made a felony by Lord Ellenborough's Act; that accordingly what came to be the common form direction that an intention to do grievous bodily harm constituted "malice aforethought" was, whether those who used it realised the fact or not, only justified by the doctrine of constructive malice and that, whether or not it realised what it was doing, Parliament when it abolished constructive malice by the Homicide Act 1957 in effect swept away the existing law of "malice aforethought" in cases in which an intent to kill could not be proved and left it to the courts to redefine the mental element requisite in such cases to support a conviction for murder. My noble and learned friend may be right. On the other hand, my noble and learned friend, Viscount Dilhorne, whose speech I have also had the advantage of reading, thinks that he is wrong—and he may be right in so thinking. All that I am certain of is that I am not prepared to decide between them without having heard the fullest possible argument on the point from counsel on both sides—especially as a decision that *R.* v. *Vickers* [*ante*, p. 370] was wrongly decided might have serious repercussions since the direction approved in that case must have been given in many homicide cases in the last 17 years. For my part, therefore, I shall content myself with saying that *on the footing that R. v. Vickers was rightly decided* the answer to the question put to us should be "Yes" and that this appeal should be dismissed.

LORD KILBRANDON: . . ., having had the advantage of reading the speech of my noble and learned friend, Lord Diplock, I have no difficulty in coming to the conclusion that to kill with the intention of causing grievous bodily harm is murder only if grievous bodily harm means some injury which is likely to cause death: if murder is to be found proved in the absence of an intention to kill, the jury must be satisfied from the nature of the act itself or from other evidence that the accused knew that death was a likely consequence of the act and was indifferent whether that consequence followed or not. It is because I regard the adoption of a fresh definition of the intention, beyond an intention to kill, necessary to support a charge of murder as inevitably called for by the passing into law of the Homicide Act 1957 that I have come to the conclusion that this House is entitled to declare the common law basis upon which the rule laid down by Parliament rests, rather than leaving it to Parliament itself to do so. It is a satisfaction to me to be able to say that in my opinion such a declaration would be in conformity with the common law of Scotland, where constructive malice has never formed part of the law of murder.

My Lords, it is not so easy to feel satisfaction at the doubts and difficulties which seem to surround the crime of murder and the distinguishing from it of the crime of manslaughter. There is something wrong when crimes of such gravity, and I will say of such familiarity, call for the display of so formidable a degree of forensic and judicial learning as the present case has given rise to. I believe this to show that a more radical look at the problem is called for, and was called for immediately upon the passing of the Murder (Abolition of Death Penalty) Act of 1965. Until that time the content of murder—and I am not talking about the definition of murder—was that form of homicide which is punishable with death. (It is not necessary to notice the experimental period during which capital murder and non-capital murder existed side by side). Since no homicides are now punishable with death, these many hours and days have been occupied in trying to adjust a definition of that which has no content. There does not appear to be any good reason why the crimes of murder and manslaughter should not both be abolished, and the single crime of unlawful homicide substituted; one case will differ from another in gravity, and that can be taken care of by variation of sentences downwards from life imprisonment. It is no longer true, if it was ever true, to say that murder as we now define it is necessarily the most heinous example of unlawful homicide. The present case could form an excellent example exhibiting as it does, assuming it to be capable of classification as manslaughter, a degree of cold-blooded cruelty exceeding that to be found in many an impulsive crime which could never, on our present law, be so classified.

My Lords, since the passage in the summing up of the learned judge which was particularly noticed is not consistent with the common law as it has now, as I agree, been shown to be, and the proviso was not relied on, it follows that this appeal should be allowed.

Appeal dismissed

Question

Lord Hailsham suggests at one point that it is the absence of intention which absolves the heart surgeon. He later suggests that the surgeon does "wilfully expose" the patient to the risk of death but does so "without lawful excuse." Are these statements compatible?

Note

Extracting a ratio from *Hyam* has not been easy. It has now become clear that whatever was said in that case about intention and foresight of probabilities is confined only to murder, see *R.* v. *Mohan*, *R.* v. *Belfon*, *ante*, p. 63. Even thus confined, there are problems in deciding what degree of foresight of probability is required (high, merely probable, likely?).

Williams, Textbook of Criminal Law, p. 216

"All that *Hyam* decides is that a direction to the jury in terms of knowledge of high probability is valid. It does not decide (because the point was not before the House) whether a direction in terms of some lesser degree of probability may not be sufficient. Three law lords out of five favoured probability or likelihood, which seem to indicate such lesser degree.

The risk of confusion in applying the rule in *Hyam* is obvious. Let us suppose, to simplify the argument, that eventually the courts decide between the various words used in *Hyam*, and agree to speak of probability; and let us suppose, purely as a theoretical matter, that the defendant admits under cross-examination that he knew that death would probably be caused. The judge directs the jury that they may bring in a conviction if they feel sure that the defendant knew that death would probably be caused. Here the defendant may have used the word 'probable' to cover a probability of .2, the judge may mean a probability of .6, and the jury may understand a probability of .8. It is true that the application of any of these figures will involve only a very rough guess. But the inaccuracy involved in the guesswork is compounded if, in addition, there is disagreement about the meaning of the language in which the law is expressed.

In practice a defendant will rarely make these admissions. What he foresaw, the risk of which he knew, is inferred from the obviousness of the risk to the ordinary man, taking into account, however, any special circumstances of the case, and any explanations, etc. given by the defendant. The jury are directed to ask themselves whether anyone in the defendant's shoes must have known the risk, and if so they may infer that the defendant knew it. Even in this situation, misunderstanding is possible. In practice the jury in estimating what an ordinary man would have foreseen will proceed on their opinion of what they themselves would have foreseen, if in the position of the defendant. But here again it is important that the jury should understand whether by 'probable' the judge means 'an appreciable risk' (*e.g.* .1 or .2), or 'more likely than not' (.5), or substantially more likely than not (say .7). Perhaps the reasonable meaning to attach to 'probable' is 'more likely than not.'

These problems could be largely avoided if the notion of recklessness were used, with its variable standard dependent (it is here suggested) on the known risk that a reasonable man would regard it as acceptable to take. But to say that all reckless risk-taking can involve liability for murder would be a great extension of that crime.

Murder by risk-taking is in fact an example of Orwellian 'doublethink'; it is a principle applied against those who are thought to deserve it, but is never contemplated in relation to those who do not. Prosecutions based on it are rare. Killing by taking risks is the typical province of the law of manslaughter, not of murder. As was said just now, even killing by a violent attack is often charged as manslaughter—particularly killing by parents of young children. Where a person whose life has been gambled with does not die, penalties are often very light. It is not at all uncommon for fleeing bandits or even ordinary motorists to drive recklessly at policemen and others to make them jump out of the way; if no death or injury occurs the driver is charged merely with reckless or careless driving and when convicted is often treated with astonishing leniency. But if a policeman were killed in this way the driver would quite likely be charged with and convicted of murder.

On an ordinary charge of murder where there is clear evidence of intention (to cause death or grievous bodily harm), the trial judge is well advised not to direct the jury on risk-taking, since this would complicate the issues unnecessarily."

Note

For a discussion of possible differences of meaning between "probable" and "likely" see *R.* v. *Gush* [1981] N.Z.L.R. 92, in which it is suggested that the former means "more probable than not" while the latter may mean "such as could well happen."

The House of Lords in *Hyam* were also ambivalent on the question of whether foresight of grievous bodily harm as [highly] probable is sufficient. Two of the majority (Lord Hailsham and Viscount Dilhorne) thought it was, the two dissenting Law Lords (Lords Diplock and Kilbrandon) thought it was not. With the lightest of touches, Lord Cross of Chelsea tipped the balance in favour.

R. v. Cunningham
[1981] 2 All E.R. 863
House of Lords

The appellant suspected (wrongly) that the victim was associating with the woman he planned to marry. The victim died from blows struck by the appellant with a chair. He appealed against his conviction for murder on the grounds that to tell the jury that intending really serious harm was sufficient for murder was a misdirection. The Court of Appeal dismissed his appeal but certified that a point of law of general public importance was involved.

Lord Hailsham of St. Marylebone L.C., with whom Lords Wilberforce, Simon of Glaisdale and Bridge of Harwich agreed;

. . . It is, of course, common ground that malice aforethought at least includes an intention to kill. The question is how nearly to this intention malice must be confined to constitute the offence of murder. The Homicide Act 1957 abolished the species of malice known as "constructive" but it has hitherto been accepted doctrine that the 1957 Act did not abolish the doctrine, in my view rather unfortunately, known as "implied malice": see s. 1 (1) of the Act, *R.* v. *Vickers*, [*ante*, p. 370], and *Hyam, above*. I call the label unfortunate because the "malice" in an intention to cause grievous bodily harm is surely express enough. The question is whether the fact that it falls short of an intention to kill and may fall short of an intent to endanger life is enough to exclude an unlawful killing resulting from an act inspired by this intention from the ambit of the crime of murder. The intermediate doctrine which adds on an intention to endanger life to the positive intention to kill as sufficient mens rea to complete the offence need not be considered until I consider Lord Diplock's dissenting speech in *Hyam*. At the other end of the spectrum, it is established that since s. 8 of the Criminal Justice Act 1967, the test whether malice is express or implied is subjective (see *Hyam*). The definition of grievous bodily harm means "really serious bodily harm" in current English usage. . . .

Counsel for the appellant understandably founded his case on the powerful dissenting opinion of Lord Diplock in *Hyam*, concurred in by Lord Kilbrandon, and asked, if necessary, your Lordships to avail themselves of the practice direction on judicial precedent (*Note* [1966] 1 W.L.R. 1234) to give effect to it. I say "if necessary", because counsel properly drew our attention to the somewhat Delphic italicised phrase employed by Lord Cross [1975] A.C. 55 at 98 [*ante*, p. 383] in adding his weight to the opinions of what became the majority in an otherwise equally divided House. In order to dispose first of this minor point I do not believe that your Lordships could give effect to the submission of counsel that *R.* v. *Vickers* was wrongly decided without invoking the practice direction. However apparently ambiguous the italicised phrase, there is no doubt on which side Lord Cross's vote was cast, and, even if there were any doubt about this, *Vickers* was effectively indorsed by your Lordships' House in *D.P.P.* v. *Smith*, which for this purpose has not been overtaken by the Criminal Justice Act 1967. In order to determine the appeal in favour of the appellant and to give effect to Lord Diplock's opinion it would be necessary, in my view, not merely to override *Vickers* but to disregard the indorsement of it in *Smith* and *Hyam* notwithstanding that the exact point in *Hyam* was concerned with the proposition formulated in art 264 (b) in Stephen's Digest of the Criminal Law (9th Edn, 1950, p. 212), whilst the present case is concerned with the part of the proposition in art 264 (a).

This brings me to Lord Diplock's dissenting opinion which is really central to the appellant's case. Like myself, he is offended by the express/implied terminology, which is, however, inescapable in discussing the previous learning. For this terminology Lord Diplock substitutes the far more convenient "actual malice" and "constructive malice". I do not myself consider that this innovation, by itself an improvement, necessarily affects the validity, or otherwise, of his argument, though it does enable him to skate over the difficulty created by the express retention by the draftsman of the "implied" category in s 1 (1) of the 1957 Act.

The real nerve of Lord Diplock's argument, however, does, as it seems to me, depend on the importance to be attached to the passing in 1803 of Lord Ellenborough's Act (43 Geo 3 c 58) by which, for the first time, wounding with the intent to inflict grievous bodily harm became a felony. This, Lord Diplock believes, rendered it possible to apply the doctrine of "felony murder" as defined in Stephen's category (c), abolished in 1957, to all cases of felonious wounding, where death actually ensued from the wound. The abolition of "felony murder" in 1957 was thus seen to enable the judiciary to pursue the mental element in murder behind the curtain imposed on it by the combined effect of the statutory crime of felonious wounding and the doctrine of constructive malice, and so to arrive at a position in which the mental element could be redefined in terms either of an intention to kill, or an intention actually to endanger human life, to correspond with the recommendations of the Fourth Report of Her Majesty's Commissioners on Criminal Law (8th March 1839).

It seems to me, however, that this highly ingenious argument meets with two insuperable difficulties. I accept that it appears to be established that the actual phrase "grievous bodily harm", if not an actual coinage by Lord Ellenborough's Act, can never be found to have appeared in print before it, though it has subsequently become current coin, and has passed into the general legal jargon of statute law, and the cases decided thereon. But counsel, having diligently carried us through the institutional writers on homicide, starting with Coke, and ending with East, with several citations from the meagre reports available, only succeeded in persuading me at least that, even prior to Lord Ellenborough's Act of 1803, and without the precise label "grievous bodily harm", the authors and the courts had consistently treated as murder, and therefore unclergiable, any killing with intent to do serious harm, however described, to which the label "grievous bodily harm", as defined by Viscount Kilmuir LC in *D.P.P.* v *Smith* [1961] AC 290 at 334 [*ante* p. 372] reversing the "murder by pinprick" doctrine arising from *R* v *Ashman* (1858) 1 F & F 88, could properly have been applied.... There is a second difficulty in the way of treating Lord Ellenborough's Act as providing the kind of historical watershed demanded by Lord Diplock's speech and contended for in the instant appeal by the appellant's counsel. This consists in the fact that, though the nineteenth century judges might in theory have employed the felony-murder rule to apply to cases where death ensued in the course of a felonious wounding, they do not appear to have done so in fact. No case was cited where they did so. On the contrary, there appears to be no historical discontinuity between criminal jurisprudence before and after 1803. Stephen never so treated the matter (either in his text, or except in the last few lines, in his Note XIV). It was not so treated in the Australian case of *La Fontaine* v *R* (1976) 136 CLR 62 (after *Hyam*, but in a jurisdiction in which the constructive malice rule still applied)....

Counsel for the appellant used one further ground, not found in Lord Diplock's opinion, for supporting the minority view in *Hyam*. This was the difficulty which, as he suggested, a jury would find in deciding what amounted to an intention to inflict "grievous bodily harm" or "really serious bodily harm" as formulated in *Smith*. I do not find this argument convincing. For much more than a hundred years juries have constantly been required to arrive at the answer to precisely this question in cases falling short of murder (eg the s 18 cases). I cannot see that the fact that death ensues should render the identical question particularly anomalous, or its answer, though admittedly more important, any more difficult. Nor am I persuaded that a reformulation of murder so as to confine the mens rea to an intention to endanger life instead of an intention to do really serious bodily harm would either improve the clarity of the law or facilitate the task of juries in finding the facts. On the contrary, in cases where death has ensued as the result of the infliction of really serious injuries I can see endless opportunity for fruitless and interminable discussion of the question whether the accused intended to endanger life and thus expose the victim to a probable danger of death, or whether he simply intended to inflict really serious injury. . . . One cannot but feel sympathy with Lord Kilbrandon's plea (*Hyam*, above) for a single, and simplified, law of homicide especially since the death penalty for murder has been abolished. But I venture to think that the problem involves difficulties more serious than is supposed. Few civilised countries have identical laws on the subject of homicide or apply them in the same way. To name only two broad issues of policy, are we to follow s 5 of the Homicide Act 1957 and categorise certain classes of murder in which the prohibited act is arbitrarily adjudged to be worse than in others? The fate of s 5 after the abolition of the death penalty, and its history before that, do not encourage emulation. Or, are we to follow Lord Kilbrandon's inclination and create a single offence of homicide and recognise that homicides are infinitely variable in heinousness, and that their heinousness depends very largely on their motivation, with the result that the judge should have absolute discretion to impose whatever sentence he considers just from a conditional discharge to life imprisonment? I can see both difficulty and danger in this for the judiciary. After conviction of the new offence of homicide, judges would have to be the judges of fact for themselves, unaided by any precise jury verdict as to the exact facts found or any guidance from the legislature as to the appropriate penalty. I doubt whether in practice they would relish the responsibility with greater enthusiasm than that with which Parliament would be eager to entrust them with it.

In the meantime we must administer the law as we consider it to be without either the zeal of the reformer or the unwillingness to admit error which characterises the reactionary. In my opinion, *Vickers* was a correct statement of the law as it was after amendment by the Homicide Act 1957, and in *Smith* and *Hyam* your Lordships were right to indorse *Vickers*. . . .

LORD EDMUND-DAVIES: The minority dissents of Lord Diplock and Lord Kilbrandon, in *Hyam*, above, were based on their conclusions that the law as to intent in murder had been incorrectly stated by this House in *Smith* and that exposure of the error should lead to a quashing of Hyam's conviction for murder. In the present case, on the other hand, your Lordships have unanimously concluded and now reiterate that the law as to murderous intent was correctly stated in *R* v *Vickers*. Even so, is now the time and is this House the place to reveal and declare (so as to "avoid injustice") what ought to be the law and, in the light of that revelation, here and now to recant from its former adoption of *Vickers*?

My lords, I would give a negative answer to the question. I say this despite the fact that, after much veering of thought over a period of years, the view I presently favour is that there should be no conviction for murder unless an intent to kill is established, the wide range of punishment for manslaughter being fully adequate to deal with all less heinous forms of homicide. I find it passing strange that a person can be convicted of murder if death results from, say, his intentional breaking of another's arm, an action which, while undoubtedly involving the infliction of "really serious harm" and, as such, calling for severe punishment, would in most cases be unlikely to kill. And yet, for the lesser offence of attempted murder, nothing less than an intent to kill will suffice. But I recognise the force of the contrary view that the outcome of intentionally inflicting serious harm can be so unpredictable that anyone prepared to act so wickedly has little ground for complaint if, where death results, he is convicted and punished as severely as one who intended to kill.

So there are forceful arguments both ways. And they are arguments of the greatest public consequence, particularly in these turbulent days when, as Lord Hailsham LC has vividly reminded us, violent crimes have become commonplace. Resolution of that conflict cannot, in my judgment, be a matter for your Lordships' House alone. It is a task for none other than Parliament, as the constitutional organ best fitted to weigh the relevant and opposing factors. Its solution has already been attempted extra-judicially on many occasions, but with no real success. My Lords, we can do none other than wait to see what will emerge when the task is undertaken by the legislature, as I believe it should be when the time is opportune. . . .

Appeal dismissed

3. SPECIAL DEFENCES

Note

A killing which would otherwise amount to murder will be reduced to manslaughter if the defendant was provoked or suffered from diminished responsibility.

i. Provocation

Homicide Act 1957, section 3

"Where on a charge of murder there is evidence on which the jury can find that the person charged was provoked (whether by things done or by things said or by both together) to lose his self control, the question whether the provocation was enough to make a reasonable man do as he did shall be left to be determined by the jury; and in determining that question the jury shall take into account everything both done and said according to the effect which, in their opinion, it would have on a reasonable man."

Although provocation is usually raised by the defence the onus of proof, that the situation was not one of provocation, lies on the prosecution and this must be made clear to the jury, *R.* v. *Cascoe* [1970] 2 All E.R. 833.

(a) *The reasonable man*

R. v. Camplin
[1978] A.C. 705
House of Lords

The facts appear in the speech of Lord Diplock, below, in which Lords Fraser of Tullybelton and Scarman concurred.

LORD DIPLOCK: The respondent, Camplin, who was 15 years of age, killed a middle-aged Pakistani, Mohammed Lal Khan, by splitting his skull with a chapati pan, a heavy kitchen utensil like a rimless frying pan. At the time, the two of them were alone together in Khan's flat. At Camplin's trial for murder before Boreham J. his only defence was that of provocation so as to reduce the offence to manslaughter. According to the story that he told in the witness box but which differed materially from that which he had told the police, Khan had buggered him in spite of his resistance and had then laughed at him. Whereupon Camplin had lost his self-control and attacked Khan fatally with the chapati pan.

In his address to the jury on the defence of provocation Mr. Baker, who was counsel for Camplin, had suggested to them that when they addressed their minds to the question whether the provocation relied on was enough to make a reasonable man do as Camplin had done, what they ought to consider was not the reaction of a reasonable adult but the reaction of a reasonable boy of Camplin's age. The judge thought that this was wrong in law. So in his summing up he took pains to instruct the jury that they must consider whether:

> "... the provocation was sufficient to make a reasonable man in like circumstances act as the defendant did. Not a reasonable boy, as Mr. Baker would have it, or a reasonable lad; it is an objective test—a reasonable man."

The jury found Camplin guilty of murder. On appeal the Court of Appeal (Criminal Division) allowed the appeal and substituted a conviction for manslaughter upon the ground that the passage I have cited from the summing up was a misdirection. The court held that

> "... the proper direction to the jury is to invite the jury to consider whether the provocation was enough to have made a reasonable person of the same age as the defendant in the same circumstances do as he did."

The point of law of general public importance involved in the case has been certified as being:

> "Whether on the prosecution for murder of a boy of 15, where the issue of provocation arises, the jury should be directed to consider the question under section 3 of the Homicide Act 1957 whether the provocation was enough to make a reasonable man do as he did by reference to a 'reasonable adult' or by reference to a 'reasonable boy of 15' ".

My Lords, the doctrine of provocation in crimes of homicide has always represented an anomaly in English law. In crimes of violence which result in injury short of death, the fact that the act of violence was committed under provocation which had caused the accused to lose his self-control does not affect the nature of the offence of which he is guilty. It is merely a matter to be taken into consideration in determining the penalty which it is appropriate to impose. Whereas in homicide provocation effects a change in the offence itself from murder for which the penalty is fixed by law (formerly death and now imprisonment for life) to the lesser offence of manslaughter for which the penalty is in the discretion of the judge.

The doctrine of provocation has a long history of evolution at common law. Such changes as there had been were entirely the consequence of judicial decision until Parliament first intervened by passing the Act of 1957. Section 3 deals specifically with provocation and alters the law as it had been expounded in the cases, including three that had been decided comparatively recently in this House, viz., *Mancini* v. *D.P.P.* [*post*, p. 400]; *Holmes* v. *D.P.P.* [1946] A.C. 588 and *Bedder* v. *D.P.P.* [1954] 1 W.L.R. 1119. One of the questions of this appeal is to what extent propositions as to the law of provocation that are laid down in those cases and in particular in *Bedder* ought to be treated as being of undiminished authority despite the passing of the Act....

[W]ith two exceptions actual violence offered by the deceased to the accused remained the badge of provocation right up to the passing of the Act of 1957. The two exceptions were the discovery by a husband of his wife in the act of committing adultery and the discovery of a father of someone committing sodomy on his son; but these apart, insulting words or gestures unaccompanied by physical attack did not in law amount to provocation.

The "reasonable man" was a comparatively late arrival in the law of provocation. As the law of negligence emerged in the first half of the 19th century he became the anthropomorphic embodiment of the standard of care required by the law. It would appear that Keating J. in *R.* v. *Welsh* (1869) 11 Cox C.C. 336 was the first to make use of the reasonable man as the embodiment of the standard of self-control required by the criminal law of persons exposed to provocation; and not merely as a criterion by which to check the credibility of a claim to have been provoked to lose his self-control made by an accused who at that time was not permitted to give evidence himself. This had not been so previously and did not at once become the orthodox view. In his *Digest of the Criminal Law* published in 1877 and his *History of the Criminal Law of England* published in 1883 Sir James Fitzjames Stephen makes no reference to the reasonable man as providing a standard of self-control by which to decide the question whether the facts relied upon as provocation are sufficient to reduce the subsequent killing to manslaughter. He classifies and defines the kinds of conduct of the deceased that alone are capable in law of amounting to provocation; and appears to treat the questions for the jury as being limited to (1) whether the evidence establishes conduct by the deceased that falls within one of the defined classes; and, if so, (2) whether the accused was thereby actually deprived of his self-control.

The reasonable man referred to by Keating J. was not then a term of legal art nor has he since become one in criminal law. . . . At least from as early as 1914 (see *R.* v. *Lesbini* [1914] 3 K.B. 1116) the test of whether the defence of provocation is entitled to succeed has been a dual one; the conduct of the deceased to the accused must be such as (1) might cause in any reasonable or ordinary person and (2) actually causes in the accused a sudden and temporary loss of self-control as the result of which he commits the unlawful act that kills the deceased. But until the Act of 1957 was passed there was a condition precedent which had to be satisfied before any question of applying this dual test could arise. The conduct of the deceased had to be of such a kind as was incapable in law of constituting provocation; and whether it was or not was a question for the judge, not for the jury. This House so held in *Mancini* v. *D.P.P.* [*post*, p. 400], where it also laid down a rule of law that the mode of resentment, as for instance the weapon used in the act that caused the death, must bear a reasonable relation to the kind of violence that constituted the provocation.

It is unnecessary for the purposes of the present appeal to spend time on a detailed account of what conduct was or was not capable in law of giving rise to a defence of provocation immediately before the passing of the Act of 1957. It had remained much the same as when Stephen was writing in the last quarter of the nineteenth century. What, however, is important to note is that this House in *Holmes* v. *D.P.P.* [1946] A.C. 588 had recently confirmed that words alone, save perhaps in circumstances of a most extreme and exceptional nature, were incapable in law of constituting provocation.

My Lords, this was the state of law when *Bedder* v. *D.P.P.* [1954] 1 W.L.R. 1119 fell to be considered by this House. The accused had killed a prostitute. He was sexually impotent. According to his evidence he had tried to have sexual intercourse with her and failed. She taunted him with his failure and tried to get away from his grasp. In the course of her attempts to do so she slapped him in the face, punched him in the stomach and kicked him in the groin; whereupon he took a knife out of his pocket and stabbed her twice and caused her death. The struggle which led to her death thus started because the deceased taunted the accused with his physical infirmity; but in the state of the law as it then was taunts unaccompanied by any physical violence did not constitute provocation. The taunts were followed by violence on the part of the deceased in the course of her attempt to get away from the accused, and it may be that this subsequent violence would have a greater effect upon the self-control of an impotent man already enraged by the taunts than it would have had upon a person conscious of possessing normal physical attributes. So there might have been some justification for the judge to instruct the jury to ignore the fact that the accused was impotent when they were considering whether the deceased's conduct amounted to such provocation as would cause a reasonable or ordinary person to lose his self-control. This indeed appears to have been the ground on which the Court of Criminal Appeal had approved the summing up when they said, at p. 1121:

> "no distinction is to be made in the case of a person who, though it may not be a matter of temperament, is physically impotent, is conscious of that impotence, *and therefore mentally liable to be more excited unduly* if he is 'twitted' or attacked on the subject of that particular infirmity."

This statement, for which I have myself supplied the emphasis, was approved by Lord Simonds L.C. speaking on behalf of all the members of this House who sat on the appeal; but he also went on to lay down the broader proposition, at p. 1123, that

> "It would be plainly illogical not to recognise an unusually excitable or pugnacious temperament in the accused as a matter to be taken into account but yet to recognise for that purpose some unusual physical characteristic, be it impotence or another."

. . . [Section 3 of the 1957 Act] was intended to mitigate in some degree the harshness of the common law of provocation as it had been developed by recent decisions in this House. It recognises and retains the dual test: the provocation must not only have caused the accused to lose his self-control but must also be such as might cause a reasonable man to react to it as the accused did. Nevertheless it brings about two important changes in the law. The first is: it abolishes all previous rules of law as to what can or cannot amount to provocation and in particular the rule of law that, save in the two exceptional cases I have mentioned, words unaccompanied by violence could not do so. Secondly it makes it clear that if there was any evidence that the accused himself at the time of the act which caused the death in fact lost his self-control in consequence of some provocation however slight it might appear to the judge, he was bound to leave to the jury the question, which is one of opinion not of law: whether a reasonable man might have reacted to that provocation as the accused did.

I agree with my noble and learned friend Lord Simon of Glaisdale that since this question is one for the opinion of the jury the evidence of witnesses as to how they think a reasonable man would react to the provocation is not admissible.

The public policy that underlay the adoption of the "reasonable man" test in the common law doctrine of provocation was to reduce the incidence of fatal violence by preventing a person relying upon his own exceptional pugnacity or excitability as an excuse for loss of self-control. The rationale of the test may not be easy to reconcile in logic with more universal propositions as to the mental element in crime. Nevertheless it has been preserved by the Act of 1957 but falls to be applied now in the context of a law of provocation that is significantly different from what it was before the Act was passed.

Although it is now for the jury to apply the "reasonable man" test, it still remains for the judge to direct them what, in the new context of the section, is the meaning of this apparently inapt expression, since powers of ratiocination bear no obvious relationship to powers of self-control. Apart from this the judge is entitled, if he thinks it helpful, to suggest considerations which may influence the jury in forming their own opinion as to whether the test is satisfied; but he should make it clear that these are not instructions which they are required to follow; it is for them and no one else to decide what weight, if any, ought to be given to them.

As I have already pointed out, for the purposes of the law of provocation the "reasonable man" has never been confined to the adult male. It means an ordinary person of either sex, not exceptionally excitable or pugnacious, but possessed of such powers of self-control as everyone is entitled to expect that his fellow citizens will exercise in society as it is today. A crucial factor in the defence of provocation from earliest times has been the relationship between the gravity of provocation and the way in which the accused retaliated, both being judged by the social standards of the day. When Hale was writing in the seventeenth century, pulling a man's nose was thought to justify retaliation with a sword; when *Mancini* v. *D.P.P.* [*post*, p. 400] was decided by this House, a blow with a fist would not justify retaliation with a deadly weapon. But so long as words unaccompanied by violence could not in law amount to provocation the relevant proportionality between provocation and retaliation was primarily one of degrees of violence. Words spoken to the accused before the violence started were not normally to be included in the proportion sum. But now that the law has been changed so as to permit of words being treated as provocation even though unaccompanied by any other acts, the gravity of verbal provocation may well depend upon the particular characteristics or circumstances of the person to whom a taunt or insult is addressed. To taunt a person because of his race, his physical infirmities or some shameful incident in his past may well be considered by the jury to be more offensive to the person addressed, however equable his temperament, if the facts on which the taunt is founded are true than it would be if they were not. It would stultify much of the mitigation of the previous harshness of the common law in ruling out verbal provocation as capable of reducing murder to manslaughter if the jury could not take into consideration all those factors which in their opinion would affect the gravity of taunts or insults when applied to the person to whom they are addressed. So to this extent at any rate the unqualified proposition accepted by this House in *Bedder* v. *D.P.P.* [1954] 1 W.L.R. 1119 that for the purposes of the "reasonable man" test any unusual physical characteristics of the accused must be ignored requires revision as a result of the passing of the Act of 1957.

That he was only 15 years of age at the time of the killing is the relevant characteristic of the accused in the instant case. It is a characteristic which may have its effects on temperament as well as physique. If the jury think that the same power of self-control is not to be expected in an ordinary, average or normal boy of 15 as in an older person, are they to treat the lesser powers of self-control possessed by an ordinary, average or normal boy of 15 as the standard of self-control with which the conduct of the accused is to be compared?

It may be conceded that in strict logic there is a transition between treating age as a characteristic that may be taken into account in assessing the gravity of the provocation addressed to the accused and treating it as a characteristic to be taken into account in determining what is the degree of self-control to be expected of the ordinary person with whom the accused's conduct is to be compared. But to require old heads upon young shoulders is inconsistent with the law's compassion to human infirmity to which Sir Michael Foster ascribed the doctrine of provocation more than two centuries ago. The distinction as to the purposes for which it is legitimate to take the age of the accused into account involves considerations of too great nicety to warrant a place in deciding a matter of opinion, which is no longer one to be decided by a judge trained in logical reasoning but is to be decided by a jury drawing on their experiences of how ordinary human beings behave in real life. . . .

In my view *Bedder*, like *Mancini* v. *D.P.P.* [*post*, p. 400], and *Holmes* v. *D.P.P.* [1946] A.C. 588, ought no longer to be treated as an authority on the law of provocation.

In my opinion a proper direction to a jury on the question left to their exclusive determination by section 3 of the Act of 1957 would be on the following lines. The judge should state what the question is using the very terms of the section. He should then explain to them that the reasonable man referred to in the question is a person having the power of self-control to be expected of an ordinary person of the sex and age of the accused, but in other respects sharing such of the accused's characteristics as they think would affect the gravity of the provocation to him; and that the question is not merely whether such a person would in like circumstances be provoked to lose his self-control but also whether he would react to the provocation as the accused did.

I accordingly agree with the Court of Appeal that the judge ought not to have instructed the jury to pay no account to the age of the accused even though they themselves might be of opinion that the degree of self-control to be expected in a boy of that age was less than in an adult. So to direct them was to impose a fetter on the right and duty of the jury which the Act accords to them to act upon their own opinion on the matter.

I would dismiss this appeal.

Lord Morris of Borth-y-Gest: [His Lordship read section 3 and continued:] One big change enacted was that things said could, either alone or in conjunction with things done, constitute provocation. It will first be for the court to decide whether, on a charge of murder, there is evidence on which a jury can find that the person charged was provoked to lose his self-control; thereafter, as it seems to me, all questions are for the jury. It will be for the jury to say whether they think that whatever was or may have been the provocation, such provocation was in their view enough to make a reasonable man do as the accused did: the jury must take into account everything both done and said according to the effect which they think there would have been on a reasonable man. Who then or what then is the "reasonable man" who is referred to in the section? It seems to me that the courts are no longer entitled to tell juries that a reasonable man has certain stated and defined features. It is for the jury to consider all that the accused did: it is for them to say whether the provocation was enough to make a "reasonable man" do as the accused did. The jury must take into account "everything both done and said". What do they think would have been the effect on a reasonable man? They must bring their "collective good sense" to bear. As Lord Goddard C.J. said in *R.* v. *McCarthy* [1954] 2 Q.B. 105, 112:

> No court has ever given, nor do we think ever can give, a definition of what constitutes a reasonable or an average man. That must be left to the collective good sense of the jury, and what no doubt would govern their opinion would be the nature of the retaliation used by the provoked person."

So in relation to the facts in *Bedder* v. *D.P.P.* [1954] 1 W.L.R. 1119 apart from the painful physical kick, a jury would now have to consider the effect of the things said on a reasonable man. If an impotent man were taunted about his impotence the jury would not today be told that an impotent man could not be a reasonable man as contemplated by the law. The jury would be entitled to decide that the accused man acted as a "reasonable man" in being provoked as he was and in doing as he did.

It seems to me that as a result of the changes effected by section 3 a jury is fully entitled to consider whether an accused person, placed as he was, only acted as even a reasonable man might have acted if he had been in the accused's situation. There may be no practical difference between, on the one hand, taking a notional independent reasonable man but a man having the attributes of the accused and subject to all the events which surrounded the accused and then considering whether what the accused did was only what such a person would or might have done, and, on the other hand, taking the accused himself with all his attributes and subject to all the events and then asking whether there was provocation to such a degree as would or might make a reasonable man do what he (the accused) in fact did.

In my view it would now be unreal to tell a jury that the notional "reasonable man" is someone without the characteristics of the accused: it would be to intrude into their province. A few examples may be given. If the accused is of particular colour or particular ethnic origin and things are said which to him are grossly insulting it would be utterly unreal if the jury had to consider whether the words would have provoked a man of different colour or ethnic origin—or to consider how such a man would have acted or reacted. The question would be whether the accused if he was provoked only reacted as even any reasonable man in his situation would or might have reacted. If the accused was ordinarily and usually a very unreasonable person, the view that on a particular occasion he acted just as a reasonable person would or might have acted would not be impossible of acceptance.

It is not disputed that the "reasonable man" in section 3 could denote a reasonable person and so a reasonable woman. If words of grievous insult were addressed to a woman, words perhaps reflecting on her chastity or way of life, a consideration of the way in which she reacted would have to take account of how other women being reasonable women would or might in like circumstances have reacted. Would or might she, if she had been a reasonable woman, have done what she did?

In the instant case the considerations to which I have been referring have application to a question of age.... The jury had to consider whether a young man of about the same age as the accused but placed in the same situation as that which befell the accused could, had he been a reasonable young man, have reacted as did the accused and could have done what the accused did. For the reasons which I have outlined the question so to be considered by the jury would be whether they considered that the accused, placed as he was, and having regard to all the things that they found were said, and all the things that they found were done, only acted as a reasonable young man might have acted, so that, in compassion, and having regard to human frailty, he could to some extent be excused even though he had caused a death.

I consider that the Court of Appeal came to the correct conclusion and agreeing with what my noble and learned friend Lord Diplock has said as to the direction to a jury I would dismiss the appeal.

LORD SIMON OF GLAISDALE: ... [I]t is accepted that the phrase "reasonable man" really means "reasonable person", so as to extend to "reasonable woman" (see, specifically, *Holmes* v. *D.P.P.* [1946] A.C. 588, 597). So, although this has never yet been a subject of decision, a jury could arguably, consistently with *Bedder* and its precedent authorities, take the sex of the accused into account in assessing what might reasonably cause her to lose her self-control. (A "reasonable woman" with her sex eliminated is altogether too abstract a notion for my comprehension or, I am confident, for that of any jury. In any case, it hardly makes sense to say that an impotent man must be notionally endowed with virility before he ranks within the law of provocation as a reasonable man, yet that a normal woman must be notionally stripped of her femininity before she qualifies as a reasonable woman). If so, this is already some qualification on the "reasonable person" as a pure abstraction devoid of any personal characteristics, even if such a concept were of any value to the law. This qualification might be crucial: take the insult "whore" addressed respectively to a reasonable man and a reasonable woman. Nevertheless, as counsel for the appellant sternly and cogently maintained, *Bedder* would preclude the jury from considering that the accused was, say, pregnant (*R.* v. *Smith* (1914) 11 Cr. App. R. 36) or, presumably, undergoing menstruation or menopause.

Such refinements, anomalies and affronts to common sense invite courts to distinguish an authority. In the instant case the Court of Appeal distinguished *Bedder* [1954] 1 W.L.R. 1119 on the ground that age is a universal quality not a personal idiosyncrasy. It is certainly not a "physical infirmity or disability". This distinction is, further, arguably justified by the implications of the "reasonable woman" as a standard. It could be said that the law, in distinguishing from personal idiosyncrasy something universal like age, was doing no more than it had already done in distinguishing implicitly something universal like sex.

Nevertheless, the distinction drawn by the Court of Appeal leads to great difficulties. If youth is to be considered (and, presumably, advanced years too), what about immaturity in a person of full years or premature senility? These would seem to fall on the other, on the *Bedder*, side of the line. One calls to mind what Lord Reid said in *R.* v. *National Insurance Commissioner, Ex parte Hudson* [1972] A.C. 944, 966: "It is notorious that where an existing decision is disapproved but cannot be overruled courts tend to distinguish it on inadequate grounds." The fine distinctions and the anomalies inherent in distinguishing *Bedder* are such as, in my judgment, to make it incumbent to face the issue whether it should be followed or is so inconvenient an authority that it should be regarded as no longer representing the law. . . .

[His Lordship then discussed the effect of section 3].

In the exceptional circumstances whereby the reasoning of a decision of your Lordships' House, and that of the authorities on which it was founded, has been undermined by a subsequent Act of Parliament (even though the decision has not been clearly and expressly abrogated), I think that your Lordships are justified in saying that *Bedder* should no longer be followed. I think that the law as it now stands in this country is substantially the same as that enacted in the New Zealand Crimes Act 1961, section 169 (2), as explained by the Court of Appeal of New Zealand in *R.* v. *McGregor* [1962] N.Z.L.R. 1069.

I think that the standard of self-control which the law requires before provocation is held to reduce murder to manslaughter is still that of the reasonable person (hence his invocation in section 3); but that, in determining whether a person of reasonable self-control would lose it in the circumstances, the entire factual situation, which includes the characteristics of the accused, must be considered.

There is only one other matter which I would desire to add. It was suggested on behalf of the Director of Public Prosecutions that if what his counsel called the "completely objective test" as established by *Bedder* were modified, so that it was open to the jury to consider such mental or physical characteristics of the defendant as might affect his self-control in the relevant situation, the jury might require evidence as to how a person of reasonable self-control would be likely to react in such circumstances—or at least that it would be open to either side to call such evidence. In other words, evidence would be required, or alternatively be admissible, to show, for example, how a pregnant woman or a 15 year old boy or a hunchback would, exercising reasonable self-control, react in the circumstances. I cannot agree. Evidence of the pregnancy or the age or the malformation would be admissible. But whether the defendant exercised reasonable self-control in the totality of the circumstances (which would include the pregnancy or the immaturity or the malformation) would be entirely a matter for consideration by the jury without further evidence. The jury would, as ever, use their collective common sense to determine whether the provocation was sufficient to make a person of reasonable self-control in the totality of the circumstances (including personal characteristics) act as the defendant did. I certainly do not think that that is beyond the capacity of a jury. I have heard nothing to suggest that juries in New Zealand find the task beyond them.

My Lords, for those reasons I would dismiss the appeal.

I have had the privilege of reading in draft the speech prepared by my noble and learned friend on the Woolsack; and I agree with what he proposes as the appropriate direction to the jury.

Appeal dismissed

Note

The main impact of *Camplin* is on the notional "reasonable person." Lord Diplock's suggested direction to the jury contains two kinds of characteristics which the "reasonable person" might acquire: universal qualities, such as age or sex, and personal idiosyncracies, for example impotence. It is already clear that some "personal" characteristics will be ignored—hot-temperedness, for example. In *Newell*, below, the Court of Appeal added chronic alcoholism to the list of excluded characteristics. This case also suggests a restricted role for those personal characteristics which can be included, *i.e.* that they will only be relevant where the provocation was directed at them.

R. v. Newell
(1980) 71 Cr. App. R. 331
Court of Appeal

The appellant was a chronic alcoholic who battered a friend to death. He claimed that he was provoked by disparaging remarks about his former cohabitee made by the victim. The trial judge told the jury that they had to assume that the remarks were made to a sober man, and to ask themselves whether any of them would have so reacted.

Lord Lane L.C.J.: . . . Mr. Ashe Lincoln [counsel for the appellant] submits that the learned judge should have directed the jury in these terms: "Do you consider that the accused, being emotionally depressed and upset, as he was, and in the physical condition of a chronic alcoholic, was reasonably provoked by the words used and reacted in a way in which he might reasonably be expected to have acted, on the basis that he had had a very large amount to drink and had had a suicidal overdose of drugs four days previously, and that he was in a state of toxic confusion."

It seems to us that to ascertain the meaning of the speeches in *D.P.P.* v. *Camplin* (above) it is necessary to consider the meaning of the word "characteristics" as used in those speeches. To do so we find it helpful to refer, as we were invited to do by Mr. Crespi, to *McGregor* [1962] N.Z.L.R. 1069, referred to by Lord Simon of Glaisdale. First, we would read the material parts of section 169 of the New Zealand Crimes Act 1961: "(1) Culpable homicide that would otherwise be murder may be reduced to manslaughter if the person who caused the death did so under provocation. (2) Anything done or said may be provocation if—(*a*) In the circumstances of the case it was sufficient to deprive a person having the power of self-control of an ordinary person, but otherwise having the characteristics of the offender, of the power of self-control; and (*b*) It did in fact deprive the offender of the power of self-control and thereby induced him to commit the act of homicide. (3) Whether there is any evidence of provocation is a question of law. (4) Whether, if there is evidence of provocation, the provocation was sufficient as aforesaid, and whether it did in fact deprive the offender of the power of self-control and thereby induced him to commit the act of homicide, are questions of fact."

In *McGregor* (*supra*) the judgment of the court was delivered by North J., and contains the following passage which appears to us to be entirely apt to the situation in the instant case: "The Legislature has given us no guide as to what limitations might be imposed, but perforce there must be adopted a construction which will ensure regard being had to the characteristics of the offender without wholly extinguishing the ordinary man. The offender must be presumed to possess in general the power of self-control of the ordinary man, save in so far as his power of self-control is weakened because of some particular characteristic possessed by him. It is not every trait or disposition of the offender than can be invoked to modify the concept of the ordinary man. The characteristic must be something definite and of sufficient significance to make the offender a different person from the ordinary run of mankind, and have also a sufficient degree of permanence to warrant its being regarded as something constituting part of the individual's character or personality. A disposition to be unduly suspicious or to lose one's temper readily will not suffice, nor will a temporary or transitory state of mind such as a mood of depression, excitability or irascibility. These matters are either not of sufficient significance or not of sufficient permanency to be regarded as 'characteristics' which would enable the offender to be distinguished from the ordinary man. The 'unusually excitable or pugnacious individual' spoken of in *Lesbini* [1914] 3 K.B. 1116 is no more entitled to special consideration under the new section than he was when that case was decided. Still less can a self-induced transitory state be relied upon, as where it arises from the consumption of liquor. The word 'characteristics' in the context of this section is wide enough to apply not only to physical qualities but also to mental qualities and such more indeterminate attributes as colour, race and creed. It is to be emphasised that of whatever nature the characteristic may be, it must be such that it can fairly be said that the offender is thereby marked off or distinguished from the ordinary man of the community. Moreover, it is to be equally emphasised that there must be some real connection between the nature of the provocation and the particular characteristic of the offender by which it is sought to modify the ordinary man test. The words or conduct must have been exclusively or particularly provocative to the individual because, and only because, of the characteristic. In short, there must be some direct connection between the provocative words or conduct and the characteristic sought to be invoked as warranting some departure from the ordinary man test. Such a connection may be seen readily enough where the offender possesses some unusual physical peculiarity. Though he might in all other respects be an ordinary man, provocative words alluding for example to some infirmity or deformity from which he was suffering might well bring about a loss of self-control. So too, if the colour, race or creed of the offender be relied on as constituting a characteristic, it is to be repeated that the provocative words or conduct must be related to the particular characteristic relied upon. Thus, it would not be sufficient, for instance, for the offender to claim merely that he belongs to an excitable race, or that members of his nationality are accustomed to resort readily to the use of some lethal weapon. Here again, the provocative act or words require to be directed at the particular characteristic before it can be relied upon. Special difficulties, however, arise when it becomes necessary to consider what purely mental peculiarities may be allowed as characteristics.

In our opinion it is not enough to constitute a characteristic that the offender should merely in some general way be mentally deficient or weak-minded. To allow this to be said would, as we have earlier indicated, deny any real operation to the reference made in the section to the ordinary man, and it would, moreover, go far towards the admission of a defence of diminished responsibility without any statutory authority in this country to sanction it. There must be something more, such as provocative words or acts directed to a particular phobia from which the offender suffers. Beyond that, we do not think it is advisable that we should attempt to go."

That passage, and the reasoning therein contained, seem to us to be impeccable. It is not only expressed in plain, easily comprehended language; it represents also, we think, the law of this country as well as that of New Zealand. In the present case the only matter which could remotely be described as a characteristic was the appellant's condition of chronic alcoholism. Assuming that that was truly a characteristic (and we expressly make no determination as to that), nevertheless it had nothing to do with the words by which it is said that he was provoked. There was no connection between the derogatory reference to the appellant's girl friend and the suggestion of a possible homosexual act and his chronic alcoholism. It had nothing at all to do with the words by which it is said that he was provoked.

If the test set out in *McGregor* (*supra*) is applied, the learned judge in the instant case was right in not inviting the jury to take chronic alcoholism into account on the question of provocation.

The other matters advanced by Mr. Ashe Lincoln as being characteristics which the jury should have been invited to consider, in examining what a reasonable man might or would have done, are not characteristics at all. The appellant's drunkenness, or lack of sobriety, his having taken an overdose of drugs and written a suicide note a few days previously, his grief at the defection of his girl friend, and so on, are none of them matters which can properly be described as characteristics. They were truly transitory in nature, in the light of the words and reasoning of North J., in *McGregor's* case (*supra*). . . .

Appeal dismissed

Questions

1. In *Newell*, above, the Court of Appeal adopted a passage from *McGregor* which talked of the need for "some direct connection between the provocation" and the special characteristic before that characteristic can become relevant. Was there a connection in *Camplin*? Can *Camplin* be explained using the distinction between universal qualities and personal oddities, on the basis that the former must be attached to the "reasonable person" in every case but the latter only when the direct connection exists?

2. If the distinction suggested in question 1, above, is accepted, how does one determine a "universal quality"? The passage from *McGregor* suggests that race would only be a relevant factor if the provocation were so directed. But is not race as "universal" as age or sex?

3. Lord Simon, in *Camplin*, suggested that a female defendant's being pregnant, menopausal or menstrual might be characteristics with which the reasonable person could be endowed for the purposes of establishing

provocation. Would these be "universal" like age, or idiosyncratic, like impotence? Can these states of a woman's uterus be peculiarities?

b. *The reasonable relationship factor*

Mancini v. Director of Public Prosecutions
[1942] A.C. 1
House of Lords

The appellant was the manager of a club. He stabbed a member with a sharp dagger-knife. He claimed that the stabbing was done in self-defence. He was convicted and appealed.

VISCOUNT SIMON L.C.: Although the appellant's case at the trial was in substance that he had been compelled to use his weapon in necessary self-defence—a defence which, if it had been accepted by the jury, would have resulted in his complete acquittal—it was undoubtedly the duty of the judge, in summing up to the jury, to deal adquately with any other view of the facts which would reduce the crime from murder to manslaughter. The fact that a defending counsel does not stress an alternative case before the jury (which he may well feel it difficult to do without prejudicing the main defence) does not relieve the judge from the duty of directing the jury to consider the alternative, if there is material before the jury which would justify a direction that they should consider it. Thus, in *R.* v. *Hopper* [1915] 2 K.B. 431, at a trial for murder the prisoner's counsel relied substantially on the defence that the killing was accidental, but Lord Reading C.J., in delivering the judgment of the Court of Appeal, said: "We do not assent to the suggestion that as the defence throughout the trial was accident, the judge was justified in not putting the question as to manslaughter. Whatever the line of defence adopted by counsel at the trial of a prisoner, we are of opinion that it is for the judge to put such questions as appear to him properly to arise upon the evidence, even although counsel may not have raised some question himself. In this case it may be that the difficulty of presenting the alternative defences of accident and manslaughter may have actuated counsel in saying very little about manslaughter, but if we come to the conclusion, as we do, that there was some evidence—we say no more than that—upon which a question ought to have been left to the jury as to the crime being manslaughter only, we think that this verdict of murder cannot stand."

To avoid all possible misunderstanding, I would add that this is far from saying that in every trial for murder, where the accused pleads not guilty, the judge must include in his summing-up to the jury observations on the subject of manslaughter. The possibility of a verdict of manslaughter instead of murder only arises when the evidence given before the jury is such as might satisfy them as the judges of fact that the elements were present which would reduce the crime to manslaughter, or, at any rate, might induce a reasonable doubt whether this was, or was not, the case. Murder by secret poisoning, for example, does not give room for the defence that, owing to provocation received, the administration of the poison should be treated as manslaughter. On the other hand, if the defence to a charge of murder by poisoning was that the accused never administered the poison at all, the judge might very well be obliged to direct the jury on the alternative view that the administration was accidental, if the facts proved reasonably admitted this as a possible interpretation, even though the defence had not relied on the alternative.

In the present case, the appellant's counsel contended that the learned judge should have directed the jury as to what would amount to provocation sufficient to reduce the felonious act to manslaughter, and should have told them that, if they took the view that the appellant's act was provoked in this sense, they should acquit him of murder, and moreover that if, without being satisfied on the point, they felt a reasonable doubt whether the act was or was not so provoked, the appellant was still entitled to be acquitted of murder and should be found guilty only of manslaughter. All this, however, depends on the view that there was evidence before the jury which might, if believed, be regarded as amounting to sufficient provocation. It is here, I think, that the contention for the appellant breaks down.

It is not all provocation that will reduce the crime of murder to manslaughter. Provocation, to have that result, must be such as temporarily deprives the person provoked of the power of self control, as the result of which he commits the unlawful act which causes death. "In deciding the question whether this was or was not the case, regard must be had to the nature of the act by which the offender causes death, to the time which elapsed between the provocation and the act which caused death, to the offender's conduct during that interval, and to all other circumstances tending to show the state of his mind": Stephen's *Digest of the Criminal Law*, art. 317. The test to be applied is that of the provocation on a reasonable man, as was laid down by the Court of Criminal Appeal in *R.* v. *Lesbini* [1914] 3 K.B. 1116, so that an unusually excitable or pugnacious individual is not entitled to rely on provocation which would not have led an ordinary person to act as he did. In applying the test, it is of particular importance (a) to consider whether a sufficient interval has elapsed since the provocation to allow a reasonable man time to cool, and (b) to take into account the instrument with which the homicide was effected, for to retort, in the heat of passion induced by provocation, by a simple blow, is a very different thing from making use of a deadly instrument like a concealed dagger. In short, the mode of resentment must bear a reasonable relationship to the provocation if the offence is to be reduced to manslaughter. . . .

Appeal dismissed

[Self-Defence is discussed *post*, p. 411]

Question

The effect of section 3 of the Homicide Act 1957 on the "reasonable relationship rule" in *Mancini*, above, is that it is no longer a rule to be applied by the judge but is a factor to which the jury's attention should be drawn. Is it possible, logically, to apply objective standards to a situation involving, by definition, loss of control?

An argument on these lines was rejected by the Privy Council in *Phillips* v. *R.* [1969] 2 A.C. 130. For a contrary view see Brett, "The Physiology of Provocation," [1970] Crim. L.R. 634.

(c) *Self-induced provocation*

Note

An unusual question was raised in *Edwards* v. *R.* [1973] 1 All E.R. 152: can a defendant rely on this defence where his or her behaviour has induced the provocative conduct? E. had been blackmailing his victim, C. When pressed for payment, C. swore at E. and began attacking him with a knife. E. retaliated in what he described as a fit of "white hot" passion. Lord Pearson, for the Privy Council, at p. 158: "No authority has been cited with regard to what may be called 'self-induced provocation.' On principle it seems reasonable to say that (1) a blackmailer cannot rely on the predictable results of his own blackmailing conduct as constituting provocation sufficient to reduce his killing of the victim from murder to manslaughter, and the predictable results may include a considerable degree of hostile reaction by the person sought to be blackmailed, for instance vituperative words and even some hostile action such as blows with a fist; (2) but if the hostile reaction by the person sought to be blackmailed goes to extreme lengths it might constitute sufficient provocation even for the blackmailer; (3) there would in many cases be a question of degree to be decided by the jury.

In the present case, if the appellant's version of the facts be assumed to be correct, Dr. Coombe, the person sought to be blackmailed, did go to extreme lengths, in that he made a violent attack on the appellant with a knife, inflicting painful wounds and putting the appellant's life in danger. There was evidence of provocation and it was fit for consideration by the jury."

ii. Diminished Responsibility

Homicide Act 1957, section 2

"(1) Where a person kills or is a party to the killing of another, he shall not be convicted of murder if he was suffering from such abnormality of mind (whether arising from a condition of arrested or retarded development of mind or any inherent causes or induced by disease or injury) as substantially impaired his mental responsibility for his acts and omissions in doing or being a party to the killing.

(2) On a charge of murder, it shall be for the defence to prove that the person charged is by virtue of this section not liable to be convicted of murder.

(3) A person who but for this section would be liable, whether as principal or as accessory, to be convicted of murder shall be liable instead to be convicted of manslaughter."

Criminal Procedure (Insanity) Act 1964, section 6

"Where on a trial for murder the accused contends

(*a*) that at the time of the alleged offence he was insane so as not to be responsible according to law for his actions; or

(*b*) that at that time he was suffering from such abnormality of mind as is specified in subsection (1) of section (2) of the Homicide Act 1957 (diminished responsibility)

the court shall allow the prosecution to adduce or elicit evidence tending to prove the other of those contentions, and may give directions as to the stage of the proceedings at which the prosecution may adduce such evidence."

Note

As with insanity, the onus of proof which the defence have to discharge is on a balance of probabilities: *R.* v. *Dunbar* [1958] 1 Q.B. 1. This partial defence has largely replaced insanity as a defence to murder. In 1977, for example, there was a successful plea of diminished responsibility in 92 cases, as opposed to one finding of not guilty by reason of insanity, and in 1978 the figures were 78 and 0. (See Appendix 9 of the Butler Report

(Cmnd. 6244, 1975) for a table comparing the number of insanity pleas before and after 1957.)

The limitations of the insanity defence have already been discussed, *ante*, p. 166. Williams, T.C.L. 623, 624, says of section 2 both that it "has had highly beneficial results" and that it contains "as embarrassing a formula for a scientifically-minded witness as could be devised." The success of the formula lies in the fact that it uses neither exclusively "legal" nor exclusively "medical" concepts. "Abnormality of mind" is imprecise and has been given a wide interpretation by the courts, see *Byrne*, below. "Mental responsibility," as the Butler report comments, is "either a concept of law or a concept of morality; it is not a clinical fact relating to the defendant. . . . [Y]et psychiatrists commonly testify to impaired 'mental responsibility' under section 2." (§ 19.5). This Heath Robinson approach to reducing murder to manslaughter is perhaps best explained by the fact that section 2 has two, not always compatible, functions. On the one hand, it is "a device for . . . untying the hands of the judge in murder cases" (Butler Report, § 19.8), while on the other it allows for a display of public sympathy for the domestic, one-off murderer. Problems arise when the sympathy is absent, but the defendant is clearly mentally abnormal within the section. Diminished responsibility is a question of fact but if the jury is perverse in the face of fact and medical evidence, the Court of Appeal will upset the verdict: *R.* v. *Matheson* [1958] 1 W.L.R. 474, and *Walton* v. *R., post*, p. 407. Difficulties have also arisen where the court, with the prosecution's consent, agrees to accept the defence plea of diminished responsibility. See *R.* v. *Vinagre, post*, p. 409 and the discussion following it.

R. v. Byrne

[1960] 2 Q.B. 396

Court of Criminal Appeal

The appellant admitted murder but raised the defence of diminished responsibility. The defence failed and he appealed against the verdict of misdirection in the summing-up.

Lord Parker C.J.: The appellant was convicted of murder before Stable J. at Birmingham Assizes and sentenced to imprisonment for life. The victim was a young woman whom he strangled in the Y.W.C.A. hostel, and after her death he committed horrifying mutilations upon her dead body. The facts as to the killing were not disputed, and were admitted in a long statement made by the accused. The only defence was that in killing his victim the accused was suffering from diminished responsibility as defined by section 2 of the Homicide Act, 1957, and was, accordingly, guilty not of murder but of manslaughter.

Three medical witnesses were called by the defence, the senior medical officer at Birmingham Prison and two specialists in psychological medicine. Their uncontradicted evidence was that the accused was a sexual psychopath, that he suffered from abnormality of mind, as indeed was abundantly clear from the other evidence in the case, and that such abnormality of mind arose from a condition of arrested or retarded development of mind or inherent causes. The nature of the abnormality of mind of a sexual psychopath, according to the medical evidence, is that he suffers from violent perverted sexual desires which he finds it difficult or impossible to control. Save when under the influence of his perverted sexual desires he may be normal. All three doctors were of opinion that the killing was done under the influence of his perverted sexual desires, and although all three were of opinion that he was not insane in the technical sense of insanity laid down in the M'Naghten Rules it was their view that his sexual psychopathy could properly be described as partial insanity.

In his summing-up the judge, after summarising the medical evidence, gave to the jury a direction of law on the correctness of which this appeal turns. He told the jury that if on the evidence they came to the conclusion that the facts could be fairly summarised as follows:

"(1) from an early age he has been subject to these perverted violent desires, and in some cases has indulged his desires; (2) the impulse or urge of these desires is stronger than the normal impulse or urge of sex to such an extent that the subject finds it very difficult or perhaps impossible in some cases to resist putting the desire into practice; (3) the act of killing this girl was done under such an impulse or urge; and (4) that setting aside these sexual addictions and practices this man was normal in every other respect"; those facts with nothing more would not bring a case within the section, and do not constitute such abnormality of mind as substantially to impair a man's mental responsibility for his acts. "In other words," he went on, "mental affliction is one thing. The section is there to protect them. The section is not there to give protection where there is nothing else than what is vicious and depraved."

Taken by themselves these words are unobjectionable, but it is contended on behalf of the appellant that the direction taken as a whole involves a misconstruction of the section, and had the effect of withdrawing from the jury an issue of fact which it was peculiarly their province to decide.

Section 2 of the Homicide Act, 1957, is dealing with the crime of murder in which there are at common law two essential elements: (1) the physical act of killing another person, and (2) the state of mind of the person who kills or is a party to the killing, namely, his intention to kill or to cause grievous bodily harm. Subsection (1) of section 2 does not deal with the first element. It modified the existing law as respects the second element, that is, the state of mind of the person who kills or is a party to the killing.

Before the passing of the Homicide Act, 1957, a person who killed or was party to a killing could escape liability for murder—as for any other crime requiring *mens rea*—if he showed that at the time of the killing he was insane within the meaning of the M'Naghten Rules, that is, "that he was labouring under such a defect of reason from disease of the mind as not to know the nature and quality of the act that he was doing, or if he did know it that he did not know that he was doing wrong." If established, this defence negatives *mens rea* and the accused was and still is entitled to a special verdict of "guilty of the act but insane" at the time of doing the act, which is an acquittal of any crime. The test is a rigid one: it relates solely to a person's intellectual ability to appreciate: (a) the physical act that he is doing, and (b) whether it is wrong. If he has such intellectual ability, his power to control his physical acts by exercise of his will is irrelevant.

The ability of the accused to control his physical acts by exercise of his will was relevant before the passing of the Homicide Act, 1957, in one case only—that of provocation. Loss of self-control on the part of the accused so as to make him for the moment not master of his mind had the effect of reducing murder to manslaughter if: (i) it was induced by an act or series of acts done by the deceased to the accused, and (ii) such act or series of acts would have induced a reasonable man to lose his self-control and act in the same manner as the accused acted. (See *R.* v. *Duffy* [1949] 1 All E.R. 932n. (C.C.A.)).

Whether loss of self-control induced by provocation negatived the ordinary presumption that a man intends the natural ordinary consequences of his physical acts so that, in such a case, the prosecution had failed to prove the essential mental element in murder (namely, that the accused intended to kill or to inflict grievous bodily harm) is academic for the purposes of our consideration. What is relevant is that loss of self-control has always been recognised as capable of reducing murder to manslaughter, but that the criterion has always been the degree of self-control which would be exercised by a reasonable man, that is to say, a man with a normal mind.

It is against that background of the existing law that section 2 (1) of the Homicide Act, 1957, falls to be construed. To satisfy the requirements of the subsection the accused must show: (a) that he was suffering from an abnormality of mind, and (b) that such abnormality of mind (i) arose from a condition of arrested or retarded development of mind or any inherent causes or was induced by disease or injury and (ii) was such as substantially impaired his mental responsibility for his acts in doing or being a party to the killing.

"Abnormality of mind," which has to be contrasted with the time-honoured expression in the M'Naghten Rules "defect of reason," means a state of mind so different from that of ordinary human beings that the reasonable man would term it abnormal. It appears to us to be wide enough to cover the mind's activities in all its aspects, not only the perception of physical acts and matters, and the ability to form a rational judgment as to whether an act is right or wrong, but also the ability to exercise will power to control physical acts in accordance with that rational judgment. The expression "mental responsibility for his acts" points to a consideration of the extent to which the accused's mind is answerable for his physical acts which must include a consideration of the extent of his ability to exercise will power to control his physical acts.

Whether the accused was at the time of the killing suffering from any "abnormality of mind" in the broad sense which we have indicated above is a question for the jury. On this question medical evidence is no doubt of importance, but the jury are entitled to take into consideration all the evidence, including the acts or statements of the accused and his demeanour. They are not bound to accept the medical evidence if there is other material before them which, in their good judgment, conflicts with it and outweighs it.

The aetiology of the abnormality of mind (namely, whether it arose from a condition of arrested or retarded development or any inherent causes, or was induced by disease or injury) does, however, seem to be a matter determined on expert evidence.

Assuming that the jury are satisfied on the balance of probabilities that the accused was suffering from "abnormality of mind" from one of the causes specified in the parenthesis of the subsection, the crucial question nevertheless arises: was the abnormality such as substantially impaired his mental responsibility for his acts in doing or being a party to the killing? This is a question of degree and essentially one for the jury. Medical evidence is, of course, relevant, but the question involves a decision not merely as to whether there was some impairment of the mental responsibility of the accused but whether such impairment can properly be called "substantial", a matter upon which juries may quite legitimately differ from doctors.

Furthermore, in a case where the abnormality of mind is one which affects the accused's self-control the step between "he did not resist his impulse" and "he could not resist his impulse" is, as the evidence in this case shows, one which is incapable of scientific proof. *A fortiori* there is no scientific measurement of the degree of difficulty which an abnormal person finds in controlling his impulses. These problems which in the present state of medical knowledge are scientifically insoluble, the jury can only approach in a broad common sense way. This court has repeatedly approved directions to the jury which have followed directions given in Scots cases where the doctrine of diminished responsibility forms part of the common law. We need not repeat them. They are quoted in *R.* v. *Spriggs*

[1958] 1 Q.B. 270. They indicate that such abnormality as "substantially impairs his mental responsibility" involves a mental state which in popular language (not that of the M'Naghten Rules) a jury would regard as amounting to partial insanity or being on the borderline of insanity.

It appears to us that the judge's direction to the jury that the defence under section 2 of the Act was not available even though they found the facts set out in Nos. 2 and 3 of the judge's summary, amounted to a direction that difficulty or even inability of an accused person to exercise will power to control his physical acts could not amount to such abnormality of mind as substantially impairs his mental responsibility. For the reasons which we have already expressed we think that this construction of the Act is wrong. Inability to exercise will power to control physical acts, provided that it is due to abnormality of mind from one of the causes specified in the parenthesis in the subsection is, in our view, sufficient to entitle the accused to the benefit of the section; difficulty in controlling his physical acts depending on the degree of difficulty it may be. It is for the jury to decide on the whole of the evidence whether such inability or difficulty has, not as a matter of scientific certainty but on the balance of probabilities, been established, and in the case of difficulty whether the difficulty is so great as to amount in their view to a substantial impairment of the accused's mental responsibility for his acts. The direction in the present case thus withdrew from the jury the essential determination of fact which it was their province to decide.

As already indicated, the medical evidence as to the appellant's ability to control his physical acts at the time of the killing was all one way. The evidence of the revolting circumstances of the killing and the subsequent mutilations as of the previous sexual history of the appellant pointed, we think plainly, to the conclusion that the accused was what would be described in ordinary language as on the borderline of insanity or partially insane. Properly directed, we do not think that the jury could have come to any other conclusion than that the defence under section 2 of the Homicide Act was made out.

The appeal will be allowed and a verdict of manslaughter substituted for the verdict of murder. The only possible sentence having regard to the tendencies of the accused is imprisonment for life. The sentence will, accordingly, not be disturbed.

Appeal allowed

Note

The review of Scots cases by Lord Goddard in *R.* v. *Spriggs*, referred to above, is as follows (see [1958] 1 Q.B. 274):

"I had in mind *H.M. Advocate* v. *Braithwaite*, 1945 S.C. (J.) 55, where Lord Cooper, Lord Justice-Clerk, gave this charge to the jury with regard to diminished responsibility: 'Now I have got to give you the most accurate instruction I can on this delicate question. The Solicitor-General read to you a passage from the charge of the Lord Justice-Clerk in the case of *Savage*, 1923, S.C. (J.) 49, and I am going to read a sentence or two again, because it seems to me to give as explicit and clear a statement of the sort of thing which you have to look for as I can find. He says: 'It is very difficult to put it in a phrase'—and I respectfully agree—'but it has been put in this way; that there must be aberration or weakness of mind; that there must be some form of mental unsoundness; that there must be a state of mind which is bordering on, though not amounting to, insanity; that there must be a mind so affected that responsibility is diminished from full responsibility to partial responsibility—in other words, the prisoner in question must be only partially accountable for his actions.' And then he adds: 'And I think one can see running through the cases that there is implied . . . that there must be some form of mental disease.' The matter has been put in different words by other judges. I notice in a later case (*Muir* v. *H.M. Advocate*, 1933 S.C. (J.) 46, 49) that the condition was referred to for short as "partial insanity"; and that this was explained as meaning 'that weakness or great peculiarity of mind which the law has recognised as possibly differentiating a case of murder from one of culpable homicide.' And, finally, to give you one last test, the question as put by the late Lord Clyde in the same case, quoting from a charge to a jury by Lord Moncrieff, was stated thus: 'Was he, owing to his mental state, of such inferior responsibility that his act should have attributed to it the quality not of murder but of culpable homicide?' You will see, ladies and gentlemen, the stress that has been laid in all these formulations upon weakness of intellect, aberration of mind, mental unsoundness, partial insanity, great peculiarity of mind, and the like' ".

Question

Can it be argued that in *Byrne*, Lord Parker is suggesting that medical evidence is conclusive on "abnormality of mind" but not on whether that resulted in "substantial impairment"? Do the cases below provide any elucidation? See M. D. Cohen, "Medical Evidence and Diminished Responsibility" [1981] N.L.J. 667.

Walton v. The Queen
(1978) 66 Cr. App. R. 25
Privy Council

The appellant was driving home with his girlfriend and her mother when he stopped the car. His girlfriend thought he was "acting funny" and flagged down another car. The appellant shot and killed a passenger in a car which stopped. His defence to murder was diminished responsibility (which, in the Barbadian legislation, was identical with section 2 of the 1957 Act). He called two psychiatrists and a psychologist in his support. The Crown led no medical evidence. There was no evidence of any history of mental disorder. The jury convicted him of murder. The conviction was upheld by the Court of Appeal of Barbados. On appeal to the Privy Council.

Lord Keith of Kinkel delivered the judgment of the Board: . . . It was argued by Mr. Murray, for the appellant, that in the light of the uncontradicted medical evidence to the effect that the appellant suffered from an abnormality of mind which substantially impaired his mental responsibility for his acts, the jury was bound to accept that the defence of diminished responsibility had been established, and that the trial judge should have so directed them. Mr. Murray relied upon *R.* v. *Matheson* [1958] 1 W.L.R. 474 and *R.* v. *Bailey* (1978) 66 Cr. App. Rep. 31n. In the first of these cases the accused, who had a long recorded history of conduct indicative of mental abnormality, had killed a 15 year old boy under peculiarly revolting circumstances. Three medical witnesses testified at the trial that they were satisfied that the accused's mind was so abnormal as substantially to impair his mental responsibility, giving their reasons for that view, and no medical evidence was led in rebuttal. The jury returned a verdict of guilty of murder. The Court of Criminal Appeal quashed that verdict and substituted one of manslaughter. Lord Goddard C.J., delivering the judgment of the Court, having referred to the medical evidence, said (at p. 478): "What then were the facts or circumstances which would justify a jury in coming to a conclusion contrary to the unchallenged evidence of these gentlemen? While it has often been emphasised, and we would repeat, that the decision in these cases, as in those in which insanity is pleaded, is for the jury and not for doctors, the verdict must be founded on evidence. If there are facts which would entitle a jury to reject or differ from the opinions of the medical men, this Court would not, and indeed could not, disturb their verdict, but if the doctor's evidence is unchallenged and there is no other on this issue, a verdict contrary to their opinion would not be 'a true verdict in accordance with the evidence'". After considering other circumstances of the case Lord Goddard continued, at p. 479: "If then there is unchallenged evidence that there is abnormality of mind and consequent substantial impairment of mental responsibility and no facts or circumstances appear that can displace or throw doubt on that evidence, it seems to the Court that we are bound to say that a verdict of murder is unsupported by the evidence."

In *R.* v. *Bailey* the appellant, who was just 17 years of age at the time, had met a girl aged 16 years and with no apparent motive had battered her to death with an iron bar. In support of a defence of diminished responsibility the evidence of three medical witnesses was led, including a senior prison medical officer. All expressed the opinion that the appellant suffered from epilepsy, which substantially impaired his mental responsibility. The prison medical officer thought it highly probable that the appellant was at the time of the killing in an epileptic upset or fit. The Court of Criminal Appeal substituted a verdict of manslaughter for the jury's verdict of murder. Lord Parker C.J., delivering the judgment of the Court, said (p. 32): "This Court has said on many occasions that of course juries are not bound by what the medical witnesses say, but at the same time they must act on evidence, and if there is nothing before them, no facts and no circumstances shown before them which throw doubt on the medical evidence, then that is all that they are left with, and the jury, in those circumstances, must accept it."

These cases make clear that upon an issue of diminished responsibility the jury are entitled and indeed bound to consider not only the medical evidence but the evidence upon the whole facts and circumstances of the case. These include the nature of the killing, the conduct of the accused before, at the time of and after it and any history of mental abnormality. It being recognised that the jury on occasions may properly refuse to accept medical evidence, it follows that they must be entitled to consider the quality and weight of that evidence. As was pointed out by Lord Parker C.J. in *R.* v. *Byrne* [*ante*, p. 403], what the jury are essentially seeking to ascertain is whether at the time of the killing the accused was suffering from a state of mind bordering on but not amounting to insanity. That task is to be approached in a broad common sense way.

In the present case their Lordships are of opinion that, in so far as they can judge of the medical evidence from the trial judge's notes, the jury were entitled to regard it as not entirely convincing. Dr. Patricia Bannister, whose evidence was subjected to quite lengthy cross-examination, expressed an opinion as to the appellant's state of mind which in terms satisfied the statutory definition. The particular mental abnormality which she identified was that of an extremely immature personality. Mr. Browne, the clinical psychologist, found the appellant to be of average intellectual ability with good observational ability and clear thinking. He supported Dr. Patricia Bannister's evidence by describing the appellant as having an inadequate personality enhanced by emotional immaturity and a low tolerance level. The evidence of Dr. Lawrence Bannister was merely to the effect that he treated the appellant for depression, with disappointing results. It is plain that the quality and weight of this medical evidence fell a long way short of that in *Matheson's* case and in *Bailey's* case. The jury also had before them evidence about the conduct of the appellant before, during and after killing, including that of a number of conflicting statements about it made by him to the police and to Dr. Patricia Bannister. They may well have thought there was nothing in that evidence indicative of a man whose mental state bordered on insanity. There was also the appellant's unsworn statement regarding his having suffered in the past from severe headache, blackouts, sleeplessness and lack of memory, supported to some extent by Miss Watson, but no objective evidence of any history of mental disorder. In both these aspects the case is in marked contradistinction to *Matheson's* case.

Having carefully considered the relevant evidence, their Lordships have come to be of opinion that in all the circumstances the jury were entitled not to accept as conclusive the expression of opinion by Dr. Patricia Bannister that the appellant's mental condition satisfied the statutory definition of diminished responsibility, and to conclude, as they did, that the defence had not on a balance of probabilities been established.

Their Lordships will therefore humbly advise Her Majesty that the appeal should be dismissed.

Appeal dismissed

R. v. Vinagre
(1979) 69 Cr. App. R. 104
Court of Appeal

The appellant, who suspected his wife of infidelity, stabbed her to death. His plea of diminished responsibility was accepted by the trial judge who sentenced him to life imprisonment. It was against this that he appealed. The Court of Appeal considered the wider issue of when such a plea should be accepted.

LAWTON L.J.: . . . In this case there were medical examinations of the accused by psychiatrists. Two medical reports were produced. We find them rather unusual documents, because the substance of them was this, that the appellant at the material time was suffering from a mental condition which was described in picturesque, if inaccurate, language as the "Othello syndrome," which was defined as being "morbid jealousy for which there was no cause."

One of the two psychiatrists, whose reports were before the Court, said this:

> "This case would seem to hinge on whether indeed Mrs. Vinagre was being unfaithful to her husband by having sex relationships with the plain clothes policeman Michael. If there was no such liaison then the possibility of a jealous spouse or Othello syndrome may be raised whereby the accused became so overwhelmed by his jealous suspicion that after having not slept the night before and only two hours that morning, later that day after a violent argument with his wife he attacked her with fatal consequences.
>
> On the other hand if there is evidence that his wife was indeed unfaithful, then it would be difficult to offer the same psychiatric defence. A good deal will therefore depend on the evidence of the Court as to whether his wife was, as he claimed her to be, the victim of his pathological jealousy."

One would have thought that in those circumstances, it would have been necessary, if justice was to be done, to find out whether, on the basis of this report, there had been any sexual relationship between the wife and Michael, because this doctor was saying that if there had been, it was a straightforward case of a jealous husband. It was only if there was not any evidence—and it was not for him to say whether there was any evidence or not—that the so-called "Othello syndrome" could be called in aid. The other doctor, who was the prison medical officer, was of the same opinion.

This Court wishes to say that however much the concept of the Othello syndrome may have entered modern psychiatric medicine, it is not one which appeals to this Court.

This however is to be said. Such medical evidence as was before the Court came from the Crown. In those circumstances there was not much point in the defence producing any other psychiatric evidence. Indeed there was a danger that they might have produced a hard-headed psychiatrist who would not have had much use for the Othello syndrome.

As a result, when the case came before the trial judge, Mr. Baker, on behalf of the accused, was able to tender the plea to manslaughter on the grounds of diminished responsibility on the basis that that was what the Crown themselves were saying. The learned judge, as I have already stated, accepted the plea.

We wish to call attention to the history of the acceptance of pleas on grounds of diminished responsibility. After the passing of the Homicide Act 1957, the question arose as to whether Courts could accept pleas to manslaughter on grounds of diminished responsibility. The Court of Criminal Appeal decided in *R.* v. *Matheson* [1958] 1 W.L.R. 474, that that was not to be done. After that decision until 1962 in all cases of this kind the verdict of the jury had to be taken. The wording of the Homicide Act 1957 indicates that that may well have been the intention of Parliament, because the burden of proving diminished responsibility was upon the defendant. Between 1957 and 1962 there were distressing cases in which a distraught woman (or sometimes a man but usually a distraught woman) had to sit in the dock listening to hours of evidence of what she had done when she was in a state of mental imbalance. Some judges thought that that was wrong. As a result in 1962 the judges decided that pleas to manslaughter on grounds of diminished responsibility could be accepted.

Thompson J. and I were both judges at the time and we are sure that it was never intended that pleas should be accepted on flimsy grounds. As Scarman L.J. pointed out two or three years ago in *R.* v. *Ford* (1976) (*unrep.*) cases are tried by the Courts and not by psychiatrists. It seems to us that pleas to manslaughter on the grounds of diminished responsibility should only be accepted when there is clear evidence of mental imbalance. We do not consider that in this case there was clear evidence of mental imbalance. There was clear evidence of a killing by a jealous husband which, until modern times, no one would have thought was anything else but murder.

Be that as it may, Park J. did accept the plea and he listened to the submissions by Mr. Baker on behalf of the appellant as to how the case should be disposed of. . . .

Having been told by the psychiatrist that he was satisfied that there would be no recurrence, Mr. Baker so informed the learned judge, who was somewhat sceptical about this and in the course of sentencing the appellant he said: "I am told that you are in no danger; you are no longer any danger to the public but for my part, I am not able to say when you will be fit to resume your place in society." . . .

The way things happened has put this Court in a difficulty because if this man is suffering from the Othello syndrome, he may suffer from it again. In other words he is in a state of mental imbalance which may at some future date make him a danger to the public. On the other hand there was some assertion before Park J. that, whatever he may have been suffering from at the time when he killed his wife, he was not likely to suffer from it in the future. That was left unresolved, the judge taking a different view to that which was being urged upon him by Mr. Baker.

We feel that we have no alternative but to approach this case on the basis that Mr. Baker's instructions were correct. In those circumstances the appellant at the time of the trial, and certainly today, is not suffering from the kind of mental imbalance which would justify keeping him in custody until such time as the

Home Secretary and the parole board think that it is safe to release him. Accordingly we quash the sentence of life imprisonment and substitute for it a sentence of seven years' imprisonment. To that extent the appeal against sentence is allowed.

Appeal allowed
Sentence varied

Note

In *R.* v. *Cox* [1968] 1 W.L.R. 308, at 310, Winn L.J. for the Court of Appeal "[F]rom the very onset of the trial it was quite clear . . . that the medical evidence available . . . showed perfectly plainly that [the plea of diminished responsibility] was a plea which it would have been proper to accept. . . . The Court desires to say yet again . . . that there are cases where, on an indictment for murder, it is perfectly proper, where the medical evidence is plainly to this effect, to treat the case as one of substantially diminished responsibility and accept, if it be tendered, a plea to manslaughter on that ground, and avoid a trial for murder."

Both the Butler Committee on Abnormal Offenders (Cmnd. 6244, 1975, § 19.19) and the Criminal Law Revision Committee (14th Report, Offences Against the Person, Cmnd. 7844, 1980, §§ 95, 96) recommend that, in clear cases, it should be possible to avoid indicting for murder at all so that the period between committal and trial is not spent under the shadow of an unrealistic charge.

However, *R.* v. *Vinagre*, above, and the trial of *Peter Sutcliffe* (at the Old Bailey, April-May 1981, *The Times* May 23, 1981) illustrate the difficulties of, on the one hand, pursuing a humane procedure to protect the mentally disordered and, on the other, striving to preserve the public interest in murderers being convicted as such. Sutcliffe tendered pleas of diminished responsibility to 13 charges of murder. The psychiatric reports were unanimous in suggesting that Sutcliffe was a paranoid schizophrenic. The judge, however, deemed it to be in the public interest that a jury should determine this matter and the trial proceeded. The jury returned convictions for murder. The case highlights, if nothing else, the extent to which murder and manslaughter are divided not by the niceties of legal definitions but by public gut-reaction. And this raises the question of the proper roles of prosecution, judge and jury. Who is to be the arbiter of the place which any particular homicide is to take on the scale of heinousness?

4. SELF-DEFENCE

Note

This term is used here in its broad sense and covers not only defence of self, but defence of others, defence of property and prevention of crime. Any of these can arise in non-fatal offences against the person but most of the appellate cases concern homicide. It is difficult to avoid describing self-defence as a "defence" but it should be emphasised that killing or otherwise injuring in these circumstances is not *unlawful* and therefore, strictly, there is no onus for the defendant to discharge. Winn L.J. in *R.* v. *Wheeler* [1967] W.L.R. 1531, at p. 1533:

"... wherever there has been a killing, or indeed the infliction of violence not proving fatal, in circumstances where the defendant puts forward a justification such as self-defence, such as provocation, such as resistance to a violent felony, it is very important and indeed quite essential that the jury should understand, and that the matter should be so put before them that there is no danger of their failing to understand, that none of those issues of justification are properly to be regarded as defences: unfortunately there is sometimes a regrettable habit of referring to them as, for example, the defence of self-defence. In particular, where a judge does slip into the error or quasi error of referring to such explanations as defences, it is particularly important that he should use language which suffices to make it clear to the jury that they are not defences in respect of which any onus rests upon the accused, but are matters which the prosecution must disprove as an essential part of the prosecution case before a verdict of guilty is justified"

(Reiterated in *R.* v. *Abraham* [1973] 1 W.L.R. 1270.)

This section is divided as follows:

i. The different situations in which "self-defence" can arise.
ii. How far section 3 of the Criminal Justice Act 1967 (force in the prevention of crime) has replaced the common law.
iii. The common requirement of reasonableness.
iv. Whether, in cases of homicide, excessive force should give rise to a partial defence.

i. Scope of the Defence

(a) *Defence of self*

R. v. Bull
(1839) 9 C. & P. 22; 173 E.R. 723
Central Criminal Court

The deceased was one of a party of six who had been drinking at several public-houses. They were going along a road when they met the defendant who stabbed the deceased with a knife in the armpit. There was some discrepancy in the testimony as to the conduct of the deceased and his friends previous to the infliction of the wound. The defendant was charged with murder but maintained that he was defending himself.

VAUGHAN J.: It was not justifiable homicide unless there was an intention on the part of the deceased and his companions to rob or murder the prisoner or to do some dreadful bodily injury to him; and that it was not the law that a man would be justified in taking away the life of another, merely because he feared that he might be assaulted, or indeed if he were actually assaulted. His Lordship told the jury that the question for their consideration was, whether the conduct of the party made it necessary for the prisoner to inflict that blow which almost immediately terminated in the death of the deceased—whether he inflicted the wound in self-defence to save his own life, which was in danger, or to protect himself from some dreadful bodily injury.

Verdict: Guilty

R. v. Scully

(1824) C. & P. 319; 171 E.R. 1213
Gloucester Assizes

The defendant was set to watch his master's premises. He saw a man on the garden wall and hailed him. This man said to another, "Tom, why don't you fire?" The defendant hailed the man on the wall again and he said, "Shoot and be d——d," whereupon he shot at the man on the wall, aiming at his legs. He missed and shot the deceased whom he had not seen. The defendant was charged with manslaughter.

GARROW B.: Any person set by his master to watch a garden or yard, is not at all justified in shooting at or injuring in any way persons who may come into those premises, even in the night: and if he saw them go into his master's hen roost, he would still not be justified in shooting them. He ought first to go and see if he could not take measures for their apprehension. But here the life of the prisoner was threatened and if he considered his life in actual danger, he was justified in shooting the deceased as he had done; but, if not considering his own life in danger, he rashly shot that man, who was only a trespasser, he would be guilty of manslaughter.

Verdict: Not guilty

Note

Is there a duty to retreat?

In *R.* v. *Julien* (1969) 1 W.L.R. 843 Widgery L.J. said: "... The third point taken by Mr. McHale is that the deputy chairman was wrong in directing the jury before the appellant could use force in self-defence he was required to retreat. The submission here is that the obligation to retreat before using force in self-defence is an obligation which only arises in homicide cases. As the court understands it, it is submitted that if the injury results in death then the accused cannot set up self-defence except on the basis that he had retreated before he resorted to violence. On the other hand, it is said that where the injury does not result in death (as in the present case) the obligation to retreat does not arise.

The sturdy submission is made that an Englishman is not bound to run away when threatened, but can stand his ground and defend himself where he is. In support of this submission no authority is quoted, save that Mr. McHale has been at considerable length and diligence to look at the textbooks on the subject, and has demonstrated to us that the textbooks in the main do not say that preliminary retreat is a necessary prerequisite to the use of force in self-defence. Equally, it must be said that the textbooks do not state the contrary either; and it is, of course, well known to us all that for very many years it has been common form for judges directing juries where the issue of self-defence is raised in any case (be it a homicide case or not) to say that the duty to retreat arises.

It is not, as we understand it, the law that a person threatened must take to his heels and run in the dramatic way suggested by Mr. McHale; but what is necessary is that he should demonstrate by his actions that he does not want to fight. He must demonstrate that he is prepared to temporise and disengage and perhaps to make some physical withdrawal; and that that is necessary as a feature of the justification of self-defence is true, in our opinion, whether the charge is a homicide charge or something less serious. Accordingly, we reject Mr. McHale's third submission."

In *R.* v. *McInnes* [1971] 1 W.L.R. 1600, the Court of Appeal accepted *Julien*, above, as an accurate statement of the law, but Edmund-Davies L.J.

(as he then was) suggested at p. 1608, that "a failure to retreat is only an *element* in the considerations upon which the reasonableness of an accused's conduct is to be judged."

If there is a duty to retreat, it does not extend so far as to require D. to remove himself or herself from an attack which is anticipated but has not yet occurred: *R.* v. *Field* [1972] Crim. L.R. 435

Fletcher, Rethinking Criminal Law, p. 866

"Anglo-American law has undergone several stages in the evolution of its posture toward the duty to retreat, particularly in cases of deadly force. Prior to the nineteenth century, the excuse of *se defendendo* coexisted with the justification recognised in the Statute of 1532. [24 Hen. VIII, c. 5, which allowed deadly force against murderers, robbers and burglars].

The former implied a duty to retreat; the latter, the principle of autonomy and the right not to "give way to a thief." In the course of the nineteenth century, the distinction between justifiable and excusable homicide lost its procedural manifestations, and thus the impulse was to fashion a single body of principles covering cases of both *se defendendo* and justifiable homicide. But if there was to be only one law of necessary defense, the question was whether it would incorporate the duty to retreat from *se defendendo* or follow the principle of autonomy implicit in the law of justifiable homicide."

Ashworth argues in "Self-Defence and The Right to Life" [1975] C.L.J. 282, 302, that the duty to retreat justifiably reflects the difference between self-defence and prevention of crime: "[T]he central case of prevention of crime (*i.e.* intervention by a police officer) involves aggressive acts for a positive purpose, whereas self-defence and defence of property typically involve defensive acts for a negative purpose. An individual under attack might be able to avoid further violence by withdrawing, but a police officer who sees an offence being committed has a duty to go forward and intervene."

The A.L.I. Model Penal Code, § 3.04 (2) (b) ii incorporates a duty to retreat except where the attack is at a person's home or place of work. Fletcher, p. 868, commenting on this:

"The special position of someone attacked in his private quarters continues to express our respect for personal autonomy, but it is harder to understand extending this theory to one's place of work. If, in general, there should be a duty to retreat rather than kill, the same preference for life should prevail whether one is attacked at work or at play."

(b) *Defence of others*

"Under the excuse of self-defence, the principal civil and natural relations are comprehended; therefore master and servant, parent and child, husband and wife, killing an assailant in the necessary defence of each other respectively, are excused: the act of the relation, assisting being construed the same as the act of the party himself": 4 Bl. Co. 186, and see 1 Hale 484.

R. v. Rose
(1884) 15 Cox 540
Oxford Assizes

The defendant was a weakly young man of 22; his father was a powerful man. Recently the father had been drinking excessively and whilst intoxicated he was of the opinion that his wife had been unfaithful to him. He had threatened her life and she was so frightened that she had frequently hidden everything in the house that could be used as a weapon. On the night in question the family had retired to separate bedrooms when the father had started abusing and arguing with his wife, threatening to murder her. He rushed from his room, seized his wife, and forced her up against the balusters in such a way as to give the impression that he was cutting her throat. The daughter and the mother shouted "murder," whereupon the defendant ran from his room. He is said to have fired a gun to frighten his father—no trace of his shot was found, and then he fired again, hitting his father in the eye and killing him. On arrest he said, "Father was murdering mother. I shot on one side to frighten him: he would not leave her, so I shot him." He was charged with murder.

LOPES J.: Homicide is excusable if a person takes away the life of another in defending himself, if the fatal blow which takes away life is necessary for his preservation. The law says not only in self-defence such as I have described may homicide be excusable, but also it may be excusable if the fatal blow inflicted was necessary for the preservation of life. In the case of parent and child, if the parent had reason to believe that the life of a child is in imminent danger by reason of an assault by another person, and that the only possible, fair and reasonable means of saving the child's life is by doing something which will cause the death of that person, the law excuses that act. It is the same of a child with regard to a parent; it is the same in the case of husband and wife. Therefore, I propose to lay the law before you in this form: If you think, having regard to the evidence, and drawing fair and proper inferences from it, that the prisoner at the Bar acted without vindictive feeling towards his father when he fired the shot, if you think that at the time he fired that shot he honestly believed, and had reasonable grounds for the belief, that his mother's life was in imminent peril, and that the fatal shot which he fired was absolutely necessary for the preservation of her life, then he ought to be excused, and the law will excuse him, from the consequences of the homicide. If, however, on the other hand, you cannot come to this conclusion, if you think, and think without reasonable doubt, that it is not a fair inference to be drawn from the evidence, but are clearly of opinion that he acted vindictively, and had not such a belief as I have described to you, or had not reasonable grounds for such a belief, then you must find him guilty of murder.

Verdict: Not guilty

R. v. Duffy

[1967] 1 Q.B. 63
Court of Criminal Appeal

The appellant's sister was fighting. It was the appellant's case that she went to rescue her sister and that this was justifiable as self-defence. They were both convicted of unlawful wounding.

EDMUND DAVIES J.: . . . defending counsel throughout relied upon the plea that the appellant was acting in self-defence, a plea which he submitted extended to the action of the appellant in seeking to rescue her sister. It is established that such a defence is not restricted to the person attacked. It has been said to extend to "the principal civil and natural relations." Hale's Pleas of the Crown, Vol. 1, p. 484, gives as instances master and servant, parent and child, and husband and wife who, if they even kill an assailant in the necessary defence of each other, are excused, the act of the relative assisting being considered the same as the act of the party himself. But no reported case goes outside the relations indicated, although the editor of Kenny's Outlines of Criminal Law, 18th ed. (1962), p. 198, says that "... perhaps the courts will now take a still more general view of this duty of the strong to protect the weak." Be that as it may, the judge seems to have found himself limited by the fact that no reported decision extended self-defence to a case where, as here, a sister went to the rescue of a sister, and the direction given to the jury as far as this appellant is concerned was this: "So far as I can see, members of the jury, in this case, the defence of self-defence is not open to Lilian Duffy. There is no suggestion whatever that she personally was attacked and it is my direction to you to approach this case on the footing that it is no defence for Lilian Duffy to say she was going to the assistance of her sister...."

The source of error in this case, as it appears to this court is, as we have said, that everyone, including counsel at the trial and again before us, seems to have overlooked that in reality and in law the case of Lilian Duffy was not trammelled by any technical limitations on the application of the plea of self-defence, and this court is not here concerned to consider what those limitations are. Quite apart from any special relations between the person attacked and his rescuer, there is a general liberty even as between strangers to prevent a felony. That is not to say, of course, that a newcomer may lawfully join in a fight just for the sake of fighting. Such conduct is wholly different in law from that of a person who in circumstances of necessity intervenes with the sole object of restoring the peace by rescuing a person being attacked. That, credible or otherwise, was the basic defence advanced by the appellant. She herself tied no lawyer's label to her tale. It is true that the judge said: "I need only remind you again that it is Lilian Duffy's case that she was going to the rescue of her sister and that was why she hit Akbar with a bottle, she could not get him off her sister." But his earlier directions had indicated that such a case afforded no defence in law. We think that this was a misdirection. The necessity for intervening at all and the reasonableness or otherwise of the manner of intervention were matters for the jury. It should have been left to them to say whether, in view of the appellant's proved conduct, such a defence could possibly be true, they being directed that the intervener is permitted to do only what is necessary and reasonable in all the circumstances for the purpose of rescue....

Appeal allowed

See also *Devlin* v. *Armstrong, post,* p. 419.

(c) *Defence of property*

R. v. Hussey

(1924) 18 Cr. App. R. 160

Court of Criminal Appeal

The appellant given an invalid notice to quit his rooms by his landlady, refused to do so. The landlady with two friends, armed with a hammer, a spanner, a poker and a chisel, tried to break down the door to the appellant's room which he had barricaded. A panel of the door was broken and the appellant fired through the hole wounding the friends of the landlady. He was charged with unlawfully wounding them and convicted. He appealed on the ground that the distinction between self-defence and defence of one's house had not been drawn to the attention of the jury.

LORD HEWART C.J.: No sufficient notice had been given to the appellant to quit his room, and therefore he was in the position of a man who was defending his house. In Archbold's Criminal Pleading, Evidence and Practice, 26th ed., p. 887, it appears that: "In defence of a man's house, the owner or his family may kill a trespasser who would forcibly dispossess him of it, in the same manner as he might, by law, kill in self-defence a man who attacks him personally; with the distinction, however, that in defending his home he need not retreat, as in other cases of self-defence, for that would be giving up his house to his adversary." [See now 40th ed., § 2472.] That is still the law, but not one word was said about that distinction in the summing-up, which proceeded on the foundation that the defence was the ordinary one of self-defence. The jury, by their verdict, negatived felonious intent, and with a proper direction they might have come to a different conclusion. The appeal must therefore be allowed.

Conviction quashed

Questions

1. Consider the limitations of this wider rule. Does the burglar fall under it? Defence against intruders in the form of man-traps is dealt with in section 31 of the Offences against the Person Act, 1861:

> "Whosoever shall set or place, or cause to be set or placed any spring-gun, man trap, or other engine calculated to destroy human life or inflict grievous bodily harm with intent that the same or whereby the same may destroy life or inflict grievous bodily harm upon a trespasser or other person coming into contact therewith, shall be guilty of a misdemeanour. . . ."

[But exceptions are allowed for traps set with the intention of destroying vermin or man-traps set in a dwelling-house for its protection by day, and by *R.* v. *Munks* [1964] 1 Q.B. 304 the section has been restricted to mechanical contrivances, excluding electric wires, which were involved in that case.]

2. The common practice of fixing broken glass on wall tops could conceivably cause death—what would be the position of the landowner who fixed the glass? Would it make any difference to the position if the intruder came to turn out the landowner rather than to steal goods from the property?

Note

The landlady in *Hussey*, above, would now be committing an offence under the Protection from Eviction Act 1977, s. 1, and under the Criminal Law Act 1977, s. 6 (although this latter is not yet in force). Had the case arisen today, Hussey could have relied on the defence of prevention of crime.

In *Taylor* v. *Mucklow* [1973] Crim. L.R. 750 the owner of a house threatened with a loaded airgun a builder who began knocking down the extension he had built for him but for which he had not paid. The magistrates did not accept that he had a reasonable excuse for use of the gun in the circumstances. The Divisional Court agreed and added that for anyone to argue nowadays that a loaded firearm was a suitable way of restraining the kind of bad temper exhibited by the builder was to show a lack of appreciation of modern trends and dangers. Professor Smith in his commentary suggests that the dictum in *Hussey* "should be regarded with caution."

(d) *Prevention of crime*

Criminal Law Act 1967, section 3

"(1) A person may use such force as is reasonable in the circumstances in the prevention of crime, or in effecting or assisting in the lawful arrest of offenders or suspected offenders or of persons unlawfully at large.

(2) Subsection (1) above shall replace the rules of common law on the question when force used for a purpose mentioned in the subsection is justified by that purpose."

Section 3 of the Criminal Law Act (Northern Ireland) 1967 is in similar terms and was considered by the House of Lords in the civil case of *Farrell* v. *Secretary of State for Defence* [1980] 1 W.L.R. 172. Viscount Dilhorne said, at p. 178: "[Section 3 (1)] may provide a defence for a person accused of a crime. It also may provide a defence for a person sued. In each case when such a defence is put forward the question to be determined is whether the person who is accused or sued used such force as was reasonable in the circumstances *in which he was placed* in the prevention of crime or in bringing about a lawful arrest of an offender or suspected offender. Section 3 (1) . . . can only provide a defence for those who used force. . . ." (emphasis added). The facts were that four soldiers had been instructed by their commanding officer to set up an ambush in anticipation of an expected bomb attack on a bank. Three men whom the soldiers suspected were about to plant a bomb, failed to halt when asked, and were shot and killed by the soldiers. It later emerged that none of them was armed, nor were any carrying a bomb. The action was brought by the widow of one of the men. The Court of Appeal in Northern Ireland ordered a new trial on the ground, *inter alia*, that "in the circumstances" meant the circumstances in which an operation was conceived and planned as well as those in which the actual act took place. The House of Lords rejected this view and allowed the Secretary of State's appeal against the ordering of the new trial. See the note by Walker at (1980) 43 M.L.R. 591.

ii. Section 3 and the common law

Ashworth, "Self-Defence and The Right to Life" (1975) C.L.J. 282, 284

"Does the English criminal law on self-defence consist of a number of rules and exceptions laid down at common law, or is it governed by a general standard of 'reasonableness' laid down by statute? At first blush it seems extraordinary that such an elementary point should remain in doubt, not least because the statute in question (the Criminal Law Act 1967) has been in force for several years. Professors Smith and Hogan state, in their influential work [Criminal Law, now 4th ed. (1978) p. 325], that the common law rules no longer represent English law; the practice of the courts suggests otherwise. What are, or were, these rules? The two principal requirements are that the force should have been necessary for self-defence and reasonable in the circumstances. The requirement of necessity supports two separate limitations. The first is that it should have been necessary to use force rather than employing non-violent means of self-protection. From this limitation derives the so-called 'duty to retreat': when an individual's purpose in a threatening situation is to save himself from injury or death, it cannot be necessary for him to inflict harm on his assailant if there is a safe avenue of withdrawal open to him. To this duty there have always been certain exceptions. A second limitation is that the amount of force should have been no more than necessary for the purpose of self-defence. Courts have occasionally merged this with the requirement of reasonableness, which demands a sense of proportion between the harm inflicted and the harm thereby prevented, but the two requirements are theoretically distinct.

What are the grounds for arguing that the common law has been overruled by section 3 of the Criminal Law Act 1967? The section enacts that 'a person may use such force as is reasonable in the circumstances in the prevention of crime,' and that this provision 'shall replace the rules of the common law' on the justifiability of force used in the prevention of crime. Smith and Hogan argue that 'self-defence and defence of others invariably arise out of an attempt to commit a crime by the assailant and thus consist in the use of force to prevent the commission of the crime.' It therefore follows that cases of self-defence should be decided according to the general test of reasonableness laid down by section 3, and that all the old common law authorities should be regarded as repealed. Now, even on the assumption that the conflation of the two grounds of justification would be logical and desirable, there are good reasons why it is unacceptable as an analysis of English law. In the first place, section 3 was not intended to alter the law on self-defence. Furthermore, the courts continue to deal with cases by reference to the common law. Indeed in not one of the appellate decisions reported since 1967 has there been even a passing reference to section 3 as relevant to self-defence."

CLRC, 14th Report, Offences Against the Person, § 281: "Section 3 applies to most cases of self-defence . . . however, in a few cases the attacker may not be committing a crime because, for example, he is a child under 10 years old, insane, in a state of automatism, or under a material mistake of fact."

See also Harlow, "Self-Defence: Public Right or Private Privilege" [1974] Crim. L.R. 528.

Note

The case below is unusual not only because of its facts but also for the explicit discussion of the relationship between the common law and section 3 (or its Northern Irish equivalent).

Devlin v. Armstrong
[1971] N.I. 13
Court of Appeal for Northern Ireland

The case arose out of serious disturbances in Londonderry in August 1969. The appellant exhorted a crowd of people, who had been stoning the police, to build barricades and to fight the police with petrol bombs. Her grounds of appeal against four convictions of riotous behaviour and incitement to riotous behaviour were that she reasonably believed that the police were about to act unlawfully in assaulting people and damaging property and so her behaviour was justified.

Lord MacDermott L.C.J., with whom Curran and McKeigh L.JJ. agreed, after describing the events in some detail:

The findings of the case indicate that the state of disorder which I have described involved a violent and aggressive resistance to constitutional authority, and if the relevant facts and considerations ended with the tale of events already told, the inescapable conclusion would be that the appellant and those associated with her in opposing the police by the means described were participants in a riot and guilty of riotous behaviour.

As I have stated, the answer to this, as advanced on behalf of the appellant, is one of justification. She did what she did, it was submitted, because she believed honestly and reasonably that the police were about to assault people and damage property in the Bogside. The learned resident magistrate did not accept the factual basis of this submission, but that finding has become entwined with one respecting the admissibility of certain evidence which the appellant sought to adduce in support of this plea and I shall, therefore, assume for present purposes that in fact, the appellant did honestly and reasonably believe that the police were about to behave unlawfully in the manner mentioned. Thus arises what I have called the principal issue. Does this plea of justification afford a defence to the charges? At this point I do not need to distinguish between the offences of inciting to riotous behaviour and behaving riotously. If this defence meets one of these offences it must, in the circumstances, meet the other.

The conclusion I have reached on this issue is against the appellant. In my opinion the submission under discussion fails as an answer to any of the charges. Since there is a dearth of authority on the point and various principles have been invoked on one side and the other, I shall enumerate the reasons which, separately and in conjunction, have led me to this view.

1. At any rate one common purpose of the rioters and the appellant was, beyond any question, to keep the police from entering or establishing themselves in the Bogside and to achieve this by force. The appellant's contention that the honesty and reasonableness of her apprehensions (as I have assumed them to be for the sake of the argument) robbed her actions of the mens rea necessary to constitute the offences charged must, to my mind, fail once the nature of this common purpose has been demonstrated. If it were conceded that her apprehensions supplied a motive for her actions and incitements, that in itself would fall well short of neutralising her intentions as manifested by the manner of her participation.

2. Reliance was also placed upon the doctrine of self-defence. The general nature of this doctrine may be taken as described in Russell on Crime, 12th ed. (1964) vol. I, p. 680, thus:

> "The use of force is lawful for the necessary defence of self or others or of property; but the justification is limited by the necessity of the occasion, and the use of unnecessary force is an assault."

The plea of self-defence may afford a defence where the party raising it uses force, not merely to counter an actual attack, but to ward off or prevent an attack which he has honestly and reasonably anticipated. In that case, however, the anticipated attack must be imminent: see *R.* v. *Chisam* (1963) 47 Cr. App. R. 130, 134, and the excerpt from Lord Normand's judgment in *Owens* v. *H.M. Advocate*, 1946 S.C. (J) 119, which is there quoted and which runs:

> "In our opinion self-defence is made out when it is established to the satisfaction of the jury that the panel believed that he was in imminent danger and that he held that belief on reasonable grounds. Grounds for such belief may exist though they are founded on a genuine mistake of fact."

That there was a distinction between the right of self-defence and the right to prevent a felony appears from *R.* v. *Duffy*, [*ante,* p. 415], but the latter right has gone with the abolition of the distinctions between felony and misdemeanour and its place is now taken in this jurisdiction by section 3 of the Criminal Law Act (Northern Ireland), 1967, subsection (1) of which says:

> "A person may use such force as is reasonable in the circumstances in the prevention of crime. . . ."

However reasonable and convinced the appellant's apprehensions may have been, I find it impossible to hold that the danger she anticipated was sufficiently specific or imminent to justify the actions she took as measures of self-defence. The police were then in the throes of containing a riot in the course of their duty, and her interventions at that juncture were far too aggressive and premature to rank as justifiable effort to prevent the prospective danger of the police getting out of hand and acting unlawfully which, as I have assumed, she anticipated.

3. Where force is used either in exercise of the right of self-defence or, under section 3 of the Act of 1967, in the prevention of crime, it must be reasonable in the circumstances. This consideration alone seems to me fatal to the appellant's plea of justification. Whatever her fears and however genuine they may have been, to organise and encourage the throwing of petrol bombs was, I would hold, an utterly unwarranted and unlawful reaction. The night of 12 August had demonstrated the capacity of these lethal weapons to injure and destroy and nothing that had happened or was likely to happen could excuse the appellant in facilitating and encouraging their use.

4. The plea of justification, whether based on the doctrine of self-defence or the statutory right to prevent crime, appears to me to place a further difficulty when the offence sought to be justified is that of inciting others to riotous behaviour. While there was evidence of a general fear of the police amongst people of the Bogside, there is nothing in the findings or facts of the case to show that those who were exhorted by the appellant to riot were actuated by any honest and reasonable apprehension of unlawful violence on the part of the police such as she is assumed to have had. Her incitements were, therefore, directed to encouraging others to do what for them was prima facie unlawful. It cannot be taken for granted that those she addressed were opposing the police for what she says were her reasons, and this all the more as the rioting had started in opposition to the parade and before the police had entered the Bogside. In my opinion the plea of self-defence cannot be availed of where what is sought to be justified is an incitement to unjustifiable crime. I know of no authority to the contrary, and on this ground as well I would hold that the plea fails.

5. As I understood his argument Sir Dingle Foot at one stage sought, in the alternative, to broaden the appellant's plea of justification by putting it on the basis of a collective right of self-defence arising out of some collective necessity. He frankly admitted that there was no clear authority for such a concept, but drew our attention to a passage from the judgment of Lord Mansfield in *R.* v. *Stratton and Ors.* (1779) 21 St. Tr. 1045 at 1224, which is mentioned by Mr. Justice Stephen in his *History of the Criminal Law* (1883), vol. ii, 109, in relation to the plea of compulsion by necessity. In that case the accused, who were charged for deposing Lord Pigot from the Government of Madras, defended themselves on the ground that Lord Pigot's conduct had been such that it was necessary for them to do so in the interests of the Madras Presidency. After speaking of cases of natural necessity, such as self-defence, Lord Mansfield continued:

> "As to civil necessity, none can happen in corporations, societies, and bodies of men deriving their authority under the Crown and therefore subordinate; no case ever did exist in government to which they can apply, they have a superior at hand, and therefore I cannot be warranted to put to you any case of civil necessity that justifies illegal acts, because the case not existing, nor being supposed to exist, there is not authority in the law books nor any

adjudged case upon it. Imagination may suggest, you may suggest so extraordinary a case as would justify a man by force overturning a magistrate and beginning a new government all by force, I mean in India, where there is no superior nigh them to apply to; in England it cannot happen; but in India you may suppose a possible case, but in that case it must be imminent, extreme, necessity; there must be no other remedy to apply to for redress; it must be very imminent, it must be very extreme, and in the whole they do, they must appear clearly to do it with a view of preserving the society and themselves—with a view of preserving the whole."

On this aspect Sir Dingle pressed his suit with a delicate circumspection, leaving it to the court to apply such part of Lord Mansfield's words as might be considered appropriate. I need only say that I can find nothing in the passage quoted to justify the actions of the appellant or the rioters whom she incited. It is one thing to act for the best in some case of extreme necessity, where the forces of law and order are absent or have ceased to act in that capacity. It is quite another to fight against and seek to expel a lawfully constituted constabulary while acting as such in the execution of its proper functions.

6. The ambit of the doctrine of self-defence may be wider than it once was, but when considered apart from the statutory right to which I have referred, some special nexus or relationship between the party relying on the doctrine to justify what he did in aid of another, and that other, would still appear to be necessary. Without attempting to define that factor, I cannot accept, on the material available, that it existed as between the appellant and the people of the Bogside. There is nothing to suggest that she belonged to or had property or a home in that district, and her status as a Member of Parliament would not, of itself, afford her protection by supplying a special relationship. It would seem as though she came in as a visitor and made common cause with the rioters, but I cannot regard that as an adequate relationship on which to found a defence of justification by way of self-defence.

7. Finally, the outbreak of rioting on 12 and 13 August imposed a duty on more than the constabulary. The private citizen has authority in law to help in the suppression of riots, and it is his common law duty to assist the constabulary to this end: see Russell on Crime, 12th ed. (1964), p. 270 et seq., and, in particular, the *Bristol Riots* case (1832) 3 St. Tr. (N.S.) 1 at 4 and 5, and *R.* v. *Pinney* (1832) 3 St. Tr. (N.S.) 11. That obligation, which rested upon the appellant as well as others, made it impossible, in my opinion, for her to find any legal justification for her conduct in aiding and encouraging the rioters as she undoubtedly did.

Appeals dismissed

R. v. *McInnes* [1971] 1 W.L.R. 1600, Edmund-Davies L.J. at p. 1610: "Section 3 (1) of the Criminal Law Act 1967 provides that "A person may use such force as is reasonable in the circumstances in the prevention of crime . . ." and in our judgment the degree of force permissible in self-defence is similarly limited."

iii. Reasonable Force

R. v. Shannon
(1980) 71 Cr. App. Rep. 192
Court of Appeal

The appellant was charged with murder by stabbing while being attacked. He worked for the same firm as the deceased and there had been some history of friction between them. It was alleged that he stabbed in revenge, punishment, retaliation or pure aggression. His defence was self-defence and absence of intent to cause grievous bodily harm. After being directed on the intent for murder, the jury were asked to consider on the issue of self-defence: "Did the defendant use more force than necessary in the circumstances?" The jury returned a verdict of guilty of manslaughter. He appealed against conviction.

ORMROD L.J., for the court: Mr. Fox Andrews, Q.C. for the appellant has criticised the learned judge's summing up on the basis of the well-known passage in the speech of Lord Morris of Borth-y-Gest giving the advice of the Privy Council in *Palmer* v. *R.* [1971] AC. 814, 831, 832, *post*, p. 430. He submits that the learned judge overlooked one important sentence in that advice, which reads thus: "If a jury thought that in a moment of unexpected anguish a person attacked had only done what he honestly and instinctively thought was necessary, that would be most potent evidence that only reasonable defensive action had been taken."

This proposition is, as it were, a bridge between what is sometimes referred to as "the objective test," that is what is reasonable judged from the viewpoint of an outsider looking at a situation quite dispassionately, and "the subjective test," that is the viewpoint of the accused himself with the intellectual capabilities of which he may in fact be possessed and with all the emotional strains and stresses to which at the moment he may be subjected.

The learned judge dealt fully with the relevant evidence and the law, and finally left this question to the jury: "Has the prosecution satisfied you that Mr. Shannon used more force than was reasonable in the circumstances?, because that goes solely to the question: Did he lawfully kill Mr. Meredith?" This summarises the burden of his direction to the jury. Mr. Fox Andrews argues that the judge ought to have invited the jury to consider whether the appellant, at the moment of stabbing, "honestly and instinctively thought that this action was necessary" to his defence and to have told them that if they thought that that was right and provided an adequate reason for the stabbing, it would be strong evidence that only reasonable defensive action had been taken.

Mr. Fox Andrews in effect urged that the learned judge had concentrated so much on the state of the appellant's mind in relation to the intent necessary to establish the charge of murder that he had, unwittingly, obscured this subjective element in self-defence. Taken in isolation it is not an easy concept to explain to a jury, or for a jury to understand and apply, although Lord Morris regarded the defence of self-defence as "one which can and will be readily understood by any jury." It is however easier to understand in its context. [His Lordship then quoted the passage in full, see *post*, p. 434.]

The whole tenor of this statement of the law is directed to the distinction which has to be drawn between acts which are essentially defensive in character and acts which are essentially offensive, punitive, or retaliatory in character. Attack may be the best form of defence, but not necessarily in law. Counter-attack within limits is permissible; but going over to the offensive when the real danger is over is another thing. This, we think, is the distinction which Lord Morris was endeavouring to explain, and which he thought a jury would readily understand.

Various indicators are used by judges to enable juries to make this crucial distinction. If the act or acts go beyond what the jury think reasonably necessary for defensive purposes, that points to the offensive rather than the defensive character of the act; if the attack is finished, the subsequent employment of force may be, in Lord Morris's words, "by way of revenge or punishment or by way of paying off an old score or may be pure aggression"; if other people have come to the assistance of the person attacked before some act of violence is done to the assailant, this too may indicate that the victim has gone over to the offensive. But these are only indicators to be used by the jury in making their common sense assessment on the facts as they find them; they are not conclusive tests in themselves of self-defence on the one hand or of aggression on the other. This is where Lord Morris's references come in to "a person defending himself cannot weigh to a nicety the exact measure of his necessary defensive action" and to such a person's "honest and instinctive" belief that his act was necessary. These considerations, depending on the facts of the particular case, may have to be weighed by the jury before coming to their conclusion "self-defence" or "no self-defence".

The learned judge, in the course of his summing up, used verbatim several extracts from Lord Morris's statement of the law in *Palmer* v. *R. (supra)*, but throughout the summing up, and at the end he left the jury with the bald question, "Are you satisfied that the appellant used more force than was necessary in the circumstances?" without Lord Morris's qualification that if they came to the conclusion that the appellant honestly thought, without having to weigh things to a nicety, that what he did was necessary to defend himself, they should regard that as "most potent evidence" that it was actually reasonably necessary. In other words, if the jury came to the conclusion that the stabbing was the act of a desperate man in extreme difficulties, with his assailant dragging him down by the hair, they should consider very carefully before concluding that the stabbing was an offensive and not a defensive act, albeit it went beyond what an onlooker would regard as reasonably necessary. . . .

In the judgment of this Court the evidence of the appellant, if accepted by the jury, raised the questions (a) whether the stabbing was in fact the act of a desperate man trying to defend himself and to force his assailant to let go of his hair and (b) whether, although not reasonably necessary by an objective standard, nonetheless, to use Lord Morris's words, the appellant honestly and instinctively thought that it was; in which case his honest belief would be "most potent evidence" that he had only taken defensive action; in other words, in the circumstances the stabbing was essentially defensive in character. The case for the prosecution, on the other hand, if accepted by the jury, was a perfect illustration of a man going over to the offensive and stabbing by way of revenge, punishment, retaliation or pure aggression.

The learned judge touched on this aspect of the matter when he was directing the jury on the issue of intent in relation to the charge of murder. At the end of the summing up he said this: "If you think that he lashed out because he lost his temper, having been treated in this painful, humiliating, frightening way, then you may think—it is a matter for you—that because he lost his temper in those circumstances he gave little or no thought to what might be the consequences of lashing out and in those circumstances he did not form the intent suggested. This is the matter which you must consider, clearly. The more a man loses his temper, the less likely he may be to consider what are likely to be the consequences of his acts even though when he is in a balanced state of mind he realises that if you lash out with scissors and it lands and you do it with force then it is going to do a lot of personal injury." But on the issue of self-defence he, effectively, excluded the state of the accused's mind. In other words, by leaving that issue to the jury on the bald basis of "Did the appellant use more force than was necessary in the circumstances?" the learned judge may have precluded the jury from considering the real issue, which, to paraphrase Lord Morris in *Palmer* v. *R.* was "Was this stabbing within the conception of necessary self-defence judged by the standards of common sense, bearing in mind the position of the appellant at the moment of the stabbing, or was it a case of angry retaliation or pure aggression on his part."

It is, we think, significant that in relation to intent, that is applying the test of what was in the accused's mind, the jury concluded that it was not murder but only manslaughter on the basis of no intent to cause really serious bodily harm, but seem to have excluded the appellant's state of mind in considering self-defence.

In those circumstances the Court came to the conclusion, not without considerable hesitation and anxiety, that the verdict of manslaughter was unsafe and unsatisfactory and ought to be quashed, which was done on April 15, 1980.

Appeal allowed
Conviction quashed

Att.-Gen. for Northern Ireland's Reference
[1977] A.C. 105
House of Lords

The reference was based on a case in which a soldier was charged with murder after shooting at the deceased in the mistaken belief that he was a member of the I.R.A., a proscribed organisation.

Lord Diplock: To kill or wound another person is *prima facie* unlawful. There may be circumstances, however, which render the act of shooting and any killing which results from it lawful; and an honest and reasonable belief by the accused in the existence of facts which if true would have rendered his act lawful is a defence to any charge based on the shooting. So for the purposes of the present reference one must ignore the fact that the deceased was an entirely innocent person and must deal with the case as if he were a member of the Provisional I.R.A. and a potentially dangerous terrorist, as the accused honestly and reasonably believed him to be. . . .

What amount of force is 'reasonable in the circumstances' for the purpose of preventing crime is, in my view, always a question for the jury in a jury trial, never a 'point of law' for the judge.

The form in which the jury would have to ask themselves the question in a trial for an offence against the person in which this defence was raised by the accused, would be: Are we satisfied that no reasonable man a) with knowledge of such facts as were known to the accused or reasonably believed by him to exist b) in the circumstances and time available to him for reflection c) could be of the opinion that the prevention of the risk of harm to which others might be exposed if the suspect were allowed to escape justified exposing the suspect to the risk of harm to him that might result from the kind of force that the accused contemplated using?

To answer this the jury would have first to decide what were the facts that did exist and were known to the accused to do so and what were mistakenly believed by the accused to be facts. In respect of the latter the jury would have had to decide whether any reasonable man on the material available to the accused could have shared that belief. . . .

The jury would have also to consider how the circumstances in which the accused had to make his decision whether or not to use force and the shortness of the time available to him for reflection, might affect the judgment of a reasonable man. In the facts that are to be assumed for the purposes of the reference there is material upon which a jury might take the view that the accused had reasonable grounds for apprehension of imminent danger to himself and other members of the patrol if the deceased were allowed to get away and join armed fellow-members of the Provisional I.R.A. who might be lurking in the neighbourhood, and that the time available to the accused to make up his mind what to do was so short that even a reasonable man could only act intuitively. This being so, the jury in approaching the final part of the question should remind themselves that the postulated balancing of risk against risk, harm against harm, by the reasonable man is not undertaken in the calm analytical atmosphere of the court-room after counsel with the benefit of hindsight have expounded at length the reasons for and against the kind of degree of force that was used by the accused; but in the brief second or two which the accused had to decide whether to shoot or not and under all the stresses to which he was exposed.

In many cases where force is used in the prevention of crime or in effecting an arrest there is a choice as to the degree of force to use. On the facts that are to be assumed for the purposes of the reference the only options open to the accused were either to let the deceased escape or to shoot at him with a service rifle. A reasonable man would know that a bullet from a self-loading rifle if it hit a human being, at any rate at the range at which the accused fired, would be likely to kill him or to injure him seriously. So in one scale of the balance the harm to which the deceased would be exposed if the accused aimed to hit him was predictable and grave and the risk of its occurrence high. In the other scale of the balance it would be open to the jury to take the view that it would not be unreasonable to assess the kind of harm to be averted by preventing the accused's escape as even graver—the killing or wounding of members of the patrol by terrorists in ambush, and the effect of this success by members of the Provisional I.R.A. in encouraging the continuance of the armed insurrection and all the misery and destruction of life and property that terrorist activity in Northern Ireland has entailed. The jury would have to consider too what was the highest degree at which a reasonable man could have assessed the likelihood that such consequence might follow the escape of the deceased if the facts had been as the accused knew or believed them reasonably to be.

Albert v. Lavin
[1981] 1 All E.R. 628
Queen's Bench Division

> A. caused a disturbance in a bus queue while attempting to board a bus. L., an off-duty police officer in plain clothes, restrained him. A struggle ensued, during which L. told A. that he was a police officer and threatened to arrest him. L. was unable to produce his warrant card because of the struggle. A. continued to hit him and was arrested and charged with assaulting a police officer in the execution of his duty. The magistrates convicted A. after finding that he had caused a breach of the peace, that the arrest was lawful, and that A. had no reasonable grounds for his belief that L. was not a police officer.

HODGSON J. stated the facts and confirmed the magistrates' finding that a police officer who reasonably believes that a breach of the peace is about to take place is entitled to take such steps as are necessary to prevent it, including the reasonable use of force:

The second argument presented to us by counsel is a much more difficult one....

The short question is whether in the circumstances set out a person's belief (the added words 'honest' or 'genuine' may be useful emphasis but in fact add nothing) is of itself sufficient to render him not guilty or whether that belief must be reasonable belief or, which is the same thing, a belief based on reasonable grounds.

But, before I come to deal with this difficult question for which, surprisingly, no direct authority cited to or known to me provides an answer, I must make two things clear. First, it is not of course contended that it is necessary that the appellant should have known that the man he was hitting was a police officer before he could be guilty of assaulting a police officer in the execution of his duty.

On the wording of s 51 of the Police Act 1964 it is now trite law that that is not so. What is in issue here is whether the appellant is guilty of an assault at all.

I turn now to deal with this most important question in this appeal. As I have said, there appears to be no reported instance of a man being convicted of an assault (or aggravated assault) when he acted, as he believed, in self-defence, but the belief was held to be unreasonable. However nearly all the authorities when considering self-defence require that a mistaken belief must be reasonable.

In *R.* v. *Weston* (1879) 14 Cox CC 346 at 351 Cockburn CJ, in directing the jury on the law relating to self-defence, said:

> '. . . if under such circumstances, the prisoner resorted to the gun in order to defend himself from serious violence, or under a reasonable apprehension of it, and so used it in necessary self-defence he would be justified.'

In *R.* v. *Rose* (1884) [*ante*, p. 414] Lopes J told the jury that they were entitled to acquit on the ground of self-defence only—

> 'if you think that at the time he [the defendant] fired that shot he honestly believed, and had reasonable grounds for the belief, that his mother's life was in imminent peril . . .'

In 10 Halsbury's Laws (3rd Edn) 721, para 1382 the rule (in relation to murder) was formulated thus:

> 'Where a forcible and violent felony is attempted upon the person of another, the party assaulted . . . is entitled to repel force by force, and, if necessary, to kill the aggressor. There must be reasonable necessity for the killing, or at least an honest belief based upon reasonable grounds that there is such necessity . . .'

In *R.* v. *Chisam* (1963) 47 Cr App R 130 this statement of the law was expressly approved. That case held that, where a man is charged with the killing of another and alleges that the killing took place in defence of a relative or friend, in order that the defence of self-defence may be available, he must have believed that that relative or friend was in imminent danger and the belief must have been based on reasonable grounds. Reasonable grounds for such belief may, however, exist though they are founded on a genuine mistake of fact. In giving the judgment of the court Lord Parker CJ cited with approval a passage from the direction of the Lord Justice-General (Lord Normand) in *Owens* v. *HM Advocate* 1946 JC 119 at 125:

> 'In our opinion self-defence is made out when it is established to the satisfaction of the jury that the panel believed that he was in imminent danger and that he held that belief on reasonable grounds. Grounds for such belief may exist though they are founded on a genuine mistake of fact.'

The requirement of reasonableness is also to be found in *R.* v. *Fennell* [1971] 1 Q.B. 428.

So far as self-defence is concerned the only dictum which recognises what may be called the subjective view which I have been able to find is *R.* v. *Porritt* [1961] 1 W.L.R. 1372. That was a case of capital murder and the point at issue was whether, where there was evidence of facts which could amount to provocation but that partial defence had not been raised, the issue should have been left to the jury. In giving the judgment of the Court of Criminal Appeal, Ashworth J said ([1961] 1 W.L.R. 1372 at 1375):

> 'At the trial it was conceded on behalf of the Crown that if the jury took the view that the firing was done in the honest belief that it was necessary for the protection of his stepfather, then the proper verdict was one of not guilty, and a similar concession was made in regard to the possibility of an honest belief that it was reasonably necessary to protect the house by shooting.'

It may be that the facts were thought to be so strong by the prosecution (the defendant was found guilty of capital murder by the jury) that they felt able to go further than they needed to in regard to self-defence. All that can be said is that Ashworth J did not say that the concessions had gone further than was necessary.

The rule that only a reasonable mistake may constitute a ground for the defence of self-defence has (both before and since *Director of Public Prosecutions* v. *Morgan ante,* p. 101] been vigorously criticised (see Glanville Williams, Criminal Law—The General Part (2nd Edn, 1961, para 73, pp 208–209); Kenny, Outlines of Criminal Law (19th Edn, 1966, pp 59–60); Russell on Crime (12th Edn, 1964, pp 75–76); Smith and Hogan, Criminal Law (4th Edn, 1978, pp 328–329, 364–365)). Whilst *Morgan* was on its way from the Court of Appeal to the House of Lords, Professor Smith wrote a comment on the Court of Appeal decision in which he strongly contended for the subjective test (see [1975] Crim LR 40). Perhaps the most cogent recent criticism of the objective test is to be found in Professor Glanville Williams's Textbook of Criminal Law (1978, pp 451 ff). He concludes a lengthy and extremely persuasive argument with the words: 'The law must be prepared, so far as it can do so, to look into the mind of the defendant and give him the benefit of the facts as they appeared to him.'

Counsel for the appellant has asked us to look again at the requirement of reasonableness in the light of the decision of the House of Lords in *Morgan*. Professor Glanville Williams warns that that decision is a formidable obstacle to any argument in favour of the subjective rule. He goes on to say, correctly:

> '. . . but here again it may be said that the question of *mens rea* in relation to defences was not before the House, it being held that the question of consent in rape was not a matter of defence but an ingredient of the offence.'

[He then cited from the speeches in *Morgan* [1976] A.C. 182: from Lord Hailsham, at pp. 213–214, and from Lord Simon, at p. 219.]

The reason why the House of Lords was able to reach the decision which it did in *Morgan* without overruling the authorities on self-defence was because they distinguished between the mens rea required for the basic or definitional elements of an offence and that required for a defence. It is said that the offence of assault requires an attack on a person (definitional element) but that the question whether the attack had to be made by the defendant in self-defence is a defence element, and the question of fault is not the same. It is this double test of a defendant's state of mind which has been the subject of vigorous academic criticism.

But counsel for the appellant submits that, despite the long line of authority some of which I have cited and the obiter dicta in *Morgan*, the ratio decidendi itself of *Morgan* leads one, in respect of self-defence, to a different conclusion as to what the law is. The argument goes thus. He accepts that to decide, in respect of any offence, whether the objective or subjective test should be applied to mistake it is necessary first of all to see what the definitional elements of the offence are. Citing Archbold, Pleading, Evidence and Practice in Criminal Cases (40th Edn, 1979, para 2634) he submits that the definition of assault is the actual or intended use of unlawful force to another without that other's consent, and that, just as lack of consent is one of the essential ingredients, so the unlawfulness of the assault is another. Applying the reasoning in *Morgan*, he says that the intention which the prosecution has to prove in assault is an intention to use or threaten actual force unlawfully and without the consent of the victim. It follows that if a man believes that what he is doing is not unlawful it avails him just as much as if he believes that he has the consent of his victim.

The further contention is that to make the difference between the objective and subjective test of mistake depend on where the evidential burden lies is unreal and illogical. At the end of the evidence all the facts are before the tribunal of fact which has then to direct itself or be directed as to the burden of proof and (with few exceptions) in respect of common law offences that burden lies on the prosecution. It matters not where the evidence has come from nor whether any issue has been specifically raised; if it is an issue the resolution of which in the defendant's favour would be to his advantage it must be left to the jury (or magistrates must consider it): see *R.* v. *Porritt* [1961] 1 W.L.R. 1372.

Support for the contention that the question whether the subjective or objective test should be applied does not depend on where the evidential burden as to any issue lies can be found in the comparatively recent decision of the Court of Appeal, Criminal Division, in *R* v. *Smith* [1974] Q.B. 354 *ante*, p. 100.

[After quoting from Professor Smith's comment on the Court of Appeal decision in *Morgan* [1975] Crim. L.R. 40 at pp. 43–44]:

I agree with the criticism voiced . . . in that passage and I do not think that the test whether the objective or subjective test of mistake applies can depend on where in respect of the relevant issue the evidential burden lies or may, in any particular case, lie.

But in my judgment counsel's ingenious argument for the appellant fails at an earlier stage. It does not seem to me that the element of unlawfulness can properly be regarded as part of the definitional elements of the offence. In defining a criminal offence the word 'unlawful' is surely tautologous and can add nothing to its essential ingredients. The requirement in the Criminal Damage Act 1971 that the property should be that of another is however clearly part of the definition of the statutory offence.

It seems to me that the law is that one has to distinguish between the mens rea required for the basic elements of the offence and that required for a defence. In the absence of express words in any offence created by statute (e g the Criminal Damage Act 1971, s 5) where the issue is whether a defence is made out then mistake avails a defendant nothing if it is an unreasonable (and therefore negligent) one. And, no matter how strange it may seem that a defendant charged with assault can escape conviction if he shows that he mistakenly but unreasonably thought his victim was consenting but not if he was in the same state of mind whether his victim had a right to detain him, that in my judgment is the law.

That being so this appeal fails. . . .

I would only add this. In *Morgan* Lord Edmund-Davies felt that he was constrained by authority to dismiss the appeal but he felt strongly that the law (as he would have held it to be) ought to be changed. However he thought that if change was to come it should be brought about by legislation. He referred to a passage from Smith and Hogan, Criminal Law (3rd Edn, 1973, p. 150):

> 'It is now established by s. 8 of the Criminal Justice Act 1967 that a failure to foresee the material *results* of one's conduct is a defence whether reasonable or not. It is odd that a different rule should prevail with respect to circumstances, the more particularly since foresight of results frequently depends on knowledge of circumstances. . . . Such a distinction seems unjustifiable. Its existence points in favour of a rule allowing as a defence any honest mistake which negatives *mens rea*, whether reasonable or not.'

In March 1980 the Criminal Law Revision Committee (of which Lord Edmund-Davies was, for many years, chairman) published its 14th report, Offences Against the Person (Cmnd 7844). The committee considered self-defence (paras 281–288). Their proposal is summarised in Part IX. It recommends adoption of the subjective test. Paragraph 72 (a) reads:

> 'The Common Law defence of self-defence should be replaced by a statutory defence providing that a person may use such force as is reasonable in the

circumstances as he believes them to be in the defence of himself or any other person, or in the defence of his property or that of any other person.'

Paragraph 72 (e) reads:

'There should be a provision that, in considering whether the defendant believed he or another or his property or that of another was under attack, the presence or absence of reasonable grounds for such a belief is a matter to which the court or jury is to have regard in conjunction with any other relevant matters.'

DONALDSON L.J. agreed, adding:
However, an ill-founded but completely honest and genuine belief removes all or much of the culpability involved in the offence. It therefore provides powerful mitigation and in an appropriate case would justify a court granting an absolute discharge.

Appeal dismissed

Note

The Divisional Court certified the following question of law of general public importance: "Whether a person charged with an offence of assault may properly be convicted if the court finds that he acted in the belief that facts existed which if true would justify his conduct on the basis of self-defence but that there were in fact no reasonable grounds for believing." The House of Lords [1981] 3 All E.R. 878 dismissed the appeal without considering the question on the ground that it was hypothetical. Lord Diplock: "Every citizen in whose presence a breach of the peace is being, or reasonably appears to be about to be, committed, has the right to take reasonable steps to make the person who is breaking . . . the peace refrain from doing so. . . . Even if Albert's belief that Lavin was a private citizen and not a constable had been correct, it would not have made his resistance to Lavin's restraint of him lawful."

See the discussion following *Morgan, ante,* p. 114.

iv. Excessive Force

Palmer v. The Queen
[1971] A.C. 814
Privy Council

A group of men, including the appellant went to buy ganja. The accused had a gun. A dispute arose and the men left with the ganja but without paying. A chase ensued and a man was shot. The appellant was charged with murder and claimed self-defence. He was convicted of murder and appealed.

LORD MORRIS OF BORTH-Y-GEST: . . . On behalf of the appellant it was contended that if where self-defence is an issue in a case of homicide a jury came to the conclusion that an accused person was intending to defend himself then an intention to kill or to cause grievous bodily harm would be negatived: so it was contended that if in such a case the jury came to the conclusion that excessive force had been used the correct verdict would be one of manslaughter: hence it was argued that in every case where self-defence is left to a jury they must be directed that there are the three possible verdicts, viz. guilty of murder, guilty of manslaughter, and not guilty. But in many cases where someone is intending to defend himself he will have had an intention to cause serious bodily injury or even to kill, and if the prosecution satisfy the jury that he had one of these intentions in circumstances in which or at a time when there was no justification or excuse for having it—then the prosecution will have shown that the question of self-defence is eliminated. All other issues which on the facts may arise will be unaffected.

An issue of self-defence may of course arise in a range and variety of cases and circumstances where no death has resulted. The tests as to its rejection or its validity will be just the same as in a case where death has resulted. In its simplest form the question that arises is the question: Was the defendant acting in necessary self-defence? If the prosecution satisfy the jury that he was not then all other possible issues remain.

It was claimed that support for the contention of the appellant could be found in the judgments of the High Court of Australia in *R.* v. *Howe* (1958) 100 C.L.R. 448—judgments to which their Lordships pay the highest respect. They therefore feel that the facts should be set out in some detail.

On November 13, 1957, Howe had killed a man named Millard. He did so after a bout of drinking at the end of which Millard made an alleged indecent assault upon Howe which Howe repelled. They had driven to the scene of these events in a car. After the alleged indecent assault and its repulse, there was some slight scuffle between the two, at the end of which Howe took a rifle out of the car, and shot Millard dead. He was standing some eight or nine paces away from Howe at the time, and with his back to him. Thereafter Howe took Millard's wallet from Millard's pocket, abstracted the money from it and threw the wallet away. His evidence as to his reason for shooting Millard was that he thought that Millard was about to attack him sexually and that he did not think that he could keep Millard off with his hands.

"I intended to stop him from further attacks. That's what I say now. I didn't think at all about whether I was likely to kill him. The thought never came into my mind. I was afraid of him. I was angry with him. I didn't think about what I was going to do. It all just came as soon as he grabbed me." (100 C.L.R. 448, 459).

It is to be noted that in this account there is no suggestion made that Howe considered that it was essential to his own self-defence that he should kill Millard. He didn't think about it. He was afraid. He didn't think about what he was going to do. Had he done so the obvious solution would have occurred to him—to get into the car and drive away. Nor was any explanation given for taking Millard's money. Small wonder is it in these circumstances that Taylor J. in the High Court of Australia thought the evidence in support of a plea of self-defence "flimsy in the extreme."

The course which the proceedings against Howe took were these:

He was tried for murder before a judge and jury in the Supreme Court of South Australia. He pleaded not guilty and pleaded self-defence against a sodomitical attack by Millard. The defence of provocation was also raised. The jury found him guilty, adding a recommendation to mercy. The judge sentenced him to death.

Howe appealed to the Full Court of the Supreme Court of South Australia sitting as a Court of Criminal Appeal. That court allowed the appeal, quashed the conviction and ordered a new trial. They did so on the ground that the following direction to the jury given by the trial judge was a misdirection in law: "where a person charged with the murder of an assailant relies on self-defence, he cannot succeed, and has no defence at all, if the jury are satisfied that the killing took place either (1) when the accused has not retreated as far as possible having regard to the attack; or (2) if he has used more force than is necessary for mere defence, the result in both cases being that the person who kills is guilty of murder." (100 C.L.R. at p. 460).

The Full Court gave guidance to the effect that a failure to retreat is only an element in the considerations upon which the reasonableness of an accused's conduct is to be judged: and in regard to the matters now relevant stated their view of the law as follows at p. 456: "We have come to the conclusion that it is the law that a person who is subjected to a violent and felonious attack and who, in endeavouring, by way of self-defence, to prevent the consummation of that attack by force exercises more force than a reasonable man would consider necessary in the circumstances, but no more force than he honestly believes to be necessary in the circumstances, is guilty of manslaughter and not of murder.

The Crown appealed to the High Court of Australia against this ruling. It was natural enough that the Crown should emphasise the requirement of the ruling that the accused should be acting in self-defence, and that the evidence in the case showed that Howe was not. But the High Court declined to entertain the question of the applicability of the principle to the case before it, and treated the appeal as raising an abstract point of law.

Dixon C.J. agreed in substance with the opinion of the Full Court: and McTiernan J. and Fullager J. did the same without delivering separate judgments.

Taylor J. recognised that the ruling of the Full Court might justifiably be thought to pose a somewhat unreal or artificial question of fact for the jury. "Indeed," he said, at p. 466, "it may be thought only remotely possible that a jury, having satisfied itself beyond reasonable doubt that an accused person had used more force in self-defence than he could reasonably have thought necessary, would, thereafter, be prepared to entertain the view that the degree of force used was no greater than the accused, in fact, honestly believed to be necessary."

It was not surprising in his view, therefore, that there was no expressed authority on the point. Favouring the view that the test should be whether what the accused did was done primarily for the purpose of defending himself he stated his final conclusion thus, at p. 469: ". . . I prefer to state the test as being whether the respondent used more force than on reasonable grounds he could have believed to be necessary and not whether he used more force than on reasonable grounds he actually believed to be necessary."

Menzies J.'s view, at p. 477, was: ". . . I have reached the conclusion that the law is that it is manslaughter and not murder if the accused would have been entitled to acquittal on the ground of self-defence except for the fact that in honestly defending himself he used greater force than was reasonably necessary for his self-protection and in doing so killed his assailant."

He was of the opinion that it would be a very unusual case in which a jury would come to the conclusion that an accused person in defending himself from a violent and felonious attack killed his attacker by the use of force which notwithstanding his honest belief that it was necessary for his self-protection was force in excess of that which on reasonable grounds he could have believed was necessary for that purpose.

It will thus be seen that the Full Court of South Australia had posed two questions as being the relevant questions where a plea of self-defence would succeed in toto but for the use of excessive force by the person attacked:

1. Was more force used than a reasonable man would consider necessary?
2. If so, did the accused nevertheless honestly believe that such excessive force was necessary?

and both questions would have to be answered in the affirmative to justify a verdict of manslaughter.

Three members of the High Court of Australia (Dixon C.J., McTiernan and Fullager JJ.) agreed in substance with the Full Court.

On the assumption that an attack of a violent and felonious nature, or at least of an unlawful nature, was made or threatened so that a person under attack or threat of attack reasonably feared for his life or the safety of his person from injury, violation or indecent or insulting usage so that occasion had arisen entitling a person to resort to force to repel force or apprehended force, then Dixon C.J. stated (see pp. 460–461) that the law was as follows: "Had he used no more force than was proportionate to the danger in which he stood, or reasonably supposed he stood, although he thereby caused the death of his assailant he would not have been guilty either of murder or manslaughter. But assuming that he was not entitled to a complete defence to a charge of murder, for the reason only that the force or violence which he used against his assailant or apprehended assailant went beyond what was needed for his protection or what the circumstances could cause him reasonably to believe to be necessary for his protection, of what crime does he stand guilty? Is the consequence of the failure of his plea of self-defence on that ground that he is guilty of murder or does it operate to reduce the homicide to manslaughter? There is no clear and definite judicial decision providing an answer to this question but it seems reasonable in principle to regard such a homicide as reduced to manslaughter, and that view has the support of not a few judicial statements to be found in the reports."

Taylor J. and Menzies J. expressed themselves independently. It would appear as though they favoured the single objective test implied in question No. 1.

Their Lordships must disregard for present purposes the obvious deficiencies in Howe's plea of self-defence. The question for them now is simply whether the majority or minority view in the High Court of Australia represents the English common law, or whether neither does.

In the year before *R.* v. *Howe* was decided occurred the case of *R.* v. *McKay* [1957] V.R. 560. This was a trial for murder in the State of Victoria though no issue as to self-defence arose in the case. McKay was caretaker of a poultry farm outside Melbourne belonging to his father. For a considerable time there had been nightly thefts of fowls from the farm, and a system of alarm bells was installed which would ring in the farmhouse if an intruder entered the pens. The bells did so ring on the morning of September 9, 1956, as daylight was breaking. McKay rose, took a loaded rifle with him, and saw a man named Wicks some 50 yards away carrying away some fowls. He fired one shot at him, intending he said to hit Wicks in the leg. Wicks ran away, and when he had run some five yards McKay fired another shot at him. Wicks thereupon dropped the fowls, but continued running. McKay fired another three shots, and later discovered Wicks behind a hedge either dead or in a dying condition. It seemed probable that one of the last three shots had killed him by penetrating the heart. To a neighbour who by this time had joined him, McKay said "Serve him right. He was pinching fowls." He added that when he fired he did not care whether he killed the man or not. To the police, however, he said that he only meant to wound the man and not to kill him, and he fired because he did not want the man to get away. He again made this assertion in a statement from the dock at his trial.

The trial judge directed the jury that if they thought that McKay fired with the intention of killing Wicks and that when he fired he did so out of feelings of revenge or a desire to punish, he was guilty of murder. But that if McKay was honestly exercising his legal right to prevent the escape of a man who had committed a felony, and that the killing was unintentional, but the means used were far in excess of what was proper in the circumstances, then McKay was guilty of manslaughter. He was convicted of manslaughter.

McKay appealed to the Supreme Court of Victoria alleging a misdirection upon the law which had deprived him of the chance of an acquittal. The appeal was, by a majority of two to one, dismissed. An application by McKay to the High Court of Australia for special leave to appeal was also dismissed.

In giving the leading judgment in the Supreme Court of Victoria, Lowe J. formulated six propositions dealing with the law relating to justifiable homicide. The sixth was in these terms, at p. 563: "If the occasion warrants action in self-defence or for the prevention of felony or the apprehension of the felon, but the person taking action acts beyond the necessity of the occasion and kills the offender, the crime is manslaughter—not murder."

This proposition was quoted with approval by the High Court in *Howe's* case, 100 C.L.R. 448. Taylor J., however, pointed out, at p. 467, that the proposition so formulated was not in any way limited to cases where it appears that the accused entertained an honest belief that the force used, though excessive on any reasonable view, was necessary. "This distinction," he added, "is of significance and reflection upon it provides grounds for thinking that the test proposed by the Full Court is erroneous."

A wholly different line was taken in *De Freitas* v. *The Queen* (1960) 2 W.I.R. 523 which was an appeal from the Supreme Court of British Guiana to the West Indian Federal Supreme Court. After a review of many authorities the court preferred not to follow the development of the law propounded in *Howe's* case, 100 C.L.R. 448. They sought to avoid the necessity of requiring a jury to go through a complicated and difficult process. An accused who has done no more than was in the opinion of the jury reasonably necessary in self-defence was entitled to be acquitted. If he has gone further then considerations as to provocation may reduce an offence so that the verdict should be one of manslaughter. In 1966, *Howe's* case and *De Freitas'* case were considered in the careful judgment in *Johnson* v. *The Queen* (1966) 10 W.I.R. 402 in the Court of Criminal Appeal of Trinidad and Tobago. That case followed in *R.* v. *Hamilton* (1967) 11 W.I.R. 309 in the Court of Appeal of Jamaica.

Because of the conclusion which their Lordships will express it does not become necessary for them to refer fully to these and to various other cases which were cited.

In their Lordships' view the defence of self defence is one which can be and will be readily understood by any jury. It is a straightforward conception. It involves no abstruse legal thought. It requires no set words by way of explanation. No formula need be employed in reference to it. Only common sense is needed for its understanding. It is both good law and good sense that a man who is attacked may defend himself. It is both good law and good sense that he may do, but may only do what is reasonably necessary. But everything will depend upon the particular facts and circumstances. Of these a jury can decide. It may in some cases be only sensible and clearly possible to take some simple avoiding action. Some attacks may be serious and dangerous. Others may not be. If there is some relatively minor attack it would not be common sense to permit some action of retaliation which was wholly out of proportion to the necessities of the situation. If an attack is serious so that it puts someone in immediate peril then immediate defensive action may be necessary. If the moment is one of crisis for someone in imminent danger he may have to avert the danger by some instant reaction. If the attack is all over and no sort of peril remains then the employment of force may be by way of revenge or punishment or by way of paying off an old score or may be pure aggression. There may no longer be any link with a necessity of defence. Of all these matters the good sense of a jury will be the arbiter. There are no prescribed words which must be employed in or adopted in a summing up. All that is needed is a clear exposition, in relation to the particular facts of the case, of the conception of necessary self-defence. If there has been no attack then clearly there will have been no need for defence. If there has been attack so that defence is reasonably necessary it will be recognised that a person defending himself cannot weigh to a nicety the exact measure of his necessary defensive action. If a jury thought that in a moment of unexpected anguish a person attacked had only done what he honestly and instinctively thought was necessary that would be most potent evidence that only reasonable defensive action had been taken. A jury will be told that the defence of self-defence, where the evidence makes its raising possible, will only fail if the prosecution show beyond doubt that what the accused did was not by way of self-defence.

Appeal dismissed

Note

In *Viro* v. *R.* (1976–1978) 141 C.L.R. 88, the High Court of Australia, in an appeal from the Supreme Court of New South Wales, considered the effect of *Palmer*. By a majority of four to three it was decided that *Palmer* should not be followed: Mason J. at p. 139:

> "[T]he doctrine enunciated in *R.* v. *Howe* . . ., supra, is not a novel development in the criminal law without any previous foundation in judicial decisions. There are to be found in the cases a number of indications that excessive force used by an accused person in defending himself against an aggressor should result in a conviction for manslaughter, not murder. These cases are referred to in the judgments of the Court in *R.* v. *Howe* and by Morris and Howard in their Studies in Criminal Law, pp. 127–136. Although they do not themselves furnish a decisive or authoritative answer to the question, these cases are sufficient to dispose of the suggestion that the doctrine emerged of a sudden, so to speak, without benefit of reputable antecedents in the law. In *R.* v. *Howe* the view was taken, and in my opinion correctly taken, that the weight of authority pointed to the existence of the doctrine. Not that the weight of authority was so strong as to be irresistible. When *R.* v. *Howe* came to be decided, the issue was very much an open question the answer to which depended more upon an evaluation of the considerations inherent in murder and manslaughter than upon the force of previous authority.
>
> The underlying rationale of *R.* v. *Howe* is to be found in a conviction that the moral culpability of a person who kills another in defending himself but who fails in a plea of self-defence only because the force which he believed to be necessary exceeded that which was reasonably necessary falls short of the moral culpability ordinarily associated with murder. The notion that a person commits murder in these circumstances should be rejected on the ground that the result is unjust. It is more consistent with the distinction which the criminal law makes between murder and manslaughter that an error or judgment on the part of the accused which alone deprives him of the absolute shield of self-defence results in the offence of manslaughter.
>
> In *Palmer* v. *The Queen* [above], these considerations were dismissed as illusory. The possibility that a jury would distinguish between the accused's belief as to the degree of force which was reasonably necessary and that which a reasonable man placed in the accused's situation would believe to be necessary was held to be academic or hypothetical, a possibility which is never likely to arise, because, so it was said, a jury which finds that the accused honestly believed that the force which he used was necessary will always find that the degree of force which he used was reasonably necessary. I am not persuaded that juries will always come to this conclusion or that there is any sound basis on which a prediction to this effect can confidently be made.
>
> The principle that the jury may take into account and give weight to the accused's belief as to what was necessary in deciding what a reasonable man in his situation would believe to be necessary itself acknowledges that there

is a distinction between the accused's subjective belief and the objective standard which may in a given case prove decisive. If it be correct to say that *R.* v. *Howe* is erroneous, and this because in all cases the jury will invariably find an exact correspondence between the accused's subjective belief and the objective standard, then one would expect the law to acknowledge an identity between the two by formulating the principle in terms of the accused's belief or by requiring that the jury be instructed accordingly. Such an approach is denied by *Palmer* v. *The Queen* for the acknowledgement that the accused's belief is "most potent evidence" of the objective standard does not completely bridge the gap. Indeed, the more one reflects upon the approach taken in *Palmer* v. *The Queen* the less reason there would appear to be for retaining the standard as an element in the defence. Apart from the sense of continuity which it provides by way of a link with earlier authority, it serves little purpose if it is no more than a reflection of the accused's honest belief."

and at p. 146:

"There is a distinction between (a) the person who kills in self-defence; (b) the person who kills through resorting to excessive force for his own protection; and (c) the person who does not kill at all. The store which we set by the preservation of human life requires that the act of killing through an excessive degree of force, though in self-protection, should be adjudged unlawful and that the offence is of a lesser order than murder."

Having lost on this point, the minority concurred with the majority that the direction to the jury should be as Mason J. described, at p. 146:

"1. (a) It is for the jury first to consider whether when the accused killed the deceased the accused reasonably believed that an unlawful attack which threatened him with death or serious bodily harm was being or was about to be made upon him.

(b) By the expression 'reasonably believed' is meant, not what a reasonable man would have believed, but what the accused himself might reasonably believe in all the circumstances in which he found himself.

2. If the jury is satisfied beyond reasonable doubt that there was no reasonable belief by the accused of such an attack no question of self-defence arises.

3. If the jury is not satisfied beyond reasonable doubt that there was no such reasonable belief by the accused, it must then consider whether the force in fact used by the accused was reasonably proportionate to the danger which he believed he faced.

4. If the jury is not satisfied beyond reasonable doubt that more force was used than was reasonably proportionate it should acquit.

5. If the jury is satisfied beyond reasonable doubt that more force was used, then its verdict should be either manslaughter or murder, that depending upon the answer to the final question for the jury—did the accused believe that the force which he used was reasonably proportionate to the danger which he believed he faced?

6. If the jury is satisfied beyond reasonable doubt that the accused did not have such a belief the verdict will be murder. If it is not satisfied beyond reasonable doubt that the accused did not have that belief the verdict will be manslaughter."

The CLRC, 14th Report, favoured the introduction of a partial defence along the Australian lines, see *post*, p. 469.

5. INVOLUNTARY MANSLAUGHTER

Note

Manslaughter which has been reduced from murder because of provocation or diminished responsibility (often called "voluntary" manslaughter) has been dealt with in the preceding section. "Involuntary" manslaughter, with which this section is concerned, is a generic term comprising those homicides which occupy "the shifting sands between the uncertain ... definition of murder and the unsettled boundaries of excusable or accidental death." (Hogan, "The Killing Ground: 1964–73" [1974] Crim. L.R. 387, 391).

"Involuntary" manslaughter can be divided into manslaughter by unlawful act and gross negligence manslaughter. The same case will often give rise to a consideration of both: see *Andrews* v. *D.P.P.*, *R.* v. *Church* and *R.* v. *Lamb*, below. In *R.* v. *Larkin* (1944), 29 Cr. App. Rep. 18, a case where the jury's verdict of manslaughter could have been based on a finding of provocation or of unlawful act, the Court of Criminal Appeal deprecated the practice of asking the foreman to explain the basis of the jury's verdict. Humphreys J., for the court, at p. 27:

"As we in this country think, trial by jury is the best method yet devised for dealing with serious criminal cases, and the jury is the best possible tribunal to decide whether a man is guilty and, if he is guilty, of what he is guilty, subject to the direction in law of the judge; but no one has ever suggested that a jury is composed of persons who are likely to be able to give at a moment's notice a logical explanation of how and why they arrived at their verdict. That was what Oliver, J., was inviting the jury to do in this case, and, as has been already observed, inviting the foreman to do so, and accepting from the foreman something with which, perhaps, the other eleven did not agree. The unhappy result was that the foreman, no doubt thoroughly confused, gave two totally inconsistent answers. That incident cannot, in our opinion, be of any importance whatever from the point of view of this appeal against conviction. It was something which happened after the trial was over, so far as the jury were concerned, and if it has any effect at all, it must be an effect upon the sentence. But it must be understood that this court deprecates questions being put to a jury upon the meaning of the verdict which they have returned. If the verdict appears to be inconsistent, proper questions may be put by a judge to invite the jury to explain what they mean, but where a verdict has been returned which is perfectly plain and unambiguous, it is most undesirable that the jury should be asked any further questions about it at all."

The table below indicates the frequency with which homicides initially charged as murder result in convictions for manslaughter. In the accompanying commentary, it is noted that: "From table 9. 11 it may be calculated that in the period 1968–78 about one-quarter of persons indicted for murder were in the event convicted of murder, and nearly as many were convicted of manslaughter under Section 2, Homicide Act 1957, where the only or principle defence was that of 'diminished responsibility.' In each year between 10 and 20 per cent. of persons indicted for homicide have been acquitted of all charges relating to the incident." Criminal Statistics, England and Wales, 1978, Cmnd. 7670.

Table 9.11 Persons indicted for homicide by outcome of precedings

England and Wales — Number of persons

Outcome	1968	1969	1970	1971	1972	1973	1974	1975	1976	1977	1978
Indicted for											
Murder	277	266	293	336	354	342	420	412	428	356	367
Manslaughter	73	89	78	63	77	77	100	87	93	94	63
Infanticide	23	12	14	18	17	8	14	2	8	4	6
Total	373	367	385	417	448	427	534	501	529	454	436[1]
Outcome	**1968**	**1969**	**1970**	**1971**	**1972**	**1973**	**1974**	**1975**	**1976**	**1977**	**1978**
Not convicted of homicide[2]											
Not tried—count to remain on file[3]				2	3	3	3	3	4	3	1
Found unfit to plead	3	9	3	7	6	4	3	4	3	–	2
Found not guilty by reason of insanity	3	–	2	1	2	1	2	1	2	1	–
Convicted of lesser offence	24	32	33	26	22	28	26	31	35	42	25
Acquitted on all counts	73	55	49	55	78	70	66	80	91	47	53
Sub Total	103	96	87	91	111	106	100	119	135	93	81
Convicted of homicide											
Murder	76	78	99	91	85	83	135	98	108	115	110
Sec. 2 manslaughter	49	58	65	72	85	77	96	76	93	92	78
Other manslaughter[a]	120	122	119	145	150	152	188	203	187	148	159
Infanticide	25	13	15	18	17	9	15	5	6	6	8
Sub-total	270	271	298	326	337	321	434	382	394	361	355
Total	373	367	385	417	448	427	534	501	529	454	436

[1] In addition there were 70 persons who had been committed for trial for homicide and were awaiting trial at June 1979.

[2] The offences for which these persons were indicted may nevertheless remain currently recorded as homicide.

[3] This usually implies that the suspect has been dealt with for some other serious offence.

[[a] This will include cases of successful provocation pleas.]

i. Unlawful Act Manslaughter

R. v. Franklin
(1883) 15 Cox 163
Sussex Assizes

The defendant was indicted with manslaughter. He took a box from another man's stall on West Pier, Brighton, and threw it into the sea. The box hit and killed a man who was swimming. The prosecution argued that the question of the defendant's negligence was immaterial, since it was manslaughter where death ensued in consequence of any wrongful act.

FIELD J.: I am of opinion that the case must go to the jury upon the broad ground of negligence and not upon the narrow ground proposed by the learned counsel, because it seems to me—and I may say that in this view my brother Mathew agrees—that the mere fact of a civil wrong committed by one person against another ought not to be used as an incident which is a necessary step in a criminal case. I have a great abhorrence of constructive crime. . . .

Verdict: Guilty

Note

Counsel in this case had relied upon *R.* v. *Fenton* (1830) I Lew. 179, in which Tindal C.J. had formulated this proposition: "If death ensues as the consequence of a wrongful act, an act which the party who commits it can neither justify nor excuse, it is not accidental death, but manslaughter. If the wrongful act was done under circumstances which show an attempt to kill, or do any serious injury in the particular case, or any general malice, the offence becomes that of murder. In the present instance the act was one of mere wantonness and sport, but still the act was wrongful, it was a trespass. The only question therefore is whether the death of the party is to be fairly and reasonably considered as a consequence of such wrongful act; if it followed from such wrongful act as an effect from a cause, the offence is manslaughter; if it is altogether unconnected with it, it is accidental death."

This harsh rule, which Field J. regarded as creating constructive crime, was rejected. If it had been accepted, a large number of circumstances would become manslaughter automatically without consideration of the culpability of the accused. Consider the traditional hypothetical case in this regard—a burglar accidentally turns on a gas-tap with his foot without knowing and the occupants of the house are gassed. The growth of statutory crime in recent years would have made the rule most wide. See the next case for a modern consideration and rejection of it by an appellate court after it had been used at the trial.

Andrews v. Director of Public Prosecutions
[1937] A.C. 576
House of Lords

The appellant was convicted at Leeds Assizes of manslaughter. He was driving his van at a fast speed and whilst overtaking a car in a city street knocked down and killed a man who was a few yards from the offside kerb. The appellant did not stop after the accident. The appeal was based on alleged misdirection by the trial judge in his summing-up. The Court of Criminal Appeal had dismissed the appeal.

Lord Atkin: [In the earlier authorities] expressions will be found which indicate that to cause death by any lack of due care will amount to manslaughter; but as manners softened and the law became more humane a narrower criterion appeared. [He considered the judgment in *R.* v. *Bateman, post,* p. 449, and continued:] The substance of the judgment is most valuable, and in my opinion is correct. In practice it has generally been adopted by judges in charging juries in all cases of manslaughter by negligence, whether in driving vehicles or otherwise. The principle to be observed is that cases of manslaughter in driving motor-cars are but instances of a general rule applicable to all charges of homicide by negligence. Simple lack of care such as will constitute civil liability is not enough: for purposes of the criminal law there are degrees of negligence: and a very high degree of negligence is required to be proved before the felony is established. Probably of all the epithets that can be applied "reckless" most nearly covers the case. It is difficult to visualise a case of death caused by reckless driving in the connotation of that term in ordinary speech which would not justify a conviction for manslaughter: but it is probably not all-embracing, for "reckless" suggests an indifference to risk whereas the accused may have appreciated the risk and intended to avoid it and yet shown a high degree of negligence in the means adopted to avoid the risk as would justify a conviction. If the principle of *Bateman's* case, is observed it will appear that the law of manslaughter has not changed by the introduction of motor-vehicles on the road. Death caused by their negligent driving, though unhappily much more frequent, is to be treated in law as death caused by any other form of negligence: and juries should be directed accordingly.

If this view be adopted it will be easier for judges to disentangle themselves from the meshes of the Road Traffic Acts. Those Acts have provisions which regulate the degree of care to be taken in driving motor-vehicles. They have no direct reference to causing death by negligence. Their prohibitions, while directed no doubt to cases of negligent driving, which if death be caused would justify convictions for manslaughter, extended to degrees of negligence of less gravity. Section 12 of the Road Traffic Act, 1930, imposes a penalty for driving without due care and attention. This would apparently cover all degrees of negligence. Section 11 imposes a penalty for driving recklessly or at a speed or in a manner which is dangerous to the public. There can be no doubt that this section covers driving with such a high degree of negligence as that if death were caused the offender would have committed manslaughter. But the converse is not true, and it is perfectly possible that a man may drive at a speed or in a manner dangerous to the public and cause death and yet not be guilty of manslaughter: and the legislature appears to recognise this by the provision in section 34 of the Road Traffic Act, 1934, that on an indictment for manslaughter a man may be convicted of dangerous driving. But, apart altogether from any inference to be drawn from section 34, I entertain no doubt that the statutory offence of dangerous driving may be committed, though the negligence is not of such a degree as would amount to manslaughter if death ensued. . . . It therefore would appear that in directing the jury in a case of manslaughter the judge should in the first instance charge them substantially in accordance with the general law, that is, requiring the high degree of negligence indicated in *Bateman's* case [*post*, p. 449], and then explain that such a degree of negligence is not necessarily the same as that which is required for the offence of dangerous driving, and then indicate to them the conditions under which they might acquit of manslaughter and convict of dangerous driving. A direction that all they had to consider was whether death was caused by dangerous driving within section 11 of the Road Traffic Act, 1930, and no more, would in my opinion be a misdirection.

In dealing with the summing-up in the present case I feel bound to say with every respect to the learned and very careful judge that there are passages which are open to criticism. In particular at the beginning of his charge to the jury he began with the statement that if a man kills another in the course of doing an unlawful act he is guilty of manslaughter, and then proceeded to ascertain what the unlawful act was by considering section 11 of the Road Traffic Act, 1930. If the summing-up rested there, there would have been misdirection. There is an obvious difference in the law of manslaughter between doing an unlawful act and doing a lawful act with a degree of carelessness which the legislature makes criminal. If it were otherwise a man who killed another while driving without due care and attention would *ex necessitate* commit manslaughter. But as the summing-up proceeded the learned judge reverted to, and I think rested the case on, the principles which have been just stated. On many occasions he directed the attention of the jury to the recklessness and high degree of negligence which the prosecution alleged to have been proved and which would justify them in convicting the accused. On consideration of the summing-up as a whole I am satisfied that the true question was ultimately left to the jury.

Appeal dismissed

[Sections 11 and 12 of the Road Traffic Act 1930, have been replaced by, respectively, sections 2 and 3 of the Road Traffic Act 1972 (section 2 as substituted by section 50 of the Criminal Law Act 1977).]

Note

Juries proved unwilling to convict of manslaughter in driving cases, hence the introduction in 1956 of a special offence. This is now contained in section 1 of the Road Traffic Act 1972 (as substituted by section 50 of the Criminal Law Act 1977). See *R.* v. *Lawrence, ante,* p. 78.

The Court of Appeal followed *Andrews* v. *D.P.P.* above, in *R.* v. *Lowe* [1973] 1 Q.B. 702. The defendant was charged with manslaughter and with the offence of wilfully neglecting his child (under Section 1 (1) of the Children and Young Persons Act 1933). His conviction for manslaughter was quashed because the jury were directed that a conviction on the manslaughter charge must automatically follow if they convicted of wilful neglect. Phillimore J. at p. 202: "How can mere neglect, albeit wilful, amount to manslaughter? This court feels that there is something inherently unattractive in a theory of constructive manslaughter."

Questions

1. What is the "obvious difference . . . between doing an unlawful act and doing a lawful act with a degree of a carelessness which the legislature makes criminal" to which Lord Atkin refers in *Andrews* v. *D.P.P.*, above?

2. Are negligence and neglect the same thing?

See *post,* p. 452 for manslaughter by omission.

R. v. Church

[1966] 1 Q.B. 59

Court of Criminal Appeal

> The appellant was mocked by a woman and fought with her, knocking her unconscious. He failed to revive her and in a panic threw her into a river. She drowned. The appellant was acquitted of murder but convicted of manslaughter. He appealed on the ground of misdirection as to manslaughter.

EDMUND-DAVIES J.: . . . it seems to this court that at least three possible bases of the manslaughter verdict call for consideration:

(a) Criminal negligence. A grosser case of criminal negligence it would be difficult to imagine. As the trial judge put it: "What steps did he take to find out whether she was alive or dead? He seems to have made no attempt, according to him, to find out whether she was breathing or not. He seems to have made no attempt to feel whether her heart was beating. Surely these are elementary steps. You have then nothing left but his bare unsupported statement: 'I thought she was dead.' All he had done had been to shake her and she had not recovered consciousness. Do you think that persuaded him that she was dead, or do you not?" That passage was directed to the charge of murder. As to manslaughter, the following direction was given: ". . . If, not knowing whether the woman was dead or not, and not having taken the trouble to find out whether she was dead or not, he throws her body into the river, you may (if you think fit) come to the conclusion that that was a negligent act done utterly recklessly without regard to the danger to life or limb that could be caused by it, and that would be another ground on which the throwing of the body into the river would be manslaughter."

That direction has been strongly criticised as wholly inadequate in relation to criminal negligence as expounded in *R.* v. *Bateman* [*post*, p. 449] and *Andrews* v. *D.P.P.* [above]. But the nature of the direction called for must depend on the facts of each case. In the judgment of this court, the facts in the present case were such as to render an elaborate direction unnecessary. Utter recklessness was the standard which the jury were told had to be applied, and the evidence amply justified a verdict that it had been established.

(b) Provocation. There is no room for doubt that the plea of provocation had but a flimsy basis and wholly justified the adverse summing-up on this issue . . .

(c) An unlawful act causing death. Two passages in the summing-up are here material. They are these: (1) "If by an unlawful act of violence done deliberately to the person of another, that other is killed, the killing is manslaughter even though the accused never intended either death or grievous bodily harm to result. If this woman was alive, as she was, when he threw her into the river, what he did was the deliberate act of throwing a living body into the river. That is an unlawful killing and it does not matter whether he believed she was dead or not, and that is my direction to you," and (2) "I would suggest to you, though it is of course for you to approach your task as you think fit, that a convenient way of approaching it would be to say: What do we think about this defence that he honestly believed the woman to be dead? If you think that it is true, why then, as I have told you, your proper verdict would be one of manslaughter, not murder."

Such a direction is not lacking in authority: see, for example, *Shoukatallie* v. *The Queen* [1962] A.C. 81 and Dr. Glanville Williams' Criminal Law (1961), 2nd ed., p. 173. Nevertheless, in the judgment of this court it was a misdirection. It amounted to telling the jury that, whenever any unlawful act is committed in relation to a human being which resulted in death there must be, at least, a conviction for manslaughter. This might at one time have been regarded as good law. . . . But it appears to this court that the passage of years has achieved a transformation in this branch of the law and, even in relation to manslaughter, a degree of *mens rea* has become recognised as essential. To define it is a difficult task, and in *Andrews* v. *D.P.P.* Lord Atkin spoke of the "element of 'unlawfulness' which is the elusive factor." Stressing that we are here leaving entirely out of account those ingredients of homicide which might justify a verdict of manslaughter on the grounds of (a) criminal negligence, or (b) provocation, or (c) diminished responsibility, the conclusion of this court is that an unlawful act causing the death of another cannot, simply because it is an unlawful act, render a manslaughter verdict inevitable. For such a verdict inexorably to follow, the unlawful act must be such as all sober and reasonable people would inevitably recognise must subject the other person to, at least, the risk of some harm resulting therefrom, albeit not serious harm. See, for example, *R.* v. *Franklin*, [*ante*, p. 438]; *R.* v. *Senior* [1899] 1 Q.B. 283; *R.* v. *Larkin* [1943] 1 K.B. 174 in the judgment of the court delivered by Humphrey J.; *R.* v. *Buck & Buck* (1960) 44 Cr. App. R. 213; and *R.* v. *Hall* (1961) 45 Cr. App. R. 366.

If such be the test, as we adjudge it to be, then it follows that in our view it was a misdirection to tell the jury simpliciter that it mattered nothing for manslaughter whether or not the appellant believed Mrs. Nott to be dead when he threw her in the river. But, quite apart from our decision that the direction on criminal negligence was an adequate one in the circumstances, such a misdirection does not, in our judgment, involve that the conviction for manslaughter must or should be quashed.

Appeal dismissed

Note

R. v. *Church* should be compared with *Thabo Meli* v. *R., ante,* p. 40. The cases of *Lamb* and *Newbury*, below, clarified the two parts of the unlawful act formula in *Church* holding, respectively, that the *mens rea* of the unlawful act itself must be established subjectively but that the further test of foresight of harm is objective.

R. v. Lamb
[1967] 2 Q.B. 981
Court of Appeal

> The appellant, in fun, pointed a revolver at a friend. He knew that there were two bullets in the chambers, but neither was opposite the barrel. He pulled the trigger and because of the action of the cylinder, which rotated before firing, a bullet was fired and the friend killed. He did not appreciate that the cylinder rotated automatically. The appellant was convicted of manslaughter and appealed against this.

SACHS J.: The general effect of the summing-up was that a verdict of guilty could be returned on either or both of two grounds as follows: "It is manslaughter if death results from an unlawful and dangerous act on the part of the accused. It is also manslaughter if death results from an extreme degree of carelessness, negligence, on the part of the accused. Those are both grounds on which manslaughter can be found. It is quite possible that to some extent they overlap . . ."

As regards the first of those grounds, which was pressed upon the jury very strongly indeed, in the course of his summing-up, the trial judge no doubt founded himself on that part of the judgment of Edmund-Davies J. in *R.* v. *Church* when he says: "The unlawful fact must be such as all sober and reasonable people would inevitably recognise must subject the other person to, at least, the risk of some harm resulting therefrom, albeit not serious harm."

Unfortunately, however, he fell into error as to the meaning of the word "unlawful" in that passage and pressed upon the jury a definition with which experienced counsel for the Crown had disagreed during the trial and which he found himself unable to support on the appeal. The trial judge took the view that the pointing of the revolver and the pulling of the trigger was something which could of itself be unlawful even if there was no attempt to alarm or intent to injure. This view is exemplified in a passage in his judgment which will be cited later.

It was no doubt on that basis that he had before commencing his summing-up stated that he was not going "to involve the jury in any consideration of the niceties of the question whether or not the action of the "accused did constitute or did not constitute an assault"; and thus he did not refer to the defence of accident or the need for the prosecution to disprove accident before coming to a conclusion that the act was unlawful.

Mr. Mathew [for the Crown], however, had at all times put forward the correct view that for the act to be unlawful it must constitute at least what he then termed "a technical assault." In this court moreover he rightly conceded that there was no evidence to go to the jury of any assault of any kind. Nor did he feel able to submit that the acts of the defendant were on any other ground unlawful in the criminal sense of that word. Indeed no such submission could in law be made: if, for instance, the pulling of the trigger had had no effect because the striking mechanism or the ammunition had been defective no offence would have been committed by the defendant.

Another way of putting it is that mens rea, being now an essential ingredient in manslaughter (compare *Andrews* v. *D.P.P.* and *R.* v. *Church*), that could not in the present case be established in relation to the first ground except by proving that element of intent without which there can be no assault.

It is perhaps as well to mention that when using the phrase "unlawful in the criminal sense of that word" the court has in mind that it is long settled that it is not in point to consider whether an act is unlawful merely from the angle of civil liabilities. That was first made in the "Brighton Pier" case (*R.* v. *Franklin*). . . .

Taken by themselves the directions on law in regard to the second ground were substantially correct, but this court would in any event have to proceed with caution when asked to uphold the verdict when so much of the first part of the summing-up was vitiated by misdirections . . .

The general effect of the summing-up was thus to withdraw from the jury the defence put forward on behalf of the defendant. When the gravamen of a charge is criminal negligence—often referred to as recklessness—of an accused, the jury have to consider among other matters the state of his mind, and that includes the question of whether or not he thought that that which he was doing was safe. In the present case it would, of course, have been fully open to a jury, if properly directed, to find the defendant guilty because they considered his view as to there being no danger was formed in a criminally negligent way. But he was entitled to a direction that the jury should take into account the fact that he had undisputably formed that view and that there was expert evidence as to this being an understandable view.

Strong though the evidence of criminal negligence was, the defendant was entitled as of right to have his defence considered, but he was not accorded this right and the jury was left without a direction on an essential matter. Those defects of themselves are such that the verdict cannot stand.

Appeal allowed

D.P.P. v. Newbury
[1977] A.C. 500
House of Lords

The appellants, two 15 year old boys, pushed into the path of an oncoming train a piece of paving stone which some workmen had left on the parapet of a railway bridge. The stone killed the guard of the train. They were convicted of manslaughter and their appeal was dismissed by the Court of Appeal which nevertheless certified the following point of law: "Can a defendant be properly convicted of manslaughter, when his mind is not affected by drink or drugs, if he did not foresee that his act might cause harm to another?"

Lord Salmon, Lords Diplock, Simon of, Glaisdale and Kilbrandon agreeing: . . . The learned trial judge did not direct the jury that they should acquit the appellants unless they were satisfied beyond a reasonable doubt that the appellants had foreseen that they might cause harm to someone by pushing the piece of paving stone off the parapet into the path of the approaching train. In my view the learned trial judge was quite right not to give such a direction to the jury. The direction which he gave is completely in accordance with established law, which, possibly with one exception to which I shall presently refer, has never been challenged. In *R.* v. *Larkin* (1942) 29 Cr. App. R. 18, Humphreys J. said, at p. 23:

> "Where the act which a person is engaged in performing is unlawful, then if at the same time it is a dangerous act, that is, an act which is likely to injure another person, and quite inadvertently the doer of the act causes death of that other person by that act then he is guilty of manslaughter."

I agree entirely with Lawton L.J. that that is an admirably clear statement of the law which has been applied many times. It makes it plain (a) that an accused is guilty of manslaughter if it is proved that he intentionally did an act which was unlawful and dangerous and that that act inadvertently caused death and (b) that it is unnecessary to prove that the accused knew that the act was unlawful or dangerous. This is one of the reasons why cases of manslaughter vary so infinitely in their gravity. They may amount to little more than pure inadvertence and sometimes to little less than murder.

I am sure that in *R.* v. *Church* [*ante,* p. 441] Edmund-Davies J. in giving the judgment of the court, did not intend to differ from or qualify anything which had been said in *R.* v. *Larkin*, 29 Cr. App. R. 18. Indeed he was restating the principle laid down in that case by illustrating the sense in which the word "dangerous" should be understood. Edmund-Davies J. said, at p. 70:

> "For such a verdict" (guilty of manslaughter)" inexorably to follow, the unlawful act must be such as all sober and reasonable people would inevitably recognise must subject the other person to, at least, the risk of some harm resulting therefrom, albeit not serious harm."

The test is still the objective test. In judging whether the act was dangerous the test is not did the accused recognise that it was dangerous but would all sober and reasonable people recognise its danger.

Mr. Esyr Lewis in his very able argument did not and indeed could not contend that the appellants' act which I have described was lawful but he did maintain that the law as stated in *Larkin's* case had undergone a change as a result of a passage in the judgment of Lord Denning M.R. in *Gray* v. *Barr* [1971] 2 Q.B. 554, 568 which reads as follows:

> "In manslaughter of every kind there must be a guilty mind. Without it, the accused must be acquitted [see *R.* v. *Lamb*, above]. In the category of manslaughter relating to an unlawful act, the accused must do a dangerous act with the intention of frightening or harming someone, or with the realisation that it is likely to frighten or harm someone, and nevertheless he goes on and does it, regardless of the consequences. If his act does thereafter, in unbroken sequence, cause the death of another, he is guilty of manslaughter."

I do not think that Lord Denning M.R. was attempting to revolutionise the law relating to manslaughter if his judgment is read in the context of the tragic circumstances of the case. [His Lordship then gave the facts in full. One night, finding his wife not at home, Mr. Barr decided that she must be at the home of Mr. Gray with whom she was associating. He went to Mr. Gray's house and threatened him with a shotgun in order to get past him to find his wife. The gun went off, one shot hit the ceiling, the other hit Mr. Gray and killed him. In fact, Mrs. Barr was lying unconscious in a field having tried to commit suicide.]

There was much sympathy for Mr. Barr when he was tried at the Old Bailey for murder. The summing-up read like an invitation to acquit him of both murder and manslaughter—an invitation which the jury accepted no doubt gratefully. Mrs. Gray then sued Mr. Barr for damages in respect of her husband's death to which he in reality had no defence. Mr. Barr however, in the third party proceedings which he had brought against the Prudential, claimed an indemnity under a "hearth and home" policy covering him against all sums he became liable to pay as damages in respect of bodily injury to any person caused by accident. The learned trial judge gave judgment against Mr. Barr in Mrs. Gray's favour for some £6,668 in all. He dismissed Mr. Barr's claim for an indemnity on grounds of public policy having come to the conclusion that, in spite of the jury's verdict, Mr. Barr was clearly guilty of manslaughter. Mr. Barr appealed, amongst other things, against the judgment in favour of the Prudential. That appeal was dismissed. Every member of the Court of Appeal, agreeing with the learned trial judge, found that in spite of Mr. Barr's acquittal at the Old Bailey he had been, on his own story, undoubtedly guilty of manslaughter. They also agreed with the learned trial judge that on grounds of public policy a man is not entitled to be indemnified against damages for which he became liable as a result of committing a crime of violence.

I have taken a little time dealing with the facts of Barr's case to show that the Court of Appeal was in a very different position from that of a Court of Appeal (Criminal Division). It was not considering whether a conviction could be upheld but whether an acquittal could be justified. It was concerned to decide whether the facts established by Mr. Barr's own evidence proved that he was guilty of manslaughter which, of course, they did; but this does not mean that nothing short of such facts can prove manslaughter. Lord Denning M.R.'s judgment is certainly capable of being read in a contrary sense, and indeed has been so understood by some judges, but I doubt whether he intended that it should be. If he did, then I am afraid I cannot agree with him. Neither of the other members of the court in *Gray* v. *Barr* [1971] 2 Q.B. 554 said anything in support of the proposition which some believe that Lord Denning intended to propound. Indeed, the second member of that court cited *Larkin's* case, 29 Cr. App. R. 18 with approval, see p. 576.

R. v. *Lamb* was referred to by Lord Denning M.R. for the proposition that in manslaughter there must always be a guilty mind. This is true of every crime except those of absolute liability. The guilty mind usually depends on the intention of the accused. Some crimes require what is sometimes called a specific intention, for example murder, which is killing with intent to inflict grievous bodily harm. Other crimes need only what is called a basic intention, which is an intention to do the acts which constitute the crime. Manslaughter is such a crime: see *R.* v. *Larkin,* 29 Cr. App. R. 18 and *R.* v. *Church. R.* v. *Lamb* is certainly no authority to the contrary. Two young men were playing about with a revolver which, to their knowledge, had two shells in chambers, neither of which was opposite the barrel. The defendant in jest and with no intention to harm or frighten pointed the revolver at his friend, who was also treating the incident as a joke. The revolver fired and the friend was killed. The defendant was charged with manslaughter on two grounds (a) killing by doing an unlawful and dangerous act and (b) killing by criminal negligence. The defendant was convicted but his conviction was quashed on appeal because, luckily for him, there had been a series of serious misdirections by the learned trial judge.

Lawton L.J. had observed that in manslaughter cases, some judges are now directing juries not in accordance with the law as correctly laid down in *R.* v. *Larkin,* 29 Cr. App. R. 18 and *R.* v. *Church* [1966] 1 Q.B. 59 but in accordance with the observations of Lord Denning M.R. in *Gray* v. *Barr* [1971] 2 Q.B. 554 taken in their literal sense. For the reasons I have already given they should cease to do so.

My Lords, I would dismiss the appeal.

LORD EDMUND-DAVIES: My Lords, for the reasons developed in the speech of my noble and learned friend, Lord Salmon, I concur in holding that these appeals against conviction should be dismissed.

R. v. *Church* [1966] 1 Q.B. 59 [*ante,* p. 441] which the learned trial judge adopted for the purpose of his direction to the jury, marked no new departure in relation to the offence of involuntary manslaughter. In so far as the charge was based on the commission of an unlawful act causing death, the court of Criminal Appeal was there concerned to demolish the old notion (which the direction to the jury in that case was thought to have resurrected) that, whenever any unlawful act is committed in relation to a human being which causes death, there must at least be a conviction for manslaughter. In delivering the judgment of the court, I therefore said, at p. 70:

> "Stressing that we are here leaving entirely out of account those ingredients of homicide which might justify a verdict of manslaughter on the grounds of (a) criminal negligence, or (b) provocation or (c) diminished responsibility, the conclusion of this court is that an unlawful act causing the death of another cannot, simply because it is an unlawful act, render a manslaughter verdict inevitable."

The key sentence which followed has often been quoted. I would respectfully say that Widgery L.J. (who was a member of the court in *R.* v. *Church*) was perfectly correct in observing in *R.* v. *Lipman* [1970] 1 Q.B. 152 that, "The development recognised by *R.* v. *Church* relates to the type of act from which a charge of manslaughter may result, not in the intention (real or assumed) of the prisoner."

But, in so far as *R.* v. *Church* has been regarded as laying down that for the proof of manslaughter in such circumstances what is required is no more than the intentional committing of an unlawful act of the designated type or nature, it followed a long line of authorities which the court there cited. Of these the best known is possibly *R.* v. *Larkin,* 29 Cr. App. R. 18, dealt with in detail in the speech of my noble and learned friend, Lord Salmon. Accordingly, if *R.* v. *Church* was wrong, so was its long ancestry.

I believe that *R.* v. *Church* accurately applied the law as it then existed. I believe, further, that, since it was decided, nothing has happened to change the law in relation to the constituents of involuntary manslaughter caused by an unlawful act. The Criminal Justice Act 1967 has certainly effected no such change, for, as I sought to show in *R.* v. *Majewski* [*ante,* p. 176], section 8 thereof has nothing to do with when intent or foresight or any other mental state has to be established, but simply how it is to be determined where such determination is called for.

That is not to say that a change in the law may not be opportune. If I may be permitted to introduce a personal note into a judgment, I have the best reason to know that the forthcoming working paper of the Criminal Law Revision Committee on offences against the person will afford those concerned in such important matters an opportunity to assess the cogency of the argument for a drastic change in the law applicable to such cases as at the present. But, unless and until such argument prevails and so leads on to legislation, the existing law has to be applied. I hold that the direction of the learned trial judge, Watkins J., was in strict accordance with the settled law and that these appeals should therefore be refused.

Appeal dismissed

Note

Although the cases following *Franklin* show a general softening of judicial attitudes towards constructive manslaughter, the decision in *Newbury,* above, raises again questions as to what can amount to an unlawful act. Lord Salmon speaks of "an act which was unlawful and dangerous" without mentioning the limitations introduced in *Franklin, Andrews* and *Lowe*. And in *Cato*, the facts of which appear [*ante,* p. 26] the Court of Appeal suggested that the unlawful act need not itself be a crime. Lord Widgery C.J. [1976] 1 W.L.R. 110, 118:

> "Strangely enough, . . . although the possession or supply of heroin is an offence, it is not an offence to take it, and although supplying it is an offence, it is not an offence to administer it. . . .

> Of course if the conviction on count 2 remains (that is the charge under section 23 of the Offences against the Person Act 1861 of administering a noxious thing), then that in itself would be an unlawful act. . . .
>
> But . . . had it not been possible to rely on [that] charge, . . . we think there would have been an unlawful act here, and we think the unlawful act would be described as injecting the deceased Farmer with a mixture of heroin and water which at the time of the injection and for the purposes of the injection the accused had unlawfully taken into his possession."

A further harshness in this type of manslaughter is the application of the limitations of the defence of intoxication to the unlawful act element.

Intoxication and the Unlawful Act

In *R.* v. *Lipman* [1970] 1 Q.B. 152, the defendant killed a woman while on an L.S.D. "trip." He had no recollection of the killing. The Court of Appeal approved the trial judge's direction that, for manslaughter, the Crown had to prove that ". . . he must have realised, before he got himself into the condition he did by taking the drug, that acts such as those he subsequently performed and which resulted in the death were dangerous." Widgery L.J. added, at p. 159:

> ". . . When the killing results from an unlawful act of the accused no specific intent has to be proved to convict of manslaughter and self-induced intoxication is accordingly no defence."

In *R.* v. *O'Driscoll* (1977) 65 Cr. App. R. 50, the Court of Appeal more precisely suggested that where the unlawful act in question was a crime of specific intent, the rule in *Majewski* (*ante*, p. 176) would apply and evidence of intoxication would be admitted. It is, however, in this context, hard to imagine a crime of specific intent which does not include one of basic intent. The Canadian case of *Swietlinski* v. *R.* (1981) 117 D.L.R. (3d) 285 was concerned with a similar issue, although the offence in question was murder not manslaughter. The Canadian Criminal Code provides, s. 213 (d):

> "Culpable homicide is murder where a person causes the death of a human being while committing . . . an offence mentioned in sections . . . 149 or 156 (indecent assault) . . . whether or not the person means to cause death . . . and whether or not he knows that death is likely to be caused . . . , if . . . he uses a weapon or has it upon his person (i) during or at the time he commits or attempts to commit the offence . . . and the death ensues as a consequence."

McIntyre J. for the Supreme Court, at p. 302:

> "I am of the opinion that the rule of law to the effect that voluntary or self-induced intoxication cannot negative a general intent constituting the only mental element required for an indecent assault does not apply to the offence of murder where conviction rests upon proof of the offence of indecent assault. This conclusion rests upon the proposition that the appellant was not charged with indecent assault, an offence in respect of which the defence of drunkeness would not have assisted him. He was charged with murder, an offence which cannot be complete without the proof of some mental element which, in a charge of murder resting upon proof of an underlying offence, as in s. 213 (d) of the Code, substitutes for the specific intent ordinarily required for murder. In this case proof of such mental element or

> intent can only be made by proof of an intent to commit an indecent assault and to use the knife in the commission of the assault."

Question

Could the English Courts adopt the approach of the Supreme Court in *Swietlinski* to the "underlying" unlawful act? Should they?
For intoxication generally, see *ante*, p. 176.

ii. Gross Negligence Manslaughter

Note

In many instances a jury will be invited to consider both heads of involuntary manslaughter. Reference should thus be made to *Andrews* v. *D.P.P., ante*, p. 439, *R.* v. *Church, ante*, p. 441 and *R.* v. *Lamb, ante*, p. 443. Gross negligence manslaughter, in its pure form can arise where death results from a lawful activity, such as a surgeon operating on someone, or inactivity, such as failing to summon medical help. (The circumstances in which the common law imposes a duty to act are discussed *ante*, p. 18.) The element of culpability which distinguishes such cases from accidents and converts them into unlawful homicides is "gross" or "criminal" negligence.

R. v. Bateman
(1925) 19 Cr. App. R. 8
Court of Criminal Appeal

> The appellant, who had been convicted of manslaughter, was a doctor. He was present at a difficult confinement. Three heads of negligence were alleged against him. The first two were matters of medical technique, the third that he delayed in removing the deceased to hospital.

LORD HEWART C.J.: . . . In expounding the law to juries on the trial of indictments for manslaughter by negligence, judges have often referred to the distinction between civil and criminal liability for death by negligence. If A has caused the death of B by alleged negligence, then, in order to establish civil liability, the plaintiff must prove (in addition to pecuniary loss caused by death) that A owed a duty to B to take care, that that duty was not discharged, and that the default caused the death of B. To convict A of manslaughter, the prosecution must prove the three things above mentioned and must satisfy the jury, in addition, that A's negligence amounted to a crime. In the civil action, if it is proved that A fell short of the standard of reasonable care required by law, it matters not how far he fell short of that standard. The extent of his liability depends not on the degree of negligence, but on the amount of the damage done. In a criminal court, on the contrary, the amount and degree of negligence are the determining question. There must be mens rea.

. . . In explaining to juries the test which they should apply to determine whether the negligence, in the particular case, amounted or did not amount to a crime, judges have used many epithets, such as "culpable," "criminal," "gross," "wicked," "clear," "complete." But whatever epithet be used, and whether an epithet be used or not, in order to establish criminal liability the facts must be such that, in the opinion of the jury, the negligence of the accused went beyond a mere matter of compensation between subjects and showed such disregard for the life and safety of others as to amount to a crime against the state and conduct deserving punishment. . . .

If a person holds himself out as possessing special skill and knowledge and he is consulted, as possessing such skill and knowledge, by or on behalf of a patient, he owes a duty to the patient to use due caution in undertaking the treatment. If he accepts the responsibility and undertakes the treatment accordingly, he owes a duty to the patient to use diligence, care, knowledge, skill and caution in administering the treatment. No contractual relation is necessary, nor is it necessary that the service be rendered for reward. It is for the judge to direct the jury what standard to apply and for the jury to say whether that standard has been reached. The jury should not exact the highest, or a very high standard, nor should they be content with a very low standard. The law requires a fair and reasonable standard of care and competence. This standard must be reached in all the matters above mentioned. If the patient's death has been caused by the defendant's indolence or carelessness, it will not avail to show that he had sufficient knowledge; nor will it avail to prove that he was diligent in attendance, if the patient has been killed by his gross ignorance and unskilfulness. No further observation need be made with regard to cases where the death is alleged to have been caused by indolence or carelessness. As regards cases where incompetence is alleged, it is only necessary to say that the unqualified practitioner cannot claim to be measured by any lower standard than that which is applied to a qualified man. As regards cases of alleged recklessness, juries are likely to distinguish between the qualified and the unqualified man. There may be recklessness in undertaking the treatment and recklessness in the conduct of it. It is, no doubt, conceivable that a qualified man may be held liable for recklessly undertaking a case which he knew, or should have known, to be beyond his powers, or for making his patient the subject of reckless experiment. Such cases are likely to be rare. In the case of the quack, where the treatment has been proved to be incompetent and to have caused the patient's death, juries are not likely to hesitate in finding liability on the ground that the defendant undertook, and continued to treat, a case involving the gravest risk to his patient, when he knew he was not competent to deal with it, or would have known if he had paid any proper regard to the life and safety of his patient.

The foregoing observations deal with civil liability. To support an indictment for manslaughter the prosecution must prove the matters necessary to establish civil liability (except pecuniary loss), and, in addition, must satisfy the jury that the negligence or incompetence of the accused went beyond a mere matter of compensation and showed such disregard for the life and safety of others as to amount to a crime against the state and conduct deserving punishment. . . .

[He went through the trial judge's summing-up and continued:] If the words "gross," "wicked" and "culpable" are put aside this summing-up amounts to a direction to the jury that they must draw the line between mistake or error of judgment on the one hand, and carelessness or incompetence on the other hand. If there was only mistake or error of judgment there is no liability, but if there was any falling short of a fair average degree of care or competence, then there is liability. Such a direction would be complete and accurate on the trial of an action for damages for negligence. It is not adequate on the trial of an indictment for manslaughter. There is however, in the passages dealing with the evidence, a frequent use of some of the adjectives which have always been used in explaining criminal negligence to a jury. For this reason, looking at the summing-up as a whole, this court is of the opinion that there was no misdirection. It is, nevertheless, most desirable that in trials for manslaughter by negligence it should be impressed on the jury that the issue they have to try is not negligence or no negligence, but felony or no felony. It is desirable that, as far as possible, the explanation of criminal negligence to a jury should not be a mere question of epithets. It is, in a sense, a question of degree—and it is for the jury to draw the line, but there is a difference in kind between the negligence which gives a right to compensation and the negligence which is a crime.

The learned judge was invited to withdraw the first and second charges of negligence from the jury on the ground that there was no evidence to support them. He declined to do so. . . . For this reason the conviction cannot stand.

Conviction quashed

A far less stringent attitude was adopted in the case below.

R. v. Cato
[1976] 1 W.L.R. 110

The facts appear *ante*, p. 26.

Lord Widgery C.J.: The judge left the manslaughter charge to the jury on the two alternative bases which the Crown had suggested, and it will be appreciated at once what they were. The first alternative was that the death was caused by the injection and the consequent intrusion of morphine into the body, and that was an unlawful act so that the killing was the result of an unlawful act and manslaughter on that footing. Alternatively, it was said that a verdict of guilty would be justified on the footing that there had been no unlawful act, but that the injection of heroin had been done with recklessness or gross negligence, which of course would be sufficient to sustain the conviction of manslaughter.

. . . [T]he judge on more than one occasion, as the extracts which I have read show, told the jury that Farmer's consent was quite irrelevant. Occasionally he says the consent of Farmer is no defence to the charge, but more often he says the consent of Farmer is quite irrelevant. Mr. Blom-Cooper says that that was a misdirection because he says there are two factors, two aspects of this case, which have to be considered separately. It may be that if one asks oneself whether the consent of the victim could provide a defence to a charge of manslaughter, the answer should be a vivid "no". In general, as a simple proposition, where this kind of injury is done by one person to another the consent of the person injured is not a defence. On the other hand, one of the matters which the jury at some stage had to consider in the present case was whether the appellant had acted with recklessness or gross negligence, and Mr. Blom-Cooper says, and we think rightly, that when considering that aspect of the case the consent of Farmer is something which could not be wholly excluded.

In those circumstances we have tried to look at these two aspects of the matter separately. We think that the judge, when saying so positively that the consent of Farmer was irrelevant or was no defence, was anticipating a question in the jury's mind that they might have been uncertain as to whether it would be a defence or not. One has to realise that laymen will often think that a person who dies in Farmer's circumstances will not produce a charge of manslaughter against his friend if in fact he consented to what was being done to him and the friend did not attempt to do more than that. We think it could very well have been the case that the jury might have asked the judge directly "Is consent a defence?," and if they had, he would have had to say "no," and his saying "no" in the course of his summing-up appears to be an anticipation of that kind of question in the jury's mind.

But of course in a perfect world the judge, when faced with this question, would have dealt with both aspects of the matter in contrast. He would have said "It is not a defence in the sense that merely by proving Farmer's permission the matter is at an end: but when you come to consider the questions of gross negligence or recklessness of course you must take it into account." Whether he would have gone further we very much doubt. If a persistent juror had said "Well, what do you mean by 'take into account'? What have we got to do?," it may very well be that the judge would be stumped at that point and really could not do any more than say "You must take it into account." Lawyers understand what it means, but jurors very often do not, and although I have taken more time to discuss this point than perhaps it really requires, we have come to the conclusion that there is not here any matter which gives us cause to think that the conviction may be unsafe or unsatisfactory. We support the judge in dealing head-on with the question of whether consent was a defence or not, and we do not think that he could usefully have said much more in regard to gross negligence or recklessness in order to avoid any possible confusion at that end of the scale.

... [O]n the first count is the question of recklessness. Of course if the jury convicted on the second approach the reckless approach, they must have considered whether there was recklessness. They were indeed instructed so to do. Mr. Blom-Cooper makes the complaint that the judge has not dealt sufficiently with this aspect of the case to give the jury a proper, fair and adequate direction about it. Of course he recognises, he is far too experienced, if I may say so, not to recognise, that he cannot expect every judge in the hurly-burly of every case to sum up with the polished perfection which counsel can produce in this court some months later. But even so, making all allowances for that, the complaint is made that the judge did not do anything to help the jury as to the meaning of recklessness, and in particular that the judge did not refer to one aspect of the appellant's evidence which might have proved of some importance.

The appellant when pressed as to his knowledge of the potentiality of heroin when injected, said that he knew that it might give rise to addiction, but had no idea that it could give rise to death or serious bodily harm. Of course in deciding whether the appellant had himself acted recklessly one would have to have regard to the fact, if it was accepted, that he did not know about the potentiality of the drug. It is said that this was not really sufficiently provided for in the summing-up.

We think it was. After all, recklessness is a perfectly simple English word. Its meaning is well known and it is in common use. There is a limit to the extent to which the judge in the summing-up is expected to teach the jury the use of ordinary English words. Although we have listened to Mr. Blom-Cooper on this point, with respect, we do not find that criticism justifies our concluding that the manslaughter verdict was in any measure unsafe or unsatisfactory, so we shall dismiss the appeal so far as that conviction is concerned.

Appeal dismissed

R. v. Stone and Dobinson

The facts appear *ante*, p. 22.

GEOFFREY LANE L.J.: ... Mr. Coles' second submission presents greater difficulty. It is that the judge's direction on the nature of the negligence or recklessness required was wrongly stated. This is how the matter was left to the jury:

"Have the Crown proved that either or both of these defendants was guilty of gross neglect of Fanny amounting to a reckless disregard for the health and wellbeing of that woman. Do not place your judgment on the question of recklessness as to whether she died or not. What has to be proved is not that, but that there was a reckless disregard for their duty of care. It may well be that that will involve a consideration of what they thought would be the consequences of their reckless disregard, if you found there was one. For example, if I were in charge of a person and I was guilty of some major neglect, but I genuinely did not appreciate that it would lead to any dire results, you would probably say, 'That person is not very bright, but I am not sure he is guilty of recklessness!'"

The appellants' contention is that the prosecution in order to succeed must show recklessness on the part of the defendant; that recklessness in this context means foresight of the likelihood or possibility of death or serious injury and a determination nevertheless to persist in the omission to provide care. We were referred to a number of 19th century decisions which are historically interesting but of small practical assistance. Mr. Coles relied principally on the decision of this court in *R.* v. *Lowe* [1973] Q.B. 702. In that case there were two counts, one alleging manslaughter to a child on the grounds that the defendants' cruelty alleged under the second count caused its death, and the second count charging cruelty to a child by wilfully neglecting it so as to cause unnecessary suffering or injury to health under section 1 (1) of the Children and Young Persons Act 1933. The judge had directed the jury that if they found the appellant guilty on the second count they must find him guilty under the first count of manslaughter, even though they acquitted him of recklessness. That was held to be a misdirection. Phillimore L.J., delivering the judgment of the court, went on to say, at p. 709:

> "Now in the present case the jury negatived recklessness. How then can mere neglect, albeit wilful, amount to manslaughter? This court feels that there is something inherently unattractive in a theory of constructive manslaughter. It seems strange that an omission which is wilful solely in the sense that it is not inadvertent, the consequences of which are not foreseen by the person who is neglectful should, if death results, automatically give rise to an indeterminate sentence. . . ."

Mr. Coles submits that that passage is support for his argument that there must be an appreciation by the defendant of the risk of death or serious injury before a conviction for manslaughter in these circumstances can result. We disagree. The court is saying simply that there must be proved the necessary high degree of negligence, and a direction which fails to emphasise that requirement will be defective. It is to *Andrews* v. *Director of Public Prosecutions* [*ante*, p. 439], that one must turn to discover the definition of the requisite degree of negligence. Lord Atkin cites with approval the words of Lord Hewart C.J. in *R.* v. *Bateman* [*ante*, p. 449], and goes on to say:

> "Simple lack of care such as will constitute civil liability is not enough; for purposes of the criminal law there are degrees of negligence: and a very high degree of negligence is required to be proved before the felony is established. Probably of all the epithets that can be applied 'reckless' most nearly covers the case. It is difficult to visualise a case of death caused by reckless driving in the connotation of that term in ordinary speech which would not justify a conviction for manslaughter: but it is probably not all-embracing for 'reckless' suggests an indifference to risk whereas the accused may have appreciated the risk and intended to avoid it and yet have shown such a high degree of negligence in the means adopted to avoid the risk as would justify a conviction."

It is clear from that passage that indifference to an obvious risk and appreciation of such risk, coupled with a determination nevertheless to run it, are both examples of recklessness.

The duty which a defendant has undertaken is a duty to caring for the health and welfare of the infirm person. What the prosecution have to prove is a breach of that duty in such circumstances that the jury feel convinced that the defendant's conduct can properly be described as reckless that is to say a reckless disregard of danger to the health and welfare of the infirm person. Mere inadvertence is not enough. The defendant must be proved to have been indifferent to an obvious risk of injury to health, or actually to have foreseen the risk but to have determined nevertheless to run it.

The direction given by the judge was wholly in accord with those principles. If any criticism is to be made it would be that the direction was unduly favourable to the defence.

Appeals dismissed

In *R.* v. *Smith* [1979] Crim. L.R. 251 a jury were discharged after being unable to agree on a charge of manslaughter by neglect. Griffiths J. directed that "it had to be proved that in reckless disregard of his duty to care for the deceased's health, S. failed to get medical attention, and that as a direct result of that failure she died. "Reckless disregard" meant that, fully appreciating that she was so ill that there was a real risk to her health if she did not get help, S. did not do so, either, because he was indifferent, or because he deliberately ran a wholly unjustified and unreasonable risk."

Notes

Griew, "Consistency, Communication and Codification: Reflections on Two Mens Rea Words" in Reshaping the Criminal Law, ed. Glazebrook, pp. 57, 62–63

"The language of recklessness had appeared in reported manslaughter cases before 1937. But it had done so irregularly and hardly ever as amounting to the key that might solve the jury's problem, and its use was as impressionistic and unanalysed as that of the other varied language in which judges sought to convey to juries a sense of manslaughter as felony.

Since 1937 the position has been different in one respect. From Lord Atkin's speech in *Andrews* the criterion of recklessness passed into common currency in manslaughter cases, as witness reports both of trial practice and of Court of Appeal judgments. It appears that 'criminal' or 'gross' negligence is translated for juries into recklessness. What more strikingly appears, however, is that the sense in which this expression is used by the trial judge is not explained to them. In just the period in which analysts have been engaged in revealing how difficult a word it is and in which law teachers, in particular, have been discovering from the practice of students, writers and judges how variously it is understood, the indications have been that juries are offered the word to make of it what they will. Emphatic vindication of this practice came recently in *Cato*, in which the judge's naked explanation of 'with gross negligence' as 'recklessly' was approved by the Court of Appeal. 'After all, recklessness is a perfectly simple English word. Its meaning is well known and it is in common use. There is a limit to the extent to which the judge in the summing-up is expected to teach the jury the use of ordinary English words.' Yet the question remains: what did the judge mean when he used the word?

It so happens that in the case of *Stone* a year later the Court of Appeal did attempt to spell out its understanding of recklessness for manslaughter purposes. But the judgment in *Stone* did not, alas, resolve any of the problems to which the cases from *Andrews* to *Cato* had given rise. On the contrary, it may be said to have compounded them. First, two states of mind are referred to as 'examples of recklessness'—namely, 'indifference to an obvious risk and appreciation of such risk, coupled with determination nevertheless to run it . . .' It is not at all clear what in the context is meant by 'indifference' to a risk or whether, in particular, that state of mind is not merely an example of the second state of mind mentioned. The court's statement is seriously lacking in rigour. Secondly, *Cato* was neither cited to the court nor mentioned by it. The court did not expressly resile from the position adopted in that case. The result appears to be, therefore, that the Court of Appeal has its own sense, however inadequately stated, of what the word 'recklessness' means when used specifically for the purpose of manslaughter, but that there is no need to let the jury into the secret."

It has also been argued that *Stone* greatly extends the ambit of the gross negligence principle, Dennis, "Manslaughter by Omission" (1980) C.L.P. 255, 264:

"Geoffrey Lane L.J. refers to the risk involved as being one of danger to "health and welfare" of the infirm person. These are new terms in this context and they are hardly satisfactory. 'Welfare' is an extremely vague word; as a synonym for 'health' it is unhelpful, and if it adds something to the concept of physical wellbeing then the liability is too ill defined to be acceptable. An 'obvious risk of injury to health' seems to water down the traditional test of a risk of death or serious injury very considerably, and is not warranted by anything in the authorities. If this test is taken at face value it appears that it is enough that a reasonable man would inevitably realise that there is a risk of some harm or injury resulting from neglect of the infirm person, and this of course is the same test used to assess the dangerous quality of an unlawful act in the first category of manslaughter. The result is ironic. Having expressly thrown out constructive manslaughter in *Lowe* [*ante*, p. 441], the Court of Appeal has inadvertently re-introduced it in *Stone and Dobinson*."

Questions

1. Which of the two following analyses do the cases support? One, favoured by Smith and Hogan (309 *et seq.*) is that, apart from unlawful act manslaughter there are *two* categories of involuntary manslaughter: gross negligence and reckless disregard of the possibility of harm. The other, favoured by Williams, T.C.L. (224 *et seq.*), is that there is only one category but that the courts are ambivalent as to whether the mental element is objective (as the term "gross negligence" would imply) or subjective (as the word "recklessness" would suggest).

2. Dennis, in "Manslaughter by Omission" (see above) accepts Smith and Hogan's analysis but suggests that there is now a distinction between the mental element required for positive acts as opposed to omissions. Do you agree?

3. How does the direction to the jury in *R.* v. *Smith*, above, differ from that in *Stone and Dobinson*?

6. OTHER UNLAWFUL HOMICIDES

i. Infanticide

Infanticide Act 1938, section 1

"(1) Where a woman by any wilful act or omission causes the death of her child being a child under the age of twelve months, but at the time of the act or omission the balance of her mind was disturbed by reason of her not having fully recovered from the effect of giving birth to the child or by reason of the effect of lactation consequent upon the birth of the child, then, notwithstanding that the circumstances were such that but for this Act the offence would have amounted to murder, she shall be guilty of felony, to wit of infanticide, and may for such offence be dealt with and punished as if she had been guilty of the offence of manslaughter of the child."

Note

Less than half a dozen women are convicted of this offence per year and a custodial sentence is rare.

ii. Child Destruction

Infant Life (Preservation) Act 1929, section 1

"(1) Subject as hereinafter in this subsection provided, any person who, with intent to destroy the life of a child capable of being born alive, by any wilful act causes a child to die before it has an existence independent of its mother, shall be guilty of felony, to wit, of child destruction, and shall be liable on conviction thereon to imprisonment for life: Provided that no person shall be found guilty of an offence under this section unless it is proved that the act which caused the death of the child was not done in good faith for the purpose only of preserving the life of the mother.

"(2) For the purposes of this Act, evidence that a woman had at any material time been pregnant for a period of twenty-eight weeks or more shall be prima facie proof that she was at that time pregnant of a child capable of being born alive."

Note

Neither this offence nor abortion below, are true homicides, see *ante*, p. 366. For a discussion of the proviso to subsection (1), see Abortion, particularly the case of *R.* v. *Bourne*, below.

iii. Abortion

Offences Against the Person Act 1861, section 58

"Every woman being with child, who, with intent to procure her own miscarriage, shall unlawfully administer to herself any poison or other noxious thing, or shall unlawfully use any instrument or other means whatsoever with the like intent, and whosoever, with intent to procure the miscarriage of any woman, whether she be or be not with child, shall unlawfully administer to her or cause to be taken by her any poison or other noxious thing, or shall unlawfully use any instrument or other means whatsoever with the like intent, shall be guilty of felony, and being convicted thereof shall be liable to [imprisonment] for life."

Notes

Complications follow when the women is not pregnant but does what would otherwise fall within the section. Note the cases of *Whitchurch, ante*, p. 341 and *Sockett* (1908) 24 T.L.R. 893 on conspiracy and aiding and abetting respectively, the combined effect of which is to destroy the duality of the offences in section 58. The woman who is not pregnant commits no wrong if she attempts to procure her own miscarriage unaided. If she has help, the helper is guilty under the second part of the section, they are both guilty of conspiracy and the woman herself is guilty of aiding and abetting the helper.

Various acts of preparation are made specifically criminal under the following section:

Offences Against the Person Act 1861, section 59

"Whosoever shall unlawfully supply or procure any poison or other noxious thing, or any instrument or thing whatsoever, knowing that the same is intended to be unlawfully used or employed with intent to procure the miscarriage of any woman, whether she be or not be with child, shall be guilty of a misdemeanour, and being convicted thereof shall be liable to [imprisonment] not exceeding five years."

The number of convictions for illegally procuring an abortion has greatly-diminished since the Abortion Act 1967 which allows for lawful medical termination.

Abortion Act 1967, section 1

"(1) Subject to the provisions of this section, a person shall not be guilty of an offence under the law relating to abortion when a pregnancy is terminated by a registered medical practitioner if two registered medical practitioners are of the opinion, formed in good faith—

(a) that the continuance of the pregnancy would involve risk to the life of the pregnant woman, or of injury to the physical or mental health of the pregnant woman or any existing children of her family, greater than if the pregnancy were terminated; or

(b) that there is a substantial risk that if the child were born it would suffer from such physical or mental abnormalities as to be seriously handicapped."

The 1967 Act was in some senses merely a declaration and clarification of the interpretation given by at least one Old Bailey judge to section 58: see the case below.

R. v. Bourne

[1939] 1 K.B. 687
Central Criminal Court

The accused performed an operation on a girl of 14 who was pregnant as a result of a rape. The pregnancy was terminated with the consent of the girl's parents. The accused claimed that to continue the pregnancy would have caused serious injury to the girl.

MACNAGHTEN J. in summing up the case to the jury said: . . . A man of the highest skill, openly, in one of our great hospitals, performs the operation. Whether it was legal or illegal you will have to determine, but he performs the operation as an act of charity, without fee or reward, and unquestionably believing that he was doing the right thing, and that he ought, in the performance of his duty as a member of a profession devoted to the alleviation of human suffering, to do it. That is the case that you have to try today.

It is, a case, of first instance, first impression. The matter has never, so far as I know, arisen before for a jury to determine circumstances such as these, and there was, even amongst learned counsel, some doubt as to the proper direction to the jury in such a case as this.

The defendant is charged with an offence against section 58 of the Offences against the Person Act, 1861. That section is a re-enactment of earlier statutes, the first of which was passed at the beginning of the last century in the reign of George III (43 Geo. 3, c. 58, s. 1). But long before then, before even Parliament came into existence, the killing of an unborn child was by the common law of England a grave crime, see *Bracton*, Book III (*De Corona*), fol. 121. The protection which common law afforded to human life extended to the unborn child in the womb of its mother. But, as in the case of homicide, so also in the case where an unborn child is killed, there may be justification for the act.

Nine years ago Parliament passed an Act called the Infant Life (Preservation) Act, 1929. Section 1, subsection 1, of that Act provides that "any person who, with intent to destroy the life of a child capable of being born alive, by any wilful act causes a child to die before it has an existence independent of its mother, shall be guilty of felony, to wit, of child destruction, and shall be liable on conviction thereof on indictment to penal servitude for life: Provided that no person shall be found guilty of an offence under this section unless it is provided that the act which caused the death of the child was not done in good faith for the purpose only of preserving the life of the mother." It is true . . . that this enactment provides for the case where a child is killed by a wilful act at the time when it is being delivered in the ordinary course of nature; but in my view the proviso that it is necessary for the Crown to prove that the act was not done in good faith for the purpose only of preserving the life of the mother is in accordance with what has always been the common law of England with regard to the killing of an unborn child. No such proviso is in fact set out in section 58 of the Offences Against the Person Act, 1861; but the words of that section are that any person who "unlawfully" uses an instrument with intent to procure miscarriage shall be guilty of felony. In my opinion the word "unlawfully" is not, in that section, a meaningless word. I think it imports the meaning expressed by the proviso in section 1, subsection 1, of the Infant Life (Preservation) Act, 1929, and that section 58 of the Offences against the Person Act, 1861, must be read as if the words making it an offence to use an instrument with intent to procure a miscarriage were qualified by a similar proviso.

In this case, therefore, my direction to you in law is this—that the burden rests on the Crown to satisfy you beyond reasonable doubt that the defendant did not procure the miscarriage of the girl in good faith for the purpose only of preserving her life. If the Crown fails to satisfy you of that, the defendant is entitled by the law of this land to a verdict of acquittal. If, on the other hand, you are satisfied that what the defendant did was not done by him in good faith for the purpose only of preserving the life of the girl, it is your duty to find him guilty. It is said, and I think said rightly, that this is a case of great importance to the public and, more especially, to the medical profession; but you will observe that it has nothing to do with the ordinary case of procuring abortion. . . . In those cases the operation is performed by a person of no skill, with no medical qualifications, and there is no pretence that it is done for the preservation of the mother's life. Cases of that sort are in no way affected by the consideration of the question which is put before you today.

What then is the meaning to be given to the words "for the purpose of preserving the life of the mother." There has been much discussion in this case as to the difference between danger to life and danger to health. It may be that you are more fortunate than I am, but I confess that I have found it difficult to understand what the discussion really meant, since life depends upon health, and it may be that health is so gravely impaired that death results. A question was asked by the learned Attorney-General in the course of his cross-examination of Mr. Bourne. "I suggest to you, Mr. Bourne," said the Attorney-General, "that there is a perfectly clear line—there may be border-line cases—there is a clear line of distinction between danger to health and danger to life." The answer of Mr. Bourne was: "I cannot agree without qualifying it; I cannot say just yes or no. I can say there is a large group whose health may be damaged, but whose life almost certainly will not be sacrificed. There is another group at the other end whose life will be definitely in very great danger." And then he adds: "There is a large body of material between those two extremes in which it is not really possible to say how far life will be in danger, but we find, of course, that the health is depressed to such an extent that life is shortened, such as in cardiac cases, so that you may say that their life is in danger, because death might occur within measurable distance of the time of their labour." If that view commends itself to you, you will not accept the suggestion that there is a clear line of distinction between danger to health and danger to life. Mr. Oliver wanted you to give what he called a wide and liberal meaning to the words "for the purpose of preserving the life of the mother." I should prefer the word "reasonable" to the words "wide and liberal." I think you should take a reasonable view of those words.

It is not contended that those words mean merely for the purposes of saving the mother from instant death. There are cases, we are told, where it is reasonably certain that a pregnant woman will not be able to deliver the child which is in her womb and survive. In such a case where the doctor anticipates, basing his opinion upon the experience of the profession, that the child cannot be delivered without the death of the mother, it is obvious that the sooner the operation is performed the better. The law does not require the doctor to wait until the unfortunate woman is in peril of immediate death. In such a case he is not only entitled, but it is his duty to perform the operation with a view to saving her life.

Here let me diverge for one moment to touch upon a matter that has been mentioned to you, the various views which are held with regard to this operation. Apparently there is a great difference of opinion even in the medical profession itself. Some there may be, for all I know, who hold the view that the fact that a woman desires the operation performed is a sufficient justification for it. Well, that is not the law: the desire of a woman to be relieved of her pregnancy is no justification at all for performing the operation. On the other hand there are people who, from what are said to be religious reasons, object to the operation being performed under any circumstances. That is not the law either. On the contrary, a person who holds such an opinion ought not to be an obstetrical surgeon, for if a case arose where the life of the woman could be saved by performing the operation and the doctor refused to perform it because of his religious opinions and the woman died, he would be in grave peril of being brought before this court on a charge of manslaughter by negligence. He would have no better defence than a person who, again for some religious reason, refused to call in a doctor to attend his sick child, where a doctor could have been called in and the life of the child could have been saved. If the father, for a so-called religious reason, refused to call in a doctor, he is also answerable to the criminal law for the death of his child. I mention these two extreme views merely to show that the law lies between them. It permits the termination of pregnancy for the purpose of preserving the life of the mother.

As I have said, I think those words ought to be construed in a reasonable sense, and, if the doctor is of opinion, on reasonable grounds and with adequate knowledge, that the probable consequences of the continuance of the pregnancy will be to make the woman a physical or mental wreck, the jury are quite entitled to take the view that the doctor who, under those circumstances and in that honest belief, operates, is operating for the purpose of preserving the life of the mother. . . .

Verdict: Not guilty

Note

Recently the lawfulness of the role of nurses in the conduct of abortions has been considered by the House of Lords.

Royal College of Nursing of the United Kingdom v. Department of Health and Social Security
[1981] 1 All E.R. 545
House of Lords

Medical induction has largely replaced the surgical method of terminating pregnancies of over three months. The procedure is in two stages, the second of which is carried out by nurses. The Department issued a circular to the nursing profession stating that no offence was committed by nurses who participated in this stage provided that the person who decided on the termination, initiated it and remained responsible for its overall conduct and control, was a doctor. The Royal College sought a declaration that the advice on the circular was wrong and that nurses would be contravening section 58 of the 1861 Act.

LORD DIPLOCK: The Abortion Act 1967 which it falls to this House to construe is described in its long title as 'An Act to amend and clarify the law relating to termination of pregnancy by registered medical practitioners'. The legislation of abortion, at any rate in circumstances in which the termination of the pregnancy is not essential in order to save the mother's life, is a subject on which strong moral and religious convictions are held; and these convictions straddle the normal party political lines. That, no doubt, is why the Act, which incorporates a 'conscience clause' that I shall be quoting later, started its Parliamentary life as a private member's Bill and, maybe for that reason, it lacks that style and consistency of draftsmanship both internal to the Act itself and in relation to other statutes which one would expect to find in legislation that had its origin in the office of Parliamentary counsel.

Whatever may be the technical imperfections of its draftsmanship, however, its purpose in my view becomes clear if one starts by considering what was the state of the law relating to abortion before the passing of the Act, what was the mischief that required amendment, and in what respects was the existing law unclear.

In England the 'law relating to abortion' which it was the purpose of the Act to amend and clarify, is defined in s 6 of the Act itself as meaning 'sections 58 and 59 of the Offences against the Person Act 1861'. [*ante*, p. 456.]

. . . It had long been generally accepted that abortion was lawful where it was necessary to save the pregnant woman's life; but what circumstances, if any, short of this, legitimised termination of a pregnancy does not appear to have attracted judicial notice until, in 1938, the matter was put to a sagaciously selected test by Mr Aleck Bourne, a well-known obstetrical surgeon at St Mary's Hospital, London. He there performed an abortion on a 14-year old girl who was seven weeks pregnant as a consequence of being the victim of a particularly brutal rape. He invited prosecution for having done so. The evidence at his trial was that if the girl had been allowed to bear the child she would 'be likely to have become a mental wreck'.

The summing up by Macnaghten J in *R.* v. *Bourne* resulted in an acquittal. So the correctness of his statement of the law did not undergo examination by any higher authority. It still remained in 1967 the only judicial pronouncement on the subject.

. . . Such then was the unsatisfactory and uncertain state of the law that the

Abortion Act 1967 was intended to amend and clarify. What the Act sets out to do is to provide an exhaustive statement of the circumstances in which treatment for the termination of a pregnancy may be carried out lawfully. That the statement, which is contained in s 1, is intended to be exhaustive appears from s 5 (2):

> "For the purposes of the law relating to abortion, anything done with intent to procure the miscarriage of a woman is unlawfully done unless authorised by section 1 of this Act."

This sets aside the interpretation placed by Macnaghten J in *R* v. *Bourne* on the word 'unlawfully' in ss 58 and 59 of the Offences against the Person Act 1861.

The 'conscience clause' which I have already mentioned is also worth citing before coming to the crucial provisions of s 1. It is s 4 (1) and so far as is relevant for the present purposes it reads:

> '. . . no person shall be under any duty, whether by contract or by any statutory or other legal requirement, to participate in any treatment authorised by this Act to which he has a conscientious objection. . .'

. . . I have spoken of the requirements of the Act as to the way in which 'treatment for the termination of the pregnancy' is to be carried out rather than using the word 'termination' or 'terminated' by itself, for the draftsman appears to use the longer and the shorter expressions indiscriminately, as is shown by a comparison between subsections (1) and (3) of s 1, and by the reference in the conscience clause to 'treatment authorised by this Act'. Furthermore, if 'termination' or 'terminated' meant only the event of miscarriage and not the whole treatment undertaken with that object in mind, lack of success, which apparently occurs in 1% to 2% of cases, would make all who had taken part in the unsuccessful treatment guilty of an offence under s 58 or s 59 of the Offences against the Person Act 1861. This cannot have been the intention of Parliament.

The requirement of the Act as to the way in which the treatment is to be carried out, which in my view throws most light on the second aspect of its policy and the true construction of the phrase in sub-section (1) of s 1 which lies at the root of the dispute between the parties to this appeal, is the requirement in sub-section (3) that, except in cases of dire emergency, the treatment must be carried out in a national health service hospital (or private clinic specifically approved for that purpose by the minister). It is in my view evident that, in providing that treatment for termination of pregnancies should take place in ordinary hospitals Parliament contemplated that (conscientious objections apart) like other hospital treatment, it would be undertaken as a team effort in which, acting on the instructions of the doctor in charge of the treatment, junior doctors, nurses, paramedical and other members of the hospital staff would each do things forming part of the whole treatment which it would be in accordance with accepted medical practice to entrust to a member of the staff possessed of their respective qualifications and experience.

Subsection (1) although it is expressed to apply only 'when a pregnancy is terminated by a registered medical practitioner' . . . also appears to contemplate treatment that is in the nature of a team effort and to extend its protection to all those who play a part in it. The exoneration from guilt is not confined to the registered medical practitioner by whom a pregnancy is terminated, it extends to any person who takes part in the treatment for its termination.

What limitation on this exoneration is imposed by the qualifying phrase, 'when a pregnancy is terminated by a registered medical practitioner'? In my opinion, in the context of the Act, what it requires is that a registered medical practitioner, whom I will refer to as a doctor, should accept responsibility for all stages of the treatment for the termination of the pregnancy. The particular method to be used should be decided by the doctor in charge of the treatment for termination of the pregnancy; he should carry out any physical acts, forming part of the treatment, that in accordance with accepted medical practice are done only by qualified medical practitioners, and should give specific instructions as to the carrying out of such parts of the treatment as in accordance with accepted medical practice are carried out by nurses or other members of the hospital staff without medical qualifications. To each of them, the doctor, or his substitute, should be available to be consulted or called on for assistance from beginning to end of the treatment. In other words, the doctor need not do everything with his own hands; the requirements of the subsection are satisfied when the treatment for termination of a pregnancy is one prescribed by a registered medical practitioner carried out in accordance with his directions and of which a registered medical practitioner remains in charge throughout.

My noble and learned friend Lord Wilberforce has described the successive steps taken in the treatment for termination of pregnancies in the third trimester by medical induction; and the parts played by registered medical practitioners and nurses respectively in the carrying out of the treatment. This treatment satisfies the interpretation that I have placed on the requirements of s. 1 of the Act. I would accordingly allow the appeal and restore the declaration made by Woolf J.

Lords Keith of Kinkel and Roskill delivered concurring speeches, Lords Wilberforce and Edmund-Davies dissented.

Appeal allowed

iv. Suicide

Suicide Act 1961

Section 1: "The rule of law whereby it is a crime for a person to commit suicide is hereby abrogated."

Section 2: "(1) A person who aids, abets, counsels or procures the suicide of another, or an attempt by another to commit suicide, shall be liable on conviction on indictment to imprisonment for a term not exceeding fourteen years.

(2) If on the trial of an indictment for murder or manslaughter it is proved that the accused aided, abetted, counselled or procured the suicide of the person in question, the jury may find him guilty of that offence."

Homicide Act 1957, section 4

"(1) It shall be manslaughter, and shall not be murder, for a person acting in pursuance of a suicide pact between him and another to kill the other or be a party to the other killing himself or being killed by a third person. . . .

(3) For the purposes of this section 'suicide pact' means a common agreement between two or more persons having for its object the death of all of them, whether or not each is to take his own life, but nothing done by a person who enters into a suicide pact shall be treated as done by him in pursuance of the pact unless it is done while he has the settled intention of dying in pursuance of the pact."

Notes

Any doubt as to whether it is an offence to *attempt* to aid, or abet suicide was settled in *R.* v. *McShane* (1977) 66 Cr. App. R. 97 in which Orr. L.J. said, at p. 102:

"[E]very attempt to commit an offence is an offence at common law whether the crime attempted is one by statute or at common law. . . . It follows in our judgment that the appellant was properly charged under count 1 with an offence of attempting to aid or abet, counsel or procure the suicide of Mrs Mott and none the less so because the crime defined in section 2 (1) of the Suicide Act 1961 is itself of the nature of an attempt."

An area surrounded not only by legal doubt but also by difficult, and ultimately insoluble, questions of moral philosophy is that of euthanasia. A person who kills another at that other's request will be liable for murder since consent is no defence. This is mitigated where the killing is in pursuance of a suicide pact (section 4 of the Homicide Act 1957, above), and, possibly, where a doctor administers drugs, which alleviate pain but shorten life. At the trial of Dr. Adams in 1957 Devlin J. (as he then was) said that the administration of drugs to relieve pain would not amount to legal causation. This is a grey, untested, area maintained by the turning of a blind eye by prosecuting authorities.

As far as aiding and abetting suicide is concerned the decision to prosecute rests solely with the Director of Public Prosecution whose consent is required for any proceedings (section 2 (4) of the Suicide Act 1961). "Exit," a society campaigning for voluntary euthanasia, recently published a booklet giving details of methods of committing suicide. Whether this amounts to an offence under section 2 has yet to be tested, but see Lanham, "Murder by Instigating Suicide" [1980] Crim. L.R. 215.

See generally Williams, *The Sanctity of Life and the Criminal Law*, Chap. 8; Williams, "Euthanasia" 41 *Medico Legal Journal* 14; Kennedy, "The Legal Effect of Requests by the Terminally Ill and Aged not to receive further Treatment from Doctors" [1976] Crim. L.R. 21; CLRC 14th Report, §§ 126–139 and *post*, p. 468.

7. REFORM OF THE LAW OF HOMICIDE

D. A. Thomas, "Form and Function in Criminal Law" in Reshaping the Criminal Law (ed. Glazebrook), pp. 21, 25

"No better example can be found of the failure of all those concerned with the development of the criminal law—including Parliament and the appellate judiciary as well as the advisory bodies—to see the substantive law in a functional context than the history of the definition of murder from 1960 to the present day. With few exceptions, discussions of the propriety of the objective test of intention and the proper scope of the offence have proceeded on the same lines for 18 years with only a passing reference to the fact that what was being decided by establishing a definition had utterly changed. In 1960 the questions in issue in *D.P.P.* v. *Smith* were hanging matters, and Smith was sentenced to death on his original conviction. The Law Commission's Report on Imputed Criminal Intent, which was the first attempt to clarify the implications of the case and propose amending legislation, followed the abolition of the death penalty for murder. The statute which implemented part of the Law Commission's proposals also created the Parole Board. As a result of these two developments the definition of the offence of murder was no longer concerned with the scope of liability to the death penalty, and had become a means of establishing the respective roles of judge and Parole Board in determining the period of time to be served by a person convicted of homicide and (incidentally) the manner in which that decision was to be made. This fundamental change in the nature of what was actually being decided had little obvious impact on the thinking of the House of Lords when the matter was reconsidered in 1974 [*R.* v. *Hyam, ante,* p. 374], six years after the now system of dealing with murderers had been established. With the exception of Lord Kilbrandon who (with respect) drew the wrong conclusions, their Lordships did not relate their arguments to the realities of the processes of determining the disposal of those convicted of murder and manslaughter. The problem of defining murder was essentially a formal question, to be considered and decided in terms which would have been equally relevant 100 years ago.

The results of maintaining a separation between the development of the substantive criminal law on the one hand and procedure and penal policy on the other is a system of dealing with homicide and grave personal violence which makes no sense at all in functional terms. A man strikes another with a broken glass in a public-house fight in circumstances which would normally lead to a sentence of three or four years' imprisonment for causing grievous bodily harm with intent; fortuitously the victim dies from his injuries, and unless either the prosecution or the jury will relax the law the assailant is convicted of murder and subject to a mandatory sentence of life imprisonment. In another case the defendant makes a determined attempt to kill his victim, using carefully contrived means based on thoughtful preparations; despite his best endeavours his plans miscarry and he is convicted of attempted murder: his sentence is absolutely within the discretion of the sentencing judge. Two men act in concert in the murder of a third. The first is convicted of murder and receives the mandatory sentence of life imprisonment. The second tenders evidence of psychopathic disorder and secures a reduction in his guilt to manslaughter by reason of diminished responsibility: the judge exercises his discretion to sentence him to life imprisonment. Some years pass: the first, having paid his debt (or at least made a down-payment on it) to society, is released by the Home Secretary on the recommendation of the Parole Board. His co-defendant, having established to the satisfaction of the jury—possibly in the face of prosecution evidence to the contrary—that he is suffering from psychopathic disorder—remains in custody, denied parole on the grounds that he is too dangerous to be released. What is counsel's duty in such a case? Should he advise his client to plead guilty as a sane murderer, in the hope of achieving parole within a decade, or aim for an immediate forensic victory which his client may in the long term find to be of the pyrrhic variety? A provision originally intended to mitigate the severity of the law by reducing the scope of liability to the death penalty has, in the context of changes in penal practice, become potentially a trap, at least for the accused person whose defence is based on a condition which is likely to continue and justify precautionary custody.

Other examples abound. The present definition of murder (whatever its precise terms may be) is clearly not a satisfactory basis for selecting offenders for a unique variety of sentencing procedure. In so far as the mandatory life sentence is justified by the special problems of estimating the chances of future violence by those who have killed once, the existence of special defences such as diminished responsibility and provocation, introduced in earlier times for different purposes, undermines the logic of the sentence by excepting from its scope just those offenders who are most likely to prove dangerous for the future. If the justification for the mandatory life sentence is the unique gravity of the offence and the need to emphasise the particular abhorrence of society for the murderer, that justification is at least diluted by the extension of the definition of murder to include the fortuitous killer. The extension of the definition of murder by the felony-murder rule and the recognition of an intention to inflict grievous bodily harm as a sufficient mental state for conviction may have made some sense in the days when the offence was capital, as directing the supposedly unique deterrent effect of the death sentence at the potential offender who was prepared to risk the use of grave violence to achieve his objects. Now that justification has gone, the effect of the extension of the definition of murder beyond intentional killing weakens whatever morally educative force the mandatory life sentence possesses.

A reconstruction of the law of homicide must begin with a decision on the nature of the sentencing structure which is to be attached to the offences concerned. It would clearly be absurd to design a series of definitions on the assumption that a mandatory sentence in some form will continue to exist for murder, and then enact those definitions against the background of a discretionary sentence. The present shape of the law of murder is the product of the process of reducing the scope of the death penalty; a new approach must start with sentencing structure and proceed to establish the graduations and degrees of liability necessary to the rational operation of that structure."

Report of the Committee on Mentally Abnormal Offenders (the Butler Committee) 1975, Cmnd. 6244

"*Summary of Recommendations*

§ 57 The present provision relating to diminished responsibility is unsatisfactory; our preferred solution would be the abolition of the mandatory life sentence for murder, and of the provision for diminished responsibility which would then be unnecessary. We have suggested answers to possible objections (§§ 19.15–19.16)."

Report of the Advisory Council on the Penal System, "Sentences of Imprisonment," Home Office, 1978

"§ 224 Although murder has been traditionally and distinctively considered the most serious crime, it is not a homogeneous offence but a crime of considerable variety. It ranges from deliberate cold-blooded killing in pursuit of purely selfish ends to what is commonly referred to as "mercy killing". Instead of automatically applying a single sentence to such an offence, we believe that sentences for murder should reflect this variety with correspondingly variable terms of imprisonment or, in the exceptional case, even with a non-custodial penalty. This is primarily because we do not think that anyone should, without the most specific justification, be subjected to the disadvantages which we see in indeterminate sentencing (see paragraph 226). It is also because we cannot believe that the problems of predicting future behaviour at the time of conviction are inherently more difficult in a murder case than in any other case where there is a measure of instability, or that judges are any less able to make predictions or to assess degrees of culpability in murder cases than in any others. But it is also because efforts to alleviate the harshness of the mandatory penalty have led to complications in legal proceedings for which we believe there can be no proper justification.

§ 225 The efforts at alleviation to which we refer are, first of all, the two special defences of provocation and diminished responsibility which, if successful, reduce the conviction to manslaughter. Although a conviction for manslaughter may be considered less of a stigma than a conviction for murder, to the offender the important difference often is that the lesser conviction avoids the mandatory penalty. The jurisprudence that has developed out of this defence demonstrates the conceptual difficulties of seeking to mitigate a penal consequence via the substantive law. Provocation may be a factor in any crime; it can and does properly affect the sentence passed on the offender, but only in this one case does it reduce the finding of guilt to a lesser offence. Similarly, the legal concept which enables the defence of diminished responsibility, under section 2 of the Homicide Act 1957, to reduce the crime of murder to manslaughter, creates difficulties. If the mental incapacity is not sufficient to negative the requisite mental element for murder, there are problems in describing the offence as any other crime. If judges had discretion in sentencing, the issues of provocation and diminished responsibility could be considered in their proper place, as mitigating factors in the sentencing process."

[Both the Butler Committee and the Advisory Council recognised that the question of the mandatory penalty was under consideration by the Criminal Law Revision Committee. See below for that Committee's conclusion on the matter (s. 6).]

Criminal Law Revision Committee, 14th Report, "Offences Against the Person," Cmnd. 7844, 1980

"*Summary of Recommendations*

MURDER

1. It should be murder:

(a) if a person, with intent to kill, causes death and

(b) if a person causes death by an unlawful act intended to cause serious injury and known to him to involve a risk of causing death (§§ 19–29).

In addition, if Parliament favours a provision of the type referred to in paragraphs 27 and 30, it should be on the following lines: that it should be murder if a person causes death by an unlawful act intended to cause fear (of death or serious injury) and known to the defendant to involve a risk of causing death (§ 30).

2. For killing to constitute murder (or manslaughter or infanticide) the victim should have been born and have an existence independent of the mother (§ 35).

3. There should be a special provision to secure that, if a jury are sure that either child destruction or murder (or manslaughter or infanticide) has been committed or attempted, but are not sure which, they should convict of the lesser offence (§ 36). The offence of concealing birth, contrary to section 60 of the Act of 1861, should be retained pending its examination by the appropriate departments (§ 33, footnote).

4. There should not be a statutory definition of death for the purposes of offences against the person (§ 37).

5. A killing should not amount to murder (or any other offence of homicide) unless death follows before the expiration of a year after the day on which the injury was inflicted (§ 39). Time should run from the infliction of injury as opposed to the act which causes death (§ 40).

THE PENALTY FOR MURDER

6. We are divided on this matter [the penalty for murder]. In view of the importance of the subject and the division of opinion amongst us the arguments for and against retaining the mandatory life penalty for murder have been set out in full (§§ 42–60). In the circumstances we are not in a position to recommend that there should be any change on this matter. In our consideration of other aspects of offences against the person we have assumed (unless otherwise stated) that the mandatory penalty for murder will remain.

JUDICIAL RECOMMENDATIONS UNDER SECTION 1(2) OF THE MURDER (ABOLITION OF DEATH PENALTY) ACT 1965

7. The scheme of minimum recommendations introduced in 1965 should continue (§§ 64–70).

8. If the scheme is retained, the exercise of the power to make recommendations should continue to be discretionary. However the following changes should be made:

(a) an offender should be able to appeal against a minimum recommendation in the same way as against a determinate sentence (§ 72);
(b) when making a minimum recommendation the trial judge should state publicly the factors on which he is basing his recommendation (§ 72);
(c) as a matter of practice, when minded to make a minimum recommendation the trial judge should invite the defence to make any representations they consider desirable (§ 72).

SPECIAL DEFENCES TO MURDER CHARGES—PROVOCATION AND DIMINISHED RESPONSIBILITY

9. Defences of provocation and diminished responsibility should be retained but with some changes (§ 75).

10. The test of provocation should be reformulated so that provocation is a defence to a charge of murder if, on the facts as they appeared to the defendant, it can reasonably be regarded as a sufficient ground for the loss of self-control leading the defendant to react against the victim with a murderous intent (§§ 81 and 82).

11. The defendant should be judged with due regard to all the circumstances, including any disability, physical or mental, from which he suffered (§ 83); the provocation need not be by the victim of the defendant's attack (§ 85); and the defence of provocation should not depend upon the particular mode by which the victim was injured or killed. To this extent the "reasonable relationship" test should go (§ 86).

12. The judge's discretion to decide whether there is any evidence on which the defence of provocation can properly be left to the jury should be restored (§ 88).

13. A person who kills under provocation or while suffering from diminished responsibility should continue to be guilty of manslaughter (§ 87) and the offence should be punishable with a maximum penalty of life imprisonment (§ 90).

14. The definition of diminished responsibility should be reworded. Some possible forms of rewording are suggested in §§ 92–93.

15. The burden on the defendant in respect of both provocation and diminished responsibility should only go to adducing sufficient evidence to raise an issue (§ 94).

16. Provision should be made enabling a magistrates' court, if the defendant consents, to commit for manslaughter by reason of diminished responsibility or, if he has been committed for trial on a charge of murder, allowing a defendant, with his consent, to be indicted for manslaughter by reason of diminished responsibility (§§ 95 and 96).

17. There should be an offence of attempted manslaughter by reason of provocation or diminished responsibility (§ 98).

INFANTICIDE

18. An offence of infanticide should be retained (§§ 100–104).

19. The definition should include the following:
(a) the woman's act or omission causes the death of her child being a child under the age of 12 months;
(b) the act or omission is such as would otherwise amount to murder or manslaughter;
(c) at the time of the act or omission the balance of the woman's mind was disturbed by reason of the effect of giving birth or circumstances consequent upon that birth (§§ 105 and 106).

20. If the defendant is charged with murder, attempted murder, manslaughter, or attempted manslaughter, it should be possible for her to plead to, or the jury to convict of, infanticide or attempted infanticide (§§ 106 and 113).

21. The burden resting upon the defendant to prove infanticide should only go to adducing sufficient evidence to raise an issue (§ 106).

22. The offence should be triable on indictment only and punishable with a maximum penalty of 5 years' imprisonment (§§ 108–111).

23. There should be no specific restrictions on reporting trials of infanticide (§ 112).

24. There should be an offence of attempted infanticide (§ 113).

MERCY KILLING

25. There should not be an offence of mercy killing; nor should any special sentencing discretion be given to judges in such cases (§ 115).

INVOLUNTARY MANSLAUGHTER

26. It should be manslaughter (punishable with a maximum penalty of life imprisonment) if a person causes death with intent to cause serious injury or being reckless whether death or serious injury be caused. All other forms of the existing offence of involuntary manslaughter, for example manslaughter by gross negligence, should be abolished (§§ 116–123).

TERRORISM

27. Crimes committed either directly or indirectly for political purposes, which have come to be referred to as terrorist crimes, should not be put into a special category of crime (§ 125).

KILLING BY CONSENT AND SUICIDE

28. Killing by consent should continue to be treated as murder (§ 128)

29. The offence now in section 4 of the Homicide Act 1957 should be restated as an offence of killing in pursuance of a suicide pact punishable with a maximum penalty of 7 years' imprisonment.

30. On an indictment charging murder, if it is established that the killing was in pursuance of a suicide pact a jury should be empowered to return that verdict. Similarly, if attempted murder is charged attempted killing in pursuance of a suicide pact should be returnable as an alternative verdict (§ 133).

31. The burden resting on the defendant of proving the existence of a suicide pact should only go to adducing sufficient evidence to raise an issue (§ 133).

32. Aiding, abetting, counselling or procuring suicide should continue to be an offence but should be subject to a maximum penalty of 7 years' imprisonment (§§ 134–136).

33. The consent of the Director of Public Prosecutions to the institution of proceedings for aiding, abetting, counselling or procuring suicide and killing in pursuance of a suicide pact should be necessary (§ 137).

34. On an indictment charging killing in pursuance of a suicide pact a jury should be empowered to return a verdict of aiding, abetting, counselling or procuring suicide if the facts establish that offence and vice versa (§ 137).

CAUSING DEATH BY RECKLESS DRIVING AND CAUSING BODILY HARM BY WANTON OR FURIOUS DRIVING

35. The offence of causing death by reckless driving should be abolished (§ 142).

36. There should be a provision empowering verdicts of reckless driving and careless driving to be returned on a charge of causing death recklessly (§ 143).

37. The offence of causing bodily harm by wanton or furious driving should be abolished (§ 144).

38. Consideration might be given to replacing the offence of reckless driving by a driving offence involving complete disregard for the life or safety of other persons (§§ 145 and 146).

DEFENCES

Self-defence

72. (a) The common law defence of self-defence should be replaced by a statutory defence providing that a person may use such force as is reasonable in the circumstances as he believes them to be in the defence of himself or any other person, or in the defence of his property or that of any other person (§§ 281–284).

(b) The defence should be confined to cases where the defendant feared an imminent attack (§ 286).

(c) There should be no specific provision relating to the retreat rule or the refusal to comply with an unlawful demand (§ 285).

(d) Section 3 of the Criminal Law Act 1967 should be amended so that, as regards criminal proceedings only, whether the defendant believed that force was necessary in the prevention of crime or in effecting or assisting in a lawful arrest should be decided on the facts as the defendant believed them to be, but whether the force used was reasonable should be governed by an objective test (§§ 283 and 287).

(e) There should be a provision that, in considering whether the defendant believed he or another or his property or that of another was under attack, the presence or absence of reasonable grounds for such a belief is a matter to which the court or jury is to have regard in conjunction with any other relevant matters (§§ 283 and 287).

(f) The burden on the defendant of establishing that he acted in self-defence should only go to adducing sufficient evidence to raise an issue (§ 287).

7.3 Where a person kills in a situation in which it is reasonable for some force to be used in self-defence or in the prevention of crime but the defendant uses excessive force, he should be liable to be convicted of manslaughter not murder if, at the time of the act, he honestly believed that the force he used was reasonable in the circumstances (§ 288).

Notes

See also the comments on the CLRC Report in [1980] Crim. L.R. 521 and 530 and the extract below.

Duff, "Implied and Constructive Malice in Murder" (1979) 95 L.Q.R. 418, 426 et seq

". . . I would not dissent from the principle that a man should be held guilty of a serious crime offence only if he either intends or is seriously reckless with regard to the result or state of affairs which constitutes the *actus reus* of the offence. But I will argue in the next section that the doctrines of implied and constructive malice, once suitably interpreted and properly understood, are fully consistent with this principle, once *it* is properly understood: that these doctrines embody an understanding of the moral relationship between an agent's intentional action and his responsibility for its consequences (including some consequences which he may neither intend or anticipate) which their critics often lack; that we can on this basis develop a defensible definition of murder which includes both the man who intends serious injury (whether or not he realises that this is likely to cause death) and the man who intends to expose others to a serious risk of death (whether or not he thinks it probable that death will in fact ensue); and that objections to these doctrines and to such a definition rest in part on an over-simplified and distorted understanding of the moral notions of intention and recklessness. . . .

The traditional doctrine of constructive malice was wrong in so far as it required only that the agent be engaged in some felony, which need not be directed against the person: but the moral truth in the doctrine as it came to be used by the courts, and in the doctrine of implied malice, is that a man who acts with the intention of causing or threatening serious violence against the person, realising that this may well cause death, makes himself fully responsible for such injuries as actually ensue, even if these are more serious than he intended or expected; for the effects he actually causes belong within the same moral category as those which he intends.

I have argued that malice aforethought should consist in either the express malice of the man who intends to kill or realises that his action will certainly or probably cause death; or the implied malice of the man who intends to expose another to a serious risk of death or to cause serious injury: such men intend, or are relevantly "reckless" as to, their victims' deaths. But if this is right, it also follows that we must reject the definitions of "intention" and "recklessness" proposed by the Law Commission [*ante*, p. 56]. For their definition of "intention", which takes a man to intend a result if he aims to bring about or "has no substantial doubt" that it will ensue, makes it impossible to distinguish between one who *intends* to expose another to risk and one who *knows* that his action creates a risk. And their definition of "recklessness," which requires only that the agent consciously take a risk which we judge to be unreasonable, is shown to be both too wide and too narrow: too wide in that it precludes the distinction between the man who realises that his action will *probably* cause death and the reckless driver who realises that he *might*, but probably will not, cause death; too narrow in that it requires that the agent actually realise that his action might cause death before he can be judged "reckless" as to that death—whereas I have argued that the very fact that he engages in a serious assault, intending serious injury, shows him to be reckless of his victim's life, even if (indeed partly because) he does not attend to the possibly fatal effect of his assault. It is one of the merits of Scots criminal law that it recognises that "recklessness," as a basis of criminal liability, need not be a matter of *conscious* risktaking."

Chapter 9

NON-FATAL OFFENCES AGAINST THE PERSON

	PAGE
1. Assault and Battery	471
i. *Actus Reus*	471
ii. *Mens rea*	475
iii. Consent	475
iv. Statutory Assaults	479
2. Malicious Wounding and Wounding with Intent	481
i. Malicious Wounding	481
ii. Wounding with Intent	484
3. Administering Poison	485
4. Sexual Offences	486
i. Rape	486
ii. Other Sexual Offences	491
5. Proposals for Reform	492

1. ASSAULT AND BATTERY

Note

Lord Goddard C.J. in *R.* v. *Rolfe* (1952) 36 Cr. App. R. 4: "The offence of assault is often confused with the offence of battery. An assault can be committed without touching a person. One always thinks of an assault as the giving of a blow to somebody, but that is not necessary. An assault may be constituted by a threat or a hostile act committed towards a person. . . ." The confusion is not mitigated by the use of the word assault in statutory crimes such as "assault occasioning actual bodily harm"—section 47 of the Offences against the Person Act, 1861. In everyday speech where exact precision is not essential the word "assault" has become the generic name for offences against the person less than homicide, most of which will in fact be batteries as well as assaults.

Archbold (40th ed.), § 2634: "An assault is any act which intentionally—or possibly recklessly—causes another to apprehend immediate and unlawful violence." § 2636: "The term 'battery' means the actual application of unlawful force, however slight, to another, whether directly or indirectly."

Assault and battery are both torts as well as crimes; discussion of the concepts is commonly sought in both civil and criminal cases. "Though criminal cases are no rule for civil ones, yet in trespass I think there is an analogy": *per* De Grey C.J. in *Scott* v. *Shepherd* (1773) 2 Wm. Bl. 892, 899. Presumably the vice versa position is the same.

i. Actus Reus

Tuberville v. Savage
(1669) 1 Mod. Rep. 3; 86 E.R. 684
Court of King's Bench

Action of assault, battery and wounding. The evidence to prove a provocation was, that the plaintiff put his hand upon his sword and said, "If it were not assize-time I would not take such language from you."—The question was, if that were an assault?—The court agreed that it was not; for the declaration of the plaintiff was, that he would not assault him, the judges being in town; and the intention as well as the act makes an assault. Therefore if one strike another upon the hand, or arm, or breast in discourse, it is no assault, there being no intention to assault; but if one, intending to assault, strike at another and miss him, this is an assault; so if he hold up his hand against another in a threatening manner and say nothing, it is an assault.

Judgment for the plaintiff

Note

Here the effect of the words spoken was to remove any suggestion that the aggressor might strike and this nullified the assault. In *Mead's & Belt's Case* (1823) 1 Lewin 184 Holroyd J. said "no words or singing are equivalent to an assault...." Similarly, "Mere words, however, can never amount to an assault" 1 Hawk. c. 62, but see *contra per* Lord Goddard C.J. in *R.* v. *Wilson* [1955] 1 All E.R. 745, 746: "He called out 'Get out your knives,' which would be an assault." The sentence is ambiguous and may be read as meaning either the words or the suggested action would be an assault.

Question

Consider these situations:

1. A points a weapon at B, flourishes it and says "Hands up or I shoot."
2. A is standing motionless in a room when B enters. He is covering the doorway with a weapon and without moving he says the same words.
3. A is in a darkened room when B enters. He says the same words.

Two tests are relevant to these situations. Was B frightened of an impending battery upon reasonable grounds? Had A the means of carrying out the battery? Which test is used will depend upon the definition of assault adopted—see above.
This type of problem has arisen with the unloaded gun cases.

R. v. St. George
(1840) 9 C. & P. 483; 173 E.R. 921
Shrewsbury Assizes

St. George was charged under statute with attempting to discharge loaded arms at the prosecutor. He had quarrelled with Durant and in a fight he took out a pistol, pointed it and tried to cock it. Although his finger was on the trigger he was prevented from drawing it. The question arose whether, if the full offence were not proved, the prisoner would be convicted of an assault, being an ingredient of the full offence.

LUDLOW, SERJT.: I submit that the prisoner cannot be convicted of an assault, unless the jury are satisfied that the pistol was loaded.

PARKE B.: It seems to me that it is an assault to point a weapon at a person though not loaded, but so near, that if loaded, it might do injury. I think the offence of pointing a loaded gun at another does involve an assault, unless it is done secretly; and I think that the presenting a fire-arm, which has the appearance of being loaded, as near that it might produce injury if it was loaded, and went off, is an assault.... My idea is, that it is an assault to present a pistol at all, whether loaded or not. If you threw the powder out of the pan, or took the percussion cap off, and said to the party, "This is an empty pistol," then that would be no assault; for there the party must see that it was not possible that he should be injured; but if a person presents a pistol which has the appearance of being loaded, and puts the party into fear and alarm, that is what it is the object of the law to prevent.

Verdict: Guilty of an assault

Cole v. Turner

(1705) 6 Mod. 149; 87 E.R. 907
King's Bench

"To touch another in anger, though in the slightest degree or under pretence of passing is, in law, a battery."—S. C. Holt, 108.

HOLT C.J., upon evidence in trespass for assault and battery declared: Firstly, that the least touching of another in anger is a battery. Secondly, if two or more meet in a narrow passage, and without any violence or design of harm, one touches the other gently, it will be no battery. Thirdly, if any of them use violence against the other to force his way in a rude inordinate manner, it will be a battery; or any struggle about the passage to that degree as may do hurt, will be a battery.

Note

A police officer who touches a suspect on the shoulder after the suspect has refused his request to stop is still acting in the course of his duty: *Donnelly* v. *Jackman* [1970] 1 W.L.R. 562.

Fagan v. Metropolitan Police Commissioner

[1969] 1 Q.B. 439
Divisional Court

Fagan was told by a police officer to park his car at a particular spot. He drove his car on to the policeman's foot. He refused for some time to reverse off. Fagan was convicted by the magistrates of assaulting a police officer in the execution of his duty. On appeal he maintained that the initial driving on to the foot was not an assault, because unintentional; nor was the refusal to drive off because this was not an act.

JAMES J.: In our judgment the question arising, which has been argued on general principles, falls to be decided on the facts of the particular case. An assault is any act which intentionally—or possibly recklessly—causes another person to apprehend immediate and unlawful personal violence. Although "assault" is an independent crime and is to be treated as such, for practical purposes today "assault" is generally synonymous with the term "battery" and is a term used to mean the actual intended use of unlawful force to another person without his consent. On the facts of the present case the "assault" alleged involved a "battery." Where an assault involves a battery, it matters not, in our judgment, whether the battery is inflicted directly by the body of the offender or through the medium of some weapon or instrument controlled by the action of the offender. An assault may be committed by the laying of a hand upon another, and the action does not cease to be an assault if it is a stick held in the hand and not the hand itself which is laid on the person of the victim. So for our part we see no difference in principle between the action of stepping on to a person's toe and maintaining that position and the action of driving a car on to a person's foot and sitting in the car whilst its position on the foot is maintained.

To constitute the offence of assault some intentional act must have been performed: a mere omission to act cannot amount to an assault. Without going into the question whether words alone can constitute an assault, it is clear that the words spoken by the appellant could not alone amount to an assault: they can only shed a light on the appellant's action. For our part we think the crucial question is whether in this case the act of the appellant can be said to be complete and spent at the moment of time when the car wheel came to rest on the foot or whether his act is to be regarded as a continuing act operating until the wheel was removed. In our judgment a distinction is to be drawn between acts which are complete—though results may continue to flow—and those acts which are continuing. Once the act is complete it cannot thereafter be said to be a threat to inflict unlawful force upon the victim. If the act, as distinct from the results thereof, is a continuing act there is a continuing threat to inflict unlawful force. If the assault involves a battery and that battery continues there is a continuing act of assault.

For an assault to be committed both the elements of *actus reus* and *mens rea* must be present at the same time. The "*actus reus*" is the action causing the effect on the victim's mind (see the observations of Parke B. in *R.* v. *St. George*). The "*mens rea*" is the intention to cause that effect. It is not necessary that *mens rea* should be present at the inception of the *actus reus*; it can be superimposed upon an existing act. On the other hand the subsequent inception of *mens rea* cannot convert an act which has been completed without *mens rea* into an assault.

In our judgment the Willesden magistrates and quarter sessions were right in law. On the facts found the action of the appellant may have been initially unintentional, but the time came when knowing that the wheel was on the officer's foot the appellant (1) remained seated in the car so that his body through the medium of the car was in contact with the officer, (2) switched off the ignition of the car, (3) maintained the wheel of the car on the foot and (4) used words indicating the intention of keeping the wheel in that position. For our part we cannot regard such conduct as mere omission or inactivity.

There was an act constituting battery which at its inception was not criminal because there was no element of intention but which became criminal from the moment the intention was formed to produce the apprehension which was flowing from the continuing act. The fallacy of the appellant's argument is that it seeks to equate the facts of this case with such a case as where a motorist has accidentally run over a person and, that action having been completed, fails to assist the victim with the intent that the victim should suffer.

We would dismiss this appeal.

BRIDGE J.: I fully agree with my Lords as to the relevant principles to be applied. No mere omission to act can amount to an assault. Both the elements of *actus reus* and *mens rea* must be present at the same time, but the one may be superimposed on the other. It is in the application of these principles to the highly unusual facts of this case that I have, with regret, reached a different conclusion from the majority of the court. I have no sympathy at all for the appellant, who behaved disgracefully. But I have been unable to find any way of regarding the facts which satisfies me that they amounted to the crime of assault. This has not been for the want of trying. But at every attempt I have encountered the inescapable question: after the wheel of the appellant's car had accidentally come to rest on the constable's foot, what was it that the appellant did which constituted the act of assault? However the question is approached, the answer I feel obliged to give is: precisely nothing. The car rested on the foot by its own weight and remained stationary by its own inertia. The appellant's fault was that he omitted to manipulate the controls to set it in motion again.

Neither the fact that the appellant remained in the driver's seat nor that he switched off the ignition seem to me to be of any relevance. The constable's plight would have been no better, but might well have been worse, if the appellant had alighted from the car leaving the ignition switched on. Similarly I can get no help from the suggested analogies. If one man accidentally treads on another's toe or touches him with a stick, but deliberately maintains pressure with foot or stick after the victim protests, there is clearly an assault. But there is no true parallel between such cases and the present case. It is not, to my mind, a legitimate use of language to speak of the appellant "holding" or "maintaining" the car wheel on the constable's foot. The expression which corresponds to the reality is that used by the justices in the case stated. They say quite rightly, that he "allowed" the wheel to remain.

With a reluctantly dissenting voice I would allow this appeal and quash the appellant's conviction.

Appeal dismissed

Questions

1. How much logic is there in the stand taken by Bridge J.? Is he right in refusing to accept the analogy between pressing, say, a stick into another and pressing with a car? If a deliberate driving on is (with the necessary *mens rea*) an assault, and driving off would end such an assault, why is keeping it there not continuing the assault?

2. If Bridge J. is right and there is merely an omission is the law then satisfactory in its attitude to omissions?—see *ante*, p. 18. Merely to pull away from someone (as opposed to resisting lawful arrest) is not an assault, *R.* v. *Sherriff* [1969] Crim. L.R. 260.

ii. Mens Rea

James L.J. in *R.* v. *Venna* [1976] 1 Q.B. 421, 429:

"In our view the element of *mens rea* in the offence of battery is satisfied by proof that the defendant intentionally or recklessly applied force to the person of another.... In many cases the dividing line between intention and recklessness is barely distinguishable."

iii. Consent

Fairclough v. Whipp
(1951) 35 Cr. App. R. 138
Divisional Court

> The respondent invited a girl of nine to touch his exposed person. She did so and the respondent was charged with indecent assault on the girl. The justices dismissed the case and the prosecutor appealed.

LORD GODDARD C.J.: An assault can be committed without there being battery, for instance, by a threatening gesture or a threat to use violence made against a person, but I do not know of any authority that says that, where one person invites another person to touch him, that can amount to an assault. The question of consent or non-consent arises only if this is something which, without consent, would be an assault on the latter. If that which was done to the child would have been an assault if done against her will, it would also be an assault if it was done with her consent and is of an indecent nature, because she cannot consent to an indecent assault. But before we come to the question of whether there was an indecent assault we must consider whether there was an assault, and I cannot hold that an invitation to somebody to touch the invitor can amount to an assault on the invitee.

Appeal dismissed

Note

By the Indecency with Children Act 1960, the facts in this case would now disclose a crime under that Act, but that does not effect the general point about assaults.

R. v. Donovan
[1934] 2 K.B. 498
Court of Criminal Appeal

D. was charged with caning a girl for the purpose of sexual gratification. His defence was that she consented. The jury were directed that "consent or no consent" was the vital issue, but were not told that it was for the Crown to prove absence of consent. D. was convicted of indecent assault. On appeal:

SWIFT J.: First, it was of importance that the jury should be left in no doubt as to the incidence of the burden of proof in relation to consent. In *R.* v. *May* [1912] 3 K.B. 572, 575 the principle applicable to cases of this kind was laid down by this court in these words: "The court is of opinion that if the facts proved in evidence are such that the jury can reasonably find consent, there ought to be a direction by the judge on that question, both as to the onus of negativing consent being on the prosecution and as to the evidence in the particular case bearing on the question."

We have no doubt that the facts proved in the present case were such that the jury might reasonably have found consent—it is, indeed, difficult to reconcile some of the admitted facts with absence of consent. It was therefore of importance (if consent was in issue) that there should be no possibility of doubt in the minds of the jury upon the question whether it was for the Crown to negative consent, or for the defence to prove it. . . .

[But] counsel for the Crown . . . argued that, this being a case in which it was unnecessary for the Crown to prove absence of consent, this court ought not to quash the conviction. . . .

No person can license another to commit a crime. So far as the criminal law is concerned, therefore, where the act charged is in itself unlawful, it can never be necessary to prove absence of consent on the part of the person wronged in order to obtain the conviction of the wrongdoer. There are, however, many acts in themselves harmless and lawful which become unlawful only if they are done without the consent of the person affected. What is, in one case, an innocent act of familiarity or affection, may, in another, be an assault, for no other reason than that, in the one case there is consent, and in the other consent is absent. As a general rule, although it is a rule to which there are well-established exceptions, it is an unlawful act to beat another person with such a degree of violence that the infliction of bodily harm is a probable consequence and when such an act is proved, consent is immaterial. . . .

There are, as we have said, well-established exceptions to [this] general rule. . . . One of them is dealt with by Sir Michael Foster in the chapter just cited [Crown Law, 3rd ed., p. 259], where he refers to the case of persons who in perfect friendship engage by mutual consent in contests, such as "cudgels, foils, or wrestling," which are capable of causing bodily harm. . . . Another exception to the general rule . . . is to be found in cases of rough and undisciplined sport or play, where there is no anger and no intention to cause bodily harm. . . . In such cases the act is not in itself unlawful, and it becomes unlawful only if the person affected by it is not a consenting party.

. . . [I]t was not in dispute that the motive of the appellant was to gratify his own perverted desires. . . . Nothing could be more absurd or more repellant to the ordinary intelligence than to regard his conduct as comparable with that of a participant in one of those 'manly diversions' of which Sir Michael Foster wrote. . . .

[In this case] in our view, on the evidence given at the trial, the jury should have been directed that, if they are satisfied that the blows struck by the prisoner were likely or intended to do bodily harm to the prosecutrix they ought to convict him, and that it was only if they were not so satisfied, that it became necessary to consider the further question whether the prosecution had negatived consent. For this purpose we think that "bodily harm" has its ordinary meaning and includes any hurt or injury calculated to interfere with the health or comfort of the prosecutor. Such hurt or injury need not be permanent, but must, no doubt, be more than merely transient and trifling.

[He concluded that as the jury, properly directed, might have found that the assault was such that consent was material, and if so, might have been in some doubt as to where the onus lay, the conviction could not stand.]

Conviction quashed

Questions

1. Is caning not "likely . . . to cause bodily harm"?
2. If Donovan's behaviour was "perverted" why should the issue of consent be relevant even if bodily harm was unlikely or unintended

The case below suggests a stricter approach to the issue of consent.

Attorney General's Reference (No. 6 of 1980)
[1981] 2 All E.R. 1057
Court of Appeal

The reference made by the Attorney General under section 36 of the Criminal Justice Act 1972 was as follows: "Where two persons fight (otherwise than in the course of sport) in a public place can it be a defence for one of these persons to a charge of assault arising out of the fight that the other consented to fight?"

Lord Lane C.J. for the court: The facts out of which the reference arises are these. The respondent, aged 18, and a youth aged 17 met in a public street and argued together. The respondent and the youth decided to settle the argument there and then by a fight. Before the fight the respondent removed his watch and handed it to a bystander for safe keeping and the youth removed his jacket. The respondent and the youth exchanged blows with their fists and the youth sustained a bleeding nose and bruises to his face caused by blows from the respondent.

Two issues arose at the trial: (1) self-defence and (2) consent. The judge directed the jury in part as follows:

"Secondly, if both parties consent to a fight then that fight may be lawful. In that respect I disagree with [counsel for the prosecution's] description of the law. It may well be that a fight on the pavement is a breach of the peace or fighting in public or some other offence but it does not necessarily mean that both parties are guilty of an assault. So that if two people decide to fight it out

> with their fists then that is not necessarily an assault. If they use weapons or something of that nature, other considerations apply. So you have to consider those two matters in this case. Was [the youth] acting in self-defence? Was this a case of both parties agreeing to fight and using only reasonable force"

Thus the jury were directed that the respondent would, or might, not be guilty of assault if the victim agreed to fight, and the respondent only used reasonable force. The respondent was acquitted.

Leading counsel who appeared for the Attorney General at the hearing of the reference submitted that this direction was incorrect, that the answer to the point of law was No, and that if an act (ordinarily constituting an assault) is unlawful per se no amount of consent can render it lawful. Thus an act committed in public might, he submitted, be an assault, even though it would not be if committed in private, since if committed in public it would be a breach of the peace and for that reason unlawful.

Counsel as amicus curiae drew the attention of the court to the relevant authorities and textbooks. He pointed out that though the conclusions in the case are reasonably consistent the reasons for them are not.

For convenience we use the word 'assault' as including 'battery', and adopt the definition of James J in *Fagan* v. *Metropolitan Police Comr.* [*ante*, p. 473] namely 'the actual intended use of unlawful force to another person without his consent', to which we would respectfully add 'or any other lawful excuse'.

We think that it can be taken as a starting point that it is an essential element of an assault that the act is done contrary to the will and without the consent of the victim; and it is doubtless for this reason that the burden lies on the prosecution to negative consent. Ordinarily, then, if the victim consents, the assailant is not guilty.

But the cases show that the courts will make an exception to this principle where the public interest requires: see *R* v. *Coney* (1882) 8 QBD 534 (the prize-fight case). The eleven judges were of the opinion that a prize-fight is illegal, that all persons aiding and abetting were guilty of assault, and that the consent of the actual fighters was irrelevant. Their reasons varied as follows: Cave J, that the blow was struck in anger and likely to do corporal hurt, as opposed to one struck in sport, not intended to cause bodily harm; Mathew J, the dangerous nature of the proceedings; Stephen J, what was done was injurious to the public, depending on the degree of force and the place used; Hawkins J, the likelihood of a breach of the peace, and the degree of force and injury; Lord Coleridge CJ, breach of the peace and protection of the public.

The judgement in *R* v. *Donovan* [*ante*, p. 476] . . . the reasoning in which seems to be tautologous, proceeds on a different basis, starting with the proposition that consent is irrelevant if the act complained of is 'unlawful . . . in itself', which it will be if it involves the infliction of bodily harm.

Bearing in mind the various cases and the views of the textbook writers cited to us, and starting with the proposition that ordinarily an act consented to will not constitute an assault, the question is: at what point does the public interest require the court to hold otherwise?

In answering this question the diversity of view expressed in the previous decisions, such as the two cases cited, make some selection and a partly new approach necessary. Accordingly we have not followed the dicta which would make an act (even if consensual) an assault if it occurred in public, on the ground that it constituted a breach of peace, and was therefore itself unlawful. These dicta reflect the conditions of the times when they were uttered, when there was little by way of an established police force and prize-fights were a source of civil disturbance. Today, with regular policing, conditions are different. Statutory offences, and indeed byelaws, provide a sufficient sanction against true cases of public disorder, as do the common law offences of affray etc. Nor have we followed the Scottish case of *Smart* v *HM Advocate* 1975 SLT 65, holding the consent of the victim to be irrelevant on a charge of assault, guilt depending on the 'evil intent' of the accused, irrespective of the harm done.

The answer to this question, in our judgment, is that it is not in the public interest that people should try to cause or should cause each other actual bodily harm for no good reason. Minor struggles are another matter. So, in our judgment, it is immaterial whether the act occurs in private or in public; it is an assault if actual bodily harm is intended and/or caused. This means that most fights will be unlawful regardless of consent.

Nothing which we have said is intended to cast doubt on the accepted legality of properly conducted games and sports, lawful chastisement or correction, reasonable surgical interference, dangerous exhibitions etc. These apparent exceptions can be justified as involving the exercise of a legal right, in the case of chastisement or correction or as needed in the public interest, in the other cases.

Our answer to the point of law is No, but not (as the reference implies) because the fight occurred in a public place, but because, wherever it occurred, the participants would have been guilty of assault (subject to self-defence) if (as we understand was the case) they intended to and/or did cause actual bodily harm.

The point of law referred to us by the Attorney General has revealed itself as having been the subject of much interesting legal and philosophical debate, but it does not seem that the particular uncertainty enshrined in the reference has caused practical inconvenience in the administration of justice during the last few hundred years. We would not wish our judgment on the point to be the signal for unnecessary prosecutions.

Determination accordingly

Note

Self-defence can also justify an assault: see *ante*, p. 411. Similarly, a lawful arrest will justify an assault and a false imprisonment. The circumstances in which arrest without warrant is lawful are contained in section 2 of the Criminal Law Act 1967.

iv. Statutory Assaults

Note

The general law of assault is amplified by a considerable number of statutory provisions creating special assault offences all of which embrace the basic assault but have some added aggravation. A comprehensive study of these is inappropriate here. The majority of them are to be found in the Offences Against the Person Act 1861. The two most common are assaulting a police officer in the execution of his duty and assault occasioning actual bodily harm.

Offences Against the Person Act 1861, section 38

"Whosoever shall assault any person with intent to resist or prevent the lawful apprehension or detainer of himself or of any other person for any offence, shall be guilty of a [an offence] . . . and shall be liable . . . [to a maximum penalty of two years' imprisonment]."

Assaulting a police officer in the execution of his duty was formerly in this section but now, by an unhappy piece of rationalisation, it appears as

Police Act 1964, section 51

"(1) Any person who assaults a constable in the execution of his duty, or a person assisting a constable in the execution of his duty shall be guilty of an offence. . . ."

Note

It does not matter that the defendant does not know that the person assaulted is a policeman: see *Forbes* and *Webb* (1865) 10 Cox 362, and the discussion in relation to mistake, *ante*, p. 101.

Offences Against the Person Act 1861, section 47

"Whosoever shall be convicted upon an indictment of any assault occasioning actual bodily harm shall be liable [to a maximum penalty of five years' imprisonment]."

"Actual bodily harm"

R. v. Miller [1954] Q.B. 282, Lynskey J. at 292:
"The bodily harm alleged is said to be the result of the prisoner's actions, and that is . . . that he threw the wife down three times. There is evidence that afterwards she was in a hysterical and nervous condition. . . . Actual bodily harm . . . includes 'any hurt or injury calculated to interfere with the health or comfort of the prosecutor' [Archbold, 32nd Edn., p. 959]. There was a time when shock was not regarded as bodily hurt, but . . . it seems to be now that if a person is caused hurt or injury resulting, not in any physical injury, but in an injury to her state of mind for the time being, that is within the definition of actual bodily harm, and on that point I would leave the case to the jury."

Taylor v. Grainville [*1978*] *Crim. L.R. 482:* the Divisional Court dismissed an appeal against a conviction under section 47 which was based on the justices' finding that the defendant struck his victim in the face. It was a justifiable inference that this must have caused at least a bruise.

Note

The injury can arise indirectly. *R.* v. *Roberts* (1971) 56 Cr. App. R. 95: a young girl who was a passenger in R.'s car injured herself by jumping out of the car while it was moving. Her evidence was that she had been assaulted and threatened by R., and jumped out to save herself. In dismissing R.'s appeal against his conviction under section 47, Stephenson L.J. said the test is:

"Was it [the jumping out] the natural result of what the alleged assailant said and did, in the sense that it was something that could reasonably have been foreseen as the consequence of what he was saying or doing? As it was put in one of the old cases, it had got to be shown to be his act, and if of course the victim does something so 'daft,' in the words of the appellant in this case, or so unexpected, not that this particular assailant did not actually foresee it but that no reasonable man could be expected to foresee it, then it is only in a very remote and unreal sense a consequence of his assault, it is really occasioned by a voluntary act on the part of the victim which could not reasonably be foreseen and which breaks the chain of causation between the assault and the harm or injury."

2. MALICIOUS WOUNDING AND WOUNDING WITH INTENT

i. Malicious Wounding

Offences Against the Person Act 1861, section 20

"Whosoever shall unlawfully and maliciously wound or inflict any grievous bodily harm upon any other person, either with or without any weapon or instrument, shall be guilty of [an offence and liable to a maximum penalty of five years' imprisonment]."

"Grievous Bodily Harm"

The Court of Criminal Appeal in *R.* v. *Metharam* [1961] 3 All E.R. 200, adopted the dictum of Viscount Kilmuir in *D.P.P.* v. *Smith, ante,* p. 371, that "bodily harm" needs no explanation and "grievous" means no more and no less than "really serious."

"Inflict"

R. v. Clarence
(1888) 22 Q.B.D. 23
Court for Crown Cases Reserved

C. was charged both under section 20 and section 47 of the Offences Against the Person Act 1861. He was alleged to have had intercourse with his wife when he was suffering from a venereal disease, which was communicated to her. She would not have consented to intercourse had she known of his condition. He was convicted on both counts; on a case being reserved it was held by all the judges that because of the wife's consent, there was no assault on her, but they differed on whether an assault was necessary for the conviction under section 20, and by a majority of nine to four quashed the conviction.

STEPHEN J.: The question in this case is whether a man who knows that he has gonorrhoea, and who by having connection with his wife, who does not know it, infects her, is or is not guilty of an offence either under section 20 of 24 and 25 Vict. c. 100, or under section 47 of the same Act. Section 20 punishes everyone who "unlawfully and maliciously inflicts any grievous bodily harm upon any other person." Section 47 punishes everyone who is convicted of "an assault occasioning actual bodily harm to any person." . . .

If the present conviction is right it is clear that unless some distinction can be pointed out which does not occur to me, the sections must be held to apply, not only to venereal diseases, but to infection of every kind which is in fact communicated by one person to another by any act likely to produce it. A man who knowing that he has scarlet fever or small-pox shakes hands with a friend and so infects him may be said to fall under section 20 or section 47 as much as the prisoner in this case. To seize a man's hand without his consent is an assault; but no one would consent to such a grasp if he knew that he risked small-pox by it, and if consent in all cases is rendered void by fraud, including suppression of the truth, such a gesture would be an assault occasioning actual bodily harm as much as the conduct of the prisoner in this case.

Not only is there no general principle which makes the communication of infection criminal, but such authority as exists is opposed to such a doctrine in relation to any disease. . . .

I now come to the construction of the precise words of the statute.

Section 20 punishes "every one who unlawfully and maliciously wounds or inflicts any grievous bodily harm upon any other person either with or without any weapon or instrument." . . . Is there an "infliction of bodily harm either with or without any weapon or instrument"? I think there is not, for the following reasons.

The words appear to me to mean the direct causing of some grievous injury to the body itself with a weapon, as by a cut with a knife, or without a weapon, as by a blow with the fist, or by pushing a person down. Indeed, though the word "assault" is not used in the section, I think the words imply an assault and battery of which a wound or grievous bodily harm is the manifest immediate and obvious result. This is supported by *R.* v. *Taylor*, L.R. 1 C.C.R. 194, in 1869, in which it was held that a prisoner could upon an indictment under that section be convicted of a common assault, because each offence, "wounding" and "inflicting grievous bodily harm," "necessarily includes an assault," though the word does not occur in the section. It is further illustrated by reference to the 14 & 15 Vict. c. 19, s. 4, of which the present section is a re-enactment. Section 4 of the earlier Act begins with the preamble, "And whereas it is expedient to make further provision for the punishment of aggravated assaults," and then proceeds in the words of the present section, with a trifling and unimportant difference in their arrangement.

Infection by the application of an animal poison appears to me to be of a different character from an assault. The administration of poison is dealt with by section 24, which would be superfluous if poisoning were an "infliction of grievous bodily harm either with or without a weapon or instrument." The one act differs from the other in the immediate and necessary connection between a cut or a blow and the wound or harm inflicted, and the uncertain and delayed operation of the act by which infection is communicated. If a man by a grasp of the hand infects another with small-pox, it is impossible to trace out in detail the connection between the act and the disease, and it would, I think, be an unnatural use of language to say that a man by such an act, "inflicted" small-pox on another. It would be wrong in interpreting an Act of Parliament to lay much stress on etymology, but I may just observe that "inflict" is derived from "infligo," for which, in *Facciolati's Lexicon* three Italian and three Latin equivalents are given, all meaning "to strike," viz. "dare, ferire and percuotere" in Italian, and "infero, impingo and percutio" in Latin.

There is authority for the propositioin that poisoning is not an assault. [His Lordship reviewed certain first instance rulings and then continued.] Upon these grounds I am of opinion that section 20 does not apply to the case.

Is the case, then, within section 47, as "an assault occasioning actual bodily harm"? The question here is whether there is an assault. It is said there is none, because the woman consented, and to this it is replied that fraud vitiates consent, and that the prisoner's silence was a fraud. Apart altogether from this question, I think that the act of infection is not an assault at all, for the reasons already given. Infection is a kind of poisoning. It is the application of an animal poison, and poisoning as already shewn, is not an assault. Apart, however, from this, is the man's concealment of the fact that he was infected such a fraud as vitiated the wife's consent to his exercise of marital rights, and converted the act of connection into an assault? It seems to me that the proposition that fraud vitiates consent in criminal matters is not true if taken to apply in the fullest sense of the word, and without qualification. It is too short to be true, as a mathematical formula is true. If we apply it in that sense to the present case, it is difficult to say that the prisoner was not guilty of rape, for the definition of rape is having connection with a woman without her consent; and if fraud vitiates consent, every case in which a man infects a woman or commits bigamy, the second wife being ignorant of the first marriage, is also a case of rape. Many seductions would be rapes, and so might acts of prostitution procured by fraud, as for instance by promises not intended to be fulfilled. These illustrations appear to shew clearly that the maxim that fraud vitiates consent is too general to be applied to these matters as if it were absolutely true. I do not at all deny that in some cases it applies though it is often used with reference to cases which do not fall within it. For instance, it has nothing to do with such cases as assaults on young children. A young child who submits to an indecent act no more consents to it than a sleeping or unconscious woman. The child merely submits without consenting. The only cases in which fraud indisputably vitiates consent in these matters are cases of fraud as to the nature of the act done. As to fraud as to the identity of the person by whom it is done the law is not quite clear. In *R.* v. *Flattery* (1877) 2 Q.B.D. 410, in which consent was obtained by reporting the act as a surgical operation, the prisoner was held to be guilty of rape. In the case where consent was obtained by the personation of a husband, there was before the passing of the Criminal Law Amendment Act of 1885 a conflict of authority. The last decision in England, *R.* v. *Barrow* (1868) L.R. 1 C.C.R. 158, decided that the act was not rape, and *R.* v. *Dee* (1884) 14 L.R. Ir. 486, decided in Ireland in 1884, decided that it was. The Criminal Law Amendment Act of 1885 "declared and enacted" that thenceforth it should be deemed to be rape, thus favouring the view taken in *R.* v. *Dee*. I do not propose to examine in detail the controversies connected with these cases. The judgments in the case of *R.* v. *Dee* examine all of them minutely, and I think they justify the observation that the only sorts of fraud which so far destroy the effect of a woman's consent as to convert a connection consented to in fact into a rape are frauds as to the nature of the act itself, or as to the identity of the person who does the act. There is abundant authority to shew that such frauds as these vitiate consent both in the case of rape and in the case of indecent assault. I should myself prefer to say that consent in such cases does not exist at all, because the act consented to is not the act done. Consent to a surgical operation or examination is not a consent to sexual connection or indecent behaviour. Consent to connection with a husband is not consent to adultery. . . .

The woman's consent here was as full and conscious as consent could be. It was not obtained by any fraud either as to the nature of the act or as to the identity of the agent. The injury done was done by a suppression of the truth. It appears to me to be an abuse of language to describe such an act as an assault. . . .

HAWKINS J. (one of the minority): . . . In my opinion the legislature, in framing the various sections of the statute already and hereafter referred to, used the words "inflict," "cause" and "occasion" as synonymous terms for the following among other reasons. Let me begin by calling attention to the language of the eighteenth section, which runs thus: "whosoever shall unlawfully and maliciously by any means whatsoever wound or *'cause'* any grievous bodily harm to any person, etc., with intent, etc. shall be guilty of felony." If the prisoner had been indicted under this section, could anybody doubt that upon proof of his intention to cause the grievous bodily harm he in fact occasioned, he would have fallen within not only the spirit but the precise language of the section according to the strictest interpretation which could be applied to it? I next ask myself what was the object of the twentieth section? Clearly it was to provide for cases in which the grievous bodily harm mentioned in section 18, though unlawfully and maliciously caused, was unaccompanied by the felonious intent, which is the aggravating feature of the felony created by that section, and accordingly section 20 made such last-mentioned offence a misdemeanour only, by enacting as follows, "whosoever shall unlawfully or maliciously wound or *inflict* any grievous bodily harm upon any person either with or without any weapon or instrument shall be guilty of a misdemeanour." Surely the object of these two sections could only have been to make the doing of grievous bodily harm with intent, a felony, without intent, a mere misdemeanour, and to hold that no man could be convicted under section 20 without proof of an assault would practically amount to holding that maliciously to do grievous bodily harm to another without felonious intent is unpunishable, unless such harm is done through the medium of an assault. It is impossible the legislature could have intended this.

I must refer now to section 47, which enacts that "whosoever shall be convicted upon an indictment of an assault" occasioning "actual bodily harm, shall be liable, etc." Here it will be observed that where the legislature intends that an assault shall be that foundation of the offence, it says so in express terms. If in using the word "inflict in section 20 it had intended that it should be interpreted as "cause by means of an assault," section 47 would have been superfluous for by merely substituting the word "actual" for "grievous" in section 20, the whole object of both sections would have been attained; for the punishment awarded in each is the same, and "actual" harm of necessity includes "grievous" harm, and if for any reason, which I am unable to discover, the legislature had thought fit to separate the two sections, applying one to an assault causing "grievous," the other to an assault causing "actual" harm, I should at least have expected it to use the same phraseology in each. If, on the other hand, it intended the twentieth section to bear the construction I put upon it, I should expect to find that which I do, viz., difference in the language.

Conviction quashed

Question

Should the sexual transmission of a disease be an offence? See Lynch "Criminal Liability for Transmitting Disease" [1978] Crim.L.R. 612.

Note

In most cases arising under section 20 the grievous bodily harm will be the result of an assault *and* battery. But either will do. For assault-only cases see, for example, *R.* v. *Halliday* (1889) 61 L.T. 701, *R.* v. *Beech* (1912) 7 Cr. App. R. 197 (V. frightened into jumping out of a window). *R.* v. *Martin, ante,* p. 124, is an example of a battery-only case. This means that neither an assault nor a battery can be said to be *necessary* to a conviction under section 20, with the apparent result that an alternative verdict of common assault cannot be returned under the provisions of section 6 (3) of the Criminal Law Act 1967: see *R.* v. *Beasley* [1981] Crim. L.R. 635, and the commentary thereon.

"Unlawfully" and "Maliciously"

"Unlawfully": see the discussion on consent, above.

"Maliciously" is discussed in Chapter 3, p. 81.

ii. Wounding with Intent

Offences Against The Person Act 1861, section 18
(as amended by the Criminal Law Act 1967, Sched. 3)

"Whosoever shall unlawfully and maliciously by any means whatsoever wound, or cause any grievous bodily harm to any person, with intent . . . to do some grievous bodily harm to any person, or with intent to resist or prevent the lawful apprehension or detainer of any person, shall be guilty of [an offence and shall be liable . . . to imprisonment for life. . .]"

Note

See *ante,* p. 483 for the meaning of grievous bodily harm.

The chief difference between sections 18 and 20 is that the former requires specific intent, and the latter only general *mens rea.*

R. v. Mowatt [1968] 1 Q.B. 421, Diplock L.J. at 426:

"In section 18 the word 'maliciously' adds nothing. The intent expressly required by that section is more specific than such element of foresight of consequences as is implicit in the word 'maliciously' and in directing a jury about an offence under this section, the word 'maliciously' is best avoided."

In *R.* v. *Belfon, ante,* p. 65, the Court of Appeal declined to adopt the wider meaning given to the *mens rea* of murder in *R.* v. *Hyam, ante,* p. 374. In *Belfon,* Wien J. said [1976] 1 W.L.R. 741, 748: "We do not find . . . in *Hyam's* case anything which obliges us to hold that the 'intent' in wounding with intent is proved by foresight that serious injury is likely to result from a deliberate act. There is certainly no authority that recklessness can constitute an intent to do grievous bodily harm. . . . Foresight and recklessness are evidence from which intent may be inferred but they cannot be equated either separately or in conjunction with intent to do grievous bodily harm."

3. ADMINISTERING POISON

Offences Against The Person Act 1861, section 23

"Whosoever shall unlawfully and maliciously administer to or cause to be administered to or taken by any person any poison or other destructive or noxious thing, so as thereby to endanger the life of such person, or so as thereby to inflict upon such person any grievous bodily harm, shall be guilty of [an offence] . . . and shall be liable . . . [to a maximum penalty of 10 years' imprisonment]."

Offences Against The Person Act 1861, section 24

"Whosoever shall unlawfully and maliciously administer to or cause to be administered to or taken by any other person any poison or other destructive or noxious thing, with intent to injure, aggrieve, or annoy such person, shall be guilty of [an offence] . . . and shall be liable . . . [to a maximum penalty of 5 years' imprisonment]."

"Poison or noxious thing"

R. v. Cramp (1880) 5 Q.B.D. 307, Lord Coleridge C.J. at p. 309:

"But what is a poison? It is something which when administered is injurious to health or life. There is hardly any active drug which taken in large quantities may not be so, and, on the other hand, there is hardly any poison which may not in small quantities be useful and salutary. It is therefore in each case a question of the quantity and the circumstances in which the drug is administered."

R. v. Cato [1976] 1 W.L.R. 110, Lord Widgery C.J. at 119:
"The authorities show that an article is not to be described as noxious for present purposes merely because it has a potentiality for harm if taken in an overdose. There are many articles of value in common use which may be harmful in overdose and it is clear on the authorities . . . that one cannot describe an article as noxious merely because it has that aptitude."

Note

No authorities were cited by Lord Widgery C.J. to support the above proposition and it was distinguished in *R.* v. *Marcus* [1981] Crim. L.R. 490. The Court of Appeal held that the concept of the "noxious thing" involved not only the quality or nature but also the quantity administered or sought to be administered and that it was for the jury to decide as a question of fact in all the circumstances whether the thing was noxious.

"Maliciously"
See *ante*, p. 81.

4. SEXUAL OFFENCES

Note

Sexual offences are consolidated in the Sexual Offences Act 1956. Section 37 and the Second Schedule provide a comprehensive list of the offences under the Act.

A definition important to many of this range of offences is to be found in section 44:

"Where, on trial of any offence under this Act, it is necessary to prove sexual intercourse (whether natural or unnatural), it shall not be necessary to prove the completion of the intercourse by the emission of seed, but the intercourse shall be deemed complete upon proof of penetration only."

It was held in *R.* v. *Kaitamaki* [1980] N.Z.L.R. 59 that rape is committed where the defendant fails to withdraw following an initially consensual penetration.

i. Rape

Sexual Offences Act 1956, section 1 (1)

"It is [an offence] for a man to rape a woman."

Sexual Offences (Amendment) Act 1976, section 1 (1)

"For the purposes of section 1 of the Sexual Offences Act 1956 . . . a man commits rape if—

(a) he has unlawful sexual intercourse with a woman who at the time of the intercourse does not consent to it; and

(b) at that time he knows that she does not consent to the intercourse or he is reckless as to whether she consents to it;

and references to rape in other enactments . . . shall be construed accordingly."

[s. 1 (2) contains a declaration that one of the matters for consideration by the jury is the existence or otherwise of reasonable grounds for belief in the woman's consent, see *D.P.P.* v. *Morgan*, *ante*, p. 101.]

Note

It is not necessary for the prosecution to prove that the consent of the victim was vitiated by force, the fear of force or fraud, but merely that the victim did not in fact consent: *R.* v. *Olugboja* [1981] 3 All E.R. 443. Dunn L.J., for the Court of Appeal, said at p. 448:

"We do not think that the issue of consent should be left to a jury without some further direction. What this should be will depend on the circumstances of each case . . . . They should be directed that consent, or the absence of it, is to be given its ordinary meaning and if need be, by way of example, that there is a difference between consent and submission; every consent involves a submission, but it by no means follows that a mere submission involves consent. . . ."

Intercourse with a woman made drunk by the defendant is without consent (*R.* v. *Camplin* (1845) 1 Den. 89) as also is intercourse with a sleeping woman (*R.* v. *Mayers* (1872) 12 Cox 311 and *R.* v. *Young* (1878) 14 Cox 114).

Marriage is taken as implied consent by the wife to sexual intercourse with her husband but limitations have been imposed, see the case below.

R. v. Steele
(1977) 65 Cr. App. Rep. 22
Court of Appeal

The appellant and his wife, the complainant, were living apart. In proceedings commenced by the wife, the appellant undertook not to molest her and not to approach or enter the nurses' home where she was living. Four days later the appellant entered the home and had intercourse with his wife, she alleged it was without her consent and he was convicted of rape. He appealed on the ground, *inter alia*, that their marriage was a bar to a conviction for rape against her.

Geoffrey Lane L.J.: As a general principle, there is no doubt that a husband cannot be guilty of rape upon his wife. The reason in Sir Matthew Hale's Pleas of the Crown, Vol. 1 at p. 639 is stated in this way: ". . . by their mutual matrimonial consent and contract the wife hath given up herself in this kind unto her husband, which she cannot retract." No doubt in times gone by there were no circumstances in which the wife could be held to have retracted that overall consent which, by the marriage ceremony, she gave to sexual intercourse with her husband. Researchers have failed to reveal any exception to the general rule until 1949: that was the case of *R.* v. *Clarke* (1949) 33 Cr. App. R. 216 decided by Byrne J. In *R.* v. *Clarke,* there was in existence at the time of alleged rape, a separation order on the grounds of the prisoner's persistent cruelty towards his wife. That separation order was in force and it contained a clause that the wife was no longer bound to cohabit with the prisoner. Cohabitation had not been resumed. The learned judge ruled that in those circumstances the wife's consent had been revoked. He said at p. 218: "The position, therefore, was that the wife, by process of law, namely, by marriage, had given consent to the husband to exercise the marital right during such time as the ordinary relations created by the marriage contract subsisted between them, but by a further process of law, namely, the justices' order, her consent to marital intercourse was revoked."

The next case in point of time was the decision by Lynskey J. in *R.* v. *Miller* [1954] 2 Q.B. 282. In that case, the only relevant action which the wife had taken was to file a petition for divorce on the grounds of adultery. There had been, it seems, some sort of hearing of that petition in which the wife had given evidence but the hearing was adjourned for the attendance of the husband. Subsequently, the husband met her and had sexual intercourse with her without her consent. He was indicted for rape and also for assault occasioning actual bodily harm. Lynskey J. at p. 290 held that the mere filing of a petition for a divorce, even though there had been a partial hearing of that petition, without any order from the Court at all, was not sufficient to revoke the wife's consent and consequently the husband was entitled to have intercourse, albeit by force, with his wife without being guilty of rape although, in certain circumstances, he might be guilty of inflicting harm and violence upon her.

The third decision is that of *R.* v. *O'Brien*, a decision of Park J. reported in [1974] 3 All E.R. 663. In that case, the wife was granted a decree nisi and it was after that decree that the husband had intercourse with her by force. It was held by the learned judge that the decree nisi effectively terminated the wife's consent to marital intercourse. Therefore, the husband was liable to be convicted of rape.

In this case, the circumstances are of course different from any of those in the three cases to which I have referred. Here there has been no decree of the Court, here there has been no direct order of the Court compelling the husband to stay away from his wife. There has been an undertaking by the husband not to molest his wife. The question which the Court has to decide is this. Have the parties made it clear, by agreement between themselves, or has the Court made it clear by an order or something equivalent to an order, that the wife's consent to sexual intercourse with her husband implicit in the act of marriage, no longer exists? A separation agreement with a non-cohabitation clause, a decree of divorce, a decree of judicial separation, a separation order in the justices' court containing a non-cohabitation clause and an injunction restraining the husband from molesting the wife or having sexual intercourse with her are all obvious cases in which the wife's consent would be successfully revoked. On the other hand, the mere filing of a petition for divorce would clearly not be enough, the mere issue of proceedings leading up to a magistrates' separation order or the mere issue of proceedings as a preliminary to apply for an *ex parte* injunction to restrain the husband would not be enough but the granting of an injunction to restrain the husband would be enough because the Court is making an order wholly inconsistent with the wife's consent and an order, breach of which would or might result in the husband being punished by imprisonment.

What then of the undertaking in lieu of an injunction? It is, in the judgment of this Court, the equivalent of an injunction. It is given to avoid, amongst other things, the stigma of an injunction. Breach of it is enforceable by the Court and may result in imprisonment. It is, in effect equivalent to the granting of an injunction. Indeed, whether one considers this as equivalent to the order of the Court or the equivalent of an agreement between the parties, it does not matter. It may indeed have aspects of both. The effect is to eliminate the wife's matrimonial consent to intercourse. That is the judgment of the Court on that first point. Therefore, there is no bar to this man being found guilty of rape if the other ingredients of the offence are successfully proved by the prosecution....

Appeal allowed on other grounds

Questions

1. Why should "the mere filing of a petition for divorce" not be sufficient to revoke a wife's implied consent?

2. Is a statement made by Hale 300 years ago an appropriate starting point for a consideration of a husband's immunity for rape? See Mitra "...

For she Has no Right or Power to Refuse Her consent." [1979] Crim. L.R. 558 and Matthews, "Marital Rape" [1980] 10 Fam. Law 22.

Note

The Supreme Court of Israel has recently rejected the English common law on marital rape, holding that the doctrine of "submission" is sufficient to "outrage human conscience and reason in an enlightened country in our times." (noted [1981] 55 A.L.J. 59). The Criminal Law Revision Committee's Working Paper on Sexual Offences provisionally concluded that prosecution for marital rape should be allowed with the consent of the D.P.P. (1980, §§ 28–43).

Fraud and Consent

On the effect of fraud on consent at common law, see the authorities discussed by Stephen J., in *R.* v. *Clarence, ante*, p. 481. But see now the following statutory provisions, and *R.* v. *Williams*, below.

Sexual Offences Act 1956

Section 1 (2): "A man who induces a married woman to have sexual intercourse with him by impersonating her husband commits rape."

Section 3 (1): "It is an offence for a person to procure a woman, by false pretences or false representations, to have unlawful sexual intercourse in any part of the world."

The effect of section 3 (1) (formerly section 3 (2) of the Criminal Law Amendment Act 1885) on the common law of rape was considered in the case below.

R. v. Williams

[1923] 1 K.B. 340

Court of Criminal Appeal

W., a singing master, had sexual intercourse with a pupil aged 16 by pretending to her that it was a method of training her voice. The girl made no resistance, as she believed him and did not know that he was having sexual intercourse with her. He was convicted of rape and appealed.

LORD HEWART C.J.: Mr. Gorst has today taken one point and one point only on behalf of the appellant—namely, that in view of the evidence the appellant ought not to have been convicted of the crime of rape. In support of that argument the attention of the court has been directed to *R.* v. *O'Shay* (1898) 19 Cox 76, and to the provisions of the Criminal Law Amendment Act, 1885. There is no doubt that before the passing of the Act of 1885 a man who by fraudulent pretence succeeded in obtaining sexual intercourse with a woman might be guilty of rape. For example, in *R.* v. *Case* (1850) 4 Cox 220, a medical practitioner had sexual connection with a girl of fourteen years of age upon the pretence that he was treating her medically and the girl made no resistance owing to a bona fide belief that she was being medically treated. It was held that he was properly convicted of an assault and might have been convicted of rape. In *R.* v. *Flattery* (1877) 2 Q.B.D. 410 the same principle was affirmed. But it has been argued that the position has been changed by the passing of the Criminal Law Amendment Act, 1885. Mr. Gorst, when the question was specifically put to him, did not contend that that Act would prevent the laying of an indictment for rape in such a case as *R.* v. *Flattery*, but he said that that Act made an indictment for rape impossible in the present case. The argument is based upon the provisions of section 3, subsection (2), of the Act of 1885, which provides that "any person who . . . by false pretences or false representations procures any woman or girl, not being a common prostitute or of known immoral character, to have any unlawful carnal connection, either within or without the Queen's dominions . . . shall be guilty of a misdemeanour . . ." It is obvious that those words go beyond a case of rape. It is easy to imagine a case which would come within the comprehensive scope of those words and yet fail to come within the charge of rape. No doubt in *R.* v. *O'Shay*, Ridley J. did appear to say that after the passing of Criminal Law Amendment Act *R.* v. *Flattery* was no longer law. . . . It is, however, quite clear when one looks at the report of the case that the attention of the judge was not directed to section 16 of the Act of 1885. That section makes it plain that the provisions of the statute were not in the least intended to interfere with the liability of a person for an offence punishable at common law, but were intended to supplement the offences punishable at common law. In my opinion of this court the decision in *R.* v. *O'Shay* was given under a misapprehension.

Reference has been made in the course of the argument to *R.* v. *Dicken* (1877) 14 Cox 8, which was tried at the Stafford Assizes in 1877. In that case a man was charged with rape upon a girl above the age of twelve and under the age of thirteen years. Mr. C. J. Darling (as he was then) argued that the prisoner could not be convicted of felony. He said that the prisoner "was charged with rape. That offence consisted of his unlawfully and carnally knowing the girl against her will, i.e. without her consent. But such an offence was now defined in 38 & 39 Vict., c. 94, s. 4, and thereby declared to be a misdemeanour. Consequently, with respect to girls between the age of twelve and thirteen the earlier statutes making that offence a felony were repealed." That argument depended upon the words in the statute: "whether with or without her consent." Mellor J., who was the judge trying the case, said: "The carnal abuse of children having excited the attention of the legislature, they have been specially protected by Acts of Parliament. 24 & 25 Vict., c. 100, s. 51, enacted that "Whosoever shall unlawfully and carnally know and abuse any girl being above the age of ten years and under the age of twelve years, shall be guilty of a misdemeanour." Under this provision an offender was punishable, whether the girl did or did not consent to his act. In 1875 it was thought desirable that further protection should be given to young girls, and the limit of ten years was extended, by 38 & 39 Vict., c. 94, s. 4, declaring that 'Whosoever shall unlawfully and carnally know and abuse any girl being above the age of twelve years, and under the age of thirteen, whether with or without her consent, shall be guilty of misdemeanour.' *Ex abundanti cautela* the words 'whether with or without her consent' were inserted in the later enactment; but, save in respect of the alteration in the age of the girl, the law remained exactly as it was previously—that is to say, if she consented, the prisoner might be convicted of the statutory misdemeanour; if she did not, *a fortiori* he might be so. But if she did not consent, his offence would amount also to a higher crime—the felony—of rape, and he might be indicted and tried for it quite irrespective of the modern statutes throwing special protection around children. The present indictment is for rape, and therefore if the girl consented to the carnal knowledge, the act was not done 'against her will,' and the crime is not made out. It would be preposterous to suppose that Parliament intended to repeal the law of rape as to girls of the very age during which extra statutory protection is cast over them, and I am clearly of the opinion that no such repeal has been effected." . . .

In the present case the argument on behalf of the appellant must amount to this—if it be a sound argument at all—that after the passing of the Act of 1885 it is no longer possible to indict a man for rape in such cases as *R.* v. *Case* and *R.* v.

Flattery. That is to say that inasmuch as there is a statute which makes the obtaining of carnal connection with a woman by false pretences a misdemeanour that offence can no longer be rape. That propositioin cannot be the law, for the same reason as that stated by Mellor J. in *R.* v. *Dicken*, even if section 16 of the Act of 1885 be disregarded, but in view of that section the proposition is obviously untenable. Branson J. stated the law in the course of the summing-up in the present case in accurate terms. He said: "The law has laid it down that where a girl's consent is procured by the means which the girl says this prisoner adopted, that is to say, where she is persuaded that what is being done to her is not the ordinary act of sexual intercourse but is some medical or surgical operation in order to give her relief from some disability from which she is suffering, then it is rape although the actual thing that was done was done with her consent, because she never consented to the act of sexual intercourse. She was persuaded to consent to what he did because she thought it was not sexual intercourse and because she thought it was a surgical operation."

Appeal dismissed

ii. Other Sexual Offences

Unlawful Sexual Intercourse

Sexual Offences Act 1956

Section 5: "It is an [an offence] for a man to have unlawful sexual intercourse with a girl under the age of thirteen."

Section 6 (1): "It is an offence, subject to the exceptions mentioned in this section, for a man to have unlawful sexual intercourse with a girl . . . under the age of sixteen."

Section 6 (3):"A man is not guilty of an offence under this section because he has unlawful sexual intercourse with a girl under the age of sixteen, if he is under the age of twenty-four and has not previously been charged with a like offence, and he believes her to be of the age of sixteen or over and has reasonable cause for the belief.

In this subsection, 'a like offence' means an offence under this section or an attempt to commit one, or an offence under paragraph (1) of section five of the Criminal Law Amendment Act, 1885 (the provision replaced for England and Wales by this section)."

Indecent Assault

This can be committed against a woman (s. 14 of the Sexual Offences Act 1956) or against a man (s. 15). Consent can be a defence to indecent assault (subject to the qualifications indicated in *R.* v. *Donovan, ante*, p. 476 and *A-G's Reference No. 6 of* 1980, *ante*, p. 477). A person under 16 cannot give a valid consent and there is no defence corresponding to that provided by section 6 (3), above: *R.* v. *McCormack* [1969] 3 All E.R. 371.

Indecent assault is an assault or battery "accompanied by circumstances of indecency." The act has to have an overt sexual aspect and an otherwise "decent" assault accompanied by an indecent motive, such as touching a person's shoe to satisfy a foot fetish, is not indecent: *R.* v. *George* [1956] Crim. L.R. 52. Nor is it an indecent assault to touch a boy to indicate a pose for the purpose of taking obscene photographs: *R.* v. *Sutton* [1977] 1

W.L.R. 1086 (although this would be an offence under the Protection of Children Act 1978).

5. PROPOSALS FOR REFORM

Criminal Law Revision Committee, 14th Report

"Summary of Recommendations

GRIEVOUS BODILY HARM, UNLAWFUL WOUNDING AND ACTUAL BODILY HARM

39. The existing offences under section 18, 20 and 47 of the Act of 1861 should be replaced by the three following offences:

(1) causing serious injury with intent to cause serious injury punishable with a maximum penalty of life imprisonment and triable on indictment only;

(2) causing serious injury recklessly punishable with a maximum penalty of 5 years' imprisonment and triable either way.

(3) causing injury recklessly or with intent to cause injury punishable with a maximum penalty of 3 years' imprisonment and triable either way but made an arrestable offence (§§ 152–153 and 155).

40. We do not propose that there should be a definition of injury or serious injury except a provision that injury includes unconsciousness (§ 154).

41. A magistrates' court should be empowered to convict, without separate information being laid, of causing injury recklessly or with intent on a charge of causing serious injury recklessly (§ 156).

ASSAULT (INCLUDING ASSAULT ON A CONSTABLE AND SECTIONS 36–40 OF THE ACT OF 1861)

42. Assault should remain an offence and the definition should continue to be left to the common law (§§ 159 and 160).

43. No new offences of threatening assault or unlawful force should be created (§ 159).

44. Assault should be triable summarily only and should be punishable with a maximum penalty of 6 months' imprisonment or a fine of £1,000 or both. There should be a provision empowering a jury to convict of assault on a charge of causing injury recklessly or with intent to cause injury, causing serious injury recklessly or causing serious injury with intent to cause serious injury. Similarly, a magistrates' court should be empowered to convict of assault, without separate information being laid, on a charge of causing serious injury recklessly or causing injury recklessly or with intent to cause injury (§§ 161 and 162).

45. Sections 42–47 of the Act of 1861 should be repealed without replacement (§§ 163–165).

46. There should continue to be an offence of assaulting a constable in the execution of his duty or a person assisting a constable in the execution of his duty (§§ 170 and 171).

47. In addition to having to prove that the constable assaulted was acting in the execution of his duty, the prosecution should be required to prove that the defendant knew or was reckless as to whether he was a constable (§ 172).

48. The offence should remain triable summarily only with a maximum penalty of 6 months' imprisonment or a fine or £1,000 or both (§§ 173–176).

49. There should be a provision empowering magistrates' courts to convict without separate information having to be laid, of the offence of assault on a charge of assaulting a constable or a person assisting a constable (§ 177).

50. Sections 36, 37, 39, and 40 of the Act of 1861 should be repealed without replacement (§§ 179 and 180).

51. It should continue to be an offence for a person to assault another with

intent to resist or prevent the lawful arrest of himself or any other person. The offence should be punishable with a maximum penalty of 2 years' imprisonment and triable either way (§§ 181 and 182).

52. There should also be a provision empowering a jury to convict of assault on a charge of assault with intent to resist or prevent a lawful arrest and similarly a magistrates' court should be empowered to convict of assault, without separate information being laid, on a charge of assault with intent to resist or prevent a lawful arrest (§ 182).

ADMINISTRATION OF POISON AND OTHER NOXIOUS SUBSTANCES

53. Section 23 of the Act of 1861 should be repealed without replacement (§ 185).

54. Section 24 of the Act of 1861 should be repealed by a provision along the following lines. It should be an offence for a person to administer to another without consent and without lawful excuse any substance which in the circumstances is capable, and which that person knows may be capable, of interfering substantially with the other's bodily functions (§§186–188).

55. The offence should be punishable with 3 years' imprisonment and triable either way (§ 189)."

Note

The Criminal Law Revision Committee is currently considering the reform of sexual offences and issued a Working Paper in 1980. See Richard Card [1981] Crim. L.R. 361.

Report of the Advisory Council on the Penal System, "Sentences of Imprisonment, A Review of Maximum Penalties," 1978

This Report recommended that, for the ordinary offender, new maximum penalties should be fixed at the level below which 90 per cent. of sentences of immediate imprisonment passed by the Crown Court have fallen between 1974 and 1976 (§ 170). It further proposed that those maxima should only be exceeded where the court is of the opinion that a custodial sentence of exceptional length is necessary for the protection of the public against serious harm (§ 207). In such cases a determinate sentence of any length could be imposed (§ 213). The following proposed maxima for offences against the person are taken from Appendix A of the Report:

	Existing Penalty	*New Maximum*
Common Assault	12 months	12 months
Assault occasioning actual bodily harm	5 years	2 years
Unlawful wounding	5 years	3 years
Wounding with intent	Life	5 years
Administering poison endangering life	10 years	5 years
Administering poison with intent	5 years	3 years
Rape	Life	7 years
Sexual intercourse with a girl under 13	Life	5 years
Sexual intercourse with a girl under 16	2 years	2 years
Indecent assault		
—on a woman	2 years	2 years
—on a girl under 13	5 years	3 years
—on a man	10 years	5 years

Chapter 10

THEFT AND ROBBERY

	PAGE		PAGE
1. Theft	494	1. Theft—(*contd.*)	
i. Appropriation	495	v. "Temporary Deprivation"	544
ii. "Property"	504	vi. "Dishonestly"	555
iii. "Belonging to Another"	515	vii. A New Approach	562
iv. "With the Intention of Depriving permanently"	534	2. Robbery	566

1. THEFT

Note

Before 1969, the law about dishonest acquisition of the property of another was contained in the Larceny Act 1916, which was a codification of a number of common law rules with certain piecemeal statutory amendments mostly occurring in the Victorian era. The principal offence was larceny, but it was a highly technical crime, too narrowly defined to cover certain quite common cases of dishonesty. The crime was tinkered with both by statute and by judicial innovation, but the basis of the crime was such that no amount of tinkering would enable it to cover the whole range of dishonest conduct involving the property of another. The basis of the offence was that the accused should take and carry away property in the possession of another; it therefore failed to cover an accused person who dishonestly misappropriated that of which he already had lawful possession, and the offences of embezzlement and fraudulent conversion had to be invented to fill some of this gap. Moreover, the law's insistence that the crime was a wrong against possession, not against ownership, meant that the law was complicated by the need to reflect the intricacies of the English law of possession. The offence of fraudulent conversion, which, in its modern form, was first created by statute in 1901, was tied neither to taking and carrying away by the accused, nor to possession as the invaded interest of the victim. It consisted essentially of the accused fraudulently converting to his own use or benefit or to the use or benefit of any other person the property of the victim. When it was decided to replace larceny, embezzlement and fraudulent conversion by a single new offence of theft, the offence of fraudulent conversion was the model taken for the new definition in section 1. See Criminal Law Revision Committee's Eighth Report, on Theft and Related Offences, Cmnd. 2977, paras. 15–39. What might be called "swindling," *i.e.* obtaining by false pretences and certain other offences of fraud, was not swept into the new definition, and was treated separately by both the Report, § 38, and the Act, which contains a range of new offences of swindling. See next Chapter, where these offences are dealt with. However in spite of this separate treatment, the offence of theft has been held to be wide enough to cover virtually all cases of obtaining property by deception: *Lawrence* v. *Commissioner of Police*, *post*, p. 496.

Theft Act 1968, section 1

"(1) A person is guilty of theft if he dishonestly appropriates property belonging to another with the intention of permanently depriving the other of it; and 'thief' and 'steal' shall be construed accordingly.

(2) It is immaterial whether the appropriation is made with a view to gain, or is made for the thief's own benefit.

(3) The four following sections of this Act shall have effect as regards the interpretation and operation of this section (and, except as otherwise provided by this Act, shall apply only for purposes of this section)."

Note

The *actus reus* of Theft is (i) appropriating (ii) property (iii) belonging to another. All three elements are given extended definitions by Sections 3, 4 and 5 respectively. In addition, the concepts of "appropriation" and "belonging to another" are heavily affected by *Lawrence* v. *Commissioner of Police* (see below).

i. Appropriation

Theft Act 1968, section 3

(1) Any assumption by a person of the rights of an owner amounts to an appropriation, and this includes, where he has come by the property (innocently or not) without stealing it, any later assumption of a right to it by keeping or dealing with it as owner.

(2) Where property or a right or interest in property is or purports to be transferred for value to a person acting in good faith, no later assumption by him or rights which he believed himself to be acquiring shall, by reason of any defect in the transferor's title, amount to theft of the property.

Glanville Williams, Textbook of Criminal Law, p. 726

"The phrase 'any assumption of the rights of an owner' [in Section 3 (1), *supra*] is a remarkable juristic invention. Except in special situations that the framers of the Act were probably not thinking of, it is impossible for anyone to 'assume the rights of an owner' by way of theft, in the sense of actually acquiring rights of ownership. Thieves do not normally acquire rights against the owner. One may steal a watch, but one cannot generally steal rights of ownership in the watch. The thief may act in a way that would be lawful *if* he had the rights of an owner, or *if* he were acting by authority of the owner; but he does not by stealing give himself those rights. Obviously the word 'assumption' in this context means, generally, a *usurpation* of rights. (The word 'usurpation' is given as one of the meanings of 'assumption' in the OED). What appears to be intended by this cloudy definition is that an appropriation is (or includes) anything done in relation to property by a non-owner that only the owner could lawfully do or authorise."

Notes

1. However, not every usurpation, even a dishonest one, is theft, because to be such it must be with intent to deprive the owner permanently of his property. An unjustified borrowing is an appropriation (a

usurpation of the owner's right to use or possess the property) but it is not usually theft. (But see s. 6 (1), *post*, p. 537.)

2. Implicit in the idea of "usurpation" is the idea of one occupying a place which he is not entitled to occupy, exercising those rights which an owner is entitled to exercise but which the usurper is not. It might appear to follow that if the owner puts the accused in the position of owner, there is no appropriation, and that one who in the eye of the civil law is made the owner cannot appropriate the property, at any rate under the provisions now being considered. However the next case shows that this is not necessarily so.

Lawrence v. Commissioner of Police
[1972] A.C. 626
House of Lords

The facts appear from the speech of Viscount Dilhorne

VISCOUNT DILHORNE: My Lords, the appellant was convicted on December 2, 1969, of theft contrary to section 1 (1) of the Theft Act, 1968. On September 1, 1969, a Mr. Occhi, an Italian who spoke little English, arrived at Victoria Station on his first visit to this country. He went up to a taxi driver, the appellant, and showed him a piece of paper on which an address in Ladbroke Grove was written. The appellant said it was very far and very expensive. Mr. Occhi got into the taxi, took £1 out of his wallet and gave it to the appellant who then, the wallet being still open, took a further £6 out of it. He then drove Mr. Occhi to Ladbroke Grove. The correct lawful fare for the journey was in the region of 10s. 6d. [52½p]. The appellant was charged with and convicted of the theft of the £6.

In cross-examination, Mr. Occhi, when asked whether he had consented to the money being taken, said that he had "permitted." He gave evidence through an interpreter and it does not appear that he was asked to explain what he meant by the use of that word. He had not objected when the £6 was taken. He had not asked for the return of any of it. It may well be that when he used the word "permitted," he meant no more than he had allowed the money to be taken. It certainly was not established at the trial that he had agreed to pay to the appellant a sum far in excess of the legal fare for the journey and so had consented to the acquisition by the appellant of the £6.

The main contention of the appellant in this House and in the Court of Appeal was that Mr. Occhi had consented to the taking of the £6 and that, consequently, his conviction could not stand. In my opinion, the facts of this case to which I have referred fall far short of establishing that Mr. Occhi had so consented.

Prior to the passage of the Theft Act, 1968, which made radical changes in and greatly simplified the law relating to theft and some other offences, it was necessary to prove that the property alleged to have been stolen was taken "without the consent of the owner" (Larceny Act, 1916, s. 1 (1)).

These words are not included in section 1 (1) of the Theft Act, but the appellant contended that the subsection should be construed as if they were, as if they appeared after the word "appropriates." Section 1 (1) reads as follows: "A person is guilty of theft if he dishonestly appropriates property belonging to another with the intention of permanently depriving the other of it; and 'thief' and 'steal' shall be construed accordingly."

I see no ground for concluding that the omission of the words "without the consent of the owner" was inadvertent and not deliberate, and to read the subsection as if they were included is, in my opinion, wholly unwarranted. Parliament by the omission of these words has relieved the prosecution of the burden of establishing that the taking was without the owner's consent. That is no longer an ingredient of the offence.

Megaw L.J., delivering the judgment of the Court of Appeal, said ([1971] 1 Q.B. 373, 376) that the offence created by section 1 (1) involved four elements: "(i) a dishonest (ii) appropriation (iii) of property belonging to another (iv) with the intention of permanently depriving the owner of it."

I agree. That there was appropriation in this case is clear. Section 3 (1) states that any assumption by a person of the rights of an owner amounts to an appropriation. Here there was clearly such an assumption. That an appropriation was dishonest may be proved in a number of ways. In this case it was not contended that the appellant had not acted dishonestly. Section 2 (1) provides, *inter alia*, that a person's appropriation of property belonging to another is not to be regarded as dishonest if he appropriates the property in the belief that he would have the other's consent if the other knew of the appropriation and the circumstances of it. *A fortiori*, a person is not to be regarded as acting dishonestly if he appropriates another's property believing that with full knowledge of the circumstances that other person has in fact agreed to the appropriation. The appellant, if he believed that Mr. Occhi, knowing that £7 was far in excess of the legal fare, had nevertheless agreed to pay him that sum, could not be said to have acted dishonestly in taking it. When Megaw L.J. said that if there was true consent the essential element of dishonesty was not established, I understand him to have meant this. Belief or the absence of belief that the owner had with such knowledge consented to the appropriation is relevant to the issue of dishonesty, not to the question whether or not there has been an appropriation. That may occur even though the owner has permitted or consented to the property being taken. So proof that Mr. Occhi had consented to the appropriation of £6 from his wallet without agreeing to paying a sum in excess of the legal fare does not suffice to show that there was not dishonesty in this case. There was ample evidence that there was.

I now turn to the third element "property belonging to another." Mr. Back Q.C. for the appellant, contended that if Mr. Occhi consented to the appellant taking the £6, he consented to the property in the money passing from him to the appellant and that the appellant had not, therefore, appropriated property belonging to another. He argued that the old distinction between the offence of false pretences and larceny had been preserved. I am unable to agree with this. The new offence of obtaining property by deception created by section 15 (1) of the Theft Act also contains the words "belonging to another." "A person who by any deception dishonestly obtains property belonging to another, with the intention of permanently depriving the other of it" commits that offence. "Belonging to another" in section 1 (1) and in section 15 (1) in my view signifies no more than that, at the time of the appropriation or the obtaining, the property belonged to another, with the words "belonging to another" having the extended meaning given by section 5. The short answer to this contention on behalf of the appellant is that the money in the wallet which he appropriated belonged to another, to Mr. Occhi.

There was no dispute about the appellant's intention being permanently to deprive Mr. Occhi of the money.

The four elements of the offence of theft as defined in the Theft Act were thus clearly established and, in my view, the Court of Appeal was right to dismiss the appeal.

Having done so, they granted a certificate that a point of law of general public importance was involved and granted leave to appeal to this House. Under the Criminal Appeal Act, 1968, s. 33 (2) (which replaced section 1 (2) of the Administration of Justice Act, 1960), they have power to grant such leave if they think that a point of law of general public importance is involved and also that the point is one which ought to be considered by this House. The certificate granted does not state that they thought that the point was one which ought to be considered by this House but I infer that they were of that opinion from the fact that leave to appeal was granted.

The first question posed in the certificate was: "Whether section 1 (1) of the Theft Act, 1968, is to be construed as though it contained the words 'without having the consent of the owner' or words to that effect." In my opinion, the answer is clearly No.

"Whether the provisions of section 15 (1) and of section 1 (1) of the Theft Act, 1968, are mutually exclusive in the sense that if the facts proved would justify a conviction under section 15 (1) there cannot lawfully be a conviction under section 1 (1) on those facts." Again, in my opinion, the answer is No. There is nothing in the Act to suggest that they should be regarded as mutually exclusive and it is by no means uncommon for conduct on the part of an accused to render him liable to conviction for more than one offence. Not infrequently there is some overlapping of offences. In some cases the facts may justify a charge under section 1 (1) and also a charge under section 15 (1). On the other hand, there are cases which only come within section 1 (1) and some which are only within section 15 (1). If in this case the appellant had been charged under section 15 (1), he would, I expect, have contended that there was no deception, that he had simply appropriated the money and that he ought to have been charged under section 1 (1). In my view, he was rightly charged under that section. . . .

Appeal dismissed

Notes

1. Viscount Dilhorne holds that Parliament, by the omission of the words "without the consent of the owner," has relieved the prosecution of the burden of establishing that the taking was without the owner's consent. This could mean that the consent of the owner is always entirely irrelevant to the question of whether there is an appropriation. Two comments can be made on this.

(a) The cases below seem to establish an exception to the *Lawrence* rule if what the owner consents to is a bailment of the property of which the accused intends to deprive him.

R. v. Skipp [1975] Crim. L.R. 114: S. was convicted on a count which charged the theft of 450 boxes of oranges and 50 bags of onions. Posing as a genuine haulage contractor he obtained instructions to collect two loads of oranges and one load of onions from three different places in London and deliver them to customers in Leicester. Having collected the goods he made off with them. It was submitted that as S had the intention to steal the goods from the outset the count was bad for duplicity in that there were three separate appropriations.

Held, dismissing the appeal, . . . the three loads were properly included in the one count. An assumption of the rights of an owner over property did not necessarily take place at the same time as an intent permanently to deprive the owner of it. There might be many cases in which a person having formed the intent was lawfully in possession of the goods and could not be said to have assumed the rights of an owner because he had not done something inconsistent with those rights. In the present case it was proper to take the view that up to the point when all the goods were loaded, and probably up to the point when the goods were diverted from their true destination, there had been no assumption of rights, and so there was only one appropriation. There was no conceivable prejudice to S.

R. v. Hircock (1978) 67 Cr. App. R. 278: H. obtained possession of a car under a hire-purchase agreement, using a false name and intending permanently to deprive the owner. A fortnight later he sold the car to a third party. He was convicted of obtaining the car by deception (in respect of the hiring) and of theft (in respect of the sale to a third party). These double convictions were upheld by the Court of Appeal, on the footing that the first occasion was not one of theft. "There was clearly evidence here, upon which the jury could find that the appellant had obtained possession of this car dishonestly, by giving a false name, that he had no intention of paying and that he had the intention permanently to deprive the owner of that car. In these circumstances, the appellant had acquired the car by deception and not necessarily by stealing since he was the purported hirer of the car and, on the face of it, entitled to possession, even though he intended to deprive the owners permanently of the car. . . . It is significant that at the time of the deception he expressly acknowledged that he was not the owner. In fact he signed the hire-purchase agreement as a bailee. In the case of theft there has to be an appropriation. . . ."

(b) These cases may be wrong, being inconsistent with *Lawrence*, or it may be that *Lawrence* is distinguishable in that it dealt with the case of A tricking ownership and possession out of B, and not with a case where A tricks possession only out of B. But it is clear that *Lawrence* did not purport to deal with cases other than where B's consent was tricked out of him. It was not concerned with the position where B truly consents to A doing what he did. Usually there will be no question of theft in such a case, because A will be acting honestly. If he is not, usually he will deceive B, by concealing his dishonest motive, and the case will be like *Lawrence.* But occasionally, there will be a case where A will be acting in a way that B consented to, A will be dishonest (because he has decided to deprive B) but he will not have tricked B into consenting, because A became dishonest after B consented. For example, A is about to draw out of his account some money which belongs to B which he intends to give to B. He decides to deprive B of it, and then draws out the money intending to "lose" it in a fake robbery he has arranged. This happened in *R.* v. *Meech* [1974] Q.B. 549 (*post*, p. 526). The Court of Appeal rejected an argument that the theft occurred when Meech withdrew the money with dishonest intent. "We think the judge's direction when he said that the time of the appropriation was the time of the fake robbery was right. A dishonest intention was formed before the money was withdrawn, but the misappropriation only took place when these three men divided up the money at the scene of the fake robbery. It was then that the performance of the obligation by Meech [to restore the proceeds to the owner] finally became impossible by the dishonest act of these three men acting in concert together."

Another example is where a shopper in a supermarket, intending to steal, picks up an article displayed for sale and puts it in a basket provided by the shopkeeper. It was held in *Eddy* v. *Niman* [1981] Crim. L.R. 502 (D.C.) that, as the *act* was with the shopkeeper's implied consent, it could not be held to be an appropriation. The accused must do something with the article that he is not authorised to do, such as put it in his own bag: *R.* v. *McPherson* [1973] Crim. L.R. 191 (C.A.), or switch price tags on it: *Anderton* v. *Wish* [1980] Crim. L.R. 319 (D.C.), or take it beyond the check-out without paying the full price. And see *Kaur* v. *Chief Constable of*

Hampshire [1981] 1 W.L.R. 578 (D.C.) where the accused picked up obscurely labelled goods and carried them to the check-out girl, dishonestly hoping that the latter would make a mistake and charge the wrong price, which in fact happened. It was assumed in the decision that there was no appropriation until the check-out was reached, and, as to the assumption of ownership involved in walking away from the checkout with the goods, since they now belonged to the accused under a voidable contract of sale, the Court left open whether this could properly be described as an "appropriation."

2. The implications of Viscount Dilhorne's dictum seem to have been studiously ignored in decisions since *Lawrence* v. *Commissioner of Police.* The main question raised by the dictum is whether A's behaviour with regard to B's property, although completely lawful as far as the civil law is concerned, is turned into theft by reason of A's intention to deprive B permanently. There are powerful arguments against making the reach of the criminal law more extensive than that of the civil law, the counter-argument being that the civil law of ownership, contract and tort is complex and highly technical; it would be unfortunate if the complexities were introduced into a criminal trial, and wrong if a dishonest man escaped a conviction of theft because of some civil law technicality.

Glanville Williams, Theft, Consent and Illegality [1977] Crim. L.R. 127, 129

"Theft should be regarded in general as requiring a *mis*appropriation—an appropriation that is contrary to the general law (meaning the civil law), except that an appropriation is to be accounted illegal for this purpose although the owner consents to it in fact, if as a result of the defendant's dishonesty the owner's consent is defective in the sense of being voidable by the owner. *Lawrence* is not a conclusive authority to the contrary, because the question whether an otherwise wholly lawful appropriation can be theft was not presented to their lordships for decision.

Reasons against the prevailing opinion are, first, that it puts too much weight on dishonesty, which is an acceptable notion for restricting the law of theft but not for enabling it to range over the whole field of 'appropriations'. It would be wrong to make a conviction of theft depend entirely on the defendant's dishonesty of purpose, when from the owner's point of view there is nothing wrong with the transaction. Alternatively, it would be wrong to make the conviction depend upon a purely moral judgment, when the general law pronounces that the defendant's conduct is legally unobjectionable.

Secondly, there is the desirability of legal consistency. Consider the following hypotheticals.

(1) *Insider trading.* The director of a company sells or buys a large block of its shares, having private information affecting their value. Most share transactions are highly impersonal, but we may suppose that in this instance the transaction is face-to-face.

(2) *Doorstep selling.* A man calling himself a roof repairer persuades an old person living alone to have the roof repaired. The man inspects the roof, correctly states what is to be done, and gives a quotation that is grossly excessive for the work involved; but he does the work contracted to be done and receives the payment. Other doorstep conmen persuade gullible people to buy 'investment antiques', 'giveaway jewellery', patent medicines and so on, while refraining from actual deception.

(3) *The golden handshake.* A firm, wishing to rid itself of a director, agrees to

pay him compensation for accepting early retirement. Unknown to the firm, the director has committed breaches of his contract of employment that would have entitled the firm to dismiss him without compensation; the director knows this when he accepts the compensation.

The law of contract is always in course of development, and one can never be sure that new remedies will not be allowed by the civil courts as justice and conscience demand. But it can be said that on the ancient principles of the common law and equity none of the above transactions involves a civil wrong, or is affected by any invalidity, except in some cases under head 2 where the victim is in a peculiarly vulnerable position. If conviction in a criminal case depends upon the view taken of the civil law, then that law should be interpreted conservatively in the defendant's favour; new developments in the civil law should not take place in the criminal courts. Let us assume, then, that a civil court would regard the contracts as valid. Nevertheless, a jury in a criminal court might well find the party who was guilty of morally questionable conduct to have been dishonest. Does he commit theft of what he receives? There may be a social case for punishing his conduct in some instances: proposals have been made for legislation on insider trading, and we should perhaps control all house-to-house sales of goods and services by a licensing system. But it would surely be inapt to effect the control by an elastic interpretation of the law of theft, particularly when the civil law regards the transaction as valid.

For the criminal law to make the dishonest party guilty of theft, in holding on to his bargain, implies a judgment that he acts wrongly in receiving the money. For the civil law to say that he can enforce the bargain and need not give the money back implies a judgement that there is no sufficient reason to make him give it back: that the public interest in the security of transactions is sufficiently strong to outweigh elements of disquiet with the particular facts. This would be a contradiction. If the question is a borderline one, with a slight balance of argument against the defendant, surely the position should be that he is civilly but not criminally liable.

The law of contract has its own means of avoiding conflict with the criminal law. A contract involving illegality is void. So if the Theft Act were interpreted to make the dishonest doorstep seller guilty of theft, he would not be able to enforce the contract (the civil court would obviously not give him judgment for the contract remuneration, when his receipt of it would be theft). The result would be that the free-ranging notion of dishonesty would spread from the criminal law to the law of contract. Would it be acceptable, in the law of contract, to say that a bargain is unenforceable by anyone who is accounted morally dishonest?

Thirdly, the argument that some rules of the criminal law punish conduct that is not a civil wrong (carrying offensive weapons, for instance), is not sufficient to support the contention that the Theft Act, s. 1 (1), should be construed to do so. The rules in question are based on notions of public order or other matters of public interest and are not directed merely to the protection of property. The object of the law of theft is to protect property; one object of the law of tort is to protect property; presumptively, therefore, they should be governed by the same rules, unless a clear statutory provision or a clear reason of policy supports a distinction. One such reason of policy dictates that theft, unlike the torts of trespass and conversion, is limited to dishonest acts. But why should theft be *wider* than the law of tort?

Fourthly, the argument based on the simplification of issues in the criminal trial overlooks the fact that the Theft Act requires theft to be of 'property belonging to another'. The civil and criminal law do not conflict on what is meant by the property of another, apart from the modification made by section 5 (4). This means that the criminal courts are potentially involved in investigating a vast number of technicalities relating to the civil law: in particular, the difficult distinction between debtors and trustees, and the rules of following and tracing property. The Theft Act has a simplified provision of these particular matters (s. 5 (3)), which, however, can hardly be understood and applied except in the light of the more detailed rules of the law of property."

Questions

Is there an appropriation by A in the following cases?

1. A, at B's self-service petrol station, sees a notice "Help yourself: pay at the booth." He fills his tank, intending not to pay. (See *R.* v. *MacHugh* (1976) 64 Cr. App. R. 92.)
2. As question 1, but A *does* intend to pay when he fills his tank. He then discovers he has no money and drives off without paying. (See *Edwards* v. *Ddin, post*, p. 516.)
3. A asks for a can of oil, intending to pay for it. B hands him a can. A discovers he has no money, and drives off with the can and without paying.
4. A is lent a book by B to revise for a certain examination. After the day of the examination, A decides to keep the book and tells B that it has been accidentally destroyed.
5. Same question as 4, except that it is before the day of the examination when A tells B the book has been accidentally destroyed. (See *R.* v. *Meech, supra*.)
6. A, in possession of B's goods with authority to sell for cash or on credit, sells them for cash to C, intending to keep the cash and record the sale as a credit one.
7. A, knowing that B is not at home, takes C to B's house and offers to sell him the furniture. (See *R.* v. *Pitham & Heyl* (1976) 65 Cr. App. R. 45, at p. 49, *post*, p. 608.)
8. A, a casual passerby, hearing C admiring a horse in a roadside field, offers to sell it to him for £100. C pays A and leads the horse away. The horse belongs to B.
9. A, falsely pretending that B owes him £10, is given £10 by B. (See *Lawrence*.)
10. A is asked by B to deliver a case of wine to C at his house. A agrees, although he intends to consume the wine himself. B gives him the case. (See *R.* v. *Skipp*.)
11. A hires a television set from B. He agrees to pay a weekly hire charge, and not to part with possession of the set. In fact he fully intends to sell the set at once. (See *R.* v. *Hircock*.)
12. A, having already stolen B's property, gives it to C. (See s. 3(1), *ante*.)
13. A secretly takes a photograph of B's jewels, in order to make replicas which can be substituted for the genuine ones, which he intends to steal.

Glanville Williams: Appropriation: A Single or Continuous Act? [1978] Crim. L.R. 69

"A man steals a watch, and two weeks later sells it. In common sense and ordinary language he is not guilty of a second theft when he sells it. Otherwise it would be possible, in theory, to convict a thief of theft of a silver teapot every time he uses it to make the tea.

This view is suggested also by several provisions of the Act. Section 3 (1) says that where a person comes by a thing *without* stealing it, a subsequent assumption of right can be an appropriation, and so theft. This implies that if he comes by the thing theftously no subsequent act by him in relation to it can amount to theft. If Parliament had wished merely to say that a person who is in possession of property, whether lawfully or not can steal it, it could have said simply that.

The definition of robbery in section 8 is that a person 'steals, and immediately before or at the time of doing so, and in order to do so, he uses force' etc. This implies that force used by the thief to defend his possession after the theft is not robbery. Consequently, it implies that the time of the stealing does not extend into the time when the thief is in possession of the article after the first appropriation.

The definition of handling stolen goods in section 22 excludes acts done 'in the course of the stealing.' If a thief who, having taken goods, later sells them to a receiver, is guilty of a continuous appropriation from the taking to the sale, the receiver presumably receives the goods 'in the course of the stealing.' But this was not the intention of the Act, and the courts do not construe it in such a way. If a thief sells the property, even if only a few seconds after the theft, the buyer can be convicted of handling. (*R.* v. *Pitham, post,* p. 608.) This strongly implies that appropriation is a single event, not a continuous proceeding.

The Criminal Law Revision Committee proposed that the former offence of receiving stolen goods should be widened to include other people who without receiving the goods, helped the thief to dispose of them, because otherwise they might not be guilty of any offence. Hence the new offence of handling, which appears in the Act. Now if later acts done by the thief with the stolen goods could be regarded as new theftous appropriations, persons assisting him to do these acts would be accessories to the new thefts, and there would have been no real need to widen the old law of receiving. The fact that it was widened shows that the legislature like the Committee, assumed that there could be only one theftous appropriation. [*Meech* (*ante,* p. 499) and *Skipp* (*ante,* p. 498) bear out this conclusion]. . . .

The arguments in favour of a continuous-appropriation rule turn on policy rather than authority. A single-appropriation rule might enable a person charged with theft at a stated time to defend himself impudently by showing that he had appropriated the article earlier. . . . Another inconvenience of the single-appropriation rule may be illustrated as follows. D steals an article in Germany (which would not be punishable by our law, being out of the jurisdiction). He brings the article to this country and sells it, appropriating the proceeds. On the single-appropriation rule he still cannot be touched in this country; and a recorder has so ruled (*R.* v. *Figures* [1976] Crim. L.R. 744). It would be convenient if he could be, but an amendment to the Act would be required to secure this result.

On balance, these arguments favour the view that the single-appropriation rule represents the present law, but that if the Theft Act comes to be reconsidered it might well be amended to adopt the concept of continuous appropriation. This might enable the offence of handling, with all its complexities, to be abolished."

Note

The implication of single appropriation in the words of section 8, referred to by Williams, has since been rejected by the Court of Appeal, holding that, in robbery at least, appropriation is a continuous act: *R.* v. *Hale* (1978) 68 Cr. App. R. 415, *post*, p. 568.

ii. "Property"

Theft Act 1968, section 4

"(1) 'Property' includes money and all other property, real or personal, including things in action and other intangible property.

(2) A person cannot steal land, or things forming part of land and severed from it by him or by his directions, except in the following cases, that is to say—

(a) when he is a trustee or personal representative, or is authorised by power of attorney, or as liquidator of a company, or otherwise, to sell or dispose of land belonging to another, and he appropriates the land or anything forming part of it by dealing with it in breach of the confidence reposed in him; or

(b) when he is not in possession of the land and appropriates anything forming part of the land by severing it or causing it to be severed, or after it has been severed; or

(c) when, being in possession of the land under a tenancy, he appropriates the whole or part of any fixture or structure let to be used with the land.

For purposes of this subsection 'land' does not include incorporeal hereditaments; 'tenancy' means a tenancy for years or any less period and includes an agreement for such a tenancy, but a person who after the end of a tenancy remains in possession as statutory tenant or otherwise is to be treated as having possession under the tenancy, and 'let' shall be construed accordingly.

(3) A person who picks mushrooms growing wild on any land, or who picks flowers, fruit or foliage from a plant growing wild on any land, does not (although not in possession of the land) steal what he picks, unless he does it for reward or for sale or other commercial purpose.

For purposes of this subsection 'mushroom' includes any fungus, and 'plant' includes any shrub or tree.

(4) Wild creatures, tamed or untamed, shall be regarded as property; but a person cannot steal a wild creature not tamed nor ordinarily kept in captivity, or the carcase of any such creature, unless either it has been reduced into possession by or on behalf of another person and possession of it has not since been lost or abandoned, or another person is in course of reducing it into possession."

Notes

Section 4 replaces the common law definition of things capable of being stolen, which in general included only tangible moveable objects. There are however still some things which are not or not completely within the concept of stealable things.

1. *Land*. Land, and things attached to or growing on land could not in general be stolen, and although the Criminal Law Revision Committee were pressed to equate land with other property exactly, in the end they decided that the position should remain broadly as it was previously: Cmnd. 2977, paras. 44, 47.

Questions

1. Is theft involved in any of the following cases?

A moves the fence between his own land and that of his neighbour B, so as to take in a strip of B's land.

C, a licensee of D's land, strips off some antique wooden panelling and sells it as firewood.

E, tenant of F, cuts down a wood on the land and sells it as firewood.

G enters H's land and uproots a Christmas tree growing wild, with intention of taking it home to decorate his own home.

J is given 10p. by K to collect enough wild mushrooms from L's land to make a breakfast for K.

2. Is a charge of criminal damage available in any of these cases? Compare section 10 (1) of the Criminal Damage Act 1971, *post*, p. 654.

Notes

2. *Wild animals*, while alive and free, were not the subject of larceny. Dead animals were larcenable but not, ordinarily, by the person who killed them; in other words, poaching was not larceny. The Committee, on the grounds that poaching was not popularly regarded as stealing and that to make it theft would increase the maximum penalty too greatly, decided against equating wild animals with other things.

Various provisions making summary offences of taking deer and fish were contained in the Larceny Act 1861, which the Theft Act repeals entirely. In order to preserve these offences pending a comprehensive reform of the law of poaching, they are re-enacted substantially unchanged in Schedule 1 to the Theft Act. There are also other poaching statutes, *e.g.* the Deer Act 1963, the Salmon and Freshwater Fisheries Act 1975. Moreover, legislation not concerned with protecting anyone's property in the creatures involved protects wild birds, their nests and eggs (Protection of Birds Act 1954) and endangered species (Conservation of Wild Creatures and Wild Plants Act 1975).

Question

A rounds up wild ponies from the moorland where they are born and reared, in order to sell them at auction. B, who disapproves of this, releases them from the auction pen and one escapes. C captures it and refuses to return it to A or to pay for it. Can the actions of A or B or C amount to theft?

Notes

3. *Things in action and other intangible property*. Before the Theft Act, to be stealable, property had to be tangible. Other things of value, such as a legal right, could not be stolen, and a prosecutor was driven to such shifts as charging the stealing of the piece of paper which evidenced such a right. There is now no need to do that in many cases as a result of the wide definition of property in section 4 (1); but if a piece of paper is involved and changes hands, it may still be convenient to charge the theft of the paper, because the attempt in section 4 (1) to widen the concept of stealable property is not without its difficulties.

3a. *Things in Action*. A thing in action (or chose in action) is property which does not exist in a physical state, and cannot be enjoyed physically (looked at, listened to, eaten, worn, ridden, etc.), but can only be claimed by legal action. Examples are a debt, shares in a company, a copyright, a trade-mark, insurance cover. These things can be stolen by one who appropriates them with intent to deprive the owner permanently, *e.g.* a trustee or personal representative; the legal owner of shares beneficially owned by X, dishonestly assigning them to Y; or a cashier with power to draw cheques on P's account drawing one dishonestly in favour of his own creditor Q. When this cheque is presented and met, P will have lost part of his debt against his bankers (see *R.* v. *Kohn*, below).

R. v. Kohn
(1979) 69 Cr. App. R. 395
Court of Appeal

K was a director of Panelservice Ltd., with authority to make payments on its behalf by drawing cheques against its bank account. He drew cheques against the account for his own purposes. He was convicted of theft of the things in action, which the cheques represented, and of the cheques themselves. He appealed.

GEOFFREY LANE L.J.: The way the indictment was drawn, broadly speaking, with one or two exceptions which need not concern us at this stage, was to allege each alleged defalcation by way of two counts. The first of the two counts in each case alleged the theft of a thing in action, namely a debt in the sum of £x owed by the National Westminster Bank Ltd. to Panelservice Ltd.; and the other of the two counts in each case alleged that the defendant on or about such and such a date stole a cheque No. so and so the property belonging to Panelservice Ltd.

The counts, as appears from what I have already stated, alleged these events on various dates and, not surprisingly, the state of the particular account at the National Westminster Bank varied from time to time, with the result, again as will emerge when one comes to examine the notice of appeal in detail, that some of the cheques were drawn or presented at a time when the account was in credit, some of the cheques were drawn or presented when the account was in overdraft but within the limits of the overdraft facility, and there was one count, count 7, in which the cheque was drawn or presented at a time when the account was first of all in overdraft, and secondly beyond the agreed limit of the overdraft, that is to say the limit agreed between the bank and Panelservice. . . .

So far as the first situation is concerned, when the account is in credit, the prosecution say that, where an account is in credit the relationship of debtor and creditor exists between the bank and the customer. The customer is the creditor, the bank is the debtor. The debt is owing by the bank to the customer. That debt is something which cannot be physically handled, it is not a thing or chose in possession; it is a thing in action, namely something which can only be secured by action and, goes the argument, this is a case of a thing in action par excellence, and if it be proved that the defendant has stolen, in other words appropriated that thing in action, then the offence is made out.

[After considering reported decisions on the meaning of "chose in action"]: So the prosecution start off with the advantage of the fact that that expression is plainly one which covers a multitude of matters and over the history of English law has spread really far beyond its original concept. So at first blush it would seem that the appellant's contentions on this point are a little difficult to sustain.

But what Mr. Tyrrell submits is this—since we are not sure we have followed the argument, we quote what he says verbatim: "The very act done which is relied on as interfering with the owner's rights destroys the subject matter of the theft and so there has been no appropriation. Nothing has ever come into the possession of the appellant." What he says, we think, is that the thing in action has been destroyed before any appropriation and therefore there has been no theft.

It seems to us that the argument is quite untenable. First of all, is there a thing in action, and the answer is undoubtedly yes. Secondly, has the appellant appropriated it? The answer is yes. Was the intention permanently to deprive the owner, and again there was ample evidence upon which the jury properly directed could come to the conclusion that it was. Was it dishonest? Again there was ample evidence on which the jury could come to that conclusion.

A submission was made at the close of the prosecution case similar to that made to us, which the judge rejected. We think that he was right to reject it.

Mr. Tyrrell has frankly said that his researches have brought to light no authorities which give any support to his proposition. In so far as there is authority it is against his contentions. It is contained in the writings of two eminent academic lawyers: first of all Professor Griew in his book *The Theft Acts 1968 and 1978* (3rd ed. 1978), paras. 2–11, where one finds this:

> "The case of an employee (D) who has authority to draw on his employer's (P's) bank account and who dishonestly draws on it for unauthorised purposes seems also to be theft (assuming the account to be in credit), D has in some manner appropriated the debt owed by the bank to P. Although nothing in the transaction operates as an assignment of that debt to D, it would seem that D has appropriated the debt or part of it by causing P's credit balance to be diminished, or at the very least taking the risk of such diminution. The case is analogous to the theft of a chattel by destruction."

The whole of that passage, and particularly the last sentence, if it is correct, as we think it is, sounds the death knell to this particular submission on behalf of the appellant. . . .

We now turn to the counts which cover the situation where the account was overdrawn, but the amount of the cheque was within the agreed limits of the overdraft. So far as this aspect of the matter is concerned, Mr. Tyrrell submits that the grant of facilities for an overdraft does not create a debt. [After considering authorities holding that specific performance is not possible on a contract to lend money, and holding that to that extent the contract does not constitute a debt] [But] if the account is in credit . . . there is an obligation to honour the cheque. If the account is within the agreed limits of the overdraft facilities, there is an obligation to meet the cheque. In either case it is an obligation which can only be enforced by action. For purposes of this case it seems to us that that sufficiently constitutes a debt. . . . It is a right of property which can properly be described as a thing in action and therefore potentially a subject of theft under the provisions of the 1968 Act. The cheque is the means by which the theft of this property is achieved. The completion of the theft does not take place until the transaction has gone through to completion. . . .

[In] *William Rouse* v. *Bradford Banking Co. Ltd* [1894] A.C. 586, 596, Lord Herschell L.C. said:

> ". . . It may be that an overdraft does not prevent the bank who have agreed to give it from at any time giving notice that it is no longer to continue, and that they must be paid their money. This I think at least it does; if they have agreed to give an overdraft they cannot refuse to honour cheques or drafts, within the limit of that overdraft, which have been drawn and put in circulation before any notice to the person to whom they have agreed to give the overdraft that that limit is to be withdrawn. . ."

Finally the passage of Sir John Donaldson P. in *Eckman* v. *Midland Bank Ltd.* [1973] Q.B. 519, 529 a decision of the National Industrial Relations Court, Sir John Donaldson sitting as President with two other lay members:

> "If, however, a bank has contracted with the contemnor in terms which entitle him to draw on the bank up to a limit and that limit has not been

reached, this facility is part of the property of the contemnor which the sequestrators are entitled to have transferred to them and which they can operate by authority of the writ of sequestration."

It seems to us, in the light of those authorities and in the light of the wording of the Theft Act 1968, that in this situation, when the order to the bank is within the agreed limits of the overdraft, a thing in action certainly exists and accordingly the judge was right in rejecting the submission. The appeal so far as those particular counts are concerned must fail.

That leads us to the third situation, which affects only count 7, that being, it will be remembered, the count which dealt with the cheque presented to the bank at a time when the account was over the agreed overdraft limit which had been imposed by the bank.

The situation here is that there is no relationship of debtor and creditor, even notionally. The bank has no duty to the customer to meet the cheque. It can simply mark the cheque "Refer to drawer." It can decline to honour the cheque. The reasons for that are obvious. If then a bank declines to honour a cheque, there is no right of action in the customer. If they do as a matter of grace—that is all it can be—honour the cheque then that is a course which does not retrospectively create any personal right of property in the customer and does not create any duty retrospectively in the bank. It seems, therefore, on that bald statement of principle, that this count which alleges a theft of a thing in action when the account was over the agreed limit must be quashed, unless some external reason can be found for saving it. . . .

We turn now to the next matter which has been urged before us, and that was a matter which was raised for the first time by a supplementary notice of appeal which has been placed before us. The supplementary grounds of appeal read as follows: "The appellant will seek leave to argue as a supplementary ground of appeal that the convictions on counts 4, 6, 8, 10, 12, 14, 16, 20 and 24 of the indictment (theft of cheques) were unsafe and unsatisfactory and proceeded on a misdirection of law. The case for the appellant is that it was not possible in law for him to steal the cheques as alleged in that: (a) he himself wrote and drew the cheques; (b) there was no possibility of Panelservice Ltd. being permanently deprived of the cheques in their character as pieces of paper since they had that character both before and after the appellant drew them; (c) there was no possibility of Panelservice Ltd. being permanently deprived of the cheques in their character as things in action since they did not acquire that character until the appellant wrote and drew them."

This point was not argued at the trial and one suspects this is the brainchild of Mr. Rose, who argued this matter before us and argued, if we may say so, most attractively. The way he put it is as follows: first of all he submits that if the cheque is treated as a piece of paper *simpliciter*, rather than in its character as a thing in action, it is not proved, he suggests, that there was any intention permanently to deprive the owner. It would be likely to go back to the company, and he submits that the provisions of section 6 (1), which I have already read, do not in those circumstances bite. He submits that the decision of this Court in *Duru and Asghar* [1974] 1 W.L.R. 2 (*post*, p. 540) does not apply, because that case was dealing with a different section of the Theft Act 1968, namely section 15. Furthermore in that case the cheque, he suggests, was being treated in its capacity as a thing in action. He submits further that the defendant here in no way assumed the rights of an owner, if one is viewing the cheque simply as a piece of paper. He represented himself, so the argument goes, as agent of the company to draw a cheque and that is not acting as owner.

One of the difficulties in considering these arguments is that, by reason of the fact that the point was not raised in the Court below the issues never became crystallised. So that one has to search the transcript in order to try to discover the way in which, under these counts, the cheque was being viewed by counsel before the judge and consequently before the jury.

The matter seems to us to become reasonably clear so far as that is concerned, if one looks at p. 21 of the first volume of the transcript. Here the learned judge said to the jury: "What is represented by the cheque is, of course, the right of the person named in it, the payee, to receive the payment represented by that cheque. So far as that cheque itself is concerned, true it is a piece of paper but it is a piece of paper which changes its character completely once it is paid because then it receives a rubber stamp or, in this case, the perforated stamp saying that it has been paid and it then also ceases to be a thing in action. That is a bill of exchange which is a thing in action as I have told you. The cheque is the same thing. It ceases to be that or, at any rate, it ceases to be in its substance the same thing as it was before. That is an instrument on which payment falls to be made." It seems tolerably clear from that that the judge, counsel and the jury were not considering the cheque in its capacity as a piece of paper *simpliciter*, even if one can view a cheque properly in that light. They were looking at it as a negotiable instrument in the way that the judge described.

Even if that was the way the matter was being considered, said Mr. Rose, the drawing of a cheque in favour of a third party does not amount to treating oneself as an owner and therefore there is no appropriation sufficient to satisfy the requirements of section 1.

We do not consider that those submissions can be supported. The way in which the matter should be approached, we think, is as Miss Goddard submitted to us, which was this. A cheque is not a piece of paper and no more. In no circumstances, in this type of situation, can it be so considered. It is a piece of paper with certain special characteristics.

The sequence of events in this case can be brought down to a simple series of facts. The defendant starts with a cheque book in his possession. It is the cheque book of the company and he is plainly in lawful possession of that book with cheques inside it. He apparently had the habit, as we have already indicated, at least occasionally, of removing blank cheques from the book, tearing out the cheque leaving the counterfoil in position, putting the cheque in his pocket and filling it in at a later stage. Still nothing wrong at all in that. He is still acting lawfully, although it may be somewhat unusual. He then makes up his mind to fill in a cheque with the amount, then the payee and the date and so on. The third party in whose favour the cheques were being made were *ex hypothesi* not entitled to those sums. The appellant was therefore using the company's cheques and the company's bank account for his own purposes. Miss Goddard suggests that there was a gradual appropriation as the events moved on in this way.

The next stage is this. He says to himself, "I am now going to make the cheque payable to E.P. or Happy Pets or whoever it may be." That action is unknown to Mr. Aust. It is *ex hypothesi* once again contrary to the interests of the company. It is contrary to the will of the company and it is dishonest. This is dealing with the cheque not as the agent of the company duly authorised, but is dealing with the cheque as if it were his own. That seems to us is sufficient to amount to an appropriation under the Act.

So when the writing gets on to the cheque, it becomes a bill of exchange and becomes a necessary demand upon the bank to honour the bank's obligations to the customer, which is the company. But that is being done for the defendant's own purposes, and when he sends it on to the company, to Happy Pets or to E.P., it has come to the point where he has made the cheque his own. For the purposes of the Theft Act he has appropriated the cheque, and given that the other elements of the crime are present, which one must assume for purposes of this argument, the offence is complete. Be it noted it is not a matter of what happens to the document thereafter.

Consequently for purposes of these counts, that is to say the even numbered counts, the "cheque" counts rather than the "thing in action" counts, it does not matter whether the account of the company is in credit, it does not matter whether it is within its overdraft limits, it does not matter whether it is outside the overdraft limits, the offence is nevertheless complete.

Now to deal with the further question of whether there is an intent permanently to deprive the owner? Here we would wish to do what the judge did, simply to cite the passage from Megaw L.J.'s judgment in *Duru and Asghar* [*post*, p. 540] "In the view of this Court there can be no doubt that the intention of both of these appellants, as would necessarily have been found by the jury if the matter had been left to the jury on a proper direction of law (a direction which would no doubt have been given if the pleas of guilty had not been entered), was permanently to deprive the Greater London Council of that thing in action, that cheque; that piece of paper, in the sense of a piece of paper carrying with it the right to receive payment of the sum of £6,002.50 which is the amount concerned in count 3. So far as the cheque itself is concerned, true it is a piece of paper. But it is a piece of paper which changes its character completely once it is paid, because then it receives a rubber stamp on it saying it has been paid and it ceases to be a thing in action, or at any rate it ceases to be, in its substance, the same thing as it was before: that is, an instrument on which payment falls to be made. It was the intention of the appellants, dishonestly and by deception, not only that the cheques should be made out and handed over, but also that they should be presented and paid, thereby permanently depriving the Greater London Council of the cheques in substance as their things in action. The fact that the mortgagors were under an obligation to repay the mortgage loans does not affect the appellant's intention permanently to deprive the council of these cheques."

Consequently so far as the counts involved in these supplementary grounds of appeal are concerned, particulars of which have already been detailed, the appeal must fail. The appellant was assuming the rights of the owner, that is to say the rights of the creditor vis-à-vis the bank, that is the rights of the company to demand that the bank should hand over the money. He is assuming the right to do what he likes with that part of the company's debt with which he is dealing.

The learned Lord Justice then dealt with the further grounds of appeal, discussed them and concluded: For the reasons which we have indicated it seems to us, apart from the conviction on count 7 which must be quashed, this appeal must be dismissed.

Conviction on count 7 quashed. Appeal dismissed on other counts

Notes

There may be three different choses in action involved with regard to a cheque.

1. There is the chose represented by the bank account (the bank's debt to the customer). Dishonestly causing the cheque to be met appropriates part of this chose.

2. There is the chose consisting in the contractual right to have overdrawings met, *i.e.* a right to have the bank advance money on the customer's behalf. Dishonestly causing an overdrawn cheque to be met appropriates part of this chose.

3. There is the right in the payee of the cheque to sue the drawer (the customer) for the amount of the cheque if it is not met.

So far as concerns a cheque drawn when the amount is overdrawn beyond the agreed limit, things in action (1) and (2) do not exist; the only possible chose is (3).

Kohn holds that a cheque is not a piece of paper only; it has special characteristics, *i.e.* it constitutes the chose in action (3). The case also holds that dishonestly converting a piece of paper into a bill of exchange is an appropriation, and if done with intent to deprive is theft. The fact that choses in action (1) and (2) are not involved is immaterial. The only question is, how does one permanently deprive the customer of the appropriated property? One answer is to say that the customer has to "buy" it back, by meeting the cheque, by paying Happy Pets the amount specified in the cheque. It is clear that the owner of property is permanently deprived if he is only to get it back by buying it back [see, *post*, p. 542]. However the Court adopts another view (formulated in *R.* v. *Duru, post*, p. 540) that what the owner, Panelservice, gets back is something entirely different from what was taken from it. What was taken was a thing in action, "a piece of paper carrying with it the right to receive payment of a sum of money," and what was returned was a mere piece of paper (a cancelled cheque). The inference is that it has been stripped of all or most of its value to P. It is not at first sight clear what has been removed from the cheque which is of value to P, since its obvious value is a duty in P to pay a sum of money to the payee. Removal of this "value" does not prejudice P. The answer appears to be that while it was a cheque, P could exchange it for goods or other value. Now he has only a worthless piece of paper. However it does not seem accurate to say that P is deprived of a thing in action, because that thing in action, being a right to sue P for money, could never have been owned by P.

Questions

1. *Which* thing in action (No. 1, 2 or 3) is Geoffrey Lane L.J. referring to when he says at the end of his judgment "He is assuming the right to do what he likes with that part of the company's debt with which he is dealing?"

2. A, who has the right to draw cheques on B's account to pay for expenses incurred by A in B's business, dishonestly draws a cheque in his own favour for £100 although he has incurred no expenses. A presents the cheque, his own account is credited with £100, and B's account is debited. What is the most appropriate and provable charge to bring against A?

Notes

Kohn was able to cause Panelservice to lose part of the debt owed to it by its bankers. In most cases, however, the wrongdoer has no power to affect the victim's right in any way, and it is difficult to see how he can steal it. For example, a copyright is an exclusive right to publish a book or picture or to perform publicly a play. Suppose A dishonestly reproduces a picture, the copyright of which is in B, and sells copies to the public. B still has what he had before A's activities, *i.e.* the exclusive right to publish. Nothing A can do can take away that right. No doubt A has usurped that right by doing what only B is permitted to do, but it is only a temporary usurpation, as A must know, and such temporary misuse of property is not usually theft. Suppose A dishonestly purports to sell B's copyright to C. This does at least *purport* to be a permanent usurpation, but it must be wholly without legal effect. It is true that with *any* kind of property, a thief usually cannot legally deprive the owner; and loss of legal title by the owner has never been a requirement of theft. But with tangible property, at least the wrongdoer can deprive the owner physically, whereas with a copyright or other intangible he can deprive him *neither* legally *nor* physically. It is difficult to see how he can steal such property.

Question

Section 6 (1), *post*, p. 537, provides that a person not intending the other permanently to lose the thing itself is nevertheless regarded as having that intention if he intends "to treat the thing as his own to dispose of regardless of the other's rights." Does this subsection meet the difficulties mentioned above as to infringement or purported sale of a copyright? See Smith, § 27; Griew, § 2.54.

Notes

3b. *Other intangible property.* Some intangible things can be valuable, without being a right of action against anyone. Examples are, an idea, news, "know-how," secrets, especially trade secrets. Industrial espionage is rife nowadays and such valuables are often "stolen," in popular parlance at least. If such things were property, similar difficulties would arise as with things in action, but it seems that such are not anyway comprehended in the statutory phrase "other intangible property."

Oxford v. Moss
(1978) 68 Cr. App. R. 183
Queens Bench Division

The facts appear in the judgment of Smith J.

SMITH J.: This is a prosecutor's Appeal by way of Case Stated.

On May 5, 1976, an information was preferred by the prosecutor against the defendant alleging that the defendant stole certain intangible property, namely, confidential information being examination questions for a Civil Engineering Examination to be held in the month of June 1976 at Liverpool University, the information being the property of the Senate of the University, and the allegation being that the Respondent intended permanently to deprive the said Senate of the said property.

The facts can be stated very shortly indeed. They were agreed facts. They are set out in the case and they are as follows. In May 1976 the defendant was a student at Liverpool University. He was studying engineering. Somehow (and this Court is not concerned precisely how) he was able to acquire the proof of an examination paper for an examination in Civil Engineering to be held in the University during the following month, that is to say June 1976. Without doubt the proof, that is to say the piece of paper, was the property of the University. It was an agreed fact, as set out in the case, that the respondent at no time intended to steal what is described as "any tangible element" belonging to the paper; that is to say it is conceded that he never intended to steal the paper itself.

In truth and in fact, and in all common sense, what he was about was this. He was borrowing a piece of paper hoping to be able to return it and not be detected in order that he should acquire advance knowledge of the questions to be set in the examination and thereby, I suppose, he would be enabled to have an unfair advantage as against other students who did not possess the knowledge that he did.

By any standards, it was conduct which is to be condemned, and to the layman it would readily be described as cheating. The question raised is whether it is conduct which falls within the scope of the criminal law.

The learned stipendiary magistrate at Liverpool was of the opinion that, on the facts of the case, confidential information is not a form of intangible property as opposed to the property in the proof examination paper itself, that is the paper and the words printed thereon. He was of the opinion, further, that confidence consisted in the right to control the publication of the proof paper and was a right over property other than a form of intangible property.

Finally, he was of the opinion that by his conduct the respondent had gravely interfered with the owner's right over the paper. He had not permanently deprived the owner of any intangible property. Accordingly, the learned stipendiary magistrate dismissed the charge.

The prosecutor appeals. The question for this Court, shortly put, is whether confidential information can amount to property within the meaning of the Theft Act 1968. By section 1 (1) of the statute: "A person is guilty of theft if he dishonestly appropriates property belonging to another with the intention of permanently depriving the other of it; . . ."

By section 4 (1): "'property' includes money and all other property, real or personal, including things in action and other intangible property."

The question for this Court is whether confidential information of this sort falls within that definition contained in section 4 (1). We have been referred to a number of authorities emanating from the area of trade secrets and matrimonial secrets. In particular, we were referred to *Peter Pan Manufacturing Corporation* v. *Corsets Silhouette Ltd.* [1963] 3 All E.R. 402, to *Seager* v. *Copydex Ltd.* [1967] 2 All E.R. 415, to the case of *Argyll* v. *Argyll* [1965] 2 W.L.R. 790, and *Fraser* v. *Evans* 3 W.L.R. 1172.

Those are cases concerned with what is described as the duty to be of good faith. They are clear illustrations of the proposition that, if a person obtains information which is given to him in confidence and then sets out to take an unfair advantage of it, the courts will restrain him by way of an order of injunction or will condemn him in damages if an injunction is found to be inappropriate. It seems to me, speaking for my part, that they are of little assistance in the present situation in which we have to consider whether there is property in the information which is capable of being the subject of a charge of theft. In my judgment, it is clear that the answer to that question must be no. Accordingly, I would dismiss the Appeal.

(Lord Widgery C.J. and Wien J. agreed.)

Appeal dismissed

Questions

1. Would it have made any different if Moss had been a confidential secretary employed by the University and had utilized his knowledge of the examination paper to help some student?

2. It was conceded that he never intended to steal the paper itself. On the agreed facts need this concession have been made? See s. 6 (1), *post*,

p. 537, and J. R. Spencer, *The Metamorphosis of Section 6 of the Theft Act*, *post*, p. 539.

Notes

A right over property is not necessarily intangible property itself. Even if (as must be the case if it *is* a right) it is protected by the law in some ways (*e.g.* by injunction, or by damages for its misuse) it does not follow that it ought to be protected by the criminal law, or by the law of theft specifically. It is not said how Moss obtained the proof. If he got it from a servant of the University, it might be conspiracy to defraud (see *Scott* v. *M.P.C. ante*, p. 546) or corruption (see s. 1 of the Prevention of Corruption Act 1906: *R.* v. *Barrett* [1976] 1 W.L.R. 946.)

Electricity is valuable but intangible. It is not included in the definition of property, because the dishonest use or wasting or diverting of it is made a special offence in s. 13. See *Low* v. *Blease* [1975] Crim. L.R. 513.

4. *Unspecific Property*

If A is charged with stealing a watch, he cannot be convicted of stealing an umbrella (see Cockburn C.J. in *R.* v. *McPherson* (1858) D. & B. 197, 200). He must be shown to have stolen the specific property he is charged with stealing, although not necessarily the whole of it.

Machent v. Quinn [1970] 2 All E.R. 255 (Q.B.D.): Q. was charged with stealing 35 shirts, 9 pairs of trousers, four sweaters, two beach sets and two cardigans, to the total value of £199. It was proved that he stole four sweaters only, valued at £25. *Held*, he could be convicted as charged, (but his sentence was to relate to the four sweaters only).

It would be different if all that could be shown was that Q. had stolen some articles from the list, but not which articles. However if the articles are identical (or undifferentiated in the indictment, *i.e.* described as "goods"), it is no objection that the stolen ones cannot be identified.

R. v. Tideswell [1905] 2 K.B. 273 (C.C.C.R.): T. had permission to help himself to ashes in P.'s yard, paying for the weight taken. In collusion with P.'s servant, he took 32 tons 13 cwts., knowing that the servant had recorded the sale as of 31 tons 3 cwts. only. *Held* T. could be convicted on an indictment charging him with larceny of 1 ton 10 cwts.

And if it is impossible to show which particular articles A stole and when, but only that goods or money to a certain total value was appropriated in a certain period (*e.g.* between two stock-takings), he may be charged with, and convicted of, stealing the general deficiency. *R.* v. *Tomlin* [1954] 2 Q.B. 274.

In charges of attempted theft, or burglary with intent to commit theft, it is not necessary to charge or prove that the accused had any particular property in mind: *Re A-G's References (Nos.* 1 *and* 2 *of* 1979) [1980] Q.B. 180 (C.A.).

5. *The Human Body and its Parts*

Griew, The Theft Acts 1968 and 1978

"§ 2.13 There could be no larceny of a corpse at common law; for there could be no property in a dead body. The latter principle probably survives to limit the modern offence of theft. It is true that an executor, for instance, may have possession of a dead body, or a right to possession of it, until burial. But he cannot be said to 'own' it; and 'property' within the Act is probably limited to that which is capable of ownership. If that is so, the theft sanction will not, without amendment of the Act, protect the possession of an executor or, for instance, that of a licensed anatomist receiving the body under the Anatomy Act 1832, s. 10. Nor can a buried corpse be stolen. On the other hand, it has been argued (correctly, it is submitted) that modern medical advances make the body's 'spare parts' important potential subjects of theft; and that this result at least can be achieved without legislation. (A. T. H. Smith, "Stealing the Body and its Parts" [1976] Crim. L.R. 622.)

Products of the living body have been treated in practice as capable of theft—at least in the limited context of specimens provided to the police for laboratory examination: *R.* v. *Welsh* [1974] R.T.R. 478 (urine); *R.* v. *Rothery* [1976] Crim. L.R. 691 (blood)."

iii. "Belonging to Another"

Theft Act 1968, section 5

"(1) Property shall be regarded as belonging to any person having possession or control of it, or having in it any proprietary right or interest (not being an equitable interest arising only from an agreement to transfer or grant an interest).

(2) Where property is subject to a trust, the persons to whom it belongs shall be regarded as including any person having a right to enforce the trust, and an intention to defeat the trust shall be regarded accordingly as an intention to deprive of the property any person having that right.

(3) Where a person receives property from or on account of another, and is under an obligation to the other to retain and deal with that property or its proceeds in a particular way, the property or proceeds shall be regarded (as against him) as belonging to the other.

(4) Where a person gets property by another's mistake, and is under an obligation to make restoration (in whole or in part) of the property or its proceeds or of the value thereof, then to the extent of that obligation the property or proceeds shall be regarded (as against him) as belonging to the person entitled to restoration, and an intention not to make restoration shall be regarded accordingly as an intention to deprive that person of the property or proceeds.

(5) Property of a corporation sole shall be regarded as belonging to the corporation notwithstanding a vacancy in the corporation."

Notes

A person can only steal what belongs to another. "Belonging to another" is given an extended meaning, and covers persons who have only minor interests in the property (possession, control, any proprietory right or interest). If B has such a minor interest in property, that property can be stolen from him by A, and it matters not whether A is also entitled to a minor (or indeed major) interest in the same property. Moreover, even if A is the entire owner, and B has no interest which the civil law will recognise, it may still be possible for A to steal the property if A got the property under an obligation or by B's mistake, or dishonestly.

The "belonging to another" factor, extended as it is, must exist at the time when the accused did the act which is said to be theft. If *before* he dishonestly does an act with regard to the property, it has ceased to belong to another and belongs to the accused, that act cannot be theft. See *Edwards* v. *Ddin*, below. But if the dishonest act *results* in the property belonging to the accused, that act is an appropriation of property belonging to another, and can be theft. See *Lawrence* v. *Commissioner of Police*, *ante*, p. 496.

Edwards v. Ddin
[1976] 1 W.L.R. 942
Queen's Bench Division

The facts appear in the judgment of Croom-Johnson J.

Croom-Johnson J. This is an appeal by way of case stated from the magistrates' court sitting at Amersham in which the defendant had an information preferred against him that he stole three gallons of petrol and two pints of oil together of the value of £1.77, the property of Mamos Garage Amersham, contrary to section 1 of the Theft Act 1968.

On the facts as found by the justices the following things happened. The defendant arrived with a motor car and he asked for some petrol and oil to be placed in his car. Petrol and oil to the value as stated £1.77, was placed into the car at his request by the garage attendant. When he ordered the petrol and oil the defendant impliedly made to the attendant the ordinary representation of an ordinary customer that he had the means and the intention of paying for it before he left. He was not in fact asked to pay and he did not in fact pay, but the moment when the garage attendant was doing something else he simply drove away. The justices also found, as one would think was perfectly obvious, that whilst the petrol and oil had been placed in the car, either in the tank or in the sump, it could not reasonably be recovered by the garage in default of payment.

The questions therefore which have to be resolved in order to satisfy section 1 of the Act were two in number. First of all, was the defendant dishonest? It appears that the justices must have considered that that was so. Secondly, had he appropriated property belonging to another with the intention of permanently depriving the other of it? Upon that point the defence submitted successfully that at the time when the car was driven away the petrol and oil which had got into the tank or sump were in fact not the property of the garage any more but were the property of the defendant. On that basis the justices said that that particular essential ingredient of theft under section 1 of the Act had not been fulfilled and dismissed the information.

The whole question therefore was: whose petrol and oil was it when the defendant drove away? Property passes under a contract of sale when it is intended to pass. In such transactions as the sale of petrol at a garage forecourt ordinary common sense would say that the garage and the motorist intended the property in the petrol to pass when it is poured into the tank and irretrievably mixed with the other petrol that is in it, and I think that is what the justices decided.

But the prosecutor has appealed and has based his appeal on a consideration of the Sale of Goods Act 1893 and the provisions of that Act, and seeks a ruling that transfer of the petrol was conditional only and that therefore until payment the petrol remained the property of the garage.

But if one considers the provisions of the Sale of Goods Act 1893 one comes out at the same answer as common sense would dictate.

The prosecution argument went this way, that when the motorist arrives at the garage and says "will you fill me up, please?" or "will you give me two gallons?", then there is a contract for the sale of unascertained goods by description. In such circumstances when does the property in the petrol pass? Nothing will have been said between the motorist and the pump attendant about that, so one is thrown back on section 18 of the Sale of Goods Act 1893 and rules made under it in order to ascertain the intention of the parties.

By pouring the petrol into the tank the goods have been appropriated to the contract with the assent of both parties. If that is done unconditionally, then the property in the petrol passes to the motorist: rule 5 (1). The prosecution argument then goes on that, however, there is a condition which is waiting to be fulfilled, namely, payment, and says that under section 19 of the Sale of Goods Act 1893 the garage reserves the right of disposal of the petrol until the payment has been made and that therefore the property has not passed under rule 5 (1).

It is at this point that the argument breaks down. The garage owner does not reserve the right to dispose of the petrol once it is in the tank, nor is it possible to see how effect could be given to any such condition wherever petrol has been put in and is all mixed up with what other petrol is already there. Consequently one passes back to rule 5 (2) of section 18, which says that where a seller delivers the goods to the buyer and does not reserve the right to dispose of them, he is deemed to have unconditionally appropriated the goods to the contract and in those circumstances the property has passed to the buyer in accordance with rule 5 (1).

Reference was also made by the prosecutor to section 5 of the Theft Act 1968 which deals with one of the subsidiary definitions arising under section 1, which is the initial section dealing with theft. Section 5, which deals with but is not definitive of the expression "belonging to another," is concerned with all manner of interests in property. It was urged upon us that the motorist is under an implied obligation to retain his car with the petrol in its tank on the garage premises and not to take it away until such time as he has paid for it, and that until that has been done the garage owner retains some proprietary interest in the petrol in the tank.

The relevant part of section 5, which is in subsection (3), reads:

> "Where a person receives property from or on account of another, and is under an obligation to the other to retain and deal with that property or its proceeds in a particular way, the property or proceeds shall be regarded (as against him) as belonging to the other."

That section in my view is not apt to cover a case such as the present where there has been an outright sale of the goods and the property in the goods has passed and the seller is only waiting to be paid. Therefore the provisions of section 5 do not affect the conclusion in the present case.

I do not enter into any discussion for the purposes of this judgment of what might have been the position if the charge had been brought under some other section of the Theft Act 1968, or if the appropriation for the purposes of section 1 had been said to have arisen at an earlier stage of the events which took place. On the facts as found and on the case as it was presented to the magistrates, in my view the magistrates reached a correct conclusion in law and I would dismiss the appeal.

Appeal dismissed

Questions

1. The fact that the owner had consented to pass the property to the accused saved Ddin but did not save Lawrence from conviction. What is the distinction between the cases?

2. The Court leaves open the position if the appropriation had been said to have arisen at an earlier stage of the events. *Could* the appropriation have been said to have arisen earlier than the act of driving the car away? If yes, what difference should it have made to the result?

3. Would it have made any difference if the garage had *expressly* reserved the right of disposal pending payment? Consider the effect of the following condition of sale: "The seller supplies petrol on the understanding that from the moment of delivery until the amount supplied has been paid for, the whole of the petrol in the customer's tank shall be the property of the seller."

4. Of what offence could Ddin have been convicted if the facts had occurred in 1979? See, *post*, p. 597.

5. A, at a petrol station owned by B, mentions jokingly that the night before he saw B having sexual intercourse with a girl aged 15 (which is an offence). B, looking frightened, says, "Please don't spread it around—I'll fill your tank for nothing." A, knowing that B is giving him the petrol solely because he is frightened of being exposed, allows him to do so and drives off without paying. Is this theft by A?

(See *R.* v. *Bruce* [1975] 1 W.L.R. 1252; *R.* v. *Chapman* [1974] Crim. L.R. 488; Smith, § 43; Griew, § 2.52.)

6. A in a pub approaches B, who works at a local garage, and says he will make it worth B's while if he "forgets" to ask for any money when he fills his vehicle with petrol. B consults his employer, who instructs B to pretend to play A's game and arranges for the police to be present. Next day, A asks B to fill his tank and when that has been done starts to drive off without paying, but is apprehended. Is this theft by A?

(See Williams, *Theft Consent and Illegality: Some Problems* [1977] Crim. L.R. 327; Williams, *Textbook*, Chap. 34, § 7; Smith and Hogan, p. 521; Griew, § 2.46).

7. (i) A sees an old car parked on the central reservation of a motorway. It is the same model as A's car, for which he has found difficulty in obtaining spares. A removes a part from the parked car, which A thinks has merely broken down but which in fact has been abandoned there by B. Is this theft by A?

(ii) Is it attempted theft by A? See, *ante*, p. 325.

(iii) Would it make any difference if the car had been abandoned in Q's barn? See next case.

R. v. Woodman

[1974] Q.B. 758

Court of Appeal

A was the owner of a disused factory. He sold all the scrap metal in the place to B. B entered the factory and removed all the scrap metal which he could easily reach, but left some which was in such an inaccessible position as to be not worth the trouble of getting. A, who thought that all the metal had been removed by B, then put a barbed wire fence around the factory to exclude trespassers. W entered the factory and removed the remaining metal. He was convicted of theft, and appealed on the ground that no-one had possession or control of the metal.

LORD WIDGERY C.J.: . . . [Theft Act 1968], Section 1 (1) provides: "A person is guilty of theft if he dishonestly appropriates property belonging to another." I need not go further because the whole of the debate turns on the phrase "belonging to another." Section 5 (1) of the Act expands the meaning of the phrase in these terms:

> "Property shall be regarded as belonging to any person having possession or control of it, or having in it any proprietary right or interest . . ."

The recorder took the view that the contract of sale between English China Clays and the Bird group had divested English China Clays of any proprietary right to any scrap on the site. It is unnecessary to express a firm view on that point, but the court are not disposed to disagree with that conclusion that the proprietary interest in the scrap had passed. The recorder also took the view on the relevant facts that it was not possible to say that English China Clays were in possession of the residue of the scrap. It is not quite clear why he took that view. It may have been because he took the view that difficulties arose by reason of the fact that English China Clays had no knowledge of the existence of this particular scrap at any particular time. But the recorder did take the view that so far as control was concerned there was a case to go to the jury on whether or not this scrap was in the control of English China Clays, because if it was, then it was to be regarded as their property for the purposes of a larceny charge even if they were not entitled to any proprietary interest.

The contention before us today is that the recorder was wrong in law in allowing this issue to go to the jury. Put another way, it is said that as a matter of law English China Clays could not on these facts have been said to be in control of the scrap.

We have formed the view without difficulty that the recorder was perfectly entitled to do what he did, that there was ample evidence that English China Clays were in control of the site and had taken considerable steps to exclude trespassers as demonstrating the fact that they were in control of the site, and we think that in ordinary and straightforward cases if it is once established that a particular person is in control of a site such as this, then prima facie he is in control of articles which are on that site.

The point was well put in an article written by no lesser person than Mr. Wendell Holmes in his book *The Common Law* (1881), at pp. 222, 223–224, dealing with possession. Considering the very point we have to consider here, he said, and I take the extract from *Hibbert* v. *McKiernan* [1948] 2 K.B. 142, 147:

> "'There can be no animus domini unless the thing is known of; but an intent to exclude others from it may be contained in a larger intent to exclude others from the place where it is, without any knowledge of the object's existence. . . . In a criminal case, the property in iron taken from the bottom of a canal by a stranger was held well laid in the canal company, although it does not appear that the company knew of it, or had any lien upon it. The only intent concerning one thing discoverable in such instances is the general intent which the occupant of land has to exclude the public from the land, and thus, as a consequence, to exclude them from what is upon it.'"

So far as this case is concerned, arising as it does under the Theft Act 1968, we are content to say that there was evidence of English China Clays being in control of the site and prima facie in control of articles upon the site as well. The fact that it could not be shown that they were conscious of the existence of this or any particular scrap iron does not destroy the general principle that control of a site by excluding others from it is prima facie control of articles on the site as well.

There has been some mention in argument of what would happen if in a case like the present, a third party had come and placed some article within the barbed-wire fence and thus on the site. The article might be an article of some serious criminal consequence such as explosives or drugs. It may well be that in that type of case the fact that the article has been introduced at a late stage in circumstances in which the occupier of the site had no means of knowledge would produce a different result from that which arises under the general presumption to which we have referred, but in the present case there was, in our view, ample evidence to go to the jury on the question of whether English China Clays were in control of the scrap at the relevant time. Accordingly, the recorder's decision to allow the case to go to the jury cannot be faulted and the appeal must be dismissed.

Appeal dismissed

Questions

1. "In my judgment, it is quite clear that a person cannot be said to be in possession of some article which he or she does not realise is, or may be, in her handbag, in her room, or in some other place over which she had control": *per* Lord Parker C.J., in *Lockyer* v. *Gibb* [1967] 2 Q.B. 243, a prosecution for the offence of being in possession of a controlled drug. Is this *dictum* inconsistent with the decision in *R.* v. *Woodman*?

2. Suppose W, when stripping the factory of metal, had discovered and taken away a cache of controlled drugs abandoned there by X. If, consistent with Lord Parker's dictum English China Clays were held not to have possession of the drugs, could W be convicted of stealing them?

Subsection 1: Possession, control or any proprietary right or interest

R. v. Bonner
[1970] 1 W.L.R. 838
Court of Appeal

B. took metal from the house of W., with whom he was in partnership as demolition contractors. B. said the metal was partnership property and he took it in order not to deprive W. of it permanently but hold it as security for what was due to him from W. out of the partnership profits. B. was convicted of theft but his appeal was allowed on the ground that verdict was in all the circumstances unsafe and unsatisfactory. However the Court of Appeal thought it right to deal with the legal point certified by the trial judge, *viz.* whether the jury was misdirected on the law relating to the theft by a partner of partnership property. The direction in question is quoted in the judgment of Edmund Davies L.J. below.

EDMUND DAVIES L.J.: . . . Mr. Inglis-Jones has . . . submitted that in the circumstances of this case a mere taking away of partnership property, even with the intention of keeping the other partner permanently out of possession of it would not *per se* suffice to amount to theft; there would have to be something like destruction of the metal or its sale in market overt, which would have the effect (provided there was innocence in the buyer) of transferring a good title to him and so defeating the title of the deprived partner. Defending counsel summarised the matter by submitting that for there to be an "appropriation" within the Theft Act, 1968, there must be a "conversion" of the property by one or other of the foregoing methods, neither of which was resorted to here. Therefore, so it is submitted, there was no theft.

Rejecting that submission, Judge Ranking directed the jury in these terms:

> "... even if you are satisfied that there was a full partnership between Webb and Bonner, a partner has no right to take any partnership property with the intention of permanently depriving the other of his share. Therefore, even if Bonner was a partner of Webb, if he took that lead, which was partnership property, intending to deprive Webb permanently of his share and when he did it, he knew perfectly well that he had no legal right to take it, then he is guilty of theft; he is guilty of the theft of the whole property and not just guilty of the theft of Webb's share, because the whole of it was partnership property and it had not been divided ... and if one partner takes it he is guilty of stealing the whole of it."

Was this a misdirection? This court is clearly of the opinion that it was not. Sections 1, 3 and 5 of the Theft Act, 1968, are here relevant. Section 1 (1) reads:

> "A person is guilty of theft if he dishonestly appropriates property belonging to another with the intention of permanently depriving the other of it; and 'thief' and 'steal' shall be construed accordingly."

Section 3 defines the word "appropriates" in these terms:

> "Any assumption by a person of the rights of an owner amounts to an appropriation ..." Section 5 defines the phrase, "belonging to another," used in section 1.

Mr. Inglis-Jones has boldly submitted that, since the basic requirement of theft is the appropriation of property belonging to another, there can be no such appropriation by one co-owner of property which is the subject matter of the co-ownership or partnership; and that there can be no "assumption ... of the rights of an owner" in a case like the present, where one is dealing with (as Bonner claims) property belonging to a partnership.

The whole object of the Theft Act, 1968, was to get away from the technicalities and subtleties of the old law. Mr. Inglis-Jones has not repeated before us an interesting submission which he made below; but, since we are dealing with this topic, we think that it might be helpful if we resurrect it and attempt to dispose of it now. His submission below went something on these lines: The Larceny Act, 1916, had a special provision (section 40 (4)) that:

> "If any person, who is a member of any co-partnership or is one of two more beneficial owners of any property, steals or embezzles any such property of or belonging to such co-partnership or to such beneficial owners he shall be liable to be dealt with, tried, and punished as if he had not been or was not a member of such co-partnership or one of such beneficial owners."

The parent of that provision was the Larceny Act, 1868, a one-section statute, and in *R.* v. *Jesse Smith* (1870) 1 C.C.R. 266 Bovill C.J. said, referring to the Larceny Act, 1861, at p. 269:

> "At the time that Act (Larceny Act, 1861 (24 & 25 Vict. c. 96) was passed theft by a partner of the goods of the firm did not fall within the criminal law, either common or statute. This defect was supplied by the Larceny and Embezzlement Act, 1868 (31 & 32 Vict. c. 116), which, after reciting that 'it is expedient to provide for the better security of the property of co-partnerships and other joint beneficial owners against offences by part-owners thereof, and further to amend the law as to embezzlement,' proceeds to enact, by the first section, that if a partner, or one of two or more beneficial owners, shall steal, etc., any property of such co-partnership or such joint beneficial owners, 'every such person shall be liable to be dealt with, tried, convicted,

> and punished for the same as if such person had not been or was not a member of such co-partnership, or one of such beneficial owners.'"

Mr. Inglis-Jones submitted that, there having been a special provision in the Larceny Act, 1916, following upon the earlier Act, dealing with the position of a partner wrongfully treating partnership property, and there being no repetition of that statutory provision in the Theft Act, 1968, the inference is that the law has been changed and that it is no longer theft for a partner to deprive a co-partner of any of the partnership property even if it be done dishonestly and intending permanently to deprive.

I said a little earlier that the object of the Theft Act, 1968, was to get rid of the subtleties and, indeed, in many cases the absurd anomalies of the pre-existing law. The view of this court is that in relation to partnership property the provisions in the Theft Act, 1968, have the following result: provided there is the basic ingredient of dishonesty, provided there be no question of there being a claim of right made in good faith, provided there be an intent permanently to deprive, one partner can commit theft of partnership property just as much as one person can commit the theft of the property of another to whom he is a complete stranger.

Early though these days are, this matter has not gone without comment by learned writers. Professor Smith in his valuable work on the Theft Act, 1968, expresses his own view quite clearly in paragraph 80 under the heading "Co-owners and partners" in this way:

> "D and P are co-owners of a car. D sells the car without P's consent. Since P has a proprietary right in the car, it belongs to him under section 5 (1). The position is precisely the same where a partner appropriates the partnership property."

In the joint work of Professor Smith and Professor Hogan, the matter is thus dealt with (Smith and Hogan's *Criminal Law*, 2nd ed. (1969), p. 361):

> "... D and P ... may ... be joint owners of property. Obviously there is no reason in principle why D should not be treated as a thief if he dishonestly appropriates P's share, and he is so treated under the Theft Act."

We thus have no doubt that there may be an "appropriation" by a partner within the meaning of the Act, and that in a proper case there is nothing in law to prevent his being convicted of the theft of partnership property. But this *excursus* is of an academic kind in the present case for we have already indicated our view regarding the unsatisfactory and unsafe nature of the verdicts returned against each of these accused. In these circumstances, all four appeals are allowed.

Appeals allowed

[Three other men who had helped Bonner had been charged with him.]

R. v. Turner (No. 2)
[1971] 1 W.L.R. 901
Court of Appeal

> T. took his car to a garage to have it repaired. Those repairs having been practically completed, the car was left in the road outside the garage. T. called at the garage and told the proprietor that he would return the following day, pay him, and take the car; instead he took the car, using his spare key, without paying for the repairs. Later he lied about the matter to the police. He was convicted of theft of the car.

Lord Parker C.J.: The words "belonging to another" are specifically defined in section 5 of the Act, subsection (1) of which provides: "Property shall be regarded as belonging to any person having possession or control of it, or having in it any proprietary right or interest." The sole question was whether Mr. Brown [the garage proprietor] had possession or control.

This court is quite satisfied that there is no ground whatever for qualifying the words "possession or control" in any way. It is sufficient if it is found that the person from whom the property is taken, or to use the words of the Act, appropriated, was at the time in fact in possession or control. At the trial there was a long argument as to whether that possession or control must be lawful, it being said that by reason of the fact that this car was subject to a hire-purchase agreement, Mr. Brown could never even as against the defendant obtain lawful possession or control. As I have said, this court is quite satisfied that the judge was quite correct in telling the jury they need not bother about lien, and that they need not bother about hire purchase agreements. The only question was whether Mr. Brown was in fact in possession or control.

The second point that is taken relates to the necessity for proving dishonesty. Section 2 (1) provides that: "A person's appropriation of property belonging to another is not to be regarded as dishonest (*a*) if he appropriates the property in the belief that he has in law the right to deprive the other of it, on behalf of himself or of a third person";

The judge said in his summing up: "Fourth and last, they must prove that the defendant did what he did dishonestly and this may be the issue which lies very close to the heart of the case." He then went on to give them a classic direction in regard to claim of right, emphasising that it is immaterial that there exists no basis in law for such belief. He reminded the jury that the defendant had said categorically in evidence: "I believe that I was entitled in law to do what I did." At the same time he directed the jury to look at the surrounding circumstances. He said this: "The prosecution say that the whole thing reeks of dishonesty, and if you believe Mr. Brown that the defendant drove the car away from Carlyle Road, using a duplicate key, and having told Mr. Brown that he would come back tomorrow and pay, you may think the prosecution are right." On this point Mr. Herbert says that if in fact you disregard lien entirely, as the jury were told to do, then Mr. Brown was a bailee at will and this car could have been taken back by the defendant perfectly lawfully at any time whether any money was due in regard to repairs or whether it was not. He says, as the court understands it, first that if there was that right, then there cannot be theft at all, and secondly that if and in so far as the mental element is relevant, namely belief, the jury should have been told that he had this right and be left to judge, in the light of the existence of that right, whether they thought he may have believed, as he said, that he did have a right.

The court, however, is quite satisfied that there is nothing in this point whatever. The whole test of dishonesty is the mental element of belief. No doubt, though the defendant may for certain purposes be presumed to know the law, he would not at the time have the vaguest idea whether he had in law a right to take the car back again, and accordingly when one looks at his mental state, one looks at it in the light of what he believed. The jury were properly told that if he believed that he had a right, albeit there was none, he would nevertheless fall to be acquitted. This court, having heard all that Mr. Herbert has said, is quite satisfied that there is no manner in which this summing up can be criticised, and that accordingly the appeal against conviction should be dismissed.

Appeal dismissed

Questions

1. A's overcoat was taken by some person unknown from the cloakroom of a restaurant. A few days later, it turned up again on one of the pegs. A took it away. Was this theft by A? Would it make any difference if he thought that the law gave him no right to repossess himself of the coat but required him to report the matter to the police and leave them to take steps to get the coat back?

(Refer to the discussion on attempting the impossible, *ante*, pp. 316 *et seq*.

2. Is the following case distinguishable from *R.* v. *Turner* (*No.* 2)?

In *R.* v. *Meredith* [1973] Crim. L.R. 253, M.'s car was impounded by the police while he was at a football match and removed to the police station yard, where it was left locked. When M. went to the police station, he found it crowded and so, rather than wait, he took his car away from the yard without contacting any policeman. He was charged with stealing the car. Under the Disposal and Removal of Vehicles Regulations 1968, the owner was liable to pay the statutory charge of £4 if his car had been causing an obstruction. On going to the police he could (i) admit obstruction and pay £4, or (ii) refuse to pay and face prosecution for obstruction, or (iii) agree to pay and receive a bill for £4. In any event he would be allowed to take the car away for the regulations gave the police no power to retain it as against him. It was held by a Crown Court judge that M. had no case to answer.

Subsection 3: An obligation to retain and deal with the property or its proceeds in a particular way

R. v. Hall

[1973] 1 Q.B. 126
Court of Appeal

> H., a travel agent, received money from certain clients as deposits and payments for air trips to America. He paid the money so received into his firm's general account. None of the projected flights materialised and none of the money was refunded. He was convicted of theft. He appealed on the ground that he had not, within the meaning of section 5 (3), been placed under an obligation to retain and deal with in a particular way the sums paid to him.

EDMUND DAVIES L.J.: Two points were presented and persuasively developed by the appellant's counsel: (1) that, while the appellant has testified that all moneys received had been used for business purposes, even had he been completely profligate in its expenditure he could not in any of the seven cases be convicted of "theft" as defined by the Theft Act, 1968; there being no allegation in any of the cases of his having *obtained* any payments by deception, counsel for the appellant submitted that, having received from a client, say, £500 in respect of a projected flight, as far as the criminal law is concerned he would be quite free to go off immediately and expend the entire sum at the races and forget all about his client; . . .

Point (1) turns on the application of section 5 (3) of the Theft Act, 1968, which provides: "Where a person receives property from or on account of another, and is under an obligation to the other to retain and deal with that property or its proceeds in a particular way, the property or proceeds shall be regarded (as against him) as belonging to the other."

Counsel for the appellant submitted that in the circumstances arising in these seven cases there arose no such "obligation" on the appellant. He referred us to a passage in the Eighth Report of the Criminal Law Revision Committee which reads as follows: "*Subsection* (3) provides for the special case where property is transferred to a person to retain and deal with for a particular purpose and he misapplies it or its proceeds. An example would be the treasurer of a holiday fund. The person in question is in law the owner of the property; but the subsection treats the property, as against him, as belonging to the persons to whom he owes the duty to retain and deal with the property as agreed. He will therefore be guilty of stealing from them if he misapplies the property or its proceeds."

Counsel for the appellant . . . submits that the position of a treasurer of a holiday fund is quite different from that of a person like the appellant, who was in general (and genuine) business as a travel agent, and to whom people pay money in order to achieve a certain object—in the present cases, to obtain charter flights to America. It is true, he concedes, that thereby the travel agent undertakes a contractual obligation in relation to arranging flights and at the proper time paying the airline and any other expenses. Indeed, the appellant throughout acknowledged that this was so, although contending that in some of the seven cases it was the other party who was in breach. But what counsel for the appellant resists is that in such circumstances the travel agent "is under an obligation" to the client "to retain and deal with . . . in a particular way" sums paid to him in such circumstances.

What cannot of itself be decisive of the matter is the fact that the appellant paid the money into the firm's general trading account. As Widgery J. said in *R.* v. *Yule* [1964] 1 Q.B. 5, 10, decided under section 20 (1) (iv) of the Larceny Act, 1916: "The fact that a particular sum is paid into a particular banking account . . . does not affect the right of persons interested in that sum or any duty of the solicitor either towards his client or towards third parties with regard to disposal of that sum." Nevertheless, when a client goes to a firm carrying on the business of travel agents and pays them money, he expects that in return he will, in due course, receive the tickets and other documents necessary for him to accomplish the trip for which he is paying, and the firm are "under an obligation" to perform their part to fulfil his expectation and are liable to pay him damages if they do not. But, in our judgment, what was not here established was that these clients expected them "to retain and deal with that property or its proceeds in a particular way," and that an "obligation" to do so was undertaken by the appellant. We must make clear, however, that each case turns on its own facts. Cases could, we suppose, conceivably arise where by some special arrangement (preferably evidenced by documents), the client could impose on the travel agent an "obligation" falling within section 5 (3). But no such special arrangement was made in any of the seven cases here being considered. It is true that in some of them documents were signed by the parties; thus, in respect of counts one and three incidents there was a clause to the effect that the People to People organisation did not guarantee to refund deposits if withdrawals were made later than a certain date; and in respect of counts six, seven and eight the appellant wrote promising "a full refund" after the flights paid for failed to materialise. But neither in those nor in the remaining two cases (in relation to which there was no documentary evidence of any kind) was there, in our judgment, such a special arrangement as would give rise to an obligation within section 5 (3).

It follows from this that, despite what on any view must be condemned as scandalous conduct by the appellant, in our judgment on this ground alone this appeal must be allowed and the convictions quashed. But as, to the best of our knowledge, this is one of the earliest cases involving section 5 (3), we venture to add some observations.

(A) It is . . . essential for the purposes of [s. 2 (1) (b) of the Act] that dishonesty should be present at the time of appropriation. We are alive to the fact that to establish this could present great (and maybe insuperable) difficulties when sums are on different dates drawn from a general account. Nevertheless, they must be overcome if the Crown is to succeed.

(B) Where the case turns, wholly or in part, on section 5 (3) a careful exposition of the subsection is called for. Although it was canvassed by counsel in the present case, it was nowhere quoted or even paraphrased by the commissioner in his summing-up. Instead he unfortunately ignored it and proceeded on the assumption that, as the appellant acknowledged the purpose for which clients had paid him money, *ipso facto* there arose an "obligation . . . to retain and deal with" it for that purpose. He therefore told the jury: "The sole issue to be determined in each count is this. Has it been proved that the money was stolen in the sense I have described, dishonestly appropriated by him for purposes other than the purpose for which the moneys were handed over? Bear in mind that this is not a civil claim to recover money that has been lost." We have to say, respectfully, that this will not do, as cases under section 20 (1) (iv) of the Larceny Act, 1916, illustrate. Thus in *R.* v. *Sheaf* (1927) 134 L.T. 127, it was held that whether money had been "entrusted" to the defendant for and on account of other persons was a question of fact for the jury and must therefore be the subject of an express direction. . . .

(C) Whether in a particular case the Crown has succeeded in establishing an "obligation" of the kind coming within section 5 (3) of the new Act may be a difficult question. Happily, we are not called on to anticipate or solve for the purposes of the present case the sort of difficulties that can arise. But, to illustrate what we have in mind, mixed questions of law and fact may call for consideration. For example, if the transaction between the parties is wholly in writing, is it for the judge to direct the jury that, as a matter of law, the defendant had thereby undertaken an "obligation" within section 5 (3)? On the other hand, if it is wholly (or partly) oral, it would appear that it is for the judge to direct them that, if they find certain facts proved, it would be open to them to find that an "obligation" within section 5 (3) had been undertaken—but presumably not that they must so find, for so to direct them would be to invade their territory. In effect, however, the commissioner unhappily did something closely resembling that in the present case by his above-quoted direction that the only issue for their consideration was whether the appellant was proved to have been actuated by dishonesty.

We have only to add that counsel for the Crown submitted that, even if the commissioner's failure to deal with section 5 (3) amounted to a misdirection, this was a fitting case to apply the proviso. But point (1) successfully taken by defence counsel, is clearly of such a nature as to render that course impossible. We are only too aware that, in the result, there will be many clients of the appellant who, regarding themselves as cheated out of their money by him, will think little of a law which permits him to go unpunished. But such we believe it to be, and it is for this court to apply it.

Conviction quashed

R. v. Meech
[1974] Q.B. 549
Court of Appeal

M. agreed with McCord to cash through his own bank account a cheque in McCord's favour drawn by X, and hand the proceeds to McCord. M.

paid the cheque in but, before he drew out the proceeds, discovered that McCord had obtained the cheque from X by means of a forged instrument. M. then dishonestly planned to deprive McCord of the proceeds by arranging with P. and J. to stage a fake robbery of himself. P. and J. took the proceeds, leaving M. as the apparent victim. When charged with theft of the proceeds, they argued that as McCord's cheque was dishonestly obtained, M. was under no legal obligation to return the cheque or pay over the proceeds. They were convicted and appealed.

ROSKILL L.J.: There can be no doubt that Meech dishonestly misappropriated this money. We leave for later consideration the separate question which was argued on behalf of Parslow and Jolliffe whether they also misappropriated this money dishonestly in conjunction with Meech. The submission was the whatever Meech's position might be, they were not guilty of dishonest misappropriation.

Counsel for all the defendants relied strongly on the series of recent decisions that "obligation" means "legal obligation." The judge so directed the jury. In giving this direction he no doubt had in mind the successive decisions of this court in *R.* v. *Hall* (*ante*, p. 524) *R.* v. *Gilks* (post, p. 532) and *R.* v. *Pearce* (unreported), November 21, 1972 (both the court and counsel were supplied with copies of the judgment). Reliance was also placed on paragraph 76 of Professor Smith's *The Law of Theft*, 2nd ed. (1972)—a passage written just before the decisions referred to. Since the judge so directed the jury, we do not find it necessary further to consider those decisions beyond observing that the facts of those cases were vastly different from those of the present case.

Starting from this premise—that "obligation" means "legal obligation"—it was argued that even at the time when Meech was ignorant of the dishonest origin of the cheque, as he was at the time when he agreed to cash the cheque and hand the proceeds less the £40 to McCord, McCord could never have enforced that obligation because McCord had acquired the cheque illegally. In our view this submission is unsound in principle. The question has to be looked at from Meech's point of view, not McCord's. Meech plainly assumed an "obligation" to McCord which, on the facts then known to him, he remained obliged to fulfil and, on the facts as found, he must be taken at that time honestly to have intended to fulfil. The fact that on the true facts if known McCord might not and indeed would not subsequently have been permitted to enforce that obligation in a civil court does not prevent that "obligation" on Meech having arisen. The argument confuses the creation of the obligation with the subsequent discharge of that obligation either by performance or otherwise. That the obligation might have become impossible of performance by Meech or of enforcement by McCord on grounds of illegality or for reasons of public policy is irrelevant. The opening words of section 5 (3) clearly look to the time of the creation of or the acceptance of the obligation by the bailee and not to the time of performance by him of the obligation so created and accepted by him.

It is further to be observed in this connection that this subsection deems property (including the proceeds of property) which does not belong to the bailor to belong to the bailor so as to render a bailee who has accepted an obligation to deal with the property or to account for it in a particular way but then dishonestly fails to fulfil that obligation, liable to be convicted of theft whereas previously he would have been liable to have been convicted of fraudulent conversion though not of larceny. It was not seriously disputed in argument that before 1968 Meech would have had no defence to a charge of fraudulent conversion.

The first branch of the argument therefore clearly fails. The second argument (as already indicated) was that even if Meech initially became under an obligation to McCord, that obligation ceased to bind Meech once Meech discovered McCord had acquired the cheque by fraud. It was argued that once Meech possessed this knowledge, performance of his pre-existing obligation would have involved him in performing an obligation which he knew to be illegal. Thus, it was said, he was discharged from performance and at the time of his dishonest misappropriation had ceased to be bound by his obligation, so that he could not properly be convicted of theft by virtue of section 5 (3).

This submission was advanced at considerable length before the judge. It is not necessary to relate those arguments more fully. The judge rejected the arguments and he directed the jury in the following terms so far as relevant. After saying that there were three considerations which Meech said affected his mind and led him not to carry out his agreement with McCord, the judge dealt correctly with the first two of the three matters. He continued as follows:

> "Thirdly, he says that he was worried about being involved in the offence of obtaining money by fraud; that he knew this to be, as he described it, a 'dodgy' cheque—knew not at the time that he was handed it, but knew before he drew the cash; that he alleges that from inquiries made on September 11 and 12 he discovered what was seemingly common knowledge among some motor dealers of High Wycombe, that McCord was involved in a dishonest transaction. His knowledge of this was limited and inaccurate, since he thought that there was a name Harris involved. He is not entitled in law to repudiate his agreement merely on the basis of suspicions about McCord. The only basis on which he was entitled to refuse payment was that he refused because if he had honoured the agreement he, Meech, would have committed a criminal offence, or that was his belief. Only if that was the basis—or if you thought on the evidence that may have been the basis—was there no obligation to pay. Otherwise, although you may well think many people had a better right than McCord, so far as Meech was concerned it was his obligation to deal with the proceeds of the cheque in the way that he had agreed with McCord that he would."

The judge thus emphasised that the obligation to McCord remained but that Meech would be excused performance if performance would have involved commission of a criminal offence. Of course if Meech acted as he did honestly and had an honest reason for not performing his obligation and for claiming relief from performance of that obligation, this would clearly be the end of any criminal charge against him. But the jury, as already pointed out, clearly negatived any such honest intention or belief on Meech's part. The argument before this court was that even though he was found to have acted dishonestly, he still could not be convicted of theft . . .

The answer to the main contention is that Meech being under the initial obligation already mentioned the proceeds of the cheque continued as between him and McCord to be deemed to be McCord's property so that if Meech dishonestly misappropriated those proceeds he was, by reason of section 5 (3), guilty of theft even though McCord could not have enforced performance of that obligation against Meech in a civil action. Some reliance was placed on a passage in Professor Smith's *The Law of Theft*, p. 31, para. 76:

> "Thus there is no redress in civil or criminal law against a client who is accidentally overpaid by a bookmaker. The same principle no doubt governs other cases where the transaction is void or illegal by statute or at common law. If this is a defect in the law, the fault lies with the civil law and not with the Theft Act. If the civil law says that the defendant is the exclusive owner of the money and under no obligation to repay even an equivalent sum, it would be incongruous for the criminal law to say he had stolen it."

It must be observed that that passage was written with reference to section 5 (4) of the Theft Act 1968 and not with reference to section 5 (3) of that Act. It immediately follows a discussion of the Gaming Act cases. We do not think the author had a case such as the present in mind. On no view could it be said in the present case that the common law would regard Meech as the "exclusive owner" of the original cheque or of its proceeds. The true owner of the proceeds was the hire-purchase finance company. They could have sued Meech to judgment for the full value of the original cheque. But Meech having received the original cheque from McCord under the obligation we have mentioned, the criminal law provides that as between him and McCord the cheque and its proceeds are to be deemed to be McCord's property so that a subsequent dishonest misappropriation of the cheque or its proceeds makes Meech liable to be convicted of theft. We are therefore clearly of the view that Meech was properly convicted of theft just as under the old law he would have been liable to have been convicted of fraudulent conversion. We therefore think that the judge was quite right in leaving this case to the jury and that the direction which he gave was correct. If it be open to criticism at all, the criticism might be that the direction was arguably too favourable to the defendants.

Two other separate points were argued on behalf of Parslow and Jolliffe. First, it was said that the £1,410 obtained by Meech from his bank by cashing his own cheque were not "the proceeds" of the original cheque but of Meech's own cheque. The answer to that contention is that it is clear that the money received by Meech when he cashed his own cheque plainly emanated from the original cheque and can properly be regarded on the facts of this case as the proceeds of the original cheque.

Secondly, it was argued for Parslow and Jolliffe that there was a misdirection in relation to appropriation. The judge said:

> "As I direct you in law, the time of the appropriation was the time of the fake robbery. Up to that moment, although Meech had drawn the money from the bank, it was still open to him to honour the agreement which he had made with McCord and to pay it over, in due course to McCord; but once the fake robbery had taken place, that was no longer possible."

It was argued that Meech alone had dishonestly misappropriated the proceeds of the cheque when he drew the money from the bank and that thereafter Parslow and Jolliffe were not guilty of dishonest misappropriation since Meech had already dishonestly misappropriated that money once and for all. It was said that Parslow and Jollife were thereafter only liable to be convicted, if at all, of dishonest handling, an offence with which neither was charged.

We think that the judge's direction when he said that the time of the appropriation was the time of the fake robbery was right. A dishonest intention had been formed before the money was withdrawn but the misappropriation only took place when the three men divided up the money at the scene of the fake robbery. It was then that the performance of the obligation by Meech finally became impossible by the dishonest act of these three men acting in concert together.

The convictions must all be affirmed and the appeals dismissed. Meech's application for leave to appeal against sentence is formally refused.

Appeals dismissed

Notes

1. This subsection is to a large extent redundant, because in the vast majority of cases where there is an obligation to retain and deal with the property in a particular way, the person to whom the obligation is owed

will have a proprietary right or interest in the property. Thus with a bailment, the property "belongs to" the bailor, and with a trust, the property "belongs to" the beneficiary, under subsection 1, and in the case of misappropriation by the bailee or trustee there is no need of subsection 3 to secure a conviction. There are so many difficulties involved in subsection 3 that it is unwise of a prosecutor to rely on it unless it is absolutely necessary to do so, which is rarely if ever the case.

2. It is said that the obligation must be a legal one, not a merely moral one (see *R.* v. *Gilks*, *post*, p. 532, a case on subsection 4: "In a criminal statute, where a person's criminal liability is made dependant on his having an obligation, it would be quite wrong to construe that word so as to cover a moral or social obligation as distinct from a legal one"). However an unenforceable obligation arising under a domestic arrangement not intended to have legal force has been held to be enough (*R.* v. *Cullen* 1974, unreported: Smith, § 68). Moreover, according to *R.* v. *Meech* above, an obligation which the accused incorrectly thinks is enforceable against him may be enough. Further, *R.* v. *Meech* appears to hold that the relevant moment is when the accused *undertakes* the obligation; the fact that he is no longer under an obligation at the moment of dishonest appropriation does not save him from conviction. But see section 1 (1): "a person is guilty of theft if he *dishonestly appropriates property belonging to another*. . . ." On the other hand, if the accused is under an obligation at the moment of appropriation, he is not within the words of subsection 3 unless he received the property from or on account of the person to whom he now owes the obligation.

3. The obligation must be to retain and deal with *that property or its proceeds* in a particular way. This excludes an obligation to perform some service or do some act in return for being given the property, *e.g.* where B pays A £500 in return for A's promise to paint his house, A is not obliged to do anything *with* the £500. It is the same, in most cases, if B lends A money. The only obligation in the borrower A is to repay the loan to B, not to do anything with the money lent. A owes B the amount of the loan, but a simple debtor—creditor relationship is not enough. A debtor who dishonestly puts himself in a position to be unable to pay his creditor does not commit theft. "The essential notion is that D must be under a fiduciary obligation with regard to the property which he receives. The idea of fiduciary obligation conveys accurately the essential requirement; the property, though it may be owned solely by D, must be earmarked in D's hands for certain purposes of P's": Smith and Hogan, p. 508.

The sort of situation which might be within the subsection is where A asks B for payment in advance so that he can use the money to buy paint and hire scaffolding for the job on B's house; or where B gives money to A his office boy, so that he can go to the post office and buy stamps for the office. This is not strictly a bailment, since B does not require A to use the very notes and coins; A can mix them with his own money in his wallet, but B does entrust A with the money and in no sense can it be said that A's only duty is to repay B. He must use the money to buy stamps. Similarly if A receives money on behalf of B, and merely has to keep an account of payments received and pay B an amount representing the total received, he is not bound to do anything with the money, and it does not belong to

B: *R.* v. *Robertson* [1977] Crim. L.R. 629. *Aliter*, if he has a duty to keep the money separate from his own before paying it over to B; *R.* v. *Lord* [1905] 69 J.P. 467.

Difficult questions arise where B has the right to sue A in respect of some transaction involving the misuse by A of B's property, or the misuse by A of his position as B's servant or representative. The mere duty to account for an improper profit (*i.e.* to pay over the amount of the profit) does not make the money received property belonging to B. In *R.* v. *Cullum* (1873) L.R. 2 C.C.R. 28, A, the skipper of a muck barge owned by B, in defiance of instructions used the barge for his own purposes and kept the freight thus illegitimately earned. It was held that A was not guilty of embezzlement and he would not today be guilty of theft. In *Powell* v. *MacRae* [1977] Crim. L.R. 971 (D.C.) a servant took a bribe of £2 in connection with his master's business and kept it. It was held that he did not steal the £2 although he could undoubtedly have been sued for £2 by the master. It seems that the accused must be not merely the debtor of, but a constructive trustee for, the prosecutor, in which case the latter will anyway have a proprietory right or interest in the property under subsection 1.

4. Although the obligation is a legal one it is a question of fact whether it exists in any particular case. The judge can rule in accordance with the principles outlined above that there is no obligation of the relevant kind, and direct an acquittal. But he must not rule that there *is* an obligation. *R.* v. *Hayes* (1976) 64 Cr. App. R. 82 (C.A.) was concerned with an estate agent who took deposits from intending purchasers of houses. Widgery L.C.J., in allowing H.'s appeal: "The judge [was] making it perfectly plain that in his view as a matter of law there is an obligation owed by the estate agent either to the vendor or the purchaser according to the way events turn out. We can add, of course, there is an obligation in civil law in such circumstances in favour of one party or the other, but that is not what this question is all about. What this question is all about is whether there is an obligation within the meaning of s. 5 (3) for the purposes of a charge of theft . . . A conviction based on s. 5 (3) is something which should be based upon a verdict of the jury and not some preconceived notion of the judge that in a situation of this kind there must as a matter of law be an obligation" (pp. 85, 87).

In cases where a written contract expressly puts the accused under an appropriate obligation with regard to the property, the only question for the jury will be whether the obligation has been waived by the person to whom it is owed: *R.* v. *Brewster* (1979) 69 Cr. App. R. 375. In other cases, the jury must ask, did the payers *expect* the accused to retain and deal with the property in a particular way: see Edmund Davies L.J. in *R.* v. *Hall*, (*ante*, p. 525). In many cases, such as *R.* v. *Hall* itself where the payers were the multitudinous clients of a travel agency, it will be impossible to discover any general expectation, and any proved particular expectation by an individual client might be unreasonable and unassented to by the accused. The normal practice of traders in the accused's line of business would appear to be a better guide; but even if such were proved and was to the effect that clients' money was usually kept separate, it does not follow that the clients knew of the practice and expected the accused to follow it. In sum, although the judge, as a result of the cases, is confined to offering guidelines to the jury, it will often be far from clear what guidelines can properly be offered.

Subsection 4: Property got by another's mistake

Note

This subsection was passed in order to avoid the result of one particular case—*Moynes* v. *Coopper* [1956] 1 Q.B. 439 (See Smith, § 75). Like subsection 3, it is largely redundant because in most cases where A obtains property from B as a result of B's mistake, the result will be that B will have a proprietory right or interest in the property. A clear case would be if the transaction were void. In such a case there is no need to rely on subsection 4 to convict A if he dishonestly keeps the property: s. 3 (1), *ante*, p. 495. (See *R.* v. *Gilks*, below). Cases where the mistaken transaction is *not* void appear to be what the subsection is aimed at, but for the difficulties which may arise, see Griew, *post*, p. 534.

R. v. Gilks
[1971] 1 W.L.R. 1341
Court of Appeal

> G. in a betting shop bet on various horses, including a horse called Fighting Scot. Some bets won and some lost, but the bet on Fighting Scot lost, that race being won by Fighting Taffy. The betting shop clerk paid G. his winnings and by mistake included a sum of £106 in respect of the bet on Fighting Scot. When he was being paid, G. realised the clerk's mistake, but he took all the money and refused to return any. He was convicted of stealing £106 and appealed.

CAIRNS L.J.: The questions of law arises under the following sections of the Theft Act, 1968 [His Lordship read s. 1 (1), s. 2 (1) and s. 5 (4)].

The deputy chairman gave rulings in law to the following effect: he ruled that at the moment when the money passed it was money "belonging to another" and that that ingredient in the definition of theft in section 1 (1) of the Act of 1968 was therefore present. Accordingly section 5 (4) had no application to the case. If he was wrong about that then, he said, "obligation" in the sub-section included an obligation which was not a legal obligation. He told the jury that it was open to them to convict the defendant of theft in respect of the mistaken overpayment. . . .

The main foundation of one branch of the defendant's case at the trial and in this court was the decision of the Court of Appeal in *Morgan* v. *Ashcroft* [1938] 1 K.B. 49. In that case a bookmaker, by mistake, overpaid a client £24. It was held that the bookmaker was not entitled to recover the money by action because that would involve taking an account of gaming transactions which were void under the Gaming Act, 1845. The argument proceeded as follows: when Ladbrokes paid the defendant they never supposed that they were discharging a legal liability; even if he had won they need not, in law, have paid him. They simply made him a gift of the money. The deputy chairman was wrong in saying that at the moment of payment the money "belonged to another." At that very moment its ownership was transferred and therefore the defendant could not be guilty of theft unless the extension given by section 5 (4) of the Theft Act, 1968, to the meaning of the words "belonging to another" could be brought into play. But section 5 (4) had no application because under the rule in *Morgan* v. *Ashcroft* the defendant had no obligation to repay.

The deputy chairman did not accept this line of argument. He held that it was unnecessary for the prosecution to rely on section 5 (4) of the Act of 1968 because the property in the £106.63 never passed to the defendant. In the view of this court that ruling was right. Section 5 (4) introduced a new principle into the law of theft but long before it was enacted it was held in *R.* v. *Middleton* (1873) L.R. 2 C.C.R. 38 that where a person was paid by mistake (in that case by a Post Office clerk) a sum in excess of that properly payable, the person who accepted the overpayment with knowledge of the excess was guilty of theft. Mr. Gilpin seeks to distinguish the present case from that one on the basis that in *R.* v. *Middleton*, the depositor was entitled to withdraw ten shillings (50p) from his post office savings bank account and the clerk made a mistake in thinking he was entitled to withdraw more than £8, whereas in the present case there was no mistake about the defendant's rights—whether his horse won or lost he had no legal right to payment. In our view this argument is fallacious. A bookmaker who pays out money in the belief that a certain horse has won, and who certainly would not have made the payment but for that belief, is paying by mistake just as much as the Post Office clerk in *R.* v. *Middleton*.

The gap in the law which section 5 (4) of the Theft Act, 1968, was designed to fill was, as the deputy chairman rightly held, that which is illustrated by *Moynes* v. *Coopper* [1956] 1 Q.B. 439. There a workman received a pay packet containing £7 more than was due to him but did not become aware of the overpayment until he opened the envelope some time later. He then kept the £7. This was held not to be theft because there was no *animus furaandi* at the moment of taking, and *R.* v. *Middleton* was distinguished on that ground. In *Moynes* v. *Coopper* it was observed that the law as laid down in *R.* v. *Middleton*, was reproduced and enacted in section 1 (2) (i) of the Larceny Act, 1916. It would be strange indeed if section 5 (4) of the Theft Act, 1968, which was designed to bring within the net of theft a type of dishonest behaviour which escaped before, were to be held to have created a loophole for another type of dishonest behaviour which was always within the net.

An alternative ground on which the deputy chairman held that the money should be regarded as belonging to Ladbrokes was that "obligation" in section 5 (4) meant an obligation whether a legal one or not. In the opinion of this court that was an incorrect ruling. In a criminal statute, where a person's criminal liability is made dependent on his having an obligation, it would be quite wrong to construe that word so as to cover a moral or social obligation as distinct from a legal one. As, however, we consider that the deputy chairman was right in ruling that the prosecution did not need to rely on section 5 (4) of the Act of 1968, his ruling on this alternative point does not affect the result. . . .

Appeal dismissed

Note

Middleton was the subject of acute controversy, and it is at least doubtful whether civil lawyers would agree that the mistake made by the bookmaker's clerk in *Gilks* made the purported transfer of the money to the defendant void. If it did, however, it would seem that the bookmaker could have sued in conversion for the return of money which belonged to him (notwithstanding *Morgan* v. *Ashcroft*, which proceeded on the footing that the property in the money *had* passed to the defendant). If so, Gilks' obligation to restore can hardly be described as a mere moral or social, as opposed to a legal, obligation.

Griew: The Theft Acts 1968 and 1978

"§ 2–27 The subsection presents difficulties of a number and degree that far outstrip its importance, among them the following. First, although no doubt all quasi-contractual obligations at common law to repay money paid under a mistake of fact are covered by section 5 (4), it is not satisfactory that the precise ambit of the subsection should depend upon anything as uncertain as the law of quasi-contract. For instance, the quasi-contractual obligation may turn on difficult distinctions between mistakes of fact and mistakes of law, the former founding a claim to restoration, the latter not. Whether such distinctions should be relevant to criminal liability may be doubted. Secondly, section 5 (4) is not necessarily limited to *common law* obligations to restore money paid by mistake. It is possible, for instance, that D is guilty of theft if he knows that money has been wrongly paid to him under a will (whether the mistake is one of fact or of law) and decides against repaying it. If there is here 'an obligation to make restoration' within the meaning of section 5 (4), the 'person entitled to restoration' may not be the same as the person who paid the money in error; but the sub-section does not require that he should be. The difficult problems attending claims in equity in respect of money paid under a mistake may thus infect the law of theft.

§ 2–28 Thirdly, there has been controversy as to whether the effect of section 5 (4) may be to make guilty of theft (as well as of obtaining property by deception) a person who induces another by deception to transfer ownership of property to him and who appropriates that property, intending not to restore it or its value. Such a person, it would seem, 'gets property by another's mistake.' Where D by deception induces P to make a payment in circumstances giving P a quasi-contractual right to recover money paid under a mistake of fact, there should be no difficulty. If, for example, D falsely stated facts which would have the effect that money was due under an existing contract, and P paid that money, the money would no doubt be 'got' by mistake and a duty to make restoration of it would exist; section 5 (4) would apply. But where P pays money or delivers property under a contract (say for the sale of goods) which is itself voidable because of D's fraud, it is said [in Smith, § 80] that D has no obligation to make restoration unless and until the contract is avoided by a disaffirming act on P's part, and that on that ground section 5 (4) does not apply to such a case. It is odd, if it be the case, that D is not under an obligation to restore what he has obtained by fraud until the fraud is discovered. Nevertheless, to reject this view would involve giving an unduly wide effect to a provision with a limited purpose, or would require a very artificial reading of the sub-section in order to avoid that result."

Note

Whatever the outcome of the controversy referred to in Griew, § 2–28 above, it seems that wherever A fraudulently induces B's mistake, he will be guilty of theft anyway by virtue of the decision in *Lawrence* v. *Commissioner of Police, ante*, p. 496.

iv. "With the Intention of Depriving Permanently"

Note

The definition of theft in section 1 requires that the appropriation should be with the *intention of permanently depriving the owner of it.* The italicised words are the same as those in the definition of larceny in section 1 of the Larceny Act, 1916.

The intention to deprive must be a settled one at the time of the appropriation. As to an intention to deprive if and only if the goods on examination turn out to be what the taker wants, see next case.

R. v. Easom
[1971] 2 Q.B. 315
Court of Appeal

E. took a handbag, searched through it, found nothing to interest him, and left it with contents intact near the owner, who repossessed it. E. was convicted of theft of the bag and its detailed contents.

EDMUND DAVIES L.J.: This is an appeal by the appellant against his conviction at the Inner London Quarter Sessions last October on an indictment charging him with theft, the particulars of the charge being that, on December 27, 1969, he "stole one handbag, one purse, one notebook, a quantity of tissues, a quantity of cosmetics and one pen, the property of Joyce Crooks."

The circumstances giving rise to the charge may be shortly stated. In the evening of December 27, 1969, woman Police Sergeant Crooks and other plainclothes officers went to the Metropole cinema in Victoria. Sergeant Crooks sat in an aisle seat and put her handbag (containing the articles enumerated in the charge) alongside her on the floor. It was attached to her right wrist by a piece of black cotton. Police Constable Hensman sat next to her on the inside seat. When the house lights came on during an interval, it was seen that the appellant was occupying the aisle seat in the row immediately behind Sergeant Crooks and that the seat next to him was vacant. Within a few minutes of the lights being put out, Sergeant Crooks felt the cotton attached to her wrist tighten. She thereupon gave Police Constable Hensman a pre-arranged signal. The cotton was again pulled, this time so strongly that she broke it off. Moments later the officers could hear the rustle of tissues and the sound of her handbag being closed. Very shortly afterwards the appellant left his seat and went to the lavatory. The officers then turned round and found Sergeant Crook's handbag on the floor behind her seat and in front of that which the appellant had vacated. Its contents were intact. When the appellant emerged from the lavatory and seated himself in another part of the cinema, he was approached by the police officers. When the offence of theft was put to him, he denied it.

... In every case of theft the appropriation must be accompanied by the intention of permanently depriving the owner of his property. What may be loosely described as a "conditional" appropriation will not do. If the appropriator has it in mind merely to deprive the owner of such of his property as, on examination, proves worth taking and then, finding that the booty is valueless to the appropriator, leaves it ready to hand to be re-possessed by the owner, the appropriator has not stolen. If a dishonest postal sorter picks up a pile of letters, intending to steal any which are registered, but on finding that none of them are, replaces them, he has stolen nothing, and this is so notwithstanding the provisions of section 6 (1) of the Theft Act, 1968. In the present case the jury were never invited to consider the possibility that such was the appellant's state of mind or the legal consequences flowing therefrom. Yet the facts are strongly indicative that this was exactly how his mind was working, for he left the handbag and its contents entirely intact and to hand, once he had carried out his exploration. For this reason we hold that conviction of the full offence of theft cannot stand.

In so concluding, we have not overlooked that counsel for the Crown has, since the trial, altered his view of the case and now shares that expressed by the deputy chairman that the appellant should either have been convicted of the full offence charged or acquitted completely. Indeed he now submits that conviction for the full offence was justified. In support of this changed view we were referred to a passage in 1 Hale P.C. (1778 ed.), p. 533, which reads: "So if A without drawing his weapon requires B to deliver his purse, who doth deliver it, and finding but two shillings in it gives it to him again, this is a taking by robbery. 20 Eliz. Crompt. 34." But in our judgment counsel seeks to attach excessive weight to this short reference, and the true approach thereto is to be found in *Archbold's Criminal Pleading, Evidence and Practice*, 37th ed. (1969), p. 558 para. 1469, in the following words: "Returning the goods . . . can be considered merely as evidence of the defendant's intention when he took them; for *if it appears that he took them originally with the intent of depriving the owner of them, and of appropriating them to his own use,*" [my italics] "his afterwards returning them will not purge the offence."

So once more, one is driven back to consider with what intention the appellant embarked upon the act of taking. This court, in *R.* v. *Stark* (unreported), October 5, 1967, quashed the conviction for larceny of a man caught in the act of lifting a tool-kit from the boot of a car, the judge having misdirected the jury by telling them: "Was Stark intending, if he could get away with it, and if it was worthwhile, to take that tool-kit when he lifted it out? If he picked up something, saying 'I am sticking to this—if it is worthwhile,' then he would be guilty." But does it follow from all this that the appellant (as to whose identity and physical acts the verdict establishes that the jury entertained no doubt) has to go scot-free? Can he not, as the Crown originally submitted, be convicted at least of attempted theft? Even though the contents of the handbag, when examined, held no allure for him, why was he not as guilty of attempted theft as would be the pickpocket who finds his victim's pocket empty (see *R.* v. *Ring* (1892) 61 L.J.M.C. 116). Does a conditional intention to steal count for nothing? In his *Criminal Law (The General Part)*, 2nd ed. (1961), p. 52, para. 23, Professor Glanville Williams says: "A conditional intention is capable of ranking as intention for legal purposes. Thus it is no defence to an apparent burglar that his intention was merely to steal a certain paper if it should happen to be there." He then cites the American Model Penal Code, s. 2.02(6) (T.D. No. 4 pp. 14, 129), which states that: "When a particular purpose is an element of an offence, the element is established although such purpose is conditional, unless the condition negatives the harm or evil sought to be prevented by the law defining the offence."

But as to this, all, or, at least, much, depends upon the manner in which the charge is framed. Thus, "if you indict a man for stealing your watch, you cannot convict him of attempting to steal your umbrella" (*per* Cockburn C.J. in *R.* v. *M'Pherson* (1857) D. & B. 197, 200)—unless, of course, the court of trial has duly exercised the wide powers of amendment conferred by section 5 of the Indictment Act, 1915. In our judgment, this remains the law and it is unaffected by the provisions of section 6 of the Criminal Law Act, 1967. No amendment was sought or effected in the present case, which accordingly has to be considered in relation to the articles enumerated in the theft charge and nothing else. Furthermore, it is implicit in the concept of an attempt that the person acting intends to do the act attempted, so that the *mens rea* of an attempt is essentially that of the complete crime (see *Smith and Hogan, "Criminal Law,"* 2nd ed. (1969), p. 163). That being so, there could be no valid conviction of the appellant of attempted theft on the present indictment unless it were established that he was animated by the same intention permanently to deprive Sergeant Crooks of the goods enumerated in the particulars of the charge as would be necessary to establish the full offence. We hope that we have already made sufficiently clear why we consider that, in the light of the evidence and of the direction given, it is impossible to uphold the verdict on the basis that such intention was established in this case.

For these reasons, we are compelled to allow the appeal and quash the conviction.

Appeal allowed

Note

"What may be loosely described as a conditional appropriation will not do. If the appropriator has it in mind merely to deprive the owner of such of his property as, on examination, proves worth taking and then, finding that the booty is valueless to the appropriator, leaves it ready to hand to be repossessed by the owner, the appropriator has not stolen." For the subsequent history of this dictum of Edmund-Davies L.J. (above), which caused difficulties in burglary with intent to steal, see *Attorney-General's References* (*Nos.* 1 *and* 2 *of* 1979), *post*, p. 641.

Questions

1. "If a dishonest postal sorter picks up a pile of letters, intending to steal any which are registered, but on finding that none of them are, replaces them, he has stolen nothing." Is this hypothetical case put by Edmund-Davies L.J. indistinguishable from what Easom did? See Glanville Williams, *Textbook*, Chap. 29, § 6.

2. Is there a distinction between A, who resolves "I intend to return this article unless it proves worth stealing," and B, who resolves "I intend to keep this article if it proves worth stealing?" Could the law sensibly treat one of these cases as an intent to steal without treating the other similarly?

3. If the postal sorter had authority to pick up the letters, could he, in the hypothetical case, be said to have appropriated them? See, *ante*, p. 499. See generally, Koffman, *Conditional Intent to Steal*, [1980] Crim. L.R. 463. Greenwood, *Intention to Steal Reconsidered* (1980) 39 C.L.J. 17, 21.

Note

Edmund-Davies L.J. says that his hypothetical sorter was not guilty of theft "notwithstanding the provisions of Section 6 (1) of the Theft Act 1968." Nevertheless, that section does apparently make theft of *some* cases of conditional intent to deprive permanently.

Theft Act 1968, section 6

"(1) A person appropriating property belonging to another without meaning the other to lose the thing itself is nevertheless to be regarded as having the intention of permanently depriving the other of it if his intention is to treat the thing as his own to dispose of regardless of the other's rights; and a borrowing or lending of it may amount to so treating it if, but only if, the borrowing or lending is for a period and in circumstances making it equivalent to an outright taking or disposal.

(2) Without prejudice to the generality of subsection (1) above, where a person, having possession or control (lawfully or not) of property belonging to

another, parts with the property under a condition as to its return which he may not be able to perform, this (if done for purposes of his own and without the other's authority) amounts to treating the property as his own to dispose of regardless of the other's rights."

R. v. Warner

(1970) 55 Cr. App. R. 93
Court of Appeal

W. took a bag of tools belonging to T. and hid it. W. said that the employees of W.'s firm had a dispute with the employees of T.'s firm, and he took the bag in order to annoy T., meaning to return it in about an hour. He was convicted of theft and appealed.

EDMUND-DAVIES L.J.: . . . The one point involved in the appeal is whether the Crown established that the appellant intended permanently to deprive the owner of certain goods which he unquestionably took. That was also the sole issue at the trial, and a direction to the jury in homely language regarding the effect of section 1 (1) of the Theft Act, 1968, was all that was called for from the Chairman. But the matter became elaborated in such a way that we have come to the conclusion that there is no alternative but to allow this appeal. . . .

There was a clear issue accordingly as to whether the appellant had or did not have the necessary criminal intention of permanently depriving Mr. Thorne of his tools. It was the only issue which learned counsel on both sides desired to have left to the jury.

But the learned Chairman unfortunately did not leave it in that clear way. Instead, there came a stage when he made reference to section 6 of the Theft Act. Mr. Turner, appearing for the Crown, made it quite clear that in his view section 6 had no bearing upon the case. Reference to it was certainly not calculated to enlighten the jury in the discharge of their task.

The Theft Act, 1968, aspired to remove legal subtleties devoid of merit. Although it makes new law in certain respects, nowhere does it abandon the basic conception both of the common law and of earlier legislation that there can be no theft without the intention of permanently depriving another of his property. Section 1 (1) declares that intention an essential ingredient, and nothing to be found elsewhere in the Act justifies a conviction for theft in its absence.

The learned Chairman began with a direction which was both clear and correct, saying, "There is one big question of fact for you and it is this: did the defendant, who undoubtedly did what the Crown witnesses say he did and what he himself admits he did, do it dishonestly with the intention of permanently depriving the owner of his property?" But unfortunately his direction later became confused by his references to section 6, the object of which he may himself have misunderstood. There is no statutory definition of the words "intention of permanently depriving" but section 6 seeks to clarify their meaning in certain respects. Its object is in no wise to cut down [*sic*: *semble*, expand] the definition of "theft" contained in section 1. It is always dangerous to paraphrase a statutory enactment, but its apparent aim is to prevent specious pleas of a kind which have succeeded in the past by providing, in effect, that it is no excuse for an accused person to plead absence of the necessary intention if it is clear that he appropriated another's property intending to treat it as his own, regardless of the owner's rights. Section 6 thus gives illustrations, as it were, of what can amount to the dishonest intention demanded by section 1 (1). But it is a misconception to interpret it as watering down section 1.

The first passage in the summing-up which may well have confused the jury in this regard was in the following terms: "So far as 'appropriating property belonging to another' is concerned, you have got to be satisfied that he had the intention of permanently depriving the other of it, and there are indications in the statute that 'permanently depriving the other of it' may be 'indefinitely' depriving the other of it, because who shall say when something has become permanent rather than indefinite? The justification for such an approach to section 1 is to be found in section 6 of the same Act. . . ." [His Lordship quoted an exchange between the Chairman and counsel for the accused, which included the following:] Mr. Green: "There is one further point. When you were discussing the intention, you did make some remarks about 'indefinitely.' I would be grateful if you could tell the jury merely that, if he intended to give it back, that would be a complete defence." The Chairman: "Yes, but the only question is when? That is why I referred to section 6, because if it is his intention to treat the thing as his own to dispose of, regardless of the owner's rights, and if you dispose of them by putting them in a box covered with scarves so that the other man loses the use of his tools indefinitely, it seems that there is no difference between that and 'permanently. . . .'"

We are troubled by the use made by the Chairman of section 6 and particularly of his interpretation of the word "dispose" in the phrase "if his intention is to treat the thing as his own to dispose of regardless of the other's rights" in subsection (1) thereof. The real mischief, as it seems to us, lies in the following passage: ". . . if you dispose of them . . ." (that is, the tools which were the subject-matter of the charge) ". . . by putting them in a box covered with scarves *so that the other man loses the use of his tools indefinitely*, it seems that there is no difference between that and 'permanently.'" To imply that putting the tools in a box of itself indicated an intention to keep them indefinitely begs the essential question in the case. One of the basic issues at the trial was when and why they were put into the box at all, the defence evidence being that this was not done until after the police arrived on the scene and that it was then done purely out of panic.

What does not, we think, clearly emerge from the passage just quoted is that the essential question was whether the accused man had *ever* formed the intention to deprive the owner indefinitely of the use of his tools. If he had, then he could in certain circumstances be regarded as intending to treat the thing as his own to dispose of, regardless of the other's rights, within the meaning of section 6 (1). But if this was not so, if, for example, his intention was to deprive the owner of the use of his goods for a limited period, the precise length of which he had not yet decided upon, but fully intending to return them to their owner in due course, this would not necessarily justify conviction for theft and in the majority of cases probably would not do so. This, we think, is clearly brought out by the second part of section 6 (1), which, harking back to the earlier words, continues: ". . . a borrowing or lending is for a period and in circumstances making it equivalent to an outright taking or disposal." We do not think that this essential point was made clear to the jury.

Appeal allowed

J. R. Spencer, "The Metamorphosis of Section 6 of the Theft Act" [1977] Crim. L.R. 653

"An 'intention to deprive' was, of course an element of the crime of larceny. Over the course of many years, the concept had been interpreted in numerous cases. Generally, an *intention* to deprive, rather than mere recklessness, was necessary. Thus abandoning another person's property knowing there was a risk that he would never get it back was not larceny, unless the person who did so actually desired the owner to lose it, or (presumably) foresaw the virtual certainty that he would do so. However, there were three judge-made extensions of 'intention permanently to deprive' where mere recklessness, or something like it, was sufficient. (a) There was the 'ransom principle,' whereby it counted as an intention permanently to deprive if the idea was to return the property to the owner only if he was prepared to pay for it. (b) There was the 'essential quality principle,' whereby it counted as an intention permanently to deprive if the idea was to return the property only after it had undergone some fundamental change of character: a live horse taken but a dead horse returned, a valid ticket taken but a cancelled ticket returned. And (c) there was the 'pawning principle,' where it counted as an intention permanently to deprive if a person pawned another's property without his consent, hoping to be able to redeem the pledge, but knowing he might be unable to do so. The Criminal Law Revision Committee heartily approved of 'intention permanently to deprive' as so elaborated by the courts, and it was the one element of larceny which the Committee thought could be transplanted into the new crime of theft without any alteration. The Committee assumed that the old case-law would automatically be applied if the phrase were enacted in the definition of theft without any attempt at further elaboration. It therefore opposed putting a section into the Theft Act elaborating 'intention of permanently depriving,' and carefully omitted any such clause from the Draft Theft Bill which it appended to its Eighth Report. However, somebody who had the ear of the Government thought otherwise . . . [after tracing the tangled Parliamentary history of the new clause]; Not surprisingly, the courts have so far failed to spot Parliament's real intention through the obscure verbiage in which Parliament has dressed it up. To date, they have been quite mystified by the section. . . .

A fair summary of the Court of Appeal's interpretation of section 6 in [*R.* v. *Warner*] would be the following.

> "The section was enacted to extend 'intention permanently to deprive' beyond its previous interpretation; however, it was only meant to do so to some infinitesimal degree, and we are not prepared to say in which direction; any judge who drags section 6 into his summing-up can expect to be reversed on appeal."

It has certainly not crossed anybody's mind that section 6 was designed to *preserve* the existing case law. In *Duru* (see below) the Court of Appeal applied the 'essential quality' principle, but did so without reference to section 6. And in *Easom* (*ante*, p. 535) Edmund Davies L.J. indicated that a conditional intention to deprive was insufficient for theft, notwithstanding section 6; whereas the 'pawning principle' and the 'ransom principle,' which section 6 was intended to preserve, are obvious instances of conditional intention.

Thus, as a result of section 6, the present meaning of 'intention of permanently depriving' in theft is doubly in doubt. The expression is thought to be extended beyond its literal meaning by section 6, but we do not know how far or in what direction. And we do not know how far, if at all, the pre-1968 case law on 'intention permanently to deprive' can be relied on."

R. v. Duru

[1974] 1 W.L.R. 2

Court of Appeal

D., on behalf of X, submitted to the Greater London Council an application for an advance on mortgage, in which D. knowingly mistated X's income. As a result, a cheque for £6,002.50 was obtained from the Council and paid to solicitors acting for X and the Council. D. was convicted of obtaining property by deception (which offence requires an intention to deprive permanently: see *post*, p. 573). On appeal:

MEGAW L.J.: ... Was there any intention on the part of the appellants ... permanently to deprive the Greater London Council of property? What is said there is this. The charge as laid was the charge of obtaining property, namely, a cheque. That cheque must be treated either as being the piece of paper, or as being the money which was represented by the cheque as being the money that would be paid by the Greater London Council's bank on the due presentation to it of the cheque. It is said that there was no intention on the part of either of the appellants that the Greater London Council should be permanently deprived of the cheque in any of these cases for the simple reason that the cheque itself would ultimately, after it had been paid by the Greater London Council's bank on presentation, go back and become available to the Greater London Council. Therefore, it is said, in accordance with the contemplation of the appellants, there was not going to be a permanent depriving of the property because if their intention was duly carried out, the cheques themselves, the pieces of paper, would go back to the Greater London Council.

Alternatively, it is said, if the relevant property is to be regarded as the money payable by virtue of the cheque, there was never any intention to deprive the Greater London Council permanently of that money, because these transactions of mortgage were transactions involving a loan of the money and it was intended by everybody concerned that the money represented by the cheques, when it was received by the solicitors and passed on in due course by them to the mortgagors, would be merely loans, and the money in due time would be repaid. Therefore, again, there was no intention to deprive the Greater London Council permanently of the money.

In the view of this court again there is a simple answer to both those points, which are devoid of legal merit as much as they are of any substantial merit. A cheque is a common instance of a 'thing in action', as it is called. The definition of 'property' in s. 4(1) of the Theft Act 1968 says:

'"Property" includes money and all other property, real or personal, including things in action and other intangible property.'

Count 3, which has been read, and the other corresponding counts, use the word 'cheque' as being the property which the appellants obtained by deception. 'Cheque' there was meant, and would be understood by anybody in the ordinary use of language to mean, what in law is described as a thing in action: the legal right which is conveyed to persons who are entitled to deal with that cheque by having possession of it and having obtained it lawfully.

In the view of this court there can be no doubt that the intention of both of these appellants, as would necessarily have been found by the jury if the matter had been left to the jury on a proper direction of law (a direction which would no doubt have been given if the pleas of guilty had not been entered), was permanently to deprive the Greater London Council of that thing in action, that cheque; that piece of paper, in the sense of a piece of paper carrying with it the right to receive payment of the sum of £6,000.50, which is the amount concerned in count 3.

So far as the cheque itself is concerned, true it is a piece of paper. But it is a piece of paper which changes its character completely once it is paid, because then it receives a rubber stamp on it saying it has been paid and it ceases to be a thing in action, or at any rate it ceases to be, in its substance, the same thing as it was before: that is, an instrument on which payment falls to be made. It was the intention of the appellants, dishonestly and by deception not only that the cheques should be made out and handed over, but also that they should be presented and paid, thereby permanently depriving the Greater London Council of the cheque in substance as their things in action. The fact that the mortgagors were under an obligation to repay the mortgage loans does not affect the appellants' intention permanently to deprive the council of these cheques.

If it were necessary to look to s. 6(1) of the Theft Act 1968, this court would have no hesitation in saying that that subsection, brought in by the terms of s. 15(3), would also be relevant, since it is plain that the appellants each had the intention of causing the cheque to be treated as the property of the person by whom it was to be obtained, to dispose of, regardless of the rights of the true owner.

Appeal dismissed

Notes

1. For the difficulties involved in holding that the property was a thing in action belonging to the G.L.C., see notes to *R.* v. *Kohn, ante*, p. 511.

2. The Court of Appeal in *R.* v. *Duru* applied the "essential quality" principle (as Spencer calls it, *ante*, p. 540) without reference to section 6. No doubt, in the same way, the section is not necessary for the application of the "ransom" principle, for an example of which see next case.

R. v. Hall
(1849) 2 C. & K. 947
Court for Crown Cases Reserved

A took fat from the loft of B, a tallow-melter, and brought it to B's candle-room, and placed it on a scale, and wished B to buy it as fat sent by a butcher named R. He was convicted of larceny of the fat.

LORD DENMAN C.J.: The question here is, whether there was an intent to deprive the owner of his property permanently. How could it be done more effectually than by selling it? It is no matter to whom it is sold. I am clearly of the opinion that the direction of the learned Recorder was perfectly right.

PARKE B.: The intent of the party here was not only to deprive the owner of his goods but to commit the impudent fraud of making him buy his own goods and pay for them.

ALDERSON B.: Here the owner is never to get his goods again, but by paying the full value for them.

Conviction confirmed

R. v. Holloway
(1849) 2 C. & K. 942
Court for Crown Cases Reserved

A, who was in the employ of B, a tanner, took skins from a warehouse of B to C, the foreman of B, at another part of the premises, pretending that he had done work on them for which he had not been paid. A intended to return the skins to his master when he had been paid for his pretended work on them. He was convicted of larceny of the skins.

LORD DENMAN C.J.: But for the cases, I should have thought that there was much to be said. In the case I have put, of a horse taken away for a year, and then to be returned, it would seem to be rather singular if the law did not make that larceny. But if we were to hold, that wrongfully borrowing a thing for a time, with an intention to return it would constitute a larceny, many very venial offences would be larcenies. In late cases there has been an understanding that, to constitute larceny, it is essential that there should be an intent to deprive the owner permanently of his property. It is certainly an odd excuse for a person who is challenged with his master's property, that he meant to return it, after having cheated his master, in the first place, and his fellow-workman, in the second; still, a man can hardly do this without committing some offence, although it be not larceny.

Conviction quashed

Questions

1. What would be A's offence today?
2. If A had been a supplier of skins to B, and had moved some from the place in the warehouse where B put skins for which he had already paid A to the place where he kept skins for which he had not yet paid, with intent to receive payment twice over, would this be theft? See *R.* v. *Manning* (1852) Dears. 21.

Notes

1. The language of section 6 (1) appears to relieve the Court in some cases from the trouble of investigating the accused's real intention, by providing that in those cases, he "is to be regarded as having the intention of permanently depriving the other of it." But it is held not to have this effect. In *R.* v. *Cocks* (1976), 63 Cr. App. R. 79, the direction to the jury was to the effect that if it was clear that C's intention was to treat the thing as his own to dispose of regardless of the owner's rights, there was no need to consider whether he meant to deprive the owner permanently. This was held to be a misdirection, and the conviction was quashed. After quoting Edmund-Davies L.J.'s dictum in *R.* v. *Warner* (*ante*, p. 538), that section 6's "apparent aim is to prevent specious pleas of a kind which have succeeded in the past by providing, in effect, that it is no excuse for an accused person to plead absence of the necessary intention if it is clear that he appropriated another's property intending to treat it as his own, regardless of the owner's rights," the Court of Appeal criticised the judge's direction as leaving the jury to disregard whether at the taking of the property from the victim, C had formed the intention of permanently depriving her of it, a matter which it was essential for them to consider in coming to a true and just verdict in the case. But if absence of the necessary intention is "no excuse," it is hard to see why it should be essential for the jury to consider the matter. *R.* v. *Cocks* adds force to the opinion of Griew (§ 2.59) that section 6 should be referred to in exceptional cases only.

2. Indeed it is difficult to envisage exceptional cases where section 6 needs to be resorted to. Even wrongful pawning (the third "principle" mentioned by Spencer, *ante*, p. 540), which is dealt with separately in section 6 (2), is probably comprehended in the expression "intention to deprive permanently." In *R.* v. *Phetheon* (1840) 9 C. & P. 552, 553, Gurney B. scouted the idea that it was not such an intention with the words "A more glorious doctrine for thieves it would be difficult to discover, but a

more injurious doctrine for honest men cannot be well imagined." But from *R.* v. *Medland* (1851) 5 Cox 292, it appeared that it might not be theft if, in addition to an intention to redeem the pawn, there was a well-founded expectation in the accused that he would be able to do so. It is possible that this is one case which is made theft by virtue of section 6.

Question

A, a rich man temporarily short of funds, pawns B's property to C, intending and expecting to redeem it at the end of the week. Is A to be regarded as having the intention of permanently depriving B? Consider section 6 (2) (*ante*, p. 537), and in particular the opening words.

Note

If the answer to the above question is Yes, A might still escape conviction if he is not acting dishonestly: see, *post*, p. 555.

v. "Temporary Deprivation"

Criminal Law Revision Committee's Eighth Report, Cmnd. 2977

§ 56 ". . . We considered whether temporary deprivation of property in general should be included in theft or made a separate offence under the Bill. There is certainly a case for making temporary deprivation punishable in circumstances in which it may involve dishonesty comparable with that involved in theft and may cause serious loss or hardship. The taker gets the benefit of the property without payment, and the owner is correspondingly deprived. The property may be lost or damaged, or it may be useless to the owner by the time it is returned. . . . But the committee generally are against extending theft to include temporary deprivation or creating a general offence of temporary deprivation of property. The former course seems to them wrong because in their view an intention to return the property, even after a long time, makes the conduct essentially different from stealing. Apart from this either course would be a considerable extension of the criminal law, which does not seem to be called for by any existing serious evil. It might moreover have undesirable social consequences. Quarrelling neighbours and families would be able to threaten one another with prosecution. Students and young people sharing accommodation who might be tempted to borrow one another's property in disregard of a prohibition by the owner would be in danger of acquiring a criminal record. Further, it would be difficult for the police to avoid being involved in wasteful and undesirable investigations into alleged offences which had no social importance. It is difficult to see how the provision could be framed in a way which would satisfactorily exclude trivial cases and meet these objections. If cases of temporary deprivation should become common, or if it should become too easy a defence to a charge of theft that the intention was to return the property in the end, it might be necessary, notwithstanding these formidable difficulties, to create an offence of temporary deprivation with a high enough maximum penalty for serious cases."

Note

The Committee nevertheless identified two particular cases where temporary deprivation should be an offence. They are articles in places open to the public, and conveyances. Special offences in relation to them appear in sections 11 and 12 of the Theft Act 1968 respectively.

For criticism of the details of both of these special offences, and of the general principle that temporary deprivation should not be theft, see, *post*, p. 553.

(a) *Removal of Articles from Places open to the Public*

Criminal Law Revision Committee's Eighth Report, Cmnd. 2977

§ 57 "A striking recent instance is the removal from the National Gallery of Goya's portrait of the Duke of Wellington. The portrait, before being returned, was kept for four years, during which there was evidence that the man who took it tried to make it a condition of his returning it that a large sum should be paid to charity. He was acquitted of stealing the portrait (but convicted of stealing the frame, which was never recovered and which, if his initial statement was true, he destroyed soon after taking it). In another case an art student took a statuette by Rodin from an exhibition, intending, as he said, to live with it for a while, and returned it over four months later. (Meanwhile the exhibitors, who had insured the statuette, had paid the insurance money to the owners, with the result that the statuette, when returned, became the property of the exhibitors.) Yet another case was the removal of the Coronation Stone from Westminster Abbey. There is obviously a substantial question whether conduct of this kind should be made criminal. Many people may think that taking in cases of these kinds should be punishable, if not as theft, then as a special offence. Churches, art galleries, museums and other places open to the public may contain articles of the greatest importance and value, many of them irreplaceable. They cannot always be protected as well as in private premises and, if removed, may easily be lost or damaged. Against this it can be argued that serious cases of the kind are rare and, judging from the cases mentioned, that offenders are more eccentric than genuinely criminal. Before the Goya case few people would have said that there was an evil unprovided for and serious enough to require the creation of a new offence: and there are objections to extending the criminal law because of isolated occurrences. There may also be the danger that the taker will be less likely to return the property eventually if he is liable to punishment for having removed it. We have come to the conclusion that the situation, especially in view of the Goya case, is serious enough to justify the creation of a special offence in spite of the possible objections. . . ."

Note

The Committee felt that the offence ought to be designed as one of criminal damage, so did not draft a clause in their Bill. Nevertheless section 11 was inserted during the Theft Bill's passage through Parliament.

Theft Act 1968, section 11

"(1) Subject to subsections (2) and (3) below, where the public have access to a building in order to view the building or part of it, or a collection or part of a collection housed in it, any person who without lawful authority removes from the building or its grounds the whole or part of any article displayed or kept for display to the public in the building or that part of it or in its grounds shall be guilty of an offence.

For this purpose 'collection' includes a collection got together for a temporary purpose, but references in this section to a collection do not apply to a collection made or exhibited for the purpose of effecting sales or other commercial dealings.

(2) It is immaterial for purposes of subsection (1) above, that the public's access to a building is limited to a particular period or particular occasion; but where anything removed from a building or its grounds is there otherwise than as forming part of, or being on loan for exhibition with, a collection intended for permanent exhibition to the public, the person removing it does not thereby commit an offence under this section unless he removes it on a day when the public have access to the building as mentioned in subsection (1) above.

(3) A person does not commit an offence under this section if he believes that he has lawful authority for the removal of the thing in question or that he would have it if the person entitled to give it knew of the removal and the circumstances of it.

(4) A person guilty of an offence under this section shall, on conviction on indictment, be liable to imprisonment for a term not exceeding five years."

R. v. Barr [1978] *Crim. L.R. 244:* B for a joke took a cross and a ewer from a Victorian church, and placed them at the head and feet of C, who was sleeping in the churchyard, so that C, on awakening, thought he was dead. B then returned the articles to the church. The public were admitted for devotional purposes only, and the articles were placed in the church to complete the furnishings and as symbols to aid devotion. *Held* (Bristol Crown Court) (1) "access . . . in order to view . . . the collection" was a reference to the purposes of the occupier of the building, not the persons who had access, and (2) the articles were not "displayed," which meant exhibited in the sense in which an art gallery exhibits a painting. No case to answer.

R. v. Durkin [1973] *1 Q.B. 786:* An art gallery had more pictures than it could display at one time, and displayed them in rotation, those not being displayed at any time being kept in store. D. removed a picture from the walls of the gallery on a Sunday, when the gallery was closed, and demanded, as the price of its return, *inter alia*, that the gallery should open on Sundays and that a pair of the mayor's underpants should be raffled and the proceeds given to charity. *Held* (Court of Appeal), in subsection 2, a " collection intended for permanent exhibition" included one which was permanently available for exhibition, even if particular paintings were not displayed on some occasions when the gallery was open. The fact that the taking took place on a day when the gallery was closed was therefore immaterial.

Questions

1. Would it have made any difference if the painting had been in store in the cellar when Durkin took it?
2. Could Durkin have been convicted of theft?
3. Would it be an offence under section 11 to remove an elephant from London Zoo?

(b) *Taking Conveyances*

Note

If A took goods from B and later abandoned them in a position whence it would naturally be expected that B would eventually recover them, it was difficult to prove that the taking was with intent to deprive B. The fact that abandoned motor-cars are invariably returned, through the system of universal registration of motor vehicles, to their registered owners, made it difficult to convict a "joy-rider" of larceny of the motor car. The legislature therefore invented a crime for motor vehicles (see section 217 of the Road Traffic Act 1960) which could be described as larceny without intention permanently to deprive. Boats were covered by the Vessels Protection Act 1967, and the offence was widened still further by section 12 of the Theft Act, under which aircraft are covered for the first time.

Theft Act 1968, section 12

"(1) Subject to subsections (5) and (6) below, a person shall be guilty of an offence if, without having the consent of the owner or other lawful authority, he takes any conveyance for his own or another's use, or, knowing that any conveyance has been taken without such authority, drives it or allows himself to be carried in or on it.

(2) A person guilty of an offence under subsection (1) above shall on conviction on indictment be liable to imprisonment for a term not exceeding three years.

(3) Offences under subsection (1) above and attempts to commit them shall be deemed for all purposes to be arrestable offences within the meaning of section 2 of the Criminal Law Act, 1967.

(4) If on the trial of an indictment for theft the jury are not satisfied that the accused committed theft, but it is proved that the accused committed an offence under subsection (1) above, the jury may find him guilty of the offence under subsection (1).

(5) Subsection (1) above shall not apply in relation to pedal cycles; but, subject to subsection (6) below, a person who, without having the consent of the owner or other lawful authority, takes a pedal cycle for his own or another's use, or rides a pedal cycle knowing it to have been taken without such authority, shall on summary conviction be liable to a fine not exceeding fifty pounds.

(6) A person does not commit an offence under this section by anything done in the belief that he has lawful authority to do it or that he would have the owner's consent if the owner knew of his doing it and the circumstances of it.

(7) For purposes of this section—

(a) 'conveyance' means any conveyance constructed or adapted for the carriage of a person or persons whether by land, water or air, except that it does not include a conveyance constructed or adapted for use only under the control of a person not carried in or on it, and 'drive' shall be construed accordingly; and

(b) 'owner' in relation to a conveyance which is the subject of a hiring agreement or hire-purchase agreement, means the person in possession of the conveyance under that agreement."

R. v. Bow
(1976) 64 Cr. App. R. 54
Court of Appeal

B. and A., in A.'s car, were stopped in a narrow private road by gamekeepers who suspected them of poaching. In order to stop A. driving away before the arrival of the police, who had been sent for, a gamekeeper blocked the road with his Land Rover. B. got into the Land Rover, released the brake and coasted down the road for 200 yards, which enabled A.'s car to be driven off. B. was convicted of taking the

Land Rover, and appealed on the ground that there was no evidence that he took it "for his own or another's use."

BRIDGE L.J.: Mr. Toulson, for whose interesting and careful argument we are extremely grateful, makes two submissions in summary. First, he submits that the case should have been withdrawn from the jury on the footing that there was indeed no evidence that the taking of the Land Rover was for the appellant's own use. Secondly, and alternatively, if he is wrong on the first submission he says that in any event the issue raised a question of fact which should have been left by the judge to be determined by the jury.

It is convenient to say at the outset that no point turns in this appeal on the fact that the Land Rover's engine was not used by the appellant. Mr. Toulson does not suggest that the case falls to be decided any differently because the appellant was able to coast downhill for 200 yards than if he had driven 200 yards using the engine.

It is appropriate to recall that the present statutory offence created by section 12 of the Act of 1968 is defined in two respects in significantly different language from the language which was used in earlier statutes, the latest embodiment prior to 1968 having been in section 217 of the Road Traffic Act 1960. Under the Act the offence was defined as committed by "a person who takes and drives away a motor vehicle without having either the consent of the owner or other lawful authority." . . .

Mr. Toulson's basic submission is in these terms. He contends that if a person moves a vehicle for the sole reason that it is in his way and moves it no further than is necessary to enable him to get past the obstruction, he is not taking that vehicle for his own use. The starting point of the argument is the decision of this court in *R.* v. *Bogacki* [1973] 1 Q.B. 832. In that case the three defendants were charged with attempting to take without authority a motor bus. The evidence showed that they had gone to a bus garage late at night and attempted to start the engine of a bus without success. The trial judge directed the jury as follows, adverting specifically to the change of language between section 12 of the Act of 1968 and section 217 of the Act of 1960. He said: "The offence is not, I repeat, the offence is not taking and driving away, it is merely taking and 'taking', members of the jury, means assuming possession of an object for your own unauthorised use, however temporary that assumption of possession might be. May I give you an example. Suppose that you left your motorcar parked in the car park behind a cinema, and you forgot to lock the door but you shut the door, and suppose that a man and a woman, some time later, when the motorcar was unattended, came along, opened the door, got into the car, and had sexual intercourse in the car. This particular offence would then have been committed by them." Later he said with respect to the defendants before him: "The question is: Did they without the permission of the owners, acquire possession, for however short a time, for their unauthorised purpose? That is the question."

In giving the judgment of this Court in that case Roskill L.J. said at p. 837: "The word 'take' is an ordinary simple English word and it is undesirable that where Parliament has used an ordinary simple English word elaborate glosses should be put upon it. What is sought to be said is that 'take' is the equivalent of 'use' and that mere unauthorised user of itself constitutes an offence against section 12. It is to be observed that if one treats 'takes' as a synonym for 'uses,' the subsection has to be read in this way: 'if . . . he uses any conveyance for his own or another's use. . . .' That involves the second employment of the word 'use' being tautologous, and this court can see no justification where Parliament has used the phrase 'if . . . he takes any conveyance for his own or another's use' for construing this language as meaning if he 'uses any conveyance for his own or another's use,' thus giving no proper effect to the words 'for his own or another's use.' For those reasons the court accepts Mr. Lowry's submission that there is still built in, if I may use the phrase, to the word 'takes' in the subsection the concept of movement and that before a man can be convicted of the completed offence under section 12(1) it must be shown that he took the vehicle, that is to say, that there was an unauthorised taking possession or control of the vehicle by him adverse to the rights of the true owner or person otherwise entitled to such possession or control, coupled with some movement, however small . . . of that vehicle following such unauthorised taking."

Basing himself on that decision, Mr. Toulson submits, cogently as we think, that since the concept of taking in the definition of the offence already involves moving the vehicle taken, the words "for his own or another's use" must involve something over and above mere movement of the vehicle. What then is the concept embodied in this phrase "for his own or another's use"?

On this point the argument ranged widely, but we hope that at the end of the day it is an adequate summary of the final submission made on it by Mr. Toulson to say that he contends that what is involved is that the conveyance should have been used as a conveyance, *i.e.* should have been used as a means of transport. That submission seems to us to be well-founded. Mr. Toulson points out that the mischief at which this section is aimed has been appropriately defined as "stealing a ride." The interpretation of the phrase "for his own or another's use" as meaning "for his own or another's use as a conveyance" would fall into line, we think, with the discriminations suggested in *Smith and Hogan's Criminal Law*, 3rd ed. (1973) at p. 462, where the following passage occurs: "But subject to the requirement of taking, the offence does seem, in essence, to consist in stealing a ride. This seems implicit in the requirement that the taking be for 'his own or another's *use*.' Thus if D releases the handbrake of a car so that it runs down an incline, or releases a boat from its moorings so that it is carried off by the tide this would not as such be an offence within the section."

Pausing at that point in the quotation from the textbook, the reason why neither of those examples would constitute an offence within the section would be that in neither case, although the conveyance had been moved, would it have been used as a conveyance.

The quotation from the textbook goes on: "The taking must be for D's use or the use of another and if he intends to make no use of the car or boat there would be no offence under section 12. But it would be enough if D were to release the boat from its moorings so that he would be carried downstream in the boat." In that case, since he would be carried downstream in the boat there would be a use of the boat as a conveyance, as a means of transporting him downstream."

So far the court is in agreement with Mr. Toulson's submissions. But then the next step has to be taken. The next step is, as Mr. Toulson submits, that merely to move a vehicle which constitutes an obstruction so that it shall be an obstruction no more cannot involve use of the vehicle as a conveyance. It is at this point that the submission requires to be carefully analysed.

Clearly one can envisage instances in which an obstructing vehicle was merely pushed out of the way a yard or two which would not involve any use of it as a conveyance. But the facts involved in the removal of the obstructing vehicle must be examined in each case.

Mr. Matheson, for the Crown, meets this submission squarely by pointing to the circumstance that here the Land Rover was in the ordinary sense of the English language driven for 200 yards. Attention has already been drawn to the fact that no distinction was relied upon by Mr. Toulson between a vehicle driven under its own power and a vehicle driven by being allowed to coast down hill. Mr. Matheson says that again, as a matter of ordinary use of English, in the course of driving the vehicle a distance of 200 yards the appellant was inevitably using it as a conveyance and that his motive for so doing is immaterial. This submission for the Crown, it is pointed out to us, is in line with another suggestion by Professor Smith in his textbook on the *Law of Theft*, 3rd ed. (1972), paragraph 317, where he says: "Probably driving, whatever the motive, would be held to be 'use'."

In reply, Mr. Toulson submits that even if it be right that the appellant had in the ordinary sense of the word to drive the Land Rover for 200 yards, and even if that did involve its use as a conveyance, nevertheless the offence was still not made out because the purpose of the taking was not to use the conveyance as a conveyance but merely to remove it as an obstruction. He emphasises that the words of the section are: "takes for his own use," not "takes and uses." This is in our judgment a very subtle and refined distinctly and if it were admitted it would open a very wide door to persons who take conveyances without authority and use them as such to dispute their guilt on the ground that the motive of the taking was something other than the use of the conveyance as such.

The short answer, we think, is that where as here, a conveyance is taken and moved in a way which necessarily involves its use as a conveyance, the taker cannot be heard to say that the taking was not for that use. If he has in fact taken the conveyance and used it as such, his motive in so doing is, as Mr. Matheson submits, quite immaterial. It follows, in our judgment, that the trial judge was right, not only to reject the submission of no case, but also to direct the jury, as he did, that on the undisputed facts the appellant had taken the Land Rover for his own use. Accordingly the appeal will be dismissed.

Appeal dismissed

Note

"Some movement, however small . . ." is also required for the other offence in section 12 "allowing himself to be carried in or on it": *R.* v. *Miller* [1976] Crim. L.R. 147; *R.* v. *Diggin* [1980] R.T.R. 83.

Questions

1. Is it the "taking" or the contemplated "use" which must be "as a conveyance?"

2. In *R.* v. *Pearce* [1973] Crim. L.R. 321 (C.A.), P was held rightly convicted of the offence when he picked up a rubber dinghy, put it on a trailer and drove away with it. Is this decision inconsistent with *R.* v. *Bow*?

See, generally, White, "Taking the Joy out of Joy-Riding" [1980] Crim. L.R. 609.

McKnight v. Davies
[1974] R.T.R. 4
Queen's Bench Division

M. was a lorry driver, his duty being to deliver goods from his employer's depot to shops, and on completion of deliveries to return the lorry to the depot. On completion of his deliveries, M. was driving back to the depot when he damaged the lorry by driving it under a low bridge. He was scared, drove to a public house and had a drink. After that he drove three men to their homes on the outskirts of the city, drove back to the centre and had another drink. He then drove home and parked the lorry overnight near his home, returning it to the depot next morning. He was convicted of an offence under section 12 and appealed.

LORD WIDGERY C.J.: There can, I think, be little doubt that the lorry was being used, following the accident with the bridge, for the defendant's own use, and the argument centres on whether on the facts found he can be said to have 'taken' the conveyance at all.

A similar question arose under section 28 of the Road Traffic Act 1930 in *Mowe* v. *Perraton* [1952] 1 All E.R. 423. In that case a lorry driver had made an unauthorised deviation from his route in the course of his working day in order to pick up a radiogram and take it to the address of a friend. He had no authority from his employers to use the vehicle for a private purpose of that character, and he was charged with a breach of the corresponding provision in the Road Traffic Act 1930. In this court it was held that he had not committed the offence charged, Lord Goddard C.J. pointing out that section 28 of the Act of 1930—and, I quote, 35 Cr. App. R. 194, 196:

> '. . . was intended to deal with a case where a person takes a motor car which does not belong to him, drives it away and then abandons it . . . This is a case of a man who took and drove a motor vehicle during his work. What he did was an unauthorised thing, but that does not make the taking or the driving away a criminal offence under section 28.'

That authority on its face suggests that the offence could not be committed by a man who was lawfully entrusted with a vehicle for a limited purpose, but subsequently used it in excess of the purpose for which it had been given to him.

The point was next raised in this Court in *R.* v. *Wibberley* [1966] 2 Q.B. 214 where a driver employed to drive a vehicle had taken it home at the end of the day and parked it outside his house. It was within the authority of his employers to leave the vehicle outside overnight instead of taking it back to the depot. Having so parked it, and after an interval, the defendant took the vehicle out on a private mission of his own, and it was held that he was properly convicted of taking the vehicle for the purpose of the present legislation. The earlier decision in *Mowe* v. *Perraton* was distinguished on the footing that, since the driver had finished his working day and parked the vehicle in the place where it should be parked for the night, it was possible to say that when he returned to the vehicle and began to drive it he had taken it for present purposes.

The third authority to which I would refer is *R.* v. *Phipps* [1970] R.T.R. 209 a decision of the Court of Appeal. That case fell to be decided under section 12 of the Theft Act 1968, and I will read the headnote, in (1970) 54 Cr. App. R. 300:

> 'Where a defendant has been given permission by the owner of a motor vehicle to take and use it for a limited purpose, but on completion of that purpose fails to return it and thereafter uses it without any reasonable belief that the owner would consent, the defendant is guilty of taking the vehicle without the consent of the owner, contrary to section 12 of the Theft Act 1968.'

That decision, as I understand it, is inconsistent with the judgment of Lord Goddard C.J. in *Mowe* v. *Perraton.* In *R.* v. *Phipps* the Court of Appeal clearly rejected the argument that a lawful acquisition of possession or control of the vehicle meant that an unauthorised use by the driver could never amount to a taking for the purpose of section 12.

In my judgment we must choose between those two decisions, and I have no hesitation in saying that we should follow the decision of the Court of Appeal in *R.* v. *Phipps.* It is therefore, not in itself an answer in the present case for the defendant to say that he was lawfully put in control of the vehicle by his employers. The difficulty which I feel is in defining the kind of unauthorised activity on the part of the driver, whose original control of the vehicle is lawful, which will amount to an unlawful taking for the purpose of section 12. Not every brief, unauthorised diversion from his proper route by an employed driver in the course of his working day will necessarily involve a 'taking' of the vehicle for his own use. If, however, as in *R.* v. *Wibberley* he returns to the vehicle after he has parked it for the night and drives it off on an unauthorised errand, he is clearly guilty of the offence. Similarly, if in the course of his working day, or otherwise while his authority to use the vehicle is unexpired, he appropriates it to his own use in a manner which repudiates the rights of the true owner, and shows that he has assumed control of the vehicle for his own purposes, he can properly be regarded as having taken the vehicle within section 12.

As Professor Smith puts it (in *Smith's Law of Theft* 2nd ed. (1972) p. 113) he has:

> '. . . altered the character of his control over the vehicle, so that he no longer held as servant but assumed possession of it in the legal sense.'

In the present case I think that the defendant took the vehicle when he left the first public house. At that point he assumed control for his own purposes in a manner which was inconsistent with his duty to his employer to finish his round and drive the vehicle to the depot. I think that the justices reached the correct conclusion and I would dismiss the appeal.

Appeal dismissed

R. v. Peart
[1970] 2 Q.B. 672
Court of Appeal

> P. obtained the loan of a car to drive to Alnwick. In fact he did not go to Alnwick, but to Burnley, a journey which he knew the owner would not have consented to. He was convicted of an offence under Section 12 and appealed.

SACHS L.J.: . . . Whilst, however, reserving the point as to whether in regard to section 12(1) of the Theft Act, 1968, a fundamental misrepresentation can vitiate consent, this court has today to deal with a false pretence of the most usual category, no different in principle to the false pretences which come before the courts on a great variety of occasions. If this court acceded to the submission put forward by the Crown, it would have some far-reaching consequences which can hardly have been within the intention of the legislature. If, for instance, the false representation induced someone to enter into a hiring agreement or a hire-purchase agreement by reason of which alone the representor obtained possession of and licence to take away a vehicle, that would then result in an offence which falls within the ambit of section 12(1). That does not, however, appear to this court to be the mischief aimed at by the legislature. So to hold would in effect be inventing a fresh crime of obtaining possession by false pretences, an offence unknown to the law except when accompanied by intent to deprive the owner permanently of possession. It is a feature of the law of this country that unless there is an intent permanently to deprive of possession, temporary deprivation of an owner of his property is in general no offence. . . .

Appeal allowed

Note

Since most fraud does not vitiate consent to the original taking (*Peart*), but since use in excess of a limited permission constitutes a fresh taking without consent (*Phipps*) an anomalous distinction can arise. If A, who borrows a car ostensibly to go to Beachy Head, and then return, goes to

Beachy Head and does not return but goes on to Birmingham, he commits the offence. But if A, who borrows a car ostensibly to go to Beachy Head, goes at once to Birmingham and nowhere near Beachy Head, he does not commit the offence. It makes a difference, but surely ought not to do so, whether A goes to Birmingham by way of Beachy Head. Some commentators prefer *Phipps* to *Peart* (see Smith, § 287), but perhaps it can be said that the trouble really arises because the Courts have jettisoned Lord Goddard's opinion (in *Mowe* v. *Perraton, ante,* p. 551) that the offence was intended to deal with a case where a person takes a motor car which does not belong to him, drives it away and then abandons it.

Questions

1. A took B's car without B's knowledge, without believing that B would consent if he knew of the taking. When B found out about the taking, he said he would have consented had he known. Is A guilty of an offence under section 12? See *R.* v. *Ambler* [1979] R.T.R. 217.

2. A took B's horse from a field, saddled and bridled it, and rode it away. Has A taken a conveyance? See s. 12 (7), and *Neal* v. *Gribble* (1978) 68 Cr. App. R. 9.

(c) *Criticism*

Glanville Williams: Temporary Appropriation Should be Theft [1981] Crim. L.R. 129

"That the law of theft, taken by itself, would be inadequate is recognised not only by the survival of conspiracy to defraud but by the creation of special statutory offences. It is an offence under the Post Office Act 1953, s. 53 unlawfully to take a postal packet in course of transmission by post, without any necessity for an intent to deprive the owner permanently. The same is true for the taking and concealment of judicial documents. It is an offence to take fish even though the angler throws them back immediately upon catching them. Blackmail for the purpose of making a temporary acquisition of property can be punished as blackmail (see *post,* p. 630) but a robbery for the same purpose is not robbery in law, this offence being dependent on the definition of theft. Better-known exceptions are those created by sections 11 and 12 of the Theft Act 1968 (the former inserted in response to the public indignation at the outcome of the *Goya* case). But the exceptions are rather arbitrary. Why should it be an offence to make off temporarily with a cart but not with a horse, or with a statuette from a public museum but not from an auction sale-room when the public have been invited to view the articles or from a private collection that specific people have been invited to view? Why should the statutory offence be committed by going off with a valuable duck from the grounds of a zoo if the zoo houses some of its exhibits in a building open to the public (*e.g.* a parrot-house) but not if the public are left entirely in the open air? Is a church a building 'where the public have access in order to view the building or part of it, or a collection or part of a collection housed in it,' or is it exclusively a place of worship? In *Barr* (*ante,* p. 546) it was ruled in the Crown Court that public access is given for devotional purposes only, and not 'in-order to view'. If that is correct for the ordinary church, what about Westminster Abbey? It may be remembered that during the early hours of Christmas morning, 1950, some Glasgow students took the Stone of Scone from the Abbey, subsequently leaving it at Arbroath Abbey; so the point may not be wholly without practical importance.

The special offences do not mesh with other offences involving the concept of theft. For example, it is not burglary to break into a public musuem to remove an exhibit for temporary enjoyment, or to break into a garage to take off a car for a temporary criminal purpose. . . .

Suppose that a person removes a small piece of sculpture from a private exhibition, or a valuable book from a University library, and returns it after a year. During that time it has of course been lost to its owner; and both the owner and the police have been put to trouble. (If the owner has made a claim upon an insurer or bailee, and been compensated on the basis of total loss, he may even find that the insurer or bailee claims the right to sell the article when it is recovered, so that the owner loses it). The taker of the article may use it in such a way as to put it at risk, or he may make a profit from it, or he may return it in an impaired condition; and if he is a person of no substance the owner's civil remedy against him will be an insufficient penalty. . . .

As in the case of the missing Goya, the temporary removal of a thing may be done with the intention of causing loss to the owner, or with an intention that necessarily involves such loss. Another example of this relates to copyright and industrial espionage. It is not theft or any other offence to remove a paper that is due to be set in an examination in order to read it and then return it (See *Oxford* v. *Moss*, *ante*, p. 512) even though the result is that the examining body has to go to the expense of setting another paper. Nor is it an offence to remove a film unlawfully in order to make pirated copies, or to remove a secret document in order to copy it and sell the copy to a trade rival. A conspiracy to do these things may be punished as a conspiracy to defraud (see *Scott* v. *M.P.C.*, *ante*, p. 346), but is it right that the criminal law should take no notice of this behaviour by individuals? . . .

Yet it is not only a question of the risk of *losing* the article. When an article is unlawfully taken, even if only for a temporary purpose and without substantial risk of permanent loss of the article, the owner suffers an immediate loss, namely in respect of the use of it. . . .

One of the principle arguments for changing the law is that the value of articles lies in their use. More and more things are used by way of hiring, for longer or shorter periods, instead of by ownership. Many articles of use have comparatively short useful 'lives'. In a few years they wear out or become unfashionable or technically obsolete. Therefore, to deprive the owner of the article even for a short period is to deprive him of an appreciable part of its utility. Besides, the owner is in the dilemma of either being without the article for that time or putting himself to the expense of buying another—an expense that may turn out to have been unnecessary if the article is returned. The loss of the article will be particularly annoying if the owner has relied upon having the article for a particular purpose, which becomes frustrated. . . .

Particular trouble is caused to the police and others when dangerous articles are taken, as when in 1966 a Cobalt 60 isotope was taken from a factory by someone who broke in and then dumped it in a barrel of water in the factory area; shortly afterwards the same isotope was taken again. The fact that such a dangerous article is returned reduces but by no means eliminates the danger to the public and the nuisance of those responsible for the article when it is unlawfully carried off. . . .

Only two arguments against making the proposed extension of the Theft Act are worth consideration. The first, that it would be contrary to tradition, or that people would not recognise temporary appropriations as theft, can perhaps be answered by pointing to the legal systems that have this concept already. Many of the illustrations given in this article would, I think, readily be regarded as theft by many people. For example, it would, I am sure, generally be regarded as theft for a person to take a bicycle, use it for several weeks, and then abandon it on the street, even if the owner eventually recovers it. In the debate on the Theft Bill in the House of Lords, Viscount Dilhorne made the interesting point that none of the definitions of the word 'steal' in the *Oxford English Dictionary* required an intent to deprive the owner permanently; they spoke only of the dishonest taking or appropriating of the property of another. In one respect the definition of theft has always gone far beyond popular usage; the slightest moving of the article with the necessary intent is traditionally theft, though the ordinary man would not regard the theft as complete at that stage. Under the Theft Act it seems to be sufficient merely to touch the article, since touching is one of 'the rights of an owner' within section 3(1). It is strange to swallow this camel while straining at the gnat of saying that it is theft to decamp with someone's valuable article and to conceal it from him dishonestly for what may be a considerable period of time.

It may be that the reader, while accepting some of the arguments in this article, has throughout been afflicted by one other doubt. Is it seriously suggested that trivial cases of dishonestly using the property of another should be subject to prosecution as theft?

The argument about trivial cases is frequently used to oppose extensions of the law, but it is never conclusive in itself, because practically every offence covers *some* trivial matters. If an offence is needed to deal with serious misconduct, that is sufficient to justify it. Even the present law could be abused by prosecuting for trivial thefts, but in practice a sensible discretion is generally exercised. The Canadian experience bears out the view that a law of *furtum usus* is unlikely to be used oppressively. . . . The question has generally arisen in Canada in connection with people who walk off with articles of furniture from beer parlours or hotels; and I see no injustice or oppression in convicting them of theft, even though they aver, after being found out, that they were about to come back with the article. . . .

My main legislative proposal is that the word 'permanently' should be repealed in section 1(1) of the Theft Act 1968. It should also be repealed in section 15(1), since it was put there only out of supposed logical necessity after being put in section 1(1). There is no reason of policy why a cheat who obtains the hire of a car by deception should not be guilty of obtaining property by deception. The fact that this conduct can now be brought, somewhat awkwardly, within the offence of obtaining services under the Theft Act 1978, s. 1 is no argument for not making this change in the Act of 1968. . . ."

vi. "Dishonestly"

Theft Act 1968, section 2

"(1) A person's appropriation of property belonging to another is not to be regarded as dishonest—

(a) if he appropriates the property in the belief that he has in law the right to deprive the other of it, on behalf of himself or of a third person; or

(b) if he appropriates the property in the belief that he would have the other's consent if the other knew of the appropriation and the circumstances of it; or

(c) (except where the property came to him as trustee or personal representative) if he appropriates the property in the belief that the person to whom the property belongs cannot be discovered by taking reasonable steps.

(2) A person's appropriation of property belonging to another may be dishonest notwithstanding that he is willing to pay for the property."

Criminal Law Revision Committee, Eighth Report, Cmnd. 2977

§ 39 "The word 'dishonestly' in the definition in clause 1(1) is very important, as dishonesty is a vital element in the offence. The word replaces the requirement in 1916 section 1(1) that the offender should take the property 'fraudulently and without a claim of right made in good faith'. 'Dishonestly' seems to us a better word than 'fraudulently'. The question 'Was this dishonest?' is easier for a jury to answer than the question 'Was this fraudulent?' 'Dishonesty' is something which laymen can easily recognise when they see it, whereas 'fraud' may seem to involve technicalities which have to be explained by a lawyer. The word 'dishonestly' could probably stand without a definition and some members of the committee would have preferred not to define it. But we decided to include the partial definition in clause 2 in order to preserve specifically two rules of the present law. The first is the rule mentioned above that a 'claim of right made in good faith' is inconsistent with theft; this rule is preserved in different language in paragraph (a) of clause 2(1). The second is the rule in 1916 section 1(2)(d) that a finder of property cannot be guilty of stealing it unless he 'believes that the owner can be discovered by taking reasonable steps'; this rule is reproduced in slightly different language in paragraph [c] of clause 2(1)."

Note

Paragraph (*b*) of section 2 (1) clarifies what was not clear before, namely, whether it is an offence where the accused knows that he has no consent to what he is doing but believes that he would have been given consent if the owner had been asked.

Question

In *R.* v. *Thurborn* (1849) 1 Den. 387, T. found in the street a banknote with no means of identification on it. As soon as he picked it up, he resolved to appropriate it to his own use, but before he could spend it, he was told who the owner was. He nevertheless disposed of the note and was held not guilty of larceny, because he did not, at the time he found the note, know how the owner could be found. In view of sections 2 (1) (*c*) and 3 (1) (*ante*, pp. 495, 555) would T. today be guilty of theft? At what stage did he assume the rights of an owner? Does section 5 (4) (*ante*, p. 515) offer any assistance?

Note

A situation not precisely covered by section 2 is the case of a man who takes property (*e.g.* money) without any colour of right, knowing that the owner does not and would not consent, but intending to restore the equivalent (*e.g.* other coins to the value of the money taken). Section 2 (2) covers the case but not conclusively, saying that such an appropriation *may* be dishonest. See next case.

R. v. Feely
[1973] Q.B. 530
Court of Appeal

F. was the manager of a bookmaker's betting shop. His employers wrote to all their managers stating that the practice of borrowing from tills was to stop. He nevertheless took £30 for his own purposes. He claimed that he always meant to return the money. He was convicted of stealing the money and appealed.

LAWTON L.J.: The appeal raises an important point of law, namely, can it be a defence *in law* for a man charged with theft and proved to have taken money to say that when he took the money he intended to repay it and had reasonable grounds for believing and did believe that he would be able to do so? The trial judge, Judge Edward Jones, adjudged that such a defence is not available. If the law recognises such a defence the question arises whether the decisions of this court in *R.* v. *Cockburn*, [1968] 1 W.L.R. 281 and its predecessor in *R.* v. *Williams* [1953] 1 Q.B. 660 are applicable to a charge of theft under section 1 of the Theft Act, 1968, and, if they are, whether those cases were correctly decided. The court wishes at the outset to stress that the problem we have had to consider has been whether there can be such a defence *in law*. The experience of all of us has been that persons who take money from tills, safes or other receptacles, knowing full well that they have no right to do so, are usually and rightly convicted of theft. Nothing in this judgment should lead anyone, particularly those tempted to put their hands into other people's tills, to think that for the future the prospects of acquittal will be substantially improved. . . .

The trial judge ended his summing-up with these words: "As a matter of law, members of the jury, I am bound to direct you, even if he were prepared to pay back the following day and even if he were a millionaire, it makes no defence in law to this offence. If he took the money, that is the essential matter for you to decide". At no stage of his summing-up did he leave the jury to decide whether the prosecution had proved that the defendant had taken the money dishonestly. This was because he seems to have thought that he had to decide as a matter of law what amounted to dishonesty and he expressed his concept of dishonesty as follows: ". . . if someone does something deliberately knowing that his employers are not prepared to tolerate it, is that not dishonest?"

Should the jury have been left to decide whether the defendant had acted dishonestly? The search for an answer must start with the Theft Act, 1968, under section 1 of which the defendant had been indicted. The long title of this Act starts with these words: "An Act to revise the law of England and Wales as to theft and similar or associated offences. . . ." The draftsman seems to have searched the statute book for all the statutes dealing with offences of dishonesty and it is probable that all the old enactments have been repealed so as to enable the Theft Act to deal comprehensively with this branch of the law. The design of the new Act is clear, nearly all the old legal terms to describe offences of dishonesty have been left behind; larceny, embezzlement and fraudulent conversion have become theft; receiving stolen goods has become handling stolen goods; obtaining by false pretences has become obtaining pecuniary advantage by deception. Words in everyday use have replaced legal jargon in many parts of the Act. This is particularly noticeable in the series of sections (1 to 6) defining theft.

"Theft" itself is a word known and used by all and is defined, in what the marginal note to section 1 of the Act of 1968 describes as the basic definition, as follows: "A person is guilty of theft if he dishonestly appropriates property belonging to another with the intention of permanently depriving the other of it. . . ." These words swept away all the learning which over the centuries had gathered round the common law concept of larceny and in more modern times around the statutory definition of that offence in section 1 (1) of the Larceny Act, 1916.

In section 1 (1) of the Act of 1968, the word "dishonestly" can only relate to the state of mind of the person who does the act which amounts to appropriation.

Whether an accused person has a particular state of mind is a question of fact which has to be decided by the jury when there is a trial on indictment, and by the magistrates when there are summary proceedings. The Crown did not dispute this proposition, but it was submitted that in some cases (and this, it was said, was such a one) it was necessary for the trial judge to define "dishonestly" and when the facts fell within the definition he had a duty to tell the jury that if there had been appropriation it must have been dishonestly done.

We do not agree that judges should define what "dishonestly" means. This word is in common use whereas the word "fraudulently" which was used in section 1(1) of the Larceny Act, 1916, had acquired as a result of case law a special meaning. Jurors, when deciding whether an appropriation was dishonest can be reasonably expected to, and should, apply the current standards of ordinary decent people. In their own lives they have to decide what is and what is not dishonest. We can see no reason why, when in a jury box, they should require the help of a judge to tell them what amounts to dishonesty. We are fortified in this opinion by a passage in the speech of Lord Reid in *Cozens* v. *Brutus* [1973] A.C. 854, a case in which the words "insulting behaviour" in section 5 of the Public Order Act, 1936, had to be construed. The Divisional Court had adjudged that the meaning of the word "insulting" in this statutory context was a matter of law. Lord Reid's comment was as follows, at p. 861: "In my judgment that is not right. The meaning of an ordinary word of the English language is not a question of law. The proper construction of a statute is a question of law. If the context shows that a word is used in an unusual sense the court will determine in other words what that unusual sense is. But here there is in my opinion no question of the word 'insulting' being used in any unusual sense. . . . It is for the tribunal which decides the case to consider, not as law but as fact, whether in the whole circumstances the words of the statute do or do not as a matter of ordinary usage of the English language cover or apply to the facts which have been proved".

When this trenchant statement of principle is applied to the word "dishonestly" in section 1 (1) of the Theft Act, 1968, and to the facts of this case, it is clear in our judgment that the jury should have been left to decide whether the defendant's alleged taking of the money had been dishonest. They were not, with the result that a verdict of guilty was returned without their having given thought to what was probably the most important issue in the case.

This would suffice for the appeal were it not for the two decisions to which reference has already been made. In *R.* v. *Williams* [1953] 1 Q.B. 660, the two appellants, who were husband and wife, carried on a general shop, part of which was a sub-post office. The wife was the sub-postmistress. The business of the shop got into difficulties and in order to get out of them the wife, with the knowledge of her husband, took money from the Post Office till to discharge some of the debts of the business. In her evidence, which was supported by that of her husband, she said that she thought she would be able to repay the money out of her salary from the Post Office and from sales from the business. The husband said that he knew it was wrong to do what they had done, but he thought that it would come right in the end. They were found guilty on a number of counts and in respect of two the jury added a rider that the appellants had intended to repay the money and honestly believed that they would be able to do so, but in respect of three counts, although they intended to repay, they had no honest belief that they would be able to do so. The main ground of the appeal was that the jury had been misdirected as to the word "fraudulently" in section 1 (1) of the Larceny Act, 1916.

The judgment of the Court of Criminal Appeal was delivered by Lord Goddard C.J. It is pertinent to point out that he considered that the appellants' own evidence had established fraudulent behaviour as they had admitted putting false accounts forward to disguise and conceal what they had been doing. The question in the case which is relevant for the purposes of this appeal was whether the facts found by the jury and recorded in their riders afforded any defence. This required the court to construe the words "fraudulently and without a claim of right made in good faith" in section 1 (1) of the Larceny Act, 1916, which unlike the Theft Act, 1968, was never intended to alter the law but to consolidate and simplify it: see its long title. Lord Goddard C.J. in [1953] 1 Q.B. 660 at 665 rejected the opinion of Parke B. in *R.* v. *Holloway* (1848), 3 Cox C.C. 241, that the word "fraudulently" meant "without a claim of right" and went on to say, at p. 666: "The court thinks that the word 'fraudulently' does add, and is intended to add, something to the words 'without a claim of right', and that it means (though I am not saying that the words I am about to use will fit every case, but they certainly will fit this particular case) that the taking must be intentional and deliberate, that is to say, without mistake."

In so far as Lord Goddard C.J. adjudged that a meaning had to be given to the word "fraudulently" he was clearly right; and on the facts of the case with which he was dealing the rest of what he said was right; but if and in so far as he sought to lay down principles applicable in *all* cases we feel bound to say that we do not agree with him. For example, he said, at p. 668: "They knew that they had no right to take the money which they knew was not their money. The fact that they may have had a hope or expectation in the future of repaying that money is a matter which at most can go to mitigation and does not amount to a defence."

It is possible to imagine a case of taking by an employee in breach of instructions to which no one would, or could reasonably, attach moral obloquy; for example, that of a manager of a shop, who having been told that under no circumstances was he to take money from the till for his own purposes, took 40p from it, having no small change himself, to pay for a taxi hired by his wife who had arrived at the shop saying that she only had a £5 note which the cabby could not change. To hold that such a man was a thief and to say that his intention to put the money back in the till when he acquired some change was at the most a matter of mitigation would tend to bring the law into contempt. In our judgment a taking to which no moral obloquy can reasonably attach is not within the concept of stealing either at common law or under the Theft Act, 1968. . . .

If the law drifted off course in *R.* v. *Williams* because of the strong inference of fraud arising on the facts of that case, it got on to the wrong tack in *R.* v. *Cockburn* [1968] 1 W.L.R. 281 in which the manager of a shop took money from the till on a Saturday intending, so he said, to replace it with a cheque drawn by his daughter. Before he did so he was dismissed, and when the deficiency of cash was discovered and he was asked by telephone about it, he did not then put forward the explanation which was his defence to a charge of larceny as a servant. At his trial the jury were not directed that it would be a good defence to the charge if the accused were to satisfy them that he intended to replace the money with its currency equivalent. On the facts the accused had a lot to explain and such hope or expectation of repaying, if any, as he had probably could only have gone to mitigation, and this must be so in most cases of this kind. Winn L.J. delivered the judgment of the court. After setting out the facts he said, at p. 283: "The point raised by [counsel for the defendant] is that it is a good defence in law to a charge of larceny of a sum of money if the defendant is able to satisfy the jury, or if it remains open in the minds of the jury as a reasonable possibility, that he intended to replace the money taken with its currency equivalent and had resources available to him which would enable him to make the replacement. The court is quite satisfied that the submission of [counsel] is founded upon, and very ill-founded upon, a passage in reports of *R.* v. *Williams*."

Winn L.J. was referring to the passage to which reference has already been made. He went on to express the hope that it would for the future be entirely disregarded by the Bar—a hope which is now not likely to be fulfilled. He continued, at p. 284: "But the fact of the matter is this, that whereas larceny may vary very greatly indeed to the extent, one might say, of the whole heavens between grave theft and a taking which, whilst technically larcenous, reveals no normal obloquy, and does no harm at all it is nevertheless quite essential always to remember what are the elements of larceny and what are the complete and total elements of larceny, that is to say, taking the property of another person against the will of that other person without any claim of right so to do, and with the intent at the time of taking it permanently to deprive the owner of it. If coins, half a crown, a 10s. note, a £5 note, whatever it may be, are taken in all the circumstances which I have already indicated with the intention of spending or putting away somewhere those particular coins or notes, albeit not only hoping but intending and expecting reasonably to be able to replace them with their equivalent, nevertheless larceny has been committed because with full appreciation of what is being done, the larcenous person, the person who commits the offence, has taken something which he was not entitled to take, had no claim of right to take, without the consent of the owner, and is in effect trying to force upon the owner a substitution to which the owner has not consented."

We find it impossible to accept that a conviction for stealing, whether it be called larceny or theft, can reveal no moral obloquy. A man so convicted would have difficulty in persuading his friends and neighbours that his reputation had not been gravely damaged. He would be bound to be lowered in the estimation of right thinking people. Further, no reference was made by Winn L.J. to the factor of fraud which Lord Goddard C.J. in *R.* v. *Williams* had said had to be considered. It is this factor, whether it is labelled "fraudulently" or "dishonestly", which distinguishes a taking without consent from stealing.

If the principle enunciated in *R.* v. *Cockburn* was right, there would be a strange divergence between the position of a man who obtains cash by passing a cheque on an account which has no funds to meet it and one who takes money from a till. The man who passes the cheque is deemed in law not to act dishonestly if he genuinely believes on reasonable grounds that when it is presented to the paying bank there will be funds to meet it: see *Halstead* v. *Patel* [1972] 1 W.L.R. 661, *per* Lord Widgery C.J. at p. 665. But, according to the decision in *R.* v. *Cockburn*, the man who takes money from a till intending to put it back and genuinely believing on reasonable grounds that he will be able to do so (see Winn L.J. at p. 469) should be convicted of theft. Lawyers may be able to appreciate why one man should adjudged to be a criminal and the other not; but we doubt whether anyone else would. People who take money from tills and the like without permission are usually thieves; but if they do not admit that they are by pleading guilty, it is for the jury, not the judge, to decide whether they have acted dishonestly....

Appeal allowed

J. C. Smith: The Law of Theft (4th ed.)

"§ 117 Accepting *Feely* as the present law, it does not follow that the jury or magistrates will always have an unfettered discretion. The usual judicial controls over the finding of facts will apply. The jury may not find to be dishonest a state of mind which, in the view of the judge, no reasonable man could properly so describe; and—it is submitted—they must find a state of mind to be dishonest if no reasonable man, in the view of the judge, could fail so to find. The effect of *Feely* depends very greatly on the extent to which the judges are prepared to exert their powers of control. The present trend is to give the jury a very free hand.

On the facts of *Feely*, it must be taken that a reasonable jury could go either way. If, however, Robin Hood were to tell the court that he took P's money to give it to

Q because P is very rich and Q is very poor and he, Robin, does not consider that to be dishonest, is the judge really to leave it to the jury to say whether Robin's state of mind is dishonest or not? This example may not appear so fanciful when it is recalled that there are many people who think it right to go to extreme lengths to raise money for political causes in which they believe. If *Feely* leaves too much to the jury, two later cases go even further. In Gilks (*ante,* p. 532) D agreed that it would be dishonest if his grocer gave him too much change and he kept it but he said bookmakers are "a race apart" and there was nothing dishonest about keeping the overpayment in the case. The judge invited the jury to "try and place yourselves in [D's] position at that time and answer the question whether in your view he thought he was acting dishonestly"; and the Court of Appeal thought this a proper and sufficient direction, agreeing apparently that the prosecution had not established dishonesty if D did have the belief he claimed to have. This goes beyond *Feely* in that it applies the accused's own standards and not "the current standards of ordinary decent people"; and it goes too far. It might have been hoped that this departure from *Feely* was an oversight but in *Boggeln* v. *Williams* [1978] 2 All E.R. 1061, the court expressly rejected an argument that a man's belief as to his own honesty was irrelevant and held that, on the contrary, it was crucial. D, whose electricity had been cut off, reconnected the supply through the meter. He knew the electricity board did not consent to his doing so, but he notified them and believed, not unreasonably, that he would be able to pay at the due time. It was held that the crucial question was whether the defendant believed that his conduct was honest.

It may be that, on any test, Williams would have been found not to be dishonest; but it is easy to envisage cases in which the defendant's standards of honesty fall far below those of the community generally. If such a person is to be acquitted of dishonesty, it is indeed a case of "Everyman his own legislator." It is submitted that the law should take a firm stand in such cases. It is the business of the law to establish standards. If a belief that bookmakers are "fair game" is to be allowed as a defence it will not be long before bookmakers *are* fair game; yet the bookmakers are as much entitled to the protection of the law for their property as anyone else. The danger does not stop there. A belief has sometimes prevailed in the army and other large organisations that it is "alright" to take small items of property belonging to the organisation. Such a belief by D does not necessarily amount to a defence under *Feely* for the jury may well be satisfied that, by the "current standards of ordinary decent people", this is dishonest but under *Boggeln* v. *Williams* D must be acquitted unless the prosecution can prove that *he* did not hold the belief. It is submitted, however, that it would be preferable if the judge could direct the jury that the pilferer was acting dishonestly, certainly where, as will usually be the case, he knows that he has no right in law to take the property."

See Griew: *Dishonesty and the Jury* (Leicester University Press, 1974); Elliott: *Law and Fact in Theft Act Cases* [1976] Crim. L.R. 707.

Note

The cases which in Smith's view (above) go even further than *R.* v. *Feely* in leaving too much to the jury have since been joined by others. In *R.* v. *Landy* (1981) 72 Cr. App. R. 237 (C.A.) it was held that the defendant's own view of the honesty of his conduct was what counted in a prosecution for conspiracy to defraud. In *R.* v. *McIvor* [1972] 1 All E.R. 491 (C.A.), a theft case, it was held that, although the jury's view of the current standards of ordinary decent people was what counted, it was wrong to direct them that the defendant's view was neither here nor there. His view had to be given such weight as the jury thought fit. In *R.* v. *Ghosh, The Times,* April 7, 1982 (C.A.), also a theft case, it was held that this meant that the jury should ask, was his conduct dishonest according to the standards of ordinary decent people? If not, the prosecution failed. If so, the jury had to go on and ask whether the defendant *realised* that what he was doing was by their standards dishonest. "It was dishonest for a person to act in a way in which he knew ordinary people considered to be dishonest, even if he asserted or genuinely believed that he was morally justified in acting as he had acted": *per* Lane L.C.J. The implication is that if he did *not* realise this, he is to be acquitted, even if the jury think that according to the standards of ordinary decent people what he did was dishonest.

In Victoria, where the relevant provisions of the Crimes Act 1958 (as amended by the Crimes (Theft) Act 1973), are in all material respects the same as those in the Theft Act 1968, the persuasive authority of *R.* v. *Feely* has been entirely rejected, in so far as that case decides that the statute leaves the meaning of "dishonestly" at large, to be decided by the jury in each particular case. See *R.* v. *Salvo* [1980] V.R. 401; *R.* v. *Brow* [1981] V.R. 783; *R.* v. *Bonollo* [1981] V.R. 633. According to Fullagar J. in [1980] V.R. at p. 432, as a matter of law "dishonestly" means "with disposition to defraud, *i.e.* with disposition to withhold from a person what is his right." *R.* v. *Williams* and *R.* v. *Cockburn* were expressly approved.

vii. A New Approach

Canadian Law Reform Commission Working Paper No. 19 (1977)

"Criminal law should support morality, not contradict it. As we said, *Our Criminal Law,* the prime function of the "real" criminal law is to bolster values. But law must underline, not caricature, those values.

The value here is honesty. This, however, is such a basic value that everyone understands its import: everyone knows roughly what is meant by theft and fraud. To underline, not caricature, this value the law must be so devised as to highlight the basic principles involved, to concentrate on the vast majority of "run of the mill" dishonest actions and to avoid devoting all its efforts to the marginal case. In short, the law should make the value and the principles clear enough to underwrite the citizen's general understanding of dishonesty while also providing guidelines for judicial interpretation in border-line cases. The law, therefore, should clearly prohibit only acts commonly reckoned dishonest and avoid prohibiting any act commonly reckoned legitimate. So dishonesty becomes a necessary, but not sufficient, condition of criminality.

This leaves the marginal cases. Cases, for instance, where property law makes it doubtful whether what is stolen counts as *property*. Or cases where the law on representations makes it dubious whether there has been a *false pretence.* How should a clear and single law of theft provide for these?

Our answer is as follows. The more our criminal law serves to bolster values, the less significant is the marginal case. For bolstering values means condemning all those acts and only those acts that are clearly considered wrongful and leaving untouched all acts thought legitimate. Marginal cases, therefore,—acts considered neither clearly wrong nor clearly right—will then require to be dealt with pragmatically.

Here pragmatism means three things. First, it means recognizing the inevitability of marginal cases. Second, it means being concrete. And third, it means operating by the light of principle.

First then, we have to recognize the inevitability of marginal cases. However we define our terms, there will be a hazy border-line. For one thing, language has an open-texture and descriptions necessarily have blurred edges. For another, life is uncertain and we can't provide for everything in advance. Marginal cases, then, are unavoidable in any kind of drafting even the drafting of our present law. Our approach recognizes this and therefore worries less about it.

Second, pragmatism means being concrete. We can't judge marginal cases in the abstract. The wrongfulness of any border-line behaviour can only be determined in the light of all the actual circumstances. This of course is the rationale of the common law.

Third, pragmatism here involves using not rules but principles. Whereas rules simply lay down the law, principles do more than this: a principle articulates the reason for that law—in other words by being based on common sense and common morality it elucidates, explains and justifies that law. In this way principles point the way to the solution of border-line problems. So here the principles stemming from the value of honesty can guide our approach to marginal cases in the law of theft, fraud and similar offences.

On marginal cases, then, our view is this: the legislator has to leave them to the trial court or jury. Only these know all the facts. Only these can properly measure such cases against the moral standard.

This doesn't mean, however, that each decision must necessarily make new law. Otherwise, the law would soon become as complex as it is today. Instead, border-line cases will be decided by the judge or jury on their own particular facts although courts of appeal will occasionally lay down that certain facts cannot fall within the words of the section. That is generally what happens today. No form of expression in a statute can completely encompass all possible cases.

This does, however, mean that in such cases there will be considerable uncertainty. If all such cases are to be decided on the facts as they arise, we cannot know until the trial court tells us, whether the act is criminal or not. But that is surely right. In moral terms the act is doubtful, on the border-line. The law can't be more precise without being artificial and out of touch with ordinary morality. Where there is moral uncertainty, that surely has to be reflected in the criminal law.

This is our strategy for marginal cases of dishonesty. Don't seek to solve them all by legislation in advance. Leave it rather to the trial court to decide each border-line case in the light of its particular circumstances. Applying the measuring-rod of honesty, the court must ask: *did the accused's conduct fall short of the recognized standard of honesty*? This is no mere objective question, for conduct isn't just an external act but an act accompanied by a state of mind. The question is subjective. We have to ask: *did the accused mean to act dishonestly*? This, however, is answered not by looking at the offender's mind—as Bryan C.J. remarked in the 15th century, "the intention of a man cannot be tried; the devil himself knows not the intention of a man". It is answered by reference to objective tests of evidence. If at the end of the day, there remains a doubt, acquit; for given a doubt, defendant's act hasn't clearly violated the principle of honesty.

But what if the uncertainty—the marginality of the case—arises, not from the law, but from the defendant's ignorance of the law? What if the defendant didn't realize that theft law prohibited his act? In such a case his act will obviously have been dishonest, otherwise it wouldn't be prohibited by law. That being so, he must have known he shouldn't do it; he can't therefore complain that he didn't know the law. Accordingly, with "real" crimes, including theft and fraud, ignorance of law is no excuse. Everyone is required to live up to the common teachings of ordinary morality. Disregard them and he acts at his peril.

This strategy will achieve sufficient clarity, certainty and comprehensiveness. Clarity, because the law will now clearly underline the value of honesty. Certainty, because it will prohibit and condemn those acts and those acts only that contravene this value. And comprehensiveness, because all acts that are obviously dishonest will fall within its scope. Meanwhile the marginal cases won't become the tail that wags the dog.

. . . Theft law can and should be clear and simple. Though "property" and "taking" may be terms of art, the ordinary person knows well enough when another's property is being taken. This is sufficient for the criminal law. After all, criminal law is not like property law or contract, where the law must be certain enough to ensure that transactions completed according to the rules are valid and effective. In criminal law, by contrast, we need to be certain (1) that if we do what is ordinarily thought legitimate, we won't be liable to prosecution; and (2) that if we are prosecuted for an alleged illegality, we know exactly what we have to defend ourselves against. What we need to be sure of, then, is that we will only be penalized for doing acts which ordinary people would consider wrong. Where ordinary people, given all the circumstances, would still be doubtful, the criminal law must hold its hand. This is the essence of our new approach.

Applying this approach then, we have tried to produce *a simpler law of theft and fraud. It is simpler than the present law, we think, in three respects. First, marginal cases are left to be decided on the facts, and this avoids a mass of details. Second, this leaves us free to concentrate on the bare bones of theft and fraud and make the underlying principles obvious in our arrangement. Third, it enables us to use a simpler, more straightforward drafting style.*

. . . The main feature of our draft is simplicity. First we avoid trying to take care of all marginal cases, and so paint with a comparatively broad brush. Second, we forbear from defining our most basic terms.

Basic terms are known to all. As such they can only be defined by other words less well known. But why define the known by the unknown? After all, all definition must stop somewhere. Our draft, therefore, deliberately leaves undefined such words as "taking", "using" and "dishonestly".

Particularly important is the case of "dishonestly". Indeed it is crucial to our whole approach. "Dishonestly" is the fundamental *mens rea* term, as in the English *Theft Act* 1968, section 1 (1) of which provides that "a person is guilty of theft if he dishonestly appropriates property belonging to another with the intention of permanently depriving the other of it". Like the draftsman of that Act, we don't define "dishonestly" in terms of "fraudulently", "claim of right" or "colour of right" because "dishonestly" is better understood than any of these. Indeed, we don't define it at all—no draftsman could. We all know what it is to take another's things dishonestly. It means *taking them when we know we oughtn't*. We don't define it further.

Accordingly, we introduce "dishonestly" as a measuring-rod or standard for courts and juries to apply. But this is only to write into the letter of the law what happens all the time in practice. Judge after judge has told us that he tells the jury that in the end they have to ask themselves: "Did the accused behave dishonestly?" Indeed a well-known work for judicial directions in criminal cases instructs the judge in case of theft to ask the jury to consider whether the defendant acted fraudulently or deceitfully or dishonestly. As an English Appeal Court Judge recently observed, "Jurors when deciding whether an appropriation was dishonest can be reasonably expected to, and should, apply the current standards of ordinary decent people. In their own lives they have to decide what is and what is not dishonest. We can see no reason why, when in a jury box, they should require the help of a Judge to tell them what amounts to dishonest".

In short, what we have done is to effect a paper change. We have made the written law reflect what judges do in practice. We have brought form into harmony with substance.

Draft Statute

Section 1.1. *Theft*

A person commits theft who dishonestly appropriates another's property without his consent.

Section 1.2. *Without Consent*

For the purposes of section 1.1, appropriation by violence or threat of immediate violence is appropriation without consent.

Section 1.3. *Appropriating Property*

"Appropriating property" means

(a) taking, with intent to treat as one's own, tangible movables including immovables made movable by the taking;

(b) converting property of any kind by acting inconsistently with the express or implied terms on which it is held; or

(c) using electricity, gas, water, telephone, tele-communication or computer services, or other utilities.

Section 1.4. *Another's Property*

For the purposes of section 1.1 property is another's if he owns it, has possession, control or custody of it or has any legally protected interest in it.

Section 2. *Dishonest Taking*

A person commits dishonest taking who dishonestly and without consent takes another's property though without intent to permanently deprive.

Section 3. *Robbery*

A person commits robbery who for the purposes of theft uses violence or threats of immediate violence to person or property.

Section 4. *Blackmail*

A person commits blackmail who threatens another with injury to person, property or reputation in order to extort money, property or other economic advantage.

Section 5.1. *Definition of Fraud*

A person commits fraud who dishonestly by

(a) deceit, or

(b) unfair non-disclosure, or

(c) unfair exploitation,

either induces any person including the public to part with any property or causes him to suffer a financial loss.

Section 5.2. *Deceit*

For the purpose of Section 5.1 "deceit" means any false representation as to the past, present or future.

Section 5.3. *Puffing*

Deceit does not include mere exaggerated commendation or depreciation of the quality of anything.

Section 5.4. *Unfair Non-Disclosure*

For the purpose of Section 5.1 non-disclosure is unfair where a duty to disclose arises from

(a) a special relationship entitling the victim to rely on the offender, or

(b) conduct by the offender creating a false impression in the victim's mind, or

(c) circumstances where non-disclosure would create a false impression in the mind of any reasonable person.

Section 5.5. *Unfair Exploitation*

For the purpose of Section 5.1 "unfair exploitation" means exploitation

(a) of another person's mental deficiency;

(b) of another person's mistake intentionally or recklessly induced by the offender;

(c) of another person's mistake induced by the unlawful conduct of a third party acting with the offender.

Section 5.6. *Parting with Property*

"Parting with Property" means relinquishing ownership, possession, control or other interest in it.

Section 6. *Dishonest Obtaining*

A person commits dishonest obtaining if he dishonestly obtains food, lodging, transport or services without paying."

Note

Compare with the English law of robbery, below, and blackmail and fraud, which is dealt with in succeeding chapters of this book.

Questions

1. The Commission say that in pursuance of their policy on marginal cases of dishonesty, "We have made the written law reflect what the judges do in practice." Does their written law have the practical effect of English law as reflected in section 2 of the Theft Act, 1968 and *R.* v. *Feely*?

2. What is their policy on other marginal cases, *e.g.* marginal cases of property, and taking? Is this policy at variance with that advocated by Glanville Williams in *Theft, Consent and Illegality*, *ante*, p. 500?

2. ROBBERY

Theft Act 1968, section 8

(1) A person is guilty of robbery if he steals, and immediately before or at the time of doing so, and in order to do so, he uses force on any person or puts or seeks to put any person in fear of being then and there subjected to force.

(2) A person guilty of robbery, or of an assault with intent to rob, shall on conviction on indictment be liable to imprisonment for life.

Corcoran v. Anderton

(1980) 71 Cr. App. R. 104
Queen's Bench Division

A. intending to steal a handbag from V. struck her in the back, took hold of and tugged at the bag, causing her to release it. It fell to the ground.

A. ran away. C. who was present and assisting A. was convicted of robbery. The magistrates stated a case, with the question whether C. was rightly convicted.

Watkins J.: They were asked to state a case. They did and asked this Court this question: "Could the tugging at the handbag, accompanied by force, amount to robbery, notwithstanding the fact that the co-accused did not have sole control of the bag at any time?

I think it is a trifle unfortunate that the question does not arise more fully and appropriately out of the facts found by the justices. The justices found explicitly that not only did Partington tug at the handbag, but he tugged so successfully that Mrs. Hall was forced to release her grasp upon it, so that it fell to the ground. Therefore if the question had been properly posed, it should have taken some such form as this: "Could the fact that the handbag had been snatched from the grasp of Mrs. Hall so that it fell from her grasp to the ground amount to an appropriation?" However I will face the question as it stands and the full circumstances as found.

. . . So confining myself to the facts as found by the justices in the instant case, I think that an "appropriation" takes place when an accused snatches a woman's handbag completely from her grasp, so that she no longer has physical control of it because it has fallen to the ground. What has been involved in such activity as that, bearing in mind the dishonest state of mind of the accused, is an assumption of the rights of the owner, a taking of the property of another. If one had to consider the definition of "theft" as contained in the Larceny Act 1916, it is inevitable, so it seems to me, that there was here a sufficient taking and carrying away to satisfy the definition of "theft" in that Act. In my judgment there cannot possibly be, save for the instance where a handbag is carried away from the scene of it, a clearer instance of robbery than that which these justices found was committed.

Turning to the actual question posed to this Court, "Could the tugging at the handbag, accompanied by force, amount to robbery, notwithstanding the fact that the co-accused did not have sole control of the bag at any time?" in my opinion, which may be contrary to some notions of what constitutes a sufficient appropriation to satisfy the definition of that word in section 3 (1) of the Theft Act, the forcible tugging of the handbag of itself could in the circumstances be a sufficient exercise of control by the accused person so as to amount to an assumption by him of the rights of the owner, and therefore an appropriation of the property.

Accordingly if the question had been properly put, my answer would have been unequivocally and certainly in the affirmative. The question as put to us is academic. Had it been founded upon fact I feel sure I should have answered that too affirmatively.

For these reasons I would dismiss this appeal.

Eveleigh L.J.: I agree. Each, that is to say the lady and the defendant, was trying to exclude the other from exclusive claim to the bag. The lady was treating the bag as hers, as indeed it was, and resisting any efforts of his to deprive her of it. He, on the other hand, was treating the bag as his and seeking to overcome her efforts to retain it. He was thereby exercising the rights which belonged to the owner. She too was doing so. She was doing it lawfully, he was doing it unlawfully. He was, in my view, appropriating that bag.

I agree that this appeal should be dismissed.

Appeal dismissed

Notes

1. See "appropriation," *ante*, p. 495. There must be a theft; claim of right negates theft (see next note); and the force used must be immediately before or at the time of the theft (see *R.* v. *Hale*, below).

2. In *R.* v. *Robinson* [1977] Crim. L.R. 173 (C.A.) it was held that the law as laid down in *R.* v. *Skivington* [1968] 1 Q.B. 166 had not been altered by the Theft Act. In *R.* v. *Skivington*, S threatened with a knife his wife's employer in order to collect wages due to her which he had her authority to collect. The judge directed the jury that before S could maintain a defence to a charge of robbery, they must be satisfied that he had an honest belief that he was entitled to take the money in the way in which he did take it. Lord Goddard C.J.: "In the opinion of this court the matter is plain, namely that a claim of right is a defence to robbery . . . and that it is unnecessary to show that the defendant must have had an honest belief also that he was entitled to take the money in the way that he did." *Conviction quashed.*

Question

Is robbery involved in the following cases?

A, needing the use of a car to escape pursuit by the police, takes B's car from him at gun point.

C is lent a lawnmower by his neighbour D. When D asks for its return, C drives him away with blows, saying he is going to keep it for a further week.

R. v. Hale
(1978) 68 Cr. App. R. 415
Court of Appeal

H. and M. entered the house of Mrs. C. wearing stocking masks. H. put his hand over her mouth to stop her screaming. M. went upstairs and came back with her jewellery box. They then tied up Mrs. C. and threatened harm to her child if she told the police within five minutes of their leaving. H. was convicted of robbery and appealed.

EVELEIGH L.J.: . . . On behalf of the appellant it is submitted that the learned judge misdirected the jury in that the passages quoted above could indicate to them that if an accused used force in order to effect his escape with the stolen goods that would be sufficient to constitute the crime of robbery. In so far as the facts of the present case are concerned, counsel submitted that the theft was completed when the jewellery box was first seized and any force thereafter could not have been "immediately before or at the time of stealing" and certainly not "in order to steal". The essence of the submission was that the theft was completed as soon as the jewellery box was seized. . . .

Section 8 of the Theft Act 1968 begins: "A person is guilty of robbery if he steals. . . ." He steals when he acts in accordance with the basic definition of theft in section 1 of the Theft Act; that is to say when he dishonestly appropriates property belonging to another with the intention of permanently depriving the other of it. It thus becomes necessary to consider what is "appropriation" or, according to section 3, "any assumption by a person of the rights of an owner". An assumption of the rights of an owner describes the conduct of a person towards a particular article. It is conduct which usurps the rights of the owner. To say that the conduct is over and done with as soon as he lays hands upon the property, or when he first manifests an intention to deal with it as his, is contrary to common-sense and to the natural meaning of words. A thief who steals a motor car first opens the door. Is it to be said that the act of starting up the motor is no more a part of the theft?

In the present case there can be little doubt that if the appellant had been interrupted after the seizure of the jewellery box the jury would have been entitled to find that the appellant and his accomplice were assuming the rights of an owner at the time when the jewellery box was seized. However, the act of appropriation does not suddenly cease. It is a continuous act and it is a matter for the jury to decide whether or not the act of appropriation has finished. Moreover, it is quite clear that the intention to deprive the owner permanently, which accompanied the assumption of the owner's rights, was a continuing one at all material times. This Court therefore rejects the contention that the theft had ceased by the time the lady was tied up. As a matter of common-sense the appellant was in the course of committing theft; he was stealing.

There remains the question whether there was robbery. Quite clearly the jury were at liberty to find the appellant guilty of robbery relying upon the force used when he put his hand over Mrs. Carrett's mouth to restrain her from calling for help. We also think that they were also entitled to rely upon the act of tying her up provided they were satisfied (and it is difficult to see how they could not be satisfied) that the force so used was to enable them to steal. If they were still engaged in the act of stealing the force was clearly used to enable them to continue to assume the rights of the owner and permanently to deprive Mrs. Carrett of her box, which is what they began to do when they first seized it....

Appeal dismissed

Notes

1. Compare C.L.R.C.'s Eighth Report, Cmnd. 2977, § 65: "The force will have to be used for the purpose of stealing; force used only to get away after committing a theft does not seem naturally to be regarded as robbery (though it could be charged as a separate offence in addition to the stealing)."

2. See *Appropriation: A Single or Continuous Act, ante*, p. 502.

R. v. Dawson
(1976) 64 Cr. App. R. 170
Court of Appeal

D. and two others came alongside a sailor, and nudged him from side to side. While he was trying to keep his balance, one of the three was enabled to take his wallet. They were convicted of robbery and appealed.

LAWTON L.J.: Mr. Locke had submitted at the end of the prosecution's case that what had happened could not in law amount to the use of force. He called the learned judge's attention to some old authorities and to a passage in *Archbold* ... based on the old authorities, and submitted that because of those old authorities there was not enough evidence to go to the jury. He sought before this Court to refer to the old authorities. He was discouraged from doing so because this Court is of the opinion that in these cases what judges should now direct their attention to is the words of the statute. This had been said in a number of cases since the Theft Act 1968.

The object of that Act was to get rid of all the old technicalities of the law of larceny and to put the law into simple language which juries would understand and which they themselves would use. That is what has happened in section 8 which defines "robbery". That section is in these terms: "A person is guilty of robbery if he steals and immediately before or at the time of doing so, and in order to do so, he uses force on any person or puts or seeks to put any person in fear of being then and there subjected to force."

The choice of the word "force" is not without interest because under the Larceny Act 1916 the word "violence" had been used, but Parliament deliberately on the advice of the Criminal Law Revision Committee changed that word to "force". Whether there is any difference between "violence" or "force" is not relevant for the purposes of this case; but the word is "force". It is a word in ordinary use. It is a word which juries understand. The learned judge left it to the jury to say whether jostling a man in the way which the victim described to such an extent that he had difficulty in keeping his balance could be said to be the use of force. The learned judge, because of the argument put forward by Mr. Locke, went out of his way to explain to the jury that force in these sort of circumstances must be substantial to justify a verdict.

Whether it was right for him to put that adjective before the word "force" when Parliament had not done so we will not discuss for the purposes of this case. It was a matter for the jury. They were there to use their common sense and knowledge of the world. We cannot say that their decision as to whether force was used was wrong. They were entitled to the view that force was used.

Other points were discussed in the case as to whether the force had been used for the purpose of distracting the victim's attention or whether it was for the purpose of overcoming resistance. Those sort of refinements may have been relevant under the old law, but so far as the new law is concerned the sole question is whether the accused used force on any person in order to steal. That issue in this case was left to the jury. They found in favour of the Crown.

We cannot say that this verdict was either unsafe or unsatisfactory. Accordingly the appeal is dismissed.

Appeal dismissed

Compare *R.* v. *Feely, ante*, p. 556. If the threat is not seeking to put any person in fear of being then and there subjected to force (*e.g.* a threat to wound at some future time, or a threat to reveal the victim's misdeeds to the authorities) that is not robbery according to the wording of section 8 (1). Nor is it *assault* with intent to rob under section 8 (2). But it will almost certainly be blackmail (see, *post*, p. 621), which will also cover cases where a robbery *is* committed. If there is no threat, but an actual application of force, an assault crime of some sort will be committed. If the theft is not consummated, it will be not only assault with intent to rob but also, usually, an attempt to steal.

See J. A. Andrews, "Robbery under the Theft Bill" [1966] Crim. L.R. 524.

Question

In view of the other offences almost necessarily involved in a robbery situation, is there any justification for robbery existing as a separate crime?

CHAPTER 11

FRAUD

	PAGE
1. Obtaining Property by Deception	572
i. Obtaining Property Belonging to Another with Intention Permanently to Deprive	573
ii. Deception	573
iii. The Obtaining must be by the Deception	580
iv. Dishonesty	591
2. Obtaining Pecuniary Advantage by Deception	592
3. Obtaining Services by Deception	593
4. Evasion of Liability by Deception	594
5. Making off Without Payment	597

Note

The law of larceny did not, even in its latter-day expanded form, cover all offences of dishonesty connected with property. The law always drew a distinction between a thief and a swindler, the former being one who took the goods of another without any colour of consent and the latter being one who fraudulently persuaded the victim to make him (the swindler) the owner. The swindler was originally not punished by the common law at all in ordinary cases, and when statute invented the crime of obtaining by false pretences to cover him, it maintained a sharp distinction between the thief and the swindler, the former being in all cases a felon while the latter, except in cases where personation or forged documents were involved in the swindle, was guilty of misdemeanour only. By 1916, there was a range of offences covering various forms of swindling, see, *e.g.* the Forgery Act 1861, s. 3; the Debtors Act 1869, s. 13; the False Personation Act 1874, s. 1, and the Larceny Act 1916, s. 32, the principal offence being obtaining by false pretences under section 32 (1) of the Larceny Act 1916.

Criminal Law Revision Committee's Eighth Report, Cmnd. 2977

"§ 38 The sub-committee for a considerable time proposed that the general offence of theft should be made to cover the present offence of obtaining by false pretences under 1916, s. 32 (1). It might seem appropriate to extend theft in this way in order to make it cover as many ways as possible of getting property dishonestly. But in the end the sub-committee gave up the idea (to the regret of some members), and the full committee agreed. In spite of its attractions, it seemed to the majority of the committee that the scheme would be unsatisfactory. Obtaining by false pretences is ordinarily thought of as different from theft, because in the former the owner in fact consents to part with his ownership; a bogus beggar is regarded as a rogue but not as a thief, and so are his less petty counterparts. To create a new offence of theft to include conduct which ordinary people would find difficult to regard as theft would be a mistake. The unnaturalness of including obtaining by false pretences in theft is emphasised by the difficulty of drafting a satisfactory definition to cover both kinds of conduct. . . ."

Note

In spite of this expression of policy, *Lawrence* v. *Commissioner of Police* (*ante*, p. 496) appears to have blurred the distinction between theft and obtaining property by deception. In *R.* v. *Lawrence* [1971] 1 Q.B. 373, in the Court of Appeal, Megaw L.J., in dismissing Lawrence's appeal, said (at p. 478) "It may be that a result of our decision is that in any case where the facts would establish a charge under section 15 [obtaining by deception], they would also establish a charge under section 1 (1) [theft]." In the House of Lords, where the Court of Appeal decision was upheld (see *ante*, p. 496), Viscount Dilhorne said (*ante*, p. 498): "Not infrequently there is some overlapping of offences. In some cases the facts may justify a charge under section 1 (1) and also a charge under section 15 (1). On the other hand there are cases which only come within section 1 (1) and some which are only within section 15 (1)." It is easy to imagine a case where there is theft but no obtaining by deception, *e.g.* a forcible taking or a surreptitious appropriation without the victim's knowledge; but it is almost impossible to imagine a case which is obtaining by deception but not theft (other than the wholly exceptional one where land is the property concerned, because land is not normally covered by section 1, but is covered by section 15: see section 34 (1)). It must therefore be borne in mind that in almost every case of obtaining property by deception, a charge of theft would also succeed.

1. OBTAINING PROPERTY BY DECEPTION

Theft Act 1968, section 15

"(1) A person who by any deception dishonestly obtains property belonging to another, with the intention of permanently depriving the other of it, shall on conviction on indictment be liable to imprisonment for a term not exceeding ten years.

(2) For purposes of this section a person is to be treated as obtaining property if he obtains ownership, possession or control of it, and 'obtain' includes obtaining for another or enabling another to obtain or to retain.

(3) Section 6 above shall apply for purposes of this section, with the necessary adaptation of the reference to appropriating, as it applies for purposes of section 1.

(4) For purposes of this section 'deception' means any deception (whether deliberate or reckless) by words or conduct as to fact or as to law, including a deception as to the present intentions of the person using the deception or any other person."

Note

This is the principal swindling crime, and differs from the others dealt with in this chapter in that *property* is obtained *with intent to deprive permanently*.

i. Obtaining Property Belonging to Another with Intention Permanently to Deprive

Notes

1. By section 34 (1) "property" in this offence is given the same meaning as that given by section 4 (1) for the purposes of theft (*ante*, p. 504). The limitations and exceptions as to land and wild animals imposed by section 3 (2)–(4) relating to theft have no application to the present offence. "Belonging to another" is given the same meaning as that given by section 5 (1) for the purposes of theft (*ante*, p. 515). The remaining subsections of section 5 do not apply to the present offence.

2. On intention permanently to deprive, see *ante*, pp. 534–544. The need for this intention means that obtaining by lies the *loan* of an article which one intends to return is not an offence under this section. It is different with a loan of money, however, because there is usually no intention to return the precise coins or notes lent. In such a case the question of guilt will turn on what view the jury take of the accused's honesty. (See *post*, p. 591.)

ii. Deception

Note

Deception is needed for this crime, as it is also for obtaining pecuniary advantage (*post*, p. 592) obtaining services, and evasion of liability (*post*, p. 593). The definition in section 15 (4) is made to apply to these other offences by the Theft Act 1968, s. 16 (3) and the Theft Act 1978, s. 5 (1). The principal offence of obtaining pecuniary advantage was that contained in the Theft Act 1968, s. 16 (2) (*a*). This provision was repealed by the Theft Act 1978, s. 5 (5), a fact which must be borne in mind in considering many of the cases following, which are reproduced as authorities on deception and on the need for the deception to cause the obtaining.

Director of Public Prosecutions v. Ray

[1974] A.C. 370
House of Lords

R., and others, entered a restaurant and ordered a meal. R. did not have enough money to pay, but one of his companions agreed to lend him enough to pay. After eating the meal, while the waiter was still in the dining room, the men decided not to pay and to run out of the restaurant. Ten minutes later they did so while the waiter was absent in the kitchen. The Divisional Court quashed R.'s conviction for obtaining a pecuniary advantage by deception contrary to section 16 (2) (*a*) of the Theft Act (since repealed). The prosecution appealed to the House of Lords.

LORD REID: ... If a person induces a supplier to accept an order for goods or services by a representation of fact, that representation must be held to be a continuing representation lasting until the goods or services are supplied. Normally it would not last any longer. A restaurant supplies both goods and services:

it supplies food and drink and the facilities for consuming them. Customers normally remain for a short time after consuming their meal, and I think that it can properly be held that any representation express or implied made with a view to obtaining a meal lasts until the departure of the customers in the normal course.

In my view, where a new customer orders a meal in a restaurant, he must be held to make an implied representation that he can and will pay for it before he leaves. In the present case the accused must be held to have made such a representation. But when he made it it was not dishonest: he thought he would be able to borrow money from one of his companions.

After the meal had been consumed the accused changed his mind. He decided to evade payment. So he and his companions remained seated where they were for a short time until the waiter left the room and then ran out of the restaurant.

Did he thereby commit an offence against section 16 of the Theft Act 1968? It is admitted, and rightly admitted, that if the waiter had not been in the room when he changed his mind and he had immediately run out he would not have committed an offence. Why does his sitting still for a short time in the presence of the waiter make all the difference?

The section requires evasion of his obligation to pay. That is clearly established by his running out without paying. Secondly, it requires dishonesty: that is admitted. There would have been both evasion and dishonesty if he had changed his mind and run out while the waiter was absent.

The crucial question in this case is whether there was evasion "by any deception". Clearly there could be no deception until the accused changed his mind. I agree with the following quotation from the judgment of Buckley J. in *In re London and Globe Finance Corporation Ltd.* [1903] 1 Ch. 728, 732:

> "To deceive is, I apprehend, to induce a man to believe that a thing is true which is false, and which the person practising the deceit knows or believes to be false."

So the accused, after he changed his mind, must have done something intended to induce the waiter to believe that he still intended to pay before he left. Deception, to my mind, implies something positive. It is quite true that a man intending to deceive can build up a situation in which his silence is as eloquent as an express statement. But what did the accused do here to create such a situation? He merely sat still. . . . The magistrates stated that they were of opinion that

> ". . . having changed his mind as regards payment, by remaining in the restaurant for a further 10 minutes as an ordinary customer who was likely to order a sweet or coffee, the appellant practised a deception."

I cannot read that as a finding that after he changed his mind he intended to deceive the waiter into believing that he still intended to pay. And there is no finding that the waiter was in fact induced to believe that by anything the accused did after he changed his mind. I would infer from the case that all that he intended to do was to take advantage of the first opportunity to escape and evade his obligation to pay.

Deception is an essential ingredient of the offence. Dishonest evasion of an obligation to pay is not enough. I cannot see that there was, in fact, any more than that in this case.

I agree with the Divisional Court [1973] 1 W.L.R. 317, 323:

> "His plan was totally lacking in the subtlety of deception and to argue that his remaining in the room until the coast was clear amounted to a representation to the waiter is to introduce an artificiality which should have no place in the Act."

I would therefore dismiss this appeal.

LORD MACDERMOTT: . . . Two questions [are left] for consideration. First, do the facts justify a finding that the respondent practised a deception? And secondly, if he did, was his evasion of the debt obtained by that deception?

The first of these questions involves nothing in the way of words spoken or written. If there was deception on the part of the respondent it was by his conduct in the course of an extremely common form of transaction which, because of its nature, leaves much to be implied from conduct. Another circumstance affecting the ambit of this question lies in the fact that, looking only to the period *after* the meal had been eaten and the respondent and his companions had decided to evade payment, there is nothing that I can find in the discernible conduct of the respondent which would suffice in itself to show that he was then practising a deception. No doubt he and the others stayed in their seats until the waiter went into the kitchen and while doing so gave all the appearance of ordinary customers. But, in my opinion, nothing in this or in anything else which occurred *after* the change of intention went far enough to afford proof of deception. The picture, as I see it, presented by this last stage of the entire transaction, is simply that of a group which had decided to evade payment and were awaiting the opportunity to do so.

There is, however, no sound reason that I can see for restricting the inquiry to this final phase. One cannot, so to speak, draw a line through the transaction at the point where the intention changed and search for evidence of deception only in what happened before that or only in what happened after that. In my opinion the transaction must for this purpose be regarded in its entirety, beginning with the respondent entering the restaurant and ordering his meal and ending with his running out without paying. The different stages of the transaction are all linked and it would be quite unrealistic to treat them in isolation.

Starting then, at the beginning one finds in the conduct of the respondent in entering and ordering his meal evidence that he impliedly represented that he had the means and the intention of paying for it before he left. That the respondent did make such a representation was not in dispute and in the absence of evidence to the contrary it would be difficult to reach a different conclusion. If this representation had then been false and matters had proceeded thereafter as they did (but without any change of intention) a conviction for the offence charged would, in my view, have had ample material to support it. But as the representation when originally made in this case was not false there was therefore no deception at that point. Then the meal is served and eaten and the intention to evade the debt replaces the intention to pay. Did this change of mind produce a deception?

My Lords, in my opinion it did. I do not base this conclusion merely on the change of mind that had occurred for that in itself was not manifest at the time and did not amount to "conduct" on the part of the respondent. But it did falsify the representation which had already been made because that initial representation must, in my view, be regarded not as something then spent and past but as a continuing representation which remained alive and operative and had already resulted in the respondent and his defaulting companions being taken on trust and treated as ordinary, honest customers. It covered the whole transaction up to and including payment and must therefore, in my opinion, be considered as continuing and still active at the time of the change of mind. When that happened, with the respondent taking (as might be expected) no step to bring the change to notice, he practised, to my way of thinking, a deception just as real and just as dishonest as would have been the case if his intention all along had been to go without paying.

Holding for these reasons that the respondent practised a deception, I turn to what I have referred to as the second question. Was the respondent's evasion of the debt obtained by that deception?

I think the material before the justices was enough to show that it was. The obvious effect of the deception was that the respondent and his associates were treated as they had been previously, that is to say as ordinary, honest customers whose conduct did not excite suspicion or call for precautions. In consequence the waiter was off his guard and vanished into the kitchen. That gave the respondent the opportunity of running out without hindrance and he took it. I would therefore answer this second question in the affirmative.

I would, accordingly, allow the appeal and restore the conviction.

Lord Morris of Borth-y-Gest: For a deception to take place there must be some person or persons who will have been deceived. "Deception" is a word which is well understood. As Buckley J. said in *In re London and Globe Finance Corporation Ltd.* (1903] 1 Ch. 728, 732:

> "To deceive is, I apprehend, to induce a man to believe that a thing is true which is false, and which the person practising the deceit knows or believes to be false."

In the present case the person deceived was the waiter. Did the respondent deceive the waiter as to what were his intentions? Did the respondent so conduct himself as to induce the waiter to believe that he (the respondent) intended to pay his bill before he left the restaurant whereas at the relevant time he did not so intend? . . .

The situation may perhaps be unusual where a customer honestly orders a meal and therefore indicates his honest intention to pay but thereafter forms a dishonest intention of running away without paying if he can. Inherent in an original honest representation of an intention to pay there must surely be a representation that such intention will continue.

In the present case it is found as a fact that when the respondent ordered his meal he believed that he would be able to pay. One of his companions had agreed to lend him money. He therefore intended to pay. So far as the waiter was concerned the original implied representation made to him by the respondent must have been a continuing representation so long as he (the respondent) remained in the restaurant. There was nothing to alter the representation. Just as the waiter was led at the start to believe that he was dealing with a customer who by all that he did in the restaurant was indicating his intention to pay in the ordinary way, so the waiter was led to believe that the state of affairs continued. But the moment came when the respondent decided and therefore knew that he was not going to pay: but he also knew that the waiter still thought that he was going to pay. By ordering his meal and by his conduct in assuming the role of an ordinary customer the respondent had previously shown that it was his intention to pay. By continuing in the same role and behaving just as before he was representing that his previous intention continued. That was a deception because his intention, unknown to the waiter, had become quite otherwise. The dishonest change of intention was not likely to produce the result that the waiter would be told of it. The essence of the deception was that the waiter should not know of it or be given any sort of clue that it (the change of intention) had come about. Had the waiter suspected that by a change of intention a secret exodus was being planned, it is obvious that he would have taken action to prevent its being achieved.

It was said in the Divisional Court that deception under section 16 should not be found unless an accused has actively made a representation by words or conduct which representation is found to be false. But if there was an original representation (as, in my view, there was when the meal was ordered) it was a representation that was intended to be and was a continuing representation. It continued to operate on the mind of the waiter. It became false and it became a deliberate deception. The prosecution do not say that the deception consisted in not informing the waiter of the change of mind; they say that the deception consisted in continuing to represent to the waiter that there was an intention to pay before leaving.

On behalf of the respondent it was contended that no deception had been practised. It was accepted that when the meal was ordered there was a representation by the respondent that he would pay but it was contended that once the meal was served there was no longer any representation but that there was merely an obligation to pay a debt: it was further argued that thereafter there was no deception because there was no obligation in the debtor to inform his creditor that payment was not to be made. I cannot accept these contentions. They ignore the circumstance that the representation that was made was a continuing one: its essence was that an intention to pay would continue until payment was made: by its very nature it would not cease to operate as a representation unless some new arrangement was made....

The final question which arises is whether, if there was deception and if there was pecuniary advantage, it was by the deception that the respondent obtained the pecuniary advantage. In my view, this must be a question of fact and the magistrates have found that it was by his deception that the respondent dishonestly evaded payment. It would seem to be clear that if the waiter had thought that if he left the restaurant to go to the kitchen the respondent would at once run out, he (the waiter) would not have left the restaurant and would have taken suitable action. The waiter proceeded on the basis that the implied representation made to him (i.e. of an honest intention to pay) was effective. The waiter was caused to refrain from taking certain courses of action which but for the representation he would have taken. In my view, the respondent during the whole time that he was in the restaurant made and by his continuing conduct continued to make a representation of his intention to pay before leaving. When in place of his original intention he substituted the dishonest intention of running away as soon as the waiter's back was turned, he was continuing to lead the waiter to believe that he intended to pay. He practised a deception on the waiter and by so doing he obtained for himself the pecuniary advantage of evading his obligation to pay before leaving. That he did so dishonestly was found by the magistrates who, in my opinion, rightly convicted him.

I would allow this appeal.

LORD HODSON: ... The vital question is whether by sitting in the restaurant for 10 minutes after having consumed the meal the respondent was guilty of deception when he departed without paying. If he had no intention of paying at the outset cadit quaestio. If, on the other hand, his representation made at the outset was honest, I find it difficult to accept that the effect of the original representation continues so as to make subsequent failure to pay his creditor, automatically, so to speak, an evasion of debt obtained by deception.

Whether any evidence was given by a waiter is not disclosed. The case states that the waiter had gone to the kitchen and that during his absence the respondent and his four companions ran out of the restaurant after having been there for nearly an hour and maintaining the demeanour of ordinary customers. Would the reasonable man say that a deception had been practised on him? Evade the debt the respondent did, but no more than any other debtor who, having originally intended to pay for a pecuniary advantage, subsequently changes his mind and evades his contractual obligation by not paying.

In order to succeed the prosecution must rely on the original representation honestly made by the respondent when he entered the restaurant as a continuing representation which operated and lulled the restaurant proprietor into a sense of security so that the respondent was enabled to leave as he did. I do not recollect that the prosecution put the case in this way but I think it is most formidable if so presented, for if the representation continued it was falsified by the change of mind of the respondent.

It is trite law and common sense that an honest man entering into a contract is deemed to represent that he has the present intention of carrying it out but if, as in this case, having accepted the pecuniary advantage involved in the transaction, he does not necessarily evade his debt by deception if he fails to pay his debt. Nothing he did after his change of mind can be characterised as conduct which would indicate that he was then practising a deception. To rely on breach of a continuous representation I suggest that in administering a criminal statute this is going too far and seems to involve that the ordinary man who enters into a contract intending to carry it out can be found guilty of a criminal offence if he changes his mind after incurring the obligation to pay unless he has taken a step to bring the change of mind to the notice of his creditor.

The appellant sought to support the argument, that there was a duty on the respondent to correct his original representation, by authority. *With* v. *O'Flanagan* [1936] Ch. 575 is good authority for the proposition that if a person who makes a representation, which is not immediately acted upon, finds that the facts are changing he must, before the representation is acted upon, disclose the change to the person to whom he has made the representation. That case concerned the sale of a medical practice. The seller, a doctor, represented that his practice was profitable. This was true when the representation was made but by the time the contract was signed the practice had dwindled to practically nothing. This was not disclosed to the purchaser who, on discovery, sought rescission. It was held that the statement made, though true at the time, had become untrue during the negotiations and that there was an obligation to disclose the fact to the purchaser.

The earlier case of *Traill* v. *Baring* (1864) 4 De G.J. & Sm. 318 was cited [1936] Ch. 575, 583. It contains the following passage from the judgment of Turner L.J., at p. 329:

> "I take it to be quite clear, that if a person makes a representation by which he induces another to take a particular course, and the circumstances are afterwards altered to the knowledge of the party making the representation, but not to the knowledge of the party to whom the representation is made, and are so altered that the alteration of the circumstances may affect the course of conduct which may be pursued by the party to whom the representation is made, it is the imperative duty of the party who has made the representation to communicate to the party to whom the representation has been made the alteration of those circumstances; and that this court will not hold the party to whom the representation has been made bound unless such a communication has been made."

This authority does not assist the appellant as to continuity of representation generally. The position there taken was based upon a duty to communicate a change of circumstances which had occurred after a representation, true when made, had been falsified by the time the contract was entered into. Here no contract was entered into following a deception of any kind.

The respondent was in breach of his obligation to pay his debt but I agree with the conclusion of the Divisional Court that there was no evidence that he evaded it by deception.

I would dismiss this appeal.

LORD PEARSON: . . . The essential feature of this case, in accordance with the magistrates' findings and opinions as I understand them, is that there was a continuing representation to be implied from the conduct of the respondent and his companions. By "continuing representation" I mean in this case not a continuing effect of an initial representation, but a representation which is being made by conduct at every moment throughout the course of conduct. The course of conduct consisted of: (i) entering the restaurant, sitting down at a table and probably looking at the menu; (ii) giving to the waiter an order for a main course to be served; (iii) eating the main course; (iv) remaining at the table for about 10 minutes. The remaining at the table for that time was consistent in appearance with continuing their conversation and deciding whether or not to order another course. In my opinion all those actions can properly be regarded as one course of conduct continuing up to but not including the running out of the restaurant without paying. That is where the course of conduct was broken off. Up to the moment of running out they were behaving ostensibly as ordinary customers of the restaurant, and the ordinary customers of such a restaurant intend to pay for their meals in the appropriate manner before leaving the restaurant. . . .

In my view, the magistrates could and did reasonably imply from the course of conduct a representation by the respondent that he had a present intention of paying for his meal before leaving the restaurant. It was a continuing representation in the sense that I have indicated, being made at every moment throughout the course of conduct. In so far as it was being made before the decision to run out without paying, it was according to the magistrates' finding a true representation of the respondent's then present intention. In so far as it was being made after that decision, it was a false representation of the respondent's then present intention, and of course false to his knowledge. That false representation deceived the waiter, inducing him to go to the kitchen, whereby the respondent, with his companions, was enabled to make his escape from the restaurant and so dishonestly evade his obligation to pay for his meal. Thus by deception he obtained for himself the pecuniary advantage of evading the debt.

In my opinion, the respondent was rightly convicted by the magistrates. I would allow the appeal and restore the conviction and sentence.

Appeal allowed

Questions

1. Is the misrepresentation of a person in Ray's position (a) that he intends to pay for the meal, or (b) that his original representation that he would pay for the meal is still true? Can it ever matter which it is?
2. A, after consuming his meal, discovers that his wallet is empty and realises that he cannot pay. Is he under a duty at once to own up to the waiter? If not, how is he to be distinguished from Ray? If so, how is he to be distinguished from the ordinary man (referred to by Lord Hodson) who enters into a contract intending to carry it out but fails to take steps to bring the change of mind to the notice of his creditor?
3. Does it follow from *D.P.P.* v. *Ray* that failure to correct a mistaken impression in the other party before he transfers property to the accused counts as a deception? A, a private person, orders goods from P, a wholesaler, making no representation express or implied as to his own status. During the negotiations, he becomes aware that P thinks that he (A) is a retailer and will only sell to retailers. A fails to correct the misapprehension. Is he guilty of obtaining the goods by deception?
4. A sold a car to B, representing it as a "beautiful car." It was of beautiful appearance, but was not roadworthy. Is A guilty of obtaining B's money by deception? See *Robertson* v. *Dicicco* [1972] R.T.R. 431.

Note

In *R.* v. *Staines* (1974) 60 Cr. App. R. 160 (C.A.), a case of A signing cheques on B's behalf not *knowing* that B's account was overdrawn, James L.J. said (at p. 162) "This Court accepts the contention put forward that in this section 'recklessly' does mean more than being careless, does mean more than being negligent, and does involve an indifference to or disregard of the feature of whether a statement be true or false."

Compare "recklessly" in other parts of the law, *ante*, p. 71.

Griew, The Theft Acts 1968 and 1978

"§ 6–21 (i) *What state of mind must the representation induce?* "To deceive is, I apprehend, to induce a man to believe that a thing is true which is false." This well-known statement by Buckley J. in *Re London and Globe Finance Corporation* [1903] 1 Ch. 728 at 832, was cited with approval in *D.P.P.* v. *Ray* (*ante*, p. 576). It appears at first sight to state the obvious and require no elaboration. Yet there is, on reflection, a good deal of uncertainty attaching to the notion of 'believing that a thing is true'; and there has been no judicial consideration of what amounts to 'believing' for this purpose. It is submitted that, if indeed 'believing' is an appropriate word in this context, it should not be understood only in the sense of firmly accepting the truth of the statement in question. The deception offences can hardly be limited to cases in which P is induced to hold a strong positive belief. P may be well aware he does not know D, that there are rogues and liars abroad and that D may be one of them. He may act 'on the strength' of D's assertion and in reliance upon it, but without any positive sense either believing or disbelieving it. If D is lying, P is surely 'deceived' for the purpose of section 15. It may in fact be better to abandon the word 'believe' and say that to deceive is to induce a man to act in reliance upon a false representation."

iii. The Obtaining must be *by* the Deception

R. v. Aston and Hadley

[1970] 1 W.L.R. 1584
Court of Appeal

In a betting shop, A handed the counter clerk a betting slip for £70 to win on a particular dog. The bet was rung up on the till and the clerk was prepared to hand over the receipt. A counted out a bundle of bank notes with extreme slowness, and before he had finished, the progress of the race, which could be followed in the shop on a broadcast relay, made it obvious that the dog A bet on could not possibly win. A thereupon gathered up his money and left the shop. A and his confederate H were convicted of obtaining pecuniary advantage by deception, namely, the evasion of a debt by the deception that A intended to pay immediately the £70 for which he had made a bet. They appealed.

MEGAW L.J.: ... In the opinion of this court, in addition to other possible difficulties in attempting to force the facts of this case into the framework of section 16 (2) (a), the conduct of the appellants in the slow counting of the money could not safely or satisfactorily be presented to, or accepted by, the jury as a deception involving a representation that, as it was put, the appellants intended to pay "immediately." Whatever representation the slow counting might be thought to involve, it could hardly be a representation of an intention to make an immediate payment. Moreover, to be relevant, the deception, for the purposes of section 16 (2) (a), must at least normally be a deception which operates on the mind of the person deceived so as to influence him to do or to refrain from doing something whereby the debt is deferred or evaded. It would require an unacceptable stretch of the imagination, on the evidence in this case, to reach the conclusion that the counting of the money operated, whether or not the slowness is taken into account, on Mr. Hine's mind in such a way as to bring about the evasion of the debt.

There was accordingly a misdirection, which followed initially from the acceptance of the prosecution's submissions that the facts proved could bring the case within the terms of the indictment as framed by reference to section 16 (2) (a).

That does not mean the dishonest conduct of this sort falls outside the scope of the criminal law or that it can be resorted to with impunity. The difficulties which have arisen could have been avoided and an inassailable conviction might well have resulted, as counsel for the appellants was prepared to concede, if the Particulars of the indictment had been framed by reference to paragraph (c) instead of paragraph (a) of section 16 (2) of the Theft Act....

Had the indictment been framed by reference to that paragraph, a jury might well have had no difficulty, on the facts in evidence, in finding that there was a deception. When someone seeks to place a bet in a cash betting shop, a jury might well take the view that he is representing, and intending to be understood to represent, that it is his intention to pay the stake in cash as soon as his bet has been accepted. A jury might well have found by reference to what happened thereafter—the slow counting and the walk out when the failure of the Trap 1 dog was apparent—that that representation was untrue; that it amounted to a deception; and that that deception (not the slow counting, but the original representation of intention) had operated on Mr. Hine's mind so as to influence him to allow the bet to be placed: and thereby to give the appellants the opportunity to win money by betting.... This approach puts the slow counting of money in its right place. It was strong evidence of an earlier deception, rather than being itself a deception.

However, though the appellants might well have been convicted on a differently drawn indictment, this is not a case in which the powers of the court either under section 3 or the proviso to section 2 (1) of the Criminal Appeal Act, 1968, are applicable.

Accordingly, as the court has previously pronounced, the convictions of both the appellants are quashed. They, and other persons, would, however, be ill-advised to act in this way in future, as they might find it difficult to escape from the teeth of section 16 (2) (c), should a jury be convinced of their dishonesty.

Convictions quashed

Note

For section 16 (2) (*c*), see *post*, p. 593.

R. v. Mills (1857) 8 Cox 263: M. claimed money from P. for work done which had not been done as M. well knew. P. also knew this but sent the money to M. for the purpose of entrapping him. Held (CCCR), the representation was not what caused P. to send the money, but the desire to entrap M.

R. v. Laverty [1970] 3 All E.R. 432 (C.A.): A reconstructed an old car, and substituted for the original number plates, plates from another car he had broken up. A sold the car with the false plates to B. *Held*, since B took no notice of the plates and bought because he thought A was the owner, A was not guilty of obtaining the price by deception.

R. v. Collis-Smith [1971] *Crim. L.R. 716:* A drove his private car into a service station and asked for petrol, which was put into his tank. The attendant then asked if he was paying for it, and A said it was to be booked to his employer although, as A well knew, he had no authority to pledge his employer's credit for petrol. He was convicted of obtaining the petrol by deception, the deception being that his employer would pay. His appeal was allowed; the petrol had already been obtained before the deception took place. The court emphasised that it was dealing with a particular situation where petrol had been put in the tank of a vehicle, and would be difficult to recover, and not with different situations, such as a person putting goods into a shopping basket and being stopped before leaving the shop.

Questions

1. Why would it make a difference if the property, instead of being petrol in the tank of a car, had been goods in a shopping basket in a shop? See *Edwards* v. *Ddin, ante,* p. 516.

2. If the deception alleged had been an implied representation that he (the defendant) would pay, might the result have been different?

3. On the deception actually alleged (that his employers would pay), could Collis-Smith have been convicted of theft? See *R.* v. *McHugh* [1977] R.T.R. 1 and J. C. Smith [1977] Crim. L.R. 175.

R. v. Doukas
[1978] 1 W.L.R. 372
Court of Appeal

D., a waiter at a hotel, was found with bottles of wine not of a type sold by the hotel. He admitted that he intended, when a customer ordered wine, to substitute his own bottle for his employer's, make out a separate bill and pocket the money paid by the customer. He was convicted of going equipped to cheat, contrary to section 25 of the Theft Act 1968. He applied for leave to appeal against conviction.

Geoffrey Lane L.J. . . . The offence of going equipped to cheat is to be found in section 25 of the Theft Act 1968. It reads:

> "(1) A person shall be guilty of an offence if, when not at his place of abode, he has with him any article for use in the course of or in connection with any . . . cheat . . . (5) For purposes of this section . . . 'cheat' means an offence under section 15 of this Act."

Section 15 concerns obtaining property by deception. . . .

Combining those two sections of the Theft Act—section 25 and section 15—which are apposite, one reaches this result: a person shall be guilty of an offence if, when not in his place of abode, he has with him any article for use in the course of or in connection with any deception, whether deliberate or reckless, by words or conduct, as to fact or as to law, for purposes of dishonestly obtaining property belonging to another with the intention of permanently depriving the other of it.

If one analyses that combined provision, one reaches the situation that the following items have to be proved. First of all, that there was an article for use in connection with the deception: here the bottles. Secondly, that there was a proposed deception: here the deception of the guests into believing that the proffered wine was hotel wine and not the waiter's. Thirdly, an intention to obtain property by means of the deception, and the property here is the money of the guests which he proposes to obtain and keep. Fourthly, dishonesty.... Fifthly, there must be proof that the obtaining would have been, wholly or partially, by virtue of the deception. The prosecution must prove that nexus between the deception and obtaining. It is this last and final ingredient which, as we see it in the present case, is the only point which raises any difficulty....

We have, as in the notice of appeal, been referred to the decision in *R.* v. *Rashid* [1977] 1 W.L.R. 298, which was a decision by another division of this court. That case concerned not a waiter in a hotel, but a British Rail waiter who substituted not bottles of wine for the railway wine but his own tomato sandwiches for the railway tomato sandwiches; and it is to be observed that the basis of the decision in that case was that the summing up of the judge to the jury was inadequate. On that basis the appeal was allowed. But the court went on to express its views obiter on the question whether in those circumstances it could be said that the obtaining was by virtue of deception, and it came to the conclusion, as I say obiter, that the answer was probably no.

Of course each case of this type may produce different results according to the circumstances of the case and according, in particular, to the commodity which is being proffered. But, as we see it, the question has to be asked of the hypothetical customer, "Why did you buy this wine, or, if you had been told the truth, would you or would you not have bought the commodity?" It is, at least in theory, for the jury in the end to decide that question.

Here, as the ground of appeal is simply the judge's action in allowing the case to go to the jury, we are answering that question, so to speak, on behalf of the judge rather than the jury. Was there evidence of the necessary nexus fit to go to the jury? Certainly so far as the wine is concerned, we have no doubt at all that the hypothetical customer, faced with the waiter saying to him: "This of course is not hotel wine, this is stuff which I imported into the hotel myself and I am going to put the proceeds of the wine, if you pay, into my own pocket," would certainly answer, so far as we can see, "I do not want your wine, kindly bring me the hotel carafe wine." Indeed it would be a strange jury that came to any other conclusion, and a stranger guest who gave any other answer for several reasons. First of all, the guest would not know what was in the bottle which the waiter was proffering. True, he may not know what was in the carafe which the hotel was proffering, but he would at least be able to have recourse to the hotel if something was wrong with the carafe wine, but he would have no such recourse with the waiter; if he did, it would be worthless.

It seems to us the matter can be answered on a much simpler basis. The hypothetical customer must be reasonably honest as well as being reasonably intelligent and it seems to us incredible that any customer, to whom the true situation was made clear, would willingly make himself a party to what was obviously a fraud by the waiter upon his employers. If that conclusion is contrary to the obiter dicta in *R.* v. *Rashid* then we must respectfully disagree with those dicta....

Application refused

Note

"It seems to us incredible that any customer ... would willingly make himself a party to what was obviously a fraud by the waiter on his employers." This idea has proved to be important in securing convictions in the not uncommon case where A obtains things from B by proffering a cheque and cheque card, or a credit card, when the bank has withdrawn his authority to use the card. Since the giving of an ordinary unbacked cheque by A implies a representation that he has funds or an arrangement with his bank under which the cheque will be honoured, B will obviously rely on the representation of credit-worthiness in deciding whether to give A goods or credit. If he makes a mistake he will lose. The obtaining is thus clearly caused by the representation in all ordinary cases. But where a cheque and apparently valid cheque card, or an apparently valid credit card, is presented by A, B will be paid anyway whatever the state of A's finances, and it becomes difficult to say that B relies on the representation of credit-worthiness in giving A goods on credit. This led to opinions that where B really is indifferent to the credit-worthiness of A, no inducement can be found: Smith, § 158; Williams, *Textbook*, pp. 846–847; *R.* v. *Lambie* [1981] 1 All E.R. 332 (C.A.). However it has been held that the relevant representation in this sort of case is not as to credit-worthiness (which may well be a matter of indifference to B), but as to *authority to present the card*, which cannot be a matter of indifference to B.

R. v. Lambie
[1981] 2 All E.R. 776
House of Lords

L. obtained a credit card from a bank giving her credit facilities up to a limit of £200. The bank entered into contracts with retailers by which the bank guaranteed any purchase made with the credit card provided the retailer complied with certain conditions relating to the validity of the card. L., when well over her credit limit of £200, purchased goods from a shop using her credit card. The shop complied with the conditions of a credit card purchase and, since the amount involved was less than the amount for which special authorisation was required from the bank, made no enquiry of the bank as to L.'s credit standing. L. was charged with obtaining a pecuniary advantage by deception contrary to section 16 (1) of the Theft Act 1968. The judge asked the jury whether the shop keeper relied on the presentation of an apparently valid credit card as being due authority to use the card. The jury convicted, L.'s appeal to the Court of Appeal was allowed, and the prosecution appealed to the House of Lords.

Lord Roskill: ... My Lords, at the close of the case for the prosecution, learned counsel for the respondent invited the learned judge to withdraw both counts from the jury on, it seems, from reading the learned judge's clear ruling upon this submission, two grounds, first, that as a matter of law there was no evidence from which a jury might properly draw the inference that the presentation of the card in the circumstances I have described was a representation by the respondent that she was authorised by the bank to use the card to create a contract to which the bank would be a party, and secondly, that as a matter of law there was no evidence from which a jury might properly infer that Miss Rounding [the departmental manager at Mothercare] was induced by any representation which the respondent might have made to allow the transaction to be completed and the respondent to obtain the goods. The foundation for this latter submission was that it was the existence of the agreement between Mothercare and the bank that was the reason for Miss Rounding allowing the transaction to be completed and the goods to be taken by the respondent, since Miss Rounding knew of the arrangement with the bank, so that Mothercare was in any event certain of payment. It was not, it was suggested, any representation by the respondent which induced Miss Rounding to complete the transaction and to allow the respondent to take the goods.

My Lords, the learned judge rejected these submissions. He was clearly right to do so, as indeed was conceded in argument before your Lordships' House, if the decision of this House in *Commissioner of Police for the Metropolis* v. *Charles* [1977] A.C. 177 is of direct application. In that appeal this House was concerned with the dishonest use, not as in the present appeal of a credit card, but of a cheque card. The appellant defendant was charged and convicted on two counts of obtaining a pecuniary advantage by deception, contrary to section 16 of the Theft Act 1968. The Court of Appeal (Criminal Division) and your Lordships' House both upheld those convictions. Your Lordships unanimously held that where a drawer of a cheque which is accepted in return for goods, services or cash, uses a cheque card he represents to the payee that he has the actual authority of the bank to enter on its behalf into the contract expressed on the card that it would honour the cheque on presentation for payment.

My Lords, I venture to quote in their entirety three paragraphs from the speech of my noble and learned friend, Lord Diplock, at pages 182 and 183 of the report, which as I venture to think, encapsulate the reasoning of all those members of your Lordships' House who delivered speeches:

> "When a cheque card is brought into the transaction, it still remains the fact that all the payee is concerned with is that the cheque should be honoured by the bank. I do not think that the fact that a cheque card is used necessarily displaces the representation to be implied from the act of drawing the cheque which has just been mentioned. It is, however, likely to displace that representation at any rate as the main inducement to the payee to take the cheque, since the use of the cheque card in connection with the transaction gives to the payee a direct contractual right against the bank itself to payment on presentment, provided that the use of the card by the drawer to bind the bank to pay the cheque was within the actual or ostensible authority conferred upon him by the bank.
>
> By exhibiting to the payee a cheque card containing the undertaking by the bank to honour cheques drawn in compliance with the conditions endorsed on the back, and drawing the cheque accordingly, the drawer represents to the payee that he has actual authority from the bank to make a contract with the payee on the bank's behalf that it will honour the cheque on presentment for payment.
>
> It was submitted on behalf of the accused that there is no need to imply a representation that the drawer's authority to bind the bank was actual and not merely ostensible, since ostensible authority alone would suffice to create a contract with the payee that was binding on the bank; and the drawer's possession of the cheque card and the cheque book with the bank's consent would be enough to constitute his ostensible authority. So, the submission goes, the only representation needed to give business efficacy to the transaction would be true. This argument stands the doctrine of ostensible authority on its head. What creates ostensible authority in a person who purports to enter into a contract as agent for a principal is a representation made to the other party that he has the actual authority of the principal for whom he claims to be acting to enter into the contract on that person's behalf. If (1) the other party has believed the representation and on the faith of that belief has acted upon it and (2) the person represented to be his principal has so conducted himself towards that other party as to be estopped from denying the truth of the representation, then, and only then, is he bound by the contract purportedly made on his behalf. The whole foundation of liability under the doctrine of ostensible authority is a representation, believed by the person to whom it is made, that the person

> claiming to contract as agent for a principal has the actual authority of the principal to enter into the contract on his behalf."

If one substitutes in the passage at page 182G the words "to honour the voucher" for the words "to pay the cheque", it is not easy to see why *mutatis mutandis* the entire passages are not equally applicable to the dishonest misuse of credit cards as to the dishonest misuse of cheque cards.

But the Court of Appeal in a long and careful judgment delivered by Cumming-Bruce L.J. felt reluctantly impelled to reach a different conclusion. The crucial passage in the judgment which the learned Lord Justice delivered reads thus:

> "We would pay tribute to the lucidity with which the learned judge presented to the jury the law which the House of Lords had declared in relation to deception in a cheque card transaction. If that analysis can be applied to this credit card deception the summing-up is faultless. But, in our view, there is a relevant distinction between the situation described in *Charles* and the situation devised by Barclays Bank for transactions involving use of their credit cards. By their contract with the bank, Mothercare had bought from the bank the right to sell goods to Barclaycard holders without regard to the question whether the customer was complying with the terms of the contract between the customer and the bank. By her evidence Miss Rounding made it perfectly plain that she made no assumption about the appellant's credit standing at the bank. As she said 'the Company rules exist because of the Company's agreement with Barclaycard'. The flaw in the logic is in our view demonstrated by the way in which the Judge put the question of the inducement of Miss Rounding to the jury:
>
> > 'Is that a reliance by her, Miss Rounding of Mothercare, upon the presentation of the card as being due authority *within the limits as at that time* as with count one?'
>
> In our view, the evidence of Miss Rounding could not found a verdict that necessarily involved a finding of fact that Miss Rounding was induced by a false representation that the appellant's credit standing at the bank gave her authority to use the card."

I should perhaps mention, for the sake of clarity, that the person referred to as the appellant in that passage is the present respondent.

It was for that reason that the Court of Appeal (Criminal Division) allowed the appeal, albeit with hesitation and reluctance. That court accordingly certified the following point of law as of general public importance, namely:

> "In view of the proved differences between a cheque card transaction and a credit card transaction, were we right in distinguishing this case from that of *Commissioner of Metropolitan Police* v. *Charles* [1977] A.C. 177 upon the issue of inducement?"

My Lords, as the appellant says in paragraph 9 of his printed case, the Court of Appeal Criminal Division laid too much emphasis upon the undoubted, but to my mind irrelevant fact that Miss Rounding said she made no assumption about the respondent's credit standing with the bank. They reasoned from the absence of assumption that there was no evidence from which the jury could conclude that she was "induced by a false representation that the appellant's credit standing at the bank gave her authority to use the card". But, my Lords, with profound respect to the learned Lord Justice, that is not the relevant question. Following the decision of this House in *Charles*, it is in my view clear that the representation arising from the presentation of a credit card has nothing to do with the appellant's credit standing at the bank but is a representation of actual authority to make the contract with, in this case, Mothercare on the bank's behalf that the bank will honour the voucher upon presentation. Upon that view, the existence and terms of the agreement between the bank and Mothercare are irrelevant, as is the fact that Mothercare, because of that agreement, would look to the bank for payment.

That being the representation to be implied from the respondent's actions and use of the credit card, the only remaining question is whether Miss Rounding was induced by that representation to complete the transaction and allow the respondent to take away the goods. My Lords, if she had been asked whether had she known the respondent was acting dishonestly and, in truth, had no authority whatever from the bank to use the credit card in this way, she (Miss Rounding) would have completed the transaction, only one answer is possible—no. Had an affirmative answer been given to this question, Miss Rounding would, of course, have become a participant in furtherance of the respondent's fraud and a conspirator with her to defraud both Mothercare and the bank. Leading counsel for the respondent was ultimately constrained, rightly as I think, to admit that had that question been asked of Miss Rounding and answered, as it must have been, in the negative, this appeal must succeed. But both he and his learned junior strenuously argued that, as my noble and learned friend, Lord Edmund-Davies, pointed out in his speech in *Charles* at pages 192 and 193 of the report, the question whether a person is or is not induced to act in a particular way by a dishonest representation is a question of fact, and since what they claimed to be the crucial question had not been asked of Miss Rounding, there was no adequate proof of the requisite inducement. In her deposition, Miss Rounding stated, no doubt with complete truth, that she only remembered this particular transaction with the respondent because some one subsequently came and asked her about it after it had taken place. My Lords, credit card frauds are all too frequently perpetrated, and if conviction of offenders for offences against sections 15 or 16 of the Theft Act 1968 can only be obtained if the prosecution are able in each case to call the person upon whom the fraud was immediately perpetrated to say that he or she positively remembered the particular transaction and, had the truth been known, would never have entered into that supposedly well-remembered transaction, the guilty would often escape conviction. In some cases, of course, it may be possible to adduce such evidence if the particular transaction is well remembered. But where as in the present case no one could reasonably be expected to remember a particular transaction in detail, and the inference of inducement may well be in all the circumstances quite irresistible, I see no reason in principle why it should not be left to the jury to decide, upon the evidence in the case as a whole, whether that inference is in truth irresistible as to my mind it is in the present case. In this connection it is to be noted that the respondent did not go into the witness box to give evidence from which that inference might conceivably have been rebutted.

My Lords, in this respect I find myself in agreement with what was said by Humphreys J. giving the judgment of the Court of Criminal Appeal in *R. v. Sullivan* (1945) 30 Cr. App. R. 132 at 136:

> "It is, we think, undoubtedly good law that the question of the inducement acting upon the mind of the person who may be described as the prosecutor is not a matter which can only be proved by the direct evidence of the witness. It can be, and very often is, proved by the witness being asked some question which brings the answer: 'I believed that statement and that is why I parted with my money'; but it is not necessary that there should be that question and answer if the facts are such that it is patent that there was only one reason which anybody could suggest for the person alleged to have been defrauded parting with his money, and that is the false pretence, if it was a false pretence."

It is true that in *R.* v. *Laverty* [1970] 3 All E.R. 432 at 434, Lord Parker C.J. said that the Court of Appeal Criminal Division was anxious not to extend the principle in *Sullivan* further than was necessary. Of course, the Crown must always prove its case and one element which will always be required to be proved in these cases is the effect of the dishonest representation upon the mind of the person to whom it is made. But I see no reason why in cases such as the present, where what Humphreys J. called the direct evidence of the witness is not, and cannot reasonably be expected to be available, reliance upon a dishonest representation cannot be sufficiently established by proof of facts from which an irresistible inference of such reliance can be drawn.

My Lords, I would answer the certified question in the negative and would allow the appeal and restore the conviction of the respondent upon the second count in the indictment which she faced at Bedford Crown Court.

Appeal allowed: Conviction restored

Davies v. Flackett
[1973] R.T.R. 8
Queen's Bench Division

The facts appear in the judgment of Bridge J.

BRIDGE J.: This is a prosecutor's appeal by case stated from a decision of Newcastle under Lyme Justices, who on 27th January 1972 dismissed an information which had been preferred by the prosecutor against the defendant for an offence of dishonestly obtaining for himself a pecuniary advantage by deception.

The facts are short. The defendant drove his motor car on to a car park operated by the Newcastle Borough Council. There was no attendant at the car park. The system in use for securing the payment by patrons of the car park of the charge of 5p. which was levied by the corporation for its use, was that a machine guarded the exit from the car park; the machine operated a barrier. The car park patron approaching the exit barrier drove his car to a point where he inserted the appropriate coin into a slot, and that had the effect of causing the barrier arm to rise to permit him to drive away. In this case the defendant had the good fortune, it appears, to find as he drove to the exit barrier, that some stranger was holding it up, and he took advantage of that situation and did not put his coin into the machine. He was thereupon stopped by a police officer and an official of the corporation. On those facts the justices concluded that the offence of dishonestly obtaining a pecuniary advantage by deception had not been proved against the defendant.

There is no doubt, of course, that the defendant was dishonest; there is no doubt that he obtained for himself a pecuniary advantage. The question is: did he practise a deception, and was that deception effective in securing him the pecuniary advantage which he obtained?

The form of the question which is raised in the case stated is as follows:

> "... whether an act of deception directed towards a machine in the absence of any human agent is sufficient to support a prima facie case in the preferred information."

If the question is asked in that form, it is as it seems to me inevitable that it must be answered in the negative, but it may well be that that is not the proper form in which the question should be asked.

It is plain to my mind on those facts that, until the moment when the defendant was approaching the barrier and saw the fortuitous opportunity presented to him by the third party's action to drive out without paying, there was no evidence of any dishonest intent on the part of the defendant, no evidence that when he drove on to the car park he had not intended to pay his 5p. when leaving. But it is argued by Mr. Gosling, who has said everything that could be said on behalf of the appellant prosecutor, that at the moment when the opportunity to drive away without paying presented itself, the defendant, by taking advantage of that opportunity, was resiling from his intention to pay, and from that moment on was practising a dishonest deception, and according to the argument it is immaterial that there was no one present as representing the corporation who could in fact be deceived.

The fallacy in the argument to my mind, assuming that it is well founded in all other respects, is that it overlooks the circumstance that, to establish an offence under section 16 of the Theft Act 1968, it is necessary to show not only that there was a deception practised, but also that the deception was effective in securing for the offender the pecuniary advantage which he obtained. The offence is dishonestly obtaining a pecuniary advantage *by* deception. To my mind on those facts, even if it is possible for a deception to be practised so as to establish that ingredient of the offence under section 16 without there being a human mind to be deceived, which I am prepared to assume (though for myself I doubt it) in favour of Mr. Gosling's argument, nevertheless it is clear that here the deception was not effective to secure any pecuniary advantage. It could not possibly be said here that a pecuniary advantage was obtained by deception. Accordingly I would dismiss this appeal.

MELFORD STEVENSON J.: I agree. I wish to emphasise and perhaps to repeat that the form of the question at the end of the case stated does not disclose the real point raised by the facts which are set out. The question as stated was:

> "... whether an act of deception directed towards a machine in the absence of any human agent is sufficient to support a prima facie case in the preferred information."

What happened here was that the driver of the car, who for all that appears in the case entered this car park with a perfectly honest intention to perform his obligation of paying his 5p. on leaving, finding himself faced with the fortuitous opportunity of a barrier held up by a third person, drove out. That seems to me to be very far from establishing the offence which is described in the information of avoiding a lawful debt by a deception, namely, that he intended to pay the sum of 5p. for the use of a controlled car park. All the facts set out in the case are consistent with an intention to carry out the obligation, at least until the moment when he was provided with an opportunity of leaving as a result of the fortuitous raising of the barrier. True he obtained a pecuniary advantage, but I cannot satisfy myself that the obtaining of that advantage was by any deception, and in those circumstances it appears to me that this appeal must be dismissed.

ACKNER J.: I agree. This case does not raise the question whether an act of deception directed towards either a machine or the owner of a machine can support a prima facie case of a breach of section 16. When such case arises, no doubt it will be dealt with. Nothing which I say expressing my agreement that this appeal should be dismissed in any way suggests that an offence cannot be committed where there is any mishandling of a machine, and thereby an advantage is obtained.

Appeal dismissed with costs

Questions

1. What extra fact would be needed properly to raise the question the justices asked?

2. A puts a stolen cash card into a cash dispenser, presses the right combination of buttons and receives £10 in cash. Has he committed any offence? See, *ante*, p. 496, and *R.* v. *Hands* (1887) 16 Cox 188.

Note

See, *post*, p. 597, on making off without payment.

R. v. Clucas
[1949] 2 K.B. 226
Court of Criminal Appeal

C. induced a bookmaker to bet with him by falsely representing that he was acting as agent for many people at his place of work. The bet was successful and C. was paid the winnings. C. was convicted of obtaining money by false pretences.

LORD GODDARD C.J.: The main point which arises in the case . . . may be stated in this way: Does a man who induces a bookmaker to bet with him by making false pretences as to his identity or as to the capacity in which he is putting on the bets, obtain money by false pretences if he is fortunate enough, having made those pretences, to back a winning horse so that the bookmaker pays him? The case as it was argued originally before a court consisting of three judges raised this point, and the court showed when they adjourned the hearing, that there was not unanimity at that stage, consequently they adjourned it to be heard before a full court, for which reason five judges have now heard it.

In the opinion of the court it is impossible to say that there was an obtaining of the money by the false pretences which were alleged, because the money was obtained not by reason of the fact that the people falsely pretended that they were somebody else or acting in some capacity which they were not; it was obtained because they backed a winning horse and the bookmaker paid because the horse had won. No doubt the bookmaker might never have opened an account with these men if he had known the true facts, but we must distinguish in this case between one contributing cause and the effective cause which led the bookmaker to pay the money.

The effective cause which led the bookmaker to pay the money was the fact that these men had backed a winning horse. . . . Although these two men induced the bookmaker to bet with them by means of a false pretence, what the court cannot see is that that false pretence was the false pretence which led to the payment of the money. What led to the payment of the money was the fact that these men backed a winning horse by inducing the bookmaker to bet with them. They put themselves in the position that if they backed the horse and lost, they had to pay the bookmaker and if they backed the horse and won they were entitled to receive the money. In the opinion of the court, therefore, it cannot be said that the money was obtained by false pretences within the meaning of section 32, subsection (1), of the Larceny Act, 1916.

Mr. Boileau has called the attention of the court to certain cases, and no doubt the nearest case to this one and the only one which I think it is necessary to mention is *R.* v. *Button* [1900] 2 Q.B. 597. In that case the defendant, by representing that he was a person of the name Sims, who was a very moderate performer in athletic sports and was not known as a likely winner of races, managed to obtain from the committee of some athletic sports which were to be held in Lincoln a very substantial handicap in a race. He was in fact a man who had won a great many races and had the truth been known he would have received either no handicap at all or a very moderate handicap instead of the very substantial handicap which he obtained. Indeed, after the race was won by him he repeated the false pretence to the secretary and obtained a prize, but it was not only on account of the repetition of the false pretence that he obtained the prize. The court held that by falsely representing himself to be someone he was not, thereby obtaining a substantial handicap, he obtained the prize on false pretences because it was a matter directly connected with the winning or not winning of the prize. He obtained for himself a winning chance. He got the handicap which he would not otherwise have got, and thereby enabled himself to win the race. We think that that case on the facts is clearly distinguishable from this case.

Conviction on this count quashed

Note

In fact Button did not actually receive the prize and the charge was attempting to obtain property by false pretences.

The distinction between the two cases appears to be that in *Clucas* the placing of the bet was merely a *causa sine qua non* of the obtaining; without making the bet, he could not have received any winnings, but that applies equally to all sorts of other factors such as the fact that the bookmaker had a telephone which enabled C to get in touch with him and place the bet; these are merely contributing causes; the *causa causans*, the one cause which above all others produces the payment of winnings was the fact that the horse that C backed was first past the post. But in *Button*, the one effective cause, the *causa causans* was the fact that he had been given a big start in the race. Since the false pretences produced the *causa causans* it can be said that (had the crime been complete) the false pretence produced the handing over of the prize.

Today a man in the position of Clucas would be guilty of obtaining a pecuniary advantage by deception. See section 16, below.

iv. Dishonesty

Criminal Law Revision Committee's Eighth Report, Cmnd. 2977

§ 88 "The provision in [section 15 (1)] making a person guilty of criminal deception if he 'dishonestly obtains' the property replaces the provision in 1916, s. 32 (1), making a person guilty of obtaining by false pretences if he 'with intent to defraud, obtains' the things there mentioned. The change will correspond to the change from 'fraudulently' to 'dishonestly' in the definition of stealing which is discussed in § 39. (*Ante*, p. 556.) 'Dishonestly' seems the right word to use in relation to criminal deception also. Owing to the words 'dishonestly obtains' a person who uses deception in order to obtain property to which he believes himself entitled will not be guilty; for though the deception may be dishonest, the obtaining is not. In this respect also the offence will be in line with theft, because a belief in a legal right to deprive an owner of property is for the purpose of theft inconsistent with dishonesty and is specifically made a defence by the partial definition of 'dishonesty' in [section] 2 (1)."

Notes

1. Nevertheless, the Theft Act neglects to apply section 2 (*ante*, p. 555) to any offence other than theft.

2. In *R.* v. *Greenstein* [1975] 1 W.L.R. 1353, a case under section 15, the

Court of Appeal applied *R.* v. *Feely* (*ante*, p. 556) and held that the question of dishonesty was one of fact for the jury.

R. v. Williams (1836) 7 C. & P. 354: W. told lies to X's wife in order to get two of X's sacks of malt. X owed W.'s master a debt which he would not pay, and W.'s object in getting the sacks of malt was to gain for his master the amount of the debt. He was acquitted of obtaining by false pretences after Coleridge J. had directed the jury "if in this case you are satisfied that the prisoner did not intend to defraud [X] but only to put it in his master's power to compel him to pay a just debt, it will be your duty to find him not guilty."

R. v. Carpenter (1911) 22 Cox 618 (a trial for obtaining by false pretences): C. procured deposits of money by representing that he intended to apply that money for a particular purpose. Channell J.'s direction to the jury contained the following passage: "If the defendant made statements of fact which he knew to be untrue, and made them for the purpose of inducing persons to deposit with him money which he knew they would not deposit but for their belief in the truth of his statements, and if he was intending to use the money so obtained for purposes different from those for which he knew the depositors understood from his statements that he intended to use it, then, gentlemen, we have the intent to defraud, although he may have intended to repay the money if he could, and although he may have honestly believed, and may even have had good reason to believe, that he would be able to repay it . . . it is the fraud in the mode of getting the money, because you may by fraud get hold of money, even if you mean to repay it, and thoroughly believe that you can repay it—you are still defrauding the depositor."

In *R.* v. *McCall* (1970) 55 Cr. App. R. 175, this passage was confirmed by the Court of Appeal and applied to a case of obtaining money by deception, when the defendant by lies obtained a loan, which he genuinely intended to treat as a loan, although he lied as to his reasons for wanting it.

R. v. Potger (1970) 55 Cr. App. R. 42, 47: A, by lies about his personal position, obtained from victims cash with orders for certain goods, which would be and were duly delivered and which were well worth the money. Sachs J. said, "Once the jury had come to the conclusion that these were deliberate lies intended to induce the various persons to do acts which would benefit the appellant and that they were or would have been induced so to act by these lies, it was inevitable that the jury should reach the conclusion at which they did in fact, arrive" [*i.e.* that the appellant was dishonest].

Questions

1. Would directions on the lines of those given in *R.* v. *Williams* and *R.* v. *Carpenter*, or implied as correct in *R.* v. *Potger*, be correct today?
2. A and B both have what they think are justifiable claims to be paid £10 by P. A, by force, takes £10 from P. B, by lies, gets P to give him £10. Should there be, and is there, any difference in the way the issue of their honesty should be summed up to the juries who are trying them for theft and obtaining by deception respectively?

2. Obtaining Pecuniary Advantage by Deception

Theft Act 1968, section 16

"(1) A person who by any deception dishonestly obtains for himself or another any pecuniary advantage shall on conviction on indictment be liable to imprisonment for a term not exceeding five years.

(2) The cases in which a pecuniary advantage within the meaning of this section is to be regarded as obtained for a person are cases where—

(a) [repealed by Theft Act 1978, Section 5 (5)]

(b) he is allowed to borrow by way of overdraft, or to take out any policy of insurance or annuity contract, or obtains an improvement of the terms on which he is allowed to do so; or

(c) he is given the opportunity to earn remuneration or greater remuneration in an office or employment, or to win money by betting.

(3) For purposes of this section 'deception' has the same meaning as in section 15 of this Act."

Notes

1. No pecuniary advantage need in fact be obtained. If the situation comes within the two cases in subsection 2 a pecuniary advantage "is to be regarded as obtained." On the other hand, the two cases are exhaustive, and no other case of a *de facto* pecuniary advantage is comprehended in the offence. See *D.P.P.* v. *Turner* [1974] A.C. 357.

2. For "deception," "dishonestly," and the need for the deception to cause the obtaining, see *ante*, pp. 573–592, and for a situation coming under case (c), see *R.* v. *Aston & Hadley, ante*, p. 580.

3. The principal case of obtaining pecuniary advantage was until 1978 contained in section 16 (1) (*a*). It was the case where "any debt or charge for which he makes himself liable or is or may become liable (including one not legally enforceable) is reduced or in whole or part evaded or deferred." This short passage caused such difficulties of interpretation that it was repealed by the Theft Act 1978. Its replacement, founded on the 13th Report of the Criminal Law Revision Committee, Cmnd. 6733 but amended in Parliament, consists of the three offences mentioned below, which have not so far attracted much elucidation by the Courts.

3. OBTAINING SERVICES BY DECEPTION

Theft Act 1978, section 1

(1) A person who by any deception dishonestly obtains services from another shall be guilty of an offence.

(2) It is an obtaining of services where the other is induced to confer a benefit by doing some act, or causing or permitting some act to be done, on the understanding that the benefit has been or will be paid for.

Notes

1. For punishment see section 4, below.

2. For "deception", "dishonestly" and the need for the deception to cause the obtaining, see *ante*, pp. 573–592; and on the offence generally see Smith, §§ 219–231, and Spencer, "*The Theft Act 1978*" [1979] Crim. L.R. 26–30.

Questions

1. If the facts of *R.* v. *Potger, ante*, p. 592, arose today, would the present offence be disclosed?

2. A, by falsely pretending that he has no money with him, induces B, a taxi-driver, to give him a free ride. Is this the present offence? And see, section 2 (1) (*c*) below.

3. A, a non-resident using the restaurant at a hotel, by representing that he is a resident guest, persuades a waiter to allow him to enter the television room and to watch the television, services which are available only to resident guests. Is this an offence under section 1?

4. EVASION OF LIABILITY BY DECEPTION

Theft Act 1978, section 2

"(1) Subject to subsection (2) below, where a person by any deception—

(a) dishonestly secures the remission of the whole or part of any existing liability to make a payment, whether his own liability or another's; or

(b) with intent to make permanent default in whole or in part on any existing liability to make a payment, or with intent to let another do so, dishonestly induces the creditor or any person claiming payment on behalf of the creditor to wait for payment (whether or not the due date for payment is deferred) or to forgo payment; or

(c) dishonestly obtains any exemption from or abatement of liability to make a payment;

he shall be guilty of an offence.

(2) For purposes of this section 'liability' means legally enforceable liability; and subsection (1) shall not apply in relation to a liability that has not been accepted or established to pay compensation for a wrongful act or omission.

(3) For purposes of subsection (1) (b) a person induced to take in payment a cheque or other security for money by way of conditional satisfaction of a pre-existing liability is to be treated not as being paid but as being induced to wait for payment.

(4) For purposes of subsection (1) (c) 'obtains' includes obtaining for another or enabling another to obtain."

Notes

1. For punishment, see section 4 below.

2. For "deception", "dishonestly" and the need for the deception to cause the remission, inducement or obtaining, see, *ante*, pp. 573–592.

Spencer, The Theft Act 1978 [1979] Crim. L.R. 34

"There seems little practical need for 2 (1) (a). Where it applies, D has been fraudulent and dishonest, but his conduct is unlikely to have done P any harm. In theory harm has been caused: P used to own a debt against D; by deceiving P into waiving it, D has deprived him of it. So, it may be said, D ought to be punished just as if he had deprived P of any other item of his property—his car, for example—by deception. But the analogy is false. Where D obtains P's car by deception, P once had a car, and is left with a civil remedy against D which usually is worthless. Where D secures the remission of a debt by deception, P is also left with a probably worthless civil remedy. He can rescind the remission for fraud, and then enforce the debt—but D probably has no assets with which to pay it. However, in this case what did P have *before* D deprived him of it by deception? Merely a debt—a right to sue D for the money. It is possible that D had the money to pay at the time of the deception, and spent it on beer after the debt was remitted; but this is most unlikely. Usually, the reason why D deceived P will be that D had no money but lacked the effrontery to say so. Therefore, as a result of D's deception, P is unlikely to be any the worse off. The only result of fining and imprisoning D if he is caught will be to make P's civil remedy against D worthless in the rare case where D was, before the prosecution, worth powder and shot.

Section 2 (1) (b) seems to have little more rhyme or reason to it. It is said to be aimed mainly at those who knowingly write dud cheques in purported settlement of existing liability—conduct which frequently does the creditor good rather than harm [because the creditor can sue on the cheque as well as on the debt]. It is harmful in only two ways. First, the payee may unsuspectingly draw against the cheque and so overdraw his own bank account. If this is the mischief aimed at, however, 2 (1) (b) is too narrow, because the offence is only committed where D intends never to pay, and P is equally likely to overdraw whatever D's intentions. Secondly, tendering the cheque may enable D to disappear without trace. However, the mischief here is only the same as that involved in 'making off without payment.' Why should running away after telling lies carry a sentence of five years' imprisonment under 2 (1) (b), when running away without telling lies—which is more harmful, because D is likely to be harder to trace—only carries a sentence of two years under section 3? Furthermore, as against any dubious benefits to society which 2 (1) (b) may provide, there is the uncomfortable fact that because of it, anyone who, however innocently, tenders a cheque which is dishonoured, can be threatened with a prosecution which is likely to get past the committal stage.

The only part of section 2 which seems to strike accurately at an evil worthy of criminal sanction is 2 (1) (c), which applies to the evasion of future liability by deception. Although originally intended partly to cover obtaining services cheap or free by deception, and now in that respect redundant, [because section 1 as finally enacted has a wider scope than clause 1 as proposed by the C.L.R.C.], it still covers conduct which is really harmful to the victim and amounts to no other criminal offence. Take for example the case of the council-house tenant who by deception has his rent halved by way of rent rebate. The council will thereafter fail to collect half his rent as it would otherwise have fallen due. If the fraud is not discovered for several years, the council may lose thousands of pounds. On discovery of the fraud, the council will have in theory a right to sue the tenant for the money, but whereas he could have paid it in instalments over the years, the chance of his ever finding it now—in addition to future rent at the proper rate—is remote. This sort of conduct surely does deserve a prosecution.

A final criticism of section 2 is that it is complicated. Long, expensive hours will be spent in the courts discussing arid procedural questions resulting from a failure to specify what the relationship between the three main clauses is, and whether they are three offences or one. It is an ill wind of legal change which blows no barrister any good."

R. v. Holt
(1981) 2 All E.R. 854
Court of Appeal

The charge and facts appear from the judgment of Lawson J.

LAWSON J.: Victor Reginald Holt and Julian Dana Lee apply to the full court for leave to appeal against their convictions at the Crown Court at Liverpool on 16th July 1980 of attempting, contrary to the common law, to evade liability by deception, that is to say, an attempt to commit an offence contrary to s 2 (1) of the

Theft Act 1978. This court granted leave to appeal and treated the hearing of the application as the hearing of the appeal.

The charge on which they were convicted was as follows. The statement of the offence was attempted evasion of liability by deception, contrary to common law. The particulars of the offence were that the appellants, on 9th December 1979, by deception with intent to make permanent default on an existing liability, did attempt to induce Philip Parkinson, servant of Pizzaland Restaurants Ltd., to forgo payment of £3.65 by falsely representing that payment had been made by them to another servant of the said Pizzaland Restaurants Ltd.

From the use of the expressions "with intent to make permanent default" and "to induce (the creditor's agent) to forgo payment", it is clear that the attempt charged was one to commit the offence defined by s 2 (1) (*b*) of the 1978 Act.

The facts of the case were that in the evening of 9th December 1979, the appellants consumed meals costing £3.65 in the Pizzaland Restaurant in Southport. There was a police officer off duty also having a meal in the restaurant and he overheard the appellants planning to evade payment for their meals by the device of pretending that a waitress had removed a £5 note which they had placed on the table. When presented with their bill, the appellants advanced this deception and declined payment. The police officer concerned prevented them from leaving the restaurant and they were shortly afterwards arrested and charged.

At the close of the prosecution case in the Crown Court counsel who has also conducted this appeal, made a submission which was overruled, the main point of which was that assuming the facts as we have recounted them to be correct, the attempt to evade thus emerging was an attempt to commit an offence not under s 2 (1) (*b*) as charged but under s 2 (1) (*a*) of the 1978 Act since, he submitted, had the attempt succeeded, the appellants' liability to pay for their meals would have been "remitted" and not just "forgone", to use the contrasting terms contained in the respective subsections.

Counsel further developed his submission before us. As we understand it, he submits that the vital differences between the two offences defined in the first two paragraphs of s 2 (1) of the Act are that "remission" involves that, first, the creditor who "remits" the debtor's existing liability must communicate his decision to the debtor and, second, the legal consequence of the "remission" is to extinguish the debt, whereas the "forgoing of an existing liability", to use the words of sub-s 2 (1) (*b*), need not be communicated to the debtor and has not the consequence in law of extinguishing such liability. We find great difficulty in introducing these concepts into the construction of the subsection. We will later return to the matter.

Counsel further submitted that the effect of s 2 (1) of the Act was to create three different offences but conceded that there could be situations in which the conduct of the debtor or his agent could fall under more than one of the three paragraphs of s 2 (1).

The elements of the offence defined by s 2 (1) (*b*) of the Act relevant to the present case are clearly these: first, the defendant must be proved to have the intent to make permanent default on the whole or part of an existing liability. This element is unique to s 2 (1) (*b*); it has no application to the offences defined in s 2 (1) (*a*) or (*c*). Second, given such intent, he must use deception. Third, his deception must be practised dishonestly to induce the creditor to forgo payment.

It must always be remembered that in the present case, whatever offence was being attempted, the attempt failed. The creditor was not induced by the dishonest deception and did not forgo payment. It is clear on the evidence that the appellants' conduct constituted an attempt to evade liability by deception, and the jury, who were properly directed, clearly concluded that the appellants' conduct was motivated by the intent to make permanent default on their supper bill. Thus, all the elements needed to enable an attempt to commit the offence defined in s 2 (1) (*b*) were found to be present, so that the appellants were rightly convicted as charged.

Reverting to the construction of s 2 (1) of the Act, as to which the commentators are not at one, we are not sure whether the choice of expressions describing the consequences of deception employed in each of its paragraphs, namely in para (*a*) "secures the remission of any existing liability", in para (*b*) "induces a creditor to forgo payment" and in para (*c*) "obtains any exemption from liability", are simply different ways of describing the same end result or represent conceptual differences.

Whilst it is plain that there are substantial differences in the elements of the three offences defined in s 2 (1), they show these common features: first, the use of deception to a creditor in relation to a liability, second, dishonesty in the use of deception, and third, the use of deception to gain some advantage in time or money. Thus the differences between the offences relate principally to the different situations in which the debtor-creditor relationship has arisen.

The practical difficulty which counsel's submissions for the appellants failed to confront is strikingly illustrated by cases of attempting to commit an offence under s 2 (1) (*a*) or s 2 (1) (*b*). If, as he submits, s 2 (1) (*a*) requires communication of remission to the debtor, whereas s 2 (1) (*b*) does not require communication of the "forgoing of payment" but, as the case is a mere attempt, the matter does not *end* in remission of liability or forgoing of payment, then the prosecution would be in a dilemma since it would either be impossible to charge such an attempt or the prosecution would be obliged to charge attempts in the alternative in which case, since any attempt failed, it would be quite uncertain which of the alternatives it was.

These appeals are accordingly dismissed.

Applications for leave to appeal granted. Appeals dismissed

R. v. Andrews & Hedges [1981] *Crim. L.R. 106* (C.C. Ct.: Mr. Recorder Sherrard Q.C.: Defendants were charged with inducing creditors to wait for payment by deception contrary to section 2 (1) (b) of the Theft Act 1978. The creditors had in the course of dealing supplied large quantities of meat to the defendants on credit terms of up to three weeks for which payments were duly made by cheques which were met. The dishonesty relied upon by the prosecution was that thereafter having obtained meat from suppliers in a later period the defendants issued cheques unsupported by funds in their bank account which were not met on presentation, and induced the creditors to wait for payment. The deception relied on in each case was the false representation that the cheque in question was a good and valid order and that in the ordinary course, the cheque would be met.

Held, there was no inducement to wait for payment where the parties had traded together previously and where credit terms had been allowed and where payment by cheque was accepted in the ordinary course of dealing between the parties; for section 2 (1) (b) only applied where a creditor is induced to accept a cheque instead of cash, and only then did section 2 (3) operate as a matter of law to treat the creditor as having been induced to wait for payment. There was no evidence that the creditors had asked for cash and no evidence that they had been induced to accept cheques or to wait for payment. Accordingly, there was no case to answer.

5. MAKING OFF WITHOUT PAYMENT

Theft Act 1978, section 3

"(1) Subject to subsection (3) below, a person who, knowing that payment on the spot for any goods supplied or service done is required or expected from him, dishonestly makes off without having paid as required or expected and with intent to avoid payment of the amount due shall be guilty of an offence.

(2) For the purposes of this section 'payment on the spot' includes payment at the time of collecting goods on which work has been done or in respect of which service has been provided.

(3) Subsection (1) above shall not apply where the supply of the goods or the doing of the service is contrary to law, or where the service done is such that payment is not legally enforceable.

(4) Any person may arrest without warrant anyone who is, or whom he, with reasonable cause, suspects to be, committing or attempting to commit an offence under this section."

Note

No deception is needed; only dishonesty. Nor is it material whether ownership of goods has been transferred to the defendant, nor whether he was dishonest before or after any goods were supplied or service done. Many difficulties in the way of a prosecution for theft or obtaining property by deception are thus avoided, but the wording of the present offence is not without its own difficulties, *e.g.* as to "goods supplied," "makes off" "without having paid."

Questions

1. A, in a self-service store, picks up an article, puts it in his pocket and dishonestly departs without paying for it. Can the article be described as "goods supplied"?

2. A, having eaten a meal at B's restaurant, persuades B to let him go without paying by falsely promising to return next day with the money. Is this "making off" by A? Compare section 2 (1) (b) above.

3. On facts such as occurred in *R.* v. *Lambie, ante*, p. 584, where a credit card is dishonestly presented to a supermarket cashier, does the customer make off "without payment"?

Theft Act 1978, section 4

"(1) Offences under this Act shall be punishable either on conviction on indictment or on summary conviction.

(2) A person convicted on indictment shall be liable—

(a) for an offence under section 1 or section 2 of this Act to imprisonment for a term not exceeding five years; and

(b) for an offence under section 3 of this Act, to imprisonment for a term not exceeding two years.

(3) A person convicted summarily of any offence under this Act shall be liable—

(a) to imprisonment for a term not exceeding six months; or

(b) to a fine not exceeding the prescribed sum for the purposes of section 28 of the Criminal Law Act 1977 (punishment on summary conviction of offences triable either way: £1,000 or other sum substituted by order under that Act),

or to both."

Chapter 12

HANDLING

	PAGE
i. Stolen Goods	599
ii. Otherwise than in the Course of Stealing	608
iii. Forms of Handling	611
iv. Knowing or Believing them to be Stolen Goods	616
v. Dishonesty	620

Theft Act 1968, section 22

"(1) A person handles stolen goods if (otherwise than in the course of stealing) knowing or believing them to be stolen goods he dishonestly receives the goods, or dishonestly undertakes or assists in their retention, removal, disposal or realisation by or for the benefit of another person, or if he arranges to do so.

(2) A person guilty of handling stolen goods shall on conviction on indictment be liable to imprisonment for a term not exceeding fourteen years."

Note

The offence created by this section replaces the offence of receiving stolen goods contained in section 33 of the Larceny Act 1916 and section 97 of the Larceny Act 1861. The new offence is wider than the old. Receiving was confined to cases where a man took into his possession goods which he knew had been obtained unlawfully. Handling, however, "will punish not only receivers, but also those who knowingly convey stolen goods to any place after the theft, those who take charge of them and keep them on their premises or hide them on the approach of the police, those who negotiate for the sale of the goods and the like. The definition will also include a person who in the course of his otherwise innocent employment knowingly removes the goods from place to place, for example a driver employed by dishonest transport owners. If the driver knows that the goods are stolen and that in conveying them he is helping in their disposal, it seems right that he should be guilty of the offence. The fact that he is acting in the course of his ordinary employment may go in mitigation." (Cmnd. 2977, 128.)

i. Stolen Goods

Attorney-General's Reference (No. 1 of 1974)
[1974] Q.B. 744
Court of Appeal

The facts appear in the Court's opinion

Lord Widgery C.J.: This is a reference to the court by the Attorney-General on a point of law seeking the opinion of the court pursuant to section 36 of the Criminal Justice Act 1972. . . .

The facts of the present case, which I take from the terms of the reference itself, are these:

> "A police constable found an unlocked, unattended car containing packages of new clothing which he suspected, and which in fact subsequently proved to be stolen. The officer removed the rotor arm from the vehicle to immobilise it, and kept observation. After about ten minutes, the accused appeared, got into the van and attempted to start the engine. When questioned by the officer, he gave an implausible explanation, and was arrested."

Upon those facts two charges were brought against the respondent: one of stealing the woollen goods, the new clothing, which were in the back of the car in question and secondly and alternatively of receiving those goods knowing them to be stolen. The trial judge quite properly ruled there was no evidence to support the first charge, and that he would not leave that to the jury, but an argument developed as to whether the second count should be left to the jury or not. Counsel for the respondent in the court below had submitted at the close of the prosecution case that there was no case to answer, relying on section 24 (3) of the Theft Act 1968. That provides as follows:

> ". . . no goods shall be regarded as having continued to be stolen goods after they have been restored to the person from whom they were stolen or to other lawful possesssion or custody. . . ."

The rest of the subsection is not relevant and I do not read it. It was therefore contended in the court below on the facts to which I have already referred that by virtue of section 24 (3) the goods had been restored to other lawful possession or custody, namely the custody or possession of the police officer before the respondent appeared on the scene and sought to drive the car away. If that argument was sound of course it would follow that there was no case for the respondent to answer, because if in fact the police constable had restored the stolen goods to his own lawful possession or custody before the act relied upon as an act of receiving occurred, it would follow that they would not be stolen goods at the material time.

After hearing argument, the judge accepted the submission of the respondent and directed the jury that they should acquit on the receiving count. That has resulted in the Attorney-General referring the following point of law to us for an opinion under section 36 of the Criminal Justice Act 1972. He expresses the point in this way:

> "Whether stolen goods are restored to lawful custody within the meaning of section 24 (3) of the Theft Act 1968 when a police officer, suspecting them to be stolen, examines and keeps observation on them with a view to tracing the thief or a handler."

One could put the question perhaps in a somewhat different way by asking whether upon the facts set out in the reference the conclusion as a matter of law was clear to the effect that the goods had ceased to be stolen goods. In other words, the question which is really in issue in this reference is whether the trial judge acted correctly in law in saying that those facts disclosed a defence within section 24 (3).

Subsection (3) is not perhaps entirely happily worded. It has been pointed out in the course of argument that in the sentence which I have read there is only one relevant verb, and that is "restore". The section contemplates that the stolen goods should be restored to the person from whom they were stolen or to other lawful possession or custody. It is pointed out that the word "restore" although it is entirely appropriate when applied to restoration of the goods to the true owner, is not really an appropriate verb to employ if one is talking about a police officer stumbling upon stolen goods and taking them into his own lawful custody or possession.

We are satisfied that despite the absence of another and perhaps more appropriate verb, the effect of section 24 (3) is to enable a defendant to plead that the goods had ceased to be stolen goods if the facts are that they were taken by a police officer in the course of his duty and reduced into possession by him.

Whether or not section 24 (3) is intended to be a codification of the common law or not, it certainly deals with a topic upon which the common law provides a large number of authorities. I shall refer to some of them in a moment, although perhaps not all and it will be observed that from the earliest times it has been recognised that if the owner of stolen goods resumed possession of them, reduced them into his possession again, that they thereupon ceased to be stolen goods for present purposes and could certainly not be the subject of a later charge of receiving based on events after they had been reduced into possession. It is to be observed that at common law nothing short of a reduction into possession, either by the true owner or by a police officer acting in the execution of his duty, was regarded as sufficient to change the character of the goods from stolen goods into goods which were no longer to be so regarded.

I make that assertion true by a brief reference from the cases to which we have been referred. The first is *R.* v. *Dolan* (1855) 6 Cox C.C. 449. The facts there were that stolen goods were found in the pocket of a thief by the owner. The owner sent for a policeman, and the evidence given at the subsequent trial showed that after the policeman had taken the goods from the thief, the thief, the policeman and the owner went towards the shop owned and occupied by the prisoner at which the thief had asserted that he was hoping to sell the stolen goods. When they got near the shop the policeman gave the goods to the thief, who then went on ahead into the shop with a view to selling the goods, closely followed by the owner and the policeman, who proceeded to arrest the shop keeper. It was held there

> "that the prisoner was not guilty of feloniously receiving stolen goods; inasmuch as they were delivered to him under the authority of the owner by a person to whom the owner had bailed them for that purpose."

Put another way, one can explain that decision on the broad principle to which I have already referred: the goods had already been returned to the possession of the owner before they were then released by him into the hands of the thief in order that the thief might approach the receiver with a view to the receiver being arrested. The principle thus enunciated is one which, as I have already said, is to be found in the other authorities to which we have been referred.

The next one which is similar is *R.* v. *Schmidt* (1866) L.R. 1 C.C.R. 15. The reference in the headnote suffices:

> "Four thieves stole goods from the custody of a railway company, and afterwards sent them in a parcel by the same company's line addressed to the prisoner. During the transit the theft was discovered; and, on the arrival of the parcel at the station for its delivery, a policeman in the employ of the company opened it, and then returned it to the porter whose duty it was to deliver it, with instructions to keep it until further orders. On the following day the policeman directed the porter to take the parcel to its address, when it was received by the prisoner, who was afterwards convicted of receiving the goods knowing them to be stolen, . . ."

And it was held by the Court for Crown Cases Reserved "that the goods had got back into the possession of the owner, so as to be no longer stolen goods and that the conviction was wrong." Again unquestionably they had been reduced into the possession of the owner by the hand of the police officer acting on his behalf. They had not been allowed to continue their course unaffected. They had been taken out of circulation by the police officer, reduced into the possession of the owner or of the officer, and it matters not which, and thus had ceased to be stolen goods for present purposes. . . .

Then there is a helpful case, *R.* v. *Villensky* [1892] 2 Q.B. 597. Again it is a case of a parcel in the hands of carriers. This parcel was handed to the carriers in question for conveyance to the consignees, and whilst in the carriers' depot it was stolen by a servant of the carriers who removed the parcel to a different part of the premises and placed upon it a label addressed to the prisoners by a name by which they were known and a house where they resided. The superintendent of the carriers on receipt of information as to this and after the inspection of the parcel, directed it to be placed in the place from which the thief had removed it and to be sent with a special delivery receipt in a van accompanied by two detectives to the address shown on the label. At that address it was received by the prisoners under circumstances which clearly showed knowledge on their part that it had been stolen. The property in the parcel was laid in the indictment in the carriers and an offer to amend the indictment by substituting the names of the consignees was declined. The carriers' servant pleaded guilty to a count for larceny in the same indictment. It was there held by the Court for Crown Cases Reserved

> "that as the person in which the property was laid"—that is the carriers—"had resumed possession of the stolen property before its receipt by the prisoners, it had then ceased to be stolen property, and the prisoners could not be convicted of receiving it knowing it to have been stolen."

On p. 599 there is a brief and valuable judgment by Pollock B. in these terms:

> "The decisions in *Dolan*, and *Schmidt*, are, in my judgment, founded on law and on solid good sense, and they should not be frittered away. It is, of course, frequently the case that when it is found that a person has stolen property he is watched; but the owner of the property, if he wishes to catch the receiver, does not resume possession of the stolen goods; here the owners have done so, and the result is that the conviction must be quashed."

We refer to that brief judgment because it illustrates in a few clear words what is really the issue in the present case. When the police officer discovered these goods and acted as he did, was the situation that he had taken possession of the goods, in which event, of course, they ceased to be stolen goods? or was it merely that he was watching the goods with a view to the possibility of catching the receiver at a later stage? I will turn later to a consideration of those two alternatives.

Two other cases should, I think, be mentioned at this stage. The next one is *R.* v. *King* [1938] 2 All E.R. 662. We are now getting to far more recent times. The appellant here was convicted with another man of receiving stolen goods knowing them to have been stolen. A fur coat had been stolen and shortly afterwards the police went to a flat where they found the man Burns and told him they were enquiring about some stolen property. He at first denied that there was anything there but finally admitted the theft and produced a parcel from a wardrobe. While a policeman was in the act of examining the contents of the parcel, the telephone bell rang. Burns answered it and the police heard him say: "Come along as arranged." The police then suspended operations and about 20 minutes later the appellant arrived, and, being admitted by Burns, said "I have come for the coat. Harry sent me". This was heard by the police, who were hiding at the time. The coat was handed to the appellant by Burns, so that he was actually in possession of it. It was contended that the possession by the police amounted to possession by the owner of the coat and that, therefore, the coat was not stolen property at the time the appellant received it. Held by the Court of Criminal Appeal: that the coat had not been in the possession of the police and it was therefore still stolen when the appellant received it. . . .

The most recent case on the present topic, but of little value in the present problems is *Haughton* v. *Smith* [*ante*, p. 318], in the House of Lords. The case being of little value to us in our present problems, I will deal with it quite briefly. It is a case where a lorry load of stolen meat was intercepted by police, somewhere in the North of England, who discovered that the lorry was in fact full of stolen goods. After a brief conference they decided to take the lorry on to its destination with a view to catching the receivers at the London end of the affair. So the lorry set off for London with detectives both in the passenger seat and in the back of the vehicle, and in due course was met by the defendant at its destination in London. In that case before this court it was conceded, as it had been conceded below, that the goods had been reduced into the possession of the police when they took possession of the lorry in the North of England, so no dispute in this court or later in the House of Lords was raised on that issue. It is, however, to be noted that three of their Lordships, when the matter got to the House of Lords, expressed some hesitation as to the propriety of the prosecution conceding in that case that the goods had been reduced to the possession of the police when the lorry was first intercepted. Since we cannot discover on what ground those doubts were expressed either from the report of the speeches or from the report of the argument, we cannot take advantage of that case in the present problem.

Now to return to the present problem again with those authorities in the background: did the conduct of the police officer, as already briefly recounted, amount to a taking of possession of the woollen goods in the back seat of the motor car? What he did, to repeat the essential facts, was: that seeing these goods in the car and being suspicious of them because they were brand new goods and in an unlikely position, he removed the rotor arm and stood by in cover to interrogate any driver of the car who might subsequently appear. Did that amount to a taking possession of the goods in the back of the car? In our judgment it depended primarily on the intentions of the police officer. If the police officer seeing these goods in the back of the car had made up his mind that he would take them into custody, that he would reduce them into his possession or control, take charge of them so that they could not be removed and so that he would have the disposal of them, then it would be a perfectly proper conclusion to say that he had taken possession of the goods. On the other hand, if the truth of the matter is that he was of an entirely open mind at that stage as to whether the goods were to be seized or not and was of an entirely open mind as to whether he should take possession of them or not, but merely stood by so that when the driver of the car appeared he could ask certain questions of that driver as to the nature of the goods and why they were there, then there is no reason whatever to suggest that he had taken the goods into his possession or control. It may be, of course, that he had both objects in mind. It is possible in a case like this that the police officer may have intended by removing the rotor arm both to prevent the car from being driven away and to enable him to assert control over the woollen goods as such. But if the jury came to the conclusion that the proper explanation of what had happened was that the police officer had not intended at that stage to reduce the goods into his possession or to assume the control of them, and at that stage was merely concerned to ensure that the driver, if he appeared, could not get away without answering questions, then in that case the proper conclusion of the jury would have been to the effect that the goods had not been reduced into the possession of the police and therefore a defence under section 24 (3) of the Theft Act 1968 would not be of use to this particular defendant.

In the light of those considerations it has become quite obvious that the trial judge was wrong in withdrawing the issue from the jury. As a matter of law he was not entitled to conclude from the facts which I have set out more than once that these goods were reduced into the possession of the police officer. What he should have done in our opinion would have been to have left that issue to the jury for decision, directing the jury that they should find that the prosecution case was without substance if they thought that the police officer had assumed control of the goods as such and reduced them into his possession. Whereas on the other hand, they should have found the case proved, assuming that they were satisfied about its other elements, if they were of the opinion that the police officer in removing the rotor arm and standing by and watching was doing no more than ensure that the driver should not get away without interrogation and was not at that stage seeking to assume possession of the goods as such at all. That is our opinion.

Opinion accordingly

Note

It is not always a question of fact whether the owner or police have reduced the goods into possession. In *M.P.C.* v. *Streeter* (1980) 71 Cr. App. R. 113, the owner's security officer initialled the goods and alerted the police, who kept watch and followed the defendant when he picked up the goods. It was held by the Divisional Court that the magistrate was wrong to conclude that this was a reduction into the possession of the owner, and the case was sent back with a direction to convict.

Questions

1. Do you think that the prosecution in *Haughton* v. *Smith* ought to have made the concession it did make?

2. In *Haughton* v. *Smith* the lorry was "met by the defendant at its destination in London." If this was evidence of a pre-arranged plan between the thieves and the defendant, could the latter have been charged with handling in respect of a time *before* the police took possession? See section 22 (1), *ante*, p. 599, and *Forms of Handling*, below.

3. A, by arrangement with the thief, picks up goods which the latter had stolen but which the owner had reduced into possession. Is this *theft* by A? See, *ante*, p. 495, and *M.P.C.* v. *Streeter*, above, at p. 119.

Theft Act 1968, sections 24 (2), (4), 34 (2)

"*Section 24:* (2) . . . references to stolen goods shall include, in addition to the goods originally stolen and parts of them (whether in their original state or not),—

(a) any other goods which directly or indirectly represent or have at any time represented the stolen goods in the hands of the thief as being the proceeds of any disposal or realisation of the whole or part of the goods stolen or of goods so representing the stolen goods; and

(b) any other goods which directly or indirectly represent or have at any time represented the stolen goods in the hands of a handler of the stolen goods or any part of them as being the proceeds of any disposal or realisation of the whole or part of the stolen goods handled by him or of goods so representing them.

(4) For purposes of the provisions of this Act relating to goods which have been stolen (including subsections (1) to (3) above) goods obtained in England or Wales or elsewhere either by blackmail or in the circumstances described in section 15 (1) of this Act shall be regarded as stolen; and 'steal,' 'theft' and 'thief' shall be construed accordingly.

Section 34: (2) For the purposes of this Act—

(b) 'goods', except in so far as the context otherwise requires, includes money and every other description of property except land, and includes things severed from the land by stealing."

Attorney General's Reference (No. 4 of 1979)
(1980) 71 Cr. App. R. 341
Court of Appeal

The facts appear in the Court's opinion

LORD WIDGERY C.J.: This reference by the Attorney-General arises out of a case in which the accused was indicted on one count which alleged that she dishonestly received certain stolen goods, namely a cheque for £288.53 knowing or believing the same to be stolen goods.

After a submission on behalf of the accused at the end of the prosecution case, the trial judge directed the jury to acquit. There was no issue as to the receipt by the accused of the cheque, nor was it in dispute that the person who paid the cheque had previously obtained sums of money by dishonest deception, but the judge ruled that there was no evidence that the cheque so paid to the accused was in law stolen goods.

The facts of the case were these. Over a period of six months in 1976 and 1977, a fellow-employee of the accused obtained by deception from their employer certain cheques. It is convenient, for brief reference, to refer to that fellow-employee as "thief". The thief paid those fraudulently obtained cheques into her bank account.

During the same period the thief also paid into her bank account other cheques which she had lawfully received from her employer and which represented, first, amounts earned by and due to fellow-employees which she was required to pay on to those employees; and, secondly, sums lawfully earned by the thief.

The total of the sums paid into the bank account by the thief as sums dishonestly obtained by deception from the employer was £859.70.

The thief had duly paid out to the other employees the amounts she had received for such payments.

On the date when the thief handed to the defendant the cheque for £288.53, the state of the thief's bank account was a credit balance of £641.32.

The total amount lawfully received into the account by the thief for payment to other employees, which had been paid out to them, exceeded that balance of £641.32. The total amount lawfully received by the thief in respect of her own earnings and paid into the account had also exceeded £641.32. The Court has no information as to the nature or purpose of other disbursements made from the account by the thief and assumes there was no evidence.

There was evidence that the defendant had admitted that she knew of the obtaining by deception of the £859.70 by the thief. It is said that there was evidence from which it would have been open to the jury to conclude that, for the continued deceptions of the thief to succeed, the co-operation, or at least acquiescence, of the defendant was necessary. Whatever the reason it was thought more appropriate to charge her with handling than with obtaining by deception.

The defendant was asked about the cheque paid to her by the thief. One question asked of her was this: "Was that your share?" She replied: "I suppose it was." She added, according to the evidence which the jury was invited to consider: "I suppose you could call it guilt but I haven't touched it."

The judge at trial was invited to rule that there was no evidence upon which the jury could conclude that the cheque given to the defendant by the thief amounted in law to stolen goods within the meaning of the Theft Act 1968.

Two points were taken on behalf of the defendant by counsel. First, that the offence of handling stolen goods could not be committed with reference to a stolen thing in action, or to a thing in action representing stolen goods; secondly, that on the evidence before the court the offence of handling stolen goods could not be proved.

As to the first point, the judge rejected the submission. As to the second, the judge ruled that since the thief's bank account had been fed by payments in the three categories described above, namely: (i) sums lawfully obtained for payment on to other employees; (ii) sums lawfully obtained as money earned by the thief; and (iii) the £859.70 dishonestly obtained by deception; it was impossible for the prosecution to prove that the payment made to the defendant was in law stolen goods.

In reaching his conclusion the judge said this: "I have to consider whether or not the cheque which the thief paid to the accused's account indirectly represents the stolen goods in the hands of the thief. It is very tempting to say that if the drawer of the cheque and the recipient of the cheque intend that the money represented by the cheque shall represent that part of the choses in action owed by the bank to the account holder which is stolen money that that is sufficient for these purposes. But in my view the Act does not say that. It does not imply it and I consider that as I have to construe this part and every part of the Act strictly that if Parliament had intended to provide for such a case it would have said so."

It is from this conclusion on the second point that the point of law referred to this Court arises. The point of law referred to us under section 36 (1) of the Act of 1972 is as follows: "Where a payment is made out of a fund constituted by a mixture of money amounting to stolen goods within the meaning of section 24 of the Theft Act 1968, and money not so tainted, or of a bank account similarly constituted, in such a way that the specific origin of the sum paid cannot be identified with either portion of the fund, is a jury entitled to infer that the payment represented stolen goods within the meaning of section 24 (2) of the Act, from the intention of the parties that it should represent the stolen goods or a share thereof?"

. . . We can begin the statement of our opinion upon the point of law referred to us by observing that the cheque which the accused was alleged to have received was, plainly, not part of the goods originally stolen or obtained. In order to succeed, therefore, the prosecution had to bring the case within the terms of section 24 (2) of the Theft Act 1968, which defines the scope of offences relating to the handling of stolen goods. The relevant provisions are contained in section 24 (2) (a), which reads as follows: ". . . references to stolen goods shall include . . . any other goods which directly or indirectly represent or have at any time represented the stolen goods in the hands of the thief as being the proceeds of any disposal or realisation of the whole or part of the goods stolen. . . ." By section 24 (4) the reference to "goods which have been stolen" includes goods which have been obtained by deception.

It was submitted that the language of section 24 (2) (a) afforded some support for the first point made on behalf of the accused, namely, that a thing in action cannot be handled by receiving within section 22 of the Theft Act. By section 34 (2) (b), however, the interpretation section of this Act, "goods", except where the context otherwise requires, includes money and every other description of property except land and includes things severed from the land. Further by the combined effect of section 4 (1) and section 34 (2), "property" includes money and all other property real and personal including things in action.

In our judgment therefore it is clear from that extended definition of "goods" that a cheque obtained by deception constitutes stolen goods for the purposes of sections 22 and 24 of the Act.

Next, it is clear that a balance in a bank account, being a debt, is itself a thing in action which falls within the definition of goods and may therefore be goods which directly or indirectly represent stolen goods for the purposes of section 24 (2) (a).

Further where, as in the present case, a person obtains cheques by deception and pays them into her bank account, the balance in that account may, to the value of the tainted cheques, be goods which "directly represent the stolen goods in the hands of the thief as being the proceeds of the disposal or realisation of the goods stolen . . . ," within the meaning of section 24 (2) (a).

If, however, the prosecution is to prove dishonest handling by receiving, it is necessary to prove that what the handler received was in fact the whole or part of the stolen goods within the meaning of section 24 (2) (a). To prove that, the prosecution must prove (i) that at the material time, namely, at the time of receipt by the handler, in such a case as this, the thief's bank balance was in fact comprised, at least in part, of that which represented the proceeds of stolen goods; and (ii) that the handler received, at least in part, such proceeds.

In some cases no difficulty will arise. For example, if the thief opened a new account and paid into it only dishonestly obtained cheques, then the whole balance would constitute stolen goods within the meaning of section 24 (2) (a). If then the thief transferred the whole balance to an accused, that accused would, in our opinion, have received stolen goods.

By the same reasoning, if at the material time the whole of the balance in an account consisted only of the proceeds of stolen goods, then any cheque drawn on that account would constitute stolen goods within section 24 (2) (a).

We have no doubt that when such a cheque is paid, so that part of such a balance in the thief's account is transferred to the credit of the receiver's account, the receiver has received stolen goods because he has received a thing in action which ". . . directly represents . . . the stolen goods in the hands of the thief . . . as being the proceeds of . . . realisation of the . . . goods stolen. . . ."

The same conclusion follows where the receiver directly cashes the cheque drawn on the thief's account and receives money from the paying bank.

The allegation in this case was that the defendant received stolen goods when she received the thief's cheque. Mr. Lee, in the course of argument, was disposed to accept a suggestion from a member of the Court that a cheque drawn by the thief, directed to her bank, and intended to enable the accused to obtain transfer of part of the thief's credit balance, or cash, might not itself be stolen goods within the meaning of section 24 (2) (a). This point is not necessary for decision on the point of law referred to us and it has not been fully argued. It appears to us that there is much to be said in favour of the proposition that receipt of such a cheque, drawn in circumstances wherein it is plain that it must serve to transfer the proceeds of stolen goods, would constitute receiving stolen goods on the grounds that such a cheque would directly or indirectly represent the stolen goods within section 24 (2) (a).

In the present case the prosecution sought such proof, as to the nature of the payment received by the defendant, from the statement which the defendant made as to her understanding and intention when the payment was made. She had said that she regarded the payment to her as "her share".

In our opinion, such an admission could not by itself prove either that part of the thief's bank balance did or could represent stolen goods within section 24 (2) (a), or that part of such stolen goods was received by the defendant. Her admission was, of course, plainly admissible on the issue of her knowledge that the payment represented stolen goods, and as to her honesty in receiving the money. On the issue of fact, however, as to whether the cheque received by her represented stolen goods, the primary rule is that an accused can only make a valid and admissible admission of a statement of fact of which the accused could give admissible evidence: see *Surujpaul* v. *R.* [1958] 1 W.L.R. 1050. It is not necessary in this case to examine the limits of, or the extent of any exceptions from, that primary rule.

In our opinion Mr. Nicholl was right in his submission when he acknowledged that the prosecution must, in such a case as this, prove in the first place that any payment out of a mixed account *could*, by reference to payments in and out, be a payment representing stolen goods. Unless she had personal knowledge of the working of the thief's account, the defendant could make no valid admission as to that.

It is to be noted that the point of law referred to us contains the words: "Is a jury entitled to infer . . . from the intention of the parties. . . ." The use of the plural "parties" is misleading. There was no direct evidence in this case of what the intention of the thief might have been, only of that of the receiver. It may perhaps be that a payment can be proved to have been a payment of money representing stolen goods, even where there was enough honest money in the account to cover the payment, if there is proof direct or by way of necessary inference of the intention of the paying thief to pay out the stolen money. That problem can be decided when it arises. It does not do so here. The prosecution did not advance their case on such a basis.

The only question arising on the facts here is whether a jury is entitled to infer that the payment represented stolen goods within section 24 (2) from the intention or belief of the receiver that it should or did. The answer is "No".

Declaration accordingly

Question

A stole goods and deposited them in the warehouse of B, an innocent man. A delivered B's receipt for the goods to C, so that C, who knew the goods were stolen, could obtain them from B. Before C could present the receipt of B, he was arrested: Is he guilty of handling?

Note

Section 24 (2) was explained by the CLRC, § 138 as follows; "It may seem technical; but the effect will be that the goods which the accused is charged with handling must, at the time of the handling or at some previous time, (i) have been in the hands of the thief or of a handler, and (ii) have represented the original stolen goods in the sense of being the proceeds direct or indirect, of a sale or other realisation of the original goods."

Question

A, having stolen a car, sold it to B, an innocent man, for £10,000. B later sold the car to C, also innocent, for £8,000. A gave the £10,000 to D and B gave the £8,000 to E. Both D and E knew the full circumstances. Are they guilty of handling?

ii. Otherwise than in the Course of Stealing

R. v. Pitham and Hehl
(1976) 65 Cr. App. R. 45
Court of Appeal

P. and H. were charged with burglary along with M. M. was convicted of burglary but P. and H. were acquitted, when it appeared that M. had invited them into the victim's house and offered them the victim's furniture. They paid him for it and took it away. P. and H. were also charged with handling stolen goods and were convicted of this. They appealed on the ground that the handling was not "otherwise than in the course of the stealing."

LAWTON L.J.: Section 22 (1) of the Theft Act provides: "A person handles stolen goods if (otherwise than in the course of the stealing)"—I emphasise the words "otherwise than in the course of the stealing"—"knowing or believing them to be stolen goods he dishonestly receives the goods, or dishonestly undertakes or assists in their retention, removal, disposal or realisation by or for the benefit of another person, or if he arranges to do so." Now, the two conflicting academic views can be summarised in this way. Professor Smith's view in his book on *The Theft Act 1968* (2nd ed., 1974) § 400, seems to be that "in the course of the stealing" can be a very short time or it can be a very long period of time. Professor Griew in his book *The Law of Theft* (3rd ed., 1977) §§ 8–18, 8–19, seems to be of the opinion that, "in the course of the stealing", embraces not only the act of stealing as defined by section 1 of the Theft Act 1968, but in addition making away with the goods. In the course of expounding their differing views in their books on the Theft Act the two professors have both referred to ancient authorities. Both are of the opinion that the object of the words, "otherwise than in the course of the stealing", was to deal with the situation where two men are engaged in different capacities in a joint enterprise. In those circumstances, unless some such limiting words as those to which I have referred were included in the definition of handling, a thief could be guilty of both stealing and receiving. An illustration of the sort of problem which arises is provided by Professor Smith's reference to the old case of *R.* v. *Coggins* (1873) 12 Cox C.C. 517. In his book on the Theft Act at paragraph 400, he summarises the facts of *R.* v. *Coggins* in these terms: "If a servant stole money from his master's till and handed it to an accomplice in his master's shop, the accomplice was guilty of larceny and not guilty of receiving." He added another example. It was the case of *R.* v. *Perkins* (1852) 5 Cox C.C. 554. He summarises that case as follows: "Similarly, if a man committed larceny in the room in which he lodged and threw a bundle of stolen goods to an accomplice in the street, the accomplice was guilty of larceny and not guilty of receiving."

In our judgment the words to which I have referred in section 22 (1), were designed to make it clear that in those sorts of situations a man could not be guilty under the Theft Act of both theft and handling. As was pointed out to Mr. Murray by my brother, Bristow J., in the course of argument, the Theft Act in section 1 defines theft. It has been said in this Court more than once that the object of that definition was to make a fresh start so as to get rid of all the subtle distinctions which had arisen in the past under the old law of larceny. Subsection (1) of section 1 has a side heading, "Basic definition of theft". That definition is in these terms: "A person is guilty of theft if he dishonestly appropriates property belonging to another with the intention of permanently depriving the other of it; and 'thief' and 'steal' shall be construed accordingly." What Parliament meant by "appropriate" was defined in section 3 (1): "Any assumption by a person of the rights of an owner amounts to an appropriation, and this includes, where he has come by the property (innocently or not) without stealing it, any later assumption of a right to it by keeping or dealing with it as owner."

Mr. Murray's submission—a very bold one—was that the general words with which section 3 (1) opens, namely, "Any assumption by a person of the rights of an owner amounts to an appropriation" are limited by the words beginning "and this includes." He submitted that those additional words bring back into the law of theft something akin to the concept of asportation, which was one of the aspects of the law of larceny which the Theft Act 1968 was intended to get rid of. According to Mr. Murray, unless there is something which amounts to "coming by" the property there cannot be an appropriation. We disagree. The final words of section 3 (1) are words of inclusion. The general words at the beginning of section 3 (1) are wide enough to cover *any* assumption by a person of the rights of an owner.

What was the appropriation in this case? The jury found that the two appellants had handled the property *after* Millman had stolen it. That is clear from their acquittal of these two appellants on count 3 of the indictment which had charged them jointly with Millman. What had Millman done? He had assumed the rights of the owner. He had done that when he took the two appellants to 20 Parry Road, showed them the property and invited them to buy what they wanted. He was then acting as the owner. He was then, in the words of the statute, "assuming the rights of the owner". The moment he did that he appropriated McGregor's goods to himself. The appropriation was complete. After this appropriation had been completed there was no question of these two appellants taking part, in the words of section 22, in dealing with the goods "in the course of the stealing".

It follows that no problem arises in this case. It may well be that some of the situations which the two learned professors envisage and discuss in their books may have to be dealt with at some future date, but not in this case. The facts are too clear.

Mr. Murray suggested the learned judge should have directed the jury in some detail about the possibility that the appropriation had not been an instantaneous appropriation, but had been one which had gone on for some time. He submitted that it might have gone on until such time as the furniture was loaded into the appellants' van. For reasons we have already given that was not a real possibility in this case. It is no part of a judge's duty to give the jury the kind of lecture on the law which may be appropriate for a professor to give to a class of undergraduates. We commend the judge for not having involved himself in a detailed academic analysis of the law relating to this case when on the facts it was as clear as anything could be that either these appellants had helped Millman to steal the goods, or Millman had stolen them and got rid of them by sale to these two appellants. We can see nothing wrong in the learned judge's approach to this case and on that particular ground we affirm what he did and said. . . .

Appeal dismissed

Questions

1. Does it follow that Millman, the thief, was also guilty of handling? See forms of handling below.
2. If he was guilty, is that a satisfactory result? see below.

Criminal Law Revision Committee's Eighth Report, Cmnd. 2977

"§ 131 [Justifying the phrase "otherwise than in the course of the stealing] Under the definition a thief may be liable for handling if, after the theft is complete, he does some of the things mentioned in the definition for someone else, for example if he helps a receiver to dispose of the goods. Since it might be thought too severe to make a thief guilty of handling in such a case, we thought of providing that a thief should not be guilty of handling by reason of doing any of the things mentioned in the definition in respect of goods which he has himself stolen. But we decided not to include the provision. If after the theft is complete the thief takes part in a separate transaction for the disposal of the goods, it seems right that he should be guilty of handling like anybody else involved in the transaction."

Questions

1. In *R.* v. *Hale*, on robbery (see *ante*, p. 568) it was held that force used on the victim in a downstairs room after a jewellery box had been taken from an upstairs room was used at the time of the stealing. (See also *Appropriation: A Single or Continuous Act? ante*, p. 502.) Is it possible to distinguish *R.* v. *Pitham & Hehl* and *R.* v. *Hale* on the ground that section 22 uses the words "in the course of the stealing," whereas section 8 (on robbery) uses the words "at the time of doing so" (*i.e.* stealing)?

2. If no distinction can be founded on the words, is it justifiable for the law to take two different views on when a theft occurs in order to catch both handlers and robbers?

3. If in *R.* v. *Pitham & Hehl*, the victim had been actually present when Millman sold the goods to them, and Pitham had physically restrained the victim while Hehl picked up the goods, could Pitham at one and the same time have been guilty of handling and robbery?

iii. Forms of Handling

Notes

1. The offence is no longer confined to "receiving," as before 1968. It can be committed either by "receiving" or by "undertaking or assisting in the goods' retention, removal, disposal or realisation by or for the benefit of another person," or "arranging" to do any of those things. These are all one offence, but in order to give the defendant notice of what he has to meet, the better practice is to have one count for receiving and one count for all the other forms of handling: *R.* v. *Willis* [1972] 1 W.L.R. 1605. If the defendant is charged with receiving only, he cannot be convicted of some other form of handling: *R.* v. *Nicklin* [1977] 1 W.L.R. 403.

2. Receiving may be entirely on the accused's own account; but if the form of handling alleged is one of the other matters mentioned in section 22 (1), it must "by or for the benefit of another person." For some of the difficulties posed by these words, see Blake, *"The Innocent Purchaser and Section 22 of the Theft Act"* [1972] Crim. L.R. 494.

R. v. Pitchley
(1972) 57 Cr. App. R. 30
Court of Appeal

P.'s son handed P. £150 in order that P. should look after it for him. According to P., he paid it into his post office savings account, and then later became aware that the £150 was stolen. Because he did not wish to give his son away, P. did nothing about the money in the account until he was interviewed some days later by the police. He was convicted of "dishonestly handling goods, namely the sum of £150 . . . knowing or believing the same to be stolen goods." He appealed.

CAIRNS L.J.: The indictment . . . simply charged handling stolen goods without specifying whether it was under the first limb or under the second limb, and if the latter, under which part of the second limb of section 22 (1) of the Theft Act; but the case that was presented by the prosecution at the trial was clearly presented in the alternative, that it was either under the first limb of receiving, or under the second limb for assisting in the retention of stolen goods. . . .

The main point that has been taken by Mr. Kalisher, who is appearing for the appellant in this court, is that, assuming that the jury were not satisfied that the appellant received the money knowing it to have been stolen, and that is an assumption which clearly it is right to make, then there was no evidence after that, that from the time when the money was put into the savings bank, that the appellant had done any act in relation to it. His evidence was, and there is no reason to suppose that the jury did not believe it, that at the time when he put the money into the savings bank he still did not know or believe that the money had been stolen—it was only at a later stage that he did. That was on the Saturday according to his evidence, and the position was that the money had simply remained in the savings bank from the Saturday, to the Wednesday when the police approached the appellant. It is fair to say that from the moment when he was approached he displayed the utmost frankness to the extent of correcting them when they said it was £100 to £150 and telling them where the post office savings book was so that the money could be got out again and restored to its rightful owner.

But the question is: Did the conduct of the appellant between the Saturday and the Wednesday amount to an assisting in the retention of this money for the benefit of his son Brian? The court has been referred to the case of *Brown* (1969) 53 Cr. App. R. 527 which was a case where stolen property had been put into a wardrobe at the appellant's house and when police came to inquire about it the appellant said to them: "Get lost." The direction to the jury had been on the basis that it was for them to consider whether in saying: "Get lost," instead of helping the police constable, he was dishonestly assisting in the retention of stolen goods. This court held that that was a misdirection but there are passages in the judgment in the case of *Brown* (*supra*) which, in the view of this court, are of great assistance in determining what is meant by "retention" in this section. I read first of all from p. 528 setting out the main facts a little more fully: "A witness named Holden was called by the prosecution. He gave evidence that he and others had broken into the café and had stolen the goods, and that he had brought them to the appellant's flat, where, incidentally, other people were sleeping, and had hidden them there; and he described how he had taken the cigarettes out of the packets, put them in the plastic bag and hidden them in the wardrobe. Holden went on to say that later and before the police arrived he told the appellant where the cigarettes were; in other words, he said that the appellant well knew that the cigarettes were there and that they had been stolen." There was no evidence that the appellant had done anything active in relation to the cigarettes up to the time when the police arrived. The Lord Chief Justice, Lord Parker, in the course of his judgment at p. 530 said this: "It is urged here that the mere failure to reveal the presence of the cigarettes, with or without the addition of the spoken words 'Get lost,' was incapable itself of amounting to an assisting in the retention of the goods within the meaning of the subsection. The court has come to the conclusion that that is right. It does not seem to this court that the mere failure to tell the police, coupled if you like with the words 'Get lost,' amounts in itself to an assisting in their retention. On the other hand, those matters did afford strong evidence of what was the real basis of the charge here, namely, that knowing that they had been stolen, he permitted them to remain there or, as it has been put, provided accommodation for these stolen goods in order to assist Holden to retain them." Having said that the direction was incomplete the Lord Chief Justice went on to say: "The Chairman should have gone on to say: 'But the fact that he did not tell the constable that they were there and said "Get lost" is evidence from which you can infer, if you think right, that this man was permitting the goods to remain in his flat, and to that extent assisting in their retention by Holden.'" In this present case there was no question on the evidence of the appellant himself, that he was permitting the money to remain under his control in his savings bank book, and it is clear that this court in the case of *Brown* regarded such permitting as sufficient to constitute retention within the meaning of retention. That is clear from the passage I have already read, emphasised in the next paragraph, the final paragraph of the judgment, where the Lord Chief Justice said (at p. 531): "It is a plain case in which the proviso should be applied. It seems to this court that the only possible inference in these circumstances, once Holden was believed is that this man was assisting in their retention by housing the goods and providing accommodation for them, by permitting them to remain there." It is important to realise that that language was in relation to a situation where there was no evidence that anything active had been done by the appellant in relation to the goods.

In the course of the argument, Nield J. cited the dictionary meaning of the word "retain"—keep possession of, not lose, continue to have. In the view of this court, that is the meaning of the word "retain" in this section. It was submitted by Mr. Kalisher that, at any rate, it was ultimately for the jury to decide whether there was retention or not and that even assuming that what the appellant did was of such a character that it could constitute retention, the jury ought to have been directed that it was for them to determine as a matter of fact, whether that was so or not. The court cannot agree with that submission. The meaning of the word "retention" in the section is a matter of law in so far as the construction of the word is necessary. It is hardly a difficult question of construction because it is an ordinary English word and in the view of this court, it was no more necessary for the Deputy Chairman to leave the jury the question of whether or not what was done amounted to retention than it would be necessary for a judge in a case where goods had been handed to a person who knew that they had been stolen for him to direct the jury it was for them to decide whether or not that constituted receiving.

We are satisfied that no complaint of the summing-up which was made can be sustained and that there is no other ground on which this verdict could be said to be unsafe or unsatisfactory. The appeal is therefore dismissed.

Appeal dismissed

Note

The court held that the meaning of "retain"—"an ordinary English word"—was a matter of law for the court. But compare *Cozens* v. *Brutus* on "insulting behaviour" and *R.* v. *Feely* on "dishonestly," *ante*, p. 558.

Questions

1. What exactly were the "goods" which Pitchley was guilty of retaining? See sections 24 (2) and 34 (2), *ante*.
2. Was Pitchley guilty of assisting an offender? See *ante*, p. 283.
3. A, after stealing a gold watch from B, deposits it in the potting shed of his friend C. Later C and D, another friend, notice the watch, recognise it as stolen, and guess that A will return and remove it when he has the opportunity. Because they do not wish to "shop" A, both C and D reply "Get lost" when asked by a policeman if they have seen the watch. Is either of them guilty of handling?

R. v. Sloggett
[1972] 1 Q.B. 430
Court of Appeal

S. was indicted for handling in that knowing or believing certain goods to be stolen he dishonestly received them. Before arraignment a second, and alternative, count for handling was added; the particulars being that knowing or believing the goods to be stolen he dishonestly assisted in their retention. The prosecution relied on the evidence of D. who at first said that S. was one of a number of men who brought the goods to her house but later changed her story, and admissions by S. that he found the goods in the house, realised they were stolen and concealed them to protect D. The judge gave the jury a copy of section 22 (1) of the Theft Act, 1968, but did not in his direction refer to the words "by or for the benefit of another person." The jury were unable to agree on count 1 but convicted on count 2. S. appealed on the ground that the direction was defective, it being submitted that the omission might have led the jury to conclude that if S. acted for his own benefit that was sufficient even though his actions fell short of possession for the purpose of count 1.

Roskill L.J.: . . . The crucial question is whether the omission in the summing up of all reference to the words in section 22 (1) "by or for the benefit of another person" is fatal to the conviction on count two especially in view of the omission of those words from count two itself. It was faintly argued before us that the words "by or for the benefit of another person" did not govern "retention" or "removal" but only governed "disposal or realisation" or possibly only "realisation". Both the grammar and punctuation of this part of subsection (1) lead us unhesitatingly to reject this argument. It seems clear that the adverb "dishonestly" governs both the verb "undertakes" and the words "assists in" and that the following four nouns namely "retention", "removal", "disposal" and "realisation" are in their turn all governed by the crucial words "by or for the benefit of another person".

We reach this conclusion purely as a matter of construction of section 22 (1). But we are fortified in that conclusion by the knowledge that our construction agrees with the views of Professor J. C. Smith in his admirable book, *The Law of Theft*, 1st ed. (1968), p. 160, para. 605, where the author says, "The undertaking, assisting or arranging must be shown to be [the italics are the author's] *for the benefit of another person*. If it were not for this qualification almost all thieves would be handlers as well".

It may be that this view leads to the conclusion that a man who innocently receives stolen goods but subsequently becomes aware or believes those goods to be stolen is not guilty of any criminal offence at least so long as he retains those goods himself. This was the law before the passing of the Theft Act, 1968. But we see no reason to think that he does not in any event subsequently become guilty of an offence under the second part of the subsection if after he becomes aware of their stolen origin, he thereupon dishonestly undertakes or assists in their retention, removal, disposal or realisation by or for the benefit of another or if he arranges to do so. However, this question does not now arise for final decision and we only mention the point lest omission to do so might lead to a mistaken impression of the scope of our decision upon the construction of this subsection.

Clearly therefore both the particulars in count two and the summing up were defective, the former omitting the crucial words and the latter making no reference to them. . . . As to the latter, clearly it would have been better had the chairman's direction dealt with the point. But we cannot believe that the jury can have been under any misapprehension. Most of the text of section 22 (1) was read to them and they had the benefit of the chairman's explanation upon that part which was read to them. The jury had the whole text of the whole subsection in front of them. If the defendant did dishonestly assist in the retention of these admittedly stolen goods, it was clearly for the benefit of Mrs. Day and not for his own benefit. The evidence well justified the jury in taking the view that, even upon his own story, what he did fell precisely within the plain language of the latter part of section 22 (1). . . .

Appeal dismissed

Question

Suppose V, in possession of goods which he knows are stolen, sells them to P. Can it be said that V undertakes the disposal or realisation of the goods for the benefit of P? See below.

R. v. Bloxham
[1982] 1 All E.R. 582
House of Lords

B. agreed to buy a car which, unknown to him, had been stolen. Several months later, he became convinced that it had been stolen, because his vendor failed to produce the registration documents. B. therefore sold the car to a man he did not know who was prepared to buy it without the documents. B. was charged with handling stolen goods contrary to section 22 of the Theft Act 1968. After a ruling by the trial judge that the sale was a dishonest realisation of the car for the benefit of another person, B. pleaded guilty. He appealed on the ground that the judge's ruling was wrong in law.

LORD BRIDGE OF HARWICH: The critical words to be construed are "undertakes . . . their . . . disposal or realization . . . for the benefit of another person". Considering these words first in isolation, it seems to me that, if A sells his own goods to B, it is a somewhat strained use of language to describe this as a disposal or realization of the goods for the benefit of B. True it is that B obtains a benefit from the transaction, but it is surely more natural to say that the disposal or realization is for A's benefit than for B's. It is the purchase, not the sale, that is for the benefit of B. It is only when A is selling as agent for a third party C that it would be entirely natural to describe the sale as a disposal or realization for the benefit of another person.

But the words cannot, of course, be construed in isolation. They must be construed in their context. . . . The . . . words contemplate four activities (retention, removal, disposal, realization). The offence can be committed in relation to any one of these activities in one or other of two ways. First, the offender may himself undertake the activity *for the benefit* of another person. Second, the activity may be undertaken *by* another person and the offender may assist him. . . . If the analysis holds good it must follow, I think, that the category of other persons contemplated by the subsection is subject to the same limitations in whichever way the offence is committed. Accordingly, a purchaser, as such, of stolen goods cannot, in my opinion, be 'another person' within the subsection, since his act of purchase could not sensibly be described as a disposal or realization of the stolen goods *by* him. Equally, therefore, even if the sale to him could be described as a disposal or realization for his benefit, the transaction is not, in my view, within the ambit of the subsection. . . .

Appeal allowed: conviction quashed

Question

What offence was committed by B. if (i) the purchaser from him knew or believed that the car was stolen, (ii) the purchaser did not know or believe that?

iv. Knowing or Believing Them to be Stolen Goods

Notes

1. *R. v. McCullum (1973) 57 Cr. App. R. 645:* M. was charged with handling by assisting in the retention of stolen guns and ammunition. The guns and ammunition were in a suitcase in her possession. Part of her case was that she did not know what was in the suitcase. A direction by the trial judge that knowledge on belief that the suitcase contained stolen goods without knowledge of the nature of the goods was sufficient, was upheld by the Court of Appeal, even though the indictment had specified the goods as guns and ammunition.

2. *R. v. Hulbert (1979) 69 Cr. App. R. 243 (C.A.):* H. was charged with handling stolen clothes. H. admitted to the police that she bought them at low prices in public houses from persons who told her they were stolen. *Held*, the information from the sellers was evidence that she knew they were stolen, but no evidence that they were stolen (being hearsay). However, her appeal was dismissed because the *circumstances*, admitted by her, (namely purchases in public houses at low prices) were *prima facie* evidence that the goods were stolen. See also A-G's Reference (*No.* 4 *of* 1979), *ante*, p. 605.

3. The previous law required the accused to receive "knowing" that the goods were stolen. The CLRC, Cmnd. 2977 § 134, justified the addition of the alternative "or believing" as follows:

"It is a serious defect of the present law that actual knowledge that the property was stolen must be proved. Often the prosecution cannot prove this. In many cases indeed guilty knowledge does not exist, although the circumstances of the transaction are such that the receiver ought to be guilty of an offence. The man who buys goods at a ridiculously low price from an unknown seller whom he meets in a public house may not *know* that the goods were stolen, and he may take the precaution of asking no questions. Yet it may be clear on the evidence that he *believes* that the goods were stolen. In such cases the prosecution may fail (rightly, as the law now stands) for want of proof of guilty knowledge. We consider that a person who handles stolen goods ought to be guilty if he believes them to be stolen. A purchaser who is merely careless, in that he does not make sufficient inquiry, will not be guilty of the offence under the new law any more than under the old."

4. *R. v. White (1859) 1 F. & F. 665:* W. was charged with receiving lead, he well knowing it to have been stolen. Bramwell B. (to the jury): "The knowledge charged in this indictment need not be such knowledge as would be acquired if the prisoner had actually seen the lead stolen; it is sufficient if you think the circumstances were such, accompanying the transaction, as to make the prisoner believe that it had been stolen." Since a receiver or handler can only rarely "know" about the history of the goods, this direction may be thought to be only common sense. The question is, what is added by the inclusion of the words "or believing" in section 22?

5. *Haughton v. Smith* [1975] *A.C. 485 (H.L.) (ante,* p. 317): Viscount Dilhorne, at p. 503: "It is, in my opinion, clear that Section 22 (1) of the Theft Act 1968 does not make the handling of goods which are not stolen goods an offence if a person believes them to have been stolen. The offence created by that section is in relation to goods which are stolen and it is an ingredient of the offence that the acccused must know or believe them to have been stolen. The word 'believing'

was, I think, inserted to avoid the possibility of an accused being acquitted when there was ample evidence that he believed the goods stolen, but no proof that he knew they were."

6. *Atwal v. Massey [1971] 56 Cr. App. R. 6 (Div. Ct.):* Lord Widgery C.J., at p. 7: "If when the justices said that the appellant ought to have known that the kettle was stolen they meant that any reasonable man would have realised that it was stolen, then that was not the right test. It is not sufficient to establish an offence under section 22 that the goods were received in circumstances which would have put a reasonable man on his inquiry. The question is a subjective one: was the appellant aware of the theft or did he believe the goods to be stolen or did he, suspecting the goods to be stolen, deliberately shut his eyes to the consequences?"

7. *R. v. Griffiths (1974) 60 Cr. App. R. 14 (C.A.):* James L.J., at p. 18: "It is inconceivable that the Lord Chief Justice [in *Atwal* v. *Massey*, above] would have sought to introduce an additional alternative mental element into the statutory definition which is restricted to "knowing or believing". *Atwal* v. *Massey* is to be read as the judgment of the Divisional Court dealing with the approach which justices, as judges of fact, may adopt in order to arrive at their decision as to the knowledge or belief of the defendant. There is a danger in the adoption of the passage cited from the judgment in *Atwal* v. *Massey* as the direction to a jury unless great care is taken to avoid confusion between the mental element of knowledge or belief and the approach by which the jury may arrive at a conclusion as to knowledge or belief. To direct the jury that the offence is committed if the defendant, suspecting that the goods were stolen, deliberately shut his eyes to the circumstances as an alternative to knowing or believing the goods were stolen is a misdirection. To direct the jury that, in common sense and in law, they may find that the defendant knew or believed the goods to be stolen because he deliberately closed his eyes to the circumstances is a perfectly proper direction." [On "wilful blindness," see, degrees of knowledge, *ante*, p. 69.]

8. *R. v. Reader (1977) 66 Cr. App. R. 33:* Waller L.J. at p. 36: "We are clearly of opinion that to have in mind that it is more likely that they are stolen than that they are not, which is the test which the judge told the jury to apply, is not sufficient to comply with the terms of the section. To believe that the goods are probably stolen is not to believe that the goods are stolen, and in our view this was a misdirection by the learned judge and one which was not a misdirection which was in favour of the appellant but which was against him. The jury were being told to accept a lower state of guilty mind than the section actually requires. Our attention was drawn to two cases, *R.* v. *Grainge* (1973) 59 Cr. App. R. 3, and *R.* v. *Griffiths* [above] where two other directions about suspicion were considered by this Court. In the case of *R.* v. *Grainge* (above) in giving the judgment of the Court, Eveleigh J. pointed out that where there are simple words it is undesirable for the judge to try to explain what those words mean, and we entirely agree with that. If the learned judge had left the word "belief" entirely alone and left the jury to decide what is belief, that is something which everybody is concerned with almost every day of their lives and they would have been able to come to a proper conclusion without any explanation being given. In his mistaken attempt to give an explanation he erred. He erred in a sense in two ways, not only by putting the degree of belief wrong, but also in confusing the jury in our view by adding balance of probabilities into the concept which they had to be satisfied about. Accordingly there was in our view a material misdirection in this case."

Questions

1. Has the CLRC's object of removing a serious defect in the pre-1968 law been achieved?

2. Would a direction in the terms of that given in *R.* v. *White* still be appropriate today?

3. A, a dealer in second-hand goods, bought a £30 watch from a youth for £5. In fact the watch was stolen. Interviewed by the police, A said, "In buying that watch, I knew I was taking a chance." At A's trial for handling the watch, how ought the judge to direct the jury on the issue of A's knowledge or belief? See *R.* v. *Ismail* [1977] Crim. L.R. 557.

Griew: Consistency, Communication and Codification, in Reshaping the Criminal Law (ed. Glazebrook) 1978, 57, 69

"There are several kinds of context in the criminal law in which the use is made of the notion of "believing" something to be the case. It will be convenient in discussing that notion to adopt the shorthand of philosophers, who refer to "a belief that *p*" where "*p*" is some proposition of fact ("my husband is dead"; "the goods are stolen").

. . . Unlike the other important *mens rea* expressions, it has received almost no attention either in the literature or in the case law. It is declared that a belief that *p* shall found criminal liability or exempt from it. Yet between this declaration and the act of judgment there intervenes no elucidation, no elaboration of what will count for the purposes of the rule as a belief that *p*. Now it may be said that analysis or elaboration is plainly not called for. Here is an "ordinary word" *par excellence*. It is enough that operations (analysis of facts, legal argument, jury-direction) are conducted in terms of the rule as expressed in the language of belief. There is neither need for, nor indeed possibility of, reduction to plainer terms. My purpose is not to challenge this view to the extent of suggesting that "belief" should be accorded a general definition in the criminal code. That would not be possible. I wish, rather, to use this common word as a means of drawing attention to some further problems of communication. . . . And I do so on the basis that "belief" is in fact a very difficult word, loosely and variably used in popular speech—even, possibly, a word not in the working vocabulary of the majority of people in anything like the sense in which it is used in this or that criminal law context.

I begin with a brief, rather dogmatic summary of what, in general and in the abstract, the word "belief" may be taken to refer to. A person will typically be said to believe a proposition ("*p*") when he is disposed to say: "Yes, it is 'to my mind' the case that *p*." What justifies the statement that he believes *p* is, as philosophers have pointed out, not that he *now* assents to *p*, but that he has a disposition to do so (just now he may not be thinking about the matter, yet he cannot be said to have ceased to believe it). But he must at some time have entertained the proposition—had it present "to his mind"; or at least it must be a proposition implied by some other thing known or believed by him. Assent to the proposition may be justified or unjustified (these epithets admit of degrees). In law we call false beliefs reasonable and unreasonable; but even true beliefs may be held on adequate or inadequate evidence, perhaps on no evidence at all.

The assent given to *p* may be more or less strong. At one extreme it may be a passionate conviction, perhaps experienced exactly like knowledge. How hesitant and uncertain a sense that *p* can be, at the other extreme, and still be called "belief that *p*," is an important question on which dogmatic statement would be improper. According to common usage,

> belief admits of degrees. You may believe something very firmly or fairly firmly, or mildly. A rough scale of degrees of belief may be constructed, raging from conviction at the top end to suspecting at the bottom end, with

> various degrees of opinion somewhere in the middle. (Price, H. H., *Belief* (London 1969) p. 39.)

That is one account of the way people speak generally. And the bottom of the scale referred to itself "admits of degrees"—there is strong suspicion and slight or mild suspicion. Others would deny that any state of mere suspicion qualifies, according to general usage, for the title of "belief". Belief, they would say, involves something in the way of a commitment to the proposition believed (with rational reservations, no doubt; *p may* not be the case); a willingness to stake something on the proposition; a tendency or inclination to act, in more or less weighty matters, on the basis of it—to behave "as if *p*"—where, if *p* were not the case, the action would be unsafe, imprudent, illogical or out of character. On this view belief is an opinion held with some confidence. A middle position is possible. Strong suspicion, though not mild suspicion, under certain conditions justifies—in some cases even demands—the forming of an opinion of a tentative or provisional kind; a person tempted (or compelled) to act may (or must) choose as best he can between *p* and not-*p*, and his strong suspicion warrants the assumption that *p*—some would say, as a "belief".

These are some of the ways in which people will debate how the word "belief" is generally or properly used. That "belief admits of degrees," that beliefs are held with varying amounts of confidence, is accepted by almost everyone. Beyond that there is much room for dispute.

Such controversies, or differences of linguistic usage, are relevant to the interpretation of the formulas to be found in statutes and judicial dicta. Parliament provides that a person will be guilty or not guilty if he believes that *p*. Or it may be laid down in a code or by judicial decision that belief that *p*, such that if *p* were the case no offence would be committed, entails an acquittal. In either case the scope of the prescription (if not spelt out in the statement of the rule) depends in part upon the view of the notion of "believing that *p*" taken, for the purpose of the matter in hand, by the person or body giving effect to the prescription.

To the limited extent that lawyers bear the responsibility of decision (as when a judge must decide whether there is a case to answer, or whether a particular count should be left to the jury, or whether the accused has done enough to get a defence on its feet), the absence of a verbal definition will be felt to be made good by a shared professional sense of what is intended by the prescriptive formula. This feeling will be based on the possession of a common professional diction, on a common involvement with the criminal law as a whole, and on a common practical experience of how cases in their variety are in fact disposed of; and it may be no mere illusion. But it may well be illusion to suppose that a lay application of the same formula will reflect that professional sense of what the formula connotes. A random collection of laymen, who may represent all shades of popular linguistic usage, are quite likely to nurse, unwittingly, substantially different ideas of the states of mind embraced by the undefined legal formula.

At present, however, a jury directed in terms of a particular rule that employs the language of belief cannot expect from the court any firm indication as to the sense in which that language is to be taken. . . . The Court of Appeal has refused to sanction attempts to explain what is meant by "believing" goods to be stolen in the offence of handling in the Theft Act 1968, s. 22. For "except in most unusual cases juries are capable of understanding what is meant" for themselves. (*R.* v. *Smith* (1976) Cr. App. R. 217, 220.) Not that the jury will necessarily be left entirely without help. Where the evidence justifies such a course, it is "perfectly proper" to direct them "that, in common sense and in law, they may find that the defendant knew or believed the goods to be stolen because he deliberately closed his eyes to the circumstances." (*R.* v. *Griffiths, supra*.) But this, the Court of Appeal insists, is only to say that proof of reasonable suspicion and "wilful blindness" justifies an *inference* that the defendant believed the goods to be stolen. It does not mean—and the jury must not be directed—that such proof is proof *of* a case of belief. (*R.* v. *Smith*.) This, it is submitted, is unsatisfactory. If a judge uses a phrase such as "wilful blindness" or "deliberately closed his eyes to the circumstances", he should be at pains to make very clear what he means by it. When he has done so he will have described behaviour (including a state of mind) of which it should be possible to say either that it is within the handling rule or that it is not. That way lies clarity. The present judicial approach, on the contrary, is obscurantist. It permits information to the jury as to how they may (if they choose) detect what they seek, but leaves them to determine for themselves the full specification of the thing sought."

v. Dishonestly

Notes

1. Dishonesty must exist at the time of the act alleged to constitute handling. On dishonesty in Theft, see *R.* v. *Feely*, *ante*, p. 556.

2. For a case where it was held that a person who, on instructions from the owner, arranged with the thieves for the return of the goods, was not guilty of *dishonestly* assisting in the goods disposal, see Harvey, *What Does Dishonesty Mean?* [1972] Crim. L.R. 213.

Questions

1. In *R.* v. *Matthews* [1950] 1 All E.R. 137, M. received what he well knew were stolen goods, intending to hand them over to the police. Later, he changed his mind and did not hand them over. It was held that this did not amount to receiving stolen goods. If a similar case arose again today, would M. be guilty of handling? See forms of handling, above.

2. B owed A £10. Being short of cash, A broke into B's desk and helped himself to £10. He later admitted to the police that he knew he had no right to do this. A shared the money with C. C knew how A got the money, but thought that since B owed A £10, A was entitled to help himself. A was convicted of theft. Ought C to be convicted of handling?

CHAPTER 13

BLACKMAIL

Theft Act 1968, section 21

"(1) A person is guilty of blackmail if, with a view to gain for himself or another or with intent to cause loss to another, he makes any unwarranted demand with menaces; and for this purpose a demand with menaces is unwarranted unless the person making it does so in the belief—

(a) that he has reasonable grounds for making the demand; and

(b) that the use of the menaces is a proper means of reinforcing the demand.

(2) The nature of the act or omission demanded is immaterial, and it is also immaterial whether the menaces relate to action to be taken by the person making the demand.

(3) A person guilty of blackmail shall on conviction on indictment be liable to imprisonment for a term not exceeding fourteen years."

i. Demand with Menaces

Notes

Neither "demand" nor "menaces" are defined by the Act. "Menaces," where it was used in the statutory predecessor of the present section (*i.e.* s. 29 (1) of the Larceny Act 1916) had acquired a definite meaning, being exactly synonymous with threat.

Thorne v. *Motor Trade Association* [1937] *A.C. 797:* Lord Atkin (at p. 806), "If the matter came to us for decision for the first time I think there would be something to be said for a construction of 'menace' which connoted threats of violence and injury to person or property, and a contrast might be made between 'menaces' and 'threats', as used in other sections of the various statutes. But in several cases it has been decided that 'menace' in this subsection and its predecessors is simply equivalent to threat."

But "threat" was regarded as too wide by the draftsmen of the Theft Act 1978.

Cmnd. 2977, §123: "We have chosen the word 'menaces' instead of 'threats' because notwithstanding the wide meaning given to 'menaces' in *Thorne's* case . . . we regard that word as stronger than 'threats' and the consequent slight restriction of the scope of the offence seems to us right."

R. v. Lawrence and Pomroy
(1971) 57 Cr. App. R. 64
Court of Appeal

L. and P. were convicted of blackmail in that on January 20, with a view to gain for themselves they made an unwarranted demand of £70 from T. with menaces. P. had done some work for T. T., not being satisfied with the work, had paid part only of the contract price and had indicated that the balance of £70 would be paid when the work was completed to his satisfaction. On January 16, P. had asked T. for the £70 and, on being refused, said that unless T. paid up, he had better look over his shoulder whenever he went out. On January 20, P. again visited T., this time in company with L., a big man. The conversation on that occasion is set out in the judgment of Cairns L.J., below. L. and P. appealed on the grounds that the judge failed to give (a) a definition of menaces and (b) a direction on proviso (*b*) of section 21 (1).

CAIRNS L.J.: Detective Constable Walters said that in company with other officers he was concealed behind the door of Thorn's house when the appellants arrived on January 20. He heard a conversation about the £70 which ended with Lawrence saying: "Now listen, I've got an interest in the £70, see," and then after a pause: "Come out of the house and we'll sort this lot out now." Thorn said: "No" and Lawrence said: "Come on mate, come outside." The police officers then revealed themselves and Walters said that he saw the appellants outside the door. He said to Lawrence: "What is your name?" and Lawrence said: "Leave off, what do you want to know for?" Pomroy said: "Yes it's all right, we only want my money." Lawrence said: "Leave me out, I've only come to help my mate," and when asked gave his name to the police. The appellants were told that they were being arrested for demanding money from Thorn. After caution Lawrence said: "That's nice, we've been well set up." Pomroy said: "But he does owe me money. . . ."

The first point we deal with is the contention that the judge gave the jury no definition of what constitutes a menace. It is said that they should have been directed in accordance with *R.* v. *Clear* [1968] 1 Q.B. 670, that they must consider what the effect would be in the mind of a reasonable man of the words and actions of the two defendants. The word "menaces" is an ordinary English word which any jury can be expected to understand. In exceptional cases where because of special knowledge in special circumstances what would be a menace to an ordinary person is not a menace to the person to whom it is addressed, or where the converse may be true, it is no doubt necessary to spell out the meaning of the word. But, in our view, there was no such necessity here. The judge made it abundantly clear that the issue for the jury was whether the two men had gone to Thorne's house merely to ask reasonably for payment, on Pomroy's part to ask reasonably for payment and on Lawrence's part merely as a companion, or whether they had gone to threaten and frighten him into paying. That was quite a sufficient explanation of what is meant by menaces.

Next, should the judge have directed the jury on the proviso to section 21 (1) (b) of the Theft Act: that is to say, as to whether the accused believed that what they did was a proper way of enforcing the debt? Neither of them suggested at the trial that, if menaces were used by them, it was a proper means of enforcement. It is true that the police evidence was that when Pomroy's statement was read to him, Lawrence said: "That's about it, what's wrong with that?" but he repudiated that in his evidence and said that his reaction had been "It's a lot of nonsense."

Where on the face of it the means adopted to obtain payment of a debt is not the proper way of enforcing it and where the accused does not at his trial set up the case that he believed it to be, there is no need for any direction to be given on the proviso. . . .

Appeals dismissed

R. v. Harry [1972] Crim. L.R. 32 (Chelmsford Crown Court): H. sent letters to 115 local shopkeepers asking them to buy indemnity posters by contributing to a Student Rag Fund in aid of charity; the purpose of a poster was to "protect you from any Rag Activity which could in any way cause you inconvenience." The poster read "These premises are immune from rag '73 activities whatever they may be". In directing an acquittal of blackmail, Judge Petre said "Menaces is a strong word. You may think that menaces must be of a fairly stern nature to fall within the definition."

Treacy v. Director of Public Prosecutions
[1971] A.C. 537
House of Lords

T. wrote and posted in England a letter addressed to a woman in Germany, which letter contained a demand. T. argued that he was not triable in England, not having made the demand in England.

LORD DIPLOCK: . . . Arguments as to the meaning of ordinary everyday phrases are not susceptible of much elaboration. The Theft Act, 1968, makes a welcome departure from the former style of drafting in criminal statutes. It is expressed in simple language as used and understood by ordinary literate men and women. It avoids so far as possible those terms of art which have acquired a special meaning understood only by lawyers in which many of the penal enactments which it supersedes were couched. So the question which has to be answered is: Would a man say in ordinary conversation: "I have made a demand" when he had written a letter containing a demand and posted it to the person to whom the demand was addressed? Or would he not use those words until the letter had been received and read by the addressee?

My answer to that question is that it would be natural for him to say "I have made a demand" as soon as he had posted the letter, for he would have done all that was in his power to make the demand. He might add, if it were the fact: "but it has not reached X yet," or: "I made a demand but it got lost in the post." What, at any rate, he would not say is: "I shall make a demand when X receives my letter," unless he contemplated making some further demand after the letter had been received.

I see nothing in the context or in the pupose of the section to indicate that the words bear any other meaning than that which I have suggested they would bear in ordinary conversation. . . .

As respects the purpose of the section, I see no reason for supposing that Parliament did not intend to punish conduct which is anti-social or wicked—if that word is still in current use—unless the person guilty of the conduct achieves his intended object of gain to himself or loss caused to another. The fact that what a reasonable man would regard as an unwarranted demand with menaces after being posted by its author goes astray and never reaches the addressee, or reaches him but is not understood by him, or because of his unusual fortitude fails to disturb his equanimity, as was the case in *R.* v. *Clear* [1968] 1 Q.B. 670, may be a relevant factor in considering what punishment is appropriate but does not make the conduct of the author himself any less wicked or anti-social or less meet to be deterred.

My Lords, all that has to be decided upon this aspect of the instant appeal is whether the appellant "made a demand" when he posted his letter to the addressee. In the course of the argument many other and ingenious ways in which a blackmailer might choose to send his demand to his victim have been canvassed, and many possible, even though unlikely, events which might intervene between the sending of the demand by the blackmailer and its receipt and comprehension by the victim have been discussed. These cases which so far are only imaginary may fall to be decided if they ever should occur in real life. But unless the purpose of the new style of drafting used in the Theft Act, 1968, is to be defeated they, too, should be decided by answering the question: "Are the circumstances of this case such as would prompt a man in ordinary conversation to say: 'I have made a demand'?"

For both the reasons which I have given I would dismiss this appeal.

Appeal dismissed

Notes

1. A possible danger in "the new style of drafting used in the Theft Act, 1968," is illustrated by the fact that of the five Law Lords concerned in *Treacy's* case, three thought that posting a letter containing a demand was making a demand, but two thought that no demand was made until the letter reached the addressee. A technical term at least has the merit that its meaning is precise and can be the subject of a precise direction to a jury. See also *R.* v. *Feely, ante,* p. 556.

2. Both demand and menaces may be implicit, rather than explicit. See next case.

R. v. Collister and Warhurst

(1955) 39 Cr. App. R. 100

Court of Criminal Appeal

> C. and W., who were police officers, were charged with demanding money with menaces, under section 30 of the Larceny Act 1916. C. told W., in the presence of the prosecutor, that the prosecutor had been importuning him. The prosecutor protested, but W. said to him, "This is going to look very bad for you." They arranged to meet him on the next day, W. telling C. in the prosecutor's hearing to type out a report on the matter but to hold it up and use it only if the prosecutor failed to keep the appointment. When they met next day, W. asked the prosecutor whether he had brought anything with him, and the prosecutor handed over five one pound notes.

PILCHER J. directed the jury: What you have got to be satisfied with in this case is that these two men, working in concert, intended to convey, and did in fact convey, to Mr. Jeffries in the first place that they, being police officers, intended to take him to the West Central Police Station on a charge of importuning, or to put in a report about him, unless Jeffries then or later paid them money. That, I think, is putting it as simply as I can put it. You need not be satisfied that there was an express demand for money in words. You need not be satisfied that any express threats were made, but if the evidence satisfies you that, although there was no such express demand or threat, the demeanour of the accused and the circumstances of the case were such that an ordinary reasonable man would understand that a demand for money was being made upon him and that that demand was accompanied by menaces—not perhaps direct, but veiled menaces—so that his ordinary balance of mind was upset, then you would be justified in coming to the conclusion that a demand with menaces had been made. . . .

They were convicted and on appeal this direction was held to be perfectly proper

ii. Unwarranted

Criminal Law Revision Committee: Eighth Report, Cmnd. 2977

"§118 As to the illegality of making the demand we are decidedly of the opinion that the test should be subjective, namely whether the person in question honestly believes that he has the right to make the demand. This means in effect adopting the test of whether there is a claim of right, as in 1916, s. 30, and not the test whether there is in fact a reasonable cause for making the demand, as in 1916, s. 29 (1) (i). Since blackmail is in its nature an offence of dishonesty, it seems wrong that a person should be guilty of the offence by making a demand which he honestly believes to be justified. Moreover to adopt the objective test seems to involve almost insuperable difficulty. It would be necessary either to set out the various kinds of demand which it was considered should be justified or to find an expression which would describe exactly these kinds but not others. The former course might in theory be possible; but the provision would have to be very elaborate, and it would involve the risk which attends any attempt to list different kinds of conduct for the purpose of a criminal offence—that of including too much or too little. Moreover there is much room for disagreement as to what kinds of demand should or should not be treated as justified. The latter course seems impossible having regard to the results which have followed from making liability depend on the absence of a 'reasonable or probable cause.' Any general provision would probably have to use some such uninformative expression, and it would be almost bound to cause similar difficulty and uncertainty.

§ 119 It is in relation to the question when it is permissible to employ threats in support of a demand that differences of opinion become most acute. Several situations are possible. A may be owed £100 by B and be unable to get payment. Perhaps A needs the money badly and B is in a position to pay; or perhaps A can easily afford to wait and B is in difficulty. Should it be blackmail for A to threaten B that, if he does not pay, A will assault him—or slash the tyres of his car—or tell people that B is a homosexual, which he is (or which he is not)—or tell people about the debt and anything discreditable about the way in which it was incurred? On one view none of these threats should be enough to make the demand amount to blackmail. For it is no offence merely to utter the threats without making the demand (unless for some particular reason such as breach of the peace or defamation); nor would the threat become criminal merely because it was uttered to reinforce a demand of a kind quite different from those associated with blackmail. Why then should it be blackmail merely because it is uttered to reinforce a demand for money which is owed? On this view no demand with menaces would amount to blackmail, however harsh the action threatened unless there was dishonesty. This is a tenable view, though an extreme one. In our opinion it goes too far and there are some threats which should make the demand amount to blackmail even if there is a valid claim to the thing demanded. For example, we believe that most people would say that it should be blackmail to threaten to denounce a person, however truly, as a homosexual unless he paid a debt. It does not seem to follow from the existence of a debt that the creditor should be entitled to resort to any method, otherwise non-criminal, to obtain payment. There are limits to the methods permissible for the purpose of enforcing payment of a debt without recourse to the courts. For example, a creditor cannot seize the debtor's goods; and in *Parker* (1910) 74 J.P. 208, it was held . . . that a creditor who forged a letter from the Admiralty to a sailor warning him to pay a debt was guilty of forgery notwithstanding the existence of the debt.

§ 120 If it is agreed that some threats should make a demand amount to blackmail, the difficulty is to draw the line between different kinds of threats in a way which would be generally accepted. It may be thought that a threat to cause physical injury or damage to property should always be sufficient, even though one does not ordinarily think of such threats in connection with blackmail. A threat to injure a person in relation to his business, for example by cutting off supplies to a retailer if he will not pay a debt or persists in breaking an agreement, would probably not be regarded as rightly included in blackmail. Some might think that any threat to disclose a matter not connected with the circumstances giving rise to the debt should be included; but opinion may differ widely about threats to disclose some discreditable conduct which resulted in the debt being incurred. Probably most people would say that the offence should not extend to a threat to disclose the existence of a debt. For example, it is not blackmail to threaten to post the name of a betting defaulter at Tattersalls (see *Russell on Crime*, 12th edition, pp. 881–882). As in the case of demands, the possible courses seem to be to lay down a subjective test, depending on whether the person who utters the threat believes in his right to do so, or an objective test, whether by specifying the kinds of threats which should or should not be permissible or by means of a general provision to cover the latter. For reasons similar to those given in paragraph 118 concerning the demand we think that the only satisfactory course would be to adopt a subjective test and to make criminal liability depend on whether the person who utters the threat believes in the propriety of doing so.

§ 122 At first we proposed to include a requirement that a person's belief that he has reasonable grounds for making the demand or that the use of the menaces is proper should be reasonable belief. There would be a case for this in policy; for it may be thought that a person who puts pressure on another by menaces of a kind which any reasonable person would think ought to be blackmail should not escape liability merely because his moral standard is too low, or his intelligence too limited, to enable him to appreciate the wrongness of his conduct. The requirement might also make the decision easier for a jury; for if they found that the demand was unwarranted or that the menaces were improper, they would not have to consider whether the accused believed otherwise. But we decided finally not to include the requirement. To require that an honest belief, in order to be a defence, should be reasonable would have the result that the offence of blackmail could be committed by mere negligence (for example, in not consulting a lawyer or, as did Bernhard, in consulting the wrong kind of lawyer). [See *R.* v. *Bernhard* [1938] 2 K.B. 264.]"

Sir Bernard MacKenna, Blackmail: a Criticism [1966] Crim. L.R. 466

"5. A man's belief that he has reasonable grounds for making a demand depends on two matters:

(a) his belief that the facts of the case are such-and-such; and
(b) his opinion upon these facts that it would be reasonable to make the demand.

In a particular case one man's belief that there are reasonable grounds for making a demand may differ from another's because of a difference in their beliefs about the facts (one believing the facts to be X, the other to be Y), or because of a difference in their opinions upon the same facts (one opinion that those facts give a reasonable ground for making the demand, the other that they do not).

6. 'Reasonable grounds' in [section 21 (1) (a)] cannot be limited to such as are believed to give a legally enforceable claim. To many it would seem reasonable to demand satisfaction of a claim recognised by the law as valid though unenforceable by legal action for some technical reason, such as the want of a writing or the expiration of the period of limitation. To some it would seem equally reasonable to demand payment of a claim incapable in any circumstances of being enforced by action, such as the claim to be paid a winning bet. There may be many other cases in which a moral, as distinct from a legal, right would seem to some at least a reasonable ground for making a demand. On these questions there could be differences of opinion, particularly as to whether on the facts of the case the person demanding had a moral right to the thing demanded. There could be similar 'moral' differences about the propriety of using threats.

7. The Committee intend that the test shall be subjective in both the respects indicated in 5 above: (i) the facts shall be taken to be those which the defendant believed to exist, and (ii) his opinion as to whether those facts gave him a reasonable ground for making a demand (or made it proper for him to use threats) will be the only relevant one. His own moral standards are to determine the rightness or wrongness of his conduct. This appears from a sentence in paragraph 122 where the Committee discuss (and dismiss) the possible objection to [section 21 (1) (a)] that 'it may be thought that a person who puts pressure on another by menaces of a kind which any reasonable person would think ought to be blackmail should not escape liability merely because his moral standard is too low, or his intelligence too limited, to enable him to appreciate the wrongness of his conduct.'

8. That a sane man's guilt or innocence should depend in this way on his own opinion as to whether he is acting rightly or wrongly is, I think, an innovation in our criminal law.

9. The claim of right which excuses a taking that might otherwise be theft under section 1 of the Larceny Act 1916, may of course be a mistaken claim, and the mistake may be one of law or of fact. A man's mistaken belief that the rules of the civil law make him the owner of a certain thing is as good an excuse as his mistaken belief that the thing is X when it is in fact Y. But [section 21 (1)] goes further than this, and gives efficacy to the defendant's moral judgments whatever they may be. That is surely something different. It is one thing to hold that the defendant is excused if he believes the civil law to be X when it is Y. It is another to excuse him in any case where he thinks that what he is doing is morally right, though according to ordinary moral notions he may be doing something very wrong."

Note

Professor Smith (*Law of Theft*, 4th ed., §§ 325–328) argues that by choosing the word "proper," the CLRC imposed some minimal objective standards as to what is permissible in the way of menaces. "Where D admits that he knew that the act he threatened to do was a crime, it is submitted that the judge would be within his rights if he withdrew the defence from the jury. What is criminal cannot be 'proper' within the meaning of a statute and if D knows the act to be a crime he cannot believe it to be 'proper'." See next case.

R. v. Harvey
(1980) 72 Cr. App. R. 139
Court of Appeal

H. and others paid £20,000 to S. for what was thought to be a consignment of cannabis, but in fact was a load of rubbish. They kidnapped S.'s wife and small child and told S. they would maim and kill his family unless he gave them their money back. They were convicted of blackmail and appealed.

BINGHAM J.: The learned judge in his direction to the jury quoted the terms of the subsection and then continued as follows: "Now where the defence raise this issue, in other words, where they say that the demand is warranted and where they say they believe they had reasonable cause for making the demand and that the use of the menaces was a proper way of reinforcing the demand, it is for the prosecution to negative that allegation. It is not for the defendants to prove it once they have raised it. It is for the prosecution to prove that they had no such belief. Now is that clear? It is not easy and I do not want to lose you on the way. It has been raised in this case so you have got to ask yourself this. Has the prosecution disproved that these defendants or those who have raised the matter believed that they had *reasonable* grounds for making the demand? Certainly you may say to yourselves that they had been ripped off to the tune of £20,000. They had been swindled.... As I say, on this question of reasonable ground for making a demand, you may say to yourselves: 'Well, they did have reasonable ground for making the demand in this sense, that they had put money into this deal, they had been swindled by Scott, and it was reasonable to demand the return of their money.' So you may say: 'Well, the prosecution have not negatived that but what about the second leg of the proviso, the belief that the use of menaces is a proper method of reinforcing the demand?' Now it is for you to decide what, if any, menaces were made, because that is a question of evidence. If you decide that the threats or menaces made by these accused, or any of them, were to kill or to maim or to rape, or any of the other matters that have been mentioned in evidence—I mention about three that come into my mind—then those menaces or threats are threats to commit a criminal act, a threat to murder, a threat to rape, or a threat to blow your legs or kneecaps off, those are threats to commit a criminal offence and surely everybody in this country, including the defendants, knows those are criminal offences. The point is that this is a matter of law. It cannot be a proper means of reinforcing the demand to make threats to commit serious criminal offences. So I say to you that if you look at these two counts of blackmail and you decide that these defendants, or any of them, used menaces, dependent upon the menaces you decide were used, the threats that were used, but if you decide that these threats were made by these men to commit criminal offences against Scott, they cannot be heard to say on this blackmail charge that they had reasonable belief that the use of those threats was a proper method of reinforcing their demand."

Later, when prosecuting counsel drew attention to the learned judge's erroneous reference to "reasonable" belief, he added the following: "I do not think it affects the point I was seeking to make, that where the demand or the threat is to commit a criminal offence, and a serious criminal offence like murder and maiming and rape, or whatever it may be, it seems hard for anybody to say that the defendants had a belief that was a proper way of reinforcing their demand. That is the point."

For the appellants it was submitted that the learned judge's direction, and in particular the earlier of the passages quoted, was incorrect in law because it took away from the jury a question properly falling within their province of decision, namely, what the accused in fact believed. He was wrong to rule as a matter of law that a threat to perform a serious criminal act could never be thought by the person making it to be a proper means. While free to comment on the unlikelihood of a defendant believing threats such as were made in this case to be a proper means, the judge should nonetheless (it was submitted) have left the question to the jury. For the Crown it was submitted that a threat to perform a criminal act can never as a matter of law be a proper means within the subsection, and that the learned judge's direction was accordingly correct. Support for both these approaches is to be found in academic works helpfully brought to the attention of the Court.

The answer to this problem must be found in the language of the subsection, from which in our judgment two points emerge with clarity: (1) the subsection is concerned with the belief of the individual defendant in the particular case: "... a demand with menaces is unwarranted unless *the person making it* does so in the belief ..." (added emphasis). It matters not what the reasonable man, or any man other than the defendant, would believe save in so far as that may throw light on what the defendant in fact believed. Thus the factual question of the defendant's belief should be left to the jury. To that extent the subsection is subjective in approach, as is generally desirable in a criminal statute. (2) In order to exonerate a defendant from liability his belief must be that the use of the menaces is a "proper" means of reinforcing the demand. "Proper" is an unusual expression to find in a criminal statute. It is not defined in the Act, and no definition need be attempted here. It is, however, plainly a word of wide meaning, certainly wider than (for example) "lawful". But the greater includes the less and no act which was not believed to be lawful could be believed to be proper within the meaning of the subsection. Thus no assistance is given to any defendant, even a fanatic or a deranged idealist, who knows or suspects that his threat, or the act threatened, is criminal, but believes it to be justified by his end or his peculiar circumstances. The test is not what he regards as justified, but what he believes to be proper. And where, as here, the threats were to do acts which any sane man knows to be against the laws of every civilised country no jury would hesitate long before dismissing the contention that the defendant genuinely believed the threats to be a proper means of reinforcing even a legitimate demand.

It is accordingly our conclusion that the direction of the learned judge was not strictly correct. If it was necessary to give a direction on this aspect of the case at all (and in the absence of any evidence by the defendants as to their belief we cannot think that there was in reality any live issue concerning it) the jury should have been directed that the demand with menaces was not to be regarded as unwarranted unless the Crown satisfied them in respect of each defendant that the defendant did not make the demand with menaces in the genuine belief both—(a) that he had had reasonable grounds for making the demand; and (b) that the use of the menaces was in the circumstances a proper (meaning for present purposes a lawful, and not a criminal) means of reinforcing the demand.

The learned judge could, of course, make appropriate comment on the unlikelihood of the defendants believing murder and rape or threats to commit those acts to be lawful or other than criminal.

On the facts of this case we are quite satisfied that the misdirection to which we have drawn attention could have caused no possible prejudice to any of the appellants. Accordingly, in our judgment, it is appropriate to apply the proviso to section 2 (1) of the Criminal Appeal Act 1968, and the appeals are dismissed.

Appeals against conviction dismissed

Note

On the judge's duty to leave to the jury issues of fact which can have only one answer, see *D.P.P.* v. *Stonehouse*, *ante*, p. 313.

Questions

1. What exactly was the issue of fact which the judge had failed to leave to the jury in *R.* v. *Harvey*?

2. A wishes to ride his bicycle at night but has no lights for it. A seeks the loan of a light for it from B and B at first refuses. A says: "Riding a bike at night without lights is a crime. Unless you lend me your light, I will certainly commit this crime. You wouldn't want that on your conscience, would you?" As a result of this threat, B lends him the light. At his trial for blackmail, A contends that he thought his request and threat were perfectly justified. How ought the judge to deal with the issue in his direction to the jury?

Theft Act 1968, section 34

"... (2) For the purposes of this Act—

(a) 'gain' and 'loss' are to be construed as extending only to gain or loss in money or other property, but as extending to any such gain or loss whether temporary or permanent; and

(i) 'gain' includes a gain by keeping what one has, as well as a gain by getting what one has not; and

(ii) 'loss' includes a loss by not getting what one might get, as well as a loss by parting with what one has."

R. v. *Parkes* [1973] Crim. L.R. 358 (Sheffield Crown Court). D was charged with blackmail (*inter alia*). The evidence adduced by the prosecution showed that in one instance the money demanded was undoubtedly money owed to D by the complainant and, indeed, long overdue. In the other instance there was some issue as to whether or not the money demanded was a debt but the submission was made and ruled upon the basis that it *was* a debt owing by the complainant to D.

It was submitted that to demand that what is lawfully owing to you was not a demand "with a view to gain" within the meaning of section 21 (1) of the Theft Act 1968, as interpreted by section 32 (2) (a) of that Act. Judge Dean Q.C. ruled that by demanding money lawfully owing to him D did have a view to "gain". Section 34 (2) (a) (i) defines gain as including "getting what one has not"; by intending to obtain hard cash as opposed to a mere right of action in respect of the debt D *was* getting more than he already had and accordingly the submission failed.

Note

See also *R.* v. *Lawrence and Pomroy*, *ante*, p. 621.

Question

"Since blackmail is in its nature an offence of dishonesty, it seems wrong that a person should be guilty of the offence by making a demand which he honestly believes to be justified": Cmnd. 2977, §118, *ante*, p. 625. Is the CLRC giving the same meaning to "dishonesty" as it bears in, *e.g.* theft?

Chapter 14

BURGLARY AND KINDRED OFFENCES

	PAGE		PAGE
1. Burglary	631	3. Going Equipped	649
2. Aggravated Burglary	647		

1. BURGLARY

Theft Act 1968, section 9

"(1) A person is guilty of burglary if—

(a) he enters any building or part of a building as a trespasser and with intent to commit any such offence as is mentioned in sub-section (2) below; or

(b) having entered any building or part of a building as a trespasser he steals or attempts to steal anything in the building or that part of it or inflicts or attempts to inflict on any person therein any grievous bodily harm.

(2) The offences referred to in subsection (1) (a) above are offences of stealing anything in the building or part of a building in question, of inflicting on any person therein any grievous bodily harm or raping any woman therein, and of doing unlawful damage to the building or anything therein.

(3) References in subsections (1) and (2) above to a building shall apply also to an inhabited vehicle or vessel, and shall apply to any such vehicle or vessel at times when the person having a habitation in it is not there as well as at times when he is.

(4) A person guilty of burglary shall on conviction on indictment be liable to imprisonment for a term not exceeding fourteen years."

Note

The range of conduct prohibited by this section was before the Theft Act distributed between the offences of burglary, housebreaking and sacrilege, and the law was found in sections 25, 26 and 27 of the Larceny Act 1916. There were many intricate and confusing differences between the different offences; burglary proper needed a dwelling-house, a breaking and entering, and an intention to commit a felony, and it had to be committed in the night. Any kind of building is now covered, and vehicles and vessels are also covered provided they are dwelt in. The offence may take place at any time of day. However, the two parts of subsection (1) create two separate offences, and on an indictment for one there can be no conviction of the other: *R.* v. *Hollis* [1971] Crim. L. R. 525.

i. Entry

Note

Breaking, round which a great number of technicalities clustered, is no longer necessary, but entry is still required. This, too, was a highly technical concept, and as entry is not defined in the Act, it is quite possible that the pre-existing meaning will be adhered to.

R. v. Hughes
(1785) 1 Leach 406
Old Bailey Sessions

H. with intent to steal property from a house, inserted a centre bit into a door near the bolt. The end of the bit penetrated the door but no part of the prisoner's body entered the house. He was indicted for burglary. On the question of whether there was an entry:

COUNSEL FOR THE PRISONER: It has been held that the smallest degree of entry whatever is sufficient to satisfy the law. Putting a hand, or a foot, or a pistol over the threshold of the door, or a hook or other instrument through the broken pane of a window . . . have been decided to be burglarious entries; but the principle of all these new determinations is, that there has been such a previous breaking of the castle of the proprietor, as to render his property insecure. . . . And in those cases where an instrument has formed any part of the question, it has always been taken to mean, not the instrument by which the breaking was made, but the instrument, as a hook, a fork or other thing by which the property was capable of being removed, introduced subsequent to the act of breaking. . . . In the present case, the introduction of the instrument is part of the act of breaking, but it is impossible to conceive that it was introduced for the purpose of purloining property, for it is incapable of performing such an office.

The prisoner was acquitted

Note

But the insertion of a *hand* was an entry, whether the purpose of the insertion was to commit the ulterior felony or merely to effect entry: see *R.* v. *Bailey* (1818) R. & R. 341. However, see now *R.* v. *Collins*, below, particularly the following remark of Edmund Davies L.J.: "Unless the jury were entirely satisfied that the defendant made *an effective and substantial entry* into the bedroom without the complainant doing or saying anything to cause him to believe that she was consenting to his entering it, he ought not to be convicted of the offence charged." (Italics supplied.)

Smith, The Law of Theft, §§ 334, 335

§334 "Even if the courts are willing to follow the common law in holding that the intrusion of any part of the body is an entry, they may be reluctant to preserve these technical rules regarding instruments, for they seem to lead to outlandish results. Thus it seems to follow from the common law rules that there may be an entry if a stick of dynamite is thrown into the building or if a bullet is fired from outside the building into it. What then if a time bomb is sent by parcel post? Has D 'entered', even though he is not on the scene at all—perhaps even abroad and outside the jurisdiction? Whether D enters or not can hardly depend on how far away he is and the case seems indistinguishable from the others put. Yet this is hardly an "entry" in the simple language as used and understood by ordinary literate men and women in which the Act is said to be written (*per* Lord Diplock, in *Treacy* v. *D.P.P.* [*ante*, p. 623]).

§335 "There is, however, a cogent argument in favour of the common law rules which may be put as follows. If D sends a child, under the age of ten, into the building to steal, this is obviously an entry by D, through an 'innocent agent', under ordinary principles. Suppose that, instead of a child, D sends in a monkey. It is hard to see that this should not equally be an entry by D. But if that point be conceded, it is admitted that the insertion of an animate instrument is an entry; and are we to distinguish between animate and inanimate instruments? Unless we are, the insertion of the hooks, etc., must also be an entry."

Question

Suppose D puts a child under 10 through the window, not to steal but to open a door and admit D, who will himself steal. Is that entry by D?

ii. As a Trespasser

R. v. Collins
[1973] 1 Q.B. 100
Court of Appeal

C. was convicted of burglary with intent to commit rape in the circumstances outlined in the judgment below.

EDMUND DAVIES L.J.: . . . Let me relate the facts. Were they put into a novel or portrayed on the stage, they would be regarded as being so improbable as to be unworthy of serious consideration and as verging at times on farce. At about 2 o'clock in the early morning of Saturday, July 24, 1971, a young lady of 18 went to bed at her mother's home in Colchester. She had spent the evening with her boyfriend. She had taken a certain amount of drink, and it may be that this fact affords some explanation of her inability to answer satisfactorily certain crucial questions put to her at the trial.

She has the habit of sleeping without wearing night apparel in a bed which is very near the lattice-type window of her room. At one stage in her evidence she seemed to be saying that the bed was close up against the window which, in accordance with her practice, was wide open. In the photographs which we have before us, however, there appears to be a gap of some sort between the two, but the bed was clearly quite near the window.

At about 3.30 or 4 o'clock she awoke and she then saw in the moonlight a vague form crouched in the open window. She was unable to remember, and this is important, whether the form was on the outside of the window sill or on that part of the sill which was inside the room, and for reasons which will later become clear, that seemingly narrow point is of crucial importance.

The young lady then realised several things: first of all that the form in the window was that of a male; secondly, that he was a naked male; and thirdly, that he was a naked male with an erect penis. She also saw in the moonlight that his hair was blond. She thereupon leapt to the conclusion that her boyfriend, with whom for some time she had been on terms of regular and frequent sexual intimacy, was paying her an ardent nocturnal visit. She promptly sat up in bed, and the man descended from the sill and joined her in bed and they had full sexual intercourse. But there was something about him which made her think that things were not as they usually were between her and her boyfriend. The length of his hair, his voice as they had exchanged what was described as "love talk", and other features led her to the conclusion that somehow there was something different. So she turned on the bed-side light, saw that her companion was not her boyfriend and slapped the face of the intruder, who was none other than the defendant. He said to her, "Give me a good time tonight," and got hold of her arm, but she bit him and told him to go. She then went into the bathroom and he promptly vanished.

The complainant said that she would not have agreed to intercourse if she had known that the person entering her room was not her boyfriend. But there was no suggestion of any force having been used upon her, and the intercourse which took place was undoubtedly effected with no resistance on her part.

The defendant was seen by the police at about 10.30 later that same morning. According to the police, the conversation which took place then elicited these points: He was very lustful the previous night. He had taken a lot of drink. . . . He went on to say that he knew the complainant because he had worked around her house. On this occasion, desiring sexual intercourse—and according to the police evidence he added that he was determined to have a girl, by force if necessary, although that part of the police evidence he challenged—he went on to say that he walked around the house, saw a light in an upstairs bedroom, and he knew that this was the girl's bedroom. He found a step ladder, leaned it against the wall and climbed up and looked into the bedroom. He could see through the wide-open window a girl who was naked and asleep. So he descended the ladder and stripped off all his clothes, with the exception of his socks, because apparently he took the view that if the girl's mother entered the bedroom it would be easier to effect a rapid escape if he had his socks on than if he was in his bare feet. That is a matter about which we are not called upon to express any view, and would in any event find ourselves unable to express one.

Having undressed, he then climbed the ladder and pulled himself up on to the window sill. His version of the matter is that he was pulling himself in when she awoke. She then got up and knelt on the bed, she put her arms around his neck and body, and she seemed to pull him into the bed. He went on: "I was rather dazed because I didn't think she would want to know me. We kissed and cuddled for about 10 or 15 minutes and then I had it away with her but found it hard because I had had so much to drink."

The police officer said to the defendant: "It appears that it was your intention to have intercourse with this girl by force if necessary, and it was only pure coincidence that this girl was under the impression that you were her boyfriend and apparently that is why she consented to allowing you to have sexual intercourse with her." It was alleged that he then said, "Yes, I feel awful about this. It is the worst day of my life, but I know it could have been worse." Thereupon the officer said to him—and he challenges this: "What do you mean, you know it could have been worse?," to which he is alleged to have replied: "Well, my trouble is drink and I got very frustrated. As I've told you, I only wanted to have it away with a girl and I'm only glad I haven't really hurt her."

Then he made a statement under caution, in the course of which he said: "When I stripped off and got up the ladder I made my mind up that I was going to try and have it away with this girl. I feel terrible about this now, but I had too much to drink. I am sorry for what I have done."

In the course of his testimony, the defendant said that he would not have gone into the room if the girl had not knelt on the bed and beckoned him into the room. He said that if she had objected immediately to his being there or to his having intercourse he would not have persisted. While he was keen on having sexual intercourse that night, it was only if he could find someone who was willing. He strongly denied having told the police that he would if necessary, have pushed over some girl for the purpose of having intercourse. . . .

Now, one feature of the case which remained at the conclusion of the evidence in great obscurity is where exactly Collins was at the moment when, according to him, the girl manifested that she was welcoming him. Was he kneeling on the sill outside the window or was he already inside the room, having climbed through the window frame, and kneeling upon the inner sill? It was a crucial matter, for there were certainly three ingredients that it was incumbent upon the Crown to establish. Under section 9 of the Theft Act, 1968, which renders a person guilty of burglary if he enters any building or part of a building as a trespasser and with the intention of committing rape, the entry of the accused into the building must first be proved. Well, there is no doubt about that, for it is common ground that he did enter this girl's bedroom. Secondly, it must be proved that he entered as a trespasser. We will develop that point a little later. Thirdly, it must be proved that he entered as a trespasser with intent at the time of entry to commit rape therein.

The second ingredient of the offence—the entry must be as a trespasser—is one which has not, to the best of our knowledge, been previously canvassed in the courts. Views as to its ambit have naturally been canvassed by the textbook writers, and it is perhaps not wholly irrelevant to recall that those who were advising the Home Secretary before the Theft Bill was presented to Parliament had it in mind to get rid of some of the frequently absurd technical rules which had been built up in relation to the old requirement in burglary of a "breaking and entering." The cases are legion as to what this did or did not amount to, and happily it is not now necessary for us to consider them. But it was in order to get rid of those technical rules that a new test was introduced, namely, that the entry must be "as a trespasser."

What does that involve? According to the editors of *Archbold Criminal Pleading Evidence & Practice*, 37th ed. (1969), para. 1505: "Any intentional, reckless or negligent entry into a building will, it would appear, constitute a trespass if the building is in the possession of another person who does not consent to the entry. Nor will it make any difference that the entry was the result of a reasonable mistake on the part of the defendant, so far as trespass is concerned." If that be right, then it would be no defence for this man to say (and even were he believed in saying), "Well, I honestly thought that this girl was welcoming me into the room and I therefore entered, fully believing that I had her consent to go in." If *Archbold* is right, he would nevertheless be a trespasser, since the apparent consent of the girl was unreal, she being mistaken as to who was at her window. We disagree. We hold that, for the purposes of section 9 ot the Theft Act, a person entering a building is not guilty of trespass if he enters without knowledge that he is trespassing or at least without acting recklessly as to whether or not he is unlawfully entering.

A view contrary to that of the editors of *Archbold* was expressed in Professor Smith's book on *The Law of Theft*, 1st ed. (1968), where, having given an illustration of an entry into premises, the author comments, at paragraph 462: "It is submitted that ... D should be acquitted on the ground of lack of *mens rea*. Though, under the civil law, he entered as a trespasser, it is submitted that he cannot be convicted of the criminal offence unless he knew of the facts which caused him to be a trespasser or, at least, was reckless."

The matter has also been dealt with by Professor Griew, who in paragraph 4–05 of his work *The Theft Act* 1968 has this passage: "What if D wrongly believes that he is not trespassing? His belief may rest on facts which, if true, would mean that he was not trespassing: for instance, he may enter a building by mistake, thinking that it is the one he has been invited to enter. Or his belief may be based on a false view of the legal effect of the known facts: for instance, he may misunderstand the effect of a contract granting him a right of passage through a building. Neither kind of mistake will protect him from tort liability for trespass. In either case, then, D satisfies the literal terms of section 9 (1): he 'enters . . . as a trespasser'. But for the purposes of criminal liability a man should be judged on the basis of the facts as he believed them to be, and this should include making allowances for a mistake as to rights under the civil law. This is another way of saying that a serious offence like burglary should be held to require *mens rea* in the fullest sense of the phrase: D should be liable for burglary only if he knowingly trespasses or is reckless as to whether he trespasses or not. Unhappily it is common for Parliament to omit to make clear whether *mens rea* is intended to be an element in a statutory offence. It is also, though not equally, common for the courts to supply the mental element by construction of the statute."

We prefer the view expressed by Professor Smith and Professor Griew to that of the editors of *Archbold*. In the judgment of this court there cannot be a conviction for entering premises "as a trespasser" within the meaning of section 9 of the Theft Act unless the person entering does so knowing that he is a trespasser and nevertheless deliberately enters, or, at the very least, is reckless as to whether or not he is entering the premises of another without the other party's consent.

Having so held, the pivotal point of this appeal is whether the Crown established that this defendant at the moment that he entered the bedroom knew perfectly well that he was not welcome there or, being reckless as to whether he was welcome or not, was nevertheless determined to enter. That in turn involves consideration as to where he was at the time that the complainant indicated that she was welcoming him into her bedroom. If, to take an example that was put in the course of argument, her bed had not been near the window but was on the other side of the bedroom, and he (being determined to have her sexually even against her will) climbed through the window and crossed the bedroom to reach her bed, then the offence charged would have been established. But in this case, as we have related, the layout of the room was different, and it became a point of nicety which had to be conclusively established by the Crown as to where he was when the girl made welcoming signs, as she unquestionably at some stage did.

How did the judge deal with this matter? We have to say regretfully that there was a flaw in his treatment of it. Referring to section 9, he said "There are three ingredients. First is the question of entry. Did he enter into that house? Did he enter as a trespasser? That is to say, was the entry, if you are satisfied there was an entry, intentional or reckless? And, finally, and you may think this is the crux of the case as opened to you by Mr. Irwin, if you are satisfied that he entered as a trespasser, did he have the intention to rape this girl?"

The judge then went on to deal in turn with each of these three ingredients. He first explained what was involved in "entry" into a building. He then dealt with the second ingredient. But here he unfortunately repeated his earlier observation that the question of entry as a trespasser depended on "was the entry intentional or reckless?" We have to say that this was putting the matter inaccurately. This mistake may have been derived from a passage in the speech of counsel for the Crown when replying to the submission of "no case". Mr. Irwin at one stage said: "Therefore, the first thing that the Crown have got to prove, my Lord, is that there has been a trespass which may be an intentional trespass, or it may be a reckless trespass." Unfortunately the judge regarded the matter as though the second ingredient in the burglary charged was whether there had been an intentional or reckless entry, and when he came to develop this topic in his summing up that error was unfortunately perpetuated. The judge told the jury: "He had no right to be in that house, as you know, certainly from the point of view of the girl's parent. But if you are satisfied about entry, did he enter intentionally or recklessly? What the prosecution say about that is, you do not really have to consider recklessness because when you consider his own evidence he intended to enter that house, and if you accept the evidence I have just pointed out to you, he in fact did so. So, at least, you may think, it was intentional. At the least, you may think it was reckless because as he told you he did not know whether the girl would accept him."

We are compelled to say that we do not think the judge by these observations made sufficiently clear to the jury the nature of the second test about which they had to be satisfied before this young man could be convicted of the offence charged. There was no doubt that his entry into the bedroom was "intentional". But what the accused had said was, "She knelt on the bed, she put her arms around me and then I went in." If the jury thought he might be truthful in that assertion, they would need to consider whether or not, although entirely surprised by such a reception being accorded to him, this young man might not have been entitled reasonably to regard her action as amounting to an invitation to him to enter. If she in fact appeared to be welcoming him, the Crown do not suggest that he should have realised or even suspected that she was so behaving because, despite the moonlight, she thought he was someone else. Unless the jury were entirely satisfied that the defendant made an effective and substantial entry into the bedroom without the complainant doing or saying anything to cause him to believe that she was consenting to his entering it, he ought not to be convicted of the offence charged. The point is a narrow one, as narrow maybe as the window sill which is crucial to this case. But this is a criminal charge of gravity and, even though one may suspect that his intention was to commit the offence charged, unless the facts show with clarity that he in fact committed it he ought not to remain convicted.

Some question arose as to whether or not the defendant can be regarded as a trespasser *ab initio*. But we are entirely in agreement with the view expressed in *Archbold*, again in paragraph 1505, that the common law doctrine of trespass *ab initio* has no application to burglary under the Theft Act, 1968. One further matter that was canvassed ought perhaps to be mentioned. The point was raised that, the complainant not being the tenant or occupier of the dwelling house and her mother being apparently in occupation, this girl herself could not in any event have extended an effective invitation to enter, so that even if she had expressly and with full knowledge of all material facts invited the defendant in, he would nevertheless be a trespasser. Whatever be the position in the law of tort, to regard such a proposition as acceptable in the criminal law would be unthinkable.

We have to say that this appeal must be allowed on the basis that the jury were never invited to consider the vital question whether this young man did enter the premises as a trespasser, that is to say knowing perfectly well that he had no invitation to enter or reckless of whether or not his entry was with permission. . . .

Appeal allowed

R. v. Jones and Smith
[1976] 3 All E.R. 54
Court of Appeal

J. and S. were convicted of burglary contrary to section 9 (1) (*b*) of the Theft Act 1968. They had entered the house of S's father and stolen two television sets. S's father had reported the theft to the police at the time, but at the trial, he gave evidence to the effect that he had given S unreserved permission to enter the house, stating that S. "would not be a trespasser in the house at any time." J. and S. appealed.

JAMES L.J.: The next ground of appeal relied on by Counsel for the appellants in his argument is that which is put forward in the first of each of the defendants' grounds. It is the point upon which Counsel had laid the greatest stress in the course of his argument. The argument is based upon the wording of the Theft Act 1968, section 9 (1) (*b*) which is this:

> "(1) A person is guilty of burglary if— . . . (*b*) having entered any building or part of a building as a trespasser he steals or attempts to steal anything in the building or that part of it or inflicts or attempts to inflict on any person therein any grievous bodily harm."

The important words from the point of view of the arguments in this appeal are "having entered any building . . . as a trespasser". This is a section of an Act of Parliament which introduced a novel concept. Entry as a trespasser was new in 1968 in relation to criminal offences of burglary. It was introduced in substitution for, as an improvement upon, the old law which required considerations of breaking and entering and involved distinctions of nicety which had bedevilled the law for some time.

Counsel for the appellants argues that a person who had a general permission to enter premises of another person cannot be a trespasser. His submission is as short and as simple as that. Related to this case he says that a son to whom a father has given permission generally to enter the father's house cannot be a trespasser if he enters it even though he had decided in his mind before making the entry to commit a criminal offence of theft against the father once he had got into the house and had entered that house solely for the purpose of committing that theft. It is a bold submission. Counsel frankly accepts that there has been no decision of the court since this Act was passed which governs particularly this point. He has reminded us of the decision in *Byrne* v. *Kinematograph Renters Society Ltd.* [1958] 1 W.L.R. 762, which he prays in aid of his argument. In that case persons had entered a cinema by producing tickets not for the purpose of seeing the show, but for an ulterior purpose. It was held in the action, which sought to show that they entered as trespassers pursuant to a conspiracy to trespass, that in fact they were not trespassers. The important words in the judgment are (at p. 776): 'They did nothing that they were not invited to do . . .' That provides a distinction between that case and what we consider the position to be in this case.

Counsel has also referred us to one of the trickery cases, *R.* v. *Boyle,* (1954) 2 Q.B. 292, and in particular to a passage in the judgment of that case (at p. 295). He accepts that the trickery cases can be distinguished from such a case at the present because in the trickery cases it can be said that that which would otherwise have been consent to enter was negatived by the fact that consent was obtained by a trick. We do not gain any help in the particular case from that decision.

We were also referred to *R.* v. *Collins* [*ante,* p. 633], and in particular to the long passage of Edmund Davies L.J., where he commenced the consideration of what is involved by the words 'the entry must be "as a trespasser"'. Again it is unnecessary to cite that long passage in full; suffice it to say that this court on that occasion expressly approved the view expressed in Professor Smith's book on the Law of Theft, and also the view of Professor Griew in his publication on the Theft Act 1968 on this aspect of what is involved in being a trespasser.

In our view the passage there referred to is consonant with the passage in the wellknown case of *Hillen and Pettigrew* v. *I.C.I. (Alkali) Ltd.* [1936] A.C. 65 where, in the speech of Lord Atkin, these words appear:

> 'My Lords, in my opinion this duty to an invitee only extends so long as and so far as the invitee is making what can reasonably be contemplated as an ordinary and reasonable use of the premises by the invitee for the purposes for which he has been invited. He is not invited to use any part of the premises for purposes which he knows are wrongfully dangerous and constitute an improper use. As Scrutton L.J. has pointedly said (*The Calgarth, the Otarama* [1927] P. 93 at 110) "When you invite a person into your house to use the stair case you do not invite him to slide down the banisters."'

The decision in *R.* v. *Collins* in this court, a decision on the criminal law, added to the concept of trespass as a civil wrong only the mental element of *mens rea,* which is essential to the criminal offence. Taking the law as expressed in *Hillen and Pettigrew* v. *I.C.I. (Alkali) Ltd.* and *R.* v. *Collins,* it is our view that a person is a trespasser for the purpose of s. 9 (1) (*b*) of the Theft Act 1968 if he enters premises of another knowing that he is entering in excess of the permission that has been given to him, or being reckless whether he is entering in excess of the permission that has been given to him to enter, providing the facts are known to the accused which enable him to realise that he is acting in excess of the permission given or that he is acting recklessly as to whether he exceeds that permission, then that is sufficient for the jury to decide that he is in fact a trespasser.

In this particular case it was a matter for the jury to consider whether, on all the facts, it was shown by the prosecution that the appellants entered with the knowledge that entry was being effected against the consent or in excess of the consent that had been given by Mr. Alfred Smith to his son Christopher. The jury were, by their verdict, satisfied of that. It was a novel argument that we heard, interesting but one without, in our view, any foundation. . . .

Finally, before parting with the matter, we would refer to a passage of the summing-up to the jury which I think one must read in full. In the course of that the recorder said:

> 'I have read out the conversation they had with Detective Sergeant Tarrant and in essence Smith said, "My father gave me leave to take these sets and Jones was invited along to help". If that account may be true, that is an end of the case, but if you are convinced that that night they went to the house and entered as trespassers and had no leave or licence to go there for that purpose and they intended to steal these sets and keep them permanently themselves, acting dishonestly, then you will convict them. Learned counsel for the prosecution did mention the possibility that you might come to the conclusion that they had gone into the house with leave or licence of the father and it would be possible for you to bring in a verdict simply of theft but, members of the jury, of course it is open to you to do that if you felt that the entry to the house was as a consequence of the father's leave or licence, but what counts of course for the crime of burglary to be made out is the frame of mind of each person when they go into the property. If you go in intending to steal, then your entry is burglarious, it is to trespass because no one gave you permission to go in and steal in the house.'

Then the recorder gave an illustration of the example of a person who is invited to go into a house to make a cup of tea and that person goes in and steals the silver and he went on:

> 'I hope that illustrates the matter sensibly. Therefore you may find it difficult not to say, if they went in there they must have gone in order to steal because they took elaborate precautions, going there at dead of night, you really cannot say that under any circumstances their entry to the house could have been other than trespass'.

In that passage that I have just read the recorder put the matter properly to the jury in relation to the aspect of trespass and on this ground of appeal as on the others we find that the case is not made out, that there was no misdirection, as I have already indicated early in the judgment, and in those circumstances the appeal will be dismissed in the case of each of the appellants.

Appeals dismissed

Questions

1. Smith was not residing with his father at the time of the theft. Would it have made any difference if he had been so residing?

2. A knocks on the door of his neighbour, Miss B. Miss B, recognising him and thinking his call is purely social, invites him in, and he goes in. In fact A's intention is to rape Miss B. On the question of whether A is guilty of burglary, do the cases of *Collins*, and *Jones and Smith* give different answers?

3. A approached B, the servant of C, and asked for C's keys so that he could enter C's shop at night and steal therein. B reported to C who, with

the object of entrapping A, instructed him to let A have the keys. B gave the keys to A, who used them to enter the shop. He was immediately arrested by a policeman waiting inside. Is A guilty of burglary? See *R.* v. *Chandler* [1913] 1 K.B. 125.

iii. Buildings or Parts of Buildings

Notes

1. The word "building" in statute law has had many different meanings given to it. Under the Malicious Damage Act 1861, the word was held to cover a house which was unfinished but substantially complete and with a roof on; *R.* v. *Manning* (1871) L.R. 1 C.C.R. 338. In *Stevens* v. *Gourlay* (1859) 7 C.B. (N.S.) 99, the CCCR held that both the ordinary meaning and the presumed intention of the legislature must be looked at. Thus a wooden structure intended as a shop was held to be a building for the purposes of the Metropolitan Building Act 1855, the court holding that an object of the Act was to prevent the metropolis from being covered by combustible structures. The ordinary meaning was held to require a structure of considerable size and intended to be permanent or at least to endure for a considerable time. This dictum was apparently used in *B. and S.* v. *Leathley* [1979] Crim. L.R. 314 (Carlisle Crown Court) to hold that burglary applied to a freezer container, 25 feet long with 7 ft. square cross-sections, left standing in a farm yard for two or three years, notwithstanding that it was portable. It seems to be agreed that tents are not buildings (the CLRC did not envisage that they were: Cmnd. 2977, § 78), and that portability alone does not prevent a structure from being a building. Apart from that, little can be said with confidence, and puzzles such as a bandstand, or telephone kiosk, will have to be elucidated as and when cases arise.

2. Entry as a trespasser into a "part" of a building, *either* with intent to commit a relevant crime in that part, *or* followed by the commission of a relevant crime in that part is also burglary, even if there is no trespassory entry of the building as a whole. Most "parts" of buildings, *e.g.* rooms, cause no difficulty, but doubt might be caused by less differentiated areas, *e.g.* separate counters in a department store. It seems that there must be at least some physical demarcation for an area to be a "part" for the purposes of the law of burglary.

R. v. Walkington (1979) 1 W.L.R. 1169, 1175: W. was convicted of burglary by entering a part consisting of a movable three-sided enclosure round a till in a department store. On appeal: Geoffrey Lane L.J. One really gets two extremes, as it seems to us. First of all you have the part of the building which is shut off by a door so far as the general public is concerned, with a notice saying "Staff Only" or "No admittance to customers." At the other end of the scale you have for example a single table in the middle of the store, which it would be difficult for any jury to find properly was a part of the building, into which the licensor prohibited customers from moving.

Here, it seems to us, there was a physical demarcation. Whether there was sufficient to amount to an area from which the public were plainly excluded was a matter for the jury. It seems to us that there was ample evidence on which they could come to the conclusion (a) that the management had impliedly prohibited customers entering that area and (b) that this particular defendant knew of that prohibition.

iv. Intent to Commit an Offence in the Building

Attorney General's References (Nos. 1 and 2 of 1979)
[1980] Q.B. 180
Court of Appeal

The references arose out of two cases in each of which the judge directed an acquittal.

In Case 1, A was discovered ascending the stairs to the private rooms above a grocer's shop, where he had no right to be. He said he was looking for money to steal. He was charged with burglary with intent to steal.

In Case 2, B at 3.15 a.m. was discovered by a householder trying to force the french windows of her house. He said he wasn't going to damage anything, only to see if there was anything lying around. He was charged with attempting to enter the house with intent to steal therein.

Roskill L.J.: The matters arising for determination are of wide general importance for the administration of justice both in the Crown Court and in magistrates' courts. There appears from what we have been told by counsel and from an admirable memorandum prepared by the Law Commission for the assistance of the court on these references, to be a question of law which is causing and has caused considerable confusion, and has led to what would appear to be unjustified acquittals as a result of circuit judges or their deputies in the Crown Court and also magistrates' courts acceding to submissions that there was no case to answer, the submission being based on a single sentence in the judgment of this court in *R.* v. *Husseyn* (Note) (1977) 67 Cr. App. R. 131, decided on December 8, 1977, the court consisting of Viscount Dilhorne, Lord Scarman and the late Cusack J. The Attorney-General has referred two such cases decided in the Crown Court to this court in order that a decision may be obtained whether the acquittals with which we are immediately concerned, and also certain other acquittals of which we have been told, were in fact justified.

The question referred in Reference No. 1 is:

> "Whether a man who has entered a house as a trespasser with the intention of stealing money therein is entitled to be acquitted of an offence against section 9 (1) (a) of the Theft Act 1968 on the grounds that his intention to steal is conditional upon his finding money in the house."

The answer of this court to this question is "No". In the second reference the question is:

> "Whether a man who is attempting to enter a house as a trespasser with the intention of stealing anything of value which he may find therein is entitled to be acquitted of the offence of attempted burglary on the ground that at the time of the attempt his said intention was insufficient to amount to 'the intention of stealing anything' necessary for conviction under section 9 of the Theft Act 1968."

The answer of this court to this question is also "No".

Since it is essential to have regard to the language of the relevant statute, we begin by reading section 9 of the Theft Act 1968, under the rubric "Burglary":

"(1) A person is guilty of burglary if—(a) he enters any building or part of a building as a trespasser and with intent to commit any such offence as is mentioned in subsection (2) below . . ."—I need not read paragraph (b)—"(2) The offences referred to in subsection (1) (a) above are offences of stealing anything in the building or part of a building in question. . . ." As is well known, that subsection goes on: ". . . of inflicting on any person therein any grievous bodily harm or raping any woman therein, and of doing unlawful damage to the building or anything therein."

Now section 9 (2) includes a reference to the offence of stealing, and that takes one back to section 1 (1) which bears the rubric "Basic definition of theft" and reads:

"A person is guilty of theft if he dishonestly appropriates property belonging to another with the intention of permanently depriving the other of it; and 'thief' and 'steal' shall be construed accordingly."

How the present problem arises is told with admirable clarity in the Law Commission's memorandum. There are certain passages which I read in full, because it would be impossible, if I may say so, to improve upon them:

"10. In turning to the problems raised by these references, it is desirable to say something about the term 'conditional intention'. From the letter from counsel for the appellant in the July 1978 issue of the Criminal Law Review—[1978] Crim. L.R. 444–446—it appears that during argument in *R.* v. *Husseyn* Viscount Dilhorne expressed strong disapproval of the use of 'conditional intention'. This is certainly understandable. The content of the criminal law should be kept as clear and simple as is consonant with reality and any development which required magistrates to think or Crown Court judges to sum up to juries in terms of all the verbal complexities which such pseudo-philosophical or psychological concepts as conditional intent would involve could only be accepted if no other way could be found of enabling a fair and accurate description of the appropriate mental element in these crimes to be conveyed to those who have to decide such questions of fact."

Thus far this court whole-heartedly and emphatically agrees.

"Nevertheless, it is a convenient term in which to describe collectively a variety of mental states in argument before an appellate court, and its use in the text books, in *R.* v. *Easom* (*ante*, p. 535) and *R.* v. *Husseyn*, and academic discussion of these and subsequent cases and in the present reference themselves necessitate the use of this term in this memorandum. 'Conditional intent' is used here to describe any state of mind falling short of an intention permanently to deprive a person of property of his, which property at the time of the intention is specific and identifiable in the mind of the accused. It means that the accused does not know what he is going to steal but intends that he will steal whatever he finds of value or worthwhile stealing."

We respectfully agree with Viscount Dilhorne's stated strong disapproval of the phrase, but if it is to be used, it should only be used for that limited purpose set out in the last sentence which I have read. In paragraph 13 the paper goes on:

"The doctrine finds its first expression in the statement of Lord Scarman in *R.* v. *Husseyn*, 67 Cr. App. R. 131, 132, that 'it cannot be said that one who has it in mind to steal only if what he finds is worth stealing has a present intention to steal'. *R.* v. *Husseyn* was a case of attempted theft and, taken literally, the statement means that a conditional intent to steal in the sense of an intention to steal whatever the accused may find worth stealing or of value is insufficient to ground a charge of attempted theft. It follows from this that a charge or indictment for attempted theft must necessarily be quashed as bad in law if it specifies the mental element as 'intending, at that time, to steal whatever he might find worth stealing (or of value) therein'. Thus, wherever the prosecution has to establish an intention to steal as one of the constituents of a theft-related offence, it must prove a fixed and settled intention, contemporaneous with the act forming the other (actus reus) element of the offence, on the part of the accused permanently to deprive someone of a specified identifiable object which either exists or is believed by the accused to exist in or near the scene of his operations (or 'the target', as the references aptly describe it). This is self-evident in cases of completed theft or 'successful' burglary or robbery where, ex hypothesi, the accused is charged with having appropriated a specific identifiable object. The importance of the doctrine lies in the field of attempted theft or other cases where, although an intention to steal is required, the relevant actus reus does not postulate that anything should necessarily have been appropriated. These offences include burglary, attempted burglary, assault with intent to rob, or, as a suspected person, loitering with intent to steal or rob."

Thus the so called doctrine of "conditional intention" is described.

It will be useful to go through some of the cases to show how this so called doctrine has developed and to explain, as each member of this court is satisfied is the position, that the whole problem arises from a misunderstanding of a crucial sentence in Lord Scarman's judgment, which must be read in the context in which it was uttered, namely an indictment which charged an attempt to steal a specific object.

[His Lordship then considered *R.* v. *Stark* (unreported, October 5, 1967), *R.* v. *Eason* (*ante*, p. 535), *R.* v. *Husseyn*, and continued] Lord Scarman [in *R.* v. *Husseyn*] dealt with the law relating to attempts at p. 132 and said that in that respect there was no misdirection by the judge. But his Lordship then went on:

"Very different considerations apply when one comes to consider the way the learned judge summed up the issue of intention. The learned judge said that the jury could infer that what the young men were about was to look into the holdall and, if its contents were valuable, to steal it. In the view of this court that was a misdirection. What has to be established is an intention to steal at the time when the step is taken, which constitutes or which is alleged to constitute, the attempt. Edmund Davies L.J. put the point in *R.* v. *Easom* [*ante* p. 535]: 'In every case of theft the appropriation must be accompanied by the intention of permanently depriving the owner of his property. What may be *loosely* described as a 'conditional' appropriation will not do. If the appropriator has it in mind merely to deprive the owner of such of his property as, on examination, proves worth taking and then, finding that the booty is valueless to the appropriator, leaves it ready to hand to be repossessed by the owner, the appropriator has not stolen'. The direction of the learned judge in this case is exactly the contrary. It must be wrong, for it cannot be said that one who has it in mind to steal only if what he finds is worth stealing has a present intention to steal."

We were asked to say that either that last sentence was wrong or that it was *obiter*. We are not prepared to do either. If we may say so with the utmost deference to any statement of law by Lord Scarman, if this sentence be open to criticism, it is because in the context it is a little elliptical. If one rewrites that sentence, so that it reads: "It must be wrong, for it cannot be said that one who has it in mind to steal only if what he finds is worth stealing has a present intention to steal *the specific item charged*," (our emphasis added), then the difficulties disappear, because, as already stated, what was charged was attempted theft of a specific object, just as what had been charged in *R.* v. *Easom* had been the theft of a number of specific objects.

[His Lordship then considered *R.* v. *Hector* (1978) 67 Cr. App. R. 224, and continued]. So we have these four cases: Stark, Easom, Husseyn and Hector. In each the charge related to specific objects and in each the conviction was quashed because there had been a misdirection or because the Crown was not in a position to prove that there was on the part of the accused person or persons at the relevant time an intent to steal or to attempt to steal the specific objects which were the subject of the charges or for both those reasons. None of those cases is authority for the proposition that if a charge is brought under section 9 (1) of entering any building or part of a building as a trespasser with intent to steal, the accused is entitled to acquittal unless it can be shown that at the time he entered he had the intention of stealing specific objects.

The last case to which it is necessary to refer is *R.* v. *Walkington* [1979] 1 W.L.R. 1169. Mr. Tudor Price for the Attorney-General and Mr. Simon Brown, who has appeared as *amicus curiae*, both agree that if *R.* v. *Walkington* is right, as they submitted and as we think it clearly is, that decision is conclusive as to the answer in Reference No. 1, for the reasons given by Geoffrey Lane L.J. in giving the judgment of the court. . . .

In *R.* v. *Walkington* the indictment was for burglary. At the beginning of his judgment Geoffrey Lane L.J. set out the indictment, at p. 1171:

> "Statement of offence: Burglary, contrary to section 9 (1) (a) of the Theft Act 1968. Particulars of offence: Terence Walkington on January 15th, 1977, entered as a trespasser part of a building known as Debenhams Store with intent to steal therein."

Be it noted there was no averment in those particulars of any intention to steal any specific or identified objects. Geoffrey Lane L.J., after dealing with the first point which is presently irrelevant, dealt with the second and relevant point, at p. 1176:

> . . . "These submissions are based upon the decision of this court in *R.* v. *Husseyn*: if we may say so respectfully, a most powerful court, because it consisted of Viscount Dilhorne, Lord Scarman and Cusack J."

The Lord Justice then read the headnote and the passage in Lord Scarman's judgment upon which we have already commented. Geoffrey Lane L.J. said, at pp. 1177–1178:

> "What Mr. Osborne suggests to us is that that last passage—the last two sentences—meets the situation in this case and that if the facts were that the defendant in this case had it in mind only to steal if what he found was worth stealing, then he had no intention to steal. That is the way he put it.
>
> "First of all we would like to say that the particulars of offence in *R.* v. *Husseyn* were that the two men '. . . attempted to steal a quantity of sub-aqua equipment'. Plainly what considerations have to be applied to a charge of attempting to steal a specific article are different considerations from those which have to be applied when one is considering what a person's intent or intention may be under section 9 of the Theft Act 1968. That, we feel, is sufficient to distinguish our case from *R.* v. *Husseyn*."

Then the Lord Justice read what Lord Scarman himself had said about *R.* v. *Husseyn* in *D.P.P.* v. *Nock* [*ante*, p. 319]—I will return to this shortly—and said, at p. 1178:

> "In this case there is no doubt that the defendant was not on the evidence in two minds as to whether to steal or not. He was intending to steal when he

went to that till and it would be totally unreal to ask oneself, or for the jury to ask themselves, the question, what sort of intent did he have? Was it a conditional intent to steal if there was money in the till or a conditional intention to steal only if what he found there was worth stealing? In this case it was a cash till and what plainly he was intending to steal was the contents of the till, which was cash. The mere fact that the till happened to be empty does not destroy his undoubted intention at the moment when he crossed the boundary between the legitimate part of the store and the illegitimate part of the store. The judge's direction which we have cited already covered that point, and the matter was accurately left to the jury.

It has again been pointed out to us, and it is right that we should make reference to it, that that decision in *R.* v. *Husseyn* has apparently been causing some difficulty to judges of the Crown Court."

The Lord Justice then referred to two cases reported in the Criminal Law Review and said that the brief report in the latter case would suffice to demonstrate the difficulties which had arisen. After reading that report Geoffrey Lane L.J. went on, at p. 1179:

"A reading of that would make the layman wonder if the law had taken leave of its senses, because, if that is the proper interpretation to be applied to section 9 (1) (a), there will seldom, if ever, be a case in which section 9 (1) (a) will bite. It seems to this court that in the end one simply has to go back to the words of the Act itself which we have already cited, and if the jury are satisfied, so as to feel sure, that the defendant has entered any building or part of a building as a trespasser, and are satisfied that at the moment of entering he intended to steal anything in the building or that part of it, the fact that there was nothing in the building worth his while to steal seems to us to be immaterial. He nevertheless had the intent to steal. As we see it, to hold otherwise would be to make a nonsense of this part of the Act and cannot have been the intention of the legislature at the time when the Theft Act 1968 was passed. Nearly every prospective burglar could no doubt truthfully say that he only intended to steal if he found something in the building worth stealing.

So, whilst acknowledging that these recent decisions do provide difficulties which have been pointed out to us clearly by Mr. Osborne, it seems to us in the end that one must have regard to the wording of the Act. If that is done, the meaning, in our view, is clear."

I come back to what Lord Scarman himself said in *D.P.P.* v. *Nock* [1978] A.C. 979. The relevant passage is at pp. 999 to 1000. His Lordship, after referring to the decision of the House of Lords in *Haughton* v. *Smith* [*ante*, p. 318] said at p. 1000:

"We were invited by the Crown to express an opinion as to the correctness or otherwise of three decisions of the Court of Appeal, *R.* v. *Easom, Partington* v. *Williams* (1975) 62 Cr. App. R. 220 and *R.* v. *Husseyn. Easom* and *Husseyn* (to which I was a party) were, I think, correctly decided: but each, like every other criminal appeal, turned on its particular facts and on the way in which the trial judge directed the jury on the law. In *Easom* Edmund Davies L.J. emphasised that in a case of theft the appropriation must be accompanied by the intention of permanently depriving the owner of his property. This, of course follows from the definition of theft in section 1 (1) of the Theft Act 1968. All that *Husseyn* decided was that the same intention must be proved when the charge is one of attempted theft. Unfortunately in *Husseyn* the issue of intention was summed up in such a way as to suggest that theft, or attempted theft, could be committed by a person who had not yet formed the intention which the statute defines as a necessary part of the offence. An

> intention to steal can exist even though, unknown to the accused, there is nothing to steal: but, if a man be in two minds as to whether to steal or not, the intention required by the statute is not proved."

We venture to draw particular attention to the opening part of that last sentence: "An intention to steal can exist even though, unknown to the accused, there is nothing to steal. . . ."

We had an interesting discussion, with the help of Mr. Tudor Price and Mr. Simon Brown, how, in these cases of burglary or theft or attempted burglary or theft, it is in future desirable to frame indictments. Plainly it may be undesirable in some cases to frame indictments by reference to the theft or attempted theft or specific objects. Obviously draftsmen of indictments require the maximum latitude to adapt the particulars charged to the facts of the particular case, but we see no reason in principle why what was described in argument as a more imprecise method of criminal pleading should not be adopted, if the justice of the case requires it, as for example, attempting to steal some or all of the contents of a car or some or all of the contents of a handbag. The indictment in *R.* v. *Walkington* is in no way open to objection. There is no purpose in multiplying further examples. It may be that in some cases further particulars might be asked for and if so the prosecution could in a proper case no doubt give them without difficulty. The important point is that the indictment should correctly reflect that which it is alleged that the accused did, and that the accused should know with adequate detail what he is alleged to have done.

Taking as an example the facts in *R.* v. *Easom*, plainly what the accused intended was to steal some or all of the contents of the handbag if and when he got them into his possession. It seems clear from the latter part of Edmund Davies L.J.'s judgment that, if he had been charged with an attempt to steal some or all of the contents of that handbag, he could properly have been convicted, subject of course to a proper direction to the jury.

It follows that this court respectfully and whole-heartedly adopts Geoffrey Lane L.J.'s judgment on the second question in *R.* v. *Walkington* which, as I have already said, is conclusive of the answer in the first reference.

So far as the answer in the second reference is concerned, it would, as Mr. Simon Brown very properly agreed, be very strange if a different answer had to be given in the second reference, which is concerned with attempted burglary from that given in the first reference. In our view, notwithstanding the argument that Mr. Shepherd attempted to advance in the first of the two Divisional Court cases, it is impossible to justify giving different answers according to whether the charge is burglary or attempted burglary, theft or attempted theft or loitering with intent to commit an arrestable offence, which in most cases will be theft. In our view both principle and logic require the same answers in all these cases.

For those reasons the answers in the two references will be, as I have already indicated, "no" in the first and "no" in the second.

Opinions accordingly

Note

On conditional intent in theft, see *ante*, p. 535.

v. The Ulterior Offence

Note

It will be noted that the list of possible ulterior offences is different according as whether the charge is entering with intent under section 9 (1) (*a*) or entering and committing under section 9 (1) (*b*). Thus if A enters B's house with the intention of quarrelling with B, and in the course of the quarrel he deliberately breaks B's priceless Ming vase, A is not guilty of burglary, but he *is* guilty of burglary if he punches B and breaks his nose. And he is guilty of burglary if, when he entered, he intended to do either of these two things. A conspicuous absentee from either list of offences is obtaining property by deception under section 15. This is not as important an omission as might be thought. See following question.

Question

A, an encyclopedia salesman, calls at B's house and gets B to admit him by falsely stating that he is a student, who has been promised a scholarship if he sells a certain quantity of books. After further discussion inside the house, B buys the books, paying A cash on account of the price. (See *R.* v. *Potger* (1970) 55 Cr. App. R. 42: *ante*, p. 592.)

Is A guilty of burglary? See *Lawrence* v. *Commissioner of Police, ante*, p. 496 and also *ante*, p. 572.

2. AGGRAVATED BURGLARY

Theft Act 1968, section 10

"(1) A person is guilty of aggravated burglary if he commits any burglary and at the time has with him any firearm or imitation firearm, any weapon of offence, or any explosive; and for this purpose—

(a) 'firearm' includes an airgun or air pistol, and 'imitation firearm' means anything which has the appearance of being a firearm, whether capable of being discharged or not; and
(b) 'weapon of offence' means any article made or adapted for use for causing injury to or incapacitating a person, or intended by the person having it with him for such use; and
(c) 'explosive' means any article manufactured for the purpose of producing a practical effect by explosion, or intended by the person having it with him for that purpose.

(2) A person guilty of aggravated burglary shall on conviction on indictment be liable to imprisonment for life."

Notes

1. *"Has with him."* A enters a building with intent to steal, wearing a mackintosh which he has just stolen from a restaurant. Unknown to A, there is an automatic pistol in the pocket of the mackintosh. Is he guilty of aggravated burglary?

B enters a building with intent to destroy an old master painting hanging therein. For this purpose, he has with him an aerosol container which he thinks contains indelible yellow paint which he means to spray all over the painting. In fact, his supplier has made a mistake and the aerosol contains tear gas. Is B guilty of aggravated burglary?

See *R.* v. *Warner* [1969] 2 A.C. 256; *R.* v. *Cugullere* [1961] 1 W.L.R. 858; *R.* v. *Pierre* [1963] Crim. L.R. 513.

2. *"Intended by the person having it with him for such use."* If an article is not made or adapted for use for causing injury to or incapacitating a person, it

is nevertheless a weapon of offence if "intended by the person having it with him for such use." If A has with him a coil of rope with which he intends to tie up a watchman on the premises, the rope is a weapon of offence and if burglary is involved it will be aggravated burglary. Less certain is the position where A has with him an article, not otherwise a weapon of offence, which he does not intend to use for injuring or incapacitating, but which, perhaps on the spur of the moment, he does in fact use for such purposes. A has a rope which he intends to use to lower stolen goods out of a window, but on being surprised by a watchman B, uses the rope to tie B up. Does A have with him an article intended for such use? No cases on this point have been decided on the present section, but there are relevant cases on similar wording in the Prevention of Crimes Act 1953, s. 1, which makes it an offence for any person to have with him in a public place an offensive weapon.

Woodward v. Koessler [1958] *1 W.L.R. 1255:* A was attempting to break into premises with a boy scout sheath knife, but when challenged by a caretaker, threatened him with the knife. The knife was held not to have been made or adapted for causing injury, but A was nevertheless held to have committed the offence under section 1 of the Prevention of Crime Act 1953, Donovan J.: . . . Counsel for the accused founds himself on the words "having it with him," and says that the accused must be found to have taken the weapon out with him with the intention of causing injury. Counsel says that in this case the accused took it for the purpose of breaking into the cinema. I do not agree with that narrow interpretation of the words "having it with him". All that one has to do for the purpose of ascertaining what the intention is is to look and see what use was in fact made of it. If it is found that the accused did in fact make use of it for the purpose of causing injury he had it with him for that purpose. I think that the evidence shows that the accused in this case did have it with him for the purpose of causing injury. (See also *R.* v. *Powell* [1963] Crim. L.R. 511.)

R. v. Dayle [1974] *1 W.L.R. 181:* A was alleged to take implements from the boot of his car and throw them at B. It was held that both *Woodward* v. *Koessler* and *Powell* had to be reconsidered in the light of section 8 of the Criminal Justice Act 1967 (*ante,* p. 373). The use made of an article might, not must, lead to the inference that the defendant had the article for such use. The terms of section 1 of the Prevention of Crimes Act 1953, were apt to cover a person who went out with an offensive weapon and also a person who deliberately selected an article such as the stone in *Harrison* v. *Thornton* [1966] Crim. L.R. 388. But if an article already possessed lawfully and for good reason was used offensively to cause injury such use did not necessarily prove the intent which the Crown must prove in respect of articles not offensive weapons *per se.*

Ohlson v. Hylton [1975] *2 All E.R. 490 (Q.B.D.):* On a station platform H., a carpenter, had an altercation with another passenger M. while attempting to board an overcrowded train. H., who had with him a bag containing the tools of his trade, took out a hammer and hit M. with it. On a charge under the Prevention of Crime Act, it was held that as M. was carrying an article not made or adapted for causing injury, it had to be shown that he had formed the intention to use it for the purpose of causing injury at some time before the occasion for that use occurred. Prosecutor's appeal dismissed.

Questions

1. Assuming that these decisions are applicable to the offence under section 10 of the Theft Act, is aggravated burglary committed in the

following cases? A enters a building with a large bunch of keys, intending to steal from locked cupboards and drawers. When disturbed by the occupant, he throws the bunch of keys at the latter's head, injuring him.

B enters a building with intent to steal. When disturbed by the occupant he snatches a Zulu knobkerry which is hanging on the wall as a trophy and strikes the occupant with it.

C enters a building with intent to steal. Coming upon the occupant from behind, C takes off his overcoat and throws it over the occupant's head in order to escape unseen before the latter can extricate himself.

2. In the first two cases does it make any difference whether the burglary alleged is under section 9 (1) (a) or under section 9 (1) (b)?

3. GOING EQUIPPED

Theft Act 1968, section 25

"(1) A person shall be guilty of an offence if, when not at his place of abode, he has with him any article for use in the course of or in connection with any burglary, theft or cheat.

(2) A person guilty of an offence under this section shall on conviction on indictment be liable to imprisonment for a term not exceeding three years.

(3) Where a person is charged with an offence under this section, proof that he had with him any article made or adapted for use in committing a burglary, theft or cheat shall be evidence that he had it with him for such use.

(4) Any person may arrest without warrant anyone who is, or whom he, with reasonable cause, suspects to be, committing an offence under this section.

(5) For purposes of this section an offence under section 12 (1) of this Act of taking a conveyance shall be treated as theft, and 'cheat' means an offence under section 15 of this Act."

i. Has with him

Note

See the cases cited on similar wording in section 10 (1) (aggravated burglary), *supra*.

Question

A and B are apprehended while trying to break into a warehouse at night. When B is searched he is found to possess a banker's credit card which does not apparently belong to him. There is no evidence that A knew that B was carrying this article. Are A and B guilty of an offence under section 25? Would it make any difference if the article was not a credit card, but a jemmy? See next case.

R. v. Lester and Byast

(1955) 39 Cr. App. R. 157
Court of Criminal Appeal

L. and B. were convicted of being found by night having in their possession implements of housebreaking. Most of the implements were found in the boot of a car owned and driven by B., but some were found on B's person. L was a passenger in the car. The police had seen both L and B in the act of stealing petrol from another car, but there was no evidence of joint participation on their part in any enterprise of housebreaking.

HALLETT J.: It seems to us that the housebreaking implements found in the boot of the car were found in the possession of Byast within the meaning of section 28 [of the Larceny Act 1916], and we would refer to what was said in *Thompson* (1869) 11 Cox 362, more particularly in the interpolations at p. 364, where Lush J. says, "Or if a burglar were to hire a little boy to carry his implements, could he not be convicted under [the relevant section]?" and Blackburn J. says, "Or if the implements were in a pannier on an ass's back, could the donkey be said to be in possession of them?" That case was decided by a very powerful court, and those two interpolations seem to us to indicate what the learned judges concerned would have thought to be the true view when the implements were being carried, not by a little boy or by an ass, but by the more modern method of a boot of a motor-car. . . .

With regard to Lester, on the other hand, somewhat different considerations arise. As we understand it, the case made against him is twofold. In the first place it is said that the implements of housebreaking which were found in the car were in his possession as well as in the possession of Byast. There was, however, a distinction between the facts proved in the case of Byast and those proved in the case of Lester. Whatever suspicions may be entertained—and certainly strong suspicions can be entertained— the only evidence is that Lester was a passenger in the car belonging to and driven by Byast, in the cubbyhole of which were two pairs of gloves and a piece of celluloid, and in the boot of which were other housebreaking implements. In our view, the *mere* fact that a man is a passenger in a car which contains housebreaking implements is not sufficient to show that he is in possession of them, whatever may be the case as regards the owner and driver of the car.

The alternative ground on which it is suggested that Lester should have been found guilty is that he was a participant with Byast in a housebreaking expedition, and that in such a case, where one of the participants is found in possession of housebreaking implements, his possession can be attributed in law to the other participant also, the authority for that proposition being *Thompson, supra*. We do not doubt that, if a common participation in a housebreaking expedition had been established by the evidence, the principle of *Thompson, supra*, would apply and the conviction of Lester would be upheld on that ground. The difficulty which we all feel in this case is that . . . there is . . . a lack of evidence, . . . that the common enterprise in which Lester was engaged with Byast was an enterprise of housebreaking. It may very well have been, but we can see no evidence to establish that it was.

Byast's appeal dismissed
Lester's conviction quashed

ii. When Not at his Place of Abode

R. v. Bundy [1977] 2 All E.R. 382 (C.A.). B was convicted under s. 25 Theft Act, in respect of articles found in a car he was driving. He appealed on the ground that for several weeks he had been living in the car, which was therefore his place of abode.

LAWTON L.J. (at p. 384): We must construe the phrase in the context in which it appears in s. 25 (1) of the Theft Act 1968. In that context it is manifest that no offence is committed if a burglar keeps the implements of his criminal trade in his 'place of abode'. He only commits an offence when he takes them from his 'place of abode'. The phrase 'place of abode', in our judgment, connotes, first of all, a site. That is the ordinary meaning of the word 'place'. It is a site at which the occupier intends to abide. So, there are two elements in the phrase 'place of abode', the element of site and the element of intention. When the appellant took the motor car to a site with the intention of abiding there, then his motor car on that site could be said to be his 'place of abode', but when he took it from that site to move it to another site where he intended to abide, the motor car could not be said to be his 'place of abode' during transit.

When he was arrested by the police he was not intending to abide on the site where he was arrested. It follows that he was not then at his 'place of abode'. He may have had a 'place of abode' the previous night, but he was away from it at the time of his arrest when in possession of articles which could be used for the purpose of theft. It follows, in our judgment, that there is no substance in the point . . .

iii. For Use in the Course of or in Connection with any Burglary, Theft or Cheat

R. v. Ellames
[1974] 3 All E.R. 130
Court of Appeal

> After a robbery had taken place, E disposed of a bag containing articles used at the robbery, including a sawn-off shotgun, and ammonia in spray containers. He was charged under section 25 Theft Act. The judge directed that the fact that the theft was over did not prevent him from having the articles for the purposes of theft. E was convicted and appealed.

BROWNE J.: In our judgment the construction of the section suggested by the Crown would produce many problems, anomalies and absurdities, and it is impossible to give it that construction having regard to the words used.

In our judgment, the words in s. 25 (1) of the 1968 Act: 'has with him any article for use' mean 'has with him for the purpose' (or 'with the intention') 'that they will be used'. The effect of s. 25 (3) is that if the article is one 'made or adapted for use in committing a burglary, theft or cheat', that is evidence of the necessary intention, though not of course conclusive evidence. If the article is not one 'made or adapted' for such use, the intention must be proved on the whole of the evidence—as it must be in the case of an article which is so made or adapted, if the defendant produces some innocent explanation. We agree with the learned authors of Smith and Hogan's Criminal Law (3rd. ed. p. 484) that s. 25 is directed against acts preparatory to burglary, theft or cheat; that

> 'Questions as to D's knowledge of the nature of the thing can hardly arise here, since it must be proved that he intended to use it in the course of or in connection with [burglary, theft or cheat]';

and that the *mens rea* for this offence includes 'an intention to use the article in the course of or in connection with any of the specific crimes'.

An intention to use must necessarily relate to use in the future. If any support is needed for this view, we think it is found in the recent decision of this court in *R.* v. *Allamby, R.* v. *Medford* [1974] 3 All E.R. 126, decided under the Prevention of Crime Act 1953. It seems to us impossible to interpret s. 25 (1) of the 1968 Act as if it read: 'has with him any article for use or *which has been used* in the course of or in connection with any burglary, theft or cheat'. Equally, it is impossible to read s. 25 (3) as if it said: 'had it with him for *or after* such use'.

In our judgment the words 'for use' govern the whole of the words which follow. The object and effect of the words 'in connection with' is to add something to 'in the course of'. It is easy to think of cases where an article could be intended for use 'in connection with' though not 'in the course of' a burglary etc., e.g. articles intended to be used while doing preparatory acts or while escaping after the crime (see Smith and Hogan).

In our view, to establish an offence under s. 25 (1) the prosecution must prove that the defendant was in possession of the article, and intended the article to be used in the course of or in connection with some future burglary, theft or cheat. But it is not necessary to prove that he intended it to be used in the course of or in connection with any *specific* burglary, theft or cheat; it is enough to prove a general intention to use it for *some* burglary, theft or cheat; we think that this view is supported by the use of the word 'any' in s. 25 (1). Nor, in our view, is it necessary to prove that the defendant intended to use it himself; it will be enough to prove that he had it with him with the intention that it should be used by someone else. For example, if in the present case it had been proved that the defendant was hiding away these articles, which had already been used for one robbery, with the intention that they should later be used by someone for some other robbery, he would be guilty of an offence under s. 25 (1).

It follows from our conclusion as to the true construction of s. 25 (1) that in our judgment the judge should have upheld the appellant's submission of no case on count 2 and that the conviction must be quashed.

We come to this conclusion with some regret. But our conclusion that a person who is in possession only after a burglary, theft or cheat of articles which had been used in the crime is not guilty of an offence under s. 25 (1) of the 1968 Act, does not mean that he cannot be guilty of some other offence—the obvious possibility is an offence under s. 4 of the Criminal Law Act 1967 of impeding apprehension or prosecution. It may be that if this appellant had been charged under that section he could properly have been convicted, but he was not charged under that section.

Accordingly, this appeal must be allowed and the conviction quashed.

Appeal allowed; conviction quashed

Note

For section 4 of Criminal Law Act 1967, see *ante*, p. 283.

Chapter 15

CRIMINAL DAMAGE

	PAGE		PAGE
1. Destroying or Damaging Property	653	B. The Aggravated Offence	660
A. The Simple Offence	654	2. Other Offences	661

Note

The criminal law protects owners of property not only from the unjustified appropriation of their property, but also from the unjustified destruction or damage of that property. Appropriation is the subject of the crime of theft and related offences; until 1971, damage was the subject of the Malicious Damage Act 1861. This Act made it an offence unlawfully and maliciously to damage property. If the damage was setting fire to a house or things in a house with intent to set fire to the house, it was called arson; otherwise the offence was called malicious damage. The Act of 1861 dealt specifically with a large number of different types of property. It is now almost entirely repealed by the Criminal Damage Act 1971, which does not particularise, but establishes a small number of wide general offences. The principal offence is now called criminal damage, except that damaging property by fire is still called arson. It appears in two forms, simple and aggravated.

1. DESTROYING OR DAMAGING PROPERTY

Criminal Damage Act 1971, sections 1 and 4

Section 1: "(1) A person who without lawful excuse destroys or damages any property belonging to another intending to destroy or damage any property or being reckless as to whether any such property would be destroyed or damaged shall be guilty of an offence.

(2) A person who without lawful excuse destroys or damages any property, whether belonging to himself or another:

(a) intending to destroy or damage any property or being reckless as to whether any property would be destroyed or damaged; and

(b) intending by the destruction or damage to endanger the life of another or being reckless as to whether the life of another would be thereby endangered;

shall be guilty of an offence.

(3) An offence committed under this section by destroying or damaging property by fire shall be charged as arson."

Section 4: "(1) A person guilty of arson under section 1 above or of an offence under section 1 (2) above (whether arson or not) shall on conviction on indictment be liable to imprisonment for life."

(2) A person guilty of any other offence under this Act shall on conviction on indictment be liable to imprisonment for a term not exceeding ten years.

Note

There are two offences in section 1, a simple offence and an aggravated one. The differences between them are connected with the expressions "belonging to another" and "without lawful excuse" (see below), and with the additional *mens rea* required for the aggravated offence. The common features are the destroying or damaging of any property. "Destroy" may be surplusage since it is hardly possible to destroy property without damaging it. "Damage" is not defined, but the word was the subject of many decisions under Malicious Damage Act 1861, which presumably still apply. Dismantling a machine so that it is no longer in a workable condition is undoubtedly damaging it (see *R.* v. *Tacey* (1821) R. & R. 452) even if the various parts are themselves undamaged (see *R.* v. *Woolcock* [1977] Crim. L.R. 104, 161); as is polluting a thing so that it is less valuable, *e.g.* adulterating milk with water (see *Roper* v. *Knott* [1898] 1 Q.B. 868). Any deleterious change in the condition should be enough. The fact that the property can be repaired is usually immaterial.

In *A (a juvenile)* v. *R.* [1978] Crim. L.R. 689, a crown court judge held that a policeman's cape was not damaged by being spat on, because it appeared that all that was needed to render it perfect was a wipe with a damp cloth. It would apparently have been different if it had had to be sent to a dry cleaner, because during that time it would be "rendered inoperative," one of the dictionary definitions of being damaged.

Criminal Damage Act 1971, section 10

"(1) In this Act 'property' means property of a tangible nature, whether real or personal, including money and:

(a) including wild creatures which have been tamed or are ordinarily kept in captivity, and any other wild creatures or their carcasses if, but only if, they have been reduced into possession which has not been lost or abandoned or are in the course of being reduced into possession; but

(b) not including mushrooms growing wild on any land or flowers, fruit or foliage of a plant growing wild on any land.

For the purpose of this subsection, 'mushroom' includes any fungus and 'plant' includes any shrub or tree."

[Compare the definition of property in section 4 of the Theft Act 1968, *ante*, p. 504.]

A. THE SIMPLE OFFENCE: WITHOUT DANGER TO LIFE

i. Belonging to Another

Criminal Damage Act 1971, section 10

"(2) Property shall be treated for the purposes of this Act as belonging to any person:

(a) having the custody or control of it;

(b) having in it any proprietary right or interest (not being an equitable interest arising only from an agreement to transfer or grant an interest); or

(c) having a charge on it.

(3) Where property is subject to a trust, the persons to whom it belongs shall be so treated as including any person having a right to enforce the trust.

(4) Property of a corporation sole shall be so treated as belonging to the corporation notwithstanding a vacancy in the corporation."

Note

Before the Act, a person was criminally responsible for destroying or damaging his or her own property, if he or she did so with the intention of defrauding anyone. This is not now the case, the relaxation in the law being for the reasons given below.

Law Commission Paper No. 29

"§ 19 Offences of dishonesty have been recently reviewed and (apart from forgery and perjury) they are now contained in the Theft Act, 1968. The provisions of that Act are less complicated and may be expected to contain fewer technical traps than the corresponding provisions of the Larceny Acts, 1861 and 1916 which they replace. For the purposes of this discussion the word "dishonesty", which, though not defined except by way of limitation, is used throughout the Theft Act, may be regarded as synonymous with "with intent to defraud".

§ 20 The meaning of the expression "with intent to defraud" is uncertain, but at all events in the law of forgery, and probably also in other dishonesty offences, it means "with intent to prejudice rights or to obstruct duties or with recklessness in regard to the risk of such prejudice or obstruction". By section 15 of the Theft Act (which does not use the expression "with intent to defraud") it is an offence dishonestly to obtain property (including money) by deception, and, of course, it is equally an offence to attempt to do so. Thus a man who burns down his own house in order to make a fraudulent insurance claim will, if he takes any step towards his purpose beyond the burning, almost inevitably have attempted to commit an offence of dishonesty. He will not, however, as the law of attempt stands, be guilty if all he does is to burn down his house. Thus, elimination of the offence of dishonest destruction will create a gap in the law. Nevertheless, for the reasons indicated below we are persuaded that the disadvantages of retaining the offence outweigh the limited advantages. The gap in the law is in any event limited, because cases in which there is proof of dishonesty, and yet no step has been taken to put the fraud into effect beyond the destruction of the offender's own property, must be rare. On the other hand, if the offence were retained, it would be necessary to consider the scope of "dishonesty" or "intent to defraud" in this context. We think it right that the expression should mean the same thing wherever it occurs. If it were to bear the wide meaning indicated earlier in this paragraph, a man who burned down his house or felled his scheduled tree to circumvent planning legislation would be guilty of an offence carrying the maximum period of imprisonment which we propose for the simple offence (ten years' imprisonment). We do not favour this result. To take any other course (by limiting the meaning of dishonesty, as we suggested in the Working Paper) would have two disadvantages. In the first place it would involve reaching a decision about an important concept in a context in which it is of marginal importance. Secondly, the most obvious limitation, which is that used in sections 17 and 20 of the Theft Act, has itself been subjected to a certain amount of criticism. We express no view on the question whether the criticism is or is not well founded, but we are sure that the law of damage to property is not the right place to consider the meaning of dishonesty."

Question

Is A guilty of criminal damage in the following cases?

(1) A, the owner of a fine Georgian house, bulldozes part of the house

in order to persuade a local preservation group to pay him to preserve the house.

(2) A, the tenant for life of *Blackacre*, dismantles the mansion house in order to spite the remainderman B.

(3) A, the owner of a china shop, allows his customers to walk round and handle his goods. Seeing a customer B holding a vase, A creeps up behind him, and startles B into dropping the vase, which shatters. A's object is to charge B with the value of the vase.

(4) A, a gardener, in order to spite his master B, on a frosty night, fails to stoke the boiler to B's greenhouse, so that B's orchids are killed by the frost.

ii. Without Lawful Excuse

Criminal Damage Act 1971, section 5

"(1) This section applies to any offence under section 1 (1) above and any offence under section 2 or 3 above other than one involving a threat by the person charged to destroy or damage property in a way which he knows is likely to endanger the life of another or involving an intent by the person charged to use or cause or permit the use of something in his custody or under his control so to destroy or damage property.

(2) A person charged with an offence to which this section applies shall, whether or not he would be treated for the purpose of this Act as having a lawful excuse apart from this subsection, be treated for those purposes as having a lawful excuse:

(a) if at the time of the act or acts alleged to constitute the offence he believed that the person or persons whom he believed to be entitled to consent to the destruction of or damage to the property in question had so consented, or would have so consented to it if he or they had known of the destruction or damage and its circumstances; or

(b) if he destroyed or damaged or threatened to destroy or damage the property in question or, in the case of a charge of an offence under section 3 above, intended to use or cause or permit the use of something to destroy or damage it, in order to protect property belonging to himself or another or a right or interest in property which was or which he believed to be vested in himself or another, and at the time of the act or acts alleged to constitute the offence he believed:

(i) that the property, right or interest was in immediate need of protection; and

(ii) that the means of protection adopted or proposed to be adopted were or would be reasonable having regard to all the circumstances.

(3) For the purpose of this section it is immaterial whether a belief is justified or not if it is honestly held.

(4) For the purpose of subsection (2) above a right or interest in property includes any right or privilege in or over land, whether created by grant, licence or otherwise.

(5) This section shall not be construed as casting doubt on any defence recognised by law as a defence to criminal charges."

Notes

1. "Without lawful excuse" replaces "unlawfully" in the offence of malicious damage. Section 5, above, gives particular cases which count as

lawful excuse, but the definition is not exhaustive: see section 5 (5). Thus any general defence to a crime avails on a charge of criminal damage, *e.g.* duress, impossibility, prevention of crime, advancement of justice. Mistake, in relation to malicious damage, was the subject of some confusing cases: see *Smith and Hogan*, Chap. 17, section 2. In relation to the new offence it is separately and explicitly dealt with by subsections (2) and (3) of section 5. These subsections, it must be noted, apply only to the simple offence, and not to the aggravated offence where danger to life is intended or foreseen.

2. The fact that subsections 2 and 3 deal specifically with mistaken belief in consent of owner and mistaken belief in a right to be protected has been held to mean that such mistakes can ground a defence even though they arise as a result of self-induced intoxication: see *Jaggard* v. *Dickinson* [1980] 3 All E.R. 716. See *ante*, p. 187.

iii. Intending to Destroy or Damage any such Property or Being Reckless as to Whether any such Property would be Destroyed or Damaged

R. v. Smith
[1974] Q.B. 354
Court of Appeal

S., a tenant of a flat, installed some stereo equipment and, with the consent of the landlord, put in certain roofing, wall panels and flooring to mask the electric wiring. These fixtures thereupon belonged to the landlord by law, but S. did not know this. When he was given notice to quit he damaged the fixtures in order to remove the wiring. He said he thought he was damaging his own property. He was convicted of an offence under section 1 (1) Criminal Damage Act 1971, and appealed.

JAMES L.J.: The appellant's defence was that he honestly believed that the damage he did was to his own property, that he believed that he was entitled to damage his own property and therefore he had a lawful excuse for his actions causing the damage. In the course of his summing up the deputy judge directed the jury in these terms:

"Now, in order to make the offence complete, the person who is charged with it must destroy or damage that property belonging to another, 'without lawful excuse', and that is something that one has got to look at a little more, members of the jury, because you have heard here that, so far as each defendant was concerned, it never occurred to them, and you may think, quite naturally never occurred to either of them, that these various additions to the house were anything but their own property.... But members of the jury, the Act is quite specific, and so far as the defendant David Smith is concerned lawful excuse is the only defence which has been raised. It is said that he had a lawful excuse by reason of his belief, his honest and genuinely held belief that he was destroying property which he had a right to destroy if he wanted to. But, members of the jury, I must direct you as a matter of law, and you must, therefore, accept it from me, that belief by the defendant David Smith that he had the right to do what he did is not lawful excuse within the meaning of the Act. Members of the jury, it is an excuse, it may even be a reasonable excuse, but it is not, members of the jury, a lawful excuse, because, in law, he had no right to do what he did. Members of the jury, as a matter of law, the evidence, in fact, discloses, so far as David Smith

> is concerned, no lawful excuse at all, because, as I say, the only defence which he has raised is the defence that he thought he had the right to do what he did. I have directed you that that is not a lawful excuse, and, members of the jury, it follows from that that so far as David Smith is concerned, I am bound to direct you as a matter of law that you must find him guilty of this offence with which he is charged."

It is contended for the appellant that that is a misdirection in law, and that, as a result of the misdirection, the entire defence of the appellant was wrongly withdrawn from the jury.

Section 1 of the Criminal Damage Act 1971 reads:

> "(1) A person who without lawful excuse destroys or damages any property belonging to another intending to destroy or damage any such property or being reckless as to whether any such property would be destroyed or damaged, shall be guilty of an offence."

The offence created includes the elements of intention or recklessness and the absence of lawful excuse. There is in section 5 of the Act a partial "definition" of lawful excuse. . . .

[After reading Section 5 (2), (3), (5), his Lordship continued]

It is argued for the appellant that an honest, albeit erroneous, belief that the act causing damage or destruction was done to his own property provides a defence to a charge brought under section 1 (1). The argument is put in three ways. First, that the offence charged includes the act causing the damage or destruction and the element of *mens rea*. The element of *mens rea* relates to all the circumstances of the criminal act. The criminal act in the offence is causing damage to or destruction of "property belonging to another" and the element of *mens rea*, therefore, must relate to "property belonging to another". Honest belief, whether justifiable or not, that the property is the defendant's own negatives the element of *mens rea*. Secondly, it is argued that by the terms of section 5, in particular the words of subsection (2), "whether or not he would be treated for the purposes of this Act as having a lawful excuse apart from this subsection", and the words in subsection (5), the appellant had a lawful excuse in that he honestly believed he was entitled to do as he did to property he believed to be his own. This it seems is the way the argument was put at the trial. Thirdly, it is argued, with understandable diffidence, that if a defendant honestly believes he is damaging his own property he has a lawful excuse for so doing because impliedly he believes that he is the person entitled to give consent to the damage being done and that he has consented: thus the case falls within section 5 (2) (a) of the Act.

We can dispose of the third way in which it is put immediately and briefly. Mr. Gerber for the Crown argues that to apply section 5 (2) (a) to a case in which a defendant believes that he is causing damage to his own property involves a tortuous and unjustifiable construction of the wording. We agree. In our judgment, to hold that those words of section 5 (2) (a) are apt to cover a case of a person damaging the property of another in the belief that it is his own would be to strain the language of the section to an unwarranted degree. Moreover, in our judgment, it is quite unnecessary to have recourse to such a construction.

Mr. Gerber invited our attention to *Cambridgeshire and Isle of Ely County Council* v. *Rust* [1972] 2 Q.B. 426, a case under section 127 of the Highways Act 1959, concerning the pitching of a stall on a highway without lawful excuse. The case is cited as authority for the proposition that in order to establish a lawful excuse as a defence it must be shown that the defendant honestly but mistakenly believed on reasonable grounds that the facts were of a certain order, and that if those facts were of that order his conduct would have been lawful. Applying that proposition to the facts of the present case, Mr. Gerber argues that the appellant cannot be said to have had a lawful excuse because in law the damaged property was part of the house and owned by the landlord. We have no doubt as to the correctness of the decision in the case cited. The proposition is argued here in relation to the appellant's contention that he had a lawful excuse and does not touch the argument based on absence of *mens rea*.

It is conceded by Mr. Gerber that there is force in the argument that the element of *mens rea* extends to "property belonging to another". But, it is argued, the section creates a new statutory offence and that it is open to the construction that the mental element in the offence relates only to causing damage to or destroying property. That if in fact the property damaged or destroyed is shown to be another's property the offence is committed although the defendant did not intend or foresee damage to another person's property.

We are informed that so far as research has revealed this is the first occasion on which this court has had to consider the question which arises in this appeal.

It is not without interest to observe that, under the law in force before the passing of the Criminal Damage Act 1971, it was clear that no offence was committed by a person who destroyed or damaged property belonging to another in the honest but mistaken belief that the property was his own or that he had a legal right to do the damage. In *R.* v. *Twose* (1879) 14 Cox C.C. 327 the prisoner was indicted for setting fire to furze on a common. Persons living near the common had occasionally burned the furze in order to improve the growth of grass but without the right to do so. The prisoner denied setting fire to the furze and it was submitted that even if it were proved that she did she could not be found guilty if she *bona fide* believed she had a right to do so whether the right were a good one or not. Lopes J. ruled that if she set fire to the furze thinking she had a right to do so that would not be a criminal offence.

Upon the facts of the present appeal the charge, if brought before the Act of 1971 came into force, would have been laid under section 13 of the Malicious Damage Act 1861, alleging damage by a tenant to a building. It was a defence to a charge under that section that the tenant acted under a claim of right to do the damage.

If the direction given by the deputy judge in the present case is correct, then the offence created by section 1 (1) of the Act of 1971 involves a considerable extension of the law in a surprising direction. Whether or not this is so depends upon the construction of the section. Construing the language of section 1 (1) we have no doubt that the *actus reus* is "destroying or damaging any property belonging to another". It is not possible to exclude the words "belonging to another" which describes the "property". Applying the ordinary principles of *mens rea*, the intention and recklessness and the absence of lawful excuse required to constitute the offence have reference to property belonging to another. It follows that in our judgment no offence is committed under this section if a person destroys or causes damage to property belonging to another if he does so in the honest though mistaken belief that the property is his own, and provided that the belief is honestly held it is irrelevant to consider whether or not it is a justifiable belief.

In our judgment, the direction given to the jury was a fundamental misdirection in law. The consequence was that the jury were precluded from considering facts capable of being a defence to the charge and were directed to convict. . . .

Appeal allowed

Questions

1. In *Jaggard* v. *Dickinson* (ante, p. 187), the accused, because she was drunk, thought that the owner of the property had consented to her

damaging it. It was held that since the case came under section 5 (2) (*a*), she was entitled to be acquitted notwithstanding that her mistake was due to self-induced intoxication. But in *R.* v. *Smith*, the Court rejected the argument, advanced "with understandable diffidence" (*ante*, p. 658) that his case came under section 5 (2) (*a*). Does this mean that if Miss Jaggard thought it was her *own* window she was breaking, her drunken mistake would not have saved her?

2. If the two cases are inconsistent, which of them is to be preferred? (ignoring the fact that one is in the Court of Appeal and the other in the Divisional Court).

3. A, employed by B, the owner of a mill, burned it down in the belief that B had asked him to do so, so that he (B) could make a fraudulent claim on his insurances. If A is charged with an offence under section 1 (1):

(i) is his belief lawful excuse? or
(ii) is he to be treated as having lawful excuse under section 5 (2)? or
(iii) is he guilty as charged?

(See *R.* v. *Denton* [1982] 1 All E.R. 65.)

iv. Intending ... or being Reckless as to Whether any such Property would be Destroyed or Damaged

See *R.* v. *Caldwell*, *ante*, p. 71, on recklessness.

B. THE AGGRAVATED OFFENCE: WITH DANGER TO LIFE

Note

See sections 1 (2) and 5 (1) above and *R.* v. *Caldwell*, *ante*, p. 71. The property damaged need not belong to the accused, the extended meaning of "without lawful excuse" does not apply, and in addition to the *mens rea* required for the simple offence he must intend to endanger the life of another or be reckless as to whether another's life is endangered.

Question

In which of the following cases is the aggravated offence committed?

A set fire to B's house meaning to endanger the lives of the occupants. No one was in fact in the house, but a fireman risked his life to discover whether the house was empty.

C cleared certain scrubland belonging to himself by setting fire to it. C knew that courting couples often used the scrubland, but was indifferent to the risk to such persons. In fact no one was in the scrub at the time.

D's dog was savaging a flock of sheep belonging to E. D chased the dog in an effort to pull it away. E witnessed this from the edge of the field and, believing that the only way to save his sheep was to shoot the dog, fired and hit D.

F, out walking on open land, was set on by an imperfectly trained guard dog being exercised by G. F shot several times at the dog and one shot hit G. F realised he was endangering G, but considered that shooting was the only way to save himself from injury.

2. OTHER OFFENCES

Criminal Damage Act 1971, sections 2 and 3

"2. A person who without lawful excuse makes to another a threat, intending that that other would fear it would be carried out—

(a) to destroy or damage any property belonging to that other or a third person; or

(b) to destroy or damage his own property in a way which he knows is likely to endanger the life of that other or a third person;

shall be guilty of an offence.

3. A person who has anything in his custody or under his control intending without lawful excuse to use it or cause or permit another to use it—

(a) to destroy or damage any property belonging to some other person; or

(b) to destroy or damage his own or the user's property in a way which he knows is likely to endanger the life of some other person;

shall be guilty of an offence."

i. In a Way which He Knows is Likely to Endanger Life

Question

What is the difference between this and "being reckless as to whether the life of another would be endangered" in section 1 (2)?

ii. In his Custody or Control Intending to Use it

Note

The Law Commission rejected "in his possession" because of the difficulties in that concept underlined by *Warner* v. *Commissioner of Police* [1969] A.C. 256.

Questions

1. Since these difficulties all centre round the question of when a person can be said to be in possession of something without knowing, they can be said to be purely academic anyway in the case of section 3. Why is this?

2. A and B, on strike, come upon a car which they recognise as belonging to a workmate C, who has continued working. A and B pick up stones and throw them at the car but miss. Are they guilty of an offence under section 3? See (1972) 36 J.C.L. 185, and refer to the discussion of "has with him" in connection with aggravated burglary, *ante*, p. 647.

INDEX

ABORTION,
  statutory definition of, 456
  "unlawfully," meaning of, in, 457

ABSOLUTE OFFENCES. *See* STRICT LIABILITY.

ACCOMPLICES. *See also* DEGREES OF RESPONSIBILITY.
  Law Commission proposals on, 281
  mens rea of secondary party, 255
  no principal offender, where, 278
  principals and accessories, 246
  secondary party not convictable as a principle, where, 274

ACT,
  definitions of, 14-15

ACTUS REUS,
  causation, 24-39
  coincidence with *mens rea*, 40
  omissions, 18
  unconscious actions, 16
  voluntary conduct, 14

AIDING AND ABETTING. *See* ACCOMPLICES.

APPEAL, 3, 4
  proviso to s. 4, Criminal Appeal Act, 1907...3, 392
  writ of error, by, 2

ARSON. *See* CRIMINAL DAMAGE.

ASSAULT AND BATTERY. *See also* ASSAULTS, STATUTORY.
  actus reus, 471
  consent, in, 475
  mens rea, 475
  self-defence, as a defence, 479

ASSAULTS, STATUTORY,
  grievous bodily harm, with intent to commit, 484
  Indecent. *See* SEXUAL OFFENCES.
  malicious wounding, 481
  occasioning actual bodily harm, 480
  policeman, of, 480
  proposals for reform of, 492

ASSISTING AN OFFENDER, 283

ATTEMPTS,
  actus reus of, 305
  impossible result, at, 317
  Law Commission's proposals, 304, 317, 328
  mental element in, 328
  theories of, 305

ATTORNEY GENERAL'S REFERENCES, 10

AUTOMATISM, 167

BLACKMAIL,
  demand, 623
  gain or loss in, 630
  menaces, 621
  subjective test in, 624
  "unwarranted," 624

BURGLARY,
  aggravated, 647
  buildings, 640
  entering in, 631
  intent in, 641
  statutory definition of, 631
  trespassory entry, 633

BUTLER COMMITTEE, 196

CANADIAN LAW REFORM COMMISSION,
  proposals on theft, 562

Causation, 24
  imputability, 28
  intervening causes, 34
  sine qua non, 26

CAUSING DEATH BY RECKLESS DRIVING, 78
  proposals on, 468

CHEAT. *See* FRAUD.

CHILD DESTRUCTION, 456

CONCEALING OFFENCES, 288

CONCEPT OF CRIME, 1-7

CONSPIRACY, 331-360
  agreement, constituted by, 333
  common law, at, 343
    corrupt public morals, to, 350
    defraud, to, 346
  impossible ends, to do, 359
  jurisdiction over, 336
  parties, 339
    at least two, 339
    exempt, 340
  statute, under, 357

CORPORATIONS, 296

CREDIT CARD,
deception by using, 584

CRIME,
definition of, 1-4

CRIMINAL APPEAL,
Court of, 9

CRIMINAL DAMAGE,
arson, 653
lawful excuse, 656
mens rea, 657
with danger to life, 660
without danger to life, 654

CRIMINAL LAW REVISION COMMITTEE, 11

DECEPTION. *See also* FRAUD.
credit card, as to, 584
machine, of, 588
what is, 573

DEFENCES, 201-245
duress, 201
entrapment, 233
necessity, 227

DEGREES OF RESPONSIBILITY, 246-302
accomplices, 246
arresting an offender, 283
concealing information, 288
corporations, 296
vicarious liability, 288

DIMINISHED RESPONSIBILITY. *See* MURDER.

DISHONESTY,
obtaining by deception in, 591
theft, in, 555

DRUNKENNESS. *See* INTOXICATION.

DURESS, 201
Law Commission's views on, 225
murder, in, 203

ENTRAPMENT, 233
Law Commission's proposals on, 224

FALSE INFORMATION, GIVING, 288

FALSE PRETENCES, OBTAINING BY, 571

FORM OF ENGLISH CRIMINAL LAW, 7-12

FRAUD,
evasion of liability by deception, 594
obtaining by deception,
pecuniary advantage, 592
property, 573
services, 593

GOING EQUIPPED FOR CRIME, 649

HANDLING,
definition of, 599
forms of, 611
guilty knowledge in, 616
otherwise than in the course of stealing, 608
recaptured goods, 599
stolen goods, what are, 604
undertaking etc. in retention etc., 611

HOMICIDE, 366-469. *See also* MANSLAUGHTER; MURDER.
actus reus of,
defined, 366
life in being, in, 366
"year and a day" rule in, 367
infanticide, 455
necessity, and, 227
reform of, 463
self-defence in, 411
excessive force, in, 430
reasonable force, what is, 422
suicide, 365

HOUSE OF LORDS, 10, 11

INCHOATE OFFENCES,
attempts, 303-331
conspiracy, 331-360
incitement, 360-365

INCITEMENT, 360

INSANITY, 158
criminal liability, as negating, 162
unfitness to plead, as, 159

INTENTION. *See* MENS REA.

INTOXICATION, 176
"basic" and "specific" intent, 176

KNOWLEDGE. *See* MENS REA.

LARCENY, 494

LAW COMMISSION, 11

MAKING OFF WITHOUT PAYMENT, 597

MALICE. *See* MENS REA.

MALICIOUS WOUNDING, 481

MANSLAUGHTER,
negligence, by, 449
unlawful act, by 438
voluntary, 437

MENS REA, 43-155
  Law Commission's proposals on, 56
  judicial approaches to, 62-94
    common law *mens rea*, 62
    intention, 63
    knowledge, 68
    maliciousness, 81
    recklessness, 71
    wilfulness, 83
  meaning of terms, 46-62
    intention, 47
    knowledge, 50
    negligence, 54
    recklessness, 50
  mistakes, 98
  motive, contrasted with, 94
  requirement of, 43
  strict liability, 128

MENTAL INCAPACITY, 157-200
  automatism, 167
  defences in general, and, 157
  insanity, 158
  intoxication, 176
  proposals for reform, 195
  unfitness to plead, 159

MISTAKE,
  law, of, 122
  irrelevant, 120
  mens rea, negativing, 116
  strict liability, and, 121
  transferred malice, and, 122

MOTIVE, 94

MURDER,
  diminished responsibility,
    burden of proof as to, 402
    duress in, 203
    reform of, 467
    what amounts to, 403
  mens rea in,
    malice, constructive, 368, 370, 469
      abolition of, 369
    malice implied, as, 371, 374
      grevious bodily harm,
        intent to do, 371, 386
        probability of, 374
  penalty for, 368
  provocation, 389
    objective test applied in judging, 389, 400
    reform of, 467
    self-induced, 401
  reform of, 466

NECESSITY,
  homicide, no defence to, 227
  Law Commission's recommendations on, 231
  offences other than homicide, and, 230

NEGLIGENCE. *See* MENS REA.

OMISSIONS, 18

POISON, ADMINISTERING, 485

PREVENTION OF CRIME, 418

PROVOCATION. *See* MURDER.

QUEEN'S BENCH DIVISION, 9

RAPE,
  definition of, 486
  fraud, as affecting consent in, 487
  husband, by, on wife, 487

REASONABLE MAN,
  provocation in, 389

RECKLESS DRIVING, 78

RECKLESSNESS. *See* MENS REA.

ROBBERY, 566-570

SELF-DEFENCE,
  assault in, 479
  others, defence of, 414
  prevention of crime, and, 418
  property, defence of, 416
  reform of, 469

SEXUAL OFFENCES. *See also* RAPE.
  indecent assault, 491
  procurement by fraud, 489
  sexual intercourse, meaning of, 491

STRICT LIABILITY, 128-156
  critique of, 151
  evolution of, 128
  mistake and, 121
  present uncertainty of, 129
  proposals for reform of, 154
  regulating offences, in, 147

SUICIDE, 462

THEFT,
  appropriation in, 495
  definition of, 495
  dishonesty in, 555
  human body, of, 514
  intent to deprive in, 534
  land, of, 504
  property in, 504
    belonging to another, 515
    intangible, 512

THEFT—*cont.*
  temporary deprivation, by, 544, 553
    articles in a collection, of, 545
    conveyances, of, 546
  things in action, of, 505
  wild creatures, of, 505

TRANSFERRED MALICE, 122

UNCONSCIOUS ACTIONS,
  voluntary conduct, whether, 16

UNFITNESS TO PLEAD, 159

VICARIOUS LIABILITY, 288
  delegation principle, and, 290

VOLUNTARINESS, 14
  Unconsciousness, and, 16

WILFULNESS. *See* MENS REA.

WOUNDING WITH INTENT, 484